WEST'S
FEDERAL PRACTICE
DIGEST 4th

Volume 45

FEDERAL CIVIL PROCEDURE ⚷ 1741 to 1820

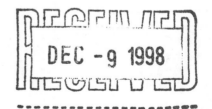
ST. PAUL, MN

WEST GROUP

Closing with Cases Reported In

COPYRIGHT © 1998

By

WEST GROUP

PRINTED ON 10% POST CONSUMER RECYCLED PAPER

PREFACE

WEST'S FEDERAL PRACTICE DIGEST 4th responsive to the continuing expansion of federal case law, provides a convenient index directly supplementing WEST'S FEDERAL PRACTICE DIGEST 3d. Key number classification has been expanded and refined to reflect recent developments in the law.

Additional case history to cases in earlier editions of the Federal Practice Digest may be found in the main volumes and pocket parts of this digest.

New topics and key numbers have been provided for many areas including bankruptcy, civil rights, civil service, criminal law, double jeopardy, ERISA, farm labor, federal preemption, habeas corpus, intoxication tests, RICO, searches and seizures, and warranties.

FEDERAL PRACTICE DIGEST 3d will continue to provide coverage of federal case law from 1975 to the beginning of FEDERAL PRACTICE DIGEST 4th.

FEDERAL PRACTICE DIGEST 2d is the index to cases reported from 1961 to November 1975. WEST'S MODERN FEDERAL PRACTICE DIGEST covers federal case law from 1939 to 1961. The FEDERAL DIGEST is the index for reported cases prior to 1939.

LIBRARY REFERENCES to Corpus Juris Secundum and other publications are included throughout. They provide access to a broad field of text research.

WESTLAW and the Decennial Digests may also be consulted for cases from other jurisdictions.

The TABLE OF CASES lists alphabetically the title of each case, the volume and page of the reports in which each is published, the subsequent case history, and the digest Topic and Key Number under which each point of law is digested.

The DEFENDANT–PLAINTIFF TABLE provides an effective and additional aid in the search for legal precedents when used in connection with the Plaintiff-Defendant Table of Cases. It is devoted to a complete listing in alphabetical order by name of defendant, of all the cases included in the Digest.

The WORDS AND PHRASES section lists alphabetically words or phrases that have been judicially defined in the cases indexed by the Digest, and sets out the titles and citations of the cases in which such definitions appear.

A comprehensive DESCRIPTIVE–WORD INDEX has been specially prepared, providing immediate and convenient access to the case law within the scope of this new Digest.

PREFACE

UPDATING WITH WESTLAW

WESTLAW provides easy and quick access to those cases reported after the latest available digest supplementation.

The WESTLAW query is entered in any appropriate case law data base of interest. The query format used substitutes a numerical equivalent for the digest topic name and adds the key number through the use of "K" as illustrated in the search for later Contracts ⚖ 155 cases published after December 31, 1997.

ad(after 12-31-97) & 95K155.

A list of topics and their numerical equivalents may be found in the DIGEST TOPICS section of this volume, in the WESTLAW Reference Manual or in the WESTLAW Directory.

THE PUBLISHER

December, 1998

ABBREVIATIONS OF COURTS

ACMR --------------------------- United States Court of Military Review
—Army
AFCMR ----------------------- United States Court of Military Review
—Air Force
Bkrtcy. --------------------------------- United States Bankruptcy Court
Bkrtcy.App. ------------------------------------ United States Bankruptcy
Appellate Panel
C.A. --- United States Court of Appeals
C.A.D.C. ------------------------------ United States Court of Appeals for
District of Columbia Circuit
C.A.Fed. ---------------------------------- United States Court of Appeals,
Federal Circuit
C.C.P.A. ---------------------------- United States Court of Customs and
Patent Appeals
CGCMR ----------------------- United States Court of Military Review
—Coast Guard
CIT ------------------------- United States Court of International Trade
Fed.Cl. --------------------------- United States Court of Federal Claims
Cl.Ct. --- United States Claims Court
CMA --------------------------- United States Court of Military Appeals
Ct.Cl. -- United States Court of Claims
Cust. & Pat.App. ---------------------- United States Court of Customs
and Patent Appeals
Cust.Ct. ---------------------------------- United States Court of Customs
D.C. --- United States District Courts
Em.App. ------------------------- United States Temporary Emergency
Court of Appeals
Jud.Pan.Mult.Lit. ---------- Judicial Panel on Multidistrict Litigation
NMCMR ----------------- United States Court of Military Review Navy
—Marine Corps Court of Military Review
U.S. ----------------------------------- Supreme Court of the United States
Vet.App. ----------------------- United States Court of Veterans Appeals

OUTLINE OF THE LAW

*Digest Topics are arranged for your convenience by Seven Main Divisions of Law.
Complete alphabetical list of Digest Topics with topic numbers follows this section.*

---

1. **PERSONS**
2. **PROPERTY**
3. **CONTRACTS**
4. **TORTS**
5. **CRIMES**
6. **REMEDIES**
7. **GOVERNMENT**

1. PERSONS

RELATING TO NATURAL PERSONS IN GENERAL

Civil Rights
Dead Bodies
Death
Domicile
Drugs and Narcotics
Food
Health and Environment
Holidays
Intoxicating Liquors
Names
Seals
Signatures
Sunday
Time
Weapons

PARTICULAR CLASSES OF NATURAL PERSONS

Absentees
Aliens
Chemical Dependents
Children Out-of Wedlock
Citizens
Convicts
Indians
Infants
Mental Health
Slaves
Spendthrifts

PERSONAL RELATIONS

Adoption
Attorney and Client
Employers' Liability
Executors and Administrators
Guardian and Ward
Husband and Wife
Labor Relations
Marriage
Master and Servant
Parent and Child
Principal and Agent
Workers' Compensation

ASSOCIATED AND ARTIFICIAL PERSONS

Associations
Beneficial Associations
Building and Loan Associations
Clubs
Colleges and Universities
Corporations
Exchanges
Joint-Stock Companies and Business Trusts
Partnership
Religious Societies

PARTICULAR OCCUPATIONS

Accountants
Agriculture
Auctions and Auctioneers
Aviation
Banks and Banking
Bridges
Brokers

3. CONTRACTS

NATURE, REQUISITES, AND INCIDENTS OF AGREEMENTS IN GENERAL

Contracts
Customs and Usages
Frauds, Statute of
Interest
Usury

PARTICULAR CLASSES OF AGREEMENTS

Bailment
Bills and Notes
Bonds
Breach of Marriage Promise
Champerty and Maintenance
Compromise and Settlement
Covenants
Deposits and Escrows
Exchange of Property
Gaming
Guaranty
Implied and Constructive Contracts
Indemnity
Joint Adventures
Lotteries
Pensions
Principal and Surety
Public Contracts
Rewards
Sales
Subscriptions
Vendor and Purchaser

PARTICULAR CLASSES OF IMPLIED OR CONSTRUCTIVE CONTRACTS OR QUASI CONTRACTS

Account Stated
Contribution
Implied and Constructive Contracts

PARTICULAR MODES OF DISCHARGING CONTRACTS

Novation
Payment
Release
Subrogation
Tender

4. TORTS

Assault and Battery
Collision

Conspiracy
False Imprisonment
Forcible Entry and Detainer
Fraud
Libel and Slander
Malicious Prosecution
Negligence
Nuisance
Products Liability
Seduction
Torts
Trespass
Trover and Conversion
Waste

5. CRIMES

Abortion and Birth Control
Adulteration
Adultery
Arson
Bigamy
Breach of the Peace
Bribery
Burglary
Compounding Offenses
Counterfeiting
Criminal Law
Disorderly Conduct
Disorderly House
Disturbance of Public Assemblage
Embezzlement
Escape
Extortion and Threats
False Personation
False Pretenses
Fires
Forgery
Homicide
Incest
Insurrection and Sedition
Kidnapping
Larceny
Lewdness
Malicious Mischief
Mayhem
Neutrality Laws
Obscenity
Obstructing Justice
Perjury
Prostitution
Racketeer Influenced and Corrupt
  Organizations
Rape
Receiving Stolen Goods
Rescue
Riot
Robbery

DIGEST TOPICS

See, also, Outline of the Law by Seven Main Divisions of Law,
preceding this section

The topic numbers shown below may be used in WESTLAW searches for cases
within the topic and within specified key numbers.

DIGEST TOPICS

FEDERAL CIVIL PROCEDURE

SUBJECTS INCLUDED

Generally, the civil procedure, other than appellate, of the District Courts of the United States and the former Circuit Courts of the United States

More particularly, procedure under the Federal Rules of Civil Procedure

SUBJECTS EXCLUDED AND COVERED BY OTHER TOPICS

Appellate procedure, see FEDERAL COURTS

Criminal procedure, see CRIMINAL LAW

District of Columbia, procedure in municipal court, see FEDERAL COURTS

Particular fields of federal jurisdiction, procedure in, see ADMIRALTY, BANK-RUPTCY, INTERNAL REVENUE and other specific topics

For detailed references to other topics, see Descriptive-Word Index

---

Analysis

I. IN GENERAL.

(A) IN GENERAL.

    ☞1. In general.

    2. Power of Congress.

    3. Constitutional and statutory provisions.

    4. Commencement of actions.

    5. Defenses.

    5.1. —— In general.

    6. —— Equitable defenses.

    7. —— Hearing before trial.

    8. Consolidation of actions.

    8.1. —— In general.

    9. —— Multidistrict litigation, consolidation for pretrial proceedings.

(B) RULES OF COURT IN GENERAL.

    1. IN GENERAL.

    ☞21. In general.

    22. Admiralty rules.

    23. Criminal rules.

    24. Equity rules.

    25. Local rules of District Courts.

    2. RULES OF CIVIL PROCEDURE.

    ☞31. In general.

    32. Power of Supreme Court.

    33. Validity.

    34. Purpose.

    35. Construction and operation in general.

    36. Liberal or strict construction.

I. **IN GENERAL.**—Continued.

(B) RULES OF COURT IN GENERAL.—Continued.

2. RULES OF CIVIL PROCEDURE.—Continued.

37. Rules as having effect of statutes.

38. Construction of Rules together.

39. Substantive rights, effect of Rules on.

40. Jurisdiction and venue, effect of Rules on.

41. Federal statutes superseded.

42. State statutes and Rules superseded.

43. United States, application of Rules to.

44. Retroactive operation of Rules.

(C) CONFORMITY TO STATE PRACTICE IN GENERAL.

⊕51. In general.

52. Degree of conformity.

53. Effect of United States statutes regulating procedure.

54. Jurisdiction.

55. Admiralty cases.

56. Criminal cases.

57. Equity cases.

58. Appeal and error.

(D) NATURE AND FORM OF REMEDY.

⊕71. In general.

72. Legal or equitable nature.

72.1. —— In general.

73. —— Abolition of distinction between law and equity.

(E) JOINDER OF CLAIMS AND REMEDIES.

⊕81. In general.

82. Grounds of claims.

82.1. —— In general.

83. —— Tort and contract claims.

84. Nature of remedies sought.

84.1. —— In general.

85. —— Legal and equitable remedies.

86. Parties involved.

II. **PARTIES.**

(A) IN GENERAL.

⊕101. In general.

102. Formal and nominal parties.

103. Proper parties in general.

103.1. Standing.

103.2. —— In general; injury or interest.

103.3. —— Causation; redressability.

103.4. —— Rights of third parties or public.

103.5. —— Pleading.

103.6. Government; officers.

103.7. Class actions.

II. PARTIES.—Continued.

(D) CLASS ACTIONS.—Continued.

2. PROCEEDINGS.—Continued.

177.1. —— In general.

178. —— Parties responsible; expense.

179. —— Sufficiency.

180. Options; withdrawal.

3. PARTICULAR CLASSES REPRESENTED.

⚷181. In general.

181.5. Antitrust plaintiffs.

182. Bondholders.

182.5. Consumers, purchasers, borrowers, and debtors.

183. Creditors.

184. Employees.

184.5. —— In general.

184.10. —— Discrimination and civil rights actions in general.

184.15. —— Sex discrimination actions.

184.20. —— Age discrimination actions.

184.25. —— Prior administrative proceeding, use or availability; limitations.

184.30. —— Public agency actions.

185. Heirs and testamentary beneficiaries.

186. Landowners.

186.5. Members of corporations, associations, or unions.

186.10. Prisoners and inmates.

186.15. Racial, religious, or ethnic groups in general.

187. Stockholders, investors, and depositors.

187.5. Students, parents, and faculty.

188. Trust beneficiaries.

189. Welfare and social security claimants.

(E) NECESSARY JOINDER.

1. IN GENERAL.

⚷201. In general.

202. Who are necessary parties.

203. Who are indispensable parties.

2. PARTICULAR, NECESSARY OR INDISPENSABLE PARTIES.

⚷211. In general.

212. Assignors and assignees.

213. Automobile owners, drivers and occupants.

214. Contractors and subcontractors and sureties thereof.

215. Corporations and officers and stockholders thereof.

216. Creditors.

217. Employers, employees and labor unions.

218. Executors and administrators.

219. Governmental bodies and officers thereof.

220. Guardians and wards.

221. Heirs and testamentary beneficiaries.

222. Insurers and insureds.

223. Joint obligors and joint obligees in general.

VII. PLEADINGS AND MOTIONS.—Continued.

(A) PLEADINGS IN GENERAL.—Continued.

(B) COMPLAINT.

1. IN GENERAL.

2. PARTICULAR ACTIONS.

VII. PLEADINGS AND MOTIONS.—Continued.

(H) DEFECTS IN AND OBJECTIONS TO PLEADINGS IN GENERAL.—Continued.

(I) MOTIONS IN GENERAL.

(J) BILL OF PARTICULARS; MORE DEFINITE STATEMENT.

1. IN GENERAL.

2. PARTICULAR CASES.

X. DEPOSITIONS AND DISCOVERY.—Continued.

(D) WRITTEN INTERROGATORIES TO PARTIES.—Continued.

1. IN GENERAL.—Continued.

1484.1. —— In general.

1485. —— Leave of court, necessity for.

1486. Motion for leave to submit, and proceedings thereon.

1487. Service or filing.

1488. Number, form and importance.

1488.1. —— In general.

1489. —— Specificity and definiteness.

1490. Striking out interrogatories.

1491. Effect.

2. SCOPE.

☞1501. In general.

1502. Grounds of claim or defense.

1503. Relevancy and materiality.

1504. Probable admissibility at trial of evidence sought.

1505. Admitted matters and matters already known or available.

1506. Adverse party's case, matters relating to in general.

1507. Circumstances of accident or injury or cause thereof.

1508. Documents, examination involving.

1509. Extent of injury or damage.

1510. Events after beginning of action.

1511. Evidentiary matters.

1512. Identity and location of witnesses and others.

1513. Opinions, conclusions and matters unknown.

1514. Privileged matters.

1514.1. —— In general.

1515. —— Results of investigation or of preparation for litigation or trial.

1516. —— Secret processes, developments or research.

3. ANSWERS; FAILURE TO ANSWER.

☞1531. In general.

1532. Duty to answer.

1532.1. —— In general.

1533. —— Inability to answer.

1534. Sufficiency.

1535. Striking out.

1536. Use.

1537. Failure to answer.

1537.1. —— In general.

1538. —— Order compelling answer.

1539. —— Payment of expenses.

1540. —— Facts taken as established or denial precluded.

1541. —— Striking out defaulting party's pleading.

1542. —— Contempt.

XI. DISMISSAL.—Continued.

(A) VOLUNTARY DISMISSAL.—Continued.

(B) INVOLUNTARY DISMISSAL.

1. IN GENERAL.

2. GROUNDS IN GENERAL.

XVII. JUDGMENT.—Continued.

  (C) SUMMARY JUDGMENT.—Continued.

    2. PARTICULAR CASES.—Continued.

2483.5. Aliens, actions involving.

2484. Antitrust and price discrimination cases.

2484.5. Armed services, actions involving.

2485. Automobile cases.

2486. Bankruptcy trustees, cases involving.

2487. Banks, cases involving.

2488. Bills and notes, cases involving.

2489. Bonds and evidences of indebtedness, cases involving.

2490. Brokers, cases involving.

2491. Carriers and warehousemen, actions involving.

2491.5. Civil rights cases in general.

2492. Contract cases in general.

2493. Copyright, trademark, and unfair competition cases.

2494. Customs cases.

2495. Decedents' estates, cases involving.

2496. Divorce cases.

2497. Employees and employment discrimination, actions involving.

2497.1. —— In general.

2498. —— Fair Labor Standards Act cases.

2498.5. Food and drug regulations, actions involving.

2499. Indian cases.

2500. Infants and other incompetents, cases involving.

2500.5. Injunction and declaratory judgment cases in general.

2501. Insurance cases.

2502. Interpleader.

2503. Judgments, actions on.

2504. Land, cases involving in general.

2505. Landlord and tenant cases.

2506. Mines and minerals, cases involving.

2507. Mortgage cases.

2507.5. National emergency regulations, actions involving.

2508. Patent cases.

2509. Public utility cases.

2510. Sales cases in general.

2511. Securities cases in general.

2512. Shipping and seamen, cases involving.

2512.5. Social security and public welfare, actions involving.

2513. Stock and stockholders, cases involving.

2514. Tax cases.

2515. Tort cases in general.

2516. Trust cases.

    3. PROCEEDINGS.

      ⚎2531. In general.

2532. Time for motion.

2533. Motion.

2533.1. —— In general.

2534. —— By both parties.

For detailed references to other topics, see Descriptive-Word Index

TABLE 1

KEY NUMBER TRANSLATION TABLE

FEDERAL CIVIL PROCEDURE TO EVIDENCE AND WITNESSES

Former Key Number Federal Civil Procedure	Present Key Number Evidence
1161	1 et seq.; Federal Courts 416
1162	1–52
1163	27–33, 35
1164	37
1165	53–89
1166	91–98
1167	96
1181, 1182	99 et seq.; Federal Courts 416
1183	99–156
1184	118–128
1185	157–187
1186	188–198
1187	200–313
1188	314–324
1189	325–383
1190	325–337
1191, 1192	351
1193	384–469
1194	470–574
1195	505–574
1196	575–583
1211, 1212	584–601
1213	588–590
1214	595
1215	596–598

Former Key Number Federal Civil Procedure	Present Key Number Witnesses
1221	1 et seq.; Federal Courts 416

Former Key Number Federal Civil Procedure	Present Key Number Witnesses
1222	1–34
1223–1225	7, 8
1226	9, 10
1227	14
1228	11
1229	13, 15
1230	8
1231	17–22
1232–1239	16
1240	17–22
1241	23–34
1242	35–223
1243	80–124
1244	125–183.5
1245	184–223
1246	224–310
1247	276
1248	266–310
1249	269
1250	276
1251	292–310
1252	311–332
1253	311–397
1254	398–409
1255	410–416

XI. DISMISSAL.—Cont'd

(B) INVOLUNTARY DISMISSAL.—Cont'd

2. GROUNDS IN GENERAL.

Research Notes

Dismissal and nonsuit, see West's Federal Forms.

See Wright & Miller, Federal Practice and Procedure: Civil.

⚷1741. In general.

Library references

C.J.S. Federal Civil Procedure §§ 486, 796 et seq.

U.S.Ind. 1989. Rule permitting dismissal for failure to state claim does not countenance dismissal based on judge's disbelief of complaint's factual allegations. Fed.Rules Civ.Proc. Rule 12(b)(6), 28 U.S.C.A.

 Neitzke v. Williams, 109 S.Ct. 1827, 490 U.S. 319, 104 L.Ed.2d 338.

U.S.Nev. 1996. If claimant's unwillingness to appear in person in civil forfeiture case resulted in noncompliance with legitimate order of court respecting pleading, discovery, presentation of evidence, or other matters, he would be exposed to same sanctions as any other uncooperative party. Fed.Rules Civ.Proc.Rule 37, 41(b), 28 U.S.C.A.

 Degen v. U.S., 116 S.Ct. 1777, 517 U.S. 820, 135 L.Ed.2d 102, on remand U.S. v. Real Property Located at Incline Village, 87 F.3d 400, on remand 958 F.Supp. 482.

Federal court has at its disposal array of means to enforce its orders, including dismissal in appropriate case; its powers include those furnished by federal rule, and by inherent authority. Fed.Rules Civ.Proc.Rule 37, 41(b), 28 U.S.C.A.

 Degen v. U.S., 116 S.Ct. 1777, 517 U.S. 820, 135 L.Ed.2d 102, on remand U.S. v. Real Property Located at Incline Village, 87 F.3d 400, on remand 958 F.Supp. 482.

U.S.Or. 1989. As general rule, if action is barred by terms of statute, it must be dismissed.

 Hallstrom v. Tillamook County, 110 S.Ct. 304, 493 U.S. 20, 107 L.Ed.2d 237, rehearing denied 110 S.Ct. 761, 493 U.S. 1037, 107 L.Ed.2d 777.

C.A.D.C. 1998. As justification to support use of dismissal or default judgment as sanction for misconduct, (1) court may decide that errant party's behavior has severely hampered other party's ability to present his case, and that other party has been so prejudiced by misconduct that it would be unfair to require him to proceed further, (2) court may take account of prejudice caused to judicial system when party's misconduct has put intolerable burden on district court

by requiring court to modify its own docket and operations in order to accommodate delay, and (3) court may consider need to sanction conduct that is disrespectful to the court and to deter similar misconduct in future; sanction imposed pursuant to any of these considerations must be based on findings supported by record.

 Webb v. District of Columbia, 146 F.3d 964, 331 U.S.App.D.C. 23.

C.A.D.C. 1996. Fact that civil enforcement proceeding brought by Federal Election Commission (FEC) against computerized database service, alleging illegal use of FEC information, was initiated prior to appellate court decision holding that FEC was unauthorized to bring such proceedings, because composition of FEC was unconstitutional under separation of powers doctrine, did not require dismissal of proceeding against service, as FEC reconstituted itself and ratified earlier decision to proceed with litigation against service; although remedy of dismissal was warranted in intervening decision, ratification by reconstituted FEC was valid alternate way of curing constitutional violation, reducing prejudice against service, and it was unlikely that FEC would reach different outcome if it repeated administrative process from beginning.

 Federal Election Com'n v. Legi-Tech, Inc., 75 F.3d 704, 316 U.S.App.D.C. 122, on remand 967 F.Supp. 523.

C.A.D.C. 1989. Failing to heed district court's order that allowed claim for benefits under group health plan and amending complaint to add claims for failure to supply summary plan description and failure to implement adequate procedures for review of claims did not support dismissal of proper claims that former employer failed to provide summary plan description and that former employee and spouse were entitled to benefits. Employee Retirement Income Security Act of 1974, §§ 3(16)(A)(i, ii), (16)(B)(i), 104(b)(1), 502(a, c), 503, 29 U.S.C.A. §§ 1002(16)(A)(i, ii), (16)(B)(i), 1024(b)(1), 1132(a, c), 1133; Fed.Rules Civ. Proc.Rules 6, 15, 15(a), 41(b), 28 U.S.C.A.

 Davis v. Liberty Mut. Ins. Co., 871 F.2d 1134, 276 U.S.App.D.C. 394.

C.A.D.C. 1987. Lawsuit against law firm plaintiff had paid to represent her son in litigation before bankruptcy court had to be dismissed for failure to comply with an order to show cause; law firm requested order to show cause why complaint should not be dismissed for apparent failure to abide by terms of injunction in son's prior litigation requiring that leave of District Court for District of Connecticut be secured prior to institution of any lawsuit by son and persons "acting at his behest," and plaintiff had deliberately elected and announced her intention not to comply with court orders in

For references to other topics, see Descriptive-Word Index

any respect. Fed.Rules Civ.Proc.Rule 41(b), 28 U.S.C.A.

> Martin-Trigona v. Gellis & Melinger, 830 F.2d 367, 265 U.S.App.D.C. 219.

C.A.D.C. 1987. Where a claimant makes a reasonable effort to notify federal agencies of a claim in accordance with administrative filing procedures set forth in the Federal Tort Claims Act, and Government takes no action to apprise claimant of objections to presentment within six-month time period it has to make final disposition of claim, such delay qualifies the force of the Government's objections when it subsequently moves for dismissal on the ground that the presentment was inadequate for its investigative purposes. 28 U.S.C.A. §§ 1346(b), 2675, 2675(a).

> GAF Corp. v. U.S., 818 F.2d 901, 260 U.S.App.D.C. 252.

C.A.D.C. 1984. Where complaint alleged presence of federal question jurisdiction over claims against corporate defendants, court could dismiss complaint for lack of subject-matter jurisdiction only if claim clearly appeared to be immaterial and made solely for purpose of obtaining jurisdiction or if the claim was wholly insubstantial or frivolous. (Per Wald, Circuit Judge, with one Judge concurring in part and one Judge concurring in part and dissenting in part.) 28 U.S.C.A. § 1331.

> Reuber v. U.S., 750 F.2d 1039, 242 U.S.App.D.C. 370, appeal after remand 787 F.2d 599, 252 U.S.App.D.C. 43.

C.A.D.C. 1984. Brandon v. District of Columbia Bd. of Parole, 734 F.2d 56, 236 U.S.App.D.C. 155, certiorari denied 105 S.Ct. 811, 469 U.S. 1127, 83 L.Ed.2d 804, on remand 631 F.Supp. 435, affirmed 823 F.2d 644, 262 U.S.App.D.C. 236.

C.A.D.C. 1971. Carter v. Carlson, 447 F.2d 358, 144 U.S.App.D.C. 388, certiorari granted District of Columbia v. Carter, 92 S.Ct. 683, 404 U.S. 1014, 30 L.Ed.2d 661, reversed 93 S.Ct. 602, 409 U.S. 418, 34 L.Ed.2d 613, rehearing denied 93 S.Ct. 1411, 410 U.S. 959, 35 L.Ed.2d 694, on remand 489 F.2d 1272, 160 U.S.App.D.C. 148, vacated in part 489 F.2d 1272, 160 U.S.App.D.C. 148.

C.A.6 1991. Courts have inherent power to dismiss and/or enter default when party disobeys court order or otherwise interferes with efficient administration of justice.

> Smith v. C.I.R., 926 F.2d 1470, rehearing denied.

C.A.7 1991. No court should dismiss case on ground of attorney's retroactive lack of authority because counsel omitted argument that would have been to client's benefit—even argu-

ment that client expressly instructs lawyer to advance.

> Slavin v. C.I.R., 932 F.2d 598.

C.A.Fed. (Ind.) 1993. Suit that may have been subject to state immunity at time it was filed can continue to be prosecuted when immunity is legislatively lifted; requiring dismissal would be wasteful to both parties and courts, since case could at once be refiled. U.S.C.A. Const.Amend. 11.

> Genentech, Inc. v. Eli Lilly and Co., 998 F.2d 931, rehearing denied, and rehearing denied, in banc suggestion declined, certiorari denied Regents of University of California v. Genentech, Inc., 114 S.Ct. 1126, 510 U.S. 1140, 127 L.Ed.2d 434.

C.A.11 (Ala.) 1994. When lack of standing is raised in motion to dismiss, issue is properly resolved by reference to allegations of complaint.

> Church v. City of Huntsville, 30 F.3d 1332.

C.A.11 (Ala.) 1991. District court may dismiss in forma pauperis suit for frivolity only when legal claim is indisputably meritless, facts are farfetched or baseless, or both. 28 U.S.C.A. § 1915(d).

> Cofield v. Alabama Public Service Com'n, 936 F.2d 512.

Dismissing all inmate's pending federal suits brought in forma pauperis was not abuse of discretion; all suits were frivolous, with some suits alleging the fantastic, such as a conspiracy by prison officials to bribe inmate into investigating improper behavior by other prison officials and subjection of inmate to administrative detention when he refused bribe, while other suits were merely meritless, as suit challenging cost of phone calls as too high. 28 U.S.C.A. § 1915(d).

> Cofield v. Alabama Public Service Com'n, 936 F.2d 512.

C.A.11 (Ala.) 1985. Inability of state officials to actually receive damages from state prisoner even if successful on their abuse of process claim did not warrant dismissal of claim.

> Harmon v. Berry, 776 F.2d 259, rehearing denied 781 F.2d 905.

C.A.9 (Alaska) 1995. Complaint is "frivolous" where none of legal points are arguable on their merits.

> Whitmore v. Federal Election Com'n, 68 F.3d 1212, as amended, certiorari denied 116 S.Ct. 1543, 517 U.S. 1155, 134 L.Ed.2d 646.

C.A.9 (Alaska) 1993. Courts have inherent power to dismiss actions for nonpayment of costs in prior actions and this power extends to litigant's failure to pay previously imposed sanctions.

> Hymes v. U.S., 993 F.2d 701, on reconsideration 2 F.3d 1157.

C.A.9 (Ariz.) 1998. Where a court suspends proceedings in order to give preliminary deference to an independent adjudicating body but further judicial proceedings are contemplated, then jurisdiction should be retained by a stay of proceedings, not relinquished by a dismissal.

> Shapiro v. Paradise Valley Unified School Dist. No. 69, 152 F.3d 1159, as amended.

C.A.9 (Ariz.) 1992. District court may dismiss action for failure to comply with any order of court.

> Ferdik v. Bonzelet, 963 F.2d 1258, as amended, certiorari denied 113 S.Ct. 321, 506 U.S. 915, 121 L.Ed.2d 242.

C.A.9 (Ariz.) 1985. Dismissal on ground that plaintiff investor failed to purge himself of contempt was not an abuse of discretion.

> Hatch v. Reliance Ins. Co., 758 F.2d 409, certiorari denied 106 S.Ct. 571, 474 U.S. 1021, 88 L.Ed.2d 555.

C.A.8 (Ark.) 1996. District court may dismiss case even though circumstances in which local rule calls for dismissal do not exist.

> Norman v. Arkansas Dept. of Educ., 79 F.3d 748.

C.A.8 (Ark.) 1991. District court presiding over action alleging that insurance company failed to pay commissions to former agent did not abuse its discretion in dismissing former agent's tort claim and claim for punitive damages by reason that, under Ohio law, claims sounded purely in contract, not in tort.

> Hicks v. Capitol American Life Ins. Co., 943 F.2d 891, rehearing denied.

C.A.8 (Ark.) 1985. Dismissal of insurer's claim against insured by intervention as of right in insured's action against tort-feasor, seeking lien against insured's settlement from tort-feasor, was abuse of discretion, under circumstances that insurer's intervention was completely ancillary to insured's claim, that following tort-feasor's settlement with insured, no questions of fact remained, and that only lack of jurisdictional amount made invocation of doctrine of ancillary or pendent jurisdiction necessary. Ark.Stats. § 66–4019; Fed.Rules Civ.Proc.Rule 24(a), 28 U.S.C.A.; 28 U.S.C.A. §§ 1331, 1332(a)(1).

> Curtis v. Sears, Roebuck & Co., 754 F.2d 781, 76 A.L.R. Fed. 163.

C.A.9 (Cal.) 1996. Since harshness is key consideration in district judge's exercise of discretion in dismissing case with prejudice for violation of court order, it is appropriate that judge consider strength of plaintiff's case, if such information is available, before determining whether dismissal with prejudice is appropriate. Fed.Rules Civ.Proc.Rule 41(b), 28 U.S.C.A.

> McHenry v. Renne, 84 F.3d 1172.

Although complaint is not defective for failure to designate statute or other provision of law violated, district judge may in his or her discretion, in response to motion for more definite statement, require such detail as may be appropriate in particular case, and may dismiss complaint if order is violated. Fed.Rules Civ. Proc.Rules 12(e), 41(b), 28 U.S.C.A.

> McHenry v. Renne, 84 F.3d 1172.

District court did not abuse its discretion in dismissing third amended complaint with prejudice for violation of general pleading rules and court's prior orders requiring short, clear statement of claims sufficient to allow defendants to prepare responsive pleading, in light of district court's prior unsuccessful use of less drastic alternatives by allowing repleading twice, court's consideration of strength of plaintiffs' case by referring matter for extensive analysis by magistrate, and court's consideration of extensive burden imposed on defendants by same plaintiffs in related litigation; 53-page third amended complaint was written more as a press release and failed to obey court's prior orders to identify which defendants were liable on which claims. Fed.Rules Civ.Proc.Rules 8, 41(b), 28 U.S.C.A.

> McHenry v. Renne, 84 F.3d 1172.

C.A.9 (Cal.) 1996. Before imposing dismissal as sanction for failure to prosecute or comply with rules of civil procedure, district court must weigh several factors: public's interest in expeditious resolution of litigation; court's need to manage its docket; risk of prejudice to defendants; public policy favoring disposition of cases on their merits; and availability of less drastic sanctions. Fed.Rules Civ.Proc.Rule 41(b), 28 U.S.C.A.

> Dahl v. City of Huntington Beach, 84 F.3d 363.

Dismissal is so harsh a penalty it should be imposed as sanction only in extreme circumstances. Fed.Rules Civ.Proc.Rule 41(b), 28 U.S.C.A.

> Dahl v. City of Huntington Beach, 84 F.3d 363.

Dismissal of civil rights action due to refusal by plaintiffs' attorneys to pay sanctions in the manner prescribed by court, one attorney's failure to pay sanctions altogether and attorney's failure to timely file joint exhibit and witness list was improper; public policy strongly favored resolution of dispute on merits, outright dismissal penalized only one of two parties guilty of discovery abuse, and dismissal severely penalized plaintiffs for their counsels' bad behavior. Fed.Rules Civ.Proc.Rule 41(b), 28 U.S.C.A.

> Dahl v. City of Huntington Beach, 84 F.3d 363.

In cases that implicate important public policy concerns, court should weigh public interest in case and preference for disposing of cases on their merits prior to granting dismissal. Fed.Rules Civ.Proc.Rule 41(b), 28 U.S.C.A.

> Dahl v. City of Huntington Beach, 84 F.3d 363.

C.A.9 (Cal.) 1990. Agricultural producers' settlement of lien claims against food processor's customers did not violate any order of court and did not warrant involuntary dismissal of remaining claims; bankruptcy court's order that nonsettling defendants should have opportunity to examine proposed settlement did not prohibit submission of proposed settlement. Fed.Rules Civ.Proc.Rule 41(b), 28 U.S.C.A.; Bankruptcy Rule 7041, 11 U.S.C.A.

> In re T.H. Richards Processing Co., 910 F.2d 639.

C.A.9 (Cal.) 1989. State secret privilege could provide adequate, independent ground for upholding district court's dismissing claim of homosexual employee of government contractor that contractor's decision not to submit his application for security clearance deprived him of constitutional rights; government asserted that privilege in its motion to dismiss as one of two alternative grounds for dismissal and trial court order plainly reflected that state secret privilege ruling was a separate ground for dismissal order, independent of due process and mootness issues argued on appeal by employee. U.S.C.A. Const.Amend. 14.

> Weston v. Lockheed Missiles & Space Co., 881 F.2d 814.

C.A.9 (Cal.) 1988. Failure to exhaust non-judicial remedies should be raised in motion to dismiss or be treated as such if raised on motion for summary judgment.

> Ritza v. International Longshoremen's and Warehousemen's Union, 837 F.2d 365.

C.A.9 (Cal.) 1987. Before dismissing an action for failure to comply with order of court, district court judge should first be certain that other less drastic alternatives are not available. Fed.Rules Civ.Proc.Rule 41(b), 28 U.S.C.A.

> Eldridge v. Block, 832 F.2d 1132.

C.A.9 (Cal.) 1987. Courts have inherent equitable powers to dismiss actions or enter default judgments for failure to prosecute, contempt of court, or abuse of litigation practices.

> TeleVideo Systems, Inc. v. Heidenthal, 826 F.2d 915.

C.A.9 (Cal.) 1986. Action may be dismissed to ensure orderly administration of justice and integrity of district court's orders only in extreme circumstances, where party's deceptive conduct is willful, in bad faith or relates to matters in controversy in such a way as to interfere with rightful decision of case.

> U.S. v. National Medical Enterprises, Inc., 792 F.2d 906.

Before dismissing action for party's alleged deceptive conduct, district court should consider whether other party has suffered prejudice or irreparable harm.

> U.S. v. National Medical Enterprises, Inc., 792 F.2d 906.

C.A.9 (Cal.) 1986. Courts have inherent power to dismiss action if party has willfully deceived court and engaged in conduct utterly inconsistent with orderly administration of justice.

> North American Watch Corp. v. Princess Ermine Jewels, 786 F.2d 1447.

Sanctions of dismissal or default for deceiving the court are generally reserved for those extreme circumstances where deception is willful, in bad faith, or relates to matters in controversy that interfere with rightful decisions of a case.

> North American Watch Corp. v. Princess Ermine Jewels, 786 F.2d 1447.

C.A.9 (Cal.) 1985. District court did not err in dismissing action where pretrial order confirmed that plaintiff in the action was bound by misconduct, consisting of willful and deliberate disobediance of discovery order, willful concealment of evidence, and attempted fabrication of false evidence, of defendants in another action.

> Shearson Loeb Rhoades, Inc. v. Quinard, 751 F.2d 1102.

C.A.9 (Cal.) 1984. Buss v. Western Airlines, Inc., 738 F.2d 1053, certiorari denied 105 S.Ct. 968, 469 U.S. 1192, 83 L.Ed.2d 972.

C.A.9 (Cal.) 1982. Where court suspends proceedings in order to give preliminary deference to independent adjudicating body but further judicial proceedings are contemplated, then jurisdiction should be retained by stay of proceedings, not relinquished by a dismissal.

> Northern California Dist. Council of Hod Carriers, Bldg. and Const. Laborers, AFL-CIO v. Opinski, 673 F.2d 1074.

C.A.9 (Cal.) 1982. Forro Precision, Inc. v. International Business Machines Corp., 673 F.2d 1045, appeal after remand 745 F.2d 1283, certiorari denied 105 S.Ct. 2664, 471 U.S. 1130, 86 L.Ed.2d 280.

C.A.10 (Colo.) 1998. Dismissal of inmate's § 1983 action for violation of court rules and orders in connection with inmate's request to proceed under pseudonym rather than her true name was not abuse of discretion, as inmate's noncompliance interfered with judicial process, fair warning was given that case would be dismissed, and there was no reason to believe that lesser sanctions would be effective in compelling compliance with court's orders. 42 U.S.C.A. § 1983.

M.M. v. Zavaras, 139 F.3d 798.

C.A.10 (Colo.) 1994. Involuntary dismissals for failure to comply with court orders should be determined by reference to same criteria as dismissals for discovery violations. Fed.Rules Civ.Proc.Rules 37(b)(2), 41(b), 28 U.S.C.A.

Mobley v. McCormick, 40 F.3d 337, on remand 160 F.R.D. 599, affirmed 69 F.3d 548.

C.A.10 (Colo.) 1986. Under liberal rules applicable to pro se complaints, action is frivolous and subject to dismissal, if plaintiff cannot make rational argument on law and facts in support of his claim. 28 U.S.C.A. § 1915(d).

Van Sickle v. Holloway, 791 F.2d 1431.

District court did not abuse its discretion in dismissing, as frivolous and malicious, pro se complaint alleging that several state and federal judges violated and conspired to violate plaintiff's civil rights by intentionally failing to rule on his slander claim. 42 U.S.C.A. §§ 1983, 1985.

Van Sickle v. Holloway, 791 F.2d 1431.

C.A.10 (Colo.) 1985. Difficulties of fashioning relief should not result in the dismissal of a complaint at the pleading stage. Fed.Rules Civ.Proc.Rule 12(b)(6), 28 U.S.C.A.

Martinez v. Winner, 771 F.2d 424, opinion modified on denial of rehearing 778 F.2d 553, certiorari granted, vacated Tyus v. Martinez, 106 S.Ct. 1787, 475 U.S. 1138, 90 L.Ed.2d 333, on remand 800 F.2d 230.

C.A.10 (Colo.) 1985. Record demonstrated that district court, which dismissed civil suit after being advised by plaintiff state Attorney General that he had been unable to obtain from state court the business records of the defendant corporate entities which were the basis for a state criminal prosecution against individual defendants, and that he could not proceed to trial without them, did not understand that it had the power to order the release of the state court records; therefore, dismissal of federal civil case was not a proper exercise of the district court's discretion.

U.S. ex rel. Woodard v. Tynan, 757 F.2d 1085, on rehearing 776 F.2d 250.

C.A.2 (Conn.) 1998. District court abused its discretion in dismissing individual-capacity § 1983 claims against former employees of state-run juvenile secure facility based on plaintiff's failure to comply with court orders requiring him to supply former employees' addresses, since there was no clear "failure" on plaintiff's part to comply with court orders, especially considering that he was proceeding pro se from correctional institution, and he reasonably believed that he had complied with orders by filing motions for extension of time and for assistance in obtaining relevant information. 42 U.S.C.A. § 1983; Fed.Rules Civ.Proc.Rule 41(b), 28 U.S.C.A.

Spencer v. Doe, 139 F.3d 107.

Dismissals for failure to prosecute or failure to follow court order are "harsh remedy" that are appropriate only in extreme circumstances, and district courts should be especially hesitant to dismiss for procedural deficiencies where failure is by pro se litigant. Fed.Rules Civ.Proc. Rule 41(b), 28 U.S.C.A.

Spencer v. Doe, 139 F.3d 107.

Correctness of dismissal for failure to prosecute or failure to follow court order is determined in light of record as whole and in consideration of: (1) duration of plaintiff's failure to comply with court order; (2) whether plaintiff was on notice that failure to comply would result in dismissal; (3) whether defendants are likely to be prejudiced by further delay in proceedings; (4) balancing of court's interest in managing its docket with plaintiff's interest in receiving fair chance to be heard; and (5) whether judge has adequately considered sanction less drastic than dismissal; generally, no factor is dispositive. Fed.Rules Civ.Proc.Rule 41(b), 28 U.S.C.A.

Spencer v. Doe, 139 F.3d 107.

C.A.2 (Conn.) 1991. In some cases, effect of invocation of state secrets privilege may be so drastic as to require dismissal.

Zuckerbraun v. General Dynamics Corp., 935 F.2d 544.

If proper assertion of state secrets privilege precludes access to evidence necessary for plaintiff to state prima facie claim, dismissal is appropriate.

Zuckerbraun v. General Dynamics Corp., 935 F.2d 544.

Removal of information subject to state secrets privilege from wrongful death action against manufacturers, designers, and testers of weapon systems for wrongful death of sailor who was killed when his ship was fired on by foreign aircraft required dismissal; very subject matter of action was state secret and removal of privileged information left no evidence available to establish prima facie case.

> Zuckerbraun v. General Dynamics Corp., 935 F.2d 544.

C.A.2 (Conn.) 1988. Civil rights suit against Commissioner of Connecticut Department of Income Maintenance claiming that Commissioner violated federal law by failing to use state's true standard of need in calculating period of ineligibility following receipt of lump-sum payment raised claim capable of repetition yet evading review, and fact that AFDC applicants and recipients were no longer eligible for benefits pursuant to statute did not require dismissal for mootness. Social Security Act, § 402(a)(17), as amended, 42 U.S.C.A. § 602(a)(17); C.G.S.A. § 17–2(a, b); U.S.C.A. Const.Amend. 11; 42 U.S.C.A. § 1983.

> Mont v. Heintz, 849 F.2d 704.

C.A.11 (Fla.) 1996. District courts have broad discretion under Federal Rules of Civil Procedure to impose sanctions for failure to comply with court orders.

> Florida Power & Light Co. v. Allis Chalmers Corp., 85 F.3d 1514, rehearing denied.

C.A.11 (Fla.) 1995. Because dismissal is considered drastic sanction, district court may only dismiss action for failure to comply with local rules as last resort, when party engages in clear pattern of delay or willful contempt and district court specifically finds that lesser sanctions would not suffice. Fed.Rules Civ.Proc. Rule 41(b), 28 U.S.C.A.

> World Thrust Films, Inc. v. International Family Entertainment, Inc., 41 F.3d 1454, on remand 1996 WL 605957.

C.A.11 (Fla.) 1991. Dismissals of federal action in deference to concurrent proceeding in state or federal court, where traditional abstention principles are inapplicable, are strongly disfavored absent clearest of justifications to warrant dismissal; pendency of action in state court is generally no bar to proceedings concerning same matter in federal court having jurisdiction.

> Adams v. Sewell, 946 F.2d 757.

C.A.11 (Fla.) 1989. Although district court possesses inherent power to police its docket, and may impose sanctions ranging from reprimand to dismissal with prejudice, dismissal is warranted only upon clear record of delay or willful contempt and finding that lesser sanctions would not suffice.

> Mingo v. Sugar Cane Growers Co-op. of Florida, 864 F.2d 101.

C.A.11 (Fla.) 1986. District court has discretion to dismiss case with prejudice where plaintiff has in bad faith filed false affidavit of poverty. 28 U.S.C.A. § 1915(d).

> Dawson v. Lennon, 797 F.2d 934, rehearing denied 805 F.2d 1043.

Plaintiff's behavior in attempting to claim indigent status while failing to draw court's attention to previous authoritative determinations of other courts of his lack of indigency was sufficient evidence of bad faith to support district court's exercise of discretion to dismiss the case with prejudice, notwithstanding plaintiff's claim that he attempted to pay filing fees and withdrew his request for in forma pauperis status before district court adopted magistrate's report and dismissed the case with prejudice.

> Dawson v. Lennon, 797 F.2d 934, rehearing denied 805 F.2d 1043.

C.A.11 (Fla.) 1986. Invocation of in forma pauperis statute to dismiss prisoner's pro se complaint was inappropriate, where prisoner had paid required filing fee. 28 U.S.C.A. § 1915(d).

> Rodriguez-Mora v. Baker, 792 F.2d 1524.

C.A.11 (Ga.) 1993. Dismissal of § 1983 action was abuse of discretion, as it was based upon clearly erroneous factual determination that plaintiff had not kept court informed of his address changes; record clearly demonstrated that plaintiff filed three formal changes of address after being advised of his duty to do so. Fed.Rules Civ.Proc.Rule 41(b), 28 U.S.C.A.; U.S.Dist.Ct.Rules N.D.Ga., Civil Rule 230–2(c); 42 U.S.C.A. § 1983.

> Kilgo v. Ricks, 983 F.2d 189.

C.A.11 (Ga.) 1989. While dismissal is an extraordinary remedy, dismissal upon disregard of an order, especially where litigant has been forewarned, generally is not an abuse of discretion.

> Moon v. Newsome, 863 F.2d 835, rehearing denied 874 F.2d 821, certiorari denied 110 S.Ct. 180, 493 U.S. 863, 107 L.Ed.2d 135, rehearing denied 110 S.Ct. 380, 493 U.S. 960, 107 L.Ed.2d 364.

C.A.11 (Ga.) 1986. Not every inaccuracy in affidavit of poverty, no matter how minimal, should be construed as false allegation of poverty so as to cause loss of in forma pauperis eligibility and dismissal of complaint. 28 U.S.C.A. § 1915.

> Camp v. Oliver, 798 F.2d 434.

Purpose of statute governing affidavits of poverty for in forma pauperis proceedings that permits dismissal if affidavit of poverty is untrue is not to punish litigant whose affidavit contains insignificant discrepancy, but to weed out litigant who falsely understates his net worth in order to obtain in forma pauperis status to which he is not entitled based upon his true financial worth. 28 U.S.C.A. § 1915.

Camp v. Oliver, 798 F.2d 434.

Automatic dismissal of inmate's civil rights action with prejudice based upon determination that allegations of poverty in affidavit of poverty were untrue was improper; district court should first have determined whether considering facts as whole, inmate's inaccuracy foreclosed in forma pauperis eligibility, and if it so found, court should then have applied less severe sanctions such as revoking in forma pauperis status and accepting partial payment of filing fees or allowing inmate reasonable time in which to pay entire fee before dismissing petition with prejudice, or alternatively dismissing without prejudice, where there was no finding of bad faith, litigiousness, or manipulative tactics by inmate. 28 U.S.C.A. § 1915.

Camp v. Oliver, 798 F.2d 434.

C.A.11 (Ga.) 1986. District court may dismiss complaint of plaintiff seeking to proceed in forma pauperis if action is maliciously brought; however, district court must have reason to believe that suit was not brought in good faith.

Wright v. Newsome, 795 F.2d 964.

C.A.11 (Ga.) 1985. Failure of plaintiff to amend his defective complaint was not justified by fact that district court reminded plaintiff of the "basis in fact" requirement of federal rule and warned that sanctions would follow if the complaint were amended falsely or recklessly. Fed.Rules Civ.Proc.Rule 11, 28 U.S.C.A.

Friedlander v. Nims, 755 F.2d 810.

C.A.9 (Guam) 1988. Generally, district court must consider less severe alternatives and discuss them if it elects to dismiss the case for procedural violations.

U.S. for Use and Ben. of Wiltec Guam, Inc. v. Kahaluu Const. Co., Inc., 857 F.2d 600.

C.A.7 (Ill.) 1998. Trial court did not abuse its discretion in granting automobile manufacturer's motion for involuntary dismissal of action brought by former owner of dealership where owner had failed to comply with conditions court had placed on owner's voluntary dismissal of his prior action against manufacturer, which required that owner pay manufacturer's attorney fees and costs incurred for trial preparation in first action, that rulings and orders in first action would apply in subsequent actions, and that parties would stand ready for trial upon refiling. Fed.Rules Civ.Proc.Rule 41(b), 28 U.S.C.A.

LeBlang Motors, Ltd. v. Subaru of America, Inc., 148 F.3d 680.

Actions of plaintiff, whose initial action had been voluntarily dismissed on condition that all pretrial rulings and orders would apply in subsequently filed case, in bringing interlocutory pretrial appeal of orders after filing second action, violated condition of prior voluntary dismissal and warranted involuntary dismissal of second action. Fed.Rules Civ.Proc.Rule 41(b), 28 U.S.C.A.

LeBlang Motors, Ltd. v. Subaru of America, Inc., 148 F.3d 680.

C.A.7 (Ill.) 1997. Dismissal of plaintiff's § 1983 action as sanction was not abuse of discretion where sanction was based on repeated misconduct including communicating directly with court, failing to timely produce discoverable documents, inaccurately verifying that his document production was complete and thereafter using undisclosed documents as exhibits in deposition, improperly threatening to bring criminal charges against defendants if settlement demands were not met, and attempting to directly contact individual defendants in violation of court order. 42 U.S.C.A. § 1983; Fed.Rules Civ.Proc.Rules 37(b)(2)(C), 41(b), 28 U.S.C.A.

Ladien v. Astrachan, 128 F.3d 1051.

C.A.7 (Ill.) 1995. Facts that plaintiff did not have counsel and that district court judge did not expressly call to plaintiff's attention local rule requiring plaintiff to pay docket fee within 15 days of denial of application to proceed in forma pauperis (IFP) did not compel finding that district court could not dismiss suit for delay in payment. U.S.Dist.Ct.Rules N.D.Ill., Rule 11, subd. D.

Williams-Guice v. Board of Educ. of City of Chicago, 45 F.3d 161, rehearing denied.

C.A.7 (Ill.) 1995. Properly certified class action survives mootness of original representative's claims, while individual action must be dismissed in identical circumstances.

Nelson v. Murphy, 44 F.3d 497, rehearing denied, certiorari denied 116 S.Ct. 671, 516 U.S. 1027, 133 L.Ed.2d 521.

C.A.7 (Ill.) 1994. At pleading stage, general factual allegation of injury resulting from defendant's conduct is sufficient to overcome motion to dismiss for lack of standing, for on motion to dismiss court presumes that general allegations embrace those specific facts that are necessary to support claim. U.S.C.A. Const. Art. 3, § 2, cl. 1 et seq.

Doe v. County of Montgomery, Ill., 41 F.3d 1156, on remand 915 F.Supp. 32.

C.A.7 (Ill.) 1994. Plaintiff's failure to comply with court's orders interferes with conduct of litigation and justifies dismissal.

U.S. v. Golden Elevator, Inc., 27 F.3d 301.

C.A.7 (Ill.) 1993. Frivolousness is independent jurisdictional basis for dismissing suit.

Harrell v. U.S., 13 F.3d 232.

For references to other topics, see Descriptive-Word Index

C.A.7 (Ill.) 1993. As general rule, federal suit may be dismissed for reasons of wise judicial administration whenever it is duplicative of parallel action already pending in another federal court.

Serlin v. Arthur Andersen & Co., 3 F.3d 221.

District courts are accorded a great deal of latitude and discretion in determining whether one action is duplicative of another, but generally, suit is duplicative if claims, parties, and available relief do not significantly differ between the two actions.

Serlin v. Arthur Andersen & Co., 3 F.3d 221.

C.A.7 (Ill.) 1993. While court is not necessarily required to take less severe action before imposing sanction of dismissal, dismissal should be employed only if district court has determined that it could not fashion equally effective but less drastic remedy.

Ball v. City of Chicago, 2 F.3d 752, suggestion for rehearing denied.

C.A.7 (Ill.) 1990. District court's dismissal of employment discrimination action as sanction for noncompliance with court rules and orders was not abuse of discretion; employees were aware that conduct by attorneys might result in dismissal given fact that employees appeared before district court where they heard judge vent his frustration over their counsel's delays and further, motion to dismiss complaint as sanction for failure to comply with pretrial procedures was pending for ten months before it was finally granted.

Anderson v. United Parcel Service, 915 F.2d 313.

C.A.7 (Ill.) 1990. Although ground upon which Court of Appeals affirms dismissal should be one raised by appellee, exception exists where waived ground makes suit frivolous; frivolous suit, because it is a complete waste of judicial effort, can be dismissed even if parties did not recognize its frivolousness.

Frederick v. Marquette Nat. Bank, 911 F.2d 1.

When statute expressly confines liability to X's and defendant is a Y, suit is frivolous and may be dismissed as such.

Frederick v. Marquette Nat. Bank, 911 F.2d 1.

C.A.7 (Ill.) 1989. Court need not impose sanction less severe than dismissal for plaintiff's lack of prosecution or failure to comply with court orders, where record of plaintiff's dilatory conduct is clear. Fed.Rules Civ.Proc.Rule 41(b), 28 U.S.C.A.

Pyramid Energy, Ltd. v. Heyl & Patterson, Inc., 869 F.2d 1058.

Court need not consider meritorious nature of action, prior to dismissing suit based on plaintiff's lack of prosecution or failure to comply with orders of court. Fed.Rules Civ.Proc. Rule 41(b), 28 U.S.C.A.

Pyramid Energy, Ltd. v. Heyl & Patterson, Inc., 869 F.2d 1058.

C.A.7 (Ill.) 1988. Conflict of interest arising from fact that attorney and special assistant for EEOC involved in bringing Title VII suit against national retailer were members of women's organization which had campaigned against retailer was not cured by attorney's and assistant's severance of connection with organization, where attorney was left in charge of case, but conflicts did not require dismissal of suit; conflicts occurred before trial, although it was possible that influence of conflicts at least to some extent carried over to trial, attorney did not try case, and all issues were fairly aired in entirety before two impartial judges. Civil Rights Act of 1964, § 701 et seq., as amended, 42 U.S.C.A. § 2000e et seq.

E.E.O.C. v. Sears, Roebuck & Co., 839 F.2d 302.

C.A.7 (Ill.) 1987. Frivolous suit does not engage subject matter jurisdiction of federal courts; dismissal of such suit is therefore jurisdictional.

Cronson v. Clark, 810 F.2d 662, certiorari denied 108 S.Ct. 199, 484 U.S. 871, 98 L.Ed.2d 151.

C.A.7 (Ill.) 1983. Redding v. Fairman, 717 F.2d 1105, certiorari denied 104 S.Ct. 1282, 465 U.S. 1025, 79 L.Ed.2d 685, appeal after remand Akbar v. Fairman, 788 F.2d 1273.

C.A.7 (Ind.) 1989. Denial of RICO defendant's motion to dismiss plaintiffs' common-law fraud claim, on ground that plaintiffs had indicated their intent to seek dismissal of claim two weeks earlier, was not abuse of discretion, where claim had been in pleadings for more than one year and defendant was not prejudiced as result.

Ashland Oil, Inc. v. Arnett, 875 F.2d 1271.

C.A.7 (Ind.) 1988. Plaintiff's inability to identify individual defendants by name does not warrant dismissal of claim as frivolous if allegations in complaint allow for specific persons to be subsequently identified with reasonable certainty. 28 U.S.C.A. § 1915(d).

Smith-Bey v. Hospital Adm'r, 841 F.2d 751.

C.A.7 (Ind.) 1987. A court reviewing dismissal of action or claim for failure of plaintiff to prosecute or to comply with procedural rules or court order must consider procedural history of case as well as status of case at time of dismissal. Fed.Rules Civ.Proc.Rule 41(b), 28 U.S.C.A.

> Roland v. Salem Contract Carriers, Inc., 811 F.2d 1175.

C.A.7 (Ind.) 1984. When plaintiff elects form of abstention in which plaintiff goes to state court just to pursue his state claims, the state court decides no federal questions, and plaintiff comes back to federal court to finish his suit, the stay of federal proceedings is a genuine stay, and not a form of dismissal.

> Mazanec v. North Judson-San Pierre School Corp., 750 F.2d 625, appeal decided 763 F.2d 845, on remand 614 F.Supp. 1152, affirmed 798 F.2d 230.

C.A.7 (Ind.) 1984. Skillern v. Bolger, 725 F.2d 1121, certiorari denied 105 S.Ct. 129, 469 U.S. 835, 83 L.Ed.2d 70.

C.A.5 (La.) 1989. After jury verdict that railroad was not negligent in connection with injury sustained by plaintiff in attempt to open railroad's boxcar, court properly dismissed with prejudice railroad's third-party complaint against plaintiff's employer for cost of defense, despite indemnity agreement by which employer agreed to defend railroad in such actions, and despite fact that jury failed to apportion fault to other possible actors; although plaintiff's and employer's alleged fault, if any, was submitted to jury, jury did not resolve those issues because interrogatories, which railroad's counsel approved, instructed them not to do so.

> Rouillier v. Illinois Cent. Gulf R.R., 886 F.2d 105.

C.A.5 (La.) 1988. Court could dismiss prisoner's civil rights case, after ordering prisoner to exhaust prison remedies on pain of dismissal with prejudice, when prisoner failed during the interim to pursue the prison grievance procedure. 28 U.S.C.A. § 1915(d); 42 U.S.C.A. §§ 1983, 1997e.

> Lay v. Anderson, 837 F.2d 231.

C.A.5 (La.) 1987. Dismissal of former college administrator's civil rights action with prejudice due to plaintiff's counsel's tardy response to discovery request, his late submission of pretrial order, and his failure to make timely filings during two weeks before trial date was not justified, where aggregate delay caused by misconduct did not amount to significant period of total inactivity, counsel was fully ready for trial on date court set, and plaintiff himself was innocent of any misconduct. Fed.Rules Civ. Proc.Rule 16(f), 28 U.S.C.A.

> John v. State of La., 828 F.2d 1129, appeal after remand 899 F.2d 1441, rehearing denied.

C.A.5 (La.) 1987. District court has power under in forma pauperis statute to dismiss action for forgery of signature on affidavit attesting to poverty, in view of the fact that such conduct is directly related to litigant's privilege to proceed at expense of government, despite the fact that litigant's allegation of poverty is true. 28 U.S.C.A. § 1915(d).

> Lay v. Justices-Middle Dist. Court, 811 F.2d 285.

C.A.5 (La.) 1986. In forma pauperis suit filed by federal prisoner against presiding federal trial judge, prosecutors, and several witnesses at his trial for conspiring to violate civil rights of a person by murdering him was properly dismissed as being frivolous or malicious, in light of immunity given judicial officers in performance of their duties, affirmance of prisoner's conviction on direct appeal, and rejection of prisoner's collateral attack upon his conviction. 28 U.S.C.A. §§ 1915(d), 2255.

> Kimble v. Beckner, 806 F.2d 1256.

C.A.5 (La.) 1985. When a plaintiff files a second complaint alleging same cause of action as a prior, pending, related action, second complaint may be dismissed.

> Oliney v. Gardner, 771 F.2d 856.

C.A.1 (Me.) 1990. Litigant commits "fraud on court" when litigant and attorney concoct some unconscionable scheme calculated to impair court's ability fairly and impartially to adjudicate dispute.

> Sandstrom v. ChemLawn Corp., 904 F.2d 83.

C.A.4 (Md.) 1990. Mere claim in complaint that right exists under federal law suffices to avoid summary dismissal unless it is facially insubstantial or frivolous, and even nonfrivolous claim that remedy may be implied from federal statute will suffice.

> Ridenour v. Andrews Federal Credit Union, 897 F.2d 715, rehearing denied, on remand 1990 WL 56489.

C.A.4 (Md.) 1986. Shareholder's individual securities fraud claim was properly dismissed after she was offered full amount of damages to which she claimed to be entitled, although she was not offered attorney fees and offer of judgment ignored her "class/derivative" claim.

> Zimmerman v. Bell, 800 F.2d 386.

C.A.4 (Md.) 1985. State secrets privilege warranted dismissal of defamation action brought by individual who worked on government marine mammal project against publisher of article which allegedly libelously charged the former with espionage, specifically, unauthorized sale of top secret marine mammal weapons system to other countries, where the Navy interposed military secrets objection to calling of certain witnesses as experts and there was no way the case could be tried without compromising sensitive military secrets.

> Fitzgerald v. Penthouse Intern., Ltd., 776 F.2d 1236.

C.A.1 (Mass.) 1996. District court has broad authority to enforce pre-trial discipline and to dismiss case for failure to obey pre-trial orders after considering pertinent circumstances, including severity of violation, legitimacy of party's excuse, repetition of violations, deliberateness of misconduct, mitigating excuses, prejudice, and adequacy of lesser instructions. Fed.Rules Civ.Proc.Rules 16(f), 41(b), 28 U.S.C.A.

> Robson v. Hallenbeck, 81 F.3d 1.

Repeated disobedience of scheduling order is inherently prejudicial, when determining whether pattern of misconduct justifies dismissal, in light of resulting disruption of court's schedule and preparation of other parties. Fed. Rules Civ.Proc.Rules 16(f), 41(b), 28 U.S.C.A.

> Robson v. Hallenbeck, 81 F.3d 1.

Succession of pre-trial scheduling order violations, indicating general unwillingness to comply with court order, may justify dismissal. Fed.Rules Civ.Proc.Rules 16(f), 41(b), 28 U.S.C.A.

> Robson v. Hallenbeck, 81 F.3d 1.

C.A.1 (Mass.) 1995. Exclusion of health care provider from Medicare provider rolls had been based solely on fact that his medical license had been revoked in New York for professional misconduct and, thus, exclusion did not confer additional stigma or result in collateral consequences supporting exception from mootness doctrine otherwise requiring dismissal of suit challenging exclusion after reinstatement to Medicare provider rolls.

> Friedman v. Shalala, 46 F.3d 115, certiorari denied 115 S.Ct. 2287, 515 U.S. 1127, 132 L.Ed.2d 289.

C.A.1 (Mass.) 1992. When evidence of "fraud on the court" is adduced prior to trial, district court may fashion appropriate pretrial remedy to cure effect of any misconduct.

> Fernandez v. Leonard, 963 F.2d 459, opinion modified.

District court's choice of remedy for "fraud on the court" is committed to broad discretion of trial court, and Court of Appeals reviews such decisions for abuse only.

> Fernandez v. Leonard, 963 F.2d 459, opinion modified.

Dismissal of prosecution for fraud on the court based on pretrial motion is extreme remedy which should not lightly be engaged.

> Fernandez v. Leonard, 963 F.2d 459, opinion modified.

Denying motion to dismiss made on grounds of fraud on the court allegedly resulting from government's tampering with witness was not abuse of discretion; letting allegations of misconduct to go before jury and lodging complaint of government abuse with Department of Justice were adequate remedies.

> Fernandez v. Leonard, 963 F.2d 459, opinion modified.

Declining to make pretrial finding of fraud on the court resulting from government's alleged witness tampering was not in error since allegations of misconduct turned on witness' credibility and referring credibility issues to jury was appropriate.

> Fernandez v. Leonard, 963 F.2d 459, opinion modified.

C.A.1 (Mass.) 1989. Although dismissal for abuse of judicial process need not be preceded by other, less drastic sanctions, it is extreme remedy, and should not lightly be engaged.

> Aoude v. Mobil Oil Corp., 892 F.2d 1115.

Before dismissing for abuse of judicial process, judge should carefully balance policy favoring adjudication on merits with competing policies such as need to maintain institutional integrity and desirability of deterring future misconduct.

> Aoude v. Mobil Oil Corp., 892 F.2d 1115.

"Fraud on the court," upon which dismissal of action can be based, occurs where it can be demonstrated, clearly and convincingly, that party has sentiently set in motion some unconscionable scheme calculated to interfere with judicial system's ability impartially to adjudicate matter by improperly influencing trier or unfairly hampering presentation of opposing party's claim or defense.

> Aoude v. Mobil Oil Corp., 892 F.2d 1115.

Service station operator's conduct in fabricating purchase agreement, and in allowing his counsel to annex bogus agreement to complaint seeking to force franchisor to accept his operation of station, constituted "fraud on the court," warranting dismissal of action.

> Aoude v. Mobil Oil Corp., 892 F.2d 1115.

Federal district court can order dismissal or default where litigant has stooped to level of fraud on the court.

> Aoude v. Mobil Oil Corp., 892 F.2d 1115.

Fraud on court practiced in original suit warranted dismissal of second suit based on parallel grounds and filed when fraud was discovered.

> Aoude v. Mobil Oil Corp., 892 F.2d 1115.

C.A.6 (Mich.) 1998. Dismissal of civil rights action as result of plaintiffs' failure to timely respond to defendants' summary judgment motions, pursuant to local rule, was abuse of discretion, absent specific finding of either bad faith by plaintiffs or prejudice to defendants as result of delay or notice that court was contemplating dismissal. Fed.Rules Civ.Proc. Rule 41(b), 28 U.S.C.A.; U.S.Dist.Ct.Rules E.D.Mich., Rule 7.1(c).

> Stough v. Mayville Community Schools, 138 F.3d 612.

When contemplating involuntary dismissal of action, court must consider: (1) whether party's failure to cooperate is due to willfulness, bad faith, or fault; (2) whether adversary was prejudiced by dilatory conduct of party; (3) whether dismissed party was warned that failure to cooperate could lead to dismissal; and (4) whether less drastic sanctions were imposed or considered before dismissal was ordered. Fed. Rules Civ.Proc.Rule 41(b), 28 U.S.C.A.

> Stough v. Mayville Community Schools, 138 F.3d 612.

C.A.6 (Mich.) 1997. Voters' failure to comply with National Voter Registration Act's (NVRA) notice provision before suing state of Michigan and various State officials for their failure to comply with Act did not warrant dismissal; purpose of notice provision was to provide states in violation of Act opportunity to attempt compliance before facing litigation, but Michigan had already received actual notice of its noncompliance, and already made clear its refusal to comply. National Voter Registration Act of 1993, § 11(b), 42 U.S.C.A. § 1973gg–9(b).

> Association of Community Organizations for Reform Now v. Miller, 129 F.3d 833.

C.A.6 (Mich.) 1994. Upon entry of summary judgment in corporation's favor on its breach of contract claims, district court could dismiss as moot breach-of-fiduciary-duty and conversion claims asserted by corporation as alternate basis for recovery, notwithstanding corporation's desire to litigate those claims to establish the nondischargeability of judgment debt in event that defendant filed for bankruptcy; district court's dismissal of the claims as moot would not have any res judicata or collateral estoppel effect on dischargeability issues if defendant subsequently filed for bankruptcy.

> In re Dollar Corp., 25 F.3d 1320.

C.A.6 (Mich.) 1985. Case may be dismissed on jurisprudential considerations if court has no present ability to provide meaningful remedy; in making this decision, court should determine whether it has ability to provide any effective remedy, not just remedy demanded by plaintiff in its pleadings. Fed.Rules Civ.Proc.Rule 54(c), 28 U.S.C.A.

> Detroit, Toledo and Ironton R. Co. v. Consolidated Rail Corp., 767 F.2d 274.

C.A.8 (Minn.) 1992. Plaintiff's threats against defendant's witnesses did not require dismissal where court considered plaintiff's troubled psychiatric background and issued a restraining order backed with the assurance that the suit would be dismissed if the restraining order were disobeyed.

> Frumkin v. Mayo Clinic, 965 F.2d 620.

C.A.8 (Minn.) 1991. District court did not err in dismissing age discrimination claim on ground that opt-in plaintiffs knowingly and voluntarily released his rights under the Age Discrimination in Employment Act (ADEA) when he signed negotiated termination agreement, district court found that employee had access to agreement for considerable time, chose not to consult an attorney, was able to negotiate addition of favorable terms to agreement, and stated that agreement was written in clear simple language, granted employee severance benefits in excess of those required by contract or statute, and that employee decided to sign agreement of his own free will. Age Discrimination in Employment Act of 1967, §§ 2–17, as amended, 29 U.S.C.A. §§ 621–634.

> Ulvin v. Northwestern Nat. Life Ins. Co., 943 F.2d 862, certiorari denied 112 S.Ct. 970, 502 U.S. 1073, 117 L.Ed.2d 135.

C.A.8 (Minn.) 1984. Pursuant to Social Security Disability Benefits Reform Act, which directed court to remand to Secretary of Health and Human Services cases of persons whose social security disability benefits were terminated and who were unnamed members of class action relating to medical improvement pending as of September 19, 1984, class action concerning medical improvement cases would be dismissed. Social Security Disability Benefits Reform Act of 1984, § 2(d)(3, 4, 5), 98 Stat. 1794.

> Polaski v. Heckler, 751 F.2d 943, on remand 606 F.Supp. 549, certiorari granted, vacated Bowen v. Polaski, 106 S.Ct. 2885, 476 U.S. 1167, 90 L.Ed.2d 974, on remand 804 F.2d 456, certiorari denied 107 S.Ct. 3211, 482 U.S. 927, 96 L.Ed.2d 698.

C.A.5 (Miss.) 1996. District court abused its discretion in dismissing pro se prisoner's suit without prejudice for failure of plaintiff to return disclosure form in timely manner; because of operation of statute of limitations, dismissal operated as dismissal with prejudice, which was appropriate only if failure to comply with order was result of purposeful delay or contumaciousness, and if lesser sanctions were employed before dismissing action; however, record contained no indication that plaintiff failed to comply with court order to secure delay or out of contumaciousness, and district court did not employ lesser sanctions before dismissing action.

> Long v. Simmons, 77 F.3d 878.

C.A.8 (Mo.) 1998. Sanction imposed by district court for failure to prosecute claim or comply with court orders must be proportionate to litigant's transgression.

> Rodgers v. Curators of University of Missouri, 135 F.3d 1216.

Dismissal of university student's discrimination action against university with prejudice on ground that student's conduct constituted wilful disregard of court orders was not abuse of discretion, in view of multiple instances of student's noncompliance with court orders and dilatory tactics, notwithstanding student's cognitive disabilities that resulted from head injury. Fed.Rules Civ.Proc.Rule 41(b), 28 U.S.C.A.

> Rodgers v. Curators of University of Missouri, 135 F.3d 1216.

District court did not abuse its discretion in dismissing student's discrimination claims against university, based on student's failure to prosecute and comply with court orders, without first imposing lesser sanctions or explaining why lesser sanctions would have been ineffective, as any lesser sanction would have involved further delay or forced university to try its case without completing discovery.

> Rodgers v. Curators of University of Missouri, 135 F.3d 1216.

C.A.8 (Mo.) 1997. District court has power to dismiss litigant's cause of action when litigant fails to comply with court's orders or for intentional delay, and need only find that litigant acted deliberately rather than accidentally, and need not find bad faith. Fed.Rules Civ. Proc.Rule 41(b), 28 U.S.C.A.

> Hutchins v. A.G. Edwards & Sons, Inc., 116 F.3d 1256.

Dismissal with prejudice is extreme sanction that should be used only in cases of willful disobedience of court order, or where litigant exhibits pattern of intentional delay. Fed.Rules Civ.Proc.Rule 41(b), 28 U.S.C.A.

> Hutchins v. A.G. Edwards & Sons, Inc., 116 F.3d 1256.

District court considering whether to dismiss cause of action involuntarily should weigh its need to advance its burdened docket against consequence of irrevocably extinguishing litigant's claim and consider whether less severe sanction could remedy effect of litigant's transgressions on court and resulting prejudice to opposing party. Fed.Rules Civ.Proc.Rule 41(b), 28 U.S.C.A.

> Hutchins v. A.G. Edwards & Sons, Inc., 116 F.3d 1256.

Employees' persistent refusal to properly answer interrogatories in employment discrimination case or pay sanctions, and their disregard of district court's orders made clear that their conduct was deliberate rather than acci-

dental and warranted extreme sanction of dismissal with prejudice, where employees failed to respond to less severe sanctions, including numerous extensions of time. Fed.Rules Civ. Proc.Rule 41(b), 28 U.S.C.A.

> Hutchins v. A.G. Edwards & Sons, Inc., 116 F.3d 1256.

C.A.8 (Mo.) 1997. To protect important interests in expeditious treatment of cases in district courts and right of parties not to suffer prejudice as result of opposing party's dilatory conduct, district court has power to dismiss cases when parties fail to comply with its rules. Fed.Rules Civ.Proc.Rule 41(b), 28 U.S.C.A.

> Mann v. Lewis, 108 F.3d 145.

Dismissal with prejudice for failure to comply with court order is extreme sanction and should be used only in cases of willful disobedience of court order or persistent failure to prosecute complaint. Fed.Rules Civ.Proc.Rule 41(b), 28 U.S.C.A.

> Mann v. Lewis, 108 F.3d 145.

In deciding whether to dismiss case for failure to comply with court order, district court should weigh court's need to advance its heavy docket against consequence of irreversibly extinguishing litigant's claim and consider whether any less-severe sanction could adequately remedy effect of delay on court and prejudice to opposing party. Fed.Rules Civ.Proc.Rule 41(b), 28 U.S.C.A.

> Mann v. Lewis, 108 F.3d 145.

Although sanctions were warranted by medical malpractice plaintiff's failure to comply with pretrial order that directed parties to comply with number of requirements not less than ten days before trial, and plaintiff's failure to comply with order requiring him to provide by certain date answers that his expert had refused to provide at his deposition, dismissal with prejudice was excessive, as plaintiff did not himself engage in any conduct designed to delay proceedings or frustrate defendants' preparations for trial, but rather, failure to comply was due solely to plaintiff's attorney's lack of diligence; proper remedy was to dismiss case without prejudice, and to assess costs against plaintiff's counsel personally. Fed.Rules Civ.Proc. Rule 41(b), 28 U.S.C.A.

> Mann v. Lewis, 108 F.3d 145.

C.A.8 (Mo.) 1996. Case is properly dismissed as "moot" if it has lost its character as present, live controversy of kind that must exist to avoid advisory opinions on abstract questions of law.

> St. Louis Fire Fighters Ass'n Intern. Ass'n of Fire Fighters Local 73 v. City of St. Louis, Mo., 96 F.3d 323.

C.A.8 (Mo.) 1996. When defendant seeks to dismiss action by putative class representative by offering payment for any damages putative class representative could prove, judgment should be entered against putative class representative on defendant's offer of payment only where class certification has been properly denied and offer satisfies representative's entire demand for injuries and costs of suit.

> Alpern v. UtiliCorp United, Inc., 84 F.3d 1525.

C.A.8 (Mo.) 1994. Action may be dismissed under rule providing for dismissal for failure to prosecute or comply with rules or order of court if plaintiff has failed to comply with any order of court. Fed.Rules Civ.Proc. Rule 41(b), 28 U.S.C.A.

> Aziz v. Wright, 34 F.3d 587, certiorari denied 115 S.Ct. 752, 513 U.S. 1090, 130 L.Ed.2d 652.

C.A.8 (Mo.) 1992. Fraud on court is grounds for dismissal with prejudice.

> Peerless Indus. Paint Coatings Co. v. Can-am Steel Corp., 979 F.2d 685.

C.A.8 (Mo.) 1991. District court properly dismissed products liability action against snap hook manufacturer due to plaintiff's fraud on the court; plaintiff had used homemade hook at time of his accident, undermining entire theory of his claim, and had repeatedly lied under oath regarding presence of homemade hook and changed his story only after four people, including his own lawyer, contradicted his testimony.

> Nichols v. Klein Tools, Inc., 949 F.2d 1047.

C.A.8 (Mo.) 1988. Dismissal of products liability action with prejudice due to counsel's failure to follow court orders was excessive sanction; though counsel failed to keep court apprised of defendant's bankruptcy as requested, monetary or practice sanction against counsel would have been more appropriate.

> Dennis v. A.H. Robins Co., Inc., 860 F.2d 871.

C.A.8 (Mo.) 1988. Dismissal of prison inmates' § 1983 action with prejudice, as Rule 11 sanction, was not abuse of discretion where inmates had submitted voluminous amount of frivolous documents and had intentionally refused to comply with court order to file amended complaint. Fed.Rules Civ.Proc.Rule 11, 28 U.S.C.A.; 42 U.S.C.A. § 1983.

> American Inmate Paralegal Assoc. v. Cline, 859 F.2d 59, certiorari denied Tyler v. Cline, 109 S.Ct. 565, 488 U.S. 996, 102 L.Ed.2d 590.

C.A.8 (Mo.) 1986. District court may dismiss action on its own initiative for plaintiff's failure to comply with court order; dismissal with prejudice, however, is drastic sanction which should be exercised sparingly. Fed.Rules Civ.Proc.Rule 41(b), 28 U.S.C.A.

> Brown v. Frey, 806 F.2d 801.

C.A.8 (Mo.) 1985. Action may not be dismissed as frivolous unless it is beyond doubt that petitioner can prove no facts in support of his claim which would entitle him to relief.

> Murphy v. Missouri Dept. of Correction, 769 F.2d 502.

C.A.8 (Mo.) 1984. Hechenberger v. Western Elec. Co., Inc., 742 F.2d 453, certiorari denied 105 S.Ct. 1182, 469 U.S. 1212, 84 L.Ed.2d 330.

C.A.8 (Mo.) 1975. Brennan v. McDonnell Douglas Corp., 519 F.2d 718, on remand Houghton v. McDonnell Douglas Corp., 413 F.Supp. 1230, reversed 553 F.2d 561, certiorari denied 98 S.Ct. 506, 434 U.S. 966, 54 L.Ed.2d 451, on remand 474 F.Supp. 193, affirmed in part, reversed in part 627 F.2d 858, on remand 553 F.Supp. 16, reversed 716 F.2d 526.

C.A.9 (Nev.) 1998. After government defendant validly invokes state secrets privilege, plaintiff's case goes forward based on evidence not covered by privilege, but, if, after further proceedings, plaintiff cannot prove prima facie elements of her claim with nonprivileged evidence, then court may dismiss claim .

> Kasza v. Browner, 133 F.3d 1159.

Notwithstanding plaintiff's ability to produce nonprivileged evidence, if very subject matter of action is state secret, then court should dismiss plaintiff's action based solely on invocation of state secrets privilege.

> Kasza v. Browner, 133 F.3d 1159.

C.A.9 (Nev.) 1995. Inmate's pro se civil rights action was properly dismissed for inmate's violation of local rule by failing to file opposition to motion to dismiss; record indicated that inmate was given proper notice and ample opportunity to respond. U.S.Dist.Ct. Rules D.Nev., Rule 140–6.

> Ghazali v. Moran, 46 F.3d 52, certiorari denied 116 S.Ct. 119, 516 U.S. 838, 133 L.Ed.2d 69.

Failure to follow district court's local rules is proper ground for dismissal.

> Ghazali v. Moran, 46 F.3d 52, certiorari denied 116 S.Ct. 119, 516 U.S. 838, 133 L.Ed.2d 69.

C.A.9 (Nev.) 1991. An actual intent to harass or abuse the defendants was not required for application of rule that two voluntary dismissals of claims against the defendant operated as an adjudication on the merits. Fed.Rules Civ.Proc.Rules 41, 41(a), 28 U.S.C.A.

> Lake at Las Vegas Investors Group, Inc. v. Pacific Malibu Development Corp., 933 F.2d 724, rehearing denied, certiorari denied 112 S.Ct. 1295, 503 U.S. 920, 117 L.Ed.2d 518.

Dismissal of all defendants was not necessary for application of rule that two voluntary dismissals of claims against the defendant operated as an adjudication on the merits. Fed. Rules Civ.Proc.Rules 41, 41(a), 28 U.S.C.A.

> Lake at Las Vegas Investors Group, Inc. v. Pacific Malibu Development Corp., 933 F.2d 724, rehearing denied, certiorari denied 112 S.Ct. 1295, 503 U.S. 920, 117 L.Ed.2d 518.

Wholly-owned subsidiary and partnership in which that subsidiary was the general partner could invoke rights of subsidiary's parent for purposes of res judicata under rule allowing two voluntary dismissals of claims against a defendant to operate as an adjudication on the merits. Fed.Rules Civ.Proc.Rule 41(a)(1), 28 U.S.C.A.

> Lake at Las Vegas Investors Group, Inc. v. Pacific Malibu Development Corp., 933 F.2d 724, rehearing denied, certiorari denied 112 S.Ct. 1295, 503 U.S. 920, 117 L.Ed.2d 518.

C.A.9 (Nev.) 1987. Ordinarily, federal jurisdiction is not negated by likelihood that complaint may fail to state cause of action, inasmuch as that is grounds for dismissal on merits and not for lack of jurisdiction, but dismissal for want of jurisdiction may occur where claim is wholly insubstantial and frivolous.

> Pratt v. Sumner, 807 F.2d 817.

Felony prisoner's action seeking, inter alia, declaratory judgment that notice and hearing were required prior to return of printed materials sent to prisoners and that soft-cover books could not be banned on "publisher or bookstore only" basis was not frivolous, and district court thus had jurisdiction over action, given that neither Supreme Court nor Ninth Circuit had addressed constitutionality of total ban on felony prisoner's receipt of books, including all soft-cover legal materials, from sources other than publishers and bookstores. 28 U.S.C.A. § 1915(c, d); 28 U.S.C.(1976 Ed.) § 1343(3).

> Pratt v. Sumner, 807 F.2d 817.

C.A.1 (N.H.) 1993. District court has power to dismiss complaint when plaintiff fails to comply with Federal Rules of Civil Procedure, including "short and plain statement" requirement of rule governing pleading. Fed.Rules Civ.Proc.Rule 8(a)(2), 28 U.S.C.A.

> Kuehl v. F.D.I.C., 8 F.3d 905, rehearing denied, certiorari denied 114 S.Ct. 1545, 511 U.S. 1034, 128 L.Ed.2d 196.

C.A.3 (N.J.) 1992. Dismissal of class action is required when claims of named plaintiffs become moot before class certification. Fed. Rules Civ.Proc.Rule 23, 28 U.S.C.A.

> Lusardi v. Xerox Corp., 975 F.2d 964.

C.A.3 (N.J.) 1989. Because meritorious claims or defenses may be precluded, dismissal for procedural default should be imposed only as sanction of last resort.

> Livera v. First Nat. State Bank of New Jersey, 879 F.2d 1186, rehearing denied, certiorari denied 110 S.Ct. 332, 493 U.S. 937, 107 L.Ed.2d 322.

C.A.2 (N.Y.) 1996. Former probationary corrections officer's state law claims for retaliatory discharge were properly dismissed, in the former officer's § 1983 action against county undersheriff for alleged discharge in violation of First Amendment, after jury awarded the former officer back pay through date of verdict on her § 1983 claim and made factual determination that reinstatement was inappropriate; state law provided no theory for additional damages. U.S.C.A. Const.Amend. 1; 42 U.S.C.A. § 1983; N.Y.McKinney's Civil Service Law § 75–b.

> Sagendorf-Teal v. County of Rensselaer, 100 F.3d 270.

C.A.2 (N.Y.) 1996. District court erred in dismissing pro se litigant's supplemental complaint for violation of court order requiring its filing within 60 days, where noncompliance was no more than 39 days, defendants did not complain about tardiness, litigant was not warned that failure to comply would result in dismissal, delay did not prejudice defendants or congest district court's docket. Fed.Rules Civ.Proc.Rule 41(b), 28 U.S.C.A.

> Lucas v. Miles, 84 F.3d 532, on remand 1997 WL 677155.

C.A.2 (N.Y.) 1995. Relator's qui tam claims under False Claims Act would be dismissed with prejudice, as opposed to without prejudice, since relator's failure to file complaint under seal and serve United States frustrated statutory purpose underlying those requirements; government could not determine whether complaint might interfere with ongoing investigation or whether government should intervene, any settlement value that might have arisen from complaint's sealed status was eliminated, any possibility of ameliorating predisclosure government decision not to pursue claim was aborted by relator's premature publication of allegations through communication with reporter, and relator's counsel did not act in good faith in attempting to comply with requirements. 31 U.S.C.A. § 3730(b)(2).

> U.S. ex rel. Pilon v. Martin Marietta Corp., 60 F.3d 995.

C.A.2 (N.Y.) 1995. District court has power to dismiss complaint for failure to comply with court order, treating noncompliance as failure to prosecute. Fed.Rules Civ.Proc.Rule 41(b), 28 U.S.C.A.

> Simmons v. Abruzzo, 49 F.3d 83, on remand 1996 WL 79321, affirmed 104 F.3d 350.

Prisoner's pro se § 1983 complaint should not have been dismissed for failure to file "clear and concise statement of his claims" as ordered by court; filing of clear and concise statement of claims was only condition precedent to further request for appointment of counsel and prisoner was not required to renew his counsel application. Fed.Rules Civ.Proc.Rule 41(b), 28 U.S.C.A.

> Simmons v. Abruzzo, 49 F.3d 83, on remand 1996 WL 79321, affirmed 104 F.3d 350.

C.A.2 (N.Y.) 1994. Request for nominal damages would not be read into students' complaint challenging constitutionality of state university regulation barring private commercial businesses from engaging in sales demonstrations in students' dormitory rooms, so as to stave off dismissal for mootness based upon fact that students were no longer enrolled at university, as it appeared that available Eleventh Amendment and qualified immunity defenses would have precluded any successful claim for money damages and there was no final judgment pursuant to which complete relief could be granted. U.S.C.A. Const. Art. 3, § 2, cl. 1; Amends. 1, 11; Fed.Rules Civ.Proc.Rule 54(c), 28 U.S.C.A.

> Fox v. Board of Trustees of State University of New York, 42 F.3d 135, certiorari denied 115 S.Ct. 2634, 515 U.S. 1169, 132 L.Ed.2d 873.

Students challenging constitutionality of state university regulation barring private commercial businesses from engaging in sales demonstrations in students' dormitory rooms would not be regarded as having litigated case in representational capacity, so as to stave off dismissal for mootness based upon fact that students were no longer enrolled at university, where students did not make any attempt to have class certified and in fact never alleged in their pleadings that they were bringing action on behalf of themselves and all others similarly situated. U.S.C.A. Const. Art. 3, § 2, cl. 1; Fed.Rules Civ.Proc.Rule 23, 28 U.S.C.A.

> Fox v. Board of Trustees of State University of New York, 42 F.3d 135, certiorari denied 115 S.Ct. 2634, 515 U.S. 1169, 132 L.Ed.2d 873.

Once case was moot, it was no longer justiciable in federal court and had to be dismissed, and plaintiffs could not be permitted to amend their complaint to add additional parties. U.S.C.A. Const. Art. 3, § 2, cl. 1.

> Fox v. Board of Trustees of State University of New York, 42 F.3d 135, certiorari denied 115 S.Ct. 2634, 515 U.S. 1169, 132 L.Ed.2d 873.

C.A.2 (N.Y.) 1994. Although dismissal for failure to comply with court order is matter committed to discretion of district court, dismissal is harsh remedy to be utilized only in extreme situations. Fed.Rules Civ.Proc.Rule 41(b), 28 U.S.C.A.

> Jackson v. City of New York, 22 F.3d 71.

Action for false arrest should not have been dismissed for failure to comply with court order absent showing that discovery delays were plaintiff's fault, that plaintiff was on notice that actions would result in dismissal, that defendants were prejudiced by any delays, that length of delay was significant, that plaintiff was given fair chance to be heard, and that judge considered lesser sanctions. Fed.Rules Civ.Proc.Rule 41(b), 28 U.S.C.A.

> Jackson v. City of New York, 22 F.3d 71.

C.A.2 (N.Y.) 1992. While ordinarily the voluntary cessation of allegedly illegal conduct does not deprive federal court of jurisdiction, such action does bear on whether court should, in exercise of its discretion, dismiss case as moot.

> Harrison & Burrowes Bridge Constructors, Inc. v. Cuomo, 981 F.2d 50.

While defendant bears heavy burden when it seeks to have case dismissed as moot, whether it should be dismissed or not lies within sound discretion of district court and strong showing of abuse must be made to reverse it.

> Harrison & Burrowes Bridge Constructors, Inc. v. Cuomo, 981 F.2d 50.

District court did not abuse its discretion in dismissing white male contractors' challenge to New York's disadvantaged businesses program governing wholly state-funded construction projects as moot, where emergency regulation enacted suspended application of minority enterprise goals on state-funded contracts. N.Y.McKinney's Executive Law §§ 311, subd. 3(a), 313, subd. 1.

> Harrison & Burrowes Bridge Constructors, Inc. v. Cuomo, 981 F.2d 50.

C.A.2 (N.Y.) 1989. After determining that third-party complaint was moot, district court should have dismissed complaint, instead of denying third-party's summary judgment motion as moot and placing matter in court's suspense docket. Fed.Rules Civ.Proc.Rule 54(b), 28 U.S.C.A.

> St. Paul Fire and Marine Ins. Co. v. Pepsi-Co, Inc., 884 F.2d 688.

C.A.2 (N.Y.) 1985. When plaintiff lacks standing court must dismiss case on that ground, and it is unnecessary to intimate a view as to merits of claim.

Matter of Appointment of Independent Counsel, 766 F.2d 70, certiorari denied Schiavone v. United States, 106 S.Ct. 569, 474 U.S. 1020, 88 L.Ed.2d 554.

C.A.2 (N.Y.) 1982. Oneida Indian Nation of New York v. State of N.Y., 691 F.2d 1070, on subsequent appeal Oneida Indian Nation of Wisconsin v. State of N.Y., 732 F.2d 259, on remand 102 F.R.D. 450, cause remanded Oneida of Thames Band v. State of N.Y., 757 F.2d 19, motion to recall mandate denied 771 F.2d 51, certiorari denied 106 S.Ct. 78, 474 U.S. 823, 88 L.Ed.2d 64, on remand 649 F.Supp. 420, affirmed 860 F.2d 1145, certiorari denied 110 S.Ct. 200, 493 U.S. 871, 107 L.Ed.2d 154, certiorari denied 110 S.Ct. 200, 493 U.S. 871, 107 L.Ed.2d 154.

C.A.2 (N.Y.) 1981. Vishipco Line v. Chase Manhattan Bank, N.A., 660 F.2d 854, 62 A.L.R. Fed. 501, certiorari denied 103 S.Ct. 313, 459 U.S. 976, 74 L.Ed.2d 291, on remand 1984 WL 679, reversed 754 F.2d 452.

C.A.2 (N.Y.) 1973. Schein v. Chasen, 478 F.2d 817, certiorari granted Lehman Brothers v. Schein, 94 S.Ct. 568, 414 U.S. 1062, 38 L.Ed.2d 467, vacated 94 S.Ct. 1741, 416 U.S. 386, 40 L.Ed.2d 215.

C.A.6 (Ohio) 1993. Where named plaintiff's claim becomes moot before class certification, dismissal of action is required.

Brunet v. City of Columbus, 1 F.3d 390, rehearing denied, certiorari denied 114 S.Ct. 1190, 510 U.S. 1164, 127 L.Ed.2d 540, appeal after remand 58 F.3d 251, rehearing and suggestion for rehearing denied.

C.A.6 (Ohio) 1990. District court did not abuse its discretion by dismissing action by workers for alleged injuries resulting from exposure to Toluene Di-Isocyanate for failure to comply with the court's orders and for want of prosecution and making condition of refiling that workers have proved payment of costs incurred by manufacturers, filed signed certificate stating that workers were ready and willing to prosecute claim expeditiously and had made adequate financial provisions for discovery, and paid sanctions levied against workers for failure to complete discovery. Fed.Rules Civ.Proc.Rule 41(b), 28 U.S.C.A.

Pollitt v. General Motors Corp., 894 F.2d 858.

C.A.10 (Okl.) 1998. Although district court may dismiss action as sanction for plaintiff's failure to follow federal procedural rules, court's dismissal of complaint would not be upheld on that basis, where court deemed one defendant's motion to dismiss complaint and other defendants' motion to dismiss amended complaint confessed, pursuant to local rule, but closing of entire case went beyond court's ruling on motions to dismiss. Fed.Rules Civ.Proc. Rule 41(b), 28 U.S.C.A; U.S.Dist.Ct.Rules E.D.Okl., Rule 7.1, subd. B.

Murray v. Archambo, 132 F.3d 609.

C.A.10 (Okl.) 1988. Dismissal is usually appropriate only where lesser sanction would not serve interest of justice.

Meade v. Grubbs, 841 F.2d 1512.

C.A.10 (Okl.) 1982. Joplin v. Southwestern Bell Telephone Co., 671 F.2d 1274, appeal after remand 753 F.2d 808.

C.A.3 (Pa.) 1996. If developments occur during course of adjudication that eliminate plaintiff's personal stake in outcome of suit or prevent court from being able to grant requested relief, case must be dismissed as moot.

Blanciak v. Allegheny Ludlum Corp., 77 F.3d 690.

C.A.3 (Pa.) 1992. Decision to dismiss complaint with prejudice as sanction for flagrant violation of court orders is exercise of district court's discretion and is subject to great deference by Court of Appeals. Fed.Rules Civ. Proc.Rules 16(f), 37(b)(2), 41(b), 28 U.S.C.A.

Mindek v. Rigatti, 964 F.2d 1369.

C.A.3 (Pa.) 1991. District court can grant motion to dismiss for lack of subject matter jurisdiction based on legal insufficiency of claim, but dismissal is proper only if claim clearly appears to be immaterial and made solely for purpose of obtaining jurisdiction or is wholly insubstantial and frivolous. Fed.Rules Civ.Proc.Rule 12(b)(1, 6), 28 U.S.C.A.

Kehr Packages, Inc. v. Fidelcor, Inc., 926 F.2d 1406, rehearing denied, certiorari denied 111 S.Ct. 2839, 501 U.S. 1222, 115 L.Ed.2d 1007.

C.A.3 (Pa.) 1990. Sanction of dismissal of action for plaintiff's failure to comply with district court's order is reserved for those cases in which plaintiff has caused delay or engaged in contumacious conduct. Fed.Rules Civ.Proc. Rule 41(b), 28 U.S.C.A.

Guyer v. Beard, 907 F.2d 1424, rehearing denied.

Even when plaintiff has caused delay or engaged in contumacious conduct, before district court dismisses complaint for plaintiff's failure to comply with district court order, district court must consider whether ends of justice would be better served by lesser sanction. Fed.Rules Civ.Proc.Rule 41(b), 28 U.S.C.A.

Guyer v. Beard, 907 F.2d 1424, rehearing denied.

C.A.3 (Pa.) 1989. District court has discretion to dismiss frivolous or malicious in forma pauperis complaints; however, that discretion is limited in every case by language of statute itself which restricts its application to complaints found to be frivolous or malicious; dismissal is appropriate when claims are based on indisputably meritless legal theories or on clearly baseless factual contentions, but complaint is not automatically frivolous merely because it fails to state claim under Federal Rule of Civil Procedure 12(b)(6). 28 U.S.C.A. § 1915(d); Fed.Rules Civ.Proc.Rule 12(b)(6), 28 U.S.C.A.

> Wilson v. Rackmill, 878 F.2d 772, on remand 1990 WL 63504, reconsideration denied 1990 WL 82117, on reconsideration 1990 WL 87316.

Civil rights complaint brought by in forma pauperis parolee alleging that various federal probation officers, parole examiners and regional commissioner of United States Parole Commission had conspired to cause his arrest, made improper investigations and probable cause findings and conducted unfair parole revocation hearing in order to have plaintiff returned to prison should not have been dismissed as frivolous; although it was arguable whether plaintiff had stated cause of action under *Bivens*, claims alleged were not clearly legally meritless, even if they would later be subject to dismissal under Federal Rule of Civil Procedure 12(b)(6). U.S.C.A. Const.Amend. 5; 28 U.S.C.A. § 1915(d); Fed.Rules Civ.Proc.Rule 12(b)(6), 28 U.S.C.A.

> Wilson v. Rackmill, 878 F.2d 772, on remand 1990 WL 63504, reconsideration denied 1990 WL 82117, on reconsideration 1990 WL 87316.

C.A.3 (Pa.) 1986. Prisoner's pro se complaint against warden and related parties alleging violations of constitutional rights and seeking injunctive relief and compensatory and punitive damages should not have been dismissed for failure to exhaust administrative remedies based solely upon allegations of pleading and without service, answer or preliminary hearing on question.

> Veteto v. Miller, 794 F.2d 98.

C.A.3 (Pa.) 1984. Greenfield v. Heublein, Inc., 742 F.2d 751, certiorari denied 105 S.Ct. 1189, 469 U.S. 1215, 84 L.Ed.2d 336.

C.A.3 (Pa.) 1982. In proper case, court may dismiss entirely claim of party who will not cooperate in discovery. Fed.Rules Civ.Proc. Rule 33(c), 28 U.S.C.A.

> In re Fine Paper Antitrust Litigation, 685 F.2d 810, certiorari denied Alaska v. Boise Cascade, 103 S.Ct. 801, 459 U.S. 1156, 74 L.Ed.2d 1003.

C.A.1 (Puerto Rico) 1988. Mortgagor's failure to comply with court order requiring mortgagor to pay accrued property taxes or post security bond for accrued tax liability warranted district court in dismissing mortgagor's cross complaint and striking its defense to mortgagee's counterclaim in foreclosure action. Fed. Rules Civ.Proc.Rule 41(b), 28 U.S.C.A.

> HMG Property Investors, Inc. v. Parque Indus. Rio Canas, Inc., 847 F.2d 908.

When noncompliant litigant has manifested disregard for orders of district court and been suitably forewarned of consequences of continued intransigence, district judge need not first exhaust milder sanctions before resorting to dismissal. Fed.Rules Civ.Proc.Rule 41(b), 28 U.S.C.A.

> HMG Property Investors, Inc. v. Parque Indus. Rio Canas, Inc., 847 F.2d 908.

C.A.1 (R.I.) 1983. Almonte v. National Union Fire Ins. Co., 705 F.2d 566, appeal after remand 787 F.2d 763.

C.A.5 (Tex.) 1996. There was no error in district court's order dismissing environmental organization's second complaint as duplicative of its first, particularly as organization had filed second complaint to achieve procedural advantage by circumventing rules pertaining to amendment of complaints.

> Friends of the Earth, Inc. v. Crown Cent. Petroleum Corp., 95 F.3d 358, rehearing denied.

When plaintiff files second complaint alleging same cause of action as prior, pending, related action, second complaint may be dismissed, particularly where plaintiff files second complaint to achieve procedural advantage by circumventing rules pertaining to amendment of complaint.

> Friends of the Earth, Inc. v. Crown Cent. Petroleum Corp., 95 F.3d 358, rehearing denied.

C.A.5 (Tex.) 1995. Complaint is "frivolous" if it lacks arguable basis in either law or fact.

> Grant v. Cuellar, 59 F.3d 523.

C.A.5 (Tex.) 1992. Court may dismiss, rather than stay, case when all of the claims must be submitted to arbitration. 9 U.S.C.A. § 3.

> Alford v. Dean Witter Reynolds, Inc., 975 F.2d 1161.

C.A.5 (Tex.) 1992. Effect of state secret privilege is generally to exclude privileged evidence from the case; plaintiff's case then goes forward without privileged information and would be dismissed only if remaining information were insufficient to make out prima facie case.

> Bareford v. General Dynamics Corp., 973 F.2d 1138, opinion vacated in part on denial of reargument, certiorari denied 113 S.Ct. 1843, 507 U.S. 1029, 123 L.Ed.2d 468.

State secret doctrine required dismissal of action against defense contractor based on deaths and injuries of sailors in missile attack allegedly caused by defectively manufactured and designed weapons system; although plaintiffs came forward with evidence of system's general performance limits, they could not prove that system was intended to destroy enemy missiles in circumstances encountered by sailors' vessel without revealing state secrets. Fed.Rules Civ.Proc.Rule 12(b)(6), 28 U.S.C.A.

> Bareford v. General Dynamics Corp., 973 F.2d 1138, opinion vacated in part on denial of reargument, certiorari denied 113 S.Ct. 1843, 507 U.S. 1029, 123 L.Ed.2d 468.

C.A.5 (Tex.) 1989. Dismissal and an award of double costs in addition to damages of $500 were appropriate sanctions against a former postal service employee whose frivolous complaint was part of an ongoing pattern of vexatious, multiplicious, and frivolous litigation extending over more than four years, despite prior dismissals and admonishments against further frivolous actions. F.R.A.P.Rule 38, 28 U.S.C.A.

> Buren v. U.S. Postal Service, 883 F.2d 429.

C.A.5 (Tex.) 1989. In forma pauperis proceeding may be dismissed as frivolous if claim has only slight chance of ultimate success, claim has no arguable basis in law or fact, and it is clear plaintiff can prove no set of facts in support of claim. 28 U.S.C.A. § 1915(d).

> Moody v. Miller, 864 F.2d 1178, rehearing denied.

Prison inmate's in forma pauperis § 1983 complaint could be dismissed with prejudice prior to service as frivolous; inmate, in about his 23rd § 1983 complaint filed in last three years, failed to state claims for violation of due process rights. 28 U.S.C.A. § 1915(d); U.S.C.A. Const.Amends. 5, 14.

> Moody v. Miller, 864 F.2d 1178, rehearing denied.

C.A.5 (Tex.) 1988. A prisoner's claim of unconstitutional discrimination which amounted to no more than a protest that he was not being moved up the trusty ladder as fast as he felt he was entitled to, with no factual support

for that assertion, was frivolous and properly dismissed with prejudice. 42 U.S.C.A. § 1983.

> Whittington v. Lynaugh, 842 F.2d 818, certiorari denied Johnson v. Lynaugh, 109 S.Ct. 108, 488 U.S. 840, 102 L.Ed.2d 83.

C.A.5 (Tex.) 1988. Dismissal of action as frivolous is appropriate where it is clear that the plaintiff can prove no set facts in support of the claim, the claim has no arguable basis in law or fact, or there is little realistic chance of ultimate success. 28 U.S.C.A. § 1915(d).

> Beck v. Lynaugh, 842 F.2d 759.

C.A.5 (Tex.) 1988. Any rights which veteran's widow, as estate representative, had to seek administrative waiver of debt for overpayment of veterans' benefits were unaffected by pendency of action to collect the debt; therefore, widow's desire to obtain administrative waiver could not form basis for granting dismissal or stay of the action. 38 U.S.C.A. §§ 3102, 3102(a).

> U.S. v. Estate of Payne, 836 F.2d 914.

C.A.5 (Tex.) 1986. Inmate's claim that former wife's wrongful filing of his income tax return and cashing of resulting refund check deprived him of his constitutional rights was frivolous, as was appeal thereof, absent connection between former wife and any tortious governmental action.

> Patterson v. Patterson, 808 F.2d 357.

C.A.5 (Tex.) 1986. Proper remedy for failure of nickel owner to send adequate demand letter to warehouseman for loss of nickel was not dismissal of Texas Deceptive Trade Practices claims, but, rather, abatement of suit until notice requirement was satisfied. V.T.C.A., Bus. & C. § 17.50A(a).

> International Nickel Co., Inc. v. Trammel Crow Distribution Corp., 803 F.2d 150.

C.A.5 (Tex.) 1986. Ex-husband's civil rights action against state judge, who was acting within scope of his judicial duties at all material times during divorce action and who was therefore absolutely immune from suit, was frivolous. 42 U.S.C.A. § 1983.

> Brinkmann v. Johnston, 793 F.2d 111.

Ex-husband's complaint against ex-wife and her attorney and his son's attorney did not state any factual basis to support civil rights conspiracy charges and was therefore frivolous. 42 U.S.C.A. § 1983.

> Brinkmann v. Johnston, 793 F.2d 111.

C.A.5 (Tex.) 1986. Credibility assessments are within sound discretion of district court making determination of frivolousness under statute authorizing dismissal of in forma pauperis proceeding if the court is satisfied that the action is frivolous; however, the most important consideration in such credibility assessment is inherent plausibility of complaint's allegations based on objective factors, rather than demeanor of witnesses or a witness' prior criminal record. 28 U.S.C.A. § 1915(d).

Cay v. Estelle, 789 F.2d 318.

C.A.5 (Tex.) 1986. Dismissal of a plaintiff's lawsuit for failing to comply with the district court's orders is an extreme sanction which is warranted only where a clear record of delay or contumacious conduct by plaintiff exists.

Day v. Allstate Ins. Co., 788 F.2d 1110.

C.A.5 (Tex.) 1986. Sanction dismissal of plaintiff's case under Federal Rule 41(b), governing involuntary dismissals, was inappropriate where, inter alia, the hour was late when plaintiff's last available witness finished testifying and plaintiff had one more witness whom counsel had attempted to subpoena that day and who was not present; the case had not been reached when first set, had been continued once because of illness of counsel, and had been reset upon one-day notice, when counsel acted promptly to subpoena the witness, whom he had listed in pretrial order. Fed.Rules Civ. Proc.Rule 41(b), 28 U.S.C.A.

Taylor v. Combustion Engineering, Inc., 782 F.2d 525.

C.A.5 (Tex.) 1986. District court's requirement that plaintiff, a veteran pro se litigator bringing action under the Freedom of Information Act, post $500 bond as security for costs should he lose on merits of case was reasonable, and thus, failure of plaintiff to post bond warranted dismissal with prejudice, where many of suits previously filed by plaintiff were repetitious or of doubtful legal merit, and plaintiff had failed to pay any of costs assessed against him in previous actions brought against same defendant. U.S.Dist.Ct.Rules W.D.Texas, Rule 300–3; 5 U.S.C.A. § 552.

Ehm v. Amtrak Bd. of Directors, 780 F.2d 516.

C.A.5 (Tex.) 1982. Jureczki v. City of Seabrook, Tex., 668 F.2d 851, appeal after remand 760 F.2d 666, rehearing denied 765 F.2d 1120, certiorari denied 106 S.Ct. 1261, 475 U.S. 1045, 89 L.Ed.2d 571.

C.A.4 (Va.) 1990. District court did not abuse its discretion when it dismissed civil rights complaint for plaintiff's failure to comply with court order; plaintiff failed to oppose defendants' motions to dismiss and for summary judgment even after district court extended time to respond, and plaintiff's counsel failed to appear at hearing on defendants' motions. Fed. Rules Civ.Proc.Rule 41(b), 28 U.S.C.A.

Simpson v. Welch, 900 F.2d 33.

C.A.4 (Va.) 1987. Students' challenge to banning of school's Confederate logo was not clearly foreclosed by authoritative precedent, did not have such tenuous connection with federal question that no possible facts would entitle students to relief, and, therefore, could not be dismissed by district court sua sponte for frivolousness. U.S.C.A. Const.Amends. 1, 14.

Crosby by Crosby v. Holsinger, 816 F.2d 162, appeal after remand 852 F.2d 801, rehearing denied.

C.A.9 (Wash.) 1989. Prisoner's complaint challenging application of jail time credit to his sentence should have been stayed pending exhaustion of state remedies, rather than dismissed, in order to avoid forcing prisoner to wait to file § 1983 claim until limitations period had expired. 42 U.S.C.A. § 1983.

Young v. Kenny, 907 F.2d 874, rehearing denied, certiorari denied Bressman v. Farrier, 111 S.Ct. 1090, 498 U.S. 1126, 112 L.Ed.2d 1194.

C.A.9 (Wash.) 1988. Notice in addition to that provided by local rule, which conferred discretion on court to dismiss pro se plaintiff's action if plaintiff failed to keep court apprised of his correct address, was not required and would have been futile gesture, given district court's prior mailing to pro se plaintiff which was returned as undeliverable. U.S.Dist.Ct.Rules W.D.Wash., Civil Rule 41(b)(2).

Carey v. King, 856 F.2d 1439.

Federal district court did not abuse its discretion in failing to impose alternative sanction, less drastic than dismissal without prejudice, for plaintiff's violation of local rule which required pro se litigants to keep court informed of their current mailing addresses and which permitted court to dismiss action if pro se plaintiff did not communicate with court within 60 days after date upon which mail was returned by post office as undeliverable. U.S.Dist.Ct.Rules W.D.Wash., Civil Rule 41(b)(2).

Carey v. King, 856 F.2d 1439.

It was not abuse of discretion to dismiss pro se plaintiff's action for failure to keep court apprised of its current mailing address as required by local rule, permitting dismissal 60 days after mail is returned by post office as undeliverable, on theory that delay in prosecution was not unreasonable or intentional; it would have been absurd to require district court to hold case in abeyance while attempting to contact plaintiff who failed to keep court apprised of his address to determine whether reasons for not prosecuting lawsuit were reasonable. U.S.Dist.Ct.Rules W.D.Wash., Civil Rule 41(b)(2).

Carey v. King, 856 F.2d 1439.

C.A.9 (Wash.) 1986. Parties' representations to district court in malpractice action against attorney that they agreed to settle, agreed as to dollar amount and agreed that dismissal would be with prejudice warranted dismissal of action, even though there was no written stipulation of dismissal. Fed.Rules Civ. Proc.Rules 41, 41(a)(1)(ii), 28 U.S.C.A.

Eitel v. McCool, 782 F.2d 1470.

C.A.4 (W.Va.) 1993. Under its inherent power, court may issue orders, punish for contempt, vacate judgments obtained by fraud, conduct investigations as necessary to exercise power, bar persons from courtroom, assess attorney's fees, and dismiss actions.

U.S. v. Shaffer Equipment Co., 11 F.3d 450.

Because order dismissing actions is most severe exercise of court's inherent powers, such orders must be entered with greatest caution.

U.S. v. Shaffer Equipment Co., 11 F.3d 450.

Court has inherent power to dismiss case for misconduct of counsel.

U.S. v. Shaffer Equipment Co., 11 F.3d 450.

C.A.7 (Wis.) 1993. After finding that fraudulent misrepresentation claim relating to franchise agreement was subject to arbitration, proper disposition was to stay action pending arbitration rather than dismissal of action.

Kroll v. Doctor's Associates, Inc., 3 F.3d 1167.

C.A.7 (Wis.) 1992. Where loss is not only small but also indefinite, so that substantial resources would have to be devoted to determining whether there was any loss at all, courts will invoke doctrine of "de minimis non curat lex" and dismiss case, even if it raises constitutional issues; cost of such litigation would overwhelm benefits.

Hessel v. O'Hearn, 977 F.2d 299.

C.A.7 (Wis.) 1986. Sanction of dismissal with prejudice must be infrequently resorted to by district courts in their attempt to control their dockets and extirpate nuisance suits; only when interests of justice are best served by dismissal can this harsh sanction be consonant with role of courts.

Schilling v. Walworth County Park & Planning Com'n, 805 F.2d 272.

C.A.7 (Wis.) 1986. Action brought by purchasers under land contract against vendors, vendors' attorneys in state foreclosure action, as well as judges in state and federal court proceedings was properly dismissed for abuse of judicial process where purchasers' motions were meant solely to harass judiciary and opposing litigants in wake of legitimate ruling unfavorable to their case.

Glick v. Gutbrod, 782 F.2d 754.

C.A.10 (Wyo.) 1987. District court should not indiscriminately dismiss action based on plaintiffs' alleged failure to exhaust administra-

tive remedies, where dismissal would not promote avoidance of premature interruption of administrative process, deference to bodies possessing expertise in areas outside conventional experience of judges, recognition of executive and administrative autonomy, or development of factual record.

Park County Resource Council, Inc. v. U.S. Dept. of Agriculture, 817 F.2d 609.

M.D.Ala. 1997. Prejudicial dismissal of insured's complaint, rather than stay, was appropriate since arbitration was required for all issues.

Clayton v. Woodmen of World Life Ins. Soc., 981 F.Supp. 1447.

M.D.Ala. 1996. Employees' 26–year-old class action alleging racially discriminatory employment policies by Alabama Cooperative Extension Service (ACES), which had been operated by first university, would be dismissed, where ACES no longer existed in that it had been replaced, pursuant to court order in separate federal action seeking desegregation of Alabama's institutions of higher education, by Alabama Cooperative Extension System which was to be operated jointly by first and second universities, where System's employment actions were to be supervised by court which had issued such order, and where desegregation in ACES had been achieved.

Strain v. Muse, 940 F.Supp. 302.

N.D.Ala. 1980. Armour v. City of Anniston, 89 F.R.D. 331, affirmed 654 F.2d 382.

D.Ariz. 1990. Plaintiff's failure to obtain leave of court before filing amendment changing parties did not justify dismissal of amended complaint, as such failure could be corrected. Fed.Rules Civ.Proc.Rule 21, 28 U.S.C.A.

Karsten Mfg. Corp. v. U.S. Golf Ass'n, 728 F.Supp. 1429.

E.D.Ark. 1987. Pro se complaint concerning plaintiff's commitment to state mental hospital, filed on same day as dismissal by another United States district judge of another complaint based on the same incident, was subject to sua sponte dismissal as frivolous. 28 U.S.C.A. § 1915(d).

Cook v. Williams, 651 F.Supp. 350, affirmed 822 F.2d 1093.

C.D.Cal. 1996. When plaintiff's personal stake in outcome of controversy ceases to exist during course of litigation, there is no longer live controversy and case generally should be dismissed as moot. U.S.C.A. Const. Art. 3, § 2, cl. 1.

In re Di Giorgio, 200 B.R. 664, vacated 134 F.3d 971.

C.D.Cal. 1993. If proper assertion of state secrets privilege precludes access to evidence necessary for plaintiff to state prima facie claim, dismissal is appropriate; similarly, if court determines that privilege so impairs defendant in establishing valid defense that trier is likely to reach erroneous conclusion, dismissal is also proper.

> Bentzlin v. Hughes Aircraft Co., 833 F.Supp. 1486.

C.D.Cal. 1987. Once court makes finding that decision was void, it must proceed simultaneously to dismiss action on which decision was made.

> Gregorian v. Izvestia, 658 F.Supp. 1224, affirmed in part, reversed in part 871 F.2d 1515, certiorari denied 110 S.Ct. 237, 493 U.S. 891, 107 L.Ed.2d 188.

E.D.Cal. 1995. In order to be "capable of repetition yet evading review," so as to avoid dismissal on ground of mootness, two requirements must be met: challenged action must be too short in duration to be fully litigated prior to its cessation or expiration, and there must be reasonable expectation that same plaintiffs will be subjected to same action again.

> Westlands Water Dist. v. Patterson, 900 F.Supp. 1304, reversed 100 F.3d 94.

E.D.Cal. 1994. Dismissal for failure to state a claim upon which relief can be granted is proper where there is either lack of cognizable legal theory or absence of sufficient facts alleged under cognizable theory. Fed.Rules Civ.Proc.Rule 12(b)(6), 28 U.S.C.A.

> Fonovisa, Inc. v. Cherry Auction, Inc., 847 F.Supp. 1492, reversed 76 F.3d 259.

E.D.Cal. 1985. Government counsel's misconduct in attempting to improperly influence a neutral witness for the Government warranted dismissal of the Government's action with prejudice.

> U.S. v. National Medical Enterprises, Inc., 107 F.R.D. 628.

N.D.Cal. 1994. Failure to properly allege standing is ground for dismissal for failure to state claim on which relief can be granted. Fed.Rules Civ.Proc.Rule 12(b)(6), 28 U.S.C.A.

> MAI Systems Corp. v. UIPS, 856 F.Supp. 538.

N.D.Cal. 1991. Motion to dismiss directed at a form of relief requested by plaintiff is improper.

> Pratt v. Rowland, 769 F.Supp. 1128.

N.D.Cal. 1988. Publisher of business directory would be required to pay competitor's legal expenses and out-of-pocket costs, and publisher's copyright infringement action against competitor would be dismissed as Rule 11 sanctions for filing action without reasonable factual inquiry; publisher claimed that false information or "seeds" that appeared in its directory also appeared in competitor's directory, but failed to check accuracy of purported seeds. Fed.Rules Civ.Proc.Rule 11, 28 U.S.C.A.

> Business Guides, Inc. v. Chromatic Communications Enterprises, Inc., 121 F.R.D. 402, affirmed in part, vacated in part 892 F.2d 802, certiorari granted 110 S.Ct. 3235, 497 U.S. 1002, 111 L.Ed.2d 746, affirmed 111 S.Ct. 922, 498 U.S. 533, 112 L.Ed.2d 1140.

S.D.Cal. 1986. Even where federal question exists, lack of private cause of action, either express or implied, requires dismissal of lawsuit. 28 U.S.C.A. § 1331.

> Guinto v. Marcos, 654 F.Supp. 276.

D.Colo. 1995. Involuntary dismissal of an action for plaintiff's failure to comply with the Federal Rules of Civil Procedure or court orders is an extreme sanction which is appropriate only in cases of willful misconduct. Fed.Rules Civ.Proc.Rule 41(b), 28 U.S.C.A.

> Mobley v. McCormick, 160 F.R.D. 599, affirmed 69 F.3d 548.

Involuntary dismissal with prejudice of employment discrimination action was appropriate based on former employee's failure to comply with the Federal Rules of Civil Procedure or court orders; result of former employee's actions in ignoring procedural requirements, failing to attend scheduled conferences and resisting and refusing to produce requested and necessary information had been unnecessary delay and cost to employer, former employee's actions interfered with and impeded judicial process, former employee's actions constituted bad faith and willful and intentional disobedience of court orders, former employee was aware that dismissal could result from his conduct, and lesser sanctions would not have been effective as former employee had repeatedly ignored court orders. Fed.Rules Civ.Proc.Rule 41(b), 28 U.S.C.A.

> Mobley v. McCormick, 160 F.R.D. 599, affirmed 69 F.3d 548.

D.Colo. 1986. Conduct of plaintiffs' attorney in evading discovery efforts by defendant to ascertain true facts in products liability case as to whether bald tires were on front and rear left of automobile in question, thus rebutting rear brake lock-up hypothesis, did not require sanction of dismissal in absence of prejudice, but did require sanction of striking individual's appearance as attorney for plaintiffs, removing him from case, and prohibiting him from appearing further. Fed.Rules Civ.Proc.Rules 37, 37(a)(3), (b, d), 28 U.S.C.A.; ABA Code of Prof.Resp., Canons 7, 9; DR1–102(A), (A)(4–7), (B)(2).

> Schmidt v. Ford Motor Co., 112 F.R.D. 216.

D.Conn. 1996. Rehiring of some of deputy clerk union's members did not moot union's

§ 1983 claims for relief since union sought damages as well as the reinstatement of its members who were not rehired by chief court administrator of the State of Connecticut and thus, union's § 1983 claims alleging that administrator terminated its members' employment without due process and discriminated against them on the basis of their union activities would not be dismissed as moot. 42 U.S.C.A. § 1983.

> Local 749, AFSCME, Council 4, AFL-CIO v. Ment, 945 F.Supp. 30.

D.Conn. 1991. If plaintiff is unable to establish prima facie case without information subject to state secrets privilege, or if state secrets are so central to subject matter of litigation that any attempt to proceed will threaten disclosure of privileged matters, dismissal of case is appropriate; if, however, plaintiff has sufficient admissible evidence to allow judgment in his favor without privileged information, case may go forward.

> Clift v. U.S., 808 F.Supp. 101.

D.Conn. 1990. If plaintiff is unable to establish prima facie case without information subject to state secrets privilege or if sensitive military secrets are so central to subject matter of litigation that any attempt to proceed will threaten disclosure of privilege, dismissal of case is appropriate.

> Zuckerbraun v. General Dynamics Corp., 755 F.Supp. 1134, affirmed 935 F.2d 544.

Upon successful invocation of state secrets privilege, action against weapon systems manufacturers, designers, and testers for wrongful death of sailor who was killed when his ship was fired on by foreign aircraft would be dismissed where maintenance of the case would require disclosure of classified state secrets in order to establish prima facie case.

> Zuckerbraun v. General Dynamics Corp., 755 F.Supp. 1134, affirmed 935 F.2d 544.

D.Conn. 1987. Counts which plaintiffs conceded should be dismissed would be dismissed.

> Stengel v. City of Hartford, 652 F.Supp. 572.

D.Conn. 1977. Alexander v. Yale University, 459 F.Supp. 1, affirmed 631 F.2d 178.

D.Del. 1996. Plaintiff willfully and deliberately ignored court orders, where he did not heed court warnings that continued delays would not be tolerated and would be interpreted as willful disregard for court's authority. Fed.Rules Civ.Proc.Rule 41(b), 28 U.S.C.A.

> Guy v. City of Wilmington, 169 F.R.D. 593.

Plaintiff's deliberate pattern of reckless disregard for orders and rules of court compelled ultimate sanction of dismissal; as both party and lawyer, he was fully responsible for those violations, he had been warned twice before of potential consequences of his lack of diligence, and he not only chose to ignore that warning, but also subsequent court orders. Fed.Rules Civ.Proc.Rule 41(b), 28 U.S.C.A.

> Guy v. City of Wilmington, 169 F.R.D. 593.

D.Del. 1995. "First-filed" rule, whereby in all cases of federal concurrent jurisdiction, court which first has possession of the subject must decide it, is based on principles of equity and comity, and empowers trial judge to exercise his discretion and dismiss an action, where action involving same issues between the same parties is already pending in another forum; however, rule is not hard and fast.

> Moore Corp. Ltd. v. Wallace Computer Services, Inc., 898 F.Supp. 1089.

D.Del. 1994. Landowner's action challenging county zoning ordinance was not ripe for review, notwithstanding contention that if landowner waited for state zoning Board of Adjustment to make final determination as to validity of ordinance, action might be barred by Delaware's 60–day statute of limitations for challenging zoning law; court was required to dismiss action for lack of case or controversy, regardless of dictates of state statute of limitations, and, in any event, constitutional challenges to zoning ordinances were not governed by statute of limitations at issue. 10 Del.C. § 8126(a).

> Baldini West, Inc. v. New Castle County, 852 F.Supp. 251.

If there is no case or controversy before federal court, it must dismiss action, regardless of dictates of state statute of limitations. U.S.C.A. Const. Art. 3, § 2, cl. 1.

> Baldini West, Inc. v. New Castle County, 852 F.Supp. 251.

D.D.C. 1995. Where named individual plaintiff's claims had become moot and plaintiff organization was dismissed due to lack of standing, pending motion for class certification did not preclude case from being dismissed as moot; because named plaintiffs' claims had become moot, no case or controversy existed on which to append a class of plaintiffs or new individual plaintiffs.

> Legal Assistance for Vietnamese Asylum Seekers v. U.S. Dept. of State, Bureau of Consular Affairs, 909 F.Supp. 1, reversed 74 F.3d 1308, 316 U.S.App.D.C. 47, suggestion for rehearing declined, and mandate stayed, certiorari granted 116 S.Ct. 2521, 518 U.S. 1003, 135 L.Ed.2d 1046, vacated 117 S.Ct. 378, 519 U.S. 1, on remand 104 F.3d 1349, 323 U.S.App.D.C. 1.

D.D.C. 1995. For district court to dismiss plaintiff's claims as moot, two conditions had to be met: court had to find that there was no reasonable expectation that alleged violation would recur, and it had to be clear that interim relief or events had completely and irrevocably eradicated effects of alleged violation.

> Amoco Production Co. v. Fry, 908 F.Supp. 991.

D.D.C. 1993. Dismissal for counsel's misconduct is justified only in cases involving prejudice to defendant or to judicial system, or where dismissal would serve interest of deterrence and punishment.

> John Akridge Co. v. Travelers Companies, 837 F.Supp. 6.

D.D.C. 1987. Defendants' motion to dismiss plaintiff's case was not barred by fact that defendants had not moved to dismiss two companion cases, and plaintiff was not entitled to attorneys fees incurred in responding to motion as Rule 11 sanction; plaintiff elected to file three separate actions, and could not subsequently complain of hardship involved in litigating each action separately. Fed.Rules Civ.Proc. Rules 11, 12(g), 28 U.S.C.A.

> Johnson v. Computer Technology Services, Inc., 670 F.Supp. 1036.

D.D.C. 1984. Amended complaint adding three defendants in action centering on dispute between plaintiff and defendants over license for radio station in Massachusetts was a new action, and as such, plaintiff was bound to comply with terms of another district court's order imposing permanent injunction upon plaintiff from instituting any action in the federal courts without first obtaining permission from that court; since plaintiff had failed to comply with terms of that order, those defendants would be dismissed. Fed.Rules Civ.Proc. Rule 15(c), 28 U.S.C.A.

> Martin-Trigona v. Acton Corp., 600 F.Supp. 1193, affirmed 818 F.2d 95, 260 U.S.App. D.C. 229.

D.D.C. 1984. Synanon Church v. U.S., 579 F.Supp. 967, affirmed 820 F.2d 421, 261 U.S.App.D.C. 13.

D.D.C. 1982. Powell v. Nigro, 543 F.Supp. 1044, case remanded 711 F.2d 420, 229 U.S.App.D.C. 142, certiorari denied 104 S.Ct. 149, 464 U.S. 846, 78 L.Ed.2d 139, on remand 601 F.Supp. 144.

M.D.Fla. 1995. In exercising its discretion to dismiss for disobedience of court orders, trial court should maintain scrupulous regard for rights of parties to action, even when court acts sua sponte.

> In re Metas, 183 B.R. 290.

M.D.Fla. 1994. When litigant has failed to obey direct order of court, dismissal is appro-

priate. Fed.Rules Civ.Proc.Rule 41(b), 28 U.S.C.A.

> Sussman v. Salem, Saxon and Nielsen, P.A., 154 F.R.D. 294.

M.D.Fla. 1993. District court generally may dismiss, transfer, or stay action so that issues presented can be resolved first in earlier filed action pending in another district court. Fed.Rules Civ.Proc.Rule 13(a), 28 U.S.C.A.

> New England Machinery, Inc. v. Conagra Pet Products Co., 827 F.Supp. 732.

M.D.Fla. 1991. Sanction of dismissal for failure to comply with court order was not warranted even though second amended complaint contained same allegations and requested much the same relief as complaint that had previously been dismissed with leave to amend in accordance with court's instruction; second amended complaint differed from dismissed complaint in that it did not refer to or seek remedy under inapplicable statute. Fed.Rules Civ.Proc.Rule 41(b), 28 U.S.C.A.

> Dimuccio v. D'Ambra, 779 F.Supp. 1318.

M.D.Fla. 1990. Stay, rather than dismissal, because of pending state court proceeding is preferable, as it is possible that state court proceeding might not address all issues before the federal court.

> Nacol v. Keith Wood Agency, Inc., 750 F.Supp. 1128.

S.D.Fla. 1997. Legal standard to be applied, in deciding whether to dismiss action under Federal Rule of Civil Procedure based on party's failure to prosecute or to obey court order or federal rule, is whether there is clear record of delay or willful contempt and a finding that lesser sanctions would not suffice. Fed.Rules Civ.Proc.Rule 41(b), 28 U.S.C.A.

> In re Southeast Banking Corp. Securities and Loan Loss Reserves Litigation, 212 B.R. 397.

"Willful" conduct, of kind which will permit court to dismiss action under Federal Rule of Civil Procedure based on party's failure to prosecute or to obey court order or federal rule, implies a conscious or intentional failure to act, as distinguished from accidental or involuntary noncompliance, and no wrongful intent need generally be shown. Fed.Rules Civ.Proc.Rule 41(b), 28 U.S.C.A.

> In re Southeast Banking Corp. Securities and Loan Loss Reserves Litigation, 212 B.R. 397.

Party's simple negligence or other action grounded in misunderstanding of court order does not rise to level of "willful" conduct, of kind which will permit court to dismiss action under Federal Rule of Civil Procedure based on party's failure to prosecute or to obey court order or federal rule. Fed.Rules Civ.Proc.Rule 41(b), 28 U.S.C.A.

> In re Southeast Banking Corp. Securities and Loan Loss Reserves Litigation, 212 B.R. 397.

In deciding whether to dismiss action under Federal Rule of Civil Procedure based on party's failure to prosecute or to obey court order or federal rule, court does not take into account the probable merit of party's case. Fed.Rules Civ.Proc.Rule 41(b), 28 U.S.C.A.

> In re Southeast Banking Corp. Securities and Loan Loss Reserves Litigation, 212 B.R. 397.

S.D.Fla. 1992. Homeowners associations' claim against estate in federal civil rights action could not be dismissed on grounds claim against estate had not been timely filed in state probate proceeding, absent showing that associations had actual notice of probate proceedings. West's F.S.A. § 733.702; Fed.Rules Civ.Proc. Rule 25(a)(1), 28 U.S.C.A.; U.S.C.A. Const. Amend. 14.

> Lake Lucerne Civic Ass'n, Inc. v. Dolphin Stadium Corp., 801 F.Supp. 684.

S.D.Fla. 1990. As part of its inherent equitable powers, court may dismiss actions for abusive litigation practices, though such sanction is proper only in extraordinary situations and court exceeds proper bounds of its power when it fails to consider whether less extreme sanctions might maintain integrity of court and deter future misconduct.

> U.S. v. Eighty-Eight (88) Designated Accounts Containing Monies Traceable to Exchanges for Controlled Substances, 740 F.Supp. 842.

Government's apparent violations of Right to Financial Privacy Act in obtaining order freezing hundreds of bank accounts did not require dismissal of action seeking forfeiture of accounts allegedly containing funds derived from controlled substance transactions, though claimants were entitled to seek suppression of evidence as remedy for alleged misconduct. Financial Institutions Regulatory and Interest Rate Control Act of 1978, §§ 1102(1), 1113(e), 12 U.S.C.A. §§ 3402(1), 3413(e).

> U.S. v. Eighty-Eight (88) Designated Accounts Containing Monies Traceable to Exchanges for Controlled Substances, 740 F.Supp. 842.

Government's conduct during discovery phase of forfeiture proceeding was not so outrageous as to constitute due process violation mandating dismissal; Government seemingly attempted to use protective order provisions of criminal forfeiture statute as discovery tool in connection with frozen bank accounts and apparently violated the Right to Financial Privacy

Act in obtaining order freezing accounts. Financial Institutions Regulatory and Interest Rate Control Act of 1978, §§ 1102(1), 1113(e), 12 U.S.C.A. §§ 3402(1), 3413(e); U.S.C.A. Const.Amend. 14.

> U.S. v. Eighty-Eight (88) Designated Accounts Containing Monies Traceable to Exchanges for Controlled Substances, 740 F.Supp. 842.

S.D.Fla. 1980. Haitian Refugee Center v. Civiletti, 503 F.Supp. 442, modified 676 F.2d 1023.

M.D.Ga. 1985. Decision whether to dismiss case when in forma pauperis plaintiff has submitted false poverty affidavit is committed to discretion of court. 28 U.S.C.A. § 1915(d).

> Camp v. Oliver, 609 F.Supp. 718, vacated 798 F.2d 434.

Where inmate had $63.65 in his prison account on day he signed his affidavit in support of request to proceed in forma pauperis, indicating he had no money in his prison account, inmate did not attempt to explain why he gave incorrect information, and even if inmate did not know exact amount of money in his account, he knew he had some money, dismissal with prejudice of inmate's civil right litigation was proper.

> Camp v. Oliver, 609 F.Supp. 718, vacated 798 F.2d 434.

N.D.Ga. 1994. Taxpayer's failure to file motion for rule nisi, as required by local rule, warranted dismissal without prejudice of action seeking review of jeopardy tax assessment. 26 U.S.C.A. § 7429; U.S.Dist.Ct.Rules N.D.Ga., Rule 325–1.

> Vax v. C.I.R., 156 F.R.D. 272.

N.D.Ga. 1988. A dismissal or stay of federal court action because of pending state court action can only be based on limited grounds.

> First Nat. Bank of Atlanta v. Licari, 706 F.Supp. 876.

Decision to stay or dismiss case under exceptional circumstances test must be evaluated in light of court's strong obligation not to dismiss in the absence of exceptional circumstances, and most important factor is that circumstances be exceptional.

> First Nat. Bank of Atlanta v. Licari, 706 F.Supp. 876.

Simply because state court is more appropriate court in which to bring action is not sufficient to justify dismissal of federal action under *Colorado River.*

> First Nat. Bank of Atlanta v. Licari, 706 F.Supp. 876.

N.D.Ga. 1988. District court would not reconsider jurisdictional ruling, but rather would vacate entire order, upon plaintiffs' motion to voluntarily dismiss action as moot; portion of prior order for which defendant sought reconsideration was only tangentially considered by court in reaching decision on subject matter jurisdiction.

> Government Finance Officers Ass'n v. Baker, 686 F.Supp. 901.

N.D.Ga. 1988. Any action brought in federal district court is subject to dismissal for failure or refusal to obey lawful court order under local rules. U.S.Dist.Ct.Rules N.D.Ga., Civil Rule 230–3(a)(2).

> Chapman v. Misdom-Frank & Sklar, 124 F.R.D. 233.

N.D.Ga. 1987. On motion to dismiss, defendant may, in addition to basing motion on lack of subject matter jurisdiction, assert any other defenses or objections which may be available; however, when motion is based on more than one ground, district court should first consider challenge to subject matter jurisdiction. Fed.Rules Civ.Proc.Rule 12(b)(1), 28 U.S.C.A.

> Shared Network Technologies, Inc. v. Taylor, 669 F.Supp. 422.

N.D.Ga. 1985. Unsuccessful litigant's pro se complaint against various attorneys, judges, and others involved in his prior actions for alleged malpractice, obstruction of justice, and antitrust violations, was subject to dismissal as frivolous; named federal judges were entitled to absolute judicial immunity for their acts in connection with prior litigation, litigant had no standing to assert antitrust injury merely by virtue of certain defendants' refusal to represent him, certain claims had already been fully litigated in prior suits, and remaining parties were not of diverse citizenship. 28 U.S.C.A. § 1915(d).

> Patterson v. Aiken, 628 F.Supp. 1068, affirmed 784 F.2d 403.

N.D.Ga. 1985. Civil rights complaint seeking damages for loss of pair of shoes by pretrial detainee was subject to dismissal as frivolous; conduct alleged was not sufficiently egregious to amount to independent constitutional tort, and to extent that it was construed as alleging violation of procedural due process, state had provided adequate postdeprivation remedy. 28 U.S.C.A. § 1915(d); 42 U.S.C.A. § 1983; U.S.C.A. Const.Amends. 5, 14.

> Vincent v. Lynch, 626 F.Supp. 801.

S.D.Ga. 1997. Sanction of involuntary dismissal is imposed only in extreme circumstances. Fed.Rules Civ.Proc.Rule 41(b), 28 U.S.C.A.

> Direct Media Corp. v. Camden Tel. and Tel. Co., 989 F.Supp. 1211.

If defendant has suffered prejudice or delay, sanction of involuntary dismissal is often warranted. Fed.Rules Civ.Proc.Rule 41(b), 28 U.S.C.A.

> Direct Media Corp. v. Camden Tel. and Tel. Co., 989 F.Supp. 1211.

Legal standard for determining whether involuntary dismissal is appropriate is whether there is clear record of delay or willful contempt, and finding that lesser sanction would not suffice. Fed.Rules Civ.Proc.Rule 41(b), 28 U.S.C.A.

> Direct Media Corp. v. Camden Tel. and Tel. Co., 989 F.Supp. 1211.

Involuntary dismissal of claim was not warranted, even though plaintiff's counsel stated in deposition that claim in question would be withdrawn; such statement was insufficient to warrant dismissal of claim without appropriate motion from plaintiff, and defendants failed to show any significant prejudice as result of any reliance on that statement. Fed.Rules Civ.Proc. Rule 41(b), 28 U.S.C.A.

> Direct Media Corp. v. Camden Tel. and Tel. Co., 989 F.Supp. 1211.

S.D.Ga. 1988. By not responding to standard interrogatories, and by failing to associate counsel who was a member of the district court's bar, plaintiff failed to comply with local rules of the district court, warranting dismissal of suit. U.S.Dist.Ct.Rules S.D.Ga., § 1, Rule 8.6; § 4, Rule 4.

> Howard v. Brown, 738 F.Supp. 508.

D.Hawai'i 1995. To justify dismissal for failure to comply with court order, district court must consider (1) public's interest in expeditious resolution of litigation, and (2) court's need to manage its docket, (3) risk of prejudice to defendants, (4) public policy favoring disposition of cases on their merits, and (5) availability of less drastic alternatives. Fed.Rules Civ.Proc. Rule 41(b), 28 U.S.C.A.

> Lui Ciro, Inc. v. Ciro, Inc., 895 F.Supp. 1365.

Court would exercise its discretion not to dismiss Racketeer Influenced and Corrupt Organizations Act (RICO) claim based on failure to comply with standing order requiring a RICO case statement within 30 days of filing of complaint; order was not part of most recent copy of local rules, adversary had not cited actual order in motion to dismiss, and there had been a problem in counsel obtaining notice of order's existence. 18 U.S.C.A. § 1961 et seq.; Fed. Rules Civ.Proc.Rule 41(b), 28 U.S.C.A.

> Lui Ciro, Inc. v. Ciro, Inc., 895 F.Supp. 1365.

D.Idaho 1992. Before a federal court can dismiss a case as moot, two conditions must be satisfied; court must conclude there is no reasonable expectation that the alleged violation will recur; and it must be clear from the record that the interim relief or events have completely and irrevocably eradicated the effects of the alleged violation.

> Doremus v. U.S., 793 F.Supp. 942.

N.D.Ill. 1996. School district's claim against state agencies for reimbursement for full costs of severely disabled child's residential placement was moot and dismissed for lack of subject matter jurisdiction; state agencies had previously offered full reimbursement. Fed. Rules Civ.Proc.Rule 12(b)(1), 28 U.S.C.A.

> Barbara Z. v. Obradovich, 937 F.Supp. 710.

School district's claim against state agencies for injunctive relief compelling state agencies to comply with Individuals with Disabilities Education Act (IDEA) by developing and implementing required intergovernmental agreement was moot and dismissed for lack of subject matter jurisdiction; after state agency offered to fund severely disabled child's residential placement, lack of interagency agreement was no longer live issue so far as damages were concerned; rather, all damages incurred after that point were independent of any interagency agreement of lack thereof. Individuals with Disabilities Education Act, § 613(a)(13), as amended, 20 U.S.C.A. § 1413(a)(13); Fed.Rules Civ.Proc.Rule 12(b)(1), 28 U.S.C.A.

> Barbara Z. v. Obradovich, 937 F.Supp. 710.

N.D.Ill. 1996. Claim is moot and dismissal is required when dispute between parties no longer rages or when one of the parties loses his personal interest in claim.

> Yellow Cab Co. v. City of Chicago, 919 F.Supp. 1133.

Dismissal for mootness is not warranted if plaintiff shows that its claim, although no longer alive, is capable of repetition yet evading review, which requires plaintiff to prove that it will again be subject to alleged illegality; there must be reasonable expectation or demonstrable probability that same controversy will recur involving same parties, and mere physical or theoretical possibility of such recurrence is not sufficient. U.S.C.A. Const.Amend. 14.

> Yellow Cab Co. v. City of Chicago, 919 F.Supp. 1133.

N.D.Ill. 1995. Federal suit may be dismissed in interest of judicial administration whenever it is duplicative of parallel action already pending in another court; although courts have great discretion to determine whether one suit is duplicative of another, generally, suit is considered duplicative if claim, parties, and available relief do not significantly differ between two actions.

> Black and Decker Corp. v. Vermont American Corp., 915 F.Supp. 933.

N.D.Ill. 1995. Under "first-filed doctrine," as a general rule, federal suit may be dismissed for reasons of wise judicial administration whenever it is duplicative of parallel action pending in another federal court.

> Cherry Communications, Inc. v. Coastal Telephone Co., 906 F.Supp. 452.

N.D.Ill. 1995. Client may not avoid dismissal merely because of negligence of its freely selected attorney. Fed.Rules Civ.Proc.Rule 12(b)(6), 28 U.S.C.A.

> Aircraft Gear Corp. v. Kaman Aerospace Corp., 875 F.Supp. 485.

N.D.Ill. 1994. Illinois statute providing that defendant may move for dismissal of action on ground that there is another action pending between the same parties for the same cause did not require dismissal of railroad employee's federal action under ADA, a federal question case, because of prior pendency in state court of employee's FELA action as there might be if ARA action were before district court via diversity jurisdiction. Americans with Disabilities Act of 1990, §§ 2–514, 42 U.S.C.A. §§ 12101–12213; Federal Employers' Liability Act, §§ 1–10, as amended, 45 U.S.C.A. §§ 51–60; S.H.A. 735 ILCS 5/2–619(a)(3).

> Jones v. Illinois Cent. R. Co., 859 F.Supp. 1144.

N.D.Ill. 1993. In order for suit to survive, actual controversy must exist at all stages of federal litigation; cases in which dispute has been resolved must be dismissed as moot.

> Schmidt v. Reich, 835 F.Supp. 435.

N.D.Ill. 1992. Although stay is generally the proper procedural mechanism for district court to employ when deferring to parallel state court proceeding under *Colorado River* doctrine, in the interest of judicial economy and administration, district court would dismiss federal proceedings without prejudice and with leave to reinstate within 45 days of completion of state court proceedings.

> U.S. ex rel. Hartigan v. Palumbo Bros., Inc., 797 F.Supp. 624.

N.D.Ill. 1991. Sua sponte dismissal of suit brought against police officer alleging violation of constitutional rights was warranted; after pro se complainant's attempt to recover attorney's fees as attorney of record was barred, he advertised for an attorney who would say that he was attorney of record, promising to divide legal fees with attorney, thus showing that his interest was in attorney fees and not merits of case.

> Roby v. Skupien, 762 F.Supp. 813, appeal dismissed 972 F.2d 352, rehearing denied, certiorari denied 113 S.Ct. 474, 506 U.S. 978, 121 L.Ed.2d 380.

N.D.Ill. 1989. Whether complaint was subject to dismissal for failure to join a necessary party was a matter of federal, rather than state, law. Fed.Rules Civ.Proc.Rule 19(b), 28 U.S.C.A.

> Aetna Cas. & Sur. Co. v. Chicago Ins. Co., 123 F.R.D. 589.

N.D.Ill. 1988. District court would decline to exercise jurisdiction over franchisees' action against franchisor and related individuals for breach of franchise agreement and violations of Illinois Franchise Disclosure Act, in favor of pending Colorado state court action by franchisor against franchisees, which involved identical parties, claims, and issues; although discovery was near completion in Illinois action, order of filing, potential for piecemeal litigation, and inconvenience of simultaneously litigating claims in Colorado and Illinois weighed heavily in favor of dismissal, and there was no strong federal interest in action. S.H.A. ch. 110 ¶ 2–619(a)(3); ch. 121½, ¶ 1701 et seq.

> Schiller v. Packaging Store, Inc., 690 F.Supp. 711.

N.D.Ill. 1986. Where codefendants have prevailed on merits of a case in which jointly liable or similarly situated defendant has not answered, latter should be dismissed as well.

> Tavarez v. O'Malley, 642 F.Supp. 291.

N.D.Ill. 1985. Although attorney for law firm for debtors in possession was enlisted to write bankruptcy judge's opinion on a motion without knowledge of opposing parties, dismissal of debtors in possession's counterclaim was too drastic a remedy.

> In re Wisconsin Steel Corp., 48 B.R. 753.

N.D.Ill. 1984. Because it was clearly unreasonable for anybody to read provision of securities fraud complaint as setting forth a claim under section 78i(b), the cited section, rather than under 78j(b), counsel's argument that the claim was under the former section raised a strong inference of improper purpose with respect to motion to dismiss. Securities Exchange Act of 1934, §§ 9(b), 10(b), 15 U.S.C.A. §§ 78i(b), 78j(b); Fed.Rules Civ.Proc. Rule 11, 28 U.S.C.A.

> Miller v. Affiliated Financial Corp., 600 F.Supp. 987.

N.D.Ill. 1984. Pursuant to plaintiffs' motion, class action brought on behalf of disabled persons whose social security and medicaid assistance had been denied or terminated by an Illinois agency would be dismissed, as proceedings in the Illinois court system, including statewide class action in several individual cases, might have resolved all of the plaintiffs' claims. Fed.Rules Civ.Proc.Rule 41(a)(2), 28 U.S.C.A.

> Dixon v. Miller, 599 F.Supp. 395.

N.D.Ill. 1981. Yakin v. University of Illinois, Chicago Circle Campus, 508 F.Supp. 848, affirmed 760 F.2d 270.

N.D.Ill. 1980. Marrese v. American Academy of Orthopaedic Surgeons, 496 F.Supp. 236, on reconsideration 524 F.Supp. 389, reconsideration denied 1981 WL 2207, reversed 726 F.2d 1150, certiorari granted in part 104 S.Ct. 3553, 467 U.S. 1258, 82 L.Ed.2d 854, reversed 105 S.Ct. 1327, 470 U.S. 373, 84 L.Ed.2d 274, rehearing denied 105 S.Ct. 2127, 471 U.S. 1062, 85 L.Ed.2d 491, on remand 628 F.Supp. 918, cause remanded 767 F.2d 927.

N.D.Ill. 1980. Loctite Corp. v. Fel-Pro Inc., 94 F.R.D. 1, affirmed and remanded 667 F.2d 577.

N.D.Ill. 1969. Shakman v. Democratic Organization of Cook County, 310 F.Supp. 1398, reversed 435 F.2d 267, certiorari denied 91 S.Ct. 1383, 402 U.S. 909, 28 L.Ed.2d 650, on remand 356 F.Supp. 1241.

S.D.Ill. 1970. Shirck v. Thomas, 315 F.Supp. 1124, reversed 447 F.2d 1025, certiorari granted, vacated 92 S.Ct. 2848, 408 U.S. 940, 33 L.Ed.2d 764, on remand 486 F.2d 691, certiorari granted, vacated 92 S.Ct. 2848, 408 U.S. 940, 33 L.Ed.2d 764, on remand 486 F.2d 691.

N.D.Ind. 1991. Plaintiff may not avoid dismissal for failure to state claim merely by attaching bare legal conclusions to narrated facts which fail to outline basis of his claims. Fed. Rules Civ.Proc.Rule 12(b)(6), 28 U.S.C.A.

> Patrick v. Staples, 780 F.Supp. 1528.

N.D.Ind. 1991. Plaintiff corporation purposefully misused Declaratory Judgment Act, and therefore plaintiff corporation's suit would be dismissed for forum shopping, where plaintiff corporation had copy of defendant corporations' complaint which they intended to file in different district court if plaintiff corporation did not respond to their demands, plaintiff corporation filed declaratory judgment action three days before defendants filed their action, and plaintiff's action was not proper declaratory judgment action because damage had already accrued to defendants and early adjudication of plaintiff's rights was not necessary. 28 U.S.C.A. §§ 2201, 2202.

> Patton Elec. Co., Inc. v. Rampart Air, Inc., 777 F.Supp. 704.

N.D.Ind. 1990. Pro se state inmate's civil rights suit against officers, alleging improper denial of his medical needs postarrest, would be dismissed with prejudice as sanction for inmate's misconduct of loud cursing during opponent's closing argument; simple entry of judgment on verdict for officers would leave inmate's misconduct without consequence, and such sanction was warranted by inmate's willful disregard of court orders. Fed.Rules Civ. Proc.Rule 41(b), 28 U.S.C.A.; 42 U.S.C.A. § 1983.

Thompson v. Holmes, 738 F.Supp. 318.

N.D.Ind. 1986. Dismissal is appropriate sanction where there is clear record of delay or willful contempt and finding that lesser sanctions will not suffice, where there is clear record of contumacious conduct, or where one party's conduct prejudices other party so severely that it would be unfair to make other party proceed; dismissal may also be appropriate to alleviate burden that party's misconduct places on judicial system, or to punish abuse of system and deter future misconduct. Fed.Rules Civ.Proc.Rule 41(b), 28 U.S.C.A.

Hilgeford v. Peoples Bank, Inc., Portland, Ind., 113 F.R.D. 161.

Dismissal with prejudice was necessary sanction due to failure of lesser sanctions to adequately serve interests of justice, plaintiffs' manifesting willful contempt for court, and fact that current case was third lawsuit filed by plaintiffs imposing upon same defendants burden of defending themselves against outlandish claims supported only by vague and irrelevant notions of law and twisted and self-manufactured facts; to allow lawsuit to continue, in view of plaintiffs' history, their blatant disregard for court, and inadequacy of less drastic sanctions, would severely prejudice defendants and burden court. Fed.Rules Civ.Proc.Rule 41(b), 28 U.S.C.A.

Hilgeford v. Peoples Bank, Inc., Portland, Ind., 113 F.R.D. 161.

N.D.Ind. 1985. Dismissal of claims for breach of employment contract and abusive discharge was not warranted because plaintiff's counsel mistakenly asserted that Michigan, rather than Indiana law, governed contract in question and claims made pursuant to contract, as claims themselves set forth legal theory upon which they were based and basic thrust of the case was not changed, prejudicing defendant.

Thibodeau v. Foremost Ins. Co., 605 F.Supp. 653.

S.D.Ind. 1990. Rule providing that action shall be dismissed without prejudice if effective service is not obtained within 120 days of filing and plaintiff cannot show good cause is mandatory, but defense under the rule can be waived. Fed.Rules Civ.Proc.Rules 4, 4(j), 12(h), 28 U.S.C.A.

Patterson v. Brady, 131 F.R.D. 679, 108 A.L.R. Fed. 847, affirmed 89 F.3d 838, certiorari denied 117 S.Ct. 245, 136 L.Ed.2d 173.

N.D.Iowa 1995. District court has authority in its discretion to dismiss action with preju-dice for failure to comply with court orders or federal rules of civil procedure. Fed.Rules Civ. Proc.Rules 16, 37, 41(b), 28 U.S.C.A.

Waitek v. Dalkon Shield Claimants Trust, 908 F.Supp. 672.

N.D.Iowa 1995. District court has authority, in its discretion, to dismiss action with prejudice for failure to comply with court orders or Federal Rules of Civil Procedure. Fed. Rules Civ.Proc.Rule 41(b), 28 U.S.C.A.

Dahl v. Kanawha Inv. Holding Co., 161 F.R.D. 673.

N.D.Iowa 1994. District court has authority, in its discretion, to dismiss action with prejudice for failure to comply with court orders or the Federal Rules of Civil Procedure. Fed.Rules Civ.Proc.Rule 41(b), 28 U.S.C.A.

Tyler v. Iowa State Trooper Badge No. 297, 158 F.R.D. 632.

N.D.Iowa 1994. To prevent dismissal on basis of mootness, named plaintiff in class action must present live case or controversy at time complaint is filed and at time of certification. Fed.Rules Civ.Proc.Rule 23, 28 U.S.C.A.

Perley by Perley v. Palmer, 157 F.R.D. 452.

S.D.Iowa 1986. Mere fact that state penitentiary inmate had not been afforded same procedural protections at Iowa State Penitentiary as he would have been in Kansas prison did not constitute colorable claim of denial of due process for purposes of civil rights action, and thus, that claim would be dismissed as frivolous. U.S.C.A. Const.Amend. 5; 42 U.S.C.A. § 1983.

Stewart v. McManus, 647 F.Supp. 1024.

State penitentiary inmate's claim that he had been denied equal protection because he had not been afforded same disciplinary proceeding at Iowa State Penitentiary as he would have been were he imprisoned in Kansas, from where he was transferred, would be dismissed as frivolous, where inmate had failed to allege he had been treated dissimilarly from those similarly situated. U.S.C.A. Const.Amend. 14.

Stewart v. McManus, 647 F.Supp. 1024.

D.Kan. 1993. Question whether state law claims involving failure to disclose termination date for coverage under health plan subject to ERISA was barred by preemption provisions of ERISA could be raised on motion to dismiss. Fed.Rules Civ.Proc.Rule 12(b)(6), 28 U.S.C.A.; Employee Retirement Income Security Act of 1974, § 2 et seq., as amended, 29 U.S.C.A. § 1001 et seq.

Van Hoove v. Mid-America Bldg. Maintenance, Inc., 811 F.Supp. 609.

D.Kan. 1993. Diversity action was not subject to dismissal due to plaintiff's failure to pay filing fee within six months of dismissal of plaintiff's first action, where plaintiff deposited complaint with court within six month period and filed in forma pauperis application in lieu of paying filing fee, court denied plaintiff's application after six month period had run, and district does not have local rule requiring parties to prepay filing fee. Rules Civ.Proc., K.S.A. 60–203(a); K.S.A. 60–518; 28 U.S.C.A. § 1914.

Burnett v. Perry Mfg., Inc., 151 F.R.D. 398.

D.Kan. 1992. Because district court held that allegations of fraud as pled in amended petition comported with requirements of rules of civil procedure, defendant's motion to dismiss or for a more definite statement would be denied as moot. Fed.Rules Civ.Proc.Rule 9(b), 28 U.S.C.A.

Norton v. National Research Foundation, 141 F.R.D. 510.

D.Kan. 1989. Dismissal was proper sanction for failure of claimant to file response to motion to dismiss complaint seeking determination of dischargeability of debt. Bankr.Code, 11 U.S.C.A. § 523(c); U.S.Dist.Ct.Rules, D.Kan., Civil Rule 206(g).

Burger King Corp. v. Wilkinson, 98 B.R. 550, affirmed in part, vacated in part In re Wilkinson, 961 F.2d 221.

D.Kan. 1986. Shareholder's failure to make demand upon corporate directors to instigate suit themselves prior to her filing derivative action against directors based on alleged waste of corporate assets required that action be dismissed without prejudice. Fed.Rules Civ. Proc.Rule 23.1, 28 U.S.C.A.

Kaufman v. Kansas Gas and Elec. Co., 634 F.Supp. 1573.

E.D.Ky. 1986. Dismissal of insured horse owner's counterclaim for recovery under horse mortality policy was warranted by fraud practiced upon court by insured when insured introduced letters backdated to dates prior to horse's death in order to establish value of horse, and insured encouraged witness to perjure himself in order to authenticate letter; declining to follow *Young v. Curgil*, 358 So.2d 58 (Fla.App. 3 Dist.); *Lockwood v. Bowles*, 46 F.R.D 625 (D.C.Cir.)

Eppes v. Snowden, 656 F.Supp. 1267.

E.D.La. 1990. Contractor's disregard of orders and deliberate refusal to specify claims and facts upon which it relied in its civil Racketeer Influenced and Corrupt Organizations Act (RICO) claim against owner of property of failed construction project warranted imposition of dismissal with prejudice as sanction. 18 U.S.C.A. §§ 1961 et seq., 1962(c); Fed.Rules Civ.Proc.Rule 37(b), 28 U.S.C.A.

Newport Ltd. v. Sears, Roebuck & Co., 739 F.Supp. 1078, vacated 941 F.2d 302, rehearing denied 946 F.2d 893, certiorari denied 112 S.Ct. 1175, 502 U.S. 1096, 117 L.Ed.2d 420, on remand 1992 WL 245557, reversed 6 F.3d 1058, suggestion for rehearing denied 15 F.3d 1081, certiorari denied 114 S.Ct. 2710, 512 U.S. 1221, 129 L.Ed.2d 836, on remand 1995 WL 626188.

E.D.La. 1987. Plaintiffs' contumacious refusal to comply with court orders to file amended complaint to indicate against which harbor police officers they intended to proceed warranted dismissal of complaint with prejudice.

Lynch v. Cannatella, 122 F.R.D. 195, appeal dismissed 844 F.2d 786, affirmed 860 F.2d 651.

M.D.La. 1987. Conduct by attorney, in taking depositions of litigants in bankruptcy case, and bringing his own action against litigants during pendency of depositions, but failing to notify them of his action until after depositions were taken, did not require dismissal of attorney's action, but in interest of justice, parties in attorney's action would not be allowed to use depositions taken pursuant to order granted by bankruptcy judge, and all summaries of depositions and notes taken during depositions must also be submitted to court. Rules Bankr.Proc.Rule 2004, 11 U.S.C.A.

Collins v. Polk, 115 F.R.D. 326.

M.D.La. 1984. Filing of a suit pro se does not give plaintiff the right to proceed frivolously. Fed.Rules Civ.Proc.Rule 11, 28 U.S.C.A.; 28 U.S.C.A. § 2412.

McKinney v. Regan, 599 F.Supp. 126.

D.Me. 1986. Dismissal of action by physician whose emergency room privileges were allegedly reduced because of his age would unfairly punish physician for shortcomings of his attorney's performance in responding to motion to dismiss where motion to dismiss was based on failure to allege employee status. Age Discrimination in Employment Act of 1967, §§ 2–17, 29 U.S.C.A. §§ 621–634; Fed.Rules Civ.Proc.Rules 56(e), 59(e), 28 U.S.C.A.

Kuck v. Bensen, 649 F.Supp. 68.

D.Me. 1986. Discharged postal carrier's state law tort claims of defamation and tortious interference with contractual relationship would be dismissed, based upon considerations of judicial economy, comity, and promotion of justice, following dismissal of civil rights claims in federal court.

Springer v. Seaman, 639 F.Supp. 1137, affirmed in part, reversed in part 821 F.2d 871, on remand 117 F.R.D. 487.

D.Me. 1985. Dismissal of medical malpractice action was warranted where plaintiff filed action within two-year limitations period but failed to provide prelitigation notice of claim as required by 24 M.R.S.A. § 2903 within that period. 14 M.R.S.A. § 753.

Houk v. Furman, 613 F.Supp. 1022.

D.Md. 1996. Dismissal for lack of injury is appropriate where claimed injury is not cognizable as a legal matter, but not where claimed injury is not easily susceptible to proof.

In re American Honda Motor Co., Inc. Dealerships Relations Litigation, 941 F.Supp. 528.

D.Md. 1995. District court would, in exercise of discretion, dismiss action rather than stay action pending arbitration pursuant to National Association of Securities Dealers (NASD) code, in broker's action against competitor alleging common law trademark infringement, "passing off," and false designation of origin, absent apparent reason why complete relief would not be available to broker in arbitration proceeding.

Lombard Securities Inc. v. Thomas F. White & Co., Inc., 903 F.Supp. 895.

D.Mass. 1992. Where jurisdictional basis of claim becomes moot, but other aspects of claim remain live, court has discretion to dismiss case.

New Bank of New England, N.A. v. Tritek Communications, Inc., 143 F.R.D. 13.

D.Mass. 1988. Plaintiff's counsel's extrajudicial statements to news media on very date that trial of case was scheduled to begin did not require dismissal of case, as any prejudice to defendant caused by the publication could be eradicated on voir dire. Mass.S.J.C.Rule 3:07, Code of Prof.Resp., DR 7–107(G).

Bushkin Associates, Inc. v. Raytheon Co., 121 F.R.D. 5.

D.C.Mass. 1985. Claims, which contained only conclusory allegations and failed to allege any facts which would afford a basis for granting of relief, would be dismissed as to nonjudicial and nonprosecutorial defendants for failure to state a claim; furthermore, case against one defendant asserted by plaintiff, who sought retaliation by instituting litigation against everyone who had even the most tenuous relationship to his arrest, conviction and incarceration, would be dismissed as being both frivolous and malicious. 28 U.S.C.A. § 1915(d).

Papas v. Bertrum, 600 F.Supp. 174, affirmed 782 F.2d 1023.

E.D.Mich. 1994. Determination whether to apply mootness doctrine to dismiss lawsuit involves close appraisal of facts with discretionary determination of need for present decision.

Strout v. U.S. Parole Com'n, 842 F.Supp. 948, affirmed 40 F.3d 136.

E.D.Mich. 1990. In most instances, action against an absolutely immune defendant may be dismissed on motion setting out defendant's status as well as an allegation of action within official capacity.

Bennett v. Batchik, 743 F.Supp. 1245, affirmed 936 F.2d 572.

W.D.Mich. 1997. Accounting firm's counterclaims seeking contribution were moot in corporation's malpractice action based on firm's audit, and therefore, dismissal of such claims was warranted; counterclaims were expressly contingent on district court's denial of accounting firm's then-pending motion to dismiss corporation's claim for contribution against firm, and court dismissed such claim.

Ameriwood Industries Intern. Corp. v. Arthur Andersen & Co., 961 F.Supp. 1078.

W.D.Mich. 1994. Dismissal for failure to state a claim is proper if complaint fails to allege an element necessary for relief or if affirmative defense or other bar to relief is apparent from face of complaint, such as official immunity of defendant. Fed.Rules Civ. Proc.Rule 12(b)(6), 28 U.S.C.A.

Torrie By and Through Torrie v. Cwayna, 841 F.Supp. 1434.

W.D.Mich. 1988. Failure of securities broker and its principal to retain counsel and amend complaint to comply with requirements for shareholder derivative suit as ordered by court warranted dismissal of complaint against NASD and officials. Fed.Rules Civ.Proc.Rule 23.1, 28 U.S.C.A.

Prevatte v. National Ass'n of Securities Dealers, Inc., 682 F.Supp. 913.

W.D.Mich. 1976. Thompson v. Board of Ed. of Romeo Community Schools, 71 F.R.D. 398, adhered to 519 F.Supp. 1373, reversed 709 F.2d 1200.

D.Minn. 1994. Once state secrets privilege is successfully invoked, if plaintiff is, or will be, unable to establish prima facie case without privileged information, or if privileged information is so central to subject matter of litigation that any attempt to proceed will threaten disclosure of privileged matters, dismissal or summary judgment is appropriate. Fed.Rules Civ. Proc.Rule 56, 28 U.S.C.A.

Black v. U.S., 900 F.Supp. 1129.

Individual's claim against federal government under Federal Tort Claims Act (FTCA) for intentional infliction of emotional distress had to be dismissed after government's successful invocation of state secrets privilege respecting information as to identities of any government agents who might have contacted individual, nature and purposes of contacts, and locations of contacts; individual would not have access to facts necessary to establish whether alleged wrongdoers were employees or agents of government, and factual allegations in complaint were so tied to privileged information that further litigation would constitute undue threat that privileged information would be disclosed. 28 U.S.C.A. §§ 1346(b), 2674.

Black v. U.S., 900 F.Supp. 1129.

Once state secrets privilege is successfully invoked, dismissal of claim is warranted if no measure of security or diligence could ensure that information falling within privilege will not be disclosed.

Black v. U.S., 900 F.Supp. 1129.

Individual's *Bivens* claim against federal government agents for injuries caused by agents having deprived individual of his Fourth Amendment rights had to be dismissed after government's successful invocation of state secrets privilege respecting information as to identities of any government agents who might have contacted individual, nature and purposes of contacts, and locations of contacts; litigating claim would present continuing and substantial threat that privileged information would be disclosed, and individual's inability to acquire information concerning identity of alleged wrongdoers and nature of their actions precluded him from establishing prima facie case.

Black v. U.S., 900 F.Supp. 1129.

In circumstances in which state secrets privilege is upheld, dismissal may be appropriate even though government is not named party to cause of action.

Black v. U.S., 900 F.Supp. 1129.

D.Minn. 1994. To survive motion to dismiss based on lack of standing, plaintiffs need only state general factual allegations of injury resulting from defendant's conduct.

Ben Oehrleins and Sons and Daughter, Inc. v. Hennepin County, Minn., 867 F.Supp. 1430.

For purposes of motion to dismiss, solid waste haulers suffered economic injury as result of impermissible burden that county ordinance governing waste management placed on interstate commerce, and, thus, they had standing to bring constitutional challenge against ordinance, where haulers alleged that ordinance forced them to forego alternative disposal facilities and pay county's higher tipping fees. U.S.C.A. Const. Art. 1, § 8, cl. 3; Hennepin County, Minn., Ordinance 12.

Ben Oehrleins and Sons and Daughter, Inc. v. Hennepin County, Minn., 867 F.Supp. 1430.

D.Minn. 1990. Dismissal of class action for management reasons is never favored. Fed. Rules Civ.Proc.Rule 23, 28 U.S.C.A.

In re Workers' Compensation, 130 F.R.D. 99.

D.Minn. 1989. Debenture holder's claims for class certification and constructive trust would be dismissed for failure to comply with terms of "no action" clause of indenture, where clause restricted rights of holders of less than 25% of aggregate principal amount of debentures to bring suit on their own and holder held approximately 19% of the debenture principal.

Alleco, Inc. v. IBJ Schroder Bank & Trust Co., 745 F.Supp. 1467.

N.D.Miss. 1996. When exhaustion of administrative remedies is statutorily required, district court must dismiss plaintiff's case for failing to exhaust administrative remedies, even when sending plaintiff back to administrative remedy process would be futile.

Calhoun v. USDA Farm Service Agency, 920 F.Supp. 696.

N.D.Miss. 1988. Under Mississippi law, dismissal without prejudice of libel suit was warranted by plaintiff's failure to comply with retraction statute prior to filing thereof. Miss. Code 1972, § 95–1–5.

Pannell v. Associated Press, 690 F.Supp. 546.

S.D.Miss. 1985. When personal claims of named plaintiff are moot and no class has been certified, general rule is that action will be dismissed for mootness.

K v. Complaints Committee of Mississippi State Bar, 618 F.Supp. 307.

E.D.Mo. 1984. Action is frivolous and may be dismissed if it fails to state claim upon which relief can be granted. 28 U.S.C.A. § 1915(d).

Harvey v. Three Doctors from India, 598 F.Supp. 739.

E.D.Mo. 1983. McClure v. Esparza, 556 F.Supp. 569, affirmed 732 F.2d 162, certiorari denied 105 S.Ct. 2111, 471 U.S. 1052, 85 L.Ed.2d 477.

E.D.Mo. 1982. Alexander Grant & Co. v. Tiffany Industries, Inc., 563 F.Supp. 35, reversed 742 F.2d 408, motion denied Kahn v. Alexander Grant & Company, 105 S.Ct. 1164, 469 U.S. 1205, 84 L.Ed.2d 316, certiorari granted, vacated 105 S.Ct. 3550, 473 U.S. 922, 87 L.Ed.2d 673, on remand 770 F.2d 717, certiorari denied 106 S.Ct. 799, 474 U.S. 1058, 88 L.Ed.2d 776, certiorari denied 106 S.Ct. 799, 474 U.S. 1058, 88 L.Ed.2d 776, certiorari granted, vacated 105 S.Ct. 3551, 473 U.S. 922, 87 L.Ed.2d 673, on remand 770 F.2d 717, certiorari denied 106 S.Ct. 799, 474 U.S. 1058, 88

L.Ed.2d 776, certiorari denied 106 S.Ct. 799, 474 U.S. 1058, 88 L.Ed.2d 776.

W.D.Mo. 1989. Federal civil rule authorizing court to order payment of costs for previously dismissed action which included same claim as currently asserted against same defendant and stay proceedings until compliance did not authorize dismissal of case. Fed.Rules Civ. Proc.Rule 41(d), 28 U.S.C.A.

    Fisher v. Chevron Chemical Co., 716 F.Supp. 1283.

W.D.Mo. 1984. Gale v. Moore, 587 F.Supp. 1491, affirmed as modified 763 F.2d 341.

D.Mont. 1986. Dismissal of federal suit seeking injunctive relief with regard to distribution of water by reservation irrigation project administered by the Bureau of Indian Affairs in favor of state proceedings was not justified by wise judicial administration and efficiency, where there was no state forum available for parties to air their differences over water management problems existing on reservation.

    Joint Bd. of Control of Flathead, Mission and Jocko Irr. Dist. v. U.S. of America, 646 F.Supp. 410, reversed Joint Bd. of Control of Flathead, Mission and Jocko Irr. Districts v. U.S., 832 F.2d 1127, certiorari denied 108 S.Ct. 1732, 486 U.S. 1007, 100 L.Ed.2d 196.

D.Nev. 1997. Action that is premature should be dismissed without prejudice.

    Martin v. State Farm Mut. Auto. Ins. Co., 960 F.Supp. 233.

D.Nev. 1996. Military and state secrets privilege alone can be basis for dismissal of entire case; dismissal is appropriate where it is clear that national security interests prevent plaintiff from establishing prima facie case.

    Frost v. Perry, 919 F.Supp. 1459, affirmed Kasza v. Browner, 133 F.3d 1159.

Plaintiffs bringing citizen suit under Resource Conservation and Recovery Act (RCRA) regarding classified Air Force site could not provide essential evidence to establish prima facie case for any of their claims, due to defendants' assertion of military and state secrets privilege, thus warranting dismissal of case. Solid Waste Disposal Act, § 7002, as amended, 42 U.S.C.A. § 6972.

    Frost v. Perry, 919 F.Supp. 1459, affirmed Kasza v. Browner, 133 F.3d 1159.

D.Nev. 1986. District court may dismiss in forma pauperis action that is frivolous or malicious. 28 U.S.C.A. § 1915(a, d).

    Williams v. Sumner, 648 F.Supp. 510.

D.Nev. 1986. Action in which defendant tried to renew dismissed action by amending its answer and adding third party to its counterclaim required dismissal in that defendant was required to file new third-party action or move court for leave to do so. Fed.Rules Civ.Proc. Rule 4(j), 28 U.S.C.A.

    Mainline Industries, Inc. v. Palco Linings, Inc., 113 F.R.D. 148.

D.N.J. 1996. Inmates' complaint would be dismissed since inmates neither petitioned court to proceed in forma pauperis nor paid the requisite filing fee; however, the dismissal would be without prejudice.

    Robinson v. Fauver, 932 F.Supp. 639.

D.N.J. 1995. Lack of standing is more appropriately characterized as absence of subject matter jurisdiction, rather than failure to state claim and can be raised by court on its own initiative for purpose of dismissal. Fed. Rules Civ.Proc.Rule 12(b)(1, 6), 28 U.S.C.A.

    Kessler Institute for Rehabilitation, Inc. v. Mayor and Council of Borough of Essex Fells, 876 F.Supp. 641.

D.N.J. 1993. Claims under New Jersey law for private nuisance, public nuisance, negligence, fraudulent concealment, waste of property, trespass, and unjust enrichment by property owner against former lessee of property for environmental contamination did not "parrot" claim for strict liability so as to warrant dismissal of claims as duplicative.

    Mayor and Council of Borough of Rockaway v. Klockner & Klockner, 811 F.Supp. 1039.

D.N.J. 1992. Upholding government's claim of state secrets privilege did not entitle Eastern European emigre to dismissal of denaturalization proceeding for concealing propaganda efforts on behalf of Nazis; the most significant material relating "disinformation" defense was voluntarily released by government, disclosure of withheld information would pose substantial risk of compromising intelligence sources, and government offered to stipulate to information in withheld documents.

    U.S. v. Koreh, 144 F.R.D. 218.

E.D.N.Y. 1995. Court would dismiss civil rights claim and vacate appointment of pro bono counsel where plaintiff was fugitive from justice, having failed to report to parole officer.

    Griffin v. City of New York Correctional Com'r, 882 F.Supp. 295.

E.D.N.Y. 1993. Generally, fact that complaint does not cite relevant statutory provision does not require dismissal; as long as complaint contains set of facts for which relief may be granted, it survives motion to dismiss for failure to state a claim. Fed.Rules Civ.Proc. Rule 12(b)(6), 28 U.S.C.A.

    Thomas v. New York City, 814 F.Supp. 1139.

E.D.N.Y. 1991. Plaintiffs' failure to oppose motion to dismiss could, in and of itself, have been grounds to grant dismissal motion by default. Fed.Rules Civ.Proc.Rule 12(b)(6), 28 U.S.C.A.; U.S.Dist.Ct.Rules E.D.N.Y., Civil Rule 3(b).

> Laverpool v. New York City Transit Authority, 760 F.Supp. 1046.

E.D.N.Y. 1988. Defendant was not entitled to dismissal of civil RICO action on ground that his age, ill-health and mental condition, combined with Government's delay in bringing action, made prosecution of the action a denial of his due process rights. 18 U.S.C.A. § 1961 et seq.; U.S.C.A. Const.Amend. 14.

> U.S. v. Bonanno Organized Crime Family of La Cosa Nostra, 695 F.Supp. 1426.

E.D.N.Y. 1976. Woe v. Mathews, 408 F.Supp. 419, dismissed in part, remanded in part 556 F.2d 563, affirmed 562 F.2d 40, certiorari denied 98 S.Ct. 895, 434 U.S. 1048, 54 L.Ed.2d 799.

N.D.N.Y. 1998. Failure of inmate bringing § 1983 action against state prison officials to notify district court of his new address after being released from prison warranted dismissal of inmate's action. 42 U.S.C.A. § 1983; U.S.Dist.Ct.Rules N.D.N.Y., Local Rule 10.1(b).

> Fenza v. Conklin, 177 F.R.D. 126.

N.D.N.Y. 1998. Plaintiff's failure to inform court of his current address warranted dismissal of complaint. U.S.Dist.Ct.Rules N.D.N.Y., Civil Rule 41.2.

> Morgan v. Dardiz, 177 F.R.D. 125.

N.D.N.Y. 1997. Dismissal of United States corporation's action against Canadian corporation in federal district court for misappropriation of trade secrets, trade dress infringement, and Canadian law copyright infringement was not warranted on ground of comity; plaintiff was not collaterally attacking Canadian bankruptcy proceedings that led to transfer of intellectual property to defendant, as alleged by defendant, but was instead challenging failure to return intellectual property that had allegedly been lent to another corporation by plaintiff.

> Frink America, Inc. v. Champion Road Machinery Ltd., 961 F.Supp. 398.

N.D.N.Y. 1995. There was no authority for dismissing for failure to state a cause of action complaint alleging violations of state law, based on ruling that foreign law applied. Fed.Rules Civ.Proc.Rule 12(b)(6), 28 U.S.C.A.

> Elgin Sweeper Co. v. Melson Inc., 884 F.Supp. 641.

N.D.N.Y. 1994. Pro se civil litigant's § 1983 claim against state would be dismissed for failure to respond to motion, where final adjournment notices sent to pro se litigant contained warning, in layman's terms, that if opposition papers were not filed in timely fashion it could result in granting of relief requested; under circumstances, all possible leeway was given to litigant, and he had over three months to file the required papers. Fed.Rules Civ.Proc. Rule 12(b), (b)(1, 6), 28 U.S.C.A.

> Hall v. Ruggeri, 841 F.Supp. 484.

N.D.N.Y. 1993. Allegation in complaint that amount in controversy exceeded sum of $10,000, exclusive of interest and costs, did not adequately put defendants on notice that plaintiffs were seeking nominal damages, and, thus, did not preclude dismissal of action on mootness grounds; jurisdiction in case was not predicated on diversity of citizenship.

> Fox v. Board of Trustees of State University of New York, 148 F.R.D. 474, affirmed 42 F.3d 135, certiorari denied 115 S.Ct. 2634, 515 U.S. 1169, 132 L.Ed.2d 873.

Fact that "wherefore" clause in complaint requested such other relief as court would deem just and proper was not sufficient to show that civil rights plaintiffs were seeking nominal damages, and, thus, did not preclude dismissal of complaint on mootness grounds.

> Fox v. Board of Trustees of State University of New York, 148 F.R.D. 474, affirmed 42 F.3d 135, certiorari denied 115 S.Ct. 2634, 515 U.S. 1169, 132 L.Ed.2d 873.

When action becomes moot, it no longer presents live case or controversy, and, thus, federal court must dismiss that case because it lacks subject-matter jurisdiction to entertain it. U.S.C.A. Const. Art. 3, § 1 et seq.

> Fox v. Board of Trustees of State University of New York, 148 F.R.D. 474, affirmed 42 F.3d 135, certiorari denied 115 S.Ct. 2634, 515 U.S. 1169, 132 L.Ed.2d 873.

Action brought by students to challenge constitutionality of state university's resolution prohibiting group sales demonstrations in dormitories had to be dismissed when action became moot because plaintiff students had graduated.

> Fox v. Board of Trustees of State University of New York, 148 F.R.D. 474, affirmed 42 F.3d 135, certiorari denied 115 S.Ct. 2634, 515 U.S. 1169, 132 L.Ed.2d 873.

N.D.N.Y. 1984. Interests of justice and preservation of court responsibility for efficient control of its litigation warranted and compelled grant of motion to dismiss employment discrimination action of pro se plaintiff for failure to diligently prosecute the action and for failure to comply with directions of the court where plaintiff kept court in turmoil for several months after his dismissal of his competent attorneys, with telephone calls, mailgrams and letters, requested list of trial judge's law clerks, prosecuted the action from long distance, ignored express directions of court to appear in court, and took more than a year to file reply to pending motions without applying for stay to permit such delay. Fed.Rules Civ.Proc.Rule 41(b), 28 U.S.C.A.

> Silver v. Mohasco Corp., 103 F.R.D. 614.

S.D.N.Y. 1996. Plaintiff's repeated failures to comply with discovery orders justified dismissal of suit, regardless of whether automatic bankruptcy stay precluded dismissal based on failure to pay discovery sanctions; plaintiff failed to comply with order directing answer to interrogatories despite four-month delay, had been repeatedly warned that failure to comply with court orders could result in dismissal, defendants were likely to be prejudiced due to failure of plaintiff to identify possible witnesses, court's interest in managing its docket outweighed plaintiff's interest in being heard on the merits, and sanction less drastic than dismissal was not appropriate. Bankr.Code, 11 U.S.C.A. § 362(a); Fed.Rules Civ.Proc.Rules 37, 41(b), 28 U.S.C.A.

> Georgiadis v. First Boston Corp., 167 F.R.D. 24.

S.D.N.Y. 1995. Equal protection claim raised in complaint would be dismissed as abandoned, where plaintiffs advanced no argument and offered no evidence in its support. U.S.C.A. Const.Amend. 14.

> Irwin v. City of New York, 902 F.Supp. 442.

S.D.N.Y. 1995. Claim alleging that former employer violated Title VII by denying plaintiff leave to attend doctor's appointment, and by putting final warning letter in his file in reference to requested leave, could not be dismissed as moot based on employer's contention that final warning letter was later removed from employee's personnel file pursuant to arbitration award in employee's favor, since whether letter was removed from employee's personnel file was not apparent from face of complaint. Civil Rights Act of 1964, § 701 et seq., as amended, 42 U.S.C.A. § 2000e et seq.

> Humphrey v. Council of Jewish Federations, 901 F.Supp. 703.

S.D.N.Y. 1995. Dismissals for lack of standing may be made pursuant to rule providing for dismissal due to failure to state claim upon which relief may be granted. Fed.Rules Civ.Proc.Rule 12(b)(6), 28 U.S.C.A.

> Red Ball Interior Demolition Corp. v. Palmadessa, 874 F.Supp. 576.

In area of Racketeer Influenced and Corrupt Organizations Act (RICO), standing is issue appropriate for consideration on motion to dismiss for failure to state claim upon which relief

may be granted. 18 U.S.C.A. § 1964; Fed. Rules Civ.Proc.Rule 12(b)(6), 28 U.S.C.A.

> Red Ball Interior Demolition Corp. v. Palmadessa, 874 F.Supp. 576.

District court may dismiss action for lack of standing, and do so on its own motion. Fed. Rules Civ.Proc.Rule 12(b)(6), (h)(3), 28 U.S.C.A.

> Red Ball Interior Demolition Corp. v. Palmadessa, 874 F.Supp. 576.

District court could dismiss action brought under Racketeer Influenced and Corrupt Organizations Act (RICO) for plaintiffs' lack of standing, even though defendants had not expressly raised question of standing, if lack of subject matter jurisdiction was apparent. 18 U.S.C.A. § 1964; Fed.Rules Civ.Proc.Rule 12(b)(6), (h)(3), 28 U.S.C.A.

> Red Ball Interior Demolition Corp. v. Palmadessa, 874 F.Supp. 576.

S.D.N.Y. 1994. Issues presented by pro se litigants raising matters of public concern should be addressed on merits, if appropriate, even if action could be dismissed on procedural grounds for abusive repetitive litigation.

> Glendora v. Dolan, 871 F.Supp. 174, affirmed 48 F.3d 1212, certiorari denied 115 S.Ct. 1827, 514 U.S. 1098, 131 L.Ed.2d 748.

S.D.N.Y. 1994. In seeking to have case dismissed as moot, defendant must demonstrate that it is absolutely clear that allegedly wrongful behavior could not reasonably be expected to recur.

> Orange Environment, Inc. v. County of Orange, 860 F.Supp. 1003.

S.D.N.Y. 1993. Claims describing fantastic or delusional scenarios are subject to sua sponte dismissal as frivolous, even though plaintiff asserting claims is not proceeding in forma pauperis, but, rather has paid filing fee. Fed.Rules Civ.Proc.Rule 12(b)(6), 28 U.S.C.A.

> Tyler v. Carter, 151 F.R.D. 537, affirmed 41 F.3d 1500.

District court would, sua sponte, dismiss as frivolous plaintiff's claims against federal agencies, president and former president, private corporations, and private individuals alleging conspiracy to reinstitutionalize slavery and oppress political dissidents; claims described fantastic or delusional scenarios. Fed.Rules Civ. Proc.Rule 12(b)(6), 28 U.S.C.A.

> Tyler v. Carter, 151 F.R.D. 537, affirmed 41 F.3d 1500.

S.D.N.Y. 1992. Private right of action allegedly implied by statute governing personal liability of directors or officers of insured depository institutions, which holders of notes issued by federally chartered savings bank did not assert in their complaint, could not properly be presented through argument on motion to dismiss in their fiduciary duty action against bank's directors based on failure to make payments due on notes. Fed.Rules Civ.Proc.Rule 12(b)(1), 28 U.S.C.A.; Federal Deposit Insurance Act, § 2[11](k), 12 U.S.C.A. § 1821(k); 28 U.S.C.A. § 1331.

> Curiale v. Reissman, 798 F.Supp. 141.

S.D.N.Y. 1992. Although assertion that implied private right of action under federal statute provides federal subject matter jurisdiction for the claim, claim should nevertheless be dismissed if court determines that private cause of action does not in fact exist under statute. Fed.Rules Civ.Proc.Rule 12(b)(6), 28 U.S.C.A.

> Platzer v. Sloan-Kettering Institute for Cancer Research, 787 F.Supp. 360, affirmed 983 F.2d 1086, certiorari denied 113 S.Ct. 1648, 507 U.S. 1006, 123 L.Ed.2d 270.

S.D.N.Y. 1988. When consideration of record as whole makes it clear that plaintiff lacks standing, court should dismiss action on that basis alone.

> Strykers Bay Neighborhood Council, Inc. v. City of New York, 695 F.Supp. 1531.

S.D.N.Y. 1987. Dismissal is permissible because of deception only when deception relates to matters in controversy in action, and even then is so harsh a remedy that it should be imposed only in the most extreme circumstances.

> Bower v. Weisman, 674 F.Supp. 109.

Plaintiff's perjury as to whether she had sexual relations with others than defendant during period in question did not warrant dismissal of action alleging breach of contract between nonmarital partners relating to nonsexual personal services; plaintiff had already testified as to having sexual relations with males other than defendant during period in issue, belated addition of three more affairs had little effect on merits of action.

> Bower v. Weisman, 674 F.Supp. 109.

S.D.N.Y. 1987. Counterclaim for almost $150,000 in consultancy fees which defendant originally claimed to have paid would be dismissed in light of defendant's abandonment of any claims to damages after plaintiff presented copies of defendant's letter repudiating its obligations under consultancy agreement and partial summary judgment from Washington state court.

> Cross & Cross Properties, Ltd. v. Everett Allied Co., 664 F.Supp. 713.

S.D.N.Y. 1987. Court would not dismiss counterclaim on grounds that plaintiffs had filed a separate proceeding, to which the defen-

dant was not a party, in another country involving the same subject matter.

> Summit, Ltd. v. Levy, 660 F.Supp. 708.

S.D.N.Y. 1987. Plaintiff's failure to comply with court order to post a bond for costs in the amount of $2,500 warranted dismissal of her suit with prejudice in view of her continuing abuse of the courts by bringing repeated and usually baseless litigation. Fed.Rules Civ.Proc. Rule 41(b), 28 U.S.C.A.; U.S.Dist.Ct.Rules S.D.N.Y., Civil Rule 39.

> Zerman v. E.F. Hutton & Co., Inc., 656 F.Supp. 1225.

S.D.N.Y. 1987. Dismissal should not be granted for mere technical defects or ambiguities. Fed.Rules Civ.Proc.Rule 12(b)(6), (c), 28 U.S.C.A.

> Morse/Diesel, Inc. v. Trinity Industries, Inc., 655 F.Supp. 346, on reargument 664 F.Supp. 91, reversed 859 F.2d 242.

S.D.N.Y. 1987. Investor's federal securities action was subject to dismissal under Rule 11; investor testified that he closed his account with a broker other than defendant before coming to defendant and that he had never had and never intended to have margin account with that broker but it was established at trial that investor continued to maintain account with broker after setting up account with defendant, including a margin account. Fed.Rules Civ. Proc.Rule 11, 28 U.S.C.A.

> Murray v. Dominick Corp. of Canada, Ltd., 117 F.R.D. 512.

S.D.N.Y. 1986. Inmate's failure to report veterans benefits or prison salary on his application for in forma pauperis status did not require dismissal of inmate's civil rights action, where there was no evidence that inmate acted in bad faith, and inmate would have been eligible for in forma pauperis status even if his assets were taken into account. 28 U.S.C.A. §§ 1915, 1915(d).

> Acevedo v. Reid, 653 F.Supp. 347.

S.D.N.Y. 1986. Plaintiff's failure to submit statement pursuant to court rule with respect to defendants' cross motion for summary judgment on plaintiff's claims required dismissal of claims. U.S.Dist.Ct.Rules S.D.N.Y., Civil Rule 3(g).

> Aldon Industries, Inc. v. Brown, 647 F.Supp. 1558.

S.D.N.Y. 1984. In section 1983 action challenging constitutionality of various policies enforced in detention house's maximum security section, claims of two pretrial detainees who were no longer housed in detention house and had not participated in action for more than one year were dismissed on grounds of mootness and failure to prosecute; defendants' summary judgment motion directed at the two pretrial detainees was denied on the ground that it too was moot. 42 U.S.C.A. § 1983.

> Arrango v. Ward, 103 F.R.D. 638.

S.D.N.Y. 1979. Haberman v. Tobin, 480 F.Supp. 425, affirmed 626 F.2d 1101.

S.D.N.Y. 1979. Avigliano v. Sumitomo Shoji America, Inc., 473 F.Supp. 506, certification granted 1979 WL 286, amended 1979 WL 58, on reargument 1979 WL 58, affirmed 638 F.2d 552, certiorari granted 102 S.Ct. 501, 454 U.S. 962, 70 L.Ed.2d 377, vacated and remanded 102 S.Ct. 2374, 457 U.S. 176, 72 L.Ed.2d 765, on remand 103 F.R.D. 562.

W.D.N.Y. 1995. Appropriate procedure where plaintiff had not exhausted remedies in tribal court system for challenging jurisdiction of tribal courts was to hold matter in abeyance pending development of further tribal court proceedings, rather than dismissal, where, if tribal court's exercise of jurisdiction was upheld on appeal within the tribal court system, plaintiff could challenge that ruling in district court.

> AG Organic, Inc. v. John, 892 F.Supp. 466.

W.D.N.Y. 1993. State inmate's motion seeking injunctive relief based on alleged wrongful conduct at two correctional facilities would be dismissed as moot in inmate's § 1983 action; inmate had been transferred to at least two different correctional facilities since he filed motion and failed to show demonstrated probability that he was likely to be retransferred and subject to same alleged conduct. 42 U.S.C.A. § 1983.

> Klos v. Haskell, 835 F.Supp. 710, affirmed 48 F.3d 81.

E.D.N.C. 1987. Trial judges have broad discretionary power to keep dockets streamlined by dismissing case if action is malicious. 28 U.S.C.A. § 1915(d).

> Spencer v. Rhodes, 656 F.Supp. 458, affirmed 826 F.2d 1061, affirmed 826 F.2d 1061.

In determining whether pro se complaint should be dismissed as malicious, judge may consider not only printed words, but circumstances of history that surrounds filing, tone of allegations, and whether probative facts vital to life of lawsuit have been alleged. 28 U.S.C.A. § 1915(d).

> Spencer v. Rhodes, 656 F.Supp. 458, affirmed 826 F.2d 1061, affirmed 826 F.2d 1061.

Dismissable claim that is "frivolous or malicious" is one that can range from attempted litigation of truly de minimus (non curat lex) matter to abuse of judicial process, but neither pole should constitute bright line incapable of being crossed when justice so requires. 28 U.S.C.A. § 1915(d).

> Spencer v. Rhodes, 656 F.Supp. 458, affirmed 826 F.2d 1061, affirmed 826 F.2d 1061.

North Carolina inmate's civil rights action seeking $748 million in damages for harm done to his marriage, and another $748 million for punitive damages, and $748 million in damages to compensate for "illegal activity," was obviously attempt to harass defendants merely to satisfy desire for vengeance and not to rectify any wrong, and was thus "malicious" and subject to dismissal. 28 U.S.C.A. § 1915(d).

> Spencer v. Rhodes, 656 F.Supp. 458, affirmed 826 F.2d 1061, affirmed 826 F.2d 1061.

Inmate's suit is "malicious" and thus subject to dismissal when there is no recital of credible probative facts that support allegations inmate is attempting to make, inmate sues those involved in securing his incarceration, and tone of all inmate's allegations indicates that he is bringing his suit merely to satisfy his desire for vengeance against defendants and not to rectify any wrong done to him. 28 U.S.C.A. § 1915(d).

> Spencer v. Rhodes, 656 F.Supp. 458, affirmed 826 F.2d 1061, affirmed 826 F.2d 1061.

M.D.N.C. 1985. A "frivolous claim" by a pro se party may properly be dismissed; to be characterized as "frivolous," court must conclude beyond doubt and under any arguable construction, both in law and in fact, of substance of plaintiff's claim that he would not be entitled to relief.

> Waller v. Butkovich, 605 F.Supp. 1137.

W.D.N.C. 1984. Because Eleventh Amendment prohibits federal courts from adjudicating pendent claims against state officials based on those officials' alleged violations of state law, all pendent state law claims in civil rights action in federal district court against state officials would be dismissed, but claims against state officials based on their alleged violation of federal law would be entertained. N.C.G.S. §§ 35–1.28, 122–24.1; U.S.C.A. Const.Amends. 11, 14.

> Thomas S. by Brooks v. Morrow, 601 F.Supp. 1055, affirmed as modified and remanded 781 F.2d 367, certiorari denied Kirk v. Thomas S. by Brooks, 106 S.Ct. 1992, 476 U.S. 1124, 90 L.Ed.2d 673, certiorari denied Childress v. Thomas S., 107 S.Ct. 235, 479 U.S. 869, 93 L.Ed.2d 161.

D.N.D. 1994. When administrative agency withdraws offending order but continues to maintain that its action was legal, repetition is likely, and, therefore, case should not be dismissed as moot.

> Minn-Dak Farmers Co-op. v. Espy, 851 F.Supp. 1423.

N.D.Ohio 1990. Dismissal of pro se plaintiff's civil rights action was justified by absence of activity on plaintiff's part except for requests for continuances for almost three years after filing suit and refusal by plaintiff to obey court orders, including orders to respond to motion to dismiss and to personally appear, but dismissal would be without prejudice. Fed.Rules Civ. Proc.Rule 41, 28 U.S.C.A.

> Vesely v. Cuyahoga Metropolitan Housing Authority, 130 F.R.D. 83.

N.D.Ohio 1989. Attorney and litigant have continuing obligation to review and reevaluate their pleadings, motions, and other papers, and upon learning that these papers may be without merit, appropriate course is to dismiss the action.

> Costanzo v. Plain Dealer Pub. Co., 715 F.Supp. 1380.

N.D.Ohio 1983. If dock owner, which was alleging a conspiracy by railroads to monopolize business of providing dock services for iron ore and other goods moving over docks in the lower Great Lakes, and that the alleged conspiracy was carried out through a series of anticompetitive activities, including the fixing and maintaining of dock and railroad rates and charges, intended to prove damages by establishing a hypothetical line-haul rate or hypothetical handling charges, that claim would be dismissed, as the court would lack authority to ascertain such hypothetical rates and would not be able to refer the question to the Interstate Commerce Commission for determination; therefore, dock owner was directed to file written statement declaring whether or not it intended to ask court to make those determinations.

> Pinney Dock & Transport Co. v. Penn Cent. Corp., 600 F.Supp. 859, dismissed in part, remanded in part 838 F.2d 1445, certiorari denied 109 S.Ct. 196, 488 U.S. 880, 102 L.Ed.2d 166.

S.D.Ohio 1984. Unavailability of particular remedy should not lead to dismissal of complaint, provided such remedy is not sole remedy sought.

> Pierce v. Apple Valley, Inc., 597 F.Supp. 1480.

D.Or. 1997. A case is "moot" when the issues presented are no longer "live" or the parties lack a legally cognizable interest in the outcome, but federal court may not dismiss an action for mootness unless it concludes with assurance that there is no reasonable expectation that the alleged violation will recur and it is plain that interim relief or events have completely and irrevocably eradicated the effects of the alleged violation.

> Bonnichsen v. U.S., Dept. of Army, 969 F.Supp. 628.

D.Or. 1994. Federal court will not dismiss claim merely because it is incorrectly labeled.

> Plumb v. Prinslow, 847 F.Supp. 1509.

D.Or. 1990. Once it is shown that court lacks subject matter jurisdiction, all other motions in case become moot and case must be dismissed. Fed.Rules Civ.Proc.Rule 12(b)(1), 28 U.S.C.A.

> Pineros Y Campesinos Unidos del Noroeste v. Goldschmidt, 790 F.Supp. 216.

E.D.Pa. 1997. Heavy burden of demonstrating mootness of case is on party moving for dismissal.

> Lanning v. Southeastern Pennsylvania Transp. Authority, 176 F.R.D. 132.

E.D.Pa. 1996. When complaint's allegations are defective but it appears that they can be cured, courts should not dismiss, but should grant leave to amend to cure defects.

> Clarke v. Whitney, 934 F.Supp. 148.

E.D.Pa. 1996. Injunctive element of inmate's § 1983 civil rights action against court clerk and court reporter for failing for over 15 months to fulfill request for trial documents was dismissed, where inmate had received requested documents since filing action. 42 U.S.C.A. § 1983.

> Johnson v. Miller, 925 F.Supp. 334.

E.D.Pa. 1994. Determination of whether complaint states cause of action is distinct from determination of federal court's subject matter jurisdiction. Fed.Rules Civ.Proc.Rule 12(b)(1, 6), 28 U.S.C.A.

> Lake v. First Nationwide Bank, 156 F.R.D. 615.

E.D.Pa. 1993. If events subsequent to filing of complaint resolve dispute, case should be dismissed as moot.

> Carlough v. Amchem Products, Inc., 834 F.Supp. 1437, certification denied 1993 WL 441720.

E.D.Pa. 1993. Dismissal for failure to prosecute or to comply with rules or court order should be reserved for cases where there is clear record of delay or contumacious conduct by plaintiff, and it is necessary for district courts to consider whether lesser sanctions would better serve ends of justice. Fed.Rules Civ.Proc.Rule 41(b), 28 U.S.C.A.

> Riddle v. National R.R. Passenger Corp., 831 F.Supp. 442.

E.D.Pa. 1993. Claims asserted by plaintiff who did not address defendant's arguments for dismissal of those claims or otherwise defend viability of claims were subject to dismissal.

Seal v. Riverside Federal Sav. Bank, 825 F.Supp. 686.

E.D.Pa. 1993. Motion to dismiss for lack of subject-matter jurisdiction is appropriate vehicle when plaintiff has failed to exhaust administrative remedies that are prerequisite to suit. Fed.Rules Civ.Proc.Rule 12(b)(1), 28 U.S.C.A.

Oshiver v. Levin, Fishbein, Sedran and Berman, 818 F.Supp. 104, affirmed in part, reversed in part 38 F.3d 1380, on remand 910 F.Supp. 225, affirmed 96 F.3d 1434.

E.D.Pa. 1991. Without live controversy before court, appropriate procedure is dismissal of action without prejudice.

Dancu v. Coopers & Lybrand, 778 F.Supp. 832, affirmed 972 F.2d 1330.

E.D.Pa. 1990. Even though a corporation ordinarily must employ an attorney to appear for it and represent it before the court, a defendant corporation's motion to dismiss for lack of in personam jurisdiction filed in proper person was not denied due to the technical error that an attorney had not been employed, where the plaintiff did not object to the motion on basis of defendant's failure to employ an attorney, defendant had retained counsel, who had recently entered an appearance, and denying motion because of technical error would likely result in further delay. 28 U.S.C.A. § 1654.

Mickleburgh Machinery Co., Inc. v. Pacific Economic Development Co., 738 F.Supp. 159.

E.D.Pa. 1987. In forma pauperis civil rights suit against federal attorneys by plaintiff who alleged that attorneys used their positions to obstruct complaints filed against judges, officials, and attorneys allegedly stealing from estate of plaintiff's uncle, was subject to dismissal as frivolous, as there was no specification that either attorney failed to perform a required duty or improperly performed required duty. 28 U.S.C.A. § 1915(d).

Keno v. Mvros, 113 F.R.D. 634.

E.D.Pa. 1984. Since fact issue existed as to whether doctors would be indemnified from damages resulting solely from their negligence under their contract with hospital, court would not dismiss third-party complaint brought against doctors by hospital, which was named as a defendant in a medical malpractice action.

DiLorenzo v. Saint Agnes Medical Center, 103 F.R.D. 546.

M.D.Pa. 1991. Factors to be balanced in determining whether to dismiss case for failure to comply with district court's orders include: extent of party's personal responsibility; prejudice to adversary; history of dilatoriness; whether attorney's conduct was willful or in bad faith; alternative sanctions; and meritoriousness of the claim or defense.

Sweeney v. St. Joseph's Hosp., 769 F.Supp. 747, affirmed 980 F.2d 724.

M.D.Pa. 1991. Defendants were not entitled to dismissal of products liability action due to continuous failure to comply with procedural rules and deadlines by plaintiffs' counsel in the absence of any suggestion that plaintiffs were personally responsible for their attorneys' conduct; rather, it was more appropriate to impose on plaintiffs' counsel costs, including attorney fees, for preparing motions and briefs which were prompted by dilatory conduct.

Niklaus v. Vivadent, Inc., U.S.A., 767 F.Supp. 94, affirmed 986 F.2d 1409.

W.D.Pa. 1988. Action in injunction would not be dismissed for plaintiffs' failure to file briefs where court did not order filing of briefs, suggesting only that if parties wished to file briefs they could do so within certain periods of time.

Hudak v. Woods, 91 B.R. 718.

W.D.Pa. 1985. Where derivative plaintiff's financial security interest in outcome of suit is minimal, defendant's protection from alleged "strike suit" is to request court to order plaintiff to post security for costs or expenses, not to have action dismissed.

Recchion on Behalf of Westinghouse Elec. Corp. v. Kirby, 637 F.Supp. 284.

W.D.Pa. 1985. Plaintiff's failure to satisfy demand requirement of Federal Rule of Civil Procedure governing derivative claims required dismissal of derivative count. Fed.Rules Civ. Proc.Rule 23.1, 28 U.S.C.A.

Recchion v. Westinghouse Elec. Corp., 606 F.Supp. 889.

D.Puerto Rico 1992. Where injury and causation element are not clear for standing purposes, plaintiff must plead such with specificity in complaint or, upon leave granted, supplement and/or amend complaint with additional facts; thereafter, in event that entire record is inadequate to support plaintiff's standing, action must be dismissed.

In re San Juan Dupont Plaza Hotel Fire Litigation, 802 F.Supp. 624, affirmed 989 F.2d 36.

D.Puerto Rico 1992. When plaintiff acts pro se, complaint should not be dismissed merely because the allegations do not support the legal theory on which he intends to proceed, and court is under duty to examine the complaint to determine if the allegations provide relief under any possible theory.

Bermudez Zenon v. Restaurant Compostela, Inc., 790 F.Supp. 41.

D.C.Puerto Rico 1984. Castro v. U.S., 584 F.Supp. 252, affirmed 775 F.2d 399.

M.D.Tenn. 1990. District court could not dismiss claim that plaintiff did not bring. Fed. Rules Civ.Proc.Rule 12(b)(6), 28 U.S.C.A.

French by Pickard v. Wilgus, 742 F.Supp. 434.

E.D.Tex. 1997. Failure to pay filing fee within reasonable time, or bad faith failure to pay fee, may constitute ground for dismissing case.

Lowery v. Carrier Corp., 953 F.Supp. 151.

E.D.Tex. 1993. Prior to considering whether defendant is entitled to qualified immunity, district court must first address threshold consideration of whether plaintiff's complaint even states violation of constitutional right; if plaintiff fails to meet this burden, then district court must dismiss case.

Idoux v. Lamar University System, 828 F.Supp. 1252, affirmed in part 37 F.3d 632.

S.D.Tex. 1996. Federal court lacks authority to give opinions upon moot questions or abstract propositions, or to declare principles or rules of law which cannot affect matter in issue in case before it; thus, if challenged action has already taken place, or event occurs that prevents court from granting any effectual relief, claim is "moot" and must be dismissed. U.S.C.A. Const. Art. 3, § 2, cl. 1.

Center for Marine Conservation v. Brown, 917 F.Supp. 1128.

W.D.Tex. 1987. Jail inmate's civil rights action against state judge for alleged discrimination in refusing to allow inmate to proceed pro se in a state cause of action was subject to dismissal where inmate had delayed the cause by disobeying court orders and engaging in contumacious conduct and where lesser sanction would not suffice. Fed.Rules Civ.Proc.Rule 41(b), 28 U.S.C.A.

Gill v. Neaves, 657 F.Supp. 1394.

W.D.Tex. 1986. Although court cannot and will not tolerate sexual discrimination, federal employee's repeated failure to abide by procedural requirements of Title VII and federal rules of civil procedure mandated dismissal. Civil Rights Act of 1964, § 717(c), as amended, 42 U.S.C.A. § 2000e–16(c); Fed.Rules Civ.Proc. Rules 12(b)(1), 56(c, e), 28 U.S.C.A.

Polisoto v. Weinberger, 638 F.Supp. 1353.

D.Utah 1994. South Carolina order dismissing defendant's claims to sole exclusive use and ownership of equipment furnished by plaintiff had same effect as plaintiff's claims for injunctive relief in federal action and, thus, to avoid needless duplication and/or relitigation of issues already determined, plaintiff's federal claims for injunctive relief would be dismissed as moot; although South Carolina order was not final until entire state court action was finalized and all avenues of appeal exhausted, the order was nevertheless enforceable.

Recovery Processes Intern., Inc. v. Hoechst Celanese Corp., 857 F.Supp. 863.

E.D.Va. 1994. Dispute over whether coastal state could review activities wholly in another state for compliance with coastal state's coastal management plan was rendered moot, and would be dismissed, once United States Department of Commerce overruled coastal state's objection. Coastal Zone Management Act of 1972, § 307(c)(3)(A), as amended, 16 U.S.C.A. § 1456(c)(3)(A).

City of Virginia Beach, Va. v. Brown, 858 F.Supp. 585.

E.D.Va. 1994. If plaintiff cannot demonstrate a distinct and palpable injury, no other inquiry is relevant to consideration of standing, and complaint should be dismissed. U.S.C.A. Const. Art. 3, § 1 et seq.

Charles E. Smith Management, Inc. v. Aspin, 855 F.Supp. 852.

E.D.Va. 1990. Court can dismiss action where plaintiff fails to comply with Federal Rules of Civil Procedure or court orders; whether to do so is a matter for the court's discretion, which involves balancing public policy of deciding cases on their merits against considerations of sound judicial administration. Fed.Rules Civ.Proc.Rule 41(b), 28 U.S.C.A.

Claitt v. Newcomb, 138 F.R.D. 72.

In determining whether dismissal for failure to comply with rules or court orders is appropriate sanction, district court must consider: degree of personal responsibility of plaintiff; amount of prejudice caused defendant; existence of history of deliberately proceeding in a dilatory fashion; and existence of sanctions less drastic than dismissal. Fed.Rules Civ.Proc.Rule 41(b), 28 U.S.C.A.

Claitt v. Newcomb, 138 F.R.D. 72.

Dismissal with prejudice of action alleging malicious prosecution and other torts was warranted based on plaintiff's failure to supplement response to defendant's interrogatory on damages in a timely fashion, twice filing revised witness lists in an untimely manner, failing to notify defendant in a timely fashion of waiver of prior demand for jury trial, and supplementing exhibit list in an untimely manner, all to the severe prejudice of defendant in attempt to prepare for trial. Fed.Rules Civ.Proc.Rule 41(b), 28 U.S.C.A.

Claitt v. Newcomb, 138 F.R.D. 72.

E.D.Va. 1985. Plaintiff's six lawsuits against numerous defendants would be dismissed, and plaintiff would be enjoined from filing further groundless actions, in light of frivolous nature of plaintiff's claims and since pattern of plaintiff's lawsuits indicated that they were brought to abuse judicial process.

> Klimek v. Hunter, 624 F.Supp. 886, affirmed in part, vacated in part 819 F.2d 1138.

W.D.Va. 1993. Substantial justice would not be done if complaint filed by out-of-state attorney who had not yet been admitted to practice before district court pro hac vice was dismissed; failure to be admitted was mere technical defect and was promptly cured when attorney associated himself with local counsel and was admitted pro hac vice. Fed.Rules Civ.Proc.Rules 8(f), 11, 28 U.S.C.A.; U.S.Dist. Ct.Rules W.D.Va., Rule 5.

> Wolford v. Budd Co., 149 F.R.D. 127.

D.C.Virgin Islands 1983. Wells v. Rockefeller, 97 F.R.D. 42, affirmed in part, vacated in part 728 F.2d 209, certiorari denied 105 S.Ct. 2343, 471 U.S. 1107, 85 L.Ed.2d 858.

N.D.W.Va. 1992. Government's motion, based on immunity provision of Flood Control Act, to dismiss Federal Tort Claims Act suit would be entertained by district court under rule governing motions to dismiss for lack of subject matter jurisdiction, even though it would have been more appropriate to file motion under rule governing dismissal for failure to state claim upon which relief can be granted; parties seemed to assume that motion fell under rule governing subject matter jurisdiction, and distinction would not affect decision on motion. 33 U.S.C.A. § 702c; 28 U.S.C.A. §§ 1331, 2674; Fed.Rules Civ.Proc.Rule 12(b)(1, 6), 28 U.S.C.A.

> Cox v. U.S., 827 F.Supp. 378.

S.D.W.Va. 1984. As complaint appeared frivolous on its face, dismissal was appropriate. 28 U.S.C.A. § 1915(d).

> Duncan v. State of W.Va., 597 F.Supp. 1195.

E.D.Wis. 1986. Allegation that religious university's refusal to hire applicant as associate professor of theology violated state law and university's own policies regarding academic freedom was properly dismissed, where First Amendment precluded District Court from examining hiring decisions made by theology department at religious university, particularly where applicant failed to provide authority to support position that either policies of university or state law required principles of academic freedom to be extended to hiring decisions. U.S.C.A. Const.Amend. 1.

> Maguire v. Marquette University, 627 F.Supp. 1499, affirmed in part, vacated in part 814 F.2d 1213.

E.D.Wis. 1985. Parties' stipulation to application of Illinois law to securities fraud action brought in Wisconsin was insufficient basis upon which to dismiss plaintiffs' third count alleging violation of Wisconsin securities law. Wis.St.1983, § 551.01 et seq.; Securities Act of 1933, § 12(2), 15 U.S.C.A. § 77l (2); Securities Exchange Act of 1934, § 10(b), 15 U.S.C.A. § 78j(b).

> Pikofsky v. Jem Oil, 607 F.Supp. 727.

Bkrtcy.D.Ariz. 1995. If court rules for party, but cannot grant effective relief, matter is dismissed as "moot."

> In re Circle K Corp., 181 B.R. 457.

Bkrtcy.W.D.Va. 1997. If seasonably raised and properly brought into question, attorney may always be called upon to produce satisfactory evidence of authority to take all lawful steps for protection of client's interest, and, upon failure to produce such authority, suit or proceeding instituted by such attorney should be dismissed.

> In re Goodman, 208 B.R. 145.

⚷**1742. Want of jurisdiction.**

Library references

> C.J.S. Federal Civil Procedure §§ 799–803.

⚷**1742(1). In general.**

U.S.Ill. 1998. Dismissal for lack of subject-matter jurisdiction because of inadequacy of federal claim is proper only when claim is so insubstantial, implausible, foreclosed by prior decisions of Supreme Court, or otherwise completely devoid of merit as not to involve federal controversy. U.S.C.A. Const. Art. 3, § 2, cl. 1.

> Steel Co. v. Citizens for a Better Environment, 118 S.Ct. 1003, 140 L.Ed.2d 210, on remand 151 F.3d 1032.

C.A.D.C. 1986. Pro se complaint may not be dismissed on its face on grounds it is frivolous solely on the ground that the court lacks jurisdiction over the defendants. 28 U.S.C.A. § 1915(d).

> Anger v. Revco Drug Co., 791 F.2d 956, 253 U.S.App.D.C. 54.

Pro se complaint may not be dismissed as frivolous on its face on the basis that venue is improper. 28 U.S.C.A. § 1915(d).

> Anger v. Revco Drug Co., 791 F.2d 956, 253 U.S.App.D.C. 54.

C.A.D.C. 1983. International Ladies' Garment Workers' Union v. Donovan, 722 F.2d 795, 26 Wage & Hour Cas. (BNA) 829, 232 U.S.App.D.C. 309, on remand 26 Wage & Hour Cas. (BNA) 1165, remanded 733 F.2d 920, 26 Wage & Hour Cas. (BNA) 1214, 236 U.S.App. D.C. 89, certiorari denied Breen v. International Ladies' Garment Workers Union, 105 S.Ct. 93, 469 U.S. 820, 26 Wage & Hour Cas. (BNA) 1494, 83 L.Ed.2d 39.

C.A.9 1989. Subject matter jurisdiction is fundamental; defense of lack of subject matter jurisdiction cannot be waived, and court is under continuing duty to dismiss action whenever it appears that court lacks jurisdiction.
Billingsley v. C.I.R., 868 F.2d 1081.

C.A.Fed. 1995. Dismissal for lack of subject matter jurisdiction means that subject matter of the dispute is one that court is not empowered to hear and decide.
Gould, Inc. v. U.S., 67 F.3d 925.

C.A.11 (Ala.) 1998. Federal court may dismiss federal question claim for lack of subject matter jurisdiction only if: (1) alleged claim under Constitution or federal statutes clearly appears to be immaterial and made solely for purpose of obtaining jurisdiction, or (2) such claim is wholly insubstantial and frivolous.
Fed.Rules Civ.Proc.Rule 12(b)(1), 28 U.S.C.A.
Blue Cross & Blue Shield of Alabama v. Sanders, 138 F.3d 1347.

Claim is wholly insubstantial and frivolous, and thus may be dismissed for lack of subject matter jurisdiction, if it has no plausible foundation, or if court concludes that prior Supreme Court decision clearly forecloses claim. Fed. Rules Civ.Proc.Rule 12(b)(1), 28 U.S.C.A.
Blue Cross & Blue Shield of Alabama v. Sanders, 138 F.3d 1347.

C.A.11 (Ala.) 1997. Motion to dismiss is appropriately granted if plaintiffs failed to allege element necessary for subject matter jurisdiction.
Crayton v. Callahan, 120 F.3d 1217, rehearing and suggestion for rehearing denied 132 F.3d 48.

C.A.11 (Ala.) 1986. Where complaint seeks relief under Constitution or laws of United States, dismissal must be for failure to state claim, not for want of jurisdiction, unless claim is immaterial and made solely for purpose of obtaining jurisdiction or claim is wholly insubstantial and frivolous. Fed.Rules Civ.Proc.Rule 12(b), (b)(1), (h)(3), 28 U.S.C.A.
Marine Coatings of Alabama, Inc. v. U.S., 792 F.2d 1565, on remand 674 F.Supp. 819, reversed 932 F.2d 1370, appeal after remand 71 F.3d 1558.

When complaint is drawn so as to seek recovery under admiralty laws, federal court may not dismiss for lack of jurisdiction, unless claim is immaterial and made solely for purpose of obtaining jurisdiction or claim is wholly insubstantial and frivolous; in normal course, dismissal may only be for failing to state claim for which relief can be granted. Fed.Rules Civ.Proc.Rule 12(b), (b)(1), (h)(3), 28 U.S.C.A.
Marine Coatings of Alabama, Inc. v. U.S., 792 F.2d 1565, on remand 674 F.Supp. 819, reversed 932 F.2d 1370, appeal after remand 71 F.3d 1558.

C.A.9 (Cal.) 1995. On motion to dismiss for lack of personal jurisdiction, plaintiff must show that: (1) defendants purposefully availed themselves of privilege of conducting activities in forum state, thereby invoking benefits and protections of its laws; (2) his claims arise out of defendants' activities in forum state; and (3) exercise of jurisdiction would be reasonable.
Ziegler v. Indian River County, 64 F.3d 470.

C.A.9 (Cal.) 1989. Motion raising ripeness issue is treated as motions to dismiss for lack of subject matter jurisdiction, even if brought as motion to dismiss for failure to state claim upon which relief can be granted. Fed.Rules Civ. Proc.Rule 12(b)(1, 6), 28 U.S.C.A.
St. Clair v. City of Chico, 880 F.2d 199, certiorari denied 110 S.Ct. 541, 493 U.S. 993, 107 L.Ed.2d 539.

Motion to dismiss for lack of subject matter jurisdiction can attack substance of complaint's jurisdictional allegations despite their formal sufficiency and, in so doing, can rely on affidavits or any other evidence properly before the court. Fed.Rules Civ.Proc.Rule 12(b)(1), 28 U.S.C.A.
St. Clair v. City of Chico, 880 F.2d 199, certiorari denied 110 S.Ct. 541, 493 U.S. 993, 107 L.Ed.2d 539.

C.A.9 (Cal.) 1987. Upon motion to dismiss for lack of jurisdiction in action in which jurisdictional issue and substantive claims are so intertwined that resolution of jurisdictional question is dependent on factual issues going to the merits, district court should grant motion only if material jurisdictional facts are not in dispute and moving party is entitled to prevail as matter of law; intertwined jurisdictional facts must otherwise be resolved at trial. Fed. Rules Civ.Proc.Rules 12, 12(b)(6), 28 U.S.C.A.
Rosales v. U.S., 824 F.2d 799.

C.A.9 (Cal.) 1987. Complaint will only be dismissed for lack of subject matter jurisdiction where plaintiff's claims are clearly insubstantial because law is clear or plaintiff has persistently failed to allege essential element.
Republic of Philippines v. Marcos, 818 F.2d 1473, rehearing granted 832 F.2d 1110, on rehearing 862 F.2d 1355, certiorari denied 109 S.Ct. 1933, 490 U.S. 1035, 104 L.Ed.2d 404.

C.A.9 (Cal.) 1986. Dismissal for lack of personal jurisdiction is appropriate only if plaintiff has not made prima facie showing of jurisdiction where district court rules on issue relying on affidavits and discovery materials without evidentiary hearing.

> Fields v. Sedgwick Associated Risks, Ltd., 796 F.2d 299.

C.A.9 (Cal.) 1985. Because jurisdiction is not defeated by mere possibility that complaint might fail to state claim upon which recovery can be had, failure to state valid claim is not the equivalent of lack of subject matter jurisdiction, but calls for judgment on the merits rather than for dismissal for lack of jurisdiction.

> Brock v. Writers Guild of America, West, Inc., 762 F.2d 1349.

C.A.9 (Cal.) 1982. Capitol Industries-EMI, Inc. v. Bennett, 681 F.2d 1107, certiorari denied EMI Limited v. Bennett, 102 S.Ct. 1438, 455 U.S. 943, 71 L.Ed.2d 655, certiorari denied 102 S.Ct. 1438, 455 U.S. 943, 71 L.Ed.2d 655, on remand 560 F.Supp. 134, affirmed 738 F.2d 994, certiorari denied 105 S.Ct. 567, 469 U.S. 1073, 83 L.Ed.2d 508, certiorari denied 103 S.Ct. 570, 459 U.S. 1087, 74 L.Ed.2d 932, certiorari denied 103 S.Ct. 1189, 459 U.S. 1203, 75 L.Ed.2d 435.

C.A.9 (Cal.) 1976. Timberlane Lumber Co. v. Bank of America, N.T. and S.A., 549 F.2d 597, 40 A.L.R. Fed. 314, on remand 574 F.Supp. 1453, affirmed 749 F.2d 1378, certiorari denied Timberlane Lumber Company v. Bank of America National Trust and Savings Association, 105 S.Ct. 3514, 472 U.S. 1032, 87 L.Ed.2d 643.

C.A.2 (Conn.) 1990. Claim alleging federal subject-matter jurisdiction may be dismissed if claim is patently without merit. 28 U.S.C.A. § 1331.

> Town of West Hartford v. Operation Rescue, 915 F.2d 92, rehearing denied, on remand 792 F.Supp. 161, vacated in part 991 F.2d 1039, certiorari denied Syversen v. Summit Women's Center West, Inc., 114 S.Ct. 185, 510 U.S. 865, 126 L.Ed.2d 144.

C.A.11 (Fla.) 1997. When jurisdictional motion to dismiss depends on the assertion of right created by federal statute, court should dismiss for lack of jurisdiction only if right claimed is so insubstantial, implausible, foreclosed by prior decisions, or otherwise devoid of merit as not to involve federal controversy. Fed.Rules Civ.Proc.Rule 12(b)(1, 2), 28 U.S.C.A.

> Republic of Panama v. BCCI Holdings (Luxembourg) S.A., 119 F.3d 935.

In analyzing motion to dismiss for lack of personal jurisdiction, court first determines whether applicable statute potentially confers jurisdiction over defendant, and then determines whether exercise of jurisdiction comports with due process. U.S.C.A. Const.Amend. 5; Fed.Rules Civ.Proc.Rule 12(b)(2), 28 U.S.C.A.

> Republic of Panama v. BCCI Holdings (Luxembourg) S.A., 119 F.3d 935.

C.A.11 (Fla.) 1996. If court in which action is brought has no subject matter jurisdiction, suit must be dismissed; such dismissal is not a determination of the claim, but rather a refusal to hear it, and plaintiff is free to pursue it in appropriate forum.

> Sewell v. Merrill Lynch, Pierce, Fenner & Smith, Inc., 94 F.3d 1514.

C.A.11 (Fla.) 1994. Motion to dismiss for lack of subject matter jurisdiction can be based on lack of jurisdiction on face of complaint.

> Sea Vessel, Inc. v. Reyes, 23 F.3d 345.

C.A.5 (Fla.) 1981. Stanley v. Central Intelligence Agency, 639 F.2d 1146, on remand 549 F.Supp. 327, withdrawn 552 F.Supp. 619, adhered to in part 574 F.Supp. 474, order clarified 587 F.Supp. 1071, affirmed in part, reversed in part 786 F.2d 1490, rehearing denied 794 F.2d 687, certiorari granted U.S. v. Stanley, 107 S.Ct. 642, 479 U.S. 1005, 93 L.Ed.2d 699, reversed in part, vacated in part 107 S.Ct. 3054, 483 U.S. 669, 97 L.Ed.2d 550, on remand 828 F.2d 1498, certiorari denied Board of Regents of University of Maryland v. Stanley, 107 S.Ct. 3262, 483 U.S. 1020, 97 L.Ed.2d 761.

C.A.11 (Ga.) 1994. In addition to constitutional requirements, district court must consider, in ruling on motion to dismiss for lack of standing, whether plaintiff's complaint falls within zone of interest protected by statute or constitutional provision at issue, whether complaint raises abstract questions amounting to generalized grievances, and whether plaintiff is asserting his or her own legal rights and interests rather than legal rights and interests of third parties. Fed.Rules Civ.Proc.Rule 12, 28 U.S.C.A.

> Harris v. Evans, 20 F.3d 1118, certiorari denied 115 S.Ct. 641, 513 U.S. 1045, 130 L.Ed.2d 546.

C.A.11 (Ga.) 1993. Appropriate procedure for district court to follow when it determines that it lacks jurisdiction is to transfer case to court with jurisdiction, rather than dismissing case, provided such action is in interest of justice.

> George Kabeller, Inc. v. Busey, 999 F.2d 1417, rehearing denied 9 F.3d 122.

C.A.11 (Ga.) 1985. A court which does not have subject matter jurisdiction over a money claim, or authority to transfer it to another court having such jurisdiction, can do nothing with it but dismiss it.

> Rhodes v. U.S., 760 F.2d 1180.

C.A.11 (Ga.) 1982. Bracewell v. Nicholson Air Services, Inc., 680 F.2d 103, appeal after remand 748 F.2d 1499, rehearing denied 755 F.2d 176.

C.A.7 (Ill.) 1997. In ruling on motion to dismiss for lack of personal jurisdiction, three distinct obstacles to personal jurisdiction must generally be examined: state statutory law, state constitutional law, and federal constitutional law.

    RAR, Inc. v. Turner Diesel, Ltd., 107 F.3d 1272.

C.A.7 (Ill.) 1994. If court determines that claim is wholly insubstantial and frivolous, court does not have power to decide case and complaint must be dismissed for lack of subject matter jurisdiction.

    Gammon v. GC Services Ltd. Partnership, 27 F.3d 1254, on remand 162 F.R.D. 313.

C.A.7 (Ill.) 1993. Court must dismiss case without ever reaching the merits if it concludes that it has no jurisdiction.

    Capitol Leasing Co. v. F.D.I.C., 999 F.2d 188.

C.A.7 (Ill.) 1993. While court may dismiss case at any time for lack of subject matter jurisdiction, once defendant has waived objections based on insufficiency of process and submitted generally to jurisdiction of court, court is powerless to dismiss suit for lack of personal jurisdiction.

    O'Brien v. R.J. O'Brien & Associates, Inc., 998 F.2d 1394.

C.A.7 (Ind.) 1996. Failure to include necessary jurisdictional allegations in complaint, even after opportunity to amend, usually means dismissal.

    Denlinger v. Brennan, 87 F.3d 214.

C.A.7 (Ind.) 1996. If district court finds itself without jurisdiction based upon presentation made by litigant with respect to its motion for relief from default judgment for lack of jurisdiction, then court is obligated to dismiss case because it has no authority over litigant and the default judgment is void. Fed.Rules Civ.Proc.Rule 60(b), 28 U.S.C.A.

    Swaim v. Moltan Co., 73 F.3d 711, certiorari denied Gurley v. Swaim, 116 S.Ct. 2499, 517 U.S. 1244, 135 L.Ed.2d 191.

C.A.7 (Ind.) 1995. Claim purporting to rest on federal law comes within federal jurisdiction unless it is frivolous, and even claims that look frivolous may have enough substance to be dismissed on merits rather than for lack of jurisdiction.

    Mid-American Waste Systems, Inc. v. City of Gary, Ind., 49 F.3d 286, rehearing and suggestion for rehearing denied, appeal after remand 78 F.3d 586.

C.A.5 (La.) 1986. Court may dismiss for lack of subject-matter jurisdiction on any one of three different bases: the complaint alone; the complaint supplemented by undisputed facts in the record; or the complaint supplemented by undisputed facts plus the court's resolution of disputed facts.

    Voisin's Oyster House, Inc. v. Guidry, 799 F.2d 183.

C.A.5 (La.) 1986. To avoid dismissal under Rule 12(b)(1) for lack of subject-matter jurisdiction under 28 U.S.C.A. § 1331, governing federal question jurisdiction, question "arising under" a federal law must be substantial; complaint's allegations are "insubstantial" if they are obviously without merit or if prior decisions foreclose controversy on the subject. Fed.Rules Civ.Proc. Rule 12(b)(1), 28 U.S.C.A.

    New Orleans Public Service, Inc. v. City of New Orleans, 782 F.2d 1236, opinion withdrawn in part 798 F.2d 858, certiorari denied 107 S.Ct. 1910, 481 U.S. 1023, 95 L.Ed.2d 515.

C.A.4 (Md.) 1990. If it is determined that federal court's jurisdiction fails because no federal claim exists, proper disposition is to dismiss on merits for failure to state claim rather than for want of subject matter jurisdiction.

    Ridenour v. Andrews Federal Credit Union, 897 F.2d 715, rehearing denied, on remand 1990 WL 56489.

C.A.6 (Mich.) 1995. On motion to dismiss for lack of subject matter jurisdiction, the issue is not whether plaintiff will ultimately prevail but whether plaintiff is entitled to offer evidence to support the claim, and indeed it may appear on the face of the pleadings that a recovery is very remote and unlikely but that is not the test.

    Kroll v. U.S., 58 F.3d 1087.

C.A.5 (Miss.) 1998. Motion to dismiss for lack of subject matter jurisdiction should be granted only if it appears certain that the plaintiff cannot prove any set of facts in support of his or her claim that would entitle him or her to relief. Fed.Rules Civ.Proc.Rule 12(b)(1), 28 U.S.C.A.

    Home Builders Ass'n of Mississippi, Inc. v. City of Madison, Miss., 143 F.3d 1006.

    Case is properly dismissed for lack of subject matter jurisdiction when the court lacks statutory or constitutional power to adjudicate the case. Fed.Rules Civ.Proc.Rule 12(b)(1), 28 U.S.C.A.

    Home Builders Ass'n of Mississippi, Inc. v. City of Madison, Miss., 143 F.3d 1006.

C.A.8 (Mo.) 1996. Dismissal for lack of subject matter jurisdiction will not be granted lightly; however, dismissal is proper when facial attack on complaint's alleged basis for subject matter jurisdiction shows there is no basis for jurisdiction.

> Wheeler v. St. Louis Southwestern Ry. Co., 90 F.3d 327.

C.A.8 (Mo.) 1989. Dismissal of complaint for either lack of subject matter jurisdiction or for failure to state claim upon which relief can be granted is on pleadings and should be granted sparingly and with caution. Fed.Rules Civ. Proc.Rules 12(b)(1, 6), 56, 28 U.S.C.A.

> Huelsman v. Civic Center Corp., 873 F.2d 1171.

C.A.3 (N.J.) 1997. Threshold to withstand a motion to dismiss for lack of subject matter jurisdiction is lower than that required to withstand motion to dismiss for failure to state a claim. Fed.Rules Civ.Proc.Rule 12(b)(1, 6), 28 U.S.C.A.

> Suber v. Chrysler Corp., 104 F.3d 578, as amended.

C.A.2 (N.Y.) 1997. Where jurisdictional challenge is addressed to complaint, in antitrust action, analyses under rule governing motions to dismiss for lack of subject matter jurisdiction and rule governing motions to dismiss for failure to state claim merge, and critical inquiry is into adequacy of plaintiffs' allegations that challenged conduct affects interstate commerce. Fed.Rules Civ.Proc.Rule 12(b)(1, 6), 28 U.S.C.A.

> Hamilton Chapter of Alpha Delta Phi, Inc. v. Hamilton College, 128 F.3d 59.

C.A.2 (N.Y.) 1997. Before discovery, plaintiff may defeat motion to dismiss for lack of personal jurisdiction with legally sufficient allegations of jurisdiction; however, where parties have conducted jurisdictional discovery but have not held evidentiary hearing, plaintiff must allege facts that, if credited, would suffice to establish jurisdiction over defendant. Fed. Rules Civ.Proc.Rule 12(b)(2), 28 U.S.C.A.

> Chaiken v. VV Pub. Corp., 119 F.3d 1018, certiorari denied 118 S.Ct. 1169, 140 L.Ed.2d 179.

C.A.2 (N.Y.) 1996. As a general rule, failure to state proper cause of action calls for judgment on merits and not for dismissal for want of jurisdiction.

> Merchant v. Levy, 92 F.3d 51, certiorari denied 117 S.Ct. 943, 136 L.Ed.2d 833.

C.A.2 (N.Y.) 1996. Case is properly dismissed for lack of subject matter jurisdiction when court lacks statutory or constitutional power to adjudicate case. Fed.Rules Civ.Proc. Rule 12(b)(1), 28 U.S.C.A.

> Nowak v. Ironworkers Local 6 Pension Fund, 81 F.3d 1182.

C.A.2 (N.Y.) 1995. If a party fails to exhaust administrative remedies, then court may

dismiss action because subject matter jurisdiction does not exist.

> Howell v. I.N.S., 72 F.3d 288.

C.A.2 (N.Y.) 1993. Challenge to court's subject matter jurisdiction may be raised at any time during the course of litigation. Fed.Rules Civ.Proc.Rule 12(h)(3), 28 U.S.C.A.

> Maryland Cas. Co. v. W.R. Grace and Co., 23 F.3d 617, rehearing granted, and amended, certiorari denied 115 S.Ct. 655, 513 U.S. 1052, 130 L.Ed.2d 559, on remand 1995 WL 562179.

C.A.2 (N.Y.) 1993. When complaint fairly read fails to make any claim for judgment against another party contrary to Article III's "case or controversy" requirement, it is properly dismissed for lack of subject-matter jurisdiction, and not just for failing to state a claim upon which relief can be granted. Fed.Rules Civ.Proc.Rule 12(b)(1, 6), 28 U.S.C.A.

> In re Joint Eastern and Southern Dist. Asbestos Litigation, 14 F.3d 726.

C.A.2 (N.Y.) 1990. District court should not dismiss a complaint asserting a nonfrivolous claim under federal law for lack of jurisdiction even if the complaint fails to state a claim on which relief can be granted. Fed.Rules Civ. Proc.Rule 12(b)(6), 28 U.S.C.A.

> Spencer v. Casavilla, 903 F.2d 171, on remand 839 F.Supp. 1014, affirmed in part, vacated in part 44 F.3d 74.

Complaint should not have been dismissed for lack of federal jurisdiction where it plainly sought recovery under the Federal Constitution and laws and asserted claims that were neither immaterial nor frivolous, regardless of issue as to whether complaint failed to state a federal claim on which relief could be granted.

> Spencer v. Casavilla, 903 F.2d 171, on remand 839 F.Supp. 1014, affirmed in part, vacated in part 44 F.3d 74.

C.A.4 (N.C.) 1986. Generally, when plaintiffs have failed to exhaust state remedies, actions in federal court are dismissed, thereby forcing plaintiffs to completely begin their quest for relief anew unless special circumstances make dismissal inappropriate.

> Leonard v. Hammond, 804 F.2d 838.

C.A.8 (N.D.) 1990. Court deciding motion to dismiss for lack of subject matter jurisdiction must distinguish between "facial attack," under which court restricts itself to face of pleadings and nonmoving party receives the same protections as it would defending against motion to dismiss for failure to state claim, and "factual attack," under which court considers matters outside pleadings and nonmoving party does not have benefit of motion to dismiss for failure to state claim safeguards. Fed.Rules Civ.Proc. Rule 12(b)(1, 6), 28 U.S.C.A.

> Osborn v. U.S., 918 F.2d 724.

C.A.6 (Ohio) 1996. Court disposing of motion to dismiss for lack of personal jurisdiction does not weigh controverting assertions of party seeking dismissal, because court wants to prevent non-resident defendants from regularly avoiding personal jurisdiction simply by filing affidavit denying all jurisdictional facts; dismissal on pleadings is proper only if all specific facts which plaintiff alleges collectively fail to state prima facie case for jurisdiction. Fed.Rules Civ.Proc.Rule 12(b)(2), 28 U.S.C.A.

> CompuServe, Inc. v. Patterson, 89 F.3d 1257, rehearing and suggestion for rehearing denied.

C.A.6 (Ohio) 1995. If, under Article 3 of Federal Constitution, party does not have standing to bring action, court has no jurisdiction over matter and order of dismissal must be entered. U.S.C.A. Const. Art. 3, § 2, cl. 1.

> Greater Cincinnati Coalition for the Homeless v. City of Cincinnati, 56 F.3d 710.

C.A.6 (Ohio) 1990. Where subject matter jurisdiction is challenged pursuant to the Federal Rules of Civil Procedure, the plaintiff has the burden of proving jurisdiction in order to survive the motion, and the court is empowered to resolve factual disputes when subject matter jurisdiction is challenged. Fed.Rules Civ.Proc. Rule 12(b)(1), 28 U.S.C.A.

> Moir v. Greater Cleveland Regional Transit Authority, 895 F.2d 266.

C.A.10 (Okl.) 1996. Dismissal of complaint for lack of subject matter jurisdiction would only be justified if that claim were so attenuated and unsubstantial as to be absolutely devoid of merit or frivolous.

> Cardtoons, L.C. v. Major League Baseball Players Ass'n, 95 F.3d 959.

C.A.10 (Okl.) 1996. When court's subject matter jurisdiction is dependent upon same statute that provides substantive claim in case, jurisdictional question is necessarily intertwined with merits, and such "intertwined" jurisdictional questions should be resolved either under civil procedure rule governing dismissal, or, after proper conversion into motion for summary judgment, under summary judgment rule. Fed.Rules Civ.Proc.Rules 12(b)(6), 56, 28 U.S.C.A.

> U.S. ex rel. Ramseyer v. Century Healthcare Corp., 90 F.3d 1514.

C.A.10 (Okl.) 1993. If alleged claim is clearly immaterial or asserted solely for the purpose of obtaining federal jurisdiction or if the alleged claim is insubstantial and wholly frivolous, court may dismiss for lack of subject matter jurisdiction rather than ruling on the merits even when the merits of the case and the issue of subject matter jurisdiction are intertwined.

> Tilton v. Richardson, 6 F.3d 683, certiorari denied 114 S.Ct. 925, 510 U.S. 1093, 127 L.Ed.2d 218.

C.A.10 (Okl.) 1991. Action must be dismissed at any stage of the proceedings in which it becomes apparent that subject matter jurisdiction is lacking, and thus defendant can attack jurisdiction even after final judgment has been rendered. Fed.Rules Civ.Proc.Rule 12(h)(3), 28 U.S.C.A.

> Penteco Corp. Ltd. Partnership--1985A v. Union Gas System, Inc., 929 F.2d 1519.

C.A.9 (Or.) 1981. Franklin v. State of Or., State Welfare Division, 662 F.2d 1337, on remand 563 F.Supp. 1310, affirmed in part, reversed in part 745 F.2d 1221.

C.A.3 (Pa.) 1997. District court may rule on motion to dismiss for lack of subject matter jurisdiction when, on face of pleadings, it is clear that administrative remedies have not been exhausted; however, this rule is inapplicable to resolution of disputed issues of material fact with respect to applicability of statutes of limitations. Fed.Rules Civ.Proc.Rule 12(b)(1), 28 U.S.C.A.

> Robinson v. Dalton, 107 F.3d 1018.

C.A.3 (Pa.) 1993. When federal district court dismisses jurisdictional challenges with little or no analysis and then imposes punitive damages after trial on merits, two unfortunate perceptions may be fostered in eyes of losing party, the bar, and the public; first, it may appear that court has failed to give jurisdictional issues full attention they require, and second, it may appear that court's desire to reach merits of case has obscured its judgment of its jurisdiction to do so.

> Packard v. Provident Nat. Bank, 994 F.2d 1039, rehearing denied, certiorari denied Upp v. Mellon Bank, N.A., 114 S.Ct. 440, 510 U.S. 964, 126 L.Ed.2d 373.

C.A.3 (Pa.) 1990. Procedural rule that provides that subject-matter jurisdiction can never be waived invests district court with power to dismiss action for lack of subject-matter jurisdiction, while rule that provides that court may consider such motion before trial or defer hearing and determination of motion until trial discloses when power may be exercised; thus, under authority of two rules, district court could delay until trial dismissal of class members that purportedly could not meet amount in controversy requirement. Fed.Rules Civ.Proc. Rule 12(d), (h)(3), 28 U.S.C.A.

In re School Asbestos Litigation, 921 F.2d 1310, rehearing denied, certiorari denied U.S. Gypsum Co. v. Barnwell School Dist. No. 45, 111 S.Ct. 1623, 499 U.S. 976, 113 L.Ed.2d 720.

C.A.3 (Pa.) 1989. Dismissal for lack of jurisdiction is not appropriate merely because legal theory alleged is probably false. Fed.Rules Civ. Proc.Rule 12(b)(1), 28 U.S.C.A.

Lunderstadt v. Colafella, 885 F.2d 66, rehearing denied.

C.A.3 (Pa.) 1984. Stibitz v. General Public Utilities Corp., 746 F.2d 993, certiorari denied 105 S.Ct. 1187, 469 U.S. 1214, 84 L.Ed.2d 334.

C.A.1 (Puerto Rico) 1985. Once a federal court has assumed jurisdiction over the controversy, it may then dismiss case on the merits if it determines that plaintiffs have failed to state a ground on which a federal court may grant relief; however, court may not refuse jurisdiction because plaintiffs have failed to prove substantive allegations of the complaint or because plaintiffs' ultimate recovery may be limited to tort damages.

Ortiz De Arroyo v. Barcelo, 765 F.2d 275.

C.A.4 (S.C.) 1989. Lack of overall reasonableness in an assertion of personal jurisdiction constitutes independent ground for dismissal. Fed.Rules Civ.Proc.Rule 12(b)(2), 28 U.S.C.A.

Federal Ins. Co. v. Lake Shore Inc., 886 F.2d 654.

In determining whether complaint should be dismissed due to lack of overall reasonableness in assertion of personal jurisdiction, district court should consider burden on defendants, interest of forum state, plaintiff's interest in obtaining relief in forum, interstate judicial system's interest in obtaining most efficient resolution of controversies, and shared interest of the several states in furthering fundamental substantive social policy. U.S.C.A. Const. Amends. 5, 14; Fed.Rules Civ.Proc.Rule 12(b)(2), 28 U.S.C.A.

Federal Ins. Co. v. Lake Shore Inc., 886 F.2d 654.

Assertion of personal jurisdiction by federal district court in South Carolina over nonresident vessel manufacturer and nonresident cargo winch manufacturer would be unreasonable and unfair, and thus complaint by shipper's subrogee for damages sustained after winch allegedly malfunctioned could be dismissed on that basis; witnesses and evidence relating to claims were located in other states, shipper and its subrogee were not residents of South Carolina, and subrogee failed to demonstrate why South Carolina was most convenient forum in which to litigate its subrogation claim.

U.S.C.A. Const.Amends. 5, 14; Fed.Rules Civ. Proc.Rule 12(b)(2), 28 U.S.C.A.

Federal Ins. Co. v. Lake Shore Inc., 886 F.2d 654.

C.A.8 (S.D.) 1991. To defeat motion to dismiss for lack of personal jurisdiction, nonmoving party need only make prima facie showing of jurisdiction; jurisdiction need not be proved by preponderance of evidence until trial or until court holds evidentiary hearing. Fed.Rules Civ. Proc.Rule 12(b)(2), 28 U.S.C.A.

Dakota Industries, Inc. v. Dakota Sportswear, Inc., 946 F.2d 1384, appeal after remand 988 F.2d 61.

C.A.6 (Tenn.) 1996. When motion to dismiss based on lack of subject matter jurisdiction attacks face of complaint, plaintiff's burden to prove federal question subject matter jurisdiction is not onerous, and plaintiff must show only that complaint alleges claim under federal law and that claim is substantial. Fed.Rules Civ. Proc.Rule 12(b)(1), 28 U.S.C.A.

Musson Theatrical, Inc. v. Federal Exp. Corp., 89 F.3d 1244, rehearing and suggestion for rehearing denied, amended on denial of rehearing 1998 WL 117980.

Claim under federal law is "substantial," and may potentially withstand motion to dismiss based on lack of subject matter jurisdiction, unless prior decisions inescapably render it frivolous. Fed.Rules Civ.Proc.Rule 12(b)(1), 28 U.S.C.A.

Musson Theatrical, Inc. v. Federal Exp. Corp., 89 F.3d 1244, rehearing and suggestion for rehearing denied, amended on denial of rehearing 1998 WL 117980.

When faced with challenge to face of complaint which is raised through motion to dismiss for failure to state claim, plaintiff can survive motion by showing any arguable basis in law for claim made. Fed.Rules Civ.Proc.Rule 12(b)(1), 28 U.S.C.A.

Musson Theatrical, Inc. v. Federal Exp. Corp., 89 F.3d 1244, rehearing and suggestion for rehearing denied, amended on denial of rehearing 1998 WL 117980.

C.A.6 (Tenn.) 1994. Factual attack, on motion to dismiss for lack of subject matter jurisdiction, is not challenge to sufficiency of pleading's allegations, but challenge to factual existence of subject matter jurisdiction. Fed. Rules Civ.Proc.Rule 12(b)(1), 28 U.S.C.A.

U.S. v. Ritchie, 15 F.3d 592, rehearing and suggestion for rehearing denied, certiorari denied 115 S.Ct. 188, 513 U.S. 868, 130 L.Ed.2d 121.

C.A.5 (Tex.) 1998. It is incumbent on all federal courts to dismiss action whenever it appears that subject matter jurisdiction is lacking.

> Stockman v. Federal Election Com'n, 138 F.3d 144.

C.A.5 (Tex.) 1996. Where Eleventh Amendment sovereign immunity deprives court of jurisdiction over § 1983 claim, matter can be dismissed only under Rule 12(b)(1) for lack of subject matter jurisdiction, and not with prejudice. U.S.C.A. Const.Amend. 11; Fed.Rules Civ.Proc.Rule 12(b)(1), 28 U.S.C.A.

> Warnock v. Pecos County, Tex., 88 F.3d 341, appeal after remand 116 F.3d 776.

C.A.5 (Tex.) 1986. Age discrimination claims against individual employees of defendant's employer were properly dismissed, in absence of federal statutory basis for relief or any other federal claim against those employees. Age Discrimination in Employment Act of 1967, § 2 et seq., 29 U.S.C.A. § 621 et seq.

> Slaughter v. Allstate Ins. Co., 803 F.2d 857.

C.A.5 (Tex.) 1986. Where questions concerning subject-matter jurisdiction are intertwined with the merits, district court should not dismiss for lack of subject-matter jurisdiction unless the claim is frivolous or clearly excluded by prior law; subject-matter jurisdiction and merits will normally be considered intertwined where statute provides both basis of federal court subject-matter jurisdiction and the cause of action.

> Clark v. Tarrant County, Texas, 798 F.2d 736, rehearing denied 802 F.2d 455.

C.A.5 (Tex.) 1985. If, as matter of fact or law, plaintiff fails to establish claim brought under federal statute, case is properly dismissed under Federal Civil Rules 12(b)(6) or 56, it should not be dismissed for lack of jurisdiction. Fed.Rules Civ.Proc.Rules 12(b)(6), 56, 28 U.S.C.A.

> Gonzalez v. Southern Pacific Transp. Co., 773 F.2d 637.

C.A.10 (Utah) 1996. Issue as to whether claim is ripe for review bears on court's subject matter jurisdiction under case or controversy requirement; accordingly, ripeness challenge, like most other challenges to court's subject matter jurisdiction, is treated as Rule 12(b)(1) motion to dismiss. U.S.C.A. Const. Art. 3, § 2, cl. 1; Fed.Rules Civ.Proc.Rule 12(b)(1), 28 U.S.C.A.

> Bateman v. City of West Bountiful, 89 F.3d 704.

C.A.2 (Vt.) 1996. Prior to discovery, a plaintiff may defeat a motion to dismiss based on legally sufficient allegations of jurisdiction. Fed.Rules Civ.Proc.Rule 12(b)(2), 28 U.S.C.A.

> Metropolitan Life Ins. Co. v. Robertson-Ceco Corp., 84 F.3d 560, certiorari denied 117 S.Ct. 508, 136 L.Ed.2d 398, certiorari denied 117 S.Ct. 508, 136 L.Ed.2d 398.

Cases in which existence of minimum contacts between the defendant and the forum state presents an arguably close question, but in which analysis of the five *Asahi* factors reveals that the exercise of personal jurisdiction would be decidedly unreasonable, are good candidates for dismissal.

> Metropolitan Life Ins. Co. v. Robertson-Ceco Corp., 84 F.3d 560, certiorari denied 117 S.Ct. 508, 136 L.Ed.2d 398, certiorari denied 117 S.Ct. 508, 136 L.Ed.2d 398.

C.A.2 (Vt.) 1996. As general rule, plaintiff's failure to state proper cause of action calls for judgment on merits, not dismissal for want of jurisdiction.

> Savoie v. Merchants Bank, 84 F.3d 52.

C.A.4 (Va.) 1991. In resolving motion to dismiss for lack of factual basis for subject matter jurisdiction, district court should apply standard applicable to motion for summary judgment, under which nonmoving party must set forth specific facts beyond pleadings to show that genuine issue of material fact exists.

> Richmond, Fredericksburg & Potomac R. Co. v. U.S., 945 F.2d 765, certiorari denied 112 S.Ct. 1667, 503 U.S. 984, 118 L.Ed.2d 388.

Party moving for dismissal for lack of subject matter jurisdiction should prevail only if material jurisdictional facts are not in dispute and moving party is entitled to prevail as matter of law.

> Richmond, Fredericksburg & Potomac R. Co. v. U.S., 945 F.2d 765, certiorari denied 112 S.Ct. 1667, 503 U.S. 984, 118 L.Ed.2d 388.

C.A.9 (Wash.) 1990. Where trial court's ruling, on motion to dismiss for lack of personal jurisdiction, is based solely upon review of affidavits and discovery materials, dismissal was appropriate only if plaintiff fails to make prima facie showing of personal jurisdiction.

> Shute v. Carnival Cruise Lines, 897 F.2d 377, certiorari granted 111 S.Ct. 39, 498 U.S. 807, 112 L.Ed.2d 16, reversed 111 S.Ct. 1522, 499 U.S. 585, 113 L.Ed.2d 622, on remand 934 F.2d 1091.

C.A.7 (Wis.) 1987. Complaint which fails to allege federal jurisdiction must be dismissed with or without leave to amend depending on circumstances, but if jurisdiction is alleged and question is raised by party or district judge about truth of allegation, proper course is not to dismiss outright but to determine whether federal jurisdiction in fact exists.

Hemmings v. Barian, 822 F.2d 688.

C.A.7 (Wis.) 1986. Jurisdictional rules should be as simple as possible, so that time of litigants and judges is not wasted deciding whether case should be brought and so that fully litigated cases are not set at naught.

Cote v. Wadel, 796 F.2d 981.

M.D.Ala. 1998. Dismissals for lack of subject matter jurisdiction do not involve merits of claim.

Owens v. Blue Tee Corp., 177 F.R.D. 673.

M.D.Ala. 1997. Unlike motion to dismiss for failure to state claim, dismissals for lack of subject matter jurisdiction do not involve merits of claim. Fed.Rules Civ.Proc.Rule 12(b)(1, 6), 28 U.S.C.A.

Player v. Nations Biologics, Inc., 993 F.Supp. 878.

M.D.Ala. 1996. There are two forms of attack in motion to dismiss for lack of subject matter jurisdiction, which are "facial attack," which requires court to ascertain if plaintiff has sufficiently alleged basis of subject matter jurisdiction, and "factual attack," which focuses not on pleadings but on existence of subject matter jurisdiction "in fact." Fed.Rules Civ.Proc.Rule 12(b)(1), 28 U.S.C.A.

U.S. ex rel. Sanders v. East Alabama Healthcare Authority, 953 F.Supp. 1404.

M.D.Ala. 1996. As general rule, claim cannot be dismissed for lack of subject matter jurisdiction because of absence of federal cause of action. Fed.Rules Civ.Proc.Rule 12(b)(1), 28 U.S.C.A.

Cook Oil Co., Inc. v. U.S., 919 F.Supp. 1556, affirmed 108 F.3d 344.

Exceptions to rule that claim cannot be dismissed for lack of subject matter jurisdiction because of absence of federal cause of action are narrowly drawn, and are intended to allow jurisdictional dismissals only in those cases where federal claim is clearly immaterial or insubstantial. Fed.Rules Civ.Proc.Rule 12(b)(1), 28 U.S.C.A.

Cook Oil Co., Inc. v. U.S., 919 F.Supp. 1556, affirmed 108 F.3d 344.

M.D.Ala. 1996. Unlike motion to dismiss for failure to state claim upon which relief can be granted, dismissals for lack of subject matter jurisdiction do not involve merits of claim. Fed.Rules Civ.Proc.Rule 12(b)(1, 6), 28 U.S.C.A.

Andalusia City Bd. of Educ. v. Andress, 916 F.Supp. 1179.

M.D.Ala. 1994. To invoke jurisdiction of federal district courts, complaint must affirma-tively and distinctly allege statutory basis for jurisdiction, and if complaint fails to state grounds for subject matter jurisdiction, district court may dismiss claim. Fed.Rules Civ.Proc. Rule 12(b)(1), 28 U.S.C.A.

Yeager v. Norwest Multifamily, Inc., 865 F.Supp. 768.

M.D.Ala. 1994. "Facial attack" on complaint, on motion to dismiss for lack of subject matter jurisdiction, requires district court to assess whether plaintiff has alleged sufficient basis of subject matter jurisdiction. Fed.Rules Civ.Proc.Rule 12(b)(1), 28 U.S.C.A.

Hayden v. Blue Cross and Blue Shield of Alabama, 855 F.Supp. 344.

W.D.Ark. 1997. Complaint should not be dismissed before trial for want of personal jurisdiction if there is any genuine issue as to any fact material to jurisdictional question. Fed. Rules Civ.Proc.Rule 12(b)(2), 28 U.S.C.A.

Smith v. Hobby Lobby Stores, Inc., 968 F.Supp. 1356.

W.D.Ark. 1996. Complaint should not be dismissed for want of jurisdiction before trial if there is any genuine issue as to any fact material to jurisdictional question.

Sanders v. Buch, 938 F.Supp. 532.

W.D.Ark. 1996. Complaint should not be dismissed for want of jurisdiction, before trial, if there is any genuine issue as to any fact material to jurisdictional question. Fed.Rules Civ. Proc. Rule 12(b)(2), 28 U.S.C.A.

Burkhart v. Medserv Corp., 916 F.Supp. 919.

C.D.Cal. 1997. Standard applicable to motion to dismiss complaint for failure to state claim does not apply to resolution of jurisdictional questions when issues of jurisdiction and substance are intertwined; rather, summary judgment standard applies, and moving party must establish that there are no material facts in dispute and that he or she is entitled to prevail as a matter of law. Fed.Rules Civ.Proc. Rules 12(b)(1, 6), 56, 28 U.S.C.A.

Los Angeles News Service v. Conus Communications Co. Ltd. Partnership, 969 F.Supp. 579.

C.D.Cal. 1997. If court is not conducting evidentiary hearing, dismissal for lack of personal jurisdiction is appropriate only if plaintiff fails to make prima facie showing of personal jurisdiction over defendant. Fed.Rules Civ. Proc.Rule 12(b)(3), 28 U.S.C.A.

Douglas Furniture Co. of California, Inc. v. Wood Dimensions, Inc., 963 F.Supp. 899.

C.D.Cal. 1996. Motion to dismiss for lack of subject matter jurisdiction or for failure to state claim should be granted when it is clear that plaintiff can prove no set of facts in support

of claim that would entitle him to relief. Fed. Rules Civ.Proc.Rule 12(b)(1, 6), 28 U.S.C.A.
  Cevallos v. City of Los Angeles, 914 F.Supp. 379.

N.D.Cal. 1995. Standard to be applied in evaluating motion to dismiss for lack of subject matter jurisdiction depends upon whether the motion is facial or factual attack and whether jurisdictional and substantive issues are so intertwined that question of jurisdiction depends upon factual determinations going to merits. Fed.Rules Civ.Proc.Rule 12(b)(1), 28 U.S.C.A.
  McMorgan & Co. v. First California Mortg. Co., 916 F.Supp. 966.

Motion to dismiss for lack of subject matter jurisdiction may either attack allegations of complaint (facial attack), or it may be made as speaking motion attacking existence of subject matter jurisdiction in fact (factual attack). Fed. Rules Civ.Proc.Rule 12(b)(1), 28 U.S.C.A.
  McMorgan & Co. v. First California Mortg. Co., 916 F.Supp. 966.

For purposes of determining appropriate standard to be applied in evaluating motion to dismiss for lack of subject matter jurisdiction, question of jurisdiction is normally considered intertwined with underlying facts of case where same statute provides basis of both subject matter jurisdiction and plaintiff's claim for relief. Fed.Rules Civ.Proc.Rule 12(b)(1), 28 U.S.C.A.
  McMorgan & Co. v. First California Mortg. Co., 916 F.Supp. 966.

N.D.Cal. 1995. Defense of lack of subject-matter jurisdiction cannot be waived, and court is under continuing duty to dismiss action whenever it appears that court lacks jurisdiction. Fed.Rules Civ.Proc.Rule 12(h)(3), 28 U.S.C.A.
  Noel v. U.S., 893 F.Supp. 1410.

N.D.Cal. 1994. In suit challenging alleged violation of federal statute, generally finding of no statutory violation results in dismissal for failure to state a claim rather than for lack of jurisdiction. Fed.Rules Civ.Proc.Rule 12(b)(1, 6), 28 U.S.C.A.
  Citizens for a Better Environment-California v. Union Oil Co. of California, 861 F.Supp. 889, affirmed 83 F.3d 1111, as amended, certiorari denied 117 S.Ct. 789, 136 L.Ed.2d 731.

N.D.Cal. 1994. "First to file" rule allows district court to transfer, stay or dismiss action when similar complaint has been filed in another federal court, and court must look to three threshold factors in deciding whether to apply the rule: the chronology of the two actions, the similarity of the parties, and the similarity of the issues.
  Ward v. Follett Corp., 158 F.R.D. 645.

N.D.Cal. 1986. Federal court must dismiss action for lack of federal subject-matter jurisdiction if federal claims that are basis for jurisdiction are obviously without merit or frivolous, notwithstanding rule of federal procedure that after party's first amended pleading, party may amend his pleading by leave of court freely given, when justice so requires. 26 U.S.C.A. § 7431(a)(1); Fed.Rules Civ.Proc.Rule 15(a), 28 U.S.C.A.
  Medina v. U.S., 664 F.Supp. 1318, affirmed 820 F.2d 407.

D.Colo. 1996. Court should dismiss action for failure to state claim, rather than for want of jurisdiction, if court determines that federal law does not give right that party claims. 28 U.S.C.A. § 1361.
  Saum v. Widnall, 912 F.Supp. 1384.

D.Colo. 1991. Where issue of subject matter jurisdiction is intertwined with merits, dismissal on grounds of lack of subject matter jurisdiction is proper only if claim is frivolous or clearly excluded by prior law. Fed.Rules Civ.Proc.Rule 12(b)(1), 28 U.S.C.A.
  McEndree v. Wilson, 774 F.Supp. 1292.

D.Colo. 1985. If claim is patently unsound and without merit, court may be justified in dismissing complaint for want of jurisdiction.
  Roberts v. Clark, 615 F.Supp. 1554.

D.Conn. 1998. Unlike a motion to dismiss for failure to state a claim upon which relief can be granted, dismissals for lack of subject matter jurisdiction are not predicated on the merits of the claim. Fed.Rules Civ.Proc.Rule 12(b)(1, 6), 28 U.S.C.A.
  Klein & Vibber, P.C. v. Collard & Roe P.C., 3 F.Supp.2d 167.

D.Conn. 1996. If district court lacks subject matter jurisdiction, dismissal of action is mandatory. 28 U.S.C.A. § 1331; Fed.Rules Civ.Proc.Rule 12(b)(1), 28 U.S.C.A.
  Bird v. U.S., 923 F.Supp. 338.

D.Conn. 1995. Motion to dismiss for lack of jurisdiction over subject matter must be granted if plaintiff fails to establish jurisdiction. Fed.Rules Civ.Proc.Rule 12(b)(1), 28 U.S.C.A.
  Gorman v. Hughes Danbury Optical Systems, 908 F.Supp. 107.

D.Conn. 1994. Dismissals for lack of subject matter jurisdiction are not predicated on merits of claim. Fed.Rules Civ.Proc.Rule 12(b)(1), 28 U.S.C.A.
  Connecticut Hosp. Ass'n v. Pogue, 870 F.Supp. 444, reversed 66 F.3d 413.

D.Conn. 1994. Motion to dismiss for lack of subject matter jurisdiction challenges court's statutory or constitutional power to adjudicate case, and typically alleges that federal court lacks federal question jurisdiction or that it lacks diversity jurisdiction. Fed.Rules Civ.Proc. Rule 12(b)(1), 28 U.S.C.A.

> Bleiler v. Cristwood Contracting Co., Inc., 868 F.Supp. 461, affirmed in part, reversed in part 72 F.3d 13.

D.Conn. 1993. If district court lacks subject matter jurisdiction, dismissal of action is mandatory. 28 U.S.C.A. § 1331(a); Fed.Rules Civ.Proc.Rule 12(h)(3), 28 U.S.C.A.

> Golden Hill Paugussett Tribe of Indians v. Weicker, 839 F.Supp. 130, remanded 39 F.3d 51.

D.Conn. 1993. Party seeking dismissal for lack of subject matter jurisdiction and pleading party may use affidavits and other materials beyond pleadings in support of or in opposition to challenge to subject matter jurisdiction, but dismissal is not predicated on merits of claim, unlike motion to dismiss for failure to state claim. Fed.Rules Civ.Proc.Rules 8(f), 12(b)(1, 6), 28 U.S.C.A.

> Wills v. Ferrandino, 830 F.Supp. 116.

D.Conn. 1993. Under "colorable constitutional claim" standard for determining federal court's jurisdiction in security clearance cases, court should not dismiss claims for lack of subject matter jurisdiction, even where they would have dismissed claims for failure to state claim upon which relief could be granted. Fed. Rules Civ.Proc.Rule 12(b)(1, 6), 28 U.S.C.A.

> Chesna v. U.S. Dept. of Defense, 822 F.Supp. 90.

D.Conn. 1993. In general, when motion to dismiss has more than one ground, court should first consider challenge of lack of subject matter jurisdiction. Fed.Rules Civ.Proc.Rule 12(b)(1), 28 U.S.C.A.

> State of Conn. ex rel. Blumenthal v. Tobacco Valley Sanitation Service Co., 818 F.Supp. 504.

D.Conn. 1993. Under rule that court should not dismiss federal claim for lack of subject matter jurisdiction based on pleadings unless claim clearly appears to be immaterial or claim is wholly insubstantial and frivolous, court should not dismiss claim for lack of subject matter jurisdiction, even if court would have dismissed complaint in response to motion for failure to state claim on which relief could be granted. Fed.Rules Civ.Proc.Rule 12(b)(1, 6), 28 U.S.C.A.

> Ensign-Bickford Co. v. ICI Explosives USA Inc., 817 F.Supp. 1018.

Court may dismiss facially sufficient complaint for lack of subject jurisdiction if court finds, based on affidavits or other evidence outside complaint, that asserted basis for federal jurisdiction is not sufficient. Fed.Rules Civ. Proc.Rule 12(b)(1), 28 U.S.C.A.

> Ensign-Bickford Co. v. ICI Explosives USA Inc., 817 F.Supp. 1018.

D.Conn. 1991. Party may move to dismiss action because of failure of subject matter jurisdiction at any time during course of action. U.S.C.A. Const. Art. 3, § 1 et seq.; Fed.Rules Civ.Proc.Rule 12(b)(1, 6), (h)(3), 28 U.S.C.A.

> Commonwealth Land Title Ins. Co. v. U.S., 759 F.Supp. 87.

Where federal claim is alleged on face of complaint, and the plaintiff asserts jurisdiction under general federal question statute, court will only dismiss matter when claim is so insubstantial, implausible, foreclosed by prior decisions of the Supreme Court, or otherwise completely devoid of merit as not to involve federal controversy within jurisdiction of district court. 28 U.S.C.A. § 1331(a).

> Commonwealth Land Title Ins. Co. v. U.S., 759 F.Supp. 87.

D.Conn. 1986. Motion to dismiss for lack of personal jurisdiction will be denied, if plaintiff is able to make prima facie showing that defendant's conduct was sufficient for court to exercise personal jurisdiction. Fed.Rules Civ. Proc.Rule 12(b)(2), 28 U.S.C.A.

> Hover v. Asbestos Corp., Ltd., 678 F.Supp. 370.

D.Del. 1997. Dismissal of action is mandated if federal district court lacks subject matter jurisdiction at any stage of proceedings. Fed.Rules Civ.Proc.Rule 12(h)(3), 28 U.S.C.A.

> Sanderson, Thompson, Ratledge & Zimny v. AWACS, Inc., 958 F.Supp. 947.

Prior to certification of plaintiff class in putative class action, federal court which does not possess jurisdiction over claims of the representative party must dismiss case for want of jurisdiction. Fed.Rules Civ.Proc.Rule 12(h)(3), 28 U.S.C.A.

> Sanderson, Thompson, Ratledge & Zimny v. AWACS, Inc., 958 F.Supp. 947.

D.Del. 1996. When jurisdictional issues are inextricably intertwined with merits of cause of action, courts have not dismissed federal claims for lack of subject-matter jurisdiction unless they are clearly insubstantial or immaterial. Fed.Rules Civ.Proc.Rule 12(b)(1), 28 U.S.C.A.

> Rhoades v. U.S., 950 F.Supp. 623.

D.Del. 1996. Nonmoving party presents prima facie case in support of exercise of personal jurisdiction over party moving to dismiss for lack of personal jurisdiction by establishing with reasonable particularity sufficient contacts between moving party and Delaware to satisfy Delaware's long-arm statute and Due Process

Clause of United States Constitution. U.S.C.A. Const.Amend. 14; 10 Del.C. § 3104.

> Joint Stock Soc. Trade House of Descendants of Peter Smirnoff, Official Purveyor to the Imperial Court v. Heublein, Inc., 936 F.Supp. 177.

Prior to beginning of discovery, nonmoving party may rely on good faith factual allegations of its complaint, cross claims, or counterclaims to establish personal jurisdiction over party moving to dismiss if such allegations establish sufficient contacts between moving party and Delaware. Fed.Rules Civ.Proc.Rule 12(b)(2), 28 U.S.C.A.

> Joint Stock Soc. Trade House of Descendants of Peter Smirnoff, Official Purveyor to the Imperial Court v. Heublein, Inc., 936 F.Supp. 177.

D.Del. 1989. Plaintiff can defeat motion to dismiss for lack of subject matter jurisdiction by establishing prima facie case of federal subject matter jurisdiction. Fed.Rules Civ.Proc.Rule 12(b)(1), 28 U.S.C.A.

> Fitzpatrick v. U.S., 726 F.Supp. 975.

D.Del. 1988. Broad discretion is granted to the district court as to the mode of inquiry on a motion to dismiss for lack of subject matter jurisdiction. Fed.Rules Civ.Proc.Rule 12(b)(1), 28 U.S.C.A.

> SWT Acquisition Corp. v. TW Services, Inc., 700 F.Supp. 1323.

D.Del. 1987. Rule, which permits court to dismiss action whenever subject matter jurisdiction appears to be lacking, applies when there is no case or controversy. Fed.Rules Civ.Proc. Rule 12(h)(3), 28 U.S.C.A.; U.S.C.A. Const. Art. 3, § 1 et seq.

> Akzona Inc. v. E.I. du Pont de Nemours & Co., 662 F.Supp. 603.

D.D.C. 1996. To withstand motion to dismiss for lack of personal jurisdiction, plaintiffs must prove prima facie showing of pertinent jurisdictional facts by alleging specific acts connecting defendants with forum. Fed.Rules Civ. Proc.Rule 12(b)(2), 28 U.S.C.A.

> Richard v. Bell Atlantic Corp., 946 F.Supp. 54.

At dismissal stage, court will consider all allegations of jurisdictional facts in light most favorable to assertion of personal jurisdiction, but conclusory jurisdictional statements will not suffice. Fed.Rules Civ.Proc.Rule 12(b)(2), 28 U.S.C.A.

> Richard v. Bell Atlantic Corp., 946 F.Supp. 54.

D.D.C. 1995. If a claim is unripe, federal courts lack subject matter jurisdiction and complaint must be dismissed.

> Johnson v. Greater Southeast Community Hosp. Corp., 903 F.Supp. 140, appeal held in abeyance In re Johnson, 1996 WL 174379, certiorari denied 117 S.Ct. 2514, 138 L.Ed.2d 1016, vacated in part 1996 WL 377147.

D.D.C. 1995. When government moves to dismiss on political question grounds, court must conduct a discriminating inquiry into precise facts and posture of the particular case to ensure that the lawsuit is not a bona fide controversy as to whether some "political" action exceeds constitutional authority.

> Federation for American Immigration Reform, Inc. v. Reno, 897 F.Supp. 595, affirmed 93 F.3d 897, 320 U.S.App.D.C. 234, certiorari denied 117 S.Ct. 2510, 138 L.Ed.2d 1013.

M.D.Fla. 1995. Motion to dismiss for lack of subject matter jurisdiction attacks jurisdictional sufficiency of complaint as matter of law. Fed.Rules Civ.Proc.Rule 12(b)(1), 28 U.S.C.A.

> Harris v. McDonald's Corp., 901 F.Supp. 1552.

M.D.Fla. 1994. Attacks on subject matter jurisdiction by way of motion to dismiss come in two forms: facial attacks on complaint require court merely to look and see if plaintiff has sufficiently alleged basis of subject matter jurisdiction and allegations in complaint are taken as true for purposes of motion whereas factual attacks challenging existence of subject matter jurisdiction in fact, irrespective of the pleadings, and matters outside the pleadings, such as testimony and affidavits, are considered. Fed.Rules Civ.Proc.Rule 12(b)(1), 28 U.S.C.A.

> Bowman v. U.S., 848 F.Supp. 979.

M.D.Fla. 1993. Federal district court is under mandatory duty to dismiss suit over which it has no jurisdiction. Fed.Rules Civ. Proc.Rule 12(b)(1), 28 U.S.C.A.

> First Union Nat. Bank of Florida v. North Beach Professional Office Complex, Inc., 841 F.Supp. 399.

"Facial attacks" on subject matter jurisdiction under Rule 12(b)(1) require court merely to look and see if plaintiff has alleged basis of subject matter jurisdiction in complaint, and allegations in complaint are taken as true for purposes of motion. Fed.Rules Civ.Proc.Rule 12(b)(1), 28 U.S.C.A.

> First Union Nat. Bank of Florida v. North Beach Professional Office Complex, Inc., 841 F.Supp. 399.

"Factual attacks" under Rule 12(b)(1) challenge existence of subject matter jurisdiction in fact, considering matters outside pleadings, such as testimony and affidavits. Fed.Rules Civ.Proc.Rule 12(b)(1), 28 U.S.C.A.

> First Union Nat. Bank of Florida v. North Beach Professional Office Complex, Inc., 841 F.Supp. 399.

S.D.Fla. 1997. Motion to dismiss for lack of subject matter jurisdiction raises question that may be inquired into at any stage of proceedings. Fed.Rules Civ.Proc.Rule 12(b)(1), 28 U.S.C.A.

> Slugocki v. U.S. By and Through Dept. of Labor, Office of Workers' Compensation Programs, Div. of Federal Employees' Compensation, 988 F.Supp. 1443.

S.D.Fla. 1993. Federal district court is under mandatory duty to dismiss suit over which it has no jurisdiction. Fed.Rules Civ.Proc.Rules 12(b)(1), 56, 28 U.S.C.A.

> Southeast Bank, N.A. v. Gold Coast Graphics Group Partners, 149 F.R.D. 681.

Attacks on subject matter jurisdiction under rule authorizing dismissal of claim for lack of subject matter jurisdiction, come in two forms: "facial attacks" on complaint require court merely to look and see if plaintiff has sufficiently alleged basis of subject matter jurisdiction, and allegations in complaint are taken as true for purposes of motion; "factual attacks," on other hand, challenge existence of subject matter jurisdiction in fact, irrespective of pleading, and matters outside pleadings, such as testimony and affidavits are considered. Fed.Rules Civ.Proc.Rule 12(b)(1), 28 U.S.C.A.

> Southeast Bank, N.A. v. Gold Coast Graphics Group Partners, 149 F.R.D. 681.

S.D.Fla. 1991. Federal district court must dismiss for want of jurisdiction if asserted federal claim that is basis of jurisdiction is obviously without merit or is wholly frivolous.

> Bahr v. National Ass'n of Securities Dealers, Inc., 763 F.Supp. 584.

S.D.Fla. 1985. Plaintiff's various claims should not be dismissed for lack of in personam jurisdiction unless it appears beyond doubt that plaintiff can prove no set of facts that would establish personal jurisdiction over defendants.

> Moltz v. Seneca Balance, Inc., 606 F.Supp. 612.

N.D.Ga. 1995. Attacks under rule governing dismissal for lack of subject matter jurisdiction come in two forms: (1) facial attacks, and (2) factual attacks. Fed.Rules Civ.Proc.Rule 12(b)(1), 28 U.S.C.A.

> Hulsey v. Gunn, 905 F.Supp. 1067.

N.D.Ga. 1990. Motion to dismiss for lack of personal jurisdiction should be denied if plaintiff alleges sufficient facts to support reasonable inference that defendant can be subjected to court's jurisdiction. Fed.Rules Civ.Proc. Rule 12(b)(2), 28 U.S.C.A.

> James Whiten Livestock, Inc. v. Western Iowa Farms, Co., 750 F.Supp. 529, affirmed 948 F.2d 731, affirmed 948 F.2d 731.

N.D.Ga. 1989. When motion to dismiss for lack of personal jurisdiction is to be decided at preliminary stage of proceedings without hearing, plaintiff need only show prima facie case of jurisdiction.

> Electronic Transaction Network v. Katz, 734 F.Supp. 492.

District court is obligated to deny motion to dismiss for lack of personal jurisdiction if plaintiff alleges sufficient facts to support reasonable inference that nonresident defendant can be subjected to jurisdiction of court.

> Electronic Transaction Network v. Katz, 734 F.Supp. 492.

N.D.Ga. 1989. As general rule, motion to dismiss for lack of personal jurisdiction should be denied if complaint alleges sufficient facts to support reasonable inference that defendant could be subjected to jurisdiction of court. Fed. Rules Civ.Proc.Rule 12(b)(2), 28 U.S.C.A.

> Cable News Network, Inc. v. Video Monitoring Services of America, Inc., 723 F.Supp. 765.

N.D.Ga. 1987. On motion to dismiss, defendant may, in addition to basing motion on lack of subject matter jurisdiction, assert any other defenses or objections which may be available; however, when motion is based on more than one ground, district court should first consider challenge to subject matter jurisdiction. Fed.Rules Civ.Proc.Rule 12(b)(1), 28 U.S.C.A.

> Shared Network Technologies, Inc. v. Taylor, 669 F.Supp. 422.

N.D.Ga. 1983. Stone Mountain Game Ranch, Inc. v. Hunt, 570 F.Supp. 238, affirmed 746 F.2d 761.

D.Hawai'i 1995. Motion to dismiss for lack of subject matter jurisdiction can attack substance of complaint's jurisdictional allegations despite their formal sufficiency, whereupon plaintiff must present affidavits or other evidence necessary to satisfy its burden. Fed. Rules Civ.Proc.Rule 12(b)(1), 28 U.S.C.A.

> Forsyth v. Eli Lilly and Co., 904 F.Supp. 1153.

D.Hawai'i 1988. In scrutinizing motion to dismiss based on lack of personal jurisdiction, court looks to uncontroverted allegations of complaint, affidavits, and depositions. Fed. Rules Civ.Proc.Rule 12(b)(2), 28 U.S.C.A.

> Pure, Ltd. v. Shasta Beverages, Inc., 691 F.Supp. 1274.

D.Idaho 1996. Where there is no waiver of sovereign immunity, it is appropriate for court to dismiss action against federal government for lack of subject matter jurisdiction.
Murray v. I.R.S., 923 F.Supp. 1289.

C.D.Ill. 1994. Summary judgment motions can only be considered if court has subject matter jurisdiction and dismissal is mandated if subject matter jurisdiction is lacking. Fed. Rules Civ.Proc.Rules 12(h)(3), 56, 28 U.S.C.A.
Poole v. Baker, 874 F.Supp. 222.

N.D.Ill. 1996. Motions to dismiss for lack of jurisdiction are premised on either facial attacks or factual attacks to jurisdiction; "facial attack" is challenge to sufficiency of pleading itself, while "factual attack" is not challenge to sufficiency of pleading's allegations, but challenge to factual existence of subject matter jurisdiction. Fed.Rules Civ.Proc.Rule 12(b)(1), 28 U.S.C.A.
Villasenor v. Industrial Wire & Cable, Inc., 929 F.Supp. 310.

N.D.Ill. 1995. If plaintiff is unable to establish Article III standing, court must dismiss case for lack of subject matter jurisdiction. U.S.C.A. Const. Art. 3, § 2, cl. 1 et seq.
Paramount Health Systems, Inc. v. Wright, 907 F.Supp. 1212.

N.D.Ill. 1995. Only where alleged federal claim is immaterial and brought solely to fabricate federal jurisdiction, or wholly insubstantial and frivolous, may attack on merits of claim be treated as one seeking dismissal for lack of jurisdiction; instead, if issue of jurisdiction is intertwined with merits of case, then district court should take jurisdiction and handle defendant's motion as direct attack on merits of plaintiff's case. Fed.Rules Civ.Proc.Rule 12(b)(1, 6), 28 U.S.C.A.
Mungiovi v. Chicago Housing Authority, 901 F.Supp. 261.

Because attack on plaintiff's federal claim went to its merits, complaint would be analyzed under rule providing for dismissal for failure to state claim, even though defendants sought dismissal for lack of subject matter jurisdiction. Fed.Rules Civ.Proc.Rule 12(b)(1, 6), 28 U.S.C.A.
Mungiovi v. Chicago Housing Authority, 901 F.Supp. 261.

N.D.Ill. 1995. Court must dismiss case without reaching merits if it concludes that it has no subject matter jurisdiction. Fed.Rules Civ.Proc.Rule 12(b)(1), 28 U.S.C.A.
Seber v. Unger, 881 F.Supp. 323.

N.D.Ill. 1994. In determining whether case was properly removed despite nondiverse defendant, under "fraudulent joinder" doctrine, by determining whether law of forum state would recognize cause of action against the nondiverse defendant, district court would apply in its analysis state's standard for motions to dismiss.
Katonah v. USAir, Inc., 868 F.Supp. 1031.

N.D.Ill. 1994. Lack of subject matter jurisdiction is appropriately raised in motion to dismiss. Fed.Rules Civ.Proc.Rule 12(b)(1), 28 U.S.C.A.
U.S. E.E.O.C. v. City of Evanston, 854 F.Supp. 534.

N.D.Ill. 1993. Court would grant leave to amend complaint which erroneously listed joint venture as plaintiff, rather than dismiss complaint for lack of subject matter jurisdiction, so that members of joint venture would not have to pay additional filing fee. Fed.Rules Civ.Proc. Rule 17(b), 28 U.S.C.A.; S.H.A. 735 ILCS 5/2–411.
Hawkins VMR Joint Venture v. Rowbec, Inc., 835 F.Supp. 1091.

N.D.Ill. 1993. Lack of subject-matter jurisdiction is appropriately raised in motion to dismiss. Fed.Rules Civ.Proc.Rule 12(b)(1), 28 U.S.C.A.
U.S. v. Aspen Square Management Co., Inc., 817 F.Supp. 707, vacated 1993 WL 268352.

N.D.Ill. 1992. Lack of subject matter jurisdiction is appropriately raised in motion to dismiss. Fed.Rules Civ.Proc.Rule 12(b)(1, 6), 28 U.S.C.A.
MSA Realty Corp. v. State of Ill., 794 F.Supp. 267, affirmed 990 F.2d 288.

N.D.Ill. 1992. Lack of subject matter jurisdiction is appropriately raised in motion to dismiss and may be supported by any documents needed to resolve issue. Fed.Rules Civ. Proc.Rule 12(b)(1), 28 U.S.C.A.
West Shore Pipe Line Co. v. Associated Elec. and Gas Ins. Services Ltd., 791 F.Supp. 200.

N.D.Ill. 1989. Dismissal for lack of subject matter jurisdiction is proper course, where claim is wanting in essential ingredient for federal jurisdiction.
Harris v. Johnson, 731 F.Supp. 846.

N.D.Ill. 1987. Where lack of jurisdiction is patent and also patently incurable, it is not only right but duty of court to dismiss action.
Manny v. Department of Transp. of State of Hawaii, 664 F.Supp. 1210.

N.D.Ill. 1986. Rule 12(b)(1), governing dismissal for lack of subject-matter jurisdiction, is proper vehicle for dismissing cases which are untimely and over which no subject-matter jurisdiction exists because plaintiff has failed to exhaust his administrative remedies before coming to court. Fed.Rules Civ.Proc.Rule 12(b)(1), 28 U.S.C.A.

> Gervasio v. U.S., 627 F.Supp. 428.

N.D.Ill. 1986. If jurisdictional issue is uncertain, but is at least a difficult one, with substantial argument on both sides, prudence counsels dismissal, since refiling case in court that clearly has jurisdiction is no-risk situation, while retention of case in court of questionable jurisdiction risks subsequent invalidation of judgment.

> State Sec. Ins. Co. v. Frank B. Hall & Co., Inc., 109 F.R.D. 99.

S.D.Ill. 1992. Where defendant argues that court lacks jurisdiction because complaint fails to state cause of action, proper course of action for district court is to find that jurisdiction exists and address objection as direct attack on merits of complaint. Fed.Rules Civ.Proc. Rule 12(b)(6), 28 U.S.C.A.

> Small v. Sullivan, 820 F.Supp. 1098.

District court will dismiss complaint on jurisdictional grounds only if claim appears to be immaterial and made solely for purpose of obtaining jurisdiction, or where claim is wholly insubstantial and frivolous. Fed.Rules Civ. Proc.Rule 12(b)(6), 28 U.S.C.A.

> Small v. Sullivan, 820 F.Supp. 1098.

N.D.Ind. 1995. Motion to dismiss for lack of subject matter jurisdiction usually requires nonmoving party to resolve, whether through affidavits or other relevant evidence, factual dispute regarding court's subject matter jurisdiction. Fed.Rules Civ.Proc.Rule 12(b)(1), 28 U.S.C.A.

> Crampton v. U.S., 163 F.R.D. 545.

S.D.Ind. 1996. While exhaustion of administrative remedies is prudential doctrine, not jurisdictional prerequisite, failure to exhaust administrative remedies may properly be raised on motion to dismiss for lack of subject matter jurisdiction. Fed.Rules Civ.Proc.Rule 12(b)(1), 28 U.S.C.A.

> Brown v. Metropolitan School Dist. of Lawrence Tp., 945 F.Supp. 1202.

N.D.Iowa 1997. For court to dismiss for lack of subject matter jurisdiction, complaint must be successfully challenged on its face or on factual truthfulness of its averments. Fed. Rules Civ.Proc.Rule 12(b)(1), 28 U.S.C.A.

> Med-Tec, Inc. v. Kostich, 980 F.Supp. 1315.

N.D.Iowa 1997. For court to dismiss for lack of subject matter jurisdiction, complaint must be successfully challenged on its face or on factual truthfulness of its averments. Fed. Rules Civ.Proc.Rule 12(b)(1), 28 U.S.C.A.

> Doe v. Hartz, 970 F.Supp. 1375, reversed in part, vacated in part 134 F.3d 1339.

N.D.Iowa 1996. For court to dismiss for lack of subject matter jurisdiction, complaint must be successfully challenged on its face or on factual truthfulness of its averments. Fed. Rules Civ.Proc.Rule 12(b)(1), 28 U.S.C.A.

> Slycord v. Chater, 921 F.Supp. 631.

N.D.Iowa 1995. Complaint must be successfully challenged on its face or on factual truthfulness of its averments in order for federal district court to dismiss complaint for lack of subject matter jurisdiction. Fed.Rules Civ.Proc. Rule 12(b)(1), 28 U.S.C.A.

> Quality Refrigerated Services, Inc. v. City of Spencer, 908 F.Supp. 1471.

N.D.Iowa 1995. For court to dismiss for lack of subject matter jurisdiction, complaint must be successfully challenged on its face or on factual truthfulness of its averments. Fed. Rules Civ.Proc.Rule 12(b)(1), 28 U.S.C.A.

> Laird v. Ramirez, 884 F.Supp. 1265, on reconsideration 982 F.Supp. 1345.

N.D.Iowa 1995. For court to dismiss for lack of subject matter jurisdiction, complaint must be successfully challenged on its face or on factual truthfulness of its averments. Fed. Rules Civ.Proc.Rule 12(b)(1), 28 U.S.C.A.

> Woodke v. Dahm, 873 F.Supp. 179, affirmed 70 F.3d 983.

N.D.Iowa 1994. Federal courts have duty to examine substantiality of federal claim throughout litigation, and must dismiss all claims if federal claim proves patently meritless even after trial begins. 28 U.S.C.A. § 1331.

> Thomas v. St. Luke's Health Systems, Inc., 869 F.Supp. 1413, affirmed 61 F.3d 908.

N.D.Iowa 1994. For court to dismiss for lack of subject matter jurisdiction under Federal Rules of Civil Procedure, complaint must be successfully challenged on its face or on factual truthfulness of its averments. Fed.Rules Civ. Proc.Rule 12(b)(1), 28 U.S.C.A.

> Veeder v. Omaha Tribe of Nebraska, 864 F.Supp. 889.

D.Kan. 1998. Court lacking jurisdiction must dismiss cause at any stage of proceeding in which it becomes apparent that jurisdiction is lacking. Fed.Rules Civ.Proc.Rule 12(h)(3), 28 U.S.C.A.

> Mills v. State of Kan., Eighth Judicial Dist., 994 F.Supp. 1356.

D.Kan. 1997. Federal court lacking jurisdiction must dismiss cause at any stage of proceeding in which it becomes apparent that jurisdiction is lacking. Fed.Rules Civ.Proc.Rule 12(h)(3), 28 U.S.C.A.

> Sac and Fox Nation of Missouri v. Lafaver, 979 F.Supp. 1350, reconsideration denied 993 F.Supp. 1374.

D.Kan. 1997. A court lacking jurisdiction must dismiss cause at any stage of proceeding in which it becomes apparent that jurisdiction is lacking. Fed.Rules Civ.Proc.Rule 12(h)(3), 28 U.S.C.A.

> Fitzgerald v. City of Ottawa, Kan., 975 F.Supp. 1402.

D.Kan. 1997. Court lacking jurisdiction must dismiss cause at any stage of proceeding in which it becomes apparent that jurisdiction is lacking. Fed.Rules Civ.Proc.Rule 12(h)(3), 28 U.S.C.A.

> Whayne v. City of Topeka, 959 F.Supp. 1375.

D.Kan. 1996. In analyzing motion to dismiss for lack of jurisdiction, court must apply two-part test: first, court must determine if defendant's conduct falls within one of the provisions of the forum state's long-arm statute; second, court must determine whether defendant had sufficient minimum contacts with forum states to satisfy constitutional guarantee of due process. U.S.C.A. Const.Amend. 14.

> Electronic Realty Associates, L.P. v. Paramount Pictures Corp., 935 F.Supp. 1172.

D.Kan. 1995. When federal statute serves as both basis for court's subject matter jurisdiction and plaintiff's substantive claim, motion to dismiss for lack of subject matter jurisdiction should not be granted unless claim is immaterial, insubstantial, or frivolous. Fed.Rules Civ.Proc.Rule 12(b)(1), 28 U.S.C.A.

> Fanoele v. U.S., 898 F.Supp. 822.

D.Kan. 1994. In analyzing motion to dismiss for lack of jurisdiction, court must apply two-part test; first determining whether defendant's conduct falls within provisions of forum state's long-arm statute, and second determining whether defendant had sufficient minimum contacts with forum state to satisfy constitutional guarantee of due process. U.S.C.A. Const. Amend. 14.

> Key Industries, Inc. v. O'Doski, Sellers & Clark, Inc., 872 F.Supp. 858.

D.Kan. 1993. Court lacking subject matter jurisdiction must dismiss case at any stage of proceeding in which it becomes apparent that such jurisdiction is absent.

> Jensen v. Johnson County Youth Baseball League, 838 F.Supp. 1437.

When federal statute serves as both basis for court's subject matter jurisdiction and plaintiff's substantive claim, court should assume jurisdiction and resolve issue on merits, unless alleged cause of action is immaterial, insubstantial or frivolous.

> Jensen v. Johnson County Youth Baseball League, 838 F.Supp. 1437.

D.Kan. 1989. When federal statute serves as both basis for court's subject matter jurisdiction and plaintiff's substantive claim, motion to dismiss for lack of jurisdiction should not be granted unless claim is immaterial, insubstantial or frivolous.

> St. Mary of the Plains College v. Higher Educ. Loan Program of Kansas, Inc., 724 F.Supp. 803.

Where defendant's motion to dismiss challenges both jurisdiction and existence of federal cause of action, court should find jurisdiction and determine merits of claim. Fed.Rules Civ.Proc.Rule 12(b)(6), 28 U.S.C.A.

> St. Mary of the Plains College v. Higher Educ. Loan Program of Kansas, Inc., 724 F.Supp. 803.

D.Kan. 1985. Court lacking jurisdiction cannot render judgment but must dismiss cause at any stage of proceedings in which it becomes apparent that jurisdiction is lacking.

> Gross v. Federal Deposit Ins. Corp., 613 F.Supp. 79.

M.D.La. 1997. Standard for dismissal articulated in Supreme Court's *Bell v. Hood* decision is inapplicable to motions to dismiss that do not challenge existence of federal cause of action.

> Hannover Corp. of America v. Beckner, 211 B.R. 849.

District court has power to dismiss for lack of subject matter jurisdiction based upon three separate bases: complaint alone, complaint supplemented by undisputed facts in the record, or complaint supplemented by undisputed facts plus the court's resolution of disputed facts.

> Hannover Corp. of America v. Beckner, 211 B.R. 849.

W.D.La. 1997. Where factual findings regarding subject matter jurisdiction are intertwined with the merits, motion to dismiss is treated as attack on the merits and district court employs standard applicable to motion for summary judgment; subject matter jurisdiction and merits are considered intertwined where same statute provides both basis for subject matter jurisdiction and cause of action. Fed.Rules Civ.Proc.Rule 12(b)(1), 28 U.S.C.A.

> Cupit v. U.S., 964 F.Supp. 1104.

W.D.La. 1996. Action may be dismissed for lack of subject matter jurisdiction on any one of three separate grounds: complaint standing alone, complaint supplemented by undisputed facts evidenced in record, or complaint, undisputed facts, and court's resolution of disputed facts. Fed.Rules Civ.Proc.Rule 12(b)(1), 28 U.S.C.A.

> Pleasant v. U.S., 915 F.Supp. 826.

D.Me. 1997. In order for plaintiff to withstand motion to dismiss for lack of personal jurisdiction, record must contain specific allegations of jurisdictional facts, which district court will construe in plaintiff's favor. Fed.Rules Civ.Proc.Rule 12(b)(2), 28 U.S.C.A.

Scott v. Jones, 984 F.Supp. 37.

D.Me. 1994. Failure to comply with rule requiring plaintiff to include in complaint short plain statement of basis of subject matter jurisdiction must result in dismissal unless such failure is corrected by amendment. Fed.Rules Civ.Proc.Rule 8(a)(1), 28 U.S.C.A.

Doyle v. Household Credit Services, Inc., 844 F.Supp. 13.

D.Md. 1996. Motion to dismiss for lack of subject matter jurisdiction may attack complaint on its face, in that complaint fails to allege facts upon which court can base jurisdiction, or it may attack truth of underlying jurisdictional allegations contained in complaint. Fed.Rules Civ.Proc.Rule 12(b)(1), 28 U.S.C.A.

Crosten v. Kamauf, 932 F.Supp. 676.

D.Md. 1994. "Patently insubstantial complaints," which may be dismissed for want of subject matter jurisdiction, include those that are based on indisputably meritless legal theory and those whose factual contentions are clearly baseless, as well as claims describing fantastic or delusional scenarios. Fed.Rules Civ.Proc. Rule 12(b)(1), 28 U.S.C.A.

O'Connor v. U.S., 159 F.R.D. 22, affirmed 54 F.3d 773.

D.Md. 1985. Dismissal of suit on grounds of forum non conveniens may be granted even though law applicable in alternative forum is less favorable to plaintiff's chance of recovery.

Zinsler v. Marriott Corp., 605 F.Supp. 1499.

D.Mass. 1997. Although plaintiff has burden of showing that personal jurisdiction exists, district court must determine what evidentiary showing plaintiff must make for case to survive defendant's motion to dismiss. Fed.Rules Civ. Proc.Rule 12(b)(2), 28 U.S.C.A.

Hasbro Inc. v. Clue Computing Inc., 994 F.Supp. 34.

D.Mass. 1991. Subject matter jurisdiction may be refuted by way of "facial attack," where it is asserted that complaint fails to allege facts upon which subject matter jurisdiction can be based, or by "factual attack" and where it is asserted that jurisdictional allegations of complaint are not true. Fed.Rules Civ.Proc.Rule 12(b)(1), 28 U.S.C.A.

1610 Corp. v. Kemp, 753 F.Supp. 1026.

E.D.Mich. 1996. Court will dismiss complaint for lack of subject matter jurisdiction if, assuming allegations in complaint are true and construing complaint in light most favorable to plaintiff, it appears beyond doubt that plaintiff can prove no set of facts in support of his or her claim that would entitle him or her to relief. Fed.Rules Civ.Proc.Rule 12(b)(1), 28 U.S.C.A.

Michigan Ass'n of Homes and Services for Aging, Inc. v. Shalala, 931 F.Supp. 1338, affirmed 127 F.3d 496, rehearing and suggestion for rehearing denied.

E.D.Mich. 1995. Motion to dismiss for lack of subject matter jurisdiction may be used to attack two different types of defects: (1) pleader's failure to allege facts in complaint sufficient to show subject matter jurisdiction, and (2) court's actual lack of jurisdiction over subject matter, which is defect that may exist despite formal sufficiency of allegations in complaint. Fed.Rules Civ.Proc.Rule 12(b)(1), 28 U.S.C.A.

National Rifle Ass'n of America v. Magaw, 909 F.Supp. 490, affirmed in part, reversed in part 132 F.3d 272.

W.D.Mich. 1997. If court relies solely upon affidavits submitted by parties in determining motion for dismissal for lack of personal jurisdiction, plaintiff need only make prima facie showing that personal jurisdiction exists; in such case, dismissal is proper only if all of specific facts alleged by plaintiff collectively fail to state prima facie case for jurisdiction. Fed. Rules Civ.Proc.Rule 12(b)(2), 28 U.S.C.A.

Brady v. Burtt, 979 F.Supp. 524.

W.D.Mich. 1993. Motion to dismiss for lack of subject matter jurisdiction may be decided by district court on one of three bases: complaint alone, complaint supplemented by undisputed facts evidenced in record, or complaint supplemented by undisputed facts plus court's resolution of disputed facts. Fed.Rules Civ.Proc.Rule 12(b)(1), 28 U.S.C.A.

Rospatch Jessco Corp. v. Chrysler Corp., 829 F.Supp. 224.

Facial attack on court's subject matter jurisdiction required court to review complaint to see if it sufficiently alleged basis of subject matter jurisdiction, with allegations in complaint taken as true for purposes of motion to dismiss. Fed.Rules Civ.Proc.Rule 12(b)(1), 28 U.S.C.A.

Rospatch Jessco Corp. v. Chrysler Corp., 829 F.Supp. 224.

W.D.Mich. 1987. Motion to dismiss for lack of subject matter jurisdiction is meant to test formal sufficiency of complaint to state redressable claim and, if it presents matters outside pleadings, is to be treated as motion for summary judgment in which movant must prove that there is no genuine issue of material fact. 28 U.S.C.A. § 1331; Fed.Rules Civ.Proc. Rules 12(b)(1, 6), 56, 56(a), 28 U.S.C.A.

> Doe v. Keane, 658 F.Supp. 216.

D.Minn. 1998. Court lacking jurisdiction over action must dismiss it. Fed.Rules Civ. Proc.Rule 12(b)(1), 28 U.S.C.A.

> Midwestern Machinery Co., Inc. v. Northwest Airlines, Inc., 990 F.Supp. 1128.

D.Minn. 1996. In order to obtain dismissal of action for lack of subject matter jurisdiction, challenging party must successfully attack complaint, either upon its face or upon factual truth of its averments. Fed.Rules Civ.Proc.Rule 12(b)(1), 28 U.S.C.A.

> Moubry By and Through Moubry v. Independent School Dist. No. 696 (Ely), 951 F.Supp. 867.

D.Minn. 1996. Motion to dismiss for lack of subject matter jurisdiction will prove to be successful if plaintiff should fail to allege element necessary for finding of subject matter jurisdiction. Fed.Rules Civ.Proc.Rule 12(b)(1), 28 U.S.C.A.

> Hoeffner v. University of Minnesota, 948 F.Supp. 1380.

D.Minn. 1996. "Facial attack" on subject matter jurisdiction questions sufficiency of pleading itself and is reviewed by examining only the pleadings, utilizing same standards favorable to nonmoving party as on motion to dismiss for failure to state a claim. Fed.Rules Civ.Proc.Rule 12(b)(6), 28 U.S.C.A.

> Vizenor v. Babbitt, 927 F.Supp. 1193.

D.Minn. 1990. Jurisdiction is deemed not to lie where federal claim asserted is immaterial, insubstantial or frivolous. Fed.Rules Civ. Proc.Rule 12(h)(3), 28 U.S.C.A.

> Sassower v. Dosal, 744 F.Supp. 908, affirmed 930 F.2d 583, rehearing denied.

D.Minn. 1986. Dismissal of federal action based on lack of subject-matter jurisdiction is appropriate only if the federal claims are insubstantial.

> Spring Water Dairy, Inc. v. Federal Intermediate Credit Bank of St. Paul, 625 F.Supp. 713.

S.D.Miss. 1989. Failure to comply with federal procedural rule requiring complaint to contain short and plain statement of grounds upon which court's jurisdiction depends does not mandate dismissal for lack of jurisdiction so long as complaint reveals proper basis for jurisdiction. Fed.Rules Civ.Proc.Rule 8(a)(1), 28 U.S.C.A.

> Un-Common Carrier Corp. v. Oglesby, 98 B.R. 751.

E.D.Mo. 1996. Standards applied to a motion to dismiss for lack of subject matter juris-

diction are same as those applied to motion to dismiss for failure to state a claim. Fed.Rules Civ.Proc.Rules 12(b)(1), 12(b)(6), 28 U.S.C.A.

> Vankempen v. McDonnell Douglas Corp., 923 F.Supp. 146.

E.D.Mo. 1994. Motion to dismiss under Rule 12(b)(1) may challenge either facial sufficiency or factual truthfulness of plaintiff's jurisdictional allegations. Fed.Rules Civ.Proc.Rule 12(b)(1), 28 U.S.C.A.

> Wittmann v. U.S., 869 F.Supp. 726.

When passing on facial challenge on motion to dismiss under Rule 12(b)(1), court must presume that all of the plaintiff's jurisdictional allegations are true, and motion must be granted if plaintiff has failed to allege necessary element supporting jurisdiction. Fed.Rules Civ. Proc.Rule 12(b)(1), 28 U.S.C.A.

> Wittmann v. U. S., 869 F.Supp. 726.

E.D.Mo. 1984. Sun World Lines, Ltd. v. March Shipping Corp., 585 F.Supp. 580, affirmed 801 F.2d 1066.

W.D.Mo. 1994. District court must dismiss for lack of subject matter jurisdiction case in which no diversity or supplemental jurisdiction exists, unless federal question is presented. 28 U.S.C.A. §§ 1332, 1367.

> U.S. v. Chorice, 857 F.Supp. 672.

D.Neb. 1997. To survive motion to dismiss for lack of subject matter jurisdiction, the pleadings must sufficiently evince a basis for subject matter jurisdiction. Fed.Rules Civ.Proc.Rule 12(b)(1), 28 U.S.C.A.

> Vasiliades v. U.S., 991 F.Supp. 1136.

Court should dismiss plaintiff's cause of action for lack of subject matter jurisdiction sparingly and cautiously, and only when no basis for subject matter jurisdiction exists. Fed. Rules Civ.Proc.Rule 12(b)(1), 28 U.S.C.A.

> Vasiliades v. U.S., 991 F.Supp. 1136.

D.Neb. 1985. Claim may be dismissed for lack of subject-matter jurisdiction, rather than for failure to state a claim, only when the allegations of the complaint are frivolous, where statute provides basis for both subject-matter jurisdiction of the federal court and plaintiff's substantive claim for relief.

> Jonak v. John Hancock Mut. Life Ins. Co., 629 F.Supp. 90.

D.Nev. 1997. Although court may resolve disputed factual issues in determining its own subject matter jurisdiction, where jurisdiction is so intertwined with merits that its resolution depends on resolution of merits, court should not dismiss for lack of subject matter jurisdiction unless there are no genuinely disputed issues of material fact and moving party is entitled to judgment as matter of law.

Duval Ranching Co. v. Glickman, 965 F.Supp. 1427.

D.Nev. 1995. Contests over existence of jurisdiction over defendant res are more properly resolved by motion to dismiss in civil forfeiture proceeding, rather than by motion for summary judgment.

U.S. v. 3 Parcels in La Plata County, Colo., 919 F.Supp. 1449.

D.N.H. 1996. In ruling on motion to dismiss for lack of personal jurisdiction, court must analyze contacts attributable to each individual defendant. Fed.Rules Civ.Proc.Rule 12(b)(2), 28 U.S.C.A.

Gray v. St. Martin's Press, Inc., 929 F.Supp. 40.

D.N.J. 1996. Dismissal pursuant to federal rule of civil procedure governing dismissal for lack of subject-matter jurisdiction is only proper when claim clearly appears to be immaterial. Fed.Rules Civ.Proc.Rule 12(b)(1), 28 U.S.C.A.

Watts v. I.R.S., 925 F.Supp. 271.

Threshold to withstand motion to dismiss for lack of subject-matter jurisdiction is lower than that required for motion to dismiss for failure to state claim. Fed.Rules Civ.Proc.Rule 12(b)(1, 6), 28 U.S.C.A.

Watts v. I.R.S., 925 F.Supp. 271.

D.N.J. 1996. District court may grant defendant's motion to dismiss for lack of subject matter jurisdiction based on the legal insufficiency of claim. Fed.Rules Civ.Proc.Rule 12(b)(1), 28 U.S.C.A.

Danowski by Danowski v. U.S., 924 F.Supp. 661.

D.N.J. 1995. District Court may grant motion to dismiss for lack of subject matter jurisdiction based on legal insufficiency of claim; such dismissal is proper, however, only when claim clearly appears to be immaterial and made solely for purpose of obtaining jurisdiction, or is wholly insubstantial and frivolous. Fed.Rules Civ.Proc.Rule 12(b)(1), 28 U.S.C.A.

Stehney v. Perry, 907 F.Supp. 806, affirmed 101 F.3d 925.

D.N.J. 1994. There are two types of motions to dismiss for lack of subject matter jurisdiction: those which attack complaint on its face and those which attack existence of subject matter jurisdiction in fact, apart from any pleading. Fed.Rules Civ.Proc.Rule 12(b)(1), 28 U.S.C.A.

Biase v. Kaplan, 852 F.Supp. 268.

Jurisdictional attack which does not implicate merits of any federal cause of action is not bound by standard that when basis of jurisdiction is also element in federal cause of action motion to dismiss should be dealt with on merits by finding that jurisdiction exists. Fed. Rules Civ.Proc.Rule 12(b)(1), 28 U.S.C.A.

Biase v. Kaplan, 852 F.Supp. 268.

Office of Thrift Supervision's (OTS's) motion to dismiss action brought against it by shareholder in savings and loan was attack on subject matter jurisdiction per se, where motion neither attacked amended complaint on its face nor addressed merits of amended complaint. Fed.Rules Civ.Proc.Rule 12(b)(1), 28 U.S.C.A.

Biase v. Kaplan, 852 F.Supp. 268.

D.N.J. 1993. Plaintiffs' failure to include statement regarding grounds for subject matter jurisdiction in amended complaint did not warrant dismissal of action, where it appeared that defect could be cured by amendment alleging diversity jurisdiction. Fed.Rules Civ.Proc.Rule 8(a), 28 U.S.C.A.; 28 U.S.C.A. § 1332.

Bryan v. Associated Container Transp. (A.C.T.), 837 F.Supp. 633.

D.N.J. 1993. Motion to dismiss for lack of subject matter jurisdiction differs from motion to dismiss for failure to state claim and from motion for summary judgment; challenge to court's subject matter jurisdiction entails no presumption that plaintiff's allegations are true, unless motion attacks complaint on its face, and court may consider matters outside pleadings in determining whether jurisdiction exists. Fed. Rules Civ.Proc.Rules 12(b)(1, 6), 56, 28 U.S.C.A.

Schwartz v. Medicare, 832 F.Supp. 782.

E.D.N.Y. 1998. In ruling on motion to dismiss filed by non-U.S. parties, court must be mindful that great care and reserve should be exercised when extending our notions of personal jurisdiction into international field. Fed. Rules Civ.Proc.Rule 12(b)(2), 28 U.S.C.A.

Local 875 I.B.T. Pension Fund v. Pollack, 992 F.Supp. 545.

E.D.N.Y. 1996. Dismissal for lack of jurisdiction is not appropriate merely because legal theory alleged is probably false, but only because right claimed is so insubstantial, implausible, foreclosed by prior decisions of Court of Appeals, or otherwise completely devoid of merit as not to involve federal controversy.

Maggio v. Leeward Ventures, Ltd., 939 F.Supp. 1020.

E.D.N.Y. 1993. Consideration of issue of subject matter jurisdiction is not equivalent to evaluation of merits of party's federal claim; test is whether claim is so patently without merit so as to justify dismissal based on jurisdictional grounds.

Paulsen v. Lehman, 839 F.Supp. 147.

E.D.N.Y. 1989. If motion to dismiss asserts lack of subject matter jurisdiction and failure to state claim, court should generally find jurisdiction and proceed to determine whether claim is stated. Fed.Rules Civ.Proc. Rule 12(b)(1, 6), 28 U.S.C.A.

> Pagano by Pagano v. Massapequa Public Schools, 714 F.Supp. 641.

E.D.N.Y. 1987. Federal court should be slow to dismiss for lack of jurisdiction claims purportedly made under federal law; wiser course is to take jurisdiction and dismiss for failure to state a claim.

> Banco de Ponce v. Hinsdale Supermarket Corp., 663 F.Supp. 813, motion denied 1987 WL 12846.

E.D.N.Y. 1985. Without subject matter jurisdiction, a district court has no power to order any sort of relief, but is compelled to dismiss. 28 U.S.C.A. § 1332; Fed.Rules Civ. Proc.Rule 12(h)(3), 28 U.S.C.A.

> We Try Harder v. United Press Intern. Services Co. Inc., 615 F.Supp. 556.

N.D.N.Y. 1997. Federal court must dismiss for lack of subject matter jurisdiction even if federal claim is asserted on face of complaint where federal question is so plainly insubstantial as to be devoid of any merit and thus does not present any issue worthy of adjudication; test is whether federal claim is so insubstantial, implausible, or otherwise completely devoid of merit as to not involve federal controversy.

> Schulz v. New York State Executive, Pataki, 960 F.Supp. 568, certiorari denied 119 S.Ct. 168.

N.D.N.Y. 1996. Fair legal allegations by plaintiff may be sufficient to withstand dismissal motion for lack of personal jurisdiction, but on summary judgment motion after discovery plaintiff bears burden of establishing whether jurisdiction is present.

> Murphy v. Cuomo, 913 F.Supp. 671.

N.D.N.Y. 1993. District court has considerable discretion in deciding pretrial motion to dismiss for lack of personal jurisdiction.

> Gilbert v. Wilson, 821 F.Supp. 857.

N.D.N.Y. 1988. To survive motion to dismiss for lack of personal jurisdiction, until pretrial evidentiary hearing is held or until trial, plaintiff need only make prima facie showing that jurisdiction exists.

> Pellegrino v. Stratton Corp., 679 F.Supp. 1164.

S.D.N.Y. 1998. Motion to dismiss for lack of subject matter jurisdiction may challenge either truth of jurisdictional allegations of complaint or, alternatively, legal sufficiency of allegations to support exercise of district court's jurisdiction. Fed.Rules Civ.Proc.Rule 12(b)(1), 28 U.S.C.A.

> Hayden v. New York Stock Exchange, Inc., 4 F.Supp.2d 335.

S.D.N.Y. 1998. If defendants' jurisdictional challenge precedes any pretrial discovery, plaintiff need only make legally sufficient allegations of jurisdiction to defeat motion to dismiss for lack of personal jurisdiction. Fed.Rules Civ.Proc.Rule 12(b)(2), 28 U.S.C.A.

> Kelly v. MD Buyline, Inc., 2 F.Supp.2d 420.

S.D.N.Y. 1997. Prior to discovery, party may defeat motion to dismiss for lack of subject matter jurisdiction by pleading in good faith legally sufficient allegations of jurisdiction, without having to state facts that if credited by ultimate trier of fact, would suffice to establish jurisdiction. Fed.Rules Civ.Proc.Rule 12(b)(1), 28 U.S.C.A.

> Evans Medical Ltd. v. American Cyanamid Co., 980 F.Supp. 132.

S.D.N.Y. 1997. Facially sufficient complaint may be dismissed for lack of subject matter jurisdiction if district court finds that asserted basis for federal jurisdiction is not sufficient. Fed.Rules Civ.Proc.Rule 12(b)(1), (h)(3), 28 U.S.C.A.

> Peterson v. Continental Airlines, Inc., 970 F.Supp. 246.

S.D.N.Y. 1997. Motion to dismiss based on lack of subject matter jurisdiction challenges court's statutory or constitutional power to adjudicate a case, and typically alleges that federal court lacks either federal question or diversity jurisdiction over action. Fed.Rules Civ.Proc. Rule 12(b)(1), 28 U.S.C.A.

> Moreno v. U.S., 965 F.Supp. 521.

S.D.N.Y. 1996. Motion to dismiss for lack of subject matter jurisdiction can raise facial challenge based on the pleadings or factual challenge based on extrinsic evidence; in the latter circumstance, court may conduct whatever further proceedings are appropriate to determine whether it has jurisdiction and it can decide matter on the basis of affidavits or can hold evidentiary hearing. Fed.Rules Civ.Proc. Rule 12(b)(1), 28 U.S.C.A.

> Guadagno v. Wallack Ader Levithan Associates, 932 F.Supp. 94.

S.D.N.Y. 1996. Motion to dismiss for lack of subject matter jurisdiction challenges district court's power to resolve a dispute, regardless of merits of dispute. Fed.Rules Civ.Proc.Rule 12(b)(1), 28 U.S.C.A.

> Dillard v. Runyon, 928 F.Supp. 1316, affirmed 108 F.3d 1369.

S.D.N.Y. 1995. Rule of Civil Procedure governing motion to dismiss for lack of subject matter or personal jurisdiction was not appropriate, in action seeking enforcement of foreign judgment, to challenge the jurisdiction of the foreign court. Fed.Rules Civ.Proc.Rule 12(b)(1, 2), 28 U.S.C.A.

> Canadian Imperial Bank of Commerce v. Saxony Carpet Co., Inc., 899 F.Supp. 1248, affirmed 104 F.3d 352.

S.D.N.Y. 1995. On motion to dismiss federal-question case for lack of subject matter jurisdiction, district court must determine whether plaintiffs have claimed violation of federal law and whether this claim is immaterial or insubstantial. Fed.Rules Civ.Proc.Rule 12(b)(1), 28 U.S.C.A.

> Walsh v. McGee, 899 F.Supp. 1232, reargument denied 918 F.Supp. 107.

S.D.N.Y. 1995. Failure to state proper cause of action calls for judgment on the merits and not for dismissal for want of jurisdiction. Fed.Rules Civ.Proc.Rule 12(b)(1, 6), 28 U.S.C.A.

> HBP Associates v. Marsh, 893 F.Supp. 271.

S.D.N.Y. 1995. Court may dismiss facially sufficient complaint for lack of subject matter jurisdiction if court finds, based on affidavits or other evidence outside complaint, that asserted basis for federal jurisdiction is not sufficient. Fed.Rules Civ.Proc.Rule 12(b)(1), 28 U.S.C.A.

> RAD Data Communications, Inc. v. Patton Electronics Co., 882 F.Supp. 351, dismissed 64 F.3d 675.

S.D.N.Y. 1995. On motion to dismiss for lack of personal jurisdiction, plaintiff is only obligated to allege facts sufficient to establish prima facie showing of jurisdiction.

> Eskofot A/S v. E.I. Du Pont De Nemours & Co., 872 F.Supp. 81.

S.D.N.Y. 1994. Dismissal of case based upon lack of personal jurisdiction is vital safeguard against lawsuits where neither events involved nor parties have significant connections with forum.

> Morrison Law Firm v. Clarion Co., Ltd., 158 F.R.D. 285, affirmed 60 F.3d 811.

Dismissal of case based on lack of personal jurisdiction must be approached with caution where party to be sued may have substantial connections with forum.

> Morrison Law Firm v. Clarion Co., Ltd., 158 F.R.D. 285, affirmed 60 F.3d 811.

S.D.N.Y. 1993. On motion to dismiss for lack of subject matter jurisdiction, plaintiff may establish such jurisdiction through extrapleading material. Fed.Rules Civ.Proc.Rule 12(b)(1), 28 U.S.C.A.

> Bridges v. Eastman Kodak Co., 822 F.Supp. 1020.

S.D.N.Y. 1992. Action must be dismissed, even on court's own motion, whenever it appears that court lacks subject matter jurisdiction. Fed.Rules Civ.Proc.Rule 12(h)(3), 28 U.S.C.A.

> Carlucci v. U.S., 793 F.Supp. 482.

S.D.N.Y. 1991. In order to defeat postdiscovery motion to dismiss for lack of personal jurisdiction, plaintiff must make prima facie showing of facts which, if credited by trier of fact, would suffice to establish jurisdiction over defendant; bare allegations of jurisdiction will not suffice where discovery has taken place. Fed.Rules Civ.Proc.Rule 12(b)(2), 28 U.S.C.A.

> United Bank of Kuwait, PLC v. James M. Bridges, Ltd., 766 F.Supp. 113.

S.D.N.Y. 1989. To withstand a motion to dismiss for lack of personal jurisdiction, plaintiff need make out only a prima facie case of personal jurisdiction. Fed.Rules Civ.Proc.Rule 12(b)(2), 28 U.S.C.A.

> Perez-Rubio v. Wyckoff, 718 F.Supp. 217.

S.D.N.Y. 1989. In order to prevail against motion to dismiss for lack of personal jurisdiction, plaintiff need only make out prima facie case of jurisdiction with all inferences drawn in its favor. Fed.Rules Civ.Proc.Rule 12(b)(2), 28 U.S.C.A.

> Picard v. Elbaum, 707 F.Supp. 144.

S.D.N.Y. 1988. Where motion to dismiss for lack of in personam jurisdiction is decided on the pleadings and affidavits without an evidentiary hearing, plaintiff need only make a prima facie showing that jurisdiction exists; all pleadings and affidavits are construed in a light most favorable to the plaintiff, and all doubts resolved in its favor. Fed.Rules Civ.Proc.Rule 12(b)(2), 28 U.S.C.A.

> Hedlund v. Products From Sweden, Inc., 698 F.Supp. 1087.

In ruling on motion to dismiss for lack of personal jurisdiction, court must consider whether there is a statutory basis for jurisdiction and whether the exercise of personal jurisdiction under state law comports with due process under the Fourteenth Amendment. U.S.C.A. Const.Amend. 14.

> Hedlund v. Products From Sweden, Inc., 698 F.Supp. 1087.

S.D.N.Y. 1988. On motion to dismiss for lack of personal jurisdiction, district court has considerable leeway in determining how to proceed. Fed.Rules Civ.Proc.Rule 12(b)(2), 28 U.S.C.A.

> Norma Walters & Co., Inc. v. Clothes Garden, Inc., 693 F.Supp. 1549.

S.D.N.Y. 1980. Fosen v. United Technologies Corp., 484 F.Supp. 490, affirmed 633 F.2d 203.

S.D.N.Y. 1978. Loria & Weinhaus, Inc. v. H. R. Kaminsky & Sons, Inc., 80 F.R.D. 494, motion granted 495 F.Supp. 253.

E.D.N.C. 1998. Motion to dismiss for lack of subject matter jurisdiction may attack complaint on its face, in that complaint fails to allege facts upon which court can base its jurisdiction, or it may attack truth of allegations of complaint.

Zelaya v. J.M. Macias, Inc., 999 F.Supp. 778.

M.D.N.C. 1996. To prevail against defendant's motion to dismiss for lack of personal jurisdiction, plaintiff must prove that exercise of personal jurisdiction comports with requirements of due process clause of Fifth Amendment and that relevant long-arm statute authorizes exercise of personal jurisdiction over defendant. U.S.C.A. Const.Amend. 5; Fed. Rules Civ.Proc.Rule 12(b)(2), 28 U.S.C.A.

Plant Genetic Systems, N.V. v. Ciba Seeds, 933 F.Supp. 519.

M.D.N.C. 1995. Party moving to dismiss for lack of subject matter jurisdiction should prevail only if material jurisdictional facts are not in dispute and moving party is entitled to prevail as a matter of law; complaint should not be dismissed merely because court doubts that plaintiff will ultimately prevail so long as plaintiff colorably states facts which, if proven, would entitle him to relief, assuming to be true all facts alleged in complaint and drawing in plaintiff's favor all factual inferences. Fed. Rules Civ.Proc.Rule 12(b)(1), 28 U.S.C.A.

RPR & Associates v. O'Brien/Atkins Associates, P.A., 921 F.Supp. 1457, affirmed 103 F.3d 120.

M.D.N.C. 1995. Party seeking to dismiss for lack of subject matter jurisdiction may argue that complaint fails to allege facts upon which subject matter jurisdiction can be based; in that event, all facts alleged in complaint are assumed to be true and plaintiff, in effect, is afforded same procedural protection as he or she would receive under rule governing motion to dismiss for failure to state claim. Fed.Rules Civ.Proc.Rule 12(b)(1, 6), 28 U.S.C.A.

Higgins v. U.S., 894 F.Supp. 232, affirmed 81 F.3d 149.

Party seeking to dismiss for lack of subject matter jurisdiction may assert that jurisdictional obligations of complaint are not true; then trial court may look beyond allegations of complaint to evidence to determine if there are facts to support jurisdictional allegations. Fed.Rules Civ.Proc.Rule 12(b)(1), 28 U.S.C.A.

Higgins v. U.S., 894 F.Supp. 232, affirmed 81 F.3d 149.

S.D.Ohio 1997. Motion to dismiss premised upon argument that plaintiff's claim must be submitted to arbitration is properly analyzed under as motion to dismiss for lack of subject matter jurisdiction. Fed.Rules Civ.Proc.Rule 12(b)(1), 28 U.S.C.A.

Dalton v. Jefferson Smurfit Corp. (U.S.), 979 F.Supp. 1187.

S.D.Ohio 1996. Motions to dismiss for lack of subject matter jurisdiction fall into two categories: facial attacks and factual attacks. Fed.Rules Civ.Proc.Rule 12(b)(1), 28 U.S.C.A.

Rhoades v. U.S., 953 F.Supp. 203.

Facial attack on subject matter jurisdiction challenges pleading itself. Fed.Rules Civ.Proc. Rule 12(b)(1), 28 U.S.C.A.

Rhoades v. U.S., 953 F.Supp. 203.

Factual attack on subject matter jurisdiction challenges factual existence of subject matter jurisdiction. Fed.Rules Civ.Proc.Rule 12(b)(1), 28 U.S.C.A.

Rhoades v. U.S., 953 F.Supp. 203.

S.D.Ohio 1996. "Facial attack" under rule governing motions to dismiss for lack of subject matter jurisdiction challenges pleading itself; on such attack, court must take all material allegations in complaint as true, and construe them in light most favorable to nonmoving party. Fed.Rules Civ.Proc.Rule 12(b)(1), 28 U.S.C.A.

Danis Industries Corp. v. Fernald Environmental Restoration Management Corp., 947 F.Supp. 323.

"Factual attack" under rule governing motions to dismiss for lack of subject matter jurisdiction is challenge to factual existence of subject matter jurisdiction; on such motion, no presumptive truthfulness applies to the factual allegations, and court is free to weigh the evidence and satisfy itself as to existence of its power to hear case. Fed.Rules Civ.Proc.Rule 12(b)(1), 28 U.S.C.A.

Danis Industries Corp. v. Fernald Environmental Restoration Management Corp., 947 F.Supp. 323.

S.D.Ohio 1993. When district court is confronted by motion to dismiss raising a combination of defenses, it will pass on jurisdictional issues before considering whether claim was stated by complaint. Fed.Rules Civ.Proc.Rule 12(b), 28 U.S.C.A.

Martin v. Voinovich, 840 F.Supp. 1175.

S.D.Ohio 1993. When defendant seeks dismissal of complaint both for lack of subject matter jurisdiction and for failure to state claim, district court is bound to consider jurisdictional motion first, because motion to dismiss for failure to state claim will become moot if court lacks subject matter jurisdiction. Fed.Rules Civ.Proc.Rule 12(b)(1, 6), 28 U.S.C.A.

> City of Heath, Ohio v. Ashland Oil, Inc., 834 F.Supp. 971.

In reviewing motion to dismiss complaint for lack of subject matter jurisdiction, when complaint seeks recovery directly under federal law, district court must entertain action unless claim is immaterial or wholly insubstantial and frivolous. Fed.Rules Civ.Proc.Rule 12(b)(1), 28 U.S.C.A.

> City of Heath, Ohio v. Ashland Oil, Inc., 834 F.Supp. 971.

S.D.Ohio 1993. When court is confronted by motion raising combination of Rule 12(b) defenses, it will pass on jurisdictional issues before considering whether claim was stated by complaint. Fed.Rules Civ.Proc.Rule 12(b), 28 U.S.C.A.

> City of Reynoldsburg v. Browner, 834 F.Supp. 963.

S.D.Ohio 1989. Rule 12(b)(1) of the Federal Rules of Civil Procedure may be used to attack complaint defect involving court's actual subject matter jurisdiction or pleader's failure to comply with rule dealing with allegations of jurisdiction. Fed.Rules Civ.Proc.Rules 8(a), 12(b)(1), 28 U.S.C.A.

> Carr v. French Oil Mill Machinery Co., 746 F.Supp. 700.

D.Or. 1997. Motion to dismiss for lack of subject matter jurisdiction may attack substance of complaint's jurisdictional allegations even though allegations are formally sufficient. Fed. Rules Civ.Proc.Rule 12(b)(1), 28 U.S.C.A.

> Zimmerman v. State of Or. Dept. of Justice, 983 F.Supp. 1327.

D.Or. 1997. Court's ruling on motion to dismiss for lack of subject matter jurisdiction is limited to question of whether it has jurisdiction over the controversy; determination that court has or does not have jurisdiction is not an opinion on merits of claims asserted in case. Fed.Rules Civ.Proc.Rule 12(b)(1), 28 U.S.C.A.

> Bonnichsen v. U.S., Dept. of the Army, 969 F.Supp. 614.

D.Or. 1996. Where jurisdictional issue is separable from merits of case, court may determine jurisdiction by standards of motion to dismiss for lack of jurisdiction, and in such situation, court is free to hear evidence regarding jurisdiction and to rule on that issue prior to trial, resolving factual disputes where necessary. Fed.Rules Civ.Proc.Rule 12(b)(1), 28 U.S.C.A.

> Oregon Natural Desert Ass'n v. Thomas, 940 F.Supp. 1534.

D.Or. 1994. Motion to dismiss for lack of subject matter jurisdiction may attack substance

of complainant's jurisdictional allegations even though allegations are formally sufficient. Fed. Rules Civ.Proc.Rule 12(b)(1), 28 U.S.C.A.

> Mittendorf v. Stone Lumber Co., 874 F.Supp. 292.

E.D.Pa. 1998. District court may grant motion to dismiss for lack of subject matter jurisdiction based on legal insufficiency of claim; however, dismissal is proper only when claim appears to be immaterial and made solely for purpose of obtaining jurisdiction, or is wholly insubstantial or frivolous. Fed.Rules Civ. Proc.Rule 12(b)(1), 28 U.S.C.A.

> Cohen v. Temple Physicians, Inc., 11 F.Supp.2d 733.

On motion to dismiss for lack of subject matter jurisdiction, if attack to jurisdiction is facial, to allegations of jurisdiction stated in complaint, then factual allegations of complaint are presumed to be true and complaint is reviewed to ensure that each element necessary for jurisdiction is present. Fed.Rules Civ.Proc. Rule 12(b)(1), 28 U.S.C.A.

> Cohen v. Temple Physicians, Inc., 11 F.Supp.2d 733.

On motion to dismiss for lack of subject matter jurisdiction, complaint may be dismissed only if it appears to a certainty that pleader will not be able to assert colorable claim of subject matter jurisdiction. Fed.Rules Civ.Proc.Rule 12(b)(1), 28 U.S.C.A.

> Cohen v. Temple Physicians, Inc., 11 F.Supp.2d 733.

E.D.Pa. 1998. While district court can grant motion to dismiss for lack of subject matter jurisdiction based on legal insufficiency of claim, dismissal is proper only when claim appears to be immaterial and made solely for purpose of obtaining jurisdiction or is wholly insubstantial or frivolous. Fed.Rules Civ.Proc. Rule 12(b)(1), 28 U.S.C.A.

> Tolan v. U.S., 176 F.R.D. 507.

E.D.Pa. 1997. If attack to court's jurisdiction is facial, i.e., based on allegations of jurisdiction stated in complaint, factual allegations of complaint are presumed to be true and complaint is reviewed to ensure that each element necessary for jurisdiction is present; only if it appears to certainty that pleader will not be able to assert colorable claim of subject matter jurisdiction may complaint be dismissed under those circumstances. Fed.Rules Civ.Proc.Rule 12(b)(1), 28 U.S.C.A.

> Snyder v. Garb, 988 F.Supp. 868.

E.D.Pa. 1997. District court can grant motion to dismiss for lack of subject matter jurisdiction based on legal insufficiency of plaintiff's claim, but only if claim appears to be immaterial and made solely for purpose of obtaining jurisdiction or is wholly insubstantial or frivolous. Fed.Rules Civ.Proc.Rule 12(b)(1), 28 U.S.C.A.

> Leuthe v. Office of Financial Institution Adjudication, 977 F.Supp. 357.

If motion to dismiss for lack of subject matter jurisdiction involves facial attack on court's jurisdiction, i.e., a challenge to allegations of jurisdiction stated in complaint, then factual allegations of complaint are presumed to be true, and complaint is reviewed to ensure that each element necessary for jurisdiction is present. Fed.Rules Civ.Proc.Rule 12(b)(1), 28 U.S.C.A.

> Leuthe v. Office of Financial Institution Adjudication, 977 F.Supp. 357.

Only if it appears to a certainty that pleader will not be able to assert colorable claim of subject matter jurisdiction may complaint be dismissed on facial attack to court's subject matter jurisdiction. Fed.Rules Civ.Proc.Rule 12(b)(1), 28 U.S.C.A.

> Leuthe v. Office of Financial Institution Adjudication, 977 F.Supp. 357.

E.D.Pa. 1997. On motion to dismiss for lack of subject matter jurisdiction, defendant may contend that jurisdiction was not properly pled, a "facial" attack, or that jurisdiction does not actually exist in particular case, a "factual" attack. Fed.Rules Civ.Proc.Rule 12(b)(1), 28 U.S.C.A.

> Kuestner v. Health and Welfare Fund & Pension Fund of Philadelphia Bakery Employers and Food Driver Salesmen's Union Local No. 463 and Teamsters Union Local No. 676, 972 F.Supp. 905.

E.D.Pa. 1997. Motion to dismiss for lack of subject matter jurisdiction is usually considered an appropriate vehicle when plaintiff has failed to exhaust administrative remedies that are a prerequisite to his suit. Fed.Rules Civ. Proc.Rule 12(b)(6), 28 U.S.C.A.

> McDevitt v. U.S. Postal Service, 963 F.Supp. 482.

E.D.Pa. 1996. Dismissal for legal insufficiency of claim is proper only when claim appears to be either immaterial and solely for purpose of obtaining jurisdiction, or is wholly insubstantial and frivolous. Fed.Rules Civ. Proc.Rule 12(b)(1), 28 U.S.C.A.

> Talley v. Feldman, 941 F.Supp. 501.

E.D.Pa. 1996. District court can grant motion to dismiss for lack of subject matter jurisdiction when claim clearly appears to be immaterial and made solely for basis of obtaining jurisdiction or is wholly unsubstantial and frivolous. Fed.Rules Civ.Proc.Rule 12(b)(1), 28 U.S.C.A.

> Sun Co., Inc. (R & M) v. Badger Design & Constructors, Inc., 939 F.Supp. 365.

E.D.Pa. 1996. On motion to dismiss for lack of personal jurisdiction, district court considers only whether plaintiff has proffered evidence that, if credited, is enough to support findings of all facts essential to personal jurisdiction. Fed.Rules Civ.Proc.Rule 12(b)(2), 28 U.S.C.A.

> Leonard A. Feinberg, Inc. v. Central Asia Capital Corp., Ltd., 936 F.Supp. 250.

Plaintiff can defeat motion to dismiss for lack of personal jurisdiction if it makes showing as to every fact required to satisfy both forum's long-arm statute and due process clause; this showing must be based on evidence of specific facts set forth in the record, and plaintiff must go beyond the pleadings and make affirmative proof. U.S.C.A. Const.Amend. 14; Fed.Rules Civ.Proc.Rule 12(b)(2), 28 U.S.C.A.

> Leonard A. Feinberg, Inc. v. Central Asia Capital Corp., Ltd., 936 F.Supp. 250.

E.D.Pa. 1996. Dismissal is appropriate for lack of subject-matter jurisdiction. Fed.Rules Civ.Proc.Rule 12(b)(1), 28 U.S.C.A.

> Adams v. U.S. E.E.O.C., 932 F.Supp. 660.

E.D.Pa. 1994. Dismissal for lack of subject matter jurisdiction based on legal insufficiency of claim is proper only when claim clearly appears to be immaterial and solely for purpose of obtaining jurisdiction, or is wholly insubstantial and frivolous. Fed.Rules Civ.Proc.Rule 12(b)(1), 28 U.S.C.A.

> Walnut Associates v. Saidel, 164 B.R. 487.

E.D.Pa. 1994. Dismissal for lack of subject matter jurisdiction is proper only when claim clearly appears to be immaterial and made solely for purpose of obtaining jurisdiction or wholly insubstantial and frivolous. Fed.Rules Civ.Proc.Rule 12(b)(1), 28 U.S.C.A.

> Vidovic v. Losinjska Plovidba Oour Broadarstvo, 868 F.Supp. 691.

E.D.Pa. 1994. Upon motion to dismiss for lack of subject matter jurisdiction, party asserting jurisdiction must be allowed reasonable opportunity to demonstrate jurisdiction. Fed. Rules Civ.Proc.Rule 12(b)(1), 28 U.S.C.A.

> Sitkoff v. BMW of North America, Inc., 846 F.Supp. 380.

E.D.Pa. 1994. District court is under continuing obligation to examine its subject matter jurisdiction in particular case and must dismiss case if it becomes apparent at any time that such jurisdiction is lacking. Fed.Rules Civ. Proc.Rule 12(h)(3), 28 U.S.C.A.

> Lake v. First Nationwide Bank, 156 F.R.D. 615.

E.D.Pa. 1993. When motion to dismiss is based on more than one ground, court should consider subject matter jurisdictional challenge first, since if complaint is dismissed for lack of subject matter jurisdiction, all other defenses and objections become moot. Fed.Rules Civ. Proc.Rule 12(b)(1, 6), 28 U.S.C.A.

> In re Corestates Trust Fee Litigation, 837 F.Supp. 104, affirmed 39 F.3d 61.

E.D.Pa. 1993. Lack of subject matter jurisdiction is ground for dismissal and may be raised at any time by parties or by court sua sponte.

> Walls v. Ahmed, 832 F.Supp. 940.

E.D.Pa. 1993. Mere fact that plaintiff's complaint contains conclusory allegations in support of personal jurisdiction is not sufficient to defeat defendant's motion to dismiss for lack of such jurisdiction. Fed.Rules Civ.Proc.Rule 12(b)(2), 28 U.S.C.A.

> Zecco v. Solaris Hotel and Resorts, Inc., 820 F.Supp. 962.

E.D.Pa. 1993. Action based upon alleged existence of federal question may be dismissed for lack of subject-matter jurisdiction only if allegation is made solely for purpose of obtaining jurisdiction or is wholly insubstantial and frivolous; this test does not allow court to prejudge facts alleged in complaint, however, for a court may dismiss for lack of jurisdiction only if claims are insubstantial on their face. Fed.Rules Civ.Proc.Rule 12(b)(1), 28 U.S.C.A.

> Young v. Francis, 820 F.Supp. 940.

Dismissal for lack of subject-matter jurisdiction is not warranted simply because legal theory alleged is probably false; it is appropriate only where federal claim is so insubstantial, implausible, foreclosed by prior court decisions or otherwise completely devoid of merit as not to involve federal controversy. Fed.Rules Civ. Proc.Rule 12(b)(1), 28 U.S.C.A.

> Young v. Francis, 820 F.Supp. 940.

Federal claim being reviewed for failure to state a claim does not have to be "wholly insubstantial" to be dismissed. Fed.Rules Civ. Proc.Rule 12(b)(1), 28 U.S.C.A.

> Young v. Francis, 820 F.Supp. 940.

E.D.Pa. 1992. In ruling on motion to dismiss due to lack of jurisdiction over subject matter, court is not restricted to facts pleaded in complaint. Fed.Rules Civ.Proc.Rule 12(b)(1), 28 U.S.C.A.

> Warner Cable Communications Inc. v. Borough of Schuylkill Haven, 784 F.Supp. 203.

E.D.Pa. 1988. On motion to dismiss for lack of subject matter jurisdiction, if jurisdiction is based on federal question, pleader need only show that he has alleged claim under federal

law and that case is not frivolous. Fed.Rules Civ.Proc.Rule 12(b)(1), 28 U.S.C.A.

> Kronmuller v. West End Fire Co. No. 3 Fire Dept. of Borough of Phoenixville, 123 F.R.D. 170.

E.D.Pa. 1985. Failure to state grounds upon which jurisdiction depends does not automatically result in dismissal of complaint; leave to amend complaint should be freely given in order to cure such defect.

> Barlow v. Pep Boys, Inc., 625 F.Supp. 130.

E.D.Pa. 1982. In order to dismiss complaint for lack of federal question jurisdiction, court must find that claims asserted therein are so attenuated and unsubstantial as to be absolutely devoid of merit, or clearly foreclosed by decisions of Supreme Court so as to leave no room for inference that questions sought to be raised can be subject of the controversy. 28 U.S.C.A. § 1331.

> Lawrence v. U.S., 631 F.Supp. 631.

M.D.Pa. 1998. Generally, reference to a federal question in a complaint filed in federal court precludes dismissal for lack of subject matter jurisdiction.

> McCreary v. Wilt, 11 F.Supp.2d 731.

Dismissal of complaint for lack of federal jurisdiction is not appropriate merely because the legal theory contained therein is probably false, but only if the right claimed is so insubstantial, implausible, foreclosed by prior decisions, or otherwise completely devoid of merit as not to involve a federal controversy.

> McCreary v. Wilt, 11 F.Supp.2d 731.

M.D.Pa. 1994. Complaint should not be dismissed for lack of jurisdiction if it reveals any grounds for assertion of jurisdiction. Fed. Rules Civ.Proc.Rule 12(b)(1), 28 U.S.C.A.

> Nationwide Ins. Co. v. Agway Ins. Co., 845 F.Supp. 252, reversed 77 F.3d 463.

M.D.Pa. 1993. Although courts enjoy substantial procedural flexibility in ruling on jurisdictional challenges, they should proceed cautiously in dismissing claims for lack of subject-matter jurisdiction at early stage if relevant facts are in dispute and pertinent discovery has not been conducted. Fed.Rules Civ.Proc.Rule 12(b)(1), 28 U.S.C.A.

> Koch v. U.S., 814 F.Supp. 1221.

Dismissal for lack of subject-matter jurisdiction is appropriate only if record establishes that plaintiff had opportunity to present facts by affidavit or deposition, or in evidentiary hearing, after jurisdictional challenge arose, and either exercised or waived that opportunity. Fed.Rules Civ.Proc.Rule 12(b)(1), 28 U.S.C.A.

> Koch v. U.S., 814 F.Supp. 1221.

M.D.Pa. 1992. While jurisdiction over subject matter is absolute prerequisite to maintaining action in federal district court, complaint should not be dismissed unless it is completely devoid of any ground for jurisdiction; nevertheless, once lack of subject matter jurisdiction is found, it cannot be ignored by the district court and dismissal must follow.

Rode v. U.S., 812 F.Supp. 45.

W.D.Pa. 1997. Dismissal for lack of subject matter jurisdiction is appropriate only if the right claimed is so insubstantial, implausible, foreclosed by prior decisions of this Court, or otherwise completely devoid of merit as not to involve a federal controversy.

L.C. Renninger Co., Inc. v. VIK Bros. Ins., Inc., 180 F.R.D. 272.

W.D.Pa. 1996. Dismissal for lack of subject matter jurisdiction is appropriate only if the right claimed is so insubstantial, implausible, foreclosed by prior decisions of court, or otherwise completely devoid of merit as not to involve federal controversy. Fed.Rules Civ.Proc. Rule 12(b)(1), 28 U.S.C.A.

Coxson v. Com. of Pa., 935 F.Supp. 624.

Threshold to withstand motion to dismiss for lack of subject matter jurisdiction is lower than that required to withstand motion to dismiss for failure to state claim. Fed.Rules Civ. Proc.Rule 12(b)(1, 6), 28 U.S.C.A.

Coxson v. Com. of Pa., 935 F.Supp. 624.

W.D.Pa. 1996. Motion to dismiss for lack of subject matter jurisdiction requires district court to examine legal sufficiency of a claim. Fed.Rules Civ.Proc.Rule 12(b)(1), 28 U.S.C.A.

Kennedy v. Runyon, 933 F.Supp. 480.

Dismissal of claim for lack of subject matter jurisdiction is proper only when claim clearly appears to be immaterial and made solely for purpose of obtaining jurisdiction or is wholly insubstantial and frivolous. Fed.Rules Civ. Proc.Rule 12(b)(1), 28 U.S.C.A.

Kennedy v. Runyon, 933 F.Supp. 480.

W.D.Pa. 1996. Dismissal for lack of subject matter jurisdiction is not appropriate on ground that complaint fails to state claim upon which relief can be granted, but only if right claimed is so insubstantial, implausible, foreclosed by prior decisions or court, or otherwise completely devoid of merit as not to involve federal controversy. Fed.Rules Civ.Proc.Rule 12(b)(1), 28 U.S.C.A.

Thomeier v. Rhone-Poulenc, Inc., 928 F.Supp. 548.

Threshold to withstand motion to dismiss for lack of subject matter jurisdiction is lower than that required to withstand motion to dis-

miss for failure to state a claim. Fed.Rules Civ.Proc.Rule 12(b)(1, 6), 28 U.S.C.A.

Thomeier v. Rhone-Poulenc, Inc., 928 F.Supp. 548.

W.D.Pa. 1996. When subject matter jurisdiction is challenged, plaintiff bears burden of persuasion; however, burden is not demanding because court may dismiss for lack of subject matter jurisdiction only when right claimed is so insubstantial, foreclosed by prior decisions of Supreme Court, or otherwise completely devoid of merit as not to involve federal controversy. Fed.Rules Civ.Proc.Rule 12(b)(1), 28 U.S.C.A.

Optimum, S.A. v. Legent Corp., 926 F.Supp. 530.

W.D.Pa. 1995. Dismissal for lack of subject matter jurisdiction is not appropriate on ground that complaint fails to state claim upon which relief can be granted, but only if right claimed is so insubstantial, implausible, foreclosed by prior decisions, or otherwise completely devoid of merit as not to involve federal controversy; threshold to withstand motion to dismiss for lack of subject matter jurisdiction is thus lower than that required to withstand motion to dismiss for failure to state claim. Fed. Rules Civ.Proc.Rules 12(b)(1), 12(b)(6), 28 U.S.C.A.

Saint Vincent Health Center v. Shalala, 937 F.Supp. 496, affirmed 96 F.3d 1434.

W.D.Pa. 1995. Dismissal for lack of subject matter jurisdiction is not appropriate on ground that complaint fails to state claim upon which relief can be granted, but only if right claimed is so insubstantial, implausible, foreclosed by prior decisions of Court, or otherwise completely devoid of merit as not to involve federal controversy.

Bonnett Enterprises, Inc. v. U.S., 889 F.Supp. 208.

W.D.Pa. 1993. Court may dismiss action for lack of subject matter jurisdiction at pleading stage only if it affords plaintiff safeguards of accepting all allegations of complaint as true, drawing reasonable factual inferences from complaint in plaintiff's favor, and only if it appears to certainty that pleader will not be able to assert colorable claim of subject matter jurisdiction. Fed.Rules Civ.Proc.Rule 12(b)(1, 6), 28 U.S.C.A.

Radeschi v. Com. of Pa., 846 F.Supp. 416.

W.D.Pa. 1993. Federal court may dismiss action for lack of jurisdiction if federal claim underlying action is without merit or has been foreclosed by previous court decision.

Erie City Retirees Ass'n v. City of Erie, 838 F.Supp. 1048.

W.D.Pa. 1986. Where a complaint alleges that cause of action arises under Constitution or laws of United States, court should not dismiss for lack of jurisdiction except that a suit may sometimes be dismissed for want of jurisdiction where the alleged claim under the Constitution or federal statutes clearly appears to be immaterial and made solely for purpose of obtaining jurisdiction or where such a claim is wholly insubstantial and frivolous.

> Gorman v. North Pittsburgh Oral Surgery Associates, Ltd., 110 F.R.D. 446.

D.Puerto Rico 1997. In addressing motion to dismiss for lack of personal jurisdiction over nonresident defendant, district court considers only whether plaintiff has proffered evidence that, if credited, is sufficient to support facts authorizing personal jurisdiction over nonresident defendant under both forum's long-arm statute and due process clause. U.S.C.A. Const. Amends. 5, 14; Fed.Rules Civ.Proc.Rule 12(b)(2), 28 U.S.C.A.

> De La Rosa v. Philip Morris Products, Inc., 975 F.Supp. 161.

D.Puerto Rico 1994. Nonjusticiable case must be dismissed as not presenting "case" or "controversy" under Article III of Federal Constitution. U.S.C.A. Const. Art. 3, § 1 et seq.

> Igartua de la Rosa v. U.S., 842 F.Supp. 607.

D.R.I. 1995. Federal Rules of Civil Procedure provide for dismissal of an action against an individual the court has no in personam or personal jurisdiction over. Fed.Rules Civ.Proc. Rule 12(b)(2), 28 U.S.C.A.

> Scully Signal Co. v. Joyal, 881 F.Supp. 727.

D.S.C. 1994. Motion to dismiss for lack of jurisdiction does not necessitate ruling on merits, whereas motion to dismiss for failure to state claim does. Fed.Rules Civ.Proc.Rule 12(b)(1, 6), 28 U.S.C.A.

> Richland-Lexington Airport Dist. v. Atlas Properties, Inc., 854 F.Supp. 400.

D.S.C. 1989. Where defendant's challenge to court's jurisdiction is also a challenge to existence of federal cause of action, proper procedure for district court is to find that jurisdiction exists and to determine merits of claim under rule governing failure to state a claim or rule governing summary judgment. Fed.Rules Civ.Proc.Rules 12(b)(6), 56, 28 U.S.C.A.

> Chiles v. Crooks, 708 F.Supp. 127.

D.S.D. 1993. Motion to dismiss based on lack of subject matter jurisdiction is argument that court lacks the power to hear the class of cases to which plaintiff's claim belongs, and thus if claims fall within class of cases over which court is granted jurisdiction and are not patently frivolous, court has subject matter jurisdiction regardless of the merits of the claims. Fed.Rules Civ.Proc.Rule 12(b)(1), 28 U.S.C.A.

> FGS Constructors, Inc. v. Carlow, 823 F.Supp. 1508.

E.D.Tenn. 1996. Summary dismissal for lack of jurisdiction of subject matter is appropriate where absence of jurisdiction of subject matter appears on the face of complaint, and jurisdictional defect is obviously not curable. Fed.Rules Civ.Proc.Rule 12(b)(1), 28 U.S.C.A.

> Hess v. Hess, 950 F.Supp. 226, affirmed 103 F.3d 129, certiorari denied 118 S.Ct. 53, 139 L.Ed.2d 18.

M.D.Tenn. 1997. Motion to dismiss for lack of subject matter jurisdiction may challenge complaint on its face or it may contest existence of subject matter in fact. Fed.Rules Civ.Proc.Rule 12(b)(1), 28 U.S.C.A.

> Patton v. Toshiba America Consumer Products, Inc., 967 F.Supp. 283.

If motion to dismiss for lack of subject matter jurisdiction attacks face of complaint, plaintiff need only demonstrate that complaint alleges "substantial" federal claim, meaning that prior decisions do not inescapably render claim frivolous. Fed.Rules Civ.Proc.Rule 12(b)(1), 28 U.S.C.A.

> Patton v. Toshiba America Consumer Products, Inc., 967 F.Supp. 283.

M.D.Tenn. 1996. If plaintiffs are without standing, court cannot maintain jurisdiction over dispute, and order to dismiss must be entered.

> Doe v. Sundquist, 943 F.Supp. 886, affirmed 106 F.3d 702, certiorari denied 118 S.Ct. 51, 139 L.Ed.2d 16.

W.D.Tenn. 1985. Complaint that appears to state a cause of action under a federal statute should be dismissed by federal court for lack of subject-matter jurisdiction only when the claim is clearly "immaterial" or is "wholly insubstantial and frivolous." 28 U.S.C.A. § 1331.

> Adams v. Republic Steel Corp., 621 F.Supp. 370.

N.D.Tex. 1998. On motion to dismiss for lack of jurisdiction, facial attack of complaint or cross-claim requires court merely to decide if plaintiff has correctly alleged basis for subject matter jurisdiction, and attack is valid if from face of pleadings, court can determine it lacks subject matter jurisdiction. Fed.Rules Civ.Proc. Rule 12(b)(1), 28 U.S.C.A.

> Rodriguez v. Texas Com'n of Arts, 992 F.Supp. 876.

N.D.Tex. 1997. Motion to dismiss for lack of subject matter jurisdiction may be granted on any of three separate bases: complaint alone; complaint supplemented by undisputed facts evidenced in record; or complaint supplemented by undisputed facts plus court's resolution of disputed facts. Fed.Rules Civ.Proc.Rule 12(b)(1), 28 U.S.C.A.

> U.S. ex rel. Foulds v. Texas Tech University, 980 F.Supp. 864.

N.D.Tex. 1995. In considering motion to dismiss, court would sua sponte consider reasons for lack of jurisdiction other than those given by defendant. Fed.Rules Civ.Proc.Rule 12(b)(1), 28 U.S.C.A.

Rodgers v. Scott, 901 F.Supp. 224.

S.D.Tex. 1996. Although act of state doctrine does not deprive federal court of subject matter jurisdiction over action, if court concludes that doctrine is applicable, dismissal of claims may be appropriate, if presumed validity of official acts precludes possibility of any relief for opposing party.

Hargrove v. Underwriters at Lloyd's, London, 937 F.Supp. 595.

S.D.Tex. 1996. Motion to dismiss for lack of subject matter jurisdiction should not be granted unless it appears certain that plaintiff cannot prove any set of facts in support of his claim which would entitle him to relief. Fed. Rules Civ.Proc.Rule 12(b)(1), 28 U.S.C.A.

Jolly v. Klein, 923 F.Supp. 931.

S.D.Tex. 1995. When plaintiff alleges Fifth Amendment takings claim in federal court before having unsuccessfully exhausted state remedies, case is subject to dismissal for lack of subject matter jurisdiction under ripeness doctrine. U.S.C.A. Const.Amend. 5.

Trail Enterprises, Inc. v. City of Houston, 907 F.Supp. 250.

W.D.Tex. 1994. Motion to dismiss for lack of subject matter jurisdiction may be based on complaint alone, complaint supplemented by undisputed facts evidenced in record, or complaint supplemented by undisputed facts plus court's resolution of disputed facts. Fed.Rules Civ.Proc.Rule 12(b)(1), 28 U.S.C.A.

Zuspann v. Brown, 864 F.Supp. 17, affirmed 60 F.3d 1156, certiorari denied 116 S.Ct. 909, 516 U.S. 1111, 133 L.Ed.2d 841.

Motion that attacks subject matter jurisdiction of court occurs when motion refers to matters outside pleadings, such as affidavits or testimony.

Zuspann v. Brown, 864 F.Supp. 17, affirmed 60 F.3d 1156, certiorari denied 116 S.Ct. 909, 516 U.S. 1111, 133 L.Ed.2d 841.

D.Utah 1996. Court lacking jurisdiction cannot render judgment but must dismiss cause at any stage of proceedings in which it becomes apparent jurisdiction is lacking.

Ute Distribution Corp. v. Secretary of Interior of U.S., 934 F.Supp. 1302, reversed 149 F.3d 1260.

D.Utah 1989. Failure to state grounds on which jurisdiction depends will not automatically result in dismissal of complaint if factual basis for claim is stated; leave to amend complaint in order to cure this defect is normally freely given.

Sauers v. Salt Lake County, 722 F.Supp. 676.

D.Vt. 1996. Federal court may raise issue of lack of subject matter jurisdiction sua sponte, and must dismiss where jurisdiction is lacking.

Glinka v. Abraham and Rose Co. Ltd., 199 B.R. 484.

D.Vt. 1995. Ordinarily, action which has become moot must be dismissed for lack of subject matter jurisdiction.

Randolph Union High School Dist. No. 2 v. Byard, 897 F.Supp. 174.

D.Vt. 1993. Personal jurisdiction may be waived for failure to follow certain requirements of civil rules, specifically, rule providing that defense of lack of personal jurisdiction is waived if party makes motion to dismiss but fails to raise defense of lack of personal jurisdiction in initial motion. Fed.Rules Civ.Proc.Rule 12(h)(1), 28 U.S.C.A.

Committe v. Dennis Reimer Co., L.P.A., 150 F.R.D. 495.

Defendant waived personal jurisdiction defense, even though defendant pleaded that affirmative defense in its answer to complaint, where defendant moved to dismiss for failure to state claim upon which relief could be granted, and defense of lack of personal jurisdiction was not included in that motion. Fed.Rules Civ. Proc.Rule 12(b)(6), (h)(1)(A), 28 U.S.C.A.

Committe v. Dennis Reimer Co., L.P.A., 150 F.R.D. 495.

E.D.Va. 1998. Motion to dismiss for lack of subject matter jurisdiction may attack subject matter jurisdiction in two different ways: motion may attack complaint on its face, by asserting simply that complaint fails to allege facts upon which subject matter jurisdiction can be based, or may attack existence of subject matter jurisdiction, quite apart from the pleadings. Fed.Rules Civ.Proc.Rule 12(b)(1), 28 U.S.C.A.

Wise v. U.S., 8 F.Supp.2d 535.

Where motion to dismiss for lack of subject matter jurisdiction attacks complaint on its face, asserting simply that complaint fails to allege facts upon which subject matter jurisdiction can be based, facts alleged in complaint are assumed to be true, and plaintiff, in effect, is afforded the same procedural protection as he would receive on motion to dismiss for failure to state a claim. Fed.Rules Civ.Proc.Rule 12(b)(1, 6), 28 U.S.C.A.

Wise v. U.S., 8 F.Supp.2d 535.

E.D.Va. 1998. It is within a court's sound discretion to dismiss a case for lack of personal jurisdiction, rather than grant a plaintiff's motion to transfer, where counsel should have reasonably foreseen that the district court lacked jurisdiction. 28 U.S.C.A. § 1406(a); Fed.Rules Civ.Proc.Rule 12(b)(2), 28 U.S.C.A.

> Chisholm v. UHP Projects, Inc., 1 F.Supp.2d 581.

E.D.Va. 1997. Motion to dismiss for lack of subject matter jurisdiction may attack complaint on its face, asserting simply that complaint fails to allege facts upon which subject matter jurisdiction can be based. Fed.Rules Civ.Proc.Rule 12(b)(1), 28 U.S.C.A.

> GTE South Inc. v. Morrison, 957 F.Supp. 800.

Motion to dismiss for lack of subject matter jurisdiction may challenge truth of jurisdictional allegations of complaint. Fed.Rules Civ.Proc. Rule 12(b)(1), 28 U.S.C.A.

> GTE South Inc. v. Morrison, 957 F.Supp. 800.

E.D.Va. 1996. Motion to dismiss for lack of subject matter jurisdiction may attack complaint on its face, asserting simply that complaint fails to allege facts upon which subject matter jurisdiction can be based; in such case facts alleged in complaint are assumed to be true and plaintiff, in effect, is afforded same procedural protection as he would receive under motion to dismiss for failure to state claim. Fed.Rules Civ.Proc.Rule 12(b)(1, 6), 28 U.S.C.A.

> White v. CMA Const. Co., Inc., 947 F.Supp. 231.

Motion to dismiss for lack of subject matter jurisdiction may attack existence of subject matter jurisdiction in fact, quite apart from any pleadings; in such case no presumptive truthfulness attaches to plaintiff's allegations, and existence of disputed material facts will not preclude trial court from evaluating for itself the merits of jurisdictional claims. Fed.Rules Civ.Proc.Rule 12(b)(1), 28 U.S.C.A.

> White v. CMA Const. Co., Inc., 947 F.Supp. 231.

E.D.Va. 1996. Defendant may present a motion to dismiss for lack of subject-matter jurisdiction either by contending that complaint fails to allege facts upon which subject-matter jurisdiction can be based or by contending that jurisdictional allegations of complaint are not true. Fed.Rules Civ.Proc.Rule 12(b)(1), 28 U.S.C.A.

> Oram v. Dalton, 927 F.Supp. 180.

E.D.Va. 1996. Motions to dismiss for lack of subject matter jurisdiction do not go to merits of claim, but address only jurisdictional issues. Fed.Rules Civ.Proc.Rule 12(b)(1), 28 U.S.C.A.

> Shoemaker v. Metro Information Services, 910 F.Supp. 259.

E.D.Va. 1996. When court has reason to doubt that it has subject matter jurisdiction, it is inappropriate to engage in the balancing process required by federal rule governing voluntary dismissal by order of court; dismissal is required and there is simply no discretion to be exercised. Fed.Rules Civ.Proc.Rule 41(a)(2), 28 U.S.C.A.

> Taylor v. Com. of Va., Dept. of Transp., 170 F.R.D. 10.

E.D.Va. 1996. Motion to dismiss for lack of subject matter jurisdiction may attack complaint on its face, asserting simply that complaint fails to allege facts upon which subject matter jurisdiction can be based; under this approach, facts alleged in complaint are assumed to be true and plaintiff is afforded same procedural protection he would receive under motion to dismiss for failure to state claim upon which relief can be granted. Fed.Rules Civ. Proc.Rule 12(b)(1, 6), 28 U.S.C.A.

> Materson v. Stokes, 166 F.R.D. 368.

Motion to dismiss for lack of subject matter jurisdiction can attack existence of subject matter jurisdiction in fact, quite apart from any pleadings. Fed.Rules Civ.Proc.Rule 12(b)(1), 28 U.S.C.A.

> Materson v. Stokes, 166 F.R.D. 368.

District court's very power to hear case is at issue in motion to dismiss for lack of subject matter jurisdiction, and thus trial court is free to weigh evidence to determine existence of its jurisdiction; no presumptive truthfulness attaches to plaintiff's allegations, and existence of disputed material facts will not preclude trial court from evaluating for itself the merits of jurisdictional claims. Fed.Rules Civ.Proc.Rule 12(b)(1), 28 U.S.C.A.

> Materson v. Stokes, 166 F.R.D. 368.

E.D.Va. 1995. If dispute does not fall within "case or controversy" requirement of Article III, and is therefore not ripe for judicial review, court lacks subject matter jurisdiction and must dismiss case. U.S.C.A. Const. Art. 3, § 2, Cl. 1.

> Com. of Va. v. U.S., 926 F.Supp. 537, affirmed 74 F.3d 517.

E.D.Va. 1995. Motion to dismiss for lack of subject matter jurisdiction may attack complaint on its face or truth of underlying jurisdictional allegations contained in complaint, and nonmovant has burden to allege and prove such jurisdiction. Fed.Rules Civ.Proc.Rule 12(b)(1), 28 U.S.C.A.

> Marks v. U.S. Social Sec. Admin., 906 F.Supp. 1017, affirmed in part, vacated in part 92 F.3d 1180, on remand 963 F.Supp. 517, rehearing denied 963 F.Supp. 517.

On motion to dismiss for lack of subject matter jurisdiction, district court must weigh evidence before it in order to establish its jurisdiction. Fed.Rules Civ.Proc.Rule 12(b)(1), 28 U.S.C.A.

Marks v. U.S. Social Sec. Admin., 906 F.Supp. 1017, affirmed in part, vacated in part 92 F.3d 1180, on remand 963 F.Supp. 517, rehearing denied 963 F.Supp. 517.

E.D.Va. 1995. A motion to dismiss for lack of subject matter jurisdiction may attack complaint on its face, and that complaint fails to allege facts upon which court can base jurisdiction, or it may attack truth of underlying jurisdictional allegations contained in complaint. Fed.Rules Civ.Proc.Rule 12(b)(1), 28 U.S.C.A.

Lane v. David P. Jacobson & Co., Ltd., 880 F.Supp. 1091.

E.D.Va. 1994. Motion to dismiss for lack of personal jurisdiction generally should be denied if complaint alleges sufficient facts to support reasonable inference that defendants could be subjected to jurisdiction of district court.

Holland v. Hay, 840 F.Supp. 1091.

E.D.Va. 1994. Amended complaint which clearly contained required jurisdictional allegations should not be dismissed based on original pro se complaint's failure to contain statement of jurisdictional grounds. Fed.Rules Civ.Proc. Rule 8(a)(1), 28 U.S.C.A.

Jacobi v. Blocker, 153 F.R.D. 84.

E.D.Va. 1991. Once court finds that it lacks jurisdiction in a case, the only option available to the court is dismissal.

First American Nat. Bank v. Straight Creek Processing Co., 756 F.Supp. 945.

W.D.Va. 1990. Federal court must dismiss case, upon determination that it lacks subject matter jurisdiction.

In re Woods, 130 B.R. 204.

D.Virgin Islands 1996. Where attack on federal question jurisdiction in action alleging violation of constitutional or federal statute is in essence attack on merits, dismissal for lack of subject matter jurisdiction is appropriate only where federal claim is made solely for purpose of obtaining jurisdiction or if claim is wholly insubstantial and frivolous.

Gotha v. U.S., 929 F.Supp. 207, reversed 115 F.3d 176.

E.D.Wash. 1993. When jurisdictional challenges are based solely upon complaint, district court's task in resolving motion to dismiss for lack of subject matter jurisdiction is relatively limited one, and issue is not whether plaintiff will ultimately succeed on merits, but rather whether it is entitled to offer further evidence in support of its claims. Fed.Rules Civ.Proc.Rule 12(b)(1), 28 U.S.C.A.

Hanford Downwinders Coalition, Inc. v. Dowdle, 841 F.Supp. 1050, affirmed 71 F.3d 1469, affirmed Columbia River United v. Dowdle, 76 F.3d 385.

E.D.Wash. 1993. Motions to dismiss for lack of subject matter jurisdiction are generally considered motions in abatement that do not go to merits of case. Fed.Rules Civ.Proc.Rule 12(b)(1), 28 U.S.C.A.

Washington Cent. R. Co., Inc. v. National Mediation Bd., 830 F.Supp. 1343.

E.D.Wash. 1993. Unless claim is ripe for adjudication, court lacks subject-matter jurisdiction under the case or controversy clause of Article III, and claim must be dismissed. U.S.C.A. Const. Art. 3, § 1 et seq.

W. Birkenfeld Trust v. Bailey, 827 F.Supp. 651, modified on denial of reconsideration 837 F.Supp. 1083.

W.D.Wash. 1996. Where issue of court's subject matter jurisdiction does not address merits of case, court need not accept plaintiff's allegations as true, and existence of disputed facts does not preclude resolving issue in favor of party moving to dismiss.

Cascade Conservation League v. M.A. Segale, Inc., 921 F.Supp. 692.

S.D.W.Va. 1995. In assessing plaintiff's jurisdictional allegations in context of motion to dismiss for lack of subject matter jurisdiction, district court regards allegations in pleadings as mere evidence on issue, and may consider evidence outside pleadings without converting proceeding to one for summary judgment; court should apply summary judgment standard, under which nonmoving party must set forth specific facts beyond pleadings to show genuine issue of material fact, and moving party should prevail only if material jurisdictional facts are not in dispute and moving party is entitled to prevail as matter of law. Fed.Rules Civ.Proc. Rule 12(b)(1), 28 U.S.C.A.

Johnson v. U.S., 906 F.Supp. 1100.

E.D.Wis. 1995. Lack of subject matter jurisdiction is appropriate basis for motion to dismiss. Fed.Rules Civ.Proc.Rule 12(b)(1), 28 U.S.C.A.

Strasen v. Strasen, 897 F.Supp. 1179.

D.Wyo. 1994. Motion to dismiss for lack of subject matter jurisdiction may be used to attack failure to plead sufficient facts to demonstrate federal court's jurisdiction over subject matter of case based on court's lack of jurisdiction over subject matter of case. Fed.Rules Civ.Proc.Rule 12(b)(1), 28 U.S.C.A.

Axtell v. U.S., 860 F.Supp. 795.

8th Cir.BAP (Neb.) 1998. Every court has independent obligation to determine its jurisdiction, and, if subject-matter jurisdiction does not exist, matter must be dismissed.

In re Kearns, 219 B.R. 823.

Matter may be dismissed at any stage of proceeding or appellate review if no subject matter jurisdiction exists.

In re Kearns, 219 B.R. 823.

Bkrtcy.C.D.Cal. 1990. Dismissal is appropriate remedy where there is absence of subject matter jurisdiction. Fed.Rules Civ.Proc.Rule 12(h)(3), 28 U.S.C.A.

In re Western Land Bank, Inc., 116 B.R. 721.

Bkrtcy.D.Idaho 1992. When party moving for dismissal has challenged actual existence of subject matter jurisdiction, and jurisdiction depends upon facts that also go to merits of case, applicable standard is that utilized on motion for summary judgment, as opposed to standard utilized on motion to dismiss for failure to state a claim. Fed.Rules Civ.Proc.Rule 12(b)(1), 28 U.S.C.A.

In re Western States Drywall, Inc., 145 B.R. 661.

Bkrtcy.W.D.Mo. 1981. Motion to dismiss for failure to state a claim necessarily comprehends a motion to dismiss for lack of jurisdiction as question of whether complaint states a cause of action must be decided after and not before the court has assumed jurisdiction.

Matter of Citizens Loan and Sav. Co., 15 B.R. 919.

Bkrtcy.S.D.N.Y. 1994. Motion to dismiss for lack of subject matter jurisdiction which is filed prior to defendant's answer may be granted only if plaintiff has failed to allege element necessary for subject matter jurisdiction. Fed. Rules Civ.Proc.Rule 12(b)(1), 28 U.S.C.A.

Matter of Modell, 168 B.R. 851.

Bkrtcy.S.D.N.Y. 1994. Showing that plaintiff must make to avoid dismissal for lack of personal jurisdiction heightens as court becomes more acquainted with facts of matter before it. Fed.Rules Civ.Proc.Rule 12(b)(2), 28 U.S.C.A.

In re Levant Line, S.A., 166 B.R. 221.

Bkrtcy.D.Vt. 1990. Motion to dismiss for failure to state claim upon which relief may be granted can be decided only after finding subject-matter jurisdiction, since to rule on validity of claim is in itself an exercise of jurisdiction. Fed.Rules Civ.Proc.Rule 12(b)(6), 28 U.S.C.A.

In re Kelton Motors Inc., 121 B.R. 166.

⟨⟩**1742(2). Particular cases and grounds.**

U.S.Mont. 1987. District court, in which action challenging tribal court subject matter jurisdiction was brought while matter was pending in tribal court, should not have dismissed for lack of subject matter jurisdiction but, rather, should either have stayed proceedings or dismissed pending exhaustion of tribal court remedies.

Iowa Mut. Ins. Co. v. LaPlante, 107 S.Ct. 971, 480 U.S. 9, 94 L.Ed.2d 10.

C.A.D.C. 1998. District court did not abuse its discretion in dismissing foreign radio station owner's antitrust action against competitor for lack of personal jurisdiction, without allowing owner to conduct jurisdictional discovery; there was no indication that competitor had any contacts with forum.

Caribbean Broadcasting System, Ltd. v. Cable & Wireless P.L.C., 148 F.3d 1080, 331 U.S.App.D.C. 226.

C.A.D.C. 1994. Action brought by present and former prisoners to challenge change in provider of prison drug treatment program could not be dismissed based on ground that jurisdiction was lacking because complaint was "patently insubstantial" as claims were not essentially fictitious; if district court wished to dismiss claims as frivolous, it should have dismissed for failure to state claim on which relief could be granted. Fed.Rules Civ.Proc.Rule 12(b)(1, 6), 28 U.S.C.A.

Best v. Kelly, 39 F.3d 328, 309 U.S.App. D.C. 51.

C.A.D.C. 1989. Question whether plaintiff showed that reasonable fact finder could rule in her favor was proper standard for ruling on motion to dismiss for lack of subject matter jurisdiction, where ruling was based in part upon matters outside pleadings. Fed.Rules Civ. Proc.Rules 12(b)(1, 6), 56, 28 U.S.C.A.

In re Swine Flu Immunization Products Liability Litigation, 880 F.2d 1439, 279 U.S.App.D.C. 366, on remand Kenneda v. U.S., 815 F.Supp. 926.

C.A.D.C. 1984. Where complaint alleged presence of federal question jurisdiction over claims against corporate defendants, court could dismiss complaint for lack of subject-matter jurisdiction only if claim clearly appeared to be immaterial and made solely for purpose of obtaining jurisdiction or if the claim was wholly insubstantial or frivolous. (Per Wald, Circuit Judge, with one Judge concurring in part and one Judge concurring in part and dissenting in part.) 28 U.S.C.A. § 1331.

Reuber v. U.S., 750 F.2d 1039, 242 U.S.App.D.C. 370, appeal after remand 787 F.2d 599, 252 U.S.App.D.C. 43.

C.A.D.C. 1983. National Ass'n for Mental Health, Inc. v. Califano, 717 F.2d 1451, 230 U.S.App.D.C. 394, certiorari denied Wagshal v.

Crozer-Chester Medical Center, 105 S.Ct. 85, 469 U.S. 817, 83 L.Ed.2d 32.

C.A.D.C. 1973. "Americans United" Inc. v. Walters, 477 F.2d 1169, 155 U.S.App.D.C. 284, certiorari granted 93 S.Ct. 2752, 412 U.S. 927, 37 L.Ed.2d 154, reversed Alexander v. "Americans United" Inc., 94 S.Ct. 2053, 416 U.S. 752, 40 L.Ed.2d 518.

C.A.Fed. (Ky.) 1988. Patent assignee's action for declaration of rights under patent assignment agreement was not "action arising under any Act of Congress relating to patents," so that action was properly dismissed for lack of subject matter jurisdiction; any issue regarding validity of patent would be raised, if at all, only as defense to assignor's state law action to recover payments allegedly owing under agreement. 28 U.S.C.A. § 1338(a).
Speedco, Inc. v. Estes, 853 F.2d 909.

C.A.11 (Ala.) 1990. When defendant has waived his objection to sufficient service of process or any other defect in personal jurisdiction by failing to timely object, and has thus consented to litigate action in that court, court may not, either upon defendant's motion or its own initiative, dismiss suit for lack of personal jurisdiction or insufficient service of process. Fed.Rules Civ.Proc.Rules 4(j), 12(g, h), 28 U.S.C.A.
Pardazi v. Cullman Medical Center, 896 F.2d 1313.

C.A.8 (Ark.) 1992. Federal district court did not err in dismissing insureds' class action diversity suit in favor of pending state court action for same claims.
Allison v. Security Ben. Life Ins. Co., 980 F.2d 1213.

C.A.9 (Cal.) 1998. The district court should have stayed, rather than dismiss, a False Claims Act suit pending the Department of Labor's findings, pursuant to the doctrine of primary jurisdiction, as to how a particular type of work was classified for the purposes of wage determinations. 31 U.S.C.A. § 3729 et seq.
U.S. v. Dan Caputo Co., 152 F.3d 1060.

C.A.9 (Cal.) 1990. If claim is unripe, federal courts lack subject matter jurisdiction and complaint must be dismissed.
Southern Pacific Transp. Co. v. City of Los Angeles, 922 F.2d 498, certiorari denied 112 S.Ct. 382, 502 U.S. 943, 116 L.Ed.2d 333.

C.A.9 (Cal.) 1990. District court was required to stay, rather than dismiss, action when it determined that it should defer to state court proceedings under *Colorado River* doctrine.
Coopers & Lybrand v. Sun-Diamond Growers of CA, 912 F.2d 1135.

C.A.9 (Cal.) 1987. Even if *Bivens* claims did not lie against private parties, dismissal for lack of subject-matter jurisdiction was improper; proper form of dismissal was for failure to state claim upon which relief could be granted.
Schowengerdt v. General Dynamics Corp., 823 F.2d 1328, 91 A.L.R. Fed. 201, appeal after remand 944 F.2d 483, certiorari denied 112 S.Ct. 1514, 503 U.S. 951, 117 L.Ed.2d 650.

C.A.9 (Cal.) 1987. Ordinarily, where jurisdictional issue is separable from merits of case, court may determine jurisdiction by standards of motion to dismiss for lack of jurisdiction, but standards of motion to dismiss for lack of jurisdiction are not appropriate for determining jurisdiction in case involving inmate's constitutional challenge to Parole Commission's decision-making process where issues of jurisdiction and substance are intertwined, and, in such a case, district court should apply standards applicable to 12(b)(6) motion and assume truth of allegations in complaint or habeas petition, unless controverted by undisputed facts in record, and dismiss complaint where it appears beyond doubt that plaintiff can prove no set of facts in support of claim which would entitle him to relief. Fed.Rules Civ.Proc.Rule 12(b)(1, 6), 28 U.S.C.A.
Roberts v. Corrothers, 812 F.2d 1173.

C.A.9 (Cal.) 1987. While there is no requirement that every conceivable sanction be examined, meaningful alternatives must be explored before case can be dismissed for want of prosecution.
Hamilton v. Neptune Orient Lines, Ltd., 811 F.2d 498.

C.A.9 (Cal.) 1976. Timberlane Lumber Co. v. Bank of America, N.T. and S.A., 549 F.2d 597, 40 A.L.R. Fed. 314, on remand 574 F.Supp. 1453, affirmed 749 F.2d 1378, certiorari denied Timberlane Lumber Company v. Bank of America National Trust and Savings Association, 105 S.Ct. 3514, 472 U.S. 1032, 87 L.Ed.2d 643.

C.A.11 (Fla.) 1997. Genuine issues of fact as to whether plaintiff was independent contractor or an "employee" within meaning of the ADEA and conversely whether defendant was an "employer" under the ADEA, precluded dismissal of complaint for lack of subject matter jurisdiction, as issue was one for jury. Fed. Rules Civ.Proc.Rule 12(b)(1), 28 U.S.C.A.
Garcia v. Copenhaver, Bell & Associates, M.D.'s, P.A., 104 F.3d 1256.

C.A.11 (Ga.) 1993. District court erred by dismissing claims of automobile owner suing French manufacturer of vehicle for personal injuries, based on lack of personal jurisdiction under Georgia long-arm statute and absence of minimum contacts with Georgia; jurisdiction was based under long-arm provision under Foreign Sovereign Immunities Act, as manufacturer was deemed "foreign state" due to its ownership by French government, and those state long-arm and minimum contacts requirements were inapplicable. 28 U.S.C.A. § 1330(b); U.S.C.A. Const.Amend. 14.

> Vermeulen v. Renault, U.S.A., Inc., 985 F.2d 1534, certiorari denied Regie Nationale Des Usines Renault S.A. v. Vermeulen, 113 S.Ct. 2334, 508 U.S. 907, 124 L.Ed.2d 246.

C.A.9 (Hawai'i) 1995. Case that did not fall within supplemental jurisdiction of the district court was subject to dismissal and could not instead be remanded from federal to state court, where case had not been filed in or removed from state court.

> Misischia v. Pirie, 60 F.3d 626.

C.A.9 (Idaho) 1987. Where district court decided issue of its personal jurisdiction over defendant on basis of affidavits and written discovery materials, plaintiffs in tort action needed to make only prima facie showing of jurisdictional facts in order to avoid motion to dismiss.

> Lake v. Lake, 817 F.2d 1416.

C.A.7 (Ill.) 1994. Federal prisoner's legal malpractice action against federal public defenders, for whom federal government was substituted as party defendant under Westfall Act, would be dismissed for lack of subject-matter jurisdiction because prisoner did not exhaust administrative remedies by first presenting claim to appropriate federal agency. 28 U.S.C.A. §§ 2675(a), 2679(b)(1), (d)(4).

> Sullivan v. U.S., 21 F.3d 198, certiorari denied 115 S.Ct. 670, 513 U.S. 1060, 130 L.Ed.2d 604.

C.A.7 (Ill.) 1993. Language contained in motion to dismiss, indicating that defendant could not explain its failure to respond given presumptively valid return of service, without alerting court in any way to alleged defects in summons, did not adequately raise issue of personal jurisdiction, particularly when considered with defendant's statement that it did not challenge service. Fed.Rules Civ.Proc.Rule 12, 28 U.S.C.A.

> O'Brien v. R.J. O'Brien & Associates, Inc., 998 F.2d 1394.

C.A.7 (Ill.) 1992. Under *"Colorado River* doctrine," federal court may stay or dismiss suit in exceptional circumstances when there is concurrent state proceeding and stay or dismissal would promote wise judicial administration.

> Caminiti and Iatarola, Ltd. v. Behnke Warehousing, Inc., 962 F.2d 698.

C.A.7 (Ill.) 1990. Claims asserted against counsel and his corporate persona, for allegedly advising bank not to disclose director's involvement as principal shareholder of corporation whose assets were purchased with guaranteed loan to Small Business Administration (SBA), that were based on pendent party jurisdiction were properly dismissed for lack of pendent jurisdiction when SBA's motion for summary judgment was granted.

> Heritage Bank & Trust Co. v. Abdnor, 906 F.2d 292.

C.A.7 (Ill.) 1988. Dismissal of case for lack of jurisdiction by federal courts because it is frivolous is possible—and mandatory—even if defendant fails to preserve the ground that demonstrates the suit's lack of merit.

> Crowley Cutlery Co. v. U.S., 849 F.2d 273.

C.A.7 (Ill.) 1984. Cross claim filed by tenant's purported successor in interest against tenant, seeking specific performance of power of attorney and option agreements entered after landlord sued tenant, should not have been dismissed, on subject-matter jurisdiction grounds, where cross claim related to property that was subject matter of original suit and where, although landlord and tenant settled main claim before trial, cross claim had independent jurisdictional basis, grounded on diversity of citizenship between parties and amount in controversy greater than $10,000, which was not violated by reason of fact that landlord and purported successor were both Illinois corporations, since purported successor was not indispensable party when landlord filed its complaint against tenant. Fed.Rules Civ.Proc. Rule 13(g), 28 U.S.C.A.; 28 U.S.C.A. § 1332.

> American Nat. Bank and Trust Co. of Chicago v. Bailey, 750 F.2d 577, certiorari denied Chicago Investment Corporation v. American National Bank and Trust Company of Chicago, 105 S.Ct. 2324, 471 U.S. 1100, 85 L.Ed.2d 842.

If landlord's claim against tenant's purported successor in interest was a complaint in an independent action over which court had no jurisdiction because parties were not of diverse citizenship, claim would have to be dismissed, but dismissal would not effect court's jurisdiction over underlying action between landlord and tenant.

> American Nat. Bank and Trust Co. of Chicago v. Bailey, 750 F.2d 577, certiorari denied Chicago Investment Corporation v. American National Bank and Trust Company of Chicago, 105 S.Ct. 2324, 471 U.S. 1100, 85 L.Ed.2d 842.

C.A.6 (Ky.) 1991. Proper recourse where pendent jurisdiction is not exercised is dismissal of state claims without prejudice.

Vandiver v. Hardin County Bd. of Educ., 925 F.2d 927.

C.A.5 (La.) 1992. Motion to dismiss for lack of jurisdiction may be decided by district court considering only the complaint, the complaint supplemented by undisputed facts reflected in record, or the complaint supplemented by undisputed facts plus court's resolution of disputed facts.

Meliezer v. Resolution Trust Co., 952 F.2d 879.

C.A.5 (La.) 1985. Second, identical suit which was filed while first suit was still pending and which sought to plead new facts pertaining to diversity jurisdiction would be dismissed for lack of subject matter jurisdiction due to fact that second complaint sought to do nothing more than amend allegations in initial action going to diversity jurisdiction, which would relate back to original filing of initial action where diversity of citizenship did not exist.

Oliney v. Gardner, 771 F.2d 856.

Failure to inform district court or opposing counsel of filing of second identical suit while first suit was still pending would result in dismissal of second suit, which alleged new or changed facts pertaining to diversity jurisdiction, as duplicative of first suit. U.S.Dist.Ct. Rules E.D.La., Rule 2.5; Fed.Rules Civ.Proc. Rule 15, 28 U.S.C.A.

Oliney v. Gardner, 771 F.2d 856.

C.A.1 (Me.) 1992. Most commonly used method of determining motion to dismiss for want of personal jurisdiction is for district court to consider only whether plaintiff has proffered evidence that, if credited, is enough to support findings of all facts essential to personal jurisdiction; to defeat motion to dismiss when court uses this method plaintiff must make showing as to every fact required to satisfy both forum's long-arm statute and due process clause of Constitution; this standard for deciding motion to dismiss is commonly referred to as "prima facie" or standard requiring "prima facie showing."

Boit v. Gar-Tec Products, Inc., 967 F.2d 671.

Third method of determining motion to dismiss for lack of personal jurisdiction is to apply intermediate standard between requiring only prima facie showing and requiring proof by preponderance of the evidence; thus, even though allowing evidentiary hearing and weighing evidence to make findings, court may merely find whether plaintiff has shown likelihood of existence of each fact necessary to support jurisdiction.

Boit v. Gar-Tec Products, Inc., 967 F.2d 671.

Showing of likelihood that jurisdictional facts exist pursuant to third intermediate method of determining motion to dismiss for lack of personal jurisdiction is means of assuring that circumstances justifying imposing on out-of-state defendant burden of trial in local form, in which trial issues of fact essential to establishing both jurisdiction and merits of claim will be decided by preponderance of evidence; if court finds that plaintiff has shown such justifying circumstances, court may deny motion to dismiss.

Boit v. Gar-Tec Products, Inc., 967 F.2d 671.

C.A.1 (Mass.) 1987. District court properly dismissed for lack of jurisdiction, rather than staying, action by multiemployer employee benefit fund to collect unpaid contributions following expiration of collective bargaining agreement as to which NLRB had primary jurisdiction.

New Bedford Fishermen's Welfare Fund By Its Trustees v. Baltic Enterprises, Inc., 813 F.2d 503, certiorari denied 108 S.Ct. 1074, 485 U.S. 904, 99 L.Ed.2d 234.

C.A.6 (Mich.) 1995. Federal district court in Michigan lacked personal jurisdiction over life insurance agent who lived in North Carolina, and, thus, insurance beneficiary's complaint, as it related to agent, had to be dismissed; although agent allegedly visited his children in Michigan and formerly resided there, had first discussed the issuance of the subject insurance policy while in the state and had once applied for nonresident's license to sell insurance in Michigan, that was not sufficient to bring agent under Michigan's general personal jurisdiction statute, or its limited personal jurisdiction statute. M.C.L.A. §§ 600.701, 600.705.

Simmons v. Allstate Life Ins. Co., 65 F.3d 526.

C.A.6 (Mich.) 1992. If claim is unripe, federal courts lack subject matter jurisdiction and complaint must be dismissed. U.S.C.A. Const. Art. 3, § 1 et seq.

Bigelow v. Michigan Dept. of Natural Resources, 970 F.2d 154.

C.A.6 (Mich.) 1986. Decision to dismiss claims for declaratory and equitable relief against several justices and judges of the Michigan state court system by reason of alleged violations of civil rights in connection with judgments in state cases respecting plaintiff's dispute with bankrupt defendant over possession of premises was not clearly erroneous given fact that review of final determinations in state judicial proceedings could be obtained only in the United States Supreme Court when state court judgments were not shown to have been procured through fraud, deception, accident or mistake. 28 U.S.C.A. § 1257; 42 U.S.C.A. § 1983.

> In re Sun Valley Foods Co., 801 F.2d 186.

C.A.8 (Minn.) 1994. Where federal subject matter jurisdiction is based on ERISA, but the evidence fails to establish existence of an ERISA plan, claim must be dismissed for lack of subject matter jurisdiction. Employee Retirement Income Security Act of 1974, § 2 et seq., 29 U.S.C.A. § 1001 et seq.

> Kulinski v. Medtronic Bio-Medicus, Inc., 21 F.3d 254, appeal after remand 60 F.3d 830.

C.A.8 (Minn.) 1992. Dismissal for lack of subject matter jurisdiction should be granted sparingly and cautiously.

> Bowe v. Northwest Airlines, Inc., 974 F.2d 101, certiorari denied 113 S.Ct. 1602, 507 U.S. 992, 123 L.Ed.2d 164.

C.A.8 (Minn.) 1985. Union member's failure to list any statute to support federal question jurisdiction in his pro se complaint against union did not require dismissal of complaint, where, at hearing before district court, he specifically referred to Landrum-Griffin Act as basis for his claim. Labor-Management Reporting and Disclosure Act of 1959, § 101(a)(5), 29 U.S.C.A. § 411(a)(5).

> Schmid v. United Broth. of Carpenters and Joiners of America, 773 F.2d 993, appeal after remand 827 F.2d 384, certiorari denied 108 S.Ct. 1041, 484 U.S. 1071, 98 L.Ed.2d 1004.

C.A.8 (Mo.) 1998. Issue of whether *Feres* doctrine barred medical malpractice action brought by former cadet in the United States Army Reserve Officers' Training Corps (ROTC) raised jurisdictional question, and district court should have viewed United States' motion to dismiss as motion for dismissal for want of subject matter jurisdiction, rather than as motion to dismiss for failure to state a claim. 28 U.S.C.A. §§ 1346(b), 2674; Fed.Rules Civ.Proc. Rule 12(b)(1, 6), 28 U.S.C.A.

> Brown v. U.S., 151 F.3d 800, rehearing and suggestion for rehearing denied.

C.A.8 (Mo.) 1993. Even if third-party claim of savings and loan association's directors against Resolution Trust Corporation (RTC), that they were entitled to indemnification from association with regard to original claim against them and that RTC had assumed that liability as association's receiver, was legally frivolous because there were no association assets with which RTC could satisfy judgment, directors'

claim that RTC negligently mismanaged association after it took control was not frivolous, so as to require dismissal of claim for want of federal jurisdiction. Federal Deposit Insurance Act, § 2[11](d), 12 U.S.C.A. § 1821(d).

> Kansas Public Employees Retirement System v. Reimer & Koger Associates, Inc., 4 F.3d 614, rehearing and suggestion for rehearing denied, certiorari denied 114 S.Ct. 2132, 511 U.S. 1126, 128 L.Ed.2d 862.

C.A.8 (Mo.) 1992. District court should have stayed, rather than dismissed, complaint which was identical to plaintiffs' complaint filed in another state, where defendants had refused to stipulate to personal jurisdiction in other court and plaintiffs had filed complaint in forum court in order to ensure federal forum in which to litigate their cause of action.

> Selph v. Nelson, Reabe and Snyder, Inc., 966 F.2d 411, certiorari denied 113 S.Ct. 603, 506 U.S. 1000, 121 L.Ed.2d 539.

C.A.8 (Mo.) 1984. Party's failure to allege federal jurisdiction over its affirmative claims was proper ground for federal district court's dismissal without prejudice of counterclaim. Fed.Rules Civ.Proc.Rules 8(a)(1), 13(a, b), 28 U.S.C.A.

> Shelter Mut. Ins. Co. v. Public Water Supply Dist. No. 7 of Jefferson County, Mo., 747 F.2d 1195.

C.A.1 (N.H.) 1990. Because Federal Tort Claims Act discretionary function exemption is a limitation on the waiver of sovereign immunity, cases which fall within the exception are dismissed for lack of subject matter jurisdiction. 28 U.S.C.A. §§ 1346(b), 2680(a).

> Irving v. U.S., 909 F.2d 598, on remand 1994 WL 287750, reconsideration denied 1994 WL 392614, vacated 49 F.3d 830, on remand 942 F.Supp. 1483, rehearing granted, opinion withdrawn 146 F.3d 12.

C.A.3 (N.J.) 1992. Plaintiff's claim must be live throughout entire litigation, once controversy ceases to exist court must dismiss case for lack of jurisdiction since no agreement between parties to allow federal court to hear case will rescue mooted action. U.S.C.A. Const. Art. 3, §§ 1 et seq., 2, cl. 1.

> Lusardi v. Xerox Corp., 975 F.2d 964.

C.A.10 (N.M.) 1987. Petroleum corporation's independent action, in which it sought to pay adjusted bonuses to preserve its interest in certain oil and gas leases initially awarded by Department of Interior as part of lease sales challenged by Jicarilla Apache Tribe in another suit, was properly dismissed because Tribe was essential party to litigation but was immune from suit; although Tribe's filing of its litigation may have waived its immunity with regard to petroleum corporation's intervention in that suit, filing of suit did not express waiver of immunity with regard to all subsequent actions relating to same leases, and Tribe's interest in oil leases would be directly affected by corporation's independent action.

Jicarilla Apache Tribe v. Hodel, 821 F.2d 537.

C.A.2 (N.Y.) 1994. If there was no subject matter jurisdiction over taxpayers' counterclaim in suit to recover tax deficiencies, then default judgment entered against government was void and had to be vacated, and taxpayers' counterclaim had to be dismissed. Fed.Rules Civ.Proc. Rules 12(h)(3), 60(b)(4), 28 U.S.C.A.

U.S. v. Forma, 42 F.3d 759.

C.A.2 (N.Y.) 1993. Dismissals for lack of standing should be made under procedural provision governing failure to state claim for relief rather than provision governing lack of subject matter jurisdiction. Fed.Rules Civ.Proc.Rule 12(b)(1, 6), 28 U.S.C.A.

Rent Stabilization Ass'n of City of New York v. Dinkins, 5 F.3d 591.

C.A.2 (N.Y.) 1983. Pressroom Unions-Printers League Income Sec. Fund v. Continental Assur. Co., 700 F.2d 889, 67 A.L.R. Fed. 937, certiorari dismissed 104 S.Ct. 26, 463 U.S. 1233, 77 L.Ed.2d 1449, certiorari denied 104 S.Ct. 148, 464 U.S. 845, 78 L.Ed.2d 138.

C.A.6 (Ohio) 1985. Since dismissal of pendent state law claim for tortious interference with contractual rights was required once federal claim under the Labor Management Relations Act was dismissed, district court erred in dismissing the state law claim on the merits; it should have dismissed the claim without prejudice for want of jurisdiction. Labor Management Relations Act, 1947, § 301, 29 U.S.C.A. § 185.

Service, Hosp., Nursing Home and Public Employees Union, Local No. 47, Affiliated with Service Employees Intern. Union, AFL-CIO v. Commercial Property Services, Inc., 755 F.2d 499, certiorari denied 106 S.Ct. 147, 474 U.S. 850, 88 L.Ed.2d 122.

C.A.6 (Ohio) 1984. District court did not abuse its discretion in dismissing pendent state law claims after having dismissed all federal claims prior to trial.

Marx v. Centran Corp., 747 F.2d 1536, certiorari denied 105 S.Ct. 2656, 471 U.S. 1125, 86 L.Ed.2d 273.

C.A.10 (Okl.) 1995. District court did not abuse its discretion in dismissing for lack of jurisdiction oil and gas leasehold interest owners' action against natural gas well operator, alleging operator violated duties imposed by Oklahoma Corporation Commission (OCC) by depriving owners of their fair share of gas in special allocated pool by producing from well in adjoining section, and seeking damages for conversion, rather than staying or suspending action pending Commission's resolution of question, where issue was first raised in motion for reconsideration or alternative relief, which was untimely filed. 52 Okl.St.Ann. § 87.1.

Brumark Corp. v. Samson Resources Corp., 57 F.3d 941.

C.A.3 (Pa.) 1990. Questions regarding Government's waiver of sovereign immunity from suit go directly to court's subject matter jurisdiction; accordingly, proper disposition, upon finding that Government's immunity is intact, is order dismissing case for lack of jurisdiction.

Dawson v. U.S., 894 F.2d 70.

C.A.3 (Pa.) 1987. Dismissal of claim for lack of jurisdiction is not appropriate merely because legal theory alleged is probably false, but only because right claimed is so insubstantial, implausible, foreclosed by prior court decisions, or otherwise completely devoid of merit so as not to involve a federal controversy.

Kulick v. Pocono Downs Racing Ass'n, Inc., 816 F.2d 895.

Dismissal of civil rights action for lack of jurisdiction was not appropriate on theory that claim was legally frivolous. 42 U.S.C.A. § 1983.

Kulick v. Pocono Downs Racing Ass'n, Inc., 816 F.2d 895.

C.A.1 (Puerto Rico) 1994. Where District Court lacked subject matter jurisdiction to entertain back-pay claim against Secretary of Air Force, in challenge by member of Puerto Rico Air National Guard (PRANG) to his discharge following positive test for Human Immunodeficiency Virus (HIV), and Court of Federal Claims, which was the only tribunal arguably possessed of jurisdiction over such claim, expressly held that it lacked subject matter jurisdiction where civilian technician was duly discharged from state Guard unit, claim would be dismissed for want of jurisdiction, since transfer of claim would be to no avail. 28 U.S.C.A. § 1631.

Charles v. Rice, 28 F.3d 1312.

C.A.6 (Tenn.) 1996. Allegations by shipper that air freight carrier had represented that its two-day service was cheaper than its overnight service when overnight service was in fact cheaper, and that carrier was accordingly liable for fraud under federal common law were sufficient to allege federal question jurisdiction and to withstand motion to dismiss based on lack of subject matter jurisdiction. Fed.Rules Civ.Proc. Rule 12(b)(1), 28 U.S.C.A.

> Musson Theatrical, Inc. v. Federal Exp. Corp., 89 F.3d 1244, rehearing and suggestion for rehearing denied, amended on denial of rehearing 1998 WL 117980.

C.A.5 (Tex.) 1996. Homeowners failed to meet their burden of showing personal jurisdiction over nonresident defendant and, thus, district court properly granted defendant's motion to dismiss for lack of personal jurisdiction, in homeowners' action against alleged owners, operators, and maintainers of oil and gas well located near home, alleging homeowners had suffered property damage and personal injuries from toxic chemicals emanating from well, where homeowners had almost two years to conduct discovery to determine whether defendant had any relevant contacts with forum state, but failed to take reasonable and timely steps to acquire information they needed. Fed.Rules Civ.Proc.Rule 12(b)(2), 28 U.S.C.A.

> Doddy v. Oxy USA, Inc., 101 F.3d 448.

C.A.5 (Tex.) 1995. Choice-of-forum provision contained in contract between bank and Texas corporation that had contracted to administer benefits services for bank's customers was valid and enforceable, and, therefore, federal district court in Texas improperly dismissed breach of contract action for lack of personal jurisdiction over bank, which was organized and had its principal place of business in North Carolina, where choice-of-forum provision in contract unambiguously provided that Texas law applied and that proper venue lay in Texas county, and bank failed to sufficiently prove that enforcement of that provision would be unreasonable due to fraud or overreaching.

> Kevlin Services, Inc. v. Lexington State Bank, 46 F.3d 13.

C.A.5 (Tex.) 1993. As general rule, district court should dismiss complaint for want of subject matter jurisdiction, rather than by granting defendant's motion for summary judgment, whenever it finds that conditions for waiver of governmental defendant's sovereign immunity have not been met.

> Broussard v. U.S., 989 F.2d 171.

C.A.5 (Tex.) 1991. If it appears from face of complaint that federal claim is without merit, court should dismiss for failure to state claim, and not on jurisdictional grounds; however, dismissal for want of jurisdiction is appropriate if federal claim is frivolous or mere matter of form. 28 U.S.C.A. § 1331.

> Sarmiento v. Texas Bd. of Veterinary Medical Examiners By and Through Avery, 939 F.2d 1242.

C.A.5 (Tex.) 1990. County's suit against asbestos products manufacturers and suppliers to recover costs of removal of asbestos products from buildings would be dismissed for lack of jurisdiction, where jurisdiction in original suit was predicated solely on nonexistent federal claim under CERCLA, and attempt to amend complaint to drop nondiverse party in order to obtain valid diversity jurisdiction was ineffectual in that district court had already lost jurisdiction due to pending appeal. Comprehensive Environmental Response, Compensation, and Liability Act of 1980, § 107(a), as amended, 42 U.S.C.A. § 9607(a); Fed.Rules Civ.Proc.Rules 15(a), 21, 28 U.S.C.A.

> Dayton Independent School Dist. v. U.S. Mineral Products Co., 906 F.2d 1059, rehearing denied.

C.A.5 (Tex.) 1988. After district court determined that it did not have personal jurisdiction over Virginia corporation in action for tortious interference with contract and business relations, dismissing suit against corporation for lack of jurisdiction, rather than entry of judgment on merits in favor of corporation, was appropriate.

> Southmark Corp. v. Life Investors, Inc., 851 F.2d 763.

C.A.5 (Tex.) 1986. Federal claims of Texas prison inmates, that they were deprived of property rights in funds without due process of law based upon alleged earning of interest on prisoners' money without payment of interest to prisoners, and upon alleged spending of prison commissary proceeds on items that did not benefit inmates in violation of Texas Administrative Code, were not immaterial or designed solely to obtain jurisdiction, so as to justify dismissal of federal action on grounds of lack of jurisdiction, even though prisoners had advanced claims that could only be read as grounded in state law, where they also clearly alleged violations by state officials of federal constitutional protections, and it did not appear from complaint that prisoners' federal claims were any less serious than their state claims. U.S.C.A. Const.Amends. 5, 14; 42 U.S.C.A. § 1983.

> Eubanks v. McCotter, 802 F.2d 790.

Federal claims of Texas prison inmates, that they were deprived of property rights in certain funds without due process, based upon alleged earning of interest on prisoners' funds that was not paid to prisoners, and upon alleged spending of commissary proceeds on items that did not benefit inmates in violation of Texas Administrative Code, were not wholly insubstantial or frivolous, so as to justify dismissal of prisoners' action on ground of lack of jurisdiction. U.S.C.A. Const.Amends. 5, 14; 42 U.S.C.A. § 1983.

> Eubanks v. McCotter, 802 F.2d 790.

Federal claims of Texas prison inmates, that they were deprived of property rights in certain funds without due process, based upon alleged earning of interest on prisoners' money without payment of interest to prisoners, and upon alleged expenditure of prison commissary proceeds on items that did not benefit inmates in violation of Texas Administrative Code, were improperly dismissed for lack of subject matter jurisdiction, where federal causes of action were neither immaterial nor frivolous.   U.S.C.A. Const.Amends. 5, 14; 42 U.S.C.A. § 1983.

Eubanks v. McCotter, 802 F.2d 790.

C.A.5 (Tex.) 1986.   Claim by female adult probation officers that they were Title VII employees and were not personal staff employees of elected state district court judges was not wholly insubstantial and frivolous, so that officers' Title VII claims against county adult probation department, alleging that they were paid less than men who performed similar work and had been denied promotions due to their sex, should not have been dismissed for lack of subject-matter jurisdiction.   Fed.Rules Civ.Proc. Rule 12(b)(1), 28 U.S.C.A.; Civil Rights Act of 1964, § 706(e, f), (f)(2, 4, 5), as amended, 42 U.S.C.A. § 2000e–5(f).

Clark v. Tarrant County, Texas, 798 F.2d 736, rehearing denied 802 F.2d 455.

C.A.5 (Tex.) 1985.   While dismissal on jurisdictional grounds for want of substantiality of federal claim should be applied hesitantly, student's Fourteenth Amendment challenge to five-year rule, which provided students may participate in interscholastic athletics for only five years after their first enrollment in eighth grade, was insubstantial, where claim had no plausible foundation in law and participation in interscholastic athletics was not interest protected by due process clause.   U.S.C.A. Const. Amend. 14.

Maroney v. University Interscholastic League, 764 F.2d 403.

C.A.2 (Vt.) 1996.   Proper vehicle for dismissing claim under Federal Tort Claims Act (FTCA) which is barred under *Feres* doctrine is motion for dismissal based on lack of subject-matter jurisdiction; *Feres* doctrine concerns waiver of sovereign immunity, so that issue is necessarily one of jurisdiction.   28 U.S.C.A. §§ 2671–2680;   Fed.Rules   Civ.Proc.Rule 12(b)(1), 28 U.S.C.A.

Wake v. U.S., 89 F.3d 53.

C.A.4 (Va.) 1996.   Where challenged conduct in action under Federal Tort Claims Act (FTCA) was performed by independent contractor, district court must dismiss action for want of subject matter jurisdiction.   28 U.S.C.A. § 1346(b).

Robb v. U.S., 80 F.3d 884.

C.A.4 (Va.) 1995.   Where United States was not liable for plaintiff's injury under the Federal Tort Claims Act, district court should have dismissed for want of jurisdiction rather than granting summary judgment for the United States.   28 U.S.C.A. §§ 1346(b), 2671–2680; Fed.Rules Civ.Proc.Rules 12(b)(1), 56(c), 28 U.S.C.A.

Williams v. U.S., 50 F.3d 299.

C.A.9 (Wash.) 1986.   Dismissal of civil rights action for improper venue, rather than transfer of that action to proper district, was not an abuse of discretion.   28 U.S.C.A. § 1406(a).

Costlow v. Weeks, 790 F.2d 1486.

C.A.7 (Wis.) 1992.   Conclusion that state law claims were preempted by ERISA did not require that suit be dismissed for failure to state claim.   Employee Retirement Income Security Act of 1974, § 2 et seq., 29 U.S.C.A. § 1001 et seq.;   Fed.Rules Civ.Proc.Rule 12(b)(6), 28 U.S.C.A.

Shannon v. Shannon, 965 F.2d 542, rehearing denied, certiorari denied 113 S.Ct. 677, 506 U.S. 1028, 121 L.Ed.2d 599.

C.A.7 (Wis.) 1985.   Prison inmate's pendent state claims not based upon same facts as permissible Eighth Amendment claim of intentional interference with prescribed therapy by refusing to permit inmate to attend all scheduled physical therapy sessions or equal protection claim that prison officials had implemented a double celling policy that discriminated on basis of race were properly dismissed.

Benson v. Cady, 761 F.2d 335.

M.D.Ala. 1996.   False Claims Act action would not be dismissed on jurisdictional grounds where, although defendants extensively briefed and cited jurisdictional bars to plaintiff's claims, such issues were closely related to merits of case and were, therefore, better addressed following more thorough gathering of evidence in form of discovery proceedings.   31 U.S.C.A. § 3721 et seq.;   Fed.Rules Civ.Proc.Rule 12(b)(1), 28 U.S.C.A.

U.S. ex rel. Sanders v. East Alabama Healthcare Authority, 953 F.Supp. 1404.

M.D.Ala. 1994.   District court was required to dismiss action for lack of subject matter jurisdiction after dismissing § 1983 claim upon finding that officer was entitled to qualified immunity, where action involved non-diverse parties and there was no implication of federal law.

Cofield v. Randolph County Com'n, 874 F.Supp. 1276, affirmed 90 F.3d 468.

N.D.Ala. 1992.   Taxpayers seeking to challenge county occupational tax were provided requisite opportunity to present evidence bearing on existence of federal jurisdiction prior to dismissal; court held hearing, issue of jurisdiction was thoroughly discussed, and taxpayers were allowed to furnish to court any evidence they wished. 28 U.S.C.A. § 1341.

> Richards v. Jefferson County, 789 F.Supp. 369, affirmed 983 F.2d 237.

S.D.Ala. 1990. There is no case or controversy for purposes of Article III if plaintiff's purported injuries cannot be redressed through court action; case must be dismissed if court can award no remedy. U.S.C.A. Const. Art. 3, § 1 et seq.

> Black v. Frank, 730 F.Supp. 1087.

D.Alaska 1984. Shultz v. Sundberg, 577 F.Supp. 1491, affirmed 759 F.2d 714.

C.D.Cal. 1993. When dealing with attack on court's subject matter jurisdiction by Australian defendants in copyright infringement action concerning dictionary of Austronesian languages, district court would be guided by standards set forth under rules 12(b)(1) and (2) and would evaluate disputed facts, to extent any exist, to reach merits of jurisdictional claim. Fed.Rules Civ.Proc.Rule 12(b)(1, 2), 28 U.S.C.A.

> Intercontinental Dictionary Series v. De Gruyter, 822 F.Supp. 662.

E.D.Cal. 1992. Complaint will be dismissed for lack of subject matter jurisdiction if cause does not arise under any federal law or United States Constitution, there is no case or controversy within meaning of that constitutional term, or if cause is not one described by any jurisdictional statute. Fed.Rules Civ.Proc.Rule 12(b)(1, 6), 28 U.S.C.A.

> ITSI T.V. Productions, Inc. v. California Authority of Racing Fairs, 785 F.Supp. 854.

If jurisdictional issue and merits of case are intertwined, courts must employ standard applicable to motion for summary judgment in disposing of motion to dismiss for lack of subject matter jurisdiction. Fed.Rules Civ.Proc.Rule 12(b)(1), 28 U.S.C.A.

> ITSI T.V. Productions, Inc. v. California Authority of Racing Fairs, 785 F.Supp. 854.

E.D.Cal. 1990. Complaint will be dismissed for lack of subject matter jurisdiction if cause does not "arise under" any federal law or the United States Constitution, if there is no case or controversy within meaning of constitutional term, or if cause is not one described by any jurisdictional statute. U.S.C.A. Const. Art. 3, § 2, cl. 1 et seq.; Fed.Rules Civ.Proc.Rule 12(b)(1), 28 U.S.C.A.

> Sullivan By and Through Sullivan v. Vallejo City Unified School Dist., 731 F.Supp. 947.

N.D.Cal. 1992. On motion to dismiss for lack of subject matter jurisdiction, applicable standard turns on whether attack is facial, in which case nonmoving party is entitled to same protection it would receive in defending against motion to dismiss for failure to state claim, or whether defendant is challenging veracity of jurisdictional facts underlying complaint, in which case court considers matters outside pleadings to resolve disputed jurisdictional facts. Fed.Rules Civ.Proc.Rule 12(b)(1), 28 U.S.C.A.

> Doe v. Schachter, 804 F.Supp. 53.

Where there is facial attack on court's subject matter jurisdiction, factual allegations are presumed to be true, and motion is granted only if plaintiff does not set forth elements necessary for jurisdiction; after construing allegations in light most favorable to plaintiff, complaint will be dismissed if: claim does not "arise under" federal law or Constitutions, there is no case or controversy, or cause of action is not described in any jurisdictional statute. Fed.Rules Civ. Proc.Rule 12(b)(1), 28 U.S.C.A.

> Doe v. Schachter, 804 F.Supp. 53.

Where issue of subject matter jurisdiction is separable from merits of case, court may hear evidence regarding jurisdiction, resolve existing factual disputes and rule on that issue. Fed. Rules Civ.Proc.Rule 12(b)(1), 28 U.S.C.A.

> Doe v. Schachter, 804 F.Supp. 53.

N.D.Cal. 1983. Timberlane Lumber Co. v. Bank of America Nat. Trust and Sav. Ass'n, 574 F.Supp. 1453, affirmed 749 F.2d 1378, certiorari denied Timberlane Lumber Company v. Bank of America National Trust and Savings Association, 105 S.Ct. 3514, 472 U.S. 1032, 87 L.Ed.2d 643.

S.D.Cal. 1997. When court determines that United States is immune from suit under Federal Tort Claims Act (FTCA), proper disposition is dismissal for lack of subject matter jurisdiction. 28 U.S.C.A. §§ 1346(b), 2671 et seq.; Fed.Rules Civ.Proc.Rule 12(b)(1), 28 U.S.C.A.

> LeCrone v. U.S. Navy, 958 F.Supp. 469.

S.D.Cal. 1995. Absent authority for proposition that arbitration provision may divest federal court of subject-matter jurisdiction over claims falling within the provision, district court would not dismiss employee's age, sex, and disability discrimination claims against university and other defendants, based on defendants' contention that claims were covered by mandatory arbitration clause in collective bargaining agreement, and that failure to arbitrate was failure to exhaust administrative remedies that would deprive court of subject matter jurisdiction. Civil Rights Act of 1964, § 701 et seq., as amended, 42 U.S.C.A. § 2000e et seq.

> Gallo v. Board of Regents of University of California, 916 F.Supp. 1005.

D.Colo. 1992. A district court has the power and the duty to determine its jurisdiction *sua sponte*, and must dismiss a case whenever it appears by suggestion of the parties or otherwise that the court lacks jurisdiction of the subject matter. Fed.Rules Civ.Proc.Rule 12(h), 28 U.S.C.A.

 U.S. v. Black Hawk Masonic Temple Ass'n, Inc., 798 F.Supp. 646.

D.Colo. 1990. Where RICO claim is sole federal claim and there is no other basis for jurisdiction, all pendent claims should be dismissed. 18 U.S.C.A. § 1962.

 Weiszmann v. Kirkland and Ellis, 732 F.Supp. 1540.

D.Conn. 1995. For purposes of establishing jurisdiction over corporate defendants, prima facie case that defendants were alter egos of defendants who had already admitted jurisdiction was sufficient to deny motion to dismiss for lack of jurisdiction.

 Northern Tankers (Cyprus) Ltd. v. Backstrom, 901 F.Supp. 72.

D.Del. 1996. Because personal injury plaintiff's basis for jurisdiction in action under Federal Tort Claims Act (FTCA)—negligence of federal facility and its employees—constituted very elements of plaintiff's substantive claims, court would not dismiss those claims for lack of subject matter jurisdiction unless they were "insubstantial." 28 U.S.C.A. § 1346(b); Fed.Rules Civ.Proc.Rule 12(b)(1), 28 U.S.C.A.

 Rhoades v. U.S., 950 F.Supp. 623.

D.Del. 1992. Determination of motion to dismiss for lack of jurisdiction was inappropriate in patent infringement suit prior to completion of jurisdictional discovery where jurisdictional facts that must be established were the same as those giving rise to civil action relating to patents. Fed.Rules Civ.Proc.Rule 12(b), 28 U.S.C.A.

 Metallgesellschaft AG v. Foster Wheeler Energy Corp., 143 F.R.D. 553.

D.D.C. 1997. Summary judgment motion, rather than motion to dismiss for subject matter jurisdiction, was appropriate motion for viatical settlement company to request dismissal of action by Securities and Exchange Commission (SEC) alleging that interests in life insurance policies sold by company were "securities" subject to federal securities laws. Fed.Rules Civ.Proc.Rules 12(b)(1), 56(c), 28 U.S.C.A.

 S.E.C. v. Life Partners, Inc., 986 F.Supp. 644.

D.D.C. 1994. Plaintiff's claims on alleged breaches of fiduciary duties under ERISA and common law would be dismissed where they were premised on conclusion that LMRA had been violated, and district court was without jurisdiction to hear case under LMRA. Labor Management Relations Act of 1947 § 302(e), 29 U.S.C.A. § 186(e); Employee Retirement Income Security Act of 1974, § 404, 29 U.S.C.A. § 1104.

 Mason Contractors Ass'n of America v. International Council of Employers of Bricklayers & Allied Craftsmen, 853 F.Supp. 515.

D.D.C. 1990. Plaintiff's citation to wrong statute as jurisdictional basis for employment discrimination suit did not justify dismissal where amended complaint specifically cited statutory and constitutional provisions that established his causes of action.

 Richards v. U.S. Merit Systems Protection Bd., 739 F.Supp. 657.

D.D.C. 1989. Motion to dismiss for lack of standing can only be brought as, and must be evaluated as, motion to dismiss for lack of subject matter jurisdiction. Fed.Rules Civ.Proc. Rule 12(b)(1), 28 U.S.C.A.

 Steffan v. Cheney, 733 F.Supp. 115.

D.D.C. 1984. Hastings v. Judicial Conference of U.S., 593 F.Supp. 1371, affirmed in part, vacated in part 770 F.2d 1093, 248 U.S.App.D.C. 180, certiorari denied 106 S.Ct. 3272, 477 U.S. 904, 91 L.Ed.2d 562.

M.D.Fla. 1998. On motion to dismiss for lack of personal jurisdiction, district court did not have to consider whether defendant had the required minimum contacts with forum, where plaintiff failed to present any facts in complaint to suggest that defendant had participated in any activity subjecting her to jurisdiction in Florida under Florida's long-arm statute. U.S.C.A. Const.Amends. 5, 14; West's F.S.A. § 48.193.

 Parham v. Lamar, 1 F.Supp.2d 1457.

M.D.Fla. 1995. Alleged procedural violations of Fair Housing Act (FHA) by Department of Housing and Urban Development (HUD) regarding 100–day investigation period, notification of delay, and good faith conciliation did not raise jurisdictional issues so as to warrant dismissal of action to enforce FHA for lack of subject matter jurisdiction. Civil Rights Act of 1968, § 810(b)(1), (g)(1), as amended, 42 U.S.C.A. § 3610(b)(1), (g)(1); Fed.Rules Civ. Proc.Rule 12(b)(1), 28 U.S.C.A.

 U.S. v. Sea Winds of Marco, Inc., 893 F.Supp. 1051.

M.D.Fla. 1991. Federal suit to compel arbitration was not required to be dismissed, abated or stayed in favor of suit brought in New York State Court one day earlier seeking to compel arbitration before different arbitral body; New York State Court had not taken action to expedite case and New York law was not involved, as question of arbitrability would be decided in either forum under the Federal Arbitration Act. 9 U.S.C.A. §§ 1–15.

> Luckie v. Smith Barney, Harris Upham & Co., Inc., 766 F.Supp. 1116, affirmed 999 F.2d 509.

S.D.Fla. 1994. Motion to dismiss claim for breach of collective bargaining agreement (CBA) for lack of subject matter jurisdiction was proper, even though argument appeared to have been at odds with contention that claim raised exclusively federal cause of action under RLA, as court has jurisdiction to determine its own jurisdiction. Fed.Rules Civ.Proc.Rule 12(b)(1), 28 U.S.C.A.; Railway Labor Act, § 1 et seq., 45 U.S.C.A. § 151 et seq.

> Cawthard v. Flagship Airlines, Inc., 863 F.Supp. 1567.

S.D.Fla. 1990. Transferring action was more appropriate alternative to dismissing action upon determining that personal jurisdiction could not be exercised over out-of-state defendants, where process was served and preliminary discovery was accomplished, so that dismissal would lead only to the unnecessary duplication of fees and costs. 28 U.S.C.A. § 1406(a).

> Cauff Lippman & Co. v. Apogee Finance Group, Inc., 745 F.Supp. 678.

S.D.Fla. 1983. Feldman v. Jackson Memorial Hosp., 571 F.Supp. 1000, affirmed 752 F.2d 647, certiorari denied 105 S.Ct. 3504, 472 U.S. 1029, 87 L.Ed.2d 635.

N.D.Ga. 1990. District court is obligated to deny motion to dismiss for lack of personal jurisdiction if plaintiff alleges sufficient facts to support reasonable inference that defendant can be subjected to court's jurisdiction. Fed.Rules Civ.Proc.Rule 12(b)(2), 28 U.S.C.A.

> Commercial Cas. Ins. Co., Inc. v. BSE Management, Inc., 734 F.Supp. 511.

N.D.Ga. 1988. Motion to dismiss for lack of personal jurisdiction should be denied if plaintiff has alleged sufficient facts to support reasonable inference that defendant can be subjected to jurisdiction of the court.

> Gerber Garment Technology, Inc. v. Lectra Systems, Inc., 699 F.Supp. 1576.

N.D.Ga. 1984. Morgan v. Westinghouse Elec. Corp., 579 F.Supp. 867, affirmed 752 F.2d 648.

S.D.Ga. 1996. Where insurer clearly and explicitly invoked jurisdiction of federal court pursuant to statutory interpleader alone, absence of required minimal diversity between at least two claimants required dismissal, even if insurer could have successfully invoked jurisdiction of court pursuant to interpleader rule or general diversity jurisdiction statute. 28

U.S.C.A. §§ 1332, 1335; Fed.Rules Civ.Proc. Rule 22, 28 U.S.C.A.

> Allstate Ins. Co. v. Young, 923 F.Supp. 1559.

S.D.Ga. 1990. A motion challenging district court's subject-matter jurisdiction can either be a facial attack on the complaint, requiring court merely to assess whether plaintiff has alleged a sufficient basis of subject-matter jurisdiction, which requires court to consider the allegations in plaintiff's complaint as true, or a factual attack on subject-matter jurisdiction, in which matters outside the pleadings, such as affidavits and testimony, are considered, and in which plaintiff bears burden of proof that subject-matter jurisdiction exists. Fed.Rules Civ. Proc.Rule 12(b)(1), 28 U.S.C.A.

> U.S. ex rel. Stinson, Lyons, Gerlin & Bustamante, P.A. v. Blue Cross Blue Shield of Georgia, Inc., 755 F.Supp. 1040, on reconsideration 755 F.Supp. 1055.

Motion to dismiss for lack of subject-matter jurisdiction is not the proper vehicle for defendant to claim that plaintiff has no evidence to back up its allegations; the proper context in which to make such argument is summary judgment. Fed.Rules Civ.Proc.Rule 12(b)(1), 28 U.S.C.A.

> U.S. ex rel. Stinson, Lyons, Gerlin & Bustamante, P.A. v. Blue Cross Blue Shield of Georgia, Inc., 755 F.Supp. 1040, on reconsideration 755 F.Supp. 1055.

S.D.Ga. 1988. Although it appeared that interests of justice would be served by transfer of case from Georgia federal district court, which did not have personal jurisdiction over defendant, to South Carolina court, where venue was proper and personal jurisdiction existed, case would be dismissed for lack of personal jurisdiction, where neither party had requested transfer, although action could have been transferred. 28 U.S.C.A. §§ 1404(a), 1406(a).

> Stacy v. Hilton Head Seafood Co., 688 F.Supp. 599.

D.Hawai'i 1997. Allegations by plaintiffs who asserted fraud and intentional misrepresentation claims against nonresident defendants in connection with purchase of yacht by plaintiffs were sufficient to make prima facie showing that defendants had purposely availed themselves of privilege of conducting activities in Hawai'i, as required to defeat motion to dismiss based on lack of personal jurisdiction with respect to tort claims asserted; allegations of solicitations of and communications with plaintiffs met burden of showing conduct aimed at Hawai'i, and perpetration of fraud on Hawai'i residents would foreseeably cause injury there. U.S.C.A. Const.Amends. 5, 14.

> Lung v. Yachts Intern., Ltd., 980 F.Supp. 1362.

Allegations by plaintiffs who asserted breach of contract claims against nonresident defendants in connection with purchase of yacht by plaintiffs were sufficient to make prima facie showing that defendants had purposely availed themselves of privilege of conducting activities in Hawai'i, as required to defeat motion to dismiss based on lack of personal jurisdiction with respect to contract claim; defendants had actively solicited plaintiffs, who were Hawai'i residents, and created continuing relationship and obligation with Hawai'i residents. U.S.C.A. Const.Amends. 5, 14.

Lung v. Yachts Intern., Ltd., 980 F.Supp. 1362.

D.Hawai'i 1989. If action brought against state alleging violations of due process rights in state criminal prosecution was construed as appeal from state court judgment, it was required to be dismissed for lack of subject matter jurisdiction; only United States Supreme Court is empowered to review state court judgments. 28 U.S.C.A. § 1257; U.S.C.A. Const.Amend. 14.

Au v. State of Hawaii, 735 F.Supp. 963, affirmed 899 F.2d 1224.

N.D.Ill. 1996. One-year restriction on suit under Miller Act constitutes statute of limitations rather than element of claim itself, and, thus, failure to meet that timetable cannot provide basis for motion to dismiss for lack of subject matter jurisdiction. Miller Act, § 2(b), 40 U.S.C.A. § 270b(b); Fed.Rules Civ.Proc.Rule 12(b)(1), 28 U.S.C.A.

U.S. ex rel. Automatic Elevator Co., Inc. v. Lori Const., 912 F.Supp. 398.

N.D.Ill. 1995. Plaintiff's inability to identify anything but John Doe defendants to federal claim did not require dismissal for lack of subject matter jurisdiction. 42 U.S.C.A. § 1983.

Aviles v. Village of Bedford Park, 160 F.R.D. 565.

N.D.Ill. 1994. Employer's motion to dismiss state statutory workers' compensation claim should have been raised prior to answering plaintiff employee's complaint alleging federal and state claims, and thus inclusion of motion to dismiss in summary judgment motion was disfavored, but court would nonetheless dismiss claim for want of jurisdiction, since employee could not state claim of retaliatory discharge under Illinois workers' compensation statute, and, in any event, employee did not respond to employer's argument for dismissal of statutory claim. S.H.A. 820 ILCS 305/4(h).

Flasza v. TNT Holland Motor Exp., Inc., 159 F.R.D. 672.

N.D.Ill. 1993. Ripeness being jurisdictional issue, court was free and bound to test ripeness of all counts of complaint regardless of breadth of defendants' motion to dismiss on ripeness grounds.

Kerr-McGee Chemical Corp. v. Edgar, 837 F.Supp. 927.

N.D.Ill. 1992. Stay rather than dismissal is proper mechanism for district court to apply when deferring to parallel state court proceeding under *Colorado River* doctrine.

Home Federal Bank For Sav. v. Gussin, 783 F.Supp. 363.

N.D.Ill. 1986. Defense that claim is barred by sovereign immunity may be raised by motion under Rule 12(b)(1), governing dismissal for lack of subject-matter jurisdiction, since district court has no jurisdiction over action against United States unless Government has consented to be sued. Fed.Rules Civ.Proc.Rule 12(b)(1), 28 U.S.C.A.

Gervasio v. U.S., 627 F.Supp. 428.

N.D.Ill. 1985. Claim under Illinois housing laws by applicants for subsidized housing against owners of apartment complexes would be dismissed without prejudice, where applicants' due process and § 1983 claims were dismissed, where state law claim involved issue of first impression, and where state law claim against owners was a pendent party claim not closely related to remaining federal claim against the Secretary of Housing and Urban Development. 42 U.S.C.A. § 1983; United States Housing Act of 1937, § 8, as amended, 42 U.S.C.A. § 1437f.

Price v. Pierce, 615 F.Supp. 173, affirmed 823 F.2d 1114, certiorari denied 108 S.Ct. 1222, 485 U.S. 960, 99 L.Ed.2d 422.

N.D.Ill. 1979. Taxpayers' claim that the section of the Internal Revenue Code which provides means whereby a person may challenge an Internal Revenue Service examination or investigation as improper creates a cause of action for damages for its violation was not wholly insubstantial and frivolous and, therefore, complaint wherein taxpayers alleged that IRS employees had violated their constitutional rights by intentionally and maliciously conducting tax investigations prohibited by the section could not be dismissed for want of subject matter jurisdiction. 26 U.S.C.A.(I.R.C. 1954) § 7605(b).

Dema v. Feddor, 470 F.Supp. 152, affirmed Tabcor Sales Clearing, Inc. v. Dept. of the Treasury, 661 F.2d 937, certiorari denied 102 S.Ct. 1433, 455 U.S. 941, 71 L.Ed.2d 652, affirmed 661 F.2d 937, certiorari denied 102 S.Ct. 1433, 455 U.S. 941, 71 L.Ed.2d 652, affirmed 661 F.2d 937, certiorari denied 102 S.Ct. 1433, 455 U.S. 941, 71 L.Ed.2d 652.

N.D.Ill. 1978. Plummer v. Chicago Journeyman Plumbers' Local Union No. 130, U. A.,

452 F.Supp. 1127, reversed Eggleston v. Chicago Journeymen Plumbers' Local Union No. 130, U. A., 657 F.2d 890, certiorari denied Joint Apprenticeship Committee Local No. 130, U.A. v. Eggleston, 102 S.Ct. 1710, 455 U.S. 1017, 72 L.Ed.2d 134, certiorari denied Plumbing Contractors Ass'n of Chicago & Cook County v. Plummer, 102 S.Ct. 1710, 455 U.S. 1017, 72 L.Ed.2d 134, certiorari denied 102 S.Ct. 1710, 455 U.S. 1017, 72 L.Ed.2d 134.

S.D.Ind. 1995. Disabled employee's ADA claims that employer and union had to agree to his placement in position over more senior nondisabled employee as reasonable accommodation for his disability, and that union should not have been permitted to rescind its initial agreement to employee's special placement had to be dismissed for lack of subject matter jurisdiction, as they were preempted by RLA. Railway Labor Act, § 1 et seq., 45 U.S.C.A. § 151 et seq.

> Eckles v. Consolidated Rail Corp., 890 F.Supp. 1391, affirmed 94 F.3d 1041, certiorari denied 117 S.Ct. 1318, 137 L.Ed.2d 480.

N.D.Iowa 1995. Motion to dismiss § 1983 claim brought by class of social security disability claimants presented a facial challenge to subject matter jurisdiction, not factual challenge, and, thus, complaint would be dismissed only if it appeared beyond doubt that class of claimants could prove no set of facts in support of § 1983 claim which would entitle class to relief; state agency charged with making disability determination challenged subject matter jurisdiction entirely on ground that class could not pursue its claims under § 1983 and, thus, no adjudication of facts would be necessary. 42 U.S.C.A. § 1983; Fed.Rules Civ.Proc.Rule 12(b)(1), 28 U.S.C.A.

> Laird v. Ramirez, 884 F.Supp. 1265, on reconsideration 982 F.Supp. 1345.

N.D.Iowa 1995. Although district court could dismiss for failure to plead federal question jurisdiction employee's § 1983 claim that employer deprived her of "a right protected by the Constitution or laws of the United States," court would, in interest of judicial economy and in light of investment of resources by parties, construe complaint as inartful attempt to assert plausible federal claims through § 1983 violation of federal constitutional rights to due process and equal protection under Fourteenth Amendment, or plausible claim under ADEA. U.S.C.A. Const.Amend. 14; Age Discrimination in Employment Act of 1967, § 2 et seq., as amended, 29 U.S.C.A. § 621 et seq.; 42 U.S.C.A. § 1983.

> Mummelthie v. City of Mason City, Ia., 873 F.Supp. 1293, affirmed 78 F.3d 589.

N.D.Iowa 1994. Parties could not waive defect in subject-matter jurisdiction or invoke federal jurisdiction simply by consent, and thus dismissal for race discrimination plaintiff's failure to plead federal jurisdiction was justified even though parties proceeded throughout case on assumption that federal question case had been presented for race discrimination, and had argued case as though it were one for violation of Title VII. 28 U.S.C.A. § 1331; 42 U.S.C.A. § 1981; Civil Rights Act of 1964, § 701, 42 U.S.C.A. § 2000e.

> Thomas v. St. Luke's Health Systems, Inc., 869 F.Supp. 1413, affirmed 61 F.3d 908.

N.D.Iowa 1994. Tribe made only a facial challenge to plaintiff's assertion of diversity jurisdiction, even though it argued in motion to dismiss that plaintiff erroneously assumed that tribe was citizen of Nebraska, where tribe did not present evidence or ask court for evidentiary hearing to consider evidence that it was not citizen of Nebraska, but rested on plaintiff's obligation to show that subject matter jurisdiction existed, challenging adequacy of plaintiff's allegations of diversity; therefore, general rule was applicable that complaint should not be dismissed unless it appears beyond doubt that plaintiff can prove no set of facts in support of his claim which would entitle him to relief. 28 U.S.C.A. § 1332.

> Veeder v. Omaha Tribe of Nebraska, 864 F.Supp. 889.

N.D.Iowa 1987. Interests of justice mandated transfer, rather than dismissal, of action brought against commodities broker where broker was not doing business in Iowa and where customer was never apprised that he would not be able to sue in Iowa if there was a controversy. Commodity Exchange Act, § 1 et seq., 7 U.S.C.A. § 1 et seq.; 28 U.S.C.A. §§ 1391(b, c), 1406(a).

> Hemann v. Murlas Commodities, Inc., 666 F.Supp. 1299.

D.Kan. 1996. For time being, court would not dismiss guaranty action against guarantor-corporation's officer, though officer had no personal contact with forum state, and officer's signature on guaranty was located beneath corporation's name and word "By:" was located to left of name where guaranty contained Kansas forum selection clause, and there was no explicit statement that officer was signing as corporate officer and no corporate title listed in connection with signature. U.S.C.A. Const. Amend. 5.

> Raytheon Aircraft Credit Corp. v. Pal Air Intern., Inc., 923 F.Supp. 1408.

E.D.La. 1991. Unlike rule governing dismissals for failure to state cause of action, rule governing dismissal for failure to establish jurisdiction can attack substance of complaint's jur-

isdictional allegations despite their formal sufficiency, and in so doing rely on affidavits or any
other evidence properly before court. Fed.
Rules Civ.Proc.Rule 12(b)(1, 6), 28 U.S.C.A.

In re Complaint For Exoneration From or
Limitation of Liability of Shell Oil Co.
and Shell Offshore Inc. as Owners and/or
Owners Pro Hac Vice of M/V EB II, 780
F.Supp. 1086.

W.D.La. 1995. To extent that United
States is immune from suit, federal district
courts do not have subject matter jurisdiction to
decide those cases, and dismissal for lack of
jurisdiction is then appropriate, but, if general
sovereign immunity rule has been specifically
waived by Congress, district court may have
jurisdiction. Fed.Rules Civ.Proc.Rule 12(b)(1),
28 U.S.C.A.

Woods v. U.S., 909 F.Supp. 437, affirmed
84 F.3d 432.

D.Md. 1994. Complaint alleging that Drug
Enforcement Administration (DEA) was engaging in stalking and harassment activities against
plaintiff was so attenuated and unsubstantial as
to be absolutely devoid of merit, such that
district court did not have subject matter jurisdiction, even though plaintiff's prose was lucid
and he was cognizant that allegations might
seem "fantastic and paranoid"; allegations included claims that DEA had recruited "thousands" of individuals to walk by or near plaintiff
uttering stock phrases such as "can't win" and
"I know" and using as props newspapers and
magazines with suggestive headlines or print,
book covers, clothing items with printed material and vehicles with slogans or meaningful license plates or bumper stickers. Fed.Rules
Civ.Proc.Rule 12(b)(1), 28 U.S.C.A.

O'Connor v. U.S., 159 F.R.D. 22, affirmed
54 F.3d 773.

D.Md. 1983. Vaughns v. Board of Educ. of
Prince George's County, 574 F.Supp. 1280, affirmed in part, reversed in part 758 F.2d 983.

D.Md. 1971. Henderson v. Eastern
Freight Ways, Inc., 330 F.Supp. 1287, reversed
460 F.2d 258, certiorari denied 93 S.Ct. 976,
410 U.S. 912, 35 L.Ed.2d 275.

D.Mass. 1993. United States district
courts have subject matter jurisdiction to consider allegations that state statute or rule, which
may have been applied by state court, is generally unconstitutional but, where federal plaintiffs challenge state court decisions relating to
particular case, district court must dismiss for
lack of subject matter jurisdiction.

South Boston Allied War Veterans Council
v. Zobel, 830 F.Supp. 643.

E.D.Mich. 1982. Holliday v. Xerox Corp.,
555 F.Supp. 51, affirmed 732 F.2d 548, certio-

rari denied 105 S.Ct. 294, 469 U.S. 917, 83
L.Ed.2d 229.

W.D.Mich. 1994. Motion to dismiss action
under Federal Tort Claims Act (FTCA) for lack
of subject matter jurisdiction must be denied if
genuine issue of material fact exists with respect
to whether exception to FTCA's general waiver
of immunity is applicable. 28 U.S.C.A.
§ 2680(a); Fed.Rules Civ.Proc.Rule 12(b)(1), 28
U.S.C.A.

Angle by Angle v. U.S., 931 F.Supp. 1386,
affirmed 89 F.3d 832.

W.D.Mich. 1991. Motion to dismiss for
lack of subject matter jurisdiction must be denied should pleader allege facts from which
jurisdiction may be inferred. Fed.Rules Civ.
Proc.Rule 12(b)(1), 28 U.S.C.A.

Cooper Industries, Inc. v. U.S. E.P.A., 775
F.Supp. 1027.

If there are genuine issues of material fact
at issue, decision must be made on those factual
questions before district court decides motion to
dismiss for lack of subject matter jurisdiction.
Fed.Rules Civ.Proc.Rule 12(b)(1), 28 U.S.C.A.

Cooper Industries, Inc. v. U.S. E.P.A., 775
F.Supp. 1027.

W.D.Mich. 1987. Federal claim should be
dismissed for lack of subject matter jurisdiction
only when it is clearly immaterial and brought
only for the purpose of obtaining jurisdiction.
28 U.S.C.A. § 1331; Fed.Rules Civ.Proc.Rules
12(b)(1, 6), 56, 56(a), 28 U.S.C.A.

Doe v. Keane, 658 F.Supp. 216.

D.Minn. 1990. Claims of plaintiff seeking
preliminary injunctive relief were wholly frivolous and malicious and, thus, complaint would
be dismissed for lack of subject matter jurisdiction. Fed.Rules Civ.Proc.Rule 12(h)(3), 28
U.S.C.A.

Sassower v. Dosal, 744 F.Supp. 908, affirmed 930 F.2d 583, rehearing denied.

D.Minn. 1986. Federal court would dismiss claims by debtor farmers who sought to
assert a private cause of action under the Farm
Credit Act [12 U.S.C.A. §§ 2001–2260] or its
regulations for failure to state a claim upon
which relief could be granted, rather than for
lack of subject-matter jurisdiction, where court
determined private cause of action should not
be implied under the Act, but farmers' federal
claims were not frivolous as there had been no
controlling precedent on the issue at time action
was brought.

Spring Water Dairy, Inc. v. Federal Intermediate Credit Bank of St. Paul, 625
F.Supp. 713.

D.Minn. 1985. Following grant of furniture manufacturer's motion for summary judgment with respect to distributor's antitrust

claims, dismissal of distributor's state law claims and manufacturer's counterclaims without prejudice, rather than proceeding to trial on pendent state claims, was appropriate.

Pink Supply Corp. v. Hiebert, Inc., 612 F.Supp. 1334, affirmed 788 F.2d 1313.

N.D.Miss. 1996. Judicial economy justified decision to retain uninsured motorist (UM) carrier's third-party action against alleged tortfeasor for equitable indemnification, even though cause of action had not accrued and thus there was no case or controversy; dismissing claim before carrier's liability to insured was determined would be blatant waste of judicial resources and would not facilitate resolution of controversy.

Coleman v. American Mfrs. Mut. Ins. Co., 930 F.Supp. 255.

D.Neb. 1997. Court would dismiss for lack of subject matter jurisdiction, without leave to amend or further notice, complaint that was patently frivolous and malicious, particularly as plaintiff had not sought to cure subject matter jurisdiction defect despite being placed on notice; complaint set forth no plausible basis of subject matter jurisdiction, absurdly invoking "flag" jurisdiction, it failed to give any factual basis for suit, and legal theories were unintelligible, particularly because none were explained or related to facts. Fed.Rules Civ.Proc.Rule 12(h)(3), 28 U.S.C.A.

Slangal v. Cassel, 962 F.Supp. 1214.

Any complaint predicated in whole or in part upon allegation that jurisdiction is based upon "the American Free Flag of Peace TITLE 4 U.S.C. 1 of the United States of America," or similar allegations, is frivolous, malicious and intended to harass, and any such "flag" suit will be dismissed sua sponte without notice for lack of subject matter jurisdiction.

Slangal v. Cassel, 962 F.Supp. 1214.

D.N.J. 1992. If subject matter jurisdiction is lacking, federal court must dismiss action regardless of stage of litigation. 28 U.S.C.A. § 1331; Fed.Rules Civ.Proc.Rule 12(h)(3), 28 U.S.C.A.

TM Marketing, Inc. v. Art & Antiques Associates, L.P., 803 F.Supp. 994.

D.N.J. 1987. Class action on behalf of shareholders, and shareholders' derivative action alleging securities fraud and breach of fiduciary duty by directors was rendered moot by stock purchase and tender offer made by a third party, requiring dismissal of the action with prejudice. Fed.Rules Civ.Proc.Rule 41(a)(2), 28 U.S.C.A.

Shields v. Murphy, 116 F.R.D. 600.

D.N.M. 1987. Dismissal of products liability action over which court lacked in personam jurisdiction for lack of sufficient "minimum contacts" rather than transfer, was appropriate; although patient demonstrated good-faith belief that court had in personam jurisdiction over defendants, mistake was not reasonable mistake as to some "elusive fact." 28 U.S.C.A. § 1404(a); Fed.Rules Civ.Proc.Rule 12(b)(2), 28 U.S.C.A.

Beh v. Ostergard, 657 F.Supp. 173.

E.D.N.Y. 1997. Plaintiffs in tort action involving dispute over liens on property located in Washington state failed to make prima facie showing that they suffered injury in New York, as required to establish personal jurisdiction in diversity case brought under New York's long-arm statute, and so dismissal of action was required; critical events in dispute occurred in Washington, and indirect financial consequences potentially suffered by plaintiffs in New York as result of their lower lien status were merely result of two plaintiffs' residency there and were insufficient to confer jurisdiction. Fed.Rules Civ.Proc.Rule 12(b)(2), 28 U.S.C.A.; N.Y.McKinney's CPLR 302(a), par. 3(ii).

Kowalski-Schmidt v. CLS Mortg., Inc., 981 F.Supp. 105.

E.D.N.Y. 1995. Upon determining that it lacked personal jurisdiction over defendant in defamation action, federal court in New York would dismiss action, rather than transfer it to federal court in Virginia; transfer would frustrate interest of justice, as plaintiff created false impression with court that plaintiff's purchase of Virginia property (which gave rise to defamation claim) came about as result of solicitation in New York by defendant and her agents, three out of four legal proceedings plaintiff had filed (all of which affected defendant) had been dismissed, and one had been voluntarily withdrawn, suggesting that plaintiff was intentionally using courts to harass 81–year-old defendant. 28 U.S.C.A. § 1404(a).

Williams v. Nathan, 897 F.Supp. 72, affirmed 101 F.3d 687.

E.D.N.Y. 1992. When parties present several grounds for dismissal, including lack of subject-matter jurisdiction, court must first examine grounds that allege lack of subject-matter jurisdiction because if complaint is dismissed on that basis, accompanying defenses and objections become moot. Fed.Rules Civ.Proc.Rule 12(b)(1), 28 U.S.C.A.

Complaint of Dickenson, 780 F.Supp. 974.

E.D.N.Y. 1990. If, in resolving issues presented, federal court becomes embroiled in factual disputes concerning custody and visitation matters, action must be dismissed.

Neustein v. Orbach, 732 F.Supp. 333.

Where constitutional claims arising out of domestic relations dispute are frivolous, action must be dismissed as an abortive attempt to involve federal courts in domestic matters best left to the states.

Neustein v. Orbach, 732 F.Supp. 333.

E.D.N.Y. 1986. In action by prospective tenant under the Civil Rights Act, civil rights statutes, the Fair Housing Act, and New York real property law based on failure to rent to dark-skinned Puerto Rican woman, counterclaims by apartment owners alleging libel, malicious abuse of process, and demand for punitive and exemplary damages based on prospective tenant's filing of complaint before city human rights commission and filing of action were permissive, raising issues which were not relevant to the main claim, and thus, claims had to be dismissed for lack of subject-matter jurisdiction where they did not present basis for jurisdiction independent of main action. Civil Rights Act of 1968, § 801 et seq., 42 U.S.C.A. § 3601 et seq.; 42 U.S.C.A. §§ 1981, 1982; Fed.Rules Civ.Proc.Rules 12(b)(1), 13, 28 U.S.C.A.; N.Y.McKinney's Real Property Law § 236.

Quinones v. Nescie, 110 F.R.D. 346.

E.D.N.Y. 1985. Regardless of whether utility's complaint seeking injunction to require county and its executive to fulfill their duty to exercise their governmental functions fairly by taking all reasonable steps necessary to assist utility in emergency planning for nuclear power facility stated civil rights cause of action on which utility could actually recover, claim alleged was not so patently without merit, wholly insubstantial or essentially frivolous as to warrant dismissal for lack of jurisdiction. 28 U.S.C.A. § 1331; 42 U.S.C.A. § 1983; U.S.C.A. Const.Amends. 5, 14.

Citizens for an Orderly Energy Policy, Inc. v. Suffolk County, 604 F.Supp. 1084.

N.D.N.Y. 1995. Absent plaintiff's filing of complaint with Equal Employment Opportunity Commission (EEOC) and his receipt of right to sue letter, federal district court lacked subject matter jurisdiction to entertain plaintiff's ADA claim and thus, court would dismiss ADA claim with prejudice unless time remained in which plaintiff could file claim with EEOC and receive right to sue letter; only if these events occurred, could plaintiff return to federal court and continue to prosecute suit. Americans with Disabilities Act of 1990, § 2 et seq., 42 U.S.C.A. § 12101 et seq.

Redlich v. Albany Law School of Union University, 899 F.Supp. 100.

N.D.N.Y. 1993. Plaintiff's allegations that stock sale agreement was negotiated and signed in New York constituted prima facie showing of personal jurisdiction under New York law, notwithstanding defendants' controverting allegation that contract was signed in Massachusetts,

so as to defeat defendants' pretrial motion to dismiss for lack of personal jurisdiction.

Gilbert v. Wilson, 821 F.Supp. 857.

N.D.N.Y. 1992. "Substantiality doctrine" requires that district court dismiss complaints to seek recovery under the Constitution or laws of the United States if alleged federal claim either clearly appears to be immaterial and solely made for purpose of obtaining jurisdiction or where such claim is wholly unsubstantial and frivolous. 28 U.S.C.A. § 1331.

Hotel Syracuse, Inc. v. Young, 805 F.Supp. 1073.

S.D.N.Y. 1996. Damage claims of lender which financed buyers' purchase of businesses by taking debt and equity in buyers, allegedly suffered due to sellers' misrepresentation of value of the entities, were premature, warranting dismissal without prejudice, where none of the notes at issue was due for several years and buyers may have been able to satisfy the notes when they fell due if arbitration proceedings against sellers resulted in an award.

Jackson Nat. Life Ins. Co. v. Ligator, 949 F.Supp. 200.

S.D.N.Y. 1996. Declaratory plaintiff's action against out-of-state patentee would not be dismissed for lack of personal jurisdiction despite questionable nature of court's jurisdiction, where parties had not yet frontally addressed merits of plaintiff's claims of noninfringement of patents and trade dress rights, false advertising, tortious interference with business relations, commercial disparagement, and prima facie tort.

Riviera Trading Corp. v. Oakley, Inc., 944 F.Supp. 1150.

S.D.N.Y. 1996. Federal employer's motion to dismiss federal employee's Title VII claim for alleged failure to exhaust administrative remedies within allotted time was a motion to dismiss for lack of subject matter jurisdiction. Civil Rights Act of 1964, § 701 et seq., as amended, 42 U.S.C.A. § 2000e et seq.; Fed. Rules Civ.Proc.Rule 12(b)(1), 28 U.S.C.A.

Dillard v. Runyon, 928 F.Supp. 1316, affirmed 108 F.3d 1369.

S.D.N.Y. 1995. Pendent state law claims were dismissed without prejudice for lack of subject matter jurisdiction where defendant was granted summary judgment on federal claims.

Osipova v. Dinkins, 907 F.Supp. 94.

S.D.N.Y. 1995. Where federal subject matter jurisdiction is based on ERISA, but evidence failed to establish existence of ERISA plan, claim must be dismissed for lack of subject matter jurisdiction. Employee Retirement Income Security Act of 1974, § 2 et seq., 29 U.S.C.A. § 1001 et seq.

> Fludgate v. Management Technologies, Inc., 885 F.Supp. 645.

S.D.N.Y. 1994. District Court lacked subject matter jurisdiction to review merits of Internal Revenue Service's (IRS) administrative forfeiture of owners' automobile except for claims based on procedural deficiency in administrative process and, thus, automobile owners' claims that forfeiture violated owners' rights under just compensation clause of Fifth Amendment, denied owners due process, constituted conversion under Federal Tort Claims Act (FTCA), and constituted excessive fine under Eight Amendment would be dismissed for lack of subject matter jurisdiction. U.S.C.A. Const. Amends. 5, 8; 28 U.S.C.A. § 2671 et seq.

> Lopes v. U.S., 862 F.Supp. 1178.

S.D.N.Y. 1994. Former employee chose not to appeal administrative dismissal of complaint filed with New York State Division of Human Rights, which dismissed complaint for lack of jurisdiction over Federal Reserve Bank, not for administrative convenience, and, thus, subsequent dismissal of federal court complaint did not violate due process. N.Y.McKinney's Executive Law § 297, subd. 9; U.S.C.A. Const. Amends. 5, 14.

> Moodie v. Federal Reserve Bank of New York, 861 F.Supp. 10, affirmed 58 F.3d 879.

S.D.N.Y. 1992. In determining whether cause of action should be stayed or dismissed pending disposition of related action, general rule is that suit which was filed first should have priority, absent showing of balance of convenience in favor of second action.

> Capitol Records, Inc. v. Optical Recording Corp., 810 F.Supp. 1350.

S.D.N.Y. 1992. When faced with a challenge to court's subject matter jurisdiction in context of a multipronged motion, court should consider the challenge to subject matter jurisdiction first since if it must dismiss the complaint for lack of subject matter jurisdiction, the accompanying defenses and objections become moot and do not need to be determined. Fed. Rules Civ.Proc.Rule 12(b)(1), 28 U.S.C.A.

> Koal Industries Corp. v. Asland, S.A., 808 F.Supp. 1143.

S.D.N.Y. 1992. To survive motion to dismiss for lack of subject matter jurisdiction, complaint of note holders against federally chartered savings bank's directors for alleged violation of fiduciary duties based on failure to make payments due on notes had to state cause of action actually arising under Constitution, laws or treaties of the United States. Fed.Rules Civ.Proc.Rule 12(b)(1), 28 U.S.C.A.; 28 U.S.C.A. § 1331.

> Curiale v. Reissman, 798 F.Supp. 141.

S.D.N.Y. 1992. Mootness of deaf inmate's personal constitutional claims for failure to accommodate her hearing impairment did not require dismissal of class action; other hearing-impaired inmates had sought to intervene, indicating strong likelihood that some other named plaintiff existed who would be able to represent putative class adequately. 42 U.S.C.A. § 1983; Fed.Rules Civ.Proc.Rules 23, 24(b)(2), 28 U.S.C.A.

> Clarkson v. Coughlin, 783 F.Supp. 789.

Fact that female inmate's individual claims had been dismissed as moot in civil rights action did not require dismissal from suit of superintendent of facility in which inmate had been incarcerated where lawsuit had been allowed to continue as class action; although subclass of female hearing-impaired inmates had not yet been certified, class that inmate sought to represent included deaf or hearing-impaired inmates at facility in which she had been incarcerated. 42 U.S.C.A. § 1983; Fed. Rules Civ.Proc.Rule 23(b), 28 U.S.C.A.

> Clarkson v. Coughlin, 783 F.Supp. 789.

S.D.N.Y. 1991. Conditional dismissal or stay is ordinarily appropriate response to violation of New York statute providing that foreign corporation doing business in state shall not maintain any action until it has been authorized to do business in state. N.Y.McKinney's Business Corporation Law § 1312.

> Caspian Investments, Ltd. v. Vicom Holdings, Ltd., 770 F.Supp. 880.

Relevant factors in determining whether to grant stay or dismissal because of litigation in overseas forum include similarity of parties and issues involved, promotion of judicial efficiency, adequacy of relief available in alternative forum, considerations of fairness to all parties and possible prejudice to any of them, and temporal sequence of filing for each action.

> Caspian Investments, Ltd. v. Vicom Holdings, Ltd., 770 F.Supp. 880.

Parties and claims need not be identical in order for one action to be stayed or dismissed in deference to earlier action.

> Caspian Investments, Ltd. v. Vicom Holdings, Ltd., 770 F.Supp. 880.

Action brought by British corporation against Georgia subsidiary of Irish corporation for breach of loan agreement would be dismissed in deference to previously commenced action pending in Ireland against the parent; the actions were virtually identical and involved interpretation of same loan agreements, and parent had agreed to submit to jurisdiction of

Irish court and to be bound by any determination by that court.

> Caspian Investments, Ltd. v. Vicom Holdings, Ltd., 770 F.Supp. 880.

S.D.N.Y. 1991. Motion to dismiss securities fraud complaint was properly one to dismiss for failure to state claim rather than for lack of subject matter jurisdiction absent contention that claims were frivolous and interposed to manufacturer jurisdiction. Fed.Rules Civ.Proc.Rule 12(b)(1, 6), 28 U.S.C.A.

> National Bank of Yugoslavia v. Drexel Burnham Lambert, Inc., 768 F.Supp. 1010.

S.D.N.Y. 1990. Federal securities fraud action would not be dismissed for lack of subject matter jurisdiction on basis that note and refinanced note were not "securities"; defendant had sought dismissal for failure to state a claim and for want of subject matter jurisdiction, and resolution by court of whether the Securities Exchange Act of 1934 was violated to the extent of giving rise to a private action for damages would be regarded as an adjudication on merits, binding in any subsequent litigation between parties, as contrasted with dismissal for want of subject matter jurisdiction, which would have no preclusive effect. Fed.Rules Civ.Proc.Rule 12(b)(1, 6), 28 U.S.C.A.; Securities Exchange Act of 1934, §§ 3(a)(10), 10(b), 15 U.S.C.A. §§ 78c(a)(10), 78j(b).

> Singer v. Livoti, 741 F.Supp. 1040.

S.D.N.Y. 1990. Failure of age discrimination plaintiff to wait 60 days after filing charge with Equal Employment Opportunity Commission (EEOC) before commencing civil action did not require dismissal of action based on lack of subject matter jurisdiction since dismissal for failure to comply with waiting period would have been "hypertechnical"; instead, court would suspend claims until 60-day period had expired. Age Discrimination in Employment Act of 1967, §§ 7(d), 14(b), 29 U.S.C.A. §§ 626(d), 633(b).

> Goulding v. Institute of Elec. & Electronics Engineers, Inc., 739 F.Supp. 934.

S.D.N.Y. 1988. Federal district court's lack of in personam jurisdiction under New York's long arm statute did not require dismissal of personal injury action brought against owner of recreational theme park operated in Florida as statute provided transfer of action commenced in wrong judicial district to proper district (middle district of Florida) in interest of justice. 28 U.S.C.A. § 1406(a); N.Y.McKinney's CPLR 301.

> Grill v. Walt Disney Co., 683 F.Supp. 66.

S.D.N.Y. 1988. Action brought in federal district court in New York against South Dakota corporation by former law firm would not be dismissed for lack of personal jurisdiction merely because prior action brought by corporation against law firm in South Dakota federal court had been dismissed for lack of personal jurisdiction.

> Pennie & Edmonds v. Austad Co., 681 F.Supp. 1074.

S.D.N.Y. 1985. Since employer failed to show any independent basis of federal jurisdiction for its permissive counterclaims for torts of conversion, trespass, unfair competition, breach of fiduciary duty, and tortious interference with business contracts and relationships, in employee's EEOC action, counterclaims had to be dismissed. Fed.Rules Civ.Proc.Rule 13(b), 28 U.S.C.A.

> Spencer v. Banco Real, S.A., 623 F.Supp. 1008.

S.D.N.Y. 1985. To extent that complaint filed against special prosecutor, assistant special prosecutor, and investigator implicitly alleged common-law torts or a state law wrongful death action in connection with alleged murder of decedent while he was serving as an informant for special prosecutor, those claims were subject to dismissal, in that diversity jurisdiction was not alleged and pendent jurisdiction was insufficient because underlying federal claim had been dismissed. 28 U.S.C.A. § 1332.

> Estate of Masselli by Masselli v. Silverman, 606 F.Supp. 341.

E.D.N.C. 1996. Trial court would not dismiss complaint brought by Securities and Exchange Commission (SEC) alleging securities fraud, based on claim that investment vehicle in question was not a "security" as required for there to be federal subject matter jurisdiction; appropriate procedure was to accept jurisdiction and deal with objection as attack on merits of SEC's case. Fed.Rules Civ.Proc.Rule 12(b)(1, 6), 28 U.S.C.A.

> S.E.C. v. Pinckney, 923 F.Supp. 76.

W.D.N.C. 1991. Party asserting existence of personal jurisdiction need only make prima facie showing that jurisdiction exists, in order to survive motion to dismiss for lack of jurisdiction in case in which trial court decides motion without evidentiary hearing based solely on written submissions of parties. Fed.Rules Civ. Proc.Rule 12(b)(2), 28 U.S.C.A.

> Capstar Corp. v. Pristine Industries, Inc., 768 F.Supp. 518.

Mere allegations of in personam jurisdiction are insufficient for party to make prima facie showing sufficient to survive motion to dismiss for lack of jurisdiction over person. Fed.Rules Civ.Proc.Rule 12(b)(2), 28 U.S.C.A.

> Capstar Corp. v. Pristine Industries, Inc., 768 F.Supp. 518.

S.D.Ohio 1995. Dismissal without prejudice, rather than stay, was more appropriate treatment for state law claims which could not be heard in federal court until Ohio Court of Claims exercised its exclusive jurisdiction to determine immunity of state officer from suit in his or her individual capacity. Ohio R.C. § 2743.02(F).

     Gravely v. Madden, 964 F.Supp. 260.

S.D.Ohio 1986. Issue of appropriate remedies for age discrimination under Ohio law were still arguable and better left to Ohio courts; therefore, age discrimination claims brought under Ohio law on theory of pendent jurisdiction would be dismissed.

     Foltzer v. Lodge & Shipley Co., 636 F.Supp. 843.

S.D.Ohio 1983. Where plaintiff alleged operative facts showing grounds of federal jurisdiction under statute governing deprivation of civil rights, plaintiff's failure to cite jurisdictional statute was insufficient ground to dismiss complaint for lack of subject matter jurisdiction. 42 U.S.C.A. § 1983; 28 U.S.C. (1976 Ed.) § 1343(3).

     Haines v. General Motors Corp., 603 F.Supp. 471.

N.D.Okl. 1991. Complex issues of fact and law regarding involvement of Panamanian corporation and its Delaware subsidiary in developing and marketing allegedly infringing device, including alter ego theory, barred dismissal of patent infringement action against them on grounds that they were beyond reach of Oklahoma's long-arm statute. 12 O.S.1981, § 1701.03(a)(4); Fed.Rules Civ.Proc.Rule 12(b)(2, 3, 6), 28 U.S.C.A.

     Immuno Mycologics, Inc. v. Syntex Corp., 767 F.Supp. 1112.

D.Or. 1995. Insurance agent's third party complaint against nonresident defendant, which was a holding company that did not operate as insurance broker, had to be dismissed for lack of personal jurisdiction where insurance agent presented no evidence that holding company participated in insurance placement transaction at issue and, thus, holding company could not have purposefully availed itself privilege of conducting activities in forum state of Oregon.

     Albany Ins. Co. v. Rose-Tillmann, Inc., 883 F.Supp. 1459.

Insurance agent's third party complaint against nonresident defendant, which was wholesale insurance broker, had to be dismissed for lack of personal jurisdiction where wholesale insurance broker did not purposefully avail itself of privilege of conducting business in forum state of Oregon and did not have minimum contacts with Oregon necessary to sustain personal jurisdiction; wholesale insurance broker

dealt only with insurance agent in Illinois and another agent in California, and had no contact with Oregon whatsoever.

     Albany Ins. Co. v. Rose-Tillmann, Inc., 883 F.Supp. 1459.

E.D.Pa. 1995. As discretionary function exception to government liability, under Federal Tort Claims Act, is limitation on waiver of sovereign immunity, claims falling within exception must be dismissed for lack of subject matter jurisdiction. 28 U.S.C.A. § 2680(a); Fed.Rules Civ.Proc.Rule 12(b)(1), 28 U.S.C.A.

     Garcia v. U.S., 896 F.Supp. 467.

E.D.Pa. 1993. Defendant's state law counterclaim for malicious use of process arose from instant legal proceeding, not from defendant's testimony in another proceeding, which gave rise to plaintiff's cause of action, and, thus, counterclaim was permissive and had to be dismissed for lack of independent jurisdictional basis; both plaintiff and defendant appeared to be citizens of Pennsylvania. 28 U.S.C.A. § 1332; Fed.Rules Civ.Proc.Rule 13(b), 28 U.S.C.A.

     Reitz v. Dieter, 840 F.Supp. 353.

E.D.Pa. 1993. Case is properly dismissed for lack of subject matter jurisdiction where alleged claim under Constitution clearly appears to be immaterial and made solely for purpose of obtaining jurisdiction or where such claim is wholly insubstantial and frivolous. Fed.Rules Civ.Proc.Rule 12(b)(1), 28 U.S.C.A.

     Glendon Energy Co. v. Borough of Glendon, 836 F.Supp. 1109, reconsideration denied.

Dismissal for lack of subject matter jurisdiction is proper where right claimed has been foreclosed by prior decisions of Court of Appeals. Fed.Rules Civ.Proc.Rule 12(b)(1), 28 U.S.C.A.

     Glendon Energy Co. v. Borough of Glendon, 836 F.Supp. 1109, reconsideration denied.

E.D.Pa. 1993. Inasmuch as plaintiffs' federal claims were dismissed, court would dismiss plaintiffs' claims under state law for lack of subject matter jurisdiction without prejudice to plaintiffs to refile them in proper state form, as causes of action were more suitably raised and considered in appropriate state court. 28 U.S.C.A. §§ 1331, 1367.

     Marrazzo v. Bucks County Bank and Trust Co., 814 F.Supp. 437.

E.D.Pa. 1993. At pleading stage, general factual allegations of injury resulting from defendant's conduct may suffice to withstand motion to dismiss based on lack of standing, but standing must affirmatively appear in record and cannot be inferred. U.S.C.A. Const. Art. 3, § 1 et seq.

> Delaware Valley Toxics Coalition v. Kurz-Hastings, Inc., 813 F.Supp. 1132.

E.D.Pa. 1993. Motion to dismiss for lack of subject matter jurisdiction can be granted when claim clearly appears to be material and made solely for purpose of obtaining jurisdiction or is wholly insubstantial and frivolous. Fed.Rules Civ.Proc.Rule 12(b)(1), 28 U.S.C.A.

> Johnson v. U.S., 147 F.R.D. 91.

Motion to dismiss for lack of subject matter jurisdiction is usually considered appropriate vehicle when plaintiff has failed to exhaust administrative remedies that are a prerequisite to suit. Fed.Rules Civ.Proc.Rule 12(b)(1), 28 U.S.C.A.

> Johnson v. U.S., 147 F.R.D. 91.

While court may postpone decision on jurisdictional issue to allow for presentation of evidence on that matter if none has been provided or if that which has been offered is inconclusive, once it finds that no jurisdiction exists, it should grant motion to dismiss for lack of subject matter jurisdiction. Fed.Rules Civ.Proc.Rule 12(b)(1), 28 U.S.C.A.

> Johnson v. U.S., 147 F.R.D. 91.

E.D.Pa. 1992. While federal district court had to abstain from adjudicating plaintiff's § 1983 claim for declaratory relief pending determination of state criminal action against him, court would stay, rather than dismiss, accompanying claims for damages, as such relief was not available in ongoing state criminal proceeding. U.S.C.A. Const.Amend. 4; 42 U.S.C.A. § 1983.

> Nelson v. Howard, 810 F.Supp. 161.

E.D.Pa. 1992. Challenges to jurisdiction based on legal insufficiency of claim are subject to standards of motion to dismiss for failure to state action and dismissal is warranted only if defendant shows that no claim has been stated. Fed.Rules Civ.Proc.Rule 12(b)(6), 28 U.S.C.A.

> Southeastern Pennsylvania Transp. Authority v. Pennsylvania Public Utility Com'n, 802 F.Supp. 1273.

E.D.Pa. 1992. Where motion to dismiss for lack of subject matter jurisdiction is based on claim that plaintiff's claim is not ripe for adjudication, district court may decide ripeness issue without submitting it to jury for factual findings. Fed.Rules Civ.Proc.Rule 12(b)(1), 28 U.S.C.A.

> Warner Cable Communications Inc. v. Borough of Schuylkill Haven, 784 F.Supp. 203.

E.D.Pa. 1990. In considering motion to dismiss for lack of subject matter jurisdiction, district court must use standard for dismissals developed under rule governing dismissal for failure to state a claim. Fed.Rules Civ.Proc. Rule 12(b)(1, 6), 28 U.S.C.A.

> White v. Judicial Inquiry and Review Bd. of Pennsylvania, 744 F.Supp. 658.

E.D.Pa. 1990. On defendant corporation's motion to dismiss complaint for lack of in personam jurisdiction, the plaintiff corporation was required to demonstrate that the defendant had sufficient contacts with the forum state to establish in personam jurisdiction. Fed.Rules Civ.Proc.Rules 12(b)(2), 28 U.S.C.A.

> Mickleburgh Machinery Co., Inc. v. Pacific Economic Development Co., 738 F.Supp. 159.

E.D.Pa. 1987. Dismissal of action, which was commenced in state court prior to effective date of statute which expressly repealed derivative jurisdiction doctrine and which was removed to federal court, is required where state court lacks subject-matter jurisdiction over matter. 28 U.S.C.A. § 1441(e).

> Village Imp. Ass'n of Doylestown, Pa. v. Dow Chemical Co., 655 F.Supp. 311.

Both state and federal courts possess concurrent jurisdiction to entertain civil actions brought pursuant to Racketeer Influenced and Corrupt Organizations Act; therefore, a RICO claim which was commenced in state court and removed to federal court was not subject to dismissal under doctrine of derivative jurisdiction. 18 U.S.C.A. §§ 1961–1968.

> Village Imp. Ass'n of Doylestown, Pa. v. Dow Chemical Co., 655 F.Supp. 311.

E.D.Pa. 1985. General contractor's antitrust complaint against county revealed bare bones series of interstate commerce allegations but, in view of substantive defects in the complaint and fact that amendment would certainly enable general contractor to establish jurisdictional basis, district court would decline to dismiss the case for lack of subject matter jurisdiction for general contractor's failure to sufficiently plead interstate commerce element.

> Skepton v. Bucks County, Pa., 613 F.Supp. 1013.

E.D.Pa. 1984. Defendant's counterclaim for an alleged loan did not arise out of same transaction or occurrence as that asserted by plaintiff, namely, conversion of CATSCANNERS by defendant; therefore, counterclaim was permissive and since independent jurisdictional basis did not exist, claim had to be dismissed for lack of subject-matter jurisdiction.

> Shared Diagnostic Services, Inc. v. Henningsen, 602 F.Supp. 428.

E.D.Pa. 1984. Tunis Bros. Co., Inc. v. Ford Motor Co., 587 F.Supp. 267, reversed 763 F.2d 1482, certiorari granted, vacated 106 S.Ct. 1509, 475 U.S. 1105, 89 L.Ed.2d 909, on remand 823 F.2d 49, certiorari denied 108 S.Ct. 1013, 484 U.S. 1060, 98 L.Ed.2d 979, on remand 696 F.Supp. 1056.

M.D.Pa. 1992. Suit may be dismissed for lack of jurisdiction where claim upon which federal question jurisdiction is based clearly appears to be immaterial and made solely for purpose of obtaining jurisdiction or where such claim is wholly insubstantial and frivolous.

> Pagnotti Enterprises, Inc. v. Beltrami, 787 F.Supp. 440.

Dismissal of suit based upon federal question claim is appropriate when allegations of complaint clearly demonstrate that plaintiff does not have claim.

> Pagnotti Enterprises, Inc. v. Beltrami, 787 F.Supp. 440.

W.D.Pa. 1997. On motion by non-resident defendants to dismiss for lack of personal jurisdiction in action brought in Pennsylvania, district court was required solely to inquire whether exercise of jurisdiction over defendants would be constitutional, where Pennsylvania's long-arm jurisdiction statute authorized courts to exercise jurisdiction to the fullest extent allowed under Federal Constitution. U.S.C.A. Const.Amend. 14; 42 Pa.C.S.A. § 5322(b); Fed. Rules Civ.Proc.Rules 4(e), 12(b)(6), 28 U.S.C.A.

> Penzoil Products Co. v. Colelli & Associates, Inc., 953 F.Supp. 669, reversed 149 F.3d 197.

W.D.Pa. 1994. Plaintiff's securities fraud action against issuer and former executive of issuer would be dismissed sua sponte by district court, as district court was without jurisdiction; both parties were in bankruptcy, and commencement and continuation of the suit was in violation of the automatic stay provision of Bankruptcy Code. Bankr.Code, 11 U.S.C.A. § 362.

> In re Phar-Mor, Inc. Securities Litigation, 900 F.Supp. 777.

D.Puerto Rico 1997. "Likelihood standard" governed task of trial court in ruling on motion to dismiss trade organization for cigarette manufacturers for lack of personal jurisdiction, where categorical jurisdictional determination would have required discovery as to ultimate issue of whether organization committed fraud in the jurisdiction through any public relations efforts.

> Barreras Ruiz v. American Tobacco Co., 977 F.Supp. 545.

D.Puerto Rico 1986. Failure of complaint to allege jurisdictional grounds did not require dismissal since court could exercise its discretion and accept jurisdictional allegations submitted in amended complaint. Fed.Rules Civ. Proc.Rule 8(a)(1), 28 U.S.C.A.

> Del Valle Rivera v. U.S., 626 F.Supp. 347.

D.R.I. 1995. Counterclaim of defendants, a Rhode Island corporation, and individual citizens of Rhode Island and Massachusetts, for breach of partnership agreement, against plaintiffs, a New York and Delaware corporation, would be dismissed for lack of federal subject matter jurisdiction, even though their counterclaim against a non-diverse corporation no longer existed due to merger with New York plaintiff corporation, where the plaintiff corporation's claim was dismissed as an improper attempt to create diversity jurisdiction; no independent basis for jurisdiction over counterclaims existed, and to hear counterclaim while allowing plaintiff's claim to be heard by different court would be inconsistent with efficiency policy behind Rule of Civil Procedure regarding compulsory counterclaims. 28 U.S.C.A. §§ 1332(a), 1359, 1367(a, c); R.I.Gen.Laws 1956, § 7–1.1–69; Fed.Rules Civ.Proc.Rule 13(a), 28 U.S.C.A.

> Toste Farm Corp. v. Hadbury, Inc., 882 F.Supp. 240, affirmed 70 F.3d 640.

D.R.I. 1995. Individual defendants were not entitled to dismissal on grounds that court did not have personal jurisdiction, where defendants conceded court's jurisdiction over corporation, and corporate veil would be pierced because corporation was little more than a shell, with no finances, corporate structure, or formality, and controlled by its owners in such a manner that it would be inequitable to recognize it as a separate legal entity. Fed.Rules Civ.Proc.Rule 12(b)(2), 28 U.S.C.A.

> Scully Signal Co. v. Joyal, 881 F.Supp. 727.

D.R.I. 1994. Jurisdictional challenge based on ripeness of complaint is considered motion to dismiss for lack of subject matter jurisdiction. Fed.Rules Civ.Proc.Rule 12(b)(1), 28 U.S.C.A.

> Ernst & Young v. Depositors Economic Protection Corp., 862 F.Supp. 709, affirmed 45 F.3d 530.

If claim is unripe, federal courts lack subject matter jurisdiction, and complaint must be dismissed rather than stayed.

> Ernst & Young v. Depositors Economic Protection Corp., 862 F.Supp. 709, affirmed 45 F.3d 530.

D.S.C. 1994. Absence of personal jurisdiction, absence of subject matter jurisdiction, and improper venue warranted dismissal of case, rather than transfer, since, because of defects, plaintiff's counsel could have reasonably foreseen that case was not properly filed in South Carolina.

> Jarrett v. State of N.C., 868 F.Supp. 155.

D.S.C. 1989. District court was required to dismiss nontenured, probationary college professor's civil rights action challenging his discharge due to lack of federal question jurisdiction, since professor's constitutional claims were frivolous; there was no evidence that professor's dismissal was due to exercise of his free speech rights under First Amendment, and professor had no property interest in his continued employment. U.S.C.A. Const.Amends. 1, 14; 28 U.S.C.A. § 1343(a)(3); 42 U.S.C.A. § 1983.

> Beken v. Eaglin, 711 F.Supp. 860.

D.S.D. 1992. When motion is made to dismiss complaint for lack of subject matter jurisdiction, issue to be addressed is whether court is empowered to hear class of cases in which plaintiff's claim arises. Fed.Rules Civ. Proc.Rule 12(b)(1), 28 U.S.C.A.

> Mousseaux v. U.S. Com'r of Indian Affairs, 806 F.Supp. 1433, affirmed in part, remanded in part 28 F.3d 786.

E.D.Tenn. 1992. Motion by United States to dismiss complaint filed against it pursuant to the Federal Tort Claims Act, (FTCA) on ground that plaintiff's claim is barred by doctrine of sovereign immunity under discretionary function exception, is properly treated as motion to dismiss for lack of subject matter jurisdiction. 28 U.S.C.A. §§ 2671–2680.

> Cooley v. U.S., 791 F.Supp. 1294, affirmed Myers v. U.S., 17 F.3d 890, rehearing denied.

S.D.Tex. 1997. Proper remedy for actions barred by Eleventh Amendment is dismissal of case, without prejudice, for lack of subject matter jurisdiction. U.S.C.A. Const.Amend. 11; Fed.Rules Civ.Proc.Rule 12(b)(1), 28 U.S.C.A.

> Correa v. City of Bay City, 981 F.Supp. 477.

S.D.Tex. 1991. Dismissal for failure to state claim upon which relief can be granted is appropriate if plaintiff cannot establish standing to bring claim. Fed.Rules Civ.Proc.Rule 12(b)(6), 28 U.S.C.A.

> Rockbit Industries U.S.A., Inc. v. Baker Hughes, Inc., 802 F.Supp. 1544.

S.D.Tex. 1989. If federal court must determine which parent should receive custody, what rights noncustodial parent should have, whether a previous court's decree should be modified, federal court should dismiss the case as falling within the domestic relations exception to jurisdiction.

> Thompson v. Sundholm, 726 F.Supp. 147.

W.D.Tex. 1994. Any action barred by doctrine of sovereign immunity must be dismissed for lack of subject-matter jurisdiction.

> Bob Hamric Chevrolet, Inc. v. U.S. I.R.S., 849 F.Supp. 500.

D.Utah 1992. Motions to dismiss which raise ripeness issue are treated as motions to dismiss for lack of subject matter jurisdiction.

> Anderson v. Alpine City, 804 F.Supp. 269.

Subject matter jurisdiction is absolute prerequisite for continuance of action in federal district court, and whenever it appears that subject matter jurisdiction is lacking, court is duty bound to dismiss action.

> Anderson v. Alpine City, 804 F.Supp. 269.

D.Vt. 1984. Rosenfeld v. Clark, 586 F.Supp. 1332, affirmed 760 F.2d 253.

E.D.Va. 1998. Third-party contribution/indemnification claim against German manufacturer of component that was incorporated into machine owned and operated by defendant, which machine allegedly caused personal injuries that gave rise to instant action, would be dismissed for lack of personal jurisdiction, rather than transferred to different district; defendant made obvious error in filing third-party action in federal district court in Virginia, manufacturer suffered substantial costs in having to defend in foreign and improper forum, and improper filing imposed unnecessary costs on judicial system, and thus, transfer, at no cost to defendant, would not serve interest of justice. 28 U.S.C.A. § 1406(a); Fed.Rules Civ.Proc.Rule 12(b)(2), 28 U.S.C.A.

> Chisholm v. UHP Projects, Inc., 1 F.Supp.2d 581.

E.D.Va. 1996. Eleventh Amendment restricted federal court's jurisdiction under Article III and since court lacked subject matter jurisdiction over action brought against the state of Virginia, court had no discretion to grant plaintiff's motion for voluntary dismissal and, pursuant to federal rule governing relief from judgment, court would grant the state relief from its judgment by dismissing plaintiff's claims without prejudice. U.S.C.A. Const. Art. 3, § 1 et seq.; Amend. 11; Fed.Rules Civ.Proc.Rules 12(b)(1), 60, 28 U.S.C.A.

> Taylor v. Com. of Va., Dept. of Transp., 170 F.R.D. 10.

E.D.Va. 1993. Product liability action would not be dismissed for lack of personal jurisdiction over defendant; although complaint failed to allege facts which would justify exercise of personal jurisdiction under Virginia long-arm statute, plaintiff's memorandum in opposition to defendant's motion to dismiss showed, at least in conclusory terms, that plaintiff could possibly establish jurisdiction over defendant and since defendant had not yet filed responsive pleading, plaintiff could amend his complaint as matter of right so as to state with particularity basis for personal jurisdiction over defendant. Fed.Rules Civ.Proc.Rule 15, 28

U.S.C.A.; Va.Code 1950, § 8.01–328.1, subd. A, par. 1.

> St. Jarre v. Heidelberger Druckmaschinen A.G., 816 F.Supp. 424, affirmed 19 F.3d 1430.

E.D.Va. 1992. Strict standard governs dismissal for lack of subject matter jurisdiction when the basis of jurisdiction is also an element in plaintiff's cause of action. Fed.Rules Civ. Proc.Rule 12(b)(1), 28 U.S.C.A.

> E.E.O.C. v. Alford, 142 F.R.D. 283.

E.D.Va. 1984. National Trust for Historic Preservation v. 1750 K Inv. Partnership, 100 F.R.D. 483, affirmed Fisher v. Beauchamp, 755 F.2d 927, affirmed 755 F.2d 929.

W.D.Va. 1990. Allegation of jurisdictional defects does not inevitably preclude consideration of motion for voluntary dismissal; to the contrary, voluntary dismissal may be warranted in diversity cases as means to remedy problem of subject matter jurisdiction. Fed.Rules Civ. Proc.Rule 41(a)(2), 28 U.S.C.A.

> Shortt v. Richlands Mall Associates, Inc., 130 F.R.D. 64, reversed 922 F.2d 836, on remand 781 F.Supp. 454.

Potential lack of subject matter jurisdiction does not preclude court from considering whether it should allow plaintiff voluntary dismissal. Fed.Rules Civ.Proc.Rule 41(a)(2), 28 U.S.C.A.

> Shortt v. Richlands Mall Associates, Inc., 130 F.R.D. 64, reversed 922 F.2d 836, on remand 781 F.Supp. 454.

S.D.W.Va. 1995. Although district court lacked personal jurisdiction over owners and operators of resort located in Middle District of Florida, absence of such jurisdiction did not compel outright dismissal; rather, venue would be transferred to the Middle District of Florida where a substantial part of the events or omissions giving rise to guest's slip and fall claim occurred. 28 U.S.C.A. §§ 1391(a)(2), 1406(a).

> Bashaw v. Belz Hotel Management Co., Inc., 872 F.Supp. 323.

E.D.Wis. 1996. Because requirement of Title VII and the ADEA that plaintiff name defendant as respondent in Equal Employment Opportunity Commission (EEOC) charge prior to bringing suit are not jurisdictional, a defendant's motion to dismiss for lack of subject matter jurisdiction was not appropriate. Civil Rights Act of 1964, § 706(f)(1), as amended, 42 U.S.C.A. § 2000e–5(f)(1); Age Discrimination in Employment Act of 1967, § 7(d), 29 U.S.C.A. § 626(d); Fed.Rules Civ.Proc.Rule 12(b)(1), 28 U.S.C.A.

> Secrist v. Burns Intern. Sec. Services, 926 F.Supp. 823.

W.D.Wis. 1992. If plaintiff's claim under the United States Constitution or federal law clearly appears to be immaterial and made solely for the purpose of obtaining jurisdiction where claim is wholly insubstantial and frivolous, the suit may be dismissed for lack of subject matter jurisdiction.

> Forest County Potawatomi Community of Wisconsin v. Doyle, 803 F.Supp. 1526, appeal dismissed 7 F.3d 238.

D.Wyo. 1990. Lawsuit brought against United States which is not provided for by statute or does not comply with statutory requirements must be dismissed because it is jurisdictionally defective.

> Egbert v. U.S., 752 F.Supp. 1010, affirmed 940 F.2d 1539, certiorari denied 112 S.Ct. 666, 502 U.S. 1016, 116 L.Ed.2d 756.

Bkrtcy.D.Or. 1994. Chapter 13 debtor's failure to state grounds upon which district court's jurisdiction depended in suit seeking permission to set off against tax debt owed to Internal Revenue Service (IRS) amount that Department of Housing and Urban Development (HUD) and Environmental Protection Agency (EPA) owed debtor on contract guarantee and his failure to state name, number and chapter of related bankruptcy case was basis upon which to grant EPA's and HUD's motion to dismiss for lack of subject matter jurisdiction; court had already provided debtor, over earlier motion to dismiss, opportunity to correct insufficiencies in complaint, and debtor failed to meet minimum requirements of federal pleadings in second try. Fed.Rules Bankr.Proc.Rule 7008(a), 11 U.S.C.A.; Fed.Rules Civ.Proc.Rule 8(a), 28 U.S.C.A.

> In re Gibson, 176 B.R. 910.

⊕**1742(3). Diversity of citizenship.**

C.A.D.C. 1987. So long as nondiverse party is not indispensable to action, district court may dismiss only claim against nondiverse party and retain diversity jurisdiction over rest of case at any stage of litigation, even after trial and entry of judgment. 28 U.S.C.A. § 1332(d); Fed.Rules Civ.Proc.Rule 21, 28 U.S.C.A.

> Long v. District of Columbia, 820 F.2d 409, 261 U.S.App.D.C. 1.

Court of Appeals had authority under rule of civil procedure to dismiss District of Columbia as nondiverse, but not indispensable party, while retaining jurisdiction over plaintiff's claim against electric company, to cure jurisdictional defect in plaintiff's complaint. 28 U.S.C.A. § 1332(d); Fed.Rules Civ.Proc.Rule 21, 28 U.S.C.A.

> Long v. District of Columbia, 820 F.2d 409, 261 U.S.App.D.C. 1.

Given absence of prejudice to diverse defendant electric company, Court of Appeals would exercise its authority under rule of federal procedure to dismiss District of Columbia as nondiverse, but not indispensable party, while retaining jurisdiction over plaintiff's claim against electric company. 28 U.S.C.A. § 1332(d); Fed. Rules Civ.Proc.Rule 21, 28 U.S.C.A.

Long v. District of Columbia, 820 F.2d 409, 261 U.S.App.D.C. 1.

C.A.8 (Ark.) 1992. District court should dismiss for lack of jurisdiction when it appears to legal certainty that plaintiff cannot satisfy amount in controversy requirement for diversity jurisdiction. 28 U.S.C.A. § 1332(a).

Allison v. Security Ben. Life Ins. Co., 980 F.2d 1213.

C.A.7 (Ill.) 1984. If landlord's cross claim against tenant's purported successor in interest was an amendment to landlord's complaint to add another defendant or an addition of a party and if purported successor could have been joined originally, then amendment or addition would require dismissal of entire action for lack of diversity between landlord and purported successor. Fed.Rules Civ.Proc. Rules 15(a), 21, 28 U.S.C.A.

American Nat. Bank and Trust Co. of Chicago v. Bailey, 750 F.2d 577, certiorari denied Chicago Investment Corporation v. American National Bank and Trust Company of Chicago, 105 S.Ct. 2324, 471 U.S. 1100, 85 L.Ed.2d 842.

C.A.8 (Iowa) 1998. Dismissal of plaintiff's shareholder derivative claims was proper when plaintiff failed to plead properly diversity jurisdiction over such claims and federal securities law claims upon which derivative claims depended for federal jurisdiction were properly dismissed on the pleadings. 28 U.S.C.A. § 1332.

Dubach v. Weitzel, 135 F.3d 590.

C.A.5 (La.) 1991. District court sitting in Louisiana did not abuse its discretion by dismissing diversity negligence action as barred by Louisiana prescriptive period rather than transferring case to Texas forum for convenience of parties and witnesses, in the interest of justice, inasmuch as Texas court also would have been required to apply Louisiana prescriptive period, similarly barring action, under principle that transferee court must apply choice-of-law rules of transferor court. 28 U.S.C.A. § 1404(a).

Crase v. Astroworld, Inc., 941 F.2d 265.

C.A.5 (La.) 1990. Court would treat complaint in intervention, in action in which complete diversity was lacking between plaintiff and original defendants, as if it was separate action, and would not dismiss intervention claims along with main demand, where complete diversity of citizenship existed between plaintiff and intervenor, and dismissal would only result in further delay and expense to parties.

Arkoma Associates v. Carden, 904 F.2d 5, certiorari denied Magee Drilling Co. v. Arkoma Associates, 111 S.Ct. 429, 498 U.S. 967, 112 L.Ed.2d 413.

C.A.1 (Mass.) 1992. After district court determined that diversity of citizenship was lacking in bank's action to recover deficiency on note, district court was required to dismiss case for lack of jurisdiction and did not have power to go on and decide case. 28 U.S.C.A. § 1332.

Bank One, Texas, N.A. v. Montle, 974 F.2d 220.

C.A.2 (N.Y.) 1991. Dismissal for lack of jurisdiction of related state law claims in § 1983 action against city transit authority was inappropriate, even if § 1983 claim should have been dismissed, where plaintiffs were citizens of one state and all defendants citizens of another and jurisdiction was premised on diversity of citizenship. 42 U.S.C.A. § 1983.

Ricciuti v. N.Y.C. Transit Authority, 941 F.2d 119, on remand 1991 WL 221110.

C.A.2 (N.Y.) 1991. Inactive corporation was nondiverse plaintiff required to be dismissed from action, where corporation's last principal place of business was Florida and at time lawsuit was filed its corporate charter had lapsed in Ohio but it was still corporation in good standing in Florida. 28 U.S.C.A. § 1332(c).

Wm. Passalacqua Builders, Inc. v. Resnick Developers South, Inc., 933 F.2d 131.

Fact that inactive corporation was nondiverse plaintiff required to be dismissed from corporate disregard and fraud action, did not require entire complaint to be dismissed, where corporation was not indispensable to resolution of remaining claims against defendants. 28 U.S.C.A. § 1332(c); Fed.Rules Civ.Proc.Rule 19(b), 28 U.S.C.A.

Wm. Passalacqua Builders, Inc. v. Resnick Developers South, Inc., 933 F.2d 131.

C.A.2 (N.Y.) 1985. When federal diversity jurisdiction will exist if nondiverse parties are dropped, bare fact that state court forum is available does not, by itself, make it appropriate to dismiss federal action.

Samaha v. Presbyterian Hosp. in City of New York, 757 F.2d 529.

C.A.3 (Pa.) 1987. District court erred as a matter of law when it granted defendant's second motion to reinstate an order dismissing plaintiffs' claim due to failure to adequately allege the basis for diversity jurisdiction and denied plaintiff's motion to reconsider, in which plaintiff additionally asked to be permitted to amend complaint with respect to jurisdiction;

on initial motion to dismiss, district court told plaintiffs that no immediate response was necessary, and stipulation into which parties had entered regarding jurisdictional problem did not mandate dismissal if plaintiff was unable to adequately allege diversity jurisdiction within a 30–day time period.

> Kiser v. General Elec. Corp., 831 F.2d 423, certiorari denied Parker-Hannifin Corp. v. Kiser, 108 S.Ct. 1078, 485 U.S. 906, 99 L.Ed.2d 238.

C.A.4 (S.C.) 1994. Joinder of all insurers who issued policies to insured was mandated by their nature as necessary and indispensable parties, but joinder would destroy complete diversity and district court's only basis for subject matter jurisdiction, which thus required that claims be dismissed. Fed.Rules Civ.Proc.Rule 19(a, b), 28 U.S.C.A.

> Schlumberger Industries, Inc. v. National Sur. Corp., 36 F.3d 1274.

C.A.4 (S.C.) 1993. Proper response to failure of some plaintiffs in class action suit to meet jurisdictional minimum amount in controversy is dismissal of those plaintiffs, not dismissal of entire action.

> Central Wesleyan College v. W.R. Grace & Co., 6 F.3d 177.

C.A.5 (Tex.) 1994. Action filed in district court was not dismissible under statute providing that action arising under state workers' compensation laws could not be removed to district court; although action involved state workers' compensation law, jurisdiction was still proper based on diversity of citizenship. 28 U.S.C.A. § 1445(c).

> St. Paul Ins. Co. v. Trejo, 39 F.3d 585.

C.D.Cal. 1995. When proofs adduced at trial conclusively show that plaintiff never had claim even arguably within jurisdictional range, federal diversity action must be dismissed. 28 U.S.C.A. § 1332.

> Heichman v. American Tel. & Tel. Co., 943 F.Supp. 1212.

N.D.Cal. 1991. Third-party complaint would be dismissed with regard to third-party defendants whose citizenship was not diverse from that of defendant who filed third-party complaint, but denied with respect to diverse third-party defendants, with permission to amend third-party complaint if defendant could allege facts showing that third-party complaint were derivative, so as to establish jurisdiction over nondiverse third-party defendants pursuant to rule providing for filing of third-party complaint upon nonparty who is or may be liable for all or part of plaintiff's claim against third-party plaintiff. Fed.Rules Civ.Proc.Rules 13(h), 14(a), 28 U.S.C.A.

> General American Life Ins. Co. v. Rana, 769 F.Supp. 1121.

D.Colo. 1995. Products liability action by federal penitentiary inmate would be dismissed for lack of subject matter jurisdiction on ground that inmate failed to affirmatively plead his state of citizenship (i.e. domicile) prior to his incarceration, and thus, failed to satisfy requirements of diversity jurisdiction; although inmate's response brief raised inference that inmate was citizen of California prior to his incarceration, in which case complete diversity would exist, such inference was insufficient to overcome presumption against diversity jurisdiction. 28 U.S.C.A. § 1332; Fed.Rules Civ.Proc.Rule 8(a)(1), 28 U.S.C.A.

> Robinson v. Brown & Williamson Tobacco Corp., 909 F.Supp. 824.

D.Conn. 1994. Motion to dismiss for lack of subject matter jurisdiction challenges court's statutory or constitutional power to adjudicate case, and typically alleges that federal court lacks federal question jurisdiction or that it lacks diversity jurisdiction. Fed.Rules Civ.Proc. Rule 12(b)(1), 28 U.S.C.A.

> Bleiler v. Cristwood Contracting Co., Inc., 868 F.Supp. 461, affirmed in part, reversed in part 72 F.3d 13.

D.Del. 1985. When nondiverse party intervening of right is indispensable within meaning of Rule 19, district court must dismiss entire suit for lack of jurisdiction. 28 U.S.C.A. § 1332; Fed.Rules Civ.Proc.Rule 19, 28 U.S.C.A.

> Butcher & Singer, Inc. v. Kellam, 623 F.Supp. 418.

D.D.C. 1996. Dismissal for lack of subject matter jurisdiction, rather than transfer to state court or another federal forum, was only appropriate result in action brought by partnership formed under North Carolina law against Maryland attorneys in which Maryland residence of one of partnership's limited partners defeated complete diversity; statute does not allow federal court to transfer action to state court, and no other federal court could exercise jurisdiction as diversity was only asserted basis for federal jurisdiction. 28 U.S.C.A. §§ 610, 1332, 1404(a), 1406(a), 1631.

> Kier Bros. Investments Inc. v. White, 943 F.Supp. 1, appeal dismissed 1997 WL 404856.

S.D.Fla. 1989. Addition of indispensable party to action, defeating federal diversity jurisdiction, warranted dismissal.

> Casualty Indem. Exchange v. High Croft Enterprises, Inc., 714 F.Supp. 1190.

D.Hawai'i 1993. Dismissal of nondiverse manufacturer of paragliding equipment from wrongful death action brought against premises owner, equipment provider, and manufacturer was warranted in order to maintain diversity jurisdiction, where manufacturer was not indispensable, since manufacturer could be included on special verdict form for apportionment of fault and other defendants could bring third-party complaint against manufacturer for indemnification, and dismissal would greatly prejudice decedent's widow, since statute of limitations had expired on her claims. 28 U.S.C.A. § 1332; Fed.Rules Civ.Proc.Rule 19, 28 U.S.C.A.

  Wheelock v. Sport Kites, Inc., 839 F.Supp. 730.

D.Hawai'i 1992. In diversity case, if it appears to legal certainty that amount in controversy is less than jurisdictional amount, court should dismiss case for lack of subject matter jurisdiction. 28 U.S.C.A. § 1332(a).

  Marquardt v. United Airlines, Inc., 781 F.Supp. 1487.

D.Hawai'i 1991. Although plaintiff's pleadings were technically inadequate to establish diversity jurisdiction, in that they failed to allege principal place of business of corporate defendant, plaintiff nonetheless presented sufficient evidence to demonstrate that corporation's principal place of business was, in fact, located in Hawaii; thus, complaint was not required to be dismissed for lack of diversity jurisdiction. 28 U.S.C.A. § 1332.

  Macheras v. Center Art Galleries--Hawaii, Inc., 776 F.Supp. 1436.

N.D.Ill. 1998. Diversity action had to be dismissed based on plaintiff's failure in amended complaint to invoke diversity jurisdiction by identifying citizenship of plaintiff and each defendant. 28 U.S.C.A. § 1332.

  Smith v. City of Chicago, 992 F.Supp. 1027.

N.D.Ill. 1995. Because federal supplemental jurisdiction statute did not apply to defendant who was added before that statute's effective date, and because that defendant was not diverse from plaintiffs, dismissal for lack of jurisdiction was required. 28 U.S.C.A. § 1367.

  National Organization for Women, Inc. v. Scheidler, 897 F.Supp. 1047.

N.D.Ill. 1992. For defendants to prevail on their motions to dismiss if jurisdictional amount in controversy requirement is not met, it must appear to legal certainty that claim is really for less than jurisdictional amount. 28 U.S.C.A. § 1332(a).

  ITT Commercial Finance Corp. v. Unlimited Automotive, Inc., 814 F.Supp. 664.

N.D.Ill. 1991. Dismissal of Illinois residents' tort action against a "foreign corpora-

tion" for lack of diversity jurisdiction was required where complaint merely stated that corporation was incorporated in California and did not identify corporation's principal place of business; inference that corporation's principal place of business was not in Illinois was insufficient to establish federal jurisdiction. 28 U.S.C.A. § 1332(c)(1).

  Lutkowski v. High Energy Sports, 768 F.Supp. 224.

N.D.Ill. 1985. In action brought by limited partner, a Florida citizen, against Illinois partnership for alleged breach of partnership agreement, other limited partners, some of whom were also Illinois citizens, were indispensable parties; thus, because joinder of absent parties would destroy diversity, action was subject to dismissal. Fed.Rules Civ.Proc.Rules 19, 19(b), 28 U.S.C.A.

  Schmidt v. E.N. Maisel and Associates, 105 F.R.D. 157.

N.D.Ill. 1983. Chicago Heights Venture v. Dynamit Nobel of America, Inc., 575 F.Supp. 214, affirmed 782 F.2d 723.

N.D.Ind. 1987. Dismissal of claim based on diversity jurisdiction for want of sufficient allegations of diversity is "overkill." 28 U.S.C.A. § 1332.

  Jones v. National Union Fire Ins. Co., 664 F.Supp. 440.

D.Kan. 1997. If legal impossibility of recovering $50,000 is so certain that it virtually negates plaintiff's good faith in asserting claim, district court must dismiss action for lack of diversity jurisdiction. 28 U.S.C.A. § 1332.

  Fitzgerald v. City of Ottawa, Kan., 975 F.Supp. 1402.

D.Md. 1998. Plaintiff knew to a legal certainty when he filed personal injury action that his claim did not satisfy amount required for diversity jurisdiction, and therefore, dismissal of case for lack of jurisdiction was warranted; plaintiff failed to present expert opinion evidence causally connecting his complaints and medical treatments to the accident at issue in the action. 28 U.S.C.A. § 1332.

  Pupkar v. Tastaca, 999 F.Supp. 644.

D.Mass. 1997. At least when lack of complete diversity of citizenship comes to district court's attention at early stage of litigation, dismissal for want of jurisdiction is appropriate. 28 U.S.C.A. § 1332.

  Barrows v. Robson, 993 F.Supp. 17.

W.D.Mich. 1994. In insurer's declaratory judgment action against insured and approximately 50 other insurers, district court would not dismiss action for lack of diversity, even though two of defendant insurers were citizens of same state as plaintiff insurer; two defendant

For references to other topics, see Descriptive-Word Index

insurers were dispensable parties which could be dismissed with leave to join case as plaintiffs. Fed.Rules Civ.Proc.Rules 20, 21, 28 U.S.C.A.
> Commercial Union Ins. Co. v. Cannelton Industries, Inc., 154 F.R.D. 164.

In insurer's declaratory judgment action against insured and approximately 50 other insurers, district court would not dismiss action for lack of diversity, even though plaintiff insurer's complaint left citizenship of several of defendant insurers vague, stating only that they were not citizens of same state as plaintiff insurer; however, plaintiff insurer was required to amend complaint to identify nature of each defendant insurer as partnership or corporation and citizenship of each corporation and each partner.
> Commercial Union Ins. Co. v. Cannelton Industries, Inc., 154 F.R.D. 164.

E.D.Mo. 1984. Count of complaint charging civil fraud was not subject to dismissal due to lack of diversity, despite contention that diversity was defeated by fact that an unnamed partner of bond counsel was a citizen of same state as was plaintiff, purchaser of municipal bonds, in that no one had offered support for dismissal based on failure to name an indispensable party, nor had bond counsel claimed lack of jurisdiction.
> Southgate Bank v. Public Water Supply Dist. No. 7 of Jefferson County, Mo., 601 F.Supp. 262.

W.D.Mo. 1994. District court must dismiss for lack of subject matter jurisdiction case in which no diversity or supplemental jurisdiction exists, unless federal question is presented. 28 U.S.C.A. §§ 1332, 1367.
> U.S. v. Chorice, 857 F.Supp. 672.

D.Neb. 1986. Nebraska residents' claims against national banking association located in Nebraska had to be dismissed, after federal defendants were dismissed, given the absence of diversity of citizenship. 28 U.S.C.A. § 1332(c).
> Hagebush v. U.S., 657 F.Supp. 675.

D.N.H. 1992. District court had authority to entertain alien plaintiff's motion to dismiss alien defendant in order to maintain diversity jurisdiction. 28 U.S.C.A. §§ 1332, 1332(a).
> Fox v. Bourgeois, 799 F.Supp. 1274.

E. & S.D.N.Y. 1989. Asbestos-related personal injury case would be dismissed as to nondiverse defendant that had participated in trial, without prejudice to filing of amended complaint alleging diversity. Fed.Rules Civ. Proc.Rule 21, 28 U.S.C.A.
> In re Joint Eastern and Southern Districts Asbestos Litigation, 124 F.R.D. 538, affirmed Johnson v. Celotex Corp., 899 F.2d 1281, certiorari denied 111 S.Ct. 297, 498 U.S. 920, 112 L.Ed.2d 250.

N.D.N.Y. 1998. When federal court's subject matter jurisdiction is dependent solely on diversity jurisdiction and court finds that complete diversity does not exist, court must dismiss suit. 28 U.S.C.A. § 1332(a)(1).
> Seemann v. Maxwell, 178 F.R.D. 23.

S.D.N.Y. 1991. Nondiverse limited partnership could be dismissed as defendant in securities fraud action to restore diversity jurisdiction over state securities fraud claims; there was no showing that delay in seeking dismissal prejudiced remaining defendants, and fact that amended complaint sought damages from limited partnership did not render it indispensable. Fed.Rules Civ.Proc.Rule 21, 28 U.S.C.A.
> Haggerty v. Comstock Gold Co., L.P., 770 F.Supp. 216.

S.D.N.Y. 1985. To extent that complaint filed against special prosecutor, assistant special prosecutor, and investigator implicitly alleged common-law torts or a state law wrongful death action in connection with alleged murder of decedent while he was serving as an informant for special prosecutor, those claims were subject to dismissal, in that diversity jurisdiction was not alleged and pendent jurisdiction was insufficient because underlying federal claim had been dismissed. 28 U.S.C.A. § 1332.
> Estate of Masselli by Masselli v. Silverman, 606 F.Supp. 341.

E.D.Pa. 1987. Failure to amend complaint to establish complete diversity, after being provided opportunity to do so, warranted dismissal of claim with prejudice as to two corporate defendants in asbestos case. U.S.C.A. Const. Art. 3, § 1 et seq.; 28 U.S.C.A. §§ 1332, 1332(c); Fed.Rules Civ.Proc.Rules 8, 8(a)(1), 12(h)(3), 28 U.S.C.A.
> Randazzo v. Eagle-Picher Industries, Inc., 117 F.R.D. 557.

D.Puerto Rico 1996. Subsidiary was indispensable party to lessor's action against parent corporation for breach of lease agreement, and therefore dismissal of action was required due to subsidiary's lack of diversity, where lessor's claims were against subsidiary rather than corporation, and subsidiary was signatory to agreement. Fed.Rules Civ.Proc.Rule 19, 28 U.S.C.A.
> E & E Inv., Inc. v. Simmons Co., 169 F.R.D. 467.

W.D.Va. 1990. Personal injury plaintiff was entitled to voluntary dismissal in order to pursue claim against corporate defendant in state court, after defendant raised question as to federal court's diversity jurisdiction; suit was filed in federal court in good faith, and defendant would suffer prejudice from voluntary dismissal, apart from loss of limitations defense. Fed.Rules Civ.Proc.Rule 41(a)(2), 28 U.S.C.A.

> Shortt v. Richlands Mall Associates, Inc., 130 F.R.D. 64, reversed 922 F.2d 836, on remand 781 F.Supp. 454.

W.D.Wash. 1995. District court would dismiss employee's outrage and intentional infliction of emotional distress claims against employer for lack of jurisdiction; employee's Title VII claims were only federal causes of action before court, court granted summary judgment on Title VII claims, and diversity did not exist between parties. Civil Rights Act of 1964, § 701 et seq., 42 U.S.C.A. § 2000e et seq.

> Ashworth v. Roundup Co., 897 F.Supp. 489.

S.D.W.Va. 1985. Before a court can dismiss an action for lack of jurisdictional amount under diversity statute, it must appear to a legal certainty that the plaintiff cannot recover the requisite amount. 28 U.S.C.A. § 1332(a).

> Prior Oil Well Drilling Co. v. David A. Waldron and Associates, Inc., 601 F.Supp. 778.

⚷1742(4). **Amount in controversy.**

C.A.D.C. 1993. Federal courts are obliged to include inherently nebulous unliquidated damage claims in amount in controversy calculus and to dismiss case only if it appears to legal certainty that amount in controversy barrier cannot be breached; although these obligations do not mean that diversity suits backed only by purely speculative or unsupported allegations of injury cannot be ousted from federal court, they do mean that federal courts may not toss out cases in which there are tenable claims of potentially debilitating and painful permanent injuries supported by physician's report. 28 U.S.C.A. § 1332.

> Rosenboro v. Kim, 994 F.2d 13, 301 U.S.App.D.C. 286.

C.A.8 (Ark.) 1995. Diversity action against insurer for alleged bad faith refusal to pay had to be dismissed where action only presented claim for compensatory damages totaling $25,-000, an amount insufficient to support diversity jurisdiction. 28 U.S.C.A. § 1332(a).

> Hall v. Modern Woodmen of America, 68 F.3d 1120.

C.A.11 (Fla.) 1996. Life insurer's complaint seeking cancellation of life insurance policy with face value of $100,000, on ground of misrepresentation in application, could not be dismissed for failure to meet the $50,000 minimum amount in controversy requirement, even though insured was still alive; the only fixed and definite liability of the insurer was to pay face value of the policy. 28 U.S.C.A. § 1332.

> Guardian Life Ins. Co. of America v. Muniz, 101 F.3d 93.

C.A.7 (Ill.) 1995. Standby terms capping liability at $5000 in disputes arising from environmental risk assessment by engineering firm, that were prescribed in contract for earlier job that firm had performed for property owner, governed later job performed on behalf of property owner in which firm failed to discover hazardous chemicals below property, and so warranted dismissal of breach of contract and warranty case for want of jurisdiction. 28 U.S.C.A. § 1332(a); Fed.Rules Civ.Proc.Rule 12(b)(1), 28 U.S.C.A.

> Pratt Central Park Ltd. Partnership v. Dames & Moore, Inc., 60 F.3d 350.

C.A.7 (Ill.) 1994. To warrant dismissal, it must appear to legal certainty that claim is for less than jurisdictional amount of $50,000 for purposes of diversity jurisdiction.

> National Union Fire Ins. Co. of Pittsburgh, Pa. v. Wilkins-Lowe & Co., Inc., 29 F.3d 337.

C.A.7 (Ind.) 1994. Only if district court in diversity action determines to a legal certainty that claim is really for less than the jurisdictional amount should it dismiss claim for lack of jurisdiction.

> Cincinnati Ins. Co. v. Star Financial Bank, 35 F.3d 1186.

C.A.6 (Ky.) 1996. District court should consider amount alleged in complaint and should not dismiss complaint for lack of subject matter jurisdiction unless it appears to legal certainty that plaintiff in good faith cannot claim jurisdictional amount. 28 U.S.C.A. § 1332.

> Massachusetts Cas. Ins. Co. v. Harmon, 88 F.3d 415.

C.A.6 (Ky.) 1993. If plaintiff brings action in federal court and defendant seeks dismissal on amount-in-controversy grounds, case will not be dismissed unless it appears that plaintiff's assertion of amount in controversy was made in bad faith. 28 U.S.C.A. § 1332(a).

> Gafford v. General Elec. Co., 997 F.2d 150.

C.A.3 (N.J.) 1997. Unless the law gives a different rule, the sum claimed by the plaintiff controls whether plaintiff satisfies amount in controversy requirement for federal diversity jurisdiction if the claim is apparently made in good faith; it must appear to a legal certainty that claim is really for less than the jurisdictional amount to justify dismissal. 28 U.S.C.A. § 1332.

> Suber v. Chrysler Corp., 104 F.3d 578, as amended.

C.A.2 (N.Y.) 1996. In determining whether amount in controversy satisfies threshold amount for diversity jurisdiction, sum claimed by plaintiff controls if claim is apparently made in good faith; it must appear to a legal certainty that claim is really for less than jurisdictional amount to justify dismissal. 28 U.S.C.A. § 1332(a).

> Chase Manhattan Bank, N.A. v. American Nat. Bank and Trust Co. of Chicago, 93 F.3d 1064.

Diversity plaintiff's good faith belief as to amount in controversy as of filing date may be ascertained by reference to the pleadings and any facts on that subject adduced in discovery; if, from the face of the pleadings, it is apparent, to a legal certainty, that plaintiff cannot recover amount claimed, or if, from the proofs, court is satisfied to a like certainty that plaintiff never was entitled to recover that amount, and that his claim was therefore colorable for purpose of conferring jurisdiction, diversity suit will be dismissed. 28 U.S.C.A. § 1332(a).

> Chase Manhattan Bank, N.A. v. American Nat. Bank and Trust Co. of Chicago, 93 F.3d 1064.

C.A.3 (Pa.) 1997. Plaintiff's good faith in choosing federal forum is open to challenge not only by resort to face of his complaint, but by facts disclosed at trial, and if from either source it is clear that his claim never could have amounted to sum necessary to give jurisdiction there is no injustice in dismissing suit. 28 U.S.C.A. § 1332(a).

> Spectacor Management Group v. Brown, 131 F.3d 120, certiorari denied 118 S.Ct. 1799, 140 L.Ed.2d 939.

C.A.3 (Pa.) 1996. Unless law gives different rule, sum claimed by plaintiff controls in determining whether amount in controversy requirements for diversity jurisdiction are satisfied if claim is apparently made in good faith; it must appear to legal certainty that claim is really for less than jurisdictional amount to justify dismissal. 28 U.S.C.A. § 1332(a).

> State Farm Mut. Auto. Ins. Co. v. Powell, 87 F.3d 93.

Federal court's jurisdiction ordinarily depends upon facts as they exist when complaint is filed, and thus subsequent events that reduce amount in controversy below statutory minimum do not require dismissal; however, a distinction must be made between subsequent events that change amount in controversy and subsequent *revelations* that, in fact, required amount was or was not in controversy at commencement of the action. 28 U.S.C.A. § 1332(a).

> State Farm Mut. Auto. Ins. Co. v. Powell, 87 F.3d 93.

C.A.3 (Pa.) 1995. It must appear to legal certainty that claim is really for less than juris-

dictional amount to justify dismissal on that grounds. 28 U.S.C.A. § 1332.

> Columbia Gas Transmission Corp. v. Tarbuck, 62 F.3d 538.

C.A.3 (Pa.) 1993. When it appears to legal certainty that plaintiff was never entitled to recover requisite jurisdictional amount in controversy in diversity action, case must be dismissed, even if jurisdictional deficiency becomes evident only after trial. 28 U.S.C.A. § 1332(a).

> Packard v. Provident Nat. Bank, 994 F.2d 1039, rehearing denied, certiorari denied Upp v. Mellon Bank, N.A., 114 S.Ct. 440, 510 U.S. 964, 126 L.Ed.2d 373.

C.A.3 (Pa.) 1990. Entire class action does not have to be dismissed for lack of subject-matter jurisdiction over some class members due to their inability to meet amount in controversy requirement; rather, court is required only to dismiss those class members whose claims appear to legal certainty to be less than jurisdictional amount. Fed.Rules Civ.Proc.Rule 23(b)(3), 28 U.S.C.A.

> In re School Asbestos Litigation, 921 F.2d 1310, rehearing denied, certiorari denied U.S. Gypsum Co. v. Barnwell School Dist. No. 45, 111 S.Ct. 1623, 499 U.S. 976, 113 L.Ed.2d 720.

C.A.1 (Puerto Rico) 1985. Claim should be dismissed for failure to meet jurisdictional minimum only if it appears to legal certainty that the claim is really for less than the jurisdictional amount. 28 U.S.C.A. § 1332(a).

> Duchesne v. American Airlines, Inc., 758 F.2d 27.

While it seemed unlikely that airline passenger who was struck on her head when flight attendant opened overhead luggage bin and caused metal luggage carrier to fall would recover $7,750 in pain and suffering damages so as to bring her total claim, including maximum damages of $2,250 for lost earnings and medical expenses, up to jurisdictional minimum of $10,000, such was not legally certain, since the passenger appeared to have sustained some physical injury, had consulted number of physicians, and suffered headaches and other symptoms for considerable period of time, and thus, district court erroneously dismissed the claim. 28 U.S.C.A. § 1332(a).

> Duchesne v. American Airlines, Inc., 758 F.2d 27.

C.A.1 (R.I.) 1995. For purposes of federal diversity jurisdiction amount-in-controversy requirement, plaintiff's good faith in choosing federal forum is open to challenge not only by resort to face of complaint, but by facts disclosed at trial, and if from either source it is clear that his claim never could have amounted to sum necessary to give jurisdiction, there is no injustice in dismissing suit. 28 U.S.C.A. § 1332(a).

> Coventry Sewage Associates v. Dworkin Realty Co., 71 F.3d 1.

For purposes of federal diversity jurisdiction amount-in-controversy requirement, if postcomplaint evidence shows, to a legal certainty, that damages never could have exceeded jurisdictional minimum such that claim was essentially feigned, i.e., colorable, in order to confer jurisdiction, action must be dismissed. 28 U.S.C.A. § 1332(a).

> Coventry Sewage Associates v. Dworkin Realty Co., 71 F.3d 1.

C.A.6 (Tenn.) 1988. In determining whether dismissal is justified for lack of jurisdictional amounts, sums posited by plaintiffs, provided they are made in good faith, control unless it appears to a legal certainty that their claims are, in actuality, for less.

> Sterling v. Velsicol Chemical Corp., 855 F.2d 1188, rehearing denied.

Defendant in class action failed either to assert that plaintiffs proffered bad-faith damage claims or to set forth any basis for justifying its allegation that plaintiffs' claims were for less than jurisdictional amount of $10,000; accordingly, defendant was not entitled to dismissal of action on grounds of lack of subject matter jurisdiction.

> Sterling v. Velsicol Chemical Corp., 855 F.2d 1188, rehearing denied.

D.Conn. 1992. Franchisee was not entitled to dismissal of franchisor's complaint alleging violation of franchise agreement and seeking payment for royalty, advertising, and attorney fees, interest, and other relief, on ground that amount in controversy did not exceed $50,000, as it did not prove to a legal certainty that franchisor could not recover the jurisdictional minimum amount. Fed.Rules Civ.Proc.Rule 12(c), 28 U.S.C.A.; 28 U.S.C.A. § 1332(a).

> Grease Monkey Intern., Inc. v. Watkins, 808 F.Supp. 111.

D.D.C. 1990. Plaintiff failed to state cause of action under District of Columbia law for fraud and, absent that claim, plaintiff failed to meet requisite jurisdictional amount for diversity jurisdiction warranting dismissal; plaintiff had not pointed to any false representation made by defendants. 28 U.S.C.A. § 1332; Fed. Rules Civ.Proc.Rule 12(b)(6), 28 U.S.C.A.

> McGowan v. Warnecke, 739 F.Supp. 662.

D.D.C. 1987. Plaintiff in diversity action will fail to allege appropriate amount in controversy to afford federal court subject-matter jurisdiction if claim appears to have been in bad faith, and even where good faith is present,

dismissal will still be proper if court finds to legal certainty that claim is really for less than jurisdictional amount; burden of establishing amount in controversy is upon plaintiff as party seeking jurisdiction. 28 U.S.C.A. § 1332.

> Srour v. Barnes, 670 F.Supp. 18.

N.D.Fla. 1992. Motion to dismiss for lack of subject matter jurisdiction based on plaintiff's failure to satisfy amount in controversy requirement should not be granted unless defendant shows to a legal certainty that the claim is really for less than the jurisdictional amount. 28 U.S.C.A. § 1332.

> Burke Co. v. Hilton Development Co., 802 F.Supp. 434.

S.D.Fla. 1990. Dismissal on grounds of forum non conveniens is not appropriate if plaintiff is citizen of forum, defendant resides at least part-time in forum, cause of action arose in forum, no Spanish contract or copyright rights are implicated, most witnesses reside in country, and forum law applies.

> Korman v. Iglesias, 736 F.Supp. 261.

S.D.Ga. 1996. It must appear to legal certainty that claim is really for less than amount required for diversity jurisdiction in order to justify dismissal on jurisdictional grounds. 28 U.S.C.A. § 1332(a).

> Patray v. Northwest Pub., Inc., 931 F.Supp. 865.

If, from face of pleadings, it is apparent, to legal certainty, that plaintiff cannot recover amount claimed or if, from proofs, court is satisfied to like certainty that plaintiff never was entitled to recover amount, and that his claim was therefore merely colorable for purpose of conferring diversity jurisdiction, suit will be dismissed. 28 U.S.C.A. § 1332(a).

> Patray v. Northwest Pub., Inc., 931 F.Supp. 865.

If evidence after institution of suit shows, to legal certainty, that damages never could have exceeded jurisdictional minimum such that claim was essentially feigned in order to confer diversity jurisdiction, action must be dismissed. 28 U.S.C.A. § 1332(a).

> Patray v. Northwest Pub., Inc., 931 F.Supp. 865.

N.D.Ill. 1996. Rule governing dismissal for want of jurisdiction in cases brought in federal court is that, unless law gives different rule, sum claimed by plaintiff controls as to amount in controversy if claim is apparently made in good faith.

> In re Amino Acid Lysine Antitrust Litigation, 918 F.Supp. 1181, supplemented.

N.D.Ill. 1995. In diversity action, court will not dismiss case because of jurisdictional amount deficiency unless it appears to legal certainty that plaintiff cannot meet required amount in controversy. 28 U.S.C.A. § 1332(a).

Kenebrew v. Connecticut General Life Ins. Co., 882 F.Supp. 749.

For purposes of motion to dismiss for lack of jurisdiction where compensatory damages alone do not satisfy jurisdictional amount requirement, court must determine whether punitive damages are recoverable under applicable state law; if they are found to be recoverable, then court must determine whether complaint satisfies jurisdictional amount to legal certainty. 28 U.S.C.A. § 1332(a); Fed.Rules Civ.Proc.Rule 12(b)(1), 28 U.S.C.A.

Kenebrew v. Connecticut General Life Ins. Co., 882 F.Supp. 749.

N.D.Ill. 1992. In diversity action filed in federal court, court will not dismiss action because of jurisdictional amount deficiency unless it appears to legal certainty that plaintiff cannot meet jurisdictional amount.

Navarro v. Subaru of America Operations Corp., 802 F.Supp. 191.

N.D.Ill. 1991. Motion to dismiss diversity action for lack of jurisdictional amount should be granted only when it appears to legal certainty that claim is really for less than jurisdictional amount. 28 U.S.C.A. § 1332.

Rash Ranco Corp. v. B.L.B. Inc., 762 F.Supp. 1339.

N.D.Ill. 1991. For purposes of motion to dismiss for lack of subject matter jurisdiction, amount in controversy claimed by plaintiff in good faith will be determinative on issue of jurisdictional amount, unless it appears to legal certainty that claim is for less than that required. 28 U.S.C.A. § 1332; Fed.Rules Civ. Proc.Rule 12(b)(1), 28 U.S.C.A.

Racich v. Mid Continent Builders Co., 755 F.Supp. 228.

N.D.Ill. 1990. Although defendant is not absolutely precluded from challenging plaintiff's claim that diversity jurisdiction amount-in-controversy requirement is met, it must appear to legal certainty that claim is really for less than jurisdictional amount to justify dismissal; burden is heavy one for defendant despite fact that, technically, actual burden of proof on jurisdictional issue always lies with party invoking federal jurisdiction.

Interpane Coatings, Inc. v. Australia and New Zealand Banking Group Ltd., 732 F.Supp. 909.

N.D.Iowa 1995. Procedure for disposing of motion to dismiss for lack of diversity jurisdiction on the basis of insufficient amount in controversy is that the sum claimed by plaintiff controls if it is apparently made in good faith; to justify dismissal, it must appear to a legal

certainty that claim is for less than the jurisdictional amount. 28 U.S.C.A. § 1331.

Quality Refrigerated Services, Inc. v. City of Spencer, 908 F.Supp. 1471.

N.D.Iowa 1994. Procedure for disposing of motion to dismiss for lack of subject matter jurisdiction on basis of insufficient amount in controversy, is that sum claimed by plaintiff controls if it is apparently made in good faith; to justify dismissal, it must appear to legal certainty that claim is for less than jurisdictional amount. Fed.Rules Civ.Proc.Rule 12(b)(1), 28 U.S.C.A.

Veeder v. Omaha Tribe of Nebraska, 864 F.Supp. 889.

D.Kan. 1995. Fact that motion for class certification did not include evidence that individual prospective class members met amount in controversy requirement for diversity jurisdiction was not grounds to deny class certification; appropriate procedure is to grant class certification, assuming it is proper, and subsequently dismiss those particular class members who appear to legal certainty to have insufficient claims. Fed.Rules Civ.Proc.Rule 23, 28 U.S.C.A.

Heartland Communications, Inc. v. Sprint Corp., 161 F.R.D. 111.

D.Kan. 1994. Action will not be dismissed because amount in controversy less that jurisdictional amount unless it appears to legal certainty that claim is really for less than jurisdictional amount. 28 U.S.C.A. § 1332.

Smith v. Hawkeye-Security Ins. Co., 842 F.Supp. 1373.

M.D.La. 1994. In order for court to dismiss case for lack of jurisdictional amount, it must appear to legal certainty that claim is for less than jurisdictional amount. 28 U.S.C.A. § 1332(a).

Jones v. Dow Chemical Co., 885 F.Supp. 905.

D.Md. 1998. To justify dismissal for want of jurisdiction in a diversity case based on failure to meet amount in controversy requirement, it must appear to a legal certainty that the claim is really for less than the jurisdictional amount. 28 U.S.C.A. § 1332(a).

FLF, Inc. v. World Publications, Inc., 999 F.Supp. 640.

Dismissal of diversity action must be granted where it is plain from the complaint that an amount less than the jurisdictional amount in controversy is all that is at issue. 28 U.S.C.A. § 1332(a).

FLF, Inc. v. World Publications, Inc., 999 F.Supp. 640.

D.Md. 1996. Appropriate relief for claims under jurisdictional amount for diversity jurisdiction was to grant summary judgment on hotel owner's claim to recover punitive damages for insurer's alleged breach of implied covenant of good faith and fair dealing, but to dismiss claims for compensatory damages and interest without prejudice; claims other than those related to punitive damages did not need to be reached to determine issue of jurisdictional amount, and punitive damages issue presented no disputed questions of fact.

> Schaefer v. Aetna Life & Cas. Co., 910 F.Supp. 1095.

D.Md. 1990. Complaint may be dismissed for lack of subject matter jurisdiction in diversity action if it appears to legal certainty that plaintiff's claim is for less than jurisdictional amount. 28 U.S.C.A. § 1332(a).

> Herlihy v. Ply-Gem Industries, Inc., 752 F.Supp. 1282.

D.Mass. 1997. Upon determination that borrower had no viable class claim against mortgage lender, on theory that the fees it charged for telefaxing an original and duplicate statement of payoff amount on borrower's loan were illegal "prepayment charges," and that the only matter in dispute was borrower's individual claim for recovery of this $40.00 fee as not having been voluntarily made under the facts of his particular case, borrower's lawsuit had to be dismissed, as failing to meet the "amount in controversy" requirement for district court to exercise diversity jurisdiction.

> Cappellini v. Mellon Mortg. Co., 991 F.Supp. 31.

D.Mass. 1995. Even where complaint adequately alleges jurisdictional amount for diversity jurisdiction, federal court may dismiss case if it appears to legal certainty that plaintiff, at time of complaint, could not recover amount in controversy. 28 U.S.C.A. § 1332(a).

> F.C.I. Realty Trust v. Aetna Cas. & Sur. Co., 906 F.Supp. 30.

Plaintiff's offer, in opposition to motion to dismiss, for lack of diversity jurisdiction, of repair estimate in excess of $50,000 sufficed to show that claim was not, to legal certainty, for less than jurisdictional amount, even though other estimates placed in evidence by defendant were for less than jurisdictional amount and complaint itself merely pled damages in amount not less than $42,525. 28 U.S.C.A. § 1332(a).

> F.C.I. Realty Trust v. Aetna Cas. & Sur. Co., 906 F.Supp. 30.

E.D.Mo. 1993. District court should dismiss for lack of jurisdiction when it appears to a legal certainty that plaintiff cannot satisfy jurisdictional amount in controversy requirement.

> Piper v. Kassel, 817 F.Supp. 802.

E.D.Mo. 1989. Dismissal of diversity action for failure to allege requisite jurisdictional

amount in controversy is justified only if it appears to a legal certainty that the claim is really for less than jurisdictional amount. 28 U.S.C.A. § 1332(a).

> Perma Glass Corp. v. Sasak Corp., 718 F.Supp. 742.

D.Neb. 1996. Complaint which alleges in good faith jurisdictional amount in excess of $50,000 will suffice to confer diversity jurisdiction upon court; however, where defendant questions legitimacy of alleged amount, plaintiff has burden of proving requisite amount, and if it appears to a legal certainty that claim is really for less than jurisdictional amount, complaint will be dismissed. 28 U.S.C.A. § 1332.

> Morris B. Chapman & Associates v. Union Pacific R. Co., 937 F.Supp. 870.

D.N.H. 1990. When jurisdictional amount for exercise of diversity jurisdiction is not satisfied, federal court must dismiss action for lack of subject matter jurisdiction.

> Lerer v. Ultra Scan, Inc., 770 F.Supp. 51.

Diversity action had to be dismissed for failure to satisfy jurisdictional amount-in-controversy requirement, where allegations in complaint were sufficient to satisfy amount-in-controversy requirement only if plaintiff's damages were trebled under New Hampshire Consumer Protection Act (NHCPA), and where any claim under NHCPA was plainly time barred. N.H.RSA 358–A:1 et seq.

> Lerer v. Ultra Scan, Inc., 770 F.Supp. 51.

E.D.N.Y. 1996. It is not enough to warrant dismissal of action, based on failure to meet amount in controversy requirement for diversity actions, that allegations leave grave doubt about likelihood of recovery of requisite amount; rather, it must appear to a legal certainty that allegations do not warrant award in excess of $50,000. 28 U.S.C.A. § 1332(a).

> Bennett v. Town of Riverhead, 940 F.Supp. 481.

S.D.N.Y. 1997. District court will dismiss diversity action for lack of jurisdiction on amount in controversy grounds only if it appears to a legal certainty that claim is really for less than jurisdictional amount; even where plaintiff's allegations leave grave doubt about likelihood of recovery of requisite amount, dismissal is not warranted. 28 U.S.C.A. § 1332.

> Whitney Holdings, Ltd. v. Givotovsky, 988 F.Supp. 732.

S.D.N.Y. 1996. Rule governing dismissal for want of diversity jurisdiction is that the sum claimed by plaintiff controls if claim is apparently made in good faith; it must appear to a legal certainty that claim is really less than the jurisdictional amount to justify dismissal. 28 U.S.C.A. § 1332.

> Leslie v. BancTec Service Corp., 928 F.Supp. 341.

To dismiss for want of diversity jurisdiction, federal court must find with a "legal certainty" that plaintiff's claim is for less than the jurisdictional amount required for diversity jurisdiction and although "legal certainty" test makes it difficult to achieve dismissal, there are three instances in which the standard is met: when terms of contract limit plaintiff's recovery; when statute or other law limits recovery; or when independent facts show jurisdiction amount was pled in order to avoid federal jurisdiction. 28 U.S.C.A. § 1332.

> Leslie v. BancTec Service Corp., 928 F.Supp. 341.

Federal district court could not determine with a legal certainty that employment discrimination plaintiff's claim was for less than $50,000 so as to dismiss case for lack of diversity jurisdiction; plaintiff's backpay amounted to approximately $46,168, jury who believed plaintiff could also award him thousands of dollars in compensatory damages, if plaintiff was reinstated, that would be worth the amount of years he would work at employer, also resulting in thousands of dollars, and plaintiff's requests to settle for more than $50,000 were indications of what he believed his claim was worth. 28 U.S.C.A. § 1332.

> Leslie v. BancTec Service Corp., 928 F.Supp. 341.

S.D.N.Y. 1995. Complaint alleging diversity of citizenship will be dismissed on jurisdictional amount grounds only if it appears to legal certainty that claim does not exceed jurisdictional amount. 28 U.S.C.A. § 1332(a).

> Gardiner Stone Hunter Intern. v. Iberia Lineas Aereas De Espana, S.A., 896 F.Supp. 125.

S.D.N.Y. 1995. In determining whether amount in controversy requirement allowing court to exercise jurisdiction under diversity statute has been met, court must rely on amount claimed in complaint as dispositive, unless it appears that that amount is not recoverable in good faith; court may only dismiss complaint if, to legal certainty, plaintiff's allegations do not support recovery in excess of jurisdictional amount. 28 U.S.C.A. § 1332(a).

> Kry v. Poleschuk, 892 F.Supp. 574.

S.D.N.Y. 1995. To dismiss diversity case for failure to meet jurisdictional amount, it must appear to legal certainty that claim is actually for less than jurisdictional amount. Fed.Rules Civ.Proc.Rule 12(h)(3), 28 U.S.C.A.

> Chase Manhattan Bank, N.A. v. American Nat. Bank and Trust Co. of Chicago, 889 F.Supp. 121, vacated 93 F.3d 1064.

Construction lender's suit against persons who had guaranteed cost of any renovations if building was not completed by borrower would be dismissed for lack of jurisdictional amount, where lender repossessed and sold allegedly unfinished building without incurring any renovation costs. 28 U.S.C.A. § 1332(a); Fed.Rules Civ.Proc.Rule 12(h)(3), 28 U.S.C.A.

> Chase Manhattan Bank, N.A. v. American Nat. Bank and Trust Co. of Chicago, 889 F.Supp. 121, vacated 93 F.3d 1064.

S.D.N.Y. 1991. Bank's allegations, in diversity action brought by customers seeking damages arising out of alleged unauthorized transfer of funds from money market account, that New York Uniform Commercial Code limited customers' recovery to their actual damages absent bad faith, that customers could not sustain burden of showing reasonably foreseeable damages in order to recover consequential damages under New York law, and that amount of consequential damages claimed by customers had to be limited because customers paid only a portion of funds forfeited due to dishonorment of checks, could not form basis for dismissal for lack of jurisdictional amount, since all of bank's arguments could not be resolved without addressing merits of those defenses. N.Y.McKinney's Uniform Commercial Code §§ 4–101 et seq., 4–103(5); 28 U.S.C.A. § 1332(a); Fed. Rules Civ.Proc.Rule 12(b)(1), 28 U.S.C.A.

> Reddy v. Barclays Bank of New York, N.A., 773 F.Supp. 655.

N.D.Ohio 1984. Although party must satisfy jurisdictional amount in controversy requirement, complaint will not be dismissed where made in good faith unless it is "legal certainty" that claim is actually for less than minimum amount. Fed.Rules Civ.Proc.Rule 12(b)(1), 28 U.S.C.A.

> Innovative Digital Equipment, Inc. v. Quantum Technology, Inc., 597 F.Supp. 983.

E.D.Pa. 1996. Rule governing dismissal for want of jurisdiction in diversity action on basis that plaintiff cannot satisfy jurisdictional amount in controversy requirement is that sum claimed by plaintiff controls if claim is apparently made in good faith, and it must appear to legal certainty that claim is really for less than jurisdictional amount to justify dismissal. 28 U.S.C.A. § 1332(a).

> Marino v. Sports Authority, 940 F.Supp. 792.

E.D.Pa. 1995. Dismissal for failure to meet jurisdictional amount in controversy is justified only when it appears to legal certainty that claim is really for less than jurisdictional amount. 28 U.S.C.A. § 1332(a)(1).

> Omega Sports, Inc. v. Sunkyong America, Inc., 872 F.Supp. 201.

D.Puerto Rico 1994. Claim may only be dismissed for failure to meet jurisdictional amount when it appears to "legal certainty" that, after considering applicable state law, claim is really for less than jurisdictional amount. Fed.Rules Civ.Proc.Rule 12(h), 28 U.S.C.A.

> Serrano v. Nicholson Nursery, Inc., 844 F.Supp. 73.

Plaintiffs claim was for less than $50,000 to "legal certainty" so as to support dismissal for lack of subject matter jurisdiction where allegations regarding emotional damages were too conclusory to support their recovery in breach of contract action under Puerto Rico law. Fed. Rules Civ.Proc.Rule 12(h), 28 U.S.C.A.

> Serrano v. Nicholson Nursery, Inc., 844 F.Supp. 73.

D.Puerto Rico 1989. A diversity claim should be dismissed on grounds that actual amount in controversy does not exceed a jurisdictional amount only if it appears to a reasonable certainty that claim is really for less than jurisdictional amount. 28 U.S.C.A. § 1332.

> De Jesus v. Eastern Air Lines, Inc., 708 F.Supp. 470.

D.Puerto Rico 1986. It was not legally certain that plaintiffs who asserted claim for damages incurred when they discovered cockroach in their restaurant meal would not recover in excess of $10,000 for purposes of diversity jurisdiction, and dismissal of action premised on amount in controversy would be improper. 28 U.S.C.A. § 1332.

> Tobie v. Don Pepe Corp., Inc., 646 F.Supp. 620.

D.Utah 1994. When making determination on diversity jurisdiction, federal courts base amount in controversy on plaintiff's good faith claim in complaint; to justify dismissal based on insufficient jurisdictional amount, it must appear to district court with legal certainty that claim is really for less than jurisdictional amount. 28 U.S.C.A. § 1332(a).

> Prudential Ins. Co. v. Thomason, 865 F.Supp. 762.

E.D.Wash. 1991. Each plaintiff in class action must satisfy amount required for federal jurisdiction, and any plaintiff who does not must be dismissed from case. 28 U.S.C.A. § 1332(a); Fed.Rules Civ.Proc.Rule 23(b)(3), (c)(1), 28 U.S.C.A.

> Auvil v. CBS "60 Minutes", 140 F.R.D. 450.

S.D.W.Va. 1995. Generally, in determining whether requisite jurisdictional amount is in controversy, sum claimed by plaintiff controls if claim is apparently made in good faith; it must appear to legal certainty that claim is really for less than jurisdictional amount to justify dismissal. 28 U.S.C.A. § 1332(a).

> Adkins v. Gibson, 906 F.Supp. 345.

S.D.W.Va. 1985. Although plaintiff could establish facts which would show it entitled to expectation remedy or the restitution remedy, it could not show that it was entitled to both remedies, and thus, because neither amount awardable under restitution theory or the expectation theory was in excess of $10,000, amount in controversy failed to reach jurisdictional requirement. 28 U.S.C.A. § 1332(a).

> Prior Oil Well Drilling Co. v. David A. Waldron and Associates, Inc., 601 F.Supp. 778.

⚖➣1742(5). **Improper venue.**

C.A.D.C. 1989. Clause in agreement between Italian manufacturer and American distributor under which agreement would be "determined and governed by the appropriate court of Verona, Italy" was choice-of-forum clause and not choice-of-law clause, and thus required dismissal of suit for improper venue. Fed.Rules Civ.Proc.Rule 12(b)(3), 28 U.S.C.A.

> Commerce Consultants Intern., Inc. v. Vetrerie Riunite, S.p.A., 867 F.2d 697, 276 U.S.App.D.C. 81.

C.A.9 (Ariz.) 1996. Forum selection clause in loan agreement was not rendered unreasonable and therefore would be enforced by dismissal for lack of venue, notwithstanding opposing party's subjective fear of persecution and allegations of specific acts of misconduct by particular individuals when that party was last in selected country of Mexico.

> Argueta v. Banco Mexicano, S.A., 87 F.3d 320.

C.A.9 (Ariz.) 1992. Even though federal defendants originally requested transfer rather than dismissal due to improper venue in the District of Arizona, district court did not abuse its discretion by dismissing mortgagor's action alleging civil rights violations and violation of the Truth in Lending Act; it would not be in the interests of justice to transfer case because mortgagor expressed no interest in transfer and because action smacked of harassment and bad faith on mortgagor's part in that it appeared she filed it after repeatedly losing on at least some similar claims in California. Truth in Lending

Act, § 125, 15 U.S.C.A. § 1635; 28 U.S.C.A. § 1406(a).

> King v. Russell, 963 F.2d 1301, certiorari denied 113 S.Ct. 1263, 507 U.S. 913, 122 L.Ed.2d 660, rehearing denied 113 S.Ct. 1891, 507 U.S. 1047, 123 L.Ed.2d 507.

Although venue was proper as to one defendant in District of Arizona in mortgagor's action alleging violations of civil rights laws and Truth in Lending Act since defendant did business in Arizona, after district court had dismissed the other defendants based on improper venue, district court could not proceed as to one defendant alone since its relationship to action was at best tangential; mortgagor alleged that her rights were violated by foreclosure of junior mortgage on her home, defendant held senior mortgage and mortgagor did not allege senior mortgagee had played any part in foreclosure proceedings or subsequent eviction of which she complained. 28 U.S.C.A. § 1391(c).

> King v. Russell, 963 F.2d 1301, certiorari denied 113 S.Ct. 1263, 507 U.S. 913, 122 L.Ed.2d 660, rehearing denied 113 S.Ct. 1891, 507 U.S. 1047, 123 L.Ed.2d 507.

C.A.9 (Ariz.) 1991. Although dismissal of action for improper venue is harsh penalty, dismissal is proper where filing in improper forum evidences bad faith. 28 U.S.C.A. § 1406(a).

> In re Hall, Bayoutree Associates, Ltd., 939 F.2d 802.

C.A.9 (Cal.) 1991. District court did not abuse its discretion in dismissing without prejudice Title VII action that was brought in wrong venue, rather than transferring it sua sponte, inasmuch as plaintiff did not ask court to transfer action and plaintiff refused to bring suit in proper venue. Civil Rights Act of 1964, § 701 et seq., as amended, 42 U.S.C.A. § 2000e et seq.

> Johnson v. Payless Drug Stores Northwest, Inc., 950 F.2d 586, certiorari denied 112 S.Ct. 3044, 505 U.S. 1225, 120 L.Ed.2d 911.

C.A.11 (Fla.) 1998. Motions to dismiss based upon choice-of-forum and choice-of-law clauses ordinarily are not properly brought as motions to dismiss for lack of subject matter jurisdiction, but, instead, are properly brought as motions to dismiss for improper venue; basis upon which defendants seek dismissal, namely, that parties' agreement prohibits plaintiff from bringing suit in particular forum, is unrelated to actual basis of federal subject matter jurisdiction, either federal question jurisdiction or diversity of citizenship. Fed.Rules Civ.Proc.Rule 12(b)(1, 3), 28 U.S.C.A.

> Lipcon v. Underwriters at Lloyd's, London, 148 F.3d 1285.

C.A.11 (Ga.) 1990. Although breach of reinsurance contract which was not negotiated in Northern District of Georgia, was one claim asserted by workers' compensation insurers against corporations and members of family running corporations, central claim was one against corporations to pierce corporate veil to hold corporations and family members who were located in that district responsible for allegedly squandering assets of reinsurer which they had created and for otherwise defrauding insurer; accordingly, venue was appropriate in United States District Court for the Northern District of Georgia, and it was an abuse of discretion to dismiss case for lack of venue. 28 U.S.C.A. § 1391(a).

> Home Ins. Co. v. Thomas Industries, Inc., 896 F.2d 1352.

C.A.7 (Ill.) 1997. Even assuming that corporation's counterclaim arising out of contract met requirements for compulsory counterclaim, dismissal of counterclaim was required by contract's forum-selection clause, under which claim had to be brought in Delaware; agreement would operate so as to preclude shareholder from later asserting, in Delaware, that corporation should have raised claim in instant action. Fed.Rules Civ.Proc.Rule 13(a), 28 U.S.C.A.

> Publicis Communication v. True North Communications Inc., 132 F.3d 363.

C.A.7 (Ill.) 1993. Local agents of operator of insurance underwriting market were integrally related to market operator and syndicate managing agents successfully invoking English forum selection and choice of law clauses, such that fraud and securities suit against all defendants would properly be kept in single forum, warranting dismissal of suit as to local agents also, on condition that they would agree to appear voluntarily in England if suit were refiled there.

> Bonny v. Society of Lloyd's, 3 F.3d 156, certiorari denied 114 S.Ct. 1057, 510 U.S. 1113, 127 L.Ed.2d 378.

C.A.7 (Ind.) 1989. District court may transfer action brought in wrong division or district if it is in interest of justice to do so, but must dismiss such suit if it denies transfer. 28 U.S.C.A. § 1406(a).

> Hapaniewski v. City of Chicago Heights, 883 F.2d 576, certiorari denied 110 S.Ct. 1116, 493 U.S. 1071, 107 L.Ed.2d 1023.

C.A.5 (La.) 1990. Foreign defendants' motion for discretionary dismissal under forum non conveniens doctrine was not untimely where viability of forum non conveniens defense was slim while some domestic defendants remained in case, and foreign defendants filed their motion as soon as plaintiff notified district court that he planned to dismiss all other remaining defendants; defendants timing of forum non conveniens motion could not be considered dilatory where plaintiff alone controlled joinder and dismissal of other, nonforeign defendants.

> Ikospentakis v. Thalassic S.S. Agency, 915 F.2d 176.

C.A.1 (Mass.) 1993. Although dismissal based on forum selection clause is based on failure to state a claim rather than improper venue, label employed does not bind the court. Fed.Rules Civ.Proc.Rule 12(b)(3, 6), 28 U.S.C.A.

> Lambert v. Kysar, 983 F.2d 1110.

C.A.6 (Mich.) 1998. The decision of whether to dismiss for improper venue or transfer the case to a proper venue is within the district court's sound discretion, and accordingly, Court of Appeals reviews such a decision for an abuse of discretion. 28 U.S.C.A. §§ 1391(a), 1406(a).

> First of Michigan Corp. v. Bramlet, 141 F.3d 260.

C.A.8 (Minn.) 1997. Dismissal by Minnesota district court of action arising from accident occurring in Illinois on basis of improper venue, which was entered after plaintiff withdrew her motion to transfer venue of action to Illinois, was not result of erroneous view of law or erroneous assessment of evidence, and thus, plaintiff's motion for relief based on mistake, inadvertence, or excusable neglect was properly denied; district court first concluded that it did not have personal jurisdiction over defendants, and then properly dismissed action based on improper venue, as all named defendants did not reside in Minnesota. Fed.Rules Civ.Proc. Rule 60(b), 28 U.S.C.A.

> Richards v. Aramark Services, Inc., 108 F.3d 925.

C.A.8 (Mo.) 1981. Mizokami Bros. of Arizona, Inc. v. Mobay Chemical Corp., 660 F.2d 712, appeal after remand 798 F.2d 1196.

C.A.9 (N.Mariana Islands) 1989. Motion to dismiss for improper venue was waived by virtue of having been asserted after movants filed their motion for summary judgment. Fed. Rules Civ.Proc.Rule 12(b, g, h), 28 U.S.C.A.

> Misch on Behalf of Estate of Misch v. Zee Enterprises, Inc., 879 F.2d 628.

C.A.2 (N.Y.) 1993. Whether dismissal or transfer is appropriate following finding that case laid venue in wrong division or district lies within sound discretion of district court. 28 U.S.C.A. § 1406(a).

> Minnette v. Time Warner, 997 F.2d 1023.

C.A.2 (N.Y.) 1992. Suit naming as defendants justices of the United States Supreme Court, former United States Attorney General, bankruptcy judges and others and alleging conspiracy dating back to 1963 presented "extraordinary circumstances" justifying federal district court's exercise of its power to dismiss sua sponte on ground of improper venue, where complaint's allegations were similar to those made in several cases brought by plaintiff in Ninth Circuit where he had been classified as vexatious litigant and barred from instituting new suits without leave of court. 28 U.S.C.A. §§ 1391, 1402.

> Stich v. Rehnquist, 982 F.2d 88.

C.A.10 (Okl.) 1998. In responding to motion to dismiss for improper venue, plaintiff is entitled to rely upon well pled facts of complaint only to extent that such facts are uncontroverted by defendant's affidavit.

> Pierce v. Shorty Small's of Branson Inc., 137 F.3d 1190.

C.A.1 (Puerto Rico) 1990. District court sitting in Puerto Rico did not abuse its discretion in dismissing suit by Puerto Rican distributor against Brazilian manufacturer for breach of distributorship agreement on forum non conveniens grounds; forum-selection clause in agreement, calling for resolution of disputes in Brazil, was freely negotiated by parties, and thus would be given effect.

> Royal Bed and Spring Co., Inc. v. Famossul Industria e Comercio de Moveis Ltda., 906 F.2d 45, 123 A.L.R. Fed. 739.

C.A.1 (R.I.) 1994. Although district court for district in which financial transaction occurred lacked jurisdiction over action arising from claim disallowed by Federal Deposit Insurance Corporation (FDIC), retransfer of case, rather than dismissal, was appropriate, where FDIC was responsible for transfer of case from district court with jurisdiction to district court without jurisdiction and time to refile action had expired. Federal Deposit Insurance Act, § 2[11](d)(6)(A), 12 U.S.C.A. § 1821(d)(6)(A); 28 U.S.C.A. § 1404(a).

> Lloyd v. F.D.I.C., 22 F.3d 335.

C.A.5 (Tex.) 1996. District court could dismiss, as opposed to transfer, diversity case based solely on forum selection clause, where personal jurisdiction existed and venue was otherwise proper. 28 U.S.C.A. §§ 1391(a, c), 1404(a), 1406(a).

> International Software Systems, Inc. v. Amplicon, Inc., 77 F.3d 112, rehearing denied.

C.A.5 (Tex.) 1989. After court repeatedly denied defendant's pretrial motions to dismiss or transfer claims in bellwether products liability trial in which decision to try case in the forum was adequately supported, dismissal of all claims for improper venue after jury verdict had been returned on some of those claims under provision allowing cure or waiver of defects was erroneous. 28 U.S.C.A. § 1406(a).

> Scott v. Monsanto Co., 868 F.2d 786, rehearing denied.

C.D.Cal. 1995. Interests of justice dictated that vessel passenger's personal injury suit against vessel operator be transferred to Florida district pursuant to forum-selection clause, rather than dismissed, as passenger may have had statute of limitations problem if action were dismissed. 28 U.S.C.A. § 1406(a).

> Roberson v. Norwegian Cruise Line, 897 F.Supp. 1285.

C.D.Cal. 1995. Federal court located in California would not dismiss, on forum non conveniens grounds, law suit brought by corporation against guarantor of forged stock certificates, which had its home office in Canada; guarantor had provided no facts to support claim that Canadian or other forum could afford corporation remedy, or that it would be unnecessarily burdened by defending action in California, and while guarantor pointed out that much evidence and many witnesses were in Canada, it did not list single witness that would have difficulty testifying in California, nor any problems with producing Canadian evidence in American courts, and United States had significant interest in having case adjudicated here, as there were allegedly over 700 shareholders of corporation injured by forgery.

> MTC Electronic Technologies Co., Ltd. v. Leung, 876 F.Supp. 1143.

N.D.Cal. 1994. Whether interest of justice militates in favor of transfer rather than dismissal for improper venue is judgment committed to sound discretion of the district court, but transfer is generally consistent with the interest of justice. 28 U.S.C.A. § 1406(a).

> Citizens for a Better Environment-California v. Union Oil Co. of California, 861 F.Supp. 889, affirmed 83 F.3d 1111, as amended, certiorari denied 117 S.Ct. 789, 136 L.Ed.2d 731.

Transfer rather than dismissal for improper venue was appropriate in citizen suit under the Clean Water Act. 28 U.S.C.A. § 1406(a); Federal Water Pollution Control Act Amendments of 1972, § 505(c)(1), as amended, 33 U.S.C.A. § 1365(c)(1).

> Citizens for a Better Environment-California v. Union Oil Co. of California, 861 F.Supp. 889, affirmed 83 F.3d 1111, as amended, certiorari denied 117 S.Ct. 789, 136 L.Ed.2d 731.

D.Conn. 1996. In diversity action, where venue in district is improper with respect to some claims in multi-claim action, claims for which venue is improper must either be dismissed or severed and transferred to proper venue; another alternative is to transfer entire case. 28 U.S.C.A. §§ 1391(b), 1406(a); Fed. Rules Civ.Proc.Rule 12(b)(3), 28 U.S.C.A.

> Jones v. Trump, 919 F.Supp. 583.

D.D.C. 1995. Defendant's motion to dismiss action based on improper venue was denied where defendant was amenable to suit in both district where action was brought and district in which venue was contemplated and, following dismissal of other defendants which had been named, venue was proper in either jurisdiction.

> Chung v. Chrysler Corp., 903 F.Supp. 160.

D.D.C. 1993. District court would dismiss rather than transfer breach of contract claims against Department of Housing and Urban Development (HUD) and Government National Mortgage Association (GNMA) for which exclusive jurisdiction resided in Court of Federal Claims under Tucker Acts, in light of admission that relief sought by breach of contract claims was completely duplicative of relief sought by claims which would be retained by district court. Fed.Rules Civ.Proc.Rule 12(b)(1), 28 U.S.C.A.; 28 U.S.C.A. § 1631.

> York Associates, Inc. v. Secretary of Housing and Urban Development, 815 F.Supp. 16.

D.D.C. 1991. Securities and Exchange Commission's failure to assert venue explicitly in its complaint was not basis to dismiss action for improper venue.

> S.E.C. v. Ernst & Young, 775 F.Supp. 411.

D.Hawai'i 1995. Fact issue as to whether passenger had notice of forum selection clause on back of cruise ship ticket precluded dismissal for lack of venue of action for damages against cruise line.

> Kalman v. Cunard Line, Ltd., 904 F.Supp. 1150.

N.D.Ill. 1997. Transfer, rather than dismissal, is proper remedy if convenience of parties and witnesses and interest of justice describe more appropriate forum elsewhere. 28 U.S.C.A. § 1404(a).

> Georgouses v. NaTec Resources, Inc., 963 F.Supp. 728.

N.D.Ill. 1994. District court must dismiss suit brought in wrong district if it denies transfer. 28 U.S.C.A. § 1406(a).

> Holmgren v. Allen, 886 F.Supp. 641.

N.D.Ill. 1994. Motions to dismiss on ground that forum selection clause required litigation in another jurisdiction involved only question of proper venue, and not question of subject matter jurisdiction.

> Frediani & Delgreco, S.P.A. v. Gina Imports, Ltd., 870 F.Supp. 217.

Where moving party seeks to dismiss case because appropriate forum is other than federal district court, statute which provides for transfer to a different district court is inapplicable. 28 U.S.C.A. § 1404(a).

> Frediani & Delgreco, S.P.A. v. Gina Imports, Ltd., 870 F.Supp. 217.

N.D.Ill. 1990. Transfer of suit from one federal district court to another, rather than dismissal of suit, is proper remedy if convenience of parties and witnesses and interests of justice point to different forum as more appropriate. 28 U.S.C.A. § 1404(a).

> Robinson v. Town of Madison, 752 F.Supp. 842.

N.D.Ill. 1990. Court would not grant defendant's motion to dismiss for lack of personal jurisdiction, although there were highly persuasive reasons for doing so, where granting motion would be wasteful because transfer of venue to district in which defendant resided was appropriate. 28 U.S.C.A. § 1404(a).

> Zalutsky, Pinski & DiGiacomo, Ltd. v. Kleinman, 747 F.Supp. 457.

N.D.Ill. 1986. Action by Pennsylvania resident for injuries suffered in Pennsylvania while working with machine manufactured by Japanese corporation brought against Japanese corporation in Illinois, where Japanese corporation employed one service representative, would be dismissed for lack of personal jurisdiction, despite plaintiff's request that decision be deferred until discovery was completed in Pennsylvania action based on hope that discovery would reveal more activities of Japanese corporation in Illinois, where there appeared no likelihood that plaintiff could discover quantity and quality of contacts by Japanese corporation with Illinois that he needed for suit grounded on Pennsylvania injury, and there was no reason to believe that Pennsylvania long-arm statute could not reach Japanese corporation.

> Palmer v. Kawaguchi Iron Works, Ltd., 644 F.Supp. 327.

N.D.Ill. 1985. Transfer of a civil action, rather than dismissal, is the proper remedy if the convenience of parties and witnesses and the interest of justice describe a more appropriate forum elsewhere. 28 U.S.C.A. § 1404(a).

> Van Gelder v. Taylor, 621 F.Supp. 613.

Normally, if venue is not proper in district court where action is initiated, transfer to a proper district or division is preferred over dismissal; transfer is generally considered to be more "in the interest of justice" than dismissal for improper venue and, therefore, any doubt should be resolved in favor of preserving the action, particularly where it appears that venue is proper in the transferee court.

> Van Gelder v. Taylor, 621 F.Supp. 613.

N.D.Ind. 1995. Where district court lacked personal jurisdiction over defendant, venue was also inappropriate in district court, and it could either dismiss case outright, or, in interest of justice, transfer case to any district in which the cause of action could have been brought originally. 28 U.S.C.A. § 1406.

> Charlesworth v. Marco Mfg. Co., 878 F.Supp. 1196.

N.D.Iowa 1996. It is important to distinguish between circumstances in which court is called upon to "enforce" forum selection clause by dismissing action for improper venue, and situation in which party seeks to rely upon forum selection clause as tipping balance in favor of stated forum in court's discretionary weighing of all relevant factors under statute that permits transfer of venue for convenience of parties and witnesses, in interest of justice: in former case, "mandatoriness" of forum selection clause is of critical importance; however, in latter case, it is parties' expression of preference in such clause, not its "mandatoriness," that is of critical importance, and in this latter case, transfer will only be effected to specified forum if balance of other factors also dictates that specified forum is proper, or if balance of other factors fails to indicate that one forum or another should be preferred. 28 U.S.C.A. § 1404(a).

> Terra Intern., Inc. v. Mississippi Chemical Corp., 922 F.Supp. 1334, affirmed 119 F.3d 688, rehearing and suggestion for rehearing denied, certiorari denied 118 S.Ct. 629, 139 L.Ed.2d 609.

D.Kan. 1996. Procedure to decide motion to dismiss for improper venue is generally the same as for deciding motion to dismiss for lack of personal jurisdiction.

> Electronic Realty Associates, L.P. v. Paramount Pictures Corp., 935 F.Supp. 1172.

D.Kan. 1995. District of Nebraska, rather than District of Kansas, was proper venue for Kansas resident's medical malpractice action against Nebraska physician for allegedly negligent acts that occurred in Nebraska; interests of justice required transfer to Nebraska, rather than dismissal, as there was no question that Nebraska court would have personal jurisdiction over defendant, and, according to plaintiff, statute of limitations on her action had expired and Nebraska did not have statute that would save her action from being untimely if refiled there. 28 U.S.C.A. §§ 1391(a), 1406(a).

> McDonald v. Doolittle, 885 F.Supp. 233.

If court determines that venue is not proper, and that action would be barred by statute of limitations if refiled in new venue, it is in interest of justice and particularly appropriate to transfer action, rather than dismissing it. 28 U.S.C.A. §§ 1391(a), 1406(a).

> McDonald v. Doolittle, 885 F.Supp. 233.

D.Kan. 1994. Procedure to deciding motion to dismiss for improper venue is generally the same as for deciding motion to dismiss for lack of personal jurisdiction; when motion to dismiss for lack of jurisdiction is brought before trial and supported by affidavits and other written material, plaintiff need only make prima facie showing of jurisdiction.

> M.K.C. Equipment Co., Inc. v. M.A.I.L. Code, Inc., 843 F.Supp. 679.

D.Kan. 1989. Selection between options of dismissal and transfer, for improper venue, is a matter within district court's sound discretion.

> General Elec. Capital Corp. v. Selph, 718 F.Supp. 1495.

E.D.La. 1995. Upon plaintiff's failure to show that venue in Louisiana was proper in personal injury action arising from automobile accident that occurred in Mississippi, court would not dismiss matter, but rather, would transfer it to Southern District of Mississippi. 28 U.S.C.A. § 1406(a); Fed.Rules Civ.Proc.Rule 12(b)(3), 28 U.S.C.A.

> Smith v. Fortenberry, 903 F.Supp. 1018.

M.D.La. 1995. Suit arising out of subcontract for rubber lined piping manufactured in Louisiana, but used in construction project located in Tennessee, was subject to transfer, but not dismissal, where it was initially brought in court of proper venue. 28 U.S.C.A. §§ 1404(a), 1406(a).

> Shaw Group, Inc. v. Natkin & Co., 907 F.Supp. 201.

D.Minn. 1987. On motion to dismiss on ground of improper venue, court is not presented with question of where venue would be proper, so long as it can say that the forum is not a district that constitutes the locus of the claim. 28 U.S.C.A. § 1391(b).

> Saturn Systems, Inc. v. Saturn Corp., 659 F.Supp. 865.

D.Minn. 1985. A finding that personal jurisdiction exists over a defendant does not preclude court from dismissing case because of improper venue.

> Tonka Corp. v. TMS Entertainment, Inc., 638 F.Supp. 386.

Minnesota venue was not proper with regard to suit brought by Minnesota corporation against California corporation, alleging that children's television program produced by California corporation infringed trademark of Minnesota corporation, considering that Central District of California was clearly a more convenient forum from standpoint of many of defendant's witnesses and evidence concerning

development of program; moreover, California corporation was not doing business in Minnesota for venue purposes. 28 U.S.C.A. § 1391(b, c).

> Tonka Corp. v. TMS Entertainment, Inc., 638 F.Supp. 386.

S.D.Miss. 1989. Federal district court in Mississippi would not grant natural gas marketer's motion to dismiss natural gas seller's breach of contract action, even though marketer had declaratory judgment action pending in Nebraska encompassing same issues, insofar as marketer secretly filed Nebraska action on day before settlement negotiations took place in obvious attempt to deprive seller of its choice of forum. Fed.Rules Civ.Proc.Rule 13(a), 28 U.S.C.A.

> Southmark Corp. v. PSI, Inc., 727 F.Supp. 1060.

E.D.Mo. 1992. On motion to dismiss on forum non conveniens grounds, district court must first determine whether there is adequate alternative forum available in which dispute can be resolved; if there is, court must then balance a number of private and public interest factors to determine whether they outweigh deference originally attended to plaintiff's choice of forum.

> Peabody Holding Co., Inc. v. Costain Group PLC, 808 F.Supp. 1425.

W.D.Mo. 1993. District court in improper venue should transfer, rather than dismiss, case upon finding that it is in interest of justice to do so. 28 U.S.C.A. § 1406(a).

> Naegler v. Nissan Motor Co., Ltd., 835 F.Supp. 1152.

D.N.J. 1996. Upon determination that District of New Jersey was not appropriate venue for personal injury action against Pennsylvania resident arising from accident that occurred in Pennsylvania, court would dismiss action, as transfer to Pennsylvania was not in interest of justice; plaintiff admitted that she had already filed complaint regarding same matter in Pennsylvania state court, and that such action was not successful due to running of statute of limitations in Pennsylvania. 28 U.S.C.A. § 1406(a).

> Kitces v. Wood, 917 F.Supp. 338.

Although transfer of venue may be in interest of justice if plaintiff could potentially face statute of limitations bar to suit in proper venue if court should dismiss, where it is clear that statute of limitations has run in proposed transferee district, dismissal, rather than transfer, is appropriate. 28 U.S.C.A. § 1406(a).

> Kitces v. Wood, 917 F.Supp. 338.

D.N.J. 1993. Georgia corporation correctly challenged assertion of personal jurisdiction in New Jersey, even though corporation filed motion to transfer venue rather than motion to dismiss for lack of personal jurisdiction, where corporation preserved defense of lack of personal jurisdiction in its answer, and, thus, corporation had not waived defense and could bring follow-up motion to dismiss for lack of personal jurisdiction. Fed.Rules Civ.Proc.Rule 12(h)(1), 28 U.S.C.A.

> Database America, Inc. v. Bellsouth Advertising & Pub. Corp., 825 F.Supp. 1195, reconsideration denied 825 F.Supp. 1216.

D.N.J. 1993. Enforceable contractual forum selection provision did not entitle supplier to dismissal for lack of venue of dealer's breach of contract action, even though transfer of venue would be warranted, where venue was proper in the district; fact that parties agreed to litigate disputes in another forum is not question of venue, but one of contract, which will be enforced unless fundamentally unfair. Fed. Rules Civ.Proc.Rule 12(b)(3), 28 U.S.C.A.; 28 U.S.C.A. § 1391.

> National Micrographics Systems, Inc. v. Canon U.S.A., Inc., 825 F.Supp. 671.

D.N.J. 1992. Dismissal is unfavored remedy in situations where venue is challenged and is to be avoided when another court may properly exercise jurisdiction over matter.

> Telebrands Direct Response Corp. v. Ovation Communications, Inc., 802 F.Supp. 1169.

D.N.J. 1990. After it was determined that district court did not have personal jurisdiction in medical malpractice action arising from alleged negligent acts occurring in Florida, dismissing action, rather than transferring action to Florida, was appropriate, where action would have been barred under applicable Florida statute of limitations had it been brought there. 28 U.S.C.A. § 1404(a); West's F.S.A. §§ 95.11(4)(b), (6), 766.201.

> McTyre v. Broward General Medical Center, 749 F.Supp. 102.

D.N.J. 1989. Where district court had personal jurisdiction over corporate employer, in union pension fund's withdrawal liability action, but no personal jurisdiction over employer's individual officers, directors, or shareholders, interest of justice favored transfer of case to forum where pension fund could proceed against all defendants, rather than dismissal as to individual defendants alone; all corporate assets had been distributed among shareholders and dismissal would have necessitated pursuit of claims against individual defendants individually. 28 U.S.C.A. § 1404(a).

> IUE AFL-CIO Pension Fund v. Locke Mach. Co., a Div. of U.S. Components Corp., 726 F.Supp. 561.

E.D.N.Y. 1988. Appropriate remedy, when lessors' breach of contract action was unintentionally filed in court which did not have venue, was order transferring action to court which did have venue and not dismissal of case. 28 U.S.C.A. § 1406.

> Zumft v. Doney Slate Co., 698 F.Supp. 444.

S.D.N.Y. 1993. Dismissal, rather than transfer of entire action, was appropriate when another district was appropriate venue, where district court did not have subject matter jurisdiction over part of action, which would have to proceed, if at all, in state court. 28 U.S.C.A. §§ 1391(b), 1406(a).

> Friedman v. Revenue Management of New York, Inc., 839 F.Supp. 203, affirmed 38 F.3d 668.

S.D.N.Y. 1991. New York export company's breach of contract action against Bolivian government-owned purchaser was not subject to dismissal on basis of exclusive forum clause, where no written instrument signed by parties containing choice of forum provision was produced; while it was possible that Bolivian regulations would have mandated inclusion of such clause in any formal contract, district court could not pass on validity of clause that might have been or should have been included in nonexisted document.

> Walpex Trading Co. v. Yacimientos Petroliferos Fiscales Bolivianos, 756 F.Supp. 136, reargument denied 1991 WL 79464.

S.D.N.Y. 1990. In action for violation of Racketeer Influenced and Corrupt Organizations Act, investors' allegations, upon information and belief, that Colorado resident visited New York to participate in conspiracy and that both Colorado resident and Colorado corporation transacted their affairs through offices of entities in New York were insufficient to withstand motion to dismiss for lack of venue in New York, where investors had not disclosed source of their beliefs. 18 U.S.C.A. § 1965(a).

> Morin v. Trupin, 747 F.Supp. 1051.

S.D.N.Y. 1990. Dismissal on ground of forum non conveniens presupposes at least two forums in which defendant is amenable to process, and thus motion to dismiss on that ground must be accompanied by affidavit from defendants that they will waive any defenses based on statute of limitations, make witnesses and documents available, and pay judgment rendered by transferee court.

> Gazis v. John S. Latsis (USA) Inc., 729 F.Supp. 979.

S.D.N.Y. 1989. Dismissal of medical malpractice action which was brought in wrong venue, rather than transfer, was warranted given that plaintiffs' attorneys refused to stipulate to venue transfer despite knowing for more than two months that venue was improper and plaintiffs did not attempt to explain how interests of justice might in some way point to transfer rather than dismissal.

Peckio v. Shay, 708 F.Supp. 75.

W.D.N.Y. 1997. District court has discretion to determine whether dismissal or transfer of case is appropriate if action has been brought in improper venue. 28 U.S.C.A. § 1406(a).

Daniel v. American Bd. of Emergency Medicine, 988 F.Supp. 127.

W.D.N.C. 1990. North Carolina federal district court would dismiss claims arising out of allegedly fraudulent stock transactions based on improper venue instead of transferring them, where no transfer motion was currently pending and court was unsure what district would be most convenient to litigate the suit. Fed. Rules Civ.Proc.Rule 12(b)(3), 28 U.S.C.A.; 28 U.S.C.A. § 1406(a).

Medoil Corp. v. Clark, 753 F.Supp. 592.

N.D.Ohio 1990. When subject matter jurisdiction is lacking, court must dismiss the action and cannot transfer because of improper venue. 28 U.S.C.A. § 1406.

N.A.A.C.P.-Special Contribution Fund v. Jones, 732 F.Supp. 791.

S.D.Ohio 1993. If enforceability of forum selection clause is considered for purposes of motion to dismiss, court, on submission of evidentiary materials outside pleadings, must employ standards applicable to summary judgment motion. Fed.Rules Civ.Proc.Rules 12(b)(1, 6), 56, 28 U.S.C.A.

General Elec. Co. v. G. Siempelkamp GmbH & Co., 809 F.Supp. 1306, affirmed 29 F.3d 1095.

S.D.Ohio 1993. Whether case that has been brought in district where venue is improper should be dismissed or transferred is within discretion of district court; however, doubts are usually resolved in favor of transferring action since interest of justice is generally better served by transfer than by dismissal. 28 U.S.C.A. § 1406(a).

United Liberty Life Ins. Co. v. Pinnacle West Capital Corp., 149 F.R.D. 558.

Transfer rather than dismissal was appropriate after it was determined that venue did not lie in transferor court in action for securities fraud and racketeering. Securities Exchange Act of 1934, § 27, 15 U.S.C.A. § 78aa; 28 U.S.C.A. §§ 1391, 1391(b); 18 U.S.C.A. § 1965(a).

United Liberty Life Ins. Co. v. Pinnacle West Capital Corp., 149 F.R.D. 558.

D.Or. 1990. Trademark infringement defendant's counterclaim for intentional interference with business relations was compulsory counterclaim which would not be dismissed on

ground of forum non conveniens. Fed.Rules Civ.Proc.Rule 13(a), 28 U.S.C.A.

Official Airline Guides, Inc. v. Churchfield Publications, Inc., 756 F.Supp. 1393, affirmed 6 F.3d 1385.

Trademark infringement defendant's counterclaim, even if not compulsory, would not be dismissed on ground of forum non conveniens where law of competing forums did not conflict.

Official Airline Guides, Inc. v. Churchfield Publications, Inc., 756 F.Supp. 1393, affirmed 6 F.3d 1385.

D.Puerto Rico 1993. Forum non conveniens doctrine warranted dismissal of contract claims asserted in federal district court in Puerto Rico by Puerto Rican importer retailer of automobiles against German manufacturer, in favor of German forum; forum selection clause in contract chose Germany, contract was entered into in Germany, compulsory process is available in Germany, costs for importer to obtain witness attendance was negligible, given that manufacturer had its operations in Germany, and calendar congestion in Puerto Rico was considerable.

Caribe BMW, Inc. v. Bayerische Motoren Werke Aktiengesellschaft, 821 F.Supp. 802, vacated 19 F.3d 745.

"Forum non conveniens" doctrine essentially permits discretionary dismissals on case-by-case basis where alternative forum is available in another nation which is fair to parties and substantially more convenient, and court's task is to determine whether availability of adequate alternative forum would in fairness be sufficient to overcome presumption in favor of plaintiff's choice of forum.

Caribe BMW, Inc. v. Bayerische Motoren Werke Aktiengesellschaft, 821 F.Supp. 802, vacated 19 F.3d 745.

In ruling on motion to dismiss on forum non conveniens ground, district court must consider private and public interests at stake.

Caribe BMW, Inc. v. Bayerische Motoren Werke Aktiengesellschaft, 821 F.Supp. 802, vacated 19 F.3d 745.

D.R.I. 1993. Motion to dismiss for improper venue, rather than for inconvenience, is appropriate where moving party seeks to enforce contractual forum selection clause. 28 U.S.C.A. §§ 1404(a), 1406(a).

Arrow Plumbing and Heating, Inc. v. North American Mechanical Services Corp., 810 F.Supp. 369.

D.S.C. 1995. It would be unjust to force disability discrimination plaintiff to bring suit in Tennessee, and thus court would not dismiss for improper venue based on forum selection clause in parties' employment contract, since relationship between parties was not one of sophisticated business entities negotiating at arms length, employer dictated terms of employment, enforcing forum selection clause would be so costly as to deprive employee of his day in court, and all circumstances surrounding lawsuit took place in South Carolina. 28 U.S.C.A. § 1391; Americans with Disabilities Act of 1990, § 2 et seq., 42 U.S.C.A. § 12101 et seq.; Fed.Rules Civ. Proc.Rule 12(b)(3), 28 U.S.C.A.

Scott v. Guardsmark Sec., 874 F.Supp. 117.

D.S.C. 1994. Absence of personal jurisdiction, absence of subject matter jurisdiction, and improper venue warranted dismissal of case, rather than transfer, since, because of defects, plaintiff's counsel could have reasonably foreseen that case was not properly filed in South Carolina.

Jarrett v. State of N.C., 868 F.Supp. 155.

Decision to transfer case or dismiss it is committed to sound discretion of the district court, and district court may be reversed only if it has abused its discretion.

Jarrett v. State of N.C., 868 F.Supp. 155.

M.D.Tenn. 1996. Case filed in improper venue is subject to mandatory dismissal, unless it is transferred. 28 U.S.C.A. § 1406(a).

Allied Sound, Inc. v. Dukane Corp., 934 F.Supp. 272.

Action brought by distributor in federal district court in Tennessee, against manufacturer located in Illinois, would be transferred to Illinois federal court following determination that Illinois was proper venue, rather than being dismissed; transfer is generally perceived to further interests of justice more than dismissal and manufacturer had not addressed any potential injustice resulting from transfer rather than dismissal and refiling. 28 U.S.C.A. § 1406.

Allied Sound, Inc. v. Dukane Corp., 934 F.Supp. 272.

S.D.Tex. 1997. If parties designate by contract a forum in which any litigation is to take place, any lawsuit commenced elsewhere may then be subject to dismissal for improper venue.

Kessmann and Associates, Inc. v. Barton-Aschman Associates, Inc., 10 F.Supp.2d 682.

E.D.Va. 1997. When plaintiff's attorney reasonably should have foreseen that forum in which he filed action was improper, dismissal is warranted. 28 U.S.C.A. § 1406(a).

Dee-K Enterprises, Inc. v. Heveafil Sdn. Bhd., 985 F.Supp. 640.

Although venue for antitrust action brought by end user of extruded rubber thread was improper in Eastern District of Virginia, transfer of action, rather then dismissal, was warranted, where substantial proceedings had already occurred, including initial discovery,

entry of protective orders, briefing and resolution of motions to dismiss, and the filing of answers, counterclaims, and cross claims. 28 U.S.C.A. § 1406(a).

Dee-K Enterprises, Inc. v. Heveafil Sdn. Bhd., 985 F.Supp. 640.

E.D.Va. 1992. District court, or its corresponding bankruptcy court, has only two options upon finding that case has been laid in an improper venue, to dismiss or transfer. 28 U.S.C.A. §§ 1406, 1477.

In re Great Lakes Hotel Associates, 154 B.R. 667.

S.D.W.Va. 1996. Statute, providing for dismissal for improper venue, is not correct procedural vehicle for enforcing contract forum-selection clause. 28 U.S.C.A. § 1406(a).

P.M. Enterprises v. Color Works, Inc., 946 F.Supp. 435.

If forum-selection clause requires litigation of disputes in foreign court or state court, dismissal pursuant to federal statute providing for cure or waiver of defects is warranted because federal courts lack statutory power to transfer action to those forums. 28 U.S.C.A. § 1406(a).

P.M. Enterprises v. Color Works, Inc., 946 F.Supp. 435.

E.D.Wis. 1998. Rather than dismissing buyer's action against seller on basis of forum selection clause specifying North Carolina forum, which would require buyer to refile its claim in North Carolina and perhaps subject it to applicable statute of limitations, court would transfer venue to North Carolina in interest of justice and judicial economy. 28 U.S.C.A. § 1406(a).

Polar Mfg. Corp. v. Michael Weinig, Inc., 994 F.Supp. 1012.

10th Cir.BAP (Okla.) 1998. Under improper venue statute, district court has no discretion to retain case in which venue is improper but, rather, is required to dismiss or transfer case. 28 U.S.C.A. § 1406(a).

In re Sorrells, 218 B.R. 580.

Bkrtcy.D.Colo. 1984. In re B & L Oil Co., 42 B.R. 808, appeal decided 834 F.2d 156.

Bkrtcy.M.D.Fla. 1992. Improper venue is not basis for dismissal; appropriate remedy is to transfer proceeding to proper district.

In re Hillsborough Holdings Corp., 146 B.R. 1008.

Bkrtcy.D.Mass. 1996. In First Circuit, dismissal of complaint based on forum selection clause is properly accomplished by motion to dismiss for failure to state claim, not by motion to dismiss for improper venue. Fed.Rules Civ. Proc.Rule 12(b)(3, 6), 28 U.S.C.A.

In re Healthco Intern., Inc., 195 B.R. 971.

⚷**1743. Misjoinder of claims or defenses.**

Library references

C.J.S. Federal Civil Procedure § 818.

C.A.9 (Cal.) 1998. District courts do not have inherent power to dismiss action on grounds that assertion of instant claims in separate, related action would have resulted in discovery or scheduling violations in related action, where such claims would have been permissive, not mandatory, in separate action. Fed.Rules Civ.Proc.Rule 14, 28 U.S.C.A.

Atchison, Topeka and Santa Fe Ry. Co. v. Hercules Inc., 146 F.3d 1071.

C.A.5 (Tex.) 1986. Joinder of claims of organizations on behalf of minority college students wishing to become teachers to claims of elementary and secondary school students challenging state's requirement that persons wishing to become teacher pass skills test before being permitted to take professional education courses did not require that claims on behalf of college students be dismissed, though it might have been procedural irregularity. Fed.Rules Civ.Proc.Rules 18, 24, 61, 28 U.S.C.A.; 28 U.S.C.A. § 2111.

U.S. v. LULAC, 793 F.2d 636.

M.D.Fla. 1990. Since plaintiffs were entitled to plead in alternative, fact that claim for breach of fiduciary duty was based on misrepresentations that were not distinct from fraud claim did not require dismissal; dismissal of one count or other, if necessary, could await proof at trial.

McCarthy v. Barnett Bank of Polk County, 750 F.Supp. 1119.

D.Kan. 1991. Prison inmate's claim for declaratory relief based on conditions of confinement in segregated housing unit would be dismissed from case due to inmate's standing as class member in pending class action regarding conditions of confinement in state penal system.

Dotson v. Maschner, 764 F.Supp. 163.

D.N.J. 1995. Consolidation of related actions obviates concerns of rule governing compulsory counterclaims and dismissal of such claims does not serve interest of judicial economy where actions are already consolidated. Fed.Rules Civ.Proc.Rule 13(a), 28 U.S.C.A.

Jack LaLanne Fitness Centers, Inc. v. Jimlar, Inc., 884 F.Supp. 162.

E.D.N.Y. 1990. Age discrimination plaintiff's pendent claim for violation of state age discrimination statute would not be dismissed on ground it risked jury confusion; claims involved parallel issues, both of fact and law, with efficiency, economy and fairness best served by single adjudication of dispute. Age Discrimination in Employment Act of 1967, § 2 et seq., 29

U.S.C.A. § 621 et seq.; N.Y.McKinney's Executive Law § 290 et seq.

Martel v. Dean Witter Reynolds, Inc., 738 F.Supp. 53.

⚷**1744. Parties, defects as to.**

Library references

C.J.S. Federal Civil Procedure §§ 804, 805.

⚷**1744.1. —— In general.**

C.A.D.C. 1994. Action cannot be dismissed by reason of being brought by someone other than "real party in interest" as long as party, by substantive law, has right sought to be enforced. Fed.Rules Civ.Proc.Rule 17(a), 28 U.S.C.A.

Best v. Kelly, 39 F.3d 328, 309 U.S.App. D.C. 51.

C.A.5 (Ala.) 1981. Walker v. Jim Dandy Co., 638 F.2d 1330, on remand 97 F.R.D. 505, affirmed in part, reversed in part 747 F.2d 1360, on remand Rhoades v. Jim Dandy Co., 107 F.R.D. 26.

C.A.9 (Ariz.) 1992. Inability of incarcerated pro se civil rights litigant to spell defendant's name correctly, despite plethora of indicia as to whom the named defendant refers, does not justify dismissal of complaint against that defendant. 42 U.S.C.A. § 1983.

McGuckin v. Smith, 974 F.2d 1050.

District court committed reversible error by dismissing misnamed defendant in prisoner's pro se civil rights action without advising prisoner that his complaint against that defendant was deficient and providing him with an opportunity to amend it. 42 U.S.C.A. § 1983.

McGuckin v. Smith, 974 F.2d 1050.

C.A.9 (Cal.) 1998. Once district court decided that plaintiffs lacked standing, dismissal was required.

Pareto v. F.D.I.C., 139 F.3d 696.

C.A.2 (N.Y.) 1997. Although district court retains some discretion to dismiss action where there was no semblance of any reasonable basis for naming of incorrect party, there plainly should be no dismissal where substitution of real party in interest is necessary to avoid injustice. Fed.Rules Civ.Proc.Rule 17(a), 28 U.S.C.A.

Advanced Magnetics, Inc. v. Bayfront Partners, Inc., 106 F.3d 11, on remand 1997 WL 299430.

C.A.3 (Pa.) 1998. Fictitious parties must eventually be dismissed, if discovery yields no identities.

Hindes v. F.D.I.C., 137 F.3d 148.

C.A.1 (Puerto Rico) 1998. Dismissal without prejudice of § 1983 claim, alleging that deliberate indifference to inmate's medical needs led to his premature death, was properly based on plaintiffs' failure during 17 months between filing of complaint and entry of judgment to identify and serve anonymous defendants allegedly responsible for inmate's death. 42 U.S.C.A. § 1983; Fed.Rules Civ.Proc.Rule 4(m), 28 U.S.C.A.

> Figueroa v. Rivera, 147 F.3d 77.

C.A.5 (Tex.) 1991. District court properly granted motions to dismiss filed by nonremoving nominal parties against whom plaintiff could not prevail in state court.

> Farias v. Bexar County Bd. of Trustees for Mental Health Mental Retardation Services, 925 F.2d 866, rehearing denied 931 F.2d 892, certiorari denied 112 S.Ct. 193, 502 U.S. 866, 116 L.Ed.2d 153.

C.A.5 (Tex.) 1989. Only after plaintiff has opportunity to supply more supportive facts either by amending complaint or submitting affidavit should complaint be dismissed for failure to demonstrate standing.

> Xerox Corp. v. Genmoora Corp., 888 F.2d 345.

C.A.5 (Tex.) 1978. Satterwhite v. City of Greenville, Tex., 578 F.2d 987, certiorari granted, vacated 100 S.Ct. 1334, 445 U.S. 940, 63 L.Ed.2d 773, on remand 634 F.2d 231.

C.A.7 (Wis.) 1995. In determining whether to dismiss for lack of standing qui tam action against defendants who allegedly leased gambling equipment to Indian tribe without receiving approval of Bureau of Indian Affairs or receiving license under Indian Traders Licensing Act, appropriate inquiry was whether United States suffered injury-in-fact, not whether its representatives suffered injury. U.S.C.A. Const. Art. 3, § 2, cl. 1; 25 U.S.C.A. §§ 81, 201, 264.

> U.S. ex rel. Hall v. Tribal Development Corp., 49 F.3d 1208, on remand 165 F.R.D. 83, affirmed 100 F.3d 476, rehearing and suggestion for rehearing denied.

M.D.Ala. 1997. When plaintiff with standing seeks to represent class defined too broadly, so that some members lack standing, court need not dismiss case for lack of jurisdiction; instead, court should either reform class, limiting it to those persons who have standing, or allow named plaintiff(s) to proceed individually, permitting others with like claims to request joinder. U.S.C.A. Const. Art. 3, § 2, cl.1.

> R.C. by Alabama Disabilities Advocacy Program v. Nachman, 969 F.Supp. 682, affirmed 145 F.3d 363.

M.D.Ala. 1995. Whether plaintiff has standing to bring antitrust action is question of law that may be raised by motion to dismiss.

> Florida Seed Co., Inc. v. Monsanto Co., 915 F.Supp. 1167, affirmed 105 F.3d 1372, certiorari denied 118 S.Ct. 296, 139 L.Ed.2d 228.

C.D.Cal. 1997. When deciding motion to dismiss for lack of standing, it is within trial court's power to allow or to require plaintiff to supply, by amendment to complaint or by affidavits, further particularized allegations of fact deemed supportive of plaintiff's standing; if, after this opportunity, plaintiff's standing does not adequately appear from all materials of record, complaint must be dismissed.

> National Coalition Government of Union of Burma v. Unocal, Inc., 176 F.R.D. 329.

Where standing is challenged on motion to dismiss, general factual allegations of injury resulting from defendant's conduct are sufficient, and plaintiff need not set forth specific facts proving injury.

> National Coalition Government of Union of Burma v. Unocal, Inc., 176 F.R.D. 329.

E.D.Cal. 1988. Public employees' pro se employment discrimination complaint did not have to be dismissed because employees named as defendant department which employed employees instead of secretary of that department; exacting standard of pleading government urged court to apply was at odds with both modern standards of notice pleading and liberal standard to be afforded pleadings of pro se litigants, and government failed to demonstrate prejudice.

> Hollcroft v. Department of Treasury, I.R.S., 687 F.Supp. 510, affirmed 65 F.3d 175.

D.Colo. 1995. Controlling persons of security issuer, sued by shareholder, were premature in challenging shareholder's standing as class representative by motion to dismiss for failure to state claim; appropriate vehicle was through rule requiring court to determine by order whether class action is to be maintained. Fed.Rules Civ.Proc.Rules 12(b)(6), 23(c)(1), 28 U.S.C.A.

> Schwartz v. Celestial Seasonings, Inc., 904 F.Supp. 1191, reversed 124 F.3d 1246, on remand 178 F.R.D. 545.

D.Colo. 1994. Normal and decent procedure where plaintiff has sued wrong defendant is to raise the matter by telephone call to opposing counsel and, at least, issue should be promptly and clearly raised by timely motion to dismiss.

> Barrett v. Qual-Med, Inc., 153 F.R.D. 653.

D.Colo. 1989. Defendant named in original complaint, but not in amended complaint, was entitled to be dismissed from action upon motion. Fed.Rules Civ.Proc.Rules 15, 21, 28 U.S.C.A.

> Anesthesia Advantage, Inc. v. Metz Group, 708 F.Supp. 1180.

D.Colo. 1985. Civil RICO claim against corporation would be dismissed, where plaintiffs confessed that claim was not brought against defendant corporation, despite terms of complaint. 18 U.S.C.A. § 1961 et seq.

Miller v. Calvin, 647 F.Supp. 199.

D.Conn. 1989. When basis for challenge to foreign judgment is that rendering court lacked personal jurisdiction over defendant, challenge should be made by way of motion to dismiss for lack of jurisdiction over person, particularly when federal action merely seeks enforcement of foreign default judgment after failure to appear, and personal jurisdiction of foreign court has not previously been litigated. Fed.Rules Civ.Proc.Rule 12(b)(2), 28 U.S.C.A.

Prete v. Lepore, 125 F.R.D. 572.

M.D.Fla. 1996. Complaint should be dismissed for improper party as matter of law.

Pierre v. Schlemmer, 932 F.Supp. 278.

M.D.Fla. 1993. Under liberal pleading standards of Federal Rules of Civil Procedure, absence of any factual allegation against named defendant will entitle that defendant to have complaint dismissed as to him. Fed.Rules Civ. Proc.Rule 1 et seq., 28 U.S.C.A.

Clark v. Sierra, 837 F.Supp. 1179.

When defendant is merely named in caption of complaint but is nowhere claimed to have caused plaintiff injury, complaint against him must be dismissed even under liberal construction to be given to pro se complainants.

Clark v. Sierra, 837 F.Supp. 1179.

N.D.Ga. 1997. Products liability case would be dismissed, due to denial of second motion to substitute resulting from plaintiff's death, given that appellate court, in vacating and remanding case after denial of first motion, wanted Georgia courts to decide underlying legal issues concerning appropriateness of appointment of representative for nonresident plaintiff's estate, who was party to be substituted, under Georgia law, issues were not resolved by Georgia courts prior to counsel's second motion, and dismissal would permit appellate court either to decide issues or certify case to Georgia Supreme Court, particularly when further delay to allow plaintiff's counsel to obtain clearly appropriate substitute was unwarranted. Fed.Rules Civ.Proc.Rule 25(a), 28 U.S.C.A.; O.C.G.A. § 15–9–31.

Escareno v. Noltina Crucible and Refractory Corp., 172 F.R.D. 522, question certified 139 F.3d 1456.

N.D.Ga. 1994. Dismissal of personal injury action for failure to substitute proper party, approximately 11 months after death of original plaintiff, was not unduly harsh; attorney for deceased plaintiff had approximately five months from date of plaintiff's death to locate proper substitute and instead the attorney filed motion to substitute himself as plaintiff, notwithstanding vigorous opposition to plaintiff's

proposed substitute, attorney never located proper substitute or sought extension of time to locate such substitute prior to dismissal of the case, and attorney never indicated during pendency of his motion to reconsider that he had identified proper substitute and obtained that substitute's consent to becoming a party.

Escareno v. Noltina Crucible and Refractory Corp., 172 F.R.D. 517.

N.D.Ill. 1997. If plaintiff lacked standing at time action was filed, suit must be dismissed even if plaintiff later acquired interest sufficient to support standing.

Ball v. Nationscredit Financial Services Corp., 207 B.R. 869.

N.D.Ill. 1993. Defendants who had never been named or served would be dismissed.

Vakharia v. Swedish Covenant Hosp., 824 F.Supp. 769, on reconsideration in part.

S.D.Ind. 1996. Since plaintiff could not proceed under a false name, his original complaint using false name failed to comply with federal rule providing that title of action in complaint include names of all the parties and, thus, was subject to dismissal without prejudice and with leave to amend. Fed.Rules Civ.Proc. Rule 10(a), 28 U.S.C.A.

Doe v. Indiana Black Expo, Inc., 923 F.Supp. 137.

D.Kan. 1997. Real party in interest defense can be raised as motion to dismiss for failure to state claim, stating, in effect, that because plaintiff is not the person who should be bringing suit, plaintiff has failed to state claim upon which relief can be granted. Fed. Rules Civ.Proc.Rule 12(b)(6), 28 U.S.C.A.

Classic Communications, Inc. v. Rural Telephone Service Co., Inc., 956 F.Supp. 910, reconsideration denied 1997 WL 231087.

There was insufficient factual development, on motion to dismiss for failure to state a claim, to properly dismiss, for not being real party in interest or for lack of antitrust standing, parent corporation of telephone and cable television subsidiaries, in action in which company and subsidiaries alleged that competing provider had engaged in illegal conduct and schemes designed to prevent company and subsidiaries from competing with provider. U.S.C.A. Const. Art. 3, § 1 et seq.; Fed.Rules Civ.Proc.Rules 12(b)(6), 17(a), 28 U.S.C.A.

Classic Communications, Inc. v. Rural Telephone Service Co., Inc., 956 F.Supp. 910, reconsideration denied 1997 WL 231087.

D.Kan. 1996. There was insufficient factual development, on motion to dismiss for failure to state a claim, to properly dismiss, for lack of standing, parent corporation of cable television company which was denied franchises by cities.

U.S.C.A. Const. Art. 3, § 1 et seq.; Fed.Rules Civ.Proc.Rule 12(b)(6), 28 U.S.C.A.

Classic Communications, Inc. v. Rural Telephone Service Co., Inc., 956 F.Supp. 896.

D.Kan. 1996. Court would treat "cross-claim" as third-party petition and change case's caption to reflect that designation, where both answer and "cross-claim" were made in same pleading, and third parties were not previously parties to action; redesignation, rather than dismissal, was appropriate. Fed.Rules Civ. Proc.Rules 13(g, h), 14(a), 19, 20, 28 U.S.C.A.

Raytheon Aircraft Credit Corp. v. Pal Air Intern., Inc., 923 F.Supp. 1408.

E.D.La. 1998. If, after discovery, plaintiff who used fictitious defendant as stand-in for real party in complaint is still unable to name fictitious defendant, claims against him should be dismissed. Fed.Rules Civ.Proc.Rules 4(m), 21, 28 U.S.C.A.

Richard v. City of Harahan, 6 F.Supp.2d 565.

E.D.La. 1998. If, after discovery, plaintiff is still unable to name the fictitious defendants, the claims against them should be dismissed.

Jones v. St. Tammany Parish Jail, 4 F.Supp.2d 606.

Pretrial detainee's civil rights claims and state law negligence claims against fictitious prison guard and fictitious insurance company would be dismissed without prejudice, where discovery had concluded and detainee had not ascertained identities of those parties. 42 U.S.C.A. § 1983.

Jones v. St. Tammany Parish Jail, 4 F.Supp.2d 606.

D.Me. 1995. Corporate subsidiary named as defendant was not entitled to dismissal of suit against it on ground that plaintiff failed to implicate it in alleged wrongdoing; subsidiary noted that plaintiff's complaint made only two explicit references to it, in the caption and later in description of parties, but it was unclear what exact relationship between defendant corporation and defendant wholly owned subsidiary was, plaintiff treated the two entities as one throughout the complaint, and thus his allegations were imputed to both entities, establishing potential liability against both, to the extent that plaintiff considered corporation and subsidiary as single defendant. Fed.Rules Civ.Proc.Rule 12(b)(6), 28 U.S.C.A.

Carey v. Mt. Desert Island Hosp., 910 F.Supp. 7.

D.Md. 1986. Alleged misnomer of piece of partnership property, rather than limited partnership, as defendant in employment discrimination action did not alone warrant dismissal of that action in absence of prejudice thereby;

everyone involved in action knew of and could identify entity that was being sued.

Quann v. Whitegate-Edgewater, 112 F.R.D. 649.

D.Mass. 1995. On motion to dismiss for want of standing, analysis focuses not on claim itself, but on the plaintiff bringing the claim; whether complaint could survive on the merits is irrelevant to standing inquiry.

Pagan v. Dubois, 894 F.Supp. 45.

D.Mass. 1993. Complaint did not fail to state claim against executors on the ground that it referred to them only in caption, in "Parties" portion, and in headings of six claims for relief against "All Defendants," where claims against executors were supported by factual averments concerning liability of the estates and executors had responded and replied with various affirmative defenses, counterclaims, and cross claims. Fed.Rules Civ.Proc.Rule 12(b)(6), 28 U.S.C.A.

Steego Corp. v. Ravenal, 830 F.Supp. 42.

S.D.Miss. 1997. Contractor's unsuccessful argument, that it was real party in interest in suit against pipe supplier despite subrogation agreement with its insurer because contractor retained pecuniary interest in any recovery by insurer, was not wholly lacking in any reasonable basis, and therefore, court would not dismiss suit brought by contractor but would instead allow insurer to be substituted as party plaintiff. Fed.Rules Civ.Proc.Rule 17(a), 28 U.S.C.A.

IHP Indus., Inc. v. PermAlert, ESP, 178 F.R.D. 483.

E.D.Mo. 1993. Where complaint alleges no specific act or conduct on part of defendant and complaint is silent as to defendant except for name appearing in caption, complaint is properly dismissed, even under liberal construction to be given pro se complaints.

Davis v. Sancegraw, 850 F.Supp. 809.

W.D.Mo. 1998. On motion to dismiss for lack of standing, it is within trial court's power to allow or require plaintiff to supply, by amendment to complaint or by affidavits, further particularized allegations of fact deemed supportive of plaintiff's standing; if, after all this opportunity, plaintiff's standing does not adequately appear from all materials of record, complaint must be dismissed. U.S.C.A. Const. Art. 3, § 2, cl. 1.

Gralike v. Cook, 996 F.Supp. 889.

W.D.Mo. 1988. Plaintiff had a right to file an amended petition without leave of court where the defendant had merely filed a motion to dismiss, which was not a responsive pleading under the federal rule; failure to sue the proper party, which was subsequently remedied by an amended complaint naming proper parties, did not constitute grounds for dismissal of an action. Fed.Rules Civ.Proc.Rules 7(a), 15(a), 28 U.S.C.A.

> Hantover, Inc. v. Omet, S.N.C. of Volentieri & C., 688 F.Supp. 1377.

D.Neb. 1991. Pro se plaintiff's claims against defendants should be dismissed, where in original complaint claims against defendants had been dismissed as frivolous, plaintiff had not been granted leave to file amended complaint as to those defendants, and those defendants were not discussed in amended complaint.

> Tyler v. City of Omaha, 780 F.Supp. 1266, remanded 953 F.2d 648.

D.N.J. 1991. District court, in its discretion, may dismiss third-party claims which do not satisfy federal civil rule governing third-party practice. Fed.Rules Civ.Proc.Rule 14(a), 28 U.S.C.A.

> U.S. v. Berk & Berk, 767 F.Supp. 593.

D.N.M. 1990. Complaint arising out of alleged violation of Age Discrimination in Employment Act (ADEA), which had been filed with Equal Employment Opportunity Commission (EEOC), was required to be dismissed as to previously unnamed defendants where plaintiff knew roles of unnamed defendants at time of EEOC filing, defendants had filed affidavits indicating they had not been involved in EEOC conciliation proceedings, and defendants were prejudiced by failure to be named in that they did not have opportunity to settle, hire counsel, or otherwise protect their rights.

> Buffington v. Phelps Dodge Corp., 800 F.Supp. 945.

E.D.N.Y. 1997. Whether challenge to standing in civil forfeiture action is analyzed pursuant to rule allowing court to strike insufficient defense from pleading or as dismissal for failure to state a claim, test is the same under either provision and so is the outcome. Fed. Rules Civ.Proc.Rule 12(b)(6), (f), 28 U.S.C.A.

> U.S. v. All Funds on Deposit on or Before November 8, 1994 in Citibank Account No. 42773634 in the Name Imtiaz Ahmed Kahn, 955 F.Supp. 23.

E.D.N.Y. 1996. On motion to dismiss, challenging standing of particular plaintiff, court would not address possible amendments to complaint that had not yet been sought and would not refrain from removing such plaintiff, as to whom action was moot, on ground that plaintiffs stated they intended to file motion to certify action as class action and that such plaintiff was a potential member of class. Fed. Rules Civ.Proc.Rule 23, 28 U.S.C.A.

> Mincone v. Nassau County Community College, 923 F.Supp. 398.

N.D.N.Y. 1998. Civil rights plaintiff's failure to identify and serve with process 17 John Doe defendants and one Jane Roe defendant warranted dismissal of all claims against unidentified defendants, where plaintiff had over two years to locate and serve them, and failed to locate or serve even one despite being warned by trial court that his failure to do so within reasonable time would result in dismissal of his claims.

> Pravda v. City of Albany, 178 F.R.D. 25.

N.D.N.Y. 1993. Complaint failed to meet minimal notice pleading requirements, and thus would be dismissed as to defendants not named in caption or body of complaint; complaint was entirely devoid of factual allegations against such defendants. Fed.Rules Civ.Proc.Rule 8(a), 28 U.S.C.A.

> Mason v. County of Delaware Sheriff's Dept., 150 F.R.D. 27.

S.D.N.Y. 1995. Complaint which identified defendant newspaper by name in the caption only and nowhere else mentioned it specifically was not subject to summary dismissal on that ground where newspaper was identified as a defendant and body of complaint set out numerous claims against "defendants," "defendant newspapers," and "newspaper defendants."

> AD/SAT, a Div. of Skylight, Inc. v. Associated Press, 885 F.Supp. 511, reconsideration denied 920 F.Supp. 1287.

S.D.N.Y. 1989. Court ordinarily must accept as true all material allegations of complaint, and must construe complaint in favor of plaintiffs, when ruling on motion to dismiss for lack of standing; however, plaintiffs must prove allegations on which they are relying, where defendants raise standing issue in opposition to plaintiffs' summary judgment motion.

> New York State Nat. Organization for Women v. Terry, 704 F.Supp. 1247, affirmed as modified 886 F.2d 1339, certiorari denied 110 S.Ct. 2206, 495 U.S. 947, 109 L.Ed.2d 532.

S.D.N.Y. 1987. In *Bivens* suit against FBI agents, plaintiffs' designation of defendants as unknown was appropriate and did not provide grounds for dismissal of those agents who submitted affidavits claiming they did not participate in the search which was subject of suit, where plaintiffs provided sworn testimony that violations by various agents involved in the raid did take place and discovery was not yet complete.

> Adelona v. Webster, 654 F.Supp. 968.

S.D.N.Y. 1964. Derdiarian v. Futterman Corp., 36 F.R.D. 192, application granted 38 F.R.D. 178.

N.D.Ohio 1998. Complaint filed against non-existent entity is nullity and must be dismissed because any judgment rendered against such entity would be void.

Aurora Shores Homeowners Ass'n, Inc. v. F.D.I.C., 2 F.Supp.2d 975.

N.D.Ohio 1996. Complaint must be dismissed if plaintiff's standing does not adequately appear from all materials of record.

National Air Traffic Controllers Ass'n, MEBA, AFL-CIO v. Pena, 944 F.Supp. 1337.

S.D.Ohio 1996. Dismissal for lack of standing is proper either for lack of subject matter jurisdiction or for failure to state claim upon which relief could be granted. Fed.Rules Civ.Proc.Rule 12(b)(1, 6), 28 U.S.C.A.

In re Dublin Securities, Inc., 197 B.R. 66, affirmed 133 F.3d 377, rehearing and suggestion for rehearing denied, certiorari denied Terlecky v. Hurd, 119 S.Ct. 45.

E.D.Pa. 1998. Following dismissal of § 1983 claims against city, who was employer of unknown "Doe" defendants, continuation of action against unknown defendants would have offended basic notions of due process, since it would have required unknown individuals to defend claims of which they had no knowledge. U.S.C.A. Const.Amend. 5; 42 U.S.C.A. § 1983.

Bey v. City of Philadelphia, 6 F.Supp.2d 422.

E.D.Pa. 1995. On motion to dismiss for failure to state claim, general factual allegations of injury resulting from defendant's conduct may suffice to establish plaintiff's standing, as district court presumes that general allegations embrace those specific facts which are necessary to support claim. Fed.Rules Civ.Proc.Rule 12(b)(6), 28 U.S.C.A.

Burks v. City of Philadelphia, 904 F.Supp. 421.

E.D.Pa. 1994. Court would not dismiss civil rights complaint against United States marshals for plaintiff's inability to identify the marshals by name where plaintiff would be in a better position to identify them after discovery.

Lattany v. Four Unknown U.S. Marshals, 845 F.Supp. 262.

E.D.Pa. 1993. Nondiverse party could only be dismissed if it was dispensable party; if it was indispensable party, District Court could not dismiss it, but rather was required to dismiss entire suit for lack of subject matter jurisdiction. 28 U.S.C.A. § 1332.

Enza, Inc. v. We The People, Inc., 838 F.Supp. 975.

W.D.Pa. 1994. Racketeer Influenced and Corrupt Organizations (RICO) claim against defendant would be dismissed sua sponte, even though defendant did not move for dismissal, where federal court already dismissed RICO claims against co-defendant, and holding established as matter of law that plaintiff lacked standing to bring suit against any defendants for injuries alleged, which were derivative of corporation's damages. U.S.C.A. Const. Art. 3, § 2, cl. 1 et seq.; 18 U.S.C.A. § 1961 et seq.; Fed. Rules Civ.Proc.Rule 12(h)(3), 28 U.S.C.A.

In re Phar-Mor, Inc. Securities Litigation, 900 F.Supp. 777.

W.D.Pa. 1994. Where pro se complainant failed to mention defendant in complaint other than in caption, action would be dismissed; however, in light of complainant's pro se status, he would be allowed to amend complaint to state claim against defendant.

Randolph v. Cooper Industries, 879 F.Supp. 518.

D.R.I. 1991. Amended Federal Tort Claims Act (FTCA) complaint changing defendant's name from "Defense Logistics Agency" to the "United States of America" would not be dismissed for lack of subject matter jurisdiction, even though amendment occurred after limitations period had expired, where plaintiff was merely seeking to correct a misnomer. Fed. Rules Civ.Proc.Rule 15(a), 28 U.S.C.A.; 28 U.S.C.A. §§ 2671–2680.

Boliden Metech, Inc. v. U.S., 140 F.R.D. 254.

E.D.Wis. 1997. If plaintiff fails to meet minimum constitutional requirements for standing, district court must dismiss action for failure of subject-matter jurisdiction. U.S.C.A. Const. Art. 3, § 1 et seq.

Lauer Farms, Inc. v. Waushara County Bd. of Adjustment, 986 F.Supp. 544.

E.D.Wis. 1993. *Bivens* claim that certain unknown federal agents had violated civil rights of aircraft importer, in connection with search of premises and sending of questionnaire to customers, would be dismissed following the dismissal of all claims against United States and five named government employees in their personal and official capacities; unknown agents had never been served with process or identified, and legal conclusions made in present case as basis for dismissing claims raised would apply to same claims raised against any federal defendant sued in his or her official capacity. Fed.Rules Civ.Proc.Rule 12(b), 28 U.S.C.A.

Wag-Aero, Inc. v. U.S., 837 F.Supp. 1479, affirmed 35 F.3d 569, rehearing denied.

E.D.Wis. 1990. Pretrial detainee's § 1983 action against unnamed deputy sheriffs who allegedly were personally involved in deprivation of medical treatment would be dismissed where detainee, after opportunity, remained unable to identify defendants. 42 U.S.C.A. § 1983.

> Dockerty-Bostron v. Waukesha County, 744 F.Supp. 877.

⚷1745. —— Capacity in general.

C.A.D.C. 1986. Dismissal on the pleadings for lack of standing is inappropriate, even if the extreme generality of a complaint leaves the injury in fact component of standing in doubt, where the standing requirement may be satisfied on affording an opportunity to make more definite the allegations of the complaint. U.S.C.A. Const. Art. 3, § 1 et seq.

> Action Alliance of Senior Citizens of Greater Philadelphia v. Heckler, 789 F.2d 931, 252 U.S.App.D.C. 249, on remand 1987 WL 4914, affirmed Action Alliance of Sr. Citizens of Greater Philadelphia v. Bowen, 846 F.2d 1449, 269 U.S.App.D.C. 463, certiorari granted, vacated 110 S.Ct. 1329, 494 U.S. 1001, 108 L.Ed.2d 469, on remand 930 F.2d 77, 289 U.S.App.D.C. 192, certiorari denied 112 S.Ct. 371, 502 U.S. 938, 116 L.Ed.2d 323.

C.A.D.C. 1983. Ramirez de Arellano v. Weinberger, 724 F.2d 143, 233 U.S.App.D.C. 11, rehearing granted, vacated, on rehearing 745 F.2d 1500, 240 U.S.App.D.C. 363, certiorari granted, vacated 105 S.Ct. 2353, 471 U.S. 1113, 86 L.Ed.2d 255, on remand 788 F.2d 762, 252 U.S.App.D.C. 137.

C.A.9 (Ariz.) 1992. District courts have the authority to dismiss a "nonexistent" defendant on that ground alone, even though there is no explicit basis for that authority in Federal Rules of Civil Procedure or in federal statutes. McGuckin v. Smith, 974 F.2d 1050.

C.A.11 (Fla.) 1990. Standing is threshold inquiry, and lack thereof is proper basis to dismiss complaint.

> E.F. Hutton & Co., Inc. v. Hadley, 901 F.2d 979.

Trial court resolves issue of standing in motion to dismiss without considering likelihood of success on merits, as motion to dismiss occurs at inception of litigation and standing is preliminary jurisdictional matter.

> E.F. Hutton & Co., Inc. v. Hadley, 901 F.2d 979.

C.A.7 (Ill.) 1986. If plaintiff files amended complaint adding additional parties without first obtaining leave of court, defect may be corrected and does not, in itself, justify dismissal of action.

> Ed Miniat, Inc. v. Globe Life Ins. Group, Inc., 805 F.2d 732, certiorari denied Globe Life Ins. Co. v. Ed Miniat, Inc., 107 S.Ct. 3188, 482 U.S. 915, 96 L.Ed.2d 676.

C.A.6 (Ohio) 1988. Standing is not properly the subject of motion to dismiss for failure to prosecute or for noncompliance with orders of the court. Fed.Rules Civ.Proc.Rule 41(b), 28 U.S.C.A.

> Haskell v. Washington Tp., 864 F.2d 1266, appeal after remand 891 F.2d 132.

C.A.3 (Pa.) 1988. Proper disposition of case in which putative class plaintiff lacked standing is to dismiss complaint, not to deny class certification and to avoid reaching decision on merits of claims presented.

> Hassine v. Jeffes, 846 F.2d 169.

D.D.C. 1989. While plaintiffs' factual allegations must be accepted as true for purposes of agency's motion to dismiss action for lack of standing, court must determine legal sufficiency of connections between alleged injury, challenged agency action, and remedy sought. U.S.C.A. Const. Art. 3, § 1 et seq.

> Coker v. Bowen, 715 F.Supp. 383, affirmed 902 F.2d 84, 284 U.S.App.D.C. 119.

N.D.Ga. 1985. Where plaintiff corporation has not obtained a certificate of authority to transact business in Georgia, claims which are founded on diversity of citizenship should be dismissed without prejudice. O.C.G.A. § 14–2–331(b).

> Kinetic Concepts, Inc. v. Kinetic Concepts, Inc., 601 F.Supp. 496.

D.Hawai'i 1991. Because standing to sue is matter in abatement, not going to merits of claim, it should be resolved in motion to dismiss, not motion for summary judgment.

> Paulson, Inc. v. Bromar, Inc., 775 F.Supp. 1329.

S.D.N.Y. 1992. Dismissal for failure to state claim upon which relief can be granted is proper if plaintiff lacked standing to maintain the action. Fed.Rules Civ.Proc.Rule 12(b)(6), 28 U.S.C.A.

> In re Carver, 144 B.R. 643.

E.D.Pa. 1990. Fictitious parties must eventually be dismissed, if discovery yields no identities.

> Scheetz v. Morning Call, Inc., 130 F.R.D. 34.

N.D.Tex. 1987. If court concludes that proposed class representatives lack individual standing, proper procedure is to dismiss complaint, rather than to deny class for inadequate representation or to allow other class representatives to step forward; dismissal on standing grounds is to take place before class certification issues are ever reached. Fed.Rules Civ. Proc.Rule 23, 28 U.S.C.A.

> Gabrielsen v. BancTexas Group, Inc., 675 F.Supp. 367.

Bkrtcy.W.D.Pa. 1991. Standing is threshold inquiry and lack thereof is proper basis to dismiss complaint.

In re North East Projects, Inc., 133 B.R. 59.

⚷**1746. —— Capacity in particular actions.**

C.A.D.C. 1994. Action brought by present and former prisoners to challenge change in provider of prison drug treatment program could not be dismissed for failure to be brought by "real party in interest," although program provider did have interest in action, where prisoners alleged constitutional violations which affected their rights and not program provider's. Fed.Rules Civ.Proc.Rule 17(a), 28 U.S.C.A.

Best v. Kelly, 39 F.3d 328, 309 U.S.App. D.C. 51.

C.A.10 (Colo.) 1989. Complaint would be dismissed as to unnamed individual plaintiff members of plaintiff organizations where complaint did not specify names of individual members whose rights were allegedly violated, and unnamed plaintiffs had made no request to court for permission to proceed anonymously or otherwise disclose their identities to court or defendants; absent permission by district court to proceed anonymously on conditions such as court might impose, federal courts lacked jurisdiction over unnamed parties, as case had not been commenced with respect to them. U.S.C.A. Const.Amend. 6; Fed.Rules Civ.Proc. Rule 10(a), 28 U.S.C.A.

National Commodity and Barter Ass'n, National Commodity Exchange v. Gibbs, 886 F.2d 1240, on remand 790 F.Supp. 233, affirmed in part, reversed in part National Commodity and Barter Ass'n v. Archer, 31 F.3d 1521.

Complaint would be dismissed with respect to named plaintiff individual members of plaintiff organizations where the complaint contained no direct allegations of unlawful acts against the property or rights of such named persons.

National Commodity and Barter Ass'n, National Commodity Exchange v. Gibbs, 886 F.2d 1240, on remand 790 F.Supp. 233, affirmed in part, reversed in part National Commodity and Barter Ass'n v. Archer, 31 F.3d 1521.

C.A.10 (Colo.) 1985. Department of Justice and Federal Bureau of Investigation were not juridical entities separate from the United States or individual officers and employees who directed and worked for Department and Bu-

reau and, thus, were properly dismissed as named defendants in federal civil rights action.

Martinez v. Winner, 771 F.2d 424, opinion modified on denial of rehearing 778 F.2d 553, certiorari granted, vacated Tyus v. Martinez, 106 S.Ct. 1787, 475 U.S. 1138, 90 L.Ed.2d 333, on remand 800 F.2d 230.

Complaint had to be dismissed as to defendant who died and for whom plaintiff did not request that cause be revived against defendant's estate or personal representative.

Martinez v. Winner, 771 F.2d 424, opinion modified on denial of rehearing 778 F.2d 553, certiorari granted, vacated Tyus v. Martinez, 106 S.Ct. 1787, 475 U.S. 1138, 90 L.Ed.2d 333, on remand 800 F.2d 230.

C.A.7 (Ill.) 1993. District court properly dismissed mayor, sued in his official capacity, as party to action challenging constitutionality of city's weed ordinance, since lawsuit against mayor in his official capacity was same as lawsuit against city.

Schmidling v. City of Chicago, 1 F.3d 494, certiorari denied 114 S.Ct. 555, 510 U.S. 994, 126 L.Ed.2d 456.

C.A.7 (Ill.) 1984. Since lease lapsed by its terms when tenant, without landlord's prior written authorization, granted its purported successor in interest an option to acquire tenant's interest, or, at the very least, would have lapsed if purported successor had attempted to exercise option, purported successor did not and could not acquire interest in subject matter of lawsuit between landlord and tenant; accordingly, purported successor's counterclaim against landlord, tracking allegations in counterclaim it had filed in tenant's name, was properly dismissed. Fed.Rules Civ.Proc. Rule 17(a), 28 U.S.C.A.

American Nat. Bank and Trust Co. of Chicago v. Bailey, 750 F.2d 577, certiorari denied Chicago Investment Corporation v. American National Bank and Trust Company of Chicago, 105 S.Ct. 2324, 471 U.S. 1100, 85 L.Ed.2d 842.

C.A.4 (Md.) 1985. District court's ability to protect defendants from duplicative litigation under Clean Water Act [33 U.S.C.A. § 1251 et seq.] includes consolidation, citizen intervention and intervention of government in citizen suit, but does not include dismissal of previously filed citizen suit when government subsequently files suit. Federal Water Pollution Control Act Amendments of 1972, §§ 101 et seq., 505, 505(b)(1)(B), (c)(2), as amended, 33 U.S.C.A. §§ 1251 et seq., 1365, 1365(b)(1)(B), (c)(2).

Chesapeake Bay Foundation v. American Recovery Co., Inc., 769 F.2d 207.

C.A.8 (Minn.) 1994. District court did not abuse its discretion in dismissing statutes and "unknown defendants" improperly named as defendants in *Bivens* action.

> Phelps v. U.S. Federal Government, 15 F.3d 735, certiorari denied 114 S.Ct. 2118, 511 U.S. 1114, 128 L.Ed.2d 676.

C.A.8 (Mo.) 1986. City school district was properly dismissed as a party plaintiff in school desegregation case and realigned as a defendant, in view of potential conflict between interests of students seeking to demonstrate the existence of segregative conditions in the area, and those of city school district, which would resist the introduction of incriminating evidence concerning its own past or present actions.

> Jenkins by Agyei v. State of Mo., 807 F.2d 657, certiorari denied 108 S.Ct. 70, 484 U.S. 816, 98 L.Ed.2d 34, certiorari denied Kansas City, Mo. School Dist. v. Missouri, 108 S.Ct. 70, 484 U.S. 816, 98 L.Ed.2d 34.

C.A.2 (N.Y.) 1985. Dismissal of inmate's civil rights action under 42 U.S.C.A. § 1983 against State Commissioner of the Department of Correctional Services and superintendent of a correctional facility was proper, where record did not demonstrate personal involvement of those defendants sufficient to support their liability for wrongful acts on part of correctional facility officer who allegedly permitted inmate to be injured by fellow inmate's assault even though officer allegedly had specific knowledge of impending assault by the fellow inmate.

> Ayers v. Coughlin, 780 F.2d 205.

C.A.2 (N.Y.) 1981. Vishipco Line v. Chase Manhattan Bank, N.A., 660 F.2d 854, 62 A.L.R. Fed. 501, certiorari denied 103 S.Ct. 313, 459 U.S. 976, 74 L.Ed.2d 291, on remand 1984 WL 679, reversed 754 F.2d 452.

C.A.10 (Okl.) 1992. Former prison warden was properly dismissed in his official capacity from inmate's civil rights suit after new warden replaced him, but was still required to personally defend allegations of misconduct brought against him in his individual capacity, based on his order that inmate be served reduced rations for 72 hours with further warning that punishment would again be imposed if prisoner's disruptive behavior continued. 42 U.S.C.A. § 1983.

> Green v. Johnson, 977 F.2d 1383.

C.A.5 (Tex.) 1987. Dismissal of civil rights claims against municipality, which had at earlier stage in proceedings aligned itself with plaintiffs in their requests for injunctive relief against codefendants while continuing to challenge requests for damages against itself, was no longer warranted; complaint against codefendant had been dismissed, and municipality no longer took position as plaintiff. 42 U.S.C.A. § 1983.

> Roe v. Abortion Abolition Soc., 811 F.2d 931, certiorari denied 108 S.Ct. 145, 484 U.S. 848, 98 L.Ed.2d 101.

C.A.5 (Tex.) 1984. District court erred in dismissing complaint brought by mother of adjudicated incompetent, which alleged that temporary guardian's act of having incompetent involuntarily committed to mental hospital constituted false imprisonment, on ground that mother lacked capacity to sue on her son's behalf inasmuch as incompetent was adult represented by temporary guardian; as complaint alleged conflict of interest between guardian and incompetent, district court should have exercised its authority to appoint guardian ad litem or next friend to assure that incompetent's statutory and constitutional rights were properly protected. Fed.Rules Civ.Proc.Rule 17(c), 28 U.S.C.A.

> Adelman on Behalf of Adelman v. Graves, 747 F.2d 986.

M.D.Ala. 1998. District court would dismiss student's § 1983 claims against individual school officials in their official capacities, where retention of such claims would be redundant of claims against school board as entity and had potential to confuse jury. 42 U.S.C.A. § 1983.

> Godby v. Montgomery County Bd. of Educ., 996 F.Supp. 1390.

E.D.Ark. 1989. Inasmuch as United States was not party to action brought by Federal Deposit Insurance Corporation in its corporate capacity as assignee of claims of insolvent bank, counterclaim by bank officer based on alleged negligence by FDIC was to be dismissed as matter of law.

> Federal Deposit Ins. Corp. v. Manatt, 723 F.Supp. 99.

N.D.Cal. 1994. Fact that referee in partition action had not personally incurred CERCLA response costs did not require dismissal of CERCLA action filed in referee's own name on behalf of landowners, in light of ability to cure pleading defect by amendment of complaint to substitute landowners, who had incurred response costs, as real parties in interest. Comprehensive Environmental Response, Compensation, and Liability Act of 1980, § 107(a)(1–4), (a)(4)(B), 42 U.S.C.A. § 9607(a)(1–4), (a)(4)(B); Fed.Rules Civ.Proc.Rule 17(a), 28 U.S.C.A.

> Kamb v. U.S. Coast Guard, 869 F.Supp. 793.

N.D.Cal. 1986. Since title to tidelands would revert to the United States, which did not acquire the right to convey the land to corporation, unless corporation proved an estoppel defense, the United States had an interest in the property and would not be dismissed from the action disputing title to the tidelands.

> City of Alameda v. Todd Shipyards Corp., 632 F.Supp. 333, reconsideration denied 635 F.Supp. 1447.

N.D.Cal. 1979. Tran Qui Than v. Blumenthal, 469 F.Supp. 1202, affirmed in part, remanded in part 658 F.2d 1296, certiorari denied 103 S.Ct. 487, 459 U.S. 1069, 74 L.Ed.2d 630, appeal after remand 740 F.2d 759.

D.Colo. 1985. Estate of individual fatally shot by police officer would be dismissed as plaintiff in civil rights action pursuant to Colorado law making personal representative rather than estate proper party to bring action on behalf of estate. 42 U.S.C.A. § 1988.

> Trejo v. Wattles, 636 F.Supp. 992.

D.Conn. 1998. Lessees' § 1983 action against town building official who ordered demolition of warehouse in which lessees stored business equipment, alleging official deprived lessees of due process and just compensation under Federal Constitution for taking their property, would not be dismissed to extent that complaint alleged official capacity claim; complaint did not specify whether it was against official in his official or individual capacity. U.S.C.A. Const.Amends. 5, 14; 42 U.S.C.A. § 1983.

> Kendrick v. Town of Winchester/City of Winsted, 11 F.Supp.2d 212.

D.Conn. 1990. In litigation precipitated by announcement of presence of benzene in brand of mineral water, plaintiffs' erroneous identification of defendant's registered corporate names did not warrant dismissal, without prior opportunity to amend, where defendant had not alleged any prejudice stemming from any mistaken identification and plaintiffs had requested discovery on the issue.

> In re Perrier Bottled Water Litigation, 754 F.Supp. 264.

D.D.C. 1982. Moore v. U.S. House of Representatives, 553 F.Supp. 267, affirmed 733 F.2d 946, 236 U.S.App.D.C. 115, certiorari denied 105 S.Ct. 779, 469 U.S. 1106, 83 L.Ed.2d 775.

S.D.Fla. 1991. It would have been improper to dismiss wrongful death action on ground that parents of minor decedent were named as plaintiffs in addition to named personal representative who, under Florida statute, was proper person to bring action on behalf of decedent and his survivors. West's F.S.A. § 768.20.

> Brown v. Seebach, 763 F.Supp. 574.

N.D.Ill. 1994. Village police department was merely organizational division of village without separate legal existence and, thus, ar-

restee's § 1983 claim against police department had to be dismissed with prejudice. 42 U.S.C.A. § 1983.

> Williams v. Hutchens, 870 F.Supp. 857.

N.D.Ill. 1986. Individuals who had been awarded judgment in personal injury action against insured corporations had been named as defendants in insurer's declaratory judgment action solely for purpose of preventing transfer of venue to more appropriate jurisdiction and could be dismissed; failure of individuals' counsel to act on their behalf indicated his belief that their interests could not be adversely affected by resolution of dispute between parties to policy, and insurer was not likely to be prejudiced by absence of individual defendants from case. Fed.Rules Civ.Proc.Rule 21, 28 U.S.C.A.

> Liberty Mut. Ins. Co. v. Batteast by Batteast, 113 F.R.D. 77.

District courts have power to dismiss improperly named defendants to prevent manipulation of venue provisions of judicial code in attempt to defeat ends of justice. Fed.Rules Civ.Proc.Rule 21, 28 U.S.C.A.

> Liberty Mut. Ins. Co. v. Batteast by Batteast, 113 F.R.D. 77.

N.D.Ind. 1987. State's motion to dismiss action which challenged state's maintenance of allegedly segregated school system, which was premised upon challenge to specific individual plaintiffs' standing, required denial, where grant of motion would require court to engage in factual analysis pertaining to percentage of minority students in schools. Fed.Rules Civ. Proc.Rule 12, 28 U.S.C.A.

> Parents for Quality Educ. With Integration, Inc. v. Fort Wayne Community Schools Corp., 662 F.Supp. 1475.

N.D.Iowa 1994. Plaintiff's complaint against Indian tribe would be dismissed, even though tribe waived sovereign immunity as a Section 17 federal corporation formed under IRA, and court would have subject matter jurisdiction if this entity were sued, where plaintiff failed to make a capacity stipulation in his complaint, and failed to specify which entity of tribe he was suing, the tribal governmental entity or federal corporation entity, rendering complaint inadequate on its face. Fed.Rules Civ.Proc.Rules 9(a), 12(b)(1), 28 U.S.C.A.; Indian Reorganization Act, §§ 16, 17, 25 U.S.C.A. §§ 476, 477.

> Veeder v. Omaha Tribe of Nebraska, 864 F.Supp. 889.

D.Kan. 1996. Even if Kansas Department of Corrections was entity that could not be sued, Title VII discrimination and retaliation claims against it would not be dismissed, where Department did not raise argument in pretrial order, and Department could be replaced by state without prejudice. Civil Rights Act of 1964, § 701 et seq., 42 U.S.C.A. § 2000e et seq.

> Zinn v. McKune, 949 F.Supp. 1530, affirmed 143 F.3d 1353.

D.Kan. 1993. Suit brought by members of unincorporated association of anglers alleging breach of fiduciary duties by proposed defendants to association, and not alleging any injury by members bringing suit which was not common to other members, was clearly "derivative action," rather than "direct action," and thus was required to be dismissed for failure to comply with requirements of civil rule on derivative actions; complaint was not verified, complaint did not allege that members were shareholders or members at time of transaction of which they complained, and complaint did not allege that action was not collusive. Fed.Rules Civ.Proc.Rule 23.1, 28 U.S.C.A.

> Murray v. Sevier, 145 F.R.D. 563, reconsideration denied 149 F.R.D. 638.

Complaint by member of unincorporated association against business associate of association's founder, under which member alleged no special relationship to acts complained of other than as member of association, and which sought relief on behalf of association, was "derivative action," and thus was subject to dismissal for failure to comply with requirements for derivative actions under civil rule. Fed. Rules Civ.Proc.Rule 23.1, 28 U.S.C.A.

> Murray v. Sevier, 145 F.R.D. 563, reconsideration denied 149 F.R.D. 638.

D.Md. 1993. Claim that plaintiff should have named mayor and city council as defendants with capacity to sue and to be sued, instead of city, was hypertechnical pleading defense that had to fail based on principle that purpose of pleading is to facilitate proper decision on merits.

> Neufeld v. City of Baltimore, 820 F.Supp. 963, reconsideration denied 863 F.Supp. 255, affirmed 70 F.3d 1262, certiorari denied 116 S.Ct. 1852, 517 U.S. 1222, 134 L.Ed.2d 952, affirmed 70 F.3d 1262, certiorari denied 116 S.Ct. 1852, 517 U.S. 1222, 134 L.Ed.2d 952.

D.Mass. 1998. Medical malpractice defendant was not entitled to dismissal of action on ground that plaintiff, the duly appointed executrix of patient's estate in Vermont, failed to obtain ancillary powers as executrix in Massachusetts before filing suit and before medical malpractice tribunal convened and issued its finding; although defendant raised lack of executrix capacity in his answer, he then waited, for 15 months after medical malpractice tribunal and full two and one-half years after originally pleading plaintiff's lack of executrix capacity, to advance that issue, neither party would have been able to raise at tribunal issue of plaintiff's

capacity to sue, and plaintiff did remedy any defect in her representative capacity when, in response to defendant's summary judgment motion, plaintiff filed authenticated copies of her Vermont appointment with Massachusetts court, together with copy of bond filed in Vermont and her appointment of resident agent for service of process. M.G.L.A. c. 199A, § 5.

> Bohl v. Leibowitz, 1 F.Supp.2d 67.

D.Mass. 1988. Court may dismiss derivative action because plaintiffs are inadequate representatives, but may not do so for failure to state a claim upon which relief may be granted on the ground that the plaintiffs do not allege that they are adequate representatives. Fed. Rules Civ.Proc.Rules 12(b)(6), 23.1, 28 U.S.C.A.

> Abeloff v. Barth, 119 F.R.D. 332.

D.C.Mass. 1984. Complaint of sectarian schools, their teachers, students, students' parents, and churches operating schools against local officials for enforcing Massachusetts' compulsory education laws [M.G.L.A. c. 76, §§ 1, 2] could not be dismissed on grounds of standing or ripeness where local officials, through superintendent of schools, had threatened legal action.

> Braintree Baptist Temple v. Holbrook Public Schools, 616 F.Supp. 81.

E.D.Mich. 1992. District court would dismiss state prison inmate's civil rights action against defendant state prison assistant resident unit manager who had never been served with process and "John Doe" defendant who had never been identified and had never been served with process. 42 U.S.C.A. § 1983.

> Taylor v. Foltz, 803 F.Supp. 1261, affirmed 14 F.3d 602.

W.D.Mich. 1993. Appointment of plaintiff as personal representative related back to filing of amended complaint before plaintiff had received letters of authority, and, thus, plaintiff's original lack of status as real party in interest to act on behalf of estate was no basis for dismissal. M.C.L.A. §§ 700.5, 700.311, 700.312, 700.601; Fed.Rules Civ.Proc.Rules 17, 17(a), 28 U.S.C.A.

> Lavean v. Cowels, 835 F.Supp. 375.

D.Neb. 1994. Inmate who presented no evidence that he ever applied for commutation of sentence was not proper plaintiff in suit against governor and other state officials, which alleged commutation policy for persons convicted of second-degree murder violated inmates' civil rights, and suit would be dismissed as to this plaintiff.

> Walker v. Nelson, 863 F.Supp. 1059, affirmed in part 70 F.3d 1276.

D.Neb. 1992. School's motion to dismiss for failure to state a claim would be granted with respect to claims asserting that nonparty parents of handicapped students suffered loss of services and support, and medical expenses resulting from abuse of students while at school, absent indication that students were entitled to assert parents' claims; parents did not assign their causes of action to students. Fed.Rules Civ.Proc.Rule 12(b)(6), 28 U.S.C.A.

> Geir By and Through Geir v. Educational Service Unit No. 16, 144 F.R.D. 680.

D.Nev. 1985. Inclusion of three newspapers in complaint which also named their single corporate entity as a party defendant was merely surplusage and, thus, the newspapers would be dismissed from the action under Fed.Rules Civ.Proc.Rule 17(b), 28 U.S.C.A.

> Laxalt v. McClatchy, 622 F.Supp. 737.

D.N.M. 1984. While failure to name personal representative who is bringing action on behalf of deceased's estate, on face of complaint, may have been technical defect, to dismiss for so slight an error would have been to exalt form over substance.

> Jones v. 3M Co., 107 F.R.D. 202.

E.D.N.Y. 1987. Question of whether National Credit Union Association, as guarantor against losses sustained by credit union as result of merger with financially unsound credit union, had standing to bring action alleging that funds transferred from unsound credit union for purchase and development of real properties were fraudulently transferred and not repaid, was fact intensive and was not readily answerable on motion to dismiss before discovery. Fed. Rules Civ.Proc.Rule 12(b), 28 U.S.C.A.

> U.S. v. Rivieccio, 661 F.Supp. 281 1987 WL 15271.

S.D.N.Y. 1997. Failure of complaint to specify that plaintiff asserted claims against district attorney in his individual, rather than his official, capacity did not warrant dismissal at pleading stage on grounds that suit against district attorney in his official capacity is barred by Eleventh Amendment; rather, case would be permitted to proceed against official in his individual capacity. U.S.C.A. Const.Amend. 11.

> Smith v. Gribetz, 958 F.Supp. 145.

S.D.N.Y. 1989. In shareholder derivative action that on its face does not appear to be strike suit and where failure to verify complaint was merely an oversight, district court would not dismiss complaint for failure to comply with Federal Rule of Civil Procedure 23.1, but would instead require plaintiff to submit verifying affidavit. Fed.Rules Civ.Proc.Rule 23.1, 28 U.S.C.A.

> Zucker v. Katz, 708 F.Supp. 525.

S.D.N.Y. 1984. If bulletin allegedly issued by head of Office of Management and Budget authorized or arguably compelled unlawful activity in defunding publications, publisher of journal would be entitled to its nullification, and thus head of OMB would remain in action challenging Agency for International Development's refusal to continue funding of journal.

> Alan Guttmacher Institute v. McPherson, 597 F.Supp. 1530, affirmed 805 F.2d 1088.

E.D.N.C. 1986. Civil rights action was dismissed as to "Director of Internal Affairs Division" of county, as to whom other defendants presented uncontroverted evidence that no such office existed and that no person fit that description.

> Fate v. Dixon, 649 F.Supp. 551.

W.D.N.C. 1985. Motion to dismiss United States Postal Service as defendant in employment discrimination suit would be denied, where Postal Service was referred to in caption of case merely to identify defendant postmaster general and the capacity in which he was sued. Civil Rights Act of 1964, § 701 et seq., as amended, 42 U.S.C.A. § 2000e et seq.

> Grier v. Carlin, 620 F.Supp. 1364.

S.D.Ohio 1985. Alleged business entity was properly dismissed from civil action, in light of evidence that it was in fact not legal entity, but, rather, office-sharing arrangement consisting of four independent practitioners.

> S & R, Inc. v. Unlimited Financing, Inc., 625 F.Supp. 1033.

W.D.Okl. 1990. It was but surplusage that municipal officials were named defendants in civil rights action in their representative capacities and, therefore, their motion to dismiss filed in their representative capacities would be deemed moot, where city was named defendant. 42 U.S.C.A. § 1983.

> Havens v. City of NewCastle, 746 F.Supp. 1487.

D.Or. 1995. Claims of individual administrators of residential care facilities in connection with equal protection challenge to ballot initiative that allows terminally ill adult to obtain doctor's prescription for lethal drug dosage for express purpose of ending their life were subject to dismissal to the extent that they were asserted on behalf of patients of the respective residential care facilities; corporate facilities were real parties in interest for purposes of asserting such claims. U.S.C.A. Const.Amend. 14; Or.Laws 1995, c. 3, § 1.01 et seq.

> Lee v. State of Or., 891 F.Supp. 1421.

E.D.Pa. 1995. Because court could not decipher whether counterclaim defendant was true legal entity or lacked capacity to be sued, it would deny entity's motion to dismiss claims.

> Continental Cas. Co. v. Diversified Industries, Inc., 884 F.Supp. 937.

E.D.Pa. 1986. Hybrid entity which was both a handler as defined under Agricultural Marketing Agreement Act and federation of cooperatives, qualified under Capper Volstead Act, would not be dismissed from action seeking to prohibit Secretary of Agriculture from implementing regulations which would amend milk marketing orders, where member producers could simply have brought actions in their own names. 5 U.S.C.A. §§ 556, 556(e), 557, 706(2)(A, E); Agricultural Adjustment Act, §§ 8b, 8c(4), as amended, 7 U.S.C.A. §§ 608b, 608c(4).

Lehigh Valley Farmers v. Block, 640 F.Supp. 1497, affirmed 829 F.2d 409.

E.D.Pa. 1984. Because the Racketeer Influenced and Corrupt Organization Act counterclaim was dismissed as to one defendant it had to be dismissed as to other counterclaim defendants, which were additional parties.

Shared Diagnostic Services, Inc. v. Henningsen, 602 F.Supp. 428.

D.Puerto Rico 1990. Failure of complaint to mention that deceased student's parents were suing in their representative capacity on behalf of student did not require dismissal of § 1983 complaint that included claim for loss of student's companionship; inferences could be drawn that parents were suing in representative capacity and personal capacity. 42 U.S.C.A. § 1983; U.S.C.A. Const.Amend. 14.

Arroyo v. Pla, 748 F.Supp. 56.

N.D.Tex. 1991. Where police officials were sued only in their official capacities and the respective entities they were alleged to represent were joined as party defendants, the police officials would be dismissed.

Leatherman v. Tarrant County Narcotics Intelligence and Coordination Unit, 755 F.Supp. 726, affirmed 954 F.2d 1054, certiorari granted 112 S.Ct. 2989, 505 U.S. 1203, 120 L.Ed.2d 867, reversed 113 S.Ct. 1160, 507 U.S. 163, 122 L.Ed.2d 517, on remand 993 F.2d 1177, opinion after remand 28 F.3d 1388.

E.D.Va. 1986. Complaint which did not allege that one defendant was a joint venturer and which made no specific allegations against it did not state a claim against the defendant and would be dismissed with leave to amend to assert the joint venture relationship.

Allied Towing Corp. v. Great Eastern Petroleum Corp., 642 F.Supp. 1339.

E.D.Wis. 1985. District court, unable to name successor for agency school committee and educational service agency which no longer existed, but were named as defendants in suit by city school board alleging equal protection violations and other claims arising out of suburban school districts' maintaining of dual, racially segregated school system in metropolitan area, was required to dismiss claims against those defendants for lack of capacity. Civil Rights Act of 1964, § 601, 42 U.S.C.A. § 2000d; 42 U.S.C.A. §§ 1981, 1983, 1985, 1988; U.S.C.A. Const. Art. 6, cl. 2; Amends. 13, 14; 28 U.S.C.A. §§ 2201, 2202; 28 U.S.C.(1976 Ed.) §§ 1331(a), 1343(3, 4); W.S.A. Const. Art. 1, § 1; Art. 10, § 3; W.S.A. 118.13; W.S.A. 116.51(2) (Repealed); Wis. L.1983, c. 116, § 1446; Fed.Rules Civ.Proc.Rules 9(a), 12, 17(b), 25(d), 28 U.S.C.A.

Board of School Directors of City of Milwaukee v. State of Wis., 649 F.Supp. 82.

⚷1747. —— Nonjoinder in general.

C.A.D.C. 1986. District court should be extra cautious in dismissing case for nonjoinder of indispensable party if plaintiff will not have adequate remedy elsewhere. Fed.Rules Civ. Proc.Rule 19(b), 28 U.S.C.A.

Wichita and Affiliated Tribes of Oklahoma v. Hodel, 788 F.2d 765, 252 U.S.App.D.C. 140.

C.A.Fed. (Cal.) 1998. Fact that alternative forum exists does not automatically warrant dismissal of case based on absence of indispensable party, given rule's mandate to consider all relevant factors and equities of situation. Fed. Rules Civ.Proc.Rule 19(b), 28 U.S.C.A.

Dainippon Screen Mfg. Co., Ltd. v. CFMT, Inc., 142 F.3d 1266.

C.A.9 (Ariz.) 1996. Whether action should be dismissed under compulsory joinder rule requires district court to determine, first, whether absent party is necessary and, if so, can be joined, and second, whether absent party is indispensable. Fed.Rules Civ.Proc.Rule 19, 28 U.S.C.A.

Kescoli v. Babbitt, 101 F.3d 1304.

To determine whether, in equity and good conscience, district court may allow action to proceed in absence of necessary party which cannot be joined, court balances prejudice to any party or to absent party, whether relief can be shaped to lessen prejudice, whether adequate remedy, even if not complete, can be awarded without absent party, and whether there exists alternative forum, and court should be extra cautious before dismissing action if no alternative forum exists. Fed.Rules Civ.Proc.Rule 19(b), 28 U.S.C.A.

Kescoli v. Babbitt, 101 F.3d 1304.

C.A.9 (Cal.) 1994. Court deciding whether action must be dismissed for failure to join indispensable party must first determine if absent party is "necessary" to suit; then if party cannot be joined, court must determine whether party is "indispensable" so that in equity and good conscience suit should be dismissed. Fed. Rules Civ.Proc.Rule 19, 28 U.S.C.A.

> U.S. ex rel. Morongo Band of Mission Indians v. Rose, 34 F.3d 901.

C.A.10 (Colo.) 1998. Rule governing misjoinder and non-joinder of parties allows court to dismiss parties on such terms as are just, thus granting considerable discretion to district court; however, such discretion is circumscribed because court cannot proceed without indispensable parties. Fed.Rules Civ.Proc. Rules 19(b), 21, 28 U.S.C.A.

> Lenon v. St. Paul Mercury Ins. Co., 136 F.3d 1365.

C.A.11 (Fla.) 1986. Under Fed.Rules Civ. Proc.Rule 19(b), 28 U.S.C.A., applicable where joinder is not feasible in diversity action, federal court must examine situation pragmatically and make choice between alternatives of proceeding with action in absence of particular interested persons and dismissing action.

> Tick v. Cohen, 787 F.2d 1490.

Determination of extent to which judgment rendered in person's absence might be prejudicial to him or other parties, as required by Fed.Rules Civ.Proc.Rule 19(b), 28 U.S.C.A., setting forth factors to be considered by court in deciding whether to proceed without party who cannot be joined, calls for assessment of resulting prejudice to either absent persons or to parties already joined.

> Tick v. Cohen, 787 F.2d 1490.

C.A.7 (Ill.) 1989. Once trial has occurred and judgment has been entered, much greater showing of opposing interests is required to dismiss for failure to join indispensable party. Fed.Rules Civ.Proc.Rule 19(b), 28 U.S.C.A.

> Landau & Cleary, Ltd. v. Hribar Trucking, Inc., 867 F.2d 996.

C.A.7 (Ind.) 1990. In determining whether action should be dismissed for failure to join indispensable party, court must first determine whether absent parties are persons to be joined if feasible and then analyze whether case can proceed in absence of those parties; only if it has been determined that action cannot proceed in absence of those parties may label "indispensable" be applied to them; analysis should not initiate with determination that absent parties are "indispensable" followed by determination of whether in equity and good conscience case can proceed without them. Fed.Rules Civ. Proc.Rules 19, 19(a, b), 28 U.S.C.A.

> Moore v. Ashland Oil, Inc., 901 F.2d 1445.

In determining whether plaintiffs will have adequate remedy if action is dismissed for failure to join indispensable party, plaintiffs should not be entitled to federal forum despite their inability to join party without destroying diversity jurisdiction merely because they have waited too long to file their complaints in state court. Fed.Rules Civ.Proc.Rule 19(b), 28 U.S.C.A.

> Moore v. Ashland Oil, Inc., 901 F.2d 1445.

C.A.5 (La.) 1985. Federal Rule of Civil Procedure governing consequences of failure to join indispensable party is not intended to exclude considerations that are applicable in particular case. Fed.Rules Civ.Proc.Rule 19(b), 28 U.S.C.A.

> Lone Star Industries, Inc. v. Redwine, 757 F.2d 1544.

Pragmatic and equitable considerations control analysis under Federal Rule of Civil Procedure governing consequences of failure to join indispensable party. Fed.Rules Civ.Proc. Rule 19(b), 28 U.S.C.A.

> Lone Star Industries, Inc. v. Redwine, 757 F.2d 1544.

C.A.6 (Mich.) 1993. Dismissal for failure to join indispensable party involves three-step process: court must first determine whether person is necessary to the action and should be joined if possible, and court must then consider issues of personal jurisdiction and indispensability. Fed.Rules Civ.Proc.Rules 12(b)(7), 19(a, b), 28 U.S.C.A.

> Keweenaw Bay Indian Community v. State, 11 F.3d 1341.

District court did not err in considering motion to dismiss for absence of indispensable parties before addressing plaintiff's motion for preliminary injunction. Fed.Rules Civ.Proc. Rule 19, 28 U.S.C.A.

> Keweenaw Bay Indian Community v. State, 11 F.3d 1341.

C.A.10 (Okl.) 1996. Determining whether an absent party is indispensable requires a two-part analysis: court must first determine whether the party is necessary to the suit and must therefore be joined if joinder is feasible and, if the absent party is necessary but cannot be joined, the court must then determine whether the party is indispensable such that suit must be dismissed due to failure to join party. Fed. Rules Civ.Proc.Rule 19(a, b), 28 U.S.C.A.

> Rishell v. Jane Phillips Episcopal Memorial Medical Center, 94 F.3d 1407, certiorari dismissed 117 S.Ct. 1331, 137 L.Ed.2d 491, certiorari denied Wellshear v. Rishell, 117 S.Ct. 1427, 137 L.Ed.2d 536.

In context of motion to dismiss for failure to join indispensable parties, if, as a practical matter, the interests of absent parties will be adequately represented, their interests will not be impaired and a waiver agreeing to drop state court claim becomes a mere technicality and is not required. Fed.Rules Civ.Proc.Rule 19(a), 28 U.S.C.A.

> Rishell v. Jane Phillips Episcopal Memorial Medical Center, 94 F.3d 1407, certiorari dismissed 117 S.Ct. 1331, 137 L.Ed.2d 491, certiorari denied Wellshear v. Rishell, 117 S.Ct. 1427, 137 L.Ed.2d 536.

Availability of an alternative forum is primarily of negative significance under joinder rule, i.e., while absence of an alternative forum would weigh heavily, if not conclusively, against dismissal, the existence of another forum would not have as significant an impact in favor of dismissal; therefore, courts do not view the availability of an alternative remedy, standing alone, as a sufficient reason for deciding that the action should not proceed among the parties before the court, and some additional interest of either the absent party, the other properly joined parties or entities, or the judicial system must also be present, and judicial economy and convenience do not in themselves provide adequate grounds for dismissal. Fed.Rules Civ. Proc.Rule 19, 28 U.S.C.A.

> Rishell v. Jane Phillips Episcopal Memorial Medical Center, 94 F.3d 1407, certiorari dismissed 117 S.Ct. 1331, 137 L.Ed.2d 491, certiorari denied Wellshear v. Rishell, 117 S.Ct. 1427, 137 L.Ed.2d 536.

C.A.9 (Or.) 1993. Before action can be dismissed due to infeasibility of joining a party, district court must consider: prejudice resulting to any party or to absent party; whether relief can be shaped to lessen prejudice; whether an adequate remedy, even if not complete, can be awarded without the absent party; and whether there exists an alternative forum.

> Stock West Corp. v. Lujan, 982 F.2d 1389.

C.A.3 (Pa.) 1987. If complete relief cannot be accorded in absence of particular party, or party claims interest relating to subject of action such that his absence would impair or impede his ability to protect that interest or subject other party to multiple or inconsistent obligations, court must determine whether, in equity or in good conscience, action should proceed without absent party or whether absent party is indispensable and action should be dismissed. Fed.Rules Civ.Proc.Rule 19(a, b), 28 U.S.C.A.

> Steel Valley Authority v. Union Switch and Signal Div., 809 F.2d 1006, certiorari dismissed American Standard, Inc. v. Steel Valley Authority, 108 S.Ct. 739, 484 U.S. 1021, 98 L.Ed.2d 756.

C.A.4 (S.C.) 1996. The federal rules do not authorize a defendant to compel an unwilling plaintiff to assert a claim against a second defendant; the most that the defendant can do is argue that complete relief cannot be afforded without joinder of the second defendant, and if the court agrees, the plaintiff is given the choice of amending its complaint to name the "indispensable" second defendant or suffering dismissal of the complaint. Fed.Rules Civ.Proc. Rule 19(a, b), 28 U.S.C.A.

> Stanley v. Darlington County School Dist., 84 F.3d 707.

C.A.5 (Tex.) 1988. Unless court finds that party is indispensable, it has no discretion, except in most exceptional cases, to dismiss case even if necessary party cannot be joined. Fed.Rules Civ.Proc.Rule 19, 28 U.S.C.A.

> Shelton v. Exxon Corp., 843 F.2d 212, on remand 719 F.Supp. 537, affirmed in part, reversed in part 921 F.2d 595.

C.A.9 (Wash.) 1990. To determine whether absent party has legally protected interest in suit for purposes of dismissal, absent party's interest must be more than financial stake and more than speculation about future event.

> Makah Indian Tribe v. Verity, 910 F.2d 555.

Amicus status or ability to intervene is not sufficient to lessen finding of prejudice to absent party resulting from judgment which militates toward dismissal of suit. Fed.Rules Civ.Proc. Rule 19(a)(2), (b), 28 U.S.C.A.

> Makah Indian Tribe v. Verity, 910 F.2d 555.

If no alternative forum is available to plaintiff, court should be extra cautious before dismissing suit on grounds of inability to join indispensable parties; however, lack of alternative forum does not automatically prevent dismissal of suit.

> Makah Indian Tribe v. Verity, 910 F.2d 555.

M.D.Ala. 1996. A federal district court in its discretion may dismiss action for failure to join indispensable party. Fed.Rules Civ.Proc. Rules 12(b)(7), 19, 28 U.S.C.A.

> WMX Technologies, Inc. v. Jackson, 168 F.R.D. 64.

When deciding whether party is indispensable, district court must first determine whether party in question is necessary party to action within meaning of rule; if party is necessary, but joinder would deprive court of subject matter jurisdiction, district court must then determine whether in equity and good conscience action should proceed among parties before it, or alternatively, whether it should be dismissed. Fed.Rules Civ.Proc.Rule 19(a, b), 28 U.S.C.A.

> WMX Technologies, Inc. v. Jackson, 168 F.R.D. 64.

D.Ariz. 1997. On motion to dismiss for failure to join indispensable party, once court determines that party is necessary and cannot be properly joined, it must then undertake a four-part balancing test to determine whether party is indispensable to litigation based: (1) on prejudice to any party or to absent party; (2) on whether relief can be shaped to lessen prejudice; (3) on whether adequate remedy, even if not complete, can be awarded without absent party; and (4) on whether alternative forum exists. Fed.Rules Civ.Proc.Rule 19(b), 28 U.S.C.A.

> Village of Hotvela Traditional Elders v. Indian Health Services, 1 F.Supp.2d 1022, affirmed 141 F.3d 1182.

D.Ariz. 1992. To determine whether action should be dismissed because of inability to join necessary party, court must consider prejudice to party or those who are already parties, extent to which prejudice can be lessened by protective provisions in the judgment, whether judgment would be adequate, and whether plaintiff will have adequate remedy if the action is dismissed. Fed.Rules Civ.Proc.Rule 19, 28 U.S.C.A.

> Masayesva for and on Behalf of Hopi Indian Tribe v. Zah, 792 F.Supp. 1178.

C.D.Cal. 1997. To determine whether action should be dismissed under compulsory joinder rule, court must first determine whether absent party is necessary and cannot be joined, and, if so, court must then determine whether in equity and good conscience the action should proceed among parties before it, or should be dismissed. Fed.Rules Civ.Proc.Rule 19, 28 U.S.C.A.

> National Coalition Government of Union of Burma v. Unocal, Inc., 176 F.R.D. 329.

C.D.Cal. 1995. Motion to dismiss for failure to join indispensable party will be granted only where party is "indispensable" (not merely "necessary") and party cannot be joined. Fed. Rules Civ.Proc.Rule 12(b)(7), 28 U.S.C.A.

> U.S. v. White, 893 F.Supp. 1423.

To determine whether party is "indispensable," for purposes of motion to dismiss for failure to join indispensable party, courts consider whether valid reason exists for joining absent party, whether joinder is feasible, and whether it is fair to proceed if party cannot be joined. Fed.Rules Civ.Proc.Rule 12(b)(7), 28 U.S.C.A.

> U.S. v. White, 893 F.Supp. 1423.

D.Conn. 1991. If joinder of necessary party would destroy diversity and court in equity and good conscience cannot proceed without him, action has to be dismissed. Fed.Rules Civ.Proc.Rules 19, 19(b), 19 note, 28 U.S.C.A.

> Travelers Indem. Co. v. Household Intern., Inc., 775 F.Supp. 518.

N.D.Ill. 1997. Only when absent party is deemed indispensable may court dismiss lawsuit on basis of nonjoinder. Fed.Rules Civ. Proc.Rule 19(b), 28 U.S.C.A.

> Winklevoss Consultants, Inc. v. Federal Ins. Co., 174 F.R.D. 416.

N.D.Ill. 1995. If absent party cannot be joined, court must determine whether, in equity and good conscience, action may proceed without party; if court finds action cannot proceed without absent party, party is deemed indispensable and action is dismissed. Fed.Rules Civ.Proc.Rule 19(b), 28 U.S.C.A.

> Rhone-Poulenc, Inc. v. International Ins. Co., 877 F.Supp. 1170.

N.D.Ill. 1994. Two-step inquiry applies in determining whether to dismiss action if it is not feasible to join interested person: rule governing persons to be joined if feasible lists criteria for determining whether absent party should be joined if feasible and, if plaintiff cannot join absent party who should be joined if feasible under rule, court must then determine whether, in equity and good conscience, action should proceed among parties before it or should be dismissed because absent person is indispensable. Fed.Rules Civ.Proc.Rule 19(a, b), 28 U.S.C.A.

> Shell Oil Co. v. Aetna Cas. and Sur. Co., 158 F.R.D. 395, reconsideration denied.

In deciding whether to dismiss complaint for failure to join indispensable parties, test for determining to what extent judgment tendered in omitted person's absence might be prejudicial to that person or those already parties is whether, as a practical matter, absent party may be prejudiced, although omitted persons may not be technically bound by court's ruling. Fed.Rules Civ.Proc.Rules 12(b)(7), 19(b), 28 U.S.C.A.

> Shell Oil Co. v. Aetna Cas. and Sur. Co., 158 F.R.D. 395, reconsideration denied.

In deciding whether to dismiss complaint for failure to join indispensable parties, factor of whether judgment in omitted party's absence will be adequate, concerns public interest in complete and efficient resolution of controversies by the wholes. Fed.Rules Civ.Proc.Rules 12(b)(7), 19(b), 28 U.S.C.A.

> Shell Oil Co. v. Aetna Cas. and Sur. Co., 158 F.R.D. 395, reconsideration denied.

In determining whether to dismiss manufacturer's complaint in its declaratory judgment action for failure to join indispensable parties, manufacturer was entitled to high degree of respect for its choice of forum. Fed.Rules Civ. Proc.Rules 12(b)(7), 19(a, b), 28 U.S.C.A.

> Shell Oil Co. v. Aetna Cas. and Sur. Co., 158 F.R.D. 395, reconsideration denied.

In deciding whether to dismiss complaint for failure to join indispensable parties, factor of whether plaintiff will have access to adequate forum if case is dismissed, implicates not only parties' interests, but also those of public in avoiding piecemeal litigation. Fed.Rules Civ. Proc.Rules 12(b)(7), 19(b), 28 U.S.C.A.

    Shell Oil Co. v. Aetna Cas. and Sur. Co., 158 F.R.D. 395, reconsideration denied.

In determining whether to dismiss complaint for failure to join indispensable parties, availability or unavailability of alternative forum is critical consideration in deciding whether necessary parties are so indispensable that case cannot go forward in their absence. Fed. Rules Civ.Proc.Rules 12(b)(7), 19(b), 28 U.S.C.A.

    Shell Oil Co. v. Aetna Cas. and Sur. Co., 158 F.R.D. 395, reconsideration denied.

N.D.Ind. 1995. To avoid dismissal of action for nonjoinder, judgment entered must be adequate in general, and not simply adequate to needs of those persons already parties to action. Fed.Rules Civ.Proc.Rule 19(b), 28 U.S.C.A.

    Taylor v. Chater, 907 F.Supp. 306.

N.D.Ind. 1987. Adequate remedy in state courts if action is dismissed for nonjoinder is not alone sufficient basis for dismissal. Fed. Rules Civ.Proc.Rule 19(b), 28 U.S.C.A.

    Albers v. Sprayrite Mfg. Co., 115 F.R.D. 579.

S.D.Ind. 1993. Under rule governing joinder of persons needed for just adjudication, court is only required to determine whether to proceed or dismiss for lack of indispensable party when joinder is not feasible. Fed.Rules Civ.Proc.Rules 19, 19(b), 28 U.S.C.A.

    Showtime Game Brokers, Inc. v. Blockbuster Video, Inc., 151 F.R.D. 641.

N.D.Iowa 1995. If absent party is merely a "necessary" party, proper procedure under rule governing joinder of parties is to give parties opportunity to bring in such a party, not to dismiss action. Fed.Rules Civ.Proc.Rule 19(a), 28 U.S.C.A.

    De Wit v. Firstar Corp., 879 F.Supp. 947, on reconsideration 904 F.Supp. 1476.

Court does not err by refusing to dismiss for failure to join necessary party who is within venue and jurisdiction of district court, but whom present parties fail to join. Fed.Rules Civ.Proc.Rule 19(a), 28 U.S.C.A.

    De Wit v. Firstar Corp., 879 F.Supp. 947, on reconsideration 904 F.Supp. 1476.

D.Kan. 1996. In deciding whether dismissal for nonjoinder of indispensable party is required, court must conduct practical and pragmatic, but equitable, analysis of factors in rule governing joinder of indispensable parties, weighing interest of plaintiff in its choice of forum against interests of defendant and/or ab-

sent parties in protecting their rights. Fed. Rules Civ.Proc.Rule 19(b), 28 U.S.C.A.

    Cross Timbers Oil Co. v. Rosel Energy, Inc., 167 F.R.D. 457, reconsideration denied 168 F.R.D. 649.

To assess indispensability of absent party to action, court looks to following factors: extent to which judgment rendered in party's absence might be prejudicial to absent party or those already parties, extent to which court can fashion judgment in manner to reduce or eliminate potential prejudice, whether judgment rendered in parties' absence would be adequate, and whether adequate remedy is available if present action is dismissed for nonjoinder. Fed.Rules Civ.Proc.Rule 19(b), 28 U.S.C.A.

    Cross Timbers Oil Co. v. Rosel Energy, Inc., 167 F.R.D. 457, reconsideration denied 168 F.R.D. 649.

Court decides whether absent party's interest in litigation is sufficient to render it "necessary party" based on pleadings as they appear at time of motion to dismiss. Fed.Rules Civ. Proc.Rule 19(a), 28 U.S.C.A.

    Cross Timbers Oil Co. v. Rosel Energy, Inc., 167 F.R.D. 457, reconsideration denied 168 F.R.D. 649.

Availability of alternative remedy, alone, is not sufficient reason for dismissal, under rule governing joinder of necessary and indispensable parties. Fed.Rules Civ.Proc.Rule 19, 28 U.S.C.A.

    Cross Timbers Oil Co. v. Rosel Energy, Inc., 167 F.R.D. 457, reconsideration denied 168 F.R.D. 649.

M.D.La. 1993. If person who must be joined if feasible cannot be joined, court must decide whether in equity and good conscience court may proceed without that party or must dismiss; if court finds that lawsuit cannot proceed without absent party, then that party is indispensable, and if indispensable party is also nondiverse, then the court is compelled to dismiss case for lack of subject matter jurisdiction. Fed.Rules Civ.Proc.Rule 19(b), 28 U.S.C.A.

    Shell Western E & P Inc. v. Dupont, 152 F.R.D. 82.

Factors that court must consider and weigh when determining whether to proceed or dismiss case for failure to join indispensable party include: prejudicial effect on present and absent parties of judgment rendered in absence of party who could not be joined; extent to which prejudice could be lessened or avoided by measures such as protective provisions in judgment and by shaping relief granted; adequacy of any judgment rendered in party's absence; and adequacy of any remedy plaintiff might have if action is dismissed on basis of nonjoinder. Fed. Rules Civ.Proc.Rule 19(b), 28 U.S.C.A.

> Shell Western E & P Inc. v. Dupont, 152 F.R.D. 82.

W.D.La. 1987. Dismissal for failure to join other parties is reserved for instances when absentees are found to be indispensable.

> Southern Pacific Transp. Co. v. Town of Baldwin, 685 F.Supp. 601.

E.D.Mich. 1995. Court in considering motion to dismiss due to failure to join "indispensable" parties must first determine whether persons whose joinder is requested are "necessary" under rule, and if persons are necessary court must then determine whether persons are "indispensable" parties, or whether present proceedings may, in good conscience, continue without necessary persons. Fed.Rules Civ.Proc. Rule 19, 28 U.S.C.A.

> Intercept Sec. Corp. v. Code-Alarm, Inc., 164 F.R.D. 215.

D.Minn. 1989. If necessary, party must be joined to action; however, if party is necessary but joinder would destroy diversity, court must consider number of factors to determine whether interests of justice require that case proceed absent party or be dismissed. Fed.Rules Civ. Proc.Rule 19, 28 U.S.C.A.

> Federal Deposit Ins. Corp. v. Lindquist & Vennum, 702 F.Supp. 749.

S.D.Miss. 1986. Criteria for determining whether to allow action to proceed or dismiss it in forced absence of interested party require court to examine inter alia whether continuing action in absence of interested party will work deprivation of substantive rights of any persons already parties to action. Fed.Rules Civ.Proc. Rule 19(a), 28 U.S.C.A.

> Forest Oil Corp. v. Tenneco, Inc., 626 F.Supp. 917.

D.N.J. 1994. Claim should be dismissed only if unjoined person is both necessary and indispensable. Fed.Rules Civ.Proc.Rule 19, 28 U.S.C.A.

> Estrella v. V & G Management Corp., 158 F.R.D. 575.

S.D.N.Y. 1997. In order to dismiss claim or action for failure to join indispensable party, court must undertake a two-step inquiry: first, court must determine whether absent party is necessary; if court determines that party is necessary, and for any reason that party cannot be joined, then court must proceed to second step and determine whether under the circumstances of the particular case, court could, in equity and good conscience, proceed in party's absence.   Fed.Rules Civ.Proc.Rule 19(a), 28 U.S.C.A.

> Global Discount Travel Services, LLC v. Trans World Airlines, Inc., 960 F.Supp. 701.

S.D.N.Y. 1997. On motion to dismiss for failure to join indispensable party, court must first determine whether absent party is necessary party, i.e., party to be joined if feasible; if party is necessary, but cannot be joined, court must then proceed to determine whether absent party is indispensable and action should in equity and good conscience be dismissed. Fed. Rules Civ.Proc.Rule 19(a, b), 28 U.S.C.A.

> In re Lloyd's American Trust Fund Litigation, 954 F.Supp. 656, certification granted 1997 WL 458739.

Court should generally be reluctant to dismiss case for failure to join party. Fed.Rules Civ.Proc.Rule 19, 28 U.S.C.A.

> In re Lloyd's American Trust Fund Litigation, 954 F.Supp. 656, certification granted 1997 WL 458739.

Decision whether or not to dismiss action for failure to join party ultimately rests within district court's equitable jurisdiction. Fed. Rules Civ.Proc.Rule 19, 28 U.S.C.A.

> In re Lloyd's American Trust Fund Litigation, 954 F.Supp. 656, certification granted 1997 WL 458739.

S.D.N.Y. 1996. For purposes of dismissal of action for failure to join indispensable party, immunity of necessary party from suit because of sovereign immunity alone is ordinarily sufficient to warrant dismissal of action. Fed.Rules Civ.Proc.Rule 19(a, b); 28 U.S.C.A. §§ 1603(b), 1604.

> Aquinda v. Texaco, Inc., 945 F.Supp. 625, reconsideration denied 175 F.R.D. 50, vacated Jota v. Texaco, Inc., 157 F.3d 153, vacated 157 F.3d 153.

S.D.N.Y. 1996. On motion to dismiss for failure to join indispensable party, court must first determine whether absent party is "party to be joined if feasible"; only if court determines that party is to be joined if feasible, but cannot be joined, must court proceed to determine whether action should, in equity and good conscience, be dismissed. Fed.Rules Civ.Proc.Rule 19, 28 U.S.C.A.

> Evergreen Marine Corp. v. Welgrow Intern. Inc., 942 F.Supp. 201.

Potential difficulties of proof, due to party's absence, do not prevent complete relief from being accorded without joinder of absent party. Fed.Rules Civ.Proc.Rule 19, 28 U.S.C.A.

> Evergreen Marine Corp. v. Welgrow Intern. Inc., 942 F.Supp. 201.

Rule authorizing dismissal of action for failure to join indispensable party does not protect party from logically inconsistent results, but only from inconsistent obligations. Fed. Rules Civ.Proc.Rule 19, 28 U.S.C.A.

Evergreen Marine Corp. v. Welgrow Intern. Inc., 942 F.Supp. 201.

S.D.N.Y. 1995. If court determines that case may not proceed in the absence of a party, that party is considered "indispensable" and the action should be dismissed. Fed.Rules Civ. Proc.Rule 19, 28 U.S.C.A.

German v. Federal Home Loan Mortg. Corp., 885 F.Supp. 537, decision clarified on reargument 896 F.Supp. 1385.

S.D.N.Y. 1993. In context of motion to dismiss for failure to join indispensable party, determination as to whether court can proceed in equity and good conscience without party does not have to be made unless threshold showing is made that party should be joined if feasible. Fed.Rules Civ.Proc.Rule 19(a, b), 28 U.S.C.A.

Drankwater v. Miller, 830 F.Supp. 188.

As general rule, in determining whether party is indispensable, preference is for nondismissal, and procedural rule dealing with dismissal for failure to join indispensable party should thus be applied narrowly. Fed.Rules Civ.Proc.Rule 19, 28 U.S.C.A.

Drankwater v. Miller, 830 F.Supp. 188.

S.D.N.Y. 1990. In ruling on motion to dismiss for failure to join indispensable party, court must initially determine if absent person should be joined as party and should then consider whether proceeding without person would prejudice those parties already before court. Fed.Rules Civ.Proc.Rules 12(b)(7), 19, 28 U.S.C.A.

Ashley v. American Airlines, Inc., 738 F.Supp. 783.

S.D.N.Y. 1986. Courts must try, where possible, to avoid dismissal based on failure to join indispensable parties. Fed.Rules Civ.Proc. Rule 19(b), 28 U.S.C.A.

von Bulow by Auersperg v. von Bulow, 634 F.Supp. 1284, on reargument 1986 WL 7781.

M.D.N.C. 1995. On motion to dismiss for failure to join necessary and indispensable party, court initially determines if absent party should be joined, and if absent party is necessary but cannot be joined, court will determine by analyzing factors described in joinder rule whether to proceed without the absent party or to dismiss the action, but courts are extremely reluctant to grant motion to dismiss based on nonjoinder and will do so only when defect cannot be cured and serious prejudice or ineffi-

ciency will result. Fed.Rules Civ.Proc.Rules 12(b)(7), 19(a, b), 28 U.S.C.A.

RPR & Associates v. O'Brien/Atkins Associates, P.A., 921 F.Supp. 1457, affirmed 103 F.3d 120.

M.D.N.C. 1995. In determining whether action may proceed despite absence of indispensable party, court is to consider following factors: to what extent judgment rendered in person's absence might be prejudicial to person or those already parties; extent to which, by protective provisions in judgment, by shaping of relief, or other measures, prejudice can be lessened or avoided; whether judgment rendered in person's absence will be adequate; whether plaintiff will have adequate remedy if action is dismissed for nonjoinder. Fed.Rules Civ.Proc. Rule 19(a, b), 28 U.S.C.A.

May Apparel Group, Inc. v. Ava Import-Export, Inc., 902 F.Supp. 93.

S.D.Ohio 1996. Dismissal for failure to join indispensable party involves three-step process; first, court must determine whether person is necessary to action and should be joined if possible, and court must then consider issues of personal jurisdiction and indispensability. Fed.Rules Civ.Proc.Rules 12(b)(7), 19(a, b), 28 U.S.C.A.

Dorsey v. Tompkins, 917 F.Supp. 1195.

D.Or. 1993. Dismissal of action is appropriate based on failure to join indispensable parties if there is prejudice to party or absent party, if relief cannot be shaped to lessen the prejudice, where adequate remedy cannot be afforded without absent party, and where alternative forum exists.

Pacific Northwest Generating Co-op. v. Brown, 822 F.Supp. 1479, affirmed 38 F.3d 1058.

E.D.Pa. 1993. Nondiverse party could only be dismissed if it was dispensable party; if it was indispensable party, District Court could not dismiss it, but rather was required to dismiss entire suit for lack of subject matter jurisdiction. 28 U.S.C.A. § 1332.

Enza, Inc. v. We The People, Inc., 838 F.Supp. 975.

E.D.Pa. 1993. To decide motion to dismiss for failure to join indispensable parties, court must determine whether party is necessary and then determine whether party is indispensable. Fed.Rules Civ.Proc.Rule 19, 28 U.S.C.A.

Scott Paper Co. v. National Cas. Co., 151 F.R.D. 60, opinion superseded 151 F.R.D. 577.

If it is not feasible to join necessary party, e.g., subject matter jurisdiction will be defeated by joinder, court must determine whether absent party is indispensable—whether action can continue without absent party or action must be dismissed. Fed.Rules Civ.Proc.Rule 19(b), 28 U.S.C.A.

> Scott Paper Co. v. National Cas. Co., 151 F.R.D. 60, opinion superseded 151 F.R.D. 577.

E.D.Pa. 1984. Existence of adequate remedy in state court is not enough to compel dismissal of federal court action for failure to join indispensable party.

> Clements v. Holiday Inns, Inc., 105 F.R.D. 467.

D.Puerto Rico 1998. Generally, motion to dismiss for failure to join a necessary party should be granted when there is absent party without whom complete relief will not be possible in case or whose interest in controversy is such that to proceed without this party might prejudice it or parties already present in the case. Fed.Rules Civ.Proc.Rules 12(b)(7), 19, 28 U.S.C.A.

> Rivera Rojas v. Loewen Group Intern., Inc., 178 F.R.D. 356.

D.Puerto Rico 1997. Party moving for dismissal for failure to join indispensable party must show need to join absent party. Fed.Rules Civ.Proc.Rule 19, 28 U.S.C.A.

> Kmart Corp. v. Rivera-Alejandro Architects and Engineers, 174 F.R.D. 242.

D.Puerto Rico 1997. Party moving for dismissal for failure to join indispensable party must show need to join absent party. Fed.Rule Civ.Proc.Rule 19, 28 U.S.C.A.

> Western Auto Supply Co. v. Noblex Advertising, Inc., 173 F.R.D. 338.

D.R.I. 1993. If absent parties are indispensable, entire action, including allegations against diverse party, must be dismissed. Fed. Rules Civ.Proc.Rule 19(b), 28 U.S.C.A.

> Potter v. Bennett, 826 F.Supp. 62.

D.R.I. 1990. Defense of failure to join indispensable parties is not defense against merits of case, and will only result in dismissal of case if party cannot be joined and court determines that this failure to join will result in undue prejudice to one of parties. Fed.Rules Civ.Proc. Rules 12(b)(7), 19(b), 28 U.S.C.A.

> Friends of Sakonnet v. Dutra, 738 F.Supp. 623.

W.D.Tex. 1994. Factors in rule governing whether to dismiss case for lack of indispensable party or to proceed without party do not control district court's analysis, but rather are mere guidelines to encourage district court to reach practical, well-reasoned decision and, thus, factors do not exclude additional consider-

ations. Fed.Rules Civ.Proc.Rule 19(b), 28 U.S.C.A.

> Teacher Retirement System of Texas v. Reilly Mortg. Group, Inc., 154 F.R.D. 156.

D.Utah 1996. Motion to dismiss for failure to join party will not be granted because of vague possibility that persons who are not parties may have interest in action. Fed.Rules Civ.Proc.Rule 12(b)(7), 28 U.S.C.A.

> Sunrise Financial, Inc. v. PaineWebber, Inc., 948 F.Supp. 1002.

E.D.Va. 1986. Generally, John Doe suits are permissible only against real, but unidentified, defendants; if it does not appear that true identity of unnamed party can be discovered through discovery or through intervention of the court, then court can dismiss the action.

> HMK Corp. v. Walsey, 637 F.Supp. 710, affirmed 828 F.2d 1071, certiorari denied 108 S.Ct. 706, 484 U.S. 1009, 98 L.Ed.2d 657.

E.D.Wash. 1994. In determining whether failure to join party requires dismissal of action, court must determine whether absent party is "necessary" to suit, if so, and if that party cannot be joined, court must assess whether absentee party is indispensable so that in equity and good conscience suit should be dismissed. Fed.Rules Civ.Proc.Rule 19(a, b), 28 U.S.C.A.

> Cassidy v. U.S., 875 F.Supp. 1438.

E.D.Wis. 1997. In deciding whether action should be dismissed for failure to join indispensable party, district court must initially determine whether absent party is "necessary" to the suit, and if so, and if party cannot be joined, whether absent party is "indispensable" such that equity and good conscience demand that suit be dismissed. Fed.Rules Civ.Proc.Rule 19(b), 28 U.S.C.A.

> Southeastern Sheet Metal Joint Apprenticeship Training Fund v. Barsuli, 950 F.Supp. 1406.

In deciding whether suit should be dismissed for failure to join indispensable party, district court's inquiry should be practical and fact specific, and should be designed to avoid harsh results of rigid application. Fed.Rules Civ.Proc.Rule 19(b), 28 U.S.C.A.

> Southeastern Sheet Metal Joint Apprenticeship Training Fund v. Barsuli, 950 F.Supp. 1406.

Decision as to whether suit should be dismissed for failure to join indispensable party should not be based on formalistic or mechanistic grounds, but on pragmatic analysis of effect of potential party's absence. Fed.Rules Civ. Proc.Rule 19(b), 28 U.S.C.A.

> Southeastern Sheet Metal Joint Apprenticeship Training Fund v. Barsuli, 950 F.Supp. 1406.

Absent party is "necessary," for purposes of deciding whether lawsuit should be dismissed based on his or her nonjoinder, if complete relief cannot be granted among existing parties, or if absent party has some legally protected interest that might be impeded if lawsuit proceeds in his or her absence. Fed.Rules Civ. Proc.Rule 19(b), 28 U.S.C.A.

> Southeastern Sheet Metal Joint Apprenticeship Training Fund v. Barsuli, 950 F.Supp. 1406.

In deciding whether lawsuit should be dismissed for failure to join indispensable party, district court should consider various practical factors, including: plaintiff's interest in having a forum; defendant's interest in avoiding multiple litigation, inconsistent relief or sole responsibility for liability shared with other nonparties; interests of outsiders; and public interest in complete, efficient and consistent settlement of controversies. Fed.Rules Civ.Proc.Rule 19(b), 28 U.S.C.A.

> Southeastern Sheet Metal Joint Apprenticeship Training Fund v. Barsuli, 950 F.Supp. 1406.

In deciding whether lawsuit should be dismissed for failure to join indispensable party, district court must look beyond whether absent party would technically be bound by judgment, and must consider whether judgment would, as practical matter, impair absent party's interests. Fed.Rules Civ.Proc.Rule 19(b), 28 U.S.C.A.

> Southeastern Sheet Metal Joint Apprenticeship Training Fund v. Barsuli, 950 F.Supp. 1406.

In deciding whether lawsuit should be dismissed for failure to join indispensable party, district court must not elevate form over substance. Fed.Rules Civ.Proc.Rule 19(b), 28 U.S.C.A.

> Southeastern Sheet Metal Joint Apprenticeship Training Fund v. Barsuli, 950 F.Supp. 1406.

D.Wyo. 1994. When joinder of necessary party is not feasible, court must determine whether in equity and good conscience action may go forward in party's absence or whether it must be dismissed; if court decides that action must be dismissed, absent party is regarded as "indispensable." Fed.Rules Civ.Proc.Rule 19, 28 U.S.C.A.

> Bank of Keystone v. Wagensen, 152 F.R.D. 644.

Bkrtcy.D.Mass. 1995. Court should take pragmatic approach in considering equities of dismissal when joinder of party is not feasible. Fed.Rules Civ.Proc.Rule 19(b), 28 U.S.C.A.

> In re Cambridge Biotech Corp., 186 B.R. 9, affirmed 212 B.R. 10.

Bkrtcy.E.D.Va. 1985. Person is indispensable party to proceeding only when his joinder is not feasible under Rule 19(a), and in his absence, dismissal of case is preferable to adjudication. Fed.Rules Civ.Proc.Rules 19, 19(a, b), 28 U.S.C.A.

> In re Cleveland, 53 B.R. 814.

☞**1748. —— Nonjoinder in particular actions.**

U.S.La. 1990. Doctor who performed implant surgery and hospital where surgery was performed were merely permissive parties in patient's products liability action against manufacturer of "plate and screw device" implanted in patient's lower spine, and it was error to order their joinder as indispensable parties, and to dismiss suit with prejudice for failure to join them. Fed.Rules Civ.Proc.Rule 19(a, b), 28 U.S.C.A.

> Temple v. Synthes Corp., Ltd., 111 S.Ct. 315, 498 U.S. 5, 112 L.Ed.2d 263, rehearing denied 111 S.Ct. 715, 498 U.S. 1042, 112 L.Ed.2d 704.

C.A.D.C. 1985. Failure of pro se litigant, a federal employee seeking redress for employment discrimination, to name head of agency as proper defendant did not warrant dismissal of action with prejudice; rather, a reasonable amount of time would be allowed to permit amendment of complaint to comply with procedural requirement. Civil Rights Act of 1964, §§ 701 et seq., 717(c), as amended, 42 U.S.C.A. §§ 2000e et seq., 2000e–16(c).

> Jarrell v. U.S. Postal Service, 753 F.2d 1088, 243 U.S.App.D.C. 350.

C.A.9 (Ariz.) 1996. Although adequate remedy could be awarded, in absence of Navajo Nation and Hopi Tribe, to member of Nation who challenged Interior Department's approval of settlement agreement among Nation, Tribe, Office of Surface Mining (OSM), and coal mining company, which modified special condition to mining permit governing protection of sacred and ceremonial sites, and member might not have alternative forum, concern for tribal sovereignty warranted dismissal, in light of Nation's and Tribe's interests in lease and settlement agreements and impossibility of shaping relief to minimize prejudice to those interests. Fed.Rules Civ.Proc.Rule 19(b), 28 U.S.C.A.

> Kescoli v. Babbitt, 101 F.3d 1304.

C.A.8 (Ark.) 1990. Even if carrier's alleged agent for collection purposes were necessary party in suit brought by carrier to enforce shipper's liability for unpaid freight charges, proper procedure was to give parties opportunity to bring in alleged agent, not to dismiss action, and shipper, which merely raised issue of indispensability and then moved to dismiss after joinder deadline had passed, was not entitled to have suit dismissed; alleged agent was within venue and jurisdiction of district court and could easily have been impleaded by shipper. Fed.Rules Civ.Proc.Rules 19, 19(a), (a)(2)(ii), (b), 28 U.S.C.A.; 49 U.S.C.A. § 10744.

> Ranger Transp., Inc. v. Wal-Mart Stores, 903 F.2d 1185, rehearing denied.

C.A.9 (Cal.) 1994. Federally recognized governing body of Indian tribe, which was entitled to sovereign immunity with regard to claims by group of Indian families to beneficial ownership of land held in trust by United States, was indispensable party to group's claims against United States and Secretary of the Interior, and, thus, claims had to be dismissed, since governing body would clearly suffer prejudice if group was successful in its claim for beneficial ownership, United States could not adequately represent interests of governing body, and group could not be provided adequate judgment in absence of governing body. Fed.Rules Civ.Proc.Rule 19(b), 28 U.S.C.A.

> Pit River Home and Agr. Co-op. Ass'n v. U.S., 30 F.3d 1088.

Fact that there was no alternative forum in which group of Indian families could seek declaratory and injunctive relief regarding beneficial ownership of real property held in trust by United States did not preclude determination that federally recognized governing body of Indian tribe was indispensable party to group's action against United States and Secretary of the Interior and that action had to be dismissed due to governing body's sovereign immunity, since governing body's interest in maintaining its sovereign immunity outweighed group's interest in litigating its claim. Fed.Rules Civ. Proc.Rule 19(b), 28 U.S.C.A.

> Pit River Home and Agr. Co-op. Ass'n v. U.S., 30 F.3d 1088.

C.A.9 (Cal.) 1992. Hoopa Valley and Yurok tribes had indisputable interest in outcome of action by individual Indians and coast Indian community of Yurok Indians in challenging constitutionality of Hoopa-Yurok Settlement Act, and, thus, action was properly dismissed for failure to join indispensable parties. Fed.Rules Civ.Proc.Rules 19, 19(a)(2), (a)(2)(i), 28 U.S.C.A.

> Shermoen v. U.S., 982 F.2d 1312, certiorari denied 113 S.Ct. 2993, 509 U.S. 903, 125 L.Ed.2d 688, rehearing denied 114 S.Ct. 13, 509 U.S. 940, 125 L.Ed.2d 765.

C.A.9 (Cal.) 1990. Department of Interior employee's unlawful termination complaint was not subject to dismissal, though Department, rather than Secretary, was improperly named as defendant in caption, in that allegations made in body of complaint made it plain that Secretary was intended as defendant. Rehabilitation Act of 1973, § 505(a)(1), as amended, 29 U.S.C.A. § 794a(a)(1); Civil Rights Act of 1964, § 717, as amended, 42 U.S.C.A. § 2000e–16.

> Barsten v. Department of Interior, 896 F.2d 422, appeal after remand 947 F.2d 949, certiorari denied 113 S.Ct. 287, 506 U.S. 900, 121 L.Ed.2d 212, rehearing denied 113 S.Ct. 647, 506 U.S. 1016, 121 L.Ed.2d 576.

C.A.9 (Cal.) 1986. Sanitation district's claim for injunctive relief against further discharge by defendant into disposal system of nonparty municipal water district, which emptied into sanitation district's disposal system, which sanitary district claimed violated its wastewater ordinance required dismissal for failure to join municipal water district as indispensable party whose joinder would destroy diversity jurisdiction, rather than dismissal on the merits for failure to state a claim on which injunctive relief could be granted. Fed.Rules Civ.Proc.Rules 12(b)(6), 19(a, b), 28 U.S.C.A.

> County Sanitation Dist. No. 2 of Los Angeles County v. Inland Container Corp., 803 F.2d 1074.

C.A.9 (Cal.) 1985. Where parents had adequate alternative forum, state court, in which they could obtain relief, where defendant would be subject to multiple litigation and possibly inconsistent obligations by having to defend two separate lawsuits, one by the parents and one by the child, and where there was potential prejudice to the child, who might be collaterally estopped from pursuing his state action if his parents' federal suit were allowed to proceed and was unsuccessful, district court did not abuse its discretion in dismissing parents' action upon determining that child, whose joinder would defeat diversity, was an indispensable party. Fed.Rules Civ.Proc.Rule 19(b), 28 U.S.C.A.

> Aguilar v. Los Angeles County, 751 F.2d 1089, certiorari denied 105 S.Ct. 2656, 471 U.S. 1125, 86 L.Ed.2d 273.

C.A.2 (Conn.) 1988. District court should not have dismissed official capacity civil rights claims without giving plaintiffs opportunity to amend their complaints to add municipalities as parties. 42 U.S.C.A. § 1983.

> Perez v. Ortiz, 849 F.2d 793.

C.A.11 (Fla.) 1995. Suit brought by successors in interest who claimed that predecessor's offer of dedication had never been accepted by county was not subject to dismissal based on successors' failure to join adjoining landowners as indispensable parties, despite county's contention that adjoining landowners owned property in question; adjoining landowners would not be bound by district court's order, and county failed to establish nature of their allegedly unprotected interests.

> West Peninsular Title Co. v. Palm Beach County, 41 F.3d 1490, certiorari denied 116 S.Ct. 338, 516 U.S. 932, 133 L.Ed.2d 237, rehearing denied 116 S.Ct. 586, 516 U.S. 1018, 133 L.Ed.2d 507.

C.A.11 (Fla.) 1991. In action brought by potential personal representative of estate before resolution of state probate proceedings, better course of action would have been to stay proceedings to await state court action, rather than dismissing case for inability to join estate as indispensable party; while ability of estate to be joined as party was uncertain, it was likely to be determined in near future. Fed.Rules Civ. Proc.Rules 17(b), 19, 28 U.S.C.A.; West's F.S.A. § 733.601.

> Glickstein v. Sun Bank/Miami, N.A., 922 F.2d 666.

C.A.7 (Ill.) 1989. Dismissal with prejudice of action to set aside pension election for failure to join plan participant as indispensable party was inappropriate, where district court had not ordered participant to be joined. Fed.Rules Civ.Proc.Rules 12(b)(1, 7), 19, 19(a), 28 U.S.C.A.

> Sladek v. Bell System Management Pension Plan, 880 F.2d 972, 112 A.L.R. Fed. 849.

C.A.7 (Ill.) 1986. Dismissal of claims under ADEA and Title VII which named wrong defendant was not inequitable or a denial of substantial justice where parties simply chose to not amend, even though district court told them pleadings were deficient, told them how to correct pleadings and gave them time to effect changes. Age Discrimination in Employment Act of 1967, § 2 et seq., 29 U.S.C.A. § 621 et seq.; Civil Rights Act of 1964, § 717(c), as amended, 42 U.S.C.A. § 2000e–16(c).

> Ellis v. U.S. Postal Service, 784 F.2d 835.

C.A.7 (Ind.) 1991. If district court felt, considering equities involved in Voting Rights Act case, that Indiana legislature was necessary party, proper course would have been to require joinder, rather than to dismiss. Fed.Rules Civ. Proc.Rule 19, 28 U.S.C.A.; Voting Rights Act of 1965, § 2, as amended, 42 U.S.C.A. § 1973.

> Dickinson v. Indiana State Election Bd., 933 F.2d 497.

C.A.7 (Ind.) 1990. Federal suit raising issue of ownership of oil leasehold was subject to dismissal for failure to join indispensable parties; some of parties to be joined if feasible were persons who would deprive court of diversity jurisdiction; those individuals, who claimed conflicting ownership of same leaseholds, had to be considered adverse to plaintiffs and could not be realigned in order to preserve complete

diversity. Fed.Rules Civ.Proc.Rule 19, 28 U.S.C.A.

> Moore v. Ashland Oil, Inc., 901 F.2d 1445.

C.A.5 (La.) 1986. District court did not abuse its discretion in dismissing suit against sole voting trustee of corporation by his niece, as successor to 12 and one-half percent of voting stock, for failure to join niece's sister, who was a beneficiary of a trust that held 12 and one-half percent of the voting stock, and their mother, who was a trustee along with sole voting trustee and niece, as niece's interest in the federal forum, where she sought damages for sole voting trustee's alleged breaches of fiduciary duty under voting trust agreement, was weak, relief in state court, where similar suit by niece, her sister and mother was pending, was available to her, state courts were as convenient to her and her witnesses as federal court, federal court had no special expertise in the subject of the suit, and sole voting trustee's interest in avoiding multiple litigation or inconsistent relief was clear. Fed.Rules Civ.Proc. Rule 19, 28 U.S.C.A.

> Pulitzer-Polster v. Pulitzer, 784 F.2d 1305.

C.A.1 (Me.) 1989. Insurers could not avoid dismissal of declaratory judgment action against insured for lack of indispensable party on argument that, rather, than dismissing action because parties which had entered into settlement agreements with insured were indispensable parties which could not be joined without destroying diversity, court should have joined all of the parties except the nondiverse party. Fed.Rules Civ.Proc.Rule 19(b), 28 U.S.C.A.

> Travelers Indem. Co. v. Dingwell, 884 F.2d 629.

C.A.6 (Mich.) 1993. In suit by one band of an Indian tribe against state and individual members of two other bands concerning fishing rights under treaty, the two absent bands, which could not be joined because of sovereign immunity, were indispensable parties such that, in equity and good conscience, action should be dismissed, considering, inter alia, that plaintiff would still have adequate remedy by petitioning Secretary of the Interior to promulgate federal regulations governing the fishing treaty. Fed. Rules Civ.Proc.Rule 19(b), 28 U.S.C.A.

> Keweenaw Bay Indian Community v. State, 11 F.3d 1341.

C.A.5 (Miss.) 1987. In suit on behalf of infant alleging negligent delivery, dismissal of suit for nonjoinder of infant's parents in their individual capacity was unnecessary; doctors would not thereby be protected from inconsistent state and federal court judgments as they had already won in federal court, and parents' suit was originally separate cause of action from lawsuit on behalf of their child even though they were now estopped to bring that suit. Fed. Rules Civ.Proc.Rule 19(b), 28 U.S.C.A.

Lewis v. Holden, 821 F.2d 291.

C.A.10 (N.M.) 1997. The United States was not indispensable to determination of validity of state's compact with Indian tribe under Indian Gaming Regulatory Act (IGRA), such that state's counterclaim would have to be dismissed, though compact was approved by Secretary of the Interior. Indian Gaming Regulatory Act, §§ 2–22, 25 U.S.C.A. §§ 2701–2721; Fed.Rules Civ.Proc.Rule 19(b), 28 U.S.C.A.

Mescalero Apache Tribe v. State of N.M., 131 F.3d 1379.

C.A.2 (N.Y.) 1996. Conclusion that customer who requested letter of credit was indispensable to adjudication of creditor's suit to recover on letter of credit under collection theory did not justify dismissal of entire case, where creditor also pled, in alternative, under theory of letter-of-credit against issuing bank, and negligence against advising bank, neither of which required customer as party. Fed.Rules Civ. Proc.Rules 12(b)(7), 19(b), 28 U.S.C.A.

Clarendon, Ltd. v. State Bank of Saurashtra, 77 F.3d 631.

C.A.2 (N.Y.) 1991. District court, instead of simply dismissing plaintiff's pro se actions for injunctive relief and damages against Central Intelligence Agency (CIA), Federal Bureau of Investigation (FBI), and Defense Intelligence Agency on grounds that he failed to name responsible federal government officials, should have explained correct form to plaintiff so that he could have amended his pleadings accordingly.

Platsky v. C.I.A., 953 F.2d 26, appeal after remand 990 F.2d 1251, appeal after remand 990 F.2d 1251.

C.A.2 (N.Y.) 1990. Tenant's suit against subtenant could not properly be dismissed for failure to join landlord as indispensable party, though joinder would have destroyed diversity, in that subtenant could have joined landlord by asserting compulsory counterclaim against it. Fed.Rules Civ.Proc.Rules 13(a, h), 19(b), 28 U.S.C.A.

Associated Dry Goods Corp. v. Towers Financial Corp., 920 F.2d 1121.

C.A.2 (N.Y.) 1990. Limited partnership was dispensable party in limited partners' recharacterized class action against general partner and its controlling shareholder for looting limited partnership and could be dismissed by Court of Appeals to preserve diversity jurisdiction after change in law while case was pending on appeal; judgment had already been entered against general partner and its shareholder; and district court would be able to deal with

any difficulties by protective provisions in judgment or by shaping of relief.

Curley v. Brignoli, Curley & Roberts Associates, 915 F.2d 81, certiorari denied Brignoli & Curley, Inc. v. Curley, 111 S.Ct. 1430, 499 U.S. 955, 113 L.Ed.2d 484.

C.A.6 (Ohio) 1997. Failure of doctor and abortion clinic to join county prosecutors other than prosecutor from county in which doctor performed abortions and in which abortion clinic was located did not warrant dismissal of challenge to law regulating abortion for nonjoinder; Attorney General vigorously defended constitutionality of law, and there was no showing that prosecutors who were not joined had interests different from the state.

Women's Medical Professional Corp. v. Voinovich, 130 F.3d 187, certiorari denied 118 S.Ct. 1347, 140 L.Ed.2d 496.

C.A.10 (Okl.) 1996. For purpose of motion to dismiss medical malpractice action brought by curator for incapacitated patient, interests of patient's husband and children would not be impaired such that they had to be considered necessary parties; while state law provided that husband's interest in recovering damages for loss of consortium (and presumably the children's interest with regard to loss of parental consortium) was derivative of patient's recovery, and husband thus would be barred in state court action by adverse determination in federal court, curator could adequately protect husband's interest in pursuing suit on behalf of patient. Fed.Rules Civ.Proc.Rule 19(a), 28 U.S.C.A.

Rishell v. Jane Phillips Episcopal Memorial Medical Center, 94 F.3d 1407, certiorari dismissed 117 S.Ct. 1331, 137 L.Ed.2d 491, certiorari denied Wellshear v. Rishell, 117 S.Ct. 1427, 137 L.Ed.2d 536.

C.A.9 (Or.) 1995. Trial court erred by concluding that issuer of stock was sole seller under Oregon Blue Sky Law, and that failure to include issuer in lawsuit alleging violation of Blue Sky Law required dismissal; subsidiary which had transferred stock as consideration for transfers of real property made to it, could also be a "seller" within contemplation of statute. ORS 59.015(11)(a), (1975).

West Park Associates v. Butterfield Sav. & Loan Ass'n, 60 F.3d 1452.

C.A.3 (Pa.) 1988. First partner bringing suit for share of 30% profit position pursuant to agreement with corporation under which partnership would receive 30% of profits of production and sale of art reference book by corporation was not suit asserting interests of partnership but was merely suit for partner's personal entitlement and thus second and third partners were not necessary parties and nonjoinder of second and third partners did not require dismissal. Fed.Rules Civ.Proc.Rule 19(a, b), 28 U.S.C.A.

> Abel v. American Art Analog, Inc., 838 F.2d 691.

C.A.1 (R.I.) 1997. Claim by sales representative of insolvent jewelry manufacturer for tortious interference with contractual relations against manufacturer's secured creditors, through whose foreclosure sale manufacturer's operating assets were transferred to acquiring corporation, was properly dismissed by district court for representative's failure to name secured creditors in tortious interference count, and to move to amend when omission was brought to its attention; moreover, even if representative did not abandon claim, it failed to cite case law supporting cause of action, and was not entitled to have federal court make "trailblazing" interpretation of state law.

> Ed Peters Jewelry Co., Inc. v. C & J Jewelry Co., Inc., 124 F.3d 252.

C.A.5 (Tex.) 1996. Action for consent judgment by which defendant classes agreed to judgment declaring approval of settlement agreement between insurers and asbestos manufacturer and release of insurers would not be dismissed for failure to join asbestos manufacturer as indispensable party, in light of failure of defendant classes to object and manufacturer's consent to entry of similar release in another action.

> In re Asbestos Litigation, 90 F.3d 963, rehearing en banc denied 101 F.3d 368, rehearing denied, certiorari granted, vacated Flanagan v. Ahearn, 117 S.Ct. 2503, 138 L.Ed.2d 1008, on remand 134 F.3d 668, certiorari granted Ortiz v. Fibreboard Corp., 118 S.Ct. 2339, 141 L.Ed.2d 711, certiorari granted, vacated 117 S.Ct. 2503, 138 L.Ed.2d 1008, on remand 134 F.3d 668, certiorari granted 118 S.Ct. 2339, 141 L.Ed.2d 711.

C.A.5 (Tex.) 1992. Insured would not be granted leave to file motion to dismiss its action for lack of subject matter jurisdiction on basis of failure to join necessary parties; insured had control of suit below and chose which parties to sue, insurer's answer raised issue of failure to join indispensable parties, and, thus, insured had notice other parties might be necessary; moreover, insured failed to raise issue of indispensable parties until after oral argument in Court of Appeals. Fed.Rules Civ.Proc.Rule 19, 28 U.S.C.A.

> Judwin Properties, Inc. v. U.S. Fire Ins. Co., 973 F.2d 432, rehearing denied.

C.A.5 (Tex.) 1987. Corporation failed to establish that it would be subject to multiple or inconsistent obligations if investment broker was not joined, nor did it establish that disposition of securities fraud, breach of contract and Texas Deceptive Trade Practices Act case against it would impair or impede any interest that investment broker may have had and, therefore, investors' case was not subject to dismissal for failure to join allegedly indispensible party. Fed.Rules Civ.Proc.Rules 19, 19(a), 28 U.S.C.A.

> Nottingham v. General American Communications Corp., 811 F.2d 873, certiorari denied 108 S.Ct. 158, 484 U.S. 854, 98 L.Ed.2d 113.

C.A.3 (Virgin Islands) 1987. Plaintiff-investor, although failing to effectively ratify all nonparty investors as had been ordered by the District Court, made a reasonable, good-faith effort to comply with that order, and suit should not have been dismissed; although plaintiff-investor failed to submit ratification for one nonparty investor who had an interest in the subject matter of the action, plaintiff-investor did attempt to obtain ratification of most nonparty investors indicating that plaintiff could act as their express agent and could maintain instant action on their behalf. Fed.Rules Civ. Proc.Rule 17(a), 28 U.S.C.A.

> ICON Group, Inc. v. Mahogany Run Development Corp., 829 F.2d 473.

C.A.7 (Wis.) 1996. Even though dismissal for nonjoinder of Menominee Indian Tribe, as indispensable party, of qui tam action alleging that gambling equipment leases violated federal law left qui tam relators with no other remedy, relators' interests in contracts at issue were, at best, tenuous and indirect, and their inability to seek alternative relief thus would not preclude dismissal when weighed against tribe's interest in maintaining its sovereign immunity. Fed. Rules Civ.Proc.Rule 19(b), 28 U.S.C.A.

> U.S. ex rel. Hall v. Tribal Development Corp., 100 F.3d 476, rehearing and suggestion for rehearing denied.

M.D.Ala. 1996. Subsidiaries of corporation which acquired business owner's interest in various businesses were not necessary parties in corporation's action against business owner for indemnification of certain losses and, thus, corporation's action would not be dismissed for failure to join indispensable party; business owner was not subjected to risk of double recovery from subsidiaries, since subsidiaries were not parties to acquisition agreement between corporation and business owner which contained indemnification clause. Fed.Rules Civ. Proc.Rule 19(a), 28 U.S.C.A.

> WMX Technologies, Inc. v. Jackson, 168 F.R.D. 64.

N.D.Ala. 1997. Dismissal of assignee's action against purchaser to enforce arbitration clause in assigned sales contract was warranted, where seller was indispensable party in action who could not be joined without destroying diversity jurisdiction, purchaser might be subject to conflicting obligations and multiple litigation if seller was not joined, complete relief could not be afforded by proceeding without seller and there were actions pending in state court involving arbitration clause so that assignee would have adequate remedy. Fed.Rules Civ.Proc.Rule 19(b), 28 U.S.C.A.

> Green Tree Financial Corp. v. Holt, 171 F.R.D. 313.

D.Ariz. 1997. Indian tribe which had entered into agreement with federal agencies for construction of wastewater treatment facilities on Indian reservation was "indispensable party," the nonjoinder of which required dismissal of lawsuit which was brought to prevent federal agencies from proceeding with project until environmental impact statement (EIS) had been completed; tribe, as party which might otherwise be forced to fund completion of project to prevent hundreds of tribal members from remaining without modern sanitation, had a significant interest in project which could not be relieved or minimized, and adequate judgment could not be entered in tribe's absence. Fed. Rules Civ.Proc.Rule 19(b), 28 U.S.C.A.

> Village of Hotvela Traditional Elders v. Indian Health Services, 1 F.Supp.2d 1022, affirmed 141 F.3d 1182.

D.Ariz. 1995. Proper course for bankruptcy court to take, in face of motion to dismiss for failure to join necessary party in Chapter 7 adversary proceeding, was to attempt to join necessary party, rather than to dismiss lawsuit. Fed.Rules Bankr.Proc.Rule 7019, 11 U.S.C.A.; Fed.Rules Civ.Proc.Rule 19, 28 U.S.C.A.

> In re Home America T.V.-Appliance-Audio, Inc., 193 B.R. 929.

D.Ariz. 1992. Inability, because of tribal sovereign immunity, to join Pauite Tribe in action challenging BIA's determination of tribal status for that tribe required dismissal of the action. Fed.Rules Civ.Proc.Rule 19, 28 U.S.C.A.

> Masayesva for and on Behalf of Hopi Indian Tribe v. Zah, 792 F.Supp. 1178.

E.D.Ark. 1993. Bank, which held second lien on farm equipment involved in action brought by first lender against borrowers, was an "indispensable party" and its absence mandated dismissal of action; disposition of case in the absence of bank might have impaired or impeded its ability to protect its interest in proceeds of sale of collateral, it was doubtful that there were any protective measures, judgment in favor of first lienor could bring another action or result in bank losing any chance to claim some of sale proceeds, and adequate

remedy was available in state court. Fed.Rules Civ.Proc.Rule 19(b), 28 U.S.C.A.

> Deere & Co. v. Diamond Wood Farms, Inc., 152 F.R.D. 158.

W.D.Ark. 1987. Wife's civil action against husband under electronic surveillance provisions of Omnibus Crime Control and Safe Streets Act, alleging that husband caused electronic recording device to be installed on wife's phone and that he took tape recordings of conversations between wife and third parties, was not subject to dismissal for failure to join indispensable parties, the third parties thus recorded, where husband set forth no facts to indicate that persons believed to be indispensable were subject to service of process or that there was any reason to believe that failure to join third parties would subject husband to multiple liability. 18 U.S.C.A. § 2520; Fed. Rules Civ.Proc.Rule 19, 28 U.S.C.A.

> Nations v. Nations, 670 F.Supp. 1432.

D.Conn. 1997. Lessee of municipal landfill who arranged for city to operate landfill and committee of municipalities formed to provide solid waste management for region were not indispensible parties to landowners' claims against city for injunctive relief concerning alleged hazardous waste contamination from landfill, for purposes of motion to dismiss for failure to join indispensible parties, in light of evidence that interests of committee and lessee in removal and remediation of hazardous wastes in landfill was only financial and subject to indemnity agreements so that any injunctive relief would not impair their ability to protect financial interests. Fed.Rules Civ.Proc.Rule 12(b)(7), 28 U.S.C.A.

> Albahary v. City and Town of Bristol, Conn., 963 F.Supp. 150.

D.Del. 1987. Independent contractor which ran facilities of oil company, another independent contractor which ran clinic, and physician who treated employee of first independent contractor were indispensible parties to employee's medical malpractice action against oil company, for improper medical diagnosis and treatment allegedly received in Saudi Arabia, and employee's failure to join them required dismissal of action, in that complete relief could not be accorded, ability of absent parties to protect their interests could be impeded, and multiple and inconsistent judgments could result; employee would have adequate forum in Saudi Arabia. Fed.Rules Civ.Proc. Rule 19(a)(2)(i, ii), (b), 28 U.S.C.A.

> Chadwick v. Arabian American Oil Co., 656 F.Supp. 857.

D.Del. 1985. Complete relief could be accorded between those already parties in action challenging constitutionality of at-large system for conducting city council elections in Dover,

Delaware, so that failure to join Delaware as party defendant did not require that action be dismissed, despite contention that Delaware General Assembly would have to approve any amendments to Dover's city charter pertaining to redistricting of councilmanic boundaries, where relief sought included declaration that districts were unconstitutional as well as order requiring city council to frame districts which passed constitutional muster. 64 Del.Laws, c. 5, § 16; Del.C.Ann. Const. Art. 9, § 1; Fed. Rules Civ.Proc.Rules 12(b)(7), 19(a), (a)(1), (b), 28 U.S.C.A.; Voting Rights Act of 1965 § 2 et seq., 42 U.S.C.A. § 1973 et seq.; U.S.C.A. Const.Amend. 14.

> Central Delaware Branch, N.A.A.C.P. v. City of Dover, 110 F.R.D. 239.

D.D.C. 1991. Assuming that assignor was necessary party in suit against assignee alleging that assignee had assumed an obligation of the assignor, dismissal was not proper where it was not shown that joining assignor was not feasible and that proceeding with the action without assignor would be inequitable. Fed.Rules Civ. Proc.Rules 12(b)(7), 19, 19(b), 28 U.S.C.A.

> Nofziger Communications, Inc. v. Birks, 757 F.Supp. 80.

D.D.C. 1991. Whether two former law firm employees were indispensable parties who had to be joined as defendants in a client's negligence action was question which required discovery, and, thus, dismissal of action was not justified before discovery was completed; if attorneys had to be joined, diversity jurisdiction would have been destroyed. Fed.Rules Civ. Proc.Rules 12(b), 19, 28 U.S.C.A.

> - Anderson v. Hall, 755 F.Supp. 2.

D.D.C. 1985. While holders of mining claims and mineral leases for federal lands were necessary parties to suit by environmental organization challenging lifting of protective restrictions on those lands, their absence did not compel dismissal for nonjoinder; "public rights" exception favored denial of dismissal, which would effectively end litigation for all practical purposes, whereas if case proceeded absent parties would suffer only temporary hardship. Fed.Rules Civ.Proc.Rule 19(a, b), 28 U.S.C.A.

> National Wildlife Federation v. Burford, 676 F.Supp. 271, reconsideration denied 676 F.Supp. 280, affirmed 835 F.2d 305, 266 U.S.App.D.C. 241, rehearing denied 844 F.2d 889, 269 U.S.App.D.C. 271.

S.D.Fla. 1988. Dismissal of declaratory judgment action brought by successor of insolvent excess umbrella liability insurers was warranted for failure to join asbestos fiber suppliers' corporate parents as indispensable parties; litigation of declaratory judgment action could have collateral estoppel effects on corporate parents, judgment rendered against suppliers would not be fully dispositive of issues involving corporate parents, who were coinsureds under policies, other suits were pending in state court for litigation of same issues, in which suppliers were parties, and joinder of corporate parents would destroy district court's subject matter jurisdiction. Fed.Rules Civ.Proc.Rules 19, 19(b), 19 note, 28 U.S.C.A.

> Florida Ins. Guar. Ass'n, Inc. v. Carey Canada, Inc., 123 F.R.D. 356, reversed in part, vacated in part 886 F.2d 1324.

S.D.Fla. 1984. Seller was not proper party plaintiff against common carrier for cost of spoiled tomatoes, where seller's insurer paid seller in full for tomatoes, including "cost factor" and "profit" for sale to buyer, which neither accepted nor enjoyed benefits of bargain, but outright dismissal was not appropriate until seller had opportunity to join or substitute real party in interest. West's F.S.A. § 672.320; Fed. Rules Civ.Proc.Rule 17(a), 28 U.S.C.A.

> William D. Branson, Ltd. v. Tropical Shipping & Const. Co., Ltd., 598 F.Supp. 680.

M.D.Ga. 1988. Postal employee's Title VII race discrimination action against Postal Service required dismissal; employee failed to name postmaster general as proper party defendant and was not entitled to amend complaint to name proper party as amendment was beyond 30–day limitations period prescribed by statute. Fed.Rules Civ.Proc.Rule 15(c), 28 U.S.C.A.; Civil Rights Act of 1964, §§ 704(a), 717(c), as amended, 42 U.S.C.A. §§ 2000e–3(a), 2000e–16(c).

> Coleman v. U.S. Postal Service, 683 F.Supp. 263.

N.D.Ga. 1996. ERISA breach of fiduciary duty action was not subject to dismissal for failure to join four additional individuals as cofiduciary defendants; although they could have been jointly and severally liable with named defendants, they were parties subject to permissive joinder only, and were not indispensable parties. Employee Retirement Income Security Act of 1974, §§ 2 et seq., 405(a), 29 U.S.C.A. §§ 1001 et seq., 1105(a); Fed.Rules Civ.Proc.Rules 12(b)(7), 19(a), 20, 28 U.S.C.A.

> District 65 Retirement Trust for Members of Bureau of Wholesale Sales Representatives v. Prudential Securities, Inc., 925 F.Supp. 1551.

N.D.Ga. 1989. Dismissal was required due to inability to join nonparty partners in lawsuit by certain partners against other partners to recover profits from operation of hospital in alleged violation of defaulting partners' obligations not to compete with partnership; any judgment in action would have no legally preclusive effect on nonparty partners' claims, court could not fashion complete relief in absence of all partners, possibility of relitigation rendered judgment inadequate, and parties were presently using satisfactory alternate state forum in another suit. Fed.Rules Civ.Proc.Rule 19(a), 28 U.S.C.A.

DM II, Ltd. v. Hospital Corp. of America, 130 F.R.D. 469.

D.Idaho 1986. Dismissal of Comprehensive Environmental Response, Compensation, and Liability Act action for failure to add indispensable parties, premised on uncertainty of whether joint and several liability or merely several liability, would be imposed was not required, where even if joint and several liability were not imposed, of necessity, there would be finding as to divisibility and defendant would only be liable for injury which was divisible and capable of apportionment and not run the risk of multiple liability. Comprehensive Environmental Response, Compensation, and Liability Act of 1980, § 107, 42 U.S.C.A. § 9607; Fed. Rules Civ.Proc.Rule 19, 28 U.S.C.A.

State of Idaho v. Bunker Hill Co., 635 F.Supp. 665.

C.D.Ill. 1993. Alzheimers patient was not real party in interest, and thus, her absence did not warrant dismissal of action brought by her son challenging revocation of power of attorney in favor of son and challenging creation of new power of attorney in favor of patient's stepson; son sought to recover damages sustained by him personally in legal proceedings and did not seek to recover on behalf of patient. Fed.Rules Civ. Proc.Rule 12(b)(1, 7), 28 U.S.C.A.

Matter v. Williams, 832 F.Supp. 244.

N.D.Ill. 1995. Insured's suit against insurer that issued environmental impairment liability policy containing excess clause had to be dismissed because two absent insurers, which had issued comprehensive general liability (CGL) policies to insured, could not be joined; determination of first insurer's liability, even if that insurer was ultimately not held to be excess insurer, required construction of absent insurers' CGL policies. Fed.Rules Civ.Proc.Rule 19, 28 U.S.C.A.

Rhone-Poulenc, Inc. v. International Ins. Co., 877 F.Supp. 1170.

N.D.Ill. 1994. District court would dismiss, for failure to join other insurers as indispensable parties, action brought by manufacturer of polybutylene resin used for tubing in plumbing and municipal water systems against manufacturer's primary and excess comprehensive general liability insurers, seeking declaration that insurers had to indemnify manufacturer for claims arising from failures of systems, where, to obtain diversity jurisdiction, manufacturer failed to join other insurers that were in same layer or below layer of coverage of named defendants, and absent insurers' policies had to be exhausted before defendants' policy coverage was triggered. Fed.Rules Civ.Proc.Rules 12(b)(7), 19(a, b), 28 U.S.C.A.

Shell Oil Co. v. Aetna Cas. and Sur. Co., 158 F.R.D. 395, reconsideration denied.

N.D.Ill. 1994. Debtor's rights would not be prejudiced if it was not joined as party to creditor's action against guarantor, and, thus, complaint did not have to be dismissed for failure to join necessary party, where action would be stayed pending arbitration between debtor and creditor, and arbitration proceeding would fully address debtor's rights and obligations. Fed.Rules Civ.Proc.Rules 12(b)(7), 19, 28 U.S.C.A.

Stone Distribution Co. v. Meyers, 157 F.R.D. 405.

N.D.Ill. 1993. District court would not consider defendant's motion to dismiss plaintiff's age and sex discrimination complaint for plaintiff's failure to name defendant as respondent in Equal Employment Opportunity Commission (EEOC) charge as motion to dismiss for lack of subject matter jurisdiction; identifying entities in EEOC charge was not a jurisdictional requirement. Fed.Rules Civ.Proc.Rule 12(b)(1), 28 U.S.C.A.

Otterbacher v. Northwestern University, 838 F.Supp. 1256.

In ruling on defendant's motion to dismiss plaintiff's age and sex discrimination complaint for plaintiff's failure to name defendant as respondent in Equal Employment Opportunity Commission (EEOC) charge, court would consider, even though motion to dismiss for failure to state a claim focuses on four corners of complaint, accusations made in EEOC charge as well as the investigation to determine whether plaintiff satisfied this condition precedent to filing suit and court, therefore, accepted affidavit, as well as the charge attached to the complaint and accordingly treated motion as one for summary judgment. Fed.Rules Civ.Proc.Rules 12(b)(6), 56, 28 U.S.C.A.

Otterbacher v. Northwestern University, 838 F.Supp. 1256.

N.D.Ill. 1989. Absent any indication as to residence of allegedly necessary party, suit could not be dismissed on ground the joinder of such party would defeat diversity jurisdiction. Fed.Rules Civ.Proc.Rule 19(b), 28 U.S.C.A.

Aetna Cas. & Sur. Co. v. Chicago Ins. Co., 123 F.R.D. 589.

N.D.Ill. 1986. Securities fraud action could be maintained despite inability to join securities firm that was under Chapter 11 reorganization as defendant; other defendants were presumably solvent and able to satisfy any judgment against them, so firm was not indispensable party, joinder was not mandatory as possible liability was joint and several, securities firm's liability was primarily vicarious, and no adequate alternative form existed. Securities Exchange Act of 1934, § 9(e), 15 U.S.C.A. § 78i(e); Fed.Rules Civ.Proc.Rule 19, 28 U.S.C.A.

> Morgan v. Kobrin Securities, Inc., 649 F.Supp. 1023, on reconsideration 1987 WL 8992.

N.D.Ill. 1985. In the absence of explanation by defendants as to why individual had to be joined as a party in action alleging violations of the Racketeer Influenced and Corrupt Organizations Act, dismissal was not warranted for failure to include individuals as a necessary party. 18 U.S.C.A. § 1961 et seq.

> Millonzi v. Bank of Hillside, 605 F.Supp. 140.

N.D.Ill. 1984. Absence of members of plaintiff class did not require dismissal of counterclaims filed against them. Fed.Rules Civ. Proc.Rule 13, 28 U.S.C.A.

> In re Financial Partners Class Action Litigation, 597 F.Supp. 686.

N.D.Ill. 1969. Waters v. Wisconsin Steel Works of International Harvester Co., 301 F.Supp. 663, reversed 427 F.2d 476, certiorari denied United Order of American Bricklayers and Stone Masons, Local 21 v. Waters, 91 S.Ct. 137, 400 U.S. 911, 27 L.Ed.2d 151, certiorari denied 91 S.Ct. 137, 400 U.S. 911, 27 L.Ed.2d 151, on remand 1973 WL 11545, affirmed in part, reversed in part 502 F.2d 1309, certiorari denied 96 S.Ct. 2214, 425 U.S. 997, 48 L.Ed.2d 823, certiorari denied 96 S.Ct. 2214, 425 U.S. 997, 48 L.Ed.2d 823.

N.D.Ind. 1995. Social Security claimant's failure to join, as ordered by court, mother of wage earner's stepchildren, who were receiving child's insurance benefits, required dismissal with prejudice for failure to join indispensable party of her action challenging determination that recipient's stepchildren were entitled to receive benefits, resulting in reduction of benefits paid to recipient's natural children. Social Security Act, §§ 202(d), 216(e), 42 U.S.C.A. §§ 402(d), 416(e); Fed.Rules Civ.Proc.Rule 12(b)(7), 28 U.S.C.A.

> Taylor v. Chater, 907 F.Supp. 306.

N.D.Ind. 1986. Second amended complaint, alleging that eviction procedures utilized by landlords and city housing authority deprived recipients of section 8 housing assistance payments of their right to due process of law, was dismissed for failure to join United States Department of Housing and Urban Development as a necessary party as previously ordered, in that complaint essentially contended that regulations of the Department which governed eviction procedures for section 8 housing

were inadequate. United States Housing Act of 1937, § 8, as amended, 42 U.S.C.A. § 1437f.

> Gardfrey v. Gary Housing Authority, 109 F.R.D. 338.

N.D.Iowa 1987. Juvenile court judges were not indispensable parties to § 1983 action seeking to enforce state compliance with Juvenile Justice and Delinquency Prevention Act, and claim was not subject to dismissal for failure to name an indispensable party. Fed. Rules Civ.Proc.Rule 12(b)(7), 28 U.S.C.A.; 42 U.S.C.A. § 1983; Juvenile Justice and Delinquency Prevention Act of 1974, § 101 et seq., 42 U.S.C.A. § 5601 et seq.

> Hendrickson v. Griggs, 672 F.Supp. 1126, appeal dismissed 856 F.2d 1041.

D.Kan. 1996. Nondiverse physician was indispensable party in diversity medical malpractice action, and action had to be dismissed despite plaintiffs' reliance on "phantom party" provision of state comparative negligence law as standing for proposition that individual whose joinder would eliminate diversity could never be joined as defendant even under indispensable party theory; case relied on by plaintiffs did not involve suits pending in both state and federal forums, and plaintiffs had adequate remedy in state forum, where their action against nondiverse physician was pending. Fed.Rules Civ.Proc.Rule 19(b), 28 U.S.C.A.

> Thurston v. Page, 168 F.R.D. 655.

D.Kan. 1996. Joint interest owners in gas wells operated by plaintiff holder of rights to gas production from higher zone were "indispensable parties" whose addition would destroy district court's federal diversity jurisdiction over action, action could not proceed in equity and good conscience without their joinder, and, thus, court would dismiss operator's action against holder of rights from lower zone, alleging that lower zone holder illegally extracted gas from higher zone; judgment rendered in absence of joint venturers might prove prejudicial to their interests, there was no way to fashion order enjoining future production so as to protect joint venturers' interests, resolution of operator's claim left court unable to fully adjudicate all competing interests in gas without joinder of joint venturers, and operator had adequate remedy in state courts. Fed.Rules Civ.Proc.Rules 19(a, b), 24(a), 28 U.S.C.A.

> Cross Timbers Oil Co. v. Rosel Energy, Inc., 167 F.R.D. 457, reconsideration denied 168 F.R.D. 649.

E.D.La. 1991. Complaint against fictitious insurance company would be dismissed in civil rights action alleging false arrest and malicious prosecution by sheriff and deputy where company was not served, there was no appearance made on behalf of company, sheriff was self-insured, and there was no liability insurer providing liability coverage for sheriff or his deputies. 42 U.S.C.A. § 1983.

> Williams v. Divittoria, 760 F.Supp. 564.

M.D.La. 1993. Diversity action involving dispute between lessee and one co-owner of land concerning mineral rights in co-owners' land had to be dismissed for lack of subject matter jurisdiction after co-owners could not be joined as indispensable parties where main prejudicial effect would be that decision would spawn more litigation on same issues, and there were other remedies available to parties, including allowing state court to decide issue. Fed. Rules Civ.Proc.Rule 19(b), 28 U.S.C.A.

> Shell Western E & P Inc. v. Dupont, 152 F.R.D. 82.

D.Me. 1996. Intervening plaintiff did not establish that he would be prejudiced in legally significant manner by continuation of suit in federal court in his absence, as required for him to establish that he was indispensable party without whom case must be dismissed, where disposition of case in his absence would not prevent him from pursuing his claim in alternative forum with requisite jurisdiction, and he did not demonstrate how his addition to action would protect his ability to collect on any judgment he may receive better than if he proceeded in state court. 28 U.S.C.A. § 1367(b); Fed. Rules Civ.Proc.Rule 19(a)(2), 28 U.S.C.A.

> Liberty Mut. Group v. Hillman's Sheet Metal and Certified Welding, Inc., 168 F.R.D. 90.

D.Me. 1988. Dismissal of insurers' diversity action seeking declaration that they were not required to indemnify insured for environmental cleanup liabilities was warranted, in light of inability to join indispensable, nondiverse member of group of waste generators and transporters that paid for mandated cleanup at landfill site or to make substitution of parties based on transfer of interest. Fed.Rules Civ.Proc.Rules 19(a, b), 24(a), 25(c), 28 U.S.C.A.; Comprehensive Environmental Response, Compensation, and Liability Act of 1980, § 101 et seq., 42 U.S.C.A. § 9601 et seq.

> Travelers Indem. Co. v. Dingwell, 691 F.Supp. 503, affirmed 884 F.2d 629.

D.Md. 1986. Claim that United States had failed to join all parties indispensable to just adjudication of civil action by United States under the Comprehensive Environmental Response, Compensation, and Liability Act to recover response costs United States incurred in cleaning up landfill was not valid affirmative defense. Comprehensive Environmental Response, Compensation, and Liability Act of 1980, § 101 et seq., 42 U.S.C.A. § 9601 et seq.

> U.S. v. Dickerson, 640 F.Supp. 448.

D.Md. 1986. Unavailability of reformation or rescission of directors' and officers' liability policy issued to insured savings and loan association, due to Eleventh Amendment immunity of Maryland Deposit Insurance Fund acting as receiver of insured, and availability of complete relief for insurer in state court required dismissal of insurer's federal action for reformation or rescission. Md.Code, Financial Institutions, §§ 9–708, 9–709, 10–102.

> American Cas. Co. of Reading, Pa. v. Community Sav. & Loan, Inc., 635 F.Supp. 539.

D.Mass. 1991. Even if other banks were necessary parties in action brought on notes by one member of consortium of banks which financed leveraged buyout, motion to dismiss for nonjoinder would be denied, where it was unclear whether other banks would destroy diversity if they were joined; other banks' citizenship was unstated, and it was uncertain whether they would be joined as plaintiffs or defendants. Fed.Rules Civ.Proc.Rules 12(b)(7), 19(a), 28 U.S.C.A.

> Bank One Texas, N.A. v. Leaseway Transp. Corp., 137 F.R.D. 631, affirmed 968 F.2d 94.

D.C.Mass. 1981. Crowley v. Local No. 82, Furniture and Piano Moving, Furniture Store Drivers, Helpers, Warehousemen and Packers, 521 F.Supp. 614, affirmed 679 F.2d 978, certiorari granted 103 S.Ct. 813, 459 U.S. 1168, 74 L.Ed.2d 1012, reversed 104 S.Ct. 2557, 467 U.S. 526, 81 L.Ed.2d 457, rehearing denied 105 S.Ct. 19, 468 U.S. 1224, 82 L.Ed.2d 915.

W.D.Mich. 1992. Dismissal of commercial fisherman in dispute over fishing rights was warranted by Native American Indian tribe's failure to join additional tribes as indispensable parties, in light of open question of "home waters" concept which could impair absent tribes' ability to protect their interest or subject other parties to substantial risk of incurring multiple or inconsistent obligations.

> Keweenaw Bay Indian Community v. State of Mich., 152 F.R.D. 562, affirmed 11 F.3d 1341.

D.Minn. 1986. Even if Eleventh Amendment did not bar state employees' suit against the State for alleged overwithholding of social security taxes, on basis that State might properly seek reimbursement from the United States for the overwithholding, the suit was nonetheless subject to dismissal for failure to join the United States as an indispensable party. Fed. Rules Civ.Proc.Rule 19(a), 28 U.S.C.A.; U.S.C.A. Const.Amend. 11.

> Dunlop v. State of Minn., 626 F.Supp. 1127.

D.Neb. 1991. Sufficient showing that constitutional rights have been violated is not enough to state a claim upon which relief may be granted; plaintiff must also name appropriate defendant.

Tyler v. City of Omaha, 780 F.Supp. 1266, remanded 953 F.2d 648.

D.Nev. 1997. Consumer debtor's failure to join creditor as party to her action against debt collector for its alleged violations of the Fair Debt Collection Practices Act (FDCPA) did not warrant dismissal of FDCPA action for failure to join indispensable party; there was no dispute between consumer debtor and creditor over debt, and complete relief could be afforded without joining creditor. Truth in Lending Act, § 802 et seq., as amended, 15 U.S.C.A. § 1692 et seq.; Fed.Rules Civ.Proc.Rule 19, 28 U.S.C.A.

Pittman v. J.J. Mac Intyre Co. of Nevada, Inc., 969 F.Supp. 609.

D.Nev. 1988. Air Force employee's failure to name Secretary of Air Force as one of defendants in Title VII action was mere technical deficiency which could be remedied by amendment, and which did not require dismissal of action, where employee served complaint on Department of Air Force, and Air Force did not claim material prejudice to any substantive right. Civil Rights Act of 1964, § 717(c), as amended, 42 U.S.C.A. § 2000e–16(c).

Garrison v. U.S., 688 F.Supp. 1469.

D.N.H. 1992. Plaintiff's failure to join corporation to action based on violation of covenant not to compete did not justify dismissal for failure to join necessary party; corporation did not become indispensable party simply because its rights and obligations under entirely separate contract might be affected by results of action. Fed.Rules Civ.Proc.Rule 19, 28 U.S.C.A.

Ferrofluidics Corp. v. Advanced Vacuum Components, Inc., 789 F.Supp. 1201, affirmed 968 F.2d 1463.

D.N.J. 1985. Motion to dismiss trademark infringement complaint for failure to join indispensable party would be denied, since motion was attempt to raise jus tertii defense which generally should not be allowed as defense in any trademark case.

Eagle Snacks, Inc. v. Nabisco Brands, Inc., 625 F.Supp. 571.

E.D.N.Y. 1996. Fact that employee's estate had not been joined as a party did not bar employment discrimination action, given civil rule providing that executor or administrator may sue in that person's own name without joining party for whose benefit action is brought. Fed.Rules Civ.Proc.Rule 17(a), 28 U.S.C.A.

Estwick v. U.S.Air Shuttle, 950 F.Supp. 493.

E.D.N.Y. 1990. Insolvent savings and loan association, which was "lead" bank in lending consortium, was indispensable party to subcontractor's action against consortium, and thus, complaint was subject to dismissal where court lacked subject-matter jurisdiction over savings and loan association as result of subcontractor's failure to exhaust its administrative remedies with respect to association; subcontractor would have alternative form to litigate its claims against all named defendants after exhausting its administrative remedies with respect to claims against receiver of association, other defendants had strong interest in avoiding multiple litigation and potential inconsistent relief, and remaining defendants would be unable to assert claims for contribution and indemnity without association present. Fed.Rules Civ. Proc.Rule 19(b), 28 U.S.C.A.

Circle Industries, Div. of Nastasi-White, Inc. v. City Federal Sav. Bank, 749 F.Supp. 447, affirmed 931 F.2d 7.

E.D.N.Y. 1988. Defendant's accusation that he was not mentioned in connection with original complaints and that his subsequent inclusion was "specious" could not provide basis for motion to dismiss.

U.S. v. Bonanno Organized Crime Family of La Cosa Nostra, 695 F.Supp. 1426.

E.D.N.Y. 1986. Action by New York resident alleging fraudulent inducement to marry by Massachusetts residents in inducing him to marry their Lithuanian niece was not required to be dismissed for failure to join Lithuanian niece as indispensable party. Fed.Rules Civ. Proc.Rule 12(b)(7), 28 U.S.C.A.

Gudaitis v. Adomonis, 643 F.Supp. 383.

E.D.N.Y. 1984. Even if unintelligible complaint of pro se plaintiff against New York court system, Supreme Court, judge, and file clerk had stated claim upon which relief could be granted, District Court would have had to dismiss complaint for lack of in personam jurisdiction over defendants, where not every defendant had been served, and, in those instances in which service was made, service was rendered by plaintiff himself in violation of Federal Rules of Civil Procedure. Fed.Rules Civ.Proc. Rule 4(c)(2)(A), 28 U.S.C.A.

Browne v. N.Y.S. Court System, 599 F.Supp. 36.

N.D.N.Y. 1997. Fact that author named marketing company, in addition to book warehouse, as defendant in complaint alleging claims related to use of defective books did not establish that marketing company was indispensable party, as would require dismissal of author's action against book warehouse after author's voluntary dismissal of marketing company, despite warehouse's claim that author could sue marketing company in state court and warehouse could be impleaded. Fed.Rules Civ. Proc.Rules 12(b)(7), 19, 28 U.S.C.A.

> Donovan v. H.C. Associates, Inc., 174 F.R.D. 12.

N.D.N.Y. 1996. Deputy who had accompanied police officer on visit to detainee's home was not necessary party whose absence required dismissal of detainee's civil rights claims against officer arising out of visit, where deputy did not claim interest in subject of action and officer did not claim such interest on behalf of deputy, and deputy merely had possibility of tort liability. Fed.Rules Civ.Proc.Rules 12(b)(7), 19, 28 U.S.C.A.

> Mann by Parent v. Meachem, 929 F.Supp. 622.

S.D.N.Y. 1997. Mere assertion that bank, which was not a party to refinancing and guaranty agreements upon which creditor sued, and against which creditor had not articulated any specific claims, might be necessary to lawsuit under some speculative scenario for relief, if district court decided that creditor was entitled to participate in bond exchange for which bank had acted as paying agent, was insufficient to justify its continued presence in litigation or to preclude grant of its motion to dismiss.

> Yucyco, Ltd. v. Republic of Slovenia, 984 F.Supp. 209.

S.D.N.Y. 1997. Council and Corporation of Lloyd's of London, managing agents, and members' agents were not "indispensable parties" in names' action as members of underwriting syndicates against trustee of Lloyd's American Trust Funds (LATF), and, thus, dismissal was not required; trustee had obligation to implead Council, Corporation, and agents in order to eliminate potential prejudice, even though their interests could be impaired even absent claim against them by trustee, and any inconvenience and frustration of Council, Corporation and agents in intervening was not sort of undue burden that, in equity and good conscience, required dismissal. Fed.Rules Civ. Proc.Rules 13(h), 14, 19(b), 28 U.S.C.A.

> In re Lloyd's American Trust Fund Litigation, 954 F.Supp. 656, certification granted 1997 WL 458739.

S.D.N.Y. 1997. Major league baseball team was an indispensable party in minor league team's action against acting commissioner of major league baseball organization to challenge composition of board of arbitration, which was to fix compensation to which minor league team was entitled after major league team took minor league team's territory, and

thus dismissal of action was warranted; major league team would not have been bound by holding of case, thus potentially subjecting acting commissioner to inconsistent verdicts, joining major league team would have deprived court of subject matter jurisdiction, and state court was an available forum for minor league team's action. Fed.Rules Civ.Proc.Rule 19, 28 U.S.C.A.

> Greater Miami Baseball Club Ltd. Partnership v. Selig, 171 F.R.D. 73.

S.D.N.Y. 1996. Ecuadoran state-owned oil company and Republic of Ecuador were necessary parties that could not feasibly be joined in action and, thus, Ecuador residents' failure to join them as "indispensable parties" required dismissal of their class action against oil corporation headquartered in New York, seeking relief for damage to Ecuador region allegedly caused by oil exploration and extraction activities of consortium substantially controlled at various times by corporation and company; extensive equitable relief sought by residents could not be undertaken in absence of company or Republic, neither company nor Republic was subject to suit in United States due to Foreign Sovereign Immunities Act, and, in absence of company and Republic, any order granting material part of equitable relief sought would be unenforceable and prejudicial to present and absent parties. Fed.Rules Civ.Proc.Rule 19(a, b); 28 U.S.C.A. §§ 1603(b), 1604.

> Aquinda v. Texaco, Inc., 945 F.Supp. 625, reconsideration denied 175 F.R.D. 50, vacated Jota v. Texaco, Inc., 157 F.3d 153, vacated 157 F.3d 153.

S.D.N.Y. 1995. Securities fraud case was not required to be dismissed following failure to join former chief financial officer of issuer as a defendant, even though it was claimed that absence of officer from litigation precluded defendants from obtaining necessary information and was otherwise inequitable; knowledge of information does not render an individual indispensible, and when defendants are jointly and severally liable, plaintiff may sue defendants it deems fit. Securities Exchange Act of 1934, § 20(a), 15 U.S.C.A. § 78t(a); Fed.Rules Civ. Proc.Rule 19, 28 U.S.C.A.

> Miele v. Greyling, 892 F.Supp. 107.

S.D.N.Y. 1994. Heir's claim for accounting from decedent's attorney would not be dismissed for failure to join entities that allegedly held decedent's assets, where it was attorney who indicated that decedent operated his affairs through nominees, and purpose of heir's accounting would be to find out what nominee corporations were, whether they were legitimate corporate entities, and whether they had assets; it would be precipitous to dismiss heir's accounting claims before she had opportunity to determine identity of these entities. Fed.Rules Civ.Proc.Rule 19, 28 U.S.C.A.

> Pressman v. Estate of Steinvorth, 860 F.Supp. 171.

S.D.N.Y. 1993. For purposes of claim by supplier and its officer, that suit brought against them by former employee of distributor should be dismissed for failing to join distributor, fact that neither supplier nor officer had power to reinstate employee to her former position did not mean that complete relief could not be accorded unless distributor was joined; former employee was only seeking monetary damages. Fed.Rules Civ.Proc.Rule 19(a)(1), 28 U.S.C.A.

> Drankwater v. Miller, 830 F.Supp. 188.

Allegation by supplier and its officer, that failure by former employee of distributor to join distributor as party would impair distributor's ability to protect its interests in future litigation and thus that dismissal was necessary, was not sufficient to support finding that distributor should be joined if feasible; employee's claims against supplier and its officer sounded in tort, while causes of action against distributor would arise out of employment contract, and any finding in absence of distributor would not be binding upon distributor in subsequent action since distributor was not party to instant action. Fed.Rules Civ.Proc.Rule 19(a)(2)(i), 28 U.S.C.A.

> Drankwater v. Miller, 830 F.Supp. 188.

Claims asserted by supplier and its officer, regarding risks of incurring double, multiple, or otherwise inconsistent obligations if distributor was not joined as party in distributor's former employee's lawsuit, were too speculative to warrant dismissal for failure to join distributor, despite allusion to possibility that employee might sue distributor at some time in future and that distributor might file third-party complaint against supplier and officer, and to fact that employee currently had administrative claim pending against distributor. Fed.Rules Civ. Proc.Rule 19(a)(2)(ii), 28 U.S.C.A.

> Drankwater v. Miller, 830 F.Supp. 188.

S.D.N.Y. 1992. Corporation formed to provide engineering and design services which might be engendered by cooperation agreement to demonstrate various applications of advanced armor systems technology to United States military was "indispensable party" in action brought by owner of technical information alleging breach of agreement and misappropriation of technology requiring dismissal for nonjoinder, where corporation had exclusive role in delivering technology to one of the parties to the agreement and corporation's absence from suit might subject party to double or inconsistent liability. Fed.Rules Civ.Proc.Rules 19, 19(a), (a)(2), (a)(2)(ii), (b), 28 U.S.C.A.

> N.S.N. Intern. Industry v. E.I. du Pont de Nemours & Co., Inc., 143 F.R.D. 30.

Bare allegations of bias made in prior state court action which was dismissed on forum non conveniens grounds were insufficient to show that plaintiff would be prejudiced, much less denied its day in court, following dismissal for nonjoinder of indispensable party. Fed.Rules Civ.Proc.Rules 19, 19(a), (a)(2), (a)(2)(ii), (b), 28 U.S.C.A.

> N.S.N. Intern. Industry v. E.I. du Pont de Nemours & Co., Inc., 143 F.R.D. 30.

S.D.N.Y. 1989. Dismissal of commercial tenant's suit against subtenant seeking payment of rent allegedly due on sublease was warranted in light of tenant's failure to join landlord, a nondiverse indispensable party; landlord could not be easily aligned with subtenant, nor could subtenant's dispute with landlord be encompassed within court's ancillary jurisdiction. Fed.Rules Civ.Proc.Rule 19(b), 28 U.S.C.A.

> Associated Dry Goods Corp. v. Towers Financial Corp., 127 F.R.D. 57, reversed 920 F.2d 1121.

S.D.N.Y. 1988. Absence of indispensable parties justified dismissal of claim against all defendants where adjudication as to any defendant would necessarily risk prejudicing the absent claimants.

> Rapoport v. Banco Mexicano Somex, S.A., 706 F.Supp. 207, reconsideration denied 1989 WL 46701, stay granted 1989 WL 34043.

Company which had a plain interest in the result of plaintiff's claim against defendant, an alleged guarantor of the obligations of the party, was a necessary party and, because it could not be made a party to the suit, the action was required to be dismissed for failure to join an indispensable party. Fed.Rules Civ.Proc.Rule 19(a), 28 U.S.C.A.

> Rapoport v. Banco Mexicano Somex, S.A., 706 F.Supp. 207, reconsideration denied 1989 WL 46701, stay granted 1989 WL 34043.

S.D.N.Y. 1988. Under nationwide service of process provisions of Securities Exchange Act, two persons who were not joined as parties in securities action could be joined; accordingly, dismissal of case, because two individuals were indispensable parties who could not be joined because court lacked personal jurisdiction over them, would be inappropriate. Fed. Rules Civ.Proc.Rule 19(a, b), 28 U.S.C.A.; Securities Exchange Act of 1934, § 27, 15 U.S.C.A. § 78aa.

> Steinberg & Lyman v. Takacs, 690 F.Supp. 263.

W.D.N.Y. 1994. Banished Indian tribe members' counterclaim against utility for breach of franchise agreement and state law obligations based on utility's failure to provide members with electrical service, would be dismissed for inability to join Indian tribe as indispensable party after utility's declaratory judgment action against tribe was dismissed due to tribe's sovereign immunity; tribe was "indispensable party" because determination on merits of counterclaim could impair or impede tribe's ability to exercise its claimed right under agreement to prior approval of utility's provision of electricity to reservation residents, and sovereign immunity was of paramount importance. Fed.Rules Civ.Proc.Rule 19(a, b), 28 U.S.C.A.

> Niagara Mohawk Power Corp. v. Tonawanda Band of Seneca Indians, 862 F.Supp. 995, affirmed 94 F.3d 747.

W.D.N.Y. 1983. Sierra Club v. SCM Corp., 572 F.Supp. 828, appeal dismissed 747 F.2d 99.

W.D.N.C. 1990. Employment discrimination complaint against Equal Employment Opportunity Commission (EEOC) failed to state a claim for which relief could be granted where it did not comply with statutory requirement that the employee name the chairman of the EEOC as a defendant. 5 U.S.C.A. § 7703(b)(2); Civil Rights Act of 1964, § 717(c), as amended, 42 U.S.C.A. § 2000e-16(c).

> McKenzie v. E.E.O.C./Charlotte Dist. Office, 749 F.Supp. 115.

W.D.Okl. 1992. Plaintiffs' unjust enrichment claim against working interest owners in oil and gas production unit sounded in tort, rather than contract and, therefore, failure of plaintiffs to join all of owners' partners or joint venturers did not require dismissal of claim; plaintiffs alleged that owners' actions in area surrounding oil and gas production unit constituted negligence and negligence per se and as a remedy plaintiffs sought disgorgements of gains flowing from owners' alleged wrongdoing in form of money saved by owners by not complying with state pollution laws.

> Branch v. Mobil Oil Corp., 788 F.Supp. 539.

E.D.Pa. 1990. Company that was responsible for installing door in van was not an indispensable party in products liability suit and, accordingly, dismissal of suit due to alleged impossibility of joinder was not warranted, although door manufacturer alleged that company was a necessary party in view of expert report indicating that door was improperly installed. Fed.Rules Civ.Proc.Rule 19(a, b), 28 U.S.C.A.

> Marshall v. Overhead Door Corp., 131 F.R.D. 94.

E.D.Pa. 1988. Arrestee failed to state § 1983 civil rights claim against certain unknown police officers as result of his arrest and detention; "unknown police officers" were not named among defendants in title of action found in caption of complaint, and where unknown party has been sued under fictitious name court will dismiss fictitiously named defendant. 42 U.S.C.A. § 1983; Fed.Rules Civ. Proc.Rule 10(a), 28 U.S.C.A.

> Agresta v. City of Philadelphia, 694 F.Supp. 117.

E.D.Pa. 1988. Proposed class action seeking accounting and termination of operating agreements regarding oil and gas wells would not be dismissed for failure to join indispensable parties based on failure to join minority working interest owners that had settled state court action, although judgment rendered in favor of plaintiff class would adversely impact members of class that had settled state court action; members of that class had not objected to proceeding in the state court action without members of plaintiff class that represented majority of nonworking interest owners in oil and gas wells at issue, plaintiff class members had legitimately opted out of state court action, and complete relief could be awarded to plaintiff class members in absence of minority interest owners. Fed.Rules Civ.Proc.Rule 19, 28 U.S.C.A.

> MacNeal v. Columbine Exploration Corp., 123 F.R.D. 181.

M.D.Pa. 1992. Federal inmate's failure to identify Doe defendants in his *Bivens*-type civil rights action despite extensive discovery compelled dismissal of such defendants from case; inmate had not identified single individual alleged to have violated his constitutional rights or demonstrated that further discovery was likely to be successful in such regard, and over 30 corrections officers had already been questioned, and none of them have claimed knowledge of or involvement in conduct alleged.

> Veteto v. Miller, 829 F.Supp. 1486.

M.D.Pa. 1991. Property owner's complaint against neighboring property owners would not be dismissed for failure to join indispensable party arising out of discrepancies concerning ownership of corporate stock of company which owned property; owners' failure to identify any creditor which could lay claim to lot rendered the argument speculative. Fed. Rules Civ.Proc.Rules 12(b)(7), 19, 28 U.S.C.A.

> McCormick v. Camp Pocono Ridge, Inc., 760 F.Supp. 1113.

W.D.Pa. 1990. Dismissal of breach of contract action was warranted in equity and good conscience, where joinder of necessary party to that action was prohibited by automatic stay provision of Bankruptcy Code. Bankr.Code, 11 U.S.C.A. § 362(a); Fed.Rules Civ.Proc.Rules 12(b)(7), 19(b), 28 U.S.C.A.

> F&M Distributors, Inc. v. American Hardware Supply Co., 129 F.R.D. 494.

D.Puerto Rico 1997. Rape victim was indispensable party to diversity action brought by her father against shopping center where rape occurred to recover for his emotional distress allegedly caused by rape, and thus, inability to join victim, who would have defeated diversity, required dismissal of action without prejudice; judgment either in favor of or against defendant would create significant prejudice in separate action by victim which was pending in Commonwealth Court, no protective provisions in judgment could lessen prejudice, substantial judgment in either of actions pending could affect recovery in the other, and father would have adequate remedy through his joinder to pending action. Fed.Rules Civ.Proc.Rule 19(b), 28 U.S.C.A.

> Delgado v. Plaza Las Americas, Inc., 173 F.R.D. 30, vacated 139 F.3d 1.

D.Puerto Rico 1991. Dismissal of Puerto Rico law antidiscrimination causes of action was required where plaintiff, who was citizen of Puerto Rico, failed to join any Puerto Rico subsidiaries of foreign parent corporation, which were indispensable parties; appearance of parent alone could not adequately protect interests of and avoid prejudice to Puerto Rico subsidiaries, which were directly responsible for plaintiff's employment and his eventual discharge. Fed.Rules Civ.Proc.Rule 19(a), 28 U.S.C.A.

> Gay v. AVCO Financial Services, Inc., 769 F.Supp. 51.

D.R.I. 1993. Nondiverse defendants who conducted experiment to study effects of drug upon aspirin allergic patients were "indispensable parties," such that entire wrongful death action, including allegations against diverse drug manufacturer, would be dismissed; nondiverse defendants would be prejudiced by continuation of action in federal court against manufacturer, which was diverse party, judgment absent nondiverse parties would subject manufacturer to either multiple litigation or sole responsibility, and wrongful death action could be resolved competently in Rhode Island state courts. Fed.Rules Civ.Proc.Rule 19(b), 28 U.S.C.A.; 28 U.S.C.A. § 1332.

> Potter v. Bennett, 826 F.Supp. 62.

D.S.C. 1991. Dismissal of an employer's diversity action against its former employee for breach of a noncompetition agreement was required where joinder of worker's current employer was necessary for complete adjudication but joinder would destroy diversity jurisdiction; relief sought by former employer could have significant impact on current employer, there was no reasonable means of protecting worker and current employer from prejudice they would suffer if current employer were not a party, any judgment for current employer was likely to be inadequate if current employer were

not made a party, and an alternative forum existed. Fed.Rules Civ.Proc.Rules 19, 19(b), 28 U.S.C.A.

> Torrington Co. v. Yost, 139 F.R.D. 91.

S.D.Tex. 1994. Owners of planes that crashed were indispensable parties in tort actions arising out of crashes, and action had to be dismissed due to failure to join owners; nonowner defendants argued that crashes were caused by negligence of owners and their employees, and if owners were not joined, defendants risked being prejudiced, possibly forced to pursue second action for indemnity or contribution, or having liability issue decided inconsistently. Fed.Rules Civ.Proc.Rule 19(b), 28 U.S.C.A.

> Kern v. Jeppesen Sanderson, Inc., 867 F.Supp. 525.

W.D.Tex. 1994. Trust beneficiary's alleged violation of trust agreement from failing to seek permission of trustee before suing mortgage company for its performance under trust agreement did not alone establish indispensability of trustee and require dismissal for trustee's nonjoinder, in light of beneficiary's allegations that trustee waived compliance with permission provision, and in light of ability of district court to abate proceedings until beneficiary obtained permission to file suit. Fed.Rules Civ.Proc.Rule 12(b)(7), 28 U.S.C.A.

> Teacher Retirement System of Texas v. Reilly Mortg. Group, Inc., 154 F.R.D. 156.

Potential impact on absent trustee from result of trust beneficiary's case against mortgage company would be immediate and serious enough to cause prejudice to trustee, which supported dismissal of action for nonjoinder of indispensable party, in light of possibility that trustee could be found to have breached trust agreement or to have been negligent in signing agreement, which could impair trustee's interests in separate declaratory action concerning same parties, or which could be used offensively by beneficiary in any subsequent action against trustee for breach of fiduciary duty. Fed.Rules Civ.Proc.Rule 19(b), 28 U.S.C.A.

> Teacher Retirement System of Texas v. Reilly Mortg. Group, Inc., 154 F.R.D. 156.

Dismissal of action for nonjoinder of indispensable party was supported by inability of district court to take any practical measures to avoid or mitigate potential prejudice resulting from trustee's absence in trust beneficiary's action against mortgage company; district court could not determine at pleadings stage what collateral affect judgment in case would have on trustee. Fed.Rules Civ.Proc.Rule 19(b), 28 U.S.C.A.

> Teacher Retirement System of Texas v. Reilly Mortg. Group, Inc., 154 F.R.D. 156.

Trust beneficiary was sole beneficiary and could be accorded complete relief in suit against mortgage company for its performance under trust agreement, which supported finding that nonjoinder of trustee would not require dismissal for failure to join indispensable party. Fed.Rules Civ.Proc.Rule 19(b), 28 U.S.C.A.

> Teacher Retirement System of Texas v. Reilly Mortg. Group, Inc., 154 F.R.D. 156.

Nonjoinder of nondiverse, indispensable party of trustee warranted remand of trust beneficiary's lawsuit against mortgage company, rather than dismissal or stay pending mortgage company's declaratory judgment action in another jurisdiction, in light of policy supporting plaintiff's choice of forum, and in order to avoid waste of resources of parties and judiciary if beneficiary were compelled to refile case in state court. Fed.Rules Civ.Proc.Rule 19(b), 28 U.S.C.A.; 28 U.S.C.A. § 1447(e).

> Teacher Retirement System of Texas v. Reilly Mortg. Group, Inc., 154 F.R.D. 156.

D.Utah 1996. Suit to compel payment for shares would not be dismissed, for failure to join two persons who allegedly owned some of shares in question, due to failure on part of buyers to offer evidence to contradict affidavit by representative of sellers that one individual had pledged his shares to sellers and had defaulted, even though affidavit had not conclusively determined sellers' rights to sue for all shares in question as it stated that sellers deemed themselves to be owners of pledged shares without providing further substantiation. Fed.Rules Civ.Proc.Rule 12(b)(7), 28 U.S.C.A.

> Sunrise Financial, Inc. v. PaineWebber, Inc., 948 F.Supp. 1002.

E.D.Va. 1990. Religious corporation was indispensable party in action by members of corporation's chapel against corporate directors; thus, dismissal of action for lack of subject matter jurisdiction was warranted as joinder of corporation would destroy diversity. Fed.Rules Civ.Proc.Rule 19(a), 28 U.S.C.A.; 28 U.S.C.A. § 1332.

> Bates v. Cekada, 130 F.R.D. 52.

D.Virgin Islands 1986. Failure to join investors who own condominiums as tenants in common with managing tenant in common, who were indispensable parties, warranted dismissal where any judgment secured by managing tenant in common would affect each investor and where defendants faced likelihood of repetitive lawsuits and inconsistent verdicts for alleged breach of sale-leaseback agreement. Fed.Rules Civ.Proc.Rule 19(a), 28 U.S.C.A.

> ICON Group, Inc. v. Mahogany Run Development Corp., 112 F.R.D. 201, vacated 829 F.2d 473.

Managing tenant in common of condominium owned by investors as tenants in common could not maintain suit under Racketeer Influenced and Corrupt Organizations Act in absence of coowners' joinder. Fed.Rules Civ. Proc.Rules 17(a), 19(a), 28 U.S.C.A.

> ICON Group, Inc. v. Mahogany Run Development Corp., 112 F.R.D. 201, vacated 829 F.2d 473.

W.D.Wash. 1990. Failure to join state, a necessary party, in action challenging constitutionality of makeup of governing council of metropolitan area did not require dismissal where there was no impediment to joining appropriate state officials as defendants. Fed. Rules Civ.Proc.Rule 19(a), 28 U.S.C.A.

> Cunningham v. Municipality of Metropolitan Seattle, 751 F.Supp. 885.

E.D.Wis. 1997. Even assuming that local apprenticeship training committee was "necessary party" in lawsuit against participant in apprenticeship job training program to recover for participant's alleged breach of his scholarship loan agreements, participant failed to satisfy his burden of demonstrating that lawsuit should be dismissed for plaintiffs' failure to join local committee as additional party plaintiff, where local committee, as distinguished from national and local funds that brought suit, had not expended any funds on participant's training and would not be prejudiced if case went forward in its absence, particularly since its interests were adequately represented by national and local fund. Fed.Rules Civ.Proc.Rule 19(b), 28 U.S.C.A.

> Southeastern Sheet Metal Joint Apprenticeship Training Fund v. Barsuli, 950 F.Supp. 1406.

E.D.Wis. 1996. Inability to join Menominee Indian Tribe of Wisconsin as party to qui tam action, which alleged that agreements for lease and/or purchase of gambling equipment and supplies in connection with tribal gaming enterprise violated federal law, required dismissal of action, even though qui tam plaintiffs had no other remedy, as Tribe was indispensable party to suit; rescission of agreements would prejudice Tribe, as goods and services provided under them were essential to operation of tribal casino, and would discourage merchants and vendors from transacting business with Indian casinos, judgment entered in absence of Tribe would encroach upon its sovereignty and imperil its right to self-governance, and Tribe's interests outweighed those of qui tam plaintiffs, which were tenuous and indirect. Fed.Rules Civ.Proc.Rule 19(b), 28 U.S.C.A.

U.S. ex rel. Hall v. Tribal Development Corp., 165 F.R.D. 83, affirmed 100 F.3d 476, rehearing and suggestion for rehearing denied.

D.Wyo. 1989. Federal court would dismiss injured employee's Federal Employers' Liability Act suit against employer in that state claim defendants, over whom district court lacked jurisdiction, were necessary parties; employee's injuries were caused by employer and/or state claim defendants, and failure to dismiss case raised risk of inconsistent verdicts. Fed.Rules Civ.Proc.Rule 19(a, b), 28 U.S.C.A.

Ezell v. Burlington Northern R. Co., 724 F.Supp. 863.

☞1749. —— Misjoinder in general.

C.A.10 (Colo.) 1998. Rule governing misjoinder and non-joinder of parties allows court to dismiss parties on such terms as are just, thus granting considerable discretion to district court; however, such discretion is circumscribed because court cannot proceed without indispensable parties. Fed.Rules Civ.Proc. Rules 19(b), 21, 28 U.S.C.A.

Lenon v. St. Paul Mercury Ins. Co., 136 F.3d 1365.

C.A.3 (Pa.) 1993. Holding that joinder is compulsory is necessary predicate to district court's discretionary determination that case must be dismissed because joinder of party is not feasible and party is indispensable to just resolution of controversy. Fed.Rules Civ.Proc. Rule 19(a, b), 28 U.S.C.A.

Janney Montgomery Scott, Inc. v. Shepard Niles, Inc., 11 F.3d 399.

D.Del. 1972. U. S. v. Sinclair, 347 F.Supp. 1129, appeal dismissed U. S. v. Pearce's Estate, 498 F.2d 847.

M.D.Fla. 1996. Whether complaint should be dismissed for improper party is a question of law.

Elliott v. Sherwood Manor Mobile Home Park, 947 F.Supp. 1574.

M.D.Fla. 1992. Failure of plaintiff to seek leave to add party required dismissal of party as defendant. Fed.Rules Civ.Proc.Rules 15(a), 21, 28 U.S.C.A.

O'Rear v. American Family Life Assur. Co. of Columbus, Inc., 784 F.Supp. 1561.

N.D.Ill. 1986. Misjoinder of parties is not ground for dismissal of an action as federal civil rule allows dropping a party or severing a claim. Fed.Rules Civ.Proc.Rule 21, 28 U.S.C.A.

Filippini v. Ford Motor Co., 110 F.R.D. 131.

S.D.Ind. 1967. Bowe v. Colgate-Palmolive Co., 272 F.Supp. 332, affirmed in part, reversed

in part 416 F.2d 711, opinion corrected on denial of rehearing 1969 WL 4715, appeal after remand 489 F.2d 896.

D.Kan. 1985. Misjoinder of parties is not ground for dismissal, but court may order additional deletion of any party on such terms as are just. Fed.Rules Civ.Proc.Rule 21, 28 U.S.C.A.

Petroleum Data Services, Inc. v. First City Bancorporation of Texas, Inc., 622 F.Supp. 1022.

D.Md. 1994. Prohibition on dismissal of case for misjoinder of parties does not bar court from dropping misjoined parties from case. Fed.Rules Civ.Proc.Rule 21, 28 U.S.C.A.

Aaberg v. ACandS Inc., 152 F.R.D. 498.

D.Md. 1982. Polk y. Montgomery County, Md., 548 F.Supp. 613, reversed 782 F.2d 1196.

E.D.Mich. 1991. Federal district court should dismiss resident defendant who is fraudulently joined in case merely to defeat diversity jurisdiction; joinder is not fraudulent, however, if there is reasonable basis for asserting that state law may impose liability on resident under facts alleged. 28 U.S.C.A. § 1447.

Yedla v. Electronic Data Systems, Inc., 764 F.Supp. 90.

D.Minn. 1993. Court could look beyond pleadings and examine affidavits and other documents in resolving motion to dismiss for lack of subject matter jurisdiction since joinder of allegedly indispensable party would destroy diversity jurisdiction. 28 U.S.C.A. § 1332; Fed. Rules Civ.Proc.Rules 12, 12(b)(1), 19, 28 U.S.C.A.

Dou Yee Enterprises (S) PTE, Ltd. v. Advantek, Inc., 149 F.R.D. 185.

M.D.Pa. 1984. City of Harrisburg v. International Surplus Lines Ins. Co., 596 F.Supp. 954, affirmed 770 F.2d 1067.

Bkrtcy.D.Colo. 1991. Question of whether party should be dropped or dismissed from case, if it has been improperly joined, lies within discretion of trial court.

In re M & L Business Mach. Co., Inc., 132 B.R. 433.

Bkrtcy.E.D.Mich. 1995. Parties may be dropped, rather than action dismissed, if necessary to insure subject-matter jurisdiction based on diversity of citizenship. 28 U.S.C.A. § 1332; Fed.Rules Civ.Proc.Rules 12(h)(3), 21, 28 U.S.C.A.

In re Gale, 177 B.R. 531.

☞1750. —— Misjoinder in particular actions.

C.A.D.C. 1987. Zoological society officers, against whom no relief was sought in individual capacities, were appropriately dismissed as parties to defamation and false light actions. Fed.

Rules Civ.Proc.Rules 30(b)(6), 32(a)(2), 28 U.S.C.A.

> Crane v. Carr, 814 F.2d 758, 259 U.S.App. D.C. 229, on remand 1988 WL 64926, reversed 894 F.2d 454, 282 U.S.App.D.C. 295.

C.A.9 (Cal.) 1977. Jacobson v. Tahoe Regional Planning Agency, 566 F.2d 1353, certiorari granted Lake Country Estates, Inc. v. Tahoe Regional Planning Agency, 98 S.Ct. 2843, 436 U.S. 943, 56 L.Ed.2d 784, affirmed in part, reversed in part 99 S.Ct. 1171, 440 U.S. 391, 59 L.Ed.2d 401, on remand 474 F.Supp. 901.

C.A.11 (Ga.) 1993. Dismissal of assignee's claim for damages under guaranty assigned to it, on ground that assignee was not real party in interest, was not warranted where, although state insurance commissioner had been appointed conservator of assignee, affidavit of manager for conservator ratified assignee's action in bringing counterclaim and agreed to be bound by court's determination as to counterclaim. Fed.Rules Civ.Proc.Rule 17(a), 28 U.S.C.A.

> Integon Life Ins. Corp. v. Browning, 989 F.2d 1143.

C.A.7 (Ill.) 1973. Hampton v. City of Chicago, Cook County, Ill., 484 F.2d 602, certiorari denied 94 S.Ct. 1413, 415 U.S. 917, 39 L.Ed.2d 471, certiorari denied Hanrahan v. Hampton, 94 S.Ct. 1414, 415 U.S. 917, 39 L.Ed.2d 471, appeal after remand 600 F.2d 600, certiorari granted in part, reversed in part 100 S.Ct. 1987, 446 U.S. 754, 64 L.Ed.2d 670, rehearing denied 101 S.Ct. 33, 448 U.S. 913, 65 L.Ed.2d 1176, rehearing denied Johnson v. Hampton, 101 S.Ct. 33, 448 U.S. 913, 65 L.Ed.2d 1177, on remand 499 F.Supp. 640, appeal dismissed 643 F.2d 478, on remand 522 F.Supp. 140.

C.A.1 (Mass.) 1994. District court did not abuse its discretion by dismissing with prejudice 1,000 plaintiff and 93 defendant complaint for failure to adhere to court order requiring plaintiffs to refile separate complaints conforming to Local Rules of District of Massachusetts governing joinder and specificity of pleading in asbestos litigation and alleging adequate basis for jurisdiction; not only did plaintiffs' counsel make no effort to comply with order requiring him to refile separate complaints, he made no attempt to object to that order by filing motion for reconsideration showing good cause why it should be vacated or amended, and counsel defied Local Rules, and neglected to respond to motions filed by opposing counsel. Fed.Rules Civ.Proc.Rule 41(b), 28 U.S.C.A.; Massachusetts Multiple Litigation Orders 3, 4.

> Abdullah v. Acands, Inc., 30 F.3d 264.

C.A.8 (Minn.) 1989. Physician's action challenging suspension of his hospital privileges brought against parent holding company of corporation which operated hospital was subject to dismissal, where allegedly wrongful suspension occurred in normal course of business of operating corporation; indispensable proper defendant was the operating corporation, as reinstatement or other remedy had to be accorded by exertion of judicial power upon operating corporation, although certain powers of supervision over hospitals were reserved by charter to parent company.

> Everett v. Franciscan Sisters Healthcare, Inc., 882 F.2d 1383, appeal after remand 974 F.2d 77.

C.A.5 (Miss.) 1995. Complaint adding plaintiffs by permissive joinder could not be dismissed solely on basis of prior blanket order that all subsequent suits against same defendant be filed separately, absent individual examination of whether subsequent plaintiffs had been properly joined and whether they should be allowed to continue in one action. Fed.Rules Civ.Proc.Rules 20, 21, 42(b), 28 U.S.C.A.

> Applewhite v. Reichhold Chemicals, Inc., 67 F.3d 571.

C.A.9 (Mont.) 1984. Houghton v. South, 743 F.2d 1438, appeal after remand 865 F.2d 264, appeal after remand 965 F.2d 1532.

C.A.9 (Nev.) 1977. Jacobson v. Tahoe Regional Planning Agency, 566 F.2d 1353, certiorari granted Lake Country Estates, Inc. v. Tahoe Regional Planning Agency, 98 S.Ct. 2843, 436 U.S. 943, 56 L.Ed.2d 784, affirmed in part, reversed in part 99 S.Ct. 1171, 440 U.S. 391, 59 L.Ed.2d 401, on remand 474 F.Supp. 901.

C.A.2 (N.Y.) 1986. Claims of state prison inmate for compensatory relief for denial of medical treatment, directed at persons not named in complaint, were properly dismissed. Fed.Rules Civ.Proc.Rule 12(b)(5), 28 U.S.C.A.; 42 U.S.C.A. § 1983.

> Purcell v. Coughlin, 790 F.2d 263.

C.A.6 (Ohio) 1988. District court did not abuse its discretion in dismissing antitrust and racketeering claims against one bank, after finding that claims against that bank did not arise from same transaction, occurrence or series of transactions or occurrences, as required by joinder rule, in action arising out of loan transactions with numerous other banks. Fed.Rules Civ.Proc.Rules 20(a), 21, 28 U.S.C.A.

> Michaels Bldg. Co. v. Ameritrust Co., N.A., 848 F.2d 674.

S.D.Ala. 1994. Race and sex discrimination plaintiff's § 1983 claims against school superintendents in their official capacities would be dismissed with prejudice, since plaintiff had sued county board of education directly. 42 U.S.C.A. § 1983.

> Garrett v. Clarke County Bd. of Educ., 857 F.Supp. 949.

E.D.Cal. 1993. Partner in plaintiff partnership would not be dismissed as defendant in antitrust suit brought by partnership and other partner, as defendant partner would be necessary party if court entertained supplemental dissolution action. Fed.Rules Civ.Proc.Rule 19(a), 28 U.S.C.A.

> Delbon Radiology v. Turlock Diagnostic Center, 839 F.Supp. 1388.

D.Conn. 1995. Based on student's complaint alleging only that school superintendent served as chief executive officer of school board and had responsibility for supervision of school district, it appeared that school board was real party in interest and, thus, claims against superintendent would be dismissed without prejudice; there were no specific allegations that superintendent was directly and personally responsible for any action or inaction on part of school board or teacher of student, who was allegedly sexually harassed by another pupil.

> Mennone v. Gordon, 889 F.Supp. 53.

D.D.C. 1991. District of Columbia and Board of Trustees of University of District of Columbia were not indispensable parties to worker's action to recover for injury while replacing electric motor in airhauling unit of University, and, thus, dismissal of District and Board would not entitle manufacturer of airhauling unit to dismissal.

> Krieger v. Trane Co., 765 F.Supp. 756.

D.D.C. 1985. Improperly identifying federal agency, rather than the United States, as defendant in suit brought pursuant to Federal Tort Claims Act did not warrant dismissal of action. 28 U.S.C.A. §§ 1346, 2671 et seq., 2679, 2679(a).

> Childress v. Northrop Corp., 618 F.Supp. 44, affirmed 784 F.2d 1131, 251 U.S.App. D.C. 327.

M.D.Fla. 1997. Allegedly improper joinder of city officials in their official capacity, in action to enjoin city from enforcing allegedly unconstitutional signage ordinance, was not a basis for dismissing complaint; however, names of those officials would be stricken from complaint, leaving city as remaining defendant. Fed.Rules Civ.Proc.Rule 21, 28 U.S.C.A.

> Lamar Advertising of Mobile, Inc. v. City of Lakeland, Fla., 980 F.Supp. 1455.

D.Hawai'i 1995. Plaintiffs were not properly added to complaint, and claims asserted by plaintiffs were dismissed, where existing plaintiffs did not seek leave of court to add additional plaintiffs and did not bring motion to amend complaint as required by order which had previously been issued. Fed.Rules Civ.Proc.Rule 15, 28 U.S.C.A.

> Pedrina v. Chun, 906 F.Supp. 1377, affirmed 97 F.3d 1296, certiorari denied Wong v. Chun, 117 S.Ct. 2441, 138 L.Ed.2d 201.

D.Hawai'i 1994. Individual defendants would be dismissed from suit challenging constitutionality of surveyor's license requirements, absent evidence that they were in any way involved in discrimination complained of.

> Bradford v. State of Hawaii, 846 F.Supp. 1411.

N.D.Ill. 1996. Official capacity claims against city councilman were redundant and would be dismissed in light of the fact that plaintiffs also named city itself as defendant.

> Contreras v. City of Chicago, 920 F.Supp. 1370, affirmed in part, remanded in part 119 F.3d 1286.

N.D.Ill. 1992. Inclusion of both city and mayor in his official capacity as defendants in challenge to ordinance regulating newsstands was duplicitous, so that mayor would be dismissed from suit.

> Graff v. City of Chicago, 800 F.Supp. 576, affirmed 9 F.3d 1309, certiorari denied 114 S.Ct. 1837, 511 U.S. 1085, 128 L.Ed.2d 464.

N.D.Ill. 1986. Commodities broker would be dismissed without prejudice as defendant in suit involving actions by its predecessor in interest in asset purchase agreement, where complaint failed to allege that broker agreed to assume predecessor's liability, was mere continuation of seller, or any other basis for holding it liable as successor.

> Ghouth v. Conticommodity Services, Inc., 642 F.Supp. 1325.

N.D.Ill. 1978. Johnson v. Nationwide Industries, Inc., 450 F.Supp. 948, affirmed 715 F.2d 1233.

S.D.Ind. 1983. Wilson v. Studebaker-Worthington, Inc., 582 F.Supp. 383, on reconsideration 699 F.Supp. 711.

S.D.Ind. 1967. Bowe v. Colgate-Palmolive Co., 272 F.Supp. 332, affirmed in part, reversed in part 416 F.2d 711, opinion corrected on denial of rehearing 1969 WL 4715, appeal after remand 489 F.2d 896.

D.Kan. 1996. Joinder of nondiverse physician, who was necessary party in diversity malpractice action, was not feasible in view of fact that his presence would destroy diversity and deprive federal district court of subject-matter jurisdiction so as to require dismissal of case.

Fed.Rules Civ.Proc.Rule 19(a), 28 U.S.C.A.; Rules Civ.Proc., K.S.A. 60–258a(c).

Thurston v. Page, 168 F.R.D. 655.

D.Kan. 1993. Ex-husband as recipient of military retirement pay was "necessary party" in ex-wife's mandamus action to compel Secretary of the United States Army, in accordance with Federal Uniformed Services Former Spouses' Protection Act (FUSFSPA), to make direct payments to ex-wife of share of ex-husband's military retirement income pursuant to Kansas court order and thus, ex-husband would not be dismissed from action. 10 U.S.C.A. § 1408; Fed.Rules Civ.Proc. Rule 19(a), 28 U.S.C.A.

Andrean v. Secretary of U.S. Army, 840 F.Supp. 1414.

D.Kan. 1990. Elimination of estate of insured from underinsured motorist insurance suit also involving survivor did not mandate dismissal of case; estate was not "indispensable party" under joinder rules, as a remedy could be fashioned so that in event insurer was found liable a portion of the judgment could be set aside so as to be available if estate obtained a judgment against insurer in state court. Fed. Rules Civ.Proc.Rule 19(b), 28 U.S.C.A.

Hanshew v. U.S. Fidelity and Guar. Co., 746 F.Supp. 55.

D.Kan. 1985. Complaint would be amended by deletion of parent holding company, and claims would proceed against subsidiary bank, where holding company was not necessary party to action. Fed.Rules Civ.Proc.Rule 21, 28 U.S.C.A.

Petroleum Data Services, Inc. v. First City Bancorporation of Texas, Inc., 622 F.Supp. 1022.

D.Me. 1985. Maine district court judges would be dismissed as defendants in action challenging incarceration of juveniles under allegedly unconstitutional conditions at a county jail since the judges, as neutral adjudicators, had no real stake in the litigation and since relief could be afforded to plaintiffs without their presence in the lawsuit.

Desrosiers v. Androscoggin County, 611 F.Supp. 897.

D.Mass. 1990. Executive director of Massachusetts Water Resources Authority was entitled to be dismissed from action involving depression of Boston's central artery, insofar as Authority had no statutory responsibility for depression of central artery. Mass.St.1984, c. 372, §§ 1, 7.

Zarrilli v. Salvucci, 730 F.Supp. 461.

D.C.Mass. 1985. Complaint which designated as defendant in personal injury action nonexistent ski resort corporation, and which had been served on president of different corporation, which was not named as party defendant, was subject to dismissal. Fed.Rules Civ. Proc.Rule 12(b)(4, 5), 28 U.S.C.A.

Gonzalez v. Temple Mountain Ski Resort, Inc., 613 F.Supp. 354.

W.D.Mich. 1976. Thompson v. Board of Ed. of Romeo Community Schools, 71 F.R.D. 398, adhered to 519 F.Supp. 1373, reversed 709 F.2d 1200.

D.Nev. 1975. Western Intern. Hotels v. Tahoe Regional Planning Agency, 387 F.Supp. 429, affirmed in part, vacated in part, reversed in part Jacobson v. Tahoe Regional Planning Agency, 558 F.2d 928, opinion withdrawn and superseded on denial of rehearing 566 F.2d 1353, certiorari granted Lake Country Estates, Inc. v. Tahoe Regional Planning Agency, 98 S.Ct. 2843, 436 U.S. 943, 56 L.Ed.2d 784, affirmed in part, reversed in part 99 S.Ct. 1171, 440 U.S. 391, 59 L.Ed.2d 401, on remand 474 F.Supp. 901.

E.D.N.Y. 1995. Postal Service was not proper defendant in former employee's action, asserting breach of Equal Employment Opportunity Commission (EEOC) agreement under Title VII, and, therefore, action against Postal Service would be dismissed. Civil Rights Act of 1964, § 717(c), as amended, 42 U.S.C.A. § 2000e–16(c).

Montalvo v. U.S. Postal Service, 887 F.Supp. 63, affirmed 1996 WL 935448.

Former Postmaster was not proper defendant in former employee's action, asserting breach of Equal Employment Opportunity Commission (EEOC) agreement under Title VII, and, therefore, action against former Postmaster would be dismissed. Civil Rights Act of 1964, § 717(c), as amended, 42 U.S.C.A. § 2000e–16(c).

Montalvo v. U.S. Postal Service, 887 F.Supp. 63, affirmed 1996 WL 935448.

E.D.N.Y. 1976. Woe v. Mathews, 408 F.Supp. 419, dismissed in part, remanded in part 556 F.2d 563, affirmed 562 F.2d 40, certiorari denied 98 S.Ct. 895, 434 U.S. 1048, 54 L.Ed.2d 799.

S.D.N.Y. 1996. Officers and directors of holding company and its immediate subsidiary, which were only distantly related to sixth-generation subsidiary that operated cable television system, had no connection to events giving rise to civil rights action brought by producer of public access cable television program against broadcasters planning to restructure public access programming schedule, as they were not officers or directors of cable system operator and had no responsibility for operation of cable system, and they would therefore be dismissed from suit, as permitting producer to take discovery of them would not reveal facts tying holding company or its officers and directors to decision to reallocate public access channel. Fed.Rules Civ.Proc.Rule 21, 28 U.S.C.A.

> Glendora v. Malone, 917 F.Supp. 224, motion denied 165 F.R.D. 42, motion to certify appeal denied 166 F.R.D. 6.

Although neither cable television system operator's marketing manager nor its administrative assistant at local office had decision-making authority with respect to channel allocation, and both would therefore be dismissed from civil rights action brought by producer of public access program against broadcasters proposing to reallocate public access channel, chairman of board of directors of operating company, who may have evaluated or approved reallocation decision, as well as company's vice president, interim and former general managers, and manager of production, would not be dismissed, as producer was entitled to discovery to ascertain their role in events underlying her claims. Fed. Rules Civ.Proc.Rule 21, 28 U.S.C.A.

> Glendora v. Malone, 917 F.Supp. 224, motion denied 165 F.R.D. 42, motion to certify appeal denied 166 F.R.D. 6.

S.D.N.Y. 1992. Nondiversed defendant was not indispensable party to claims for breach of contract and fraud and, therefore, on motion of plaintiff, it was appropriate to dismiss nondiverse defendant and other claims in which only it was named, where nondiverse defendant was alleged to be jointly and severably liable with diverse defendants in fraud and conspiracy to commit fraud counts, and thus was not necessary party. Fed.Rules Civ.Proc.Rule 19(a, b), 28 U.S.C.A.

> Philip Morris Capital Corp. v. Century Power Corp., 788 F.Supp. 794.

S.D.N.Y. 1990. Trust would be dismissed from securities fraud lawsuit, where person served stated by affidavit that he was not proper agent for service of trust since he was not its trustee at time of any service attempt, and investors had been permitted discovery on subject and had made no showing to the contrary. Fed.Rules Civ.Proc.Rule 4, 28 U.S.C.A.

> Morin v. Trupin, 747 F.Supp. 1051.

S.D.N.Y. 1989. If complaint names defendant in caption but contains no allegations indicating how defendant violated law or injured plaintiff, motion to dismiss complaint in regard to that defendant should be granted. Fed.Rules Civ.Proc.Rule 12(b), 28 U.S.C.A.

> Thomas v. Beth Israel Hosp. Inc., 710 F.Supp. 935.

W.D.N.Y. 1978. Gill v. Monroe County Dept. of Social Services, 79 F.R.D. 316, motion denied 95 F.R.D. 518.

W.D.Okl. 1993. State-related officials were entitled to dismissal as defendants in their individual capacities in death-row inmates' class action seeking injunctive and declaratory relief regarding policy and practice of state penitentiary as to attorney visitation with death-row inmates, as no proof was offered regarding any personal acts of defendants.

> Mann v. Reynolds, 828 F.Supp. 894, affirmed in part, reversed in part 46 F.3d 1055.

Coordinator of substance abuse/mental health services was entitled to dismissal as defendant in death-row inmates' class action seeking injunctive and declaratory relief regarding policy and practice of state penitentiary as to attorney visitation with death-row inmates, as there was no evidence concerning coordinator or his office.

> Mann v. Reynolds, 828 F.Supp. 894, affirmed in part, reversed in part 46 F.3d 1055.

E.D.Pa. 1995. Fact that county was also named as defendant in § 1983 action against members of county prison board in their official capacities did not compel finding that complaint against members should be dismissed for failure to state claim; such motion was intended to test validity of complaint, and claim that was redundant was not necessarily invalid. 42 U.S.C.A. § 1983; Fed.Rules Civ.Proc.Rule 12(b)(6), 28 U.S.C.A.

> Crighton v. Schuylkill County, 882 F.Supp. 411.

E.D.Pa. 1993. Defendant who was not named under eight counts of civil rights complaint as a responsible party was entitled to dismissal of those counts for failure to state a claim. 42 U.S.C.A. § 1983.

> Barrett v. City of Allentown, 152 F.R.D. 50.

E.D.Pa. 1984. In wrongful death suit against a hospital alleging that hospital's negligence in failing to maintain a sufficient coronary care facility and in failing to properly diagnose and treat a patient, two doctors who had been joined as third-party defendants were not entitled to dismissal of the third-party complaint on ground that hospital's motion to join third-party defendants was made more than 90 days after service of its answer as required by local rule where hospital acted within a reasonable time after learning of alleged negligence of the doctors and where the doctors would not be disadvantaged by their inclusion in the litigation. U.S.Dist.Ct.Rules E.D.Pa., Civil Rule 22.

> DiLorenzo v. Saint Agnes Medical Center, 103 F.R.D. 546.

Bkrtcy.D.Neb. 1989. Misjoinder of parties in adversary action brought in bankruptcy case is not basis for motion to dismiss. Fed.Rules

Civ.Proc.Rule 21, 28 U.S.C.A.; Rules Bankr. Proc.Rule 7021, 11 U.S.C.A.

Matter of Sanitary and Imp. Dist. No. 7 of Lancaster County, Neb., 96 B.R. 967.

⚷**1751. Process, defects in.**

Library references

C.J.S. Federal Civil Procedure §§ 797, 810.

C.A.D.C. 1992. Law firm that brought action against partnership for unpaid attorney fees failed to show "good cause" justification for failure to serve absent partner within 120 days of filing of complaint and, therefore, dismissal was appropriate, even if law firm believed in good faith that served partner had authority to represent absent partner's interests in litigation in which absent partner had not been served; law firm could not be excused from failing to comply with District of Columbia's requirement that all partners be served and law firm took no efforts to enlarge period for service or to renew its efforts to serve absent partner. Fed.Rules Civ.Proc.Rule 4(j), 28 U.S.C.A.

Pellegrin & Levine, Chartered v. Antoine, 961 F.2d 277, 295 U.S.App.D.C. 190.

C.A.D.C. 1988. Sua sponte dismissal of pro se plaintiff's cause of action for failure to execute service of process was error where plaintiff was never actually or constructively put on notice as to impending dismissal and, because of pro se status, did not move for reconsideration, eliminating all opportunity to show good cause why service had not been made within required 120–day time period. Fed. Rules Civ.Proc.Rule 4(j), 28 U.S.C.A.

Smith-Bey v. Cripe, 852 F.2d 592, 271 U.S.App.D.C. 294.

C.A.D.C. 1984. Hobson v. Wilson, 737 F.2d 1, 237 U.S.App.D.C. 219, certiorari denied Brennan v. Hobson, 105 S.Ct. 1843, 470 U.S. 1084, 85 L.Ed.2d 142, on remand 646 F.Supp. 884.

C.A.11 (Ala.) 1990. When defendant has waived his objection to sufficient service of process or any other defect in personal jurisdiction by failing to timely object, and has thus consented to litigate action in that court, court may not, either upon defendant's motion or its own initiative, dismiss suit for lack of personal jurisdiction or insufficient service of process. Fed.Rules Civ.Proc.Rules 4(j), 12(g, h), 28 U.S.C.A.

Pardazi v. Cullman Medical Center, 896 F.2d 1313.

C.A.9 (Ariz.) 1992. Dismissal of city defendants was required in mortgagor's action alleging violation of civil rights laws and Truth in Lending Act on grounds of untimely service; city defendants were served four and one-half years after filing of complaint and mortgagor

did not suggest any good cause for failure to serve those defendants in timely fashion. Fed. Rules Civ.Proc.Rule 4(j), 28 U.S.C.A.; Truth in Lending Act, § 125, 15 U.S.C.A. § 1635.

King v. Russell, 963 F.2d 1301, certiorari denied 113 S.Ct. 1263, 507 U.S. 913, 122 L.Ed.2d 660, rehearing denied 113 S.Ct. 1891, 507 U.S. 1047, 123 L.Ed.2d 507.

C.A.9 (Ariz.) 1991. In order to avoid dismissal for failure to serve complaint and summons within 120 days after filing, plaintiff must show, at minimum, excusable neglect and may be required to show that party to be served personally received actual notice of lawsuit, that defendant would suffer no prejudice, and that plaintiff would be severely prejudiced if complaint were dismissed. Fed.Rules Civ.Proc. Rules 4(j), 6(b)(2), 28 U.S.C.A.

Boudette v. Barnette, 923 F.2d 754.

C.A.8 (Ark.) 1987. Prisoner's complaint against correction officers was properly dismissed, without prejudice, where service was not made upon officers within 120 days after filing of complaint and there was no showing of good cause for failure to make timely service. Fed.Rules Civ.Proc.Rule 4(j), 28 U.S.C.A.

Ouzts v. Cummins, 825 F.2d 1276.

C.A.8 (Ark.) 1985. While the district court may at times dismiss cause of action against the United States for want of jurisdiction ascribed to defective service, district court is not without rather broad discretion in determining propriety of dismissal and ordinarily the Court of Appeals will reverse only for an abuse of that discretion.

C & L Farms, Inc. v. Federal Crop Ins. Corp., 771 F.2d 407.

C.A.9 (Cal.) 1998. District court erred in entering summary judgment in favor of defendant who was never served in inmate's § 1983 action; claim against defendant should have been dismissed without prejudice. 42 U.S.C.A. § 1983; Fed.Rules Civ.Proc.Rule 4(m), 28 U.S.C.A.

Johnson v. Meltzer, 134 F.3d 1393, certiorari denied 119 S.Ct. 102.

C.A.9 (Cal.) 1987. District court did not abuse its discretion in dismissing action for failure to comply with rule requiring service of summons and complaint upon defendants within 120 days after filing of complaint, even though the statute of limitations on plaintiff's civil rights action had run and the dismissal for untimely service was therefore effectively with prejudice; in enacting the rule Congress had determined that the possible loss of litigant's federal cause of action resulting from application of the rule was outweighed by the need to encourage diligent prosecution of law suits. Fed.Rules Civ.Proc.Rule 4(j), 28 U.S.C.A.

> Townsel v. Contra Costa County, Cal., 820 F.2d 319.

C.A.9 (Cal.) 1985. Plaintiff's disregard of warning by court to make service of process, although relevant to determining whether failure to serve within 120 days should result in dismissal, is not a prerequisite for dismissal. Fed.Rules Civ.Proc.Rule 4(j), 28 U.S.C.A.

> U.S. for Use and Benefit of DeLoss v. Kenner General Contractors, Inc., 764 F.2d 707.

Upon record showing that efforts to reach defendant within the 120–day period for service of summons and complaint were half-hearted at best, and that plaintiff knew defendant's address but did not share that information with counsel, district court did not abuse discretion in dismissing action under Rule 4(j) for failure of plaintiff to show good cause for failure to make service within such period of time. Fed.Rules Civ.Proc.Rule 4(j), 28 U.S.C.A.

> U.S. for Use and Benefit of DeLoss v. Kenner General Contractors, Inc., 764 F.2d 707.

C.A.10 (Colo.) 1997. Pro se civil rights plaintiff failed to establish proof of service, thus warranting dismissal without prejudice for failure to obtain service within 120 days after filing of complaint; although plaintiff submitted "receipts" purporting to show payment of postage for certified mail sent to both defendants and delivery of certified mail to one of them, there was no authenticating post office stamp on any receipt showing they actually passed through the mails, nothing showing actual delivery of complaint to purported defendants, and nothing indicating compliance with rule pertaining to service upon officers of United States. Fed.Rules Civ.Proc.Rule Rule 4(i, m), 28 U.S.C.A.

> Chester v. Green, 120 F.3d 1091.

C.A.10 (Colo.) 1992. Under either the "good cause" analysis or the "justifiable excuse" analysis, court did not abuse its discretion in dismissing employment discrimination action against the Postmaster General for lack of timely proper service on the Attorney General and the United States Attorney where United States Attorney had twice sent letters to the plaintiff notifying him that service did not comply with rules and had then filed a motion to dismiss which raised the deficiencies and essentially explained to the plaintiff what was necessary to properly serve the United States. Fed.Rules Civ.Proc.Rule 4(j), 28 U.S.C.A.

> Jones v. Frank, 973 F.2d 872.

C.A.3 (Del.) 1996. Summons which is not signed and sealed by clerk of the court does not confer personal jurisdiction over defendant, even if properly served, and upon proper motion, or if defendant raises matter in the responsive pleading, such suit should be dismissed. Fed.Rules Civ.Proc.Rule 12(b)(2), 28 U.S.C.A.

> Ayres v. Jacobs & Crumplar, P.A., 99 F.3d 565.

C.A.11 (Fla.) 1995. Dismissal of plaintiff's action for failure to serve process was improper because both defendants answered complaint without raising any service of process objections. Fed.Rules Civ.Proc.Rule 4(j), 28 U.S.C.A.

> World Thrust Films, Inc. v. International Family Entertainment, Inc., 41 F.3d 1454, on remand 1996 WL 605957.

C.A.11 (Fla.) 1994. District court did not abuse its discretion in dismissing Federal Torts Claim Act complaint without prejudice for failure to timely file service of summons and complaint on United States within 120 days after filing of complaint; although plaintiff timely filed complaint on final day for challenging denial of administrative claim, original complaint named incorrect defendant and service of process was not properly effected on United States until 184 days after filing of original complaint. 28 U.S.C.A. §§ 2401(b), 2679; Fed. Rules Civ.Proc.Rule 4(d)(4), 28 U.S.C.A.; Fed. Rules Civ.Proc.Rule 4(j), 28 U.S.C. (1988 Ed.)

> Hunt v. Department of Air Force, Div. of USA, 29 F.3d 583.

C.A.11 (Fla.) 1992. Where court found that there was no good cause for failure to serve complaint within 120 days and found that there had been neglect and repeated disregard for timely prosecution of the claims, it was required to dismiss the action, notwithstanding any consideration of the interests of justice. Fed.Rules Civ.Proc.Rule 4(j), 28 U.S.C.A.

> In re Cooper, 971 F.2d 640.

C.A.11 (Fla.) 1991. There was no "good cause" for discharged postal employee's improper service of discrimination complaint upon United States Attorney's office, such that improper service could be excused, where employee claimed that misplaced files prevented earlier delivery, but employee had files sufficient to allow improper service by mail on day after filing and was informed of defect months before 120–day deadline for effecting service. Fed.Rules Civ.Proc.Rule 4(d)(4), (j), 28 U.S.C.A.

> Prisco v. Frank, 929 F.2d 603.

C.A.11 (Ga.) 1991. District court did not abuse its discretion in granting judgment in favor of defendant for plaintiff's failure to properly serve defendant; dismissal was mandatory in that no showing of good cause was made for failure to perfect service within 120 days of filing complaint and plaintiff made no attempt to correct defective service or to inquire into alleged deficiency even though more than two months remained on 120–day period when defendant filed answer and indicated that sufficiency of process was at issue, and statute of limitations had expired, so that reinstatement of action was barred under Georgia law. Fed. Rules Civ.Proc.Rule 4(c)(2)(C)(ii), (j), 28 U.S.C.A.

Schnabel v. Wells, 922 F.2d 726.

C.A.9 (Hawai'i) 1985. Neither plaintiff's desire to amend his complaint before effecting service nor counsel's inadvertent failure to calendar 120–day limit qualified as good cause for plaintiff's failure to timely serve summons and complaint and employment discrimination and civil rights action was properly dismissed. Civil Rights Act of 1964, § 701 et seq., 42 U.S.C.A. § 2000e et seq.; Fed.Rules Civ.Proc.Rule 4(j), 28 U.S.C.A.

Wei v. State of Hawaii, 763 F.2d 370.

C.A.7 (Ill.) 1998. Under Illinois law, plaintiff did not exercise reasonable diligence to obtain service, thus warranting dismissal of malpractice action, where plaintiff's attorney filed initial suit on last possible day under statute of repose, let it sit in state court for eight months before voluntarily dismissing it without effecting service, and new counsel then took 11 months before refiling complaint in federal court and serving it shortly thereafter. Ill.Sup. Ct.Rules 103(b).

Hinkle v. Henderson, 135 F.3d 521.

C.A.7 (Ill.) 1996. When considering failure to effect timely service of process, district court must first inquire whether plaintiff has established good cause for failing to effect timely service; if good cause is shown, court must extend time for service for an appropriate period, and inquiry is ended; however, if good cause does not exist, court may, in its discretion, either dismiss action without prejudice or direct that service be effected within specified time; thus, if good cause is not shown, district court must consider whether permissive extension of time is warranted. Fed.Rules Civ.Proc.Rule 4(m), 28 U.S.C.A.

Panaras v. Liquid Carbonic Industries Corp., 94 F.3d 338.

Judgment of district court granting motion to dismiss without prejudice for failure to accomplish timely service of summons and complaint on defendants would be reversed and case remanded for reconsideration, where district court did not clearly consider, after determining that plaintiff failed to show good cause for failure to obtain service, whether permissive extension of time for service was warranted under facts of case. Fed.Rules Civ.Proc.Rule 4(m), 28 U.S.C.A.

Panaras v. Liquid Carbonic Industries Corp., 94 F.3d 338.

Running of statute of limitations does not require district court, in considering failure to timely effect service, to extend time for service of process under governing rule; rather, absent finding of good cause for untimely service, district court may in its discretion still dismiss case even after statute of limitations has run. Fed. Rules Civ.Proc.Rule 4(m), 28 U.S.C.A.

Panaras v. Liquid Carbonic Industries Corp., 94 F.3d 338.

Where statute of limitations would have barred new complaint in case, it was incumbent upon district court to fully consider such factor in deciding whether to dismiss suit without prejudice for failure to timely effect service, or whether to grant extension of time in which to effect service, particularly where statute of limitations was extremely short. Fed.Rules Civ. Proc.Rule 4(m), 28 U.S.C.A.

Panaras v. Liquid Carbonic Industries Corp., 94 F.3d 338.

C.A.7 (Ill.) 1994. Inmate could not have served federal prison employees, who were named as defendants in *Bivens* action, within 120 days of filing of amended complaint, and thus district court's dismissal of employees as defendants was not abuse of discretion; inmate did not provide marshal with copies of amended complaint, for service upon prison employees, until more than 120 days after it was filed. Fed.Rules Civ.Proc.Rule 4(c)(2)(B)(i), (j), 28 U.S.C.(1988 Ed.)

Del Raine v. Williford, 32 F.3d 1024.

C.A.7 (Ill.) 1993. Allegations that two named police officers engaged in unreasonable stop and frisk actions were properly dismissed, where officers were not located by either side and plaintiff failed to request discovery in district court. Fed.Rules Civ.Proc.Rule 4(j), 28 U.S.C.A.; 42 U.S.C.A. § 1983.

Daniels v. Southfort, 6 F.3d 482.

C.A.7 (Ill.) 1993. Party must include defense of insufficiency of process in its first motion to dismiss, or defense is waived. Fed. Rules Civ.Proc.Rule 12, 28 U.S.C.A.

O'Brien v. R.J. O'Brien & Associates, Inc., 998 F.2d 1394.

C.A.7 (Ill.) 1991. Dismissal of action in which plaintiff's counsel failed to perfect service of process on defendant within 120 days was justified; plaintiff did not provide defendant with essential items required under rules to permit defendant to acknowledge receipt of summons and complaint in legally recognizable way, and plaintiff also failed to observe requirement of attempting personal service on defendant when no acknowledgement was received within 20 days after service of process was mailed. Fed.Rules Civ.Proc.Rule 4(c)(2)(C)(ii), 28 U.S.C.A.

Williams v. Leach, 938 F.2d 769.

C.A.7 (Ill.) 1988. Plaintiff who failed to effect service of summons and complaint within 120 days of filing of complaint failed to establish "good cause" for such failure, and dismissal of complaint without prejudice was necessary, notwithstanding plaintiff's contention that employee of defendant's former employer led her to believe that defendant had left city of his prior residence; plaintiff's counsel did not make single phone call in effort to locate defendant, relying on inquiry with Secretary of State to determine if defendant, who was blind, had restricted driver's license, and former employer's employee, although stating that defendant would "never work in [city] again," did not tell plaintiff that defendant had left city. Fed.Rules Civ.Proc.Rule 4(j), 28 U.S.C.A.

Geiger v. Allen, 850 F.2d 330.

C.A.5 (La.) 1993. Action will be dismissed without prejudice unless plaintiff shows good cause for failure to complete service if plaintiff fails to serve defendant properly within 120 days of filing complaint, either upon motion of defendant or sua sponte by court with notice to plaintiff. Fed.Rules Civ.Proc.Rule 4(j), 28 U.S.C.A.

Peters v. U.S., 9 F.3d 344.

Dismissal of complaint for failure to timely complete service is proper, even if limitations period has run. Fed.Rules Civ.Proc.Rule 4(j), 28 U.S.C.A.

Peters v. U.S., 9 F.3d 344.

Dismissing wrongful death suit against United States, arising from death which occurred in Veterans Administration hospital, was not abuse of discretion where plaintiffs failed to timely serve summons and complaint on United States, even though statute of limitations had expired. Fed.Rules Civ.Proc.Rule 4(d)(4), 28 U.S.C.A.

Peters v. U.S., 9 F.3d 344.

Dismissing wrongful death suit against United States for failing to comply with rule for serving summons and complaint on United States did not deny plaintiffs access to court or deprive them of property without due process of law; rule for accomplishing service was easily understandable and not unconstitutionally vague. Fed.Rules Civ.Proc.Rule 4(d)(4), 28 U.S.C.A.; U.S.C.A. Const.Amends. 5, 14.

Peters v. U.S., 9 F.3d 344.

C.A.5 (La.) 1993. Dismissal of complaint, for failure to serve party within 120 days of filing of complaint, is required in absence of showing of good cause why service was not

timely made. Fed.Rules Civ.Proc.Rule 4(j), 28 U.S.C.A.

McGinnis v. Shalala, 2 F.3d 548, suggestion for rehearing denied, rehearing denied 5 F.3d 530, certiorari denied 114 S.Ct. 1293, 510 U.S. 1191, 127 L.Ed.2d 647.

Social security disability claims would be dismissed, for failure to properly serve local United States Attorney within 120 days of filing of complaints, even though government had actual knowledge of suits from service on other government parties. Fed.Rules Civ.Proc.Rule 4(j), 28 U.S.C.A.

McGinnis v. Shalala, 2 F.3d 548, suggestion for rehearing denied, rehearing denied 5 F.3d 530, certiorari denied 114 S.Ct. 1293, 510 U.S. 1191, 127 L.Ed.2d 647.

Social security disability claims would be dismissed, for failure to properly serve local United States Attorney within 120 days of filing of complaints, even though government was not prejudiced by late service. Fed.Rules Civ.Proc. Rule 4(j), 28 U.S.C.A.

McGinnis v. Shalala, 2 F.3d 548, suggestion for rehearing denied, rehearing denied 5 F.3d 530, certiorari denied 114 S.Ct. 1293, 510 U.S. 1191, 127 L.Ed.2d 647.

Social security disability claims would be dismissed, for failure to properly serve local United States Attorney within 120 days of filing of complaints, even though expiration of statute of limitations precluded refiling of suits. Fed. Rules Civ.Proc.Rule 4(j), 28 U.S.C.A.

McGinnis v. Shalala, 2 F.3d 548, suggestion for rehearing denied, rehearing denied 5 F.3d 530, certiorari denied 114 S.Ct. 1293, 510 U.S. 1191, 127 L.Ed.2d 647.

C.A.5 (La.) 1990. District court did not abuse its discretion in dismissing suit of a represented plaintiff for erroneous reliance on invalid service after receiving notice, well in advance of expiration of 120–day limit, that service was insufficient. Fed.Rules Civ.Proc.Rule 4(j), 28 U.S.C.A.

Traina v. U.S., 911 F.2d 1155, rehearing denied.

Inability to refile suit does not bar dismissal for failure to serve defendant within 120 days after filing of complaint. Fed.Rules Civ.Proc. Rule 4(j), 28 U.S.C.A.

Traina v. U.S., 911 F.2d 1155, rehearing denied.

C.A.5 (La.) 1983. Gaspard v. U.S., 713 F.2d 1097, rehearing denied 720 F.2d 677, certiorari denied Sheehan v. U.S., 104 S.Ct. 2354, 466 U.S. 975, 80 L.Ed.2d 826.

C.A.4 (Md.) 1995. If complaint is not served within 120 days after it is filed, complaint must be dismissed absent showing of good cause. Fed.Rules Civ.Proc.Rule 4(m), 28 U.S.C.A.

Mendez v. Elliot, 45 F.3d 75.

C.A.4 (Md.) 1993. Dismissal of shipper's action for damage to goods against five defendants due to untimely service on those defendants was not an abuse of discretion; district court had granted 40–day extension to effect service and when service still had not occurred, shipper was given another 20–day extension and shipper provided no reason why additional time was needed. Fed.Rules Civ.Proc.Rule 4(j), 28 U.S.C.A.

Shao v. Link Cargo (Taiwan) Ltd., 986 F.2d 700, appeal after remand Ting-Hwa Shao v. Sea Horse Container Lines, 72 F.3d 128.

C.A.4 (Md.) 1991. Despite conferral of sua sponte dismissal power on district court by rule requiring service of process within 120 days from date of commencement of action, defendant's unexcused failure to raise untimeliness of service defense by motion or answer deprives court of that power, since waiver of defense constitutes submission to personal jurisdiction of court. Fed.Rules Civ.Proc.Rules 4(j), 12(g, h), (h)(1)(A, B), 28 U.S.C.A.

Pusey v. Dallas Corp., 938 F.2d 498.

C.A.1 (Mass.) 1993. If plaintiff fails to properly serve named defendant within 120 days after filing complaint, he must show good cause why that service was not timely or face dismissal. Fed.Rules Civ.Proc.Rule 4(j), 28 U.S.C.A.

Benjamin v. Grosnick, 999 F.2d 590, certiorari denied Grosnick v. Embriano, 114 S.Ct. 1057, 510 U.S. 1112, 127 L.Ed.2d 377.

Dismissal of lawsuit for defective service of process was not required, where defective service did not prejudice defendant, who had actual notice of lawsuit and secured additional time to file answer, and dismissal would prejudice plaintiffs, since statute of limitations had already run on their federal statutory claims. Fed.Rules Civ.Proc.Rule 4(j), 28 U.S.C.A.

Benjamin v. Grosnick, 999 F.2d 590, certiorari denied Grosnick v. Embriano, 114 S.Ct. 1057, 510 U.S. 1112, 127 L.Ed.2d 377.

C.A.6 (Mich.) 1987. Summons specifications rule is flexible rule which principally requires sufficient notice to party of claims brought against party and dismissal for failure to comply with such rule is not appropriate unless party has been prejudiced. Fed.Rules Civ.Proc.Rule 4, 28 U.S.C.A.

Gottfried v. Frankel, 818 F.2d 485.

C.A.5 (Miss.) 1996. When district court entertains motion to extend time for service, it must first determine whether good cause exists, and if good cause is present, district court must extend time for service; on other hand, if good cause does not exist, court may, in its discretion, decide whether to dismiss case without prejudice or extend time for service. Fed.Rules Civ.Proc.Rule 4(m), 28 U.S.C.A.

Thompson v. Brown, 91 F.3d 20.

C.A.5 (Miss.) 1996. Federal Tort Claims Act suit was dismissed for insufficiency of service given that plaintiff failed to properly serve Attorney General, failed to correct error when government asserted insufficiency of service as defense, and failed to show good cause for defective service. Fed.Rules Civ.Proc.Rule 12(h)(1), 28 U.S.C.A.

Flory v. U.S., 79 F.3d 24.

C.A.5 (Miss.) 1990. Mere fact that statute of limitations has run does not make dismissal for failure to serve within 120 days unwarranted. Fed.Rules Civ.Proc.Rule 4(j), 28 U.S.C.A.

McDonald v. U.S., 898 F.2d 466, rehearing denied.

Dismissal for delayed service or process is not left to the general discretion of the district court but, rather, is mandatory unless good cause is shown. Fed.Rules Civ.Proc.Rule 4(j), 28 U.S.C.A.

McDonald v. U.S., 898 F.2d 466, rehearing denied.

C.A.5 (Miss.) 1988. Service of summons and complaint on manager of state employment commission's local office, rather than on either chief executive officer of commission or Attorney General as required by federal rules and state law, was improper and warranted dismissal of complaint without prejudice. Fed.Rules Civ.Proc.Rule 4(d)(6), 28 U.S.C.A.; Miss.Code 1972, § 11–45–3.

Way v. Mueller Brass Co., 840 F.2d 303.

C.A.5 (Miss.) 1983. Gaspard v. U.S., 713 F.2d 1097, rehearing denied 720 F.2d 677, certiorari denied Sheehan v. U.S., 104 S.Ct. 2354, 466 U.S. 975, 80 L.Ed.2d 826.

C.A.8 (Mo.) 1997. Inmate proceeding in forma pauperis was not required to complete waiver of service forms, but rather waiver of service was responsibility of United States Marshal, and untimely service caused by delay in completion of forms did not justify dismissal, where complaint listed all defendants and their addresses. 28 U.S.C.A. § 1915(d); Fed.Rules Civ.Proc.Rule 4(m), 28 U.S.C.A.

Moore v. Jackson, 123 F.3d 1082, rehearing denied.

C.A.8 (Mo.) 1996. If district court concludes there is good cause for plaintiff's failure to serve process on defendant within 120 days, as required by rule, court shall extend time for service, and even if plaintiff fails to show good cause, court still may extend time for service rather than dismiss case without prejudice. Fed.Rules Civ.Proc.Rule 4(m), 28 U.S.C.A.; Rule 4(j), 28 U.S.C.App.(1988 Ed.)

> Adams v. AlliedSignal General Aviation Avionics, 74 F.3d 882.

C.A.9 (Mont.) 1992. Creditor made diligent effort to achieve service on debtors by attempting service as soon as trial court declared initial default judgment void based on improper service, so that dismissal for failing to serve summons and complaint within 120 days after filing complaint was not required. Fed. Rules Civ.Proc.Rule 4(j), 28 U.S.C.A.

> Electrical Specialty Co. v. Road and Ranch Supply, Inc., 967 F.2d 309.

C.A.9 (Nev.) 1990. Incarcerated pro se plaintiff proceeding in forma pauperis is entitled to rely on United States Marshal for service of summons and complaint and, having provided necessary information to help effectuate service, plaintiff should not be penalized by having his or her action dismissed for failure to effect service where Marshal or court clerk has failed to perform duties required of each under statute and rule. 28 U.S.C.A. § 1915(c); Fed.Rules Civ.Proc.Rule 4(c)(2)(C)(ii), (d)(1, 4, 5), 28 U.S.C.A.

> Puett v. Blandford, 912 F.2d 270.

C.A.1 (N.H.) 1986. Dismissal of employee of foster care group who was not served by parents of juvenile bringing action for damages under 42 U.S.C.A. § 1983 was proper.

> Malachowski v. City of Keene, 787 F.2d 704, certiorari denied 107 S.Ct. 107, 479 U.S. 828, 93 L.Ed.2d 56, rehearing denied 107 S.Ct. 681, 479 U.S. 1022, 93 L.Ed.2d 731.

C.A.3 (N.J.) 1995. When entertaining motion to extend time for service of process, district court must proceed in the following manner: first, court should determine whether good cause exists for extension of time, and if good cause is present, court must extend time for service and inquiry is ended; if, however, good cause does not exist, court may in its discretion decide whether to dismiss case without prejudice or extend time for service. F.R.A.P.Rule 4(m), 28 U.S.C.A.

> MCI Telecommunications Corp. v. Teleconcepts, Inc., 71 F.3d 1086, certiorari denied 117 S.Ct. 64, 136 L.Ed.2d 25.

C.A.3 (N.J.) 1988. Failure of civil rights defendant to serve party defendant, without any justification for not doing so, warranted dis-missal of that defendant. Fed.Rule Civ.Proc. Rule 4(j), 28 U.S.C.A.

> Napier v. Thirty or More Unidentified Federal Agents, Employees or Officers, 855 F.2d 1080.

C.A.2 (N.Y.) 1994. In suits against either federal officials in their official capacities or against United States pursuant to Federal Tort Claims Act (FTCA), United States is real defendant and failure to serve United States as required by rules of civil procedures would warrant dismissal. Fed.Rules Civ.Proc.Rule 4(i)(1), (m), 28 U.S.C.A.; 28 U.S.C.A. §§ 1346(b), 2671–2680.

> Armstrong v. Sears, 33 F.3d 182.

C.A.2 (N.Y.) 1993. Foreign reinsurers were required to be dismissed from action to determine liability under marine reinsurance contracts, as they were not served within 120 days after filing of complaint; thus, court had diversity jurisdiction over remaining parties. 28 U.S.C.A. § 1332(a)(2).

> Mentor Ins. Co. (U.K.) Ltd. v. Brannkasse, 996 F.2d 506.

C.A.2 (N.Y.) 1990. Dismissal for failure to serve defendant properly within 120 days of filing of complaint is proper even if it occurs after expiration of applicable statute of limitations and even if dismissal's effect would bar plaintiff's claim. Fed.Rules Civ.Proc.Rule 4(j), 28 U.S.C.A.

> Frasca v. U.S., 921 F.2d 450.

C.A.2 (N.Y.) 1990. Failure of plaintiffs in tort claims suit to mail summons and complaint to Attorney General within 120 days was technical defect that did not warrant dismissal, even though plaintiffs' failure resulted from poor office procedure or ignorance of rules; Government did not disclose specific character of defective service until 14 months after commencement of suit and moved to dismiss a few days after expiration of six-month limitations period, and United States Attorney mailed copy of summons and complaint to Attorney General within 120–day time limit. Fed.Rules Civ.Proc. Rule 4(d)(4), (j), 28 U.S.C.A.

> Zankel v. U.S., 921 F.2d 432.

C.A.2 (N.Y.) 1990. Court has power to dismiss complaint after applicable statute of limitations has run for failure to comply with requirements of civil rule regarding service of process. Fed.Rules Civ.Proc.Rule 4(j), 28 U.S.C.A.

> Santos v. State Farm Fire and Cas. Co., 902 F.2d 1092.

C.A.2 (N.Y.) 1989. Dismissal of an action is mandatory under rule requiring service of a complaint within 120 days unless good cause can be shown for violation of 120–day limit. Fed.Rules Civ.Proc.Rule 4(j), 28 U.S.C.A.

> Yosef v. Passamaquoddy Tribe, 876 F.2d 283, certiorari denied 110 S.Ct. 1474, 494 U.S. 1028, 108 L.Ed.2d 611.

C.A.2 (N.Y.) 1989. District court could order dismissal of civil rights complaint based on plaintiff's lack of due diligence in serving complaint, notwithstanding defendants' failure to raise insufficiency of process in answer. 42 U.S.C.A. §§ 1983, 1985; Fed.Rules Civ.Proc. Rule 41(b), 28 U.S.C.A.

> Gleason v. McBride, 869 F.2d 688.

C.A.2 (N.Y.) 1986. Dismissal of products liability suit brought by incarcerated, in forma pauperis, pro se complainant was not mandated by failure of United States marshals to effect timely, personal service where complainant relied upon marshals to effect such service. Fed. Rules Civ.Proc.Rules 4(c)(2)(B)(i), (c)(2)(C)(i, ii), (d)(3), 12(f), 28 U.S.C.A.; 28 U.S.C.A. § 1915(c).

> Romandette v. Weetabix Co., Inc., 807 F.2d 309.

C.A.2 (N.Y.) 1985. Where service of process is insufficient, courts have broad discretion to dismiss the action or to retain the case but quash the service that has been made on defendant. Fed.Rules Civ.Proc. Rule 4(c)(2)(C)(ii), (d)(3), 28 U.S.C.A.

> Montalbano v. Easco Hand Tools, Inc., 766 F.2d 737.

Where no attempt was made to serve process in Japan, dismissal of Japanese corporation as third-party defendant for failure of original defendant to serve process upon Japanese corporation within 120 days after filing of complaint was proper; claims against Japanese corporation were dismissed until such time as original defendant or another party perfected service of a summons and complaint upon Japanese corporation. Fed.Rules Civ.Proc. Rules 4(i, j), 4 comment, 28 U.S.C.A.

> Montalbano v. Easco Hand Tools, Inc., 766 F.2d 737.

C.A.6 (Ohio) 1994. Absent showing of good cause to justify failure of timely service, dismissal is compelled. Fed.Rules Civ.Proc. Rule 4(j), 28 U.S.C.A.

> Habib v. General Motors Corp., 15 F.3d 72.

C.A.10 (Okl.) 1987. Dismissal for failure to serve within time period is without prejudice, but may operate as dismissal with prejudice when action will thereby be time barred. Fed. Rules Civ.Proc.Rules 4(j), 6(b)(2), 28 U.S.C.A.

> Putnam v. Morris, 833 F.2d 903.

C.A.3 (Pa.) 1995. Under former provision of Federal Rules of Civil Procedure governing service of process, district court was required to dismiss case if service of process was not effect-ed within 120–day period following filing of complaint, unless plaintiff showed good cause for delay. Fed.Rules Civ.Proc.Rule 4(j), 28 U.S.C.(1991 Ed.)

> Petrucelli v. Bohringer and Ratzinger, 46 F.3d 1298, rehearing and rehearing denied.

Under amended provision of Federal Rules of Civil Procedure governing time limit for service of process following filing of complaint, court is required to extend time for service if good cause is shown, and court is allowed discretion to dismiss case or extend time for service absent showing of good cause. Fed. Rules Civ.Proc.Rule 4(m), 28 U.S.C.A.

> Petrucelli v. Bohringer and Ratzinger, 46 F.3d 1298, rehearing and rehearing denied.

When entertaining motion to extend time for service of process beyond 120 days following filing of complaint, district court must first determine whether good cause exists for extension of time; if good cause is present, district court must extend time for service and inquiry is ended, but if good cause does not exist, court may in its discretion decide whether to dismiss case without prejudice or extend time for service. Fed.Rules Civ.Proc.Rule 4(m), 28 U.S.C.A.

> Petrucelli v. Bohringer and Ratzinger, 46 F.3d 1298, rehearing and rehearing denied.

Running of statute of limitations on cause of action does not require district court to extend time period for obtaining service of process beyond 120 days following filing of complaint; rather, absent finding of good cause, district court may in its discretion still dismiss case, even after considering that statute of limitations has run and refiling of action is barred. Fed.Rules Civ.Proc.Rule 4(m), 28 U.S.C.A.

> Petrucelli v. Bohringer and Ratzinger, 46 F.3d 1298, rehearing and rehearing denied.

C.A.3 (Pa.) 1992. Upon determining that process has not been properly served on defendant, district courts possess broad discretion to either dismiss complaint for failure to effect service or to simply quash service of process.

> Umbenhauer v. Woog, 969 F.2d 25.

Dismissal of complaint on ground that process was not properly served is inappropriate when there exists reasonable prospect that service may yet be obtained; in such instances, district court should, at most, quash service, leaving plaintiffs free to effect proper service.

> Umbenhauer v. Woog, 969 F.2d 25.

District court should not have dismissed complaint for failure to serve Swiss defendants; plaintiffs were likely to succeed in attempts to serve process and exceeded no time limit in unsuccessful attempts to serve process. Fed. Rules Civ.Proc.Rule 4(c)(2)(C)(i, ii), (i)(1)(B, D), 28 U.S.C.A.

Umbenhauer v. Woog, 969 F.2d 25.

C.A.3 (Pa.) 1987. Requirement that court give notice to plaintiff prior to dismissing action for failure to make timely service of process does not operate as automatic extension, and does not supplant necessity for plaintiff to demonstrate good cause for failure to comply with rule. Fed.Rules Civ.Proc.Rules 4, 6(b)(2), 28 U.S.C.A.

Braxton v. U.S., 817 F.2d 238.

Inadvertance of counsel which results in failure to make timely service of process does not constitute good cause such as would preclude dismissal of plaintiff's action as sanction. Fed.Rules Civ.Proc.Rules 4, 6, 28 U.S.C.A.

Braxton v. U.S., 817 F.2d 238.

Plaintiff's counsel's lapse in monitoring service of process coupled with private process server's unexplained failure to timely serve complaint was proper ground for dismissal of suit. Fed.Rules Civ.Proc.Rules 4, 6, 28 U.S.C.A.

Braxton v. U.S., 817 F.2d 238.

Letter sent by deputy court clerk calling counsel's attention to failure to timely serve complaint after time had run for service of complaint did not extend period for service. Fed.Rules Civ.Proc.Rules 4, 6, 28 U.S.C.A.

Braxton v. U.S., 817 F.2d 238.

C.A.1 (Puerto Rico) 1998. Dismissal without prejudice of § 1983 claim, alleging that deliberate indifference to inmate's medical needs led to his premature death, was properly based on plaintiffs' failure during 17 months between filing of complaint and entry of judgment to identify and serve anonymous defendants allegedly responsible for inmate's death. 42 U.S.C.A. § 1983; Fed.Rules Civ.Proc.Rule 4(m), 28 U.S.C.A.

Figueroa v. Rivera, 147 F.3d 77.

C.A.1 (Puerto Rico) 1995. Trial court improperly dismissed action against two groups on ground of minor, technical defect in summons, i.e., summons' failure to state name of person served; those groups had fair notice of suit at all times during proceedings, they had adequate opportunity to protect their interests, and their counsel made general appearances at every stage of proceeding and had ample opportunity to defend against claims. Fed.Rules Civ.Proc. Rule 4(h), 28 U.S.C.A.

Libertad v. Welch, 53 F.3d 428.

C.A.1 (Puerto Rico) 1988. Claims against individual codefendants were dismissible where plaintiffs failed to serve them with summonses and copies of complaint and offered no good cause for this omission. Fed.Rules Civ.Proc. Rule 4(j), 28 U.S.C.A.

Alvarado-Morales v. Digital Equipment Corp., 843 F.2d 613.

C.A.5 (Tex.) 1998. Mother of deceased inmate had sufficient time and warning prior to dismissal of her *Bivens* claims against federal prison employees who were not timely served; mother was granted several extensions and was warned that any claims against unserved defendants would be dismissed if she did not file proof of service.

McGuire v. Turnbo, 137 F.3d 321.

C.A.5 (Tex.) 1996. Plaintiff, who was proceeding in forma pauperis, showed good cause for failure to properly serve defendant, such that trial court should not have dismissed complaint, where clerk of court did not provide plaintiff with proper summons form, and trial court failed to appoint and direct U.S. marshal, deputy U.S. marshal, or some other person to serve process for plaintiff once he requested it. 28 U.S.C.(1994 Ed.) § 1915(c); Fed.Rules Civ. Proc.Rule 4(c)(2), (m), 28 U.S.C.A.

Lindsey v. U.S. R.R. Retirement Bd., 101 F.3d 444.

C.A.5 (Tex.) 1994. District court has broad discretion to dismiss action for ineffective service of process, and Court of Appeals reviews such decision only for abuse of discretion.

Kreimerman v. Casa Veerkamp, S.A. de C.V., 22 F.3d 634, certiorari denied 115 S.Ct. 577, 513 U.S. 1016, 130 L.Ed.2d 492.

C.A.5 (Tex.) 1990. Although actual notice and plaintiff's efforts to serve the United States, coupled with his pro se status, arguably provided grounds for leniency in considering technical imperfections of service, district court did not abuse its discretion in dismissing case for failure to effect proper service on the United States within 120–day period, considering that Assistant United States Attorney advised plaintiff nearly one month before statutory period was to lapse that service was defective, and additionally cited procedural rules governing service and invited plaintiff to call with any questions; instead of looking at the rules more closely or calling attorney to find out what problems were, plaintiff chose to dispute validity of service. Fed.Rules Civ.Proc.Rule 4(j), 28 U.S.C.A.

Systems Signs Supplies v. U.S. Dept. of Justice, Washington, D.C., 903 F.2d 1011.

C.A.5 (Tex.) 1986. District court enjoys broad discretion in determining whether to dismiss action for ineffective service of process.

George v. U.S. Dept. of Labor, Occupational Safety & Health Admin., 788 F.2d 1115.

District court did not abuse its discretion in dismissing action against United States for effective service of process, where plaintiff failed to serve Attorney General as required by Federal Rules of Civil Procedure. Fed.Rules Civ. Proc.Rule 4(d)(4), 28 U.S.C.A.

> George v. U.S. Dept. of Labor, Occupational Safety & Health Admin., 788 F.2d 1115.

C.A.5 (Tex.) 1985. Under Rule 4(j), dismissal is mandated upon a finding that service has not been made within the specified time period and that good cause to extend the time does not exist. Fed.Rules Civ.Proc.Rule 4(j), 28 U.S.C.A.

> Norlock v. City of Garland, 768 F.2d 654.

Because service on defendants by mail had never been perfected in civil rights suit, in that the attempted mail service included neither copies of a notice and acknowledgement of receipt of the summons and complaint nor a stamped self-addressed return envelope as required by Rule 4(c)(2)(C)(ii), and because plaintiff neither moved for additional time under Rule 6(b) nor even sought a finding of good cause for extension of time under Rule 4(j), the district court properly dismissed plaintiff's complaint without prejudice. Fed.Rules Civ.Proc.Rules 4(c)(2)(C)(ii), 4(j), 6(b), 28 U.S.C.A.

> Norlock v. City of Garland, 768 F.2d 654.

C.A.9 (Wash.) 1994. Technical defects in summons do not justify dismissal unless party is able to demonstrate actual prejudice. Fed. Rules Civ.Proc.Rule 4, 28 U.S.C.A.

> Chan v. Society Expeditions, Inc., 39 F.3d 1398, certiorari denied 115 S.Ct. 1314, 514 U.S. 1004, 131 L.Ed.2d 196.

C.A.7 (Wis.) 1986. State law negligence and fraud claims were subject to dismissal, although six-year limitations period had not yet expired, where plaintiffs failed to serve defendants within 60 days of filing as required by Wisconsin law. W.S.A. 801.02(1).

> Sentry Corp. v. Harris, 802 F.2d 229, certiorari denied 107 S.Ct. 1624, 481 U.S. 1004, 95 L.Ed.2d 199.

S.D.Ala. 1996. If plaintiff fails to comply with 120–day time period to serve summons and complaint upon defendant after filing of complaint, plaintiff may escape dismissal of complaint through showing of good cause or by convincing court that it should exercise its discretion and extend time for service even absent showing of good cause. Fed.Rules Civ.Proc. Rule 4(m), 28 U.S.C.A.

> Madison v. BP Oil Co., 928 F.Supp. 1132.

D.Ariz. 1988. Failure to comply with service requirements does not require dismissal if party to be served received actual notice, no prejudice to defendant resulted from defect in service, there is a justifiable excuse for failure to serve properly, and plaintiff would be severely prejudiced if complaint were dismissed. Fed. Rules Civ.Proc.Rule 4, 28 U.S.C.A.

> Justice v. Lyng, 716 F.Supp. 1567.

Failure to properly serve United States attorney did not warrant dismissal of declaratory judgment action brought against Secretary of Agriculture where there was actual notice to United States attorney, where failure was due to a breakdown in procedure on part of United States attorney's office and where there would be prejudice to plaintiff if case were dismissed. Fed.Rules Civ.Proc.Rule 4(j), 28 U.S.C.A.

> Justice v. Lyng, 716 F.Supp. 1567.

E.D.Ark. 1985. Negligence complaint which was not served within 120 days as required by federal rule was subject to dismissal without prejudice where plaintiff did not show good cause why service was not made within 120 days. Fed.Rules Civ.Proc.Rule 4(j), 28 U.S.C.A.

> Brown v. Rinehart, 105 F.R.D. 532.

W.D.Ark. 1987. Misstated name of defendant school district on summons, complaint, and other documents did not require dismissal, where defendant school district was actually served and was presently before district court. Fed.Rules Civ.Proc.Rules 4, 4(b), 12(b)(4, 5), 28 U.S.C.A.

> Cobb v. Stringer, 660 F.Supp. 1133, affirmed in part, reversed in part 850 F.2d 356.

C.D.Cal. 1995. Complaint would be dismissed against institutional defendants, as court had not ordered service of process on them, and they had not been timely served with process in inmate's *Bivens* suit.

> Scott v. Reno, 902 F.Supp. 1190.

N.D.Cal. 1995. If service of process is not accomplished within 120 days of filing of complaint, district court in its discretion may either dismiss the action without prejudice or order service within specified time, unless plaintiff can show good cause of an extension, in which case court must extend the time for accomplishing service. Fed.Rules Civ.Proc.Rule 4(m), 28 U.S.C.A.

> Tyson v. City of Sunnyvale, 159 F.R.D. 528.

Even if plaintiffs cannot show good cause for failure to effect service of the 120 days of filing complaint, court may, within its discretion, extend service rather than dismiss the action without prejudice. Fed.Rules Civ.Proc. Rule 4(m), 28 U.S.C.A.

> Tyson v. City of Sunnyvale, 159 F.R.D. 528.

Presumption under local rule favoring dismissal for failure to prosecute where service is not accomplished in 40 days is necessarily rebutted where the plaintiff affirmatively states his intent to accomplish or actually or substantially does accomplish service within 120 days. Fed. Rules Civ.Proc.Rule 4(m), 28 U.S.C.A.; U.S.Dist.Ct.Rules N.D.Cal., Civil Rule 235–10.

> Tyson v. City of Sunnyvale, 159 F.R.D. 528.

N.D.Cal. 1992. Insufficiency of process is not a favored defense, and if defendant files motion to dismiss and does not argue that process was insufficient, defense is deemed to have been waived. Fed.Rules Civ.Proc.Rules 12, 12(b, g), (h)(1), 28 U.S.C.A.

> Mateo v. M/S KISO, 805 F.Supp. 792.

S.D.Cal. 1989. Sufficiency of service of process should have been challenged by motion to dismiss under Rule 12(b) instead of proceeding according to California procedure via "motion to quash service of summons." Fed.Rules Civ.Proc.Rule 12(b), 28 U.S.C.A.; West's Ann. Cal.C.C.P. § 418.10(a)(1).

> Crane v. Battelle, 127 F.R.D. 174.

D.Colo. 1995. Under Colorado law, employment discrimination, breach of contract and promissory estoppel complaint would not be dismissed based on delay in service of process, where former employer had actual notice action was contemplated based upon Equal Employment Opportunity Commission (EEOC) complaint. Co.Rules Civ.Proc.Rule 3(a).

> Johnson v. N.T.I., a Div. of Colorado Springs Circuits, 898 F.Supp. 762.

D.Conn. 1996. Marshal's service on prison's paralegal specialist of complaint of pro se prisoner proceeding in forma pauperis against prison officials in *Bivens* action did not warrant dismissal of complaint for lack of personal jurisdiction, even though service was not personal, where the officials did not complain that they lacked actual notice of lawsuit or suffered prejudice, and government counsel had appeared and defended on behalf of all the officials. Fed.Rules Civ.Proc.Rule 4, 28 U.S.C.A.

> Tajeddini v. Gluch, 942 F.Supp. 772.

D.Conn. 1993. Claims against defendants who had not been personally served were subject to dismissal, without prejudice. Fed.Rules Civ.Proc.Rule 12(b)(4), 28 U.S.C.A.

> Johnson v. Meachum, 839 F.Supp. 953.

D.Conn. 1993. Pro se defendant's failure to raise issue of insufficiency of service of process in a timely manner and his omission of the issue in letter motion to dismiss were fatal to motion to set aside default; defendant waived any right to assert defense based on insufficiency of service. Fed.Rules Civ.Proc.Rule 12(b)(5), (h)(1), 28 U.S.C.A.

> Bentley v. Raveh, 151 F.R.D. 515.

D.Conn. 1987. Even if taxpayer had sued revenue officer in his individual capacity, and not in his official capacity as revenue officer, action would still require dismissal for lack of adequate service; taxpayer made no attempt at any manner of service upon either revenue officer, or proper defendant, United States. Fed.Rules Civ.Proc.Rules 4(c)(2)(C), (d)(1), 12(b)(5), 28 U.S.C.A.

> Jackman v. D'Agostino, 669 F.Supp. 43.

D.Del. 1988. Plaintiff's failure to timely serve defendant was for "good cause" and, therefore, plaintiff's complaint against defendant would not be dismissed, in view of plaintiff's efforts to effect service, which were not merely diligent, but bordered on heroic, and defendant's actual knowledge of lawsuit; plaintiff's failure to make additional application for enlargement of time in which to serve was not by itself fatal to plaintiff's efforts to establish good cause. Fed.Rules Civ.Proc.Rule 4(j), 28 U.S.C.A.

> U.S. v. Nuttall, 122 F.R.D. 163.

D.Del. 1981. Absent an indication in record that one of the directors named as a defendant in a shareholder's derivative action had been effectively served with summons and the amended complaint in a manner authorized by the rule, the complaint was subject to being dismissed as to him because the individual who was served with the summons and the amended complaint, being the vice-president and treasurer of the corporation, was not authorized by either the rule or law of Delaware to receive process on behalf of the director. Fed.Rules Civ.Proc. Rules 4(d), 23.1, 28 U.S.C.A.; 10 Del.C. §§ 3104, 3114.

> Weiss v. Temporary Inv. Fund, Inc., 516 F.Supp. 665, reargument denied 520 F.Supp. 1098, affirmed 692 F.2d 928, certiorari granted, vacated 104 S.Ct. 989, 465 U.S. 1001, 79 L.Ed.2d 224, on remand 730 F.2d 939.

D.D.C. 1996. Action would be dismissed against defendant who was never served with copy of summons and complaint within 120 days of filing of complaint unless plaintiffs provided court with proof of time of service within 21 days of date of opinion. Fed.Rules Civ.Proc. Rule 4(m), 28 U.S.C.A.

> McGlothlin v. Resolution Trust Corp., 913 F.Supp. 15, affirmed 111 F.3d 963, 324 U.S.App.D.C. 204.

D.D.C. 1995. Plaintiff's failure to counter defendant's assertion of failure to serve summons and complaint at his dwelling house or usual place of abode with anything but bare, unsubstantiated, unverified, undocumented assertion that it had complied with service requirements required dismissal of complaint. D.C.Civil Rule 4(c)(2)(C)(i, ii), (d)(1).

> Argon Financial Group v. Marro, 897 F.Supp. 568.

D.D.C. 1992. Inmate's failure to serve Attorney General by certified mail did not mandate dismissal of civil rights action against federal prison officials in their official capacities; necessary parties had actual notice of suit and government had received copies of summons and complaint and had defended itself through pretrial motion to dismiss. Fed.Rules Civ.Proc. Rule 4(d)(5), 28 U.S.C.A.

Huskey v. Quinlan, 785 F.Supp. 4.

D.D.C. 1991. Action to recover ERISA withdrawal liability would not be dismissed on basis of ineffective service, though service was attempted in Virginia on a Sunday in technical noncompliance with Virginia law and though one defendant resided in Florida but was not served there, because defendants had actual notice of suit, and because district court would have allowed amendments of service finding no material prejudice to defendants, and in interest of justice and expediency. Fed.Rules Civ.Proc. Rule 4(d)(1), (h), 28 U.S.C.A.; Employee Retirement Income Security Act of 1974, § 4001(b)(1), as amended, 29 U.S.C.A. § 1301(b)(1); Va.Code 1950, §§ 8.01–288, 8.01–289.

Connors v. Hi-Heat Coal Co., Inc., 772 F.Supp. 1.

D.D.C. 1987. Dismissal of pro se action against government officers for insufficient process was unwarranted and plaintiffs would be allowed to amend service to serve those officers, who had responded to receipt of notice of suit with motion to dismiss. Fed.Rules Civ.Proc. Rule 4(d)(1, 5), 28 U.S.C.A.

Jarrell v. Tisch, 656 F.Supp. 237.

D.D.C. 1985. Dismissal of age discrimination in employment action for insufficient process was unwarranted, where employee initiated case pro se, and employer received timely notice of suit and did in fact respond.

Dixon v. Stephenson Inc., 614 F.Supp. 60.

D.D.C. 1985. For want of service of process upon particular defendants, action was dismissed as to them. Fed.Rules Civ.Proc.Rule 12(b)(4), 28 U.S.C.A.

Provisional Government of Republic of New Afrika v. American Broadcasting Companies, Inc., 609 F.Supp. 104.

D.D.C. 1984. Where proper service of process was not made on District of Columbia partnership by serving individual partners within 120 days after filing of complaint, the complaint against the partnership was dismissed. Fed.Rules Civ.Proc.Rule 4(j), 28 U.S.C.A.

Affie, Inc. v. Nurel Enterprises, Inc., 607 F.Supp. 220.

M.D.Fla. 1995. Dismissal of six actions, in which claimant moving to proceed in forma pauperis alleged that state and federal court judges, police department, county jail officials, and others conspired to have him convicted of offense arising from alleged property dispute with his brother, was warranted; claimant did not effect service on any defendant within required time period, and actions were patently frivolous, brought for purposes of vexation, had no basis in law or fact, and arose largely from urge to contumacy. 28 U.S.C.A. § 1915(d); Fed.Rules Civ.Proc.Rule 4, 28 U.S.C.A.

In re Roy Day Litigation, 976 F.Supp. 1455.

M.D.Fla. 1994. Individual would be dismissed as defendant in employee's sexual harassment action against employer; although one paragraph of complaint referred to individual as defendant, defendant was not served with summons or complaint. Fed.Rules Civ.Proc. Rule 4(j), 28 U.S.C.A.

Caprio v. American Airlines, Inc., 848 F.Supp. 1528.

M.D.Fla. 1994. Pro se plaintiff failed to establish good cause for his failure to properly effect service within 120 days of filing of his complaint, and action was subject to dismissal; plaintiff's pro se status did not entitle him to more lenient scrutiny, and being confused and uninformed with regard to rule governing service was not "good cause." Fed.Rules Civ. Proc.Rule 4(m), 28 U.S.C.A.

Lowe v. Hart, 157 F.R.D. 550.

Pro se plaintiff must show "good cause" in order to avoid dismissal for failure to timely serve complaint. Fed.Rules Civ.Proc.Rule 4(m), 28 U.S.C.A.

Lowe v. Hart, 157 F.R.D. 550.

N.D.Fla. 1988. Plaintiff's desire not to force defendants to defend suit which he might not have financial resources to litigate, counsel's inability to obtain plaintiff's permission to serve complaint, and discontinuance of attorney-client relationship did not establish "good cause" for plaintiff's failure to serve defendants within 120-day period for service after filing complaint and, therefore, plaintiff's action would be dismissed without prejudice, though such dismissal would effectively deprive plaintiff of his day in court because of running of relevant statute of limitations. Fed.Rules Civ. Proc.Rule 4(j), 28 U.S.C.A.

Smith v. Pennsylvania Glass Sand Corp., 123 F.R.D. 648.

S.D.Fla. 1988. Dismissal for failure to effect service pursuant to order of district court was not warranted, in view of evidence of plaintiff's seeking in good faith to comply with order and lack of prejudice to defendant in short delay in service.

Dietrich v. Key Bank, N.A., 693 F.Supp. 1112, affirmed 72 F.3d 1509.

S.D.Fla. 1988. Failure to deliver summons and complaint in civil rights action to the United States attorney, and use of certified mail in the alternative, required dismissal of the action for improper service. Fed.Rules Civ.Proc.Rule 4(d)(4), 28 U.S.C.A.

Rodriguez v. Tisch, 688 F.Supp. 1530.

M.D.Ga. 1997. Evidence established that plaintiff's process server had not served defendant with complaint, but only with summons, thus requiring dismissal of plaintiff's employment discrimination action without prejudice, though process server had signed affidavit prepared by plaintiff's attorney stating that he had served employee of defendant with both complaint and summons; affidavit prepared by process server himself two days earlier stated only that he remembered reading section of the papers which mentioned "Discrimination," process server had admitted to defense counsel that he remembered serving only one sheet of paper to defendant's employee, such employee testified that she had received only the summons and had contacted docket clerk to learn case number and subject matter of suit. Fed.Rules Civ.Proc.Rule 4(m), 28 U.S.C.A.

Davis v. Belk-Hudson Co. of Tifton, Inc., 173 F.R.D. 323, affirmed 136 F.3d 142.

Fact that plaintiff may face statute of limitations problem does not prevent dismissal for failure to perfect service. Fed.Rules Civ.Proc. Rule 4(m), 28 U.S.C.A.

Davis v. Belk-Hudson Co. of Tifton, Inc., 173 F.R.D. 323, affirmed 136 F.3d 142.

N.D.Ga. 1997. In analyzing motion to dismiss for insufficiency of service of process of action removed to federal court, court examines whether plaintiff complied with state law governing process.

Ritts v. Dealers Alliance Credit Corp., 989 F.Supp. 1475.

N.D.Ga. 1995. Affidavit of employment discrimination plaintiff's former attorney stating that she mailed copies of summons and complaint to supervisor of plaintiff's supervisor and two copies of notice and acknowledgement of service, with a self-addressed envelope, that Postal Service never returned those documents to attorney, that subsequently litigation proceeded and attorneys for supervisor's supervisor never indicated that there was a problem with service failed to show good cause for failure to timely serve supervisor's supervisor, warranting dismissal of claims against supervisor without prejudice, given the absence of any evidence that attorney attempted to serve that supervisor personally or in any other manner provided for under service of process rule or state law.

Fed.Rules Civ.Proc.Rules 4, 4(c)(2)(C)(ii), (c)(2)(D), (j), 28 U.S.C.(1988 Ed.Supp.IV).

Simon v. Morehouse School of Medicine, 908 F.Supp. 959.

N.D.Ga. 1994. If plaintiff fails to effect service within 120 days following filing of complaint, complaint must be dismissed unless good cause can be shown by plaintiff for delay. Fed. Rules Civ.Proc.Rule 4(c)(2)(C)(ii), 28 U.S.C.App.(1988 Ed.)

In re Air Crash Disaster Near Brunswick, Georgia April 4, 1991, 158 F.R.D. 693.

Defendants were entitled to dismissal from action on grounds of failure to make timely service where plaintiffs failed to perfect service upon them within 120–day period following filing of complaint, plaintiffs did not attempt to serve defendants until 214 and 288 days after filing of complaint, and plaintiffs failed to show good cause for their actions.

In re Air Crash Disaster Near Brunswick, Georgia April 4, 1991, 158 F.R.D. 693.

N.D.Ga. 1994. Taxpayer's failure to timely serve original complaint did not require dismissal of action seeking review of jeopardy tax assessment, where amended complaint was timely served, evidence had not yet been developed, United States had not answered and issue had not yet been joined. Fed.Rules Civ.Proc. Rule 15(a), 28 U.S.C.A.; Rule 4(j), 28 U.S.C.(1988 Ed.)

Vax v. C.I.R., 156 F.R.D. 272.

N.D.Ga. 1993. Civil rights plaintiff's failure to perfect service within 120–day period and to demonstrate good cause for failing to perfect service required dismissal. Fed.Rules Civ.Proc.Rule 4(j), 28 U.S.C.(1988 Ed.)

Clark v. City of Zebulon, 156 F.R.D. 684.

N.D.Ga. 1985. District court has broad discretion to dismiss action or to quash service but retain case in which service was insufficient.

Thermo-Cell Southeast, Inc. v. Technetic Industries, Inc., 605 F.Supp. 1122.

Although plaintiff's attempts at service by mail were insufficient, district court elected to order that service be quashed, rather than to dismiss the action, where it appeared that defendant might be amenable to service of process under forum state's long-arm statute. Fed. Rules Civ.Proc.Rule 4(c)(2)(C)(i, ii), (f), 28 U.S.C.A.; O.C.G.A. §§ 9–10–91, 9–10–94.

Thermo-Cell Southeast, Inc. v. Technetic Industries, Inc., 605 F.Supp. 1122.

S.D.Ga. 1991. If party on whose behalf faulty service was made can show good cause as to why service was not made within prescribed 120 days, then court need not dismiss complaint. Fed.Rules Civ.Proc.Rule 4(j), 28 U.S.C.A.

Martin v. Mills, 138 F.R.D. 151.

D.Idaho 1989. Government's motion to dismiss action seeking preliminary injunction restraining deportation for lack of personal jurisdiction had to be denied, where illegal aliens corrected service deficiencies within statute of limitations and 120–day service period. Fed. Rules Civ.Proc.Rule 4(d)(4), 28 U.S.C.A.

Carrillo v. Mohrman, 832 F.Supp. 1412.

N.D.Ill. 1997. Pro se inmate could not be penalized for delay in service upon defendant, as United States Marshal informed inmate and court that defendant had been served, and thus, defendant would not be dismissed for lack of timely service. Fed.Rules Civ.Proc.Rule 4(m), 28 U.S.C.A.

Mitchell v. Shomig, 969 F.Supp. 487.

Because pro se inmates must rely on United States Marshal for service, delays in service attributable to Marshal automatically constitute "good cause" preventing dismissal for untimely service. Fed.Rules Civ.Proc.Rule 4(m), 28 U.S.C.A.

Mitchell v. Shomig, 969 F.Supp. 487.

N.D.Ill. 1995. Rule providing for dismissal without prejudice of complaint not properly served on defendant within 120 days of its filing is mandatory, but dismissal is not warranted if plaintiff can show good cause for failure to properly effect service. Fed.Rules Civ.Proc. Rule 4(m), 28 U.S.C.A.

Campbell v. Illinois Dept. of Corrections, 907 F.Supp. 1173.

Court's determination of "good cause," under rule providing for dismissal without prejudice of complaint not properly served on defendant within 120 days, unless good cause is shown, entails discretionary conclusions by district court that will not be disturbed absent abuse of discretion. Fed.Rules Civ.Proc.Rule 4(m), 28 U.S.C.A.

Campbell v. Illinois Dept. of Corrections, 907 F.Supp. 1173.

Though lack of prejudice, standing alone, is not sufficient basis for finding of good cause, under rule providing for dismissal without prejudice of complaint not properly served on defendant within 120 days, unless good cause is shown, lack of prejudice can and in many cases should be taken into account. Fed.Rules Civ. Proc.Rule 4(m), 28 U.S.C.A.

Campbell v. Illinois Dept. of Corrections, 907 F.Supp. 1173.

N.D.Ill. 1995. Court lacked jurisdiction over United States, requiring its dismissal as defendant in inmate's pro se action, where inmate did not serve United States attorney for

district in which action was brought or Attorney General. Fed.Rules Civ.Proc.Rule 4(d)(4), 28 U.S.C.App.(1988 Ed.)

Neville v. True, 900 F.Supp. 972.

N.D.Ill. 1995. Dismissal without prejudice is mandatory for failure to serve complaint within 120 days after its filing, unless plaintiff meets his burden of demonstrating "good cause." Fed.Rules Civ.Proc.Rule 4(m), 28 U.S.C.A.

Seber v. Unger, 881 F.Supp. 323.

N.D.Ill. 1995. Plaintiff's failure to identify and serve John Doe defendants within 120 days of filing his complaint did not require dismissal of action against them; rather, defendant would be directed to identify and serve John Doe defendants by a certain date or face dismissal of unidentified defendants. Fed.Rules Civ.Proc. Rule 4(m), 28 U.S.C.A.

Aviles v. Village of Bedford Park, 160 F.R.D. 565.

N.D.Ill. 1994. Former rule requiring district courts to dismiss action without prejudice if service were not made within 120 days of filing of complaint did not apply to service in foreign country, even if there had been no attempt at foreign service within that period. Fed.Rules Civ.Proc.Rule 4(j), 28 U.S.C.(1988 Ed.)

Cargill Ferrous Intern. v. M/V Elikon, 154 F.R.D. 193.

N.D.Ill. 1993. Defendants who had never been named or served would be dismissed.

Vakharia v. Swedish Covenant Hosp., 824 F.Supp. 769, on reconsideration in part.

N.D.Ill. 1993. Dismissal is mandated by rule requiring summons and complaint to be served within 120 days unless plaintiff can show good cause for failure to serve defendant within 120–day period. Fed.Rules Civ.Proc.Rule 4(j), 28 U.S.C.A.

Sullivan v. Mitchell, 151 F.R.D. 331.

N.D.Ill. 1993. Fact that plaintiff was effectively precluded from bringing suit against defendant does not prevent operation of court rule authorizing dismissal of complaint for failure to serve summons and complaint within 120 days after filing of complaint; dismissal is appropriate even where plaintiff's claim will be time barred. Fed.Rules Civ.Proc.Rules 4, 4(j), 28 U.S.C.A.

Serlin v. Arthur Andersen & Co., 145 F.R.D. 494, affirmed 12 F.3d 1101.

N.D.Ill. 1989. Service of process by certified mail rather than first-class mail was not grounds for dismissal, where notice and acknowledgment forms were enclosed and recipient signed and returned them. Fed.Rules Civ. Proc.Rule 4(c)(2)(C)(ii), 28 U.S.C.A.

> Lenoir v. Federal Deposit Ins. Corp., 709 F.Supp. 830.

N.D.Ill. 1988. Ineffectiveness of service by mail on corporations, as result of failure of their registered agents to sign and return acknowledgment forms, did not warrant dismissal; motion to dismiss would be treated as motion to quash and, as such, would be granted and, moreover, corporations would be ordered to pay cost of reserving them personally. Fed. Rules Civ.Proc.Rule 4(c)(2)(C)(ii), (c)(2)(D), 28 U.S.C.A.; Lanham Trade-Mark Act, § 1(d), 15 U.S.C.A. § 1051(d).

> Outboard Marine Corp. v. Chantiers Beneteau, 687 F.Supp. 366.

N.D.Ill. 1988. Plaintiffs in diversity action could not show good cause for failing to serve defendants within 120 days of commencement of lawsuit, warranting dismissal of the action, despite plaintiffs' claim that 120–day period was "tolled" while status of their case was uncertain due to issuance of purportedly redundant dismissal orders; plaintiffs had more than one month to serve defendants after court made clear that case had always been pending, but failed to do so. Fed.Rules Civ.Proc.Rule 4(j), 28 U.S.C.A.

> Lorentzen v. Honeywell Heating, a Div. of Minnesota Min. and Mfg., 120 F.R.D. 681.

N.D.Ill. 1983. Chronister v. Sam Tanksley Trucking, Inc., 569 F.Supp. 464, on reconsideration 109 F.R.D. 1.

N.D.Ind. 1990. Defendant failed to state claim upon which relief could be granted with respect to challenge to personal jurisdiction for improper service where court ordered defendant to appear, plead, answer or otherwise move with respect to complaint on or before certain date and ordered that notice be published in newspaper once a week for six consecutive weeks and thereafter defendant filed her answer and cross complaint/counterclaim. Fed.Rules Civ.Proc.Rule 12(b)(6), 28 U.S.C.A.

> Federal Nat. Mortg. Ass'n v. Cobb, 738 F.Supp. 1220.

N.D.Ind. 1986. Defense of insufficiency of process challenges content of summons, and defense of insufficiency of service of process challenges manner or method of service. Fed. Rules Civ.Proc.Rule 12(b), 28 U.S.C.A.

> Heise v. Olympus Optical Co., Ltd., 111 F.R.D. 1.

S.D.Ind. 1995. Under Indiana law, where plaintiff did not receive certified mail receipt for certain defendants in *Bivens* action, burden was on plaintiff to re-serve those defendants, and because he failed to attempt to do so, suit

would be dismissed as to those defendants. Ind.Trial Procedure Rule 4.1(A)(1).

> Robinson v. Turner, 886 F.Supp. 1451.

S.D.Ind. 1990. Rule requiring dismissal for failure to effect service within 120 days of filing complaint, absent good cause, requires good cause as to why service was not obtained only within the first 120 days, and failures of attorney appointed after the 120 days have expired are not controlling. Fed.Rules Civ.Proc. Rule 4(j), 28 U.S.C.A.

> Patterson v. Brady, 131 F.R.D. 679, 108 A.L.R. Fed. 847, affirmed 89 F.3d 838, certiorari denied 117 S.Ct. 245, 136 L.Ed.2d 173.

S.D.Ind. 1986. Federal employee's employment discrimination claim under Title VII could not be dismissed for inadequate service of process on Department of Army by use of improper address where service achieved purpose of notifying defendants of tenancy of action and defendants did not seriously contend that service resulted in material prejudice to some substantial right. Civil Rights of 1964, § 717(c), as amended, 42 U.S.C.A. § 2000e–16(c); Fed. Rules Civ.Proc.Rule 4(d)(5), 28 U.S.C.A.

> Dodson v. U.S. Army Finance and Accounting Center, 636 F.Supp. 894.

N.D.Iowa 1995. General rule is that when court finds that service is insufficient but curable, it generally should quash service and give plaintiff opportunity to re-serve defendants; however, dismissal may be proper without opportunity to cure where proper service would be futile. Fed.Rules Civ.Proc.Rules 4(d), 12(b)(5), 28 U.S.C.A.

> Dahl v. Kanawha Inv. Holding Co., 161 F.R.D. 673.

Dismissal for failure to state claim was appropriate as to defendants against whom plaintiffs failed to effect proper service of process, and against whom plaintiffs failed to state any factual allegations; however, plaintiffs were entitled to opportunity to cure defects in service as to six defendants against whom plaintiffs did make factual allegations. Fed.Rules Civ.Proc. Rule 12(b)(6), 28 U.S.C.A.

> Dahl v. Kanawha Inv. Holding Co., 161 F.R.D. 673.

D.Kan. 1998. The deficiency in service of process by certified mail of a city located in Kansas, due to sending the certified mail by plaintiff's counsel rather than by the sheriff, did not warrant dismissal of the action, in light of the plaintiff's attempts to effect timely service; instead, the court would extend the time for service an additional 30 days. K.S.A. 60–303,

60–304(d); Fed.Rules Civ.Proc.Rule 4(j)(2), (m), 28 U.S.C.A.

> Perkins v. City of Wichita, Kansas, 178 F.R.D. 566.

D.Kan. 1997. Summons specifications rule requires sufficient notice be given to party of claims brought against it, and dismissal is not in order unless party has been prejudiced. Fed. Rules Civ.Proc.Rule 4, 28 U.S.C.A.

> Bernstein v. Carter & Sons Freightways, Inc., 983 F.Supp. 994.

D.Kan. 1995. Complaint against prison officials would not be dismissed for insufficient service where the pro se prisoners were proceeding in forma pauperis and relied on United States marshall's service to effect service. Fed. Rules Civ.Proc.Rule 4(c)(2), 28 U.S.C.A.

> Bagguley v. Barr, 893 F.Supp. 967.

D.Kan. 1994. Complaint, which was served upon defendant one day after expiration of 120–day period for service, would not be dismissed for failure of service of process, where defendant did not allege any prejudice which would result from delayed service, defendant did not claim surprise, plaintiff asserted that defendant was sent courtesy copy of complaint on day complaint was filed, delayed service was caused by error by plaintiff's counsel in calculating 120 days, and dismissal of complaint would be pointless, as it would not bar plaintiff's claim, but would simply require plaintiff to refile and re-serve defendant. Fed.Rules Civ.Proc.Rules 4(m), 12(b)(5), 28 U.S.C.A.

> Freeze-Dry Products, Inc. v. Metro Park Warehouse, Inc., 159 F.R.D. 45, reconsideration denied 160 F.R.D. 156.

District court may consider practicalities in exercising its discretion to determine whether to dismiss complaint for failure of service of process within time limit for service. Fed.Rules Civ.Proc.Rules 4(m), 12(b)(5), 28 U.S.C.A.

> Freeze-Dry Products, Inc. v. Metro Park Warehouse, Inc., 159 F.R.D. 45, reconsideration denied 160 F.R.D. 156.

D.Kan. 1993. Dismissal of action against government was required for failure to effect timely service of summons and complaint, even if service was only one day late and government was not prejudiced by delay. Fed.Rules Civ. Proc.Rule 4(j), 28 U.S.C.A.

> Greene v. U.S., Dept. of Army, 149 F.R.D. 206.

D.Kan. 1993. First complaint was subject to dismissal based on plaintiff's failure to have issued summons in connection with that complaint; defendant she was served only with first amended complaint, which was dismissed, although she obviously had knowledge of original complaint. Fed.Rules Civ.Proc.Rule 12(b)(2), 28 U.S.C.A.

> Murray v. Sevier, 145 F.R.D. 563, reconsideration denied 149 F.R.D. 638.

D.Kan. 1992. Pro se complaint would be dismissed, and motion for default judgment would be overruled, for plaintiff's failure to make proper service of process, though plaintiff apparently never received notice and order to show cause sent to his last address of record, a municipal correctional institution, where apparent reason for nonreceipt was plaintiff's escape.

> Stevenson v. Kansas City, Kansas Jail, 793 F.Supp. 1029.

D.Kan. 1991. Law enforcement agents who were personally served in civil rights action could not obtain dismissal on argued basis of lack of service on state, even if officers were being sued in their official capacities. Fed. Rules Civ.Proc.Rule 4(d)(6), 28 U.S.C.A.; K.S.A. 60–304(d)(5).

> Kjorlie v. Lundin, 765 F.Supp. 671, reconsideration denied 1991 WL 290452.

E.D.La. 1997. When alleged defect in service is due to minor, technical error, only actual prejudice to defendant or evidence of flagrant disregard of requirements of rules justifies dismissal.

> Louisiana Acorn Fair Housing v. Quarter House, 952 F.Supp. 352.

Technical error by plaintiff who brought action against timeshare resort by improperly including term "Inc." in its identification of resort in summons which was served did not warrant dismissal of action; no evidence was presented that resort did not receive notice of action or had suffered any prejudice from technical error. Fed.Rules Civ.Proc.Rule 12(b)(4), 28 U.S.C.A.

> Louisiana Acorn Fair Housing v. Quarter House, 952 F.Supp. 352.

E.D.La. 1991. Dismissal of complaint brought against government officials in their individual capacities was warranted for plaintiffs' failure to obtain personal service on defendants, inasmuch as it was unlikely that plaintiffs were unable to serve individual defendants at their home addresses between time lawsuit and defendants' motion to dismiss were filed. Fed. Rules Civ.Proc.Rule 4(j), 28 U.S.C.A.

> Vu v. Meese, 755 F.Supp. 1375.

E.D.La. 1985. Where plaintiff can show good cause why service was not effected within 120 days after filing of complaint, dismissal is not mandated by Federal Civil Rule 4(j); however, harsh sanction of dismissal without prejudice is appropriate to those cases in which nonservice was result of mere inadvertence or heedlessness. Fed.Rules Civ.Proc.Rules 4, 4(j), 6(b), 28 U.S.C.A.

> Davis-Wilson v. Hilton Hotels Corp., 106 F.R.D. 505.

Where attorney had never been specifically appointed or authorized by defendant to receive service of process for it, plaintiff had no basis for believing that defendant had ever authorized its attorney to receive service, and plaintiff waited several weeks after being informed of defendant's correct agent for service of process before serving defendant through its correct agent, plaintiff's complaint was properly dismissed under Federal Civil Rule 12(b)(5) for failure to effect service within reasonable period of time. Fed.Rules Civ.Proc.Rule 12(b)(5), 28 U.S.C.A.

> Davis-Wilson v. Hilton Hotels Corp., 106 F.R.D. 505.

W.D.La. 1993. Rule requiring service of summons and complaint upon defendant within 120 days after filing of complaint is mandatory, and dismissal for failure to comply with this requirement is mandatory, in absence of good cause. Fed.Rules Civ.Proc.Rule 4(j), 28 U.S.C.A.

> Houser v. Rice, 151 F.R.D. 291.

Dismissal of complaint of alleging violations of Title VII and Age Discrimination in Employment Act (ADEA) for failure to serve defendants within 120 days was required, absent satisfactory explanation, much less showing of good cause, for plaintiff's failure to perfect timely service. Age Discrimination in Employment Act of 1967, § 2 et seq., as amended, 29 U.S.C.A. § 621 et seq.; Civil Rights Act of 1964, § 701 et seq., as amended, 42 U.S.C.A. § 2000e et seq.; Fed.Rules Civ. Proc.Rule 4(j), 28 U.S.C.A.

> Houser v. Rice, 151 F.R.D. 291.

W.D.La. 1991. If plaintiff fails to serve summons and copy of complaint on defendant within 120 days of filing complaint, plaintiff must show good cause in order to survive motion to dismiss. Fed.Rules Civ.Proc.Rule 4(j), 28 U.S.C.A.

> Gallien v. Guth Dairy, Inc., 136 F.R.D. 110.

Employee's Title VII and age discrimination action against employer had to be dismissed without prejudice, even if such dismissal would result in refiling of action being time barred, where employee failed to file summons within 120 days of filing of complaint, absent showing of good cause for failure to serve. Civil Rights Act of 1964, § 701 et seq., 42 U.S.C.A. § 2000e et seq.; Fed.Rules Civ.Proc. Rule 4(j), 28 U.S.C.A.

> Gallien v. Guth Dairy, Inc., 136 F.R.D. 110.

D.Md. 1998. Absent good cause for delay, federal district courts must dismiss case if plaintiff fails to serve summons and complaint within 120 days of filing, and courts lack discretion to reach contrary result. Fed.Rules Civ.Proc.Rule 4(m), 28 U.S.C.A.

> Eccles v. National Semiconductor Corp., 10 F.Supp.2d 514.

D.Md. 1996. In government employee's Title VII action against government, district court would extend time for government employee to serve summons and complaint on the United States Attorney's office, though the government employee did not argue there was good cause as to why he failed to effect service within prescribed time limit, where government employee was acting pro se at time of service, and dismissal of action without prejudice would effectively bar the employee's claim. Civil Rights Act of 1964, § 701 et seq., 42 U.S.C.A. § 2000e et seq.; Fed.Rules Civ.Proc.Rule 4(m), 28 U.S.C.A.

> Coates v. Shalala, 914 F.Supp. 110, affirmed 133 F.3d 914, certiorari denied 119 S.Ct. 117.

D.Md. 1995. When plaintiff fails to file a timely service of process and fails to show good cause for belated service, complaint must be dismissed; district court has no discretion to salvage the action. Fed.Rules Civ.Proc.Rules 4(m), 12(b)(5), 28 U.S.C.A.

> Braithwaite v. Johns Hopkins Hosp., 160 F.R.D. 75.

D.Md. 1986. Plaintiff's efforts to effect service were not sufficiently diligent or reasonable, and complaint, which was not served within 120 days after it was filed, would be dismissed without prejudice despite possibility of successful statute of limitations defense; plaintiff knew defendant's addresses and there was no evidence that defendants had evaded service within that period, plaintiff and/or his counsel had delayed almost an entire month in hiring private process server and attempting personal service after indicating awareness that mail service had been ineffective as to individual defendants, and plaintiff had not filed motion requesting extension of time for service. Fed. Rules Civ.Proc.Rules 4(j), 6(b), 28 U.S.C.A.

> Quann v. Whitegate-Edgewater, 112 F.R.D. 649.

D.Mass. 1990. Civil rights action by inmate visitor against state correctional institution supervisor would be dismissed, where supervisor was substituted for named predecessor supervisor as supervisor at time of challenged acts, but service was never effected on the substituted supervisor; court had never acquired personal jurisdiction over the substituted supervisor. Fed.Rules Civ.Proc., Rule 12(b)(5), 28 U.S.C.A.

> Smith v. Maloney, 735 F.Supp. 39.

D.Mass. 1990. Plaintiff's failure to timely serve federal entities required dismissal as to those entities. Fed.Rules Civ.Proc.Rule 4(j), 28 U.S.C.A.; Rules Civ.Proc., Rule 4(j), 43A M.G.L.A.

Zarrilli v. Salvucci, 730 F.Supp. 461.

Dismissal of parties was appropriate where there was no return of service as to those parties. Fed.Rules Civ.Proc.Rule 4(j), 28 U.S.C.A.; Rules Civ.Proc., Rule 4(j), 43A M.G.L.A.

Zarrilli v. Salvucci, 730 F.Supp. 461.

D.Mass. 1986. Motion to dismiss for insufficiency of service based upon service that was insufficient under state law would be denied, where defendant conceded it received notice of plaintiff's action and did not claim to have been prejudiced by the method of service used, and neither party asserted that the plaintiff would not be able to properly serve the defendant.

Howse v. Zimmer Mfg. Inc., 109 F.R.D. 628.

D.C.Mass. 1985. Complaint which designated as defendant in personal injury action nonexistent ski resort corporation, and which had been served on president of different corporation, which was not named as party defendant, was subject to dismissal. Fed.Rules Civ. Proc.Rule 12(b)(4, 5), 28 U.S.C.A.

Gonzalez v. Temple Mountain Ski Resort, Inc., 613 F.Supp. 354.

E.D.Mich. 1994. Party may raise defense of insufficiency of service of process in motion to dismiss. Fed.Rules Civ.Proc.Rule 12(b)(5), 28 U.S.C.A.

Frederick v. Hydro-Aluminum S.A., 153 F.R.D. 120.

E.D.Mich. 1994. Upon deciding that service of process must be quashed, district court has broad discretion either to dismiss action or to retain case and simply quash service. Fed. Rules Civ.Proc.Rule 12(b)(5), 28 U.S.C.A.

Voice Systems Marketing Co., L.P. v. Appropriate Technology Corp., 153 F.R.D. 117.

District court would exercise its discretion to dismiss plaintiff's complaint, and would not simply quash service, where plaintiff had obtained service of process through deception and trickery and not merely through inadvertent violation of rules governing service of process. Fed.Rules Civ.Proc.Rule 12(b)(5), 28 U.S.C.A.

Voice Systems Marketing Co., L.P. v. Appropriate Technology Corp., 153 F.R.D. 117.

E.D.Mich. 1992. District court would dismiss state prison inmate's civil rights action against defendant state prison assistant resident unit manager who had never been served with process and "John Doe" defendant who had never been identified and had never been served with process. 42 U.S.C.A. § 1983.

Taylor v. Foltz, 803 F.Supp. 1261, affirmed 14 F.3d 602.

E.D.Mich. 1986. Complaint would be dismissed due to trickery in obtaining service of process after official of defendant corporation entered jurisdiction without warning that process would be served after "settlement discussion," even though defendant initiated meeting and other business may have been discussed, where official was not in jurisdiction for business unrelated to meeting, plaintiff was willing to meet with him, had formulated intention to prepare complaint prior to offer, and did not provide opportunity to leave jurisdiction once settlement process broke down.

K Mart Corp. v. Gen-Star Industries Co., Ltd., 110 F.R.D. 310.

W.D.Mich. 1984. In light of fact that Title VII plaintiff filed a complaint with the EEOC and had provided notice thereby to employer, pro se plaintiff would not suffer dismissal of Title VII claim for late service. Fed.Rules Civ. Proc.Rule 4(j), 28 U.S.C.A.; Civil Rights Act of 1964, § 701 et seq., 42 U.S.C.A. § 2000e et seq.

Thompson v. Ralston Purina Co., 599 F.Supp. 756.

D.Minn. 1995. While provision of Federal Rules of Civil Procedure establishing time limit for service of process grants court discretion to either dismiss complaint that has not been served within 120 days after its filing or to allow service within specified time, provision apart from granting court discretionary authority provides that if good cause for failure to serve process is shown court shall extend time for service for appropriate period. Fed.Rules Civ. Proc.Rule 4(m), 28 U.S.C.A.

Rollerblade, Inc. v. Rappelfeld, 165 F.R.D. 92.

Plaintiff who had failed to effect service of process within 120 days after filing of complaint due to apparent confusion in office of plaintiff's counsel was properly granted additional 20 days in which to make service, and defendant's subsequent motion to dismiss action was denied, even though plaintiff had sought extension of time through ex parte letter request to court. Fed.Rules Civ.Proc.Rule 4(m), 28 U.S.C.A.

Rollerblade, Inc. v. Rappelfeld, 165 F.R.D. 92.

D.Minn. 1991. Technical defect in summons mistakenly identifying name and address of defendant could not justify dismissal, where defendant failed to demonstrate actual prejudice to substantial right. Fed.Rules Civ.Proc. Rule 4(b), 28 U.S.C.A.

> Federal Deposit Ins. Corp. v. Swager, 773 F.Supp. 1244.

D.Minn. 1985. Service on managing partner was valid only against partnership; accordingly all other defendants would be dismissed in dispute concerning validity of management contract for Indian tribe's bingo operations. Fed. Rules Civ.Proc.Rule 4(j), 28 U.S.C.A.

> U.S. ex rel. Shakopee Mdewakanton Sioux Community v. Pan American Management Co., 616 F.Supp. 1200, dismissed 789 F.2d 632.

S.D.Miss. 1989. Government's active participation in lawsuit without pursuit of service of process issue until after 120 days had expired made dismissal on grounds that United States attorney was not personally served within 120 days after filing of complaint inappropriate. Fed.Rules Civ.Proc.Rule 4(j), 28 U.S.C.A.

> Doe v. U.S., 128 F.R.D. 228.

E.D.Mo. 1995. Although service of process on executive employee had been quashed, action against him would not be dismissed; dismissal would serve no purpose, since there was nothing in the record which suggested that an employer would not be able to properly serve employee.

> May Dept. Stores Co. v. Wilansky, 900 F.Supp. 1154.

W.D.Mo. 1993. Plaintiff's failure to serve defendant with process within 120 days of filing of complaint warranted dismissal of action, despite plaintiff's allegations that until recently he had been unable to locate defendant; plaintiff never made any serious attempt to find defendant until ordered to do so by court and when finally pushed into action, plaintiff successfully obtained personal service on defendant at same address at which service by mail had been attempted three years earlier. Fed.Rules Civ. Proc.Rule 4(j), 28 U.S.C.A.

> Hoffman v. Benson, 147 F.R.D. 205.

D.Nev. 1990. Taxpayer's pro se suit would not be dismissed for failure to serve United States Attorney and Attorney General, as proper parties, particularly as taxpayer had served all proper parties at time of government's supplemental memorandum in support of motion to dismiss. Fed.Rules Civ.Proc.Rule 4(d)(4), 28 U.S.C.A.

> White v. I.R.S., 790 F.Supp. 1017.

D.Nev. 1988. Pro se plaintiffs' failure to serve defendants within 120 days of filing complaint required dismissal of action arising from aviation disaster, despite plaintiffs' alleged ignorance of 120–day rule or confusion arising from court's notice advising them of rule. Fed.Rules Civ.Proc.Rules 4(j), 6(b), 28 U.S.C.A.

> Sipes v. Galaxy Airlines, Inc., 119 F.R.D. 691.

D.Nev. 1985. If service of summons and complaint is not effected within 120 days after filing of complaint, plaintiff has burden of establishing good cause for delay, and if she fails to sustain that burden, dismissal of action is mandatory. Fed.Rules Civ.Proc.Rule 4(j), 28 U.S.C.A.

> Ruley v. Nelson, 106 F.R.D. 514.

Fact that plaintiff's counsel was "totally and completely unaware" of Federal Civil Rule 4(j), requiring service of summons and complaint within 120 days after filing of complaint, did not constitute good cause for failure to abide by that time limit in § 1983 action; failure to meet time limit for service required dismissal of action. Fed.Rules Civ.Proc.Rule 4(j), 28 U.S.C.A.

> Ruley v. Nelson, 106 F.R.D. 514.

D.N.J. 1991. Failure to serve defendant for more than ten months after sex discrimination complaint was filed required dismissal of complaint without prejudice sua sponte. Fed. Rules Civ.Proc.Rule 4(j), 28 U.S.C.A.

> Pittman v. La Fontaine, 756 F.Supp. 834.

D.N.J. 1990. Plaintiffs must show "good cause" for their failure to serve defendant within governing limitations period in order for their action to survive defendant's motion to dismiss for untimely service. Fed.Rules Civ. Proc.Rule 4(j), 28 U.S.C.A.

> Sheets v. Schlear, 132 F.R.D. 391.

D.N.J. 1985. Any error by plaintiffs in failing to serve the United States and the Attorney General in suit to clear title to property conveyed by Veterans Administration to plaintiffs was harmless, as necessary persons within the government had actual notice of the suit and suffered no prejudice from any technical defect in service. Fed.Rules Civ.Proc.Rule 4(d)(4, 5), 28 U.S.C.A.

> Donaghy v. Roudebush, 614 F.Supp. 585.

E.D.N.Y. 1994. Cases may be dismissed for untimely service only if plaintiffs fail to demonstrate good cause as to why service was not timely made. Fed.Rules Civ.Proc.Rule 4(j), 28 U.S.C.(1988 Ed.)

> Jackson v. Foley, 156 F.R.D. 545.

E.D.N.Y. 1992. Under "flexible due diligence standard" for question of timely service process in cases exempt from 120–day rule due to attempted service in foreign country, courts generally refuse to dismiss cases where delay was in range of two or three months unless that delay caused defendants hardship or prejudice. Fed.Rules Civ.Proc.Rule 4(i, j), 28 U.S.C.A.

In re Southold Development Corp., 148 B.R. 726.

E.D.N.Y. 1992. Failure of summons served on taxpayer to state time period for appearing and defending did not require dismissal of government's action to recover tax assessment; taxpayers could not claim prejudice since their counsel received an extension of time in which to answer and an answer was filed within the extended answering period, and the time period to answer a complaint was readily ascertainable from the federal rules of civil procedure. Fed.Rules Civ.Proc.Rules 4, 4(b), 12(a), 28 U.S.C.A.

U.S. v. Carney, 796 F.Supp. 700.

E.D.N.Y. 1992. For purposes of rule that dismissal is mandatory if service is not perfected within 120 days of filing absent showing of good cause, among factors court should consider in determining whether there is good cause is whether asserted inadvertence reflects easily manufactured excuse incapable of verification by court. Fed.Rules Civ.Proc.Rule 4(j), 28 U.S.C.A.

Szarejko v. Great Neck School Dist., 795 F.Supp. 81.

Teacher failed to show good cause for failure to perfect service within 120 days of filing action against school board and school district, and therefore dismissal of action against board and district was warranted; teacher's excuses, based on office moves, difficulty in receiving mail, heavy travel schedule, illness, and other personal problems, were of type easily manufactured and incapable of verification by court. Fed.Rules Civ.Proc.Rule 4(j), 28 U.S.C.A.

Szarejko v. Great Neck School Dist., 795 F.Supp. 81.

E.D.N.Y. 1990. Plaintiff's failure to serve the United States with original complaint within 120 days of filing of complaint, and late filing of amended complaint warranted dismissal. Fed. Rules Civ.Proc.Rule 4(j), 28 U.S.C.A.; 28 U.S.C.A. § 2401(b).

Reany v. U.S., 738 F.Supp. 680.

E.D.N.Y. 1986. Action would not be dismissed for failure to serve defendant in accordance with federal rule on service of process, considering advanced status of action and lack of prejudice to defendants; thus, plaintiff would be required to re-serve defendant in accordance with the rule within 60 days or complaint would be dismissed. Fed.Rules Civ.Proc.Rule 4, 28 U.S.C.A.

Kosta v. St. George's University School of Medicine, 641 F.Supp. 606.

E.D.N.Y. 1985. Civil rights complaint against individual police officer was subject to dismissal, where civil rights plaintiff did not pursue available options in diligently seeking to serve police officer with process, so that police officer was improperly served more than two years subsequent to filing of complaint and nearly one year after civil rights plaintiff learned that police department would not accept service on police officer's behalf. Fed. Rules Civ.Proc.Rule 4(j), 28 U.S.C.A.; N.Y.McKinney's CPLR 308, subd. 5.

Martin v. City of New York, 627 F.Supp. 892.

E.D.N.Y. 1985. Plaintiffs' failure to make proper service upon defendant, a California corporation, did not entitle defendant to dismissal of complaint but, rather, service would be quashed, with leave granted to plaintiffs to attempt valid service.

Daley v. ALIA, 105 F.R.D. 87.

N.D.N.Y. 1998. Civil rights plaintiff's failure to identify and serve with process 17 John Doe defendants and one Jane Roe defendant warranted dismissal of all claims against unidentified defendants, where plaintiff had over two years to locate and serve them, and failed to locate or serve even one despite being warned by trial court that his failure to do so within reasonable time would result in dismissal of his claims.

Pravda v. City of Albany, 178 F.R.D. 25.

N.D.N.Y. 1997. Although hyper-technicality of error in inmate's attempted service on "Dr. Hammock," when defendant was in fact "Dr. Hammack," may have constituted "good cause" for court to allow extension of time for service on defendant in year complaint was filed, court would not deem service to have been effected seven years later, on eve of trial, where inmate had been represented by counsel since year complaint was filed, and thus, defendant would be dismissed. Fed.Rules Civ.Proc.Rule 4(m), 28 U.S.C.A.

Webber v. Hammack, 973 F.Supp. 116.

N.D.N.Y. 1996. Prison official, in inmate's pro se and in forma pauperis civil rights action, was entitled to insist upon personal service by Marshals Service in strict compliance with procedural rule, notwithstanding fact that prison official had actual knowledge of inmate's action; however, case would not be dismissed for Marshals Service's initial failure to make proper service. Fed.Rules Civ.Proc.Rule 4(e), 28 U.S.C.A.

Hurlburt v. Zaunbrecher, 169 F.R.D. 258.

N.D.N.Y. 1995. District court would not dismiss action for failure to serve defendants within 120 days after filing of complaint; service was perfected only two days beyond 120–day period, and applicable statute of limitations would bar plaintiff's refiling of action. Fed. Rules Civ.Proc.Rule 4(m), 28 U.S.C.A.

> Board of Trustees of Trucking Employees of North Jersey Welfare Fund v. Canny, 876 F.Supp. 14.

N.D.N.Y. 1994. Requirement that action be dismissed without prejudice if service of summons and complaint is not made on defendant within 120 days of filing creates rebuttable presumption in favor of dismissal. Fed.Rules Civ.Proc.Rule 4(j), 28 U.S.C.App.(1988 Ed.)

> Knorr v. Coughlin, 159 F.R.D. 5.

New rule governing dismissal of case for failure to effect timely service, which called for increased leniency for those who attempt timely service in good faith, would not prevent dismissal where pleading was not effected in timely fashion and no good cause was shown. Fed. Rules Civ.Proc.Rule 4(m), 28 U.S.C.A.; Rule 4(j), 28 U.S.C.App.(1988 Ed.)

> Knorr v. Coughlin, 159 F.R.D. 5.

Fact that dismissal of action for failure to serve summons in timely fashion might affect statute of limitations with regard to action as whole did not compel court to excuse violation. Fed.Rules Civ.Proc.Rule 4(m), 28 U.S.C.A.; Rule 4(j), 28 U.S.C.App.(1988 Ed.)

> Knorr v. Coughlin, 159 F.R.D. 5.

N.D.N.Y. 1989. Civil rights claim against proprietor of "juice bar" would be dismissed on ground that service was mailed to him 120 days after the complaint was filed where no good cause had been shown for late service of process. Fed.Rules Civ.Proc.Rule 4(j), 28 U.S.C.A.

> Woolfolk v. Thomas, 725 F.Supp. 1281.

S.D.N.Y. 1998. Complaint would not be dismissed for failure to serve defendants within 120 days of filing, even though personal service was not accomplished until 54 days after expiration of 120-day period; service by mail gave defendants actual knowledge of suit on or about 120 days after filing. Fed.Rules Civ.Proc.Rule 4(f), 28 U.S.C.A.

> Barcher v. New York University School of Law, 993 F.Supp. 177.

S.D.N.Y. 1997. District court would dismiss pro se, in forma pauperis plaintiff's employment discrimination action sua sponte where plaintiff failed to effect service upon defendant more than 1,250 days after filing of complaint, which was 1,100 days after judge had granted extension of time, plaintiff offered no excuse for his failure to effect timely service, plaintiff did not make reasonable effort to effect timely service, and U.S. Marshal's Service was unable to effect service because of outdated information provided by plaintiff. Fed.Rules Civ.Proc.Rule 4(m), 28 U.S.C.A.

> Gowan v. Teamsters Union (237), 170 F.R.D. 356.

S.D.N.Y. 1996. City employee's claims under New York City Human Rights Law would not be dismissed for failure to serve the relevant parties prior to commencement of suit; to dismiss employee's claims and have her refile them the following day would be to exalt form over substance and employee filed copies of her original complaint with corporation counsel and Human Rights Commission (HRC) subsequent to commencing action and furthermore, she filed copies of her first amended complaint with both entities prior to service on court, such that both HRC and corporation counsel were now aware of this litigation. New York City, N.Y., Administrative Code § 8–502(c).

> McNulty v. New York City Dept. of Finance, 941 F.Supp. 452.

S.D.N.Y. 1996. If good cause is not established for failure to serve summons and complaint upon defendant within 120 days of filing of complaint, court has discretion to dismiss case without prejudice or extend time for service. Fed.Rules Civ.Proc.Rule 4(m), 28 U.S.C.A.

> Mejia v. Castle Hotel, Inc., 164 F.R.D. 343.

S.D.N.Y. 1995. Defendant in civil rights action who had never been served with process and had not answered or otherwise appeared in the action would be dismissed from the action without prejudice, absent showing by pro se civil litigant that good cause existed for failure to serve defendant. Fed.Rules Civ.Proc.Rule 4(m), 28 U.S.C.A.

> Landy v. Irizarry, 884 F.Supp. 788.

Where plaintiff is proceeding pro se in forma pauperis and has been forced to depend upon government for execution of service, care must be taken not to penalize plaintiff for failings of the government, for purposes of determining whether action should be dismissed for failure to serve defendant within time required. Fed.Rules Civ.Proc.Rule 4(m), 28 U.S.C.A.

> Landy v. Irizarry, 884 F.Supp. 788.

S.D.N.Y. 1995. If service of process is not effected within 120 days, the action must be dismissed without prejudice only in the absence of good cause. Fed.Rules Civ.Proc.Rule 4(m), 28 U.S.C.A.

> Stoenescu v. Jablonsky, 162 F.R.D. 268.

S.D.N.Y. 1992. Dismissal of complaint is mandatory, where plaintiff cannot establish "good cause" for failing to effect service in timely fashion. Fed.Rules Civ.Proc.Rule 4(j), 28 U.S.C.A.

> In re Chaus Securities Litigation, 801 F.Supp. 1257.

S.D.N.Y. 1991. Since rule of civil procedure governing time limit for service of process is aimed at ensuring diligent prosecution of civil cases, unless plaintiff can show good cause or excusable neglect for untimely service, complaint must be dismissed. Fed.Rules Civ.Proc. Rule 4(j), 28 U.S.C.A.

> Tillman v. New York State Dept. of Mental Health, 776 F.Supp. 841, affirmed 963 F.2d 1521.

S.D.N.Y. 1991. Although mailed service on city, mayor, and city human rights commission was inadequate, as service on those defendants had to be effected by personal service, dismissal was not warranted absent any showing of prejudice. Fed.Rules Civ.Proc.Rule 4(d)(6), 28 U.S.C.A.; N.Y.McKinney's CPLR 311, 312.

> Linares v. City of White Plains, 773 F.Supp. 559.

S.D.N.Y. 1990. Rule providing for dismissal of defendant not timely served when good cause for failure to timely serve defendant is not shown makes no exception for situations in which refiling of complaint would be time barred. Fed.Rules Civ.Proc.Rule 4(j), 28 U.S.C.A.

> Shaw v. Rolex Watch U.S.A., Inc., 745 F.Supp. 982.

S.D.N.Y. 1990. Petitioner's claim of violation of his civil rights was not served upon police officers within 120 days of filing of complaint, and, thus, action was subject to dismissal without prejudice. Fed.Rules Civ.Proc.Rule 4(j), 28 U.S.C.A.

> Hodge v. Ruperto, 739 F.Supp. 873.

S.D.N.Y. 1990. Dismissal is not invariably required when service of process is improper. Fed.Rules Civ.Proc.Rule 12, 28 U.S.C.A.

> Aries Ventures Ltd. v. Axa Finance S.A., 729 F.Supp. 289.

Quashing service, instead of dismissing case, was more appropriate remedy for improper service of defendant, where defendant had actual notice of action and had defended it for three years; case would not be dismissed against defendant, and plaintiffs would be directed to serve defendant properly if they wished to provide court with jurisdiction over defendant.

> Aries Ventures Ltd. v. Axa Finance S.A., 729 F.Supp. 289.

S.D.N.Y. 1990. Plaintiff demonstrated good cause for failing to serve defendant within 120 days of filing of complaint and, therefore, defendant was not entitled to have complaint dismissed; plaintiff's attorneys were reasonably diligent in retaining otherwise trusted firm to locate defendant and monitoring that firm's progress, plaintiff's attorneys attempted to seek enlargement of time for service of process demonstrating that they were aware of their obligations and were attempting to comply with them, and there was no cognizable prejudice

apparent from service of defendant, at the latest, 23 days after the 120–day period had expired. Fed.Rules Civ.Proc.Rule 4(j), 28 U.S.C.A.

> National Union Fire Ins. Co. of Pittsburgh, Pa. v. Barney Associates, 130 F.R.D. 291, 111 A.L.R. Fed. 849.

"Prejudice" under rule, providing for dismissal of action if service of summons and complaint is not made upon defendant within 120 days after filing of complaint and there is prejudice to defendant from delay, involves impairment of defendant's ability to defend on the merits, rather than merely foregoing procedural or technical advantage. Fed.Rules Civ.Proc. Rule 4(j), 28 U.S.C.A.

> National Union Fire Ins. Co. of Pittsburgh, Pa. v. Barney Associates, 130 F.R.D. 291, 111 A.L.R. Fed. 849.

S.D.N.Y. 1989. Failure of plaintiffs to offer any cause for their failure to serve remaining defendants months after having retained counsel required dismissal of plaintiffs' action against those defendants. Fed.Rules Civ.Proc. Rule 4(j), 28 U.S.C.A.

> Eggink v. City of New York Human Resources Admin., 126 F.R.D. 32.

S.D.N.Y. 1988. Plaintiff's failure to serve defendant within 120–day period, after having received notice that defendant claimed he had not been served, without showing of good cause or without seeking to enhance service period warranted dismissal of defendant for lack of service. Fed.Rules Civ.Proc.Rule 4(j), 28 U.S.C.A.

> Reed Holdings Inc. v. O.P.C. Corp., 122 F.R.D. 441.

S.D.N.Y. 1987. Federal civil rights plaintiff's claim would not be dismissed, even though plaintiff's counsel failed to show good cause for her failure to serve defendants within 120 days; plaintiff's counsel had appeared before district court previously, showing difficulty in attending conferences and meeting deadlines, and plaintiff would not be required to suffer for such conduct, particularly in view of fact that summons was served only one month late and defendants had suffered no prejudice. Fed. Rules Civ.Proc.Rule 4(j), 28 U.S.C.A.

> Baptiste v. Cavendish Club, Inc., 670 F.Supp. 108.

S.D.N.Y. 1987. Plaintiff's failure to serve defendant within 120 days of filing complaint required dismissal of action, in absence of any showing of good cause for such failure. Fed. Rules Civ.Proc.Rule 4(j), 28 U.S.C.A.

> Michelson v. Merrill Lynch, Pierce, Fenner & Smith, Inc., 669 F.Supp. 1244.

S.D.N.Y. 1987. Factual dispute as to whether service was timely affected as to certain defendants was more appropriately resolved following discovery, rather than on motion to dismiss. Fed.Rules Civ.Proc.Rules 4, 12(b)(6), 28 U.S.C.A.

> In re Gas Reclamation, Inc. Securities Litigation, 659 F.Supp. 493.

S.D.N.Y. 1987. Invalidity of attempted service of process does not necessitate dismissal of complaint; even if initial service is found to be inadequate, court has discretion to decline to dismiss in order to permit an additional attempt at service.

> Rankel v. Town of Greenburgh, 117 F.R.D. 50.

Notwithstanding failure of pro se plaintiff to properly serve municipal corporation within 120 days of filing of § 1983 action complaint as required by federal rules, action would not be dismissed in view of effectuation of prior service after 120 days, plaintiff's pro se status, his repeated, timely, though misguided, efforts at service and failure of municipal corporation to allege any prejudice due to delay in effectuation of service. 42 U.S.C.A. § 1983; Fed.Rules Civ. Proc.Rule 4(j), 28 U.S.C.A.

> Rankel v. Town of Greenburgh, 117 F.R.D. 50.

S.D.N.Y. 1987. If plaintiff fails without good cause to serve process within 120 days of filing complaint, dismissal is mandatory. Fed. Rules Civ.Proc.Rule 4(j), 28 U.S.C.A.

> Delicata v. Bowen, 116 F.R.D. 564.

S.D.N.Y. 1986. Federal civil rights claim was not subject to dismissal for insufficiency of process or failure to state claim where defendants who were previously classified as "unknown," but were subsequently named in third amended complaint, where served during permissible time period and therefore put on notice. Fed.Rules Civ.Proc.Rule 12(b), 28 U.S.C.A.; 42 U.S.C.A. § 1983.

> Surak v. Coughlin, 647 F.Supp. 97.

S.D.N.Y. 1985. Claim against Commissioner of New York State Department of Education in his individual capacity based on alleged constitutional violation in residency determination was dismissed for improper service absent indication that summons and complaint were mailed to Commissioner at his last known residence and there was no allegation of such mailing in either affidavit of service or the opposition papers, in which plaintiff made only ambiguous allegation that a copy of summons and complaint were also mailed by counsel directly to the Commissioner. Fed.Rules Civ.Proc.Rule 4(c)(2)(C)(i), 28 U.S.C.A.; N.Y.McKinney's CPLR 308, subd. 2.

> Takeall by Rubinstein v. Ambach, 609 F.Supp. 81.

S.D.N.Y. 1985. Where there was actual notice of inmate's suit, as evidenced by motion to dismiss, dismissal of prison officials in their individual capacity for insufficiency of service would be inappropriate. Fed.Rules Civ.Proc. Rules 4, 4(c)(2)(C)(ii), 28 U.S.C.A.

> Gilliam v. Quinlan, 608 F.Supp. 823.

E.D.N.C. 1985. Antitrust action was not subject to dismissal on grounds that defendant hospital had been misnamed and that complaint was served on the hospital administrator, who was not authorized to accept service for hospital, where it appeared that service could be properly made. Fed.Rules Civ.Proc.Rule 4(d)(6), 28 U.S.C.A.; N.C.Rules Civ.Proc., Rule 4(j)(5)c, G.S.§ 1A–1.

> Coastal Neuro-Psychiatric Associates, P.A. v. Onslow County Hosp. Authority, 607 F.Supp. 49.

M.D.N.C. 1996. Defendant was not entitled to dismissal for improper service of process, even though plaintiff made no attempt to serve initial summons, where plaintiff subsequently served defendant with alias and pluries summons as under North Carolina law, summons was valid process whether court treated it as original summons or as alias and pluries summons; any failure to attempt to serve original summons did not invalidate alias and pluries summons. Fed.Rules Civ.Proc.Rule 12(b)(5), 28 U.S.C.A.; N.C.Rules Civ.Proc., Rule 4(c), (d)(2), G.S. § 1A–1.

> CBP Resources, Inc. v. Ingredient Resource Corp., 954 F.Supp. 1106.

Civil defendant would not be entitled to dismissal, even if service of process was defective, as plaintiff would be allowed under federal rules to perfect service of process at time defendant challenged it. 28 U.S.C.A. § 1448; Fed. Rules Civ.Proc.Rule 12(b)(5), 28 U.S.C.A.

> CBP Resources, Inc. v. Ingredient Resource Corp., 954 F.Supp. 1106.

M.D.N.C. 1996. Motion under rule governing insufficiency of service of process is appropriate means for challenging manner or sufficiency of service of process. Fed.Rules Civ.Proc.Rule 12(b)(5), 28 U.S.C.A.

> Plant Genetic Systems, N.V. v. Ciba Seeds, 933 F.Supp. 519.

Corporate defendant was not entitled to dismissal on ground of insufficiency of service of process, despite initial insufficient service on defendant's parent corporation; after being informed of problem with service of process, plaintiff effected service on defendant by personal service on defendant's president, and defendant did not suffer any prejudice as result of initial difficulty in effecting service of process. Fed.Rules Civ.Proc.Rule 12(b)(5), 28 U.S.C.A.

> Plant Genetic Systems, N.V. v. Ciba Seeds, 933 F.Supp. 519.

Dismissal for insufficiency of service of process is not justified where it appears that service can be properly made. Fed.Rules Civ.Proc.Rule 12(b)(5), 28 U.S.C.A.

> Plant Genetic Systems, N.V. v. Ciba Seeds, 933 F.Supp. 519.

D.N.D. 1986. Where plaintiffs had not attempted to effect service on parties identified only by official title and not named, complaint would be dismissed as against those parties to the extent that suit was against them in their individual capacities.

> Lathan v. Block, 627 F.Supp. 397.

N.D.Ohio 1990. Dismissal of Racketeer Influenced and Corrupt Organizations Act (RICO) claims against foreign corporations based on improper service was premature, although RICO did not authorize foreign service of process, where it had not been determined whether service of process was proper under state long-arm statute or Foreign Sovereign Immunities Act. 18 U.S.C.A. § 1965; 28 U.S.C.A. § 1601 et seq.; Fed.Rules Civ.Proc. Rule 4(i), 28 U.S.C.A.

> Gould, Inc. v. Mitsui Min. & Smelting Co., Ltd., 750 F.Supp. 838.

E.D.Pa. 1998. District court has broad discretion in deciding whether to dismiss complaint for insufficient service. Fed.Rules Civ. Proc.Rule 12(b)(5), 28 U.S.C.A.

> Dill v. Com. of Pa., 3 F.Supp.2d 583.

Dismissal of a complaint for insufficient service is inappropriate when there exists a reasonable prospect that service may yet be obtained. Fed.Rules Civ.Proc.Rule 12(b)(5), 28 U.S.C.A.

> Dill v. Com. of Pa., 3 F.Supp.2d 583.

E.D.Pa. 1998. If good cause is shown for an extension of time in which to complete service, district court must extend time for service and inquiry is ended; however, if good cause is not shown, court may, in its own discretion, decide whether to dismiss the case without prejudice or extend the time for service. Fed.Rules Civ.Proc.Rule 4(m), 28 U.S.C.A.

> Suegart v. U.S. Customs Service, 180 F.R.D. 276.

E.D.Pa. 1993. Complaint as to one defendant was subject to dismissal without prejudice due to plaintiff's failure to serve that defendant within 120-day limit and failure to demonstrate good cause for untimely service or to show why claim of untimely service might have been waived. Fed.Rules Civ.Proc.Rules 4(j), 12(b), (h)(1), 28 U.S.C.A.

> Seal v. Riverside Federal Sav. Bank, 825 F.Supp. 686.

E.D.Pa. 1993. If no good cause can be shown for failure to accomplish service within 120 days from filing of complaint, action must be dismissed, as dictated by mandatory language "shall" in rule imposing 120–day period. Fed.Rules Civ.Proc.Rules 4(j), 6(b)(2), 28 U.S.C.A.

> Nelle v. Ciotti, 151 F.R.D. 568.

E.D.Pa. 1991. Pro se plaintiff's second amended complaint would be dismissed for insufficiency of service of process, though pursuant to in forma pauperis statute district court had ordered clerk's office to serve defendant, where docket sheet reflected no action by plaintiff for nearly a year and a half after district court ordered defendant to be served; at minimum, plaintiff should have requested service upon appropriate defendant and attempted to remedy any apparent service defects of which he had knowledge. Fed.Rules Civ.Proc.Rules 3, 4(j), 28 U.S.C.A.

> White v. SKF Aerospace, Inc., 768 F.Supp. 498.

E.D.Pa. 1991. Most appropriate remedy, after plaintiff's service of process on defendants' representatives was quashed under fraudulent inducement doctrine, because plaintiff had induced representatives to enter jurisdiction without clearly and unequivocally warning them that they might be served with process, was to permit plaintiff to determine whether it wished to attempt to serve defendants by other means or to have complaint dismissed where court could not determine on record whether plaintiff would be able to properly serve defendant corporations. Fed.Rules Civ.Proc.Rule 12(b)(5), 28 U.S.C.A.

> Henkel Corp. v. Degremont, S.A., 136 F.R.D. 88.

E.D.Pa. 1988. Inadvertence of counsel cannot provide basis for finding "good cause" so as not to require dismissal of action when service of summons and complaint is not made on defendant within 120 days of filing; nor can it provide basis for permitting extension of time to effect service. Fed.Rules Civ.Proc.Rule 4(j), 28 U.S.C.A.

> In re City of Philadelphia Litigation, 123 F.R.D. 515.

Dismissal of complaint, in action in which defendants were served with complaint but not summons within 120 days of filing, was required, despite plaintiffs' claims that defendants had actual notice of actions and suffered no prejudice and that defendants should not benefit by having withheld its objection to service until after expiration of limitations period. Fed Rules Civ.Proc.Rule 4(j), 28 U.S.C.A.

> In re City of Philadelphia Litigation, 123 F.R.D. 515.

E.D.Pa. 1988. In order for court to find "good cause" not to dismiss action when service of summons and complaint is not made on defendant within 120 days of filing, plaintiff must have taken whatever additional steps were necessary to insure that service was completed within 120 days. Fed.Rules Civ.Proc.Rule 4(j), 28 U.S.C.A.

> In re City of Philadelphia Litigation, 123 F.R.D. 512.

Complaint against former city employees, who were not served with summons and complaint within 120 days of filing, was required to be dismissed, despite plaintiff's contention that city refused to accept service on former employees' behalf. Fed.Rules Civ.Proc.Rules 4, 4(j), 28 U.S.C.A.

> In re City of Philadelphia Litigation, 123 F.R.D. 512.

W.D.Pa. 1989. Party against whom service was apparently not attempted, perhaps because it was now defunct, could be dismissed from action for breach of contract and fraud.

> Obenchain Corp. v. Corporacion Nacionale de Inversiones, 708 F.Supp. 695, appeal dismissed 884 F.2d 1384, affirmed in part, vacated in part 898 F.2d 142.

W.D.Pa. 1985. Under Federal Civil Rule 4(j), failure to effect service upon defendant within 120 days after filing of complaint, absent showing of good cause, warrants mandatory, rather than discretionary, dismissal of complaint. Fed.Rules Civ.Proc.Rule 4(j), 28 U.S.C.A.

> Shuster v. Conley, 107 F.R.D. 755.

D.Puerto Rico 1997. Court would sua sponte dismiss "Doe" defendants where complaint had been filed more than 18 months earlier and plaintiffs had not substituted fictitious defendants to be able to serve summons. Fed.Rules Civ.Proc.Rule 4(j), 28 U.S.C.A.

> Velazquez-Martinez v. Colon, 961 F.Supp. 362.

D.Puerto Rico 1997. Prison officials' failure to receive full copy of inmate's pro se complaint did not require dismissal of inmate's action, absent showing of prejudice.

> Dodson v. Reno, 958 F.Supp. 49, affirmed 125 F.3d 841.

D.Puerto Rico 1993. Failure to serve unnamed defendant with summons within 120 days of filing of complaint required dismissal of action against unnamed defendant. Fed.Rules Civ.Proc.Rules 4(j), 15(c), (c)(3), 28 U.S.C.A.

> Carmona Pacheco v. Betancourt y Lebron, 820 F.Supp. 45.

D.Puerto Rico 1991. Action claiming securities fraud, fraud, and breach of contract by plaintiff's brother and brother's wife would be dismissed without prejudice where plaintiff failed timely to perfect service on his brother, brother's wife and their conjugal partnership. Fed.Rules Civ.Proc.Rule 4(j), 28 U.S.C.A.

> Ades v. Ades, 769 F.Supp. 48.

D.Puerto Rico 1991. Claims against Puerto Rican physician whose malpractice allegedly resulted in death of seaman and against New York corporation who was allegedly seaman's employer and owner or operator of ship would be dismissed where there was no proof of service. Fed.Rules Civ.Proc.Rules 4, 4(j), 28 U.S.C.A.

> Theordros v. Farida Shipping, Inc., 762 F.Supp. 10.

D.Puerto Rico 1988. Though district courts have broad discretion to dismiss complaint for failure to effect service, dismissal is not appropriate when there exists a reasonable prospect that service can be obtained.

> Suarez v. Chairman of Bd. of Directors of Federal Deposit Ins. Corp., 692 F.Supp. 43, opinion vacated in part on reconsideration 707 F.Supp. 623.

D.Puerto Rico 1987. Plaintiff's motion to appoint a United States Marshal as a special process server did not toll the 120–day service period, and failure to serve within 120 days after first attempted service was quashed warranted dismissal of claim; despite motion for appointment of marshal, plaintiff nonetheless was aware that service had to be effectuated again upon quashing of initial service, and plaintiff made no showing of good cause as to why service was not made even after the defendant filed a motion to dismiss. Fed.Rules Civ. Proc.Rule 4(j), 28 U.S.C.A.

> Roig v. Chandris, Inc., 117 F.R.D. 324.

D.Puerto Rico 1986. Absent amendment of caption of complaint within 120 days to correct designation of defendant improperly designated and absent service of summons upon other named defendants within 120 days, civil rights action was dismissed against such defendants. Fed.Rules Civ.Proc.Rule 4(j), 28 U.S.C.A.

> Batista Malave v. Com. of Puerto Rico, 631 F.Supp. 936.

D.Puerto Rico 1986. Dismissal was mandatory, rather than discretionary, for failure to comply with 120–day limit for service of process, where good cause was not shown why such service was not made within specified time period. Fed.Rules Civ.Proc.Rule 4(j), 28 U.S.C.A.

> Barco Arroyo v. Federal Emergency Management Agency, 113 F.R.D. 46.

D.R.I. 1990. In ruling on motion to dismiss because of failure to timely effect service, court may grant some leniency to pro se plaintiff who diligently pursues his claim. Fed.Rules Civ.Proc.Rule 4(j), 28 U.S.C.A.

> D'Amario v. Russo, 750 F.Supp. 560.

E.D.Tenn. 1996. That dismissal of complaint might terminate litigation completely is not legitimate reason to disregard mandate that complaint be dismissed after expiration of 120–day period without service of process, absent showing of good cause. Fed.Rules Civ.Proc. Rule 4(m), 28 U.S.C.A.

> In re Southern Indus. Banking Corp., 205 B.R. 525, affirmed 112 F.3d 248, rehearing and suggestion for rehearing denied.

W.D.Tenn. 1991. Dismissal of complaint, even though statute of limitations has run, was required where plaintiff had no justifiable excuse for its failure personally to serve United States as required to appeal social security disability benefits denial, notwithstanding plaintiff's alleged reliance on nongovernment handbook, which stated that service might be effected upon United States by certified mail; counsel's attempt to use certified mail to serve United States could not demonstrate justifiable excuse. Fed.Rules Civ.Proc.Rule 4(d)(5), 28 U.S.C.A.

> Dowdy v. Sullivan, 138 F.R.D. 99.

Under rule requiring that action be dismissed if service of summons and complaint is not made upon defendant within 120 days after filing of complaint, plaintiff failed to show "good cause" for exception to dismissal based on its mistaken attempt to serve United States by certified mail rather than personal service, even though plaintiff allegedly relied upon handbook which erroneously stated that service might be effected by certified mail; mistake did not rise above simple inadvertence or mistake of counsel to establish "good cause." Fed.Rules Civ.Proc.Rule 4(j), 28 U.S.C.A.

> Dowdy v. Sullivan, 138 F.R.D. 99.

W.D.Tenn. 1986. No prejudice to defendant need be shown in order to dismiss action for failure to timely serve defendant pursuant to Rule 4(j). Fed.Rules Civ.Proc.Rule 4(j), 28 U.S.C.A.

> Boykin v. Commerce Union Bank of Union City, Tenn., 109 F.R.D. 344.

S.D.Tex. 1995. Rule providing that court may dismiss complaint without prejudice if service is not made within 120 days after filing of complaint did not apply where service was in a foreign county, and, in any event, plaintiff

would be allowed reasonable time within which to attempt to serve defendant in accordance with Hague Convention where plaintiff believed in good faith that he properly served defendant under state long-arm statute. Hague Convention on the Service Abroad of Judicial and Extrajudicial Documents in Civil or Commercial Matters, Art. 1 et seq.; Fed.Rules Civ.Proc.Rule 4 note, 28 U.S.C.A.; Fed.Rules Civ.Proc.Rule 4(m), 28 U.S.C.A.

> Sang Young Kim v. Frank Mohn A/S, 909 F.Supp. 474.

S.D.Tex. 1994. Court would dismiss discrimination suit against Secretary of Navy, rather than extending time to serve, where Attorney General was never served, even after that deficiency was called to plaintiff's attention by defendant's motion to dismiss. Fed.Rules Civ. Proc.Rule 4(m), 28 U.S.C.A.

> Flores v. Secretary of Navy, 159 F.R.D. 472, affirmed 51 F.3d 1044.

S.D.Tex. 1994. Plaintiff's attempted service on corporate defendant was defective, and plaintiff failed to show good cause in order to prevent dismissal, under rule in effect at time plaintiff filed complaint, where plaintiff failed to provide corporation with copy of complaint, where plaintiff left copy of summons and return of service with security guard employed by defendant, and thus, did not follow rule requiring that plaintiff serving corporate defendant deliver copy of summons and complaint to officer, managing or general agent, or to any other agent authorized by appointment or by law to receive service, and where plaintiff never properly served corporation though plaintiff had both notice that his attempted service of process on corporation was defective and an opportunity to correct defect within 120–day period. Fed.Rules Civ.Proc.Rule 4(d)(3), (j), 28 U.S.C.(1988 Ed.).

> Boltes v. Entex, 158 F.R.D. 110.

S.D.Tex. 1987. Supplemental complaint, which could not relate back to initial filing of suit and had never been served, would be dismissed for insufficiency of service; even if granting of motion for extension of time could be construed as granting of leave for filing and service of supplemental complaint, defendant would be unduly prejudiced by relation back. Fed.Rules Civ.Proc.Rule 15(c), 28 U.S.C.A.

> Ruston v. General Telephone Co. of the Southwest, 115 F.R.D. 330.

D.Utah 1995. "Good cause," such as complainant must show to avoid dismissal of complaint based on its failure to effect service in timely fashion, is not to be equated with "excusable neglect," such as party must show to be relieved of bankruptcy deadline; standards are not identical, and factors applicable to "excusable neglect" analysis are not likewise applicable in deciding whether "good cause" exists for untimely service of summons and complaint. Fed.Rules Bankr.Proc.Rules 7004(a), 9006(b)(1), 11 U.S.C.A.; Fed.Rules Civ.Proc. Rule 4(j), 28 U.S.C.App.(1988 Ed.)

> In re Kirkland, 181 B.R. 563, affirmed 86 F.3d 172.

Complainant who does not effect timely service of summons and complaint has burden of showing "good cause" for delay, in order to avoid dismissal for lack of timely service. Fed. Rules Bankr.Proc.Rule 7004(a), 11 U.S.C.A.; Fed.Rules Civ.Proc.Rule 4(j), 28 U.S.C.App.(1988 Ed.)

> In re Kirkland, 181 B.R. 563, affirmed 86 F.3d 172.

"Good cause," such as complainant must demonstrate to prevent dismissal of complaint for failure to effect timely service of process, is not to be equated with mere inadvertence or mistake. Fed.Rules Bankr.Proc.Rule 7004(a), 11 U.S.C.A.; Fed.Rules Civ.Proc.Rule 4(j), 28 U.S.C.App.(1988 Ed.)

> In re Kirkland, 181 B.R. 563, affirmed 86 F.3d 172.

D.Utah 1993. Dismissal of employment discrimination action was required by employee's failure to effectively serve employer with summons and complaint within 120 days after filing complaint, even though attorney's mistake was reason first attempt at service was ineffective; attorney's mistake was not such "good cause" as would justify relief from time requirement absent explanation from employee as to why he waited until last minute before first attempting service. Fed.Rules Civ.Proc.Rule 4(j), 28 U.S.C.A.

> Cloyd v. Arthur Anderson & Co., 151 F.R.D. 407, affirmed 25 F.3d 1056.

D.Vt. 1996. Determining whether extension of time for service based on good cause for failure to serve within 120 days is appropriate invokes two-part analysis under which, first, court must decide whether good cause exists, and, if good cause exists, plaintiff receives extension and inquiry is ended, but, if good cause is not shown, court proceeds to second part of analysis to decide whether to dismiss case without prejudice or to extend time for service. Fed.Rules Civ.Proc.Rule 4(m), 28 U.S.C.A.

> Goodstein v. Bombardier Capital, Inc., 167 F.R.D. 662.

D.Vt. 1996. Rule governing time limit for service permits court to dismiss complaint without prejudice or to direct that service be accomplished within given time period if 120–day period for service has expired. Fed.Rules Civ. Proc.Rule 4(m), 28 U.S.C.A.

> O'Keefe v. St. Lawrence & Atlantic R. Co., 167 F.R.D. 30.

E.D.Va. 1996. Under former civil procedure rule authorizing plaintiff to send copy of complaint and summons, along with form acknowledging receipt of complaint and waiving formal service, failure of defendant to sign and return acknowledgment form required that plaintiff personally serve defendant, and failure to do so constituted ground for dismissal of claims. Fed.Rules Civ.Proc.Rule 4(c)(2)(C)(ii), 28 U.S.C.A.

> Jones v. Navix Line, Ltd., 944 F.Supp. 468.

E.D.Va. 1986. Nonresident corporations were amenable to service of process by the Secretary of the Commonwealth of Virginia, and thus, declaratory judgment action seeking determination that nonresident corporations' patents were invalid, unenforceable, and not infringed did not have to be dismissed for insufficiency of process; exercise of personal jurisdiction over nonresident corporations was authorized under the Virginia long-arm statute. Fed.Rules Civ.Proc.Rule 12(b)(5), 28 U.S.C.A.; Va.Code 1950, §§ 8.01–328.1, 8.01–329.

> Furmanite America, Inc. v. Durango Associates, Inc., 662 F.Supp. 348.

W.D.Va. 1988. Even if defendants were never properly served within 120 days after filing of complaint, it would have been inappropriate to dismiss action; defendants received actual notice of pendency of action as a result of plaintiff's first three attempts at service of process. Fed.Rules Civ.Proc.Rule 4(j), 28 U.S.C.A.

> Selman v. American Sports Underwriters, Inc., 697 F.Supp. 225.

E.D.Wash. 1997. Pro se plaintiff's failure to comply with requirements for service upon United States does not require dismissal of complaint if party to be personally served had actual notice, defendant would suffer no prejudice from defect in service, there is justifiable excuse for failure to serve properly, and plaintiff would be severely prejudiced if complaint were dismissed. Fed.Rules Civ.Proc.Rule 4(i), 28 U.S.C.A.

> Humphrey v. Decker, 173 F.R.D. 529.

E.D.Wash. 1995. Taxpayers' failure to demonstrate that they made proper service of process on the United States, despite being reminded by court order, necessitated dismissal of refund or quiet title action. Fed.Rules Civ. Proc.Rules 4(i)(1, 2), 12(b)(5), 28 U.S.C.A.

> Russell v. Rook, 893 F.Supp. 949.

W.D.Wash. 1987. Dismissal for failure to properly serve summons and complaint on defendant within 120 days after filing of complaint is mandatory, rather than discretionary, unless good cause is shown. Fed.Rules Civ.Proc.Rule 4(j), 28 U.S.C.A.

> Mathis v. Boeing Co., 117 F.R.D. 167.

W.D.Wash. 1987. Dismissal of action without prejudice as to defendant is mandatory if plaintiff cannot show good cause why service of summons and complaint was not made upon defendant within 120 days. Fed.Rules Civ.Proc. Rule 4(j), 28 U.S.C.A.

Bryant v. Rohr Industries, Inc., 116 F.R.D. 530.

N.D.W.Va. 1996. In order to withstand motion to dismiss complaint for insufficiency of service of process, plaintiffs who failed to comply with time requirements for serving defendants must demonstrate that they had good cause for not meeting those requirements; trial court does not have discretion to extend time absent showing of good cause. Fed.Rules Civ. Proc.Rules 4(m), 12(b)(5), 28 U.S.C.A.

T & S Rentals v. U.S., 164 F.R.D. 422.

N.D.W.Va. 1992. Phrase "without prejudice" in rule mandating dismissal of action without prejudice absent showing of good cause for delay in service of summons and complaint does not mean "without consequence." Fed. Rules Civ.Proc.Rule 4(j), 28 U.S.C.A.

Vincent v. Reynolds Memorial Hosp., Inc., 141 F.R.D. 436.

S.D.W.Va. 1985. Normally, court should quash service of process rather than dismiss it if there is possibility that effective service can be had upon defendant.

Pittsburgh Terminal Corp. v. Mid Allegheny Corp., 110 F.R.D. 4.

District court would dismiss action where plaintiff had attempted, unsuccessfully, all probable methods of obtaining effective service of process on defendants.

Pittsburgh Terminal Corp. v. Mid Allegheny Corp., 110 F.R.D. 4.

E.D.Wis. 1993. *Bivens* claim that certain unknown federal agents had violated civil rights of aircraft importer, in connection with search of premises and sending of questionnaire to customers, would be dismissed following the dismissal of all claims against United States and five named government employees in their personal and official capacities; unknown agents had never been served with process or identified, and legal conclusions made in present case as basis for dismissing claims raised would apply to same claims raised against any federal defendant sued in his or her official capacity. Fed.Rules Civ.Proc.Rule 12(b), 28 U.S.C.A.

Wag-Aero, Inc. v. U.S., 837 F.Supp. 1479, affirmed 35 F.3d 569, rehearing denied.

E.D.Wis. 1989. Pro se plaintiff's claim against federal official would not be dismissed for improper service; justice would require court to explain to plaintiff how to serve defendant and to give plaintiff opportunity to serve defendant properly and move to vacate dismiss-

al order, and thus dismissal order would merely postpone court from hearing and deciding substantive issue. Fed.Rules Civ.Proc.Rule 4(d)(4), 28 U.S.C.A.

Fricton v. Oconto County ASCS, USDA, 723 F.Supp. 1312.

E.D.Wis. 1985. Insureds' claim against person to whom homeowners' policy was allegedly assigned would be dismissed without prejudice pursuant to Federal Civil Rule 4(j) and Local Rule 10.01, unless good cause for failure to obtain service would be demonstrated, where file contained no proof of service on such person, he had not answered or otherwise appeared, and more than six months had elapsed since claims were filed. Fed.Rules Civ.Proc. Rule 4(j), 28 U.S.C.A.; U.S.Dist.Ct.Rules E.D.Wis., Rule 10.01.

Kopke v. Miller, 611 F.Supp. 273.

9th Cir.BAP (Wash.) 1994. Plaintiff's failure to serve Chapter 13 debtor with copy of filed complaint in adversary proceeding within 120 days after filing required dismissal of proceeding. Fed.Rules Civ.Proc.Rule 4(a, j), 28 U.S.C.A.; Fed.Rules Bankr.Proc.Rule 7004(a), 11 U.S.C.A.

In re Van Meter, 175 B.R. 64.

Congress balanced hardship of having case dismissed without possibility of refiling against policy of moving cases promptly through courts when it enacted court rule providing that courts shall dismiss complaint served over 120 days after its filing, unless good cause for untimely service has been shown. Fed.Rules Civ.Proc. Rule 4(j), 28 U.S.C.A.

In re Van Meter, 175 B.R. 64.

Bkrtcy.E.D.Ark. 1988. Mere inadvertence of plaintiff's counsel does not constitute "good cause" under rule requiring dismissal of complaint if defendant is not served within 120 days, unless party required to make service shows "good cause" why service was not made. Fed.Rules Civ.Proc.Rules 4, 4(d)(3), (j), 28 U.S.C.A.; Rules Bankr.Proc.Rule 7004(b)(3), 11 U.S.C.A.

In re Hollis and Co., 86 B.R. 152.

"Good cause" existed for failure to sue proper party within time limit set out in rules requiring dismissal of action for failure to serve defendant within 120 days of filing of complaint, unless "good cause" is shown, where circumstances surrounding filing of action and resulting motions for extensions of time to file preliminary motions made it reasonable for plaintiff to believe service had been accomplished. Fed.Rules Civ.Proc.Rules 4, 4(d)(3), (j), 28 U.S.C.A.; Rules Bankr.Proc.Rule 7004(b)(3), 11 U.S.C.A.

In re Hollis and Co., 86 B.R. 152.

Bkrtcy.D.Conn. 1995. Burden to demonstrate good cause for failure to serve within 120 days after the filing of the complaint, and thereby avoid dismissal without prejudice, rests with the plaintiff. Fed.Rules Bankr.Proc.Rule 7004(a), 11 U.S.C.A.; Fed.Rules Civ.Proc.Rule 4(j), 28 U.S.C.A.

In re Anderson, 179 B.R. 401.

"Good cause" existed to excuse creditor's failure to effect proper service upon Chapter 7 debtors within 120 days after issuance date in nondischargeability proceeding and, thus, complaint did not have to be dismissed; debtors, who received actual notice of the nondischargeability proceeding through the untimely service of the summons and complaint 11 days after the issuance date and whose attorney was served with a copy of the creditor's default judgment motion within the 120–day service window, remained passive until the 120–day period expired, and this inaction was a conscious attempt to delay the proceeding and to obtain the technical windfall of a dismissal with its attendant prejudicial effect due to the expiration of the bar date for nondischargeability complaints. Fed.Rules Bankr.Proc.Rule 7004(a, f), 11 U.S.C.A.; Fed.Rules Civ.Proc.Rule 4(j), 28 U.S.C.A.

In re Anderson, 179 B.R. 401.

Chapter 7 debtors, who received actual notice of nondischargeability proceeding through the untimely service of the summons and complaint 11 days after the issuance date and whose attorney was served with a copy of the creditor's default judgment motion within the 120–day service window, waived any benefit they might otherwise achieve, under rule requiring dismissal if good cause does not exist for failing to serve the summons and complaint within the 120–day service window, by their conscious inaction in waiting until 120–day period had expired to move to vacate the default and for summary judgment. Fed.Rules Bankr.Proc. Rule 7004(a, f), 11 U.S.C.A.; Fed.Rules Civ. Proc.Rule 4(j), 28 U.S.C.A.

In re Anderson, 179 B.R. 401.

Bkrtcy.D.Md. 1991. Creditor's nondischargeability complaint had to be dismissed for failure to obtain service upon Chapter 7 debtors within 120 days after the filing of the complaint; creditor's unsuccessful attempts to obtain service by private process server and by certified mail did not fulfill the requirement of showing good cause why service was not made, when creditor did not attempt service by first class mail as permitted by the bankruptcy rules. Fed.Rules Bankr.Proc.Rules 7004, 7004(a), (b)(9), 11 U.S.C.A.; Fed.Rules Civ.Proc.Rule 4(j), 28 U.S.C.A.

In re Heinz, 131 B.R. 38.

Dismissal for failure to serve within 120 days after filing the complaint is not unwarranted simply because the limitations period has run. Fed.Rules Civ.Proc.Rule 4(j), 28 U.S.C.A.

In re Heinz, 131 B.R. 38.

When determining whether to dismiss complaint for failure to serve summons within 120 days, courts look to the reasonableness and the diligence of the efforts to serve the papers. Fed.Rules Civ.Proc.Rule 4(j), 28 U.S.C.A.

In re Heinz, 131 B.R. 38.

Bkrtcy.E.D.N.Y. 1985. There must be compliance with terms of rule [Fed.Rules Civ. Proc.Rule 4(d), 28 U.S.C.A.] governing service of process, and absent waiver, incomplete or improper service will lead court to dismiss action unless it appears that proper service may still be obtained.

In re Legend Industries, Inc., 49 B.R. 935.

Mere fact that service was improper does not require court to dismiss action; if proper service is still feasible, court, to avoid expense and delay involved in reinstituting action, may retain jurisdiction and quash defective service.

In re Legend Industries, Inc., 49 B.R. 935.

Trustee's service upon principal shareholder, who was not officer of corporation or managing or general agent or agent authorized to receive service, was not proper service upon corporation, but since proper service was still feasible, action would not be dismissed. Fed. Rules Civ.Proc.Rule 4(d), 28 U.S.C.A.

In re Legend Industries, Inc., 49 B.R. 935.

Bkrtcy.S.D.N.Y. 1994. On motion to dismiss for lack of personal jurisdiction in federal question case, court will not invoke traditional "minimum contacts" test if federal statute specifically authorizes service of process on a party not an inhabitant of or found within foreign state. Fed.Rules Civ.Proc.Rule 12(b)(2), 28 U.S.C.A.

In re Levant Line, S.A., 166 B.R. 221.

Bkrtcy.S.D.N.Y. 1992. Once 120 days have elapsed, after showing of good cause court may refrain from dismissing action and allow plaintiff additional time to serve complaint, but if plaintiff fails to justify insufficient service, complaint may be dismissed. Fed.Rules Civ. Proc.Rule 4(j), 28 U.S.C.A.

In re Rand, 144 B.R. 253.

Bkrtcy.S.D.N.Y. 1985. In determining whether there has been any defect in service of process, standards for service on individuals and corporations are to be liberally construed to further the purpose of finding personal jurisdiction in cases in which the party has received actual notice; however, there must be compliance with terms of the rule and, absent waiver, incomplete or improper service will lead court to dismiss the action unless it appears that proper service may still be obtained.

In re Outlet Dept. Stores, Inc., 49 B.R. 536.

Bkrtcy.S.D.N.Y. 1985. Though plaintiff in bankruptcy case can obtain reissuance of summons after failing to serve previously issued summons, outside date for service of summons is 120 days after filing of complaint; intentional delay in service of summons and complaint may justify dismissal within 120–day period. Fed. Rules Civ.Proc.Rule 4(j), 28 U.S.C.A.; Rules Bankr.Proc.Rule 7004(f), 11 U.S.C.A.

In re Dahowski, 48 B.R. 877.

Bkrtcy.D.N.D. 1985. Plaintiffs are required to use diligence in making service of process, and courts will dismiss an action where there is substantial delay between filing of complaint and service of summons.

In re Horob, 54 B.R. 693.

Bkrtcy.D.N.D. 1985. Dismissal is not required where service of process is ineffective; under such circumstances, court has discretion to either dismiss action or quash service but retain case.

In re Valeu, 53 B.R. 549.

While action is subject to dismissal for abuse of process, it is for trial court to determine what departures from its rules may be overlooked.

In re Valeu, 53 B.R. 549.

Bkrtcy.S.D.Ohio 1996. Summons and complaint must generally be served within 120 days of filing of complaint, or complaint may be dismissed without prejudice. Fed.Rules Civ. Proc.Rule 4(m), 28 U.S.C.A.

In re Tower Metal Alloy Co., 193 B.R. 266.

Bkrtcy.N.D.Tex. 1992. If summons and complaint is not served within 120 days after adversary complaint is filed, and party who should have served cannot show good cause why service was not made within that period, court shall dismiss as to that defendant, but dismissal should be without prejudice and with notice to party or upon motion. Fed.Rules Civ.Proc.Rule 4(j), 28 U.S.C.A.; Fed.Rules Bankr.Proc.Rule 7004(a, f), 11 U.S.C.A.

In re Cole, 142 B.R. 140.

⚷**1752. Affirmative defenses, raising by motion to dismiss.**

Library references

C.J.S. Federal Civil Procedure § 813.

⚷**1752.1. —— In general.**

C.A.11 (Ala.) 1996. In cases where defendants are entitled to qualified immunity, it is imperative that they receive benefits of that defense prior to trial through motions to dismiss for failure to state claim, for judgment on the pleadings, and for summary judgment; imperative results from nature of entitlement to qualified immunity, which is immunity from suit rather than mere defense to liability, and which like absolute immunity is effectively lost if case is erroneously permitted to go to trial. Fed. Rules Civ.Proc.Rules 12(b)(6), (c), 56(c), 28 U.S.C.A.

Cottrell v. Caldwell, 85 F.3d 1480.

C.A.9 (Ariz.) 1997. Government did not waive its right to seek equitable recoupment in estate tax dispute by failing to assert defense in motion to dismiss; motion to dismiss was not responsive pleading and was made before answer was filed. Fed.Rules Civ.Proc.Rules 8(c), 12(g), 28 U.S.C.A.

Parker v. U.S., 110 F.3d 678.

C.A.9 (Cal.) 1993. Ordinarily, defense of lack of personal jurisdiction is waived if it is not interposed in party's first motion to dismiss for failure to state claim upon which relief can be granted. Fed.Rules Civ.Proc.Rule 12(b)(6), (h)(1), 28 U.S.C.A.

Muldoon v. Tropitone Furniture Co., 1 F.3d 964.

C.A.9 (Cal.) 1990. For complaint to be dismissed because allegations give rise to affirmative defense, defense clearly must appear on face of pleading.

McCalden v. California Library Ass'n, 955 F.2d 1214, certiorari denied Simon Wiesenthal Center For Holocaust Studies v. McCalden, 112 S.Ct. 2306, 504 U.S. 957, 119 L.Ed.2d 227, certiorari denied 112 S.Ct. 2306, 504 U.S. 957, 119 L.Ed.2d 227.

C.A.9 (Cal.) 1988. Upon being served with a complaint which lacks sufficient nonconclusory allegations of evidence of unlawful discriminatory intent, a public official would ordinarily be entitled to raise a qualified immunity defense, and, if he wishes to avoid discovery, he may either move for dismissal for failure to state a claim or file an answer and move for judgment on the pleadings. U.S.C.A. Const. Amend. 1; 42 U.S.C.A. §§ 1981, 1983, 1985(3); Fed.Rules Civ.Proc.Rule 12(c), (h)(2), 28 U.S.C.A.

Gutierrez v. Municipal Court of Southeast Judicial Dist., Los Angeles County, 838 F.2d 1031, 90 A.L.R. Fed. 763, rehearing denied 861 F.2d 1187, certiorari granted, vacated 109 S.Ct. 1736, 490 U.S. 1016, 104 L.Ed.2d 174, on remand 873 F.2d 1342.

C.A.2 (Conn.) 1997. That complaint alleges facts which constitute defense to plaintiff's claim does not in all cases require dismissal of complaint.

Northrop v. Hoffman of Simsbury, Inc., 134 F.3d 41.

C.A.11 (Ga.) 1997. In considering a defendant's motion to dismiss or for judgment as a matter of law based on qualified immunity, district court must examine the complaint to determine whether, under the most favorable version of the facts alleged, defendant's actions violate clearly established law.

Nolen v. Jackson, 102 F.3d 1187.

C.A.11 (Ga.) 1993. Generally, existence of affirmative defense will not support motion to dismiss for failure to state a claim; however, district court may dismiss complaint on motion to dismiss when complaint's own allegations indicate existence of affirmative defense, so long as defense clearly appears on face of complaint. Fed.Rules Civ.Proc.Rule 12(b)(6), 28 U.S.C.A.

Fortner v. Thomas, 983 F.2d 1024.

C.A.11 (Ga.) 1984. Quiller v. Barclays American/Credit, Inc., 727 F.2d 1067, on rehearing 764 F.2d 1400, certiorari denied BarclaysAmerican/Credit, Inc. v. Quiller, 106 S.Ct. 1992, 476 U.S. 1124, 90 L.Ed.2d 673, certiorari denied 106 S.Ct. 1993, 476 U.S. 1124, 90 L.Ed.2d 673, certiorari denied 106 S.Ct. 1992, 476 U.S. 1124, 90 L.Ed.2d 673, certiorari denied 106 S.Ct. 1993, 476 U.S. 1124, 90 L.Ed.2d 673.

C.A.6 (Ky.) 1996. Qualified immunity is proper subject for dismissal based on failure to state claim. Fed.Rules Civ.Proc.Rule 12(b)(6), 28 U.S.C.A.

Levin v. Childers, 101 F.3d 44.

C.A.1 (Mass.) 1995. Plaintiff who wishes to force an up or down decision on asserted defense has the power to do so. Fed.Rules Civ.Proc.Rule 12(c, d), 28 U.S.C.A.

McIntosh v. Antonino, 71 F.3d 29.

C.A.1 (Mass.) 1988. Massachusetts recreational use statute, providing that landowner is not liable for injuries sustained by nonpaying member of public present on land, gave rise to "affirmative defense," which federal government had to plead in answer to sightseer's Federal Tort Claims Act complaint; defense could not be raised by motion to dismiss unless complaint itself supplied factual basis. Fed. Rules Civ.Proc.Rules 8(c), 12(b)(6), 28 U.S.C.A.; 28 U.S.C.A. §§ 1346, 2671 et seq.; M.G.L.A. c. 21, § 17C.

DiMella v. Gray Lines of Boston, Inc., 836 F.2d 718.

C.A.6 (Mich.) 1994. Qualified immunity defense can be raised at various stages of the litigation, including pleading stage in motion to

dismiss, after discovery in motion for summary judgment, or as affirmative defense at trial.

English v. Dyke, 23 F.3d 1086.

C.A.8 (Mo.) 1998. Dismissal on qualified immunity grounds is inappropriate unless it appears beyond doubt that plaintiffs can prove no set of facts in support of their constitutional claims which would entitle them to relief.

Central Airlines, Inc. v. U.S., 138 F.3d 333.

C.A.8 (Mo.) 1997. Court may order dismissal of § 1983 case on ground of immunity only if it appears beyond reasonable doubt that plaintiffs can prove no set of facts which would entitle them to relief. 42 U.S.C.A. § 1983.

Whisman Through Whisman v. Rinehart, 119 F.3d 1303.

C.A.8 (Mo.) 1996. Qualified immunity is affirmative defense, and will be upheld on motion to dismiss for failure to state claim only when immunity is established on face of complaint. Fed.Rules Civ.Proc.Rule 12(b)(6), 28 U.S.C.A.

Hafley v. Lohman, 90 F.3d 264, rehearing and suggestion for rehearing denied, certiorari denied 117 S.Ct. 1081, 137 L.Ed.2d 216.

C.A.8 (Neb.) 1995. Qualified immunity will be upheld on motion to dismiss for failure to state claim only when immunity is established on the face of the complaint. Fed.Rules Civ.Proc.Rule 12(b)(6), 28 U.S.C.A.

Weaver v. Clarke, 45 F.3d 1253.

C.A.3 (N.J.) 1994. Complaint may be subject to dismissal for failure to state claim when affirmative defense, like statute of frauds, appears on its face; receding from *Currier*, 442 F.2d 422. Fed.Rules Civ.Proc.Rule 12(b)(6), 28 U.S.C.A.

ALA, Inc. v. CCAIR, Inc., 29 F.3d 855.

C.A.10 (N.M.) 1991. Government officials must raise qualified immunity defense in order to benefit from substantial shield it affords; officials may do this in their answer, or in motion to dismiss or motion for summary judgment. 42 U.S.C.A. § 1983.

Quezada v. County of Bernalillo, 944 F.2d 710.

C.A.2 (N.Y.) 1998. Surgeon's complaint against insurance company itself established facts necessary to sustain insurance company's official immunity defense, and thus immunity defense could be determined at pleading stage on motion to dismiss for failure to state claim, since complaint made clear that all allegations arose out of company's role as carrier for Medicare "Part B" program, and, despite surgeon's conclusory allegations that company's conduct was negligent and fraudulent, it was also clear that acts complained of were discretionary and within scope of company's duties. Fed.Rules Civ.Proc.Rule 12(b)(6), 28 U.S.C.A.

> Pani v. Empire Blue Cross Blue Shield, 152 F.3d 67.

Affirmative defense may be raised by pre-answer motion to dismiss for failure to state a claim, without resort to summary judgment procedure, if defense appears on face of the complaint. Fed.Rules Civ.Proc.Rules 12(b)(6), 56, 28 U.S.C.A.

> Pani v. Empire Blue Cross Blue Shield, 152 F.3d 67.

Affirmative defense of official immunity should be resolved as early as possible by the court, and may be resolved by motion to dismiss for failure to state a claim if clearly established by allegations within complaint. Fed.Rules Civ. Proc.Rule 12(b)(6), 28 U.S.C.A.

> Pani v. Empire Blue Cross Blue Shield, 152 F.3d 67.

C.A.2 (N.Y.) 1996. Dismissal of civil rights claim under § 1983 was not justified by considerations of qualified immunity, inasmuch as qualified immunity was affirmative defense which defendants had burden of raising in answer and burden of establishing at trial or on motion for summary judgment. 42 U.S.C.A. § 1983.

> Black v. Coughlin, 76 F.3d 72, on remand 15 F.Supp.2d 311.

C.A.4 (N.C.) 1997. Qualified immunity may be raised in motion to dismiss. Fed.Rules Civ.Proc.Rule 12(b)(6), 28 U.S.C.A.

> Jenkins v. Medford, 119 F.3d 1156, certiorari denied 118 S.Ct. 881, 139 L.Ed.2d 869, certiorari denied 118 S.Ct. 881, 139 L.Ed.2d 869.

If complaint shows that plaintiff has not suffered deprivation of constitutional right, public official sued under § 1983 is entitled to dismissal of claim on grounds of qualified immunity. 42 U.S.C.A. § 1983; Fed.Rules Civ. Proc.Rule 12(b)(6), 28 U.S.C.A.

> Jenkins v. Medford, 119 F.3d 1156, certiorari denied 118 S.Ct. 881, 139 L.Ed.2d 869, certiorari denied 118 S.Ct. 881, 139 L.Ed.2d 869.

C.A.4 (N.C.) 1996. Although motion to dismiss for failure to a state claim invites inquiry into legal sufficiency of complaint, not analysis of potential defenses, dismissal nevertheless is appropriate when face of the complaint clearly reveals existence of meritorious affirmative defense. Fed.Rules Civ.Proc.Rule 12(b)(6), 28 U.S.C.A.

> Brooks v. City of Winston-Salem, N.C., 85 F.3d 178.

C.A.6 (Ohio) 1996. Immunity defenses may be raised in motions to dismiss, affirmative defenses or motions for summary judgment.

> Collyer v. Darling, 98 F.3d 211, rehearing and suggestion for rehearing denied, certiorari denied 117 S.Ct. 2439, 138 L.Ed.2d 199.

C.A.6 (Ohio) 1995. Dismissal of civil rights action is proper, if burden of pleading not only violation of rights, but also that those rights were so clearly established when acts were committed that any official in defendant's position, measured objectively, would have clearly understood that he was under affirmative duty to refrain from conduct is not carried by plaintiff in either original complaint or by pleading in response to defendant's assertion of qualified immunity defense.

> Veney v. Hogan, 70 F.3d 917, rehearing and suggestion for rehearing denied.

When civil rights plaintiff pleads his claim in generalized "notice" form, and defense of qualified immunity is asserted through motion to dismiss, plaintiff is required to respond to that defense; if his original complaint is deficient in that regard, he must amend his complaint to include specific, nonconclusory allegations of fact that will enable district court to determine that those facts, if proved, will overcome defense of qualified immunity.

> Veney v. Hogan, 70 F.3d 917, rehearing and suggestion for rehearing denied.

C.A.6 (Ohio) 1968. Mader v. Armel, 402 F.2d 158, 19 Ohio Misc. 97, 4 A.L.R. Fed. 1037, 46 O.O.2d 392, 48 O.O.2d 273, certiorari denied Young v. Mader, 89 S.Ct. 1188, 394 U.S. 930, 22 L.Ed.2d 459, on remand 1971 WL 261, affirmed 461 F.2d 1123, certiorari denied 93 S.Ct. 465, 409 U.S. 1023, 34 L.Ed.2d 315.

C.A.10 (Okl.) 1990. Prior to filing affirmative defense, defendant alleging qualified immunity can challenge complaint by filing either motion to dismiss or motion for summary judgment if plaintiff has failed to come forward with facts or allegations establishing that defendant violated clearly established law.

> Sawyer v. County of Creek, 908 F.2d 663.

Personal representative's inability without further discovery to allege more specific facts relating to death of patient at mental hospital did not bar prejudicial dismissal on basis of treating physician's qualified immunity. 42 U.S.C.A. § 1983.

> Sawyer v. County of Creek, 908 F.2d 663.

Prejudicial dismissal was appropriate after defense of qualified immunity was sustained, where plaintiff stated that she could not significantly amend complaint without discovery.

> Sawyer v. County of Creek, 908 F.2d 663.

C.A.3 (Pa.) 1997. On motion to dismiss for failure to state claim, affirmative defense is appropriately considered only if it presents insuperable barrier to recovery by plaintiff. Fed. Rules Civ.Proc.Rule 12(b)(6), 28 U.S.C.A.

Flight Systems, Inc. v. Electronic Data Systems Corp., 112 F.3d 124.

C.A.1 (Puerto Rico) 1996. Defendant public officials may raise defense of qualified immunity on pleadings in motion to dismiss; unless plaintiff's allegations state claim of violation of clearly established law, defendant pleading qualified immunity is entitled to dismissal before commencement of discovery.

Guzman-Rivera v. Rivera-Cruz, 98 F.3d 664.

C.A.6 (Tenn.) 1997. Defendant has right to plead immunity at dismissal stage and may immediately appeal adverse ruling before pleading immunity at summary judgment stage.

Barrett v. Harrington, 130 F.3d 246, certiorari denied 118 S.Ct. 1517, 140 L.Ed.2d 670.

C.A.6 (Tenn.) 1996. Government official is entitled to dismissal on grounds of qualified immunity before discovery is completed if the facts as alleged by plaintiff do not support claim of violation of clearly established law.

International Union, United Auto., Aerospace & Agr. Implement Workers of America, Local 737 v. Auto Glass Employees Federal Credit Union, 72 F.3d 1243, rehearing and suggestion for rehearing denied, certiorari denied 117 S.Ct. 63, 136 L.Ed.2d 24.

C.A.6 (Tenn.) 1995. Government officials are entitled to assert claims of qualified immunity prior to onset of discovery in form of motion to dismiss for failure to state claim upon which relief can be granted. Fed.Rules Civ. Proc.Rule 12(b)(6), 28 U.S.C.A.

Vaughn v. U.S. Small Business Admin., 65 F.3d 1322, rehearing denied 82 F.3d 684.

C.A.5 (Tex.) 1994. When successful affirmative defense appears on face of pleadings, dismissal for failure to state claim may be appropriate. Fed.Rules Civ.Proc.Rule 12(b)(6), 28 U.S.C.A.

Kansa Reinsurance Co., Ltd. v. Congressional Mortg. Corp. of Texas, 20 F.3d 1362.

C.A.4 (Va.) 1993. In limited circumstances where allegations of complaint give rise to affirmative defense, defense may be raised in motion to dismiss for failure to state claim on which relief can be granted, but only if affirmative defense clearly appears on face of complaint. Fed.Rules Civ.Proc.Rule 12(b)(6), 28 U.S.C.A.

Richmond, Fredericksburg & Potomac R. Co. v. Forst, 4 F.3d 244.

C.A.4 (W.Va.) 1997. Only defense that clearly appears on face of complaint may be raised in motion to dismiss for failure to state claim. Fed.Rules Civ.Proc.Rule 12(b)(6), 28 U.S.C.A.

Suarez Corp. Industries v. McGraw, 125 F.3d 222.

M.D.Ala. 1995. Issue of whether defendant is entitled to qualified immunity in civil rights action may be properly determined on pretrial motion to dismiss for failure to state claim upon which relief can be granted. Fed. Rules Civ.Proc.Rule 12(b)(6), 28 U.S.C.A.

Gorman v. Roberts, 909 F.Supp. 1493.

M.D.Ala. 1994. Existence of affirmative defense, such as qualified immunity, will not generally support motion to dismiss for failure to state claim. Fed.Rules Civ.Proc.Rule 12(b)(6), 28 U.S.C.A.

Cofield v. Randolph County Com'n, 844 F.Supp. 1499.

District court may dismiss complaint when it contains allegations that will clearly support defense on face of complaint. Fed.Rules Civ. Proc.Rule 12(b)(6), 28 U.S.C.A.

Cofield v. Randolph County Com'n, 844 F.Supp. 1499.

E.D.Ark. 1987. Affirmative defenses of res judicata, privilege, frivolity, and bad faith could not be the basis of motion to dismiss civil rights action. Fed.Rules Civ.Proc.Rule 8(c), 28 U.S.C.A.

Hollowell v. Gravett, 118 F.R.D. 473.

Res judicata, waiver and estoppel were affirmative defenses which could not be basis for motion to dismiss civil rights action alleging neglect/refusal to prevent conspiracy to deprive plaintiff of his civil rights. 42 U.S.C.A. § 1986; Fed.Rules Civ.Proc.Rule 8(c), 28 U.S.C.A.

Hollowell v. Gravett, 118 F.R.D. 473.

Res judicata, waiver, estoppel, and immunity were affirmative defenses which could not be basis of motion to dismiss civil rights action brought under conspiracy civil rights statute. 42 U.S.C.A. § 1985(3); Fed.Rules Civ.Proc.Rule 8(c), 28 U.S.C.A.

Hollowell v. Gravett, 118 F.R.D. 473.

C.D.Cal. 1994. Absolute judicial immunity may properly be raised in support of motion to dismiss for failure to state a claim.

Church of Scientology Intern. v. Kolts, 846 F.Supp. 873.

E.D.Cal. 1993. Jurisdictional defense based on discretionary function exception of Federal Tort Claims Act (FTCA) is properly raised by motion to dismiss for lack of subject matter jurisdiction, not by motion for summary judgment. 28 U.S.C.A. § 2680(a); Fed.Rules Civ.Proc.Rule 12(b)(1), 28 U.S.C.A.

> Valdez v. U.S., 837 F.Supp. 1065, affirmed 56 F.3d 1177.

N.D.Cal. 1993. For complaint to be dismissed because allegations give rise to affirmative defense, defense must clearly appear on face of pleading and defense must be complete. Fed.Rules Civ.Proc.Rule 12(b)(6), 28 U.S.C.A.

> Plessinger v. Castleman and Haskell, 838 F.Supp. 448.

N.D.Cal. 1992. Complaint is subject to dismissal for failure to state claim on which relief can be granted when its allegations indicate existence of affirmative defense, but defense must appear on face of pleading. Fed.Rules Civ.Proc.Rule 12(b)(6), 28 U.S.C.A.

> Kentucky Cent. Life Ins. Co. v. LeDuc, 814 F.Supp. 832.

D.Colo. 1996. Because doctrine of qualified immunity is not only defense to liability but immunity from suit, prior to filing affirmative defense, defendant can challenge complaint by filing either motion to dismiss or motion for summary judgment if plaintiff has failed to come forward with facts or allegations that establish that defendant has violated clearly establish law.

> Estate of Olivas By and Through Miranda v. City and County of Denver, 929 F.Supp. 1329.

D.Conn. 1987. Complaint may be dismissed for failure to state a claim when its own allegations indicate the existence of an affirmative defense, provided that defense clearly appears on the face of the complaint. Fed.Rules Civ.Proc.Rules 8(c), 12(b)(6), 28 U.S.C.A.

> Galvin v. Lloyd, 663 F.Supp. 1572.

D.D.C. 1998. United States' affirmative defenses, including the statute of limitations, estoppel, qualified immunity, res judicata, and laches, were not required to be raised in an answer before being presented in motions to dismiss in action brought by federal employee alleging statutory and tort claims.

> Mittleman v. U.S., 997 F.Supp. 1.

M.D.Fla. 1996. Qualified immunity is not required to be pleaded as an affirmative defense, and would be considered when raised by motion to dismiss, as court must seek to resolve immunity issues as early in the litigation as possible.

> Whitehead By and Through Whitehead v. School Bd. for Hillsborough County, State of Fla., 932 F.Supp. 1396.

S.D.Fla. 1993. Fact-based business judgment rule defense was not appropriately asserted, in action under Florida director liability statute, by way of motion to dismiss. West's F.S.A. § 607.0831(1).

> In re Southeast Banking Corp., 827 F.Supp. 742, reversed 69 F.3d 1539.

N.D.Ga. 1986. Motion to dismiss should be granted if an affirmative defense or other bar to relief appears on face of complaint.

> Prudential Ins. Co. of America v. Baum, 629 F.Supp. 466.

D.Hawai'i 1995. Motion to dismiss for failure to state claim should be granted if affirmative defense or other bar to relief is apparent from face of complaint, such as absolute immunity or statute of limitations. Fed.Rules Civ.Proc.Rule 12(b)(6), 28 U.S.C.A.

> Moore v. Kamikawa, 940 F.Supp. 260, affirmed 82 F.3d 423.

D.Hawai'i 1995. Motion to dismiss for failure to state claim upon which relief can be granted should be granted if affirmative defense or other bar to relief is apparent from face of complaint. Fed.Rules Civ.Proc.Rule 12(b)(6), 28 U.S.C.A.

> Forsyth v. Eli Lilly and Co., 904 F.Supp. 1153.

D.Hawai'i 1990. Failure to exhaust internal union remedies as a matter of abatement must be raised in a motion to dismiss, not in a motion for summary judgment.

> Hawaii Teamsters and Allied Workers, Local 996, IBT v. City Exp., Inc., 751 F.Supp. 1426.

N.D.Ill. 1997. Affirmative defense will only support motion to dismiss when plaintiff's allegations clearly point to existence of defense. Fed.Rules Civ.Proc.Rule 12(b)(6), 28 U.S.C.A.

> Adamczyk v. Lever Bros. Co., Div. of Conopco, 991 F.Supp. 931.

N.D.Ill. 1996. Whether affirmative defense fulfills the standard for motions to dismiss for failure to state claim depends on whether it would be impossible for defendant to prove set of facts in support of affirmative defense that would defeat complaint. Fed.Rules Civ.Proc. Rule 12(b)(6), (f), 28 U.S.C.A.

> Codest Engineering v. Hyatt Intern. Corp., 954 F.Supp. 1224.

N.D.Ill. 1996. Generally, affirmative defense will not support motion to dismiss for failure to state a claim; nevertheless, complaint may be dismissed pursuant to such motion when its own allegations indicate existence of affirmative defense, so long as defense clearly appears on face of complaint. Fed.Rules Civ.Proc.Rule 12(b)(6), 28 U.S.C.A.

> Hoopla Sports and Entertainment, Inc. v. Nike, Inc., 947 F.Supp. 347.

N.D.Ill. 1996. In moving to dismiss plaintiff's fourth amended complaint, defendants would be allowed, as matter of fairness and in light or previous opportunities accorded to plaintiffs to properly plead their case, to raise new defenses not previously submitted in connection with their earlier motions to dismiss, though plaintiffs' fourth amended complaint was mere "housecleaning" measure which was not substantively different from their unamended fourth complaint. Fed.Rules Civ.Proc.Rule 12(g), 28 U.S.C.A.

Mount v. LaSalle Bank Lake View, 926 F.Supp. 759.

N.D.Ill. 1996. When faced with motion to dismiss that includes arguments on both substance of plaintiff's claims and qualified immunity in § 1983 action, court should first address those arguments directed to substance, and, once court has determined that viable constitutional claim has been made, it examines applicability of qualified immunity on that claim. 42 U.S.C.A. § 1983.

Milazzo v. O'Connell, 925 F.Supp. 1331, affirmed 108 F.3d 129, rehearing and suggestion for rehearing denied.

N.D.Ill. 1994. Former employer's motion to dismiss terminated cookie distributor's post-termination lawsuit for failure to state claim upon which relief granted, based upon release of claims signed by cookie distributor pursuant to prior decision by court, was premature and improper, as release was neither within language of complaint nor matter of which court could take judicial notice. Fed.Rules Civ.Proc. Rule 12(b)(6), 28 U.S.C.A.

Dawson v. W. & H. Voortman, Ltd., 853 F.Supp. 1038.

N.D.Ill. 1988. Even if qualified immunity does not entitle prison officials to dismissal of inmate's § 1983 action against them at pleading stage, they may reassert immunity through properly supported motions for summary judgment and after trial. 42 U.S.C.A. § 1983.

Parker v. Lane, 688 F.Supp. 353.

N.D.Ill. 1987. Where affirmative defense or other bar to relief is apparent from face of complaint, dismissal is proper.

Bachmeier v. Bank of Ravenswood, 663 F.Supp. 1207.

D.Kan. 1997. Motion to dismiss for failure to state claim is appropriate where allegations clearly indicate existence of affirmative defense; in such cases, complaint is said to have built-in defense and is essentially self-defeating. Fed. Rules Civ.Proc.Rule 12(b)(6), 28 U.S.C.A.

Classic Communications, Inc. v. Rural Telephone Service Co., Inc., 956 F.Supp. 910, reconsideration denied 1997 WL 231087.

Privilege and immunity are examples of built-in affirmative defenses that are properly considered on motion to dismiss for failure to state claim. Fed.Rules Civ.Proc.Rule 12(b)(6), 28 U.S.C.A.

Classic Communications, Inc. v. Rural Telephone Service Co., Inc., 956 F.Supp. 910, reconsideration denied 1997 WL 231087.

D.Kan. 1996. Motion to dismiss for failure to state claim is appropriate where allegations clearly indicate existence of affirmative defense; in such cases, complaint is said to have built-in defense and is essentially self-defeating. Fed. Rules Civ.Proc.Rule 12(b)(6), 28 U.S.C.A.

Classic Communications, Inc. v. Rural Telephone Service Co., Inc., 956 F.Supp. 896.

E.D.La. 1997. Dismissal of complaint for failure to state claim is inappropriate unless pleadings on their face reveal beyond doubt that plaintiffs can prove no set of facts that would entitle them to relief, or if an affirmative defense or other bar to relief appears on face of complaint. Fed.Rules Civ.Proc.Rule 12(b)(6), 28 U.S.C.A.

Reyes v. Sazan, 981 F.Supp. 973.

W.D.La. 1986. While complaint may be dismissed for failure to state a claim due to existence of affirmative defense, defense must clearly appear on face of pleading. Fed.Rules Civ.Proc.Rule 12(b)(6), 28 U.S.C.A.

Airline Car Rental, Inc. v. Shreveport Airport Authority, 667 F.Supp. 293.

W.D.Mich. 1997. Dismissal of complaint for failure to state a claim is proper if complaint fails to allege element necessary for relief, or if an affirmative defense or other bar to relief appears on face of complaint, such as absolute immunity of defendant. Fed.Rules Civ.Proc. Rule 12(b)(6), 28 U.S.C.A.

Gibson v. Sain, 979 F.Supp. 557.

W.D.Mich. 1996. Dismissal of complaint is proper if complaint fails to allege element necessary for relief or if affirmative defense or other bar to relief is apparent from face of complaint, such as official immunity of defendant.

Emery v. U.S., 920 F.Supp. 788.

W.D.Mich. 1995. In ruling on motion to dismiss for failure to state claim, dismissal is proper if complaint fails to allege element necessary for relief, or affirmative defense or another matter precluding relief appears on face of complaint, including official immunity. Fed. Rules Civ.Proc.Rule 12(b)(6), 28 U.S.C.A.

Hilliard v. Shell Western E & P, Inc., 885 F.Supp. 169, reconsideration denied 1995 WL 549259.

N.D.Miss. 1998. While dismissal for failure to state a claim ordinarily is determined by whether the facts alleged, if true, give rise to a cause of action, a claim may also be dismissed if a successful affirmative defense appears clearly on the face of the pleadings. Fed.Rules Civ. Proc.Rule 12(b)(6), 28 U.S.C.A.

> Myers v. Guardian Life Ins. Co. of America, Inc., 5 F.Supp.2d 423.

N.D.Miss. 1995. While dismissal for failure to state claim ordinarily is determined by whether facts alleged, if true, give rise to cause of action, claim may also be dismissed if successful affirmative defense appears clearly on face of pleadings. Fed.Rules Civ.Proc.Rule 12(b)(6), 28 U.S.C.A.

> Cunningham v. Dun & Bradstreet Plan Services, Inc., 889 F.Supp. 932, affirmed 105 F.3d 655.

D.N.J. 1995. In ruling on motion to dismiss for failure to state claim, court examines facts as alleged by plaintiff for any dispositive affirmative defenses. Fed.Rules Civ.Proc.Rule 12(b)(6), 28 U.S.C.A.

> Griesenbeck v. American Tobacco Co., 897 F.Supp. 815.

D.N.J. 1983. Hauptmann v. Wilentz, 570 F.Supp. 351, affirmed 770 F.2d 1070, certiorari denied 106 S.Ct. 887, 474 U.S. 1103, 88 L.Ed.2d 922, affirmed Appeal of Hauptmann, 770 F.2d 1070.

D.N.M. 1991. Court must construe motion to dismiss affirmative defense liberally and may not dismiss defense if there is any possibility of affording relief.

> Hill v. Cray Research, Inc., 864 F.Supp. 1070.

E.D.N.Y. 1997. Qualified immunity defense was premature on motion to dismiss in security guard service's civil rights action challenging termination of its contract with housing development; issue was more appropriate for resolution on summary judgment motion. 42 U.S.C.A. § 1983.

> X-Men Sec., Inc. v. Pataki, 983 F.Supp. 101, on reconsideration.

E.D.N.Y. 1997. Although immunity from § 1983 liability constitutes affirmative defense, district court nevertheless could consider immunity argument on motion to dismiss for failure to state a claim where such defense was readily apparent on face of complaint. 42 U.S.C.A. § 1983.

> Willner v. Town of North Hempstead, 977 F.Supp. 182.

E.D.N.Y. 1996. Dismissal with right to re-plead would be granted, to determine if district attorney had qualified immunity from § 1983 claim of prisoner, alleging that attorney had violated prisoner's liberty interest in not being deprived of work release status without due process; allegation that attorney had transmitted to prison authorities false claim that prisoner had threatened mother of victim he had murdered could be interpreted to mean that attorney knew allegation was false at time he transmitted it, and if so prosecutor could not reasonably believe his conduct did not violate prisoner's due process rights. U.S.C.A. Const. Amends. 5, 14; 42 U.S.C.A. § 1983.

> Quartararo v. Catterson, 917 F.Supp. 919.

E.D.N.Y. 1995. Ordinarily, qualified immunity is resolved on motion for summary judgment; however, it is also proper to raise defense of qualified immunity on motion to dismiss, or on motions for directed verdict or judgment notwithstanding the verdict.

> Sheppard v. Beerman, 911 F.Supp. 606, vacated 94 F.3d 823.

If district court determines that defendant's alleged actions were those reasonable officer could have believed lawful, defendant public official is entitled to dismissal of civil rights case prior to discovery. 42 U.S.C.A. § 1983.

> Sheppard v. Beerman, 911 F.Supp. 606, vacated 94 F.3d 823.

E.D.N.Y. 1995. Disciplinary hearing panel members' affirmative defenses of absolute immunity, qualified immunity, collateral estoppel and failure to allege facts sufficient to state claim were apparent on face of suspended school teacher's complaint which alleged that disciplinary action violated his constitutional rights and New York antidiscrimination law, and therefore such defenses were reviewable on hearing panel members' motion to dismiss complaint for failure to state claim. Fed.Rules Civ.Proc.Rule 12(b)(6), 28 U.S.C.A.; N.Y.McKinney's Executive Law § 296.

> Taylor v. Brentwood Union Free School Dist., 908 F.Supp. 1165.

E.D.N.Y. 1994. Finding of qualified immunity can be appropriate in motion to dismiss if allegations so warrant. Fed.Rules Civ.Proc. Rule 12(b)(6), 28 U.S.C.A.

> Messina v. Mazzeo, 854 F.Supp. 116.

N.D.N.Y. 1993. Plaintiff's contention that New York Insurance Law contained a mandated-benefit law not preempted by ERISA raised for first time in response to defendant's motion to dismiss was not properly raised; despite presence in his complaint of other specific statutory basis for relief, never before had plaintiff asserted that section might also provide him grounds for relief. N.Y.McKinney's Insurance Law § 3221(k)(1)(A); Employee Retirement Income Security Act of 1974, §§ 2–4402, as amended, 29 U.S.C.A. §§ 1001–1461.

> Shackelton v. Connecticut General Life Ins. Co., 817 F.Supp. 277.

S.D.N.Y. 1997. In appropriate circumstances, affirmative defenses may be raised in motion to dismiss for failure to state claim. Fed.Rules Civ.Proc.Rule 12(b)(6), 28 U.S.C.A.

> Messner Vetere Berger McNamee Scmetterer EURO RSCG Inc. v. Aegis Group PLC, 974 F.Supp. 270, question certified 150 F.3d 194.

S.D.N.Y. 1994. Failure to raise no-action clause in trust indenture in original motion to dismiss for failure to state claim did not give rise to waiver of no-action clause as defense. Fed.Rules Civ.Proc.Rule 12(b)(6), (g), (h)(2), 28 U.S.C.A.

> McMahan & Co. v. Wherehouse Entertainment, Inc., 859 F.Supp. 743, affirmed in part, reversed in part 65 F.3d 1044, certiorari denied 116 S.Ct. 1678, 517 U.S. 1190, 134 L.Ed.2d 781.

S.D.N.Y. 1993. Exception to remedial statute normally must be pled as affirmative defense but, when facts alleged in complaint give rise to affirmative defense, it may be raised in preanswer motion to dismiss.

> Three Crown Ltd. Partnership v. Caxton Corp., 817 F.Supp. 1033.

W.D.N.Y. 1992. Futility of administrative remedies is question of fact which is inappropriate for resolution on motion to dismiss for lack of subject matter jurisdiction. Fed.Rules Civ.Proc.Rule 12(b)(1), 28 U.S.C.A.

> Abbott Radiology Associates v. Sullivan, 801 F.Supp. 1012.

S.D.Ohio 1994. Dismissal for failure to state claim upon which relief can be granted is proper when complaint demonstrates that relief requested is barred by an affirmative defense. Fed.Rules Civ.Proc.Rule 12(b)(6), 28 U.S.C.A.

> Martinez v. Western Ohio Health Care Corp., 872 F.Supp. 469.

S.D.Ohio 1987. Motion to dismiss on basis of affirmative defense can be granted only where defense appears valid from face of complaint alone.

> Olding v. Casey, 680 F.Supp. 1081.

E.D.Pa. 1998. Federal district court properly refused to dismiss state trial judge's civil rights action against state administrative judge for alleged wrongful "demotion" resulting from trial judge's exercise of his First Amendment free speech rights on basis of qualified immunity.

> Avellino v. Herron, 991 F.Supp. 730.

E.D.Pa. 1994. Qualified immunity is ordinarily issue of law to be determined by court on motion to dismiss or motion for summary judgment. 42 U.S.C.A. § 1983.

> Callahan v. Lancaster-Lebanon Intermediate Unit 13, 880 F.Supp. 319.

E.D.Pa. 1994. Claim may be dismissed for failure to state claim where defendant contends that under facts alleged he is entitled to immunity, even though immunity is generally characterized as affirmative defense. Fed.Rules Civ. Proc.Rule 12(b)(6), 28 U.S.C.A.

> Cohen v. Oasin, 863 F.Supp. 225.

E.D.Pa. 1994. Complaint may be dismissed when allegations indicate existence of affirmative defense, but defense must clearly appear on face of pleading. Fed.Rules Civ. Proc.Rule 12(b)(6), 28 U.S.C.A.

> Johnson v. Resources for Human Development, Inc., 860 F.Supp. 218.

Affirmative defense will not generally support motion to dismiss for failure to state a claim upon which relief can be granted. Fed. Rules Civ.Proc.Rule 12(b)(6), 28 U.S.C.A.

> Johnson v. Resources for Human Development, Inc., 860 F.Supp. 218.

E.D.Pa. 1990. Motion to dismiss counterclaim for failure to state claim upon which relief can be granted is governed by same standard as that applicable to dismissal of complaint. Fed.Rules Civ.Proc.Rule 12(b)(6), 28 U.S.C.A.

> U.S. v. Union Gas Co., 743 F.Supp. 1144.

M.D.Pa. 1995. Members of county board of elections who were sued under § 1983 for violating successful candidate's constitutional rights were not entitled to dismissal on grounds of qualified immunity under state law; in addition to fact that state law cannot immunize person against federal civil rights action, immunity defense would best be considered after some discovery had been conducted, not on motion to dismiss. 42 U.S.C.A. § 1983; Fed. Rules Civ.Proc.Rule 12(b)(6); 42 Pa.C.S.A. § 8546.

> Barley v. Luzerne County Bd. of Elections, 937 F.Supp. 362.

W.D.Tenn. 1997. Dismissal is proper if affirmative defense or other bar to relief is apparent from face of complaint. Fed.Rules Civ.Proc.Rule 12(b)(6), 28 U.S.C.A.

> Sanders v. Prentice-Hall Corp. System, Inc., 969 F.Supp. 481.

W.D.Tenn. 1991. After defendant government official has raised defense of qualified immunity by motion to dismiss, by affirmative defense, or by motion for summary judgment, burden of pleading facts which, if true, describe violation of clearly established statutory or constitutional right of which reasonable public official, under an objective standard, would have known, rests on plaintiff, and if plaintiff fails to meet burden of pleading sufficient facts to state a violation of clearly established law, government official pleading qualified immunity is entitled to dismissal before commencement of discovery. 42 U.S.C.A. § 1983.

> Gregory v. Hunt, 872 F.Supp. 476, order clarified 1992 WL 695478, affirmed 24 F.3d 781.

E.D.Tex. 1994. Where complaint shows on its face that it is barred by affirmative defense, court may dismiss action for failure to state claim upon which relief can be granted. Fed. Rules Civ.Proc.Rule 12(b)(6), 28 U.S.C.A.

> Sheppard v. Texas Dept. of Transp., 158 F.R.D. 592.

N.D.Tex. 1987. A motion to dismiss is an appropriate procedural device in which to raise immunity defense.

> Collin County, Tex. v. Homeowners Ass'n for Values Essential to Neighborhoods (HAVEN), 654 F.Supp. 943.

E.D.Va. 1998. Because motion to dismiss for failure to state claim is intended to test legal adequacy of complaint, not to address merits of any affirmative defenses, a defense may generally be raised under motion to dismiss only if it clearly appears on face of complaint; otherwise, affirmative defenses are more properly reserved for consideration on motion for summary judgment. Fed.Rules Civ.Proc.Rule 12(b)(6), 28 U.S.C.A.

> Settle v. S.W. Rodgers, Co., Inc., 998 F.Supp. 657.

S.D.W.Va. 1996. It is rarely appropriate to analyze affirmative defenses via motion to dismiss for failure to state claim, unless face of complaint clearly reveals existence of meritorious affirmative defense. Fed.Rules Civ.Proc. Rule 12(b)(6), 28 U.S.C.A.

> Guy F. Atkinson Const., a Div. of Guy F. Atkinson Co. v. Ohio Mun. Elec. Generation Agency Joint Venture 5, 943 F.Supp. 626.

D.Wyo. 1996. Following defendant's motion to dismiss under doctrine of qualified immunity, district judge should permit plaintiff to come forward with any additional allegations showing that defendant violated clearly established law and court must then determine whether complaint includes all of factual allegations necessary to sustain conclusion that defendant violated clearly established law. 42 U.S.C.A. § 1983; Fed.Rules Civ.Proc.Rule 12(b)(6), 28 U.S.C.A.

> Marshall v. Board of County Com'rs for Johnson County, Wyo., 912 F.Supp. 1456.

D.Wyo. 1994. Defendant may, prior to filing affirmative defense, challenge complaint for failure to state claim on ground that he or she is entitled to qualified immunity because pleaded facts fail to show that his or her conduct violated clearly established law of which reasonable person would have known; similarly, defendant could raise immunity issue in motion for summary judgment. Fed.Rules Civ.Proc.Rules 12(b)(6), 56, 28 U.S.C.A.

> Gressley v. Deutsch, 890 F.Supp. 1474.

Once defendant, prior to filing affirmative defense, challenges complaint for failure to state claim or moves for summary judgment on ground that he or she is entitled to qualified immunity, court must allow plaintiff the limited opportunity to come forward with facts or allegations sufficient to show that law was clearly established when alleged violation occurred; unless such showing is made, defendant prevails, and, if plaintiff has identified the clearly established law and conduct that violated the law, defendant as movant in motion for summary judgment bears normal burden of showing that no material issues of fact remain that would defeat his or her claim of qualified immunity. Fed.Rules Civ.Proc.Rules 12(b)(6), 56, 28 U.S.C.A.

> Gressley v. Deutsch, 890 F.Supp. 1474.

Bkrtcy.N.D.Ga. 1995. Although government officials can raise qualified immunity in motion to dismiss, presence of "clearly established rights" standard often makes that defense a difficult foundation upon which to justify motion to dismiss.

> Matter of Swift, 185 B.R. 963.

Bkrtcy.N.D.Ill. 1994. Statute of limitations defenses may properly be raised in either responsive pleading or motion to dismiss.

> In re Luria Steel and Trading Corp., 164 B.R. 293, opinion supplemented 168 B.R. 913, affirmed 189 B.R. 418.

🗝️**1753. —— Contributory negligence, assumption of risk and similar defenses.**

For other cases see earlier editions of this digest, the Decennial Digests, and WESTLAW.

🗝️**1754. —— Limitations, laches and prematurity.**

C.A.D.C. 1985. A motion to dismiss may be granted on basis that action is time barred only when it appears from face of the complaint that relevant statute of limitations bars the action.

> Doe v. U.S. Dept. of Justice, 753 F.2d 1092, 243 U.S.App.D.C. 354.

C.A.Fed. (Minn.) 1993. Dismissal of claim on ground of laches requires that there be unreasonable and unexcused delay in bringing claim, and material prejudice to defendant as result of delay.

> Advanced Cardiovascular Systems, Inc. v. Scimed Life Systems, Inc., 988 F.2d 1157, rehearing denied, in banc suggestion declined.

C.A.9 (Cal.) 1998. Inasmuch as applicability of equitable tolling doctrine often depends on matters outside pleadings, it is not generally amenable to resolution on motion to dismiss for failure to state claim; complaint cannot be dismissed unless it appears beyond doubt that plaintiff can prove no set of facts that would establish timeliness of claim. Fed.Rules Civ. Proc.Rule 12(b)(6), 28 U.S.C.A.

> Hernandez v. City of El Monte, 138 F.3d 393.

C.A.9 (Cal.) 1997. Statute of limitations question could be decided on motion to dismiss where all facts necessary to decide issue were in record.

> Estate of Blue v. County of Los Angeles, 120 F.3d 982, certiorari denied 118 S.Ct. 1042, 140 L.Ed.2d 107.

C.A.9 (Cal.) 1996. Motion to dismiss based on running of statute of limitations may be granted only if assertions in complaint, read with required liberality, would not permit plaintiff to prove that statute was tolled.

> Pisciotta v. Teledyne Industries, Inc., 91 F.3d 1326.

C.A.9 (Cal.) 1979. Jackson v. Hayakawa, 605 F.2d 1121, certiorari denied 100 S.Ct. 1601, 445 U.S. 952, 63 L.Ed.2d 787, appeal after remand 682 F.2d 1344, appeal after remand 761 F.2d 525.

C.A.11 (Fla.) 1990. Adversary complaint by guarantors seeking equitable lien or equitable subordination was subject to dismissal as being premature, where guarantors, who had not yet become liable on guarantee, did not have allowable claim. Bankr.Code, 11 U.S.C.A. §§ 502(e)(1), 510.

> In re Justice Oaks II, Ltd., 898 F.2d 1544, certiorari denied Wallis v. Justice Oaks II, Ltd., 111 S.Ct. 387, 498 U.S. 959, 112 L.Ed.2d 398.

C.A.7 (Ill.) 1995. If plaintiff pleads facts that show its suit barred by a statute of limitations, it may plead itself out of court under analysis applicable to motion to dismiss for failure to state claim upon which relief could be granted. Fed.Rules Civ.Proc.Rule 12(b)(6), 28 U.S.C.A.

> Whirlpool Financial Corp. v. GN Holdings, Inc., 67 F.3d 605, rehearing and suggestion for rehearing denied.

C.A.7 (Ind.) 1986. Motion to dismiss was wrong way to raise timeliness of race discrimination in employment complaint; proper manner would have been motion for summary judgment. Fed.Rules Civ.Proc.Rule 56(c), 28 U.S.C.A.

> Stewart v. RCA Corp., 790 F.2d 624.

C.A.1 (Me.) 1998. Granting a motion to dismiss based on a limitations defense is entirely appropriate when the pleader's allegations leave no doubt that an asserted claim is time-barred. Fed.Rules Civ.Proc.Rule 12(b)(6), 28 U.S.C.A.

> LaChapelle v. Berkshire Life Ins. Co., 142 F.3d 507.

C.A.8 (Mo.) 1992. District court did not abuse its discretion in allowing government to raise statute of limitations defense in its motion to dismiss filed two months after its answer to petition alleging employment discrimination; it was arguable that "failure to state claim" defense in government's answer preserved limitations defense, in that complaint is subject to dismissal for failure to state claim when affirmative limitations defense clearly appears on face of complaint, and court could have allowed government to amend its answer to expressly include omitted limitations defense. 5 U.S.C.A. § 7703(b)(2); Fed.Rules Civ.Proc.Rule 8(c), 28 U.S.C.A.

> Sanders v. Department of Army, 981 F.2d 990.

C.A.9 (Mont.) 1990. Where issue of limitations requires determination of when claim begins to accrue, complaint should be dismissed only if evidence is so clear that there is no genuine factual issue and determination can be made as a matter of law.

> Sisseton-Wahpeton Sioux Tribe, of Lake Traverse Indian Reservation, North Dakota and South Dakota v. U.S., 895 F.2d 588, certiorari denied 111 S.Ct. 75, 498 U.S. 824, 112 L.Ed.2d 48, appeal after remand 90 F.3d 351, certiorari denied 117 S.Ct. 516, 136 L.Ed.2d 405.

C.A.1 (N.H.) 1994. Alleged unavailability of witnesses did not prejudice school district, as needed for laches defense to apply at preliminary hearing on motion to dismiss suit under Individuals with Disabilities Education Act (IDEA), given that student's teachers testified at hearing, third witness resided within reach of court's subpoena power, former school superintendent was not shown to be unable or unwilling to testify, and school failed to take reasonable steps to refresh its witnesses' recollections. Fed.Rules Civ.Proc.Rule 12(d), 28 U.S.C.A.; Individuals with Disabilities Education Act, § 601 et seq., as amended, 20 U.S.C.A. § 1400 et seq.

> Murphy v. Timberlane Regional School Dist., 22 F.3d 1186, certiorari denied 115 S.Ct. 484, 513 U.S. 987, 130 L.Ed.2d 396.

C.A.3 (N.J.) 1993. In reviewing Rule 12(b)(6) dismissal on statute of limitations ground, court must determine whether time alleged in statement of claim shows that cause of action has not been brought within limitations period. Fed.Rules Civ.Proc.Rule 12(b)(6), 28 U.S.C.A.

> Davis v. Grusemeyer, 996 F.2d 617.

C.A.2 (N.Y.) 1993. It was inappropriate for district court to dismiss action on basis of statute of limitations without addressing issue of subject matter jurisdiction raised in motion to dismiss. Fed.Rules Civ.Proc.Rule 12(b)(1), 28 U.S.C.A.

> U.S. ex rel. Kreindler & Kreindler v. United Technologies Corp., 985 F.2d 1148, certiorari denied 113 S.Ct. 2962, 508 U.S. 973, 125 L.Ed.2d 663.

C.A.6 (Ohio) 1995. Even under lower standard of notice pleading required by Federal Civil Rule 8(a), plaintiffs' allegations that majority of acts which were basis for their suit occurred more than two years prior to its filing and that plaintiffs did not become aware of facts until date within two years of filing of complaint were insufficient to avoid motion to dismiss based on expiration of the statute of limitations. Fed.Rules Civ.Proc.Rules 8(a), 12(b)(6), 28 U.S.C.A.

> LRL Properties v. Portage Metro Housing Authority, 55 F.3d 1097, rehearing and suggestion for rehearing denied.

C.A.3 (Pa.) 1994. While rule governing pleading of affirmative defenses indicates that statute of limitations defense cannot be used in context of motion to dismiss for failure to state claim, exception is made where complaint facially shows noncompliance with limitations period and affirmative defense clearly appears on face of pleading. Fed.Rules Civ.Proc.Rule 12(b)(6), 28 U.S.C.A.

> Oshiver v. Levin, Fishbein, Sedran & Berman, 38 F.3d 1380, on remand 910 F.Supp. 225, affirmed 96 F.3d 1434.

C.A.5 (Tex.) 1994. Section 1983 claims against city were properly dismissed without prejudice, where plaintiffs offered no evidence of intentional discrimination within limitations period. 42 U.S.C.A. § 1983.

> National Ass'n of Government Employees v. City Public Service Bd. of San Antonio, Tex., 40 F.3d 698.

C.A.9 (Wash.) 1988. Genuine issue of material fact, as to when plaintiff under Privacy Act knew or had reason to know of Veterans Administration's alleged violation of federal regulations in failing to note receipt of his request that his medical records be changed, precluded dismissal of suit on statute of limitations grounds. 5 U.S.C.A. § 552a(d)(2)(B)(ii), (g)(5).

> Englerius v. Veterans Admin., 837 F.2d 895.

C.A.7 (Wis.) 1986. In view of court's determination that employee's termination was not unlawful under Title VII, any improper dismissal of discrimination claims for failure to exhaust administrative remedies was not error. Civil Rights Act of 1964, § 701 et seq., as amended, 42 U.S.C.A. § 2000e et seq.

> Germane v. Heckler, 804 F.2d 366.

M.D.Ala. 1986. Florida real estate broker who successfully sued title company for civil RICO violations, but whose award was reversed on appeal on statute of limitations grounds, was entitled to dismissal of action without prejudice so that he could sue in other forum with more favorable limitations period.

> Bowling v. Buderus, 111 F.R.D. 322, affirmed 798 F.2d 1419.

N.D.Ala. 1990. Class claims of employment discrimination were subject to dismissal upon determination that discrimination claims of employees who were named plaintiffs were time barred; class members could not proceed in face of dismissal of named plaintiffs. Civil Rights Act of 1964, § 706(d), as amended, 42 U.S.C.A. § 2000e-5(e).

> Beavers v. American Cast Iron Pipe Co., 751 F.Supp. 956, 30 Wage & Hour Cas. (BNA) 1003, affirmed in part, vacated in part, reversed in part 975 F.2d 792.

C.D.Cal. 1997. District court may grant a motion to dismiss based on the running of the statute of limitations only if it is clear from the face of the complaint and judicially noticed documents that the plaintiff cannot prevail as a matter of law on the equitable tolling issue.

> Diaz v. Carlson, 5 F.Supp.2d 809, affirmed 142 F.3d 443, certiorari denied 119 S.Ct. 225.

Motion to dismiss §1983 and civil conspiracy claims could not be granted on statute of limitations grounds where neither party addressed issue of equitable tolling under California law, and where it was not clear from face of complaint that plaintiff could not prevail as a matter of law on issue of equitable tolling. 42 U.S.C.A. §§ 1983, 1985.

> Diaz v. Carlson, 5 F.Supp.2d 809, affirmed 142 F.3d 443, certiorari denied 119 S.Ct. 225.

C.D.Cal. 1996. Statute of limitations defense may be raised by motion to dismiss or by motion for summary judgment.

> Remington Investments, Inc. v. Kadenacy, 930 F.Supp. 446.

N.D.Cal. 1990. While in general, issue of when reasonable investor should have discovered claims should be left to trier of fact, if complaint is time barred on its face, motion to dismiss may be appropriate.

> Gray v. First Winthrop Corp., 754 F.Supp. 157.

D.Colo. 1996. In order to grant motion to dismiss on limitations grounds, complaint must facially show noncompliance with limitations period. Fed.Rules Civ.Proc.Rule 12(b)(6), 28 U.S.C.A.

> Bowe v. SMC Elec. Products, Inc., 916 F.Supp. 1066.

D.Conn. 1994. Common-law fraud claims which were not filed within two years from date when investors in limited partnership received private placement memoranda (PPMs) were subject to dismissal in light of plaintiff's failure to adequately plead fraudulent concealment so as to toll limitations, where date investors received PPMs was deemed to be closing date indicated in PPMs. C.G.S.A. § 52–595.

> In re Colonial Ltd. Partnership Litigation, 854 F.Supp. 64.

D.Del. 1996. Defendants' statute of limitations defense was timely raised; defense was raised in defendants' motions to dismiss for failure to state claim, which served as responses to plaintiffs' complaints, and plaintiffs were thus put on notice of defense while suit was still in its infancy. Fed.Rules Civ.Proc.Rules 8(c), 12(b)(6), 28 U.S.C.A.

> Johnson v. Cullen, 925 F.Supp. 244.

D.Del. 1992. Statute of limitations is an affirmative defense properly raised on motion to dismiss. Fed.Rules Civ.Proc.Rule 12(b)(6), 28 U.S.C.A.

> McIntyre v. Division of Youth Rehabilitation Services, Dept. of Services for Children, Youth and their Families, State of Del., 795 F.Supp. 668.

M.D.Fla. 1995. When reviewing motion to dismiss on statute of limitations grounds, court must determine whether date alleged in statement of claim indicates that action was not brought within applicable statute of limitations. Fed.Rules Civ.Proc.Rule 12(b)(6), 28 U.S.C.A.

> Harmony Homes, Inc. v. U.S. on Behalf of Small Business Admin., 890 F.Supp. 1032.

On motion to dismiss on Florida statute of limitations grounds, district court had to accept as true mortgagee's allegations that it became holder of mortgages on certain date and that it held mortgages when suit was filed, and, thus, court could not dismiss foreclosure suit against United States, even though United States alleged that mortgagee did not become holder of mortgages until after suit was brought and until 14 days after statute of limitations ran, and, thus, that mortgagee lacked standing to sue on date that suit was brought. West's F.S.A.

§ 95.11(2)(c); Fed.Rules Civ.Proc.Rule 12(b)(6), 28 U.S.C.A.

> Harmony Homes, Inc. v. U.S. on Behalf of Small Business Admin., 890 F.Supp. 1032.

M.D.Fla. 1993. Expiration of applicable limitation period is most appropriately raised as affirmative defense in responsive pleadings, and not in motion to dismiss. Fed.Rules Civ.Proc. Rule 12(b), 28 U.S.C.A.

> Patrick Media Group, Inc. v. City of Clearwater, 836 F.Supp. 833.

M.D.Fla. 1990. Motion to dismiss based on tolling of statute of limitations can be granted only if it appears beyond a doubt that plaintiffs can prove no set of facts that toll statute.

> Knight v. E.F. Hutton and Co., Inc., 750 F.Supp. 1109.

M.D.Fla. 1990. Under Florida law, hospital's claims of laches, estoppel and waiver were affirmative defenses to be raised and proven and would not support dismissal of parents' action charging hospital with negligence and intentional misrepresentation based on alleged baby switching. West's F.S.A. § 768.28(6, 11).

> Twigg v. Hospital Dist. of Hardee County, Fla., 731 F.Supp. 469.

N.D.Fla. 1992. Ripeness goes to subject matter jurisdiction, and thus specific allegations of fact must be made so that court can be assured it has jurisdiction; for such reason, ripeness may be determined on a motion to dismiss.

> Villas of Lake Jackson, Ltd. v. Leon County, 796 F.Supp. 1477.

N.D.Ga. 1996. Generally statutes of limitations defenses cannot be raised on motion to dismiss unless complaint facially shows noncompliance with limitations period and affirmative defense clearly appears on face of pleading.

> District 65 Retirement Trust for Members of Bureau of Wholesale Sales Representatives v. Prudential Securities, Inc., 925 F.Supp. 1551.

D.Hawai'i 1995. Motion to dismiss for failure to state claim should be granted if affirmative defense or other bar to relief is apparent from face of complaint, such as absolute immunity or statute of limitations. Fed.Rules Civ. Proc.Rule 12(b)(6), 28 U.S.C.A.

> Moore v. Kamikawa, 940 F.Supp. 260, affirmed 82 F.3d 423.

N.D.Ill. 1995. Although affirmative defenses are not usually resolved at motion to dismiss stage, if plaintiff's complaint contains facts which demonstrate that his suit is barred by statute of limitations, it may be disposed on such motion. Fed.Rules Civ.Proc.Rule 12(b)(6), 28 U.S.C.A.

> Foster v. Unknown Cook County Deputy Sheriff, 914 F.Supp. 221.

N.D.Ill. 1995. In deciding employer's motion to dismiss for failure to state claim based on allegation that employee failed to timely file discrimination charge with Equal Employment Opportunity Commission (EEOC), court was required only to look at face of complaint and determine whether employee pleaded facts showing that suit was time-barred. Civil Rights Act of 1964, § 706(e)(1), as amended, 42 U.S.C.A. § 2000e–5(e)(1); Fed.Rules Civ.Proc. Rule 12(b)(6), 28 U.S.C.A.

> Shipbaugh v. Boys & Girls Clubs of America, 883 F.Supp. 295.

N.D.Ill. 1994. Statute of limitations defense was appropriate ground for dismissal, despite defendant's failure to plead it in answer, where noncompliance with statute was clearly demonstrated on face of complaint. Fed.Rules Civ.Proc.Rule 8(c), 28 U.S.C.A.

> DiBenedetto v. City of Chicago, 873 F.Supp. 106.

N.D.Ill. 1994. Where defendant alleges in motion to dismiss that action is time barred, district court's task, because it has before it only a complaint and not a factual record, is to determine whether plaintiff has pleaded herself out of court by pleading facts that show that her suit is time barred. Fed.Rules Civ.Proc.Rule 12(b)(6), 28 U.S.C.A.

> Pacourek v. Inland Steel Co., 858 F.Supp. 1393.

N.D.Ill. 1994. Running of statute of limitations, which is affirmative defense, will be appropriate ground for dismissal, if it clearly appears on face of complaint. Fed.Rules Civ. Proc.Rule 8(c), 28 U.S.C.A.

> E.E.O.C. v. Park Ridge Public Library, 856 F.Supp. 477.

In order to grant motion to dismiss on limitations grounds, complaint must facially show noncompliance with limitations period.

> E.E.O.C. v. Park Ridge Public Library, 856 F.Supp. 477.

Public library and city properly raised statute of limitations defense in their motion to dismiss age discrimination action against them, as face of complaint evinced limitations issue.

> E.E.O.C. v. Park Ridge Public Library, 856 F.Supp. 477.

N.D.Ill. 1994. Terminated cookie distributor's breach of implied in fact contract and unjust enrichment claims against former employer did not have to be dismissed pursuant to Illinois five-year statute of limitations for unwritten contracts, where there was no violation of statute of limitations on face of complaint. S.H.A. 735 ILCS 5/13–205.

> Dawson v. W. & H. Voortman, Ltd., 853 F.Supp. 1038.

N.D.Ill. 1994. Unless plaintiff pleads facts that show his cause is time barred, statute of limitations defense is best addressed on motion for summary judgment, rather than motion to dismiss for failure to state claim. Fed.Rules Civ.Proc.Rules 12(b)(6), 56(c), 28 U.S.C.A.

> Adams v. Cavanagh Communities Corp., 847 F.Supp. 1390.

N.D.Ill. 1989. Defense of statute of limitations may be raised in motion to dismiss if time alleged in complaint shows clearly that cause of action has not been brought within appropriate statute of limitations. Fed.Rules Civ.Proc.Rule 12(b)(6), 28 U.S.C.A.

> Motor Carrier Audit and Collection Co., a Div. of Delta Traffic Service, Inc. v. Lighting Products, Inc., 113 B.R. 424.

N.D.Ill. 1989. Former employer's claim that employee's suit for breach of predetermination settlement agreement entered into by employer, EEOC, and employee was barred by laches was premature and would not be resolved at pleadings stage.

> Sherman v. Standard Rate Data Service, Inc., 709 F.Supp. 1433.

N.D.Ill. 1989. Former Federal Deposit Insurance Corporation employee's failure to file suit against Chairman of the FDIC within 30 days of notice of final agency action was not a defect that could be cured by amendment and required dismissal of his Title VII claim against the FDIC, even if Chairman had constructive notice of former employee's claim; notice given to the FDIC employees of the former employee's action was effected after the 30–day notice period. Fed.Rules Civ.Proc.Rule 15(c), 28 U.S.C.A.; Civil Rights Act of 1964, § 717(c), as amended, 42 U.S.C.A. § 2000e–16(c).

> Lenoir v. Federal Deposit Ins. Corp., 709 F.Supp. 830.

N.D.Ill. 1989. Where dates in complaint show that action is barred by statute of limitations, defendant may raise this affirmative defense in preanswer motion to dismiss for failure to state claim upon which relief can be granted. Fed.Rules Civ.Proc.Rule 12(b)(6), 28 U.S.C.A.

> Sports Bar, Inc. v. Village of Downers Grove, Ill., 129 F.R.D. 161.

N.D.Ill. 1986. Rule 12(b)(1), governing dismissal for lack of subject-matter jurisdiction, is proper vehicle for dismissing cases which are untimely and over which no subject-matter jurisdiction exists because plaintiff has failed to exhaust his administrative remedies before coming to court. Fed.Rules Civ.Proc.Rule 12(b)(1), 28 U.S.C.A.

> Gervasio v. U.S., 627 F.Supp. 428.

S.D.Iowa 1996. Statute of limitations may be raised by motion to dismiss where it appears from face of complaint that limitations period has run. Fed.Rules Civ.Proc.Rule 12, 28 U.S.C.A.

> Vrban v. Deere & Co., 947 F.Supp. 410, reversed 129 F.3d 1008.

D.Kan. 1996. When complaint shows on its face that applicable statute of limitations has run, action is subject to dismissal for failure to state claim upon which relief can be granted. Fed.Rules Civ.Proc.Rule 12(b)(6), 28 U.S.C.A.

> Turner and Boisseau, Inc. v. Nationwide Mut. Ins. Co., 944 F.Supp. 842.

Failure of pleadings to readily indicate accrual date of liability insurer's breach of contract action against law firm hired to represent insured required denial of firm's motion alleging statute of limitations and seeking dismissal for failure to state claim. K.S.A. 60–512(1); Fed.Rules Civ.Proc.Rule 12(b)(6), 28 U.S.C.A.

> Turner and Boisseau, Inc. v. Nationwide Mut. Ins. Co., 944 F.Supp. 842.

Where party alleges bar of statute of limitations in motion to dismiss for failure to state claim, court's task is only to determine whether claimant has pleaded facts showing that suit is time barred. Fed.Rules Civ.Proc.Rule 12(b)(6), 28 U.S.C.A.

> Turner and Boisseau, Inc. v. Nationwide Mut. Ins. Co., 944 F.Supp. 842.

Where there is question of fact as to applicability of statute of limitations, motion to dismiss for failure to state claim should be denied. Fed.Rules Civ.Proc.Rule 12(b)(6), 28 U.S.C.A.

> Turner and Boisseau, Inc. v. Nationwide Mut. Ins. Co., 944 F.Supp. 842.

E.D.La. 1997. Motion to dismiss, filed by defendant bar owners in action by distributor of pay-per-view programming for illicit interception and televising of programming and state law tort of conversion, which expressly raised issue of prescription, provided sufficient notice to distributor to permit District Court to consider such issue in ruling on motion, despite bar owners' failure to raise defense of prescription in their answer to distributor's complaint; requiring amended answer would have been meaningless formality in light of distributor's failure to object to bar owners' failure to raise defense of prescription. Fed.Rules Civ.Proc. Rules 8(c), 12(c), 28 U.S.C.A.

> Joe Hand Promotions, Inc. v. Lott, 971 F.Supp. 1058.

E.D.La. 1995. Courts generally allow defense of statute of limitations or prescription to be raised in motion to dismiss. Fed.Rules Civ. Proc.Rule 12(b)(6), 28 U.S.C.A.

> Moore v. K-Mart Corp., 884 F.Supp. 217.

D.Md. 1997. When it appears from face of complaint itself that limitation period has run on action, limitations defense may properly be asserted through motion to dismiss; limitations defense will not be waived, however, when it is not raised in such a motion, as long as it is raised in answer. Fed.Rules Civ.Proc.Rule 12(b)(6), 28 U.S.C.A.

> Papesh v. American Nat. Can Co., 177 F.R.D. 344, affirmed 129 F.3d 117, certiorari denied 118 S.Ct. 1390, 140 L.Ed.2d 649.

D.Md. 1994. Allegations that each defendant committed predicate act within four years prior to filing of complaint under Racketeer Influenced and Corrupt Organizations Act (RICO), and that defendant's fraudulent concealment tolled applicable statute of limitations, was sufficient, at early stages of litigation, to withstand motion to dismiss on limitations grounds, but defendant could again address issue at later date by way of motion for partial summary judgment, if discovery indicated that any particular claim was barred by limitations. 18 U.S.C.A. § 1962 et seq.; Fed.Rules Civ.Proc. Rule 12(b)(6), 28 U.S.C.A.

> Lust v. Burke, 876 F.Supp. 1474.

D.Mass. 1996. Claim that has expired under applicable statute of limitations may be dismissed as frivolous.

> Ball v. Carroll, 932 F.Supp. 388, affirmed 107 F.3d 1.

D.Mass. 1991. In context of motion to dismiss for failure to state claims under §§ 11 and 12(2) of Securities Act of 1933, dismissal on statute of limitations grounds was not warranted, as court had not read study which allegedly put plaintiffs on inquiry notice of misrepresentations and omissions in prospectus. Securities Act of 1933, §§ 11, 12(2), 13, as amended, 15 U.S.C.A. §§ 77k, 77l (2), 77m; Fed.Rules Civ. Proc.Rule 12(b)(6), 28 U.S.C.A.

> Lucia v. Prospect Street High Income Portfolio, Inc., 769 F.Supp. 410, affirmed 36 F.3d 170.

D.C.Mass. 1981. Crowley v. Local No. 82, Furniture and Piano Moving, Furniture Store Drivers, Helpers, Warehousemen and Packers, 521 F.Supp. 614, affirmed 679 F.2d 978, certiorari granted 103 S.Ct. 813, 459 U.S. 1168, 74 L.Ed.2d 1012, reversed 104 S.Ct. 2557, 467 U.S. 526, 81 L.Ed.2d 457, rehearing denied 105 S.Ct. 19, 468 U.S. 1224, 82 L.Ed.2d 915.

E.D.Mich. 1997. Defense of statute of limitations may be raised on motion to dismiss, even though it is affirmative defense plaintiff is not required to negate, when it is apparent from face of complaint that time limit for bringing complaint has passed. Fed.Rules Civ.Proc.Rule 12(b)(6), 28 U.S.C.A.

> Havenick v. Network Exp., Inc., 981 F.Supp. 480.

W.D.Mich. 1995. On motion to dismiss based on claim of violation of limitations period, dismissal is appropriate only if time alleged in complaint clearly shows that action is untimely or if motion to dismiss for failure to state claim on which relief can be granted is accompanied by affidavit or other evidentiary matters demonstrating untimeliness. Fed.Rules Civ. Proc.Rule 12(b)(6), 28 U.S.C.A.

> State of Mich. ex rel. Kelley v. McDonald Dairy Co., 905 F.Supp. 447.

W.D.Mich. 1982. Naph-Sol Refining Co. v. Murphy Oil Corp., 550 F.Supp. 297, affirmed in part, reversed in part Mobil Oil Corp. v. Department of Energy, 728 F.2d 1477, certiorari denied 104 S.Ct. 3545, 467 U.S. 1255, 82 L.Ed.2d 849, certiorari denied 104 S.Ct. 3545, 467 U.S. 1255, 82 L.Ed.2d 849.

D.Minn. 1998. Granting motion to dismiss on basis of statutes of limitations would be improper in light of insureds' allegations of fraud by life insurers in connection with sales allegedly based on misrepresentations and omissions about vanishing premiums, churning, and use of policies for retirement or investment; allegations raised issues of fact that were not amenable to disposition on motion to dismiss for failure to state claim.

> Force v. ITT Hartford Life & Annuity Ins. Co., 4 F.Supp.2d 843.

D.Minn. 1995. Court would not dismiss securities fraud claim, based on argument that suit was brought more than one year after alleged fraud should have been discovered; time of discovery was factual inquiry not resolvable on motion to dismiss. Fed.Rules Civ.Proc. Rule 12(b)(6), 28 U.S.C.A.

> Brogren v. Pohlad, 933 F.Supp. 793.

E.D.Mo. 1994. Complaint does not state claim for which relief can be granted if it states claim for which applicable statute of limitations has run. Fed.Rules Civ.Proc.Rule 12(b)(6), 28 U.S.C.A.

> Resolution Trust Corp. v. Fiala, 870 F.Supp. 962.

W.D.Mo. 1997. When statute of limitations defense involves contested issues—including particularly claims of tolling—motion to dismiss is inadequate method for disposing of issue. Fed.Rules Civ.Proc.Rule 12(b), 28 U.S.C.A.

> Midland Psychiatric Associates, Inc. v. U.S., 969 F.Supp. 543, affirmed 145 F.3d 1000.

D.Nev. 1998. Defendants' failure to raise correct statute of limitations in their pre-answer motion to dismiss did not prejudice plaintiffs, and thus defendants did not waive their right to assert it as defense, where plaintiffs essentially advanced all arguments they could hope to make against correct statute of limitations when they opposed defendants' assertion of incorrect statute of limitations. Fed.Rules Civ.Proc.Rules 8(c), 12(b, g), (h)(2), 28 U.S.C.A.

> Tahoe-Sierra Preservation Council, Inc. v. Tahoe Regional Planning Agency, 992 F.Supp. 1218.

D.N.J. 1996. Although transfer of venue may be in interest of justice if plaintiff could potentially face statute of limitations bar to suit in proper venue if court should dismiss, where it is clear that statute of limitations has run in proposed transferee district, dismissal, rather than transfer, is appropriate. 28 U.S.C.A. § 1406(a).

> Kitces v. Wood, 917 F.Supp. 338.

D.N.J. 1995. Statute of limitations defense may be raised in motion to dismiss for failure to state claim upon which relief can be granted, but only if time alleged in statement of claim shows that cause of action has not been brought within statute of limitations. Fed.Rules Civ. Proc.Rule 12(b)(6), 28 U.S.C.A.

> U.S. v. Jones, 916 F.Supp. 383.

E.D.N.Y. 1997. Complaint alleging § 1983 claim that plaintiff's constitutional rights were violated by filing of inaccurate presentence report would not be dismissed on ground that applicable statute of limitations had run, as complaint did not specify when plaintiff received copy of presentence report and stated only that he requested report in 1995 but never received it, and thus did not allow ascertainment of when cause of action accrued; although plaintiff stated in his memorandum of law in opposition to motion to dismiss that he had opportunity to see report at time of sentencing on 1989, court could not consider extraneous fact. 42 U.S.C.A. § 1983; Fed.Rules Civ. Proc.Rule 12(b)(6).

> Hili v. Sciarotta, 955 F.Supp. 177, affirmed 140 F.3d 210.

E.D.N.Y. 1996. Where employee's § 1981 complaint was vague as to when employer's alleged withholding of supplies and work space occurred, district court could not hold as matter of law that claims were time-barred, since it was required to draw all inferences favorably to employee on motion to dismiss; instead, court would dismiss claims with leave to replead within 30 days the dates on which alleged acts occurred. 42 U.S.C.A. § 1981; Fed.Rules Civ. Proc.Rule 12(b)(6), 28 U.S.C.A.

> Campbell v. Grayline Air Shuttle, Inc., 930 F.Supp. 794.

N.D.N.Y. 1997. Question of inquiry notice may be addressed on motion to dismiss.

Pilarczyk v. Morrison Knudsen Corp., 965 F.Supp. 311.

N.D.N.Y. 1990. Issue of whether patent infringement action was barred by six-year limitations period would not be addressed on motion to dismiss, where issue was raised for first time in reply papers. 35 U.S.C.A. § 286.

Knight v. Storex Systems, Inc., 739 F.Supp. 739.

N.D.N.Y. 1982. Mobil Oil Corp. v. Department of Energy, 547 F.Supp. 1246, affirmed in part, vacated in part, reversed in part 728 F.2d 1477, certiorari denied Murphy Oil Corporation v. Naph-Sol Refining Company, 104 S.Ct. 3545, 467 U.S. 1255, 82 L.Ed.2d 849, certiorari denied 104 S.Ct. 3545, 467 U.S. 1255, 82 L.Ed.2d 849.

S.D.N.Y. 1998. A motion to dismiss on statute of limitations grounds is properly viewed as a motion to dismiss for failure to state a claim upon which relief can be granted. Fed. Rules Civ.Proc.Rule 12(b)(6), 28 U.S.C.A.

Marbi Corp. of New York v. Puhekker, 9 F.Supp.2d 425.

S.D.N.Y. 1997. On a motion to dismiss, when the facts alleged in the complaint indicate that, with reasonable diligence, plaintiffs should have uncovered the alleged fraud prior to the limitations period, the claim will be time-barred. Fed.Rules Civ.Proc.Rule 12(b)(6), 28 U.S.C.A.

In re Merrill Lynch Ltd. Partnerships Litigation, 7 F.Supp.2d 256, opinion affirmed 154 F.3d 56.

S.D.N.Y. 1990. Statute of limitations defense was to be considered raised, even though not pleaded in answer, on motion to dismiss; considering defense waived would have been futile, since defendant would have been permitted to amend its answer to include defense under liberal pleading policy of Federal Rules of Civil Procedure. Fed.Rules Civ.Proc.Rule 15, 28 U.S.C.A.

Williams v. Chase Manhattan Bank, N.A., 728 F.Supp. 1004.

S.D.N.Y. 1989. Statute of limitations claim, and other issues regarding whether defendant's negligence was cause of plaintiffs' harm, could not be disposed on motion to dismiss.

Cohen v. Abrahams, 710 F.Supp. 981.

S.D.N.Y. 1985. Pendent state claims may be dismissed from federal action if they are barred by relevant state statutes of limitation or conditions precedent.

Wrenn v. New York City Health and Hospitals Corp., 104 F.R.D. 553.

W.D.N.C. 1990. Where statute of limitations defect does not appear on face of complaint, motion to dismiss must be denied unless affidavits or other materials are presented to the court, in which case motion should be treated as a motion for summary judgment. Fed.Rules Civ.Proc.Rule 12(b), 28 U.S.C.A.

McKenzie v. E.E.O.C./Charlotte Dist. Office, 749 F.Supp. 115.

If question of fact exists as to statute of limitations defense, issue cannot be determined on affidavits.

McKenzie v. E.E.O.C./Charlotte Dist. Office, 749 F.Supp. 115.

W.D.N.C. 1990. Motion to dismiss for failure to state a claim can be raised when time alleged in complaint shows that action was not brought within applicable statute of limitations. Fed.Rules Civ.Proc.Rule 12(b)(6), 28 U.S.C.A.

I R Const. Products Co., Inc. v. D.R. Allen & Son, Inc., 737 F.Supp. 895.

Face of subcontractor's complaint did not support defendant contractor's contention that action for balance of contract price was barred by three-year statute of limitations, and since affidavits and documents submitted by contractor were unclear as to exactly when statute began to run, court would not consider such matters on motion to dismiss. Fed.Rules Civ. Proc.Rule 12(b)(6), 28 U.S.C.A.

I R Const. Products Co., Inc. v. D.R. Allen & Son, Inc., 737 F.Supp. 895.

N.D.Ohio 1998. Defense of limitations may be raised by a motion to dismiss for failure to state a claim when the time alleged in the complaint shows that plaintiff did not bring the action within the statutory period; however, dismissal of complaint on such ground is proper, only when the statement of the claim affirmatively shows that plaintiff can prove no set of facts that would entitle him to relief. Fed.Rules Civ.Proc.Rule 12(b)(6), 28 U.S.C.A.

City of Painesville, Ohio v. First Montauk Financial Corp., 178 F.R.D. 180.

W.D.Okl. 1985. Motion to dismiss on ground that statute of limitations barred federal securities action under applicable Oklahoma statute would be denied; cross claimants alleged that fraud was discovered less than two years before filing of action, and if cross claimants did not discover fraud more than two years before filing of cross complaint, limitations period would not act as bar. 12 O.S.1981, § 95.

Resler v. Financial Group, Inc., 668 F.Supp. 1454.

Cross defendant's motion to dismiss securities claim that cross claimants did not dispute was barred by statute of limitations would be granted.

> Resler v. Financial Group, Inc., 668 F.Supp. 1454.

E.D.Pa. 1998. Ordinarily, court may not grant motion to dismiss on basis of untimely filing; however, if it is apparent from face of complaint that applicable statute of limitations has expired, court must dismiss complaint. Fed.Rules Civ.Proc.Rule 12(b)(6), 28 U.S.C.A.

> Compton v. National League of Professional Baseball Clubs, 995 F.Supp. 554.

E.D.Pa. 1998. Motion to dismiss for failure to state claim should not be granted on limitations grounds unless complaint facially shows noncompliance with limitations period. Fed.Rules Civ.Proc.Rule 12(b)(6), 28 U.S.C.A.

> Giusto v. Ashland Chemical Co., 994 F.Supp. 587.

E.D.Pa. 1998. Normally, parties will not learn that a limitations period has expired until discovery, and thus, motion for summary judgment is generally proper vehicle for dismissal on this basis; however, if it is clear from face of pleadings that a statute of limitations has expired, dismissal for failure to state a claim is appropriate. Fed.Rules Civ.Proc.Rules 12(b)(6), 56, 28 U.S.C.A.

> Saylor v. Ridge, 989 F.Supp. 680.

E.D.Pa. 1997. Complaint may be dismissed on limitations grounds, in response to motion to dismiss for failure to state a claim, when complaint facially shows noncompliance with applicable limitations period. Fed.Rules Civ.Proc.Rule 12(b)(6), 28 U.S.C.A.

> Johnstone v. U.S., 980 F.Supp. 148.

E.D.Pa. 1996. Where it is apparent from complaint and other matters to which court may properly look in addressing motion to dismiss for failure to state claim upon which relief can be granted that discrimination plaintiff's claim is time-barred, it may be dismissed. Fed. Rules Civ.Proc.Rule 12(b)(6), 28 U.S.C.A.

> Arizmendi v. Lawson, 914 F.Supp. 1157.

E.D.Pa. 1995. Where motion to dismiss for failure to state claim is premised upon statute of limitations defense, court must determine whether time alleged in complaint shows that claim has not been brought within limitations period. Fed.Rules Civ.Proc.Rule 12(b)(6), 28 U.S.C.A.

> Warminster Tp. Mun. Authority v. U.S., 903 F.Supp. 847.

E.D.Pa. 1995. Statute of limitations defense could be considered within context of motion to dismiss purported civil rights claim; thus, most of conduct of which plaintiff complained occurred outside of limitations period and only that conduct inside limitations period

could properly form basis for § 1983 action against city. 42 U.S.C.A. § 1983; Fed.Rules Civ.Proc.Rule 12(b), 28 U.S.C.A.

> Young v. City of Allentown, 882 F.Supp. 1490, affirmed 66 F.3d 314.

E.D.Pa. 1994. Although motion for summary judgment will in most cases be proper vehicle for dismissal on limitations grounds, since parties will not learn that period has expired until discovery phase of trial, court may dismiss action on limitations grounds at pleading stage if face of pleading reveals that limitations period has expired. Fed.Rules Civ.Proc. Rules 12(b)(6), 56, 28 U.S.C.A.

> Jackson v. Nicoletti, 875 F.Supp. 1107.

E.D.Pa. 1994. Statute of limitations defense may be raised by motion to dismiss if defect appears on face of pleading. Fed.Rules Civ.Proc.Rules 8(c), 12(b)(6).

> Atlantic Paper Box Co. v. Whitman's Chocolates, 844 F.Supp. 1038.

E.D.Pa. 1993. Statute of limitations defense may be raised by motion to dismiss for failure to state a claim if affirmative defense appears clearly on face of complaint; inclusion of dates in complaint may show facial noncompliance with statute of limitations. Fed.Rules Civ.Proc.Rules 8(c), 12(b)(6), 28 U.S.C.A.

> Oshiver v. Levin, Fishbein, Sedran and Berman, 818 F.Supp. 104, affirmed in part, reversed in part 38 F.3d 1380, on remand 910 F.Supp. 225, affirmed 96 F.3d 1434.

E.D.Pa. 1993. Statute of limitations defense can be raised in motion to dismiss for failure to state claim upon which relief can be granted if affirmative defense clearly appears on face of pleadings; motion to dismiss should not be granted on limitations grounds unless complaint facially shows noncompliance with limitations period. Fed.Rules Civ.Proc.Rules 8(c), 12(b)(6), 28 U.S.C.A.

> Clark v. Sears Roebuck & Co., 816 F.Supp. 1064.

W.D.Pa. 1986. Premature filing of derivative suit after demand is made on board of directors is equivalent to a failure to make a demand and warrants dismissal. Fed.Rules Civ.Proc.Rule 23.1, 28 U.S.C.A.

> Recchion on Behalf of Westinghouse Elec. Corp. v. Kirby, 637 F.Supp. 1309.

D.R.I. 1992. Generally, it is in interest of justice to transfer case rather than to dismiss if running of statute of limitations will bar case from being brought in appropriate forum. 28 U.S.C.A. § 1631.

> Mansolillo v. F.D.I.C., 804 F.Supp. 426.

E.D.Tenn. 1996. Civil rights action was not subject to dismissal for failure to state a claim on which relief could be granted on statute of limitations grounds, but rather, discovery would be allowed to proceed to determine whether plaintiffs could allege discriminatory act within limitations period in accordance with continuing violations theory, where plaintiffs claimed that their complaint asserted continuing violation and under that theory was timely filed. Civil Rights Act of 1964, § 703, 42 U.S.C.A. § 2000e–2; 42 U.S.C.A. §§ 1981, 1981(a), 1983; West's Tenn.Code, § 28–3–104; Fed.Rules Civ.Proc.Rule 12(b)(6), 28 U.S.C.A.

    Caldwell v. Rowland, 932 F.Supp. 1018.

M.D.Tenn. 1996. Tennessee's "discovery rule" ordinarily raises issues of fact as to whether plaintiff should have known of claim for relief, and whether plaintiff exercised reasonable diligence, prohibiting resolution of issue on either motion to dismiss or motion for summary judgment.

    Craft v. Vanderbilt University, 940 F.Supp. 1185.

N.D.Tex. 1995. Defenses of limitations or laches may be asserted by motion to dismiss for failure to state claim if complaint shows affirmatively that claims are barred. Fed.Rules Civ. Proc.Rule 12(b)(6), 28 U.S.C.A.

    U.S. v. Bantau, 907 F.Supp. 988.

N.D.Tex. 1985. Dismissal of Title VII claims is proper where plaintiff fails to meet his or her burden of proving that complaint was timely filed in court. Civil Rights Act of 1964, §§ 701 et seq., 706(e), as amended, 42 U.S.C.A. §§ 2000e et seq., 2000e–5(f)(1).

    Smith v. Flagship Intern., 609 F.Supp. 58.

S.D.Tex. 1998. Court may dismiss claims on the pleadings; as being barred by applicable statute of limitations, only when face of pleadings clearly shows that claims are time-barred; dismissal is appropriate only when nothing further could be developed by pretrial discovery or by trial on merits.

    Lowrey v. Texas A&M University System, 11 F.Supp.2d 895.

S.D.Tex. 1996. Dismissal of Title VII claim is proper where plaintiff fails to demonstrate that complaint was filed with court on timely basis. Civil Rights Act of 1964, § 706(e, f), (f)(2, 4, 5), as amended, 42 U.S.C.A. § 2000e–5(f).

    Thomas v. Exxon, U.S.A., 943 F.Supp. 751, affirmed 122 F.3d 1067.

S.D.Tex. 1995. Dismissal of Title VII claim is proper where plaintiff fails to prove that complaint was filed with court on timely basis. Civil Rights Act of 1964, § 701 et seq., as amended, 42 U.S.C.A. § 2000e et seq.

    Patton v. United Parcel Service, Inc., 910 F.Supp. 1250.

S.D.Tex. 1995. Dismissal of Title VII claim is proper where employee fails to prove that complaint was filed with court on timely basis. Civil Rights Act of 1964, § 706(e), as amended, 42 U.S.C.A. § 2000e–5(f)(1).

    Lee v. Kroger Co., 901 F.Supp. 1218.

S.D.Tex. 1993. Where issue of limitations requires determination of when claim begins to accrue, complaint should be dismissed for failure to state claim upon which relief may be granted only if evidence is so clear that there is no genuine factual issue and determination can be made as matter of law. Fed.Rules Civ.Proc. Rule 12(b)(6), 28 U.S.C.A.

    Askanase v. Fatjo, 828 F.Supp. 465.

D.Utah 1994. Defense of statute of limitations may be raised by motion to dismiss; however, court may treat motion to dismiss as one for summary judgment where parties have submitted affidavits or other documents outside the pleadings. Fed.Rules Civ.Proc.Rules 12(b), 56(c), 28 U.S.C.A.

    Strickland v. General Motors Corp., 852 F.Supp. 956.

D.Vt. 1992. Defendant may bring motion to dismiss for violation of statute of limitations if violation is evident from the complaint. Fed. Rules Civ.Proc.Rule 12(b)(6), 28 U.S.C.A.

    King v. F.D.I.C., 785 F.Supp. 58.

E.D.Va. 1996. Laches is appropriate issue for motion to dismiss.

    Marshall v. Meadows, 921 F.Supp. 1490, appeal dismissed 105 F.3d 904.

E.D.Va. 1995. Statutes of limitations defenses are appropriately raised in motions to dismiss for failure to state claim. Fed.Rules Civ.Proc.Rule 12(b)(6), 28 U.S.C.A.

    Williams v. Enterprise Leasing Co. of Norfolk/Richmond, 911 F.Supp. 988.

E.D.Va. 1994. Bar of statute of limitations may be interposed by motion to dismiss when time alleged in complaint shows that action was not brought within statutory period. Fed.Rules Civ.Proc.Rule 12(b)(6), 28 U.S.C.A.

    Wamco, III, Ltd. v. First Piedmont Mortg. Corp., 856 F.Supp. 1076.

Bkrtcy.N.D.Ill. 1994. Statute of limitation defenses may be properly raised in either responsive pleading or in motion to dismiss. Fed. Rules Civ.Proc.Rule 12(b)(6), 28 U.S.C.A.; Fed. Rules Bankr.Proc.Rule 7012, 11 U.S.C.A.

    In re Superior Toy & Mfg. Co., Inc., 175 B.R. 693.

Bkrtcy.N.D.Ill. 1994. Statute of limitations defenses may be raised in responsive pleading or in motion to dismiss.

    In re Luria Steel and Trading Corp., 168 B.R. 913.

Bkrtcy.E.D.N.Y. 1995. Although applicable statute of limitations is tolled during 120 days in which plaintiff must serve summons and complaint, that applicable statute of limitations will govern if 120 days expires without service having been performed, and, should this occur, it is up to plaintiff to refile before termination of that statute of limitations period; if that period has also expired, plaintiff is then time-barred, and dismissal is warranted. Fed.Rules Civ. Proc.Rules 4(a), 4(j), 12, 28 U.S.C.A.; Fed.Rules Bankr.Proc.Rules 7004, 7012, 11 U.S.C.A.

In re Osebach, 187 B.R. 92.

Bkrtcy.S.D.N.Y. 1991. On motion to dismiss, courts should be reluctant to erect statute of limitations as insurmountable barrier where that determination turns on circumstances and intentions of parties not readily ascertainable from facts.

In re Argo Communications Corp., 134 B.R. 776.

Bkrtcy.S.D.N.Y. 1983. In re O.P.M. Leasing Services, Inc., 35 B.R. 854, affirmed in part, reversed in part 48 B.R. 824.

Bkrtcy.M.D.Pa. 1993. Motion to dismiss under Rule 12(b)(6) is proper vehicle to raise limitations defense. Fed.Rules Civ.Proc.Rule 12(b)(6), 28 U.S.C.A.

In re Taylorcraft Aviation Corp., 163 B.R. 734.

Bkrtcy.N.D.Tex. 1991. Complaint may be dismissed for failure to state claim upon which relief can be granted, where relief sought is barred by affirmative defense, such as statute of limitations.

In re Hunt, 136 B.R. 437.

⚷1755. —— **Res judicata and pendency of another action.**

C.A.11 (Fla.) 1986. Pending mortgage foreclosure action was not duplicative of civil rights suit brought by debtor against creditor and others, so as to warrant dismissal of the latter, in that additional parties were present in the civil rights suit and civil rights action involved significantly different issues and it could not be ascertained from record whether foreclosure action would involve Fourth Amendment or due process claims. U.S.C.A. Const.Amend. 14.

I.A. Durbin, Inc. v. Jefferson Nat. Bank, 793 F.2d 1541.

A suit is "duplicative" of another suit if the parties, issues and available relief do not significantly differ between the two actions.

I.A. Durbin, Inc. v. Jefferson Nat. Bank, 793 F.2d 1541.

Trial courts have broad discretion in determining whether to stay or dismiss litigation in order to avoid duplicating a proceeding pending in another federal court.

I.A. Durbin, Inc. v. Jefferson Nat. Bank, 793 F.2d 1541.

C.A.7 (Ill.) 1995. To discourage claim splitting, judges award plaintiffs the first outcome, not the better outcome; whichever suit goes to judgment first is dispositive, and doctrine of claim preclusion or res judicata requires the other court to dismiss the litigation.

Rogers v. Desiderio, 58 F.3d 299.

C.A.7 (Ill.) 1987. Res judicata is defense like any other and is not jurisdictional; if res judicata is proved, defendants are entitled to judgment on merits rather than dismissal of complaint.

White v. Elrod, 816 F.2d 1172, certiorari denied 108 S.Ct. 286, 484 U.S. 924, 98 L.Ed.2d 246, rehearing denied 108 S.Ct. 2837, 486 U.S. 1062, 100 L.Ed.2d 937.

C.A.7 (Ill.) 1985. As general practice, federal courts should stay rather than dismiss actions when they decline to proceed on merits because of pendency of related state court proceeding, since, should state court fully resolve dispute, then practical effect of stay will be identical to that of dismissal, but should issue remain, parties can revive action without statute of limitations problems since federal court would have retained its jurisdictional tie to case.

Ohio River Co. v. Carrillo, 754 F.2d 236.

C.A.1 (Me.) 1990. Even if senior mortgagees waived res judicata as affirmative defense to equitable subordination claims by junior lienholders, bankruptcy court could dismiss action sua sponte consistent with res judicata policy of avoiding judicial waste. Bankr.Code, 11 U.S.C.A. § 510(c)(1, 2); Fed.Rules Civ.Proc. Rule 8(c), 28 U.S.C.A.

In re Medomak Canning, 922 F.2d 895.

Even if defendant waives res judicata as affirmative defense, court on notice that it has previously decided issue may dismiss action sua sponte, consistent with res judicata policy of avoiding judicial waste.

In re Medomak Canning, 922 F.2d 895.

C.A.6 (Mich.) 1985. When the doctrine of res judicata applies, dismissal is appropriate.

Fellowship of Christ Church v. Thorburn, 758 F.2d 1140.

C.A.3 (N.J.) 1997. Contention that suit was barred by New Jersey's Entire Controversy Doctrine, under which all claims that party has against other party must be set forth or be deemed lost, was not motion to dismiss for lack of proper subject matter jurisdiction; rather, Doctrine was affirmative defense which did not defeat subject matter jurisdiction. Fed.Rules Civ.Proc.Rule 12(b)(1, 6), 28 U.S.C.A.

> Rycoline Products, Inc. v. C & W Unlimited, 109 F.3d 883.

Claim that New Jersey's Entire Controversy Doctrine, requiring that all claims against adverse parties be raised in one proceeding, barred suit in federal court could not be raised by motion to dismiss for failure to state cause of action; applicability of Doctrine was not obvious from face of pleadings, and court was required to either dismiss without prejudice to renew in form of motion for summary judgment, or to convert to summary judgment giving parties opportunity to supplement their presentations. Fed.Rules Civ.Proc.Rules 8(c), 12(b)(6), 56, 28 U.S.C.A.

> Rycoline Products, Inc. v. C & W Unlimited, 109 F.3d 883.

C.A.2 (N.Y.) 1993. District court properly dismissed distributor's second complaint against radio communications products manufacturer on res judicata grounds, notwithstanding distributor's claim that district court had failed to consider renewed claims because they were not mentioned explicitly in its prior decision; allegations contained in second complaint were argued in first action, parties were identical, and district court's grant of summary judgment against distributor rejected merits of contentions.

> Harriscom Svenska, AB v. Harris Corp., 3 F.3d 576.

C.A.2 (N.Y.) 1993. Failure of defendant to raise res judicata in answer does not deprive court of power to dismiss claim on that ground.

> Salahuddin v. Jones, 992 F.2d 447, certiorari denied 114 S.Ct. 278, 510 U.S. 902, 126 L.Ed.2d 229.

Even though state officials did not raise defense of res judicata in answer, court properly dismissed inmate's civil rights action on the grounds of res judicata where the precise claim was disposed of in a prior action a number of years earlier.

> Salahuddin v. Jones, 992 F.2d 447, certiorari denied 114 S.Ct. 278, 510 U.S. 902, 126 L.Ed.2d 229.

C.A.2 (N.Y.) 1992. Although generally res judicata is affirmative defense to be pleaded in defendant's answer, when all relevant facts are shown by court's own records, of which court takes notice, defense may be upheld on motion to dismiss for failure to state claim without requiring answer. Fed.Rules Civ.Proc.Rules 8(c), 12(b)(6), 28 U.S.C.A.

> Day v. Moscow, 955 F.2d 807, certiorari denied 113 S.Ct. 71, 506 U.S. 821, 121 L.Ed.2d 37.

C.A.2 (N.Y.) 1986. Pendency of action brought in federal district court in Wisconsin by promoter against company which had been client to recover finder's fee was not special circumstance requiring stay, dismissal or transfer of prior federal district court action brought by client seeking declaratory judgment that client was not liable for finder's fee.

> Fort Howard Paper Co. v. William D. Witter, Inc., 787 F.2d 784.

C.A.2 (N.Y.) 1985. Dismissal of nuisance action against county for improperly constructing and failing to maintain groins was not warranted on ground that homeowners' rights would be protected in a different pending litigation and that relief sought would be meaningless unless New York State and the United States were joined as parties, where plaintiffs in prior litigation had failed to file notice of claimants required by New York law, timeliness issue was more easily addressed in instant suit because of absence of additional causes of action and defendants, and injunction to abate nuisance would not necessarily require New York or United States to do any act or spend money.

> Rapf v. Suffolk County of New York, 755 F.2d 282.

C.A.1 (Puerto Rico) 1991. In ruling on motion to dismiss action arising from termination of yacht dealership under *Colorado River* doctrine in favor of parallel proceeding in Puerto Rico, court did not abuse its discretion in determining that factors of motivation, novel local law, relative progress of cases and piecemeal adjudication constituted "exceptional circumstances" outweighing presumption in favor of jurisdiction; district court found that lawsuit was reactive, that issue of whether claim for tortious interference with prospective business advantage existed was substantial question of Commonwealth law, that Commonwealth action was markedly more advanced, and that case involved more than routine inefficiency.

> Villa Marina Yacht Sales, Inc. v. Hatteras Yachts, 947 F.2d 529, certiorari denied 112 S.Ct. 1674, 503 U.S. 986, 118 L.Ed.2d 393.

Perfect identity of issues in federal and state action is not prerequisite for dismissal under *Colorado River* doctrine.

> Villa Marina Yacht Sales, Inc. v. Hatteras Yachts, 947 F.2d 529, certiorari denied 112 S.Ct. 1674, 503 U.S. 986, 118 L.Ed.2d 393.

District court, in ruling on motion to dismiss under *Colorado River* doctrine, was entitled to find facts relating to plaintiff's motivation for bringing suit based on plaintiff's actions, rather than upon allegedly unopposed statements in affidavit of plaintiff's president.

> Villa Marina Yacht Sales, Inc. v. Hatteras Yachts, 947 F.2d 529, certiorari denied 112 S.Ct. 1674, 503 U.S. 986, 118 L.Ed.2d 393.

Transferability of transcripts cannot automatically trump "relative progress" factor in evaluating motion to dismiss under *Colorado River* doctrine.

> Villa Marina Yacht Sales, Inc. v. Hatteras Yachts, 947 F.2d 529, certiorari denied 112 S.Ct. 1674, 503 U.S. 986, 118 L.Ed.2d 393.

Removal policy did not operate in favor of dismissal under *Colorado River* doctrine in favor of parallel proceeding in Commonwealth of Puerto Rico; losses were not identical, plaintiff's federal claims did not duplicate claims it filed in Commonwealth Court, and defendants in each suit were different.

> Villa Marina Yacht Sales, Inc. v. Hatteras Yachts, 947 F.2d 529, certiorari denied 112 S.Ct. 1674, 503 U.S. 986, 118 L.Ed.2d 393.

Fact that claims brought in federal lawsuit also could be brought in state court does not promote dismissal under *Colorado River* doctrine, but is significant only as indication that dismissal, if affirmatively warranted based on other factors, would not prejudice federal court plaintiff.

> Villa Marina Yacht Sales, Inc. v. Hatteras Yachts, 947 F.2d 529, certiorari denied 112 S.Ct. 1674, 503 U.S. 986, 118 L.Ed.2d 393.

C.A.5 (Tex.) 1987. Determination of whether to hold *Bivens* claims in abeyance or to dismiss them, based on prisoner's failure to exhaust federal habeas corpus remedies, should be based on considerations of statute of limitations problems dismissal would raise.

> Solsona v. Warden, F.C.I., 821 F.2d 1129.

C.A.5 (Tex.) 1987. In determining whether to dismiss or stay *Bivens* action against federal prison officials pending habeas corpus proceedings, court must consider whether dismissal of the claims without prejudice will preserve prisoner's opportunity to assert those claims upon resolution of a timely habeas corpus application. 28 U.S.C.A. § 2241.

> Spina v. Aaron, 821 F.2d 1126.

C.A.9 (Wash.) 1986. As soon as one of multiple actions being prosecuted by plaintiff on the same set of facts against the same defendant in different courts reaches judgment, the other cases must be dismissed.

> Taylor v. Burlington Northern R. Co., 787 F.2d 1309.

Em.App. 1986. Dismissal of case in Texas for continuation in Louisiana which had ten-year, rather than four-year, statute of limitations would produce type of prejudice that justified retaining case in Texas and giving oil buyer protection of Texas statute of limitations, where oil seller filed motion to dismiss before oil buyer filed motion for summary judgment in oil seller's action to collect payment under Emergency Petroleum Allocation Act. Emergency Petroleum Allocation Act of 1973, §§ 2 et seq., 5, 8(j)(1)(A), as amended, 15 U.S.C.A. §§ 751 et seq., 754, 757(j)(1)(A); Economic Stabilization Act of 1970, § 211(b)(2), 12 U.S.C.A. § 1904 note; Fed.Rules Civ.Proc.Rule 41(a)(1)(i), (a)(2), 28 U.S.C.A.

> Placid Oil Co. v. Ashland Oil, Inc., 792 F.2d 1127.

M.D.Ala. 1998. State employee's race discrimination lawsuit against state, state's transportation department and department's agents, following entry of consent decree in his prior race discrimination lawsuit, would not result in duplicative litigation or inconsistent adjudications and, therefore, would not be dismissed on such grounds, where employee did not request in second lawsuit any change, modification or alteration of consent decree, and consent decree did not form legal basis for employee's second lawsuit.

> Smith v. State of Alabama, 996 F.Supp. 1203.

E.D.Ark. 1984. Diversity action brought by beneficiaries, Arkansas residents, against nonresident insurer seeking recovery of accidental death benefits under life policy was dismissed where previous institute action between the same parties and involving the same issues were pending in Arkansas courts, insurer did not seek removal to federal court, entire suit turned on questions of state law and beneficiaries based their claim solely on state statute and raised no independent questions of federal law.

> Cory v. Mark Twain Life Ins. Co., 604 F.Supp. 226.

D.Colo. 1991. Colorado property owners' claim for exemplary damages in connection with releases of hazardous substances from mine would not be dismissed to extent that exemplary damages were sought for sole claim which was not barred by res judicata. West's C.R.S.A. § 13–21–102.

> Satsky v. Paramount Communications, Inc., 778 F.Supp. 505, reversed 7 F.3d 1464.

D.Del. 1992. Plaintiff's claim against defendant for negligently repairing one of plaintiff's chemical storage tanks would not be dismissed on res judicata grounds, where defendant conceded that state court dismissed plaintiff's case against defendant because plaintiff was unable to prove that defendant had performed any repairs on tank and complaint alleged that defendant fraudulently concealed fact that it had actually performed repairs on tank.

Standard Chlorine of Delaware, Inc. v. Sinibaldi, 821 F.Supp. 232.

D.Del. 1987. "Convenience" of forum, for purpose of determining whether to stay or dismiss federal court proceedings pending state court action, refers to ease of access to sources of proof, availability of compulsory process, and enforceability of judgments, among other things.

Sea Colony, Inc. v. Alcan Aluminum Corp., 653 F.Supp. 1323.

M.D.Fla. 1985. Dismissal of securities case involving claim of fraud was inappropriate even though similar state case was pending.

Olsen v. Paine Webber, Jackson & Curtis, Inc., 623 F.Supp. 17.

S.D.Fla. 1992. Factual issues existed, which precluded dismissal on res judicata grounds, on whether jail administrator and officers were in privity with county and its sheriff, against whom inmate had filed civil rights action that was identical to prior action in which inmate claimed that he was denied recreation while in county jail. 42 U.S.C.A. § 1983.

Jacobson v. McIlwain, 145 F.R.D. 595.

Factual issues existed on whether persons who appeared to be state officials, prosecutor, and police officer were in privity with county and its sheriff, for purposes of determining whether res judicata barred inmate's civil rights action claiming that he was denied recreation while in county jail. 42 U.S.C.A. § 1983.

Jacobson v. McIlwain, 145 F.R.D. 595.

N.D.Ga. 1984. Intrusion which would result from granting requested relief into matters which were still subject of divorce action in county court and within its special expertise in area of domestic relations warranted dismissal of former husband's complaint seeking appointment of receiver to oversee and effectuate sale of house and distribution of proceeds in accordance with divorce decree.

Cavalino v. Cavalino, 601 F.Supp. 74.

N.D.Ill. 1987. Employee's fraud and breach of contract actions brought in state court did not require dismissal of employee's federal RICO claim based on same facts; RICO claim named six defendants who were not parties to state action, and RICO allegation comprised distinct legal claim. 18 U.S.C.A. § 1961 et seq.

Shaw v. Williams, 676 F.Supp. 168.

D.Mass. 1991. If defense of res judicata is raised, court may dismiss action if issues which were raised or could have been raised in prior

action between parties or those in privity with them were resolved by prior judgment.

Continental Bank, Nat. Ass'n v. Village of Ludlow, 777 F.Supp. 92.

D.Minn. 1984. Rule that when an action involves a claim that should be a compulsory counterclaim in another pending federal suit the court should stay its own proceedings or dismiss the claim is only applicable when the claims filed in the subsequent suit are compulsory counterclaims to the prior-filed action. Fed.Rules Civ.Proc.Rule 13(a), 28 U.S.C.A.

Minnetonka, Inc. v. Sani-Fresh Intern., Inc., 103 F.R.D. 377.

S.D.Miss. 1988. Duplicative litigation, brought in Mississippi to preserve plaintiffs' punitive damages claims which were time barred under Louisiana statute of limitations at time plaintiffs sought to amend their complaint in Louisiana action to state additional claim for punitive damages, was subject to dismissal. 28 U.S.C.A. § 1406(a).

Washington v. Williams, 696 F.Supp. 237, affirmed 884 F.2d 576.

E.D.Mo. 1984. Dismissal of leased business personal property claim against insurer was warranted where another trial was to take place involving plaintiff and an outside party concerning plaintiff's liability for destruction of the leased items, and where granting of plaintiff's request to dismiss such issue would prevent inconsistent determinations.

Hampton Foods, Inc. v. Aetna Cas. & Sur. Co., 601 F.Supp. 58, affirmed in part, reversed in part 787 F.2d 349, appeal after remand 843 F.2d 1140.

D.N.J. 1995. While technically defendant should assert claim and issue preclusion as defenses in answer as precursor to motion to dismiss, affirmative defenses may be raised for first time in motion to dismiss complaint or on motion for summary judgment. Fed.Rules Civ. Proc.Rule 8(c), 28 U.S.C.A.

Sibert v. Phelan, 901 F.Supp. 183.

E.D.N.Y. 1997. Although res judicata is an affirmative defense, when all relevant facts are shown by court's own records, of which the court takes notice, defense of res judicata may be upheld on motion to dismiss for failure to state a claim, even if defendant has not filed an answer to complaint. Fed.Rules Civ.Proc.Rule 12(b)(6), 28 U.S.C.A.

Ramirez v. Brooklyn Aids Task Force, 175 F.R.D. 423.

E.D.N.Y. 1995. Disciplinary hearing panel members' affirmative defenses of absolute immunity, qualified immunity, collateral estoppel and failure to allege facts sufficient to state claim were apparent on face of suspended school teacher's complaint which alleged that disciplinary action violated his constitutional rights and New York antidiscrimination law, and therefore such defenses were reviewable on hearing panel members' motion to dismiss complaint for failure to state claim. Fed.Rules Civ.Proc.Rule 12(b)(6), 28 U.S.C.A.; N.Y.McKinney's Executive Law § 296.

> Taylor v. Brentwood Union Free School Dist., 908 F.Supp. 1165.

S.D.N.Y. 1998. Challenge based on *res judicata* grounds may be properly raised in a motion to dismiss for failure to state claim. Fed.Rules Civ.Proc.Rule 12(b)(6), 28 U.S.C.A.

> Clarkstown Recycling Center, Inc. v. Parker, Chapin Flattau & Klimpl, LLP, 1 F.Supp.2d 327.

S.D.N.Y. 1995. Res judicata is typically affirmative defense to be pleaded in defendant's answer, but if all relevant facts are shown by court's own records, of which court takes notice, defense may be upheld on motion to dismiss without requiring answer. Fed.Rules Civ. Proc.Rule 12(b)(6), 28 U.S.C.A.

> Meagher on Behalf of Pension Plan of Cement and Concrete Workers Dist. Council Pension Fund v. Board of Trustees of Pension Plan of Cement and Concrete Workers Dist. Pension Fund, 921 F.Supp. 161, opinion affirmed 79 F.3d 256.

S.D.N.Y. 1995. Res judicata and collateral estoppel can be raised and considered via pretrial motion to dismiss. Fed.Rules Civ.Proc. Rule 12(b)(6), 28 U.S.C.A.

> HBP Associates v. Marsh, 893 F.Supp. 271.

S.D.N.Y. 1993. Defense of res judicata or collateral estoppel may be brought, under appropriate circumstances, via either motion to dismiss or motion for summary judgment. Fed. Rules Civ.Proc.Rule 12(b)(6), 28 U.S.C.A.

> Sassower v. Abrams, 833 F.Supp. 253.

S.D.N.Y. 1986. Claim of independent, high-risk automobile policy brokers, which challenged automobile insurer's transfer of accounts obtained from independent brokers to affiliated brokers without consent of insured or broker, which could not clearly be resolved by grievance to appropriate state agency or agencies under New York automobile insurance plan for high-risk automobile policies, but which had to be pursued before committee or superintendent of plan under doctrine of primary jurisdiction, required stay, rather than dismissal. N.Y.McKinney's Insurance Law §§ 326(a), 5301, 5301(b), 5302, 5304(a), 5406.

> Azby Brokerage, Inc. v. Allstate Ins. Co., 637 F.Supp. 382.

S.D.N.Y. 1985. Action brought by insurer under financial guarantee bond for limited partnership to recover from limited partners under indemnification agreement was not subject to dismissal, although limited partners contended that they had first filed an action in Texas seeking reformation of loan agreements entered into by limited partners, where insurer was not a party to those agreements, and thus, its claim was not one that arose out of the same transaction or occurrence that was the subject matter of the Texas suit.

> National Union Fire Ins. Co. of Pittsburgh, Pa. v. R.H. Weber Exploration, Inc., 605 F.Supp. 1299.

E.D.Pa. 1995. Where state prisoner sought damages in § 1983 suit alleging that search and seizure which resulted in his arrest and conviction were unlawful, and judgment for plaintiff would necessarily imply that his conviction was invalid, doctrine of issue preclusion required that claim be dismissed without prejudice to renew if and when prisoner's state court conviction was legally invalidated on appeal. 42 U.S.C.A. § 1983.

> Shelton v. Macey, 883 F.Supp. 1047.

E.D.Pa. 1985. Given difference between legal and factual issues in the present antitrust actions and those in prior state court proceeding, doctrines of collateral estoppel and res judicata did not justify dismissal.

> S. Kane & Son, Inc. v. W.R. Grace & Co., 623 F.Supp. 162, affirmed Graveley Roofing Co. v. W.R. Grace & Co., Inc., 857 F.2d 1464, affirmed 857 F.2d 1465, affirmed Appeal of S. Kane & Son, Inc., 857 F.2d 1465.

D.R.I. 1995. Pleadings did not establish whether stipulated arbitration award was entered into unknowingly or involuntarily, and thus, even assuming award constituted negotiated settlement rather than arbitration decision, district court could not determine on motion to dismiss whether employee's Title VII claim relating to her termination would be precluded by that settlement. Civil Rights Act of 1964, § 703, 42 U.S.C.A. § 2000e–2; R.I.Gen.Laws 1956, § 28–5–7.

> Tang v. State of R.I., Dept. of Elderly Affairs, 904 F.Supp. 69.

N.D.Tex. 1988. Claims against the FDIC by a customer of a bank placed in receivership, which could have been but were not raised in the customer's previous action against the bank, were barred under the doctrine of res judicata; thus dismissal rather than transfer of the case to a proper forum was warranted. 28 U.S.C.A. § 1406(a).

> Spriggins v. Federal Deposit Ins. Corp., 683 F.Supp. 163, affirmed 877 F.2d 970, rehearing denied 881 F.2d 1071.

S.D.W.Va. 1985. Claims under West Virginia law for malicious use of civil process and abuse of process asserted by plaintiff in federal diversity action had not yet accrued and, thus, could not have been asserted by plaintiff in one of two civil actions brought by the parties in state court, so that federal action was not dismissed for failure to assert the claims as a counterclaim in one of the two state court actions. Fed.Rules Civ.Proc.Rule 13(a), 28 U.S.C.A.

Steele v. Morris, 608 F.Supp. 274.

Bkrtcy.E.D.N.Y. 1997. Normally, defenses of res judicata and collateral estoppel are affirmative defenses to be raised in an answer, but, when all relevant facts are shown by court's own records, of which court takes notice, defense may be upheld on motion to dismiss for failure to state claim, without requiring an answer. Fed.Rules Bankr.Proc.Rules 7001, 7008, 7012(b)(6), (c), 7056, 11 U.S.C.A.; Fed.Rules Civ.Proc.Rules 8(c), 12(b)(6), 28 U.S.C.A.

In re 9281 Shore Road Owners Corp., 214 B.R. 676.

Bkrtcy.S.D.N.Y. 1989. Res judicata and collateral estoppel defenses may not be raised by motion to dismiss for failure to state claim, or before responsive pleading has been filed.

In re Vinci, 108 B.R. 439.

Bkrtcy.S.D.Ohio 1986. Although creditor's second adversary complaint seeking denial of discharge and determination of dischargeability of debts, which contained two counts identical to those alleged in first complaint and two counts arising out of same transaction, was separately filed complaint rather than amended complaint, second complaint would be considered, rather than dismissed, despite debtors' contention that multiplicity of suits should not be allowed. Bankr.Code, 11 U.S.C.A. §§ 523, 727.

Matter of Schwartzman, 63 B.R. 348.

⚷1756. —— Statute of frauds.

C.A.3 (N.J.) 1994. Complaint may be subject to dismissal for failure to state claim when affirmative defense, like statute of frauds, appears on its face; receding from *Currier*, 442 F.2d 422. Fed.Rules Civ.Proc.Rule 12(b)(6), 28 U.S.C.A.

ALA, Inc. v. CCAIR, Inc., 29 F.3d 855.

C.A.3 (Pa.) 1997. Dismissal for failure to state claim based upon affirmative defense of statute of frauds could not be asserted before defendant had submitted answer since same would enable defendant to use statute of frauds as sword, in contravention of Pennsylvania law. 68 P.S. § 250.202; Fed.Rules Civ.Proc.Rule 12(b)(6), 28 U.S.C.A.

Flight Systems, Inc. v. Electronic Data Systems Corp., 112 F.3d 124.

W.D.Mo. 1984. Anselmo v. Manufacturers Life Ins. Co., 595 F.Supp. 541, affirmed 771 F.2d 417.

S.D.N.Y. 1997. Motion to dismiss may be granted if, drawing all reasonable inferences from complaint in favor of plaintiff, defendant has valid statute of frauds defense to plaintiff's claims. Fed.Rules Civ.Proc.Rule 12(b)(6), 28 U.S.C.A.

Messner Vetere Berger McNamee Scmetterer EURO RSCG Inc. v. Aegis Group PLC, 974 F.Supp. 270, question certified 150 F.3d 194.

E.D.Pa. 1994. Candy maker could raise statute-of-frauds affirmative defense on motion to dismiss where box manufacturer's complaint clearly raised statute of frauds defect on its face, as it referred only to oral negotiations creating alleged contractual obligations. Fed.Rules Civ.Proc.Rules 8(c), 12(b)(6), 28 U.S.C.A.

Atlantic Paper Box Co. v. Whitman's Chocolates, 844 F.Supp. 1038.

Statute of frauds defense may be raised by motion to dismiss complaint for failure to state claim if defect appears on face of pleading. Fed.Rules Civ.Proc.Rules 8(c), 12(b)(6), 28 U.S.C.A.

Atlantic Paper Box Co. v. Whitman's Chocolates, 844 F.Supp. 1038.

Bkrtcy.S.D.N.Y. 1991. Motion to dismiss for failure to state claim was not appropriate vehicle to raise statute of frauds defense, based on plaintiff's failure to specifically allege existence of written contract; rather, statute of frauds had to be plead as affirmative defense in defendant's answer. Fed.Rules Civ.Proc.Rules 8(c), 12(b)(6), 28 U.S.C.A.

In re Marceca, 129 B.R. 371.

⚷1757. —— Waiver and estoppel.

C.A.1 (Mass.) 1988. Defendant waived defense of lack of personal jurisdiction by failing to raise it in motion to dismiss for lack of proper venue. Fed.Rules Civ.Proc.Rules 12, 12(g), (h)(1), 28 U.S.C.A.

Pilgrim Badge & Label Corp. v. Barrios, 857 F.2d 1.

C.A.4 (Va.) 1995. Dismissal on grounds of judicial estoppel was improper where the facts alleged to have prompted prior, inconsistent position were in dispute. Fed.Rules Civ.Proc. Rule 12(b)(6), 28 U.S.C.A.

John S. Clark Co. v. Faggert & Frieden, P.C., 65 F.3d 26.

M.D.Fla. 1982. Manecke v. School Bd. of Pinellas County, Fla., 553 F.Supp. 787, affirmed in part, reversed in part 762 F.2d 912, rehearing denied 770 F.2d 1084, certiorari denied 106 S.Ct. 809, 474 U.S. 1062, 88 L.Ed.2d 784.

D.Md. 1996. Complaint cannot be dismissed on basis of affirmative defense of waiver when issue is legal sufficiency of plaintiff's complaint. Fed.Rules Civ.Proc.Rule 12(b)(6), 28 U.S.C.A.

> Keeler v. Mayor & City Council of Cumberland, 928 F.Supp. 591, motion denied 951 F.Supp. 83.

Bkrtcy.S.D.Fla. 1992. Estoppel and waiver are factual issues which cannot be raised in motion to dismiss, but rather must be pleaded and proven by defendant as affirmative defenses.

> In re Servico, Inc., 144 B.R. 557.

⚷**1758. Failure to prosecute.**

Library references

C.J.S. Federal Civil Procedure § 811.

⚷**1758.1. —— In general.**

C.A.D.C. 1986. District court abused discretion in dismissing complaint in response to plaintiff's request for continuance until essential witness, who had left country unexpectedly because of family emergency, returned to United States, even though plaintiff had failed to subpoena witness, where witness had cooperated fully throughout discovery and had promised to appear at trial, giving plaintiff no reason to believe that subpoena would be necessary.

> Grochal v. Aeration Processes, Inc., 797 F.2d 1093, 254 U.S.App.D.C. 426, vacated 812 F.2d 745, 259 U.S.App.D.C. 29.

C.A.D.C. 1986. Repeated failure of plaintiff's local counsel to attend status calls during three-week period did not warrant dismissal on grounds of punishment or deterrence absent showing of client complicity or client awareness that status calls were being missed.

> Shea v. Donohoe Const. Co., Inc., 795 F.2d 1071, 254 U.S.App.D.C. 175.

C.A.D.C. 1985. A dismissal for want of prosecution is proper if, in view of entire procedural history of case, litigant has not manifested reasonable diligence in pursuing the cause. Fed.Rules Civ.Proc.Rule 41(b), 28 U.S.C.A.

> Bomate v. Ford Motor Co., 761 F.2d 713, 245 U.S.App.D.C. 310.

Dismissal of an action for want of prosecution was not an abuse of discretion where trial court repeatedly warned plaintiff and her counsel of consequences of further delay, and record revealed repeated frustration of pretrial process caused by plaintiff's continuous refusal to cooperate with her own lawyers. Fed.Rules Civ.Proc.Rule 41(b), 28 U.S.C.A.

> Bomate v. Ford Motor Co., 761 F.2d 713, 245 U.S.App.D.C. 310.

C.A.D.C. 1985. Trial judge abused her discretion by denying continuance and dismissing

sex discrimination action with prejudice for want of prosecution, since plaintiff's delay in bringing her financial difficulties to attention of counsel and court did not warrant harsh sanction of dismissal. Civil Rights Act of 1964, § 701 et seq., 42 U.S.C.A. § 2000e et seq.; Fair Labor Standards Act of 1938, § 6, as amended, 29 U.S.C.A. § 206; Fed.Rules Civ.Proc.Rule 41(b), 28 U.S.C.A.

> Trakas v. Quality Brands, Inc., 759 F.2d 185, 245 U.S.App.D.C. 165.

C.A.4 1990. Before dismissing case for failure to prosecute, trial court must consider: plaintiff's degree of personal responsibility; amount of prejudice caused defendant; presence of drawn out history of deliberately proceeding in dilatory fashion; and effectiveness of sanctions less drastic than dismissal. Fed.Rules Civ.Proc.Rule 41(b), 28 U.S.C.A.; Tax Court Rule 123(b), 26 U.S.C.A. foll. § 7453.

> Hillig v. C.I.R., 916 F.2d 171, on remand 1991 WL 40510.

Dismissal sanction is usually inappropriate when it unjustly penalizes blameless client for attorney's behavior. Fed.Rules Civ.Proc.Rule 41(b), 28 U.S.C.A.; Tax Court Rule 123(b), 26 U.S.C.A. foll. § 7453.

> Hillig v. C.I.R., 916 F.2d 171, on remand 1991 WL 40510.

C.A.9 1994. District court is required to weigh five factors to determine whether to dismiss case for lack of prosecution: public's interest in expeditious resolution of litigation; court's need to manage its docket; risk of prejudice to defendants; public policy favoring disposition of cases on merits; and availability of less drastic sanctions. Fed.Rules Civ.Proc.Rule 41(b), 28 U.S.C.A.

> In re Eisen, 31 F.3d 1447.

In determining whether dismissal for lack of prosecution is warranted, courts weigh factor favoring disposition of cases on their merits against plaintiff's delay and prejudice suffered by defendant. Fed.Rules Civ.Proc.Rule 41(b), 28 U.S.C.A.

> In re Eisen, 31 F.3d 1447.

Under egregious circumstances, it is unnecessary, although helpful, for trial court to discuss why alternatives to dismissal for lack of prosecution are infeasible. Fed.Rules Civ.Proc. Rule 41(b), 28 U.S.C.A.

> In re Eisen, 31 F.3d 1447.

C.A.Fed. (Ill.) 1986. Plaintiff's deliberate refusal to appear at trial and prosecute his counterclaim for fraud and unjust enrichment with respect to patents authorized district judge to dismiss the counterclaim for failure to prosecute. Fed.Rules Civ.Proc.Rule 41(b, c), 28 U.S.C.A.

> Syntex Ophthalmics, Inc. v. Novicky, 795 F.2d 983.

C.A.11 (Ala.) 1995. Dismissal with prejudice for want of prosecution is sanction of last resort that is to be utilized only in extreme situations.

> Morewitz v. West of England Ship Owners Mut. Protection and Indem. Ass'n (Luxembourg), 62 F.3d 1356, certiorari denied 116 S.Ct. 915, 516 U.S. 1114, 133 L.Ed.2d 845.

C.A.11 (Ala.) 1991. Class action could be dismissed for want of prosecution, where plaintiff did not move for class certification and merely propounded one interrogatory pertinent to class certification during 15 months from filing of suit until grant of plaintiff's summary judgment motion.

> Kendrick v. Jefferson County Bd. of Educ., 932 F.2d 910, appeal after remand 13 F.3d 1510.

C.A.11 (Ala.) 1986. Dismissal of civil action for want of prosecution is appropriate sanction. Fed.Rules Civ.Proc.Rule 60(b)(6), 28 U.S.C.A.

> Clark v. James, 794 F.2d 595.

Prison inmate's action claiming variety of constitutional violations was properly dismissed for want of prosecution, where defendant failed to appear for evidentiary hearing as he had escaped from supervised intensive restitution program and remained at large at time of hearing and returned involuntarily only upon his recapture, and notwithstanding possibility that he escaped only because he faced "grisly choice" in considering whether to escape inhumane conditions of his incarceration and fact that he was recaptured eight days before dismissal and was not informed that dismissal was pending. Fed.Rules Civ.Proc.Rule 60(b)(6), 28 U.S.C.A.

> Clark v. James, 794 F.2d 595.

District court is not required to ignore litigant's voluntary absence from hearing set in his case and continuously reset hearings on chance that litigant may later decide to attend one; if it is clear that moving party deliberately failed to appear at hearing on issues he raises, dismissal is appropriate regardless of whether it further appears that it might have suited his convenience to appear should hearing be later set. Fed.Rules Civ.Proc.Rule 60(b)(6), 28 U.S.C.A.

> Clark v. James, 794 F.2d 595.

C.A.9 (Ariz.) 1986. In determining whether to dismiss action under Rule 41(b) for lack of prosecution, district court was required to weigh public's interest in expeditious resolution of litigation, court's need to manage its docket,

risk of prejudice to defendants, public policy favoring disposition of cases on their merits, and availability of less drastic sanctions. Fed. Rules Civ.Proc.Rule 41(b), 28 U.S.C.A.

> Henderson v. Duncan, 779 F.2d 1421.

District court's dismissal of action for failure to prosecute upon failure of plaintiff's counsel to submit pretrial order in accordance with local rule on or before fourth extended due date was not an abuse of discretion; plaintiff's counsel disregarded repeatedly the deadlines set by the court, court clearly warned counsel of consequences of continuing dilatory preparation, court explored and used alternative measures, including holding of status conference and establishing schedule for discovery and preparation of pretrial order, before it used final measure of dismissal and, although no specific showing of prejudice to defendants was made, integrity of the district court was involved. U.S.Dist.Ct.Rules D. Ariz., Rule 42(c); Fed. Rules Civ.Proc., Rule 41(b), 28 U.S.C.A.

> Henderson v. Duncan, 779 F.2d 1421.

Showing of bad faith is not required under court's inherent power to dismiss action for lack of prosecution under Rule 41(b). Fed. Rules Civ.Proc.Rule 41(b), 28 U.S.C.A.

> Henderson v. Duncan, 779 F.2d 1421.

C.A.8 (Ark.) 1993. Dismissal for failure to prosecute is proper when there has been clear record of delay or contumacious conduct by plaintiff. Fed.Rules Civ.Proc.Rule 41(b), 28 U.S.C.A.

> Garland v. Peebles, 1 F.3d 683, rehearing denied.

C.A.8 (Ark.) 1985. Dismissal with prejudice of employment discrimination action by white cafeteria employee of school district was abuse of discretion where there was no evidence of pattern of delay or contumacious conduct.

> Clayton v. White Hall School Dist., 778 F.2d 457.

C.A.8 (Ark.) 1985. Pattern of intentional delay by plaintiff is sufficient to warrant trial court's dismissal of action with prejudice.

> Fletcher v. Southern Farm Bureau Life Ins. Co., 757 F.2d 953.

C.A.9 (Cal.) 1998. Inasmuch as dismissal for lack of prosecution is harsh penalty, it is appropriate only in extreme circumstances of unreasonable delay.

> Hernandez v. City of El Monte, 138 F.3d 393.

C.A.9 (Cal.) 1996. Before imposing dismissal as sanction for failure to prosecute or comply with rules of civil procedure, district court must weigh several factors: public's interest in expeditious resolution of litigation; court's need to manage its docket; risk of prejudice to defendants; public policy favoring disposition of cases on their merits; and availability of less drastic sanctions. Fed.Rules Civ.Proc.Rule 41(b), 28 U.S.C.A.

> Dahl v. City of Huntington Beach, 84 F.3d 363.

C.A.9 (Cal.) 1996. In determining whether to dismiss for lack of prosecution, court must consider public's interest in expeditious resolution of litigation, court's need to manage its docket, risk of prejudice to defendant, public policy favoring disposition of cases on the merits, and availability of less drastic sanctions; there must be showing of unreasonable delay, but court is not required to make explicit findings on those factors. Fed.Rules Civ.Proc.Rule 41(b), 28 U.S.C.A.

> Al-Torki v. Kaempen, 78 F.3d 1381.

Dismissal with prejudice and default on counterclaims for willful and inexcusable failure to prosecute are proper exercises of discretion under the federal rules and the inherent power of the court. Fed.Rules Civ.Proc.Rules 16(f), 41(b), 28 U.S.C.A.

> Al-Torki v. Kaempen, 78 F.3d 1381.

Even assuming that plaintiff's case is meritorious, culpability of willful failure to appear for trial and prejudice to the defense, as well as interference with court's docket, may be held to outweigh that factor when ruling on motion to dismiss for failure to prosecute. Fed.Rules Civ. Proc.Rule 41(b), 28 U.S.C.A.

> Al-Torki v. Kaempen, 78 F.3d 1381.

Dismissal for failure to prosecute was proper based on age of the case and plaintiff's failure to appear after being directed to do so. Fed. Rules Civ.Proc.Rule 41(b), 28 U.S.C.A.

> Al-Torki v. Kaempen, 78 F.3d 1381.

C.A.9 (Cal.) 1991. Upon motion to dismiss for failure to prosecute, district court is required to weigh the following factors in arriving at decision: court's need to manage its docket, public interest in expeditious resolution of litigation, risk of prejudice to defendants from delay, and policy favoring disposition of cases on their merits. Fed.Rules Civ.Proc.Rule 41(b), 28 U.S.C.A.

> Morris v. Morgan Stanley & Co., 942 F.2d 648.

C.A.9 (Cal.) 1991. While district court may sua sponte dismiss an action for failure to prosecute, case should be dismissed only for an unreasonable failure to prosecute.

> McKeever v. Block, 932 F.2d 795.

Pro se plaintiff's refusal to file second-amended complaint in § 1983 action alleging infringement of right to a fair trial did not constitute unreasonable failure to prosecute, so as to justify dismissal; although first-amended complaint failed to specify when challenged activities occurred, dates of alleged misconduct could be readily ascertained because amended complaint referred to plaintiff's criminal trial. 42 U.S.C.A. § 1983; U.S.C.A. Const.Amend. 6.

> McKeever v. Block, 932 F.2d 795.

C.A.9 (Cal.) 1987. Taxpayer's contention that value of subject property was greater than minimum bid was not grounds to vacate dismissal of action, which sought to enjoin tax sale and declaration of taxpayer's rights with respect to subject property, for failure to prosecute such action prior to tax sale. Fed.Rules Civ.Proc. 59(e), 28 U.S.C.A.

> Thomassen v. U.S., 835 F.2d 727.

C.A.9 (Cal.) 1987. Courts have inherent equitable powers to dismiss actions or enter default judgments for failure to prosecute, contempt of court, or abuse of litigation practices.

> TeleVideo Systems, Inc. v. Heidenthal, 826 F.2d 915.

C.A.9 (Cal.) 1987. Length of time that case had been on docket and inconvenience of rescheduling court calendar did not relieve district judge of his obligation to warn plaintiff that dismissal for want of prosecution was imminent.

> Hamilton v. Neptune Orient Lines, Ltd., 811 F.2d 498.

C.A.9 (Cal.) 1986. District court did not abuse its discretion in dismissing local union officer's second cause of action against international, alleging failure to refer him to work, for failure to prosecute under local rule; even considering time that officer's attorney was out of the country, attorney still had approximately two weeks within which to ascertain nature of proceedings and to prepare for conference and had five-day period after learning true nature of National Labor Relations Board proceeding and pretrial conference date.

> Lynn v. Sheet Metal Workers' Intern. Ass'n, 804 F.2d 1472, certiorari granted 108 S.Ct. 1219, 485 U.S. 958, 99 L.Ed.2d 420, dismissal denied 108 S.Ct. 2866, 487 U.S. 1215, 101 L.Ed.2d 902, affirmed 109 S.Ct. 639, 488 U.S. 347, 102 L.Ed.2d 700.

C.A.9 (Cal.) 1986. Dismissal of defendant's counterclaim was not abuse of discretion, where defendant, following denial of motion to voluntarily dismiss without prejudice, refused to proceed with counterclaim before judge to whom care had been assigned.

> Kern Oil and Refining Co. v. Tenneco Oil Co., 792 F.2d 1380, certiorari denied 107 S.Ct. 1349, 480 U.S. 906, 94 L.Ed.2d 520.

C.A.9 (Cal.) 1986. District court did not abuse its discretion in dismissing Title VII action for failure to comply with pretrial orders and rules of district court pertaining to pretrial conference; district judge gave plaintiff abundant opportunity and incentive to prepare for pretrial conference and trial, and court's patience in granting continuances indicated that it weighed various factors required by *Henderson* before imposing sanction of dismissal. Civil Rights Act of 1964, § 701, 42 U.S.C.A. § 2000e; U.S.Dist.Ct.Rules C.D.Cal. General Rules 9.4, 9.8.1; Fed.Rules Civ.Proc. Rule 16, 28 U.S.C.A.

> Thompson v. Housing Authority of City of Los Angeles, 782 F.2d 829, certiorari denied 107 S.Ct. 112, 479 U.S. 829, 93 L.Ed.2d 60.

C.A.9 (Cal.) 1985. In considering dismissal for lack of prosecution under Federal Rule of Civil Procedure, courts will consider whether plaintiff has prosecuted action diligently and to what extent any delay has prejudiced the defendant. Fed.Rules Civ.Proc.Rule 41(b), 28 U.S.C.A.

> Olympic Sports Products, Inc. v. Universal Athletic Sales Co., 760 F.2d 910, certiorari denied Whittaker Corporation v. Olympic Sports Products, Inc., 106 S.Ct. 804, 474 U.S. 1060, 88 L.Ed.2d 780.

Decision to dismiss under Federal Rule of Civil Procedure governing discretionary dismissal for lack of prosecution is within discretion of district court. Fed.Rules Civ.Proc.Rule 41(b), 28 U.S.C.A.

> Olympic Sports Products, Inc. v. Universal Athletic Sales Co., 760 F.2d 910, certiorari denied Whittaker Corporation v. Olympic Sports Products, Inc., 106 S.Ct. 804, 474 U.S. 1060, 88 L.Ed.2d 780.

Federal Rule of Civil Procedure, not section of California Code of Civil Procedure, governs dismissals for lack of prosecution in diversity suits in federal court. West's Ann.Cal.C.C.P. § 583(b) (Repealed); Fed.Rules Civ.Proc.Rule 41(b), 28 U.S.C.A.

> Olympic Sports Products, Inc. v. Universal Athletic Sales Co., 760 F.2d 910, certiorari denied Whittaker Corporation v. Olympic Sports Products, Inc., 106 S.Ct. 804, 474 U.S. 1060, 88 L.Ed.2d 780.

C.A.9 (Cal.) 1984. Ash v. Cvetkov, 739 F.2d 493, certiorari denied 105 S.Ct. 1368, 470 U.S. 1007, 84 L.Ed.2d 387.

C.A.9 (Cal.) 1984. Toyota Landscape Co., Inc. v. Building Material and Dump Truck Drivers Local 420, Intern. Broth. of Teamsters, Chauffeurs, Warehousemen and Helpers of America, 726 F.2d 525, certiorari denied 105 S.Ct. 104, 469 U.S. 825, 83 L.Ed.2d 49.

C.A.2 (Conn.) 1998. Dismissals for failure to prosecute or failure to follow court order are "harsh remedy" that are appropriate only in extreme circumstances, and district courts should be especially hesitant to dismiss for procedural deficiencies where failure is by pro se litigant. Fed.Rules Civ.Proc.Rule 41(b), 28 U.S.C.A.

> Spencer v. Doe, 139 F.3d 107.

C.A.2 (Conn.) 1994. District court has power to dismiss action for failure to prosecute and such dismissal will be reviewed only for abuse of discretion.

> Nita v. Connecticut Dept. of Environmental Protection, 16 F.3d 482.

C.A.11 (Fla.) 1995. Incidental powers of federal courts include power to control admission to its bar, punish parties for contempt, vacate its own judgment upon proof that fraud has been perpetrated upon court, bar disruptive criminal defendant from courtroom, dismiss action on grounds of forum non conveniens, act sua sponte to dismiss suit for failure to prosecute, and assess attorney fees against counsel.

> In re Mroz, 65 F.3d 1567.

C.A.11 (Fla.) 1986. District court abused its discretion in dismissing action for failure to prosecute where there were no defects in summons or service, return of service was dated slightly over two months after plaintiff's action was filed and slightly over one month after her application to proceed in forma pauperis was denied, and where there was interval of slightly over one month between denial of application to proceed in forma pauperis and payment of filing fee. Fed.Rules Civ.Proc.Rules 4(c)(2)(B)(i), (d)(4, 5), (j), 41(b), 28 U.S.C.A.; Social Security Act, § 205(g), 42 U.S.C.A. § 405(g); Civil Rights Act of 1964, § 706(e), as amended, 42 U.S.C.A. § 2000e–5(f)(1); U.S.Dist.Ct.Rules M.D.Fla., Rule 4.07.

> Rodgers on Behalf of Jones v. Bowen, 790 F.2d 1550.

C.A.11 (Fla.) 1986. Decision to dismiss for want of prosecution lies within trial court's discretion and can be reversed only for abuse of discretion.

> McKelvey v. AT & T Technologies, Inc., 789 F.2d 1518.

Severe sanction of dismissal with prejudice or the equivalent thereof based on lack of prosecution should be imposed only in the face of a clear record of delay or contumacious conduct by plaintiff.

> McKelvey v. AT & T Technologies, Inc., 789 F.2d 1518.

Finding of extreme circumstances necessary to support sanction of dismissal with prejudice or the equivalent thereof based on lack of prosecution must, at a minimum, be based on evidence of willful delay; simple negligence does not warrant dismissal.

> McKelvey v. AT & T Technologies, Inc., 789 F.2d 1518.

Failure of plaintiff and his counsel to respond to district court's rule to show cause why the case should not be dismissed for failure to prosecute was, at most, simple negligence, and thus, sanction of dismissal which was the equivalent of a dismissal with prejudice because of limitations problems was improper, where the failure to respond was due to counsel's failure to receive a copy of the rule that was attributable to failure to substitute counsel for his predecessor as counsel of record.

McKelvey v. AT & T Technologies, Inc., 789 F.2d 1518.

C.A.11 (Fla.) 1986. District court abused its discretion in dismissing cruise passenger's negligence action for failure to obtain local counsel in accordance with district court's local rules, where case against cruise line was dismissed only three months and two days after it was transferred to proper court, passenger did attempt to retain local counsel, and court failed to consider less drastic sanctions for noncompliance.

Cohen v. Carnival Cruise Lines, Inc., 782 F.2d 923.

C.A.11 (Ga.) 1987. Normally, dismissal of prisoner's civil rights case for failure to prosecute is disfavored in that such a harsh sanction runs counter to policy of law favoring disposition of cases on merits.

Dorsey v. Edge, 819 F.2d 1066.

District court did not abuse its discretion in dismissing prisoner's § 1983 civil rights action against prison guard and warden, for want of prosecution, after court advised prisoner that he could present his testimony through deposition if warden would not permit his release to be present at hearing, but counsel failed to take prisoner's deposition and present it at hearing. 42 U.S.C.A. § 1983.

Dorsey v. Edge, 819 F.2d 1066.

C.A.11 (Ga.) 1987. District court should consider all possibilities for affording prisoner his day in court before dismissing his civil action for failure to prosecute, including appointing counsel or transferring inmate to place of trial, holding bench trial within prison, presenting evidence by depositions, or continuing case if prisoner's release is imminent.

Poole v. Lambert, 819 F.2d 1025.

Dismissal of inmate's civil action for failure to prosecute is justified only as last resort, after other possible methods of disposing of action on the merits have been fully explored, and where inmate does not cooperate with diligent efforts of district court.

Poole v. Lambert, 819 F.2d 1025.

C.A.11 (Ga.) 1986. A party should not be punished for his attorney's mistake absent a clear record of delay or willful contempt and a finding that lesser sanctions would not suffice.

Ford v. Fogarty Van Lines, Inc., 780 F.2d 1582.

A party's simple negligence in complying with a court's order does not warrant dismissal.

Ford v. Fogarty Van Lines, Inc., 780 F.2d 1582.

In view of the absence of a clear record of delay in contumacious conduct by plaintiff and the trial court's failure to explore lesser sanctions, dismissal with prejudice of a personal injury action because of plaintiff's counsel's failure to file a timely pretrial order was not warranted.

Ford v. Fogarty Van Lines, Inc., 780 F.2d 1582.

C.A.11 (Ga.) 1985. Court's power under Rule 41(b) to dismiss for failure to prosecute or obey court order or federal rule is inherent aspect of its authority to enforce its orders and insure prompt disposition of lawsuits. Fed. Rules Civ.Proc.Rule 41(b), 28 U.S.C.A.

Goforth v. Owens, 766 F.2d 1533.

Legal standard to be applied under Rule 41(b) governing dismissal for failure to prosecute or to obey court order or federal rule is whether there is clear record of delay or willful contempt and a finding that lesser sanctions would not suffice. Fed.Rules Civ.Proc.Rule 41(b), 28 U.S.C.A.

Goforth v. Owens, 766 F.2d 1533.

District court did not abuse its discretion in dismissing, under Rule 41(b), medical malpractice action due to plaintiff's counsel's pattern of delay and deliberate refusal to comply with court's direction; any lesser sanction than dismissal would not have served interests of justice. Fed.Rules Civ.Proc.Rule 41(b), 28 U.S.C.A.

Goforth v. Owens, 766 F.2d 1533.

Trial court would have been justified in dismissing, under Rule 16(f), medical malpractice action as sanction for conduct of plaintiff's counsel, who engaged in pattern of delay and deliberately refused to comply with court's directions. Fed.Rules Civ.Proc.Rule 16(f), 28 U.S.C.A.

Goforth v. Owens, 766 F.2d 1533.

C.A.7 (Ill.) 1998. Failure to pay filing fee normally leads to dismissal for want of prosecution by court in which pleading was filed.

Sperow v. Melvin, 153 F.3d 780.

C.A.7 (Ill.) 1998. Dismissal for failure to prosecute is extraordinarily harsh sanction, to which courts should resort only in extreme situations, when there is a clear record of delay or contumacious conduct, or when other less drastic sanctions have proven unavailable.

Dunphy v. McKee, 134 F.3d 1297.

General guidelines for district court's exercise of discretion to dismiss case for lack of prosecution are same in cases involving court-appointed counsel as those involving retained counsel.

Dunphy v. McKee, 134 F.3d 1297.

C.A.7 (Ill.) 1995. Dismissal for want of prosecution is harsh sanction, which should be imposed only in extreme situations when there is clear record of delay or contumacious conduct, or when other less drastic sanctions have proven unavailing.

Matter of Bluestein & Co., 68 F.3d 1022.

In all but the most egregious circumstances, proper exercise of district court's discretion is to dismiss action for want of prosecution only after giving due warning to plaintiff's attorney.

Matter of Bluestein & Co., 68 F.3d 1022.

C.A.7 (Ill.) 1994. Dismissal for failure to prosecute civil action against various officials of Illinois Department of Corrections who allegedly assaulted plaintiff while he was prisoner was not abuse of discretion; district court was not required to impose lesser sanctions before dismissing case of plaintiff who had been less than forthright in explaining his inability to attend trial.

Johnson v. Kamminga, 34 F.3d 466, rehearing and suggestion for rehearing denied, certiorari denied 115 S.Ct. 1373, 514 U.S. 1023, 131 L.Ed.2d 228.

Judge is not required to employ progressive discipline before ultimately dismissing case for want of prosecution.

Johnson v. Kamminga, 34 F.3d 466, rehearing and suggestion for rehearing denied, certiorari denied 115 S.Ct. 1373, 514 U.S. 1023, 131 L.Ed.2d 228.

C.A.7 (Ill.) 1994. A court is permitted to infer a lack of intent to prosecute a case from a pattern of failure to make court-imposed deadlines. Fed.Rules Civ.Proc.Rule 41(b), 28 U.S.C.A.

Dickerson v. Board of Educ. of Ford Heights, Ill., 32 F.3d 1114.

Where pattern of dilatory conduct is clear, dismissal for want of prosecution need not be preceded by imposition of less severe sanctions. Fed.Rules Civ.Proc.Rule 41(b), 28 U.S.C.A.

Dickerson v. Board of Educ. of Ford Heights, Ill., 32 F.3d 1114.

C.A.7 (Ill.) 1994. Ignoring deadlines and orders marks abandonment of suit, justifying dismissal as surely as filing notice of dismissal.

U.S. v. Golden Elevator, Inc., 27 F.3d 301.

C.A.7 (Ill.) 1993. Sanctions under rule dealing with pretrial conferences, rule dealing with discovery sanctions, and rule dealing with failure to prosecute are the same. Fed.Rules Civ.Proc.Rules 16(f), 37(b), 41(b), 28 U.S.C.A.

Lucien v. Breweur, 9 F.3d 26.

C.A.7 (Ill.) 1993. Drastic nature of dismissal with prejudice requires action to be used only in extreme situations when there is clear record of delay or contumacious conduct, or when other less drastic sanctions have proven unavailable.

GCIU Employer Retirement Fund v. Chicago Tribune Co., 8 F.3d 1195, on remand 1994 WL 496716, reversed 66 F.3d 862, rehearing and suggestion for rehearing denied.

District court abused its discretion by dismissing action with prejudice for failure to prosecute despite lapse of 22 months after case was dismissed by Court of Appeals; parties undertook settlement negotiations after dismissal and, although they did not inform district court of such negotiations, nothing in their conduct reflected lack of prosecutorial intent. Fed.Rules Civ.Proc.Rule 41(b), 28 U.S.C.A.; U.S.Dist.Ct.Rules N.D.Ill., General Rules 21, 21(a).

GCIU Employer Retirement Fund v. Chicago Tribune Co., 8 F.3d 1195, on remand 1994 WL 496716, reversed 66 F.3d 862, rehearing and suggestion for rehearing denied.

For purposes of dismissing case for failure to prosecute, court may infer lack of prosecutorial intent from such factors as withdrawal of an attorney, failure to appear at scheduled hearing, and failure to appear on time.

GCIU Employer Retirement Fund v. Chicago Tribune Co., 8 F.3d 1195, on remand 1994 WL 496716, reversed 66 F.3d 862, rehearing and suggestion for rehearing denied.

C.A.7 (Ill.) 1993. Standard for whether to impose default judgment, or dismissal for failure to prosecute, are very similar, as default judgment is mirror image of dismissal for failure to prosecute.

Philips Medical Systems Intern. B.V. v. Bruetman, 8 F.3d 600, rehearing denied.

C.A.7 (Ill.) 1993. Judge is not required to impose graduated sanctions before dismissing case for failure to prosecute. Fed.Rules Civ. Proc.Rule 41(b), 28 U.S.C.A.

Ball v. City of Chicago, 2 F.3d 752, suggestion for rehearing denied.

Decision to dismiss suit for failure to prosecute should not be based on judge's desire to improve his statistics or judge's dislike for class of litigants or of lawsuits, but judge may consider likely merits of suit in deciding whether to dismiss it for failure to prosecute. Fed.Rules Civ.Proc.Rule 41(b), 28 U.S.C.A.

> Ball v. City of Chicago, 2 F.3d 752, suggestion for rehearing denied.

Decision whether to dismiss suit for failure to prosecute should take full and careful account of frequency and magnitude of plaintiff's failure to comply with deadlines for prosecution, apportionment of responsibility for failures between plaintiff and his counsel, and appropriateness of sanctioning counsel rather than plaintiff, effect of failures in taxing judge's time and disrupting calendar to prejudice other litigants, prejudice to defendant from dilatory conduct, probable merits of suit, and consequences of dismissal. Fed.Rules Civ.Proc.Rule 41(b), 28 U.S.C.A.

> Ball v. City of Chicago, 2 F.3d 752, suggestion for rehearing denied.

C.A.7 (Ill.) 1991. Dismissal for failure to prosecute employment discrimination action brought by attorney pro se against her former employer was not abuse of discretion; record revealed pattern of delay and inattentiveness shown by plaintiff's unexplained failure to attend status hearing, her own deposition, scheduled discovery conference, and her failure to otherwise cooperate with discovery, and she offered inconsistent explanations for conduct. Fed.Rules Civ.Proc.Rule 41(b), 28 U.S.C.A.

> Lockhart v. Sullivan, 925 F.2d 214, rehearing denied.

C.A.7 (Ill.) 1989. Court need not impose sanction less severe than dismissal for plaintiff's lack of prosecution or failure to comply with court orders, where record of plaintiff's dilatory conduct is clear. Fed.Rules Civ.Proc.Rule 41(b), 28 U.S.C.A.

> Pyramid Energy, Ltd. v. Heyl & Patterson, Inc., 869 F.2d 1058.

Court need not consider meritorious nature of action, prior to dismissing suit based on plaintiff's lack of prosecution or failure to comply with orders of court. Fed.Rules Civ.Proc.Rule 41(b), 28 U.S.C.A.

> Pyramid Energy, Ltd. v. Heyl & Patterson, Inc., 869 F.2d 1058.

C.A.7 (Ill.) 1987. Dismissing pro se civil rights action for failure to prosecute was abuse of discretion; plaintiff was incarcerated and proceeding in forma pauperis, complaint was dismissed before plaintiff had been able to retain counsel, and delay involved was less than three months. 42 U.S.C.A. § 1983; Fed.Rules Civ.Proc.Rules 12(b)(6), 41(b), 28 U.S.C.A.

> Palmer v. City of Decatur, Ill., 814 F.2d 426.

C.A.7 (Ill.) 1987. Dismissal with prejudice for plaintiff's failure to prosecute case is appropriate where there is clear record of delay or contumacious behavior, or when other sanctions have proved unavailing. Fed.Rules Civ.Proc.Rule 41(b), 28 U.S.C.A.

> 3 Penny Theater Corp. v. Plitt Theatres, Inc., 812 F.2d 337.

Dismissal with prejudice for plaintiff's failure to prosecute case and subsequent refusal to vacate dismissal and reinstate case were not abuses of discretion, where plaintiff's counsel repeatedly failed to attend status hearings, did not inspect documents being held by defendants until nearly one year after magistrate had directed counsel to do so, refused to produce documents for inspection after agreeing to produce them for defendants, answered interrogatories after defendant's motion requesting that plaintiff answer those interrogatories was argued, and received three extensions of date for filing of pretrial materials. Fed.Rules Civ.Proc. Rules 41(b), 60(b), 28 U.S.C.A.

> 3 Penny Theater Corp. v. Plitt Theatres, Inc., 812 F.2d 337.

C.A.7 (Ill.) 1985. Dismissal with prejudice is appropriate when there is a clear record of delay or contumacious behavior. Fed.Rules Civ.Proc.Rule 41(b), 28 U.S.C.A.

> Zaddack v. A.B. Dick Co., 773 F.2d 147.

A court may infer lack of prosecutorial intent from withdrawal of an attorney, failure to appear at a scheduled hearing and failure to appear on time.

> Zaddack v. A.B. Dick Co., 773 F.2d 147.

District court did not abuse its discretion in dismissing employment discrimination action for failure to prosecute where plaintiff had specifically requested discovery be continued on three occasions and failed to file memorandum concerning class certification and where two sets of attorneys had been granted leave to withdraw from the action and plaintiff's third attorney, who had been granted additional time to complete discovery, failed to appear for a status conference on time. Fed.Rules Civ.Proc. Rule 41(b), 28 U.S.C.A.

> Zaddack v. A.B. Dick Co., 773 F.2d 147.

C.A.7 (Ind.) 1990. District court acted unreasonably in requiring civil rights plaintiff to choose between dismissal and going to trial when even plaintiff's previous attorney was not ready for trial; former attorney had not subpoenaed primary witnesses, who were in jail.

> Lowe v. City of East Chicago, Ind., 897 F.2d 272.

District court should consider less severe sanctions than dismissal for party's noncompliance with court orders or failure to prosecute his or her claim expeditiously, unless there exists clear record of delay or contumacious conduct or when less drastic sanctions have proven ineffective; Court of Appeals is reluctant to affirm dismissal when there is no sign of either client neglect of court processes or knowledge of attorney neglect.

> Lowe v. City of East Chicago, Ind., 897 F.2d 272.

C.A.7 (Ind.) 1987. A court reviewing dismissal of action or claim for failure of plaintiff to prosecute or to comply with procedural rules or court order must consider procedural history of case as well as status of case at time of dismissal. Fed.Rules Civ.Proc.Rule 41(b), 28 U.S.C.A.

> Roland v. Salem Contract Carriers, Inc., 811 F.2d 1175.

C.A.7 (Ind.) 1985. District court's dismissal of an action for want of prosecution is discretionary.

> Sisk v. U.S., 756 F.2d 497.

C.A.6 (Ky.) 1993. District court has authority to dismiss case for failure to prosecute. Fed.Rules Civ.Proc.Rule 41(b), 28 U.S.C.A.

> Little v. Yeutter, 984 F.2d 160.

Competing concerns guide whether court should dismiss action for failure to prosecute; on the one hand, there is court's need to manage its docket, public's interest in expeditious resolution of litigation, and risk of prejudice to defendant because plaintiff has failed to actively pursue its interest, while, on the other hand, there is policy favoring disposition of cases on their merits. Fed.Rules Civ.Proc.Rule 41(b), 28 U.S.C.A.

> Little v. Yeutter, 984 F.2d 160.

Order of dismissal for failure to prosecute is abuse of discretion, such that district court is limited to lesser sanctions designed to achieve compliance, absent showing of clear record of delay or contumacious conduct. Fed.Rules Civ. Proc.Rule 41(b), 28 U.S.C.A.

> Little v. Yeutter, 984 F.2d 160.

C.A.5 (La.) 1997. District court has the inherent authority to dismiss action for failure to prosecute sua sponte, with or without notice to the parties, but dismissals with prejudice are reserved for the most egregious of cases, usually where the requisite factors of clear delay and ineffective lesser sanctions are bolstered by delay resulting from intentional conduct, delay caused by the plaintiff personally, or delay causing prejudice to the defendant.

> Clofer v. Perego, 106 F.3d 678.

When attorney appointed to represent prisoner in civil rights action repeatedly failed to appear at hearings, court should not have imposed sanction of dismissal with prejudice for failure to prosecute.

> Clofer v. Perego, 106 F.3d 678.

C.A.5 (La.) 1991. Sanction of dismissal for failure to prosecute claim is generally reserved for most egregious cases, usually those cases where requisite factors of clear delay and ineffective lesser sanctions are bolstered by presence of at least one aggravating factor.

> Aucoin v. K-Mart Apparel Fashion Corp., 943 F.2d 6.

C.A.5 (La.) 1986. District court's dismissal of civil rights action for failure to prosecute was not an abuse of discretion where plaintiff's counsel failed to file pretrial order, resulting in stay, failed for over ten months to certify intent to comply with standing pretrial instructions and procedural rules after stay was continued, and failed to show up at pretrial conference after court reinstated complaint, and where, although nothing indicated that plaintiff herself was at fault and nothing showed that delay prejudiced defendant, intentional conduct was present. Fed.Rules Civ.Proc.Rules 16(f), 37(b)(2)(C), 41(b), 28 U.S.C.A.

> Price v. McGlathery, 792 F.2d 472, 90 A.L.R. Fed. 149.

C.A.5 (La.) 1985. Whether to involuntarily dismiss action under Federal Rule of Civil Procedure for failure to prosecute is inherent power of court, to be exercised in district court's discretion. Fed.Rules Civ.Proc.Rule 41(b), 28 U.S.C.A.

> Ford v. Sharp, 758 F.2d 1018, 27 Wage & Hour Cas. (BNA) 257.

In Fifth Circuit, involuntary dismissal of case with prejudice for failure to prosecute is proper only where there is clear record of delay or contumacious conduct by plaintiff and lesser sanctions would not serve best interests of justice. Fed.Rules Civ.Proc.Rule 41(b), 28 U.S.C.A.

> Ford v. Sharp, 758 F.2d 1018, 27 Wage & Hour Cas. (BNA) 257.

For purpose of determining whether to dismiss action with prejudice for failure to prosecute, Fifth Circuit Court of Appeals examines "aggravating factors" such as extent to which plaintiff, as distinguished from his counsel, was personally responsible for delay, degree of actual prejudice to defendant and whether delay was result of intentional conduct. Fed.Rules Civ.Proc.Rule 41(b), 28 U.S.C.A.

> Ford v. Sharp, 758 F.2d 1018, 27 Wage & Hour Cas. (BNA) 257.

C.A.4 (Md.) 1986. Dismissal under Civil Procedure Rule 41(b), for plaintiff's failure to prosecute or comply with rules or order of court, would have been unsupportable, absent evidence of any default by plaintiff. Fed.Rules Civ.Proc.Rule 41(b), 28 U.S.C.A.

> Andes v. Versant Corp., 788 F.2d 1033, appeal after remand 878 F.2d 147, rehearing denied.

C.A.4 (Md.) 1985. It was not abuse of discretion to dismiss, for failure to prosecute, remaining claim concerning marina permit decision of town board of wardens where plaintiff marina developer failed to comply with federal court orders to move forward with pending state suit and to file another amended complaint in federal court so that any additional claims could be brought to that court's attention and, instead, developer misrepresented status of federal court proceeding to state court judge and then asked for stay of state proceedings and never responded to state court order to amend the complaint. Fed.Rules Civ.Proc.Rule 41, 28 U.S.C.A.

> Mears v. Town of Oxford, Md., 762 F.2d 368.

C.A.1 (Mass.) 1986. Despite severity of granting dismissal for failure to prosecute, district court clearly has authority to do so when necessary to prevent unfair prejudice to defendants in a suit and undue delays in disposition of other pending cases.

> U.S. Inv. and Development Corp. v. Cruz, 780 F.2d 166.

C.A.6 (Mich.) 1991. Prisoner suing pro se was not entitled to special consideration in determining whether to dismiss complaint for failure to adhere to readily comprehended court deadlines; prisoner was well aware of deadlines and had sought and obtained two extensions, which he failed to utilize. Fed.Rules Civ.Proc. Rule 41(b), 28 U.S.C.A.

> Jourdan v. Jabe, 951 F.2d 108.

Dismissal is appropriate when pro se litigant has engaged in clear pattern of delay. Fed.Rules Civ.Proc.Rule 41(b), 28 U.S.C.A.

> Jourdan v. Jabe, 951 F.2d 108.

C.A.6 (Mich.) 1986. District court did not abuse discretion in dismissing action for racially discriminatory employment practices because of plaintiff's attorney's failure to appear on repeated occasions. Civil Rights Act of 1964, § 701 et seq., 42 U.S.C.A. § 2000e et seq.

> Coston v. Detroit Edison Co., 789 F.2d 377.

C.A.6 (Mich.) 1985. Trial court properly imposed $1,000 sanction against plaintiff's attorney for his failure to abide by court's orders, but lack of compliance with all of its orders within five days fell short of establishing basis for final dismissal of plaintiff's claim; absent clear record of delay or contumacious conduct by plaintiff, alternative sanction that would protect integrity of pretrial procedure should have been utilized. Fed.Rules Civ.Proc.Rule 41(b), 28 U.S.C.A.

> Patterson v. Grand Blanc Tp., 760 F.2d 686.

C.A.8 (Minn.) 1990. Trial court did not abuse its discretion in dismissing plaintiff's civil rights action for failure to prosecute; plaintiff had failed to comply with pretrial orders and had failed to appear for trial even though he had been informed of trial date on three occasions. Fed.Rules Civ.Proc.Rule 41(b), 28 U.S.C.A.

> DuBose v. State of Minn., 893 F.2d 169.

C.A.5 (Miss.) 1988. Discharged teacher's firing of her counsel a few days before trial, resulting in her lack of preparation on trial date, did not warrant dismissal with prejudice of teacher's discrimination action where there was no evidence that teacher fired counsel as delaying tactic or that she would have remained unprepared for trial for "significant period"; remand was required, however, to determine whether teacher's firing of counsel constituted such contumacious conduct as would warrant dismissal. Fed.Rules Civ.Proc.Rule 41(b), 28 U.S.C.A.

> McNeal v. Papasan, 842 F.2d 787.

C.A.8 (Mo.) 1998. Sanction imposed by district court for failure to prosecute claim or comply with court orders must be proportionate to litigant's transgression.

> Rodgers v. Curators of University of Missouri, 135 F.3d 1216.

District court did not abuse its discretion in dismissing student's discrimination claims against university, based on student's failure to prosecute and comply with court orders, without first imposing lesser sanctions or explaining why lesser sanctions would have been ineffective, as any lesser sanction would have involved further delay or forced university to try its case without completing discovery.

> Rodgers v. Curators of University of Missouri, 135 F.3d 1216.

C.A.8 (Mo.) 1997. District court has power to dismiss litigant's cause of action when litigant fails to comply with court's orders or for intentional delay, and need only find that litigant acted deliberately rather than accidentally, and need not find bad faith. Fed.Rules Civ. Proc.Rule 41(b), 28 U.S.C.A.

> Hutchins v. A.G. Edwards & Sons, Inc., 116 F.3d 1256.

Dismissal with prejudice is extreme sanction that should be used only in cases of willful disobedience of court order, or where litigant exhibits pattern of intentional delay. Fed.Rules Civ.Proc.Rule 41(b), 28 U.S.C.A.

> Hutchins v. A.G. Edwards & Sons, Inc., 116 F.3d 1256.

C.A.8 (Mo.) 1994. Action may be dismissed under rule providing for dismissal for failure to prosecute or comply with rules or order of court if plaintiff has failed to comply with any order of court. Fed.Rules Civ.Proc. Rule 41(b), 28 U.S.C.A.

> Aziz v. Wright, 34 F.3d 587, certiorari denied 115 S.Ct. 752, 513 U.S. 1090, 130 L.Ed.2d 652.

Action of inmate plaintiff, who twice appeared for deposition but refused each time to be deposed, would be dismissed for failure to prosecute or comply with rules or order of court; in light of fact that judge told plaintiff that judge would recommend dismissal due to plaintiff's conduct at first deposition, plaintiff's conduct at second deposition was willful disregard of court order allowing defendants to depose plaintiff. Fed.Rules Civ.Proc.Rule 41(b), 28 U.S.C.A.

> Aziz v. Wright, 34 F.3d 587, certiorari denied 115 S.Ct. 752, 513 U.S. 1090, 130 L.Ed.2d 652.

C.A.8 (Mo.) 1991. Sanction of dismissal under fugitive from justice rule should not lightly be invoked.

> Perko v. Bowers, 945 F.2d 1038, rehearing denied, certiorari denied 112 S.Ct. 1482, 503 U.S. 939, 117 L.Ed.2d 624.

C.A.8 (Mo.) 1988. Dismissal of inmates' § 1983 action was not abuse of discretion where magistrate had granted several requests for extensions of time in which to file amended complaint and inmates' refusal to comply with order to file amended complaint was intentional. Fed.Rules Civ.Proc.Rule 41(b), 28 U.S.C.A.; 42 U.S.C.A. § 1983.

> American Inmate Paralegal Assoc. v. Cline, 859 F.2d 59, certiorari denied Tyler v. Cline, 109 S.Ct. 565, 488 U.S. 996, 102 L.Ed.2d 590.

C.A.8 (Mo.) 1988. Sanction of dismissal upon plaintiff's failure on two occasions to appear at hearings scheduled by court was not an abuse of discretion.

> Mullen v. Galati, 843 F.2d 293.

C.A.8 (Mo.) 1986. District court abused its discretion in dismissing prison inmate's civil rights complaint for failure to comply with pretrial order requiring filing of certain documents with clerk of court; inmate did not engage in such course of intentional delay or contumacious conduct as to warrant that drastic sanction, but had diligently pursued lawsuit to best of his ability and delayed only because he thought attorney was to be appointed for

him. Fed.Rules Civ.Proc.Rule 41(b), 28 U.S.C.A.

> Brown v. Frey, 806 F.2d 801.

C.A.8 (Mo.) 1986. A district court has authority to dismiss action for failure to prosecute, and such a decision is reviewable only for abuse of discretion. Fed.Rules Civ.Proc.Rule 41, 28 U.S.C.A.

> Jackson v. Schoemehl, 788 F.2d 1296.

Dismissal of action for failure to prosecute was too severe sanction for plaintiffs' failure for more than two years to file proposed findings of fact and conclusions of law where there was no suggestion of deliberate disobedience or intentional action by plaintiffs to prevent resolution of lawsuit, plaintiffs were given no opportunity prior to dismissal to explain or cure their tardiness and their previous request for extensions were not so egregious as to render inactivity after trial the last straw in an unending series of vexations and delays. Fed.Rules Civ.Proc.Rule 41, 28 U.S.C.A.

> Jackson v. Schoemehl, 788 F.2d 1296.

C.A.8 (Mo.) 1985. District court may, on its own motion, dismiss action for failure of the plaintiff to comply with any order of the court, and, in reviewing the trial court's exercise of authority under the rule authorizing such dismissal, Court of Appeals considers whether district court exceeded permissible range of its discretion. Fed.Rules Civ.Proc.Rule 41(b), 28 U.S.C.A.

> Haley v. Kansas City Star, 761 F.2d 489.

Where there was no indication that plaintiff, state prisoner, was involved in his appointed attorney's noncompliance with the court's orders, dismissal of the prisoner's civil actions, against newspapers and officials involved in his conviction, was inappropriate. Fed.Rules Civ. Proc. Rule 41(b), 28 U.S.C.A.; 42 U.S.C.A. § 1983; U.S.C.A. Const.Amend. 6.

> Haley v. Kansas City Star, 761 F.2d 489.

C.A.9 (Nev.) 1992. Federal rule permitting dismissal for failure to prosecute was sufficiently coextensive with Nevada rule mandating prejudicial or nonprejudicial dismissal for failure to prosecute after five years and was applicable; federal rule raised no forum shopping concerns since no rational plaintiff would file in federal court based on expectation that dismissal would be discretionary, rather than mandatory, after five years, under both rules courts possess some discretion to account for reasonable diligence, and Nevada's rule was not integral to statute of limitations. Fed.Rules Civ.Proc.Rule 41(b), 28 U.S.C.A.; Nev.Rules Civ.Proc., Rule 41(e).

> Harvey's Wagon Wheel, Inc. v. Van Blitter, 959 F.2d 153.

C.A.3 (N.J.) 1995. Factors pertinent to exercise of discretion in considering motion to dismiss for failure to prosecute include: personal responsibility of plaintiff, prejudice to defendants, history of dilatoriness, willfulness or bad faith by plaintiff, adequacy of sanctions less drastic than dismissal, and meritoriousness of plaintiff's claims. Fed.Rules Civ.Proc.Rule 41(b), 28 U.S.C.A.

> U.S. v. USX Corp., 68 F.3d 811, as amended.

C.A.3 (N.J.) 1994. In determining whether dismissal for lack of prosecution is appropriate, Court looks to whether party bears personal responsibility for action or inaction which led to dismissal. Fed.Rules Civ.Proc.Rule 41(b), 28 U.S.C.A.

> Adams v. Trustees of New Jersey Brewery Employees' Pension Trust Fund, 29 F.3d 863.

Pension Benefit Guaranty Corporation (PBGC) was personally responsible for delay by its in-house counsel, for purposes of determining whether dismissal of claim for lack of prosecution was justified, and thus effect of dismissal on any innocent third parties was not dispositive. Fed.Rules Civ.Proc.Rule 41(b), 28 U.S.C.A.

> Adams v. Trustees of New Jersey Brewery Employees' Pension Trust Fund, 29 F.3d 863.

For purpose of motion to dismiss for lack of prosecution, extensive or repeated delay or delinquency constitutes history of dilatoriness, such as consistent nonresponse to interrogatories or consistent tardiness in complying with court orders. Fed.Rules Civ.Proc.Rule 41(b), 28 U.S.C.A.

> Adams v. Trustees of New Jersey Brewery Employees' Pension Trust Fund, 29 F.3d 863.

In evaluating dismissal for lack of prosecution, Court of Appeals looks for willful or contumacious behavior which amounts to flagrant bad faith, and involves intentional or self-serving behavior. Fed.Rules Civ.Proc.Rule 41(b), 28 U.S.C.A.

> Adams v. Trustees of New Jersey Brewery Employees' Pension Trust Fund, 29 F.3d 863.

Absence of good faith effort to prosecute does not necessarily amount to willfulness or bad faith for purposes of dismissal for lack of prosecution. Fed.Rules Civ.Proc.Rule 41(b), 28 U.S.C.A.

> Adams v. Trustees of New Jersey Brewery Employees' Pension Trust Fund, 29 F.3d 863.

Before dismissing a case with prejudice, district court should consider alternative sanc-

tions. Fed.Rules Civ.Proc.Rule 41(b), 28 U.S.C.A.

> Adams v. Trustees of New Jersey Brewery Employees' Pension Trust Fund, 29 F.3d 863.

Alternative sanctions, rather than dismissal, were appropriate for Pension Benefit Guaranty Corporation's (PBGC) more than four-year delay in pursuing claim for unfunded portion of multiemployer pension plan; it was not shown that employer's case was seriously compromised, delay caused no significant prejudice to employers, and sanctions such as favorable treatment for employers on any evidentiary issues affected by delay and payment of attorney fees or costs related to delay might be appropriate. Fed.Rules Civ.Proc.Rule 41(b), 28 U.S.C.A.

> Adams v. Trustees of New Jersey Brewery Employees' Pension Trust Fund, 29 F.3d 863.

Standard of meritoriousness when reviewing dismissal for lack of prosecution is moderate; where plaintiff makes out prima facie case but defendant raises prima facie defense, meritoriousness factor may not weigh in favor of plaintiff. Fed.Rules Civ.Proc.Rule 41(b), 28 U.S.C.A.

> Adams v. Trustees of New Jersey Brewery Employees' Pension Trust Fund, 29 F.3d 863.

Facial strength of Pension Benefit Guaranty Corporation's (PBGC) claim against employers for unfunded portions of multiemployer pension fund weighed heavily against dismissal for lack of prosecution; district court had rejected employer's statutory and constitutional defenses to liability. Fed.Rules Civ.Proc.Rule 41(b), 28 U.S.C.A.

> Adams v. Trustees of New Jersey Brewery Employees' Pension Trust Fund, 29 F.3d 863.

There was no special exception for the government from application of rule authorizing dismissal of claims for failure to prosecute. Fed.Rules Civ.Proc.Rule 41(b), 28 U.S.C.A.

> Adams v. Trustees of New Jersey Brewery Employees' Pension Trust Fund, 29 F.3d 863.

C.A.2 (N.Y.) 1997. Dismissal for lack of prosecution is harsh remedy to be utilized only in extreme circumstances. Fed.Rules Civ.Proc. Rule 41(b), 28 U.S.C.A.

> Valentin v. Dinkins, 121 F.3d 72.

Whether plaintiff could have carried out necessary research to identify police officer in period prior to sealing of his case and his incarceration did not warrant dismissing his subsequent civil rights action for failure to prosecute, due to plaintiff's failure to better identify officer, without some further inquiry; officer was not required to telescope his precomplaint investigation into shorter time frame than three-year statute of limitations permitted. Fed.Rules Civ.Proc.Rule 41(b), 28 U.S.C.A.

  Valentin v. Dinkins, 121 F.3d 72.

C.A.2 (N.Y.) 1996. District court may dismiss claim with prejudice for failure to prosecute; such authority is an inherent control necessarily vested in courts to manage their own affairs so as to achieve orderly and expeditious disposition of cases.

  Palmieri v. Defaria, 88 F.3d 136.

C.A.2 (N.Y.) 1996. When district court considers appropriate sanction for failure to prosecute action, more delay was occasioned by plaintiff's personal obstruction, or was designed to benefit plaintiff's strategic interests, more suitable is remedy of dismissal.

  Dodson v. Runyon, 86 F.3d 37, on remand 957 F.Supp. 465, affirmed 152 F.3d 917, certiorari denied 117 S.Ct. 1337, 137 L.Ed.2d 496.

District court erred in failing to consider possibility of alternative penalties before imposing drastic remedy of dismissal for failure to prosecute; there was evidence that attorney caused delay in derogation of, rather than to benefit, his client's interests.

  Dodson v. Runyon, 86 F.3d 37, on remand 957 F.Supp. 465, affirmed 152 F.3d 917, certiorari denied 117 S.Ct. 1337, 137 L.Ed.2d 496.

Dismissal is remedy that district judge should generally impose for dilatory conduct of litigants only when he is sure of impotence of lesser sanctions.

  Dodson v. Runyon, 86 F.3d 37, on remand 957 F.Supp. 465, affirmed 152 F.3d 917, certiorari denied 117 S.Ct. 1337, 137 L.Ed.2d 496.

C.A.2 (N.Y.) 1995. Dismissal of assignee's remaining state law claims for failure to prosecute, based on assignee's failure to notify court prior to expiration of court-imposed deadline as to what state law claims it desired to pursue by filing amended complaint, was not abuse of discretion, in light of prior history of litigation between parties, which included numerous separate actions, over 35 motions for reargument and reconsideration, for stays of actions, for leave to refile pleadings and for leave to appeal.

  Baker v. Latham Sparrowbush Associates, 72 F.3d 246.

C.A.2 (N.Y.) 1995. Dismissal for plaintiff's failure to prosecute is harsh remedy to be utilized only in extreme situations. Fed.Rules Civ.Proc.Rule 41(b), 28 U.S.C.A.

  Colon v. Mack, 56 F.3d 5, on remand 983 F.Supp. 496.

C.A.2 (N.Y.) 1995. District court has power to dismiss complaint for failure to comply with court order, treating noncompliance as failure to prosecute. Fed.Rules Civ.Proc.Rule 41(b), 28 U.S.C.A.

  Simmons v. Abruzzo, 49 F.3d 83, on remand 1996 WL 79321, affirmed 104 F.3d 350.

C.A.2 (N.Y.) 1994. Dismissal of claim may be appropriate sanction for failure to prosecute claim or failure to comply with discovery orders. Fed.Rules Civ.Proc.Rules 37(b)(2)(C), 41(b), 28 U.S.C.A.

  Mackensworth v. S.S. American Merchant, 28 F.3d 246.

C.A.2 (N.Y.) 1992. Dismissal for failure to prosecute is a matter committed to the discretion of the district court. Fed.Rules Civ.Proc. Rule 41(b), 28 U.S.C.A.

  Gibbs v. Hawaiian Eugenia Corp., 966 F.2d 101, on remand 1993 WL 14666.

C.A.2 (N.Y.) 1987. Vessel owner was not sufficiently prejudiced by "moderate delay" resulting from arbitration between charterer and consignee to warrant dismissal for failure to prosecute of consignee's action against vessel owner. Fed.Rules Civ.Proc.Rule 41(b), 28 U.S.C.A.

  Ali A. Tamini v. M/V Jewon, 808 F.2d 978, on remand Tamini v. M/V Jewon, 699 F.Supp. 105, affirmed 866 F.2d 741.

C.A.2 (N.Y.) 1986. Dismissal of pro se lawsuits for frustration of process of litigation by pro se plaintiffs is justified only when they do so deliberately, not when they do so through misunderstanding. Fed.Rules Civ.Proc.Rule 37(d), 28 U.S.C.A.

  Salahuddin v. Harris, 782 F.2d 1127.

C.A.6 (Ohio) 1990. District court did not abuse its discretion by dismissing action by workers for alleged injuries resulting from exposure to Toluene Di-Isocyanate for failure to comply with the court's orders and for want of prosecution and making condition of refiling that workers have proved payment of costs incurred by manufacturers, filed signed certificate stating that workers were ready and willing to prosecute claim expeditiously and had made adequate financial provisions for discovery, and paid sanctions levied against workers for failure to complete discovery. Fed.Rules Civ.Proc.Rule 41(b), 28 U.S.C.A.

  Pollitt v. General Motors Corp., 894 F.2d 858.

C.A.6 (Ohio) 1986. Dismissal of civil rights claim against city, city officials, police officers, and others for lack of prosecution based on plaintiffs' absence from voir dire on their counsel's advice was improper, where district judge failed to articulate the legal basis for his absolute requirement that plaintiffs be present throughout voir dire and did not make that requirement known to counsel, and record did not indicate that plaintiff's counsel was guilty of willfulness, bad faith, or contumacious conduct. Fed.Rules Civ.Proc.Rule 41(b), 28 U.S.C.A.

> Bishop v. Cross, 790 F.2d 38.

C.A.9 (Or.) 1990.   Because dismissal for lack of prosecution is drastic step, it is not permitted if district court could have adopted less drastic alternatives or district court did not warn plaintiff that dismissal was imminent. Fed.Rules Civ.Proc.Rule 41(b), 28 U.S.C.A.

> West Coast Theater Corp. v. City of Portland, 897 F.2d 1519.

Suit brought by owner of condemned property against city and others arising from eminent domain proceeding asserting civil rights, constitutional and antitrust claims could be dismissed for lack of prosecution; owner filed number of untimely motions, failed to appear at number of scheduled hearings, including show cause hearing on dismissal for lack of prosecution, owner never sought any discovery even though it obtained one extension, owner delayed service of complaint to last minute, and owner served a number of defendants with wrong complaint.   Fed.Rules Civ.Proc.Rule 41(b), 28 U.S.C.A.

> West Coast Theater Corp. v. City of Portland, 897 F.2d 1519.

Neither death of plaintiff's cousin prior to hearing to show cause on why action should not be dismissed for lack of prosecution nor large number of defendants purportedly preventing plaintiff from conducting discovery precluded dismissal for lack of prosecution; death of cousin was about 12 days before scheduled hearing, plaintiff neither responded in writing to hearing nor requested that hearing be rescheduled, and it was plaintiff who chose to include numerous defendants.   Fed.Rules Civ.Proc.Rule 41(b), 28 U.S.C.A.

> West Coast Theater Corp. v. City of Portland, 897 F.2d 1519.

Magistrate and district court used adequate number of alternatives short of dismissal for lack of prosecution to prompt plaintiff to end unnecessary delays, thus permitting dismissal for lack of prosecution when such measures failed; magistrate and district court denied seven untimely motions to extend time, Rule 11 sanctions were granted for filing of pleading not well grounded in fact, and magistrate explicitly warned plaintiff in show cause order that complaint could be dismissed for lack of prosecution.   Fed.Rules Civ.Proc.Rules 11, 41(b), 28 U.S.C.A.

> West Coast Theater Corp. v. City of Portland, 897 F.2d 1519.

C.A.9 (Or.) 1986.   District court properly dismissed for lack of prosecution civil rights action alleging wrongful arrest, even though court should have applied Oregon's general tort statute, rather than Oregon Tort Claims Act, where both statutes provided for two-year limitations period.   42 U.S.C.A. § 1983;   ORS 12.110(1), 30.275.

> Davis v. Harvey, 789 F.2d 1332.

C.A.3 (Pa.) 1994.   District court did not err in dismissing balance of plaintiff's case for failure to prosecute after she determined not to go forward with her racial discrimination and retaliation claims following dismissal of sexual discrimination and harassment claims.

> Spain v. Gallegos, 26 F.3d 439.

C.A.3 (Pa.) 1987.   It was error to dismiss for failure to prosecute without finding supported by record that client bore some responsibility for flagrant actions of attorney.

> Dunbar v. Triangle Lumber and Supply Co., 816 F.2d 126, on remand 1987 WL 14158.

C.A.3 (Pa.) 1984.   Client cannot always avoid consequences of acts or omissions of its counsel, and thus client's lack of responsibility for counsel's dilatory conduct is not dispositive of question of whether dismissal with prejudice is appropriate sanction for delay in pretrial procedures.

> Poulis v. State Farm Fire and Cas. Co., 747 F.2d 863.

C.A.1 (Puerto Rico) 1993.   District court may dismiss case for failure of plaintiff to prosecute but should dismiss with prejudice only when plaintiff's misconduct has been extreme and only after court had determined that no lesser sanction would truly be appropriate; finding of extreme misconduct is justified if there is extremely protracted inaction, disobedience of court orders, ignorance of warnings, contumacious conduct, or similar aggravating circumstances.   Fed.Rules Civ.Proc.Rule 41(b), 28 U.S.C.A.

> Estate of Solis-Rivera v. U.S., 993 F.2d 1.

C.A.1 (Puerto Rico) 1988.   Dismissal of complaint as penalty for delay is option only when plaintiff's misconduct is "extreme."   Fed. Rules Civ.Proc.Rule 41(b), 28 U.S.C.A.

> Enlace Mercantil Internacional, Inc. v. Senior Industries, Inc., 848 F.2d 315.

Dismissal of complaint as penalty for delay should be employed only after district court has determined that none of the lesser sanctions available to it would truly be appropriate.   Fed. Rules Civ.Proc.Rule 41(b), 28 U.S.C.A.

> Enlace Mercantil Internacional, Inc. v. Senior Industries, Inc., 848 F.2d 315.

C.A.1 (Puerto Rico) 1987. Plaintiff's settlement with two defendants, which led to filing of motion and stipulation to inform district court of settlement, was "action which advances the matter toward trial or judgment" and was substantial proceeding within meaning of rule which permitted dismissal if no "substantial proceedings" were taken within six months. U.S.Dist.Ct.Rules D.P.R., General Rule 313, subd. 1(B).

> Ruiz Varela v. Sanchez Velez, 814 F.2d 821.

"Substantial proceedings" within meaning of rule that permitted dismissal, if no substantial proceedings of record were taken for six months, referred to actions to advance case as whole, rather than actions as to each defendant individually, and, thus, service of notice of deposition of architect defendant, filing of motion for issuance of summons for service upon contractor defendant, and settling of claim against two defendants constituted "substantial proceedings." U.S.Dist.Ct.Rules D.P.R., General Rule 313, subd. 1(B).

> Ruiz Varela v. Sanchez Velez, 814 F.2d 821.

C.A.1 (Puerto Rico) 1986. Motions to dismiss and for summary judgment are "dispositive motions" within purview of Puerto Rico District Court Rule [U.S.Dist.Ct.Rules D.C.Puerto Rico, General Rule 313.1(B)] providing that cases are subject to dismissal where no substantial proceedings of record have been taken for a term of six months as shown by record docket.

> Martinez Class v. Caribe Hilton Hotel, 784 F.2d 12.

C.A.6 (Tenn.) 1997. District court did not abuse its discretion when it dismissed plaintiff's complaint for failure to prosecute and to comply with discovery order, where dismissal was ordered nearly full year after defendant served plaintiff with its discovery request, and plaintiff had failed to respond to amicable requests of defendant's counsel, defendant's motion to compel or its motion to dismiss; plaintiff's counsel was stubbornly disobedient and willfully contemptuous. Fed.Rules Civ.Proc.Rules 37(b)(2), 41(b), 28 U.S.C.A.

> Harmon v. CSX Transp., Inc., 110 F.3d 364, rehearing denied, certiorari denied 118 S.Ct. 178, 139 L.Ed.2d 119.

Conduct of plaintiff's counsel in failing to prosecute and comply with discovery order was sufficiently egregious to support district court's exercise of discretion in ordering dismissal as sanction, despite failing to expressly consider lesser sanctions. Fed.Rules Civ.Proc.Rules 37(b)(2), 41(b), 28 U.S.C.A.

> Harmon v. CSX Transp., Inc., 110 F.3d 364, rehearing denied, certiorari denied 118 S.Ct. 178, 139 L.Ed.2d 119.

C.A.5 (Tex.) 1996. Dismissal of plaintiff's action with prejudice was not abuse of discretion where case had been called to trial with no appearance by plaintiff or his counsel, plaintiff had previously failed to appear at scheduled docket calls, and trial had already been rescheduled three times in effort to accommodate plaintiff.

> Dorsey v. Scott Wetzel Services, Inc., 84 F.3d 170.

C.A.5 (Tex.) 1992. Dismissal for failure to file motion for default judgment is equivalent to dismissal for failure to prosecute.

> Berry v. CIGNA/RSI-CIGNA, 975 F.2d 1188.

District court abused its discretion by involuntarily dismissing Title VII case for failure to prosecute, merely because of plaintiff's failure to file motion for default judgment. Fed.Rules Civ.Proc.Rule 41(b), 28 U.S.C.A.; Civil Rights Act of 1964, § 701 et seq., as amended, 42 U.S.C.A. § 2000e et seq.

> Berry v. CIGNA/RSI-CIGNA, 975 F.2d 1188.

C.A.5 (Tex.) 1989. In determining whether to dismiss for want of prosecution, court examines record for aggravating factors that plaintiff personally contributed to delay, that defendant was prejudiced as result of delay, or that delay was intentional on plaintiff's part. Fed.Rules Civ.Proc.Rule 41(b), 28 U.S.C.A.

> Markwell v. County of Bexar, 878 F.2d 899.

C.A.5 (Tex.) 1988. District court's sua sponte dismissal without prejudice of pro se plaintiff's § 1983 action against state corrections officials, for failure to prosecute based upon plaintiff's critical default in failure to attend a scheduled status conference, did not prejudicially harm plaintiff and did not constitute an abuse of discretion, where there was no indication that statute of limitations on the action had run and plaintiff was not prevented from refiling his claim. 42 U.S.C.A. § 1983.

> McCullough v. Lynaugh, 835 F.2d 1126.

C.A.5 (Tex.) 1985. Dismissal of action with prejudice for want of prosecution, with each party to bear its own costs, was justified after district court properly refused to grant continuance that was sought due to unavailability of plaintiff's expert witness, where plaintiff was unable to carry his burden without such witness, dismissal without prejudice would have been futile due to running of limitations period, and plaintiff, despite 18 months of discovery, had waited until a few weeks before trial to obtain expert and provided only one week's notice to defendant. Fed.Rules Civ.Proc.Rule 41(b), 28 U.S.C.A.

> Sturgeon v. Airborne Freight Corp., 778 F.2d 1154.

C.A.5 (Tex.) 1985. Ultimate sanction of dismissal for failure to prosecute Title VII [42 U.S.C.A. § 2000e et seq.] employment discrimination case was warranted, where alternative sanction of payment of $5701.53 was assessed against employee, and employee had ability to pay sanction but failed to do so. Civil Rights Act of 1964, § 701 et seq., as amended, 42 U.S.C.A. § 2000e et seq.

> Hornbuckle v. Arco Oil and Gas Co., 770 F.2d 1321, certiorari denied 106 S.Ct. 1198, 475 U.S. 1016, 89 L.Ed.2d 312.

C.A.5 (Tex.) 1985. Where there were examples of delay attributable at least to counsel at every stage of proceedings in former employee's civil rights action against former employer and, moreover, former employee compounded those delays by commencing and then abandoning an appeal to the Court of Appeals from district court order that was itself entered because of former employee's failure to comply with the district court deadline, district court did not abuse its discretion in concluding that former employee's conduct created a clear record of delay for purposes of dismissing action for want of prosecution. Fed.Rules Civ.Proc. Rules 16(f), 41(b), 28 U.S.C.A.

> Callip v. Harris County Child Welfare Dept., 757 F.2d 1513.

Providing plaintiff with a second or third chance following a procedural default is a lenient sanction, which, when met with further default, may justify imposition of the ultimate sanction of dismissal with prejudice. Fed.Rules Civ.Proc.Rule 16(f), 28 U.S.C.A.

> Callip v. Harris County Child Welfare Dept., 757 F.2d 1513.

District court did not abuse its discretion in concluding that further default by former employee in her civil rights action against former employer in face of lesser sanctions imposed prior to dismissal justified dismissal with prejudice for want of prosecution.

> Callip v. Harris County Child Welfare Dept., 757 F.2d 1513.

District court did not abuse its discretion in dismissing with prejudice for want of prosecution former employee's civil rights complaint against her former employer, in view of clear record of delay and former employee's further default in face of lesser sanctions imposed prior to dismissal. Fed.Rules Civ.Proc.Rules 16(f), 41(b), 28 U.S.C.A.

> Callip v. Harris County Child Welfare Dept., 757 F.2d 1513.

C.A.5 (Tex.) 1983. Lewis v. Brown & Root, Inc., 711 F.2d 1287, on reconsideration 722 F.2d 209, certiorari denied 104 S.Ct. 975, 464 U.S. 1069, 79 L.Ed.2d 213, rehearing denied 726 F.2d 752, certiorari denied 104 S.Ct. 2690, 467 U.S. 1231, 81 L.Ed.2d 884.

C.A.10 (Utah) 1988. Tort action against United States was properly dismissed for lack of prosecution; merits of personal representative's survival action were weak, while his lack of diligence was manifest. 28 U.S.C.A. §§ 1346(b), 2671 et seq.

> Bills v. U.S., 857 F.2d 1404.

C.A.4 (Va.) 1991. Sanction of dismissal for failure to prosecute, when used to punish attorney misbehavior, is only appropriate in the most egregious cases. Fed.Rules Civ.Proc.Rule 41(b), 28 U.S.C.A.

> Doyle v. Murray, 938 F.2d 33.

In deciding whether to dismiss for failure to prosecute, as sanction for party's or lawyer's misconduct, district court must balance degree of party's personal responsibility, amount of prejudice caused to opponent, existence of "drawn out history of deliberately proceeding in a dilatory fashion," and existence of less drastic sanctions. 42 U.S.C.A. § 1983; Fed.Rules Civ. Proc.Rule 12(b)(6), 28 U.S.C.A.

> Doyle v. Murray, 938 F.2d 33.

Counsel's conduct in unrelated litigation did not justify dismissal for failure to prosecute as sanction for inmate's attorney's failure to attend pretrial conference; whatever attorney may have done in unrelated litigation, he did not do in inmate's civil rights action. 42 U.S.C.A. § 1983; Fed.Rules Civ.Proc.Rule 41(b), 28 U.S.C.A.

> Doyle v. Murray, 938 F.2d 33.

C.A.3 (Virgin Islands) 1990. Depending upon the record before the court, consideration of one or more of the *Poulis* factors dealing with consequences of party's failure to prosecute or defend may be required when party moves to dismiss an opponent's claim as sanction for failure to respond to discovery, when defendant moves for involuntary dismissal as sanction for failure to prosecute, or when plaintiff moves for default as sanction for failure to plead or otherwise defend. Fed.Rules Civ.Proc.Rules 37(b)(2), 41(b), 55(b), 28 U.S.C.A.

> Anchorage Associates v. Virgin Islands Bd. of Tax Review, 922 F.2d 168.

C.A.7 (Wis.) 1993. Lack of clarity in grantor's response when asked about further pursuit of breach of contract claim did not warrant dismissal for failure to prosecute, even though grantor did not file anything explicitly indicating intent to pursue claim; grantor's intent to pursue claim was indicated by motion in which grantor sought reconsideration of prior disqualification of counsel, which also requested scheduling order for discovery and hearing date on pending motions.

> Owen v. Wangerin, 985 F.2d 312, rehearing denied.

N.D.Ala. 1996. Dismissal for want of prosecution is a dismissal with prejudice.

> Morro v. City of Birmingham, 926 F.Supp. 1033, supplemented, affirmed 117 F.3d 508, rehearing and suggestion for rehearing denied 127 F.3d 42, certiorari denied 118 S.Ct. 1299, 140 L.Ed.2d 465.

E.D.Ark. 1990. Chapter 12 debtors' failure to go to trial postpetition on counterclaim they had filed against creditor warranted dismissal of counterclaim with prejudice; debtors' counsel had made misrepresentations to court, bankruptcy had been filed on eve of trial, and counsel had refused to proceed on counterclaim when informed that case would be tried as scheduled. Fed.Rules Civ.Proc.Rule 41(b), 28 U.S.C.A.

> Merchants & Farmers Bank of Dumas, Arkansas v. Hill, 122 B.R. 539.

C.D.Cal. 1997. Action may be dismissed if plaintiff has not diligently prosecuted it.

> Ramage v. Forbes Intern. Inc., 987 F.Supp. 810.

N.D.Cal. 1988. Medical malpractice action would be dismissed for lack of prosecution on part of plaintiff and plaintiff's failure to follow federal rules, local rules, and district court order; plaintiff repeatedly disregarded deadlines set by court, and plaintiff had been put on notice by court on more than one occasion that her behavior put her at risk of dismissal for lack of prosecution. Fed.Rules Civ.Proc. Rule 41, 28 U.S.C.A.

> Lebbos v. Heinrichs, 696 F.Supp. 1279.

In determining whether to dismiss case for lack of prosecution, district court is obligated to consider public's interest and expeditious resolution of litigation, court's need to manage its docket, risk of prejudice to defendant, public policy favoring disposition of cases on the merits, and availability of less drastic sanctions. Fed.Rules Civ.Proc.Rule 41, 28 U.S.C.A.

> Lebbos v. Heinrichs, 696 F.Supp. 1279.

Dismissal for lack of prosecution must be supported by showing of unreasonable delay. Fed.Rules Civ.Proc.Rule 41, 28 U.S.C.A.

> Lebbos v. Heinrichs, 696 F.Supp. 1279.

There is no requirement that every alternative remedy be exhausted before sanction of dismissal for lack of prosecution is imposed; trial court need only explore possible and meaningful alternatives. Fed.Rules Civ.Proc.Rule 41, 28 U.S.C.A.

> Lebbos v. Heinrichs, 696 F.Supp. 1279.

D.Del. 1996. Plaintiff was fully responsible for his failure to prosecute action and his delinquency in following court orders, supporting dismissal. Fed.Rules Civ.Proc.Rule 41(b), 28 U.S.C.A.

> Guy v. City of Wilmington, 169 F.R.D. 593.

Plaintiff engaged in persistent pattern of dilatoriness, supporting dismissal of his action for failure to prosecute and for his delinquency in complying with court orders. Fed.Rules Civ. Proc.Rule 41(b), 28 U.S.C.A.

> Guy v. City of Wilmington, 169 F.R.D. 593.

Alternative sanctions besides dismissal would be ineffective to cure plaintiff's delinquency, where plaintiff was attorney who was prosecuting his own case in dilatory manner. Fed.Rules Civ.Proc.Rule 41(b), 28 U.S.C.A.

> Guy v. City of Wilmington, 169 F.R.D. 593.

Claim is meritorious, for purposes of determining whether dismissal is appropriate sanction for failure to prosecute, when allegations of complaint would support recovery if those allegations were proven at trial. Fed.Rules Civ. Proc.Rule 41(b), 28 U.S.C.A.

> Guy v. City of Wilmington, 169 F.R.D. 593.

Plaintiff's claims were meritorious, weighing against dismissal as appropriate sanction for failure to prosecute, where claims were tested by motion to dismiss and survived. Fed. Rules Civ.Proc.Rule 41(b), 28 U.S.C.A.

> Guy v. City of Wilmington, 169 F.R.D. 593.

Not all factors to be considered in deciding motion to dismiss for failure to prosecute action or comply with court orders need to be met for dismissal to be warranted. Fed.Rules Civ.Proc. Rule 41(b), 28 U.S.C.A.

> Guy v. City of Wilmington, 169 F.R.D. 593.

Plaintiff's deliberate pattern of reckless disregard for orders and rules of court compelled ultimate sanction of dismissal; as both party and lawyer, he was fully responsible for those violations, he had been warned twice before of potential consequences of his lack of diligence, and he not only chose to ignore that warning, but also subsequent court orders. Fed.Rules Civ.Proc.Rule 41(b), 28 U.S.C.A.

> Guy v. City of Wilmington, 169 F.R.D. 593.

D.Del. 1985. Power to dismiss for failure to prosecute, which may be exercised with or without notice or opportunity to be heard, rests in discretion of trial court, and is part of its inherent authority to prevent undue delays in disposition of pending cases and to avoid congestion in its docket. Fed.Rules Civ.Proc.Rule 41(b), 28 U.S.C.A.

> Transportes Aereos de Angola v. Ronair, Inc., 104 F.R.D. 482.

For cited U.S.C.A. sections and legislative history, see United States Code Annotated

Considering corporate plaintiff's dilatory pursuit of its claims, its intractable refusal to pay for or cooperate with its own attorneys, its cavalier and repeated disregard of court orders requiring it to retain and appear by counsel, and admission by its president and half-owner that it had no more money available for payment of counsel, and that alternative lesser sanctions were not feasible, Court would dismiss with prejudice plaintiff's amended and supplemental complaint against defendants; moreover, defendants were entitled to entry of default on their counterclaims against plaintiff. Fed.Rules Civ.Proc.Rules 41(b), 55(a), 28 U.S.C.A.

> Transportes Aereos de Angola v. Ronair, Inc., 104 F.R.D. 482.

Defendant's cross claim against the codefendant would be dismissed for failure to cooperate in discovery, failure to prosecute cross claim, and failure to comply with court orders, considering defendant's continued willful and contumacious conduct as reflected in continuous shuffle of new attorneys, inadequate responses to request for admissions, flagrant and unexplained refusal to answer interrogatories or produce documents pursuant to request for production as well as defendant's unilateral unjustified failure to appear at resumption of his deposition. Fed.Rules Civ.Proc.Rule 37(b)(2), 28 U.S.C.A.

> Transportes Aereos de Angola v. Ronair, Inc., 104 F.R.D. 482.

D.D.C. 1994. Employee's discrimination claims against supervisors under District of Columbia Human Rights Act would be dismissed for failure to prosecute; employees did nothing to prosecute claims against supervisors for over nine months after default judgments against them were vacated, except improperly claiming damages from them in proposed order for relief several months after vacating order. D.C.Code 1981, § 1–2501 et seq.

> Shepherd v. American Broadcasting Companies, Inc., 862 F.Supp. 486, opinion supplemented 862 F.Supp. 505, vacated 62 F.3d 1469, 314 U.S.App.D.C. 137, rehearing and suggestion for rehearing denied, vacated 62 F.3d 1469, 314 U.S.App.D.C. 137, rehearing and suggestion for rehearing denied, and rehearing and suggestion for rehearing denied.

D.D.C. 1990. Dismissal of a tort suit for lack of prosecution and failure to comply with discovery requests was warranted notwithstanding plaintiff's claim that she had in fact provided some discovery and cooperated during the litigation; plaintiff had failed to produce requested documents and otherwise completely comply with discovery despite repeated extensions and warnings concerning the consequences of failure to do so. U.S.Dist.Ct.Rules

D.C., Civil Rule 211; Fed.Rules Civ.Proc.Rules 26(b)(4), 41(b), 28 U.S.C.A.

> Ford v. Washington Metropolitan Area Transit Authority, 131 F.R.D. 12, affirmed 946 F.2d 1564, 292 U.S.App.D.C. 84, rehearing denied.

D.D.C. 1987. Plaintiff's action against District of Columbia and nine metropolitan police officers, for alleged assault, battery, and violation of constitutional rights arising out of plaintiff's detention during warrantless search and subsequent arrest for disorderly conduct, would be dismissed due to plaintiff's failure to prosecute action; plaintiff's counsel failed to timely obtain writ for release of plaintiff who was serving sentence in federal prison, to appear at trial in instant action, requiring cancellation of two scheduled trial dates, and counsel subsequently failed to respond to inquiries as to why he had not even attempted to obtain writ to achieve presence of plaintiff at the third scheduled trial date; calling into doubt *Shea v. Donohue Construction Co.*, 795 F.2d 1071 (D.C.Cir.). Fed.Rules Civ.Proc.Rules 16(f), 41(b), 28 U.S.C.A.

> Tucker v. District of Columbia, 115 F.R.D. 493.

D.D.C. 1985. Action alleging breach of stock purchase agreement was subject to dismissal because of plaintiffs' failure to prosecute and blatant disregard of court orders and rules; almost a year had passed since plaintiffs were first ordered to proceed to arbitration and over six months had passed since the Court of Appeals dismissed plaintiffs' frivolous appeal of that order. Fed.Rules Civ.Proc.Rule 41(b), 28 U.S.C.A.

> Ames v. Standard Oil Co. (Indiana), 108 F.R.D. 299.

Federal courts possess undisputed authority to control their dockets and to dismiss those cases that plaintiffs fail to prosecute.

> Ames v. Standard Oil Co. (Indiana), 108 F.R.D. 299.

Dismissal of case for failure to prosecute is proper if, in view of history of litigation, litigant has failed to exercise reasonable diligence in pursuing case.

> Ames v. Standard Oil Co. (Indiana), 108 F.R.D. 299.

Single act of misconduct does not usually justify dismissal of case for future to prosecute.

> Ames v. Standard Oil Co. (Indiana), 108 F.R.D. 299.

Dismissal of case for failure to prosecute is generally not warranted where conduct in question is inadvertent or excusable.

> Ames v. Standard Oil Co. (Indiana), 108 F.R.D. 299.

Dismissal of case for failure to prosecute is appropriate sanction where litigant has engaged in course of protracted neglect which includes not only failure to pursue litigation in district court but also any failure to prosecute in an alternative forum such as agency or arbitration proceeding.

Ames v. Standard Oil Co. (Indiana), 108 F.R.D. 299.

Dismissal for failure to prosecute is particularly appropriate when failure is coupled with disobedience to court orders or disregard of established rules.

Ames v. Standard Oil Co. (Indiana), 108 F.R.D. 299.

D.D.C. 1985. Dismissal of action alleging assault by police officers and undue prepresentment delay was proper for counsel's failure to file timely pretrial brief where sanctions had previously been imposed on counsel for failing to comply with orders and where no acceptable or justifiable reason for neglect was offered. Fed.Rules Civ.Proc.Rule 41(b), 28 U.S.C.A.

Berry v. District of Columbia, 107 F.R.D. 663, affirmed in part, reversed in part 833 F.2d 1031, 266 U.S.App.D.C. 127.

S.D.Fla. 1997. Legal standard to be applied, in deciding whether to dismiss action under Federal Rule of Civil Procedure based on party's failure to prosecute or to obey court order or federal rule, is whether there is clear record of delay or willful contempt and a finding that lesser sanctions would not suffice. Fed.Rules Civ.Proc.Rule 41(b), 28 U.S.C.A.

In re Southeast Banking Corp. Securities and Loan Loss Reserves Litigation, 212 B.R. 397.

In deciding whether to dismiss action under Federal Rule of Civil Procedure based on party's failure to prosecute or to obey court order or federal rule, court does not take into account the probable merit of party's case. Fed.Rules Civ.Proc.Rule 41(b), 28 U.S.C.A.

In re Southeast Banking Corp. Securities and Loan Loss Reserves Litigation, 212 B.R. 397.

S.D.Fla. 1990. Dismissal of suit alleging violation of Real Estate Settlement Procedures Act for lack of prosecution was not warranted; statute of limitations had run and plaintiffs had complied with defendants' discovery requests, which had been basis for defendants' motions to dismiss.

Miller v. Weitzer Panache Ltd., 751 F.Supp. 980.

S.D.Fla. 1988. In view of plaintiff's failure to take default against defendant despite court's order to do so or to otherwise prosecute claim,

the defendant would be dismissed from the case for failure to prosecute.

Boron v. West Texas Exports, Inc., 680 F.Supp. 1532, affirmed 869 F.2d 1500.

S.D.Fla. 1987. Authority to dismiss action for lack of prosecution or to enter default for discovery abuses is one of inherent powers of court, and in particular, courts have inherent power to enter default judgment as punishment for defendant's destruction of documents.

Telectron, Inc. v. Overhead Door Corp., 116 F.R.D. 107.

S.D.Fla. 1985. Sanction of dismissal of civil action for failure to comply with court orders directing plaintiff to respond to pending motions, including motion to dismiss, and for not filing pleadings in accordance with reasonable diligence was too severe and, instead, counsel would be assessed $2,500 to be paid into registry of court. Fed.Rules Civ.Proc.Rules 11, 41(b), 28 U.S.C.A.

Navarro v. Cohan, 109 F.R.D. 86.

M.D.Ga. 1986. Employment discrimination action would not be dismissed for failure to prosecute where eight-year delay was based in large part on investigation of charge of discrimination by EEOC; plaintiffs had no duty to request right-to-sue letter so that judicial complaint could be filed earlier.

Calloway v. Westinghouse Elec. Corp., 642 F.Supp. 663, modification denied 115 F.R.D. 73, appeal dismissed 831 F.2d 1069.

Delays in prosecution of employment discrimination case which occurred while discovery was not ongoing were not willful and thus would not result in dismissal for failure to prosecute. Fed.Rules Civ.Proc.Rule 41(b), 28 U.S.C.A.

Calloway v. Westinghouse Elec. Corp., 642 F.Supp. 663, modification denied 115 F.R.D. 73, appeal dismissed 831 F.2d 1069.

S.D.Ga. 1994. Rule permitting dismissal for failure to prosecute is "housekeeping measure" which allows court to manage its docket, further policy of expeditious resolution of litigation, and prevent prejudice to defendant from delay. Fed.Rules Civ.Proc.Rule 41(b), 28 U.S.C.A.

Stolt-Nielsen, Inc. v. Zim Israel Navigation Co., Ltd., 879 F.Supp. 1223, vacated Stolt-Neilsen v. Zim Israel Nav. Co., 67 F.3d 314.

In considering whether to grant motion to dismiss for failure to prosecute, court considers fairness to litigants as well as policy concerns with efficient disposition and resolution of litigation. Fed.Rules Civ.Proc.Rule 41(b), 28 U.S.C.A.

> Stolt-Nielsen, Inc. v. Zim Israel Navigation Co., Ltd., 879 F.Supp. 1223, vacated Stolt-Nielsen v. Zim Israel Nav. Co., 67 F.3d 314.

When considering whether to dismiss for failure to prosecute, court balances differing interests and determines whether there is clear record of delay or willful contempt and finding that lesser sanctions would not suffice. Fed. Rules Civ.Proc.Rule 41(b), 28 U.S.C.A.

> Stolt-Nielsen, Inc. v. Zim Israel Navigation Co., Ltd., 879 F.Supp. 1223, vacated Stolt-Nielsen v. Zim Israel Nav. Co., 67 F.3d 314.

N.D.Ill. 1996. It is up to plaintiffs to move their cases forward in timely fashion.

> Grun v. Pneumo Abex Corp., 170 F.R.D. 441.

Even if, as plaintiff contended, order of dismissal was void ab initio, matter would nonetheless be dismissed for want of prosecution due to fact that no action had been taken in case for three years even though plaintiff had constructive notice of both long-past trial date and court's alleged clerical error. Fed.Rules Civ. Proc.Rule 60(b)(4), 28 U.S.C.A.; U.S.Dist.Ct. Rules N.D.Ill., General Rule 21, subd. B.

> Grun v. Pneumo Abex Corp., 170 F.R.D. 441.

Dismissal with prejudice for want of prosecution is strong sanction that must be reserved only for extreme circumstances.

> Grun v. Pneumo Abex Corp., 170 F.R.D. 441.

N.D.Ill. 1985. Dismissal for failure to prosecute under Federal Civil Rule 41(b) is within trial court's discretion and will not be disturbed on appeal absent abuse of discretion. Fed.Rules Civ.Proc.Rule 41(b), 28 U.S.C.A.

> In re Olympia Brewing Co. Securities Litigation, 613 F.Supp. 1286.

Dismissal with prejudice for failure to prosecute action alleging downward market manipulation in corporation's shares was appropriate, even though buyers claimed that they relied on discovery by plaintiffs' committee in consolidated cases, where it appeared that buyers had no intention of proceeding against seller and suspended prosecution of action pending resolution of matters in class actions, which involved different defendants and different issues. Fed. Rules Civ.Proc.Rule 41(b), 28 U.S.C.A.

> In re Olympia Brewing Co. Securities Litigation, 613 F.Supp. 1286.

N.D.Ill. 1985. Claim under Title VII for unlawful employment practice was subject to dismissal where employees could not allege timely filing of employment discrimination charges with EEOC and receipt of right-to-sue letter and did not respond in their brief to argument that they failed to exhaust their administrative remedies. Civil Rights Act of 1964, § 701 et seq., 42 U.S.C.A. § 2000e et seq.

> Gutierrez v. City of Chicago, 605 F.Supp. 973.

N.D.Ind. 1994. Plaintiffs did not demonstrate good cause for their failure to prosecute civil action for more than six months following docketing of returns of service, despite fact that they had entered into agreement with defendants' insurer for "indefinite extension" of time for defendants to respond, but dismissal of action for failure to prosecute would unfairly penalize plaintiffs where defendants were equally culpable. U.S.Dist.Ct.Rules N.D.Ind., Rules 6.1, 41.1; Fed.Rules Civ.Proc.Rule 12, 28 U.S.C.A.

> McMahan v. CCC Express Corp., 153 F.R.D. 633.

S.D.Ind. 1995. Unless there is clear record of dilatory conduct on part of attorney, dismissal was too stiff a penalty for failure to prosecute and may be properly corrected in response to motion for relief from judgment. Fed.Rules Civ.Proc.Rule 60(b), 28 U.S.C.A.

> Hayes v. U.S. Dept. of Transp., 162 F.R.D. 126.

Employee was not entitled to relief from judgment after dismissal of her action for failure to prosecute; conduct of plaintiff's counsel was sufficiently dilatory that dismissal for failure to prosecute was warranted, and motion for relief from judgment could not be used to remedy problems caused by attorney negligence. Fed.Rules Civ.Proc.Rule 60(b), 28 U.S.C.A.

> Hayes v. U.S. Dept. of Transp., 162 F.R.D. 126.

N.D.Iowa 1995. Dismissal for want of prosecution was unwarranted in action by pro se plaintiffs alleging misconduct of many kinds in making and foreclosing of various loans; although plaintiffs filed no resistances after being granted several extensions of time to respond to motions to dismiss, there was no willful disobedience of court order, as court did not require some action that plaintiffs failed to take. Fed.Rules Civ.Proc.Rule 41(b), 28 U.S.C.A.; U.S.Dist.Ct.Rules N.D.Iowa, Rule 14, subds. f, i.

> Dahl v. Kanawha Inv. Holding Co., 161 F.R.D. 673.

To determine whether dismissal for want of prosecution is appropriate, court should consider whether plaintiff willfully refused to comply with court orders. Fed.Rules Civ.Proc.Rule 41(b), 28 U.S.C.A.

> Dahl v. Kanawha Inv. Holding Co., 161 F.R.D. 673.

D.Kan. 1990. Plaintiff's failure to appear for trial, even though plaintiff was aware of trial date, warranted dismissal of action with prejudice for lack of prosecution. Fed.Rules Civ. Proc.Rule 41(b), 28 U.S.C.A.

> Betts v. Agri-Tech Services, Inc., 130 F.R.D. 143.

E.D.La. 1988. District court may dismiss for want of prosecution whenever necessary to achieve the orderly and expeditious disposition of cases. Fed.Rules Civ.Proc.Rule 41(b, c), 28 U.S.C.A.

> Sea-Land Service, Inc. v. Banca De Republica De Dominica, 697 F.Supp. 253.

Defendant's deliberate inattention to its litigation by failing to appear at status conference or to oppose motions to dismiss and failure to respond to pleadings or correspondence warranted dismissal of its counterclaims and third-party claims for failure to prosecute. Fed.Rules Civ.Proc.Rule 41(b, c), 28 U.S.C.A.

> Sea-Land Service, Inc. v. Banca De Republica De Dominica, 697 F.Supp. 253.

E.D.La. 1983. State of La., ex rel. Guste v. M/V Testbank, 564 F.Supp. 729, affirmed State of La. v. M/V Testbank, 767 F.2d 916, affirmed 767 F.2d 917.

M.D.La. 1993. Federal district court may dismiss action for failure to prosecute upon motion of defendant. Fed.Rules Civ.Proc.Rule 41(b), 28 U.S.C.A.

> U.S. v. Avondale Industries, Inc., 841 F.Supp. 180.

Authority contained in rule permitting federal district court to dismiss action for failure to prosecute is based on court's power to manage and administer its own affairs and to ensure orderly and expeditious disposition of cases. Fed.Rules Civ.Proc.Rule 41(b), 28 U.S.C.A.

> U.S. v. Avondale Industries, Inc., 841 F.Supp. 180.

Court may dismiss action with prejudice for failure to prosecute only if (1) there is clear record of delay or contumacious conduct by plaintiff, and (2) court has not expressly determined that lesser sanctions would not prompt diligent prosecution, or record shows that court employed lesser sanctions which proved to be futile. Fed.Rules Civ.Proc.Rule 41(b), 28 U.S.C.A.

> U.S. v. Avondale Industries, Inc., 841 F.Supp. 180.

Environmental cleanup action to recover response costs could not be dismissed for failure to prosecute despite alleged delay through deferring service on defendant for over 34 months where defendant was served but failed to answer to complaint, and settlement negotiations between parties continued throughout period of alleged delay.

> U.S. v. Avondale Industries, Inc., 841 F.Supp. 180.

D.Me. 1990. Action to foreclose Farmers Home Administration (FmHA) mortgage would be dismissed with prejudice for lack of prosecution, based upon government counsel's failure to take any initial action after filing complaint until precipitated to do so by order to show cause and counsel's failure to take any subsequent action to move matter forward on docket during period of almost five complete months, particularly in view of past inattention to civil matters filed in district court despite repeated admonitions.

> U.S. v. Anderson, 752 F.Supp. 45.

D.Mass. 1994. First circuit permits dismissal of action for failure to prosecute only when plaintiff's misconduct is extreme and no lesser sanction than dismissal will be appropriate.

> Lemelson v. Wang Laboratories, Inc., 874 F.Supp. 430.

E.D.Mich. 1987. Employment discrimination plaintiff's repeated failure to appear for depositions warranted dismissal of case.

> Roby v. Center Companies, 679 F.Supp. 664, appeal dismissed 848 F.2d 193, appeal dismissed 852 F.2d 1288, reversed 884 F.2d 1393.

E.D.Mich. 1985. For a court to dismiss a case under Federal Civil Rule 41(b) on account of a lack of prosecution, it is not necessary for it to find that plaintiff attempted to delay the trial. Fed.Rules Civ.Proc.Rule 41(b), 28 U.S.C.A.

> Snavley v. Redman, 107 F.R.D. 346.

W.D.Mich. 1997. Civil rights claim against prison nurses' supervisor, who had never been properly served with process, would be dismissed for lack of prosecution.

> Miller v. Michigan Dept. of Corrections Health Care Providers, 986 F.Supp. 1078.

W.D.Mich. 1986. Dismissal of employee's action against employer for breach of implied employment contract for failure of employee to prosecute and failure to respond to motion within ten days would be unjust, where employee obtained a new counsel only few weeks prior to motion for dismissal hearing, employee was present at hearing and presented argument, and employer was not prejudiced by any delay.

Fed.Rules Civ.Proc.Rule 41(b), 28 U.S.C.A.; U.S.Dist.Ct.Rules W.D.Mich., Rule 29(b).

> Richmond v. Wyeth Laboratories Div. of American Home Products Corp., 641 F.Supp. 483.

N.D.Miss. 1997. District court acted within its discretion in dismissing action based on plaintiff's failure to keep her own attorneys and court advised of her current address, her refusal to cooperate with her attorneys in prosecuting her case, her failure to attend case management conference and her general failure to prosecute, considering that plaintiff had been warned on multiple occasions that her case could be dismissed for failure to prosecute. Fed.Rules Civ. Proc.Rule 41(b), 28 U.S.C.A.

> Vance v. W.G. Yates and Sons Const. Co., 974 F.Supp. 879.

S.D.Miss. 1985. District court's authority to dismiss a cause with prejudice flows from its inherent power to control its docket and prevent undue delay in the disposition of pending cases, and such dismissal is not an abuse of discretion where there is a clear record of inexcusable delay and the court has provided plaintiff with repeated opportunities to cure procedural defaults through imposition of lesser sanctions. Fed.Rules Civ.Proc.Rules 37(b, c), 41(b), 28 U.S.C.A.

> Johnson v. Universal Life Ins. Co., 108 F.R.D. 150.

Action against insurer for bad-faith breach of an insurance contract was subject to dismissal with prejudice for failure of plaintiffs to respond to interrogatories and to insurer's motion to compel discovery, amounting to want of prosecution; failure to respond even after monetary sanctions indicated that further similar sanctions would likely be unavailing. Fed. Rules Civ.Proc.Rule 41(b), 28 U.S.C.A.

> Johnson v. Universal Life Ins. Co., 108 F.R.D. 150.

D.Neb. 1996. Party who refuses to prosecute civil case may suffer dismissal of his or her case with prejudice. Fed.Rules Civ.Proc.Rule 41(b), 28 U.S.C.A.

> McCaslin by McCaslin v. Radcliff, 168 F.R.D. 249, affirmed McCaslin v. County of York, 141 F.3d 1169.

In deciding whether to dismiss case for failure to prosecute, when infant or incompetent person is before court, test is whether there is clear record of delay or contumacious conduct by party against whom dismissal is ordered. Fed.Rules Civ.Proc.Rules 17(c), 41(b), 28 U.S.C.A.

> McCaslin by McCaslin v. Radcliff, 168 F.R.D. 249, affirmed McCaslin v. County of York, 141 F.3d 1169.

D.Nev. 1984. Hay v. Wells Cargo, Inc., 596 F.Supp. 635, affirmed 796 F.2d 478.

E.D.N.Y. 1997. Involuntary dismissal for plaintiff's failure to prosecute is matter committed to sound discretion of trial court. Fed.Rules Civ.Proc.Rule 41(b), 28 U.S.C.A.

> In re Folks, 210 B.R. 674.

Dismissal for failure to prosecute is harsh remedy to be utilized only in extreme situations. Fed.Rules Civ.Proc.Rule 41(b), 28 U.S.C.A.

> In re Folks, 210 B.R. 674.

Although reviewing court will consider five factors in determining propriety of dismissal of action for failure to prosecute, including duration of plaintiff's failures, whether plaintiff had received notice that further delays would result in dismissal, whether defendant is likely to be prejudiced by further delay, whether district judge has taken care to strike balance between alleviating court congestion and protecting party's right to due process and fair chance to be heard, and whether judge has adequately assessed efficacy of lesser sanctions, generally no one factor is dispositive. Fed.Rules Civ.Proc. Rule 41(b), 28 U.S.C.A.

> In re Folks, 210 B.R. 674.

E.D.N.Y. 1994. Factors to consider in determining whether to dismiss action for failure to prosecute include duration of failures, whether plaintiff had received notice that further delays would result in dismissal, whether defendant is likely to be prejudiced by further delay, whether district judge has taken care to strike balance between alleviating court calendar congestion and protecting party's right to due process, and whether judge has adequately assessed efficacy of lesser sanction. Fed.Rules Civ.Proc. Rule 41(b), 28 U.S.C.A.

> Giuliano v. Everything Yogurt, Inc., 152 F.R.D. 449.

Dismissal for lack of prosecution is left to the discretion of the court. Fed.Rules Civ.Proc. Rule 41(b), 28 U.S.C.A.

> Giuliano v. Everything Yogurt, Inc., 152 F.R.D. 449.

Dismissal for lack of prosecution is only appropriate when plaintiff has made no moves whatsoever to move the case to trial. Fed.Rules Civ.Proc.Rule 41(b), 28 U.S.C.A.

> Giuliano v. Everything Yogurt, Inc., 152 F.R.D. 449.

In determining whether to dismiss action for lack of prosecution, court must analyze whether plaintiff received notice that further delays would result in dismissal. Fed.Rules Civ.Proc.Rule 41(b), 28 U.S.C.A.

> Giuliano v. Everything Yogurt, Inc., 152 F.R.D. 449.

For purposes of determining whether franchisee had notice that further delays would result in dismissal of RICO (Racketeer Influenced Corrupt Organizations) action against franchisor for lack of prosecution, letter from franchisor's counsel to franchisee's counsel requesting discussion of discovery delays could not be interpreted as warning that further delays would result in dismissal. Fed.Rules Civ. Proc.Rule 41(b), 28 U.S.C.A.

> Giuliano v. Everything Yogurt, Inc., 152 F.R.D. 449.

E.D.N.Y. 1992. Motions to dismiss for failure to prosecute are within sound discretion of district court. Fed.Rules Civ.Proc.Rule 41(b), 28 U.S.C.A.

> Montalvo v. Quigley, 144 F.R.D. 21.

E.D.N.Y. 1985. Inmate's pro se complaint alleging that defendant corrections officers beat him without provocation during search of his cell would be dismissed with prejudice for failure to obey order to provide discovery; inmate's failure to provide ordered discovery resulted from willful failure to prosecute his case and certainly amounted to gross negligence. Fed. Rules Civ.Proc.Rule 37(b)(2)(C), 28 U.S.C.A.

> Williams v. Kane, 107 F.R.D. 632.

E.D.N.Y. 1985. Where plaintiff had made no good-faith effort to make discovery, had failed to respond to defendants' discovery requests and had failed to comply with direct orders of the court, while defendants in contrast had answered complaint, drafted interrogatories and otherwise complied with discovery in good faith and had moved to dismiss, dismissal of action was justified not only for failure to obey orders to provide discovery, but also for failure to prosecute. Fed.Rules Civ.Proc.Rules 37(b)(2)(C), 41(b), 28 U.S.C.A.

> Urban Elec. Supply and Equipment Corp. v. New York Convention Center Development Corp., 105 F.R.D. 92.

N.D.N.Y. 1997. Pro se plaintiff's failure to appear for his deposition, to respond to discovery, to appear at hearings, to respond to defendants' letters and telephone inquiries, and to oppose defendants' dismissal motions constituted willful failure to prosecute and warranted entry of order striking complaint and dismissing action, despite his pro se status. Fed.Rules Civ.Proc.Rule 1, 28 U.S.C.A.; U.S.Dist.Ct.Rules N.D.N.Y., Civil Rule 7.1(b), par. 3.

> Hoffman v. Scoville, 174 F.R.D. 11.

N.D.N.Y. 1984. Interests of justice and preservation of court responsibility for efficient control of its litigation warranted and compelled grant of motion to dismiss employment discrimination action of pro se plaintiff for failure to diligently prosecute the action and for failure to comply with directions of the court

where plaintiff kept court in turmoil for several months after his dismissal of his competent attorneys, with telephone calls, mailgrams and letters, requested list of trial judge's law clerks, prosecuted the action from long distance, ignored express directions of court to appear in court, and took more than a year to file reply to pending motions without applying for stay to permit such delay. Fed.Rules Civ.Proc.Rule 41(b), 28 U.S.C.A.

> Silver v. Mohasco Corp., 103 F.R.D. 614.

S.D.N.Y. 1997. Following factors are relevant in determining whether dismissal is appropriate remedy for failure to prosecute: what was duration of plaintiff's failure; whether plaintiff received notice that further delays would result in dismissal; whether defendant was likely to be prejudiced by further delay; whether judge had taken care to strike balance between alleviating court calendar congestion and protecting party's right to due process and chance to be heard; and whether judge had adequately assessed efficacy of lesser sanctions. U.S.C.A. Const.Amend. 14; Fed.Rules Civ.Proc.Rule 41(b), 28 U.S.C.A.

> Dodson v. Runyon, 957 F.Supp. 465, affirmed 152 F.3d 917.

S.D.N.Y. 1997. Dismissal for failure to prosecute action is matter committed to sound discretion of district court. Fed.Rules Civ.Proc. Rule 41(b), 28 U.S.C.A.

> Jenkins v. City of New York, 176 F.R.D. 127.

In exercising its discretion to dismiss action for failure to prosecute, district court should examine five factors: (1) duration of plaintiff's failure; (2) whether plaintiff received notice that further delay would result in dismissal; (3) whether defendant will suffer prejudice by further delay; (4) balancing of need to relieve court's calendar congestion with plaintiff's right to due process; and (5) efficacy of lesser sanctions. Fed.Rules Civ.Proc.Rule 41(b), 28 U.S.C.A.

> Jenkins v. City of New York, 176 F.R.D. 127.

In general, no one factor is dispositive in determining to dismiss action for failure to prosecute. Fed.Rules Civ.Proc.Rule 41(b), 28 U.S.C.A.

> Jenkins v. City of New York, 176 F.R.D. 127.

Only when district court is sure of impotence of lesser sanctions is drastic remedy of dismissal for failure to prosecute appropriate. Fed.Rules Civ.Proc.Rule 41(b), 28 U.S.C.A.

> Jenkins v. City of New York, 176 F.R.D. 127.

S.D.N.Y. 1997. Threshold for dismissal of action or claim for failure to prosecute is heightened where pro se litigant fails to satisfy procedural requirements. Fed.Rules Civ.Proc. Rule 41(b), 28 U.S.C.A.

Hedvat v. Rothschild, 175 F.R.D. 183.

Dismissal of action or claim for failure to prosecute is discretionary, and is harsh remedy appropriate only in extreme situations. Fed. Rules Civ.Proc.Rule 41(b), 28 U.S.C.A.

Hedvat v. Rothschild, 175 F.R.D. 183.

S.D.N.Y. 1997. Summary judgment motion may be granted by default if facts justify dismissal for failure to prosecute. Fed.Rules Civ.Proc.Rule 56, 28 U.S.C.A.

Lediju v. New York City Dept. of Sanitation, 173 F.R.D. 105.

Dismissal for lack of prosecution is matter committed to sound discretion of trial court. Fed.Rules Civ.Proc.Rule 41(b), 28 U.S.C.A.

Lediju v. New York City Dept. of Sanitation, 173 F.R.D. 105.

In determining whether to dismiss action for failure to prosecute, court is to consider (1) duration of plaintiff's failures, (2) whether plaintiffs have received notice that further delays would result in dismissal, (3) whether defendants are likely to be prejudiced by further delay, (4) balancing of need to alleviate court calendar congestion and party's right to due process, and (5) efficacy of lesser sanctions. Fed.Rules Civ.Proc.Rule 41(b), 28 U.S.C.A.

Lediju v. New York City Dept. of Sanitation, 173 F.R.D. 105.

S.D.N.Y. 1997. Pro se litigant's complaint should be dismissed for failure to prosecute where circumstances are sufficiently extreme. Fed.Rules Civ.Proc.Rule 41(b), 28 U.S.C.A.

Coss v. Sullivan County Jail Adm'r, 171 F.R.D. 68.

S.D.N.Y. 1996. In exercising its discretion as to whether to dismiss for failure to prosecute, court should examine five factors, including duration of plaintiff's failures, whether plaintiff received notice that further delays would result in dismissal, whether defendant is likely to be prejudiced by further delay, balancing of need to alleviate court calendar congestion with party's right to due process, and efficacy of lesser sanctions. Fed.Rules Civ.Proc.Rule 41(b), 28 U.S.C.A.

Daniels v. Loizzo, 175 F.R.D. 459.

S.D.N.Y. 1995. In determining whether to exercise its inherent power to dismiss for failure to prosecute, court considers the duration of plaintiff's failures, whether plaintiff had received notice that further delays would result in dismissal, whether defendant is likely to be prejudiced by further delay, whether district judge has carefully balanced the need to alleviate court calendar congestion and party's right

to due process, and whether court has assessed the efficacy of lesser sanctions; generally, no particular factor is dispositive. Fed.Rules Civ. Proc.Rule 41(b), 28 U.S.C.A.

Stoenescu v. Jablonsky, 162 F.R.D. 268.

S.D.N.Y. 1994. Federal court has power to dismiss action for failure to prosecute, and such a dismissal will be reviewed only for abuse of discretion. Fed.Rules Civ.Proc.Rule 41(b), 28 U.S.C.A.

In re Crysen/Montenay Energy Co., 166 B.R. 546.

Dismissal of action for failure to prosecute is harsh remedy to be utilized only in extreme situations. Fed.Rules Civ.Proc.Rule 41(b), 28 U.S.C.A.

In re Crysen/Montenay Energy Co., 166 B.R. 546.

Dismissal for failure to prosecute is appropriate remedy where plaintiff has shown no due diligence in prosecuting case. Fed.Rules Civ. Proc.Rule 41(b), 28 U.S.C.A.

In re Crysen/Montenay Energy Co., 166 B.R. 546.

S.D.N.Y. 1994. Pro se plaintiff's employment discrimination case would be dismissed under rule providing for sanctions for failure to make disclosure or cooperate in discovery and rule providing for dismissal for failure to prosecute or to comply with rules or any order of court; plaintiff's excuse that work related activities prevented him from complying with discovery orders was inadequate, plaintiff received adequate notice that his failure to respond would result in dismissal, defendant would be prejudiced by further delay if case were to continue, and monetary sanctions were not feasible given plaintiff's statements about his financial hardship. Fed.Rules Civ.Proc.Rules 37(b)(2)(C), 41(b).

Martin v. Metropolitan Museum of Art, 158 F.R.D. 289.

S.D.N.Y. 1993. Primary rationale for dismissal for failure to prosecute is plaintiff's failure to diligently proceed with action. Fed. Rules Civ.Proc.Rule 41(b), 28 U.S.C.A.

Acot v. New York Medical College, 153 F.R.D. 517, reargument denied.

S.D.N.Y. 1993. Action by FDIC as receiver bank alleging fraudulent conduct by defendants would be dismissed for lack of prosecution caused by failure of FDIC officials to give necessary authority to attorneys conducting litigation. Fed.Rules Civ.Proc.Rule 41(b), 28 U.S.C.A.

Dollar Dry Dock Bank v. Denning, 148 F.R.D. 124.

S.D.N.Y. 1993. Intrafamily business dispute would be dismissed without prejudice for lack of prosecution; parties had not responded to court order setting forth potential settlement procedures parties were directed to explore, or to questions concerning merits of their respective asserted claims which they were directed to answer if any of them wished to pursue the case.

Alpert v. Kramer, 145 F.R.D. 318.

S.D.N.Y. 1991. Plaintiff's strategic decision to exhaust remedies against insurer before initiating action against insurance broker for breach of agreement to procure effective coverage was not, in and of itself, type of dilatory conduct warranting dismissal for failure to prosecute. Fed.Rules Civ.Proc.Rule 41(b), 28 U.S.C.A.

Knight v. H.E. Yerkes and Associates, Inc., 135 F.R.D. 67.

Slow pace of discovery did not warrant dismissal of action for breach of agreement to procure insurance coverage on ground of failure to prosecute where it appeared that defendant had acquiesced in delay which had allegedly caused it prejudice. Fed.Rules Civ.Proc. Rule 41(b), 28 U.S.C.A.

Knight v. H.E. Yerkes and Associates, Inc., 135 F.R.D. 67.

S.D.N.Y. 1990. Determinations to grant or deny motion to dismiss for failure to prosecute turn on facts of each case.

Vaughn v. O'Donnell, 734 F.Supp. 139.

District court has inherent authority to grant motion to dismiss for failure to prosecute, but must weigh public interest in expeditious resolution of litigation against public interests in having case decided on its merits.

Vaughn v. O'Donnell, 734 F.Supp. 139.

S.D.N.Y. 1990. District judge may, sua sponte and without notice to parties, dismiss complaint for lack of prosecution, and such dismissal is largely matter of judge's discretion. Fed.Rules Civ.Proc.Rule 41(b), 28 U.S.C.A.

West v. City of New York, 130 F.R.D. 522.

It is plaintiff's obligation to move his case to trial, and should he fail to do so in reasonable manner, case may be dismissed with prejudice as sanction for unjustified conduct. Fed.Rules Civ.Proc.Rule 41(b), 28 U.S.C.A.

West v. City of New York, 130 F.R.D. 522.

Dismissal of case is warranted when there is lack of due diligence in prosecution of lawsuit by plaintiff. Fed.Rules Civ.Proc.Rule 41(b), 28 U.S.C.A.

West v. City of New York, 130 F.R.D. 522.

What constitutes failure to prosecute justifying dismissal of case depends on particular facts involved. Fed.Rules Civ.Proc.Rule 41(b), 28 U.S.C.A.

West v. City of New York, 130 F.R.D. 522.

There need not be any deliberate intent to delay prosecution of case for dismissal to be justified for failure to prosecute. Fed.Rules Civ.Proc.Rule 41(b), 28 U.S.C.A.

West v. City of New York, 130 F.R.D. 522.

Plaintiff's lack of diligence is alone enough for dismissal.

West v. City of New York, 130 F.R.D. 522.

Pro se plaintiff's inactivity in pursuing civil rights suit was not excusable for purposes of dismissal for lack of prosecution based on fact that plaintiff was incarcerated throughout lawsuit. Fed.Rules Civ.Proc.Rule 41(b), 28 U.S.C.A.

West v. City of New York, 130 F.R.D. 522.

S.D.N.Y. 1989. Dismissal for failure to prosecute was not required when plaintiffs in lawsuit contesting control over union failed to cooperate in meeting court-imposed deadline relating to proposed pretrial order, as plaintiffs suspended discovery in good faith while awaiting result of appeal, and entertained good-faith erroneous idea that appeal court's reversal of trial court's decision dismissing union from suit had rendered pretrial order moot.

Johnson v. Kay, 126 F.R.D. 16.

S.D.N.Y. 1989. Dismissal for lack of prosecution is a matter committed to the sound discretion of the trial court and district court may sua sponte dismiss an action for lack of prosecution. Fed.Rules Civ.Proc.Rule 41(b), 28 U.S.C.A.

Lukensow v. Harley Cars of New York, 124 F.R.D. 64.

It is not the duty of the court to contact plaintiffs and urge or require them to prosecute the action, nor is defense under any duty to take any steps to bring that action to trial.

Lukensow v. Harley Cars of New York, 124 F.R.D. 64.

In determining whether court should exercise its discretion and dismiss suit for failure to prosecute, court must consider the duration of plaintiffs' failures, whether plaintiffs have received notice that further delays would result in dismissal, whether defendants were likely to be prejudiced by further delay, the need to alleviate court calendar congestion as balanced against a party's right to due process, and the efficacy of lesser sanctions. Fed.Rules Civ.Proc.Rule 41(b), 28 U.S.C.A.

Lukensow v. Harley Cars of New York, 124 F.R.D. 64.

Dismissal for failure to prosecute was warranted by complete lack of prosecutorial effort on the part of plaintiffs for two years, failure of plaintiffs to contact counsel for five months prior to his withdrawal, court's lack of current address for plaintiffs, and the inefficacy of any other sanction because plaintiffs could not be contacted by the court. Fed.Rules Civ.Proc. Rule 41(b), 28 U.S.C.A.

> Lukensow v. Harley Cars of New York, 124 F.R.D. 64.

S.D.N.Y. 1988. Debtors, which brought postdischarge adversary proceeding claiming that state court action brought against debtors by defendants was based on discharged contracts and sought to enjoin prosecution of state court action and to hold defendants in contempt for bringing action, had burden of prosecuting adversary proceeding, and knowingly chose not to prosecute by doing nothing for five and one-half years, for purpose of determining whether case should be dismissed for lack of prosecution, despite debtors' claim that burden of proceeding in bankruptcy court was at least in part on defendants because defendants could do nothing further in state court action until adversary proceeding was terminated. Fed.Rules Civ.Proc.Rule 41(b), 28 U.S.C.A.

> In re United Merchants and Mfrs., Inc., 86 B.R. 764, appeal after remand 126 B.R. 149.

S.D.N.Y. 1987. Title VII action brought by EEOC on behalf of class of minority laborers against union could not be dismissed on basis of delay in adjudication of claims; union failed to demonstrate that delay was inexcusable or that EEOC was responsible, as some delay was result of administrative difficulties incident to reassignment of case during pendency of union's appeal of various orders. Civil Rights Act of 1964, § 701 et seq., as amended, 42 U.S.C.A. § 2000e et seq.

> E.E.O.C. v. Local 638, 674 F.Supp. 91.

S.D.N.Y. 1985. Although attorney's failure to correctly note date of pretrial conference on his calendar was not excusable, proper remedy was not to dismiss for failure to prosecute, but, rather, to impose sanctions of $300 in attorney fees and $200 in court costs.

> Barsoumian v. Szozda, 108 F.R.D. 426.

S.D.N.Y. 1985. Failure of Honduran company to pursue its action for 35 months, to respond to its own counsel's written communications, and even to respond to motion to dismiss for failure to prosecute warranted dismissal of action for want of prosecution. Fed.Rules Civ.Proc.Rule 41(b), 28 U.S.C.A.

> Aceros Industriales, S.A. de C.V. v. Florida Steel Corp., 106 F.R.D. 572.

District court cannot permit a litigant to abuse court's scarce resources by failing to prosecute an action while thousands of other litigants, desirous and deserving of relief, pa-

tiently await their day in court. Fed.Rules Civ.Proc.Rule 41(b), 28 U.S.C.A.

> Aceros Industriales, S.A. de C.V. v. Florida Steel Corp., 106 F.R.D. 572.

S.D.N.Y. 1985. Plaintiffs' attorney's failure to attend four pretrial conferences scheduled by court warranted dismissal of plaintiffs' remaining claims.

> Yannitelli v. Navieras De Puerto Rico, 106 F.R.D. 42.

Plaintiffs, who failed to pursue discovery and who frustrated defendants' attempts to obtain discovery of them, failed to prosecute action with due diligence and occasioned waste of too much of court's scarce time and resources, warranting dismissal with prejudice. Fed.Rules Civ.Proc.Rule 41(b), 28 U.S.C.A.

> Yannitelli v. Navieras De Puerto Rico, 106 F.R.D. 42.

S.D.N.Y. 1985. Suit was subject to dismissal for failure to prosecute in light of plaintiff's total failure to pursue the action for the past 21 months, his repeated failure to respond to his own counsel's missives, his repeated failure to respond to letters from the court and his failure to attend pretrial conference.

> Yacub v. Coughlin, 105 F.R.D. 152.

W.D.N.Y. 1996. Section 1983 action filed by inmate based upon circumstances of his confinement in prison's special housing unit (SHU) was subject to dismissal for failure to proceed, where inmate failed to comply with District Court directive to both parties to submit additional briefs.

> Brewton v. Hollister, 948 F.Supp. 244.

W.D.N.Y. 1987. Dismissal for failure to prosecute is particularly appropriate in instances of willful failure to prosecute such as where plaintiff fails to complete discovery or disobeys court orders.

> Markel v. Scovill Mfg. Co., 657 F.Supp. 1102, vacated 859 F.2d 148.

W.D.N.C. 1985. Both taxpayer's action for refund on taxes paid, and tax suit by United States against defendants would be dismissed for failure to prosecute. Fed.Rules Civ.Proc. Rule 41(b), 28 U.S.C.A.

> U.S. v. Cohen, 105 F.R.D. 164.

D.N.D. 1986. Local rule regarding failure to prosecute is advisory and it is within discretion of court to dismiss for lack of prosecution even when terms of that rule have not been met. Fed.Rules Civ.Proc.Rule 41(b), 28 U.S.C.A.; U.S.Dist.Ct.Rules D.N.D., Rule 4(c).

> Morlan v. Harrington, 658 F.Supp. 24.

N.D.Ohio 1984. Bankruptcy court did not abuse its discretion when it dismissed creditor's claim of fraud, as creditor's answers to discovery requests were evasive and inadequate, and creditor failed to even respond to motion to dismiss.

> In re D.H. Overmyer Telecasting Co., Inc., 53 B.R. 963, appeal decided 787 F.2d 589, appeal decided Hadar Leasing Intern. Co., Inc. v. D.H. Overmyer Telecasting Co., Inc., 787 F.2d 590.

N.D.Ohio 1984. Plaintiff's repeated and flagrant disregard for court orders, which at the least, was grossly negligent, warranted dismissal.

> Chapman v. Schnorf, Schnorf & Schnorf, 109 F.R.D. 253.

E.D.Pa. 1994. Factors to examine when weighing a motion to dismiss for want of prosecution include, among others, prejudice to defendant caused by plaintiff's inaction and whether that inaction revealed an absence of good faith. Fed.Rules Civ.Proc.Rule 41(b), 28 U.S.C.A.

> Mastromatteo v. Simock, 866 F.Supp. 853.

E.D.Pa. 1994. When pro se prisoner fails to adhere to readily comprehended court orders, district court has authority to dismiss pro se prisoner's action for want of prosecution. Fed.Rules Civ.Proc.Rule 41(b), 28 U.S.C.A.

> Muslim v. Frame, 854 F.Supp. 1215.

In deciding whether to dismiss case involuntarily for want of prosecution, district court should consider six factors: extent of party's personal responsibility, prejudice to the adversary, whether there has been a history of dilatoriness in case, whether conduct of party was willful or in bad faith, effectiveness of alternative sanctions, and meritoriousness of claim or defense; but all six factors need not be satisfied to justify dismissal of claim. Fed.Rules Civ. Proc.Rule 41(b), 28 U.S.C.A.

> Muslim v. Frame, 854 F.Supp. 1215.

Pro se prisoner's civil rights action against county prison officials would be involuntarily dismissed for failure to prosecute when he failed to respond to prison officials' motion for summary judgment; inmate was solely responsible for his failure to respond to summary judgment motion, prison officials were prejudiced by inmate's failure to respond to motion, inmate had not pursued case beyond mere pleadings despite being afforded ample opportunity, his conduct was willful, other alternative sanctions would result in termination of inmate's action, all but one of claims were without merit, and inmate would have recovered little or no damages if he were to prevail on only meritorious claim. 42 U.S.C.A. § 1983; Fed.Rules Civ.Proc.Rule 41(b), 28 U.S.C.A.

> Muslim v. Frame, 854 F.Supp. 1215.

E.D.Pa. 1994. Former inmate's civil rights suit against correctional officers should be dismissed with prejudice when inmate, who was proceeding pro se, failed to prosecute his claim and willfully disregarded court order by disappearing for five months without notifying officers or district court as to his whereabouts, and dismissal was only appropriate sanction due to his likely inability to pay any costs or fees assessed against him. Fed.Rules Civ.Proc.Rule 41(b), 28 U.S.C.A.

> Burns v. Glick, 158 F.R.D. 354.

E.D.Pa. 1993. Dismissal for failure to prosecute or to comply with rules or court order should be reserved for cases where there is clear record of delay or contumacious conduct by plaintiff, and it is necessary for district courts to consider whether lesser sanctions would better serve ends of justice. Fed.Rules Civ.Proc.Rule 41(b), 28 U.S.C.A.

> Riddle v. National R.R. Passenger Corp., 831 F.Supp. 442.

E.D.Pa. 1986. A pro se civil rights plaintiff who, following denial of request for appointed counsel, chooses to do nothing must, like any other litigant, be subject to certain procedural rules designed to facilitate the just but expeditious resolution of cases, including the court's inherent power to manage its docket, rules of procedure allowing dismissal as a sanction for failure to cooperate in discovery and comply with court orders, local rule allowing the Court to consider a motion uncontested in the absence of a timely response and civil rule specifying the response necessary to defeat a well-supported summary judgment motion. Fed.Rules Civ. Proc.Rules 37(b), 41(b), 56(e), 28 U.S.C.A.; U.S.Dist.Ct.Rules E.D.Pa., Civil Rule 20(c); 42 U.S.C.A. § 1983.

> Padro v. Heffelfinger, 110 F.R.D. 333.

Prisoner's pro se civil rights complaint charging police chief with using excessive force in effecting arrest was dismissed where after request for appointed counsel was denied the plaintiff did nothing and refused to respond to any of defendants' discovery requests or for motion for summary judgment, complaint made no request for medical treatment, police chief's sworn deposition stated that plaintiff was not injured and plaintiff had ample opportunity to respond. Fed.Rules Civ.Proc.Rules 37(b), 41(b), 56(e), 28 U.S.C.A.; U.S.Dist.Ct.Rules E.D.Pa., Civil Rule 20(c); 42 U.S.C.A. § 1983.

> Padro v. Heffelfinger, 110 F.R.D. 333.

M.D.Pa. 1987. Plaintiff's failure to respond to order directing parties to submit briefs addressing propriety of claim provided grounds for dismissal for failure to prosecute. Fed. Rules Civ.Proc.Rule 41(b), 28 U.S.C.A.

> Turner v. Miller, 679 F.Supp. 441.

D.Puerto Rico 1998. Dismissal for want of prosecution is a harsh sanction, which should be employed only when the district court, in the careful exercise of its discretion, determines that none of the lesser sanctions available to it would truly be appropriate. Fed.Rules Civ. Proc.Rule 41(b), 28 U.S.C.A.

> Jardines Ltd. Partnership v. Executive Homesearch Realty Services, Inc., 178 F.R.D. 365.

District court has the unquestionable authority to dismiss a case with prejudice for want of prosecution in order to prevent undue delay in the disposition of pending cases, docket congestion, and the possibility of harassment of a defendant. Fed.Rules Civ.Proc.Rule 41(b), 28 U.S.C.A.

> Jardines Ltd. Partnership v. Executive Homesearch Realty Services, Inc., 178 F.R.D. 365.

D.Puerto Rico 1986. Failure of cross claimants to prosecute their cross claims diligently warranted dismissal of cross claims, without prejudice, for lack of prosecution. Fed. Rules Civ.Proc.Rule 1, 28 U.S.C.A.

> U.S. (Small Business Admin.) v. Corsino, 648 F.Supp. 454.

D.R.I. 1985. Dismissal of action for failure to prosecute is matter committed to court's discretion, although that drastic sanction should be employed only when court determines that none of lesser sanctions available to it would truly be appropriate. Fed.Rules Civ.Proc.Rule 41(b), 28 U.S.C.A.

> Briehler v. Sylvia's, Inc., 106 F.R.D. 415, affirmed 774 F.2d 1149, certiorari denied 106 S.Ct. 1462, 475 U.S. 1083, 89 L.Ed.2d 719.

Plaintiff's pro se status is factor to be weighed in decision whether to dismiss case for failure to prosecute. Fed.Rules Civ.Proc.Rule 41(b), 28 U.S.C.A.

> Briehler v. Sylvia's, Inc., 106 F.R.D. 415, affirmed 774 F.2d 1149, certiorari denied 106 S.Ct. 1462, 475 U.S. 1083, 89 L.Ed.2d 719.

Where plaintiff failed to appear at first settlement conference, stating that he could not appear in state because of outstanding warrant for his arrest, was represented at second conference only by attorney who did not participate because of his unfamiliarity with case, had failed to retain counsel for his corporation, which was coplaintiff, and had previously litigated similar issues unsuccessfully in state court, his action for damages allegedly suffered in connection with constable's sale of his ship

was subject to dismissal for failure to prosecute. Fed.Rules Civ.Proc.Rule 41(b), 28 U.S.C.A.

> Briehler v. Sylvia's, Inc., 106 F.R.D. 415, affirmed 774 F.2d 1149, certiorari denied 106 S.Ct. 1462, 475 U.S. 1083, 89 L.Ed.2d 719.

D.S.C. 1992. Although district court had authority to dismiss an action for parties' failure to pursue arbitration, it would not do so absent sufficient information as to plaintiff's degree of personal responsibility, amount of prejudice caused defendant, presence of drawn out history of deliberately proceeding in dilatory fashion, and effectiveness of sanctions less drastic than dismissal.

> Sverdrup Corp. v. WHC Constructors, Inc., 787 F.Supp. 542, reversed 989 F.2d 148.

E.D.Tex. 1996. District court may, either sua sponte or upon motion of defendant, dismiss action with prejudice when plaintiff fails to prosecute his or her case. Fed.Rules Civ.Proc. Rule 41(b), 28 U.S.C.A.

> Gist v. Lugo, 165 F.R.D. 474.

Decision to grant motion to dismiss for failure to prosecute lies within district court's discretion and can be reversed only for abuse of that discretion. Fed.Rules Civ.Proc.Rule 41(b), 28 U.S.C.A.

> Gist v. Lugo, 165 F.R.D. 474.

Dismissal with prejudice for failure to prosecute is an extreme sanction which is to be used only when integrity of judicial process is threatened by plaintiff's conduct in such a way that court is left with no choice except to deny that plaintiff its benefits. Fed.Rules Civ.Proc.Rule 41(b), 28 U.S.C.A.

> Gist v. Lugo, 165 F.R.D. 474.

To impose sanction of dismissal with prejudice for failure to prosecute, history of particular case must disclose a clear record of delay or contumacious conduct by plaintiff, finding by district court that lesser sanction would not prompt diligent prosecution or that lesser sanctions were employed and proved futile, and that there is one of three aggravating factors of delay caused by plaintiff himself and not as attorney, actual prejudice to defendant, or delay from intentional conduct. Fed.Rules Civ.Proc.Rule 41(b), 28 U.S.C.A.

> Gist v. Lugo, 165 F.R.D. 474.

Dismissal of inmate's § 1983 action with prejudice was warranted by his contumacious conduct in ignoring at least six court orders particularly since inmate had been alerted of possibility of dismissal of case at least four times by court yet still refused to comply with court orders. Fed.Rules Civ.Proc.Rule 41(b), 28 U.S.C.A.

> Gist v. Lugo, 165 F.R.D. 474.

N.D.Tex. 1985. Failure of plaintiff to pursue entry of default judgment against defendants against whom clerk entered default required dismissal for failure to prosecute. Fed. Rules Civ.Proc.Rule 41(b), 28 U.S.C.A.; U.S.Dist.Ct.Rules N.D.Tex., Rule 3.1(g).

Fisher v. Henderson, 105 F.R.D. 515.

S.D.Tex. 1994. When considering whether to dismiss case for lack of prosecution, district court must weigh court's need to manage docket, public interest in expeditious resolution of litigation, risk of prejudice to defendants from delay, and policy favoring disposition of cases on their merits; in close cases, court also considers whether plaintiff personally contributed to delay, whether defendant was prejudiced as result of delay, and whether plaintiff intentionally caused delay. Fed.Rules Civ.Proc.Rule 41(b), 28 U.S.C.A.

Edwards v. Harris County Sheriff's Dept., 864 F.Supp. 633.

Dismissal of pro se litigant's action is proper when litigant engages in clear pattern of delay or disregards court rule or order and resulting delay is unreasonable.

Edwards v. Harris County Sheriff's Dept., 864 F.Supp. 633.

W.D.Tex. 1997. Rule governing dismissal of actions allows district court to dismiss case for failure to prosecute. Fed.Rules Civ.Proc. Rule 41(b), 28 U.S.C.A.

Hicks v. Brysch, 989 F.Supp. 797.

E.D.Va. 1991. Complaint may be involuntarily dismissed for failure to prosecute after considering: degree of personal responsibility of plaintiffs; amount of prejudice caused defendant; existence of history of deliberately proceeding in dilatory fashion; and existence of effective sanction less drastic than dismissal. Fed.Rules Civ.Proc.Rule 41(b), 28 U.S.C.A.

Zaczek v. Fauquier County, Va., 764 F.Supp. 1071, affirmed 16 F.3d 414.

D.Virgin Islands 1990. Factors to be considered in deciding motion to dismiss complaint for want of prosecution are: extent of party's personal responsibility; prejudice to adversary caused by failure to meet scheduling orders and response to discovery; history of dilatoriness; whether conduct of party or attorney was willful or in bad faith; effectiveness of sanctions other than dismissal, which entails analysis of alternative sanctions; and meritoriousness of claim or defense. Fed.Rules Civ.Proc.Rule 41(b), 28 U.S.C.A.

Andrews v. Government of Virgin Islands, 132 F.R.D. 405, affirmed 935 F.2d 1280.

Trial court need not find that all applicable factors weigh against opposing parties to find that dismissal for want of prosecution is warranted. Fed.Rules Civ.Proc.Rule 41(b), 28 U.S.C.A.

Andrews v. Government of Virgin Islands, 132 F.R.D. 405, affirmed 935 F.2d 1280.

E.D.Wis. 1988. Plaintiff's history of failure to pay costs to parties in other lawsuits resulted in court order requiring plaintiff to pay costs awarded to police officer in previous action by plaintiff before plaintiff would be allowed to proceed with case pending and, in the event that plaintiff failed to pay costs, his case would be dismissed for failure to prosecute.

Young v. Kunde, 698 F.Supp. 163.

W.D.Wis. 1988. Plaintiffs were not barred automatically from proceeding with medical malpractice suit by their former attorney's failure to complete mediation process within 90 days as provided by statute; dismissal of suit was not proper sanction where delay was due solely to dilatory conduct of attorney. W.S.A. 655.465(7).

Bertorello v. St. Joseph's Hosp. of Marshfield, Inc., 685 F.Supp. 192.

9th Cir.BAP (Cal.) 1988. In determining whether to dismiss action for lack of prosecution, trial court must consider public's interest in expeditious resolution of litigation, court's need to manage its docket, risk of prejudice to defendants, public policy favoring disposition of cases of their merits, and availability of less drastic sanctions.

In re Osinga, 91 B.R. 893.

It is plaintiff's duty to expedite his case to its final determination, and if he allows delays by defendant, he cannot complain of them on defendant's motion to dismiss for lack of prosecution.

In re Osinga, 91 B.R. 893.

Bkrtcy.E.D.Ark. 1995. Creditor's failure to appear twice for hearing on motion to compel distribution by Chapter 7 trustee without any formal or informal request for continuance or for stay, and despite three notices of hearing, including one delivered by certified mail, would generally be considered grounds for dismissal in Eighth Circuit for failure to prosecute. Fed. Rules Civ.Proc.Rule 41(b), 28 U.S.C.A.

In re Morrilton Plastics Products, Inc., 177 B.R. 622.

Bkrtcy.D.Hawai'i 1991. In situations where party is not responsible for fault of his attorney, dismissal for failure to prosecute is to be invoked only in extreme circumstances. Fed.Rules Civ.Proc.Rule 41(b), 28 U.S.C.A.

In re Daily, 124 B.R. 325, on reconsideration 125 B.R. 816, affirmed 967 F.2d 585.

Bkrtcy.E.D.Mich. 1986. Failure of debtors seeking turnover of funds in hand of Chapter 13 trustee to provide court with brief in support of motions as required by U.S.Dist.Ct.Rules E.D.Mich., Rule 17, subd. f, warranted dismissal of motion for want of prosecution.

In re Campbell, 58 B.R. 506.

Bkrtcy.D.N.J. 1985. Plaintiff's failure to file amended complaint within time granted by the Bankruptcy Court warranted dismissal of complaint charging defendants with fraud and mismanagement in conduct of affairs of debtor corporation.

Matter of Positive Directions Unlimited, Inc., 56 B.R. 421.

Bkrtcy.E.D.N.Y. 1985. When creditors and their attorneys for second time failed to appear for trial, bankruptcy court properly dismissed case for failure to prosecute, notwithstanding that debtor also failed to appear on one date, and notwithstanding lack of notice from bankruptcy court of adjourned trial dates, as debtor was ready to proceed on two other dates, and it was obligation of creditors' counsel to apprise himself of date to which trial he knew had been scheduled for first date had been adjourned.

Matter of Ksenzowski, 56 B.R. 819.

Dismissal for failure to prosecute is appropriate where a party's practices exemplify flagrant bad faith or a counsel's conduct demonstrates a callous disregard for responsibilities counsel owes to the court and to his opponents.

Matter of Ksenzowski, 56 B.R. 819.

Bkrtcy.S.D.Tex. 1990. To support dismissal with prejudice for failure to prosecute, record should reflect existence of one of the following aggravating factors: plaintiff's personal contribution to delay, defendant's actual prejudice because of delay, and delay that can be characterized as intentional.

In re Arhens, 120 B.R. 852.

Bkrtcy.E.D.Va. 1986. Failure of trustee for debtor to present his evidence at time set for trial warranted dismissal of complaint for failure to prosecute.

In re Virginia Store Fixtures, Inc., 61 B.R. 250.

☞1759. —— Length of delay in general.

C.A.D.C. 1988. Neither delay in service of process nor eight months' inactivity warranted dismissal of inmate's pro se *Bivens* cause of action for failure to prosecute where inmate was not given opportunity to explain why suit should not be dismissed and it was probable that service could be obtained through United States Marshal Service. Fed.Rules Civ.Proc. Rule 41(b), 28 U.S.C.A.

Smith-Bey v. Cripe, 852 F.2d 592, 271 U.S.App.D.C. 294.

C.A.9 1994. To dismiss case for lack of prosecution, court must find unreasonable delay. Fed.Rules Civ.Proc.Rule 41(b), 28 U.S.C.A.

In re Eisen, 31 F.3d 1447.

C.A.9 (Cal.) 1998. Dismissal of § 1983 action for lack of prosecution was abuse of discretion when plaintiffs served complaint upon defendants 113 days after filing and one day after district court's warning, which was within guideline set by rule, court's comments indicated that it perceived no unmanageable interference with docket as result of failure to serve earlier, and court failed to discuss or try less drastic alternatives, or to warn plaintiffs properly of chance of dismissal. 42 U.S.C.A. § 1983; Fed.Rules Civ.Proc.Rule 4(m), 28 U.S.C.A.

Hernandez v. City of El Monte, 138 F.3d 393.

C.A.9 (Cal.) 1984. Ash v. Cvetkov, 739 F.2d 493, certiorari denied 105 S.Ct. 1368, 470 U.S. 1007, 84 L.Ed.2d 387.

C.A.2 (Conn.) 1994. Dismissing § 1983 civil rights complaint for failure to prosecute was abuse of discretion; plaintiff was no more than two months in default in responding to defendant's motion, record contained no notice that plaintiff was on brink of dismissal for failing to respond to motions, defendants would not be prejudiced by delay, and district court failed to balance its interest in calendar against plaintiff's interest or to consider lesser sanctions.

Nita v. Connecticut Dept. of Environmental Protection, 16 F.3d 482.

C.A.7 (Ill.) 1991. Failure of Chapter 11 debtor manufacturers of asbestos, to pursue contractual liability claim against primary insurer, with regard to asbestos claims, for three years after filing complaint containing broad language about "primary liability coverage" justified dismissing claim for lack of prosecution; debtors focused on products liability during discovery and raised contractual liability for first time in proposed pretrial order.

UNR Industries, Inc. v. Continental Cas. Co., 942 F.2d 1101, rehearing denied, certiorari denied 112 S.Ct. 1586, 503 U.S. 971, 118 L.Ed.2d 305.

C.A.7 (Ind.) 1987. District court should dismiss case with prejudice for failure of plaintiff to prosecute or to comply with procedural rules or court order only when there exists clear record of delay or contumacious conduct or when less drastic sanctions have proven ineffective. Fed.Rules Civ.Proc.Rule 41(b), 28 U.S.C.A.

Roland v. Salem Contract Carriers, Inc., 811 F.2d 1175.

C.A.6 (Ky.) 1993. Evidence did not show clear record of delay or contumacious conduct, and therefore district court abused its discretion in dismissing for failure to prosecute a complaint seeking review of United States Forest Service's nonrenewal of "special use permit" to operate marina and hotel on Forest Service property; trial had been rescheduled twice due to judge's recusal and withdrawal of operator's attorneys, and operator noted repeatedly that he did not need to do any discovery. Fed.Rules Civ.Proc.Rule 41(b), 28 U.S.C.A.

> Little v. Yeutter, 984 F.2d 160.

C.A.1 (Mass.) 1986. District court did not abuse its discretion in dismissing, for failure to prosecute, suit by private developer arising out of city's refusal to issue building permit, where, since period during which disputed events occurred, housing authority's membership had completely changed and its then-executive and assistant directors had died, agreement upon which developer sought to impose liability on city had been executed nearly two decades before, and, because original complaint sought only injunctive and declaratory relief, some evidence on issue of monetary damages was not preserved by the parties.

> U.S. Inv. and Development Corp. v. Cruz, 780 F.2d 166.

C.A.6 (Mich.) 1991. Although prisoner was suing pro se, his failure to prosecute his case despite two extensions of time was unwarranted and merited dismissal. Fed.Rules Civ. Proc.Rule 41(b), 28 U.S.C.A.

> Jourdan v. Jabe, 951 F.2d 108.

C.A.8 (Mo.) 1991. Inmate's escape for less than three days while his civil rights action was pending did not mandate dismissal under "fugitive from justice rule," as escape caused no disruption to court proceedings, and action for alleged deliberate indifference to medical needs during prior incarceration was completely distinct and separate from sentence he was serving at time of his escape.

> Perko v. Bowers, 945 F.2d 1038, rehearing denied, certiorari denied 112 S.Ct. 1482, 503 U.S. 939, 117 L.Ed.2d 624.

C.A.3 (N.J.) 1994. Failure to prosecute for more than four years amounted to "history of dilatoriness" for purpose of analyzing whether claims should be dismissed for lack of prosecution. Fed.Rules Civ.Proc.Rule 41(b), 28 U.S.C.A.

> Adams v. Trustees of New Jersey Brewery Employees' Pension Trust Fund, 29 F.3d 863.

Litigant's history of dilatoriness weighed toward but did not mandate dismissal for lack of prosecution. Fed.Rules Civ.Proc.Rule 41(b), 28 U.S.C.A.

> Adams v. Trustees of New Jersey Brewery Employees' Pension Trust Fund, 29 F.3d 863.

Litigant's more than four-year delay in pursuing claim for final determination of employer's liability on remaining unfunded portions of multiemployer pension fund was mitigated by litigant's ten years of responsible litigation. Fed.Rules Civ.Proc.Rule 41(b), 28 U.S.C.A.

> Adams v. Trustees of New Jersey Brewery Employees' Pension Trust Fund, 29 F.3d 863.

Litigant's more than four-year delay in pursuing claim was not "willful" or in "bad faith" absent any indication that delay was strategic or self-serving; it instead appeared to constitute inexcusable negligent behavior. Fed.Rules Civ. Proc.Rule 41(b), 28 U.S.C.A.

> Adams v. Trustees of New Jersey Brewery Employees' Pension Trust Fund, 29 F.3d 863.

C.A.2 (N.Y.) 1997. Civil rights action against police officer by incarcerated, pro se plaintiff should not have been dismissed for failure to prosecute, due to plaintiff's failure to better identify officer, without some inquiry as to whether such officer existed and could readily be located, where plaintiff provided officer's surname, unit to which he was assigned, date and location of alleged use of excessive force, and docket number of plaintiff's case, and where plaintiff was not told of steps he would need to take to avoid dismissal, only 18 months passed since complaint was filed, and there was no balancing of plaintiff's due process rights. Fed.Rules Civ.Proc.Rule 41(b), 28 U.S.C.A.

> Valentin v. Dinkins, 121 F.3d 72.

C.A.2 (N.Y.) 1992. Fact that action lay dormant for five and one-half years did not required dismissal for failure to prosecute. Fed.Rules Civ.Proc.Rule 41(b), 28 U.S.C.A.

> Gibbs v. Hawaiian Eugenia Corp., 966 F.2d 101, on remand 1993 WL 14666.

C.A.2 (N.Y.) 1986. District court abused discretion in dismissing incarcerated, pro se, in forma pauperis complainant's products liability claim alleging harm attributable to ingesting foreign substance while eating cornflakes where only six-month hiatus in prosecution of claim was due to transfer of complainant to county facility lacking library and legal assistance resources required to pursue claim. Fed.Rules Civ.Proc.Rule 41(b), 28 U.S.C.A.

> Romandette v. Weetabix Co., Inc., 807 F.2d 309.

C.A.10 (Okl.) 1987. Trial court appropriately dismissed, for failure to prosecute, taxpayer's action seeking injunctive relief from federal tax levy on wages, restitution of monies collected pursuant to that levy, and attorney fees, where taxpayer declined to go forward at trial due to allegedly inadequate discovery, when case had been pending for over a year and a half and had been set for trial on four different occasions, and extension of time for discovery had been appropriately denied following prior extensions. Fed.Rules Civ.Proc.Rules 16(f), 41(b), 28 U.S.C.A.

Smith v. U.S., 834 F.2d 166.

C.A.1 (Puerto Rico) 1993. Medical malpractice action could be dismissed for failure to prosecute, even if medical problems had incapacitated plaintiffs' attorney for approximately five weeks, where dilatory behavior lasted for ten months, and dismissal followed plaintiffs' repeated failures to comply with reasonable discovery requests and discovery orders, district court's clear warnings that dismissal could result, and imposition of lesser sanction of $300 fine against plaintiffs' counsel. Fed.Rules Civ. Proc.Rule 41(b), 28 U.S.C.A.

Capo v. U.S., 7 F.3d 283.

C.A.1 (Puerto Rico) 1989. District court improperly dismissed breach of contract action against individual and his conjugal partnership for want of prosecution where docket reflected that within six months prior to dismissal "substantial proceedings" had taken place in case as required by local rule. U.S.Dist.Ct.Rules D.P.R., Rule 313, subd. 1(A, B).

Jardines Bacata, Ltd. v. Diaz-Marquez, 878 F.2d 1555.

C.A.1 (Puerto Rico) 1986. Complaint would not be dismissed for lack of diligent prosecution where the District Court for the District of Puerto Rico had adopted a clear-cut rule [U.S.Dist.Ct.Rules D.C.Puerto Rico, General Rule 313.1(B)] effectively proscribing dismissal when certain substantial elements have taken place within six-month period and six months had not yet transpired between date motion to dismiss was filed and when appeal was taken from judgment dismissing complaint for lack of diligent prosecution.

Martinez Class v. Caribe Hilton Hotel, 784 F.2d 12.

C.A.5 (Tex.) 1993. Court properly dismissed suit against unnamed defendants for failure to prosecute where the defendants remained unnamed for three years and plaintiffs had not filed joint pretrial order. Fed.Rules Civ.Proc.Rule 41(b), 28 U.S.C.A.

Colle v. Brazos County, Tex., 981 F.2d 237.

D.D.C. 1985. Action alleging breach of stock purchase agreement was subject to dismissal because of plaintiffs' failure to prosecute and blatant disregard of court orders and rules; almost a year had passed since plaintiffs were first ordered to proceed to arbitration and over six months had passed since the Court of Appeals dismissed plaintiffs' frivolous appeal of that order. Fed.Rules Civ.Proc.Rule 41(b), 28 U.S.C.A.

Ames v. Standard Oil Co. (Indiana), 108 F.R.D. 299.

S.D.Ga. 1994. There is no brightline time of delay which automatically warrants dismissal for failure to prosecute, although common sense dictates that the longer the delay, the more likely the prejudice. Fed.Rules Civ.Proc.Rule 41(b), 28 U.S.C.A.

Stolt-Nielsen, Inc. v. Zim Israel Navigation Co., Ltd., 879 F.Supp. 1223, vacated Stolt-Neilsen v. Zim Israel Nav. Co., 67 F.3d 314.

Dismissal for failure to prosecute damages action stemming from ship collision was warranted by record of clear delay, in form of failure to take action for three years, without excusable neglect, and showing that lesser sanctions would not remedy proportional prejudice to defendants from death of key witness. Fed. Rules Civ.Proc.Rule 41(b), 28 U.S.C.A.

Stolt-Nielsen, Inc. v. Zim Israel Navigation Co., Ltd., 879 F.Supp. 1223, vacated Stolt-Neilsen v. Zim Israel Nav. Co., 67 F.3d 314.

N.D.Ill. 1987. Even though employee's § 1981 employment discrimination claim was not time barred by application of five-year contracts limitations period, claim was dismissed for want of prosecution; employee's attorney had missed numerous court-imposed deadlines to answer motions and had not given employer proper notice of numerous motions. 42 U.S.C.A. § 1981.

Comer v. Interstate United Corp., 118 F.R.D. 79.

N.D.Ill. 1975. In shareholders' derivative suit asserting that proxy statement issued by corporation was fraudulent and misleading in omitting to state material fact, individual shareholders would be dismissed as plaintiffs and corporation placed in their stead, in view of the fact that shareholders had failed to pursue the suit for some five years after summary judgment had been granted in their favor on issue of liability and fact that corporation was apparently willing to pursue its rights. Securities Exchange Act of 1934, § 14(a), 15 U.S.C.A. § 78n(a); Fed.Rules Civ.Proc. rules 23.1, 41(b), 28 U.S.C.A.; U.S.Dist.Ct.Rules N.D.Ill., General Rule 21.

Berman v. Thomson, 403 F.Supp. 695.

D.Neb. 1996. Arrestee's action against sheriff was dismissed with prejudice for failure to prosecute, where, with 18 prospective jurors waiting, arrestee and his mother/guardian ad litem refused to proceed to trial after being advised that mother, who was not lawyer, would not be permitted to act as lawyer for arrestee during jury trial and after having also been advised that failure to proceed would result in judgment of dismissal with prejudice; case was over three years old because arrestee and mother refused to accept advice of two separate lawyers that case had no merit, and case was replete with delay caused by arrestee and mother. Fed.Rules Civ.Proc.Rules 17(c), 41(b), 28 U.S.C.A.

> McCaslin by McCaslin v. Radcliff, 168 F.R.D. 249, affirmed McCaslin v. County of York, 141 F.3d 1169.

E.D.N.Y. 1997. Dismissal of cross-claims for failure to prosecute was warranted by failure to file opposition papers for ten months after being served with dismissal motion.

> Bellovin v. U.S., 983 F.Supp. 344.

E.D.N.Y. 1994. Franchisee's RICO (Racketeer Influenced Corrupt Organizations) action against franchisor could not be dismissed for lack of prosecution based on franchisee's failure to initiate discovery within eight months of court's denial of franchisor's motion to dismiss and franchisee's unexcused two-month delay in responding to franchisor's document request; matter would be referred to magistrate who could establish discovery schedule. Fed.Rules Civ.Proc.Rule 41(b), 28 U.S.C.A.

> Giuliano v. Everything Yogurt, Inc., 152 F.R.D. 449.

E.D.N.Y. 1992. In exercise of discretion with respect to dismissal of action for failure to prosecute, among factors district court should consider are duration of plaintiff's inaction and prejudice suffered by defendant. Fed.Rules Civ. Proc.Rule 41(b), 28 U.S.C.A.

> Szarejko v. Great Neck School Dist., 795 F.Supp. 81.

E.D.N.Y. 1992. In deciding whether to dismiss for failure to prosecute, district court should view whole record and consider duration of failure to prosecute, whether plaintiff had received notice that further delays would result in dismissal, whether defendant is likely to be prejudiced by further delay, balance between alleviating court calendar congestion and protecting right to due process and fair chance to be heard, and efficacy of lesser sanctions. Fed.Rules Civ.Proc.Rule 41(b), 28 U.S.C.A.

> Montalvo v. Quigley, 144 F.R.D. 21.

Arrestee's civil rights action for alleged beating by police officers would be dismissed for failure to prosecute nine-year-old action where arrestee neither filed papers nor appeared following denial of motion to amend, he had been warned four years earlier that further delay would result in dismissal, district court

had no way to reach him or his successors to renew warning, and delay made location of potential witnesses difficult; defense counsel indicated that arrestee had died. 42 U.S.C.A. § 1983; Fed.Rules Civ.Proc.Rule 41(b), 28 U.S.C.A.

> Montalvo v. Quigley, 144 F.R.D. 21.

E.D.N.Y. 1988. Defendant was not entitled to dismissal of civil RICO action on ground that his age, ill-health and mental condition, combined with Government's delay in bringing action, made prosecution of the action a denial of his due process rights. 18 U.S.C.A. § 1961 et seq.; U.S.C.A. Const.Amend. 14.

> U.S. v. Bonanno Organized Crime Family of La Cosa Nostra, 695 F.Supp. 1426.

S.D.N.Y. 1997. Case would be dismissed for failure to prosecute; plaintiff failed to take any action to advance his claims for nearly five years, defendant's ability to defend action was compromised by plaintiff's protracted delay in prosecuting case, any claim that plaintiff's due process rights were violated could not prevail because delay and resultant dismissal of case were of plaintiff's own making, plaintiff was both aware of and contributed to lack of action in case, and lesser sanction was not warranted. U.S.C.A. Const.Amend. 14; Fed.Rules Civ.Proc. Rule 41(b), 28 U.S.C.A.

> Dodson v. Runyon, 957 F.Supp. 465, affirmed 152 F.3d 917.

S.D.N.Y. 1997. Three-year delay resulting from inmate's disappearance warranted dismissal with prejudice of his excessive force claim against prison officials and corrections officers, where inmate had been warned that failure to prosecute would result in dismissal with prejudice, and lesser sanctions, including placement of case on court's suspense docket, had been ineffective. Fed.Rules Civ.Proc.Rule 41(b), 28 U.S.C.A.

> Jenkins v. City of New York, 176 F.R.D. 127.

S.D.N.Y. 1997. Dismissal of securities fraud action against broker was warranted on grounds of failure to prosecute; two successive counsel representing plaintiff withdrew due to plaintiff's conduct, plaintiff took no action for 22 month period and could not be reached by court during such time, court expressly warned plaintiff twice that failure to prosecute could result in dismissal, 55 month delay rendered defense of case difficult or impossible and therefore prejudiced broker, and there were no lesser sanctions which could remedy plaintiff's failures. Fed.Rules Civ.Proc.Rule 41(b), 28 U.S.C.A.

> Hedvat v. Rothschild, 175 F.R.D. 183.

S.D.N.Y. 1997. Dismissal of employment discrimination suit was warranted for failure to prosecute and failure to obey court scheduling orders, where pro se plaintiff had conducted no discovery nor taken any steps to advance litigation in 17 months since filing complaint, and he obtained five extensions giving him five months to respond to summary judgment motion, he sought sixth extension despite "no further extension" ruling at time of fourth and fifth extensions, sixth extension was denied, and he had still not responded to summary judgment motion eight months after it was filed. Fed.Rules Civ.Proc.Rules 16(f), 41(b), 56, 28 U.S.C.A.

> Lediju v. New York City Dept. of Sanitation, 173 F.R.D. 105.

S.D.N.Y. 1996. Alien's petition for writ of mandamus to compel Immigration and Naturalization Service (INS) to issue work authorization in connection with his alleged application for temporary resident status as Special Agricultural Worker (SAW) would be dismissed for failure to prosecute, where he did not respond to government's interrogatories and request for admissions, or to government's motion to dismiss; his lack of substantive activity in 35 months from commencement of action, or 16 months from last order issued in action, was sufficient to support dismissal of action, with prejudice, for failure to prosecute. Fed.Rules Civ.Proc.Rule 41(b), 28 U.S.C.A.

> Ahmed v. I.N.S., 911 F.Supp. 132.

S.D.N.Y. 1995. Court's consideration of motion to dismiss for failure to prosecute diligently is guided by five factors: (1) duration of plaintiff's failures; (2) whether plaintiff had received notice that further delays would result in dismissal; (3) whether defendant was likely to be prejudiced by further delay; (4) balancing of need to alleviate court calendar congestion with a party's right to due process; and (5) efficacy of lesser sanctions. Fed.Rules Civ. Proc.Rule 41(b), 28 U.S.C.A.

> Patterson v. Newspaper and Mail Deliverers' Union of New York and Vicinity, 884 F.Supp. 869.

Evidence was sufficient to support ruling of administrator, who had been appointed to assure compliance with consent decree in civil rights litigation brought by newspaper deliverers against newspapers and union, that claims should not be dismissed for failure to prosecute; although deliverers failed to conduct discovery for seven years, and administrator admonished deliverers to resolve pending claims quickly pending termination of decree, postponing discovery was reasonable while deliverers questioned administrator's jurisdiction, newspaper's inability to locate documents was not sufficient to warrant dismissal, and admonishment did not constitute implied notice that further delay

would result in dismissal. Fed.Rules Civ.Proc. Rule 41(b), 28 U.S.C.A.

> Patterson v. Newspaper and Mail Deliverers' Union of New York and Vicinity, 884 F.Supp. 869.

Passage of time alone does not dictate dismissal of action for want of prosecution; instead, proper inquiry is whether plaintiff's delay is excusable. Fed.Rules Civ.Proc.Rule 41(b), 28 U.S.C.A.

> Patterson v. Newspaper and Mail Deliverers' Union of New York and Vicinity, 884 F.Supp. 869.

S.D.N.Y. 1995. Record as whole warranted dismissal of action for failure to prosecute where plaintiff failed to prosecute action in any manner for almost 21 months, plaintiff failed to appear at two pretrial conferences, plaintiff did not respond to defendants' motion to dismiss although she received notice of it, and any lesser sanction would be ineffective. Fed.Rules Civ.Proc.Rule 41(b), 28 U.S.C.A.

> Stoenescu v. Jablonsky, 162 F.R.D. 268.

S.D.N.Y. 1994. While actual period of delay is not necessarily dispositive in connection with motion to dismiss for failure to prosecute, it is an important factor and must be considered in light of all of the facts and circumstances. Fed.Rules Civ.Proc.Rule 41(b), 28 U.S.C.A.

> In re Crysen/Montenay Energy Co., 166 B.R. 546.

S.D.N.Y. 1993. For purposes of motion to dismiss for failure to prosecute, no single factor has talismanic significance in determining whether plaintiff has failed to discharge duty of diligence; thus, delay of particular duration will not, alone, be determinative. Fed.Rules Civ. Proc.Rule 41(b), 28 U.S.C.A.

> Acot v. New York Medical College, 153 F.R.D. 517, reargument denied.

Pro se employment discrimination action commenced more than four years earlier would not be dismissed for failure to prosecute, as plaintiff had neither manifested lack of interest in pursuing action (as evidenced by her pursuit of state proceedings arising out of same alleged underlying conduct) nor defied court orders, and defendant failed either to show that it had been prejudiced by plaintiff's inactivity or to call delay to court's attention until defendant moved for dismissal. Fed.Rules Civ.Proc.Rule 41(b), 28 U.S.C.A.

> Acot v. New York Medical College, 153 F.R.D. 517, reargument denied.

S.D.N.Y. 1991. Marine liability insurer's action would not be dismissed for failure to prosecute absent evidence that insurer deliberately proceeded in a dilatory fashion or that it failed to honor its commitments, particularly considering strong public policy favoring adjudication on the merits. Fed.Rules Civ.Proc. Rule 41(b), 28 U.S.C.A.

> Gibbs v. Hawaiian Eugenia Corp., 771 F.Supp. 638, reversed 966 F.2d 101, on remand 1993 WL 14666.

S.D.N.Y. 1991. Dismissal for failure to prosecute was justified where plaintiff's repeated requests for extension of discovery were granted, and she was afforded ample time to prepare and file opposition to defendants' motions for summary judgment, but upon each successive extension of time granted to her, plaintiff pressed for reconsideration of discovery issue rather than addressing merits of summary judgment motions pending for over two months.

> Moore v. American Telephone & Telegraph Communications, Inc., 137 F.R.D. 211.

S.D.N.Y. 1991. Delay in prosecuting suit following breach of contract plaintiff's death was not such as to require dismissal for delinquency; law firm could not take action prior to its formal retention by plaintiff's estate, and plaintiff's widow cited financial and practical difficulties in managing estate's affairs. Fed. Rules Civ.Proc.Rule 41(b), 28 U.S.C.A.

> Knight v. H.E. Yerkes and Associates, Inc., 135 F.R.D. 67.

S.D.N.Y. 1990. Where plaintiff has failed to take any specific and concrete action over length of time, his complaint may be dismissed for failure to prosecute.

> West v. City of New York, 130 F.R.D. 522.

S.D.N.Y. 1988. Failure of corporate plaintiff to secure counsel for more than two years after expiration of 30–day period granted corporation to secure counsel, after granting of motion of former attorney to be relieved, warranted dismissal of civil rights claim asserted by corporation against city for just compensation for destruction of buildings deemed unsafe. 42 U.S.C.A. § 1983.

> Friedman v. New York City Dept. of Housing and Development Admin., 688 F.Supp. 896, affirmed 876 F.2d 890, certiorari denied 110 S.Ct. 2570, 495 U.S. 961, 109 L.Ed.2d 752.

S.D.N.Y. 1987. Complaint would not be dismissed for failure to prosecute on ground that case had been pending for several years with virtually no discovery, where plaintiff had not received any prior warnings that delay would occasion dismissal, defendant had not demonstrated any prejudice, and less onerous sanction was available, in light of plaintiff's assertion that she had pursued discovery, by placing case on ready trial calendar with possibility of dismissal upon any further delay by plaintiff. Fed.Rules Civ.Proc.Rule 41(b), 28 U.S.C.A.

> Freed v. Braniff Airways, Inc., 119 F.R.D. 10.

S.D.N.Y. 1985. Suit was subject to dismissal for failure to prosecute in light of plaintiff's total failure to pursue the action for the past 21 months, his repeated failure to respond to his own counsel's missives, his repeated failure to respond to letters from the court and his failure to attend pretrial conference.

> Yacub v. Coughlin, 105 F.R.D. 152.

N.D.Ohio 1996. Civil rights action was subject to dismissal for failure to prosecute where more than four months had passed since last status conference and, in interim, neither plaintiff nor a representative had acted to further prosecution of claims, and plaintiff had not responded by brief or otherwise to motion to dismiss which had been pending for nearly a year. Fed.Rules Civ.Proc.Rule 41(b), 28 U.S.C.A.

> Davis v. Kent State University, 928 F.Supp. 729.

N.D.Ohio 1990. Dismissal of pro se plaintiff's civil rights action was justified by absence of activity on plaintiff's part except for requests for continuances for almost three years after filing suit and refusal by plaintiff to obey court orders, including orders to respond to motion to dismiss and to personally appear, but dismissal would be without prejudice. Fed.Rules Civ. Proc.Rule 41, 28 U.S.C.A.

> Vesely v. Cuyahoga Metropolitan Housing Authority, 130 F.R.D. 83.

D.Puerto Rico 1998. Parent's products liability action against automobile manufacturer for death of their son allegedly due to design defect could not be dismissed for want of prosecution, where the district court found that it was reasonable for parents to take longer than a year to be ready for trial, that parent's expert was qualified, and that spoliation of evidence was not a barrier to their claim.

> Bericochea-Cartagena v. Suzuki Motor Co., Ltd., 7 F.Supp.2d 109.

D.Puerto Rico 1998. Dismissal for want of prosecution was warranted where case has been on the docket for almost three years and the extent of plaintiffs' motion practice, after filing an answer to a counterclaim, was limited to requests for substitution and withdrawal of attorneys; moreover, plaintiffs were notified of codefendant's motion to dismiss for want of prosecution and did not oppose it. Fed.Rules Civ.Proc.Rule 41(b), 28 U.S.C.A.

> Jardines Ltd. Partnership v. Executive Homesearch Realty Services, Inc., 178 F.R.D. 365.

S.D.Tex. 1995. Plaintiff's 30–day delay in filing court ordered amended complaint in sex harassment lawsuit warranted dismissal of claims with prejudice, where plaintiff was dilatory, indifferent, haphazard, and obviously lacked interest in prosecuting those claims for more than nine years. Fed.Rules Civ.Proc.Rule 41(b), 28 U.S.C.A.

Twardowsky v. Klevenhagen, 164 F.R.D. 213.

S.D.Tex. 1994. Only unreasonable delay will support dismissal for lack of prosecution; delay is "unreasonable" if there is significant period of total inactivity by plaintiff, plaintiff fails to adhere to repeated warnings that dismissal will result from continued failure to proceed, or plaintiff fails to obey court rules and court orders. Fed.Rules Civ.Proc.Rule 41(b), 28 U.S.C.A.

Edwards v. Harris County Sheriff's Dept., 864 F.Supp. 633.

Delay is "unreasonable" for purpose of rule allowing dismissal of case for want of prosecution if defendant is actually prejudiced by delay. Fed.Rules Civ.Proc.Rule 41(b), 28 U.S.C.A.

Edwards v. Harris County Sheriff's Dept., 864 F.Supp. 633.

D.Virgin Islands 1990. Dismissal with prejudice of action for breach of contract and tortious interference with contractual relationship was appropriate sanction for continuing pattern of delay and inadequate attention to case on part of plaintiffs; plaintiffs, a lawyer and a law firm, were personally responsible for delays arising when they took no affirmative steps to move their case forward for 19–month period and failed to respond to motions for summary judgment and dismissal within allotted time, and prior sanctions, including imposition of attorney's fees, had proven ineffective. Fed.Rules Civ.Proc.Rule 41(b), 28 U.S.C.A.

Andrews v. Government of Virgin Islands, 132 F.R.D. 405, affirmed 935 F.2d 1280.

Bkrtcy.N.D.Ohio 1984. In light of rule placing affirmative duty on attorneys to take responsibility for progress of their cases, fact that the case was over a year old, delay to other parties in the case, and fact that defendant who had not been served was nonessential, action against that defendant would be dismissed without prejudice. Fed.Rules Civ.Proc.Rule 41(b), 28 U.S.C.A.

In re Miller, 45 B.R. 553.

Bkrtcy.S.D.Tex. 1990. Dismissal with prejudice for failure to prosecute of debtor's counterclaim for $10 million in damages for breach of contract and fraud was justified; debtor had failed to actively pursue any discovery or file any pleadings for four and one-half years after adversary proceeding was commenced, debtor's

filing of three notices of deposition for depositions which were not taken, filing of change of address, and making allegation of telephone inquiries did not overcome demonstrated delay, and sanctions against debtor would not overcome prejudice to claimant arising from debtor's delay.

In re Arhens, 120 B.R. 852.

⚷**1760.** —— **Prejudice from delay.**

C.A.D.C. 1986. Dismissal of plaintiff's action was not warranted by prejudice to defendant due to his counsels' failure to attend three status calls absent showing of actual prejudice to defendant resulting from three-week period in which no-shows occurred.

Shea v. Donohoe Const. Co., Inc., 795 F.2d 1071, 254 U.S.App.D.C. 175.

Repeated failure of plaintiff's counsel to attend three status calls over three-week period, while undoubtedly wasting the time of the district court and opposing counsel, was not so prejudicial to the judicial system as to warrant dismissal of action given availability of less drastic measures which could be imposed directly against attorneys involved.

Shea v. Donohoe Const. Co., Inc., 795 F.2d 1071, 254 U.S.App.D.C. 175.

C.A.9 1994. Court considers prejudice and delay together to determine whether there has been sufficient delay or prejudice to justify dismissal of plaintiff's case for lack of prosecution. Fed.Rules Civ.Proc.Rule 41(b), 28 U.S.C.A.

In re Eisen, 31 F.3d 1447.

C.A.9 (Ariz.) 1986. District court's dismissal of action for failure to prosecute upon failure of plaintiff's counsel to submit pretrial order in accordance with local rule on or before fourth extended due date was not an abuse of discretion; plaintiff's counsel disregarded repeatedly the deadlines set by the court, court clearly warned counsel of consequences of continuing dilatory preparation, court explored and used alternative measures, including holding of status conference and establishing schedule for discovery and preparation of pretrial order, before it used final measure of dismissal and, although no specific showing of prejudice to defendants was made, integrity of the district court was involved. U.S.Dist.Ct.Rules D. Ariz., Rule 42(c); Fed.Rules Civ.Proc., Rule 41(b), 28 U.S.C.A.

Henderson v. Duncan, 779 F.2d 1421.

C.A.9 (Cal.) 1998. Presumption of prejudice arising from plaintiff's failure to prosecute is rebuttable.

Hernandez v. City of El Monte, 138 F.3d 393.

C.A.9 (Cal.) 1985. In considering dismissal for lack of prosecution under Federal Rule of

Civil Procedure, courts will consider whether plaintiff has prosecuted action diligently and to what extent any delay has prejudiced the defendant. Fed.Rules Civ.Proc.Rule 41(b), 28 U.S.C.A.

> Olympic Sports Products, Inc. v. Universal Athletic Sales Co., 760 F.2d 910, certiorari denied Whittaker Corporation v. Olympic Sports Products, Inc., 106 S.Ct. 804, 474 U.S. 1060, 88 L.Ed.2d 780.

C.A.11 (Fla.) 1986. Defendant was not prejudiced by plaintiff's delay in prosecuting action so as to justify dismissal amounting to dismissal with prejudice based on lack of prosecution by running of limitations period on indispensable party, where defendant could assert that purported defense once action which had been dismissed for lack of prosecution had been reinstated.

> McKelvey v. AT & T Technologies, Inc., 789 F.2d 1518.

C.A.5 (La.) 1985. For purpose of determining whether to dismiss action with prejudice for failure to prosecute, Fifth Circuit Court of Appeals examines "aggravating factors" such as extent to which plaintiff, as distinguished from his counsel, was personally responsible for delay, degree of actual prejudice to defendant and whether delay was result of intentional conduct. Fed.Rules Civ.Proc.Rule 41(b), 28 U.S.C.A.

> Ford v. Sharp, 758 F.2d 1018, 27 Wage & Hour Cas. (BNA) 257.

C.A.5 (La.) 1985. Where record did not reflect egregious conduct and a clear record of delay, nor contain district court's factual findings and conclusions that a lesser sanction would be insufficient, suit seeking recovery under insurance policy allegedly covering vessel destroyed by fire was improperly dismissed with prejudice for failure of prosecution. Fed.Rules Civ.Proc.Rule 41(b), 28 U.S.C.A.

> Boudwin v. Graystone Ins. Co., Ltd., 756 F.2d 399.

C.A.1 (Mass.) 1986. District court did not abuse its discretion in dismissing, for failure to prosecute, suit by private developer arising out of city's refusal to issue building permit, where, since period during which disputed events occurred, housing authority's membership had completely changed and its then-executive and assistant directors had died, agreement upon which developer sought to impose liability on city had been executed nearly two decades before, and, because original complaint sought only injunctive and declaratory relief, some evidence on issue of monetary damages was not preserved by the parties.

> U.S. Inv. and Development Corp. v. Cruz, 780 F.2d 166.

C.A.3 (N.J.) 1994. For purposes of analyzing dismissal for lack of prosecution, in light of possible prejudice to adversary, prejudice to adversary includes irretrievable loss of evidence, dimming of witnesses' memories, excessive burdens and costs imposed on opponent, deprivation of information through noncooperation with discovery and costs spent obtaining court orders to force compliance with discovery, and need not be irremediable harm. Fed. Rules Civ.Proc.Rule 41(b), 28 U.S.C.A.

> Adams v. Trustees of New Jersey Brewery Employees' Pension Trust Fund, 29 F.3d 863.

In analyzing "prejudice" to adversary element of determination as to whether dismissal was warranted for lack of prosecution, interest paid on money owed did not amount to prejudice, but instead represented value of possession of money by debtor. Fed.Rules Civ.Proc. Rule 41(b), 28 U.S.C.A.

> Adams v. Trustees of New Jersey Brewery Employees' Pension Trust Fund, 29 F.3d 863.

More than four-year delay by Pension Benefit Guaranty Corporation (PBGC) in pursuing claims against employers for statutory employer indemnification for unfunded portions of multiemployer pension fund did not prejudice employers; determination involved computing, as of date of plan termination, value of plan assets and participants' guaranteed benefits and employers' proportionate share of liability for unfunded benefits, computation process was records-based determination unaffected by witness memory problems, employers did not claim that records were lost or that discovery was incomplete, and employers' principal contentions were statutory and constitutional arguments which could be made at any time. Fed.Rules Civ.Proc.Rule 41(b), 28 U.S.C.A.

> Adams v. Trustees of New Jersey Brewery Employees' Pension Trust Fund, 29 F.3d 863.

Claim by Pension Benefit Guaranty Corporation (PBGC) against employer for remaining unfunded portion of multiemployer pension plan was improperly dismissed with prejudice for lack of prosecution; although more than four-year delay was unreasonable, PBGC had personal responsibility for delay and there was history of dilatoriness, and those factors were outweighed by absence of significant prejudice to adversary and lack of willfulness or bad faith on part of PBGC, by availability of alternative sanctions and by meritoriousness of PBGC's claims. Fed.Rules Civ.Proc.Rule 41(b), 28 U.S.C.A.

> Adams v. Trustees of New Jersey Brewery Employees' Pension Trust Fund, 29 F.3d 863.

C.A.9 (Or.) 1990. Defendants, who were required to respond to plaintiff's motions, including motion to extend time for discovery, were prejudiced as a result of cost of time and money in preparation and filing of opposition memoranda to such motions and appearances at hearings, for purpose of determining whether suit should be dismissed for lack of prosecution. Fed.Rules Civ.Proc.Rule 41(b), 28 U.S.C.A.

West Coast Theater Corp. v. City of Portland, 897 F.2d 1519.

C.A.3 (Pa.) 1984. Sanction of dismissal was not warranted for dilatory conduct by counsel where tardiness, although serious, was not flagrant, where pretrial statement, although deficient, was not fatally defective, where claim was facially meritorious and where conduct of defendants could have been more productive. Fed.Rules Civ.Proc.Rule 41, 28 U.S.C.A.

Scarborough v. Eubanks, 747 F.2d 871.

C.A.1 (Puerto Rico) 1990. District court did not exceed its power in dismissing case for plaintiffs' failure to prosecute and to follow court's order to serve amended complaint on each defendant, in view of prior delays, prior motions, uncertain legal nature of underlying claims, obvious prejudice to defendants from keeping action alive indefinitely and absence of adequate cause for plaintiffs' actions. Fed. Rules Civ.Proc.Rule 41(b), 28 U.S.C.A.

Caribbean Transp. Systems, Inc. v. Autoridad De Las Navieras De Puerto Rico, 901 F.2d 196.

C.A.1 (Puerto Rico) 1987. District court's sua sponte dismissal of action for back pay and overtime for want of prosecution was too harsh a sanction for plaintiffs' failure to take any affirmative action in case for five months, since defendants were not prejudiced by delay, occasioned by pendency of petition for certiorari to United States Supreme Court, and plaintiffs did not engage in any active measures to delay the case, even though counsel for plaintiffs should have informed district court of the petition for certiorari. Fair Labor Standards Act of 1938, § 18(b)(2), 29 U.S.C.A. § 218(b)(2).

Cosme Nieves v. Deshler, 826 F.2d 1, 28 Wage & Hour Cas. (BNA) 471.

C.A.5 (Tex.) 1987. Administrative Procedure Act grants authority to reviewing courts to compel agency action unreasonably delayed, but does not grant courts authority to dismiss actions brought by agencies upon finding of unreasonable delay causing prejudice; therefore, action seeking determination that the United States was entitled to patent for method of continuous peritoneal dialysis, issued to coinvestigators on government contract, which called for intensive research into peritoneal dialysis, could not be dismissed on grounds that the lengthy delay in bringing action caused prejudice to coinvestigators; abrogating *EEOC v. Bell Helicopter Co.*, 426 F.Supp. 785 (N.D.Tex.); *EEOC v. Moore Group, Inc.*, 416 F.Supp. 1002 (N.D.Ga.); repudiating *Chromcraft Corp. v. EEOC*, 465 F.2d 745 (5th Cir.); *EEOC v. Exchange Security Bank*, 529 F.2d 1214 (5th Cir.); *Jones v. Bell Helicopter Co.*, 614 F.2d 1389 (5th Cir.); disagreeing with *Houseton v. Nimmo*, 670 F.2d 1375 (9th Cir.). 5 U.S.C.A. §§ 555(b), 706.

U.S. v. Popovich, 820 F.2d 134, certiorari denied 108 S.Ct. 487, 484 U.S. 976, 98 L.Ed.2d 485.

D.Del. 1996. Although defendants were not prejudiced in their defense by actions of plaintiff in failing to prosecute action and being delinquent in following court orders, plaintiff's conduct adversely impacted progress of case and effective administration of justice, supporting dismissal. Fed.Rules Civ.Proc.Rule 41(b), 28 U.S.C.A.

Guy v. City of Wilmington, 169 F.R.D. 593.

D.Del. 1985. Considering corporate plaintiff's dilatory pursuit of its claims, its intractable refusal to pay for or cooperate with its own attorneys, its cavalier and repeated disregard of court orders requiring it to retain and appear by counsel, and admission by its president and half-owner that it had no more money available for payment of counsel, and that alternative lesser sanctions were not feasible, Court would dismiss with prejudice plaintiff's amended and supplemental complaint against defendants; moreover, defendants were entitled to entry of default on their counterclaims against plaintiff. Fed.Rules Civ.Proc.Rules 41(b), 55(a), 28 U.S.C.A.

Transportes Aereos de Angola v. Ronair, Inc., 104 F.R.D. 482.

D.D.C. 1985. Although prejudice to opposing counsel is not a condition of dismissal due to failure to prosecute, prejudice to opposing party, in terms of time and expense, may be considered.

Ames v. Standard Oil Co. (Indiana), 108 F.R.D. 299.

S.D.Ga. 1994. Rule permitting dismissal for failure to prosecute is "housekeeping measure" which allows court to manage its docket, further policy of expeditious resolution of litigation, and prevent prejudice to defendant from delay. Fed.Rules Civ.Proc.Rule 41(b), 28 U.S.C.A.

Stolt-Nielsen, Inc. v. Zim Israel Navigation Co., Ltd., 879 F.Supp. 1223, vacated Stolt-Neilsen v. Zim Israel Nav. Co., 67 F.3d 314.

Dismissal for failure to prosecute damages action stemming from ship collision was warranted by record of clear delay, in form of failure to take action for three years, without excusable neglect, and showing that lesser sanctions would not remedy proportional prejudice to defendants from death of key witness. Fed. Rules Civ.Proc.Rule 41(b), 28 U.S.C.A.

> Stolt-Nielsen, Inc. v. Zim Israel Navigation Co., Ltd., 879 F.Supp. 1223, vacated Stolt-Nielsen v. Zim Israel Nav. Co., 67 F.3d 314.

N.D.Ill. 1997. Plaintiffs seeking class certification are not required to specify exact number of class members so long as good faith estimate is provided; however, estimated numbers cannot be purely speculative. Fed.Rules Civ.Proc.Rule 23(a)(1), 28 U.S.C.A.

> McKenzie v. City of Chicago, 175 F.R.D. 280.

N.D.Ill. 1988. Although attorney demonstrated irresponsibility in missing appointments and neglect in delaying motion to vacate default, problems were not so serious as to mandate default or dismissal of counterclaim in client's action; attorney indicated regret for errors, brought in another attorney to assist him, and there was no showing that opposing party was prejudiced by delay. Fed.Rules Civ. Proc.Rule 60(b)(1), 28 U.S.C.A.

> U.S. v. Asbestos Safety, Inc., 119 F.R.D. 391.

E.D.Mich. 1985. Failure of prison inmate to take any measures on behalf of his civil rights case for a period of over 19 months subsequent to defendants' filing of answer warranted dismissal for failure to prosecute, considering that delay undoubtedly caused prejudice to defendants and that there appeared to be no justification for inaction, giving rise to inference that inmate either abandoned claim or filed action to harass defendants. Fed.Rules Civ.Proc.Rule 41(b), 28 U.S.C.A.; U.S.Dist.Ct.Rules E.D.Mich., Rule 20.

> Snavley v. Redman, 107 F.R.D. 346.

D.Minn. 1998. District Court would not exercise its discretion to dismiss as stale government's equitable claim against state university for disgorgement of profits allegedly earned through use of federal grant money to sell investigational new drug (IND), absent any direct evidence that agency responsible for administering grant knew that university was earning profits through its sale of IND, where university actively concealed such profits from government and was not prejudiced by government's alleged delay in bringing suit.

> U.S. ex rel. Zissler v. Regents of the University of Minnesota, 992 F.Supp. 1097, reversed 154 F.3d 870.

E.D.N.Y. 1997. Although prejudice to defendants resulting from unreasonable delay may be presumed, for purposes of determining whether action should be dismissed for failure to prosecute, in cases where delay is more moderate or excusable the need to show actual prejudice is proportionally greater. Fed.Rules Civ.Proc.Rule 41(b), 28 U.S.C.A.

> In re Folks, 210 B.R. 674.

E.D.N.Y. 1994. "Actual prejudice" that might warrant dismissal for lack of prosecution refers not to stigma of being defendant in civil action, but to situations in which plaintiff's delay hinders defendant's opportunity to adequately defend claim. Fed.Rules Civ.Proc.Rule 41(b), 28 U.S.C.A.

> Giuliano v. Everything Yogurt, Inc., 152 F.R.D. 449.

E.D.N.Y. 1992. In exercise of discretion with respect to dismissal of action for failure to prosecute, among factors district court should consider are duration of plaintiff's inaction and prejudice suffered by defendant. Fed.Rules Civ. Proc.Rule 41(b), 28 U.S.C.A.

> Szarejko v. Great Neck School Dist., 795 F.Supp. 81.

E.D.N.Y. 1992. In deciding whether to dismiss for failure to prosecute, district court should view whole record and consider duration of failure to prosecute, whether plaintiff had received notice that further delays would result in dismissal, whether defendant is likely to be prejudiced by further delay, balance between alleviating court calendar congestion and protecting right to due process and fair chance to be heard, and efficacy of lesser sanctions. Fed.Rules Civ.Proc.Rule 41(b), 28 U.S.C.A.

> Montalvo v. Quigley, 144 F.R.D. 21.

S.D.N.Y. 1997. Case would be dismissed for failure to prosecute; plaintiff failed to take any action to advance his claims for nearly five years, defendant's ability to defend action was compromised by plaintiff's protracted delay in prosecuting case, any claim that plaintiff's due process rights were violated could not prevail because delay and resultant dismissal of case were of plaintiff's own making, plaintiff was both aware of and contributed to lack of action in case, and lesser sanction was not warranted. U.S.C.A. Const.Amend. 14; Fed.Rules Civ.Proc. Rule 41(b), 28 U.S.C.A.

> Dodson v. Runyon, 957 F.Supp. 465, affirmed 152 F.3d 917.

Prejudice to defendant, one of factors for determining whether dismissal is appropriate remedy for failure to prosecute, may be presumed where delay in prosecution is neither moderate nor excusable. Fed.Rules Civ.Proc. Rule 41(b), 28 U.S.C.A.

> Dodson v. Runyon, 957 F.Supp. 465, affirmed 152 F.3d 917.

S.D.N.Y. 1997. In determining whether to dismiss action for failure to prosecute, prejudice to defendant may be presumed from length of delay. Fed.Rules Civ.Proc.Rule 41(b), 28 U.S.C.A.

> Lediju v. New York City Dept. of Sanitation, 173 F.R.D. 105.

S.D.N.Y. 1997. Dismissal of inmate's actions against prison officials and sheriff was warranted for failure to prosecute; inmate's failure to prosecute extended over period of three and one-half years and continued even after motions to dismiss were filed, inmate failed to respond to any discovery demands and never filed responses to any earlier motions, inmate received ample notice from court that further delay in prosecution would result in dismissal, defendants would be prejudiced by any further delay in prosecution, balance between alleviating congestion of court calendar and protecting inmate's due process rights tipped decidedly in favor of dismissal, and no lesser sanctions other than dismissal were suitable. U.S.C.A. Const.Amend. 5; Fed.Rules Civ. Proc.Rule 41(b), 28 U.S.C.A.

> Coss v. Sullivan County Jail Adm'r, 171 F.R.D. 68.

S.D.N.Y. 1995. Court's consideration of motion to dismiss for failure to prosecute diligently is guided by five factors: (1) duration of plaintiff's failures; (2) whether plaintiff had received notice that further delays would result in dismissal; (3) whether defendant was likely to be prejudiced by further delay; (4) balancing of need to alleviate court calendar congestion with a party's right to due process; and (5) efficacy of lesser sanctions. Fed.Rules Civ. Proc.Rule 41(b), 28 U.S.C.A.

> Patterson v. Newspaper and Mail Deliverers' Union of New York and Vicinity, 884 F.Supp. 869.

S.D.N.Y. 1995. Where plaintiff has caused unreasonable delay in prosecuting action, prejudice to defendants may be presumed as a matter of law. Fed.Rules Civ.Proc.Rule 41(b), 28 U.S.C.A.

> Stoenescu v. Jablonsky, 162 F.R.D. 268.

S.D.N.Y. 1994. Investment fraud action would be dismissed without prejudice for failure to prosecute; case was four years old, plaintiffs failed to comply with order of magistrate judge setting date for submission of pretrial order despite numerous prior extensions, and defendants could be prejudiced by further delay in access to their assets placed in escrow by order of court. Fed.Rules Civ.Proc.Rule 41(b), 28 U.S.C.A.

> Schwartz v. F.S. & O. Associates, Inc., 157 F.R.D. 171.

S.D.N.Y. 1989. Prejudice to defendants from plaintiffs' failure to prosecute may be presumed from length of delay. Fed.Rules Civ. Proc.Rule 41(b), 28 U.S.C.A.

> Lukensow v. Harley Cars of New York, 124 F.R.D. 64.

Two-year delay which had no end in sight was evidence of prejudice to defendants from plaintiffs' failure to prosecute. Fed.Rules Civ. Proc.Rule 41(b), 28 U.S.C.A.

> Lukensow v. Harley Cars of New York, 124 F.R.D. 64.

Plaintiffs' due process rights were not denied by dismissal for failure to prosecute where the result could have been avoided by pressing their claim in the adversary proceeding and where there had been a complete lack of prosecutorial activity for two years. U.S.C.A. Const. Amend. 5; Fed.Rules Civ.Proc.Rule 41(b), 28 U.S.C.A.

> Lukensow v. Harley Cars of New York, 124 F.R.D. 64.

S.D.N.Y. 1988. Presumption of prejudice to defendants by debtors' delay of over five years in prosecuting adversary proceeding was proper, for purposes of determining whether adversary proceeding brought by debtors should be dismissed for lack of prosecution. Fed.Rules Civ.Proc.Rule 41(b), 28 U.S.C.A.

> In re United Merchants and Mfrs., Inc., 86 B.R. 764, appeal after remand 126 B.R. 149.

W.D.N.Y. 1997. Plaintiff's failure to respond to defendant's summary judgment motion warranted dismissal for failure to prosecute; plaintiff had not responded even five months after deadline and was notified of possibility of dismissal for failing to respond, further delay would likely prejudice defendant and counsel and court's ability to manage docket, likelihood of prejudice outweighed plaintiff's interest in receiving fair chance to be heard, and court considered full range of remedies. Fed.Rules Civ.Proc.Rule 41(b), 28 U.S.C.A.

> Monge v. O'Connor, 171 F.R.D. 55.

E.D.Pa. 1994. Factors to examine when weighing a motion to dismiss for want of prosecution include, among others, prejudice to defendant caused by plaintiff's inaction and whether that inaction revealed an absence of good faith. Fed.Rules Civ.Proc.Rule 41(b), 28 U.S.C.A.

> Mastromatteo v. Simock, 866 F.Supp. 853.

Although plaintiff asserting civil rights claim against police officer did not comply with some discovery requests, officer was not entitled to dismissal for failure to prosecute claim; defendant was not prejudiced by plaintiff's failure to respond, and plaintiff's failure to respond was because he was in prison and lacked representation and resources, and not because plaintiff was attempting, in bad faith, to obfuscate discovery process. 42 U.S.C.A. § 1983; Fed. Rules Civ.Proc.Rule 41(b), 28 U.S.C.A.

Mastromatteo v. Simock, 866 F.Supp. 853.

E.D.Pa. 1994. In deciding whether to dismiss case involuntarily for want of prosecution, district court should consider six factors: extent of party's personal responsibility, prejudice to the adversary, whether there has been a history of dilatoriness in case, whether conduct of party was willful or in bad faith, effectiveness of alternative sanctions, and meritoriousness of claim or defense; but all six factors need not be satisfied to justify dismissal of claim. Fed.Rules Civ.Proc.Rule 41(b), 28 U.S.C.A.

Muslim v. Frame, 854 F.Supp. 1215.

Pro se prisoner's civil rights action against county prison officials would be involuntarily dismissed for failure to prosecute when he failed to respond to prison officials' motion for summary judgment; inmate was solely responsible for his failure to respond to summary judgment motion, prison officials were prejudiced by inmate's failure to respond to motion, inmate had not pursued case beyond mere pleadings despite being afforded ample opportunity, his conduct was willful, other alternative sanctions would result in termination of inmate's action, all but one of claims were without merit, and inmate would have recovered little or no damages if he were to prevail on only meritorious claim. 42 U.S.C.A. § 1983; Fed.Rules Civ.Proc.Rule 41(b), 28 U.S.C.A.

Muslim v. Frame, 854 F.Supp. 1215.

D.Puerto Rico 1998. Dismissal for want of prosecution was warranted where case has been on the docket for almost three years and the extent of plaintiffs' motion practice, after filing an answer to a counterclaim, was limited to requests for substitution and withdrawal of attorneys; moreover, plaintiffs were notified of codefendant's motion to dismiss for want of prosecution and did not oppose it. Fed.Rules Civ.Proc.Rule 41(b), 28 U.S.C.A.

Jardines Ltd. Partnership v. Executive Homesearch Realty Services, Inc., 178 F.R.D. 365.

S.D.Tex. 1997. Dismissal with prejudice was just sanction after plaintiff's failure to respond to defendant's summary judgment motion and failure to appear at scheduling conference, in light of delays at every stage of process despite warnings both in state court before removal and in federal court to conform conduct and submissions to applicable rules; delays substantially prejudiced defendants, costing them unnecessary time, expense, and anguish, and needlessly inconvenienced court and caused expenditure of valuable judicial resources. Fed.Rules Civ.Proc.Rules 16, 37, 41, 28 U.S.C.A.

Riggs v. City of Pearland, 177 F.R.D. 395.

S.D.Tex. 1994. When considering whether to dismiss case for lack of prosecution, district court must weigh court's need to manage docket, public interest in expeditious resolution of litigation, risk of prejudice to defendants from delay, and policy favoring disposition of cases on their merits; in close cases, court also considers whether plaintiff personally contributed to delay, whether defendant was prejudiced as result of delay, and whether plaintiff intentionally caused delay. Fed.Rules Civ.Proc.Rule 41(b), 28 U.S.C.A.

Edwards v. Harris County Sheriff's Dept., 864 F.Supp. 633.

Delay is "unreasonable" for purpose of rule allowing dismissal of case for want of prosecution if defendant is actually prejudiced by delay. Fed.Rules Civ.Proc.Rule 41(b), 28 U.S.C.A.

Edwards v. Harris County Sheriff's Dept., 864 F.Supp. 633.

Inmate's failure to contact court or opposing counsel for over 14 months and failure to comply with rule requiring that parties notify court of changed address, and resulting prejudice to deputy, warranted dismissal of inmate's § 1983 action against deputy for want of prosecution. U.S.Dist.Ct.Rules S.D.Tex., Rule 2, subd. F; Fed.Rules Civ.Proc.Rule 41(b), 28 U.S.C.A.; 42 U.S.C.A. § 1983.

Edwards v. Harris County Sheriff's Dept., 864 F.Supp. 633.

D.Virgin Islands 1990. In determining whether to dismiss action with prejudice for failure to prosecute, "prejudice" factor does not refer to irremediable harm; rather, it can consist of extra costs of repeated delays in filing of motions necessitated by improper behavior on part of plaintiffs. Fed.Rules Civ.Proc.Rule 41(b), 28 U.S.C.A.

Andrews v. Government of Virgin Islands, 132 F.R.D. 405, affirmed 935 F.2d 1280.

Bkrtcy.N.D.Ohio 1984. In light of rule placing affirmative duty on attorneys to take responsibility for progress of their cases, fact that the case was over a year old, delay to other parties in the case, and fact that defendant who had not been served was nonessential, action against that defendant would be dismissed without prejudice. Fed.Rules Civ.Proc.Rule 41(b), 28 U.S.C.A.

In re Miller, 45 B.R. 553.

Bkrtcy.S.D.Tex. 1990. To support dismissal with prejudice for failure to prosecute, record should reflect existence of one of the following aggravating factors: plaintiff's personal contribution to delay, defendant's actual prejudice because of delay, and delay that can be characterized as intentional.

In re Arhens, 120 B.R. 852.

Dismissal with prejudice for failure to prosecute of debtor's counterclaim for $10 million in damages for breach of contract and fraud was justified; debtor had failed to actively pursue any discovery or file any pleadings for four and one-half years after adversary proceeding was commenced, debtor's filing of three notices of deposition for depositions which were not taken, filing of change of address, and making allegation of telephone inquiries did not overcome demonstrated delay, and sanctions against debtor would not overcome prejudice to claimant arising from debtor's delay.

In re Arhens, 120 B.R. 852.

⚷**1761. —— Process, delay in obtaining service of.**

C.A.D.C. 1988. If based on delay in service of process, dismissal under rule permitting dismissal for failure to prosecute is appropriate only when there is no reasonable probability that service can be obtained. Fed.Rules Civ. Proc.Rule 41(b), 28 U.S.C.A.

Smith-Bey v. Cripe, 852 F.2d 592, 271 U.S.App.D.C. 294.

Neither delay in service of process nor eight months' inactivity warranted dismissal of inmate's pro se *Bivens* cause of action for failure to prosecute where inmate was not given opportunity to explain why suit should not be dismissed and it was probable that service could be obtained through United States Marshal Service. Fed.Rules Civ.Proc.Rule 41(b), 28 U.S.C.A.

Smith-Bey v. Cripe, 852 F.2d 592, 271 U.S.App.D.C. 294.

C.A.9 (Cal.) 1987. District court did not abuse its discretion in dismissing, for failure to prosecute, tort and contract claims, where original defendants named in suit had not been served three years after suit was commenced.

Gulf Arab Medi--Arab American Film Co. v. Faisal Foundation, 811 F.2d 1260, opinion amended 832 F.2d 132.

C.A.7 (Ill.) 1990. Under Federal Rule of Civil Procedure 4(j), which provides that if defendant is not served with summons and complaint within 120 days after complaint was filed district court must dismiss action unless plaintiff demonstrates good cause for delay, district court has duty to make discretionary finding of whether plaintiff established good cause. Fed. Rules Civ.Proc.Rule 4(j), 28 U.S.C.A.

Floyd v. U.S., 900 F.2d 1045.

Fact that statute of limitations had run did not prevent dismissal for failure to effect timely service of summons and complaint. Fed.Rules Civ.Proc.Rule 4(j), 28 U.S.C.A.

Floyd v. U.S., 900 F.2d 1045.

Where plaintiff has offered no justifiable reason for his or her failure to effect timely service of summons and complaint, lack of prejudice to defendant, standing alone, does not constitute "good cause" for not dismissing complaint. Fed.Rules Civ.Proc.Rule 4(j), 28 U.S.C.A.

Floyd v. U.S., 900 F.2d 1045.

C.A.7 (Ill.) 1988. Rule of civil procedure requiring dismissal of action without prejudice if service of summons and complaint was not effected within 120 days of filing of complaint applied in plaintiff's action even though defendant was ultimately served beyond 120–day period; rule applied equally to defendants who were never served and defendants who were served after 120–day period had lapsed. Fed. Rules Civ.Proc.Rule 4(j), 28 U.S.C.A.

Geiger v. Allen, 850 F.2d 330.

C.A.5 (La.) 1987. Plaintiff proceeding in forma pauperis is entitled to rely upon service by the United States Marshals and should not be penalized for failure of the Marshal's Service to properly effect service of process, where such failure is through no fault of the litigant. Fed. Rules Civ.Proc.Rule 4(c)(2)(B)(i), 28 U.S.C.A.

Rochon v. Dawson, 828 F.2d 1107.

Failure of United States Marshal's Service to properly serve doctor, in action by incarcerated pro se litigant proceeding in forma pauperis, was due to litigant's inaction and dilatoriness, and thus, litigant's action against doctor to obtain documentary evidence to attack his rape conviction was properly dismissed for failure to prosecute; even though litigant knew that doctor had not been served, litigant failed to request the Marshal's Service to effect service on doctor. U.S.Dist.Ct.Rules W.D. La., Rule 14; Fed.Rules Civ.Proc.Rules 4(c)(2)(B)(i), 34(c), 28 U.S.C.A.

Rochon v. Dawson, 828 F.2d 1107.

C.A.5 (La.) 1985. In absence of legitimate explanation for 32–month delay in causing process to be served in personal injury diversity suit arising from crash of helicopter in Gulf of Mexico, delay was both prejudicial and unfair, warranting dismissal of suit for want of prosecution. Fed.Rules Civ.Proc.Rule 4, 28 U.S.C.A.

Fournier v. Textron, Inc., 776 F.2d 532.

C.A.5 (La.) 1985. District court properly dismissed personal injury suit after four times notifying plaintiffs' attorney that suit was subject to being dismissed because no steps had been taken to serve named defendant and four times receiving reply that service would be made "at an appropriate time," particularly in view of plaintiffs' explanation of the failure to act in the federal case, namely, belief that better settlement in state compensation claim could be obtained if named defendant had not had opportunity to develop its entire tort defense through discovery in the federal court; district court acted properly to vindicate its control of its docket and protect named defendants in cases brought in the federal court. Fed.Rules Civ.Proc.Rule 4(j), 28 U.S.C.A.

> Redding v. Essex Crane Rental Corp. of Alabama, 752 F.2d 1077.

C.A.8 (Mo.) 1985. District court did not abuse its discretion in dismissing complaint, where 170 days passed between filing of complaint and dismissal without summons and complaint having been served on any defendants, and where plaintiff was warned that complaint would be dismissed if he did not begin serving defendants. Fed.Rules Civ.Proc. Rule 4(j), 28 U.S.C.A.

> Edwards v. Edwards, 754 F.2d 298.

C.A.1 (Puerto Rico) 1989. Seller's failure to serve wholesale buyer of flowers more than three years after filing breach of contract action warranted dismissal of that defendant for want of prosecution. Fed.Rules Civ.Proc.Rule 4(j), 28 U.S.C.A.

> Jardines Bacata, Ltd. v. Diaz-Marquez, 878 F.2d 1555.

C.A.1 (Puerto Rico) 1988. In view of district court's failure to decide motion to quash service, its unconditional dismissal of complaint for failure to prosecute was excessive and an abuse of discretion; rather, appropriate sanction was conditional dismissal barring plaintiff from further efforts to serve defendant under Federal Rules, where record in case left open possibility that plaintiff was inactive for more than 18 months because of uncertainty concerning status of service. Fed.Rules Civ.Proc.Rule 41(b), 28 U.S.C.A.

> Enlace Mercantil Internacional, Inc. v. Senior Industries, Inc., 848 F.2d 315.

C.A.5 (Tex.) 1991. District court did not abuse its discretion in dismissing pro se plaintiff's claims against State of Texas for want of prosecution, after court had issued order directing plaintiff to serve State of Texas by serving the Secretary of State, and instead of following court's clear instructions, plaintiff filed motion to dismiss court's order.

> Hulsey v. State of Tex., 929 F.2d 168.

D.Colo. 1990. Failure to serve defendant with § 1983 complaint required dismissal of defendant for failure to prosecute, absent showing of good cause. 42 U.S.C.A. § 1983.

> Jacobs v. Dujmovic, 752 F.Supp. 1516, affirmed 940 F.2d 1392, certiorari denied 113 S.Ct. 123, 506 U.S. 840, 121 L.Ed.2d 78, rehearing denied 113 S.Ct. 641, 506 U.S. 1015, 121 L.Ed.2d 571.

N.D.Ill. 1990. Title VII plaintiff demonstrated "good cause" for her failure to serve complaint until 39 days after statutory deadline, based on neglect of her court-appointed attorney; Title VII complaint would not be dismissed, where defendant was large, well-managed business that would not be prejudiced by delay. Fed.Rules Civ.Proc.Rule 4(j), 28 U.S.C.A.; Civil Rights Act of 1964, § 701 et seq., 42 U.S.C.A. § 2000e et seq.

> Barner v. Ford Motor Co., 132 F.R.D. 495.

E.D.La. 1991. Service of admiralty complaint against United States 126 days after filing was not timely, necessitating dismissal absent showing of good cause. Fed.Rules Civ.Proc. Rule 4(j), 28 U.S.C.A.; Suits in Admiralty Act, § 2, 46 App.U.S.C.A. § 742.

> Diversified Marine Intern., Inc. v. U.S., 774 F.Supp. 1005.

S.D.N.Y. 1991. Record established that one of two defendants was never served with summons and complaint in action that was instituted nearly three years before it went to trial and, absent showing why service was not made, action was properly dismissed. Fed. Rules Civ.Proc.Rule 4(j), 28 U.S.C.A.

> Ariel Maritime Group, Inc. v. Zust Bachmeier of Switzerland, Inc., 762 F.Supp. 55.

S.D.N.Y. 1990. Dismissal of suit for failure to prosecute was not warranted in action brought by prospective mortgagors against prospective mortgagee; when it became apparent that original service of process was in dispute, prospective mortgagors had moved to extend time allowed for service and had responded to prospective mortgagee's motion to dismiss detailing several efforts to effect service other than by mail. Fed.Rules Civ.Proc.Rule 41(b), 28 U.S.C.A.

> Krank v. Express Funding Corp., 133 F.R.D. 14.

D.Puerto Rico 1996. Failure to properly serve defendant with summons required dismissal of claim against him for lack of prosecution. Fed.Rules Civ.Proc.Rule 4(m); U.S.Dist. Ct.Rules D.P.R., Rule 313(1)(A).

> Dibbs v. Gonsalves, 921 F.Supp. 44.

Bkrtcy.N.D.Ill. 1995. Old version of Federal Rules of Civil Procedure, permitting court to dismiss action for lack of prosecution if summons and complaint were not served within 120 days after filing with court, did not apply to service in foreign country. Fed.Rules Civ.Proc. Rule 4(j), 28 U.S.C.A.

> In re Schwinn Bicycle Co., 190 B.R. 599.

Bkrtcy.S.D.N.Y. 1986. If considerable delay occurs before summons is issued and served, complaint may be subject to motion to dismiss for failure to properly prosecute.

> In re Schwartz & Meyers, 64 B.R. 948.

Bkrtcy.S.D.N.Y. 1985. Plaintiff creditor did not fail to prosecute his action in debtor's bankruptcy by failing to appear at first scheduled pretrial conference; plaintiff had not served original summons, had requested reissued summons, and had notified court of circumstances and requested new pretrial conference date. Rules Bankr.Proc.Rule 7004(f), 11 U.S.C.A.

In re Dahowski, 48 B.R. 877.

⚷1762. —— Excuses in general.

C.A.9 1994. Financial difficulties do not excuse plaintiff's delay, for purposes of determining whether action should be dismissed for lack of prosecution. Fed.Rules Civ.Proc.Rule 41(b), 28 U.S.C.A.

In re Eisen, 31 F.3d 1447.

Plaintiff cannot use actions taken after filing of motion to dismiss for lack of prosecution as evidence of plaintiff's diligence in prosecuting suit. Fed.Rules Civ.Proc.Rule 41(b), 28 U.S.C.A.

In re Eisen, 31 F.3d 1447.

C.A.11 (Ala.) 1995. District court abused its discretion by dismissing with prejudice action seeking recovery under marine protection and indemnity policy, due to plaintiff's failure to proceed with arbitration after proceedings were stayed for that purpose, where plaintiff requested certification to Court of Appeals of district court's arbitration order prior to dismissal of action, but district court denied request; plaintiff had made conscious decision to forego any damages it might potentially recover from arbitration process in exchange for appealing, on the chance that district court erred in ordering arbitration.

Morewitz v. West of England Ship Owners Mut. Protection and Indem. Ass'n (Luxembourg), 62 F.3d 1356, certiorari denied 116 S.Ct. 915, 516 U.S. 1114, 133 L.Ed.2d 845.

C.A.8 (Ark.) 1993. District court could dismiss for failure to prosecute patient's medical malpractice action against physician alleging that he negligently failed to diagnose and treat her breast cancer; patient created ethical conflict that forced her attorneys to withdraw from her case by refusing, against advice of her attorneys, to admit that she lied in making statements about her condition, permitting patient to proceed pro se was not realistic option as she was extremely ill on day trial was to begin, action had been filed 18 months earlier and had been continued several times, and another continuance would not have guaranteed that case would go to trial and would have prolonged physician's hardship after he and his attorneys had worked diligently to be ready for

trial. Fed.Rules Civ.Proc.Rule 41(b), 28 U.S.C.A.

Garland v. Peebles, 1 F.3d 683, rehearing denied.

C.A.8 (Ark.) 1989. Civil rights plaintiff's case was properly dismissed with prejudice for failure to prosecute even though he contended that his failure to appear on scheduled trial date was due to transportation problems and that his failure to notify court of reason for his absence was due to fact that he got locked out of his house. Fed.Rules Civ.Proc.Rule 41(b), 28 U.S.C.A.

Wright v. Sargent, 869 F.2d 1175.

C.A.9 (Cal.) 1996. Dismissal for lack of prosecution was not due to mistake or misunderstanding on part of plaintiff where court determined that the plaintiff might be "doing something cute" and was systematically violating court orders, in absence of evidence that plaintiff did not know that he was supposed to be in court or that there were medical, financial, or other reasons for him not to be in court. Fed.Rules Civ.Proc.Rule 41(b), 28 U.S.C.A.

Al-Torki v. Kaempen, 78 F.3d 1381.

C.A.9 (Cal.) 1989. Before dismissing prisoner's pro se action for failure to appear due to incarceration, trial court must investigate reasonable alternatives to such severe sanction, including, for example, bench trial in the prison, trial by deposition, and compelling prisoner's prisons through ad testificandum writ.

Hernandez v. Whiting, 881 F.2d 768.

Dismissal of prisoner's pro se civil rights action for failure to appear due to incarceration was inappropriate; prisoner had pursued his case up to trial as diligently as pro se plaintiff could have been expected to perform, district court knew before trial that prisoner's imprisonment would be barrier to his attendance, prisoner's testimony was crucial, and case had survived summary judgment motion.

Hernandez v. Whiting, 881 F.2d 768.

C.A.9 (Cal.) 1987. Dismissal of pro se plaintiff's § 1983 action for failure to timely file amended complaint constituted abuse of discretion, given plaintiff's incarceration and lack of meaningful access to law library. Fed.Rules Civ.Proc.Rule 41(b), 28 U.S.C.A.; 42 U.S.C.A. § 1983.

Eldridge v. Block, 832 F.2d 1132.

C.A.11 (Fla.) 1988. It was error to dismiss action for want of prosecution because of plaintiff's refusal to arbitrate in accordance with court order where the refusal did not result from negligence on its part but, rather, from a conscious decision to forego any damages that might otherwise be able to recover in that arbitration proceeding for the chance that district court erred in ordering arbitration and that plaintiff could win a reversal of that order.

State Establishment for Agr. Product Trading v. M/V Wesermunde, 838 F.2d 1576, certiorari denied United Kingdom Mut. S.S. Assur. Ass'n (Bermuda) Ltd. v. State Establishment For Agr. Product Trading, 109 S.Ct. 273, 488 U.S. 916, 102 L.Ed.2d 262.

C.A.11 (Ga.) 1987. Dismissal of prisoner's § 1983 action against prison officials for failure to prosecute was improper where district court failed to rule on prisoner's motion for counsel and district court failed to consider whether prisoner's presence would have substantially furthered resolution of case, security risks presented by prisoner's presence, or whether suit could have been stayed without prejudice to cause asserted until prisoner was released. 42 U.S.C.A. § 1983.

Poole v. Lambert, 819 F.2d 1025.

C.A.7 (Ill.) 1990. Trial court improperly dismissed claims by some members of class for want of prosecution after class counsel withdrew from representing those members, where they were not informed of responsibilities and did not receive notice of ongoing proceedings.

Woodall v. Drake Hotel, Inc., 913 F.2d 447, rehearing denied, on remand Behr v. Drake Hotel, Inc., 1991 WL 33661.

C.A.1 (Me.) 1995. Dismissal with prejudice was too harsh a sanction for plaintiff's attorney's failure to appear at hearing or to notify district court and opposing counsel of his absence because egregiousness of counsel's conduct was mitigated in that he had apprised district court and opposing counsel of severity of his illness through two motions for enlargement of time and litigation, at time of district court's dismissal, was less than one year old and thus, sanction would be modified to dismissal without prejudice. Fed.Rules Civ.Proc. Rule 41(b), 28 U.S.C.A.

Benjamin v. Aroostook Medical Center, Inc., 57 F.3d 101.

C.A.2 (N.Y.) 1995. District court should not have dismissed inmate's § 1983 action for failure to prosecute by not appearing for jury selection, but it should have used lesser remedy of proceeding with jury selection in inmate's absence; inmate's version that he was awakened at 4:00 a.m. and told to prepare to go to hospital could not be dismissed as implausible since he alleged that he had not received prior notice of court date and did not understand English. Fed.Rules Civ.Proc.Rule 41(b), 28 U.S.C.A.

Colon v. Mack, 56 F.3d 5, on remand 983 F.Supp. 496.

C.A.2 (N.Y.) 1993. Dismissal of pro se Title VII case for failure to prosecute based upon plaintiff's failure to respond to defendant's request to dismiss was abuse of discretion, where only three months had transpired without action on plaintiff's part, plaintiff was not given notice that her action would be dismissed if she failed to respond to defendant's request to dismiss, plaintiff had been diligent in her prosecution up to that point, and there was no prejudice to defendant. Fed.Rules Civ.Proc.Rule 41(b), 28 U.S.C.A.; U.S.Dist.Ct.Rules W.D.N.Y., Local Rule 18.

Minnette v. Time Warner, 997 F.2d 1023.

C.A.6 (Ohio) 1988. Standing is not properly the subject of motion to dismiss for failure to prosecute or for noncompliance with orders of the court. Fed.Rules Civ.Proc.Rule 41(b), 28 U.S.C.A.

Haskell v. Washington Tp., 864 F.2d 1266, appeal after remand 891 F.2d 132.

C.A.9 (Or.) 1990. Plaintiff cannot avoid dismissal for lack of prosecution by arguing that he or she is innocent party who will be made to suffer for errors of attorney; faults and defaults of attorney may be imputed to, and their consequences visited upon, his or her client. Fed. Rules Civ.Proc.Rule 41(b), 28 U.S.C.A.

West Coast Theater Corp. v. City of Portland, 897 F.2d 1519.

C.A.1 (Puerto Rico) 1987. Evasion of service by putative defendant constitutes good cause for failure of service under rule, which permits district court to dismiss claim on its own initiative with notice to plaintiff, if service of summons and complaint is not made within 120 days after filing of complaint, and if party on whose behalf service is required cannot show good cause. Fed.Rules Civ.Proc.Rule 4(j), 28 U.S.C.A.

Ruiz Varela v. Sanchez Velez, 814 F.2d 821.

Plaintiff is not required to effect service by publication as prerequisite to claim that defendant's evasion is good cause for failure of personal service. Fed.Rules Civ.Proc.Rule 4(j), 28 U.S.C.A.

Ruiz Varela v. Sanchez Velez, 814 F.2d 821.

C.A.5 (Tex.) 1987. Age discrimination plaintiff's pattern of delay for more than two years in face of three warnings of dismissal if prosecution of claim were not proceeded with justified dismissal of claim for failure to prosecute, although plaintiff allegedly was unable to retain attorney to replace attorney who was permitted to withdraw and did not receive copy of order setting motion to dismiss for hearing. Fed. Rules Civ.Proc.Rule 41(b), 28 U.S.C.A.

Salinas v. Sun Oil Co., 819 F.2d 105.

S.D.Fla. 1993. Defendants were not entitled to dismissal for want of prosecution; delays in civil motion practice were necessitated by heavy caseload in district for which plaintiff bore no responsibility. U.S.Dist.Ct.Rules S.D.Fla., General Rule 41.1.

> Liberty Mut. Ins. Co. v. Electronic Systems, Inc., 813 F.Supp. 802.

S.D.Ga. 1994. Fact that court clerk's office had inadvertently treated dismissal of action against one defendant as dismissal against all did not excuse plaintiff's failure for three years to take any action against defendants who had not been dismissed. Fed.Rules Civ.Proc. Rule 41(b), 28 U.S.C.A.

> Stolt-Nielsen, Inc. v. Zim Israel Navigation Co., Ltd., 879 F.Supp. 1223, vacated Stolt-Neilsen v. Zim Israel Nav. Co., 67 F.3d 314.

A three-year period of inaction was not excused, for purposes of dismissal for failure to prosecute, by claim that plaintiffs and counsel were resolving differences between themselves about proper measure of recovery. Fed.Rules Civ.Proc.Rule 41(b), 28 U.S.C.A.

> Stolt-Nielsen, Inc. v. Zim Israel Navigation Co., Ltd., 879 F.Supp. 1223, vacated Stolt-Neilsen v. Zim Israel Nav. Co., 67 F.3d 314.

A three-year period of inaction was not excused for purposes of dismissal for failure to prosecute by claim that plaintiffs had assumed that liability as to remaining defendants had been established in earlier order dismissing action as to one defendant so that need for extensive discovery was reduced, where remaining defendants clearly were contesting liability. Fed.Rules Civ.Proc.Rule 41(b), 28 U.S.C.A.

> Stolt-Nielsen, Inc. v. Zim Israel Navigation Co., Ltd., 879 F.Supp. 1223, vacated Stolt-Neilsen v. Zim Israel Nav. Co., 67 F.3d 314.

E.D.La. 1991. Ignorance of rules does not constitute good cause for failure to timely serve process. Fed.Rules Civ.Proc.Rule 4, 28 U.S.C.A.

> Diversified Marine Intern., Inc. v. U.S., 774 F.Supp. 1005.

E.D.N.Y. 1997. Bankruptcy judge abused his discretion in dismissing Federal Deposit Insurance Corporation's (FDIC's) adversary complaint against debtor for failure to prosecute, based on FDIC's second failure to appear at pretrial conference; failure to appear resulted from confusion over reassignment of case from one judge to another, judge did not consider efficacy of lesser sanctions, FDIC did not receive notice that further delays would result in dismissal, and debtor was not likely to be prejudiced by further delay. Fed.Rules Civ.Proc. Rule 41(b), 28 U.S.C.A.

> In re Folks, 210 B.R. 674.

S.D.N.Y. 1996. Dismissal was not warranted for failure to prosecute civil rights action, since, among other things, it was prior pro bono counsel, not plaintiff arrestee, who failed to advance case over three-year period, arrestee did not know that counsel had been appointed for him and apparently believed that his case remained on suspense docket, and lesser sanction was available to vindicate court's authority to manage its affairs and achieve expeditious disposition of case. 42 U.S.C.A. § 1983; Fed. Rules Civ.Proc.Rule 41(b), 28 U.S.C.A.

> Daniels v. Loizzo, 175 F.R.D. 459.

Inaction on civil rights case during time that district court had placed case on its suspense docket could not be attributed to pro se plaintiff, especially since plaintiff had attempted to prosecute his case by serving interrogatories and document requests, but court had denied those requests as case had been held in abeyance pending appointment of counsel. Fed. Rules Civ.Proc.Rule 41(b), 28 U.S.C.A.

> Daniels v. Loizzo, 175 F.R.D. 459.

Most appropriate sanction for alleged failure to prosecute civil rights case over three-year period was to impose strict deadlines for resolution of case, rather than to dismiss case with prejudice, since plaintiff played no part in delay, and former pro bono counsel had been reprimanded for his failure to contact plaintiff and his lack of devotion to case. Fed.Rules Civ. Proc.Rule 41(b), 28 U.S.C.A.

> Daniels v. Loizzo, 175 F.R.D. 459.

S.D.N.Y. 1995. Evidence was sufficient to support ruling of administrator, who had been appointed to assure compliance with consent decree in civil rights litigation brought by newspaper deliverers against newspapers and union, that claims should not be dismissed for failure to prosecute; although deliverers failed to conduct discovery for seven years, and administrator admonished deliverers to resolve pending claims quickly pending termination of decree, postponing discovery was reasonable while deliverers questioned administrator's jurisdiction, newspaper's inability to locate documents was not sufficient to warrant dismissal, and admonishment did not constitute implied notice that further delay would result in dismissal. Fed. Rules Civ.Proc.Rule 41(b), 28 U.S.C.A.

> Patterson v. Newspaper and Mail Deliverers' Union of New York and Vicinity, 884 F.Supp. 869.

S.D.N.Y. 1993. Size or complexity of Federal Deposit Insurance Corporation (FDIC) was not an excuse for failure to delegate necessary authority to operational levels to permit its counsel to handle litigation in a timely fashion. Fed.Rules Civ.Proc.Rule 41(b), 28 U.S.C.A.

Dollar Dry Dock Bank v. Denning, 148 F.R.D. 124.

S.D.N.Y. 1990. Inmate's action based on claim of guard brutality would not be dismissed for failure to prosecute, where failure to pursue case was caused by combination of assigned attorney's court-related activities in North Carolina and inmate's incarceration, including hospitalization, in Virginia.

Vaughn v. O'Donnell, 734 F.Supp. 139.

S.D.N.Y. 1990. Pro se plaintiff's alleged inability to pursue civil rights suit due to "medical complaints" did not justify inactivity in pursuing lawsuit, for purposes of dismissal for failure to prosecute; there was no evidence of medical problems from May 1989 to January 1990, when motion to dismiss was filed, pro se plaintiff was granted 90–day extension for discovery upon request to vacate order dismissing case for lack of prosecution, but did not at that time mention medical problems or possibility that he might need further time for discovery, and pro se plaintiff did not act after being put on notice of intent to dismiss case if he did not proceed with discovery. Fed.Rules Civ.Proc. Rule 41(b), 28 U.S.C.A.

West v. City of New York, 130 F.R.D. 522.

S.D.N.Y. 1986. Attorney's explanation for failing to appear at calendar call, that attorney attempted to cover for pretrial conferences on same morning and could not be in several places at once, was unsatisfactory, since there were a number of other attorneys in firm.

C.E. Bickford & Co., Inc. v. M.V. Elly, 116 F.R.D. 195.

M.D.N.C. 1992. Involuntary dismissal of plaintiff's action was warranted due to dilatory conduct of plaintiff's president, who acted with indifference to his own counsel as well as to rules and orders of court over period of year; fact that president had been ill and out of country attending to overseas business interests during course of last year did not warrant such unreasonable delay and uncooperative behavior as has been exhibited by president. Fed.Rules Civ.Proc.Rule 41(b), 28 U.S.C.A.

Carolina Parachute Corp. v. Goodyear Aerospace Corp., 782 F.Supp. 38, affirmed in part, reversed in part Bauer v. Goodyear Aerospace Corp., 974 F.2d 1330.

E.D.Pa. 1994. Although plaintiff asserting civil rights claim against police officer did not comply with some discovery requests, officer was not entitled to dismissal for failure to prosecute claim; defendant was not prejudiced by plaintiff's failure to respond, and plaintiff's failure to respond was because he was in prison and lacked representation and resources, and not because plaintiff was attempting, in bad faith, to obfuscate discovery process. 42 U.S.C.A. § 1983; Fed.Rules Civ.Proc.Rule 41(b), 28 U.S.C.A.

Mastromatteo v. Simock, 866 F.Supp. 853.

E.D.Pa. 1993. Plaintiff's delinquence in complying with defendants' discovery requests and in obtaining replacement counsel after original counsel withdrew due to illness did not justify dismissal of complaint with prejudice for failure to prosecute. Fed.Rules Civ.Proc.Rule 41(b), 28 U.S.C.A.

Seal v. Riverside Federal Sav. Bank, 825 F.Supp. 686.

⌔**1763.** —— **Death or disability.**

C.A.7 (Ind.) 1985. After Arizona state prisoner failed to take steps to secure his own presence at trial or notify district court of his inability to do so, district court, rather than entering dismissal, should have considered other feasible alternatives for deciding prisoner's claim against the United States for the loss or theft of various items of personal property while he was temporarily confined in federal prison in Indiana, where district court was fully apprised at time it scheduled case for trial that prisoner's incarceration would likely foreclose the possibility of his appearance. Fed.Rules Civ.Proc.Rule 41(b), 28 U.S.C.A.; 28 U.S.C.A. § 1346.

Sisk v. U.S., 756 F.2d 497.

C.A.8 (Neb.) 1985. District court abused its discretion in dismissing civil rights complaint because of plaintiff's failure to appear at pretrial hearing, where plaintiff's incarceration in another state prevented him from appearing at hearing, and dismissal without prejudice could have effect of dismissal with prejudice if plaintiff's incarceration extended past applicable statute of limitations period.

Reynolds v. Foree, 771 F.2d 1179.

C.A.9 (Or.) 1990. Neither death of plaintiff's cousin prior to hearing to show cause on why action should not be dismissed for lack of prosecution nor large number of defendants purportedly preventing plaintiff from conducting discovery precluded dismissal for lack of prosecution; death of cousin was about 12 days before scheduled hearing, plaintiff neither responded in writing to hearing nor requested that hearing be rescheduled, and it was plaintiff who chose to include numerous defendants. Fed.Rules Civ.Proc.Rule 41(b), 28 U.S.C.A.

West Coast Theater Corp. v. City of Portland, 897 F.2d 1519.

C.A.1 (Puerto Rico) 1993. Medical malpractice action could be dismissed for failure to prosecute, even if medical problems had incapacitated plaintiffs' attorney for approximately five weeks, where dilatory behavior lasted for ten months, and dismissal followed plaintiffs' repeated failures to comply with reasonable discovery requests and discovery orders, district court's clear warnings that dismissal could result, and imposition of lesser sanction of $300 fine against plaintiffs' counsel. Fed.Rules Civ. Proc.Rule 41(b), 28 U.S.C.A.

> Capo v. U.S., 7 F.3d 283.

N.D.Cal. 1983. Acri v. International Ass'n of Machinists and Aerospace Workers, 595 F.Supp. 326, affirmed 781 F.2d 1393, certiorari denied 107 S.Ct. 73, 479 U.S. 816, 93 L.Ed.2d 29.

S.D.Ga. 1994. Dismissal for failure to prosecute damages action stemming from ship collision was warranted by record of clear delay, in form of failure to take action for three years, without excusable neglect, and showing that lesser sanctions would not remedy proportional prejudice to defendants from death of key witness. Fed.Rules Civ.Proc.Rule 41(b), 28 U.S.C.A.

> Stolt-Nielsen, Inc. v. Zim Israel Navigation Co., Ltd., 879 F.Supp. 1223, vacated Stolt-Neilsen v. Zim Israel Nav. Co., 67 F.3d 314.

E.D.Mich. 1985. Fact that a plaintiff is incarcerated does not absolve him of responsibility to prosecute his lawsuit in a diligent manner. Fed.Rules Civ.Proc.Rule 41(b), 28 U.S.C.A.

> Snavley v. Redman, 107 F.R.D. 346.

Failure of prison inmate to take any measures on behalf of his civil rights case for a period of over 19 months subsequent to defendants' filing of answer warranted dismissal for failure to prosecute, considering that delay undoubtedly caused prejudice to defendants and that there appeared to be no justification for inaction, giving rise to inference that inmate either abandoned claim or filed action to harass defendants. Fed.Rules Civ.Proc.Rule 41(b), 28 U.S.C.A.; U.S.Dist.Ct.Rules E.D.Mich., Rule 20.

> Snavley v. Redman, 107 F.R.D. 346.

D.Nev. 1986. Discovery by counsel that he had form of cancer, and receipt by counsel of extensive chemotherapy and radiation treatments forcing him to spend up to three days per week at hospital was "good cause" excusing failure to comply with service filing deadlines by 17 days where there was no indication of any injury to defendants despite counsel being well enough to file complaint in case during time for compliance. Fed.Rules Civ.Proc.Rules 4(j), 12, 38(b), 28 U.S.C.A.; F.R.A.P.Rule 4(a)(5), 28 U.S.C.A.

> LeMaster v. City of Winnemucca, 113 F.R.D. 37.

🔑**1764. —— Pendency of other proceedings.**

C.A.7 (Ill.) 1985. Dismissals of federal actions for want of prosecution are not proper where parties continue to actively prosecute their claims, although in state court.

> Ohio River Co. v. Carrillo, 754 F.2d 236.

In case where injured worker had filed negligence action against barge owner in state court, and barge owner had responded with federal admiralty action for exoneration or limitation of liability under Limitation of Liability Act, district court should not have dismissed barge owner's federal action without prejudice due to its inactive status, since such course raised possibility that barge owner would no longer be able to comply with Act's six-month filing requirement; better procedure was simply to stay barge owner's action pending disposition of state suit. 46 U.S.C.A. § 185.

> Ohio River Co. v. Carrillo, 754 F.2d 236.

M.D.Ga. 1985. Pendency of settlement negotiations is acceptable excuse for some delay in prosecution of case, but pendency of negotiations is not excuse where delay is unreasonably long or if it continues after it is apparent that negotiations would not be fruitful.

> E.E.O.C. v. Firestone Tire and Rubber Co., 626 F.Supp. 90.

Settlement negotiations, which had been dragged out over period of four years and were obviously "getting nowhere" because last proposal demanded greater amount in settlement than first proposal made years earlier, did not justify delay in prosecution of employment discrimination action.

> E.E.O.C. v. Firestone Tire and Rubber Co., 626 F.Supp. 90.

N.D.Ill. 1985. Dismissal with prejudice for failure to prosecute action alleging downward market manipulation in corporation's shares was appropriate, even though buyers claimed that they relied on discovery by plaintiffs' committee in consolidated cases, where it appeared that buyers had no intention of proceeding against seller and suspended prosecution of action pending resolution of matters in class actions, which involved different defendants and different issues. Fed.Rules Civ.Proc.Rule 41(b), 28 U.S.C.A.

> In re Olympia Brewing Co. Securities Litigation, 613 F.Supp. 1286.

W.D.N.Y. 1987. Securities and antitrust action would not be dismissed for failure to prosecute even though very little activity occurred for more than three years, where plaintiffs were involved in a related action in state court.

> Markel v. Scovill Mfg. Co., 657 F.Supp. 1102, vacated 859 F.2d 148.

⟳**1765. Stipulations, breach of.**

Library references

C.J.S. Federal Civil Procedure § 796.

3. PLEADING, DEFECTS IN, IN GENERAL.

Research Notes

Dismissal and nonsuit, see West's Federal Forms.

See Wright & Miller, Federal Practice and Procedure: Civil.

⟳**1771. In general.**

Library references

C.J.S. Federal Civil Procedure § 818.

C.A.D.C. 1991. If complaint's factual allegations, and reasonable inferences derived from them, would support a legal theory entitling the plaintiff to some relief, motion to dismiss for failure to state a claim should be denied. Fed. Rules Civ.Proc.Rule 12(b)(6), 28 U.S.C.A.

ACLU Foundation of Southern California v. Barr, 952 F.2d 457, 293 U.S.App.D.C. 101, rehearing denied.

Motion to dismiss for failure to state a claim does not countenance dismissals based on a judge's disbelief of a complaint's factual allegations or judge's belief that plaintiff cannot prove what the complaint asserts. Fed.Rules Civ.Proc.Rule 12(b)(6), 28 U.S.C.A.

ACLU Foundation of Southern California v. Barr, 952 F.2d 457, 293 U.S.App.D.C. 101, rehearing denied.

C.A.D.C. 1991. Trial judge is under no duty to recognize novel theory of recovery unaided by plaintiff and motion to dismiss should be granted, where complaint does not adequately inform court of plaintiff's legal theory supporting novel theory of recovery.

Kugel v. U.S., 947 F.2d 1504, 292 U.S.App. D.C. 135.

C.A.D.C. 1987. Trial court should not grant motion to dismiss for failure to state a claim or motion for judgment on the pleadings simply because it is dubious of plaintiff's ability to prove the allegations of the complaint at trial. Fed.Rules Civ.Proc.Rule 12(b)(6), (c), 28 U.S.C.A.

Haynesworth v. Miller, 820 F.2d 1245, 261 U.S.App.D.C. 66.

C.A.D.C. 1984. Brandon v. District of Columbia Bd. of Parole, 734 F.2d 56, 236 U.S.App. D.C. 155, certiorari denied 105 S.Ct. 811, 469 U.S. 1127, 83 L.Ed.2d 804, on remand 631 F.Supp. 435, affirmed 823 F.2d 644, 262 U.S.App.D.C. 236.

C.A.D.C. 1983. Sinclair v. Kleindienst, 711 F.2d 291, 229 U.S.App.D.C. 13, appeal after remand 916 F.2d 1109.

C.A.Fed. (Md.) 1991. Trial court has discretion to dismiss complaint if it simply duplicates another related pending action.

Finch v. Hughes Aircraft Co., 926 F.2d 1574.

C.A.Fed. (Minn.) 1993. Dismissal for failure to state a claim upon which relief can be granted is improper unless there is no reasonable view of facts which support claim. Fed. Rules Civ.Proc.Rule 12(b)(6), 28 U.S.C.A.

Advanced Cardiovascular Systems, Inc. v. Scimed Life Systems, Inc., 988 F.2d 1157, rehearing denied, in banc suggestion declined.

C.A.11 (Ala.) 1995. District court properly dismissed plaintiff's claim with prejudice, where court had allowed employee to amend her complaint twice in order to state claim on which relief could be granted, and employee failed to do so. Fed.Rules Civ.Proc.Rule 12(b)(6), 28 U.S.C.A.

Welch v. Laney, 57 F.3d 1004.

C.A.9 (Ariz.) 1992. Before dismissing pro se complaint, district court must provide litigant with notice of deficiencies in his complaint in order to ensure that litigant uses opportunity to amend effectively.

Ferdik v. Bonzelet, 963 F.2d 1258, as amended, certiorari denied 113 S.Ct. 321, 506 U.S. 915, 121 L.Ed.2d 242.

District court's dismissal of pro se litigant's second amended complaint for failure to timely comply with court order requiring him to change the caption of his complaint was not abuse of discretion, particularly where court demonstrated more than adequate sensitivity to pro se litigant's inexperience, by granting two opportunities to amend complaint, giving guidance necessary to submit properly amended complaint and vacating initial dismissal after litigant failed to file timely second amended complaint. Fed.Rules Civ.Proc.Rule 10(a), 28 U.S.C.A.

Ferdik v. Bonzelet, 963 F.2d 1258, as amended, certiorari denied 113 S.Ct. 321, 506 U.S. 915, 121 L.Ed.2d 242.

C.A.9 (Cal.) 1997. Rule requiring only a short and plain statement of claim showing pleader is entitled to relief contains a powerful presumption against rejecting pleading for failure to state a claim. Fed.Rules Civ.Proc.Rules 8(a), 12(b)(6), 28 U.S.C.A.

Gilligan v. Jamco Development Corp., 108 F.3d 246.

In reviewing sufficiency of complaint, issue is not whether plaintiff will ultimately prevail but whether plaintiff is entitled to offer evidence to support claims. Fed.Rules Civ.Proc.Rule 12(b)(6), 28 U.S.C.A.

> Gilligan v. Jamco Development Corp., 108 F.3d 246.

C.A.9 (Cal.) 1988. Dismissal for failure to state claim can be based on lack of cognizable legal theory or absence of sufficient facts alleged under cognizable theory. Fed.Rules Civ. Proc.Rule 12(b)(6), 28 U.S.C.A.

> Balistreri v. Pacifica Police Dept., 901 F.2d 696.

C.A.9 (Cal.) 1987. Purpose of allowing dismissals for failure to state cause of action is to enable defendants to challenge legal sufficiency of complaint without subjecting themselves to discovery. Fed.Rules Civ.Proc.Rule 12(b)(6), 28 U.S.C.A.

> Rutman Wine Co. v. E. & J. Gallo Winery, 829 F.2d 729.

C.A.10 (Colo.) 1995. Federal Rules of Civil Procedure erect powerful presumption against rejecting pleadings for failure to state a claim. Fed. Rules Civ. Proc. Rule 12(b)(6), 28 U.S.C.A.

> Maez v. Mountain States Tel. and Tel., Inc., 54 F.3d 1488.

C.A.10 (Colo.) 1994. Federal Rules of Civil Procedure erect powerful presumption against rejecting pleadings for failure to state claim upon which relief can be granted. Fed.Rules Civ.Proc.Rule 12(b)(6), 28 U.S.C.A.

> Brever v. Rockwell Intern. Corp., 40 F.3d 1119.

C.A.2 (Conn.) 1998. At stage in proceedings at which complaint is challenged for failure to state claim, issue is not whether a plaintiff is likely to prevail ultimately, but whether the claimant is entitled to offer evidence to support the claims; it may appear on the face of the pleading that a recovery is very remote and unlikely, but that is not the test. Fed.Rules Civ.Proc.Rule 12(b)(6), 28 U.S.C.A.

> Chance v. Armstrong, 143 F.3d 698.

C.A.11 (Fla.) 1989. Federal court was not bound by state court determination that certain claims did not state a cause of action under federal law.

> Floyd v. Eastern Airlines, Inc., 872 F.2d 1462, certiorari granted 110 S.Ct. 2585, 496 U.S. 904, 110 L.Ed.2d 266, reversed 111 S.Ct. 1489, 499 U.S. 530, 113 L.Ed.2d 569, on remand 937 F.2d 1555.

C.A.11 (Ga.) 1985. Although dismissal of a case for failure to comply with the pleading rules is a severe sanction, its imposition is justified when a party chooses to disregard the sound and proper directions of the district court. Fed.Rules Civ.Proc.Rule 12(b)(6), 28 U.S.C.A.

> Friedlander v. Nims, 755 F.2d 810.

C.A.7 (Ill.) 1994. Dismissal for failure to state claim is likely to be granted only where complaint shows some bar to relief on its face, or where complaint's allegations indicate existence of an affirmative defense.

> Sidney S. Arst Co. v. Pipefitters Welfare Educ. Fund, 25 F.3d 417.

C.A.7 (Ill.) 1993. Complaint may not be dismissed unless plaintiff can prove no set of facts that would allow for recovery. Fed.Rules Civ.Proc.Rule 12(b)(6), 28 U.S.C.A.

> Mid America Title Co. v. Kirk, 991 F.2d 417, rehearing denied, certiorari denied 114 S.Ct. 346, 510 U.S. 932, 126 L.Ed.2d 310, on remand 867 F.Supp. 673, affirmed 59 F.3d 719, certiorari denied 116 S.Ct. 520, 516 U.S. 990, 133 L.Ed.2d 428.

C.A.7 (Ill.) 1992. Plaintiff is free, in defending against motion to dismiss, to allege without evidentiary support any facts he pleases that are consistent with complaint, in order to show that there is state of facts within scope of complaint that if proved at trial would entitle him to judgment, and plaintiff does not have to plead those facts.

> Early v. Bankers Life and Cas. Co., 959 F.2d 75.

C.A.7 (Ill.) 1988. District court's dismissal of complaint for failure to state claim upon which relief could be granted, without first considering whether action could be properly brought as class action, was improper. Fed. Rules Civ.Proc.Rules 12(b)(6), 23(c)(1), 28 U.S.C.A.

> Rutan v. Republican Party of Illinois, 848 F.2d 1396, rehearing granted, on rehearing 868 F.2d 943, certiorari granted 110 S.Ct. 48, 493 U.S. 807, 107 L.Ed.2d 17, affirmed in part, reversed in part 110 S.Ct. 2729, 497 U.S. 62, 111 L.Ed.2d 52, rehearing denied 111 S.Ct. 13, 497 U.S. 1050, 111 L.Ed.2d 828, rehearing denied Frech v. Rutan, 111 S.Ct. 13, 497 U.S. 1050, 111 L.Ed.2d 828, on remand 916 F.2d 715.

C.A.7 (Ind.) 1992. While lack of intimation of any facts underlying claim will justify dismissal, Court of Appeals must construe pleadings liberally, and mere vagueness or lack of detail is inadequate basis for granting motion to dismiss.

> McMath v. City of Gary, Ind., 976 F.2d 1026, rehearing denied.

C.A.5 (La.) 1995. Motion to dismiss action for failure to state claim admits facts alleged in complaint, but challenges plaintiff's right to relief based upon those facts. Fed.Rules Civ.Proc.Rule 12(b)(6), 28 U.S.C.A.

> Crowe v. Henry, 43 F.3d 198, rehearing denied, appeal after remand 115 F.3d 294, appeal after remand 141 F.3d 1165.

C.A.5 (La.) 1992. In order to avoid dismissal for failure to state claim, plaintiff must plead specific facts, not mere conclusory allegations; conclusory allegations and unwarranted deductions of fact are not admitted as true by motion to dismiss.

> Guidry v. Bank of LaPlace, 954 F.2d 278.

C.A.4 (Md.) 1989. Conclusory allegations that are supported by pleaded facts should survive motion to dismiss for failure to state claim, even if actual assertions are equally consistent with contrary conclusion. Fed.Rules Civ.Proc.Rule 12(b)(6), 28 U.S.C.A.

> Revene v. Charles County Com'rs, 882 F.2d 870.

C.A.6 (Mich.) 1993. To survive motion to dismiss for failure to state claim, complaint need only give fair notice of what plaintiff's claim is and grounds upon which it rests. Fed.Rules Civ.Proc.Rule 12(b)(6), 28 U.S.C.A.

> In re DeLorean Motor Co., 991 F.2d 1236, rehearing denied.

C.A.5 (Miss.) 1989. Dismissal of complaint with prejudice for failure to state claim upon which relief could be granted was not abuse of discretion, where record did not contain any suggestion that plaintiff had new facts which might be alleged by amendment and plaintiff never tendered amended complaint or otherwise moved to amend. Fed.Rules Civ.Proc.Rule 15(a), 28 U.S.C.A.

> Mitchell v. Random House, Inc., 865 F.2d 664.

C.A.8 (Mo.) 1989. Dismissal of complaint for either lack of subject matter jurisdiction or for failure to state claim upon which relief can be granted is on pleadings and should be granted sparingly and with caution. Fed.Rules Civ.Proc.Rules 12(b)(1, 6), 56, 28 U.S.C.A.

> Huelsman v. Civic Center Corp., 873 F.2d 1171.

C.A.8 (Mo.) 1982. Miener v. State of Mo., 673 F.2d 969, certiorari denied 103 S.Ct. 215, 459 U.S. 909, 74 L.Ed.2d 171, certiorari denied Special School District of St. Louis County, Missouri v. Miener By & Through Miener, 103 S.Ct. 230, 459 U.S. 916, 74 L.Ed.2d 182, on remand 580 F.Supp. 562, opinion supplemented 607 F.Supp. 1425, affirmed in part, reversed in part 800 F.2d 749.

C.A.8 (Mo.) 1964. Highland Supply Corp. v. Reynolds Metals Co., 327 F.2d 725, on remand 238 F.Supp. 561, on reconsideration 245 F.Supp. 510.

C.A.1 (N.H.) 1993. District court has power to dismiss complaint when plaintiff fails to comply with Federal Rules of Civil Procedure, including "short and plain statement" requirement of rule governing pleading. Fed.Rules Civ.Proc.Rule 8(a)(2), 28 U.S.C.A.

> Kuehl v. F.D.I.C., 8 F.3d 905, rehearing denied, certiorari denied 114 S.Ct. 1545, 511 U.S. 1034, 128 L.Ed.2d 196.

C.A.3 (N.J.) 1996. In considering motion to dismiss for failure to state claim, court does not inquire whether plaintiffs will ultimately prevail, only whether they are entitled to offer evidence to support their claims. Fed.Rules Civ.Proc.Rule 12(b)(6), 28 U.S.C.A.

> Nami v. Fauver, 82 F.3d 63.

C.A.2 (N.Y.) 1997. In determining sufficiency of complaint, issue is not whether plaintiff will or might ultimately prevail on her claim, but whether plaintiff is entitled to offer evidence in support of allegations in complaint. Fed.Rules Civ.Proc.Rule 12(b)(6), 28 U.S.C.A.

> Hamilton Chapter of Alpha Delta Phi, Inc. v. Hamilton College, 128 F.3d 59.

C.A.2 (N.Y.) 1995. Complaint should not be dismissed simply because plaintiff is unlikely to succeed on the merits. Fed.Rules Civ.Proc.Rule 12(b)(6), 28 U.S.C.A.

> Baker v. Cuomo, 58 F.3d 814, rehearing denied, rehearing granted in part 67 F.3d 39, certiorari denied Pataki v. Baker, 116 S.Ct. 488, 516 U.S. 980, 133 L.Ed.2d 415, vacated in part on rehearing en banc 85 F.3d 919.

Dismissals for failure to state a claim are especially disfavored in cases where complaint sets forth novel legal theory that can best be assessed after factual development. Fed.Rules Civ.Proc.Rule 12(b)(6), 28 U.S.C.A.

> Baker v. Cuomo, 58 F.3d 814, rehearing denied, rehearing granted in part 67 F.3d 39, certiorari denied Pataki v. Baker, 116 S.Ct. 488, 516 U.S. 980, 133 L.Ed.2d 415, vacated in part on rehearing en banc 85 F.3d 919.

C.A.2 (N.Y.) 1993. When Court of Appeals reviews grant of motion to dismiss for failure to state claim upon which relief can be granted, it accepts as true factual allegations of complaint, and draws all inferences in favor of pleader; dismissal is proper where plaintiff cannot recover on facts he has alleged. Fed.Rules Civ.Proc.Rule 12(b)(6), 28 U.S.C.A.

> Mills v. Polar Molecular Corp., 12 F.3d 1170.

C.A.2 (N.Y.) 1993. On motion to dismiss for failure to state a claim, proper test is whether complaint states any valid ground for relief. Fed.Rules Civ.Proc.Rule 12(b)(6), 28 U.S.C.A.

Ferran v. Town of Nassau, 11 F.3d 21, certiorari denied 115 S.Ct. 572, 513 U.S. 1014, 130 L.Ed.2d 489, rehearing denied 115 S.Ct. 925, 513 U.S. 1121, 130 L.Ed.2d 804.

C.A.2 (N.Y.) 1989. When preanswer motion to dismiss is brought based on statute of limitations defense, such a motion is properly treated as motion to dismiss for failure to state cause of action, rather than motion to dismiss for lack of jurisdiction over subject matter. Fed.Rules Civ.Proc.Rule 12(b), (b)(1, 6), 28 U.S.C.A.

Ghartey v. St. John's Queens Hosp., 869 F.2d 160, on remand 727 F.Supp. 795, reconsideration denied 745 F.Supp. 125.

C.A.2 (N.Y.) 1988. Dismissal of complaint for failure to comply with requirement that it be short and plain is usually reserved for those cases in which complaint is so confused, ambiguous, vague, or otherwise unintelligible that its true substance, if any, is well disguised. Fed. Rules Civ.Proc. Rule 8, 28 U.S.C.A.

Salahuddin v. Cuomo, 861 F.2d 40.

C.A.4 (N.C.) 1975. Hospital Bldg. Co. v. Trustees of Rex Hosp., 511 F.2d 678, certiorari granted 96 S.Ct. 33, 423 U.S. 820, 46 L.Ed.2d 37, reversed 96 S.Ct. 1848, 425 U.S. 738, 48 L.Ed.2d 338, appeal after remand 691 F.2d 678, 71 A.L.R. Fed. 704, certiorari denied 104 S.Ct. 231, 464 U.S. 890, 78 L.Ed.2d 224, certiorari denied 104 S.Ct. 259, 464 U.S. 904, 78 L.Ed.2d 244, rehearing denied 104 S.Ct. 512, 464 U.S. 1003, 78 L.Ed.2d 700, appeal after remand 791 F.2d 288.

C.A.6 (Ohio) 1996. Standard for dismissals for failure to state claim on which relief can be granted is quite liberal. Fed.Rules Civ.Proc. Rule 12(b)(6), 28 U.S.C.A.

Collyer v. Darling, 98 F.3d 211, rehearing and suggestion for rehearing denied, certiorari denied 117 S.Ct. 2439, 138 L.Ed.2d 199.

C.A.3 (Pa.) 1997. In reviewing grant of motion to dismiss for failure to state claim, issue is not whether plaintiff will ultimately prevail but whether claimant is entitled to offer evidence to support claims. Fed.Rules Civ. Proc.Rule 12(b)(6), 28 U.S.C.A.

Lake v. Arnold, 112 F.3d 682, as amended.

C.A.3 (Pa.) 1993. Motion to dismiss for failure to state claim tests sufficiency of allegations contained in complaint. Fed.Rules Civ. Proc.Rule 12(b)(6), 28 U.S.C.A.

Kost v. Kozakiewicz, 1 F.3d 176.

In ruling on motion to dismiss for failure to state claim, question is whether facts alleged in

complaint, even if true, fail to support claim. Fed.Rules Civ.Proc.Rule 12(b)(6), 28 U.S.C.A.

Kost v. Kozakiewicz, 1 F.3d 176.

C.A.3 (Pa.) 1991. Challenges to jurisdiction for failure to state claim ordinarily should be made under Rule 12(b)(6) and not under Rule 12(b)(1) allowing dismissal for lack of subject matter jurisdiction. Fed.Rules Civ.Proc. Rule 12(b)(1, 6), 28 U.S.C.A.

Kehr Packages, Inc. v. Fidelcor, Inc., 926 F.2d 1406, rehearing denied, certiorari denied 111 S.Ct. 2839, 501 U.S. 1222, 115 L.Ed.2d 1007.

C.A.4 (S.C.) 1989. Motion to dismiss for failure to state claim upon which relief can be granted should be granted only in very limited circumstances. Fed.Rules Civ.Proc.Rule 12(b)(6), 28 U.S.C.A.

Rogers v. Jefferson-Pilot Life Ins. Co., 883 F.2d 324.

C.A.6 (Tenn.) 1994. "Facial attack," in connection with motion to dismiss for lack of subject matter jurisdiction, is challenge to sufficiency of pleading itself. Fed.Rules Civ.Proc. Rule 12(b)(1), 28 U.S.C.A.

U.S. v. Ritchie, 15 F.3d 592, rehearing and suggestion for rehearing denied, certiorari denied 115 S.Ct. 188, 513 U.S. 868, 130 L.Ed.2d 121.

C.A.5 (Tex.) 1997. Motion to dismiss complaint for failure to state claim is viewed with disfavor and is rarely granted. Fed.Rules Civ. Proc.Rule 12(b)(6), 28 U.S.C.A.

Lowrey v. Texas A & M University System, 117 F.3d 242, on remand 11 F.Supp.2d 895.

C.A.5 (Tex.) 1996. After trial on merits, sufficiency of allegations in complaint is irrelevant.

Bennett v. Pippin, 74 F.3d 578, rehearing denied, certiorari denied 117 S.Ct. 68, 136 L.Ed.2d 29, rehearing denied 117 S.Ct. 541, 136 L.Ed.2d 425.

C.A.5 (Tex.) 1994. To avoid dismissal for failure to state a claim, plaintiff must plead specific facts, not mere conclusory allegations. Fed.Rules Civ.Proc.Rule 12(b)(6), 28 U.S.C.A.

Tuchman v. DSC Communications Corp., 14 F.3d 1061, rehearing and rehearing denied 20 F.3d 1172.

C.A.5 (Tex.) 1991. Failure adequately to allege basis for diversity jurisdiction mandates dismissal.

Stafford v. Mobil Oil Corp., 945 F.2d 803.

C.A.5 (Tex.) 1991. Motion to dismiss for lack of subject matter jurisdiction may be decided by district court on one of three bases: complaint alone, complaint as supplemented by undisputed facts in record, or complaint as supplemented both by undisputed facts in record and by district court's resolution of disputed facts. Fed.Rules Civ.Proc.Rule 12(b)(1), 28 U.S.C.A.

> Ynclan v. Department of Air Force, 943 F.2d 1388.

C.A.10 (Utah) 1996. Granting motion to dismiss for failure to state cause of action must be cautiously studied, not only to effectuate spirit of liberal rules of pleading but also to protect interests of justice. Fed.Rules Civ.Proc. Rule 12(b)(6), 28 U.S.C.A.

> Pelt v. State of Utah, 104 F.3d 1534.

C.A.4 (Va.) 1992. In considering propriety of motion to dismiss for failure to state claim, standard of review is whether complaint, accepting allegations as true, allows recovery. Fed.Rules Civ.Proc.Rule 12(b)(6), 28 U.S.C.A.

> Waterford Citizens' Ass'n v. Reilly, 970 F.2d 1287.

C.A.7 (Wis.) 1992. All complaint need do to withstand motion to dismiss for failure to state claim is "outline or adumbrate" violation of statute or constitutional provision upon which plaintiff relies, and connect violation to named defendants; happenstance that complaint is "conclusory" does not automatically condemn it. Fed.Rules Civ.Proc.Rule 8, 28 U.S.C.A.

> Brownlee v. Conine, 957 F.2d 353.

C.A.7 (Wis.) 1989. When issues are complex and facts are uncertain, case should be tried before court applies public policy considerations to determination of whether cause of action can be maintained under Wisconsin law.

> Misany v. U.S., 873 F.2d 160.

M.D.Ala. 1996. A motion to dismiss for failure to state a claim questions legal sufficiency of a complaint; therefore, in assessing merit of motion, district court must assume that all factual allegations set forth in complaint are true. Fed.Rules Civ.Proc.Rule 12(b)(6), 28 U.S.C.A.

> Mays v. U.S. Postal Service, 928 F.Supp. 1552, affirmed 122 F.3d 43.

M.D.Ala. 1996. Motion to dismiss for failure to state claim questions legal sufficiency of complaint. Fed.Rules Civ.Proc.Rule 12(b)(6), 28 U.S.C.A.

> Nabors v. Transouth Financial Corp., 928 F.Supp. 1085.

M.D.Ala. 1996. Motion to dismiss for failure to state claim upon which relief may be granted questions legal sufficiency of complaint; in assessing merit of motion, court must assume that all factual allegations set forth in complaint are true. Fed.Rules Civ.Proc.Rule 12(b)(6), 28 U.S.C.A.

> Lynn v. United Technologies Corp., Inc., 916 F.Supp. 1217.

M.D.Ala. 1995. In considering whether plaintiff's complaint, and each count thereof, fails to state claim upon which relief can be granted, trial court looks not to whether plaintiff may ultimately prevail on merits, but to whether allegations are sufficient to allow plaintiff to conduct discovery in an attempt to prove its allegations. Fed.Rules Civ.Proc.Rule 12(b)(6), 28 U.S.C.A.

> Missildine v. City of Montgomery, 907 F.Supp. 1501.

M.D.Ala. 1995. Motion to dismiss for failure to state claim questions legal sufficiency of complaint and therefore, in assessing merit of such motion, court must assume that all factual allegations set forth in complaint are true and court must construe all factual allegations in light most favorable to plaintiff. Fed.Rules Civ. Proc.Rule 12(b)(6), 28 U.S.C.A.

> Douglas v. Evans, 888 F.Supp. 1536.

M.D.Ala. 1995. Threshold that complaint must meet to survive motion to dismiss for failure to state claim is exceedingly low. Fed. Rules Civ.Proc.Rule 12, 28 U.S.C.A.

> Lewis v. Board of Trustees of Alabama State University, 874 F.Supp. 1299.

M.D.Ala. 1995. Threshold that complaint must meet to survive motion to dismiss is exceedingly low. Fed.Rules Civ.Proc.Rule 12, 28 U.S.C.A.

> Bahadirli v. Domino's Pizza, 873 F.Supp. 1528.

M.D.Ala. 1994. Threshold that complaint must meet to survive motion to dismiss for failure to state a claim is exceedingly low. Fed.Rules Civ.Proc.Rule 12(b)(6), 28 U.S.C.A.

> Malone v. Chambers County Bd. of Com'rs, 875 F.Supp. 773, reconsideration denied.

M.D.Ala. 1994. Threshold that complaint must meet to survive motion to dismiss for failure to state claim is exceedingly low.

> Harrelson v. Elmore County, Ala., 859 F.Supp. 1465.

M.D.Ala. 1994. "Factual attack" on complaint, on motion to dismiss for lack of subject matter jurisdiction, challenges existence of subject matter jurisdiction in fact, irrespective of pleading, and, thus, matters outside pleading may be considered and district court may hear conflicting evidence and decide for itself the factual issues that determine jurisdiction. Fed. Rules Civ.Proc.Rule 12(b)(1), 28 U.S.C.A.

> Hayden v. Blue Cross and Blue Shield of Alabama, 855 F.Supp. 344.

D.Ariz. 1990. Court will not dismiss complaint merely because plaintiff's allegations do not support particular legal theory advanced, as court is under duty to examine complaint to determine if allegations provide basis for relief under any possible theory. Fed.Rules Civ.Proc. Rule 12(b)(6), 28 U.S.C.A.

    Espinoza v. Fry's Food Stores of Arizona, Inc., 806 F.Supp. 855.

E.D.Ark. 1996. Motion to dismiss for failure to state claim is not a device for testing the truth of what is asserted or for determining whether plaintiff has any evidence to back up what is in the complaint. Fed.Rules Civ.Proc. Rule 12(b)(6), 28 U.S.C.A.

    Hicks v. Brown, 929 F.Supp. 1184.

On motion to dismiss, issue is not whether plaintiff will ultimately prevail, but whether plaintiff is entitled to offer evidence to support her claims, irrespective of judge's disbelief of complaint's factual allegations or judge's belief that plaintiff cannot prove what complaint asserts. Fed.Rules Civ.Proc.Rule 12(b)(6), 28 U.S.C.A.

    Hicks v. Brown, 929 F.Supp. 1184.

C.D.Cal. 1997. Issue on motion to dismiss for failure to state claim is not whether claimant will ultimately prevail but whether claimant is entitled to offer evidence to support claims asserted. Fed.Rules Civ.Proc.Rule 12(b)(6), 28 U.S.C.A.

    National Coalition Government of Union of Burma v. Unocal, Inc., 176 F.R.D. 329.

C.D.Cal. 1996. On motion to dismiss for failure to state claim, issue is not whether plaintiff will ultimately prevail, but whether plaintiff is entitled to offer evidence in support of his claim. Fed.Rules Civ.Proc.Rule 12(b)(6), 28 U.S.C.A.

    Remington Investments, Inc. v. Kadenacy, 930 F.Supp. 446.

C.D.Cal. 1996. Motion to dismiss for failure to state claim tests legal sufficiency of claims asserted in complaint. Fed.Rules Civ. Proc.Rule 12(b)(6), 28 U.S.C.A.

    Bureerong v. Uvawas, 922 F.Supp. 1450.

Motion to dismiss for failure to state claim must be read in conjunction with federal rule requiring short and plain statement of the claim showing that pleader is entitled to relief. Fed. Rules Civ.Proc.Rules 8(a), 12(b)(6), 28 U.S.C.A.

    Bureerong v. Uvawas, 922 F.Supp. 1450.

C.D.Cal. 1994. Dismissal for failure to state a claim upon which relief can be granted is proper only in extraordinary cases. Fed. Rules Civ.Proc.Rule 12(b)(6), 28 U.S.C.A.

    Trenton v. Infinity Broadcasting Corp., 865 F.Supp. 1416.

N.D.Cal. 1996. In analyzing whether to grant motion to dismiss complaint for failure to state claim, court should keep in mind that dismissal is disfavored and should be granted only in extraordinary cases. Fed.Rules Civ. Proc.Rule 12(b)(6), 28 U.S.C.A.

    Informix Software, Inc. v. Oracle Corp., 927 F.Supp. 1283.

N.D.Cal. 1995. Dismissals for failure to state claim are reviewed de novo by appellate court, and are appropriate only in extraordinary cases. Fed.Rules Civ.Proc.Rule 12(b)(6), 28 U.S.C.A.

    Don King Productions/Kingvision v. Lovato, 911 F.Supp. 419.

N.D.Cal. 1994. Motion to dismiss for failure to state a claim is appropriate vehicle for challenging whether particular cause of action may be asserted by a particular category of plaintiff over a particular type of alleged harm, and dismissal should be granted where claim in question is one that, as matter of law, may not be asserted by the category of plaintiff at issue with respect to the type of harm alleged. Fed. Rules Civ.Proc.Rule 12(b)(6), 28 U.S.C.A.

    Arnold v. United Artists Theatre Circuit, Inc., 866 F.Supp. 433.

N.D.Cal. 1994. In ruling on motion to dismiss for failure to state claim, even if face of pleadings indicates that chance of recovery is remote, district court must allow plaintiff to develop his case at that stage of proceedings. Fed.Rules Civ.Proc.Rule 12(b)(6), 28 U.S.C.A.

    Independent Cellular Telephone, Inc. v. Daniels & Associates, 863 F.Supp. 1109.

N.D.Cal. 1994. In suit challenging alleged violation of federal statute, generally finding of no statutory violation results in dismissal for failure to state a claim rather than for lack of jurisdiction. Fed.Rules Civ.Proc.Rule 12(b)(1, 6), 28 U.S.C.A.

    Citizens for a Better Environment-California v. Union Oil Co. of California, 861 F.Supp. 889, affirmed 83 F.3d 1111, as amended, certiorari denied 117 S.Ct. 789, 136 L.Ed.2d 731.

N.D.Cal. 1994. Claim should not be dismissed unless it is certain that the law would not permit the requested relief even if all allegations in complaint were proven true.

    In re Syntex Corp. Securities Litigation, 855 F.Supp. 1086, affirmed 95 F.3d 922.

N.D.Cal. 1992. Complaint may be dismissed as matter of law for two reasons: lack of cognizable legal theory, or insufficient facts under cognizable theory. Fed.Rules Civ.Proc.Rule 12(b)(6), 28 U.S.C.A.

    Kentucky Cent. Life Ins. Co. v. LeDuc, 814 F.Supp. 832.

N.D.Cal. 1992. A complaint may be dismissed as matter of law for lacking a cognizable legal theory or insufficient facts under a cognizable theory. Fed.Rules Civ.Proc.Rule 12(b)(6), 28 U.S.C.A.

> In re Verifone Securities Litigation, 784 F.Supp. 1471, affirmed 11 F.3d 865.

N.D.Cal. 1992. Motions to dismiss for failure to state a claim are generally viewed with disfavor. Fed.Rules Civ.Proc.Rule 12(b)(6), 28 U.S.C.A.

> Singh v. Ilchert, 784 F.Supp. 759.

Question presented by motion to dismiss for failure to state a claim is not whether plaintiff will prevail in the action, but whether plaintiff is entitled to offer evidence in support of his claim. Fed.Rules Civ.Proc.Rule 12(b)(6), 28 U.S.C.A.

> Singh v. Ilchert, 784 F.Supp. 759.

N.D.Cal. 1991. While conclusory allegations unsupported by any specific facts are not sufficient under pleading rule, plaintiffs are not required to plead all their evidence in order to avoid dismissal for failure to state a claim; claim will be sufficiently pled where it provides fair notice of nature of claim and facts which underlie claim. Fed.Rules Civ.Proc.Rules 8, 8(a), (a)(2), 12, 28 U.S.C.A.

> Grid Systems Corp. v. Texas Instruments Inc., 771 F.Supp. 1033.

N.D.Cal. 1987. Failure to join a party is not a ground on which to dismiss a case for failure to state cause of action. Fed.Rules Civ. Proc.Rules 12, 19, 28 U.S.C.A.

> Northern California Dist. Council of Laborers v. Strauss Const. Co., Inc., 672 F.Supp. 430, affirmed 897 F.2d 533, rehearing denied.

S.D.Cal. 1993. Dismissal for failure to state claim upon which relief can be granted is proper only in extraordinary cases in which plaintiff's complaint lacks cognizable legal theory or sufficient facts to support cognizable legal theory. Fed.Rules Civ.Proc.Rule 12(b)(6), 28 U.S.C.A.

> Gen-Probe Inc. v. Center for Neurologic Study, 853 F.Supp. 1215.

D.Colo. 1997. Federal Rules of Civil Procedure create a strong presumption against rejecting pleadings for failure to state a claim. Fed.Rules Civ.Proc.Rule 12(b)(6), 28 U.S.C.A.

> Jefferson County School Dist. No. R-1 v. Moody's Investor's Services, Inc., 988 F.Supp. 1341.

D.Colo. 1996. Granting defendant's motion to dismiss is harsh remedy which must be cautiously studied, not only to effectuate spirit of liberal rules of pleading but also to protect interests of justice. Fed.Rules Civ.Proc.Rule 12(b)(6), 28 U.S.C.A.

> Adams v. Cyprus Amax Mineral Co., 927 F.Supp. 1407.

D.Colo. 1994. If plaintiff has pled facts that would support legally cognizable claim for relief, motion to dismiss for failure to state claim upon which relief can be granted should be denied. Fed.Rules Civ.Proc.Rule 12(b)(6), 28 U.S.C.A.

> West Pines Psychiatric Hosp. v. Samsonite Ben. Plan, 848 F.Supp. 907.

D.Colo. 1992. A motion to dismiss for failure to state a claim tests formal sufficiency of complaint and is limited to the four corners of that pleading. Fed.Rules Civ.Proc.Rule 12(b)(6), 28 U.S.C.A.

> American Cas. Co. v. Glaskin, 805 F.Supp. 866.

D.Colo. 1991. Courts should not dismiss cause of action for failure to state claim upon which relief can be granted unless court determines that beyond doubt, plaintiff can prove no set of facts that would entitle it to relief. Fed. Rules Civ.Proc.Rule 12(b)(6), 28 U.S.C.A.

> Federal Deposit Ins. Corp. v. Wise, 758 F.Supp. 1414.

So long as plaintiff offers evidence in support of legally recognized claim for relief, motion to dismiss must be denied. Fed.Rules Civ. Proc.Rule 12(b)(6), 28 U.S.C.A.

> Federal Deposit Ins. Corp. v. Wise, 758 F.Supp. 1414.

D.Conn. 1996. On motion to dismiss, issue is not whether plaintiff will prevail, but whether he or she should be afforded opportunity to offer evidence to prove his or her claims.

> Harvey v. Harvey, 931 F.Supp. 127, affirmed 108 F.3d 329.

D.Conn. 1996. Issue on motion to dismiss is not whether plaintiff will prevail, but whether he is entitled to offer evidence to support his claims. Fed.Rules Civ.Proc.Rule 12(b)(6), 28 U.S.C.A.

> Williams v. Hoffman/New Yorker, Inc., 923 F.Supp. 350.

D.Conn. 1995. Motion to dismiss for failure to state claim merely assesses legal feasibility of complaint, and does not assay weight of evidence which might be brought in support thereof. Fed.Rules Civ.Proc.Rule 12(b)(6), 28 U.S.C.A.

> Venclauskas v. State of Conn., Dept. of Public Safety, Div. of State Police, 921 F.Supp. 78.

In determining whether to dismiss complaint for failure to state claim, court must determine whether plaintiff has stated claim upon which relief may be granted. Fed.Rules Civ.Proc.Rule 12(b)(6), 28 U.S.C.A.

> Venclauskas v. State of Conn., Dept. of Public Safety, Div. of State Police, 921 F.Supp. 78.

D.Conn. 1995. Motion to dismiss for failure to state claim upon which relief can be granted merely assesses legal feasibility of complaint, and does not assay weight of evidence which might be offered in support thereof. Fed.Rules Civ.Proc.Rule 12(b)(6), 28 U.S.C.A.

> Gorman v. Hughes Danbury Optical Systems, 908 F.Supp. 107.

D.Conn. 1992. Motion to dismiss for failure to state a claim upon which relief can be granted must be decided solely on facts alleged, and should be granted only where no set of facts consistent with allegations could be proven; issue is not whether plaintiff will prevail, but whether he should be afforded opportunity to prove his claims.

> DeSalle v. A.G. Edwards & Sons, Inc., 804 F.Supp. 436.

D.Conn. 1990. Motion to state a claim must be decided solely on the facts alleged and should be granted only where no set of facts consistent with allegations could be proven which would entitle plaintiffs to relief. Fed.Rules Civ.Proc.Rule 12(b)(6), 28 U.S.C.A.

> National Union Fire Ins. Co. of Pittsburgh, Pa. v. Mastroni, 754 F.Supp. 269.

D.Del. 1998. The purpose of analysis under rule governing motions to dismiss for failure to state a claim is to determine not whether a plaintiff will ultimately prevail but whether the plaintiff is entitled to offer evidence to support the claim. Fed.Rules Civ.Proc.Rule 12(b)(6), 28 U.S.C.A.

> Parker v. State of Del., Dept. of Public Safety, 11 F.Supp.2d 467.

D.Del. 1991. Standard for deciding motion to dismiss for failure to state a claim is whether, taking all factual allegations in complaint as true, complaint states claim which would entitle plaintiff to relief. Fed.Rules Civ. Proc.Rule 12(b)(6), 28 U.S.C.A.

> Manchester v. Rzewnicki, 777 F.Supp. 319, affirmed 958 F.2d 364.

D.Del. 1988. To warrant dismissal for failure to allege jurisdictional amount, court must find plaintiffs incapable, to legal certainty, of recovering jurisdictional amount. 28 U.S.C.A. § 1332.

> Anderson v. Beneficial Mortg. Corp., 699 F.Supp. 1075.

D.D.C. 1992. For purposes of motion to dismiss for failure to state claim, dismissal is appropriate in cases in which plaintiff includes allegations that show on face of complaint that there is some insuperable bar to relief. Fed. Rules Civ.Proc.Rule 12(b)(6), 28 U.S.C.A.

> Tobey v. N.L.R.B., 807 F.Supp. 798, affirmed 40 F.3d 469, 309 U.S.App.D.C. 213.

D.D.C. 1992. While court is under duty, on motion to dismiss for failure to state a claim, to examine complaint to determine if allegations provide for relief on any possible theory, as a practical matter, dismissal is appropriate in cases in which plaintiff includes allegations that show on the face of the complaint that there is some insuperable bar to relief. Fed.Rules Civ. Proc.Rule 12(b)(6), 28 U.S.C.A.

> Franklin Asaph Ltd. Partnership v. F.D.I.C., 794 F.Supp. 402.

D.D.C. 1992. Complaint will not be dismissed for failure to state a claim merely because it does not allege with specificity every element of a cause of action, if it contains allegations from which an inference may be drawn that evidence on the essential elements will be produced.

> Johns v. Rozet, 141 F.R.D. 211.

M.D.Fla. 1996. Standard on motion to dismiss for failure to state claim is not whether plaintiff will ultimately prevail in his theories, but whether allegations are sufficient to allow them to conduct discovery in attempt to prove allegations. Fed.Rules Civ.Proc.Rule 12(b)(6), 28 U.S.C.A.

> Harris v. Iorio, 922 F.Supp. 588, affirmed 136 F.3d 139.

M.D.Fla. 1994. In deciding a motion to dismiss, district court must consider legal sufficiency of complaint, not weight of evidence which might be offered at trial. Fed.Rules Civ.Proc.Rule 12(b), 28 U.S.C.A.

> Sawinski v. Bill Currie Ford, Inc., 866 F.Supp. 1383.

M.D.Fla. 1994. Dismissal is warranted where it does not appear from allegations of complaint that cause of action exists. Fed. Rules Civ.Proc.Rule 12(b)(6), 28 U.S.C.A.

> Eidson v. Arenas, 155 F.R.D. 215.

M.D.Fla. 1993. For purposes of determining sufficiency of claim, likelihood of recovery is irrelevant; what is at issue is whether plaintiff is entitled to offer evidence to support claims.

> Morris v. Crow, 817 F.Supp. 102.

S.D.Fla. 1998. In ruling on a motion to dismiss for failure to state a claim, all facts stated in the complaint are accepted as true, factual issues are to be resolved in favor of the plaintiff, and the prospect of recovery is irrelevant. Fed.Rules Civ.Proc.Rule 12(b)(6), 28 U.S.C.A.

> Miccosukee Tribe of Indians of Florida v. U.S., 6 F.Supp.2d 1346.

S.D.Fla. 1998. Motion to dismiss merely tests the sufficiency of the complaint; it does not decide the merits of the case. Fed.Rules Civ. Proc.Rule 12, 28 U.S.C.A.

> Smith Barney, Inc. v. Scanlon, 180 F.R.D. 444.

S.D.Fla. 1996. In evaluation of sufficiency of claim on motion to dismiss, the prospect of recovery is irrelevant. Fed.Rules Civ.Proc.Rule 12(b)(6), 28 U.S.C.A.

> Tevini v. CHC Intern., Inc., 946 F.Supp. 985.

S.D.Fla. 1996. On motion to dismiss, issue is not whether plaintiff will ultimately prevail, but whether plaintiff is entitled to offer evidence to support the claims.

> Betancourt v. Marine Cargo Management, Inc., 930 F.Supp. 606.

S.D.Fla. 1996. Issue on motion to dismiss for failure to state claim is not whether plaintiff will ultimately prevail, but whether claimant is entitled to offer evidence to support claims.

> Sonnenreich v. Philip Morris Inc., 929 F.Supp. 416.

S.D.Fla. 1996. Motion to dismiss for failure to state a claim is viewed with disfavor and rarely granted. Fed.Rules Civ.Proc.Rule 12(b)(6), 28 U.S.C.A.

> Vernon v. Medical Management Associates of Margate, Inc., 912 F.Supp. 1549.

S.D.Fla. 1995. On motion to dismiss for failure to state a claim, issue is not whether plaintiff will ultimately prevail, but whether plaintiff is entitled to offer evidence to support the claims.

> Harvey M. Jasper Retirement Trust v. Ivax Corp., 920 F.Supp. 1260.

S.D.Fla. 1995. Motions to dismiss for failure to state claim are generally viewed with disfavor and rarely granted. Fed.Rules Civ. Proc.Rule 12(b)(6), 28 U.S.C.A.

> Klaskala v. U.S. Dept. of Health and Human Services, 889 F.Supp. 480.

S.D.Fla. 1994. Preanswer motions, such as motion to dismiss for failure to state claim or motion for more definite statement, may raise two distinct issues: whether plaintiff has stated his purported claim with sufficient detail and whether claim as stated is recognized by law.

> Bunger v. Hartman, 851 F.Supp. 461.

S.D.Fla. 1992. Dismissal is proper where complaint fails to state claim upon which relief can be granted; however, court is confined to review of pleadings, must accept pleaded facts as true, and must resolve any factual issues in manner favorable to nonmoving party. Fed. Rules Civ.Proc.Rule 12(b)(6), 28 U.S.C.A.

> Colonial Penn Ins. Co. v. Value Rent-A-Car Inc., 814 F.Supp. 1084.

S.D.Fla. 1992. While pleading must be sufficient to give defendant fair notice of what claim is and grounds upon which it rests, pleader is not required to set forth in detail facts upon which claim is based. Fed.Rules Civ. Proc.Rule 8(a), 28 U.S.C.A.

> City of Miami Firefighters' and Police Officers' Retirement Trust v. Invesco MIM, Inc., 789 F.Supp. 392.

In ruling upon motion to dismiss at pleading stage, issue is not whether plaintiff will ultimately prevail, but whether claimant is entitled to offer evidence to support claims.

> City of Miami Firefighters' and Police Officers' Retirement Trust v. Invesco MIM, Inc., 789 F.Supp. 392.

S.D.Fla. 1990. What plaintiff must do in his complaint is to set forth sufficient facts and information to outline his claim or to permit appropriate inferences that may be drawn from claim. Fed.Rules Civ.Proc.Rules 8(a), 12(b)(6), 28 U.S.C.A.

> Linder v. Calero Portocarrero, 747 F.Supp. 1452, reversed 963 F.2d 332.

S.D.Fla. 1988. Motion to dismiss should not be granted unless plaintiff can prove no set of facts in support of his claim entitling him to relief.

> O'Connor v. Kawasaki Motors Corp., U.S.A., 699 F.Supp. 1538.

N.D.Ga. 1986. In considering motion to dismiss for failure to plead fraud with particularity, trial court must carefully consider whether goals of rule requiring pleading of fraud with particularity will be advanced. Fed.Rules Civ. Proc.Rule 9(b), 28 U.S.C.A.

> Antilles Trading Co., S.A. v. Scientific-Atlanta, Inc., 117 F.R.D. 447.

S.D.Ga. 1995. A motion to dismiss for failure to state a claim upon which relief can be granted attacks the legal sufficiency of the complaint. Fed.Rules Civ.Proc.Rule 12(b)(6), 28 U.S.C.A.

> McCoy v. Johnson Controls World Services, Inc., 878 F.Supp. 229.

D.Hawai'i 1997. In determining whether complaint should be dismissed for failure to state claim, the issue is not whether plaintiff's success on merits is likely, but rather whether plaintiff is entitled to proceed beyond the threshold in attempting to establish his or her claims. Fed.Rules Civ.Proc.Rule 12(b)(6), 28 U.S.C.A.

> Burns-Vidlak by Burns v. Chandler, 980 F.Supp. 1144.

D.Hawai'i 1995. On motion to dismiss for failure to state claim, issue is not whether plaintiff's success on merits is likely, but rather whether plaintiff is entitled to proceed beyond threshold in attempting to establish his claims; court must determine whether it appears to a certainty under existing law that no relief can be granted under any set of facts that might be proved in support of plaintiff's claims. Fed. Rules Civ.Proc.Rule 12(b)(6), 28 U.S.C.A.

> Moore v. Kamikawa, 940 F.Supp. 260, affirmed 82 F.3d 423.

D.Hawai'i 1989. Dismissal on pleadings is proper only if moving party is clearly entitled to prevail. Fed.Rules Civ.Proc.Rule 12(c), 28 U.S.C.A.

> Morishige v. Spencecliff Corp., 720 F.Supp. 829.

C.D.Ill. 1993. For purposes of motion to dismiss, complaint must contain either direct or inferential allegations respecting all material elements necessary to sustain recovery under some viable legal theory.

> Greenley v. Meersman, 838 F.Supp. 381.

C.D.Ill. 1992. Motion to dismiss is not granted unless it appears beyond doubt that plaintiff can prove no set of facts in support of his claim which would entitle him to relief.

> Gadson v. Newman, 807 F.Supp. 1412.

C.D.Ill. 1988. Count alleging multiplicity of claims was subject to dismissal with leave to replead claims in separate counts. Fed.Rules Civ.Proc.Rule 10(b), 28 U.S.C.A.

> H.L. Miller Mach. Tools, Inc. v. Acroloc Inc., 679 F.Supp. 823.

N.D.Ill. 1998. A motion to dismiss for failure to state a claim tests the sufficiency of the complaint, not the merits of the suit. Fed.Rules Civ.Proc.Rule 12(b)(6), 28 U.S.C.A.

> Native American Arts, Inc. v. J.C. Penney Co., Inc., 5 F.Supp.2d 599.

N.D.Ill. 1997. Defendant moving to dismiss complaint for failure to state claim must meet a high standard. Fed.Rules Civ.Proc.Rule 12(b)(6), 28 U.S.C.A.

> Cemail v. Viking Dodge, Inc., 982 F.Supp. 1296.

N.D.Ill. 1997. Motion to dismiss tests sufficiency of complaint, not merits of suit. Fed. Rules Civ.Proc.Rule 12(b)(6), 28 U.S.C.A.

> Ozkaya v. Telecheck Services, Inc., 982 F.Supp. 578.

N.D.Ill. 1997. Motion to dismiss tests sufficiency of complaint, not merits of suit. Fed. Rules Civ.Proc.Rule 12(b), 28 U.S.C.A.

> Sampson v. Federal Republic of Germany, 975 F.Supp. 1108.

N.D.Ill. 1997. Motion to dismiss tests sufficiency of complaint, not merits of suit.

> McCullough v. City of Chicago, 971 F.Supp. 1247.

N.D.Ill. 1997. Motion to dismiss for failure to state claim is based on sufficiency of complaint, not merits of the case. Fed.Rules Civ.Proc.Rule 12(b)(6), 28 U.S.C.A.

> Pelfresne v. Village of Rosemont, 952 F.Supp. 589, rehearing denied 174 F.R.D. 72.

N.D.Ill. 1996. Purpose of motion to dismiss for failure to state claim is to test legal sufficiency of complaint. Fed.Rules Civ.Proc. Rule 12(b)(6), 28 U.S.C.A.

> Herzog v. NBD Bank of Highland Park, 203 B.R. 80.

N.D.Ill. 1996. Purpose of a motion to dismiss for failure to state claim is to test formal sufficiency of statement of claim for relief; motion is not procedure for resolving contest about facts or merits of the case. Fed.Rules Civ.Proc. Rule 12(b)(6), 28 U.S.C.A.

> Stepan Co. v. Winter Panel Corp., 948 F.Supp. 802.

N.D.Ill. 1996. In response to motion to dismiss or for summary judgment, legal basis for claim must be identified. Fed.Rules Civ. Proc.Rules 12(b), 56(c), 28 U.S.C.A.

> Carpenter v. City of Northlake, 948 F.Supp. 759.

N.D.Ill. 1996. Motion to dismiss tests sufficiency of complaint, not merits of suit.

> Johnstone v. First Bank System, Inc., 947 F.Supp. 1220.

N.D.Ill. 1996. Civil procedure rule governing dismissal of complaint for failure to state a claim does not provide a procedure for resolving contests about facts or merits of case; rather, it allows defendants to test formal sufficiency of statements of claims for relief. Fed.Rules Civ.Proc.Rule 12(b)(6), 28 U.S.C.A.

> R & V Pine Tree, Inc. v. Village of Forest Park, 947 F.Supp. 342.

N.D.Ill. 1996. Motion to dismiss for failure to state claim does not provide a procedure for resolving contests about facts or merits of case; rather, it allows defendants to test formal sufficiency of statements of claims for relief. Fed.Rules Civ.Proc.Rule 12(b)(6), 28 U.S.C.A.

> Schoiber v. Emro Marketing Co., 941 F.Supp. 730.

N.D.Ill. 1996. Motion to dismiss for failure to state claim is based on sufficiency of complaint, not merits of case. Fed.Rules Civ. Proc.Rule 12(b)(6), 28 U.S.C.A.

> Chisholm v. Foothill Capital Corp., 940 F.Supp. 1273.

Motion to dismiss for failure to state claim should be read in context of liberal pleading requirements of rule governing claims for relief. Fed.Rules Civ.Proc.Rules 8(a), 12(b)(6), 28 U.S.C.A.

> Chisholm v. Foothill Capital Corp., 940 F.Supp. 1273.

N.D.Ill. 1996. Motion to dismiss for failure to state claim is not test of merits of claim, but rather test of whether plaintiff has properly stated claim. Fed.Rules Civ.Proc.Rule 12(b)(6), 28 U.S.C.A.

> McMurry v. Sheahan, 927 F.Supp. 1082.

N.D.Ill. 1996. Motion to dismiss for failure to state claim tests sufficiency of complaint, not merits of suit. Fed.Rules Civ.Proc.Rule 12(b)(6), 28 U.S.C.A.

> Milazzo v. O'Connell, 925 F.Supp. 1331, affirmed 108 F.3d 129, rehearing and suggestion for rehearing denied.

N.D.Ill. 1996. Motion to dismiss tests sufficiency of complaint, not merits of suit.

> Spiegel v. City of Chicago, 920 F.Supp. 891.

N.D.Ill. 1996. Although standards for dismissal are liberal, notice pleading standards do not allow plaintiffs, much less attorneys, to shoot first and ask questions later.

> Vakharia v. Little Co. of Mary Hosp. and Health Care Centers, 917 F.Supp. 1282.

Failure to follow rule requiring short and plain statement of claim may warrant dismissal. Fed.Rules Civ.Proc.Rule 8, 28 U.S.C.A.

> Vakharia v. Little Co. of Mary Hosp. and Health Care Centers, 917 F.Supp. 1282.

N.D.Ill. 1996. Motion to dismiss tests sufficiency of complaint, not merits of suit. Fed. Rules Civ.Proc.Rule 12(b)(6), 28 U.S.C.A.

> Allied Vision Group, Inc. v. RLI Professional Technologies, Inc., 916 F.Supp. 778.

N.D.Ill. 1995. Motion to dismiss for failure to state a claim tests sufficiency of complaint, not merits of suit. Fed.Rules Civ.Proc. Rule 12(b)(6), 28 U.S.C.A.

> Montgomery Ward & Co., Inc. v. Warehouse, Mail Order, Office, Technical and Professional Employees Union, 911 F.Supp. 1094.

N.D.Ill. 1995. Test for evaluating motion to dismiss for failure to state claim is whether, accepting all well-pleaded factual allegations as true and drawing all reasonable inferences in plaintiff's favor, relief could be granted if plaintiff was able to prove facts consistent with those allegations. Fed.Rules Civ.Proc.Rule 12(b)(6), 28 U.S.C.A.

> Van Harken v. City of Chicago, 906 F.Supp. 1182, affirmed as modified 103 F.3d 1346, certiorari denied 117 S.Ct. 1846, 137 L.Ed.2d 1049.

N.D.Ill. 1995. Motion to dismiss for failure to state claim tests sufficiency of complaint, not merits of suit; only question is whether relief is possible under any set of facts that could be established consistent with allegations. Fed.Rules Civ.Proc.Rule 12(b)(6), 28 U.S.C.A.

> U.S. v. Brickman, 906 F.Supp. 1164.

N.D.Ill. 1995. In reviewing motion to dismiss for failure to state claim, court tests sufficiency of complaint, not merits of the suit. Fed.Rules Civ.Proc.Rule 12(b)(6), 28 U.S.C.A.

> Graves v. Tru-Link Fence Co., 905 F.Supp. 515.

N.D.Ill. 1995. Only where alleged federal claim is immaterial and brought solely to fabricate federal jurisdiction, or wholly insubstantial and frivolous, may attack on merits of claim be treated as one seeking dismissal for lack of jurisdiction; instead, if issue of jurisdiction is intertwined with merits of case, then district court should take jurisdiction and handle defendant's motion as direct attack on merits of plaintiff's case. Fed.Rules Civ.Proc.Rule 12(b)(1, 6), 28 U.S.C.A.

> Mungiovi v. Chicago Housing Authority, 901 F.Supp. 261.

Because attack on plaintiff's federal claim went to its merits, complaint would be analyzed under rule providing for dismissal for failure to state claim, even though defendants sought dismissal for lack of subject matter jurisdiction. Fed.Rules Civ.Proc.Rule 12(b)(1, 6), 28 U.S.C.A.

> Mungiovi v. Chicago Housing Authority, 901 F.Supp. 261.

N.D.Ill. 1995. Motion to dismiss for failure to state claim upon which relief can be granted tests sufficiency of complaint, not merits of suit. Fed.Rules Civ.Proc.Rule 12(b)(6), 28 U.S.C.A.

> Egan v. Palos Community Hosp., 889 F.Supp. 331.

N.D.Ill. 1994. Plaintiff can plead herself out of court, if she alleges facts which show that she is not entitled to judgment. Fed.Rules Civ. Proc.Rule 12(b)(6), 28 U.S.C.A.

> Cass v. American Properties, Inc., 861 F.Supp. 55.

To survive motion to dismiss for failure to state claim upon which relief can be granted, plaintiffs need not identify legal theory, nor is incorrect legal theory fatal. Fed.Rules Civ. Proc.Rules 8(a), 12(b)(6), 28 U.S.C.A.

Cass v. American Properties, Inc., 861 F.Supp. 55.

N.D.Ill. 1994. Complaint need not specify correct legal theory nor point to correct statute to survive motion to dismiss for failure to state claim on which relief can be granted. Fed. Rules Civ.Proc.Rule 12(b), 28 U.S.C.A.

Whitehead v. AM Intern., Inc., 860 F.Supp. 1280.

Complaint must state either direct or inferential allegations to establish necessary elements for recovery under chosen legal theory, in order to survive motion to dismiss for failure to state claim on which relief can be granted. Fed.Rules Civ.Proc.Rule 12(b)(6), 28 U.S.C.A.

Whitehead v. AM Intern., Inc., 860 F.Supp. 1280.

N.D.Ill. 1994. Complaint need not specify correct legal theory or point to right statute to survive motion to dismiss.

E.E.O.C. v. Park Ridge Public Library, 856 F.Supp. 477.

When defending against motion to dismiss, plaintiff may allege without evidentiary support any facts he pleases, that are consistent with the complaint, in order to show that there is state of facts within scope of complaint that if proved would entitle him to judgment.

E.E.O.C. v. Park Ridge Public Library, 856 F.Supp. 477.

N.D.Ill. 1994. On motion to dismiss for failure to state claim, court must construe pleadings liberally, and mere vagueness or lack of detail alone will not constitute sufficient grounds to dismiss complaint. Fed.Rules Civ. Proc.Rule 12(b)(6), 28 U.S.C.A.

Letisha A. by Murphy v. Morgan, 855 F.Supp. 943.

Complaint need not specify correct legal theory nor point to right statute to survive motion to dismiss for failure to state claim. Fed.Rules Civ.Proc.Rule 12(b)(6), 28 U.S.C.A.

Letisha A. by Murphy v. Morgan, 855 F.Supp. 943.

N.D.Ill. 1994. Complaint's mere vagueness or lack of detail is not sufficient to justify dismissal. Fed.Rules Civ.Proc.Rule 12(b)(6), 28 U.S.C.A.

Estate of Cassara by Cassara v. State of Ill., 853 F.Supp. 273.

N.D.Ill. 1994. To withstand motion to dismiss for failure to state a claim, complaint must allege facts sufficiently setting forth essential

elements of cause of action. Fed.Rules Civ. Proc.Rule 12(b)(6), 28 U.S.C.A.

Bergquist v. U.S. Nat. Weather Service, 849 F.Supp. 1221.

N.D.Ill. 1994. To survive motion to dismiss for failure to state claim, complaint must state either direct or inferential allegations concerning all material elements necessary for recovery under relevant legal theory. Fed.Rules Civ.Proc.Rule 12(b)(6), 28 U.S.C.A.

Adams v. Cavanagh Communities Corp., 847 F.Supp. 1390.

N.D.Ill. 1994. To survive motion to dismiss for failure to state claim, complaint must allege sufficient facts to outline cause of action. Fed.Rules Civ.Proc.Rule 12(b)(6), 28 U.S.C.A.

Bright v. Roadway Services, Inc., 846 F.Supp. 693.

N.D.Ill. 1994. For purposes of motion to dismiss, plaintiff must allege sufficient facts to outline cause of action, proof of which is essential to recovery. Fed.Rules Civ.Proc.Rule 12(b)(1), 28 U.S.C.A.

U.S. v. Beethoven Associates Ltd. Partnership, 843 F.Supp. 1257.

N.D.Ill. 1994. Federal courts simply require notice pleading and, thus, district court must construe pleadings liberally in ruling on motion to dismiss for failure to state claim; complaint need not specify correct legal theory or point to right statute to survive motion to dismiss. Fed.Rules Civ.Proc.Rule 12(b)(6), 28 U.S.C.A.

Clorox Co. v. Chromium Corp., 158 F.R.D. 120.

In construing reasonable inferences when ruling on motion to dismiss for failure to state claim, district court need not stretch allegations beyond their sensible and reasonable implications; party must allege all elements of asserted cause of action necessary for recovery.

Clorox Co. v. Chromium Corp., 158 F.R.D. 120.

For purposes of motion to dismiss for failure to state claim, plaintiff need not articulate specific provisions of statute. Fed.Rules Civ. Proc.Rule 12(b)(6), 28 U.S.C.A.

Clorox Co. v. Chromium Corp., 158 F.R.D. 120.

N.D.Ill. 1994. To withstand motion to dismiss for failure to state claim, complaint must allege facts sufficiently setting forth essential elements of the cause of action. Fed.Rules Civ.Proc.Rule 12(b)(6), 28 U.S.C.A.

Marie O. v. Edgar, 157 F.R.D. 433.

N.D.Ill. 1993. Violation of rule requiring separate claims to be stated in separate counts does not itself provide basis for dismissal of complaint. Fed.Rules Civ.Proc.Rule 10(b), 28 U.S.C.A.

> Selep v. City of Chicago, 842 F.Supp. 1068.

N.D.Ill. 1993. To survive motion to dismiss, plaintiffs need not identify legal theory, nor is incorrect legal theory fatal. Fed.Rules Civ.Proc.Rule 12(b)(6), 28 U.S.C.A.

> Heller Intern. Corp. v. Sharp, 839 F.Supp. 1297.

Motion to dismiss is directed at sufficiency of complaint, not sufficiency of proof, which is question reserved for trier of fact. Fed.Rules Civ.Proc.Rule 12(b)(6), 28 U.S.C.A.

> Heller Intern. Corp. v. Sharp, 839 F.Supp. 1297.

N.D.Ill. 1993. To withstand motion to dismiss for failure to state claim, complaint must allege facts sufficiently setting forth essential elements of cause of action. Fed.Rules Civ. Proc.Rule 12(b)(6), 28 U.S.C.A.

> O'Hern v. Delta Airlines, Inc., 838 F.Supp. 1264.

N.D.Ill. 1993. Because federal courts simply require "notice pleading," district court construes pleadings liberally and thus, mere vagueness or lack of detail of allegations is not sufficient to justify dismissal.

> Otterbacher v. Northwestern University, 838 F.Supp. 1256.

N.D.Ill. 1993. Complaint may be dismissed for failure to state claim upon which relief can be granted only if facts that plaintiff alleges shows she is not entitled to judgment.

> Ruich v. Ruff, Weidenaar & Reidy, Ltd., 837 F.Supp. 881.

N.D.Ill. 1993. In deciding motion to dismiss for failure to state claim, court must accept as true all facts alleged, together with all reasonable inferences which may be derived from those facts. Fed.Rules Civ.Proc.Rule 12(b)(6), 28 U.S.C.A.

> Madden v. Country Life Ins. Co., 835 F.Supp. 1081.

Dismissal is proper for failure to state claim only if it appears beyond a doubt that plaintiff can prove no set of facts that would entitle him to relief requested. Fed.Rules Civ.Proc.Rule 12(b)(6), 28 U.S.C.A.

> Madden v. Country Life Ins. Co., 835 F.Supp. 1081.

N.D.Ill. 1993. In defending against motion to dismiss, plaintiffs are free to allege without evidentiary support any facts they please that are consistent with complaint, in order to show that there is state of facts within scope of complaint that if proved entitle them to

judgment. Fed.Rules Civ.Proc.Rule 12(b)(6), 28 U.S.C.A.

> Barnett v. Daley, 835 F.Supp. 1063, reversed 32 F.3d 1196, rehearing denied, on remand 1995 WL 59229.

N.D.Ill. 1993. Complaint will not be dismissed based merely on vagueness or lack of detail. Fed.Rules Civ.Proc.Rule 12(b)(6), 28 U.S.C.A.

> Chemical Futures & Options, Inc. v. Resolution Trust Corp., 832 F.Supp. 1188.

N.D.Ill. 1993. Complaint need not specify correct legal theory or point to right statute in order to survive motion to dismiss.

> Sampson v. Village Discount Outlet, Inc., 832 F.Supp. 1163, affirmed 43 F.3d 1474, rehearing denied.

N.D.Ill. 1993. Complaint need not specify correct legal theory to survive motion to dismiss, but complaint must allege all elements of cause of action necessary for recovery.

> National Service Ass'n, Inc. v. Capitol Bankers Life Ins. Co., Inc., 832 F.Supp. 227.

N.D.Ill. 1993. To withstand motion to dismiss for failure to state a claim, complaint must state either direct or inferential allegations concerning all material elements necessary for recovery under relevant legal theory. Fed.Rules Civ.Proc.Rule 12(b)(6), 28 U.S.C.A.

> Eberhardt v. O'Malley, 820 F.Supp. 1090, affirmed in part, reversed in part 17 F.3d 1023.

N.D.Ill. 1993. Because federal courts simply require "notice pleading," court must construe pleadings liberally and mere vagueness or lack of detail alone will not be sufficient grounds to dismiss complaint.

> Lomas Mortg. U.S.A., Inc. v. W.E. O'Neil Const. Co., 812 F.Supp. 841.

N.D.Ill. 1992. District court must construe pleadings liberally on motion to dismiss for failure to state claim, and mere vagueness or lack of detail alone does not constitute sufficient grounds to dismiss complaint. Fed.Rules Civ. Proc.Rule 12(b)(6), 28 U.S.C.A.

> Harris v. O'Grady, 803 F.Supp. 1361.

N.D.Ill. 1992. Complaint need not specify correct legal theory nor point to right statute to survive motion to dismiss. Fed.Rules Civ.Proc. Rule 12(b)(1, 6), 28 U.S.C.A.

> MSA Realty Corp. v. State of Ill., 794 F.Supp. 267, affirmed 990 F.2d 288.

N.D.Ill. 1992. Plaintiff need not set out in detail facts upon which claim is based to survive motion to dismiss for failure to state claim, but must allege sufficient facts to outline cause of action; complaint must state either direct or inferential allegations concerning all material elements necessary for recovery under relevant legal theory. Fed.Rules Civ.Proc.Rule 12(b)(6), 28 U.S.C.A.

> Healy v. Axelrod Const. Co. Defined Ben. Pension Plan and Trust, 787 F.Supp. 838.

N.D.Ill. 1991. Generally, federal system of notice pleading does not favor dismissal for failure to state claim.

> Scott v. O'Grady, 760 F.Supp. 1288, affirmed 975 F.2d 366, rehearing denied, certiorari denied 113 S.Ct. 2421, 508 U.S. 942, 124 L.Ed.2d 643.

N.D.Ill. 1990. For purposes of motion to dismiss, complaint must state either direct or inferential allegations concerning all of material elements necessary for recovery under relevant legal theory. Fed.Rules Civ.Proc.Rule 12(b)(6), 28 U.S.C.A.

> Paist v. Town & Country Corp., 744 F.Supp. 179.

N.D.Ill. 1990. In order to avoid motion to dismiss, complaint must state either direct or inferential allegations concerning all of material elements necessary for recovery under relevant legal theory. Fed.Rules Civ.Proc.Rule 12(b)(6), 28 U.S.C.A.

> Westfield Partners, Ltd. v. Hogan, 740 F.Supp. 523.

N.D.Ill. 1990. Count seeking damages for unjust enrichment and also alleging that parties entered into oral sublicensing agreement was internally inconsistent, and subject to dismissal. Fed.Rules Civ.Proc.Rule 8(e)(2), 28 U.S.C.A.

> CEO Marketing Promotions Co. v. Heartland Promotions, Inc., 739 F.Supp. 1150.

N.D.Ill. 1988. Complaint that is confusing and redundant is subject to dismissal.

> Verlan, Ltd. v. John L. Armitage & Co., 695 F.Supp. 955.

N.D.Ill. 1988. To survive motion to dismiss, complaint must state either direct or inferential allegations concerning all material elements necessary for recovery under relevant legal theory. Fed.Rules Civ.Proc.Rule 12(b)(6), 28 U.S.C.A.

> Capalbo v. PaineWebber, Inc., 694 F.Supp. 1315.

N.D.Ill. 1987. Purpose of motion to dismiss for failure to state claim is to test sufficiency of complaint, not to decide merits. Fed. Rules Civ.Proc.Rule 12(b)(6), 28 U.S.C.A.

> Barkman v. Wabash, Inc., 674 F.Supp. 623.

N.D.Ill. 1987. Case should not be dismissed on mere ground that plaintiff has sought equitable relief when action is legal in nature; as long as plaintiff sets forth sufficient allegations to support contract action for damages, appropriateness of accounting or mandatory injunction request cannot justify dismissal, even if plaintiff does not specifically request damages.

> Cleland v. Stadt, 670 F.Supp. 814.

N.D.Ill. 1984. In order to withstand dismissal for failure to state claim, complaint must contain either direct allegations on every material point necessary to sustain recovery on any legal theory, even though it may not be theory suggested or intended by pleader, or contain allegations from which inference fairly may be drawn that evidence on these material points will be introduced at trial.

> Pempek v. Edgar, 603 F.Supp. 495.

N.D.Ind. 1994. Dismissal for failure to state claim upon which relief can be granted was not intended to be trap for unartful pleaders; rather, court looks to root of case and determines whether any set of facts could support cause of action. Fed.Rules Civ.Proc.Rule 12(b)(6), 28 U.S.C.A.

> Worthington v. Subaru-Isuzu Automotive, Inc., 868 F.Supp. 1067.

N.D.Ind. 1994. Plaintiff may not avoid dismissal for failure to state actionable claim merely by attaching bare legal conclusions to narrated facts which fail to outline basis of his claims. Fed.Rules Civ.Proc.Rule 12(b)(6), 28 U.S.C.A.

> Marozsan v. U.S., 849 F.Supp. 617, affirmed 90 F.3d 1284, rehearing and suggestion for rehearing denied, certiorari denied 117 S.Ct. 1117, 137 L.Ed.2d 317.

N.D.Ind. 1993. To prevail on his claim to dismiss, defendant must demonstrate that plaintiff's claim, as set forth by complaint, is without legal consequence.

> Schwartz v. Oberweis, 826 F.Supp. 280.

N.D.Ind. 1987. Issue of whether federal court should dismiss complaint for failure to state claim upon which relief can be granted is question of federal law even where federal court sits in diversity; dismissal is procedural device, federal rule of civil procedure is directly applicable, and federal court must follow federal law in applying federal procedural law. Fed.Rules Civ.Proc.Rule 12(b)(6), 28 U.S.C.A.

> Sheldon v. Munford, Inc., 660 F.Supp. 130.

S.D.Ind. 1996. Motion to dismiss for failure to state claim tests sufficiency of complaint and not merits of suit. Fed.Rules Civ.Proc.Rule 12(b)(6), 28 U.S.C.A.

> Love v. Bolinger, 927 F.Supp. 1131.

S.D.Ind. 1996. Motion to dismiss for failure to state claim tests sufficiency of complaint and not merits of suit. Fed.Rules Civ.Proc.Rule 12(b)(6), 28 U.S.C.A.

> Indiana State Teachers Ass'n v. Board of School Com'rs of City of Indianapolis, 918 F.Supp. 266, affirmed 101 F.3d 1179.

S.D.Ind. 1993. Complaint may be dismissed for failure to state claim upon which relief can be granted where review of complaint, taking all factual allegations in complaint as true, reveals that no viable cause of action exists. Fed.Rules Civ.Proc.Rule 12(b)(6), 28 U.S.C.A.

> Henson v. CSC Credit Services, 830 F.Supp. 1204, affirmed in part, reversed in part 29 F.3d 280.

S.D.Ind. 1993. To withstand motion to dismiss, complaint must provide short and plain statement of claim that will give defendant fair notice of what claim is and grounds upon which it rests. Fed.Rules Civ.Proc.Rule 12(b)(6), 28 U.S.C.A.

> Blanton v. City of Indianapolis, Ind., 830 F.Supp. 1198.

S.D.Ind. 1991. Court cannot dismiss complaint merely because it doubts that plaintiff can prove facts it alleges. Fed.Rules Civ.Proc.Rule 12(b)(6), 28 U.S.C.A.

> Mundell v. Beverly Enterprises-Indiana, Inc., 778 F.Supp. 459.

N.D.Iowa 1995. It is only in the unusual case where complaint on its face reveals some insuperable bar to relief that warrants dismissal for failure to state a claim upon which relief can be granted. Fed.Rules Civ.Proc.Rule 12(b)(6), 28 U.S.C.A.

> De Wit v. Firstar Corp., 879 F.Supp. 947, on reconsideration 904 F.Supp. 1476.

N.D.Iowa 1995. In ruling on motion to dismiss for failure to state claim, issue is not whether plaintiff will ultimately prevail, but rather, whether plaintiff was entitled to offer evidence in support of his or her claims. Fed. Rules Civ.Proc.Rule 12(b)(6), 28 U.S.C.A.

> Dahl v. Kanawha Inv. Holding Co., 161 F.R.D. 673.

D.Kan. 1998. Issue in reviewing the sufficiency of a complaint on a motion to dismiss for failure to state a claim is not whether plaintiff will ultimately prevail, but whether plaintiff is entitled to offer evidence to support the claim. Fed.Rules Civ.Proc.Rule 12(b)(6), 28 U.S.C.A.

> Ortega v. Nguyen, 7 F.Supp.2d 1178.

D.Kan. 1997. Issue in resolving motion to dismiss for failure to state claim is not whether plaintiff will ultimately prevail, but whether she is entitled to offer evidence to support her claims. Fed.Rules Civ.Proc.Rule 12(b)(6), 28 U.S.C.A.

> Wesley v. Don Stein Buick, Inc., 985 F.Supp. 1288, vacated in part 996 F.Supp. 1299.

D.Kan. 1997. Dismissal for failure to state claim is harsh remedy to be used cautiously so as to promote liberal rules of pleading while protecting interests of justice. Fed.Rules Civ. Proc.Rule 12(b)(6), 28 U.S.C.A.

> Whayne v. State of Kan., 980 F.Supp. 387.

D.Kan. 1997. Dismissal is harsh remedy to be used cautiously so as to promote liberal rules of pleading while protecting interests of justice. Fed.Rules Civ.Proc.Rule 12(b)(6), 28 U.S.C.A.

> Schmitt v. Beverly Health and Rehabilitation Services, Inc., 962 F.Supp. 1379.

D.Kan. 1996. Motions to dismiss for failure to state claim, including those directed at antitrust claims, are greatly disfavored by federal courts. Fed.Rules Civ.Proc.Rule 12(b)(6), 28 U.S.C.A.

> Classic Communications, Inc. v. Rural Telephone Service Co., Inc., 956 F.Supp. 896.

D.Kan. 1996. Issue in reviewing sufficiency of complaint is not whether plaintiff will ultimately prevail, but whether he is entitled to offer evidence to support his claim.

> Patrick v. City of Overland Park, Kan., 937 F.Supp. 1491.

D.Kan. 1996. To prevail on motion to dismiss for failure to state claim, moving party must meet high standard. Fed.Rules Civ.Proc. Rule 12(b)(6), 28 U.S.C.A.

> S.A.I., Inc. v. General Elec. Railcar Services Corp., 935 F.Supp. 1150.

D.Kan. 1996. Issue in resolving motion to dismiss complaint for failure to state claim is not whether plaintiff will ultimately prevail, but whether he or she is entitled to offer evidence to support claims. Fed.Rules Civ.Proc.Rule 12(b)(6), 28 U.S.C.A.

> Fusion, Inc. v. Nebraska Aluminum Castings, Inc., 934 F.Supp. 1270.

D.Kan. 1996. Issue in resolving motion to dismiss for failure to state claim is not whether plaintiff will ultimately prevail, but whether he or she is entitled to offer evidence to support claims. Fed.Rules Civ.Proc.Rule 12(b)(6), 28 U.S.C.A.

> Aguirre v. McCaw RCC Communications, Inc., 923 F.Supp. 1431.

D.Kan. 1996. Dismissal of complaint for failure to state claim upon which relief may be granted is harsh remedy to be used cautiously so as to promote liberal rules of pleading while protecting interests of justice. Fed.Rules Civ. Proc.Rule 12(b)(6), 28 U.S.C.A.

> Mounkes v. Conklin, 922 F.Supp. 1501.

D.Kan. 1996. On motion to dismiss for failure to state claim, court judges sufficiency of complaint, accepting as true the well-pleaded factual allegations and drawing all reasonable inferences in favor of plaintiff. Fed.Rules Civ. Proc.Rule 12(b)(6), 28 U.S.C.A.

Boyer v. Board of County Com'rs of County of Johnson County, 922 F.Supp. 476, affirmed 108 F.3d 1388.

Dismissal for failure to state claim is harsh remedy to be used cautiously so as to promote the liberal rules of pleading while protecting the interests of justice. Fed.Rules Civ.Proc.Rule 12(b)(6), 28 U.S.C.A.

Boyer v. Board of County Com'rs of County of Johnson County, 922 F.Supp. 476, affirmed 108 F.3d 1388.

D.Kan. 1996. Issue in resolving motion to dismiss cause of action for failure to state claim is not whether plaintiff will ultimately prevail, but whether plaintiff is entitled to offer evidence to support claim.

Henry v. F.D.I.C., 168 F.R.D. 55.

D.Kan. 1995. Issue in resolving motion to dismiss for failure to state claim is not whether plaintiff will ultimately prevail, but whether he or she is entitled to offer evidence to support claims. Fed.Rules Civ.Proc.Rule 12(b)(6), 28 U.S.C.A.

Garland Co. Inc. v. Ecology Roof Systems Corp., 895 F.Supp. 274.

D.Kan. 1995. Dismissal for failure to state claim is harsh remedy to be used cautiously so as to promote liberal rules of pleading while protecting interests of justice. Fed.Rules Civ. Proc.Rule 12(b)(6), 28 U.S.C.A.

Olds v. Alamo Group (KS), Inc., 889 F.Supp. 447.

D.Kan. 1995. Motion to dismiss for failure to state a claim tests sufficiency of complaint. Fed.Rules Civ.Proc.Rule 12(b)(6), 28 U.S.C.A.

Reidenbach v. U.S.D. No. 437, 878 F.Supp. 178.

D.Kan. 1994. Issue in resolving motion to dismiss complaint for failure to state claim is not whether plaintiff will ultimately prevail, but whether he or she is entitled to offer evidence to support claims.

Hamner v. BMY Combat Systems, 869 F.Supp. 888, reconsideration denied 874 F.Supp. 322, affirmed 79 F.3d 1156.

W.D.Ky. 1993. Dismissal of complaint is appropriate where, even accepting truth of plaintiff's allegations and reasonable inferences, plaintiff fails to state a claim.

Kinser v. Ciba-Geigy Corp., 837 F.Supp. 217.

E.D.La. 1995. Motions to dismiss for failure to state claim are viewed with disfavor and

rarely granted. Fed.Rules Civ.Proc.Rule 12(b)(6), 28 U.S.C.A.

Abramson v. Florida Gas Transmission Co., 909 F.Supp. 410.

E.D.La. 1995. Motions to dismiss for failure to state a claim are viewed with disfavor and are rarely granted. Fed.Rules Civ.Proc. Rule 12(b)(6), 28 U.S.C.A.

Laitram Machinery, Inc. v. Carnitech A/S, 901 F.Supp. 1155.

E.D.La. 1994. Strong policy considerations dictate that motion to dismiss for failure to state claim be viewed with disfavor. Fed. Rules Civ.Proc.Rule 12(b)(6), 28 U.S.C.A.

Durham, Inc. v. Vanguard Bank & Trust Co., 858 F.Supp. 617.

E.D.La. 1994. Pro se complaint should not be dismissed merely because plaintiff fails to articulate correct legal theory; rather, it is court's duty to examine complaint to determine if allegations therein support claim for relief under any possible legal theory. Fed.Rules Civ. Proc.Rule 12(b)(6), 28 U.S.C.A.

Robertson v. Burger King, Inc., 848 F.Supp. 78, reconsideration denied 155 F.R.D. 580.

W.D.La. 1986. Motion to dismiss for failure to state a claim is not favored and should rarely be granted, resolution on merits being preferred to disposition on technical grounds of failure to state a claim. Fed.Rules Civ.Proc. Rule 12(b)(6), 28 U.S.C.A.

Airline Car Rental, Inc. v. Shreveport Airport Authority, 667 F.Supp. 293.

D.Md. 1996. Motion to dismiss for failure to state claim tests legal sufficiency of plaintiff's complaint, and, if complaint is legally insufficient, authorizes court to dismiss claim on basis of dispositive issue of law. Fed.Rules Civ.Proc. Rule 12(b)(6), 28 U.S.C.A.

Keeler v. Mayor & City Council of Cumberland, 928 F.Supp. 591, motion denied 951 F.Supp. 83.

D.Mass. 1996. Motion to dismiss tests legal sufficiency of complaint, not plaintiff's likelihood of ultimate success.

Canney v. City of Chelsea, 925 F.Supp. 58.

Crucial inquiry on motion to dismiss is whether, based on allegations of complaint at issue, plaintiff is entitled to offer evidence in support of his claims.

Canney v. City of Chelsea, 925 F.Supp. 58.

D.Mass. 1996. In ruling on motion to dismiss for failure to state claim, court must carefully balance rule of simplified civil pleading against need for more than conclusory allegations, and may not accept any unsupported conclusions or interpretations of law; court is obliged neither to credit bald assertions, periphrastic circumlocutions, unsubstantiated conclusions, or outright vituperation, nor to honor subjective characterizations, optimistic predictions, or problematic suppositions. Fed.Rules Civ.Proc.Rule 12(b)(6), 28 U.S.C.A.

> Day v. Fallon Community Health Plan, Inc., 917 F.Supp. 72.

D.Mass. 1995. Burden is heavy on party moving to dismiss for failure to state claim upon which relief can be granted; appropriate inquiry is whether nonmover is entitled to offer evidence in support of claims. Fed.Rules Civ. Proc.Rule 12(b)(6), 28 U.S.C.A.

> General Elec. Co. v. Lyon, 894 F.Supp. 544.

D.Mass. 1988. Failure to verify derivative complaint is grounds for dismissal. Fed.Rules Civ.Proc.Rule 23.1, 28 U.S.C.A.

> Abeloff v. Barth, 119 F.R.D. 332.

E.D.Mich. 1997. Motion to dismiss for failure to state a claim upon which relief can be granted tests legal sufficiency of plaintiff's complaint. Fed.Rules Civ.Proc.Rule 12(b)(6), 28 U.S.C.A.

> Bomis v. Metropolitan Life Ins. Co., 970 F.Supp. 584.

E.D.Mich. 1996. Rule permitting district court to dismiss any complaint which fails "to state a claim upon which relief may be granted" allows defendant to test whether plaintiff is entitled to legal relief even if every allegation in complaint is true. Fed.Rules Civ.Proc.Rule 12(b)(6), 28 U.S.C.A.

> Tidik v. Ritsema, 938 F.Supp. 416.

E.D.Mich. 1996. Plaintiffs' failure to amend their complaint or otherwise comply with magistrate's order granting defendant's motion for a more definite statement warranted dismissal of complaint. Fed.Rules Civ.Proc. Rule 12(e), 28 U.S.C.A.

> Kratage v. Charter Tp. of Commerce, 926 F.Supp. 102.

E.D.Mich. 1995. Motion to dismiss for failure to state claim tests legal sufficiency of plaintiff's complaint. Fed.Rules Civ.Proc.Rule 12(b)(6), 28 U.S.C.A.

> Hakken v. Washtenaw County, 901 F.Supp. 1245.

E.D.Mich. 1994. On motion to dismiss for failure to state a claim upon which relief may be granted, court's inquiry is limited to whether challenged pleadings set forth allegations sufficient to make out elements of right to relief. Fed.Rules Civ.Proc.Rule 12(b)(6), 28 U.S.C.A.

> Fishbach-Natkin, Inc. v. Shimizu America Corp., 854 F.Supp. 1294.

E.D.Mich. 1993. On motion to dismiss for failure to state a claim or motion for judgment on the pleadings, trial court's inquiry is limited to whether challenged pleading set forth allegation sufficient to make out elements of right to relief. Fed.Rules Civ.Proc.Rule 12(b)(6), (c), 28 U.S.C.A.

> Greenan v. Romeo Village Police Dept., 819 F.Supp. 658.

E.D.Mich. 1992. Motion to dismiss complaint for failure to state claim upon which relief can be granted requires district court to determine whether plaintiff has pleaded cognizable claims. Fed.Rules Civ.Proc.Rule 12(b)(6), 28 U.S.C.A.

> Lindsey v. Jansante, 806 F.Supp. 651.

E.D.Mich. 1992. Inquiry upon motion to dismiss is limited to whether challenged pleadings set forth allegations sufficient to make out elements of right to relief. Fed.Rules Civ.Proc. Rule 12(b)(6), (c), 28 U.S.C.A.

> County of Oakland by Kuhn v. City of Detroit, 784 F.Supp. 1275.

W.D.Mich. 1998. In order to survive motion to dismiss for failure to state a claim, complaint must contain either direct or inferential allegations with respect to all material elements necessary to sustain a recovery under some viable legal theory. Fed.Rules Civ.Proc. Rule 12(b)(6), 28 U.S.C.A.

> Organic Chemicals Site PRP Group v. Total Petroleum, Inc., 6 F.Supp.2d 660.

W.D.Mich. 1992. An action may be dismissed if the complaint fails to state a claim upon which relief can be granted. Fed.Rules Civ.Proc.Rule 12(b)(6), 28 U.S.C.A.

> Coplin and Associates, Inc. v. U.S., 814 F.Supp. 643, affirmed 27 F.3d 566.

W.D.Mich. 1982. Naph-Sol Refining Co. v. Murphy Oil Corp., 550 F.Supp. 297, affirmed in part, reversed in part Mobil Oil Corp. v. Department of Energy, 728 F.2d 1477, certiorari denied 104 S.Ct. 3545, 467 U.S. 1255, 82 L.Ed.2d 849, certiorari denied 104 S.Ct. 3545, 467 U.S. 1255, 82 L.Ed.2d 849.

D.Minn. 1996. Proper motion when party claims that opponent's allegations do not state claim with sufficient detail is not motion to dismiss, but motion for more definite statement. Fed.Rules Civ.Proc.Rules 8, 12(b)(6), (e), 28 U.S.C.A.

> Radisson Hotels Intern., Inc. v. Westin Hotel Co., 931 F.Supp. 638.

D.Minn. 1993. On motion to dismiss for failure to state a claim, appropriate inquiry is not whether a plaintiff will ultimately prevail but whether he will be allowed to introduce evidence to support his claims. Fed.Rules Civ. Proc.Rule 12(b)(6), 28 U.S.C.A.

> Slice v. Sons of Norway, 866 F.Supp. 397, affirmed 34 F.3d 630.

N.D.Miss. 1998. Motion to dismiss for failure to state a claim is disfavored, and is rarely granted. Fed.Rules Civ.Proc.Rule 12(b)(6), 28 U.S.C.A.

Myers v. Guardian Life Ins. Co. of America, Inc., 5 F.Supp.2d 423.

N.D.Miss. 1995. Motion to dismiss for failure to state claim is disfavored, and is rarely granted. Fed.Rules Civ.Proc.Rule 12(b)(6), 28 U.S.C.A.

Cunningham v. Dun & Bradstreet Plan Services, Inc., 889 F.Supp. 932, affirmed 105 F.3d 655.

Dismissal for failure to state claim is never warranted because court believes plaintiff is unlikely to prevail on merits. Fed.Rules Civ.Proc.Rule 12(b)(6), 28 U.S.C.A.

Cunningham v. Dun & Bradstreet Plan Services, Inc., 889 F.Supp. 932, affirmed 105 F.3d 655.

N.D.Miss. 1993. Even if it appears an almost certainty that facts alleged cannot be proved to support claim, complaint may not be dismissed as long as complaint states claim. Fed.Rules Civ.Proc.Rule 12(b)(6), 28 U.S.C.A.

In re Catfish Antitrust Litigation, 826 F.Supp. 1019.

N.D.Miss. 1989. Although dismissal for failure to state claim is powerful tool in expediting judicial process, it should be applied cautiously and granted only on rare occasions. Fed.Rules Civ.Proc.Rule 12(b)(6), 28 U.S.C.A.

Mize v. Harvey Shapiro Enterprises, Inc., 714 F.Supp. 220.

S.D.Miss. 1997. Motion to dismiss for failure to state claim is disfavored, and it is rarely granted. Fed.Rules Civ.Proc.Rule 12(b)(6), 28 U.S.C.A.

Columbia Gulf Transmission Co. v. U.S., 966 F.Supp. 1453.

S.D.Miss. 1995. Purpose of motion to dismiss for failure to state claim is to test statement of claim for relief as set out in complaint. Fed.Rules Civ.Proc.Rule 12(b)(6), 28 U.S.C.A.

Pace v. Suntech, Inc., 900 F.Supp. 20.

S.D.Miss. 1993. Where plaintiff's complaint is devoid of any factual allegations suggesting basis for recovery against particular defendant, there can be no ground for concluding that claim has been stated.

Doe v. Cloverleaf Mall, 829 F.Supp. 866.

E.D.Mo. 1996. Standards applied to a motion to dismiss for lack of subject matter jurisdiction are same as those applied to motion to dismiss for failure to state a claim. Fed.Rules Civ.Proc.Rules 12(b)(1), 12(b)(6), 28 U.S.C.A.

Vankempen v. McDonnell Douglas Corp., 923 F.Supp. 146.

E.D.Mo. 1995. On motion to dismiss for failure to state claim, issue is not whether plaintiff will ultimately prevail, but whether plaintiff is entitled to present evidence in support of his or her claim. Fed.Rules Civ.Proc. Rule 12(b)(6), 28 U.S.C.A.

Swartzbaugh v. State Farm Ins. Companies, 924 F.Supp. 932.

E.D.Mo. 1992. Court must view complaint in light most favorable to plaintiff and should not dismiss it merely because court doubts that plaintiff will be able to prove all of necessary allegations; thus, motion to dismiss is likely to be granted only in unusual case in which plaintiff includes allegations that show on face of complaint that there is some insuperable bar to relief.

Logan v. U.S., 792 F.Supp. 663, affirmed 978 F.2d 1263.

E.D.Mo. 1991. Complaint is sufficient to defeat motion to dismiss if it contains allegation from which inference can be drawn that evidence on material points will be introduced at trial.

O'Dell v. McSpadden, 780 F.Supp. 639, affirmed 994 F.2d 843, certiorari denied 114 S.Ct. 260, 510 U.S. 895, 126 L.Ed.2d 212.

E.D.Mo. 1991. Motion to dismiss should not be granted merely because complaint does not state with precision every element of offense necessary for recovery. Fed.Rules Civ.Proc. Rule 12(b)(6), 28 U.S.C.A.

Cook v. Foster Forbes Glass, 776 F.Supp. 1391.

E.D.Mo. 1990. Court may grant motion to dismiss for failure to state a claim upon which relief can be granted only when appears plaintiff cannot prove any set of facts in support of its claims which would entitle plaintiff to relief. Fed.Rules Civ.Proc.Rule 12(b)(6), 28 U.S.C.A.

Hurt v. Dow Chemical Co., 759 F.Supp. 556.

E.D.Mo. 1990. Complaint is sufficient if it contains allegations from which inference fairly may be drawn that evidence on material points will be introduced at trial.

Formanek v. Arment, 737 F.Supp. 72.

E.D.Mo. 1986. Defendants' original motions to dismiss would be denied as moot, where plaintiff had filed first amended complaint which resolved issues raised in motions to dismiss.

Sykes v. Sweeney, 638 F.Supp. 274.

D.Neb. 1996. Issue in resolving motion to dismiss for failure to state claim is whether plaintiff is entitled to offer evidence in support of her claim, not whether she will ultimately prevail. Fed.Rules Civ.Proc.Rule 12(b)(6), 28 U.S.C.A.

> Karstens v. International Gamco, Inc., 939 F.Supp. 1430.

D.Nev. 1997. Issue on motion to dismiss for failure to state claim is not whether plaintiffs will ultimately prevail, but whether plaintiffs are entitled to offer evidence in support of their claims. Fed.Rules Civ.Proc.Rule 12(b)(6), 28 U.S.C.A.

> Martin v. State Farm Mut. Auto. Ins. Co., 960 F.Supp. 233.

D.N.H. 1996. Motion to dismiss for failure to state claim is one of limited inquiry, focusing not on whether plaintiff will ultimately prevail but whether claimant is entitled to offer evidence to support claims. Fed.Rules Civ.Proc. Rule 12(b)(6), 28 U.S.C.A.

> Minion Inc. v. Burdin, 929 F.Supp. 521.

D.N.H. 1996. Task of court presented with motion to dismiss for failure to state claim is necessarily a limited one; the issue is not whether plaintiff will ultimately prevail, but whether claimant is entitled to offer evidence to support claims. Fed.Rules Civ.Proc.Rule 12(b)(6), 28 U.S.C.A.

> Evans v. Work Opportunities Unlimited, Inc., 927 F.Supp. 554.

D.N.H. 1996. On motion to dismiss securities claim for failure to state cause of action, court will not render any decision as to whether particular statement is rendered misleading by particular omission; it will merely determine whether plaintiffs have sufficiently alleged circumstances under which plaintiffs could conceivably prove their claim. Fed.Rules Civ.Proc. Rule 12(b)(6), 28 U.S.C.A.

> Schaffer v. Timberland Co., 924 F.Supp. 1298.

D.N.H. 1993. Motion to dismiss for failure to state claim is one of limited inquiry, focusing not on whether plaintiff will ultimately prevail but whether claimant is entitled to offer evidence to support claims. Fed.Rules Civ.Proc. Rule 12(b)(6), 28 U.S.C.A.

> Gilbert v. Essex Group, Inc., 930 F.Supp. 683.

D.N.H. 1990. Issue before district court on motion to dismiss for failure to state claim is not whether plaintiff will ultimately prevail, but whether plaintiff is entitled to offer evidence to support her claims.

> McLean v. Gaudet, 769 F.Supp. 30.

D.N.J. 1997. In determination on motion to dismiss for failure to state claim, issue is not whether plaintiff will ultimately prevail, but rather, whether claimant is entitled to offer evidence to support claims. Fed.Rules Civ. Proc.Rule 12(b)(6), 28 U.S.C.A.

> Port Authority of New York and New Jersey v. Arcadian Corp., 991 F.Supp. 390.

D.N.J. 1997. Whether plaintiff presented, or even could present, any evidence to support its claims was irrelevant on motion to dismiss for failure to state a claim upon which relief can be granted. Fed.Rules Civ.Proc.Rule 12(b)(6), 28 U.S.C.A.

> TWC Cable Partners v. Cableworks, Inc., 966 F.Supp. 305.

D.N.J. 1997. To defeat motion to dismiss for failure to state a claim, it is not necessary for the plaintiff to plead evidence, nor must he plead the facts that serve as the basis for the claim, and question before the court is not whether the plaintiff will ultimately prevail; rather, question is whether plaintiff can prove any set of facts in support of his claim that would entitle him to relief. Fed.Rules Civ.Proc. Rule 12(b)(6), 28 U.S.C.A.

> Farmers & Merchants Nat. Bank v. San Clemente Financial Group Securities, Inc., 174 F.R.D. 572.

D.N.J. 1996. In determining whether to dismiss complaint for failure to state claim, issue is not whether plaintiff will ultimately prevail, but whether he or she is entitled to offer evidence to support the claims. Fed.Rules Civ. Proc.Rule 12(b)(6), 28 U.S.C.A.

> Tennsco Corp. v. Estey Metal Products, Inc., 200 B.R. 542.

D.N.J. 1996. Issue on motion to dismiss for failure to state claim is not whether plaintiff will ultimately prevail, but whether plaintiff is entitled to offer evidence to support claims. Fed.Rules Civ.Proc.Rule 12(b)(6), 28 U.S.C.A.

> DeJoy v. Comcast Cable Communications Inc., 941 F.Supp. 468.

D.N.J. 1996. In ruling on motion to dismiss for failure to state claim, issue is not whether plaintiff will ultimately prevail, but whether plaintiff is entitled to offer evidence to support claims. Fed.Rules Civ.Proc.Rule 12(b)(6), 28 U.S.C.A.

> SC Holdings, Inc. v. A.A.A. Realty Co., 935 F.Supp. 1354.

D.N.J. 1996. Motion to dismiss for failure to state a claim upon which relief can be granted does not attack merits of case, but merely tests legal sufficiency of complaint. Fed.Rules Civ.Proc.Rule 12(b)(6), 28 U.S.C.A.

> Schanzer v. Rutgers University, 934 F.Supp. 669.

Question before court on motion to dismiss for failure to state a claim upon which relief can be granted is not whether plaintiff will ultimately prevail; rather, it is whether she can prove any set of facts in support of her claim that would entitle her to relief. Fed.Rules Civ.Proc. Rule 12(b)(6), 28 U.S.C.A.

Schanzer v. Rutgers University, 934 F.Supp. 669.

D.N.J. 1995. District courts generally disfavor motions to dismiss for failure to state claim, as long-established federal policy of civil litigation is to decide cases on proofs. Fed. Rules Civ.Proc.Rule 12(b)(6), 28 U.S.C.A.

Caldwell Trucking PRP Group v. Spaulding Composites, Co., Inc., 890 F.Supp. 1247.

D.N.J. 1994. Question before court on motion to dismiss for failure to state claim upon which relief may be granted is not whether plaintiff will ultimately prevail, but, rather, whether he can prove any set of facts in support of his claim that would entitle him to relief. Fed.Rules Civ.Proc.Rule 12(b)(6), 28 U.S.C.A.

Morris v. Azzi, 866 F.Supp. 149.

D.N.J. 1992. Requirement that amended complaint be clear and concise is to be interpreted very liberally so that only complaints which clearly violate standard of being understandable, fair and amenable to response will be stricken; case will be dismissed only if it reaches level of outrageousness. Fed.Rules Civ.Proc. Rule 8(e), 28 U.S.C.A.

Transtech Industries, Inc. v. A & Z Septic Clean, 798 F.Supp. 1079, appeal dismissed 5 F.3d 51, certiorari denied Mayco Oil & Chemical Co. v. Transtech Industries, Inc., 114 S.Ct. 2692, 512 U.S. 1213, 129 L.Ed.2d 823.

D.N.J. 1989. Although motions to dismiss for failure to state a claim are generally viewed by the courts with disfavor and it is the policy of the federal rules to determine actions on their merits, when the allegations of the complaint are viewed in the light most favorable to the plaintiff, but still demonstrate no cognizable claim, dismissal is to be granted. Fed.Rules Civ.Proc.Rules 8(a), 12(b)(6), 28 U.S.C.A.

Panek v. Bogucz, 718 F.Supp. 1228, 113 A.L.R. Fed. 847.

D.N.J. 1987. In the absence of any indication of collusion, court would not dismiss derivative claim for noncompliance with verification requirement but, rather, would require plaintiff to file affidavit verifying complaint and serve it upon officers of corporation within ten days. Fed.Rules Civ.Proc.Rule 23.1, 28 U.S.C.A.

In re ORFA Securities Litigation, 654 F.Supp. 1449.

E.D.N.Y. 1998. On motion to dismiss for failure to state claim, appropriate inquiry is not whether plaintiff will ultimately prevail but whether plaintiff is entitled to offer evidence to support claims. Fed.Rules Civ.Proc.Rule 12(b)(6), 28 U.S.C.A.

Stordeur v. Computer Associates Intern., Inc., 995 F.Supp. 94.

E.D.N.Y. 1996. To survive motion to dismiss for failure to state claim, claimant is not required to set out in detail facts upon which he or she bases claim, but only give statement of his or her claim that will give defendant fair notice of what claim is and grounds upon which it rests. Fed.Rules Civ.Proc.Rule 12(b)(6), 28 U.S.C.A.

Greenberg v. New York State, 919 F.Supp. 637.

E.D.N.Y. 1995. As motion to dismiss for failure to state cause of action is solely concerned with sufficiency of complaint, defendants' defenses to claims are not factor in evaluation. Fed.Rules Civ.Proc.Rule 12(b)(6), 28 U.S.C.A.

City of Amsterdam v. Daniel Goldreyer, Ltd., 882 F.Supp. 1273.

E.D.N.Y. 1994. Court's function on motion to dismiss is not to weigh evidence that might be presented at trial, but merely to determine whether complaint itself is legally sufficient, and thus relevant inquiry is not whether plaintiff ultimately will prevail, but whether she is entitled to offer evidence in support of her claims. Fed.Rules Civ.Proc.Rule 12(b)(6), 28 U.S.C.A.

Alie v. NYNEX Corp., 158 F.R.D. 239.

E.D.N.Y. 1993. Motion to dismiss is addressed solely to face of pleading and court's function is merely to determine whether complaint itself is legally sufficient. Fed.Rules Civ. Proc.Rule 12(c), 28 U.S.C.A.

Tinlee Enterprises, Inc. v. Aetna Cas. & Sur. Co., 834 F.Supp. 605.

E.D.N.Y. 1992. Although pro se plaintiff's complaint is held to less stringent standards than formal pleadings drafted by lawyers, dismissal for failure to state a claim is warranted if statute or controlling precedent clearly forecloses pleadings. Fed.Rules Civ.Proc.Rule 12(b)(6), 28 U.S.C.A.

McArthur v. Bell, 788 F.Supp. 706.

E.D.N.Y. 1990. On motion to dismiss, allegations of complaint must be accepted as true and complaint must be construed in a light most favorable to the plaintiff; to prevail, defendant must prove that, under no interpretation of the facts alleged, can plaintiffs succeed.

Commerce Holding Co., Inc. v. Buckstone, 749 F.Supp. 441.

E.D.N.Y. 1989. If motion to dismiss asserts lack of subject matter jurisdiction and failure to state claim, court should generally find jurisdiction and proceed to determine whether claim is stated. Fed.Rules Civ.Proc. Rule 12(b)(1, 6), 28 U.S.C.A.

> Pagano by Pagano v. Massapequa Public Schools, 714 F.Supp. 641.

N.D.N.Y. 1996. Where underlying facts or circumstances may be proper subject of relief, plaintiff ought to be afforded opportunity to test his claim on merits.

> Clarke v. TRW, Inc., 921 F.Supp. 927.

Function of motion to dismiss for failure to state a claim is merely to assess legal feasibility of complaint, not to assay weight of evidence which might be offered in support thereof. Fed.Rules Civ.Proc.Rule 15, 28 U.S.C.A.

> Clarke v. TRW, Inc., 921 F.Supp. 927.

N.D.N.Y. 1995. Motion to dismiss for failure to state claim challenges sufficiency of facts alleged on face of complaint. Fed.Rules Civ. Proc.Rule 12(b)(6), 28 U.S.C.A.

> Beeman v. Lacy, Katzen, Ryen & Mittleman, 892 F.Supp. 405.

S.D.N.Y. 1996. District court's function on motion to dismiss for failure to state claim is to assess legal feasibility of complaint; issue is not whether plaintiff will ultimately prevail, but whether claimant is entitled to offer evidence to support claims. Fed.Rules Civ.Proc.Rule 12(b)(6), 28 U.S.C.A.

> In re St. Johnsbury Trucking Co., Inc., 199 B.R. 84.

S.D.N.Y. 1996. Merely because recovery appears remote and unlikely on face of complaint is not sufficient reason to dismiss for failure to state claim upon which relief can be granted; issue is not whether plaintiff will ultimately prevail but whether claimant is entitled to offer evidence to support claims. Fed.Rules Civ.Proc.Rule 12(b)(6), 28 U.S.C.A.

> In re TCW/DW North American Government Income Trust Securities Litigation, 941 F.Supp. 326, reconsideration denied.

S.D.N.Y. 1996. On motion to dismiss for failure to state claim, the issue is not whether plaintiff will ultimately prevail, but whether claimant is entitled to offer evidence to support claims. Fed.Rules Civ.Proc.Rule 12(b)(6), 28 U.S.C.A.

> Erbacci, Cerone, and Moriarty, Ltd. v. U.S., 939 F.Supp. 1045.

S.D.N.Y. 1996. Because purpose of motion to dismiss is merely to assess legal feasibility of complaint, not to assay weight of the evidence which might be offered in support thereof, plaintiff need not come forward with proof of his allegations; however, plaintiff must allege facts that taken as true constitute a claim.

> Johnson v. A.P. Products, Ltd., 934 F.Supp. 625.

S.D.N.Y. 1996. Issue on motion to dismiss for failure to state claim upon which relief may be granted is not whether plaintiff will ultimately prevail, but whether claimant is entitled to offer evidence to support claims. Fed.Rules Civ.Proc.Rule 12(b)(6), 28 U.S.C.A.

> Zheng v. I.N.S., 933 F.Supp. 338.

S.D.N.Y. 1996. In evaluating motion to dismiss for failure to state a claim, district court's function is to assess legal sufficiency of complaint; plaintiff's factual allegations must be accepted as true and all reasonable inferences must be drawn in plaintiff's favor. Fed. Rules Civ.Proc.Rule 12(b)(6), 28 U.S.C.A.

> Levitin v. Homburger, 932 F.Supp. 508, affirmed 107 F.3d 3.

S.D.N.Y. 1996. Motion to dismiss for failure to state a claim assumes that district court is authorized to resolve dispute and tests whether there is a legal dispute to resolve. Fed.Rules Civ.Proc.Rule 12(b)(6), 28 U.S.C.A.

> Dillard v. Runyon, 928 F.Supp. 1316, affirmed 108 F.3d 1369.

S.D.N.Y. 1996. Motion to dismiss for failure to state claim is viewed with disfavor and is rarely granted. Fed.Rules Civ.Proc.Rule 12(b)(6), 28 U.S.C.A.

> Walsh v. McGee, 918 F.Supp. 107.

S.D.N.Y. 1995. Improbability as to recovery is not the test for dismissal of complaint for failure to state a claim. Fed.Rules Civ.Proc. Rule 12(b)(6), 28 U.S.C.A.

> Cohen v. Litt, 906 F.Supp. 957.

S.D.N.Y. 1995. In deciding motion to dismiss for failure to state claim, role of district court is to assess legal feasibility of complaint, not to weigh evidence which might be offered at trial. Fed.Rules Civ.Proc.Rule 12(b)(6), 28 U.S.C.A.

> Odom v. Columbia University, 906 F.Supp. 188.

S.D.N.Y. 1995. Once defendant files motion to dismiss for failure to state a claim, federal district court must review complaint to assess legal feasibility of complaint. Fed.Rules Civ.Proc.Rule 12(b)(6), 28 U.S.C.A.

> Smith v. O'Connor, 901 F.Supp. 644.

S.D.N.Y. 1995. District court's function on motion to dismiss for failure to state a claim is to assess legal feasibility of complaint. Fed. Rules Civ.Proc.Rule 12(b)(6), 28 U.S.C.A.

> Gershon v. Wal-Mart Stores, Inc., 901 F.Supp. 128.

S.D.N.Y. 1995. Issue on motion to dismiss for failure to state claim on which relief can be granted is not whether plaintiff will ultimately prevail, but whether plaintiff is entitled to offer evidence to support claims. Fed.Rules Civ. Proc.Rule 12(b)(6), 28 U.S.C.A.

> Christopher v. Laidlaw Transit Inc., 899 F.Supp. 1224.

S.D.N.Y. 1995. Standard for determining whether to grant motion for judgment on the pleadings is the same as that governing motion to dismiss for failure to state claim. Fed.Rules Civ.Proc.Rule 12(b)(6), (c), 28 U.S.C.A.

> Mason Tenders Dist. Council of Greater New York v. Laborers' Intern. Union of North America, 884 F.Supp. 823.

S.D.N.Y. 1993. On motion to dismiss, court accepts all allegations in complaint as true, and dismisses only if, after drawing all inferences in plaintiffs' favor, it is clear that they are not entitled to relief.

> General Conference of Seventh-Day Adventists (Risk Management Services) v. AON Reinsurance Agency, Inc., 826 F.Supp. 107.

S.D.N.Y. 1993. As a general rule, motion to dismiss addresses only validity of plaintiff's allegations as they appear on face of complaint. Fed.Rules Civ.Proc.Rule 12(b)(6), 28 U.S.C.A.

> In re AES Corp. Securities Litigation, 825 F.Supp. 578.

In ruling on motion to dismiss complaint, "complaint" is deemed to include any document attached as exhibit or any document that complaint incorporates by reference. Fed. Rules Civ.Proc.Rule 12(b)(6), 28 U.S.C.A.

> In re AES Corp. Securities Litigation, 825 F.Supp. 578.

S.D.N.Y. 1991. Length is not by itself sufficient grounds for dismissal under rule requiring pleading to contain short and plain statement of claim. Fed.Rules Civ.Proc.Rule 8(a), 28 U.S.C.A.

> Citicorp Intern. Trading Co., Inc. v. Western Oil & Refining Co., Inc., 771 F.Supp. 600.

S.D.N.Y. 1989. Unsigned complaint could be dismissed.

> Helmsley-Spear, Inc. v. Westdeutsche Landesbank Girozentrale, 721 F.Supp. 43.

S.D.N.Y. 1988. A motion to dismiss for failure to state a cause of action is available to any party wishing to challenge formal sufficiency of claim whether it is made in complaint, counterclaim, cross claim, or third-party claim. Fed.Rules Civ.Proc.Rule 12(b)(6), 28 U.S.C.A.

> Telectronics Proprietary, Ltd. v. Medtronic, Inc., 687 F.Supp. 832.

S.D.N.Y. 1987. Complaint cannot be dismissed for failure to state claim on ground plaintiff is not immediately able to prove its allegations and offer witnesses in support thereof.

> Raine v. Lorimar Productions, Inc., 71 B.R. 450.

Under liberal pleading standards applicable in federal courts, fact that plaintiff's allegations do not support particular legal theory advanced should not necessarily result in dismissal for failure to state claim upon which relief can be granted, but rather, court must examine complaint to determine whether allegations provide for relief on any possible theory.

> Raine v. Lorimar Productions, Inc., 71 B.R. 450.

S.D.N.Y. 1987. Complaint should not be dismissed for failure to state claim unless it appears beyond doubt that plaintiff can prove no set of facts in support of claim that would entitle him to relief. Fed.Rules Civ.Proc.Rule 12(b)(6), (c), 28 U.S.C.A.

> Morse/Diesel, Inc. v. Trinity Industries, Inc., 655 F.Supp. 346, on reargument 664 F.Supp. 91, reversed 859 F.2d 242.

S.D.N.Y. 1981. Solargen Elec. Motor Car Corp. v. American Motors Corp., 530 F.Supp. 22, affirmed 697 F.2d 297, certiorari denied Solargen Electric Motor Car Corp. v. General Motors Corp., 103 S.Ct. 217, 459 U.S. 910, 74 L.Ed.2d 172.

S.D.N.Y. 1981. Kirshner v. Goldberg, 506 F.Supp. 454, affirmed 742 F.2d 1430.

E.D.N.C. 1997. Motions to dismiss for failure to state a claim upon which relief can be granted should only be granted in limited circumstances. Fed.Rules Civ.Proc.Rule 12(b)(6), 28 U.S.C.A.

> In re FAC Realty Securities Litigation, 990 F.Supp. 416.

E.D.N.C. 1993. Complaint should not be dismissed for failure to state claim upon which relief can be granted if complaint, accepting its allegations as true, allows a recovery. Fed. Rules Civ.Proc.Rule 12(b)(6), 28 U.S.C.A.

> Croydon Co., Inc. v. Unique Furnishings, Ltd., 831 F.Supp. 480.

E.D.N.C. 1988. A dismissal of complaint for failure to state a claim is likely to be granted only in the unusual case in which plaintiff includes allegations that show on the face of complaint that there is some insuperable bar to relief. Fed.Rules Civ.Proc.Rule 12(b)(6), 28 U.S.C.A.

> First Financial Sav. Bank, Inc. v. American Bankers Ins. Co. of Florida, Inc., 699 F.Supp. 1158.

M.D.N.C. 1996. Motion to dismiss for failure to state claim should only be granted in very limited circumstances. Fed.Rules Civ.Proc. Rule 12(b)(6), 28 U.S.C.A.

> Pardasani v. Rack Room Shoes Inc., 912 F.Supp. 187.

M.D.N.C. 1995. Motion to dismiss for failure to state claim should be granted only in very limited circumstances. Fed.Rules Civ.Proc. Rule 12(b)(6), 28 U.S.C.A.

> Turner v. Randolph County, N.C., 912 F.Supp. 182.

M.D.N.C. 1985. Allegations by a pro se party, even though inartfully pleaded, may require court to afford the party an opportunity to offer supporting evidence.

> Waller v. Butkovich, 605 F.Supp. 1137.

D.N.D. 1994. Dismissal is appropriate where complaint is labyrinthian prolixity of unrelated and vituperative charges that defies comprehension and amended complaint fails to cure prolixity and incomprehensibility. Fed. Rules Civ.Proc.Rule 8(a)(2), 28 U.S.C.A.

> Thomson v. Olson, 866 F.Supp. 1267, affirmed 56 F.3d 69.

N.D.Ohio 1996. Complaint is frivolous where plaintiff has failed to present claim with arguable or rational basis in fact or law.

> Czupih v. Card Pak Inc., 916 F.Supp. 687.

In determining whether claim is frivolous, district court need not accept as having an arguable basis in fact all allegations that cannot be rebutted by judicially noticeable facts; however, plaintiff's factual allegations must be weighted in favor of plaintiff.

> Czupih v. Card Pak Inc., 916 F.Supp. 687.

N.D.Ohio 1989. Attorney and litigant have continuing obligation to review and reevaluate their pleadings, motions, and other papers, and upon learning that these papers may be without merit, appropriate course is to dismiss the action.

> Costanzo v. Plain Dealer Pub. Co., 715 F.Supp. 1380.

S.D.Ohio 1997. Focus, on motion to dismiss for failure to state claim on which relief can be granted, is on whether plaintiff is entitled to offer evidence to support the claims, rather than on whether the plaintiff will ultimately prevail, as such a motion to dismiss is directed solely to complaint and any exhibits attached to it. Fed.Rules Civ.Proc.Rule 12(b)(6), 28 U.S.C.A.

> Tanksley & Associates v. Willard Industries, Inc., 961 F.Supp. 203.

S.D.Ohio 1994. Motion to dismiss for failure to state claim upon which relief can be granted requires court to determine whether cognizable claim has been pled in complaint. Fed.Rules Civ.Proc.Rules 8(a), 12(b)(6), 28 U.S.C.A.

> Misch v. Community Mut. Ins. Co., 896 F.Supp. 734.

S.D.Ohio 1994. Essence of court's inquiry on motion to dismiss for failure to state claim upon which relief can be granted is to determine whether allegations contained in complaint satisfy mandate that complaint contain short and plain statement of claim showing that pleader is entitled to relief. Fed.Rules Civ.Proc. Rules 8(a), 12(b)(6), 28 U.S.C.A.

> Pappas v. Bethesda Hosp. Ass'n, 861 F.Supp. 616.

S.D.Ohio 1993. Essence of district court's inquiry on motion to dismiss for failure to state a claim is to determine whether allegation contained in complaint satisfies mandate of federal rules that complaint contain short and plain statement of claim showing that pleader is entitled to relief. Fed.Rules Civ.Proc.Rules 8(a), 12(b)(6), 28 U.S.C.A.

> Martin v. Voinovich, 840 F.Supp. 1175.

S.D.Ohio 1993. Court will grant motion to dismiss complaint for failure to state claim only if there is absence of law to support claim of type made or of facts sufficient to make valid claim or if on face of complaint there is insurmountable bar to relief indicating that plaintiff does not have claim. Fed.Rules Civ.Proc.Rule 12(b)(6), 28 U.S.C.A.

> City of Heath, Ohio v. Ashland Oil, Inc., 834 F.Supp. 971.

S.D.Ohio 1992. Motion to dismiss attacks sufficiency of complaint. Fed.Rules Civ.Proc. Rule 12(b)(6), 28 U.S.C.A.

> Operation Badlaw, Inc. v. Licking County General Health Dist. Bd. of Health, 866 F.Supp. 1059, affirmed 991 F.2d 796.

S.D.Ohio 1992. Court will grant motion to dismiss complaint for failure to state claim upon which relief can be granted only if there is absence of law to support claim of type made or of facts sufficient to make valid claim, or if on face of complaint, there is insurmountable bar to relief indicating that plaintiff does not have claim. Fed.Rules Civ.Proc.Rule 12(b)(6), 28 U.S.C.A.

> Haffey v. Taft, 803 F.Supp. 121.

S.D.Ohio 1989. Standard for dismissal for failure to state a claim is quite liberal, but more than bare assertions of legal conclusions are ordinarily required to satisfy notice pleading requirement. Fed.Rules Civ.Proc.Rules 8(a), 12(b)(6), 28 U.S.C.A.

> In re U.S. Shoe Corp. Litigation, 718 F.Supp. 643.

W.D.Okl. 1991. That caption of Title VII plaintiff's action incorrectly stated that action was ex relatione suit did not warrant dismissal of complaint, inasmuch as body of complaint adequately identified state agency, rather than state, as defendant. Civil Rights Act of 1964, § 701 et seq., 42 U.S.C.A. § 2000e et seq.

Townsend v. State of Okl. ex rel. Oklahoma Military Dept., 760 F.Supp. 884.

W.D.Okl. 1987. Complaint should not be dismissed merely because plaintiff's allegations do not support a stated legal theory, as court is obligated to determine whether the allegations support relief under any possible theory. Fed. Rules Civ.Proc.Rule 12(b)(6), 28 U.S.C.A.

Farlow v. Peat Marwick Mitchell & Co., 666 F.Supp. 1500.

D.Or. 1997. Because motion to dismiss for failure to state claim requires court to rule before it receives any evidence, such motion is disfavored. Fed.Rules Civ.Proc.Rule 12(b)(6), 28 U.S.C.A.

Bonnichsen v. U.S., Dept. of the Army, 969 F.Supp. 614.

D.Or. 1993. Consideration of motion to dismiss complaint for failure to state a claim is limited to the complaint, and all allegations of material fact are taken as true and viewed in light most favorable to nonmoving party. Fed. Rules Civ.Proc.Rule 12(b)(6), 28 U.S.C.A.

Upchurch v. USTNet, Inc., 836 F.Supp. 737.

D.Or. 1992. Complaint should not be dismissed for failing to state claim merely because pleadings indicate that likelihood of recovery is remote.

Tigard Elec., Inc. v. National Elec. Contractors Ass'n, 790 F.Supp. 1498.

E.D.Pa. 1995. On motion to dismiss for failure to state a claim, issue is not whether plaintiff will ultimately prevail, but rather whether plaintiff would be entitled to relief under any set of facts consistent with claims set forth in the complaint. Fed.Rules Civ.Proc. Rule 12(b)(6), 28 U.S.C.A.

S.E.C. v. Bennett, 904 F.Supp. 435.

E.D.Pa. 1994. Motion to dismiss for failure to state a claim is appropriate method in which to challenge legal sufficiency of a claim. Fed.Rules Civ.Proc.Rule 12(b)(6), 28 U.S.C.A.

Bieros v. Nicola, 851 F.Supp. 683.

E.D.Pa. 1994. Motion to dismiss for failure to state claim upon which relief can be granted is appropriate method with which to challenge legal sufficiency of claim. Fed.Rules Civ.Proc.Rule 12(b)(6), 28 U.S.C.A.

Jones v. Hinton, 847 F.Supp. 41.

E.D.Pa. 1993. Motion for summary judgment may be filed where party wishes court to ascertain whether complaint's allegations have sufficient factual support to warrant their consideration at trial, and motion to dismiss for failure to state claim on which relief can be granted is generally employed to challenge legal sufficiency of claim or pleading filed in court. Fed.Rules Civ.Proc.Rules 12(b)(6), 56, 28 U.S.C.A.

Edwards v. U.S., 833 F.Supp. 521.

E.D.Pa. 1993. Notwithstanding plaintiff's pro se status, in face of motion to dismiss for failure to state claim, plaintiff's complaint had to set forth facts which, taken as true, stated claim as a matter of law. Fed.Rules Civ.Proc. Rule 12(b)(6), 28 U.S.C.A.

Taha v. I.N.S., 828 F.Supp. 362.

E.D.Pa. 1993. Motion to dismiss for failure to state a claim tests sufficiency of complaint. Fed.Rules Civ.Proc.Rule 12(b)(6), 28 U.S.C.A.

Friedman v. Lansdale Parking Authority, 151 F.R.D. 42.

E.D.Pa. 1992. To survive motion to dismiss for failure to state a claim, pleading need not correctly categorize legal theories giving rise to the claims, and court is under a duty to examine the pleadings to determine if the allegations provide for relief under any theory. Fed.Rules Civ.Proc.Rule 12(b)(6), 28 U.S.C.A.

Advanced Power Systems, Inc. v. Hi-Tech Systems, Inc., 801 F.Supp. 1450.

E.D.Pa. 1992. In resolving motion to dismiss, court must accept as true all well-pleaded allegations of complaint, construe complaint in light most favorable to plaintiffs, and determine whether, under any reasonable interpretation of the pleadings, the plaintiffs may be entitled to relief. Fed.Rules Civ.Proc.Rule 12(b)(6), 28 U.S.C.A.

Flohr v. Pennsylvania Power & Light Co., 800 F.Supp. 1252.

E.D.Pa. 1988. Dismissal on ground that upon facts and law plaintiff has shown no right to relief differs from directed verdict in jury trial in that court need not determine that defendant is entitled to judgment as a matter of law and instead, as finder of fact, court must weigh evidence and resolve disputed issues of fact and credibility. Fed.Rules Civ.Proc.Rule 41(b), 28 U.S.C.A. .

Lyncott Corp. v. Chemical Waste Management, Inc., 690 F.Supp. 1409.

M.D.Pa. 1989. Function of motion to dismiss for failure to state claim upon which relief can be granted is to test law of the claim, not facts which support it. Fed.Rules Civ.Proc.Rule 12(b)(6), 28 U.S.C.A.

U.S. v. Marisol, Inc., 725 F.Supp. 833.

M.D.Pa. 1987. An affirmative defense may not be raised by motion to dismiss for failure to state a cause of action unless facts giving rise to defense appear on face of complaint. Fed.Rules Civ.Proc.Rule 12(b)(6), 28 U.S.C.A.

> Federal Deposit Ins. Corp. v. Beall, 677 F.Supp. 279.

D.Puerto Rico 1997. Motions to dismiss for failure to state claim have no purpose other than to test formal sufficiency of statement of claim for relief. Fed.Rules Civ.Proc.Rule 12(b)(6), 28 U.S.C.A.

> Figueroa Echevarria v. Rivera Garcia, 977 F.Supp. 112, affirmed 147 F.3d 77.

Motions to dismiss for failure to state claim are not a procedure for resolving a contest about facts or merits of case. Fed.Rules Civ. Proc.Rule 12(b)(6), 28 U.S.C.A.

> Figueroa Echevarria v. Rivera Garcia, 977 F.Supp. 112, affirmed 147 F.3d 77.

D.Puerto Rico 1996. Dismissing complaint that fails to state claim is proper means to bring about just, speedy and inexpensive determination of every action as mandated by Federal Rules of Civil Procedure. Fed.Rules Civ.Proc.Rule 1, 28 U.S.C.A.

> Boschette v. Bach, 925 F.Supp. 100.

D.Puerto Rico 1996. On motion to dismiss for failure to state claim upon which relief can be granted, court analyzes complaint to determine whether there are factual allegations, either direct or inferential, regarding each material element necessary to sustain recovery under some actionable theory. Fed.Rules Civ.Proc. Rule 12(b)(6), 28 U.S.C.A.

> Schroeder v. De Bertolo, 912 F.Supp. 23.

D.Puerto Rico 1995. In ruling on motion to dismiss for failure to state claim, court shall analyze complaint to determine whether there are factual allegations, either direct or inferential, regarding each material element necessary to sustain recovery under some actionable theory. Fed.Rules Civ.Proc.Rule 12(b)(6), 28 U.S.C.A.

> Bonilla v. Trebol Motors Corp., 913 F.Supp. 655.

D.Puerto Rico 1995. On motion to dismiss for failure to state claim upon which relief may be granted, plaintiff has affirmative responsibility to put his best foot forward in effort to present legal theory that will support his claim. Fed.Rules Civ.Proc.Rule 12(b)(6), 28 U.S.C.A.

> Schroeder v. De Bertolo, 879 F.Supp. 173.

D.Puerto Rico 1991. Motions to dismiss for failure to state claim should be viewed with disfavor and rarely granted. Fed.Rule Civ.Proc. Rule 12(b)(6), 28 U.S.C.A.

> Padro v. Department of Navy, 759 F.Supp. 958.

D.R.I. 1996. Like a battlefield surgeon sorting the hopeful from the hopeless, a motion to dismiss invokes a form of legal triage, a paring of viable claims from those doomed by law. Fed.Rules Civ.Proc.Rule 12(b)(6), 28 U.S.C.A.

> Iacampo v. Hasbro, Inc., 929 F.Supp. 562.

D.S.C. 1994. Motion to dismiss for failure to state claim tests legal sufficiency of complaint. Fed.Rules Civ.Proc.Rule 12(b)(6), 28 U.S.C.A.

> Colleton Regional Hosp. v. MRS Medical Review Systems, Inc., 866 F.Supp. 896.

When reviewing motion to dismiss, court's inquiry is limited to whether plaintiffs' allegations constitute short and plain statement of claim showing that pleader is entitled to relief. Fed.Rules Civ.Proc.Rule 8(a)(2), 28 U.S.C.A.

> Colleton Regional Hosp. v. MRS Medical Review Systems, Inc., 866 F.Supp. 896.

D.S.C. 1994. Motion to dismiss for failure to state claim tests legal sufficiency of complaint. Fed.Rules Civ.Proc.Rule 12(b)(6), 28 U.S.C.A.

> Colleton Regional Hosp. v. MRS Medical Review Systems, Inc., 866 F.Supp. 891.

When reviewing motion to dismiss, court's inquiry is limited to whether plaintiffs' allegations constitute short and plain statement of claim showing that pleader is entitled to relief. Fed.Rules Civ.Proc.Rule 8(a)(2), 28 U.S.C.A.

> Colleton Regional Hosp. v. MRS Medical Review Systems, Inc., 866 F.Supp. 891.

D.S.C. 1994. Motion to dismiss for lack of jurisdiction does not necessitate ruling on merits, whereas motion to dismiss for failure to state claim does. Fed.Rules Civ.Proc.Rule 12(b)(1, 6), 28 U.S.C.A.

> Richland-Lexington Airport Dist. v. Atlas Properties, Inc., 854 F.Supp. 400.

E.D.Tenn. 1995. To warrant denial of motion to dismiss, complaint must articulate more than bare assertion of legal conclusions, but rather must contain either direct or inferential allegations respecting all material elements to sustain recovery under some viable legal theory. Fed.Rules Civ.Proc.Rule 12(b)(6), 28 U.S.C.A.

> Smith v. Grumman-Olsen Corp., 913 F.Supp. 1077.

E.D.Tenn. 1988. Dismissals for inadequate pleading are not favored and are not in keeping with spirit motivating federal rules, even where particularity requirements serve strong policy objectives.

> Montcastle v. American Health Systems, Inc., 702 F.Supp. 1369.

M.D.Tenn. 1997. In deciding motion to dismiss for failure to state a claim, function of district court is to test legal sufficiency of complaint.

> Southwest Williamson County Community Ass'n v. Slater, 976 F.Supp. 1119.

M.D.Tenn. 1996. Motion to dismiss for failure to state claim tests whether cognizable claim has been pleaded in complaint. Fed. Rules Civ.Proc.Rule 12(b)(6), 28 U.S.C.A.

> Craft v. Vanderbilt University, 940 F.Supp. 1185.

W.D.Tenn. 1997. Motions to dismiss for failure to state claim are not favored and should be granted sparingly and with caution. Fed. Rules Civ.Proc.Rule 12(b)(6), 28 U.S.C.A.

> Kutner v. Sprint Communications Co. L.P., 971 F.Supp. 302.

On motion to dismiss for failure to state claim, issue is not whether plaintiff will prevail, but rather, whether claimant is entitled to offer evidence to support claims. Fed.Rules Civ. Proc.Rule 12(b)(6), 28 U.S.C.A.

> Kutner v. Sprint Communications Co. L.P., 971 F.Supp. 302.

W.D.Tenn. 1995. Motion to dismiss for failure to state claim tests whether claim has been adequately stated in the complaint. Fed. Rules Civ.Proc.Rule 12(b)(6), 28 U.S.C.A.

> Scarborough v. Brown Group, Inc., 935 F.Supp. 954.

W.D.Tenn. 1988. Plaintiffs who did not sign complaint would be allowed ten days to file a verbatim copy of the complaint signed by them, providing necessary address information, or suffer sua sponte dismissal by the court. Fed.Rules Civ.Proc.Rule 11, 28 U.S.C.A.

> Duke v. Crowell, 120 F.R.D. 511.

E.D.Tex. 1994. Motion to dismiss for failure to state claim is viewed with disfavor, and is rarely granted. Fed.Rules Civ.Proc.Rule 12(b)(6), 28 U.S.C.A.

> Hawkins v. Upjohn Co., 890 F.Supp. 609.

N.D.Tex. 1998. Motion to dismiss for failure to state a claim is viewed with disfavor, and is rarely granted. Fed.Rules Civ.Proc.Rule 12(b)(6), 28 U.S.C.A.

> Maricle v. Biggerstaff, 10 F.Supp.2d 705, reconsideration denied 1998 WL 204652.

N.D.Tex. 1998. Motions to dismiss for failure to state a claim are viewed with disfavor and are rarely granted. Fed.Rules Civ.Proc. Rule 12(b)(6), 28 U.S.C.A.

> Burlington Northern & Santa Fe Ry. Co. v. Consolidated Fibers, Inc., 7 F.Supp.2d 822.

N.D.Tex. 1996. Facts pled in complaint must be specific and not merely conclusory.

> Jewel Recovery, L.P. v. Gordon, 196 B.R. 348.

N.D.Tex. 1996. Motion to dismiss complaint for failure to state claim is viewed with disfavor. Fed.Rules Civ.Proc.Rule 12(b)(6), 28 U.S.C.A.

> Roberts v. Dayton Hudson Corp., 914 F.Supp. 1421.

N.D.Tex. 1995. Motion to dismiss for failure to state a claim tests legal sufficiency of claim stated in complaint and must be evaluated solely on basis of pleadings. Fed.Rules Civ. Proc.Rule 12(b)(6), 28 U.S.C.A.

> Cook v. Fidelity Investments, 908 F.Supp. 438.

N.D.Tex. 1995. Generally, motion to dismiss for failure to state claim upon which relief can be granted is viewed with disfavor and is rarely granted. Fed.Rules Civ.Proc.Rule 12(b)(6), 28 U.S.C.A.

> U.S. v. Bantau, 907 F.Supp. 988.

N.D.Tex. 1993. Conclusory allegations and unwarranted deductions of fact are not admitted as true by motion to dismiss for failure to state claim. Fed.Rules Civ.Proc.Rule 12(b), (b)(6), 28 U.S.C.A.

> Tuchman v. DSC Communications Corp., 818 F.Supp. 971, affirmed 14 F.3d 1061, rehearing and rehearing denied 20 F.3d 1172.

S.D.Tex. 1996. Motions to dismiss for failure to state claim are viewed with disfavor and are rarely granted, and court in considering motion is to accept facts as pleaded by plaintiff as true and to construe complaint liberally. Fed.Rules Civ.Proc.Rule 12(b)(6), 28 U.S.C.A.

> U.S. ex rel. James M. Thompson v. Columbia/HCA Healthcare Corp., 938 F.Supp. 399, affirmed in part, vacated in part 125 F.3d 899, rehearing denied.

S.D.Tex. 1996. Motion to dismiss for failure to state claim tests only formal sufficiency of statements of claims for relief; it is not procedure for resolving contests about facts or merits of case. Fed.Rules Civ.Proc.Rule 12(b)(6), 28 U.S.C.A.

> Jolly v. Klein, 923 F.Supp. 931.

S.D.Tex. 1995. Motion to dismiss for failure to state claim tests only formal sufficiency of the statements of the claims for relief and is not a procedure for resolving contests about facts or merits of case. Fed.Rules Civ.Proc.Rule 12(b)(6), 28 U.S.C.A.

> Patton v. United Parcel Service, Inc., 910 F.Supp. 1250.

S.D.Tex. 1995. Motion to dismiss for failure to state a claim tests only formal sufficiency of statements of claims for relief; it is not a procedure for resolving contests about facts or merits of case. Fed.Rules Civ.Proc.Rule 12(b)(6), 28 U.S.C.A.

> Bonton v. Archer Chrysler Plymouth, Inc., 889 F.Supp. 995.

S.D.Tex. 1995. Dismissals for failure to state claim are rare. Fed.Rules Civ.Proc.Rule 12(b), 28 U.S.C.A.

> Mason v. F.D.I.C., 888 F.Supp. 799.

S.D.Tex. 1994. Motions to dismiss for failure to state claim are disfavored and may not be granted unless it appears to a certainty that plaintiff would not be entitled to recover under any state of facts which could be proved in support of its claim. Fed.Rules Civ.Proc.Rule 12, 28 U.S.C.A.

> TCA Bldg. Co. v. Northwestern Resources Co., 861 F.Supp. 1366.

S.D.Tex. 1994. To survive motion to dismiss for failure to state claim, plaintiff must allege facts, not conclusory allegations, to outline cause of action. Fed.Rules Civ.Proc.Rule 12(b)(6), 28 U.S.C.A.

> Kjellvander v. Citicorp, 156 F.R.D. 138.

S.D.Tex. 1991. Dismissal of complaint for failure to state claim upon which relief can be granted is warranted when plaintiff has failed to plead necessary elements of offenses claimed and thus could not prevail even if it could adduce evidence to support each such allegation. Fed.Rules Civ.Proc.Rule 12(b)(6), 28 U.S.C.A.

> Rockbit Industries U.S.A., Inc. v. Baker Hughes, Inc., 802 F.Supp. 1544.

S.D.Tex. 1987. Implicit in inherent power of district court to dismiss case at any time for failure to prove a claim is power to dismiss where plaintiff has failed even to state a claim, and there is no absolute requirement that such a dismissal be delayed until the close of plaintiff's case.

> Allstate Homecraft, Inc. v. Kaiser Aluminum and Chemical Sales, Inc., 672 F.Supp. 965, vacated 857 F.2d 1471.

W.D.Tex. 1987. In order to avoid dismissal for failure to state cause of action, issue presented cannot be insubstantial, or obviously without merit or foreclosed by prior decisions. Fed.Rules Civ.Proc.Rule 12, 28 U.S.C.A.

> Missouri Pacific R. Co. v. Railroad Com'n of Texas, 653 F.Supp. 617, affirmed in part, reversed in part 833 F.2d 570, rehearing denied 845 F.2d 1022, on remand 823 F.Supp. 1360, affirmed 948 F.2d 179, certiorari denied Railroad Com'n of Texas v. Missouri Pac. R.R., 113 S.Ct. 1943, 507 U.S. 1050, 123 L.Ed.2d 649.

E.D.Va. 1994. Complaint that fails to allege essential element of claim is subject to dismissal for failure to state claim upon which relief may be granted. Fed.Rules Civ.Proc.Rule 12(b)(6), 28 U.S.C.A.

> Chisolm v. Charlie Falk Auto Wholesalers, Inc., 851 F.Supp. 739, vacated 95 F.3d 331.

E.D.Va. 1993. Court should not dismiss complaint for failure to state a claim even if it appears on face of pleadings that chance of recovery is very remote. Fed.Rules Civ.Proc. Rule 12(b)(6), 28 U.S.C.A.

> B.M.H. by C.B. v. School Bd. of City of Chesapeake, Va., 833 F.Supp. 560.

E.D.Va. 1992. Motion to dismiss for lack of subject matter jurisdiction may attack the complaint on its face on grounds that it fails to allege facts upon which court can base jurisdiction, or may attack the truth of the underlying jurisdictional allegations contained in the complaint. Fed.Rules Civ.Proc.Rule 12(b)(1), 28 U.S.C.A.

> E.E.O.C. v. Alford, 142 F.R.D. 283.

W.D.Va. 1996. Dismissals for failure to state a claim are generally disfavored and are granted only when it appears beyond doubt that plaintiff can prove no set of facts in support of claim which would entitle plaintiff to relief. Fed.Rules Civ.Proc.Rule 12(b)(6), 28 U.S.C.A.

> Brzonkala v. Virginia Polytechnic and State University, 935 F.Supp. 779, reversed 132 F.3d 949, rehearing granted, opinion vacated.

D.Virgin Islands 1995. Standards for granting motion to dismiss complaint for failure to state claim differ from those for granting motion for judgment on pleadings; in considering motion to dismiss for failure to state claim, court accepts as true well-pleaded allegations in complaint, while judgment on pleadings is not proper unless undenied facts in both complaint and answer support judgment for moving party as matter of law. Fed.Rules Civ.Proc.Rule 12(b)(6), (c), 28 U.S.C.A.

> Mingolla v. Minnesota Min. and Mfg. Co., 893 F.Supp. 499.

D.Virgin Islands 1987. Bungled signature on pleading is merely technical defect and not substantive violation of Rule 11, which would warrant voiding of complaint or its dismissal. Fed.Rules Civ.Proc.Rule 11, 28 U.S.C.A.

> Edwards v. Groner, 116 F.R.D. 578.

N.D.W.Va. 1997. Motion to dismiss for failure to state a claim functions to test formal sufficiency of statement of claim for relief; it is not procedure for resolving contest about facts or merits of case. Fed.Rules Civ.Proc.Rule 12(b)(6), 28 U.S.C.A.

> Henegar v. Sears, Roebuck and Co., 965 F.Supp. 833.

N.D.W.Va. 1995. Motion to dismiss for failure to state claim should be granted only in very limited circumstances. Fed.Rules Civ. Proc.Rule 12(b)(6), 28 U.S.C.A.

Booth v. Old Nat. Bank, 900 F.Supp. 836.

E.D.Wis. 1993. Although all reasonable inferences are to be drawn in favor of plaintiffs when ruling on motion to dismiss for failure to state claim for relief, complaint must set forth factual allegations sufficient to establish elements that are crucial to recovery under plaintiffs' claims; legal conclusions without factual support are not sufficient. Fed.Rules Civ.Proc. Rule 12(b)(6), 28 U.S.C.A.

Kaufmann v. U.S., 840 F.Supp. 641.

E.D.Wis. 1993. Plaintiff may not avoid dismissal of complaint simply by attaching bare legal conclusions to narrated facts which fail to outline basis of its claim. Fed.Rules Civ.Proc. Rule 12(b), 28 U.S.C.A.

Wag-Aero, Inc. v. U.S., 837 F.Supp. 1479, affirmed 35 F.3d 569, rehearing denied.

W.D.Wis. 1993. Complaint must set forth factual allegations sufficient to establish elements that are crucial to recovery under plaintiff's claim in order to overcome motion to dismiss for failure to state a claim, even though all reasonable inferences are to be drawn in favor of plaintiff; legal conclusions without factual support are not sufficient. Fed.Rules Civ. Proc.Rule 12(b)(6), 28 U.S.C.A.

Petersen v. University of Wisconsin Bd. of Regents, 818 F.Supp. 1276.

9th Cir.BAP (Alaska) 1994. Complaint that merely recites statutory language fails to state claim upon which relief can be granted. Fed.Rules Civ.Proc.Rule 12(b)(6), 28 U.S.C.A.

In re Kubick, 171 B.R. 658.

Bkrtcy.E.D.Ark. 1996. Rule setting forth general rules of pleading is to be liberally construed, and motions to dismiss are disfavored. Fed.Rules Civ.Proc.Rule 8, 28 U.S.C.A.

In re Jagitsch, 201 B.R. 961.

Bkrtcy.D.Conn. 1995. Motion to dismiss for failure to state claim upon which relief can be granted essentially tests legal sufficiency of plaintiff's complaint. Fed.Rules Civ.Proc.Rule 12(b)(6), 28 U.S.C.A.; Fed.Rules Bankr.Proc. Rule 7012, 11 U.S.C.A.

In re Carter Hill Associates, 188 B.R. 5.

Bkrtcy.D.Del. 1993. Inconsistent pleadings is not ground to dismiss.

Matter of Century Glove, Inc., 151 B.R. 327.

Bkrtcy.D.Dist.Col. 1993. Complaint must only allege plausible grounds in order for it to survive motion to dismiss.

In re Beitzell & Co., Inc., 163 B.R. 637.

Bkrtcy.M.D.Fla. 1995. Dismissal for failure to state claim upon which relief can be granted is disfavored. Fed.Rules Civ.Proc.Rule 12(b)(6), 28 U.S.C.A.

In re Ricketson, 190 B.R. 684.

Bkrtcy.M.D.Fla. 1995. Courts generally do not favor dismissal for failure to state claim for which relief can be granted.

In re American Fabricators, Inc., 186 B.R. 526.

Bkrtcy.N.D.Ill. 1996. Alleging mere legal conclusions, without factual predicate, is inadequate to state claim for relief. Fed.Rules Civ. Proc.Rule 12, 28 U.S.C.A.; Fed.Rules Bankr. Proc.Rule 7012(b), 11 U.S.C.A.

In re Allard, 198 B.R. 715.

Bkrtcy.N.D.Ill. 1993. Plaintiff has failed to state claim upon which relief can be granted if complaint does not adequately plead some theory upon which plaintiff could recover. Fed. Rules Civ.Proc.Rule 12(b), 28 U.S.C.A.

In re Germansen Decorating, Inc., 149 B.R. 522.

Bkrtcy.D.Mass. 1996. In First Circuit, dismissal of complaint based on forum selection clause is properly accomplished by motion to dismiss for failure to state claim, not by motion to dismiss for improper venue. Fed.Rules Civ. Proc.Rule 12(b)(3, 6), 28 U.S.C.A.

In re Healthco Intern., Inc., 195 B.R. 971.

Bkrtcy.D.Mass. 1987. One vague provision in otherwise straightforward and specific complaint does not make entire complaint too ethereal to answer, nor does it justify dismissal.

In re Herbst, 76 B.R. 882.

Bkrtcy.E.D.Mich. 1991. Fact that counterclaimants' legal theory might have been mischaracterized was not sufficient to support dismissal for failure to state claim. Fed.Rules Civ.Proc.Rule 12(b)(6), 28 U.S.C.A.

In re Gaylor, 123 B.R. 236.

Bkrtcy.D.Nev. 1986. "Claim" on which relief can be granted means aggregate of operative facts which give rise to right enforceable in courts, or refers to set of facts giving rise to one or more legal rights. Fed.Rules Civ.Proc.Rule 12(b)(6), 28 U.S.C.A.

In re Baker, 66 B.R. 652.

Bkrtcy.D.N.J. 1998. Under view of flexible construction, rules governing form of pleading should be liberally construed, and motions to dismiss complaints based on pleading errors are to be disfavored. Fed.Rules Civ.Proc.Rule 8, 28 U.S.C.A.

In re Little, 220 B.R. 13.

Bkrtcy.E.D.N.Y. 1994. Motion to dismiss for failure to state claim upon which relief can be granted tests only the legal sufficiency of complaint and is not designed to assess factual basis of claim; question raised by such a motion is not whether claimant is entitled to prevail, but whether he is entitled to offer evidence in support of claim. Fed.Rules Civ.Proc.Rule 12(b)(6), 28 U.S.C.A.

In re Perez, 173 B.R. 284.

Bkrtcy.E.D.N.Y. 1993. Task of federal court on motion to dismiss for failure to state claim upon which relief can be granted is to determine legal sufficiency of complaint and not to assay factual basis of claim for relief. Fed. Rules Civ.Proc.Rule 12(b)(6), 28 U.S.C.A.

In re Gouiran Holdings, Inc., 158 B.R. 3, reversed 165 B.R. 104.

Deference accorded to plaintiff, on motion to dismiss for failure to state claim upon which relief can be granted, is not without limitation; plaintiff's pleading must provide defendant with fair notice of plaintiff's claim and of grounds upon which it rests so as to permit defendant to prepare appropriate defense. Fed.Rules Civ. Proc.Rule 12(b)(6), 28 U.S.C.A.

In re Gouiran Holdings, Inc., 158 B.R. 3, reversed 165 B.R. 104.

To withstand motion to dismiss for failure to state claim upon which relief can be granted, complaint must be well-pleaded and contain more than bald, conclusory or overly generalized statements that plaintiff has valid claim of some type against defendant. Fed.Rules Civ. Proc.Rule 12(b)(6), 28 U.S.C.A.

In re Gouiran Holdings, Inc., 158 B.R. 3, reversed 165 B.R. 104.

Bkrtcy.E.D.N.Y. 1993. Complaint should not be dismissed merely because plaintiff's allegations are not supported by specific legal theory advanced; rather, court is under duty to examine complaint to determine if any possible theory for relief exists. Fed.Rules Civ.Proc.Rule 12(b)(6), 28 U.S.C.A.

In re Perez, 155 B.R. 844.

Bkrtcy.E.D.N.Y. 1993. Although threshold pleading requirements to withstand motion to dismiss for failure to state claim are low, deference accorded plaintiff is not without limitation; defendant is entitled to fair notice of nature of plaintiff's claim and grounds upon which it rests so as to frame responsive pleading. Fed. Rules Civ.Proc.Rule 12(b)(6), 28 U.S.C.A.

In re Harvard Knitwear, Inc., 153 B.R. 617.

If threshold pleading requirements are not met, dismissal is warranted, ordinarily accompanied by leave to file amended complaint. Fed.Rules Civ.Proc.Rule 12(b)(6), 28 U.S.C.A.

In re Harvard Knitwear, Inc., 153 B.R. 617.

Bkrtcy.E.D.N.Y. 1993. Complaint should not be dismissed for failing to state claim upon which relief can be granted merely because

plaintiff's allegations are not supported by the specific legal theory advanced; rather, court is under duty to examine complaint to determine if any possible theory for relief exists. Fed. Rules Civ.Proc.Rule 12(b)(6), 28 U.S.C.A.

In re Rosen, 151 B.R. 648.

Bkrtcy.E.D.N.Y. 1992. Complaint should not be dismissed for failure to state claim merely because plaintiff's allegations are not supported by specific legal theory advanced; rather, court is under duty to examine complaint to determine if any possible theory for relief exists. Fed.Rules Civ.Proc.Rule 12(b)(6), 28 U.S.C.A.

In re Rifkin, 142 B.R. 61.

Bkrtcy.E.D.N.Y. 1992. Complaint should not be dismissed merely because plaintiff's allegations are not supported by specific legal theory advanced; instead, court is under duty to examine complaint to determine if any possible theory for relief exists.

In re Nemko, Inc., 136 B.R. 334, affirmed in part, remanded in part 202 B.R. 673, on remand 209 B.R. 590.

Bkrtcy.S.D.N.Y. 1996. On motion to dismiss for failure to state claim, focus of inquiry is whether pleading is sufficient to entitle claimant to offer evidence in support of his claims, not likelihood of plaintiff's success. Fed.Rules Civ. Proc.Rule 12(b)(6), 28 U.S.C.A.

In re Bradlees Stores, Inc., 194 B.R. 555, appeal dismissed 210 B.R. 506.

Bkrtcy.S.D.N.Y. 1995. Court's function in evaluating whether complaint states valid claim is not to weigh evidence that might be presented at trial but merely to determine whether claim is legally sufficient. Fed.Rules Civ.Proc.Rule 12(b)(6), 28 U.S.C.A.; Fed.Rules Bankr.Proc. Rule 7012, 11 U.S.C.A.

In re 72nd Street Realty Associates, 185 B.R. 460.

Bkrtcy.E.D.Pa. 1996. Motions to dismiss for failure to state claim are generally viewed with disfavor and are to be granted only in the unusual case in which plaintiff alleges facts that show on face of complaint that there is some insuperable bar to relief requested. Fed.Rules Civ.Proc.Rule 12(b)(6), 28 U.S.C.A.

In re DuFrayne, 194 B.R. 354.

When presented with motion to dismiss for failure to state claim, issue before court is not whether plaintiff ultimately will prevail, but whether plaintiff is entitled to offer evidence in support of its claims; that recovery appears to be remote or unlikely on face of pleadings in not the test. Fed.Rules Civ.Proc.Rule 12(b)(6), 28 U.S.C.A.

In re DuFrayne, 194 B.R. 354.

Bkrtcy.D.Vt. 1990. Upon motion to dismiss for failure to state claim upon which relief may be granted, court will not be influenced by mere possibility that ultimate recovery is remote or tenuous. Fed.Rules Civ.Proc.Rule 12(b)(6), 28 U.S.C.A.

> In re Kelton Motors Inc., 121 B.R. 166.

☞1772. Insufficiency in general.

Library references

> C.J.S. Federal Civil Procedure § 819 et seq.

U.S.Cal. 1993. Complaint should not be dismissed for failure to state claim on which relief can be granted unless it appears beyond doubt that plaintiff can prove no set of facts in support of his claim which would entitle him to relief. Fed.Rules Civ.Proc.Rule 12(b)(6), 28 U.S.C.A.

> Hartford Fire Ins. Co. v. California, 113 S.Ct. 2891, 509 U.S. 764, 125 L.Ed.2d 612, on remand In re Insurance Antitrust Litigation, 5 F.3d 1556.

C.A.D.C. 1997. Dismissal for failure to state claim is proper when, taking material allegations of complaint as admitted, and construing them in plaintiffs' favor, court finds that plaintiffs have failed to allege all the material elements of their cause of action. Fed.Rules Civ.Proc.Rule 12(b)(6), 28 U.S.C.A.

> Taylor v. F.D.I.C., 132 F.3d 753, 328 U.S.App.D.C. 52.

Vague and conclusory complaint may survive motion to dismiss for failure to state claim where more detail would disclose fatal weaknesses; defendants' remedy in such situation is not to move for dismissal but to serve contention interrogatories or to proceed to summary judgment. Fed.Rules Civ.Proc.Rules 12(b)(6), 56, 28 U.S.C.A.

> Taylor v. F.D.I.C., 132 F.3d 753, 328 U.S.App.D.C. 52.

C.A.D.C. 1996. While complaint may not be dismissed unless plaintiff can prove no set of facts that would entitle him or her to relief, complaint must, to survive motion to dismiss, give defendant fair notice of what plaintiff's claim is and grounds upon which it rests.

> Modderno v. King, 82 F.3d 1059, 317 U.S.App.D.C. 255, rehearing and suggestion for rehearing denied, certiorari denied 117 S.Ct. 772, 136 L.Ed.2d 717.

C.A.D.C. 1994. Claims may be dismissed, sua sponte if necessary, for failure to state claim on which relief may be granted whenever plaintiff cannot possibly win relief. Fed.Rules Civ. Proc.Rule 12(b)(6), 28 U.S.C.A.

> Best v. Kelly, 39 F.3d 328, 309 U.S.App. D.C. 51.

C.A.D.C. 1994. Complaint should not be dismissed for failure to state claim unless plaintiffs can prove no set of facts in support of their claim which would entitled them to relief. Fed. Rules Civ.Proc.Rule 12(b)(6), 28 U.S.C.A.

> Kowal v. MCI Communications Corp., 16 F.3d 1271, 305 U.S.App.D.C. 60.

C.A.D.C. 1984. While a complaint should not be dismissed unless trial court determines that the allegations do not support relief on any legal theory, complaint nonetheless must set forth sufficient information to suggest that there is some recognized legal theory upon which relief may be granted.

> District of Columbia v. Air Florida, Inc., 750 F.2d 1077, 243 U.S.App.D.C. 1.

Before a complaint may be dismissed for failure to state a claim, trial court must determine that allegations do not support relief on any possible theory.

> District of Columbia v. Air Florida, Inc., 750 F.2d 1077, 243 U.S.App.D.C. 1.

C.A.D.C. 1972. Irons v. Schuyler, 465 F.2d 608, 151 U.S.App.D.C. 23, certiorari denied 93 S.Ct. 682, 409 U.S. 1076, 34 L.Ed.2d 664, on remand 369 F.Supp. 403, cause remanded 548 F.2d 992, 179 U.S.App.D.C. 37, certiorari denied 98 S.Ct. 505, 434 U.S. 965, 54 L.Ed.2d 451, appeal after remand 670 F.2d 265, 216 U.S.App.D.C. 107.

C.A.3 1984. Pro se complaints are held to less stringent standards than formal pleadings drafted by lawyers and allegations contained therein are to be liberally construed.

> Becker v. C.I.R., 751 F.2d 146, on remand 1985 WL 15382.

C.A.Fed. 1996. When jurisdiction has been established, court must nonetheless dismiss complaint when plaintiff pleads a cause within the court's jurisdiction but does not assert a set of facts which, if proven, would support the claim.

> Aerolineas Argentinas v. U.S., 77 F.3d 1564, rehearing denied, in banc suggestion declined.

C.A.Fed. 1995. Dismissal for failure to state a claim is a decision on the merits which focuses on whether complaint contains allegations that, if proven, are sufficient to entitle party to relief.

> Gould, Inc. v. U.S., 67 F.3d 925.

C.A.Fed. 1995. Motion to dismiss for failure to state claim on which relief could be granted is appropriate where plaintiff cannot assert set of facts which would support its claim. RCFC, Rule 12(b)(4), 28 U.S.C.A.

> Highland Falls-Fort Montgomery Cent. School Dist. v. U.S., 48 F.3d 1166, certiorari denied 116 S.Ct. 80, 516 U.S. 820, 133 L.Ed.2d 38.

C.A.Fed. 1993. Motion to dismiss for failure to state claim upon which relief can be granted is appropriate where plaintiff cannot assert set of facts which would support its claim. RCFC, Rule 12(b)(4), 28 U.S.C.A.

> Mitchell Arms, Inc. v. U.S., 7 F.3d 212, certiorari denied 114 S.Ct. 2100, 511 U.S. 1106, 128 L.Ed.2d 662.

C.A.Fed. 1992. Complaint should be dismissed for failure to state claim only if it appears beyond doubt that plaintiff can prove no set of facts that would entitle him to relief. Mostowy v. U.S., 966 F.2d 668.

C.A.Fed. 1991. Under "simplified notice pleading" of Federal Rules of Civil Procedure, allegations of complaint or petition should be construed liberally and complaint should not be dismissed for failure to state claim unless it appears beyond doubt that plaintiff or petitioner can prove no set of facts in support of his claim which would entitle him to relief. Fed.Rules Civ.Proc.Rule 12, 28 U.S.C.A.

> Scotch Whisky Ass'n v. U.S. Distilled Products Co., 952 F.2d 1317.

C.A.Fed. (Cal.) 1998. Dismissal based on failure to state claim is proper only when, on complainant's version of facts, premises of cognizable claim have not been stated. Fed.Rules Civ.Proc.Rule 12(b)(6), 28 U.S.C.A.

> Bradley v. Chiron Corp., 136 F.3d 1317.

Conclusory allegations of law and unwarranted inferences of fact do not suffice to support claim, for purpose of motion to dismiss alleging failure to state claim. Fed.Rules Civ.Proc.Rule 12(b)(6), 28 U.S.C.A.

> Bradley v. Chiron Corp., 136 F.3d 1317.

C.A.Fed. (Cal.) 1988. Dismissal for failure to state claim is proper where it appears beyond doubt that plaintiff can prove no set of facts which would entitle him to relief.

> Constant v. Advanced Micro-Devices, Inc., 848 F.2d 1560, certiorari denied 109 S.Ct. 228, 488 U.S. 892, 102 L.Ed.2d 218.

C.A.11 (Ala.) 1994. Dismissal of complaint for failure to state claim is proper only if it is clear that no relief could be granted under any set of facts that could be proved consistent with allegations. Fed.Rules Civ.Proc.Rule 12(b)(6), 28 U.S.C.A.

> Blackston v. State of Ala., 30 F.3d 117, appeal after remand 117 F.3d 1432.

C.A.11 (Ala.) 1993. Complaint should not be dismissed for failure to state claim unless it appears beyond doubt that plaintiff can prove no set of facts which would entitle her to relief. Fed.Rules Civ.Proc.Rule 12(b)(6), 28 U.S.C.A.

> Cannon v. Macon County, 1 F.3d 1558, opinion modified on rehearing 15 F.3d 1022.

C.A.11 (Ala.) 1993. Court may dismiss complaint pursuant to Rule 12(b)(6) when, on basis of dispositive issue of law, no construction of factual allegations will support cause of action. Fed.Rules Civ.Proc.Rule 12(b)(6), 28 U.S.C.A.

> Marshall County Bd. of Educ. v. Marshall County Gas Dist., 992 F.2d 1171.

C.A.9 (Ariz.) 1995. Plaintiff failed to state claim upon which relief could be granted where plaintiff's claims were merely attempts to relitigate issues which were fully resolved by Ninth Circuit Court of Appeals and by other court of appeals. Fed.Rules Civ.Proc.Rule 12(b)(6), 28 U.S.C.A.

> Foster v. Skinner, 70 F.3d 1084.

C.A.8 (Ark.) 1994. A complaint should not be dismissed for failure to state a claim unless it appears beyond doubt that plaintiff can prove no set of facts in support of his claim which would entitle him to relief. Fed.Rules Civ.Proc. Rule 12(b)(6), 28 U.S.C.A.

> Coleman v. Watt, 40 F.3d 255, appeal after remand 108 F.3d 1381.

C.A.8 (Ark.) 1994. Motions to dismiss for failure to state a claim should not be granted unless it is clear beyond a doubt that there is no set of facts plaintiff could prove that would entitle him to relief. Fed.Rules Civ.Proc.Rule 12(b)(6), 28 U.S.C.A.

> Forbes v. Arkansas Educational Television Communication Network Foundation, 22 F.3d 1423, rehearing denied, and rehearing denied, and rehearing withdrawn, certiorari denied Arkansas Educational Television Com'n v. Forbes, 115 S.Ct. 500, 513 U.S. 995, 130 L.Ed.2d 409, certiorari denied 115 S.Ct. 1962, 514 U.S. 1110, 131 L.Ed.2d 853, appeal after remand 93 F.3d 497, certiorari granted 117 S.Ct. 1243, 137 L.Ed.2d 326, reversed Arkansas Educ. Television Com'n v. Forbes, 118 S.Ct. 1633, 140 L.Ed.2d 875, on remand 145 F.3d 1017, vacated 145 F.3d 1017.

C.A.8 (Ark.) 1994. Complaint may not be dismissed for failure to state claim upon which relief can be granted, unless it appears beyond doubt that plaintiff can prove no set of facts in support of claim that would entitle plaintiff to relief. Fed.Rules Civ.Proc.Rule 12(b)(6), 28 U.S.C.A.

> Smith v. St. Bernards Regional Medical Center, 19 F.3d 1254.

C.A.9 (Cal.) 1998. Conclusory allegations of law and unwarranted inferences are insufficient to defeat a motion to dismiss for failure to state a claim. Fed.Rules Civ.Proc.Rule 12(b)(6), 28 U.S.C.A.

> Parrino v. FHP, Inc., 146 F.3d 699, as amended.

C.A.9 (Cal.) 1998. Conclusory allegations of law and unwarranted inferences are not sufficient to defeat motion to dismiss for failure to state claim. Fed.Rules Civ.Proc.Rule 12(b)(6), 28 U.S.C.A.

> Pareto v. F.D.I.C., 139 F.3d 696.

C.A.9 (Cal.) 1996. Conclusory allegations of law and unwarranted inferences are insufficient to defeat motion to dismiss for failure to state claim.

> In re Syntex Corp. Securities Litigation, 95 F.3d 922.

C.A.9 (Cal.) 1996. Conclusory allegations of law and unwarranted inferences are insufficient to defeat motion to dismiss for failure to state a claim. Fed.Rules Civ.Proc.Rule 12(b)(6), 28 U.S.C.A.

> In re Stac Electronics Securities Litigation, 89 F.3d 1399, certiorari denied Anderson v. Clow, 117 S.Ct. 1105, 137 L.Ed.2d 308.

C.A.9 (Cal.) 1996. Court may dismiss complaint as matter of law for (1) lack of cognizable legal theory or (2) insufficient facts under cognizable legal claim. Fed.Rules Civ. Proc.Rule 12(b)(6), 28 U.S.C.A.

> SmileCare Dental Group v. Delta Dental Plan of California, Inc., 88 F.3d 780, certiorari denied 117 S.Ct. 583, 136 L.Ed.2d 513.

C.A.9 (Cal.) 1996. Rule requiring each averment of pleading to be simple, concise, and direct, applies to good claims as well as bad, and may be basis for dismissal independent of whether pleadings are subject to dismissal for failure to state a claim. Fed.Rules Civ.Proc. Rules 8, 12(b)(6), 28 U.S.C.A.

> McHenry v. Renne, 84 F.3d 1172.

Rights of defendants to be free from costly and harassing litigation, and rights of litigants awaiting their turns to have other matters resolved, must be considered in determining whether to dismiss prolix, confusing complaint. Fed.Rules Civ.Proc.Rule 8, 28 U.S.C.A.

> McHenry v. Renne, 84 F.3d 1172.

District court did not abuse its discretion in dismissing third amended complaint with prejudice for violation of general pleading rules and court's prior orders requiring short, clear statement of claims sufficient to allow defendants to prepare responsive pleading, in light of district court's prior unsuccessful use of less drastic alternatives by allowing repleading twice, court's consideration of strength of plaintiffs' case by referring matter for extensive analysis by magistrate, and court's consideration of ex-tensive burden imposed on defendants by same plaintiffs in related litigation; 53-page third amended complaint was written more as a press release and failed to obey court's prior orders to identify which defendants were liable on which claims. Fed.Rules Civ.Proc.Rules 8, 41(b), 28 U.S.C.A.

> McHenry v. Renne, 84 F.3d 1172.

C.A.9 (Cal.) 1996. Dismissal of complaint is appropriate when complaint fails to state claim.

> Mathis v. Pacific Gas and Elec. Co., 75 F.3d 498.

C.A.9 (Cal.) 1994. Complaint could not be dismissed for failure to state a claim upon which relief can be granted unless it appeared certain that plaintiff could prove no set of facts in support of his claim which would entitle him to relief. Fed.Rules Civ.Proc.Rule 12(b)(6), 28 U.S.C.A.

> Moyo v. Gomez, 40 F.3d 982, certiorari denied California Dept. of Corrections v. Moyo, 115 S.Ct. 732, 513 U.S. 1081, 130 L.Ed.2d 635.

C.A.9 (Cal.) 1994. Complaint may not be dismissed for failure to state claim unless it appears, taking all of plaintiff's allegations of material fact as true and construed in most favorable light, that plaintiff can prove no set of facts in support of his claim. Fed.Rules Civ. Proc.Rule 12(b)(6), 28 U.S.C.A.

> Moyo v. Gomez, 32 F.3d 1382, opinion amended 40 F.3d 982, certiorari denied California Dept. of Corrections v. Moyo, 115 S.Ct. 732, 513 U.S. 1081, 130 L.Ed.2d 635.

C.A.9 (Cal.) 1994. Dismissal for failure to state claim is proper only if it appears beyond doubt that plaintiff can prove no set of facts in support of his claim which would entitle him to relief. Fed.Rules Civ.Proc.Rule 12(b)(6), 28 U.S.C.A.

> Pillsbury, Madison & Sutro v. Lerner, 31 F.3d 924.

C.A.9 (Cal.) 1994. Complaint should not be dismissed for failure to state a claim unless it appears beyond a doubt that plaintiff can prove no set of facts in support of claim that would entitle him to relief; however, court is not required to accept conclusions cast in form of factual allegations if those conclusions cannot reasonably be drawn from facts alleged. Fed. Rules Civ.Proc.Rule 12(b)(6), 28 U.S.C.A.

> Clegg v. Cult Awareness Network, 18 F.3d 752.

C.A.9 (Cal.) 1994. Only if plaintiffs can prove no set of facts in support of claim which would entitle plaintiff to relief, is dismissal warranted. Fed.Rules Civ.Proc.Rule 12(b)(6), 28 U.S.C.A.

> Barron v. Reich, 13 F.3d 1370.

C.A.9 (Cal.) 1993. Court will not dismiss complaint unless it appears beyond doubt that plaintiff can prove no set of facts in support of his claim which would entitle him to relief. Fed.Rules Civ.Proc.Rule 12(b)(6), 28 U.S.C.A.

> Westinghouse Elec. Corp. v. Newman & Holtzinger, P.C., 992 F.2d 932, appeal after remand 46 Cal.Rptr.2d 151, 39 C.A.4th 1194, rehearing denied, and review denied.

C.A.9 (Cal.) 1991. Dismissal of complaint for failure to state a claim is improper unless it appears beyond doubt that plaintiff can prove no set of facts in support of claim which would entitle him to relief. Fed.Rules Civ.Proc.Rule 12(b)(6), 28 U.S.C.A.

> Arcade Water Dist. v. U.S., 940 F.2d 1265, appeal after remand 28 F.3d 104.

C.A.9 (Cal.) 1991. Dismissal for failure to state claim is appropriate only if plaintiff can prove no set of facts which would entitle him to relief.

> Waco v. Baltad, 934 F.2d 214, certiorari granted, reversed Mireles v. Waco, 112 S.Ct. 286, 502 U.S. 9, 116 L.Ed.2d 9, on remand 962 F.2d 865.

C.A.9 (Cal.) 1991. Pleadings which are timely filed but overly long under local rules should not be rejected without reasonable, even if conditional, opportunity to conform to local rules.

> Smith v. Frank, 923 F.2d 139.

C.A.9 (Cal.) 1990. Complaint should not be dismissed unless it appears beyond doubt that plaintiff can prove no set of facts in support of his claim which would entitle him to relief.

> Elias v. Connett, 908 F.2d 521.

C.A.9 (Cal.) 1989. In a bench trial, court may involuntarily dismiss an action when the court finds, after considering the evidence, that plaintiff has not established a prima facie case. Fed.Rules Civ.Proc.Rule 41(b), 28 U.S.C.A.

> Sepulveda v. Pacific Maritime Ass'n, 878 F.2d 1137, certiorari denied 110 S.Ct. 561, 493 U.S. 1002, 107 L.Ed.2d 556.

C.A.9 (Cal.) 1989. Dismissal for failure to state claim is proper only if it appears beyond doubt that plaintiff would be entitled to no relief under any state of facts that could be proved.

> Woodrum v. Woodward County, Okl., 866 F.2d 1121.

C.A.9 (Cal.) 1987. On motion to dismiss, issue is not whether plaintiff ultimately will prevail, but whether he is entitled to offer evidence to support his claims; trial court may not grant motion to dismiss for failure to state claim unless it appears beyond doubt that plaintiff can prove no set of facts in support of his claim which would entitle him to relief. Fed.Rules Civ.Proc.Rule 12(b)(6), 28 U.S.C.A.

> Usher v. City of Los Angeles, 828 F.2d 556.

C.A.9 (Cal.) 1985. A complaint should not be dismissed if it states a claim under any legal theory, even if plaintiff erroneously relies on a different legal theory.

> Haddock v. Board of Dental Examiners of California, 777 F.2d 462.

C.A.10 (Colo.) 1996. Complaint may be dismissed for failure to state claim only if plaintiff can prove no set of facts to support claim for relief. Fed.Rules Civ.Proc.Rule 12(b)(6), 28 U.S.C.A.

> David v. City and County of Denver, 101 F.3d 1344, rehearing denied, certiorari denied 118 S.Ct. 157, 139 L.Ed.2d 102.

C.A.10 (Colo.) 1994. Dismissal of complaint is appropriate only where it is clear that plaintiff can prove no set of facts which would entitle him to relief. Fed.Rules Civ.Proc.Rule 12(b)(6), 28 U.S.C.A.

> Smith v. Colorado Dept. of Corrections, 23 F.3d 339.

C.A.10 (Colo.) 1992. Dismissal for failure to state claim is appropriate only if plaintiffs can prove no set of facts that would entitle them to relief. Fed.Rules Civ.Proc.Rule 12(b)(6), 28 U.S.C.A.

> Daigle v. Shell Oil Co., 972 F.2d 1527.

C.A.10 (Colo.) 1991. Dismissal for failure to state claim upon which relief can be granted requires legal determination that plaintiff can prove no set of facts in support of claim to entitle him to relief. Fed.Rules Civ.Proc.Rule 12(b)(6), 28 U.S.C.A.

> Hospice of Metro Denver, Inc. v. Group Health Ins. of Oklahoma, Inc., 944 F.2d 752.

C.A.10 (Colo.) 1991. Pro se complaint should not be dismissed unless, accepting plaintiff's allegation as true, it appears beyond doubt that plaintiff can prove no set of facts to support claim for relief.

> Ruark v. Solano, 928 F.2d 947, appeal after remand 972 F.2d 357.

C.A.10 (Colo.) 1989. Dismissal of complaint for failure to state claim is proper if, taking all well-pleaded facts as true and construing them in light most favorable to plaintiff, it is clear that plaintiff can prove no set of facts in support of his claim which would entitle him to relief. Fed.Rules Civ.Proc.Rule 12(b)(6), 28 U.S.C.A.

> National Commodity and Barter Ass'n, National Commodity Exchange v. Gibbs, 886 F.2d 1240, on remand 790 F.Supp. 233, affirmed in part, reversed in part National Commodity and Barter Ass'n v. Archer, 31 F.3d 1521.

C.A.2 (Conn.) 1998. Dismissal for failure to state claim upon which relief may be granted was improper when plaintiff alleged facts that were not impossible to prove and that, if demonstrated, would state legally cognizable claim. Fed.Rules Civ.Proc.Rule 12(b)(6), 28 U.S.C.A.

> Chance v. Armstrong, 143 F.3d 698.

C.A.2 (Conn.) 1997. Under liberal pleading principles established by federal civil procedure rules, in ruling on motion to dismiss for failure to state claim, failure in complaint to cite statute, or to cite correct one, in no way affects merits of claim; factual allegations alone are what matters. Fed.Rules Civ.Proc.Rules 8, 12(b)(6), 28 U.S.C.A.

> Northrop v. Hoffman of Simsbury, Inc., 134 F.3d 41.

C.A.3 (Del.) 1992. Complaint's allegations are to be construed favorably to pleader, and complaint should not be dismissed for failure to state claim unless it appears beyond doubt that plaintiff can prove no set of facts in support of claim which would entitle him to relief.

> Williams v. New Castle County, 970 F.2d 1260.

C.A.11 (Fla.) 1994. Complaint should not be dismissed for failure to state claim unless it appears beyond doubt that plaintiff can prove no set of facts which would entitle him to relief.

> Hunnings v. Texaco, Inc., 29 F.3d 1480.

C.A.11 (Fla.) 1993. District court may dismiss complaint only if it is clear that no relief could be granted under any set of facts that could be proved consistent with allegations. Fed.Rules Civ.Proc.Rule 12(b)(6), 28 U.S.C.A.

> Gonzalez v. McNary, 980 F.2d 1418.

C.A.11 (Fla.) 1991. District court may dismiss complaint for failure to state claim only if it is clear that no relief could be granted under any set of facts that could be proved consistent with allegations. Fed.Rules Civ.Proc.Rule 12(b)(6), 28 U.S.C.A.

> Powell v. U.S., 945 F.2d 374.

C.A.11 (Fla.) 1991. Motion by defendant for dismissal on pleadings cannot be granted unless it appears beyond doubt that plaintiff can prove no set of facts in support of claim which would entitle him to relief.

> Lemon v. Dugger, 931 F.2d 1465, rehearing denied 943 F.2d 1316.

C.A.11 (Fla.) 1991. Complaint against party must not be dismissed unless plaintiff can prove no set of facts in support of any claim which would entitle him to relief.

> U.S. Fire Ins. Co. v. Caulkins Indiantown Citrus Co., 931 F.2d 744.

C.A.11 (Fla.) 1990. Motion to dismiss complaint will be denied unless it appears beyond all doubt that plaintiff can prove no set of facts in support of his claims that would entitle him to relief.

> Powell v. Lennon, 914 F.2d 1459.

C.A.11 (Ga.) 1993. Complaint may not be dismissed unless plaintiff can prove no set of facts entitling him to relief. Fed.Rules Civ. Proc.Rule 12(b)(6), 28 U.S.C.A.

> Duke v. Cleland, 5 F.3d 1399, rehearing denied 13 F.3d 411, on remand 884 F.Supp. 511, affirmed 87 F.3d 1226, rehearing denied, rehearing and suggestion for rehearing denied 98 F.3d 1355.

C.A.11 (Ga.) 1992. To succeed on motion to dismiss for failure to state a claim, plaintiff's complaint, factually accepted as correct, must evidence that there is no set of facts entitling him to relief. Fed.Rules Civ.Proc.Rule 12(b)(6), 28 U.S.C.A.

> Brown v. Crawford County, Ga., 960 F.2d 1002.

C.A.9 (Guam) 1993. Motion to dismiss for failure to state claim on which relief can be granted should not be granted unless it appears beyond doubt that plaintiff can prove no set of facts in support of claim which would entitle him to relief. Fed.Rules Civ.Proc.Rule 12(b)(6), 28 U.S.C.A.

> Figueroa v. U.S., 7 F.3d 1405, certiorari denied 114 S.Ct. 1537, 511 U.S. 1030, 128 L.Ed.2d 190.

C.A.9 (Hawai'i) 1994. Complaint should not be dismissed for failure to state claim unless it appears beyond doubt that plaintiff can prove no set of facts in support of his claim which would entitle him to relief. Fed.Rules Civ.Proc. Rule 12(b)(6), 28 U.S.C.A.

> Rabang v. I.N.S., 35 F.3d 1449, certiorari denied Sanidad v. I.N.S., 115 S.Ct. 2554, 515 U.S. 1130, 132 L.Ed.2d 809.

C.A.9 (Hawai'i) 1987. Conclusory allegations with nothing more are insufficient to defeat motion to dismiss. Fed.Rules Civ.Proc. Rule 12(b), 28 U.S.C.A.

> McCarthy v. Mayo, 827 F.2d 1310.

C.A.7 (Ill.) 1998. To withstand dismissal for failure to state claim, complaint must contain either direct or inferential allegations respecting all the material elements necessary to sustain a recovery under some viable legal theory; however, such allegations need only state a possible claim, not a winning claim. Fed.Rules Civ.Proc.Rule 12(b)(6), 28 U.S.C.A.

   Herdrich v. Pegram, 154 F.3d 362.

Complaint may not be dismissed for failure to state claim just because it omits factual allegations. Fed.Rules Civ.Proc.Rule 12(b)(6), 28 U.S.C.A.

   Herdrich v. Pegram, 154 F.3d 362.

C.A.7 (Ill.) 1997. Assertions in memorandum opposing motion to dismiss should have been accepted; dismissing complaint with leave to replead extra facts was inconsistent with federal rules.

   Albiero v. City of Kankakee, 122 F.3d 417.

C.A.7 (Ill.) 1996. While notice pleading allows for generous reading of complaint in order to resist motion to dismiss, complaint must at least set out facts sufficient to outline or adumbrate basis of claim and pleader will not be allowed to evade this requirement by attaching bare legal conclusion to facts that he narrates. Fed.Rules Civ.Proc.Rule 12(b)(6), 28 U.S.C.A.

   Panaras v. Liquid Carbonic Industries Corp., 74 F.3d 786, rehearing denied.

C.A.7 (Ill.) 1995. Suit should not be dismissed if it is possible to hypothesize facts, consistent with complaint, that would make out a claim. Fed.Rules Civ.Proc.Rule 56, 28 U.S.C.A.

   Graehling v. Village of Lombard, Ill., 58 F.3d 295.

C.A.7 (Ill.) 1995. Complaints are to be read liberally, and district court may grant motion to dismiss for failure to state claim only if it is beyond doubt that nonmovant can plead no facts that would support nonmovant's claim for relief. Fed.Rules Civ.Proc.Rules 8, 12(b)(6), 28 U.S.C.A.

   Palda v. General Dynamics Corp., 47 F.3d 872, rehearing and suggestion for rehearing denied.

Complaint which consists of conclusory allegations unsupported by factual assertions fails even liberal standard of rule governing dismissal for failure to state claim. Fed.Rules Civ. Proc.Rule 12(b)(6), 28 U.S.C.A.

   Palda v. General Dynamics Corp., 47 F.3d 872, rehearing and suggestion for rehearing denied.

C.A.7 (Ill.) 1994. If plaintiff has admitted facts showing that he is not entitled to recovery on theory he advances, dismissal of complaint is proper.

   Chakonas v. City of Chicago, 42 F.3d 1132.

C.A.7 (Ill.) 1994. Dismissal of claim is appropriate if there exists no set of facts that would support claim and entitle plaintiff to

recover. Fed.Rules Civ.Proc.Rule 12(b)(6), 28 U.S.C.A.

   Harris v. City of Auburn, 27 F.3d 1284.

C.A.7 (Ill.) 1993. Plaintiff's claims must survive motion to dismiss for failure to state claim on which relief can be granted, if relief could be granted under set of facts that could be proved consistent with allegations. Fed.Rules Civ.Proc.Rule 12(b)(6), 28 U.S.C.A.

   Hi-Lite Products Co. v. American Home Products Corp., 11 F.3d 1402.

C.A.7 (Ill.) 1993. Complaint should not be dismissed for failure to state claim upon which relief could be granted unless it is clear that no relief could be granted under any set of facts that could be proved consistent with allegations. Fed.Rules Civ.Proc.Rule 12(b)(6), 28 U.S.C.A.

   Cushing v. City of Chicago, 3 F.3d 1156.

C.A.7 (Ill.) 1993. Court can dismiss complaint for failure to state claim only if plaintiff cannot establish any set of facts upon which relief can be granted. Fed.Rules Civ.Proc.Rule 12(b)(6), 28 U.S.C.A.

   Northwest Tissue Center v. Shalala, 1 F.3d 522, rehearing and suggestion for rehearing denied.

C.A.7 (Ill.) 1992. Whether language in complaint can be interpreted as deficient is immaterial in determining whether it fails to state claim. Fed.Rules Civ.Proc.Rules 8, 12(b)(6), 28 U.S.C.A.

   Hrubec v. National R.R. Passenger Corp., 981 F.2d 962, on remand 829 F.Supp. 1502.

C.A.7 (Ill.) 1992. Dismissal is appropriate if there are no facts in well pleaded complaint which, if accepted as true, would support plaintiff's claim for recovery.

   A.O. Smith Corp. v. Lewis, Overbeck & Furman, 979 F.2d 546, rehearing denied.

C.A.7 (Ill.) 1992. Complaint should not be dismissed unless it appears beyond doubt that plaintiff can prove no set of facts in support of claim to entitle plaintiff to relief.

   Taylor v. Western and Southern Life Ins. Co., 966 F.2d 1188.

C.A.7 (Ill.) 1991. Complaint should not be dismissed unless it appears beyond a doubt that plaintiff can prove no set of facts in support of claim which would entitle him to relief. Fed. Rules Civ.Proc.Rule 12(b)(6), 28 U.S.C.A.

   Johnson v. Martin, 943 F.2d 15.

C.A.7 (Ill.) 1991. Plaintiff does not have to allege sufficient facts to establish its right to judgment in its favor to successfully oppose motion to dismiss for failure to state claim. Fed.Rules Civ.Proc.Rule 12(b)(6), 28 U.S.C.A.

> Pearman v. Norfolk & Western Ry. Co., 939 F.2d 521.

C.A.7 (Ill.) 1990. Court of Appeals will affirm dismissal of complaint only if it appears beyond doubt that plaintiff can prove no set of facts in support of his claim which would entitle him to relief. Fed.Rules Civ.Proc.Rule 12(b)(6), 28 U.S.C.A.

> Leahy v. Board of Trustees of Community College Dist. No. 508, County of Cook, State of Ill., 912 F.2d 917, rehearing denied.

C.A.7 (Ill.) 1986. Complaint cannot be dismissed merely because it includes invalid claims along with valid one.

> American Nurses' Ass'n v. State of Ill., 783 F.2d 716, on remand American Nurses' Assoc. v. State of Illinois, 1986 WL 10382.

Complaint cannot be dismissed merely because one of theories on which it proceeds, and facts alleged in support of that theory, do not make out claim for relief.

> American Nurses' Ass'n v. State of Ill., 783 F.2d 716, on remand American Nurses' Assoc. v. State of Illinois, 1986 WL 10382.

C.A.7 (Ill.) 1985. Mere vagueness or lack of detail does not constitute sufficient grounds to grant motion to dismiss for failure to state claim. Fed.Rules Civ.Proc.Rule 12(b)(6), 28 U.S.C.A.

> Strauss v. City of Chicago, 760 F.2d 765.

C.A.7 (Ill.) 1981. Briscoe v. LaHue, 663 F.2d 713, certiorari granted 102 S.Ct. 1708, 455 U.S. 1016, 72 L.Ed.2d 132, affirmed 103 S.Ct. 1108, 460 U.S. 325, 75 L.Ed.2d 96, certiorari denied Talley v. Crosson, 103 S.Ct. 1426, 460 U.S. 1037, 75 L.Ed.2d 787.

C.A.7 (Ind.) 1995. Motion for involuntary dismissal under old version of the rule merely tests legal sufficiency of plaintiff's case. Fed. Rules Civ.Proc.Rule 41(b), 28 U.S.C.A.

> Ashkin v. Time Warner Cable Corp., 52 F.3d 140.

C.A.7 (Ind.) 1994. Complaint may not be dismissed for failure to state a claim just because it omits factual allegations, but may be dismissed when plaintiffs make it clear that they do not plan to prove essential element of their case. Fed.Rules Civ.Proc.Rule 12(b)(6), 28 U.S.C.A.

> La Porte County Republican Cent. Committee v. Board of Com'rs of County of La Porte, 43 F.3d 1126.

C.A.7 (Ind.) 1994. Dismissal for failure to state claim upon which relief may be granted is appropriate only if plaintiff can establish no set of facts upon which relief can be granted. Fed. Rules Civ.Proc.Rule 12(b)(6), 28 U.S.C.A.

> Henson v. CSC Credit Services, 29 F.3d 280.

C.A.7 (Ind.) 1994. Motion to dismiss for failure to state claim will be granted only if it appears beyond doubt that plaintiff can prove no set of facts in support of claim which would entitle him to relief. Fed.Rules Civ.Proc.Rule 12(b)(6), 28 U.S.C.A.

> Hondo, Inc. v. Sterling, 21 F.3d 775.

C.A.7 (Ind.) 1992. In reviewing grant of motion to dismiss, Court of Appeals views all facts alleged in complaint, as well as any inferences reasonably drawn from them, in light most favorable to plaintiff; court will only dismiss complaint for failure to state claim if it appears beyond doubt that plaintiff cannot establish any set of facts which would entitle him to relief requested. Fed.Rules Civ.Proc.Rule 12(b)(6), 28 U.S.C.A.

> Caldwell v. City of Elwood, Ind., 959 F.2d 670.

C.A.7 (Ind.) 1989. In regard to sua sponte dismissal of complaints, district court must review face of complaint in light of relevant constitutional or statutory provisions and pertinent case law interpreting those provisions, which review may be conducted sua sponte, and which may be done at early stage of proceedings; if court determines that plaintiff's claims are sufficiently substantial to invoke federal jurisdiction, complaint may be dismissed for failure to state claim only if it appears beyond doubt that plaintiff can prove no set of facts in support of his claim which would entitle him to relief. Fed.Rules Civ.Proc.Rule 12(b)(6), 28 U.S.C.A.

> Ricketts v. Midwest Nat. Bank, 874 F.2d 1177.

C.A.7 (Ind.) 1981. Briscoe v. LaHue, 663 F.2d 713, certiorari granted 102 S.Ct. 1708, 455 U.S. 1016, 72 L.Ed.2d 132, affirmed 103 S.Ct. 1108, 460 U.S. 325, 75 L.Ed.2d 96, certiorari denied Talley v. Crosson, 103 S.Ct. 1426, 460 U.S. 1037, 75 L.Ed.2d 787.

C.A.8 (Iowa) 1993. Although complaints are to be liberally construed, they may be dismissed when it appears beyond reasonable doubt that plaintiff can prove no set of facts which entitles him to relief.

> Penn v. Iowa State Bd. of Regents, 999 F.2d 305, rehearing denied.

C.A.10 (Kan.) 1992. District court should not dismiss complaint for failing to state claim upon which relief can be granted unless it appears beyond doubt that plaintiff can prove no set of facts in support of his claim which

would entitle him to relief. Fed.Rules Civ.Proc. Rule 12(b)(6), 28 U.S.C.A.

> Olson v. Hart, 965 F.2d 940, appeal after remand 1 F.3d 1249.

C.A.6 (Ky.) 1993. To withstand motion to dismiss for failure to state cause of action, it must be established beyond doubt that plaintiff can prove no set of facts in support of his claim which would entitle him to relief. Fed.Rules Civ.Proc.Rule 12(b)(6), 28 U.S.C.A.

> Jones v. City of Carlisle, Ky., 3 F.3d 945, rehearing and suggestion for rehearing denied, certiorari denied 114 S.Ct. 1218, 510 U.S. 1177, 127 L.Ed.2d 564.

C.A.6 (Ky.) 1993. District court's grant of motion to dismiss for failure to state cause of action upon which relief could be granted is proper when there is no set of facts that would allow plaintiff to recover; all of plaintiff's factual allegations are deemed true and any ambiguities must be resolved in plaintiff's favor. Fed. Rules Civ.Proc.Rule 12(b)(6), 28 U.S.C.A.

> Carter by Carter v. Cornwell, 983 F.2d 52, rehearing denied.

C.A.6 (Ky.) 1989. Both summary judgment motion and motion to dismiss for failure to state claim are properly granted when moving party establishes that there is no genuine issue as to any material fact. U.S.C.A. Const. Amend. 4; Fed.Rules Civ.Proc.Rules 12(b)(6), 56, 28 U.S.C.A.

> Collins v. Nagle, 892 F.2d 489.

Dismissal for failure to state claim is proper when it is established beyond doubt that plaintiff cannot prove any set of facts consistent with allegations that would entitle such plaintiff to relief. Fed.Rules Civ.Proc.Rule 12(b)(6), 28 U.S.C.A.

> Collins v. Nagle, 892 F.2d 489.

C.A.5 (La.) 1997. Complaint lacks arguable basis in law, and is thus subject to dismissal, if it is based on indisputably meritless legal theory, such as allegation of legal interest which clearly does not exist.

> McCormick v. Stalder, 105 F.3d 1059.

C.A.5 (La.) 1995. Dismissal for failure to state claim cannot be upheld unless it appears beyond doubt that plaintiffs would not be entitled to recover under any set of facts that they could prove in support of their claim. Fed. Rules Civ.Proc.Rule 12(b)(6), 28 U.S.C.A.

> Crowe v. Henry, 43 F.3d 198, rehearing denied, appeal after remand 115 F.3d 294, appeal after remand 141 F.3d 1165.

C.A.5 (La.) 1985. Mere technical defects in a pleading do not provide a basis for dismissal. Fed.Rules Civ.Proc. Rules 8(f), 10(a), 28 U.S.C.A.

> Jones v. State of La. Through Bd. of Trustees for State Colleges & Universities, 764 F.2d 1183.

C.A.1 (Me.) 1997. To survive motion to dismiss for failure to state claim, complaint must set forth factual allegations, either direct or inferential, respecting each material element necessary to sustain recovery under some actionable legal theory, and, in judging adequacy of plaintiff's allegations, bald assertions, periphrastic circumlocutions, unsubstantiated conclusions, and outright vituperation carry no weight. Fed.Rules Civ.Proc.Rule 12(b)(6), 28 U.S.C.A.

> Berner v. Delahanty, 129 F.3d 20, certiorari denied 118 S.Ct. 1305, 140 L.Ed.2d 470.

C.A.4 (Md.) 1993. In general, motion to dismiss for failure to state claim should not be granted unless it appears certain that plaintiff can prove no set of facts which would support its claim and would entitle it to relief. Fed. Rules Civ.Proc.Rule 12(b)(6), 28 U.S.C.A.

> Mylan Laboratories, Inc. v. Matkari, 7 F.3d 1130, certiorari denied American Home Products Corp. v. Mylan Laboratories, Inc., 114 S.Ct. 1307, 510 U.S. 1197, 127 L.Ed.2d 658.

C.A.1 (Mass.) 1995. On motion to dismiss for failure to state claim, court must accept allegations of complaint as true, and determine whether, under any theory, allegations are sufficient to state cause of action in accordance with law. Fed.Rules Civ.Proc.Rule 12(b)(6), 28 U.S.C.A.

> Brown v. Hot, Sexy and Safer Productions, Inc., 68 F.3d 525, certiorari denied 116 S.Ct. 1044, 516 U.S. 1159, 134 L.Ed.2d 191.

C.A.1 (Mass.) 1994. When pro se complaint sets forth facts upon which relief is sought, and lenient construction demonstrates beyond doubt that plaintiff can prove no set of facts to support her claim for relief, complaint will be subject to dismissal for failure to state claim. Fed.Rules Civ.Proc.Rule 12(b)(6), 28 U.S.C.A.

> Rockwell v. Cape Cod Hosp., 26 F.3d 254.

C.A.6 (Mich.) 1994. Complaint should not be dismissed for failure to state a claim unless it appears without a doubt that plaintiff can prove no set of facts in support of claim which would entitle him to relief. Fed.Rules Civ.Proc.Rule 12(b)(6), 28 U.S.C.A.

> Vemco, Inc. v. Camardella, 23 F.3d 129, rehearing and suggestion for rehearing denied, certiorari denied 115 S.Ct. 579, 513 U.S. 1017, 130 L.Ed.2d 495.

C.A.6 (Mich.) 1994. Complaint should not be dismissed for failure to state a claim unless it appears beyond doubt that plaintiff can prove no set of facts in support of his claim which would entitle him to relief. Fed.Rules Civ.Proc. Rule 12(b)(6), 28 U.S.C.A.

> Mann v. Conlin, 22 F.3d 100, certiorari denied 115 S.Ct. 193, 513 U.S. 870, 130 L.Ed.2d 126.

C.A.6 (Mich.) 1994. Motion to dismiss for failure to state claim on which relief can be granted should be granted only if it appears beyond doubt that plaintiffs can prove no set of facts in support of their claim which would entitle them to relief. Fed.Rules Civ.Proc.Rule 12(b)(6), 28 U.S.C.A.

> Broyde v. Gotham Tower, Inc., 13 F.3d 994, certiorari denied 114 S.Ct. 2137, 511 U.S. 1128, 128 L.Ed.2d 866.

C.A.6 (Mich.) 1993. On motion to dismiss for failure to state claim upon which relief can be granted, court must construe complaint in light most favorable to plaintiff, accept all factual allegations as true, and determine whether plaintiff undoubtedly can prove no set of facts in support of claim that would entitle him to relief. Fed.Rules Civ.Proc.Rule 12(b)(6), 28 U.S.C.A.

> In re DeLorean Motor Co., 991 F.2d 1236, rehearing denied.

To survive motion to dismiss for failure to state claim upon which relief can be granted, complaint must consist of more than a bare assertion of legal conclusions. Fed.Rules Civ. Proc.Rule 12(b)(6), 28 U.S.C.A.

> In re DeLorean Motor Co., 991 F.2d 1236, rehearing denied.

To survive motion to dismiss for failure to state claim, complaint must contain either direct or inferential allegations respecting all material elements necessary to sustain recovery under some viable legal theory. Fed.Rules Civ. Proc.Rule 12(b)(6), 28 U.S.C.A.

> In re DeLorean Motor Co., 991 F.2d 1236, rehearing denied.

C.A.6 (Mich.) 1993. Fundamental purpose of pleadings under Federal Rules of Civil Procedure is to give adequate notice to parties of each side's claims and to allow cases to be decided on merits after adequate development of facts; therefore, complaints should be dismissed for failure to state claim upon which relief can be granted only if plaintiffs can allege no set of facts which entitle them to legal relief. Fed. Rules Civ.Proc.Rule 12(b)(6), 28 U.S.C.A.

> Mayer v. Mylod, 988 F.2d 635.

C.A.6 (Mich.) 1990. Complaint should not be dismissed unless it appears beyond doubt that plaintiff can prove no set of facts in support of his claim which would entitle him to relief.

> American Town Center v. Hall 83 Associates, 912 F.2d 104.

C.A.5 (Miss.) 1992. Claim may not be dismissed for failing to state claim unless it appears certain that plaintiff cannot prove any set of facts in support of claim which would entitle plaintiff to relief. Fed.Rules Civ.Proc.Rule 12(b)(6), 28 U.S.C.A.

> Benton v. U.S., 960 F.2d 19.

C.A.5 (Miss.) 1991. Complaint is not subject to dismissal for failure to state a claim for which relief can be granted, on ground of defendant's immunity unless it appears beyond doubt that plaintiff can prove no set of facts in support of his claim which would entitle him to relief. Fed.Rules Civ.Proc.Rule 12(b)(1), 28 U.S.C.A.

> Chrissy F. by Medley v. Mississippi Dept. of Public Welfare, 925 F.2d 844.

C.A.8 (Mo.) 1996. That plaintiff may fail to prove her allegations at trial is irrelevant to consideration of defendant's Rule 12(b)(6) motion to dismiss for failure to state claim. Fed. Rules Civ.Proc.Rule 12(b)(6), 28 U.S.C.A.

> Hafley v. Lohman, 90 F.3d 264, rehearing and suggestion for rehearing denied, certiorari denied 117 S.Ct. 1081, 137 L.Ed.2d 216.

C.A.8 (Mo.) 1995. On motion to dismiss for failure to state claim upon which relief can be granted, court must review complaint most favorably to nonmoving party, and may dismiss only if it is clear that no relief can be granted under any set of facts that could be proved consistent with allegations. Fed.Rules Civ. Proc.Rule 12(b)(6), 28 U.S.C.A.

> Frey v. City of Herculaneum, 44 F.3d 667.

C.A.8 (Mo.) 1992. Complaint should not be dismissed for failure to state claim upon which relief can be granted unless it appears beyond doubt that plaintiffs can prove no set of facts in support of their claim that would entitle them to relief.

> Dicken v. Ashcroft, 972 F.2d 231, rehearing denied.

C.A.8 (Mo.) 1991. In reviewing dismissal for failure to state claim upon which relief can be granted, Court of Appeals accepts allegations in complaint as true, and complaint should not be dismissed unless it appears beyond doubt that plaintiff can prove no set of facts that would entitle him to relief. Fed.Rules Civ.Proc. Rule 12(b)(6), 28 U.S.C.A.

> Mirax Chemical Products Corp. v. First Interstate Commercial Corp., 950 F.2d 566.

C.A.8 (Mo.) 1979. Thomas W. Garland, Inc. v. City of St. Louis, 596 F.2d 784, certiorari denied 100 S.Ct. 208, 444 U.S. 899, 62 L.Ed.2d 135, certiorari denied Manley Inv. Co. v. Thomas W. Garland, Inc., 100 S.Ct. 208, 444 U.S. 899, 62 L.Ed.2d 135, on remand 492 F.Supp. 402.

C.A.8 (Neb.) 1992. Court of Appeals' review of district court's dismissals for failure to state claim upon which relief can be granted is de novo, and motion to dismiss should be granted only if it is clear that no relief could be granted under any set of factual allegations. Fed.Rules Civ.Proc.Rule 12(b)(6), 28 U.S.C.A.
    Concerned Citizens of Nebraska (CCN) v. U.S. Nuclear Regulatory Com'n (NRC), 970 F.2d 421, rehearing denied.

C.A.3 (N.J.) 1996. Complaint will be deemed to have alleged sufficient facts to survive motion to dismiss for failure to state claim if it adequately put defendants on notice of essential elements of plaintiffs' cause of action. Fed.Rules Civ.Proc.Rule 12(b)(6), 28 U.S.C.A.
    Nami v. Fauver, 82 F.3d 63.

C.A.3 (N.J.) 1995. Test for reviewing motion to dismiss for failure to state claim is whether, under any reasonable reading of pleadings, plaintiff may be entitled to relief. Fed.Rules Civ.Proc.Rule 12(b)(6), 28 U.S.C.A.
    Simon v. Cebrick, 53 F.3d 17.

C.A.3 (N.J.) 1994. Unless plaintiff can prove no set of facts in support of claim that would entitled him to relief, complaint should not be dismissed for failure to state claim. Fed.Rules Civ.Proc.Rule 12(b)(6), 28 U.S.C.A.
    ALA, Inc. v. CCAIR, Inc., 29 F.3d 855.

C.A.10 (N.M.) 1991. To dismiss claim for failure to state a claim upon which relief can be granted, court must determine that plaintiff can prove no set of facts in support of claim to entitle him to relief.
    Bradley v. U.S. by Veterans Admin., 951 F.2d 268.

C.A.2 (N.Y.) 1998. Although bald assertions and conclusions of law are insufficient to survive motion to dismiss for failure to state claim upon which relief can be granted, pleading standard is nonetheless a liberal one. Fed. Rules Civ.Proc.Rule 12(b)(6), 28 U.S.C.A.
    Cooper v. Parsky, 140 F.3d 433.

C.A.2 (N.Y.) 1997. In order to survive motion to dismiss for failure to state claim upon which relief can be granted, plaintiff must assert cognizable claim and allege facts that, if true, would support claim; in evaluating whether these requirements are met, complaints prepared pro se are held to less stringent standards than formal pleadings drafted by lawyers. Fed. Rules Civ.Proc.Rule 12(b)(6), 28 U.S.C.A.
    Boddie v. Schnieder, 105 F.3d 857.

C.A.2 (N.Y.) 1996. Bald assertions and conclusions of law will not enable complaint to survive motion to dismiss for failure to state claim, even though relevant pleading standard is liberal. Fed.Rules Civ.Proc.Rule 12(b)(6), 28 U.S.C.A.
    Leeds v. Meltz, 85 F.3d 51.

C.A.2 (N.Y.) 1995. When complaint fails to comply with requirements of Federal Rules of Civil Procedure that it contain short and plain statement of claim showing pleader is entitled to relief and that each averment be concise and direct, district court has power, on motion or sua sponte, to dismiss complaint or strike such parts as are redundant or immaterial. Fed. Rules Civ.Proc.Rule 8(a)(2), (e)(1), 28 U.S.C.A.
    Simmons v. Abruzzo, 49 F.3d 83, on remand 1996 WL 79321, affirmed 104 F.3d 350.

In determining whether or not nonfrivolous claim is stated, complaint's allegations must be taken as true, and complaint should not be dismissed for failure to state claim upon which relief can be granted unless it appears beyond doubt that plaintiff can prove no set of facts in support of claim which would entitle him to relief. Fed.Rules Civ.Proc.Rule 12(b)(6), 28 U.S.C.A.
    Simmons v. Abruzzo, 49 F.3d 83, on remand 1996 WL 79321, affirmed 104 F.3d 350.

C.A.2 (N.Y.) 1994. Complaint must not be dismissed unless it appears beyond doubt that plaintiff can prove no set of facts in support of his claim which would entitle him to relief. Fed.Rules Civ.Proc.Rule 12(b)(6), 28 U.S.C.A.
    Yusuf v. Vassar College, 35 F.3d 709.

C.A.2 (N.Y.) 1994. District court must not dismiss for failure to state claim unless it appears beyond doubt that plaintiff can prove no set of facts in support of claim which would entitle him to relief. Fed.Rules Civ.Proc.Rule 12(b)(6), 28 U.S.C.A.
    Cohen v. Koenig, 25 F.3d 1168, on remand 918 F.Supp. 719, motion denied 932 F.Supp. 505.

C.A.2 (N.Y.) 1994. Dismissal of complaint for failure to state a claim is warranted only where plaintiffs can prove no set of facts in support of claim that would entitle them to relief. Fed.Rules Civ.Proc.Rule 12(b)(6), 28 U.S.C.A.
    Christ Gatzonis Elec. Contractor, Inc. v. New York City School Const. Authority, 23 F.3d 636.

C.A.2 (N.Y.) 1993. In deciding motion to dismiss for failure to state claim, district court must construe any well-pleaded factual allegations in complaint in favor of plaintiff and may dismiss only where it appears beyond doubt that plaintiff can prove no set of facts in support of claim which would entitle him to relief; that caution applies with greater force where complaint is submitted pro se or plaintiff alleges civil rights violations. Fed.Rules Civ.Proc.Rule 12(b)(6), 28 U.S.C.A.

> Sykes v. James, 13 F.3d 515, certiorari denied 114 S.Ct. 2749, 512 U.S. 1240, 129 L.Ed.2d 867.

C.A.2 (N.Y.) 1992. District court should grant motion to dismiss on pleadings only if, after viewing plaintiff's allegations in favorable light, it appears beyond doubt that plaintiff can prove no set of facts in support of claim which would entitle him to relief.

> Walker v. City of New York, 974 F.2d 293, certiorari denied 113 S.Ct. 1387, 507 U.S. 961, 122 L.Ed.2d 762, certiorari denied 113 S.Ct. 1412, 507 U.S. 972, 122 L.Ed.2d 784.

C.A.2 (N.Y.) 1991. In determining adequacy of a claim under rule governing dismissals for failure to state a claim, consideration is limited to facts stated on face of complaint, and documents appended to complaint or incorporated in complaint by reference, and to matters of which judicial notice may be taken. Fed. Rules Civ.Proc.Rule 12(b)(6), 28 U.S.C.A.

> Allen v. WestPoint-Pepperell, Inc., 945 F.2d 40.

C.A.2 (N.Y.) 1991. Principle that court should not dismiss complaint for failure to state claim or deny leave to file proposed amended complaint, unless it appears beyond doubt that plaintiff can prove no set of facts in support of his claim which would entitle him to relief, should be applied with particular strictness if plaintiff seeks to file amended complaint charging violation of civil rights. 42 U.S.C.A. § 1983; Fed.Rules Civ.Proc.Rules 8(a), 12(b)(6), 28 U.S.C.A.

> Ricciuti v. N.Y.C. Transit Authority, 941 F.2d 119, on remand 1991 WL 221110.

C.A.2 (N.Y.) 1988. When complaint does not comply with requirement that it be short and plain, district court has power, on its own initiative or in response to motion by defendant, to strike any portions that are redundant or immaterial or to dismiss complaint. Fed.Rules Civ.Proc.Rules 8, 12(f), 28 U.S.C.A.

> Salahuddin v. Cuomo, 861 F.2d 40.

C.A.4 (N.C.) 1994. Motion to dismiss for failure to state claim upon which relief may be granted should not be granted unless plaintiff can prove no set of facts to support claim and entitle plaintiff to relief. Fed.Rules Civ.Proc. Rule 12(b)(6), 28 U.S.C.A.

> Randall v. U.S., 30 F.3d 518, certiorari denied 115 S.Ct. 1956, 514 U.S. 1107, 131 L.Ed.2d 849.

C.A.6 (Ohio) 1997. While standard for surviving motion to dismiss for failure to state claim is decidedly liberal, it requires more than bare assertion of legal conclusions, and, in practice, complaint must contain either direct or inferential allegations respecting all material elements to sustain recovery under some viable legal theory. Fed.Rules Civ.Proc.Rule 12(b)(6), 28 U.S.C.A.

> Andrews v. State of Ohio, 104 F.3d 803, rehearing and suggestion for rehearing denied.

C.A.6 (Ohio) 1996. Court of Appeals reviews district court's dismissal of claims for failure to state claim upon which relief can be granted de novo, construing complaint in light most favorable to plaintiff, accepting all factual allegations as true, and determining whether plaintiff undoubtedly can prove no set of facts in support of his or her claims that would entitle plaintiff to relief. Fed.Rules Civ.Proc.Rule 12(b)(6), 28 U.S.C.A.

> Joelson v. U.S., 86 F.3d 1413.

C.A.6 (Ohio) 1995. While it is liberal, standard of review of complaint to determine whether it states claim requires more than bare assertion of legal conclusions. Fed.Rules Civ. Proc.Rule 12(b)(6), 28 U.S.C.A.

> Columbia Natural Resources, Inc. v. Tatum, 58 F.3d 1101, rehearing and suggestion for rehearing denied, certiorari denied 116 S.Ct. 1041, 516 U.S. 1158, 134 L.Ed.2d 189, rehearing denied 116 S.Ct. 1560, 517 U.S. 1163, 134 L.Ed.2d 661.

C.A.10 (Okl.) 1994. Dismissal for failure to state claim is appropriate only if plaintiff can prove no set of facts in support of her claim that would entitled her to relief. Fed.Rules Civ. Proc.Rule 12(b)(6), 28 U.S.C.A.

> Noland v. McAdoo, 39 F.3d 269.

C.A.10 (Okl.) 1994. Complaint should not be dismissed for failure to state claim merely because plaintiff's allegations do not support legal theory that plaintiff intends to proceed on, and certainly not when other theories are apparent on face of complaint. Fed.Rules Civ. Proc.Rule 12(b)(6), 28 U.S.C.A.

> Barrett v. Tallon, 30 F.3d 1296.

C.A.10 (Okl.) 1991. Complaint should not be dismissed for failure to state a claim unless it appears beyond doubt that plaintiff can prove no set of facts in support of his claim which would entitle him to relief.

> Richards v. Bellmon, 941 F.2d 1015.

C.A.10 (Okl.) 1991. Complaint cannot be dismissed unless it appears beyond all doubt that plaintiff cannot prove any facts entitling him to relief.

> Buckley Const., Inc. v. Shawnee Civic & Cultural Development Authority, 933 F.2d 853.

C.A.10 (Okl.) 1991. Complaint should not be dismissed for failure to state claim unless it appears beyond doubt that plaintiff can prove no set of facts in support of claim which would entitle him to relief. Fed.Rules Civ.Proc.Rule 12(b)(6), 28 U.S.C.A.

> Davis v. TXO Production Corp., 929 F.2d 1515.

C.A.10 (Okl.) 1989. Grant of motion to dismiss for failure to state claim upon which relief can be granted is proper only if it appears beyond doubt the plaintiff can prove no set of facts in support of his claim that would entitle him to relief. Fed.Rules Civ.Proc.Rule 12(b)(6), 28 U.S.C.A.

> Grider v. Texas Oil & Gas Corp., 868 F.2d 1147, rehearing denied, certiorari denied 110 S.Ct. 76, 493 U.S. 820, 107 L.Ed.2d 43.

C.A.3 (Pa.) 1998. A complaint will withstand a motion to dismiss for failure to state a claim if the material facts, as alleged, in addition to inferences drawn from the allegations, provide a basis for recovery. Fed.Rules Civ. Proc.Rule 12(b)(6), 28 U.S.C.A.

> Menkowitz v. Pottstown Memorial Medical Center, 154 F.3d 113.

C.A.3 (Pa.) 1996. District court did not abuse its discretion in dismissing viable portion of count of second amended complaint, without prejudice to repleading, for failure to provide "a short and plain statement of the claim showing that the pleader is entitled to relief," where second amended complaint was unnecessarily complicated and verbose, rambling for more than 600 paragraphs and 240 pages. Fed.Rules Civ.Proc.Rule 8(a)(2), 28 U.S.C.A.

> In re Westinghouse Securities Litigation, 90 F.3d 696, on remand 1998 WL 119554.

C.A.3 (Pa.) 1994. Case should not be dismissed for failure to state claim unless it clearly appears that no relief can be granted under any set of facts that could be proved consistently with plaintiff's allegations. Fed.Rules Civ.Proc. Rule 12(b)(6), 28 U.S.C.A.

> Jordan v. Fox, Rothschild, O'Brien & Frankel, 20 F.3d 1250, on remand 1995 WL 141465.

C.A.3 (Pa.) 1991. Although court ordinarily assumes jurisdiction over case before deciding legal issues on merits, dismissal for failure to state claim is not subject to that restriction; claim need not be wholly insubstantial to be dismissed. Fed.Rules Civ.Proc.Rule 12(b)(6), 28 U.S.C.A.

> Kehr Packages, Inc. v. Fidelcor, Inc., 926 F.2d 1406, rehearing denied, certiorari denied 111 S.Ct. 2839, 501 U.S. 1222, 115 L.Ed.2d 1007.

C.A.3 (Pa.) 1990. Dismissal of complaint for failure to state claim is limited to those circumstances where it is certain that no relief could be granted under any set of facts that could be proved. Fed.Rules Civ.Proc.Rule 12(b)(6), 28 U.S.C.A.

> Markowitz v. Northeast Land Co., 906 F.2d 100, 118 A.L.R. Fed. 813.

C.A.3 (Pa.) 1984. For purposes of dismissal of complaint, claim will be considered meritorious when allegations of pleading, as established at trial, would support recovery by plaintiff. Fed.Rules Civ.Proc.Rule 41, 28 U.S.C.A.

> Scarborough v. Eubanks, 747 F.2d 871.

C.A.1 (Puerto Rico) 1990. Upon determination that no private right of action is implied from federal law, as alleged in complaint, complaint should be dismissed for failure to state claim, rather than for lack of jurisdiction. Fed. Rules Civ.Proc.Rule 12(b)(6), 28 U.S.C.A.

> Arroyo-Torres v. Ponce Federal Bank, F.B.S., 918 F.2d 276.

C.A.1 (R.I.) 1988. Complaint seeking forfeiture of property on grounds that property was purchased with proceeds of drug trafficking must allege sufficient facts to provide reasonable belief that property is subject to forfeiture; failure to meet particularity standard requires dismissal of complaint, albeit without prejudice. Comprehensive Drug Abuse Prevention and Control Act of 1970, § 511(a)(6), (b), 21 U.S.C.A. § 881(a)(6), (b); Supplemental Admiralty and Maritime Claims Rule E(2)(a), 28 U.S.C.A.; U.S.C.A. Const.Amends. 5, 14.

> U.S. v. Pole No. 3172, Hopkinton, 852 F.2d 636.

C.A.6 (Tenn.) 1996. To survive motion to dismiss for failure to state claim, complaint must contain either direct or inferential allegations respecting all material elements to sustain recovery under some viable legal theory. Fed. Rules Civ.Proc.Rule 12(b)(6), 28 U.S.C.A.

> Lillard v. Shelby County Bd. of Educ., 76 F.3d 716.

C.A.5 (Tex.) 1998. Claims under Racketeer Influenced and Corrupt Organizations Act (RICO) may properly be dismissed only if it appears that no relief could be granted under any set of facts that could be proven consistent with the allegations. 18 U.S.C.A. § 1962; Fed. Rules Civ.Proc.Rule 12(b)(6), 28 U.S.C.A.

> Bonner v. Henderson, 147 F.3d 457.

C.A.5 (Tex.) 1995. Complaint is frivolous if it lacks arguable basis in law or fact. 28 U.S.C.A. § 1915(d).

Biliski v. Harborth, 55 F.3d 160, rehearing denied.

C.A.5 (Tex.) 1995. It is proper to dismiss complaint for failure to state claim if there is no allegation in complaint respecting required element necessary for obtaining relief. Fed.Rules Civ.Proc.Rule 12(b)(6), 28 U.S.C.A.

Blackburn v. City of Marshall, 42 F.3d 925.

Conclusory allegations or legal conclusions masquerading as factual conclusions will not suffice to prevent motion to dismiss for failure to state claim. Fed.Rules Civ.Proc.Rule 12(b)(6), 28 U.S.C.A.

Blackburn v. City of Marshall, 42 F.3d 925.

C.A.5 (Tex.) 1994. To prevail on motion to dismiss ordinary claim for failure to state a claim, defendant must show that plaintiff can prove no set of facts in support of claim which would entitle him to relief. Fed.Rules Civ.Proc. Rule 12(b)(6), 28 U.S.C.A.

Tuchman v. DSC Communications Corp., 14 F.3d 1061, rehearing and rehearing denied 20 F.3d 1172.

C.A.5 (Tex.) 1994. Appellate review of motion to dismiss is the same as that applied at the trial level; if plaintiff can prove no set of facts in support of her claims that would entitle her to relief, dismissal is proper.

Burns-Toole v. Byrne, 11 F.3d 1270, certiorari denied 114 S.Ct. 2680, 512 U.S. 1207, 129 L.Ed.2d 814, rehearing denied 115 S.Ct. 12, 512 U.S. 1270, 129 L.Ed.2d 912.

C.A.5 (Tex.) 1993. Plaintiff's complaint ordinarily need only be a short and plain statement that gives defendant notice of what the claim is and the grounds on which it rests and, in most cases, challenges to bare bones pleadings are doomed with respect to an attack on a failure to state a claim. Fed.Rules Civ.Proc. Rule 12(b)(6), 28 U.S.C.A.

Colle v. Brazos County, Tex., 981 F.2d 237.

C.A.5 (Tex.) 1991. Dismissal for failure to state a claim upon which relief can be granted is inappropriate unless pleadings on their face reveal beyond doubt that plaintiffs can prove no set of facts that would entitle them to relief. Fed.Rules Civ.Proc.Rule 12(b)(6), 28 U.S.C.A.

Garrett v. Commonwealth Mortg. Corp. of America, 938 F.2d 591.

C.A.5 (Tex.) 1985. Standard for determining legal sufficiency of complaint is same under either Federal Civil Rule 12 or under statute [28 U.S.C.A. § 1915(d)] authorizing dismissal of frivolous action brought in forma pauperis. Fed.Rules Civ.Proc.Rule 12, 28 U.S.C.A.

Spears v. McCotter, 766 F.2d 179.

C.A.5 (Tex.) 1978. Satterwhite v. City of Greenville, Tex., 578 F.2d 987, certiorari granted, vacated 100 S.Ct. 1334, 445 U.S. 940, 63 L.Ed.2d 773, on remand 634 F.2d 231.

C.A.10 (Utah) 1994. Dismissal of claim for failure of pleading to state claim upon which relief can be granted is appropriate if, taking all well-pleaded facts as true and construing them in light most favorable to plaintiff, it is clear that plaintiff can prove no set of facts which would entitle him to relief. Fed.Rules Civ.Proc. Rule 12(b)(6), 28 U.S.C.A.

Rocky Mountain Helicopters, Inc. v. Bell Helicopter Textron, Inc., 24 F.3d 125.

C.A.7 (Wis.) 1992. Dismissal of complaint for failure to state claim upon which relief can be granted is proper only if it appears beyond reasonable doubt that plaintiff can prove no set of facts in support of his claim which would entitle him to relief, as where complaint fails to allege essential element of plaintiff's claim.

Roots Partnership v. Lands' End, Inc., 965 F.2d 1411, rehearing denied.

C.A.10 (Wyo.) 1992. Motion to dismiss is properly granted when it appears beyond doubt that plaintiff could prove no set of facts entitling it to relief, and court must construe the complaint in favor of the plaintiff, accepting as true all material allegations.

Ash Creek Min. Co. v. Lujan, 969 F.2d 868.

M.D.Ala. 1996. Threshold is exceedingly low for complaint to survive motion to dismiss for failure to state claim.

Alfa Financial Corp. v. Key, 927 F.Supp. 423, affirmed 112 F.3d 1172.

M.D.Ala. 1996. Threshold that complaint must meet to survive motion to dismiss for failure to state claim is exceedingly low.

Gaither v. Barron, 924 F.Supp. 134.

M.D.Ala. 1996. Threshold requirement for allegations necessary in order for complaint to survive motion to dismiss for failure to state claim is exceedingly low. Fed.Rules Civ.Proc. Rule 12(b)(6), 28 U.S.C.A.

Kelley v. Troy State University, 923 F.Supp. 1494.

M.D.Ala. 1995. Threshold of sufficiency that complaint must meet to survive motion to dismiss for failure to state claim is exceedingly low. Fed.Rules Civ.Proc.Rule 12(b)(6), 28 U.S.C.A.

Florida Seed Co., Inc. v. Monsanto Co., 915 F.Supp. 1167, affirmed 105 F.3d 1372, certiorari denied 118 S.Ct. 296, 139 L.Ed.2d 228.

Motion to dismiss cannot be defeated with conclusory allegations if not supported by facts constituting legitimate claim for relief.

> Florida Seed Co., Inc. v. Monsanto Co., 915 F.Supp. 1167, affirmed 105 F.3d 1372, certiorari denied 118 S.Ct. 296, 139 L.Ed.2d 228.

M.D.Ala. 1995. Court may dismiss complaint only if it is clear that no relief could be granted under any set of facts that could be proven consistent with allegations. Fed.Rules Civ.Proc.Rule 12, 28 U.S.C.A.

> Lewis v. Board of Trustees of Alabama State University, 874 F.Supp. 1299.

M.D.Ala. 1995. A complaint may be dismissed for failure to state a claim only if it is clear that no relief could be granted under any set of facts that could be proved consistent with the allegations. Fed.Rules Civ.Proc.Rule 12(b)(6), 28 U.S.C.A.

> Knox v. U.S., 874 F.Supp. 1282.

M.D.Ala. 1995. Court may dismiss complaint only if it is clear that no relief could be granted under any set of facts that could be proven consistent with allegations. Fed.Rules Civ.Proc.Rule 12, 28 U.S.C.A.

> Bahadirli v. Domino's Pizza, 873 F.Supp. 1528.

M.D.Ala. 1994. Court may dismiss complaint only if it is clear that no relief could be granted under any set of facts that could be proven consistent with the allegations.

> Malone v. Chambers County Bd. of Com'rs, 875 F.Supp. 773, reconsideration denied.

M.D.Ala. 1994. District court may dismiss complaint for failure to state claim upon which relief may be granted only if it is clear that no relief could be granted under any set of facts that could be proven consistent with allegations; threshold that complaint must meet to survive motion to dismiss for failure to state claim upon which relief can be granted is exceedingly low. Fed.Rules Civ.Proc.Rule 12(b)(6), 28 U.S.C.A.

> Yeager v. Norwest Multifamily, Inc., 865 F.Supp. 768.

M.D.Ala. 1994. Court may dismiss complaint only if it is clear that no relief could be granted under any set of facts that could be proven consistent with allegations.

> Harrelson v. Elmore County, Ala., 859 F.Supp. 1465.

M.D.Ala. 1993. When considering motion to dismiss for failure to state claim, court must assume that factual allegations in complaint are true and may dismiss only if it is clear that no relief could be granted under any set of facts

that could be proved consistent with allegations. Fed.Rules Civ.Proc.Rule 12(b)(6), 28 U.S.C.A.

> Huckaby v. East Alabama Medical Center, 830 F.Supp. 1399.

M.D.Ala. 1993. Motion to dismiss may not be granted unless it appears beyond a reasonable doubt that no relief could be granted under any set of facts that could be proved consistent with allegations. Fed.Rules Civ.Proc.Rule 12(b)(6), 28 U.S.C.A.

> Storer Cable Communications, Inc. v. City of Montgomery, Ala., 826 F.Supp. 1338, vacated 866 F.Supp. 1376.

M.D.Ala. 1992. Court may dismiss complaint only if it is clear that no relief could be granted under any set of facts that could be proven consistent with allegations. Fed.Rules Civ.Proc.Rule 12(b)(6), 28 U.S.C.A.

> Holcomb v. Monahan, 807 F.Supp. 1526.

N.D.Ala. 1992. Court may dismiss complaint only if it is clear that no relief could be granted under any set of facts that could be proved consistent with allegations.

> Richards v. Jefferson County, 789 F.Supp. 369, affirmed 983 F.2d 237.

D.Ariz. 1996. Complaint lacking allegation regarding required element necessary to obtain relief may be dismissed for failure to state a claim. Fed.Rules Civ.Proc.Rule 12(b)(6), 28 U.S.C.A.

> Crawford v. American Institute of Professional Careers, Inc., 934 F.Supp. 335.

D.Ariz. 1994. In considering defendants' motions to dismiss, court must presume that plaintiff's allegations are true, and grant motion only if it appears "beyond doubt" that plaintiff can prove no set of facts entitling it to relief; issue is not whether plaintiff will ultimately prevail, but whether plaintiff is entitled to offer evidence to support its claim.

> Resolution Trust Corp. v. Dean, 854 F.Supp. 626.

D.Ariz. 1994. Complaint should be dismissed if it appears to be beyond doubt that plaintiff can prove no set of facts in support of claim which would entitle plaintiff to relief. Fed.Rules Civ.Proc.Rule 12(b)(6), 28 U.S.C.A.

> Lara v. Cowan, 848 F.Supp. 1456.

D.Ariz. 1993. Complaint should be dismissed for failure to state claim when, accepting all well-pleaded allegations of fact as true, and drawing all reasonable inferences in favor of plaintiff, no relief could be granted under any set of facts that might be proved. Fed.Rules Civ.Proc.Rule 12(b)(6), 28 U.S.C.A.

> In re American Continental Corporation/Lincoln Sav. & Loan Securities Litigation, 845 F.Supp. 1377.

D.Ariz. 1993. Complaint should not be dismissed for failure to state claim unless it appears beyond doubt that plaintiff can prove no set of facts in support of claim that would entitle plaintiff to relief. Fed.Rules Civ.Proc. Rule 12(b)(6), 28 U.S.C.A.

J.K. By and Through R.K. v. Dillenberg, 836 F.Supp. 694.

D.Ariz. 1993. Complaint should not be dismissed for failure to state claim unless it appears beyond doubt that plaintiff can prove no set of facts in support of claim that would entitle him to relief. Fed.Rules Civ.Proc.Rule 12(b)(6), 28 U.S.C.A.

PPG Industries, Inc. v. Pilkington plc, 825 F.Supp. 1465.

D.Ariz. 1992. Complaint should not be dismissed on the pleadings unless it appears beyond a doubt that plaintiff can prove no set of facts in support of claim which would entitle him to relief.

Still v. Michaels, 791 F.Supp. 248.

E.D.Ark. 1994. Court may grant motion to dismiss for failure to state claim only if it is patently clear that there is no set of facts which plaintiff could prove which would entitle her to relief. Fed.Rules Civ.Proc.Rule 12(b)(6), 28 U.S.C.A.

Chandler v. Fast Lane, Inc., 868 F.Supp. 1138.

E.D.Ark. 1992. Dismissal for failure to state claim is warranted only when it appears beyond doubt that plaintiff can prove no set of facts in support of claim which would entitle her to relief. Fed.Rules Civ.Proc.Rule 12(b)(6), 28 U.S.C.A.

Norfleet By and Through Norfleet v. State of Ark. Dept. of Human Services, 796 F.Supp. 1194, affirmed 989 F.2d 289.

E.D.Ark. 1992. Dismissal for failure to state claim upon which relief may be granted is warranted only when it appears beyond doubt that plaintiff can prove no set of facts in support of her claim which would entitle her to relief. Fed.Rules Civ.Proc.Rule 12(b)(6), 28 U.S.C.A.

Dorothy J. v. Little Rock School Dist., 794 F.Supp. 1405, affirmed 7 F.3d 729.

W.D.Ark. 1993. Motion to dismiss state-law claims for failure to state claim for relief could be granted had to be read as a whole and denied unless it appeared beyond doubt that plaintiff could prove no set of facts in support of claim which would entitle him to relief. Fed.Rules Civ.Proc.Rule 12(b)(6), 28 U.S.C.A.

Parsons v. Burns, 846 F.Supp. 1372.

C.D.Cal. 1997. Dismissal for failure to state claim may be based either on lack of cognizable legal theory or on absence of suffi-cient facts alleged under cognizable legal theory. Fed.Rules Civ.Proc.Rule 12(b)(6), 28 U.S.C.A.

National Coalition Government of Union of Burma v. Unocal, Inc., 176 F.R.D. 329.

C.D.Cal. 1996. Dismissal of complaint for failure to state claim is proper only where there is either a lack of a cognizable legal theory or absence of sufficient facts alleged under cognizable legal theory. Fed.Rules Civ.Proc.Rule 12(b)(6), 28 U.S.C.A.

Summit Technology, Inc. v. High-Line Medical Instruments, Co., 933 F.Supp. 918.

C.D.Cal. 1996. Dismissal for failure to state a claim is proper only where there is either lack of cognizable legal theory or absence of sufficient facts alleged under a cognizable legal theory. Fed.Rules Civ.Proc.Rule 12(b)(6), 28 U.S.C.A.

Gould v. Harris, 929 F.Supp. 353.

C.D.Cal. 1996. Dismissal for failure to state claim is proper only where there is either a lack of a cognizable legal theory or absence of sufficient facts alleged under cognizable legal theory. Fed.Rules Civ.Proc.Rule 12(b)(6), 28 U.S.C.A.

Bureerong v. Uvawas, 922 F.Supp. 1450.

Motion to dismiss for failure to state claim will not be granted merely because plaintiff requests remedy to which she is not entitled. Fed.Rules Civ.Proc.Rule 12(b)(6), 28 U.S.C.A.

Bureerong v. Uvawas, 922 F.Supp. 1450.

With respect to motion to dismiss for failure to state claim, it need not appear that plaintiff can obtain the specific relief demanded as long as court can ascertain from face of complaint that some relief can be granted. Fed. Rules Civ.Proc.Rule 12(b)(6), 28 U.S.C.A.

Bureerong v. Uvawas, 922 F.Supp. 1450.

C.D.Cal. 1995. In determining whether to grant motion to dismiss for failure to state cause of action, test is whether facts as alleged support any valid claim entitling plaintiff to relief, regardless of whether plaintiff erroneously used wrong legal theory. Fed.Rules Civ.Proc.Rule 12(b)(6), 28 U.S.C.A.

S.E.C. v. Cross Financial Services, Inc., 908 F.Supp. 718.

C.D.Cal. 1995. It is only the extraordinary case in which complaint may be dismissed for failure to state claim upon which relief can be granted. Fed.Rules Civ.Proc.Rule 12(b)(6), 28 U.S.C.A.

Grace v. Federal Emergency Management, 889 F.Supp. 394.

C.D.Cal. 1994. Complaint should not be dismissed for failure to state claim on which relief can be granted unless it appears beyond doubt that plaintiff can prove no set of facts in support of his claim which would entitle him to relief. Fed.Rules Civ.Proc.Rule 12(b)(6), 28 U.S.C.A.

> Microsoft Corp. v. A-Tech Corp., 855 F.Supp. 308.

C.D.Cal. 1993. Dismissal for failure to state claim is disfavored and should not be granted unless it appears beyond doubt that plaintiff can prove no set of facts in support of his claim which would entitle him to relief. Fed.Rules Civ.Proc.Rule 12(b)(6), 28 U.S.C.A.

> Haltman v. Aura Systems, Inc., 844 F.Supp. 544.

Dismissal is not justified unless allegations of complaint itself clearly demonstrate that plaintiff does not have a claim. Fed.Rules Civ. Proc.Rule 12(b)(6), 28 U.S.C.A.

> Haltman v. Aura Systems, Inc., 844 F.Supp. 544.

C.D.Cal. 1992. Dismissal of complaint for failure to state claim is improper unless it appears beyond doubt that plaintiff can prove no set of facts in support of claims which would entitle him to relief. Fed.Rules Civ.Proc.Rule 12(b)(6), 28 U.S.C.A.

> Sunbelt Television, Inc. v. Jones Intercable, Inc., 795 F.Supp. 333.

E.D.Cal. 1996. Plaintiff need not necessarily plead a particular fact if that fact is reasonable inference from facts properly alleged, for purposes of determination of whether to dismiss action for failure to state claim. Fed.Rules Civ.Proc.Rule 12(b)(6), 28 U.S.C.A.

> Youngberg v. Bekins Co., 930 F.Supp. 1396.

E.D.Cal. 1995. Claim may be properly dismissed for failure to state claim where plaintiff fails to allege facts which would support cognizable legal theory. Fed.Rules Civ.Proc.Rule 12(b)(6), 28 U.S.C.A.

> DePaoli v. Carlton, 878 F.Supp. 1351.

E.D.Cal. 1994. Court may not dismiss complaint for failure to state claim unless it appears beyond doubt that plaintiff can prove no set of facts in support of claim which would entitle him or her to relief. Fed.Rules Civ.Proc. Rule 12(b)(6), 28 U.S.C.A.

> Anthony v. County of Sacramento, Sheriff's Dept., 845 F.Supp. 1396.

E.D.Cal. 1992. Court may not dismiss complaint for failing to state claim upon which relief can be granted unless it appears beyond doubt that plaintiff can prove no set of facts in support of claim which would entitle him or her to relief. Fed.Rules Civ.Proc.Rule 12(b)(6), 28 U.S.C.A.

> Thacker v. New York Life Ins. Co., 796 F.Supp. 1338.

E.D.Cal. 1992. Court may not dismiss complaint for failure to state a claim unless it appears beyond doubt that plaintiff can prove no set of facts in support of claim which would entitle him or her to relief. Fed.Rules Civ.Proc. Rule 12(b)(6), 28 U.S.C.A.

> Natural Resources Defense Council v. Patterson, 791 F.Supp. 1425, affirmed and remanded 146 F.3d 1118.

E.D.Cal. 1990. Complaint may be dismissed as matter of law for lack of cognizable legal theory or insufficient facts under cognizable legal theory.

> California ex rel. Van de Kamp v. Reilly, 750 F.Supp. 433.

E.D.Cal. 1990. Complaint may not be dismissed for failure to state claim unless it appears beyond doubt that plaintiff can prove no set of facts in support of claim which would entitle him or her to relief; complaint is construed favorably to pleader. Fed.Rules Civ. Proc.Rule 12(b)(6), 28 U.S.C.A.

> Sullivan By and Through Sullivan v. Vallejo City Unified School Dist., 731 F.Supp. 947.

E.D.Cal. 1989. Motion to dismiss for failure to state claim tests legal sufficiency of complaint, not weight of evidence in support of it.

> Occupational-Urgent Care Health Systems, Inc. v. Sutro & Co., Inc., 711 F.Supp. 1016.

N.D.Cal. 1998. Complaint may be dismissed as matter of law for failure to state a claim for two reasons: (1) lack of cognizable legal theory, or (2) insufficient facts under cognizable legal theory. Fed.Rules Civ.Proc.Rule 12(b)(6), 28 U.S.C.A.

> Wenger v. Lumisys, Inc., 2 F.Supp.2d 1231.

N.D.Cal. 1996. In adjudicating motion to dismiss for failure to state claim upon which relief can be granted, court must determine that if all of facts alleged were true, that plaintiffs would be entitled to legal remedy, and if they would not be, then claim must be dismissed. Fed.Rules Civ.Proc.Rule 12(b)(6), 28 U.S.C.A.

> Davis v. City of Palo Alto, 930 F.Supp. 1375.

Absence of sufficient facts alleged under cognizable theory is proper reason for dismissal for failure to state claim upon which relief can be granted. Fed.Rules Civ.Proc.Rule 12(b)(6), 28 U.S.C.A.

> Davis v. City of Palo Alto, 930 F.Supp. 1375.

N.D.Cal. 1996. In adjudicating motion to dismiss for failure to state claim, court must determine that, if all facts alleged were true, plaintiffs would be entitled to legal remedy and if they would not be, then cause of action must be dismissed. Fed.Rules Civ.Proc.Rule 12(b)(6), 28 U.S.C.A.

> Vance v. County of Santa Clara, 928 F.Supp. 993.

Absence of sufficient facts alleged under a cognizable theory is proper reason for dismissal.

> Vance v. County of Santa Clara, 928 F.Supp. 993.

N.D.Cal. 1996. Dismissal of complaint for failure to state claim can be based on lack of a cognizable legal theory or absence of sufficient facts alleged under a cognizable legal theory. Fed.Rules Civ.Proc.Rule 12(b)(6), 28 U.S.C.A.

> Informix Software, Inc. v. Oracle Corp., 927 F.Supp. 1283.

N.D.Cal. 1995. Dismissal for failure to state a claim may be based on lack of cognizable legal theory or absence of sufficient facts alleged under cognizable theory. Fed.Rules Civ.Proc.Rule 12(b)(6), 28 U.S.C.A.

> Oona R.-S. by Kate S. v. Santa Rosa City Schools, 890 F.Supp. 1452, affirmed 122 F.3d 1207, as amended, opinion withdrawn and superseded on denial of rehearing 143 F.3d 473, affirmed 143 F.3d 473.

N.D.Cal. 1995. Court may dismiss complaint as matter of law for either (1) lack of cognizable legal theory, or (2) pleading of insufficient facts under cognizable legal theory.

> Adam v. Silicon Valley Bancshares, 884 F.Supp. 1398.

N.D.Cal. 1995. When complaint does not contain short and plain statement of claim showing that pleader is entitled to relief, court may dismiss complaint or may strike redundant or immaterial matter. Fed.Rules Civ.Proc. Rules 8(a)(2), 12(f), 28 U.S.C.A.

> In re Clearly Canadian Securities Litigation, 875 F.Supp. 1410.

N.D.Cal. 1994. Court may dismiss complaint, or any claims within it, as a matter of law for either lack of a cognizable legal theory, or insufficient facts to support cognizable legal theory. Fed.Rules Civ.Proc.Rule 12(b)(6), 28 U.S.C.A.

> In re Gupta Corp. Securities Litigation, 900 F.Supp. 1217.

N.D.Cal. 1994. Court may properly grant motion to dismiss for failure to state claim upon which relief may be granted if it is clear from face of complaint and judicially noticed documents that plaintiffs cannot prevail as matter of law. Fed.Rules Civ.Proc.Rule 12(b)(6), 28 U.S.C.A.

> Bloom v. Martin, 865 F.Supp. 1377, affirmed 77 F.3d 318, 142 A.L.R. Fed. 781.

N.D.Cal. 1994. Court may dismiss complaint as matter of law for lack of cognizable legal theory or pleading of insufficient facts under cognizable legal theory. Fed.Rules Civ. Proc.Rule 12(b)(6), 28 U.S.C.A.

> In re Cypress Semiconductor Securities Litigation, 864 F.Supp. 957.

N.D.Cal. 1994. On motion to dismiss for failure to state a claim, district court must construe complaint liberally, and dismissal should not be granted unless it appears beyond a doubt that plaintiff can prove no set of facts in support of claim which would entitle him to relief. Fed.Rules Civ.Proc.Rule 12(b)(6), 28 U.S.C.A.

> Parravano v. Babbitt, 861 F.Supp. 914, affirmed 70 F.3d 539, certiorari denied 116 S.Ct. 2546, 518 U.S. 1016, 135 L.Ed.2d 1066.

N.D.Cal. 1994. Legal issues on which actionability of claim depends can and should be resolved on motion to dismiss, and dismissal is appropriate if, as consequence of such resolution, court determines that, as matter of law, complaint's allegations fail to state a claim. Fed.Rules Civ.Proc.Rule 12(b)(6), 28 U.S.C.A.

> Citizens for a Better Environment-California v. Union Oil Co. of California, 861 F.Supp. 889, affirmed 83 F.3d 1111, as amended, certiorari denied 117 S.Ct. 789, 136 L.Ed.2d 731.

N.D.Cal. 1994. A complaint should not be dismissed for failure to state a claim upon which relief can be granted unless it appears beyond doubt that plaintiff can prove no set of facts in support of claim which would entitle him to relief. Fed.Rules Civ.Proc. Rule 12(b)(6), 28 U.S.C.A.

> Glenbrook Homeowners Ass'n v. Scottsdale Ins. Co., 858 F.Supp. 986.

N.D.Cal. 1994. Complaint should not be dismissed for failure to state claim upon which relief can be granted unless it appears beyond doubt that plaintiff can prove no set of facts in support of his claim which would entitle him to relief. Fed.Rules Civ.Proc.Rule 12(b)(6), 28 U.S.C.A.

> MAI Systems Corp. v. UIPS, 856 F.Supp. 538.

Complaint may be dismissed as matter of law for two reasons: lack of cognizable legal theory; or insufficient facts under cognizable legal theory. Fed.Rules Civ.Proc.Rule 12(b)(6), 28 U.S.C.A.

> MAI Systems Corp. v. UIPS, 856 F.Supp. 538.

N.D.Cal. 1994. Claim should not be dismissed unless it is certain that law would not permit requested relief even if all allegations in complaint were proven true.

> F.D.I.C. v. Jackson-Shaw Partners No. 46, Ltd., 850 F.Supp. 839.

N.D.Cal. 1993. Complaint may be dismissed for failure to state claim only if it appears beyond doubt that plaintiff can prove no set of facts in support of his claim which would entitle him to relief. Fed.Rules Civ.Proc.Rule 12(b)(6), 28 U.S.C.A.

> Plessinger v. Castleman and Haskell, 838 F.Supp. 448.

N.D.Cal. 1992. Motions to dismiss for failure to state claim upon which relief can be granted will be viewed with disfavor, under liberal standard according to which court must presume that plaintiff's allegations are true and grant motion only if it appears beyond doubt that plaintiff can prove no set of facts entitling it to relief. Fed.Rules Civ.Proc.Rule 12(b)(6), 28 U.S.C.A.

> Kentucky Cent. Life Ins. Co. v. LeDuc, 814 F.Supp. 832.

Complaint may be dismissed as matter of law for two reasons: lack of cognizable legal theory, or insufficient facts under cognizable theory. Fed.Rules Civ.Proc.Rule 12(b)(6), 28 U.S.C.A.

> Kentucky Cent. Life Ins. Co. v. LeDuc, 814 F.Supp. 832.

To dismiss complaint for failure to state claim on which relief can be granted, it must appear to be a certainty that plaintiff would not be entitled to relief under any set of facts that could be proved. Fed.Rules Civ.Proc.Rule 12(b)(6), 28 U.S.C.A.

> Kentucky Cent. Life Ins. Co. v. LeDuc, 814 F.Supp. 832.

N.D.Cal. 1992. In considering motion to dismiss, court must presume that plaintiffs' allegations are true, and court is to grant the motion to dismiss if it appears that plaintiffs can prove no set of facts which would entitle plaintiffs to relief. Fed.Rules Civ.Proc.Rule 12(b)(6), 28 U.S.C.A.

> In re Verifone Securities Litigation, 784 F.Supp. 1471, affirmed 11 F.3d 865.

N.D.Cal. 1991. Complaints may be dismissed as matter of law either for lack of cognizable legal theory or for insufficient facts under cognizable theory. Fed.Rules Civ.Proc. Rule 12(b)(6), 28 U.S.C.A.

> Alfus v. Pyramid Technology Corp., 764 F.Supp. 598.

N.D.Cal. 1991. Claim should not be dismissed unless it is certain that law would not permit requested relief, even if all allegations in complaint were proven true. Fed.Rules Civ. Proc.Rule 12(b)(6), 28 U.S.C.A.

> Colaprico v. Sun Microsystems, Inc., 758 F.Supp. 1335, on reconsideration 1991 WL 207480.

N.D.Cal. 1990. While plaintiff bears burden of proving suit was filed within limitations period, complaint should not be dismissed unless it appears beyond doubt that plaintiff can prove no set of facts in support of claim.

> Gray v. First Winthrop Corp., 754 F.Supp. 157.

N.D.Cal. 1989. Judgment of dismissal is appropriate if it is clear that no relief could be granted under any set of facts that could be proven consistent with allegations in complaint.

> In re Insurance Antitrust Litigation, 723 F.Supp. 464, reversed and remanded 938 F.2d 919, certiorari granted in part Hartford Fire Ins. Co. v. California, 113 S.Ct. 52, 506 U.S. 814, 121 L.Ed.2d 22, affirmed in part, reversed in part 113 S.Ct. 2891, 509 U.S. 764, 125 L.Ed.2d 612, on remand 5 F.3d 1556, certiorari denied Winterthur Reinsurance Corp. of America v. California, 113 S.Ct. 3034, 509 U.S. 921, 125 L.Ed.2d 721, certiorari denied Unionamerica Ins. Co. Ltd. v. California, 113 S.Ct. 3034, 509 U.S. 921, 125 L.Ed.2d 721.

N.D.Cal. 1988. Where claims in complaint are insufficiently supported by factual allegations, claims may be disposed of by summary dismissal.

> Stinson v. Home Ins. Co., 690 F.Supp. 882.

N.D.Cal. 1987. Motion to dismiss for failure to state claim tests formal sufficiency of statement of claim for relief. Fed.Rules Civ. Proc.Rule 12(b)(6), 28 U.S.C.A.

> Washington v. Baenziger, 673 F.Supp. 1478.

S.D.Cal. 1998. Although there need not be an elaborate recitation of every fact plaintiff may rely upon at trial in order to withstand a motion to dismiss, there must be a finding that the complaint gives defendant fair notice of what plaintiff's claim is and the grounds upon which it rests. Fed.Rules Civ.Proc.Rules 8(a), 12(b)(6), 28 U.S.C.A.

> Ricotta v. State of Cal., 4 F.Supp.2d 961.

S.D.Cal. 1998. Courts will dismiss a complaint for failing to state a claim only where complaint lacks a cognizable legal theory or sufficient facts to support a cognizable legal theory. Fed.Rules Civ.Proc.Rule 12(b)(6), 28 U.S.C.A.

> Allison v. Brooktree Corp., 999 F.Supp. 1342.

Motion to dismiss for failure to state claim authorizes court to dismiss a complaint on basis of a dispositive issue of law. Fed.Rules Civ. Proc.Rule 12(b)(6), 28 U.S.C.A.

Allison v. Brooktree Corp., 999 F.Supp. 1342.

S.D.Cal. 1996. Dismissal for failure to state a claim is proper only in extraordinary cases; court should grant relief only where plaintiff's complaint lacks cognizable legal theory or sufficient facts to support cognizable legal theory. Fed.Rules Civ.Proc.Rule 12(b)(6), 28 U.S.C.A.

Brown v. Adidas Int., 938 F.Supp. 628.

S.D.Cal. 1995. Motion to dismiss for failure of pleading to state claim upon which relief can be granted is proper only in extraordinary cases. Fed.Rules Civ.Proc.Rule 12(b)(6), 28 U.S.C.A.

Barker v. U.S., 903 F.Supp. 31.

Courts should grant motion to dismiss for failure of pleading to state claim upon which relief can be granted only where plaintiff's complaint lacks "cognizable legal theory" or sufficient facts to support cognizable legal theory. Fed.Rules Civ.Proc.Rule 12(b)(6), 28 U.S.C.A.

Barker v. U.S., 903 F.Supp. 31.

S.D.Cal. 1994. Under federal rule, court will grant motion to dismiss only when it appears beyond doubt that plaintiffs can prove no set of facts in support of their claim which would entitle them to relief. Fed.Rules Civ. Proc.Rule 12(b)(6), 28 U.S.C.A.

Employers Ins. of Wausau v. Musick, Peeler, & Garrett, 871 F.Supp. 381, opinion amended on reconsideration 948 F.Supp. 942.

S.D.Cal. 1994. Dismissal of complaint is improper unless it appears beyond doubt that plaintiff can prove no set of facts in support of his claim which would entitle him to relief. Fed.Rules Civ.Proc.Rule 12(b)(6), 28 U.S.C.A.

Allman v. Philip Morris, Inc., 865 F.Supp. 665.

S.D.Cal. 1994. In ruling upon motion to dismiss for failure to state claim, court must accept all material allegations in complaint as true and must construe implications which arise most favorably to plaintiff and must decide whether facts alleged, if true, would entitle plaintiff to some form of legal remedy and, unless answer is unequivocally no, motion must be denied. Fed.Rules Civ.Proc.Rule 12(b)(6), 28 U.S.C.A.

First San Diego Properties v. Exxon Co., 859 F.Supp. 1313.

D.Colo. 1994. Dismissal of a claim is proper if it appears beyond a doubt that plaintiff can prove no set of facts in support of his claim that would entitle him to relief.

Custodio v. U.S., 866 F.Supp. 479.

D.Colo. 1994. For purposes of determining sufficiency of complaint, complaint should not be dismissed for failure to state a claim unless it appears beyond a doubt that plaintiff can prove no set of facts in support of claim which would entitle him to relief. Fed.Rules Civ.Proc.Rule 12(b)(6), 28 U.S.C.A.

Burkins v. U.S., 865 F.Supp. 1480.

D.Colo. 1994. Claims should not be dismissed for failure to state a claim unless plaintiff can prove no set of facts in support of claims which would entitle her to relief, accepting all factual allegations as true and drawing all reasonable inferences in favor of plaintiff. Fed. Rules Civ.Proc.Rule 12(b), 28 U.S.C.A.

Allstate Ins. Co. v. U.S., 864 F.Supp. 1015.

D.Colo. 1994. Claim should not be dismissed unless plaintiff can provide no set of facts in support of her claims which would entitle her to relief. Fed.Rules Civ.Proc.Rule 12(b), 28 U.S.C.A.

Connolly v. Beckett, 863 F.Supp. 1379.

As long as plaintiff offers evidence in support of legally recognized claim for relief, motions to dismiss must be denied. Fed.Rules Civ.Proc.Rule 12(b), 28 U.S.C.A.

Connolly v. Beckett, 863 F.Supp. 1379.

D.Colo. 1994. Dismissal of claim for failure to state claim upon which relief can be granted requires legal determination that plaintiff can prove no set of facts in support of his claim to entitle him to relief. Fed.Rules Civ. Proc.Rule 12(b)(6), 28 U.S.C.A.

West Pines Psychiatric Hosp. v. Samsonite Ben. Plan, 848 F.Supp. 907.

D.Colo. 1994. Dismissal for failure to state a claim upon which relief can be granted is proper if it appears beyond doubt that plaintiff can prove no set of facts in support of her claim that would entitle her to relief. Fed.Rules Civ. Proc.Rule 12(b)(6), 28 U.S.C.A.

Galusha v. Farmers Ins. Exchange, 844 F.Supp. 1401.

D.Colo. 1994. Claims should not be dismissed unless plaintiff can prove no set of facts in support of her claims which would entitle her to relief. Fed.Rules Civ.Proc.Rule 12(b), 28 U.S.C.A.

George v. HEK America, Inc., 157 F.R.D. 489.

As long as plaintiff offers evidence in support of legally recognized claim for relief, motions to dismiss must be denied. Fed.Rules Civ.Proc.Rule 12(b), 28 U.S.C.A.

> George v. HEK America, Inc., 157 F.R.D. 489.

D.Colo. 1994. Dismissal of claim for failure to state claim is improper unless it appears beyond doubt that plaintiffs can prove no set of facts in support of their claim that would entitle them to relief. Fed.Rules Civ.Proc.Rule 12(b)(6), 28 U.S.C.A.

> Sugro, Inc. v. U.S., 156 F.R.D. 233, affirmed 57 F.3d 1081.

D.Colo. 1993. Claim should not be dismissed unless plaintiff can prove no set of facts in support of her claims which would entitle her to relief. Fed.Rules Civ.Proc.Rule 12(b), 28 U.S.C.A.

> Strub v. Public Service Co. of Colorado, 863 F.Supp. 1352.

As long as plaintiff offers evidence in support of legally recognized claim for relief, motions to dismiss must be denied. Fed.Rules Civ.Proc.Rule 12(b), 28 U.S.C.A.

> Strub v. Public Service Co. of Colorado, 863 F.Supp. 1352.

D.Colo. 1993. Dismissal is proper only when it appears beyond doubt that no set of facts will support plaintiff's right to relief. Fed. Rules Civ.Proc.Rule 12(b)(6), 28 U.S.C.A.

> KN Energy, Inc. v. Rockwell Intern. Corp., 840 F.Supp. 95.

D.Colo. 1993. Dismissal is proper only when it appears beyond doubt that no set of facts will support plaintiff's right to relief. Fed. Rules Civ.Proc.Rule 12(b)(6), 28 U.S.C.A.

> Resolution Trust Corp. v. Heiserman, 839 F.Supp. 1457, reconsideration denied 1994 WL 907409.

D.Colo. 1993. In considering motions to dismiss, district court accepted allegations as true and construed them in light most favorable to plaintiff; dismissal was proper only if plaintiff could prove no set of facts in support of his claims to entitle him to relief.

> Haney v. Castle Meadows, Inc., 839 F.Supp. 753.

D.Colo. 1993. Claim should not be dismissed for lack of subject matter jurisdiction unless it appears beyond doubt that plaintiff can prove no set of facts which would entitle him to relief and all of plaintiff's pleadings must be liberally construed. Fed.Rules Civ.Proc.Rule 12(b)(1), 28 U.S.C.A.

> Sierra Club v. Colorado Refining Co., 838 F.Supp. 1428.

D.Colo. 1993. Dismissal of claim is improper unless it appears beyond doubt that plaintiffs can establish no set of facts in support

of their claim that would entitle them to relief. Fed.Rules Civ.Proc.Rule 12(b)(6), 28 U.S.C.A.

> Rottman v. Krabloonik, Inc., 834 F.Supp. 1269.

D.Colo. 1993. Claim should not be dismissed for failure to state a claim unless plaintiff can prove no set of facts in support of claims which would entitle her to relief, accepting all allegations as true and drawing all reasonable inferences in favor of plaintiff, and liberally construing plaintiff's pleadings. Fed.Rules Civ. Proc.Rule 12(b), 28 U.S.C.A.

> Venta, Inc. v. Frontier Oil and Refining Co., 827 F.Supp. 1526.

D.Colo. 1993. Claim should not be dismissed unless plaintiff can prove no set of facts in support of his claim which would entitle him to relief. Fed.Rules Civ.Proc.Rule 12(b), 28 U.S.C.A.

> Fostvedt v. U.S., I.R.S., 824 F.Supp. 978, affirmed 16 F.3d 416.

As long as plaintiff offers evidence in support of legally recognized claim for relief, motion to dismiss must be denied. Fed.Rules Civ. Proc.Rule 12(b), 28 U.S.C.A.

> Fostvedt v. U.S., I.R.S., 824 F.Supp. 978, affirmed 16 F.3d 416.

D.Colo. 1992. Dismissal of claim is improper unless it appears beyond doubt that plaintiff can prove no set of facts in support of claim for relief.

> Mass v. Martin Marietta Corp., 805 F.Supp. 1530.

D.Colo. 1992. Complaint should not be dismissed for failure to state a claim unless it appears beyond a doubt that plaintiff can prove no set of facts that would entitle him to relief. Fed.Rules Civ.Proc.Rule 12(b)(6), 28 U.S.C.A.

> American Cas. Co. v. Glaskin, 805 F.Supp. 866.

D.Colo. 1992. Complaint should be dismissed only when it appears that plaintiff can prove no set of facts to support claims that would entitle plaintiff to relief and court must accept all well pleaded allegations in complaint as true and construe them in light most favorable to plaintiff. Fed.Rules Civ.Proc.Rule 12(b)(6), 28 U.S.C.A.

> Colorado Environmental Coalition v. Lujan, 803 F.Supp. 364.

D.Colo. 1992. Dismissal for failure to state a claim requires legal determination that plaintiff can prove no set of facts which entitle him or her to relief. Fed.Rules Civ.Proc.Rule 12(b)(6), 28 U.S.C.A.

> Brever v. Rockwell Intern. Corp., 801 F.Supp. 424, reversed 40 F.3d 1119.

D.Colo. 1991. Complaint should not be dismissed for failure to state a claim unless plaintiff can prove no set of facts in support of claims which would entitle plaintiff to relief. Fed.Rules Civ.Proc.Rule 12(b)(6), 28 U.S.C.A.

 Fry v. Board of County Com'rs of County of Baca, 837 F.Supp. 330, affirmed 7 F.3d 936, rehearing denied.

D.Colo. 1991. Cause of action should not be dismissed for failure to state a claim unless court determines that, beyond doubt, plaintiff can prove no set of facts that would entitle it to relief. Fed.Rules Civ.Proc.Rule 12(b)(6), 28 U.S.C.A.

 TV Communications Network, Inc. v. ESPN, Inc., 767 F.Supp. 1062, affirmed 964 F.2d 1022, certiorari denied 113 S.Ct. 601, 506 U.S. 999, 121 L.Ed.2d 537.

Plaintiff cannot survive motions to dismiss without pleading sufficient facts to prove each element of alleged offense; conclusory legal allegations are inadequate. Fed.Rules Civ.Proc. Rule 12(b)(6), 28 U.S.C.A.

 TV Communications Network, Inc. v. ESPN, Inc., 767 F.Supp. 1062, affirmed 964 F.2d 1022, certiorari denied 113 S.Ct. 601, 506 U.S. 999, 121 L.Ed.2d 537.

D.Colo. 1991. In ruling on motion to dismiss for failure to state a claim, motion will be granted if it appears beyond doubt that plaintiff can prove no set of facts in support of his claim that would entitle him to relief. Fed.Rules Civ.Proc.Rule 12(b)(6), 28 U.S.C.A.

 Winslow v. Romer, 759 F.Supp. 670.

D.Colo. 1990. Complaint is not subject to dismissal unless it appears to certainty that no relief can be granted under any set of facts that can be proven in support of its allegations.

 Alameda Nat. Bank v. Kanchanapoom, 752 F.Supp. 367.

D.Colo. 1990. A complaint is not subject to dismissal for failure to state a claim unless it appears to a certainty that no relief can be granted under any set of facts that can be proven in support of its allegations. Fed.Rules Civ.Proc.Rule 12(b)(6), 28 U.S.C.A.

 Wachter v. Denver Nat. Bank, 751 F.Supp. 906.

D.Colo. 1989. Court may dismiss complaint if it is clear that no relief could be granted under any set of facts that could be proved consistent with allegations. Fed.Rules Civ.Proc.Rule 12(c), 28 U.S.C.A.

 Luna v. City and County of Denver, 718 F.Supp. 854.

D.Colo. 1989. When reviewing sufficiency of complaint tested by motion to dismiss, court must accept as true complainant's allegations and view them in light most favorable to plain-

tiffs, and complaint must stand unless it appears beyond doubt that plaintiffs have alleged no facts that would entitle them to relief.

 Sullivan v. Boettcher & Co., 714 F.Supp. 1132.

D.Colo. 1988. On motion to dismiss, complaint must stand unless it appears beyond doubt that plaintiffs have alleged no set of facts that would entitle them to relief.

 Miller v. Moffat County State Bank, 678 F.Supp. 247.

D.Colo. 1987. So long as plaintiff may offer evidence to support legally recognized claim for relief, motion to dismiss should be denied. Fed.Rules Civ.Proc.Rule 12(b)(6), 28 U.S.C.A.

 Dukeminier v. K-Mart Corp., 651 F.Supp. 1322.

D.Colo. 1984. So long as plaintiff may offer evidence to support legally recognized claim for relief, motion to dismiss should be denied. Fed.Rules Civ.Proc.Rule 12(b)(6), 28 U.S.C.A.

 Hiatt v. Schreiber, 599 F.Supp. 1142.

D.Conn. 1995. Court may dismiss complaint for failure to state claim upon which relief can be granted only where it appears beyond doubt that plaintiff can prove no set of facts in support of claim which would entitle him to relief. Fed.Rules Civ.Proc.Rule 12(b)(6), 28 U.S.C.A.

 Hall v. United Technologies, Corp., 872 F.Supp. 1094.

D.Conn. 1994. Court will grant defendant's motion to dismiss for failure to state claim upon which relief can be granted only if it appears beyond doubt that plaintiff can prove no set of facts in support of claim which would entitle it to relief. Fed.Rules Civ.Proc.Rule 12(b)(6), 28 U.S.C.A.

 Connecticut Hosp. Ass'n v. Pogue, 870 F.Supp. 444, reversed 66 F.3d 413.

D.Conn. 1994. In assessing motion to dismiss for failure to state a claim, court must determine whether plaintiff, under any possible theory, has valid claim upon which relief can be granted. Fed.Rules Civ.Proc.Rule 12(b)(6), 28 U.S.C.A.

 A. Aiudi & Sons v. Town of Plainville, 862 F.Supp. 737.

D.Conn. 1994. When considering motion to dismiss for failure to state a claim upon which relief can be granted, district court is required to accept as true all factual allegations in complaint and draw inferences from these allegations in light most favorable to plaintiff; dismissal is warranted only if, under any set of facts that plaintiff can prove consistent with allegation, it is clear that no relief can be granted. Fed.Rules Civ.Proc.Rule 12(b)(6), 28 U.S.C.A.

> Companies for Fair Allocation v. Axil Corp., 853 F.Supp. 575.

D.Conn. 1994. Complaint should not be dismissed unless it appears beyond doubt that plaintiff can prove no set of facts in support of his claim which would entitle him to relief. Fed.Rules Civ.Proc.Rule 12(b)(6), 28 U.S.C.A.

> Kent v. AVCO Corp., 849 F.Supp. 833.

D.Conn. 1994. Dismissal of complaint is not warranted unless it appears beyond doubt that plaintiff can prove no set of facts in support of claim which would entitle him to relief. Fed.Rules Civ.Proc.Rule 12(b)(6), 28 U.S.C.A.

> Urashka v. Griffin Hosp., 841 F.Supp. 468.

When considering motion to dismiss, question for district court to decide is whether it appears to certainty under existing laws that no relief can be granted under any set of facts that might be proved in support of plaintiffs' claims. Fed.Rules Civ.Proc.Rule 12(b)(6), 28 U.S.C.A.

> Urashka v. Griffin Hosp., 841 F.Supp. 468.

D.Conn. 1993. Dismissal of complaint for failure to state claim is warranted only if it is clear that no relief could be granted under any set of facts that could be proved consistent with allegations. Fed.Rules Civ.Proc.Rule 12(b)(6), 28 U.S.C.A.

> Budget Rent A Car of Westchester, Inc. v. Rental Car Resources, Inc., 842 F.Supp. 614.

D.Conn. 1993. Complaint should not be dismissed for failure to state claim unless it appears beyond doubt that plaintiff can prove no set of facts in support of his claim which would entitle him to relief.

> Presnick v. Santoro, 832 F.Supp. 521.

Motion to dismiss should be denied if complaint states grounds for relief for which some set of facts could be proven which would entitle plaintiff to relief.

> Presnick v. Santoro, 832 F.Supp. 521.

D.Conn. 1993. Complaint should not be dismissed unless it appears beyond doubt that plaintiff can prove no set of facts in support of his claim which would entitle him to relief. Fed.Rules Civ.Proc.Rule 12(b), 28 U.S.C.A.

> Harris v. Wells, 832 F.Supp. 31.

D.Conn. 1993. Motions to dismiss for failure to state claim are decided solely on facts alleged and are granted only where no set of facts consistent with allegations could be proven that would entitle plaintiff to relief. Fed.Rules Civ.Proc.Rule 12(b)(6), 28 U.S.C.A.

> DiPietro-Kay Corp. v. Interactive Benefits Corp., 825 F.Supp. 459.

D.Conn. 1993. Motion to dismiss for failure to state claim upon which relief can be granted should be granted only where no set of facts consistent with allegations could be proven entitling plaintiffs to relief. Fed.Rules Civ.Proc. Rule 12(b)(6), 28 U.S.C.A.

> Aguilar v. United Nat. Ins. Co., 825 F.Supp. 456.

D.Conn. 1993. Motion to dismiss for failure to state a claim should be granted only where no set of facts consistent with allegations could be proven entitling plaintiff to relief; issue is not whether plaintiff will prevail, but whether he or she should be afforded opportunity to offer evidence to prove his or her claims. Fed.Rules Civ.Proc.Rule 12(b)(6), 28 U.S.C.A.

> Sacks v. Savings Bank of Rockville, 824 F.Supp. 317.

D.Conn. 1993. Motion to dismiss for failure to state a claim should be granted only where no set of facts consistent with allegations could be proven entitling plaintiffs to relief; issue is not whether plaintiffs will prevail, but whether they should be afforded opportunity to offer evidence to prove their claims. Fed.Rules Civ.Proc.Rule 12(b)(6), 28 U.S.C.A.

> Investors Capital Corp. v. Connecticut Nat. Bank, 824 F.Supp. 309.

D.Conn. 1993. In considering motion to dismiss for failure to state claim upon which relief can be granted, court is under duty to determine whether plaintiff has valid claim under any possible theory and motion should not be granted unless it appears beyond doubt that plaintiff cannot support claim entitling it to relief. Fed.Rules Civ.Proc.Rule 12(b)(6), 28 U.S.C.A.

> Vorvis v. Southern New England Telephone Co., 821 F.Supp. 851.

D.Conn. 1993. Complaint should not be dismissed unless it appears beyond doubt that plaintiff can prove no set of facts in support of his claim which would entitle him to relief.

> Shane v. State of Conn., 821 F.Supp. 829.

D.Conn. 1993. Motion to dismiss for failure to state claim should be granted only where no set of facts consistent with allegations could be proven that entitle plaintiff to relief. Fed. Rules Civ.Proc.Rule 12(b)(6), 28 U.S.C.A.

> Monroe v. Horwitch, 820 F.Supp. 682, affirmed 19 F.3d 9.

D.Conn. 1993. Motion to dismiss for failure to state cause of action must be decided solely on facts alleged, and should be granted only where no set of facts consistent with allegations could be proven which would entitle plaintiff to relief. Fed.Rules Civ.Proc.Rule 12(b)(6), 28 U.S.C.A.

> Chem-Tek, Inc. v. General Motors Corp., 816 F.Supp. 123.

D.Conn. 1992. In ruling on motion for judgment on the pleadings, court must view pleadings in light most favorable to, and draw all reasonable inferences in favor of, nonmoving party; court may not dismiss complaint unless plaintiff apparently cannot, beyond a doubt, prove facts to support his claim. Fed.Rules Civ.Proc.Rule 12(c), 28 U.S.C.A.

> Grease Monkey Intern., Inc. v. Watkins, 808 F.Supp. 111.

D.Conn. 1992. Motion to dismiss for failure to state a claim upon which relief can be granted must be decided solely on facts alleged, and should be granted only where no set of facts consistent with allegations could be proven; issue is not whether plaintiff will prevail, but whether he should be afforded opportunity to prove his claims.

> DeSalle v. A.G. Edwards & Sons, Inc., 804 F.Supp. 436.

D.Conn. 1992. Dismissal for failure to state claim upon which relief may be granted is warranted only if, under any set of facts that plaintiff can prove consistent with allegations, it is clear that no relief can be granted. Fed. Rules Civ.Proc.Rule 12(b)(6), 28 U.S.C.A.

> Ferber v. Travelers Corp., 802 F.Supp. 698.

D.Conn. 1992. On motion to dismiss for failure to state claim on which relief can be granted, complaint is construed liberally and dismissal will not be granted unless it appears beyond a reasonable doubt that plaintiffs can prove no set of facts in support of claim which would entitle them to relief. Fed.Rules Civ. Proc.Rule 12(b)(1), 28 U.S.C.A.

> Sean R. by Dwight R. v. Board of Educ. of Town of Woodbridge, 794 F.Supp. 467.

D.Conn. 1992. When considering motion to dismiss, court accepts as true all factual allegations in complaint and draws inferences from those allegations in light most favorable to plaintiff and dismissal is not warranted unless it appears beyond doubt that plaintiff could prove no set of facts in support of claim which would entitle him to relief. Fed.Rules Civ.Proc.Rules 9(b), 12(b)(6), 28 U.S.C.A.

> Walsche v. First Investors Corp., 793 F.Supp. 395, affirmed in part, vacated in part 981 F.2d 649.

D.Conn. 1992. Complaint should not be dismissed unless it appears beyond doubt that plaintiff can prove no set of facts in support of claim which would entitle plaintiff to relief. Fed.Rules Civ.Proc.Rule 12(b)(6), 28 U.S.C.A.

> Scharrer v. Consolidated Rail Corp., 792 F.Supp. 170.

D.Conn. 1992. Complaint should not be dismissed unless it appears beyond doubt that plaintiff can prove no set of facts in support of his claim which would entitle him to relief.

> Kemp v. Flygt Corp., 791 F.Supp. 48.

D.Conn. 1991. Dismissal is not warranted unless it appears beyond doubt that plaintiff can prove no set of facts in support of claim that would entitle him to relief. Fed.Rules Civ.Proc. Rule 12(b)(6), 28 U.S.C.A.

> Spear v. Town of West Hartford, 771 F.Supp. 521, affirmed 954 F.2d 63, certiorari denied 113 S.Ct. 66, 506 U.S. 819, 121 L.Ed.2d 33.

Question for court to decide on motion to dismiss is whether it appears to certainty under existing law that no relief can be granted under any set of facts that might be proved in support of plaintiff's claims. Fed.Rules Civ.Proc.Rule 12(b)(6), 28 U.S.C.A.

> Spear v. Town of West Hartford, 771 F.Supp. 521, affirmed 954 F.2d 63, certiorari denied 113 S.Ct. 66, 506 U.S. 819, 121 L.Ed.2d 33.

D.Conn. 1991. In considering motion to dismiss for failure to state claim upon which relief can be granted, court is under duty to determine whether plaintiff has valid claim under any possible theory; motion should not be granted unless it appears beyond doubt that plaintiff cannot support claim entitling it to relief. Fed.Rules Civ.Proc.Rule 12(b)(6), 28 U.S.C.A.

> Steiner v. Shawmut Nat. Corp., 766 F.Supp. 1236.

D.Conn. 1990. When considering motion to dismiss for failure to state claim upon which relief can be granted, court is under duty to determine whether plaintiff has valid claim under any possible theory. Fed.Rules Civ.Proc. Rule 12(b)(6), 28 U.S.C.A.

> D.P. Technology Corp. v. Sherwood Tool, Inc., 751 F.Supp. 1038.

D.Conn. 1986. Where failure to plead fraud with requisite particularity occurs after second attempt to do so, court may, in its discretion, dismiss with prejudice. Fed.Rules Civ.Proc.Rule 9(b), 28 U.S.C.A.

> Andreo v. Friedlander, Gaines, Cohen, Rosenthal & Rosenberg, 651 F.Supp. 877.

D.Del. 1993. In considering motion to dismiss, count of complaint may be dismissed for failure to state a claim only if, when accepting all factual allegations as true and drawing all reasonable inferences from these facts, no relief would be granted under any set of facts that could be proved, and in applying this standard, burden to show failure to state claim rests with moving party. Fed.Rules Civ.Proc.Rule 12(b)(6), 28 U.S.C.A.

> Smith v. ZENECA Inc., 820 F.Supp. 831, affirmed 37 F.3d 1489.

D.Del. 1993. Count of complaint may be dismissed for failure to state claim only if, when accepting all factual allegations as true and drawing all reasonable inferences from these facts, no relief would be granted under any set of facts that could be proved. Fed.Rules Civ. Proc.Rule 12(b)(6), 28 U.S.C.A.

> Tybout v. Karr Barth Pension Admin., Inc., 819 F.Supp. 371.

D.Del. 1992. Standard for deciding motion to dismiss is whether, taking all factual allegations as true, it is beyond doubt that plaintiff can prove no set of facts to support his claim which could entitle him to relief, and facts alleged, as well as all reasonable factual inferences drawn from those facts, are construed in plaintiff's favor.

> McIntyre v. Division of Youth Rehabilitation Services, Dept. of Services for Children, Youth and their Families, State of Del., 795 F.Supp. 668.

D.Del. 1991. Complaint should not be dismissed for failure to state claim unless it can be established that plaintiff can prove no set of facts in support of claim that would entitle him to relief. Fed.Rules Civ.Proc.Rule 12(b)(6), 28 U.S.C.A.

> Young v. West Coast Indus. Relations Ass'n, Inc., 763 F.Supp. 64, affirmed 961 F.2d 1570.

D.D.C. 1998. On motion to dismiss for failure to state claim, court need not accept plaintiff's legal conclusions, and thus complaint may be dismissed for lack of cognizable legal claim. Fed.Rules Civ.Proc.Rule 12(b)(6), 28 U.S.C.A.

> Slaby v. Fairbridge, 3 F.Supp.2d 22.

D.D.C. 1997. Though court deciding motion to dismiss for failure to state claim accepts well-pleaded facts as true and construes complaint liberally, granting nonmovant benefit of any reasonable inferences that can be derived from facts alleged, court is not required to accept inferences unsupported by facts alleged or legal conclusions that are cast as factual allegations. Fed.Rules Civ.Proc.Rule 12(b)(6), 28 U.S.C.A.

> U.S. v. BCCI Holdings (Luxembourg), S.A., 980 F.Supp. 21.

D.D.C. 1996. For purposes of determining whether plaintiff has failed to state cause of action, complaint must set forth sufficient information to suggest that there exists some recognized legal theory upon which relief can be granted; court must dismiss complaint where, even assuming all factual allegations are true, plaintiff has failed to establish right to relief based on those facts.

> Caudle v. Thomason, 942 F.Supp. 635.

D.D.C. 1994. In ruling on motion to dismiss for failure to state claim on which relief may be granted, court accepts as true each allegation in complaint and will not grant motion unless it appears that plaintiff can prove no set of facts entitling him to relief sought in complaint.

> Campbell-El v. District of Columbia, 874 F.Supp. 403.

D.D.C. 1994. Complaint should not be dismissed for failure to state claim upon which relief can be granted unless plaintiff can prove no set of facts entitling him or her to relief sought in complaint. Fed.Rules Civ.Proc.Rule 12(b)(6), 28 U.S.C.A.

> Mills v. Home Equity Group, Inc., 871 F.Supp. 1482.

D.D.C. 1994. Complaint should not be dismissed for failure to state claim upon which relief can be granted unless it appears beyond doubt that plaintiffs can prove no set of facts entitling them to relief sought in complaint. Fed.Rules Civ.Proc.Rule 12(b)(6), 28 U.S.C.A.

> NVMercure Ltd. Partnership v. Resolution Trust Corp., 871 F.Supp. 488.

D.D.C. 1994. Complaint should not be dismissed for failure to state claim unless it appears beyond doubt that plaintiff can prove no set of facts in support of his claim which would entitle him to relief. Fed.Rules Civ.Proc.Rule 12(b)(6), 28 U.S.C.A.

> Shoreham Hotel Ltd. Partnership v. Wilder, 866 F.Supp. 1.

D.D.C. 1994. Dismissal for failure to state claim is only appropriate if it appears beyond doubt that no set of facts proffered in support of plaintiff's claim would entitle him to relief. Fed.Rules Civ.Proc.Rule 12(b)(6), 28 U.S.C.A.

> Webb v. District of Columbia, 864 F.Supp. 175.

D.D.C. 1994. In viewing motion to dismiss or for judgment on pleadings, complaint should not be dismissed for failure to state claim unless it appears beyond doubt that plaintiff can prove no set of facts in support of his claim which would entitle him to relief. Fed.Rules Civ.Proc. Rule 12, 28 U.S.C.A.

> United Parcel Service, Inc. v. International Broth. of Teamsters, AFL-CIO, 859 F.Supp. 590.

D.D.C. 1994. District court may dismiss complaint for failure to state claim only when it appears beyond doubt that plaintiff can prove no set of facts in support of his claims that would entitle him to relief. Fed.Rules Civ.Proc. Rule 12(b)(6), 28 U.S.C.A.

> In re United Mine Workers of America Employee Ben. Plans Litigation, 854 F.Supp. 914.

D.D.C. 1994. When reviewing adequacy of complaint for purposes of motion to dismiss for failure to state claim, dismissal is only appropriate if it appears beyond doubt that no set of facts proffered in support of plaintiff's claim would entitle him to relief. Fed.Rules Civ.Proc. Rule 12(b)(6), 28 U.S.C.A.

Wiggins v. Hitchens, 853 F.Supp. 505.

D.D.C. 1994. Dismissal of complaint for failure to state a claim is only appropriate if it appears beyond doubt that no set of facts proffered in support of plaintiff's claim would entitle him to relief. Fed.Rules Civ.Proc.Rule 12(b)(6), 28 U.S.C.A.

Wiggins v. Philip Morris, Inc., 853 F.Supp. 470.

D.D.C. 1994. Dismissal of action for failure to state claim is only appropriate if it appears beyond doubt that no set of facts proffered in support of plaintiff's claim would entitle him to relief. Fed.Rules Civ.Proc.Rule 12(b)(6), 28 U.S.C.A.

Wiggins v. Philip Morris, Inc., 853 F.Supp. 458.

D.D.C. 1993. Complaint will be dismissed for failure to state claim upon which relief can be granted only if it appears beyond doubt that no set of facts proffered in support of claim would entitle plaintiff to relief.

Boggs v. Bowron, 842 F.Supp. 542, affirmed 67 F.3d 972, 314 U.S.App.D.C. 278, certiorari denied 116 S.Ct. 1417, 517 U.S. 1134, 134 L.Ed.2d 543.

D.D.C. 1993. Motion to dismiss for failure to state claim should be granted only if it is clear that no relief could be granted under any set of facts that could be proved consistent with the allegations. Fed.Rules Civ.Proc.Rule 12(b)(6), 28 U.S.C.A.

Edison Elec. Institute v. Henwood, 832 F.Supp. 413.

D.D.C. 1993. Complaint should not be dismissed for failure to state claim upon which relief can be granted unless it appears beyond doubt that plaintiff can prove no set of facts in support of his claim which would entitle him to relief. Fed.Rules Civ.Proc.Rule 12(b)(6), 28 U.S.C.A.

Guzel v. State of Kuwait, 818 F.Supp. 6.

D.D.C. 1993. Motion to dismiss for failure to state claim upon which relief can be granted should be granted only if it is clear that no relief can be granted under any set of facts that could be proved consistent with allegations. Fed. Rules Civ.Proc.Rule 12(b)(6), 28 U.S.C.A.

Martin v. Ezeagu, 816 F.Supp. 20.

D.D.C. 1991. In viewing motion to dismiss, complaint should not be dismissed for failure to state claim unless, presuming factual allegations true and liberally construing them and all favorable inferences therefrom in favor of plaintiff, it appears beyond doubt that plaintiff can prove no set of facts in support of his claim which would entitle him to relief.

Peterson Farms I v. Madigan, 782 F.Supp. 1.

D.D.C. 1991. Complaint should not be dismissed for failure to state claim unless it appears beyond doubt that plaintiff can prove no set of facts in support of claim which would entitle him to relief.

Fordyce v. Frohnmayer, 763 F.Supp. 654.

D.D.C. 1990. Standard for motion to dismiss for failure to state a claim is that dismissal is only proper when it appears beyond a doubt that plaintiff can prove no set of facts in support of claim which would entitle him to relief. Fed.Rules Civ.Proc.Rule 12, 28 U.S.C.A.

Federal Information Systems, Corp. v. Boyd, 753 F.Supp. 971.

D.D.C. 1990. To secure motion to dismiss, defendant must show beyond doubt that plaintiff can prove no set of facts in support of his claim which would entitle him to relief.

Amiri v. WUSA TV-Channel Nine, 751 F.Supp. 211, affirmed 946 F.2d 1563, 292 U.S.App.D.C. 83, certiorari denied 112 S.Ct. 1230, 502 U.S. 1117, 117 L.Ed.2d 465.

D.D.C. 1990. Dismissal rule permits dismissal of claim only if, construing allegations in complaint in favor of plaintiff, it is beyond doubt that plaintiff can prove no set of facts that would justify relief. Fed.Rules Civ.Proc.Rule 12(b)(6), 28 U.S.C.A.

Best v. District of Columbia, 743 F.Supp. 44.

D.D.C. 1990. Where motion to dismiss can be resolved on basis of pleadings, it must be dismissed if it appears beyond doubt that, under any reasonable reading of complaint, plaintiff will be unable to prove any set of facts that would justify relief; where resolution of motion requires consideration of matters outside pleadings, however, judgment must be entered against party who fails to make showing sufficient to establish existence of element essential to that party's case, and on which that party will bear burden of proof at trial. Fed.Rules Civ.Proc.Rule 12(b)(6), 28 U.S.C.A.

Red Lake Band of Chippewa Indians v. Swimmer, 740 F.Supp. 9.

M.D.Fla. 1998. Standard of review on motion to dismiss, which requires trial court to view complaint in the light most favorable to the plaintiff and accept all allegations as true, is not an absolute bar to dismissal of action when pro se complaint is confusing and essentially fails to state a claim upon which relief can be granted. Fed.Rules Civ.Proc.Rule 12(b)(6), 28 U.S.C.A.

> Woods v. Commissioner, I.R.S., 8 F.Supp.2d 1357.

M.D.Fla. 1998. Merely "labeling" claims is not sufficient to survive motion to dismiss for failure to state claim. Fed.Rules Civ.Proc.Rule 12(b)(6), 28 U.S.C.A.

> Farabee v. Rider, 995 F.Supp. 1398.

Threshold of sufficiency that complaint must meet to survive motion to dismiss for failure to state claim is exceedingly low. Fed. Rules Civ.Proc.Rule 12(b)(6), 28 U.S.C.A.

> Farabee v. Rider, 995 F.Supp. 1398.

M.D.Fla. 1997. To withstand motion to dismiss, plaintiff must allege sufficient facts in "four corners" of complaint to allow court to discern colorable claim.

> Chumbley v. Gashinski, 983 F.Supp. 1406.

M.D.Fla. 1997. To survive motion to dismiss for failure to state a claim, plaintiff may not merely "label" his or her claims but must, at a minimum, make short and plain statement of claim that gives fair notice to defendant. Fed.Rules Civ.Proc.Rules 8(a)(2), 12, 28 U.S.C.A.

> Lamar Advertising of Mobile, Inc. v. City of Lakeland, Fla., 980 F.Supp. 1455.

District court will not dismiss for failure to state a claim merely because complaint requests inappropriate relief or because it miscategorizes legal theories. Fed.Rules Civ.Proc.Rule 12(b)(6), 28 U.S.C.A.

> Lamar Advertising of Mobile, Inc. v. City of Lakeland, Fla., 980 F.Supp. 1455.

M.D.Fla. 1997. To survive motion to dismiss for failure to state claim, plaintiff may not merely "label" his or her claims. Fed.Rules Civ.Proc.Rule 12(b)(6), 28 U.S.C.A.

> Saunders v. Hunter, 980 F.Supp. 1236.

M.D.Fla. 1997. To survive motion to dismiss, plaintiff may not merely label his or her claims.

> Dantzler Lumber & Export Co. v. Bullington Lumber Co., Inc., 968 F.Supp. 1543.

Threshold of sufficiency that complaint must meet to survive motion to dismiss is exceedingly low.

> Dantzler Lumber & Export Co. v. Bullington Lumber Co., Inc., 968 F.Supp. 1543.

M.D.Fla. 1997. In deciding motion to dismiss, district court is required to view complaint in light most favorable to plaintiff, and claimant does not have to set out in detail facts upon which he basis his claim and is only required to make a short and plain statement of

the claim. Fed.Rules Civ.Proc.Rules 8(a)(2), 12(b)(6), 28 U.S.C.A.

> Unkel v. Liggett Group Inc., 172 F.R.D. 474.

M.D.Fla. 1996. To survive motion to dismiss for failure to state claim, plaintiff may not merely label his or her claims; at minimum, Federal Rules of Civil Procedure require short and plain statement of claim that will give defendant fair notice of what plaintiff's claim is and grounds upon which it rests. Fed.Rules Civ.Proc.Rule 8(a)(2), 28 U.S.C.A.

> Arenal v. City of Punta Gorda, Fla., 932 F.Supp. 1406.

M.D.Fla. 1996. To survive motion to dismiss, plaintiff may not merely label his or her claims; at minimum, procedural rules require short and plain statement of claims that will give defendant fair notice of what plaintiff's claims are and grounds upon which they rest. Fed.Rules Civ.Proc.Rule 8(a)(2), 28 U.S.C.A.

> Veltmann v. Walpole Pharmacy, Inc., 928 F.Supp. 1161.

Fact that plaintiff's complaint made general allegations against all named defendants and failed to separate each alleged act by each defendant into individually numbered paragraphs would be sufficient to grant either motion to dismiss with leave to amend or motion for more definite statement. Fed.Rules Civ. Proc.Rules 10(b), 12(e), 28 U.S.C.A.

> Veltmann v. Walpole Pharmacy, Inc., 928 F.Supp. 1161.

M.D.Fla. 1995. Complaint should be dismissed for failure to state claim when, on basis of dispositive issue of law, no construction of factual allegations of complaint will support cause of action. Fed.Rules Civ.Proc.Rule 12(b)(6), 28 U.S.C.A.

> Harris v. McDonald's Corp., 901 F.Supp. 1552.

M.D.Fla. 1995. Threshold of sufficiency that complaint must meet to survive motion to dismiss for failure to state claim is exceedingly low; plaintiff need not set forth all facts upon which claim is based, and short and plain statement is sufficient if it gives defendant fair notice of what claim is and grounds upon which it rests. Fed.Rules Civ.Proc.Rules 8(a), 12(b)(6), 28 U.S.C.A.

> Krehling v. Baron, 900 F.Supp. 1574.

M.D.Fla. 1995. On motions to dismiss, defendants must demonstrate that plaintiff cannot prove any set of facts consistent with pleadings that would entitle him to relief.

> National R.R. Passenger Corp. v. Rountree Transport and Rigging, Inc., 896 F.Supp. 1204.

M.D.Fla. 1995. On motions to dismiss for failure to state claim on which relief can be granted, defendants must demonstrate that plaintiff can prove no set of facts which would entitle her to relief. Fed.Rules Civ.Proc.Rule 12, 28 U.S.C.A.

Marshall v. Miller, 873 F.Supp. 628.

Court may dismiss claim only if it is beyond doubt that plaintiff can prove no set of facts in support of claim which would entitle him to relief. Fed.Rules Civ.Proc.Rule 12, 28 U.S.C.A.

Marshall v. Miller, 873 F.Supp. 628.

M.D.Fla. 1994. To prevail on motion to dismiss, moving party must demonstrate beyond a doubt that plaintiff can prove no set of facts in support of claim which would entitle him to relief. Fed.Rules Civ.Proc.Rule 12(b), 28 U.S.C.A.

Sawinski v. Bill Currie Ford, Inc., 866 F.Supp. 1383.

M.D.Fla. 1994. A complaint should not be dismissed for failure to state a claim unless it appears beyond a doubt that plaintiff can prove no set of facts that support a claim for relief. Fed.Rules Civ.Proc.Rule 12(b)(6), 28 U.S.C.A.

Patterson v. Downtown Medical and Diagnostic Center, Inc., 866 F.Supp. 1379.

M.D.Fla. 1994. Complaint should not be dismissed for failure to state a claim unless it appears beyond doubt that plaintiff can prove no set of facts that would entitle him to relief. Fed.Rules Civ.Proc.Rule 12(b)(6), 28 U.S.C.A.

In re Checkers Securities Litigation, 858 F.Supp. 1168.

M.D.Fla. 1994. Complaint should not be dismissed for failure to state claim unless it appears beyond reasonable doubt that plaintiff can prove no set of facts that would entitle plaintiff to relief. Fed.Rules Civ.Proc.Rule 12(b)(6), 28 U.S.C.A.

Fletcher v. State of Fla., 858 F.Supp. 169.

M.D.Fla. 1994. District court will dismiss for failure to state claim only if it appears beyond doubt that plaintiff can prove no set of facts that would entitle him to relief. Fed.Rules Civ.Proc.Rule 12(b)(6), 28 U.S.C.A.

Friedman v. South Carolina Ins. Co., 855 F.Supp. 348.

M.D.Fla. 1994. Complaint should not be dismissed for failure to state claim unless it appears beyond doubt that plaintiff can prove no set of facts that would entitle him to relief. Consolidated American Ins. Co. v. Hinton, 845 F.Supp. 1515.

M.D.Fla. 1994. Complaint should not be dismissed for failure to state claim unless it appears beyond doubt that plaintiff can prove no set of facts in support of his claim which would entitle him to relief. Fed.Rules Civ.Proc. Rule 12(b)(6), 28 U.S.C.A.

NCR Credit Corp. v. Reptron Electronics, Inc., 155 F.R.D. 690.

M.D.Fla. 1994. Complaint should not be dismissed for failure to state claim unless it appears beyond doubt plaintiff can prove no set of facts that would entitle him to relief. Fed. Rules Civ.Proc.Rule 12, 28 U.S.C.A.

Eidson v. Arenas, 155 F.R.D. 215.

M.D.Fla. 1993. Complaint should not be dismissed for failure to state claim unless it appears beyond doubt that plaintiff can prove no set of facts that would entitle him to relief.

Colodny v. Iverson, Yoakum, Papiano & Hatch, 838 F.Supp. 572.

Plaintiff's claims should not be dismissed for lack of in personam jurisdiction unless it appears beyond doubt that plaintiff can prove no set of facts that would establish personal jurisdiction over defendants.

Colodny v. Iverson, Yoakum, Papiano & Hatch, 838 F.Supp. 572.

M.D.Fla. 1993. Plaintiff's common law tort claims against defendant should not be dismissed unless it appears beyond doubt that plaintiff could prove no set of facts in support of her claim which would entitle her to relief. Fed.Rules Civ.Proc.Rule 12, 28 U.S.C.A.

Dibernardo v. Waste Management, Inc. of Florida, 838 F.Supp. 567.

M.D.Fla. 1993. Complaint should not be dismissed for failure to state a claim unless it appears beyond a doubt that plaintiff can prove no set of facts in support of claim which would entitle him to relief.

Searer v. Wells, 837 F.Supp. 1198.

M.D.Fla. 1993. Complaint should not be dismissed for failure to state claim unless it appears beyond doubt that plaintiff can prove no set of facts that would entitled him to relief. Fed.Rules Civ.Proc.Rule 12(b)(6), 28 U.S.C.A.

Eidson v. Arenas, 837 F.Supp. 1158.

M.D.Fla. 1993. Complaint should not be dismissed for failure to state a claim unless it appears beyond doubt that plaintiff could prove no set of facts that would entitle him to relief, viewing complaint in light most favorable to plaintiff and considering plaintiff's allegations as true. Fed.Rules Civ.Proc.Rule 8(a), 28 U.S.C.A.

Patrick Media Group, Inc. v. City of Clearwater, 836 F.Supp. 833.

M.D.Fla. 1993. Complaint should not be dismissed for failure to state a claim unless it appears beyond a doubt that plaintiff can prove no set of facts that would entitle plaintiff to

relief. Fed.Rules Civ.Proc.Rule 12(b)(6), 28 U.S.C.A.

> Underwood v. City of Fort Myers, 836 F.Supp. 823.

M.D.Fla. 1993. Complaint should not be dismissed for failure to state claim on which relief can be granted unless it appears beyond doubt that plaintiff can prove no set of facts that would entitle him to relief. Fed.Rules Civ.Proc. Rule 12(b)(6), 28 U.S.C.A.

> Nierenberg v. Heart Center of Southwest Florida, P.A., 835 F.Supp. 1404.

M.D.Fla. 1993. Complaint should not be dismissed for failure to state claim unless it appears beyond doubt that plaintiff can prove no set of facts that would entitle him to relief.

> Jacobs v. Blue Cross and Blue Shield of Iowa, 835 F.Supp. 1378.

M.D.Fla. 1993. Complaint should not be dismissed for failure to state claim unless it appears beyond doubt that plaintiff can prove no set of facts that would entitle him to relief. Fed.Rules Civ.Proc.Rule 8(a), 28 U.S.C.A.

> L.S.T. Inc. v. Crow, 834 F.Supp. 1355, reversed 49 F.3d 679.

M.D.Fla. 1993. Motion to dismiss should not be granted unless plaintiff would not be able to prove any set of facts in support of claim that would entitle him or her to relief.

> Hodges v. Gellerstedt, 833 F.Supp. 898.

M.D.Fla. 1993. Complaint should not be dismissed for failure to state a claim unless it appears beyond doubt that plaintiff can prove no set of facts that would entitle him to relief, viewing complaint in light most favorable to plaintiff.

> Olsen v. Lane, 832 F.Supp. 1525.

M.D.Fla. 1993. Motion to dismiss should not be granted unless plaintiff would not be able to prove any set of facts in support of his claim which would entitle him to relief. Fed.Rules Civ.Proc.Rule 12, 28 U.S.C.A.

> Venero v. City of Tampa, Fla., 830 F.Supp. 1457, affirmed 40 F.3d 389.

M.D.Fla. 1993. Complaint should not be dismissed for failure to state claim unless it appears beyond doubt that plaintiff can prove no set of facts that would entitle him to relief. Fed.Rules Civ.Proc.Rule 12(b)(6), 28 U.S.C.A.

> Mahon v. City of Largo, Fla., 829 F.Supp. 377.

M.D.Fla. 1993. Complaint should not be dismissed for failure to state claim unless it appears beyond doubt that plaintiff can prove no set of facts that would entitle him or her to relief.

> Gilbert v. Sears, Roebuck and Co., 826 F.Supp. 433.

M.D.Fla. 1993. Complaint should not be dismissed for failure to state a claim unless it appears beyond a doubt that plaintiff can prove no set of facts that would entitle him to relief.

> Morris v. Crow, 825 F.Supp. 295.

M.D.Fla. 1993. Complaint should not be dismissed for failure to state cause of action unless it appears beyond doubt that plaintiff can prove no set of facts in support of his claim which would entitle him to relief.

> Ippolito v. State of Fla., 824 F.Supp. 1562.

M.D.Fla. 1993. Because court must accept well pled allegations of complaint as true and all ambiguities or doubts concerning sufficiency of claim must be resolved in name of pleader, court cannot dismiss complaint unless it appears beyond doubt that under no set of facts can plaintiff state cause of action which would entitle it to relief.

> Perez v. City of Key West, Fla., 823 F.Supp. 934.

M.D.Fla. 1993. Complaint should not be dismissed for failure to state claim unless it appears beyond doubt that plaintiff can prove no set of facts which would entitle him to relief.

> Golden v. Complete Holdings, Inc., 818 F.Supp. 1495.

M.D.Fla. 1993. Complaint should not be dismissed for failure to state claim unless it appears beyond doubt that plaintiff can prove no set of facts that would entitle plaintiff to relief. Fed.Rules Civ.Proc.Rule 12(b)(6), 28 U.S.C.A.

> Hercules, Inc. v. Pages, 814 F.Supp. 79.

M.D.Fla. 1993. Complaint should not be dismissed for failure to state claim unless it appears beyond doubt that plaintiff can prove no set of facts in support of claim which would entitle him to relief. Fed.Rules Civ.Proc.Rule 12(b)(6), 28 U.S.C.A.

> Woodbury v. Sears, Roebuck & Co., 152 F.R.D. 229.

Pro se complaints, however inartfully pleaded, may only be dismissed for failure to state claim if it appears beyond doubt that plaintiff can prove no set of facts in support of cause of action. Fed.Rules Civ.Proc.Rule 12(b)(6), 28 U.S.C.A.

> Woodbury v. Sears, Roebuck & Co., 152 F.R.D. 229.

M.D.Fla. 1992. Complaint should not be dismissed for failure to state a claim unless it appears beyond doubt that plaintiff can prove no set of facts that would entitle him to relief.

> Ali v. City of Clearwater, 807 F.Supp. 701.

M.D.Fla. 1992. Complaint should not be dismissed for failure to state claim unless it appears beyond doubt that plaintiff can prove no set of facts that would entitle him to relief.

Azevedo v. Housing Authority of City of Sarasota, 805 F.Supp. 938, vacated in part on rehearing 147 F.R.D. 255, affirmed 39 F.3d 324.

M.D.Fla. 1992. A complaint should not be dismissed for failure to state a claim unless it appears beyond doubt that plaintiff can prove no set of facts that would entitle him to relief.

M.G.J. Industries, Inc. v. Greyhound Financial Corp., 801 F.Supp. 614.

M.D.Fla. 1992. Complaint should not be dismissed for failure to state a claim unless it appears beyond doubt that plaintiff can prove no set of facts that would entitle him or her to relief.

Rondolino v. Northwestern Mut. Life Ins. Co., 788 F.Supp. 553.

M.D.Fla. 1992. Court should not dismiss complaint unless it appears beyond doubt that plaintiff can prove no set of facts in support of his or her claim which would entitle him or her to relief. Fed.Rules Civ.Proc.Rule 12(b)(6), 28 U.S.C.A.

Marcus v. Carrasquillo, 782 F.Supp. 593.

M.D.Fla. 1992. Complaint should not be dismissed for failure to state claim unless it appears beyond doubt that plaintiff can prove no set of facts that would entitle him to relief.

Swerhun v. General Motors Corp., 141 F.R.D. 342.

M.D.Fla. 1991. Complaint should not be dismissed for failure to state claim unless it appears beyond doubt that plaintiff can prove no set of facts that would entitle him to relief.

Prentice v. Prentice Colour, Inc., 779 F.Supp. 578.

M.D.Fla. 1991. Complaint should not be dismissed for failure to state claim unless it appears beyond doubt that plaintiffs can prove no set of facts that would entitle them to relief.

California Int'l Chemical Co. v. Neptune Pool Service, Inc., 770 F.Supp. 1530.

M.D.Fla. 1990. A complaint should not be dismissed for failure to state a claim unless it appears that the plaintiff can prove no set of facts that would entitle him to relief.

Hibbing v. Sofarelli, 733 F.Supp. 1470, affirmed in part, vacated in part Sofarelli v. Pinellas County, 931 F.2d 718.

M.D.Fla. 1989. Complaint should not be dismissed for failure to state a claim unless it appears beyond doubt that plaintiff can prove no set of facts that would entitle him to relief and, in ruling on motion to dismiss, court is required to view the complaint in the light most favorable to the plaintiff.

Wright v. Manatee County, 717 F.Supp. 1493.

M.D.Fla. 1989. Complaint should not be dismissed for failure to state claim unless it appears beyond doubt that plaintiff can prove no set of facts that would entitle him to relief.

King v. Gandolfo, 714 F.Supp. 1180.

N.D.Fla. 1995. Rule on failure to state claim on which relief can be granted authorizes dismissal of complaint on dispositive issue of law. Fed.Rules Civ.Proc.Rule 12(b)(6), 28 U.S.C.A.

In re Miner, 185 B.R. 362, affirmed Miner v. Bay Bank & Trust Co., 83 F.3d 436.

N.D.Fla. 1995. Regardless of alleged facts, rule dealing with dismissal for failure to state claim does not authorize court to dismiss complaint on dispositive issue of law. Fed.Rules Civ.Proc.Rule 12(b)(6), 28 U.S.C.A.

T.W.M. v. American Medical Systems, Inc., 886 F.Supp. 842.

N.D.Fla. 1995. Motion to dismiss for failure to state a claim should not be granted unless it appears to a certainty that plaintiff can prove no set of facts that would entitle him to relief. Fed.Rules Civ.Proc.Rule 12(b)(6), 28 U.S.C.A.

Zombori v. Digital Equipment Corp., 878 F.Supp. 207, affirmed 103 F.3d 147.

N.D.Fla. 1993. Motion to dismiss for failure to state claim should not be granted unless it appears to certainty that plaintiff can prove no set of facts that would entitle him to relief. Fed.Rules Civ.Proc.Rules 11, 12(b)(6), 28 U.S.C.A.

Cooper v. Gulf Breeze Hosp., Inc., 839 F.Supp. 1538.

S.D.Fla. 1998. Court may dismiss complaint for failure to state a claim on dispositive issue of law, regardless of facts alleged in complaint. Fed.Rules Civ.Proc.Rule 12(b)(6), 28 U.S.C.A.

Mayoral-Amy v. BHI Corp., 180 F.R.D. 456.

S.D.Fla. 1997. Court may dismiss complaint on dispositive issue of law.

U.S. v. One (1) 1980 Cessna 441 Conquest II Aircraft, 989 F.Supp. 1465.

S.D.Fla. 1996. For purposes of motion to dismiss complaint in antitrust litigation, district courts must insist upon some specificity in pleading before allowing potentially massive factual controversy to proceed. Fed.Rules Civ. Proc.Rule 8(a), 28 U.S.C.A.

Aventura Cable Corp. v. Rifkin/Narragansett South Florida CATV Ltd. Partnership, 941 F.Supp. 1189.

For cited U.S.C.A. sections and legislative history, see United States Code Annotated

S.D.Fla. 1996. Complaint may not be dismissed for failure to state a claim because plaintiff's claims fail to support legal theory plaintiff relies on since court must determine if allegations provide for relief on any possible theory. Fed.Rules Civ.Proc.Rule 12(b)(6), 28 U.S.C.A.

> Vernon v. Medical Management Associates of Margate, Inc., 912 F.Supp. 1549.

S.D.Fla. 1995. Threshold of sufficiency that complaint must make to survive motion to dismiss for failure to state claim is exceedingly low. Fed.Rules Civ.Proc.Rule 8(a)(2), 28 U.S.C.A.

> Nussbaum v. Mortgage Service America Co., 913 F.Supp. 1548.

S.D.Fla. 1995. Complaint may not be dismissed because plaintiff's claims do not support the legal theory he relies upon since court must determine if allegations provide for relief or any possible theory. Fed.Rules Civ.Proc.Rule 12(b)(6), 28 U.S.C.A.

> Trustees of Hotel Industry Pension Fund v. Carol Management Corp., 880 F.Supp. 1548.

S.D.Fla. 1995. Court will not grant motion to dismiss unless plaintiff fails to prove any set of facts that would entitle plaintiff to relief, viewing complaint in light most favorable to plaintiff and accepting plaintiff's well-pleaded facts as true. Fed.Rules Civ.Proc.Rule 12, 28 U.S.C.A.

> Lugones v. Sandals Resorts, Inc., 875 F.Supp. 821.

S.D.Fla. 1994. On a motion to dismiss for failure to state a claim, district court must view complaint in light most favorable to plaintiff and may only grant motion where it appears beyond a doubt that plaintiff can prove no set of facts in support of claim which could entitle him to relief. Fed.Rules Civ.Proc.Rule 12(b)(6), 28 U.S.C.A.

> Albert v. National Cash Register Co., 874 F.Supp. 1328.

S.D.Fla. 1994. Claim is subject to dismissal on pleadings only if it is clear that no relief could be granted under any set of facts that could be proved consistent with allegations. Fed.Rules Civ.Proc.Rule 12(b)(6), 28 U.S.C.A.

> Smith v. Avino, 866 F.Supp. 1399, affirmed 91 F.3d 105.

S.D.Fla. 1994. Complaint should not be dismissed for failure to state claim unless it appears beyond doubt that plaintiff can prove no set of facts in support of claim which would entitle him to relief. Fed.Rules Civ.Proc.Rule 12(b)(6), 28 U.S.C.A.

> Boyd v. Brookstone Corp. of New Hampshire, Inc., 857 F.Supp. 1568.

S.D.Fla. 1994. Complaint must not be dismissed unless it is shown that plaintiff can prove no set of facts in support of claim which would entitle him to relief. Fed.Rules Civ.Proc. Rule 12, 28 U.S.C.A.

> In re Southeast Banking Corp., 855 F.Supp. 353, affirmed 69 F.3d 1539.

S.D.Fla. 1994. Court shall not grant motion to dismiss unless it appears beyond doubt that claimant can prove no set of facts in support of claim that would entitle him to relief, and in determining whether dismissal is warranted, material allegations of plaintiff's claims are taken as true and are liberally construed in favor of plaintiff. Fed.Rules Civ.Proc.Rule 12(b)(6), 28 U.S.C.A.

> Bensch v. Metropolitan Dade County, 855 F.Supp. 351.

S.D.Fla. 1994. Preanswer motions, such as motion to dismiss for failure to state claim or motion for more definite statement, may raise two distinct issues: whether plaintiff has stated his purported claim with sufficient detail and whether claim as stated is recognized by law.

> Bunger v. Hartman, 851 F.Supp. 461.

S.D.Fla. 1994. Courts do not grant motions to dismiss unless they are convinced that plaintiffs cannot prove a set of facts that would entitle them to relief under the claim; in analyzing motions to dismiss, courts assume that allegations in the complaint and incorporated exhibits are true, and construe the complaint in favor of plaintiffs.

> Mann v. Air Line Pilots Ass'n, 848 F.Supp. 990.

S.D.Fla. 1993. A motion to dismiss should not be granted unless plaintiff can prove no set of facts in support of its claim entitling it to relief.

> Borges v. City of West Palm Beach, 858 F.Supp. 174.

S.D.Fla. 1993. Claim may be dismissed for failure to state a claim only if it is clear that no relief could be granted under any set of facts consistent with allegations. Fed.Rules Civ. Proc.Rule 12(b)(6), 28 U.S.C.A.

> Burger King Corp. v. Holder, 844 F.Supp. 1528.

S.D.Fla. 1993. Complaint should not be dismissed for failure to state claim unless it appears beyond doubt that under no set of facts can plaintiff state cause of action which would entitle them to relief.

> Airlines Reporting Corp. v. Atlantic Travel Service, Inc., 841 F.Supp. 1166.

S.D.Fla. 1993. Court will not grant motion to dismiss unless, without a doubt, plaintiffs can prove no set of facts which would entitle relief under the claim.

> Dunn v. Air Line Pilots Ass'n, 836 F.Supp. 1574.

S.D.Fla. 1993. Complaint should not be dismissed for failure to state claim unless it appears beyond doubt that plaintiff can prove no set of facts in support of his claim which would entitle him to relief. Fed.Rules Civ.Proc. Rule 12(b), 28 U.S.C.A.

> Dearmas v. Av-Med, Inc., 814 F.Supp. 1103.

S.D.Fla. 1992. Complaint may not be dismissed on ground that plaintiff's claims do not support legal theory he relies upon, as court must determine if allegations provide for relief upon any possible theory. Fed.Rules Civ.Proc. Rule 12(b)(6), 28 U.S.C.A.

> Bender v. CenTrust Mortg. Corp., 833 F.Supp. 1525, appeal dismissed 51 F.3d 1027, opinion modified on denial of re-hearing 60 F.3d 1507.

S.D.Fla. 1992. For purposes of determining whether claim as stated is recognized by law, court accepts all plaintiff's allegations as true and will not dismiss action unless plaintiff could prove no set of facts in support of claim entitling him to relief. Fed.Rules Civ.Proc.Rule 8(a), 28 U.S.C.A.

> City of Fort Lauderdale v. Ross, Saarinen, Bolton & Wilder, Inc., 815 F.Supp. 444.

S.D.Fla. 1992. Claim is subject to dismissal under Rule 12(b)(6) only if it is clear that no relief could be granted under any set of facts that could be proved consistent with allegations. Fed.Rules Civ.Proc.Rule 12(b)(6), 28 U.S.C.A.

> Colonial Penn Ins. Co. v. Value Rent-A-Car Inc., 814 F.Supp. 1084.

S.D.Fla. 1992. District court shall not grant motion to dismiss unless it appears beyond doubt that claimant can prove no set of facts in support of claim that would entitle him to relief.

> Burger King Corp. v. Austin, 805 F.Supp. 1007.

S.D.Fla. 1992. Court cannot dismiss complaint for failure to state a claim unless it appears beyond doubt that plaintiffs can prove no set of facts in support of their claim.

> Lake Lucerne Civic Ass'n, Inc. v. Dolphin Stadium Corp., 801 F.Supp. 684.

S.D.Fla. 1992. Motion to dismiss should not be granted unless plaintiff can prove no set of facts in support of his claim entitling him to relief, and claims do not support legal theories on which he relies.

> Solano v. Southeast Bank, N.A., 796 F.Supp. 506.

S.D.Fla. 1992. On motion to dismiss for failure to state a claim upon which relief may be granted, court must view complaint in light most favorable to plaintiff, and may only grant motion where it appears beyond doubt that plaintiff can prove no set of facts in support of his or her claim which could entitle him or her to relief. Fed.Rules Civ.Proc.Rule 12(b)(6), 28 U.S.C.A.

> Stern v. Espirito Santo Bank of Florida, 791 F.Supp. 865.

S.D.Fla. 1992. Complaint should not be dismissed for failure to state claim unless it appears beyond doubt that under no set of facts can plaintiff state cause of action that would entitle them to relief.

> City of Miami Firefighters' and Police Officers' Retirement Trust v. Invesco MIM, Inc., 789 F.Supp. 392.

S.D.Fla. 1991. Complaint may not be dismissed because plaintiff's claims do not support legal theories on which he relies because court must determine if allegations form basis for relief on any possible theory.

> Thomas v. Burlington Industries, Inc., 769 F.Supp. 368.

S.D.Fla. 1991. Complaint should not be dismissed unless it appears beyond a doubt that plaintiff could prove no set of facts in support of claim which would entitle him to relief and allegations of complaint must be taken as true. Fed.Rules Civ.Proc.Rule 12(b)(6), 28 U.S.C.A.

> Rios v. Navarro, 766 F.Supp. 1158.

S.D.Fla. 1991. Complaint should not be dismissed for failure to state claim upon which relief may be granted unless it appears beyond doubt that plaintiff could prove no set of facts in support of his claim which would entitle him to relief. Fed.Rules Civ.Proc.Rule 12(b)(6), 28 U.S.C.A.

> McKenzie v. Doctors' Hosp. of Hollywood, Inc., 765 F.Supp. 1504, affirmed 974 F.2d 1347.

S.D.Fla. 1991. On motion to dismiss for failure to state a claim on which relief can be granted, court must view complaint or counterclaim in light most favorable to party seeking relief, and may only grant motion where it appears beyond doubt that party seeking relief can prove no set of facts in support of claim which would entitle him or her to relief. Fed. Rules Civ.Proc.Rule 12(b)(6), 28 U.S.C.A.

> MCI Telecommunications Corp. v. Gorman, Wells, Wilder & Associates, Inc., 761 F.Supp. 124.

S.D.Fla. 1990. Complaint should not be dismissed for failure to state claim unless it appears beyond reasonable doubt that plaintiff can prove no set of facts in support of his claim. Fed.Rules Civ.Proc.Rule 12(b)(6), 28 U.S.C.A.

> Miller v. Weitzer Panache Ltd., 751 F.Supp. 980.

S.D.Fla. 1990. Complaint may not be dismissed because plaintiff's claims do not support legal theory he relies on, since district court must determine if allegations provide for relief on any possible theory. Fed.Rules Civ.Proc. Rule 12(b)(6), 28 U.S.C.A.

> Linder v. Calero Portocarrero, 747 F.Supp. 1452, reversed 963 F.2d 332.

S.D.Fla. 1986. Complaint which shows that plaintiff is entitled to any relief which court can grant is drafted sufficiently to survive motion to dismiss, regardless of whether complaint asks for proper relief. Fed.Rules Civ.Proc.Rule 12(b)(6), 28 U.S.C.A.

> Irizarry v. Palm Springs General Hosp., 657 F.Supp. 739.

S.D.Fla. 1984. Under liberal federal rules concept of "notice pleading," a complaint is sufficient if facts state a claim under any conceivable legal theory.

> Bryant Heating and Air Conditioning Corp., Inc. v. Carrier Corp., 597 F.Supp. 1045.

M.D.Ga. 1994. Complaint should not be dismissed for failure to state a claim unless plaintiff can prove no set of facts entitling him to relief. Fed.Rules Civ.Proc.Rule 12(b)(6), 28 U.S.C.A.

> Aurelia D. v. Monroe County Bd. of Educ., 862 F.Supp. 363, affirmed in part, reversed in part Davis v. Monroe County Bd. of Educ., 74 F.3d 1186, rehearing granted, opinion vacated 91 F.3d 1418, on rehearing 120 F.3d 1390, certiorari granted in part 119 S.Ct. 29, affirmed 120 F.3d 1390, certiorari granted in part 119 S.Ct. 29.

M.D.Ga. 1994. Complaint should not be dismissed for failure to state claim unless it appears beyond doubt that plaintiffs can prove no set of facts in support of claim that would entitle them to relief. Fed.Rules Civ.Proc.Rule 12(b)(6), 28 U.S.C.A.

> Stiller v. Sumter Bank and Trust Co., 860 F.Supp. 835.

M.D.Ga. 1993. Claim should not be dismissed for failure to state claim upon which relief may be granted unless, accepting allegations in complaint as true, it appears beyond doubt that plaintiff can prove no set of facts entitling it to relief. Fed.Rules Civ.Proc.Rule 12(b)(6), 28 U.S.C.A.

> General Time Corp. v. Bulk Materials, Inc., 826 F.Supp. 471.

N.D.Ga. 1992. Motion to dismiss may be granted if it is clear that no relief could be granted under any set of facts that could be proved consistent with the allegations.

> Reeves v. U.S. Dept. of Treasury, Bureau of Alcohol, Tobacco and Firearms, 809 F.Supp. 92, affirmed 996 F.2d 1232.

N.D.Ga. 1990. To survive motion to dismiss, it must appear beyond doubt that plaintiff can prove no set of facts in support of his claim which would entitle him to relief. Fed.Rules Civ.Proc.Rule 12(b)(6), 28 U.S.C.A.

> Capital Ford Truck Sales, Inc. v. Ford Motor Co., 779 F.Supp. 1345.

S.D.Ga. 1993. Complaint should not be dismissed for failure to state claim unless it appears beyond doubt that plaintiff can prove no set of facts consistent with allegations that would entitle him to relief. Fed.Rules Civ.Proc. Rule 12(b)(6), 28 U.S.C.A.

> Sikes v. American Tel. and Tel. Co., 841 F.Supp. 1572.

Motion to dismiss for failure to state claim upon which relief can be granted will be denied if it appears that plaintiff might possibly prove set of facts supporting well-pleaded and cognizable legal claim. Fed.Rules Civ.Proc.Rule 12(b)(6), 28 U.S.C.A.

> Sikes v. American Tel. and Tel. Co., 841 F.Supp. 1572.

S.D.Ga. 1990. Court must deny defendant's motion to dismiss plaintiff's complaint unless it finds that plaintiff can prove no set of facts in support of his claim which would entitle him to relief.

> Penaranda v. Cato, 740 F.Supp. 1578.

D.Hawai'i 1997. Complaint may be dismissed as matter of law for two reasons: (1) lack of cognizable legal theory, or (2) insufficient facts under cognizable legal theory. Fed. Rules Civ.Proc.Rule 12(b)(6), 28 U.S.C.A.

> Burns-Vidlak by Burns v. Chandler, 980 F.Supp. 1144.

D.Hawai'i 1995. Complaint may be dismissed as matter of law for two reasons: lack of cognizable legal theory or insufficient facts under cognizable legal theory. Fed.Rules Civ. Proc.Rule 12(b)(6), 28 U.S.C.A.

> Moore v. Kamikawa, 940 F.Supp. 260, affirmed 82 F.3d 423.

D.Hawai'i 1995. Complaint may be dismissed as matter of law for lack of cognizable legal theory or insufficient facts under cognizable legal theory. Fed.Rules Civ.Proc.Rule 12(b)(6), 28 U.S.C.A.

> Forsyth v. Eli Lilly and Co., 904 F.Supp. 1153.

Motion to dismiss for failure to state claim upon which relief can be granted should be granted if affirmative defense or other bar to relief is apparent from face of complaint. Fed. Rules Civ.Proc.Rule 12(b)(6), 28 U.S.C.A.

> Forsyth v. Eli Lilly and Co., 904 F.Supp. 1153.

D.Hawai'i 1995. Complaint may be dismissed as matter of law for lack of cognizable legal theory, or insufficient facts under cognizable legal theory. Fed.Rules Civ.Proc.Rule 12(b)(6), 28 U.S.C.A.

> Covington v. U.S., 902 F.Supp. 1207.

D.Hawai'i 1995. Complaint should not be dismissed unless it appears to a certainty that plaintiff would be entitled to no relief under any set of facts that could be proved. Fed.Rules Civ.Proc.Rule 12(b)(6), 28 U.S.C.A.

> Erickson v. West, 876 F.Supp. 239.

D.Hawai'i 1994. Complaint should not be dismissed for failing to state claim upon which relief may be granted unless it appears to certainty that plaintiff would be entitled to no relief under any set of facts that could be proved. Fed.Rules Civ.Proc.Rule 12(b)(6), 28 U.S.C.A.

> Petro v. Jada Yacht Charters, Ltd., 854 F.Supp. 698.

D.Hawai'i 1994. Complaint should not be dismissed for failure to state claim unless it appears to a certainty that plaintiff can prove no set of facts which would entitle plaintiff to relief. Fed.Rules Civ.Proc.Rule 12(b)(6), 28 U.S.C.A.

> Bradford v. State of Hawaii, 846 F.Supp. 1411.

D.Hawai'i 1992. General rule in considering motion to dismiss for failure to state claim upon which relief can be granted is that complaint should not be dismissed on pleadings unless it appears beyond doubt that plaintiff can prove no set of facts in support of his claim which would entitle him to relief. Fed.Rules Civ.Proc.Rule 12(b)(6), 28 U.S.C.A.

> Kersting v. U.S., 818 F.Supp. 297.

D.Hawai'i 1992. In considering motion to dismiss for failure to state a claim, general rule is that complaint should not be dismissed on pleadings unless it appears beyond doubt that plaintiff can provide no set of facts in support of his or her claim which would entitle him or her to relief. Fed.Rules Civ.Proc.Rule 12(b), (b)(6), 28 U.S.C.A.

> Paulson, Inc. v. Bromar, Inc., 808 F.Supp. 736.

D.Hawai'i 1992. Plaintiff's complaint must stand unless it appears beyond doubt that

plaintiff has alleged no facts that would entitle him to relief.

> Scott v. U.S., 795 F.Supp. 1028, affirmed 70 F.3d 120, certiorari granted U.S. v. Brockamp, 116 S.Ct. 1875, 517 U.S. 1232, 135 L.Ed.2d 171, reversed 117 S.Ct. 849, 519 U.S. 347, 136 L.Ed.2d 818, on remand 112 F.3d 1024, on remand 112 F.3d 1024, reversed 112 F.3d 1024.

Complaint may be dismissed as matter of law if it lacks cognizable legal theory or contains insufficient facts under cognizable legal theory.

> Scott v. U.S., 795 F.Supp. 1028, affirmed 70 F.3d 120, certiorari granted U.S. v. Brockamp, 116 S.Ct. 1875, 517 U.S. 1232, 135 L.Ed.2d 171, reversed 117 S.Ct. 849, 519 U.S. 347, 136 L.Ed.2d 818, on remand 112 F.3d 1024, on remand 112 F.3d 1024, reversed 112 F.3d 1024.

D.Hawai'i 1990. In considering motion to dismiss for failure to state claim on which relief can be granted, court must construe allegations of complaint as true and cannot dismiss complaint unless it appears beyond doubt that plaintiff can prove no set of facts in support of his claim that would entitle him to relief. Fed. Rules Civ.Proc.Rule 12(b)(6), 28 U.S.C.A.

> Naliielua v. State of Hawaii, 795 F.Supp. 1009, affirmed 940 F.2d 1535.

D.Hawai'i 1988. Applicable standard for motion to dismiss for failure to state claim is whether plaintiff can prove no set of facts in support of his claim. Fed.Rules Civ.Proc.Rule 12(b)(6), 28 U.S.C.A.

> Pure, Ltd. v. Shasta Beverages, Inc., 691 F.Supp. 1274.

C.D.Ill. 1995. To survive motion to dismiss, although complaint is not required to contain detailed outline of claim's basis, it nevertheless must contain either direct or inferential allegations respecting all material elements necessary to sustain recovery under some viable legal theory.

> Resolution Trust Corp. v. Chapman, 895 F.Supp. 1072.

C.D.Ill. 1995. Motion to dismiss will not be granted unless it appears beyond doubt that plaintiff cannot prove any facts that will entitle him to relief.

> Obermeyer v. Gilliland, 873 F.Supp. 153.

C.D.Ill. 1994. Complaint should not be dismissed unless it appears from pleadings that plaintiff could prove no set of facts in support of its claim which would entitle it to relief.

> Resolution Trust Corp. v. S & K Chevrolet, 868 F.Supp. 1047.

C.D.Ill. 1993. Complaint should not be dismissed unless it appears from pleadings that plaintiff could prove no set of facts in support of his claims which would entitle him to relief.

> Greenley v. Meersman, 838 F.Supp. 381.

C.D.Ill. 1992. To prevail on motion to dismiss for failure to state claim, defendant must demonstrate that plaintiff's claim, as set forth by complaint, is without legal consequence. Fed. Rules Civ.Proc.Rule 12(b)(6), 28 U.S.C.A.

> Wright v. Bosch Trucking Co., Inc., 804 F.Supp. 1069.

C.D.Ill. 1990. Summary dismissal is only to be used when it is plain that the claims raised by the petitioner are groundless, but district court should not hesitate in dismissing frivolous claim.

> Yocum v. Dixon, 729 F.Supp. 616.

N.D.Ill. 1998. To withstand a motion to dismiss, a complaint must allege facts sufficiently setting forth the essential elements of the cause of action. Fed.Rules Civ.Proc.Rule 12(b)(6), 28 U.S.C.A.

> Cunningham v. Eyman, 11 F.Supp.2d 969.

Generally, mere vagueness or lack of detail does not constitute sufficient grounds for a motion to dismiss. Fed.Rules Civ.Proc.Rule 12(b)(6), 28 U.S.C.A.

> Cunningham v. Eyman, 11 F.Supp.2d 969.

N.D.Ill. 1997. In a notice pleading system, suit should not be dismissed so long as it is possible to hypothesize facts, consistent with the complaint, that would make out claim for relief.

> Petri v. Gatlin, 997 F.Supp. 956.

N.D.Ill. 1997. Even under liberal notice pleading standard of Federal Rules of Civil Procedure, complaint must include either direct or inferential allegations respecting all material elements of claims asserted in order to withstand motion to dismiss; bare legal conclusions attached to narrated facts will not suffice. Fed. Rules Civ.Proc.Rule 12(b)(6), 28 U.S.C.A.

> Sterling v. Kazmierczak, 983 F.Supp. 1186.

N.D.Ill. 1997. To withstand motion to dismiss for failure to state claim, complaint must allege facts sufficiently setting forth essential elements of cause of action. Fed.Rules Civ. Proc.Rule 12(b)(6), 28 U.S.C.A.

> Cemail v. Viking Dodge, Inc., 982 F.Supp. 1296.

Generally, mere vagueness or lack of detail does not constitute sufficient grounds for dismissing complaint as failing to state claim. Fed.Rules Civ.Proc.Rule 12(b)(6), 28 U.S.C.A.

> Cemail v. Viking Dodge, Inc., 982 F.Supp. 1296.

N.D.Ill. 1997. Pro se complaint need not specify correct legal theory, nor point to correct statute in order to survive motion to dismiss. Fed.Rules Civ.Proc.Rule 12(b)(6), 28 U.S.C.A.

> Thomas v. Chicago Housing Authority, 981 F.Supp. 558.

N.D.Ill. 1997. Complaint need not set out any legal theory in order to withstand motion to dismiss, and inclusion of an incorrect legal theory is not fatal. Fed.Rules Civ.Proc.Rule 12(b)(6), 28 U.S.C.A.

> Williams v. Ford Motor Co., 980 F.Supp. 938.

N.D.Ill. 1997. To avoid being dismissed for failure to state claim upon which relief can be granted, complaint must state either direct or inferential allegations concerning all material elements necessary to recover under chosen legal theory. Fed.Rules Civ.Proc.Rule 12(b)(6), 28 U.S.C.A.

> Lara v. City of Chicago, 968 F.Supp. 1278.

N.D.Ill. 1997. Failure to affirmatively plead compliance with applicable statute of limitations is not basis for dismissal in federal court.

> Woodard v. American Family Mut. Ins. Co., 950 F.Supp. 1382.

N.D.Ill. 1997. Where pleadings raise contested issue of material fact, motion to dismiss for failure to state claim must be denied. Fed. Rules Civ.Proc.Rule 12(b)(6), 28 U.S.C.A.

> Connor v. Ford Motor Co., 172 F.R.D. 375.

N.D.Ill. 1996. In order to survive motion to dismiss, complaint must allege sufficient facts to outline cause of action, and complaint must state either direct or inferential allegations concerning all material elements necessary for recovery under relevant legal theory. Fed.Rules Civ.Proc.Rule 12(b)(6), 28 U.S.C.A.

> Herzog v. NBD Bank of Highland Park, 203 B.R. 80.

N.D.Ill. 1996. To withstand motion to dismiss, complaint need not set out any legal theory, and an incorrect legal theory is not fatal.

> Reese v. May, 955 F.Supp. 869.

N.D.Ill. 1996. To survive motion to dismiss for failure to state claim, complaint must state either direct or inferential allegations concerning all material elements necessary for recovery under chosen legal theory. Fed.Rules Civ.Proc.Rule 12(b)(6), 28 U.S.C.A.

> Codest Engineering v. Hyatt Intern. Corp., 954 F.Supp. 1224.

N.D.Ill. 1996. Because federal courts require mere "notice pleading," district court must construe pleadings liberally, and mere vagueness or lack of detail alone is not sufficient ground for dismissal for failure to state a claim. Fed.Rules Civ.Proc.Rule 12(b)(6), 28 U.S.C.A.

> R & V Pine Tree, Inc. v. Village of Forest Park, 947 F.Supp. 342.

N.D.Ill. 1996. Because federal courts require mere notice pleading, court must construe pleadings liberally and mere vagueness or lack of detail alone cannot be sufficient grounds for dismissal of complaint for failure to state claim. Fed.Rules Civ.Proc.Rule 12(b)(6), 28 U.S.C.A.

> Schoiber v. Emro Marketing Co., 941 F.Supp. 730.

N.D.Ill. 1996. In order to survive motion to dismiss for failure to state a claim, complaint must allege sufficient facts to outline a cause of action. Fed.Rules Civ.Proc.Rule 12(b)(6), 28 U.S.C.A.

> Compton v. Chinn Enterprises, Inc., 936 F.Supp. 480, reconsideration denied 957 F.Supp. 139.

In order to survive motion to dismiss for failure to state a claim, complaint must state either direct or inferential allegations concerning all of material elements necessary for recovery under relevant legal theory. Fed.Rules Civ. Proc.Rule 12(b)(6), 28 U.S.C.A.

> Compton v. Chinn Enterprises, Inc., 936 F.Supp. 480, reconsideration denied 957 F.Supp. 139.

N.D.Ill. 1996. In order to withstand motion to dismiss for failure to state claim, complaint must allege acts sufficiently setting forth essential elements of cause of action. Fed.Rules Civ.Proc.Rule 12(b)(6), 28 U.S.C.A.

> Alexander v. Continental Motor Werks, Inc., 933 F.Supp. 715, reconsideration denied 1996 WL 529347.

N.D.Ill. 1996. If, when viewed in light most favorable to plaintiff, complaint fails to state claim upon which relief can be granted, court must dismiss case. Fed.Rules Civ.Proc. Rule 12(b)(6), 28 U.S.C.A.

> Vitello v. Liturgy Training Publications, 932 F.Supp. 1093.

N.D.Ill. 1996. As compared with pleadings drafted by attorneys, complaints written by pro se litigants are examined under less arduous standard for purposes of motion to dismiss for failure to state claim, but unsupported conclusions of fact and conclusions of law will not defeat otherwise meritorious motion to dismiss. Fed.Rules Civ.Proc.Rule 12(b)(6), 28 U.S.C.A.

> Young v. Breeding, 929 F.Supp. 1103.

N.D.Ill. 1996. Court must dismiss case if, when viewed in light most favorable to plaintiff, complaint fails to state claim upon which relief can be granted. Fed.Rules Civ.Proc.Rule 12(b)(6), 28 U.S.C.A.

> Moore v. Allstate Ins. Co., 928 F.Supp. 744.

N.D.Ill. 1996. Complaint need not specify correct legal theory nor point to the right statute to survive motion to dismiss; however, complaint will be dismissed if plaintiff cannot prove the facts on which the sought-after legal relief may be granted. Fed.Rules Civ.Proc.Rule 12(b), 28 U.S.C.A.

> Nutrasweet Co. v. X-L Engineering Corp., 926 F.Supp. 767.

N.D.Ill. 1996. To survive motion to dismiss for failure to state claim, plaintiff's complaint need not specify correct legal theory nor point to correct statute. Fed.Rules Civ.Proc. Rule 12(b)(6), 28 U.S.C.A.

> Mount v. LaSalle Bank Lake View, 926 F.Supp. 759.

District court must construe pleadings liberally, and mere vagueness or lack of detail alone will not constitute sufficient grounds to dismiss complaint. Fed.Rules Civ.Proc.Rule 12(b)(6), 28 U.S.C.A.

> Mount v. LaSalle Bank Lake View, 926 F.Supp. 759.

In response to motion to dismiss for failure to state claim upon which relief can be granted, plaintiffs are not required to prove every element of the claims they allege; all that is required is that plaintiffs give notice of their claims. Fed.Rules Civ.Proc.Rule 12(b), 28 U.S.C.A.

> Mount v. LaSalle Bank Lake View, 926 F.Supp. 759.

N.D.Ill. 1996. If, when viewed in light most favorable to plaintiff, complaint fails to state claim upon which relief can be granted, court must dismiss case. Fed.Rules Civ.Proc. Rule 12(b)(6), 28 U.S.C.A.

> Horton v. Marovich, 925 F.Supp. 540.

N.D.Ill. 1996. Complaint need not specify correct legal theory, nor point to correct statute, in order to survive motion to dismiss for failure to state a claim. Fed.Rules Civ.Proc.Rule 12(b)(6), 28 U.S.C.A.

> Thomas v. Chicago Housing Authority, 919 F.Supp. 1159.

N.D.Ill. 1996. To survive motion to dismiss, plaintiff must allege sufficient facts to outline cause of action.

> Yellow Cab Co. v. City of Chicago, 919 F.Supp. 1133.

N.D.Ill. 1996. Court must construe pleadings liberally, and mere vagueness or lack of detail alone does not constitute sufficient grounds to dismiss complaint.

> Vakharia v. Little Co. of Mary Hosp. and Health Care Centers, 917 F.Supp. 1282.

N.D.Ill. 1996. If plaintiff pleads particulars, and they show he has no claim, then he has pleaded himself out of court and, thus, where specific facts alleged in complaint demonstrate that there is no valid claim, dismissal is appropriate. Fed.Rules Civ.Proc.Rule 8(a), 28 U.S.C.A.

> Freeman v. Fairman, 916 F.Supp. 786.

N.D.Ill. 1995. In order to survive motion to dismiss for failure to state claim, complaint must allege sufficient facts to outline cause of action. Fed.Rules Civ.Proc.Rule 12(b)(6), 28 U.S.C.A.

> Erickson v. Board of Governors of State Colleges and Universities for Northeastern Illinois University, 911 F.Supp. 316.

In order to survive motion to dismiss for failure to state claim, complaint must state either direct or inferential allegations concerning all of material elements necessary under relevant legal theory. Fed.Rules Civ.Proc.Rule 12(b)(6), 28 U.S.C.A.

> Erickson v. Board of Governors of State Colleges and Universities for Northeastern Illinois University, 911 F.Supp. 316.

N.D.Ill. 1995. On a motion to dismiss for failure to state a claim, district court must construe pleadings liberally, and mere vagueness or lack of detail alone does not constitute sufficient grounds to dismiss a complaint. Fed. Rules Civ.Proc.Rule 12(b)(6), 28 U.S.C.A.

> Gupta v. Freixenet, USA, Inc., 908 F.Supp. 557.

N.D.Ill. 1995. Complaint's mere vagueness or lack of detail is not sufficient to justify dismissal; complaint need not specify correct legal theory or point to right statute to survive motion to dismiss.

> Taahira W. by McCord-Salley v. Travis, 908 F.Supp. 533.

N.D.Ill. 1995. For purposes of motion to dismiss for failure to state claim, complaint need not specify correct legal theory nor point to right statute. Fed.Rules Civ.Proc.Rule 12(b)(6), 28 U.S.C.A.

> Moran v. Ortho Pharmaceutical Corp., 907 F.Supp. 1228.

In ruling on motion to dismiss for failure to state claim, court must construe pleadings liberally, and mere vagueness and lack of detail alone does not constitute sufficient grounds to dismiss complaint. Fed.Rules Civ.Proc.Rule 12(b)(6), 28 U.S.C.A.

> Moran v. Ortho Pharmaceutical Corp., 907 F.Supp. 1228.

N.D.Ill. 1995. It is unnecessary that plaintiff correctly identified governing legal theory of claim, for purposes of motion to dismiss complaint, if facts alleged in complaint support claim. Fed.Rules Civ.Proc.Rule 12(b)(6), 28 U.S.C.A.

> Little v. State of Ill. Dept. of Revenue, Bureau of Criminal Investigation, 907 F.Supp. 280.

N.D.Ill. 1995. To survive motion to dismiss, plaintiff must allege sufficient facts to outline cause of action, proof of which is essential to recovery.

> Johnson v. Baxter Healthcare Corp., 907 F.Supp. 271.

N.D.Ill. 1995. Complaint need not specify the correct statute to defeat motion to dismiss for failure to state claim, although preferred practice by experienced counsel would be to provide court and defendant with sufficiently precise legal authority to avoid needless motion practice. Fed.Rules Civ.Proc.Rule 12(b)(6), 28 U.S.C.A.

> Graves v. Tru-Link Fence Co., 905 F.Supp. 515.

N.D.Ill. 1995. Failure to comply with requirements of Rule 8 to include short and plain statement of claim showing entitlement to relief in complaint may justify dismissal, albeit usually without prejudice. Fed.Rules Civ.Proc.Rule 8(e)(1), 28 U.S.C.A.

> Industrial Specialty Chemicals, Inc. v. Cummins Engine Co., Inc., 902 F.Supp. 805.

N.D.Ill. 1995. Plaintiff, opposing motion to dismiss for failure to state claim upon which relief could be granted, is not required to prove that he can win on the pleadings, but only that his allegations are sufficient to state cause of action. Fed.Rules Civ.Proc.Rule 12(b)(6), 28 U.S.C.A.

> Marks v. CDW Computer Centers, Inc., 901 F.Supp. 1302.

N.D.Ill. 1995. On motion to dismiss for failure to state a claim, court must construe pleadings liberally, and mere vagueness or lack of detail alone will not constitute sufficient grounds to dismiss. Fed.Rules Civ.Proc.Rule 12(b)(6), 28 U.S.C.A.

> Associated Bodywork and Massage Professionals v. American Massage Therapy Ass'n, 897 F.Supp. 1116.

Complaint need not specify correct legal theory nor point to right statute to survive motion to dismiss; rather, complaint must state, either directly or inferentially, allegations establishing the necessary elements for recovery under the chosen legal theory. Fed.Rules Civ. Proc.Rule 12(b)(6), 28 U.S.C.A.

> Associated Bodywork and Massage Professionals v. American Massage Therapy Ass'n, 897 F.Supp. 1116.

N.D.Ill. 1995. To survive motion to dismiss, complaint must allege sufficient facts to outline cause of action.

Banks v. Chicago Bd. of Educ., 895 F.Supp. 206.

To survive motion to dismiss, complaint must allege facts which, if true, would make out elements of prima facie case.

Banks v. Chicago Bd. of Educ., 895 F.Supp. 206.

N.D.Ill. 1995. Mere vagueness or lack of detail does not constitute sufficient grounds for motion to dismiss pro se complaint. Fed.Rules Civ.Proc.Rule 12(b)(6), 28 U.S.C.A.

Oswalt v. Godinez, 894 F.Supp. 1181.

N.D.Ill. 1995. To withstand a motion to dismiss for failure to state a claim, complaint need not narrate all relevant facts or recite the law; all it has to do is set out a claim for relief. Fed.Rules Civ.Proc.Rule 12(b)(6), 28 U.S.C.A.

Booker v. Ward, 888 F.Supp. 869.

N.D.Ill. 1995. Liberal standard on motion to dismiss for failure to allege sufficient facts stretches pleading requirements very far. Fed. Rules Civ.Proc.Rule 12(b)(6), 28 U.S.C.A.

Caplan v. International Fidelity Ins. Co., 885 F.Supp. 175.

N.D.Ill. 1995. Plaintiff need not set out in detail facts upon which a claim is based, but it must allege sufficient facts to outline cause of action to avoid dismissal for failure to state a claim.

E.E.O.C. v. Sears, Roebuck and Co., 883 F.Supp. 211.

N.D.Ill. 1995. Complaint need not specify correct legal theory nor point to right statute to survive motion to dismiss; rather, complaint must state, either directly or inferentially, allegations to establish necessary elements for recovery under chosen legal theory.

Fernando v. Rush-Presbyterian-St. Luke's Medical Center, 882 F.Supp. 119.

N.D.Ill. 1995. Dismissals for failure to state claim are not favored, and only question is whether relief is possible under any set of facts that could be established. Fed.Rules Civ.Proc. Rule 12(b), 28 U.S.C.A.

Indeck Power Equipment Co. v. Jefferson Smurfit Corp., 881 F.Supp. 338.

N.D.Ill. 1995. Only question for court in ruling on motion to dismiss for failure to state claim is whether relief is possible under any set of facts that could be established consistent with allegations. Fed.Rules Civ.Proc.Rule 12(b)(6), 28 U.S.C.A.

Seber v. Unger, 881 F.Supp. 323.

For purposes of motion to dismiss for failure to state claim, complaint need not set out

any legal theory, and incorrect legal theory is not fatal. Fed.Rules Civ.Proc.Rule 12(b)(6), 28 U.S.C.A.

Seber v. Unger, 881 F.Supp. 323.

N.D.Ill. 1995. In order to withstand a motion to dismiss for failure to state a claim upon which relief can be granted, plaintiff need not identify correct legal theory. Fed.Rules Civ. Proc.Rule 12(b)(6), 28 U.S.C.A.

Travis v. Boulevard Bank N.A., 880 F.Supp. 1226.

Plaintiff can withstand motion to dismiss for failure to state claim upon which relief can be granted by failing to specify which part of statute upon which plaintiff relies. Fed.Rules Civ.Proc.Rule 12(b)(6), 28 U.S.C.A.

Travis v. Boulevard Bank N.A., 880 F.Supp. 1226.

N.D.Ill. 1995. On motion to dismiss, only question is whether relief is possible under any set of facts that could be established consistent with allegations.

Arenson v. Whitehall Convalescent and Nursing Home, Inc., 880 F.Supp. 1202, reconsideration denied 161 F.R.D. 355.

N.D.Ill. 1995. Plaintiff must allege sufficient facts in complaint to outline elements of cause of action, in order to avoid dismissal, and only factual allegations will be considered because plaintiff's legal conclusions are not binding on court.

Pena v. Mattox, 880 F.Supp. 567, affirmed 84 F.3d 894.

N.D.Ill. 1995. In deciding motion to dismiss, court accepts all well-pleaded factual allegations as true, as well as reasonable inferences that may be drawn from those allegations, but complaint need not specify correct legal theory nor point to correct statute.

Ford v. Davis, 878 F.Supp. 1124.

N.D.Ill. 1995. Complaint's mere vagueness or lack of detail is not sufficient to justify dismissal for failure to state a claim. Fed.Rules Civ.Proc.Rule 12(b)(6), 28 U.S.C.A.

Pope v. Inland Property Management Inc., 878 F.Supp. 1114.

Complaint need not specify correct legal theory or point to right statute to survive motion to dismiss for failure to state a claim. Fed. Rules Civ.Proc.Rule 12(b)(6), 28 U.S.C.A.

Pope v. Inland Property Management Inc., 878 F.Supp. 1114.

N.D.Ill. 1995. While complaints drafted by pro se litigants are not held to the same standards as those written by practicing attorneys, complaints based on unsupported conclusions of fact and conclusions of law are not sufficient to withstand motion to dismiss. Fed. Rules Civ.Proc.Rule 12(b)(6), 28 U.S.C.A.

    Landfair v. Sheahan, 878 F.Supp. 1106.

N.D.Ill. 1995. On motion to dismiss, only question is whether relief is possible under any set of facts that could be established consistent with allegations.

    Cashman v. Coopers & Lybrand, 877 F.Supp. 425.

N.D.Ill. 1995. Motion to dismiss for failure to state claim upon which relief can be granted is granted only where it is beyond doubt that plaintiff is unable to prove any set of facts that would entitle him to relief. Fed.Rules Civ.Proc.Rule 12(b)(6), 28 U.S.C.A.

    James v. Professionals' Detective Agency, Inc., 876 F.Supp. 1013.

N.D.Ill. 1995. Dismissal is appropriate only if it appears beyond doubt that plaintiff can prove no set of facts consistent with complaint that would entitle it to relief it seeks.

    Howard v. Board of Educ. of Sycamore Community Unit School Dist. No. 427, 876 F.Supp. 959.

N.D.Ill. 1995. Motion for judgment on the pleadings is governed by same standard as motion to dismiss for failure to state a claim upon which relief can be granted and, thus, motion should not be granted unless it appears beyond doubt that plaintiff cannot prove any facts that would support his claim for relief, and that movant is entitled to judgment as matter of law. Fed.Rules Civ.Proc.Rule 12(b)(6), (c), 28 U.S.C.A.

    Rooding v. Peters, 876 F.Supp. 946, reversed 92 F.3d 578, on remand 173 F.R.D. 511.

N.D.Ill. 1995. Dismissal of complaint for failure to state claim is proper only if it appears beyond doubt that plaintiff can prove no set of facts in support of his claim which would entitle him to relief. Fed.Rules Civ.Proc.Rule 12(b)(6), 28 U.S.C.A.

    Matthews v. Rollins Hudig Hall Co., 874 F.Supp. 192.

N.D.Ill. 1994. Motion to dismiss should not be granted unless it appears beyond doubt that plaintiff can prove no set of facts in support of his or her claims which would entitle him or her to relief.

    Pankalla v. U.S. Dept. of Transp., 874 F.Supp. 175.

N.D.Ill. 1994. Motion to dismiss for failure to state claim should not be granted unless it appears beyond doubt that plaintiff can prove no set of facts in support of his claim which

would entitle him to relief. Fed.Rules Civ.Proc. Rule 12(b)(6), 28 U.S.C.A.

    Emery v. American General Finance, Inc., 873 F.Supp. 1116, reversed 71 F.3d 1343, rehearing and suggestion for rehearing denied, on remand 938 F.Supp. 495.

N.D.Ill. 1994. Complaint should not be dismissed for failure to state claim upon which relief can be granted, unless it appears beyond doubt that plaintiff can prove no set of facts in support of his claims which entitle him to relief. Fed.Rules Civ.Proc.Rule 12(b)(6), 28 U.S.C.A.

    Battye v. Child Support Services, Inc., 873 F.Supp. 103.

N.D.Ill. 1994. District court can dismiss for failure to state claim only if plaintiff, even with benefit of assumptions in his or her favor, cannot establish any set of facts which would enable him or her to relief requested.

    Williams v. Hutchens, 870 F.Supp. 857.

N.D.Ill. 1994. Complaint should not be dismissed for failure to state claim upon which relief can be granted unless it appears beyond doubt that plaintiff can prove no set of facts in support of his claim which would entitle him to relief. Fed.Rules Civ.Proc.Rule 12(b)(6), 28 U.S.C.A.

    Moore v. Fidelity Financial Services, Inc., 869 F.Supp. 557.

Complaint need not specify correct statute upon which plaintiff's claim is based, in order to preclude dismissal of complaint for failure to state claim upon which relief can be granted. Fed.Rules Civ.Proc.Rule 12(b)(6), 28 U.S.C.A.

    Moore v. Fidelity Financial Services, Inc., 869 F.Supp. 557.

Complaint should not be dismissed for failure to state claim upon which relief can be granted merely because plaintiff's allegations do not support particular legal theory he advances; rather, court is under duty to examine complaint to determine if allegations provide for relief on any possible theory. Fed.Rules Civ. Proc.Rule 12(b)(6), 28 U.S.C.A.

    Moore v. Fidelity Financial Services, Inc., 869 F.Supp. 557.

Neither vagueness nor lack of details constitutes sufficient ground alone to dismiss complaint for failure to state claim upon which relief can be granted. Fed.Rules Civ.Proc.Rule 12(b)(6), 28 U.S.C.A.

    Moore v. Fidelity Financial Services, Inc., 869 F.Supp. 557.

N.D.Ill. 1994. Complaint should not be dismissed unless court concludes beyond doubt that plaintiffs can prove no set of facts to support their claim which would entitle them to

relief. Fed.Rules Civ.Proc.Rule 12(b)(6), 28 U.S.C.A.

   Straka v. Francis, 867 F.Supp. 767.

N.D.Ill. 1994. Dismissal of action is appropriate only if it is clear that there is no relief that can be granted under any set of facts that can be proved consistent with the allegations.

   Reed v. City of Chicago, 867 F.Supp. 714, affirmed 77 F.3d 1049, rehearing and suggestion for rehearing denied.

N.D.Ill. 1994. Motion to dismiss will be granted only if it is clear that nonmoving party can prove no set of facts in support of his claim which would entitle him to relief. Fed.Rules Civ.Proc.Rule 12(b)(6), 28 U.S.C.A.

   Whirlpool Financial Corp. v. Sevaux, 866 F.Supp. 1097.

N.D.Ill. 1994. Motion to dismiss for failure to state a claim is granted only if facts alleged will not entitle plaintiff to judgment on claim asserted under any circumstances. Fed. Rules Civ.Proc.Rule 12(b)(6), 28 U.S.C.A.

   Adams v. City of Chicago, 865 F.Supp. 445.

N.D.Ill. 1994. Unsupported conclusions of fact and conclusions of law will not suffice to withstand motion to dismiss. Fed.Rules Civ. Proc.Rule 12(b)(6), 28 U.S.C.A.

   Doe v. Village of Oak Park, 863 F.Supp. 797.

N.D.Ill. 1994. No motion to dismiss should be granted unless court concludes that no relief could be granted under any set of facts that could be proved consistent with well-pleaded allegations. Fed.Rules Civ.Proc.Rule 12(b)(6), 28 U.S.C.A.

   D'Last Corp. v. Ugent, 863 F.Supp. 763, affirmed 51 F.3d 275.

N.D.Ill. 1994. Court should not grant motion to dismiss unless plaintiff is not entitled to relief under any set of facts that could be proved consistent with allegations.

   Comite Pro-Celebracion v. Claypool, 863 F.Supp. 682.

N.D.Ill. 1994. Dismissal of action is appropriate only if it is clear that there is no relief that can be granted under any set of facts that can be proved consistent with allegations. Fed. Rules Civ.Proc.Rule 12(b)(6), 28 U.S.C.A.

   Esmail v. Macrane, 862 F.Supp. 217, reversed 53 F.3d 176.

N.D.Ill. 1994. Court should not dismiss complaint for failure to state claim on which relief can be granted unless it appears beyond doubt that plaintiff can prove no set of facts in support of his claim which would entitle him to

relief. Fed.Rules Civ.Proc.Rule 12(b)(6), 28 U.S.C.A.

   Cass v. American Properties, Inc., 861 F.Supp. 55.

N.D.Ill. 1994. On motion to dismiss for failure to state claim on which relief can be granted, court must construe pleadings liberally, and mere vagueness or lack of detail alone will not constitute sufficient grounds to dismiss. Fed.Rules Civ.Proc.Rule 12(b)(6), 28 U.S.C.A.

   Whitehead v. AM Intern., Inc., 860 F.Supp. 1280.

N.D.Ill. 1994. Complaint's mere vagueness or lack of detail is not sufficient to justify dismissal.

   E.E.O.C. v. Park Ridge Public Library, 856 F.Supp. 477.

N.D.Ill. 1994. District court may grant motion to dismiss only if it appears beyond doubt that plaintiffs can prove no set of facts entitling them to relief. Fed.Rules Civ.Proc. Rule 12(b)(6), 28 U.S.C.A.

   In re Nuveen Fund Litigation, 855 F.Supp. 950.

N.D.Ill. 1994. Complaint will be dismissed for failure to state claim if plaintiff cannot prove facts upon which sought after legal relief is to be granted. Fed.Rules Civ.Proc.Rule 12(b)(6), 28 U.S.C.A.

   Letisha A. by Murphy v. Morgan, 855 F.Supp. 943.

Complaint must state either direct or inferential allegations to establish necessary elements for recovery under chosen legal theory, to survive motion to dismiss for failure to state claim. Fed.Rules Civ.Proc.Rule 12(b)(6), 28 U.S.C.A.

   Letisha A. by Murphy v. Morgan, 855 F.Supp. 943.

N.D.Ill. 1994. Motion to dismiss for failure to state claim upon which relief may be granted will only be granted if it is beyond doubt that plaintiff is unable to prove any set of facts that would entitle him to recover. Fed. Rules Civ.Proc.Rule 12(b)(6), 28 U.S.C.A.

   Dawson v. W. & H. Voortman, Ltd., 853 F.Supp. 1038.

N.D.Ill. 1994. Motion to dismiss for failure to state a claim should not be granted unless it appears beyond a doubt that plaintiff can prove no set of facts in support of claims which would entitle him to relief. Fed.Rules Civ.Proc.Rule 12(b)(6), 28 U.S.C.A.

   Jackson v. Doria, 851 F.Supp. 288.

N.D.Ill. 1994. Allegations of complaint should not be dismissed for failure to state a claim unless it appears beyond reasonable doubt that plaintiff can prove no set of facts in

support of his claim which would entitle him to relief. Fed.Rules Civ.Proc.Rule 12(b)(6), 28 U.S.C.A.

> Bergquist v. U.S. Nat. Weather Service, 849 F.Supp. 1221.

N.D.Ill. 1994. Motion to dismiss for failure to state claim may be granted only if it appears beyond doubt that plaintiff can prove no set of facts in support of his claim which would entitle him to relief. Fed.Rules Civ.Proc. Rule 12(b)(6), 28 U.S.C.A.

> Adams v. Cavanagh Communities Corp., 847 F.Supp. 1390.

N.D.Ill. 1994. Complaint should not be dismissed with prejudice unless it appears beyond doubt that plaintiff is unable to prove any set of facts consistent with complaint which would entitle plaintiff to relief.

> A.I. Credit Corp. v. Hartford Computer Group, Inc., 847 F.Supp. 588.

N.D.Ill. 1994. Motion to dismiss for failure to state claim may be granted if it is beyond doubt that plaintiff is unable to prove any set of facts that would entitle him to relief. Fed.Rules Civ.Proc.Rule 12(b)(6), 28 U.S.C.A.

> Bright v. Roadway Services, Inc., 846 F.Supp. 693.

N.D.Ill. 1994. Court should not dismiss complaint for failure to state claim on which relief can be granted unless it appears beyond doubt that plaintiff can prove no set of facts in support of its claim which would entitle it to relief. Fed.Rules Civ.Proc.Rule 12(b)(6), 28 U.S.C.A.

> Motion Picture Projectionists & Video Technicians, Local 110, I.A.T.S.E. and M.P.M.O. of U.S. and Canada v. Fred Corp., 845 F.Supp. 1255.

N.D.Ill. 1994. Complaint should not be dismissed with prejudice unless it appears beyond doubt that plaintiff is unable to prove any set of facts consistent with complaint which would entitle plaintiff to relief.

> Genin, Trudeau & Co., Ltd. v. Integra Development Intern., 845 F.Supp. 611.

N.D.Ill. 1994. Motion to dismiss for failure to state claim may be granted if it is beyond doubt that plaintiff is unable to prove any set of facts that would entitle it to relief. Fed.Rules Civ.Proc.Rule 12(b)(6), 28 U.S.C.A.

> Resolution Trust Corp. v. KPMG Peat Marwick, 844 F.Supp. 431.

N.D.Ill. 1994. Dismissal for failure to state a claim is not warranted unless it appears beyond doubt that plaintiff can prove no set of facts that would entitle him to relief. Fed.Rules Civ.Proc.Rule 12(b)(6), 28 U.S.C.A.

In re Scattered Corp. Securities Litigation, 844 F.Supp. 416, affirmed Sullivan & Long, Inc. v. Scattered Corp., 47 F.3d 857, rehearing and suggestion for rehearing denied, certiorari denied Harkins v. Scattered Corp., 116 S.Ct. 76, 516 U.S. 818, 133 L.Ed.2d 35.

N.D.Ill. 1994. Complaint should not be dismissed with prejudice unless it appears beyond doubt that plaintiff is unable to prove any set of facts consistent with complaint that would entitle plaintiff to relief. Fed.Rules Civ.Proc. Rule 12(b)(1), 28 U.S.C.A.

> U.S. v. Beethoven Associates Ltd. Partnership, 843 F.Supp. 1257.

N.D.Ill. 1994. Complaint should not be dismissed unless it appears, beyond doubt, that plaintiff can prove no set of facts in support of his claim that would entitle him to relief. Fed. Rules Civ.Proc.Rule 12(b)(1), 28 U.S.C.A.

> Fasco Industries, Inc. v. Mack, 843 F.Supp. 1252.

N.D.Ill. 1994. Motion to dismiss should not be granted unless it appears beyond doubt that plaintiff can prove no set of facts in support of his claims which would entitle him to relief.

> Commercial Ins. Co. of Newark, New Jersey v. Krain, 843 F.Supp. 404.

N.D.Ill. 1994. Complaint filed in federal court need not identify appropriate statute or even appropriate legal theory to survive motion to dismiss for failure to state claim; instead, what it must do is plead "claim for relief," and what court must determine is whether relief is possible under any set of facts that could be established consistent with allegations in complaint. Fed.Rules Civ.Proc.Rule 12(b)(6), 28 U.S.C.A.

> First Nat. Bank of Chicago as Trustee of Institutional Real Estate Fund F v. ACCO USA, Inc.-IBT Retirement Plan, 842 F.Supp. 311.

In ruling on motion to dismiss for failure to state claim, court must accept as true all well-pleaded factual allegations in complaint, along with all reasonable inferences drawn in favor of plaintiff, and dismiss complaint only if it is beyond doubt that plaintiff can prove no set of facts in support of its claims that will entitle it to relief. Fed.Rules Civ.Proc.Rule 12(b)(6), 28 U.S.C.A.

> First Nat. Bank of Chicago as Trustee of Institutional Real Estate Fund F v. ACCO USA, Inc.-IBT Retirement Plan, 842 F.Supp. 311.

N.D.Ill. 1994. Motion to dismiss for failure to state claim may be granted if it is beyond doubt that plaintiff is unable to prove any set of facts that would entitle it to relief. Fed.Rules Civ.Proc.Rule 12(b)(6), 28 U.S.C.A.

> City of Chicago Heights, Ill. v. LoBue, 841 F.Supp. 819.

N.D.Ill. 1994. Allegations of complaint should not be dismissed for failure to state claim unless it appears beyond reasonable doubt that plaintiff can prove no set of facts in support of his claim which would entitle him to relief. Fed.Rules Civ.Proc.Rule 12(b)(6), 28 U.S.C.A.

> Marie O. v. Edgar, 157 F.R.D. 433.

N.D.Ill. 1993. Complaint should not be dismissed unless it appears, beyond a doubt, that plaintiff can prove no set of facts in support of his claim that would entitle him to relief.

> Highsmith v. Chrysler Credit Corp., 150 B.R. 997, affirmed in part, reversed in part 18 F.3d 434, 129 A.L.R. Fed. 767.

N.D.Ill. 1993. Plaintiff fails to state claim upon which relief may be granted only if it appears beyond doubt that plaintiff can prove no set of facts in support of his claim which would entitle him to relief. Fed.Rules Civ.Proc. Rule 12(b)(6), 28 U.S.C.A.

> Israeli Aircraft Industries, Ltd. v. Sanwa Business Credit Corp., 850 F.Supp. 686.

N.D.Ill. 1993. Motions to dismiss should not be granted unless it appears beyond doubt that plaintiff can prove no set of facts in support of his claims which would entitle him to relief.

> Carbone v. Zollar, 845 F.Supp. 534.

N.D.Ill. 1993. District court will not grant motion to dismiss for failure to state claim upon which relief can be granted if there is any set of facts that would justify granting relief. Fed. Rules Civ.Proc.Rule 12(b)(6), 28 U.S.C.A.

> Knauz Continental Autos, Inc. v. Land Rover North America, Inc., 842 F.Supp. 1034.

N.D.Ill. 1993. Court grants motion to dismiss only if it is clear that plaintiff can prove no set of facts that would entitle him to relief.

> Northen v. City of Chicago, 841 F.Supp. 234.

Complaint may be dismissed for failure to state claim upon which relief can be granted only if facts that plaintiffs allege show that they are not entitled to judgment. Fed.Rules Civ. Proc.Rule 12(b)(6), 28 U.S.C.A.

> Northen v. City of Chicago, 841 F.Supp. 234.

N.D.Ill. 1993. Court should not dismiss complaint unless it appears beyond doubt that plaintiff can prove no set of facts in support of his claim which would entitle him to relief. Fed.Rules Civ.Proc.Rule 12(b)(6), 28 U.S.C.A.

> Heller Intern. Corp. v. Sharp, 839 F.Supp. 1297.

N.D.Ill. 1993. Party fails to state claim upon which relief may be granted only if that party can prove no set of facts upon which to grant legal relief. Fed.Rules Civ.Proc.Rule 12(b)(6), 28 U.S.C.A.

> Otterbacher v. Northwestern University, 838 F.Supp. 1256.

N.D.Ill. 1993. In ruling on motion for dismissal for failure to state a claim, court must presume all well-pleaded allegations of the complaint to be true and view those allegations in light most favorable to plaintiff, and dismissal is proper only if it appears beyond doubt that plaintiff can prove no set of facts in support of claim which would entitle him to relief. Fed. Rules Civ.Proc.Rule 12(b)(6), 28 U.S.C.A.

> U.S. v. $288,930.00 In U.S. Currency, 838 F.Supp. 367.

N.D.Ill. 1993. Motion to dismiss should not be granted unless it is clear that plaintiffs cannot prove any set of facts consistent with allegations which would entitle them to relief. Fed.Rules Civ.Proc.Rule 12(b)(6), 28 U.S.C.A.

> Eret v. Continental Holding, Inc., 838 F.Supp. 358.

N.D.Ill. 1993. Motion to dismiss will not be granted unless movant can show that under no set of facts can plaintiff prove claim.

> Scholes v. African Enterprise, Inc., 838 F.Supp. 349.

N.D.Ill. 1993. Motion to dismiss for failure to state claim should be granted only if allegations of complaint and all reasonable inferences drawn therefrom could not support any cause of action, interpreting ambiguities in the complaint in favor of plaintiff. Fed.Rules Civ.Proc.Rule 12(b)(6), 28 U.S.C.A.

> Wallace Computer Services, Inc. v. Adams Business Forms, Inc., 837 F.Supp. 1413.

In defending against motion to dismiss for failure to state a claim, plaintiff is free to allege without evidentiary support any facts it pleases that are consistent with complaint in order to show that there is state of facts within scope of complaint that, if proved, would entitle it to judgment. Fed.Rules Civ.Proc.Rule 12(b)(6), 28 U.S.C.A.

> Wallace Computer Services, Inc. v. Adams Business Forms, Inc., 837 F.Supp. 1413.

N.D.Ill. 1993. Motion to dismiss for failure to state claim will not be granted unless under no circumstances may complaint state

claim. Fed.Rules Civ.Proc.Rule 12(b)(6), 28 U.S.C.A.; U.S.C.A. Const. Art. 1, § 8, cl. 3.
> Kerr-McGee Chemical Corp. v. Edgar, 837 F.Supp. 927.

N.D.Ill. 1993. Dismissal of complaint is appropriate only if it is clear that no relief could be granted under any set of facts that could be proved consistent with complaint's allegations.
> Ryan v. DuPage County Jury Com'n, 837 F.Supp. 898.

N.D.Ill. 1993. Complaint will not be dismissed for failure to state valid cause of action unless it appears, beyond all doubt, that plaintiff can prove no set of facts in support of his claims which would entitle him to relief.
> Great Lakes Higher Educ. Corp. v. Austin Bank of Chicago, 837 F.Supp. 892.

N.D.Ill. 1993. Court grants motion to dismiss only if it is clear that plaintiff can prove no set of facts that would entitle him to relief.
> Ruich v. Ruff, Weidenaar & Reidy, Ltd., 837 F.Supp. 881.

N.D.Ill. 1993. Claim may be dismissed if, as a matter of law, it is clear that no relief could be granted under any set of facts that could be proved consistent with the allegations. Fed. Rules Civ.Proc.Rule 12(b)(6), 28 U.S.C.A.
> Walton v. Fairman, 836 F.Supp. 511.

N.D.Ill. 1993. Court will grant motion to dismiss for failure to state claim on which relief can be granted only if it appears beyond doubt that plaintiff can prove no set of facts entitling her to relief. Fed.Rules Civ.Proc.Rule 12(b)(6), 28 U.S.C.A.
> Janopoulos v. Harvey L. Walner & Associates, Ltd., 835 F.Supp. 459.

Complaint may be dismissed for failure to state claim on which relief can be granted only if plaintiff pleads herself out of court by alleging facts that show that she is not entitled to judgment. Fed.Rules Civ.Proc.Rule 12(b)(6), 28 U.S.C.A.
> Janopoulos v. Harvey L. Walner & Associates, Ltd., 835 F.Supp. 459.

N.D.Ill. 1993. Motion to dismiss should not be granted unless it appears beyond doubt that plaintiff can prove no set of facts in support of his claims which would entitle him to relief.
> Kaneria v. American Bd. of Psychiatry and Neurology, Inc., 832 F.Supp. 1226.

N.D.Ill. 1993. Case may be dismissed for failure to state claim upon which relief can be granted only if it is clear that plaintiffs can prove no set of facts consistent with their allegations that would entitle them to relief. Fed. Rules Civ.Proc.Rule 12(b)(6), 28 U.S.C.A.
> Admiral Theatre v. City of Chicago, 832 F.Supp. 1195.

N.D.Ill. 1993. Notice pleading in federal courts requires that district court construe pleadings liberally and complaint's mere vagueness or lack of detail is not sufficient to justify dismissal.
> National Service Ass'n, Inc. v. Capitol Bankers Life Ins. Co., Inc., 832 F.Supp. 227.

Party fails to state claim upon which relief may be granted only if that party can prove no set of facts upon which to grant legal relief.
> National Service Ass'n, Inc. v. Capitol Bankers Life Ins. Co., Inc., 832 F.Supp. 227.

N.D.Ill. 1993. Dismissal is a complaint appropriate only if it is clear that no relief could be granted under any set of facts that could be proved consistent with allegations.
> Douglas v. Tonigan, 830 F.Supp. 457.

N.D.Ill. 1993. Court will not dismiss complaint unless it is clear that there is no set of facts plaintiff could prove consistent with pleadings that would entitle him or her to relief.
> Amati v. City of Woodstock, Ill., 829 F.Supp. 998.

N.D.Ill. 1993. Court will grant motion to dismiss for failure to state claim only if allegations in complaint, and all reasonable inferences drawn therefrom, could not support any cause of action. U.S.C.A. Const. Art. 3, § 2, cl. 1; Fed.Rules Civ.Proc.Rule 12(b)(6), 28 U.S.C.A.
> St. Paul Ins. Co. of Illinois v. Great Lakes Turnings, Ltd., 829 F.Supp. 982.

N.D.Ill. 1993. Motion to dismiss should not be granted unless it appears beyond doubt that plaintiff can prove no set of facts in support of claims which would entitle him to relief.
> Allen v. City of Chicago, 828 F.Supp. 543.

N.D.Ill. 1993. Complaint will be dismissed for failure to state claim if plaintiff can prove no set of facts upon which the sought-after legal relief is to be granted.
> Sprague v. King, 825 F.Supp. 1324, affirmed 23 F.3d 185, rehearing and suggestion for rehearing denied, certiorari denied 115 S.Ct. 356, 513 U.S. 946, 130 L.Ed.2d 310.

N.D.Ill. 1993. Complaint's mere vagueness or lack of detail is not sufficient to justify dismissal.
> Smith v. Lyles, 822 F.Supp. 541.

Although party fails to state claim upon which relief may be granted only if that party can prove no set of facts upon which to grant legal relief, that party must allege all elements of asserted cause of action necessary for recovery.

> Smith v. Lyles, 822 F.Supp. 541.

N.D.Ill. 1993. Dismissal for failure to state a claim is improper unless it appears beyond a doubt that plaintiff can prove no set of facts in support of claim which would entitle him to relief. Fed.Rules Civ.Proc.Rule 12(b)(6), 28 U.S.C.A.

> Eberhardt v. O'Malley, 820 F.Supp. 1090, affirmed in part, reversed in part 17 F.3d 1023.

N.D.Ill. 1993. Complaint need not specify correct legal theory or point to right statute to survive motion to dismiss, but complaint will be dismissed if plaintiff cannot prove facts upon which sought after legal relief is to be granted. Fed.Rules Civ.Proc.Rule 12(b), 28 U.S.C.A.

> American Needle & Novelty, Inc. v. Drew Pearson Marketing, Inc., 820 F.Supp. 1072.

N.D.Ill. 1993. Only if allegations of complaint, and all reasonable inferences drawn therefrom, cannot support any cause of action may district court grant motion to dismiss for failure to state a cause of action. Fed.Rules Civ.Proc.Rule 12(b)(6), 28 U.S.C.A.

> Bercoon, Weiner, Glick and Brook v. Manufacturers Hanover Trust Co., 818 F.Supp. 1152.

N.D.Ill. 1993. Motion to dismiss should not be granted unless it appears beyond doubt that plaintiff can prove no set of facts in support of claims that would entitle plaintiff to relief. Fed.Rules Civ.Proc.Rule 12(b), 28 U.S.C.A.

> Pommier v. James L. Edelstein Enterprises, 816 F.Supp. 476, reconsideration denied.

N.D.Ill. 1993. Although mere vagueness for lack of detail alone does not constitute sufficient grounds to dismiss complaint, absence of facts to support claim renders allegations mere legal conclusions subject to dismissal; accordingly, plaintiff will not avoid dismissal if complaint merely recites bare legal conclusions.

> Ill v. Roland, 812 F.Supp. 855.

N.D.Ill. 1993. Party fails to state claim on which relief may be granted only if that party can prove no set of facts on which to grant legal relief.

> Lomas Mortg. U.S.A., Inc. v. W.E. O'Neil Const. Co., 812 F.Supp. 841.

N.D.Ill. 1992. In considering motion to dismiss, court accepts factual allegations of complaint as true and unless it appears beyond doubt that plaintiff can prove no set of facts in support of his claims which would entitle him to relief, court should not grant motion to dismiss.

> Tektel, Inc. v. Maier, 813 F.Supp. 1331.

N.D.Ill. 1992. Unless it appears beyond a doubt that plaintiffs can prove no set of facts in support of claims which would entitle him to relief, court should not grant motion to dismiss.

> In re Abbott Laboratories Securities Litigation, 813 F.Supp. 1315.

N.D.Ill. 1992. Motion to dismiss should not be granted unless it appears beyond doubt that plaintiff can prove no set of facts in support of his claim which would entitle him to relief.

> Hudson v. Sullivan, 812 F.Supp. 785.

N.D.Ill. 1992. Viability of complaint is not dependent upon the tyranny of labels, and the test is whether it is clear that no relief could be granted under any set of facts that could be proved consistent with the allegations; for purposes of motion to dismiss for failure to state a claim, it does not matter whether a pleader places any label, or even the wrong label, on the claim.

> Johnson v. Smith, 810 F.Supp. 235.

N.D.Ill. 1992. Complaint may be dismissed for failure to state claim upon which relief can be granted only if it appears beyond a doubt that plaintiff can prove no set of facts in support of his claim which would entitle him to relief. Fed.Rules Civ.Proc.Rule 12(b)(6), 28 U.S.C.A.

> Johnson v. Safeco Ins. Co. of America, 809 F.Supp. 602, affirmed 9 F.3d 112, rehearing denied.

N.D.Ill. 1992. Court should not dismiss complaint unless it appears beyond doubt that plaintiff can prove no set of facts in support of his claim which would entitle him to relief.

> Bryant v. Northeast Illinois Regional Commuter R.R. Corp., 809 F.Supp. 584.

N.D.Ill. 1992. Party fails to state claim upon which relief may be granted if that party can prove no set of facts upon which to grant legal relief. Fed.Rules Civ.Proc.Rule 12(b)(6), 28 U.S.C.A.

> Powell Duffryn Terminals, Inc. v. CJR Processing, Inc., 808 F.Supp. 652.

N.D.Ill. 1992. Dismissal for failure to state claim is proper only if nonmoving party can prove no set of facts upon which to grant legal relief. Fed.Rules Civ.Proc.Rule 12(b)(6), 28 U.S.C.A.

> Harris v. O'Grady, 803 F.Supp. 1361.

N.D.Ill. 1992. In ruling on motion to dismiss, dismissal is proper if it appears beyond doubt that plaintiffs can prove no set of facts that would entitle them to relief.

> Matter of VMS Ltd. Partnership Securities Litigation, 803 F.Supp. 179.

N.D.Ill. 1992. Motion to dismiss should not be granted unless it appears beyond doubt that plaintiff can prove no set of facts in support of claims which would entitle him to relief.

> National Paint & Coatings Ass'n v. City of Chicago, 803 F.Supp. 135.

N.D.Ill. 1992. Party fails to state claim only if that party can prove no set of facts upon which to grant legal relief. Fed.Rules Civ.Proc. Rule 12(b)(6), 28 U.S.C.A.

> Illinois Constructors Corp. v. Morency & Associates, Inc., 802 F.Supp. 185, reconsideration denied.

N.D.Ill. 1992. In analyzing motion to dismiss for failure to state claim on which relief could be granted, court will not dismiss complaint unless it is clear there is no set of facts that plaintiff could prove consistent with pleadings that would entitle him or her to relief, accepting all well-pleaded factual allegations as true and viewing allegations in light most favorable to nonmoving party. Fed.Rules Civ.Proc. Rule 12(b)(1, 6), 28 U.S.C.A.

> Freiburger v. Emery Air Charter, Inc., 795 F.Supp. 253.

N.D.Ill. 1992. Party fails to state claim upon which relief may be granted if that party can prove no set of facts upon which legal relief may be granted. Fed.Rules Civ.Proc.Rule 12(b)(1, 6), 28 U.S.C.A.

> MSA Realty Corp. v. State of Ill., 794 F.Supp. 267, affirmed 990 F.2d 288.

N.D.Ill. 1992. Dismissal for failure to state claim is appropriate if it appears beyond doubt that plaintiff could prove no set of facts in support of claim which would entitle him to relief. Fed.Rules Civ.Proc.Rule 12(b)(6), 28 U.S.C.A.

> Fittanto v. Klein, 788 F.Supp. 1451.

Complaint must state either direct or inferential allegations concerning all material elements necessary for recovery under relevant legal theory, to decide motion for dismissal for failure to state claim. Fed.Rules Civ.Proc.Rule 12(b)(6), 28 U.S.C.A.

> Fittanto v. Klein, 788 F.Supp. 1451.

N.D.Ill. 1992. Dismissal of complaint is proper if it appears beyond doubt that plaintiff cannot prove set of facts in support of his claim which would entitle him to relief. Fed.Rules Civ.Proc.Rule 12(b)(6), 28 U.S.C.A.

> Healy v. Axelrod Const. Co. Defined Ben. Pension Plan and Trust, 787 F.Supp. 838.

N.D.Ill. 1992. Dismissal for failure to state claim upon which relief can be granted is improper unless it appears beyond doubt that plaintiff can prove no set of facts in support of his claim which would entitle him to relief. Fed.Rules Civ.Proc.Rule 12(b)(6), 28 U.S.C.A.

> Procopio v. Johnson, 785 F.Supp. 1317, affirmed 994 F.2d 325.

N.D.Ill. 1992. Motion to dismiss should not be granted unless it appears beyond a doubt that plaintiff can prove no set of facts in support of claims which would entitle him to relief.

> State Farm Fire & Cas. Co. v. Frigidaire, a Div. of General Motors Corp., 146 F.R.D. 160.

N.D.Ill. 1991. Dismissal under Rule 12(b)(6) is improper unless it appears beyond doubt that plaintiff can prove no set of facts in support of his claim which would entitle him to relief. Fed.Rules Civ.Proc.Rule 12(b)(6), 28 U.S.C.A.

> Sledd v. Lindsay, 780 F.Supp. 554.

N.D.Ill. 1991. A motion to dismiss should not be granted unless it appears beyond doubt that the plaintiff can prove no set of facts in support of his claim which would entitle him to relief, taking the well-pleaded allegations of the complaint as true and viewing them, as well as all reasonable inferences therefrom, in the light most favorable to the plaintiff.

> Stephenson v. CNA Financial Corp., 777 F.Supp. 596.

N.D.Ill. 1991. On motion to dismiss, allegations of complaint as well as reasonable inferences to be drawn from them are taken to be true; if plaintiff cannot prove any set of facts that would entitle her to relief, then dismissal is proper. Fed.Rules Civ.Proc.Rule 12(b)(6), 28 U.S.C.A.

> Burgess v. Clairol, Inc., 776 F.Supp. 1278.

N.D.Ill. 1991. District court should not dismiss complaint unless it appears beyond doubt that plaintiff can prove no set of facts in support of his claim which would entitle him to relief.

> Johnson v. University of Chicago Hosp., 774 F.Supp. 510, affirmed in part, reversed in part 982 F.2d 230, rehearing denied, and as amended, on remand 1994 WL 118192.

N.D.Ill. 1991. A complaint can be dismissed for failure to state a claim if it appears beyond doubt that plaintiffs can prove no set of facts in support of a claim that would entitle them to the relief requested or if the complaint fails to allege a necessary element required to obtain relief.

> Lyne v. Arthur Andersen & Co., 772 F.Supp. 1064.

N.D.Ill. 1991. Plaintiff need not set out in detail facts upon which claim is based, but must allege sufficient facts to outline cause of action; complaint must state either direct or inferential allegations concerning all material elements necessary for recovery under relevant legal theory.

> McWright v. Alexander, 771 F.Supp. 256, reversed 982 F.2d 222.

On motion to dismiss for failure to state a claim, district court is not required to accept legal conclusions either alleged or inferred from pleaded facts. Fed.Rules Civ.Proc.Rule 12(b)(6), 28 U.S.C.A.

> McWright v. Alexander, 771 F.Supp. 256, reversed 982 F.2d 222.

Dismissal for failure to state a claim is improper unless it appears beyond a doubt that plaintiff can prove no set of facts in support of his claim which would entitle him to relief. Fed.Rules Civ.Proc.Rule 12(b)(6), 28 U.S.C.A.

> McWright v. Alexander, 771 F.Supp. 256, reversed 982 F.2d 222.

N.D.Ill. 1991. In analyzing motion to dismiss, court will not dismiss complaint unless it is clear there is no set of facts that plaintiffs could prove consistent with pleadings that would entitle them to relief.

> Oji v. PSC Environmental Management Inc., 771 F.Supp. 232, 30 Wage & Hour Cas. (BNA) 1054.

N.D.Ill. 1991. Motion to dismiss complaint filed by pro se plaintiff must be denied unless it appears beyond doubt that plaintiff can prove no set of facts in support of claim which would entitle plaintiff to relief.

> Wilbert v. City of Chicago, 768 F.Supp. 253.

N.D.Ill. 1991. Generally, federal system of notice pleading does not favor dismissal for failure to state a claim; however, dismissal is proper if it appears beyond doubt that plaintiff can prove no set of facts in support of her claim that would entitle her to the relief requested.

> Heffernan v. Pacific Dunlop GNB Corp., 767 F.Supp. 913, reversed 965 F.2d 369, on remand 1992 WL 275573.

N.D.Ill. 1991. Generally, federal system of notice pleading does not favor dismissal for failure to state a claim; however, dismissal is proper if it appears beyond a doubt that plaintiff can prove no set of facts in support of his claim that would entitle him to requested relief.

> Youker v. Schoenenberger, 763 F.Supp. 361.

If complaint fails to allege necessary element required to obtain relief, dismissal is in order.

> Youker v. Schoenenberger, 763 F.Supp. 361.

N.D.Ill. 1991. On motion to dismiss, court accepts as true all well-pleaded factual allegations of complaint and views those allegations in light most favorable to plaintiff.

> Scott v. O'Grady, 760 F.Supp. 1288, affirmed 975 F.2d 366, rehearing denied, certiorari denied 113 S.Ct. 2421, 508 U.S. 942, 124 L.Ed.2d 643.

In determining sufficiency of complaint in stating claim, court must construe pleadings liberally; vagueness or lack of detail are insufficient grounds for dismissal. Fed.Rules Civ. Proc.Rule 8, 28 U.S.C.A.

> Scott v. O'Grady, 760 F.Supp. 1288, affirmed 975 F.2d 366, rehearing denied, certiorari denied 113 S.Ct. 2421, 508 U.S. 942, 124 L.Ed.2d 643.

Dismissal for failure to state claim is proper if it appears beyond doubt that plaintiffs can prove no set of facts in support of their claim that would entitle them to requested relief.

> Scott v. O'Grady, 760 F.Supp. 1288, affirmed 975 F.2d 366, rehearing denied, certiorari denied 113 S.Ct. 2421, 508 U.S. 942, 124 L.Ed.2d 643.

N.D.Ill. 1991. Generally, federal system of notice pleading does not favor dismissal for failure to state a claim. Fed.Rules Civ.Proc. Rule 12(b)(6), 28 U.S.C.A.

> Greenberg v. Boettcher & Co., 755 F.Supp. 776.

Dismissal for failure to state a claim is proper if it appears beyond doubt that plaintiff can prove no set of facts in support of his or her claim that would entitle him or her to relief requested. Fed.Rules Civ.Proc.Rule 12(b)(6), 28 U.S.C.A.

> Greenberg v. Boettcher & Co., 755 F.Supp. 776.

Dismissal for failure to state a claim is in order if complaint fails to allege necessary elements required to obtain relief. Fed.Rules Civ. Proc.Rule 12(b)(6), 28 U.S.C.A.

> Greenberg v. Boettcher & Co., 755 F.Supp. 776.

N.D.Ill. 1990. In analyzing motion to dismiss, district court will not dismiss complaint unless it is clear that there are no set of facts that plaintiffs could prove consistent with pleadings that would entitle them to relief. Fed. Rules Civ.Proc.Rule 12(b)(6), 28 U.S.C.A.

> Garot Anderson Marketing, Inc. v. Blue Cross and Blue Shield United of Wisconsin, 772 F.Supp. 1054, 116 A.L.R. Fed. 729.

N.D.Ill. 1990. Dismissal for failure to state claim on which relief can be granted is proper where it is clear that no relief could be granted under any set of facts consistent with allegations in complaint. Fed.Rules Civ.Proc.Rule 12(b)(6), 28 U.S.C.A.

> In re VMS Securities Litigation, 752 F.Supp. 1373.

N.D.Ill. 1990. For purposes of motion to dismiss, plaintiff need not set out in detail facts upon which claim is based, but must allege sufficient facts to outline cause of action. Fed. Rules Civ.Proc.Rule 12(b)(6), 28 U.S.C.A.

> Paist v. Town & Country Corp., 744 F.Supp. 179.

Dismissal for failure to state a claim is improper unless it appears beyond doubt that plaintiff can prove no set of facts in support of his or her claim which would entitle him or her to relief. Fed.Rules Civ.Proc.Rule 12(b)(6), 28 U.S.C.A.

> Paist v. Town & Country Corp., 744 F.Supp. 179.

N.D.Ill. 1990. Dismissal is warranted if it appears beyond doubt that plaintiff could prove no set of facts in support of claim which would entitle him to relief. Fed.Rules Civ.Proc.Rules 12(b), (b)(6), 56, 28 U.S.C.A.

> Belmont Community Hosp. v. Local Union No. 9, I.B.E.W., & Outside Contractors Health & Welfare Fund, 737 F.Supp. 1034.

N.D.Ill. 1989. Complaint need not set out in detail the facts upon which claim is based, but must allege sufficient facts to outline cause of action, in order to survive motion to dismiss for failure to state cause of action upon which relief can be granted. Fed.Rules Civ.Proc.Rule 12(b)(6), 28 U.S.C.A.

> Davis v. Frapolly, 747 F.Supp. 451.

Complaint should not be dismissed for failure to state claim unless it appears beyond reasonable doubt that plaintiff can prove no set of facts in support of claim which would entitle him to relief. Fed.Rules Civ.Proc.Rule 12(b)(6), 28 U.S.C.A.

> Davis v. Frapolly, 747 F.Supp. 451.

N.D.Ill. 1989. Dismissal for failure to state a claim is improper unless it appears beyond doubt that plaintiff can prove no set of facts in support of claim which would entitle him to relief, but the court is not required to accept legal conclusions either alleged or inferred from pleaded facts. Fed.Rules Civ.Proc.Rule 12(b)(6), 28 U.S.C.A.

> Columbus, Cuneo, Cabrini Medical Center v. Travelers Ins. Co., 725 F.Supp. 396.

N.D.Ill. 1989. For purpose of ruling on motion to dismiss for failure to state claim upon which relief can be granted, allegations in plaintiffs' complaint must be taken as true and complaint may not be dismissed unless it is clear that plaintiffs are not entitled to relief under any set of the facts. Fed.Rules Civ.Proc.Rule 12(b)(6), 28 U.S.C.A.

> Skinner v. Shirley of Hollywood, a Div. of Nat. Corset Supply House, 723 F.Supp. 50.

N.D.Ill. 1989. Dismissal for failure to state a claim is improper unless it appears beyond

doubt that the plaintiff can prove no set of facts in support of his claim which would entitle him to relief. Fed.Rules Civ.Proc.Rule 12(b)(6), 28 U.S.C.A.

> Yaworski v. Pate, 717 F.Supp. 624.

N.D.Ill. 1989. Dismissal for failure to state a claim is improper unless it appears beyond doubt that plaintiff can prove no set of facts in support of his claim which would entitle him to relief. Fed.Rules Civ.Proc.Rule 12(b)(6), 28 U.S.C.A.

> Davis v. Frapolly, 717 F.Supp. 614.

N.D.Ill. 1988. Dismissal of claim is appropriate only when plaintiff cannot prevail under any set of facts alleged in complaint and any reasonable inferences therefrom.

> Creekside Associates, Inc. v. City of Wood Dale, 684 F.Supp. 201.

N.D.Ill. 1987. Motion to dismiss will not be granted merely because complaint does not state with precision every element necessary for recovery.

> Ambling v. Blackstone Cattle Co., Inc., 658 F.Supp. 1459.

N.D.Ill. 1986. In order to avoid granting of motion to dismiss for failure to state a claim, facts need not be set out in detail, but need only outline claim for relief. Fed.Rules Civ.Proc. Rule 12(b)(6), 28 U.S.C.A.

> Miller v. Advanced Studies, Inc., 635 F.Supp. 1196.

N.D.Ill. 1986. While plaintiff need not prove his entire case in his complaint to withstand motion to dismiss, he must plead sufficient facts to apprise court of nature and extent of challenged conduct. Fed.Rules Civ.Proc. Rule 12(b)(6), 28 U.S.C.A.

> Hornung v. Village of Park Forest, 634 F.Supp. 540.

N.D.Ill. 1985. Complaint must contain either direct or inferential allegations respecting all material elements necessary to sustain recovery under some viable legal theory.

> U.S. v. Iverson, 609 F.Supp. 927.

S.D.Ill. 1994. Test to be applied on motion to dismiss for failure to state claim is whether it appears beyond doubt that plaintiff can prove no set of facts in support of his claim which would entitle him to relief. Fed.Rules Civ.Proc. Rule 12, 28 U.S.C.A.

> Vickery v. Jones, 856 F.Supp. 1313, affirmed 100 F.3d 1334, certiorari denied 117 S.Ct. 1553, 137 L.Ed.2d 701.

N.D.Ind. 1998. Defendant seeking to dismiss complaint must attack sufficiency, by demonstrating that claim is without legal consequence, and defendant may not attempt to refute complaint or present different set of allegations. Fed.Rules Civ.Proc.Rule 12(b)(6), 28 U.S.C.A.

> Town of Ogden Dunes v. Bethlehem Steel Corp., 996 F.Supp. 850.

N.D.Ind. 1995. In order to prevail on motion to dismiss, defendant must demonstrate that plaintiff's claim, as set forth by complaint, is without legal consequences. Fed.Rules Civ. Proc.Rule 12(b)(1), 28 U.S.C.A.

> TJ's South, Inc. v. Town of Lowell, 895 F.Supp. 1116, opinion amended 924 F.Supp. 92.

N.D.Ind. 1994. To escape dismissal of complaint, plaintiff need not set out in detail facts upon which claim is based, but must allege sufficient facts to outline cause of action and complaint cannot be amended by briefs filed in opposition to motion to dismiss. Fed.Rules Civ.Proc.Rule 12(b)(6), 28 U.S.C.A.

> Graham v. Henderson, 897 F.Supp. 1157, affirmed 59 F.3d 173, rehearing and suggestion for rehearing denied, certiorari denied 116 S.Ct. 535, 516 U.S. 997, 133 L.Ed.2d 440.

On motion to dismiss complaint, defendant may not attempt to refute complaint or present different set of allegations in its challenge, attack must be against sufficiency of complaint and must demonstrate that claim, as set forth by complaint, is without legal consequence. Fed. Rules Civ.Proc.Rule 12(b)(6), 28 U.S.C.A.

> Graham v. Henderson, 897 F.Supp. 1157, affirmed 59 F.3d 173, rehearing and suggestion for rehearing denied, certiorari denied 116 S.Ct. 535, 516 U.S. 997, 133 L.Ed.2d 440.

N.D.Ind. 1994. Dismissal of complaint for failure to state claim upon which relief can be granted is appropriate only if plaintiff can prove no set of facts in support of his claims which would entitle him to relief. Fed.Rules Civ.Proc. Rule 12(b)(6), 28 U.S.C.A.

> Worthington v. Subaru-Isuzu Automotive, Inc., 868 F.Supp. 1067.

N.D.Ind. 1994. District court may not dismiss a complaint for failure to state a claim unless it appears beyond a doubt that plaintiff can prove no set of facts in support of claim which would entitle him to relief. Fed.Rules Civ.Proc.Rule 12(b)(6), 28 U.S.C.A.

> Methodist Hospitals, Inc. v. Indiana Family and Social Services Admin., 860 F.Supp. 1309.

To prevail on motion to dismiss for failure to state a claim, defendant must demonstrate that plaintiff's claim, as set forth by complaint,

is without legal consequence. Fed.Rules Civ. Proc.Rule 12(b)(6), 28 U.S.C.A.

> Methodist Hospitals, Inc. v. Indiana Family and Social Services Admin., 860 F.Supp. 1309.

N.D.Ind. 1994. Dismissal of complaint is appropriate only if it appears beyond doubt that plaintiffs can prove no set of facts in support of their claims which would entitle them to relief. Fed.Rules Civ.Proc.Rule 12(b)(6), 28 U.S.C.A.

> LaPorte County Republican Cent. Committee v. Board of Com'rs of County of LaPorte, 851 F.Supp. 340, reversed 43 F.3d 1126.

Dismissal for failure to state claim was not intended to be trap for unartful pleaders but, rather, district court looks to root of case and determines whether any set of facts could support cause of action. Fed.Rules Civ.Proc.Rule 12(b)(6), 28 U.S.C.A.

> LaPorte County Republican Cent. Committee v. Board of Com'rs of County of LaPorte, 851 F.Supp. 340, reversed 43 F.3d 1126.

N.D.Ind. 1994. District court may not dismiss complaint for failure to state a claim unless it appears beyond a doubt that plaintiff can prove no set of facts in support of claim which would entitle her to relief.

> Johnson v. Northern Indiana Public Service Co., 844 F.Supp. 466.

N.D.Ind. 1993. On motion to dismiss complaint for failure to state claim, no count of complaint should be dismissed unless it appears beyond doubt that plaintiff can prove no set of facts in support of his or her claim which would entitle him or her to relief. Fed.Rules Civ.Proc. Rule 12(b)(6), 28 U.S.C.A.

> Resolution Trust Corp. v. O'Bear, Overholser, Smith & Huffer, 840 F.Supp. 1270.

N.D.Ind. 1993. Complaint should not be dismissed for failure to state claim unless it appears beyond doubt that plaintiff can prove no set of facts in support of his or her claim which would entitle him or her to relief. Fed. Rules Civ.Proc.Rule 12(b)(6), 28 U.S.C.A.

> Garus v. Rose Acre Farms, Inc., 839 F.Supp. 563.

N.D.Ind. 1993. District court may not dismiss complaint for failure to state claim unless it appears beyond doubt that plaintiff can proven no set of facts in support of claim which would entitle him to relief. Fed.Rules Civ.Proc. Rule 12(b)(6), 28 U.S.C.A.

> West v. LTV Steel Co., 839 F.Supp. 559.

In order to prevail on motion to dismiss for failure to state claim, defendants must demonstrate that plaintiff's claim, as set forth in complaint, is without legal consequence. Fed.Rules Civ.Proc.Rule 12(b)(6), 28 U.S.C.A.

West v. LTV Steel Co., 839 F.Supp. 559.

N.D.Ind. 1993. Federal district court may not dismiss complaint for failure to state claim upon which relief can be granted unless it appears beyond doubt that plaintiff can prove no set of facts in support of claim which would entitle plaintiff to relief. Fed.Rules Civ.Proc. Rule 12(b)(6), 28 U.S.C.A.

Mauke v. Town of Dune Acres, 835 F.Supp. 468.

To prevail on motion to dismiss for failure to state claim upon which relief can be granted, defendants must demonstrate that plaintiff's claim, as set forth by complaint, is without legal consequence. Fed.Rules Civ.Proc.Rule 12(b)(6), 28 U.S.C.A.

Mauke v. Town of Dune Acres, 835 F.Supp. 468.

N.D.Ind. 1993. District court may not dismiss plaintiff's complaint unless it appears beyond doubt that plaintiff can prove no set of facts in support of his claim which would entitle him to relief.

Schwartz v. Oberweis, 826 F.Supp. 280.

N.D.Ind. 1993. Dismissal of complaint is appropriate only if it appears beyond doubt that plaintiff can prove no set of facts in support of claim which would entitle him to relief; however, complaint must allege sufficient facts to outline cause of action. Fed.Rules Civ.Proc. Rule 12(b)(6), 28 U.S.C.A.

Tracy For and on Behalf of Estate of Tracy v. Bittles, 820 F.Supp. 396.

N.D.Ind. 1993. Dismissal of a complaint is appropriate only if it appears beyond doubt that the plaintiff can prove no set of facts in support of his claim which would entitle him to relief. Fed.Rules Civ.Proc.Rule 12(b)(6), 28 U.S.C.A.

Washington v. Foresman, 148 F.R.D. 241.

N.D.Ind. 1992. Even under notice pleading of Federal Rules of Civil Procedure and liberal interpretation given to pro se pleadings, complaint must include allegations respecting all material elements of all claims asserted; bare legal conclusions attached to narrated facts will not suffice. Fed.Rules Civ.Proc.Rule 12(b)(6), 28 U.S.C.A.

McCrum v. Elkhart County Dept. of Public Welfare, 806 F.Supp. 203, reconsideration granted.

N.D.Ind. 1992. Dismissal of complaint is appropriate only if it appears beyond doubt that plaintiff can prove no set of facts in support of his or her claims which would entitle him or

her to relief. Fed.Rules Civ.Proc.Rule 12(b)(6), 28 U.S.C.A.

Steele by Steele v. Magnant, 796 F.Supp. 1143.

N.D.Ind. 1991. Dismissal for failure to state claim is improper unless it appears beyond doubt that plaintiff could prove no set of facts in support of claim which could entitle him to relief.

Frye v. Town of Akron, 759 F.Supp. 1320.

N.D.Ind. 1990. In ruling on motion to dismiss for failure to state a claim, district court must follow accepted rule that complaint should not be dismissed unless it appears beyond a doubt that plaintiff can prove no set of facts in support of claim which would entitle him to relief. Fed.Rules Civ.Proc.Rule 12(b)(6), 28 U.S.C.A.

Inner City Leasing and Trucking Co., Inc. v. City of Gary, Ind., 759 F.Supp. 461.

S.D.Ind. 1996. To survive motion to dismiss for failure to state claim, although plaintiff need not set out in detail all facts upon which claim is based, he or she must allege sufficient facts to outline cause of action; if plaintiff pleads facts and facts show that he or she is entitled to no relief, complaint should be dismissed. Fed.Rules Civ.Proc.Rule 12(b)(6), 28 U.S.C.A.

Indiana State Teachers Ass'n v. Board of School Com'rs of City of Indianapolis, 918 F.Supp. 266, affirmed 101 F.3d 1179.

S.D.Ind. 1995. To avoid dismissal of complaint, plaintiff need not set out in detail facts upon which claim is based, but must allege sufficient facts to outline cause of action. Fed. Rules Civ.Proc.Rule 12(b)(6), 28 U.S.C.A.

Hurd v. Monsanto Co., 908 F.Supp. 604, affirmed in part 107 F.3d 873.

S.D.Ind. 1995. For purposes of motion to dismiss pursuant to rules, plaintiff need not set out in detail facts on which claim is based, but must allege sufficient facts to outline cause of action. Fed.Rules Civ.Proc.Rule 12(b)(6), 28 U.S.C.A.

Robinson v. Howell, 902 F.Supp. 836.

S.D.Ind. 1994. Dismissal for failure to state a claim is appropriate where review of complaint, taking all factual allegations in complaint as true, reveals that no viable cause of action exists. Fed.Rules Civ.Proc.Rule 12(b)(6), 28 U.S.C.A.

Buffington v. Metcalf, 883 F.Supp. 1190.

S.D.Ind. 1994. For purposes of motion to dismiss for failure to state claim upon which relief can be granted, plaintiff need not set out in detail facts upon which claim is based, but must allege sufficient facts to outline cause of action. Fed.Rules Civ.Proc.Rule 12(b)(6), 28 U.S.C.A.

> Brown v. Secretary of Dept. of Health and Human Services, 874 F.Supp. 238, affirmed 61 F.3d 905.

S.D.Ind. 1993. In ruling on motion to dismiss for failing to state claim on which relief can be granted, district court must construe allegations of complaint in favor of pleader, and only in the exceptional circumstance, where it appears beyond doubt that plaintiff can prove no set of facts in support of its claim which would entitle him to relief, will motion be granted. Fed.Rules Civ.Proc.Rule 12(b)(6), 28 U.S.C.A.

> Baker v. Westinghouse Elec. Corp., 830 F.Supp. 1161.

S.D.Ind. 1992. Motion to dismiss should not be granted unless it appears beyond doubt that plaintiffs can prove no set of facts in support of their claim that would entitle them to relief. Fed.Rules Civ.Proc.Rule 12(b)(6), 28 U.S.C.A.

> Bradley v. Indiana State Election Bd., 797 F.Supp. 694.

S.D.Ind. 1991. In determining propriety of dismissal for failure to state a claim, district court must accept as true all well-pled factual allegations in complaint and draw all reasonable inferences therefrom in favor of plaintiff; if it appears beyond a doubt that plaintiffs can prove any set of facts consistent with allegations in complaint which would entitle them to relief, dismissal is appropriate. Fed.Rules Civ.Proc. Rule 12(b)(6), 28 U.S.C.A.

> Study v. U.S., 782 F.Supp. 1293.

S.D.Ind. 1989. Dismissal for failure to state claim is appropriate where review of complaint, taking all factual allegations in complaint as true, reveals that no viable cause of action exists.

> Implement Service, Inc. v. Tecumseh Products Co., 726 F.Supp. 1171.

N.D.Iowa 1995. It is only the unusual case where complaint on its face reveals some insuperable bar to relief that dismissal for failure to state claim upon which relief can be granted is warranted. Fed.Rules Civ.Proc.Rule 12(b)(6), 28 U.S.C.A.

> Powell v. Tordoff, 911 F.Supp. 1184.

N.D.Iowa 1995. Judge's disbelief of complaint's factual allegations does not warrant dismissal for failure to state claim. Fed.Rules Civ.Proc.Rule 12(b)(6), 28 U.S.C.A.

> Dahl v. Kanawha Inv. Holding Co., 161 F.R.D. 673.

N.D.Iowa 1992. It is only in "unusual case" where complaint on its face reveals some insuperable bar to relief that dismissal for fail-

ure to state claim is warranted. Fed.Rules Civ.Proc.Rule 12(b)(6), 28 U.S.C.A.

> Wiltgen v. U.S., 813 F.Supp. 1387.

S.D.Iowa 1994. Court may dismiss complaint if it is clear that no relief could be granted under any set of facts that could be proved consistent with allegations. Fed.Rules Civ.Proc.Rule 12(b)(6), 28 U.S.C.A.

> Accordino v. Langman Const., Inc., 862 F.Supp. 237.

S.D.Iowa 1992. In addressing motion to dismiss, allegations of complaint must be taken as true; complaint should not be dismissed for failure to state claim unless it appears beyond doubt that plaintiff can prove no set of facts in support of claim which would entitle him to relief.

> Nagle v. Merrill Lynch, Pierce, Fenner & Smith, Inc., 790 F.Supp. 203.

S.D.Iowa 1980. Health Care Equalization Committee of Iowa Chiropractic Soc. v. Iowa Medical Soc., 501 F.Supp. 970, affirmed 851 F.2d 1020, rehearing denied.

D.Kan. 1998. Pro se complaint may be dismissed if it clearly fails to state legally cognizable claim. Fed.Rules Civ.Proc.Rule 12(b)(6), 28 U.S.C.A.

> Dickerson v. Leavitt Rentals, 995 F.Supp. 1242, affirmed 153 F.3d 726.

D.Kan. 1996. On motion to dismiss for failure to state a claim, allegations of conclusions or opinions are not sufficient when no facts are alleged by way of statement of claim. Fed.Rules Civ.Proc.Rule 12(b)(6), 28 U.S.C.A.

> Huddleston v. Lumbermens Mut. Cas. Co., 942 F.Supp. 504.

D.Kan. 1996. Deferential rules governing judgment of sufficiency of complaint upon motion to dismiss for failure to state claim upon which relief may be granted do not allow court to assume that plaintiff can prove facts that it has not alleged or that defendants have violated laws in ways that have not been alleged; if facts narrated by plaintiff do not at least outline or adumbrate viable claim, his complaint cannot pass muster. Fed.Rules Civ.Proc.Rule 12(b)(6), 28 U.S.C.A.

> Mounkes v. Conklin, 922 F.Supp. 1501.

D.Kan. 1996. On motion to dismiss for failure to state claim upon which relief may be granted, allegations of conclusions or opinions are not sufficient when no facts are alleged by way of statement of claim. Fed.Rules Civ.Proc. Rules 8(a), 12(b)(6), 28 U.S.C.A.

> Shroff v. Bernardo, 920 F.Supp. 156.

D.Kan. 1995. The issue in reviewing sufficiency of complaint is not whether plaintiff will ultimately prevail, but whether claimant is entitled to offer evidence to support claims.

> Lyman v. Nabil's Inc., 903 F.Supp. 1443.

D.Kan. 1995. In ruling on a motion to dismiss for failure to state a claim, district court must determine whether party making claim would be entitled to relief under any set of facts that could be established to support his or her claim. Fed.Rules Civ.Proc.Rule 12(b)(6), 28 U.S.C.A.

> Reidenbach v. U.S.D. No. 437, 878 F.Supp. 178.

D.Kan. 1995. Court cannot dismiss complaint merely because it doubts that plaintiff can prove facts it alleges, but rather motion to dismiss can only be granted if plaintiff has failed to allege sufficient facts to entitle it to relief if facts alleged are taken as true. Fed. Rules Civ.Proc.Rule 12, 28 U.S.C.A.

> Potts v. Boeing Co., 162 F.R.D. 651.

D.Kan. 1994. Court may not dismiss cause of action for failure to state claim unless it appears beyond doubt that plaintiff can prove no set of facts in support of theory of recovery that would entitle him to relief. Fed.Rules Civ.Proc.Rule 12(b)(6), 28 U.S.C.A.

> Oyler v. Finney, 870 F.Supp. 1018, reconsideration denied, affirmed 52 F.3d 338.

Issue in reviewing sufficiency of complaint for purposes of determining whether court may dismiss cause of action for failure to state claim is not whether plaintiff will prevail, but whether he is entitled to offer evidence to support his claim. Fed.Rules Civ.Proc.Rule 12(b)(6), 28 U.S.C.A.

> Oyler v. Finney, 870 F.Supp. 1018, reconsideration denied, affirmed 52 F.3d 338.

D.Kan. 1994. Court may not dismiss cause of action for failure to state claim unless it appears beyond doubt that plaintiff can prove no set of facts in support of theory of recovery that would entitle him to relief. Fed.Rules Civ.Proc.Rule 12(b)(6), 28 U.S.C.A.

> Hamner v. BMY Combat Systems, 869 F.Supp. 888, reconsideration denied 874 F.Supp. 322, affirmed 79 F.3d 1156.

D.Kan. 1994. Court may not dismiss cause of action for failure to state claim unless it appears beyond doubt that plaintiff can prove no set of facts in support of theory of recovery that would entitle him to relief. Fed.Rules Civ.Proc.Rule 12(b)(6), 28 U.S.C.A.

> Gilmore v. List & Clark Const. Co., 866 F.Supp. 1310.

D.Kan. 1994. District court may not dismiss cause of action for failure to state a claim unless it appears beyond a doubt that plaintiff can prove no set of facts in support of theory of

recovery that would entitle him or her to relief. Fed.Rules Civ.Proc.Rule 12(b)(6), 28 U.S.C.A.

> Gilmore v. List & Clark Const. Co., 862 F.Supp. 294.

D.Kan. 1994. District court may not dismiss claim for failure to state claim upon which relief can be granted unless it determines that plaintiff can prove no set of facts in support of claim to entitle him to relief. Fed.Rules Civ. Proc.Rule 12(b)(6), 28 U.S.C.A.

> Anderson v. Marshall, 856 F.Supp. 604.

D.Kan. 1994. Court may not dismiss cause of action for failure to state claim upon which relief can be granted unless it appears beyond doubt that plaintiff can prove no set of facts in support of theory of recovery that would entitle him to relief. Fed.Rules Civ.Proc.Rule 12(b)(6), 28 U.S.C.A.

> First Nat. Bancshares of Beloit, Inc. v. Geisel, 853 F.Supp. 1337.

D.Kan. 1994. Court should not dismiss complaint for failure to state claim upon which relief can be granted unless it appears beyond doubt that plaintiff can prove no set of facts in support of his claim which would entitle him to relief. Fed.Rules Civ.Proc.Rule 12(b)(6), 28 U.S.C.A.

> Morris v. State of Kan. Dept. of Revenue, 849 F.Supp. 1421.

D.Kan. 1994. Motions to dismiss are disfavored; complaint should not be dismissed for failure to state claim unless it appears beyond doubt that plaintiff can prove no set of facts in support of his claim which would entitle him to relief. U.S.C.A. Const.Amend. 14; 42 U.S.C.A. § 1983; K.S.A. 65–4928.

> Anglemyer v. Hamilton County Hosp., 848 F.Supp. 938.

D.Kan. 1994. Complaint should not be dismissed for failure to state claim upon which relief can be granted unless it appears beyond doubt that plaintiff can prove no set of facts in support of his claim which would entitle him to relief. Fed.Rules Civ.Proc.Rule 12(b)(6), 28 U.S.C.A.

> West v. Boeing Co., 843 F.Supp. 670, opinion vacated in part on reconsideration 851 F.Supp. 395.

D.Kan. 1994. Cause of action may not be dismissed for failure to state claim unless it appears beyond doubt that plaintiff can prove no set of facts to support theory of recovery that would entitle plaintiff to relief. Fed.Rules Civ. Proc.Rule 12(b)(6), 28 U.S.C.A.

> Smith v. Hawkeye-Security Ins. Co., 842 F.Supp. 1373.

D.Kan. 1994. Court should not dismiss complaint unless it appears beyond doubt that plaintiff can prove no set of facts in support of his claim that would entitle him to relief.

> Bloesser v. Office Depot, Inc., 158 F.R.D. 168, reconsideration overruled.

D.Kan. 1993. Court may not dismiss cause of action for failure to state claim unless it appears beyond doubt that plaintiff can prove no set of facts in support of theory of recovery that would entitle her to relief.

> Andrean v. Secretary of U.S. Army, 840 F.Supp. 1414.

D.Kan. 1993. Cause of action may not be dismissed for failure to state claim unless it appears beyond doubt that plaintiff can prove no set of facts in support of theory of recovery that would entitle plaintiff to relief. Fed.Rules Civ.Proc.Rule 8(a), 28 U.S.C.A.

> Deere & Co. v. Zahm, 837 F.Supp. 346.

Pleading may not be dismissed for failure to state claim unless it appears beyond doubt that plaintiff can prove no set of fact in support of its theory.

> Deere & Co. v. Zahm, 837 F.Supp. 346.

D.Kan. 1993. Court should dismiss complaint for failure to state claim only if it appears beyond doubt that plaintiff can prove no set of facts supporting its claim that entitles it to relief. Fed.Rules Civ.Proc.Rule 12(b)(6), 28 U.S.C.A.

> Kaul v. Stephan, 828 F.Supp. 1504.

D.Kan. 1993. District court may not dismiss cause of action for failure to state a claim unless it appears beyond a doubt that plaintiff can prove no set of facts to support theory of recovery that would entitle him to relief. Fed. Rules Civ.Proc.Rule 12(b)(6), 28 U.S.C.A.

> Monarch Normandy Square Partners v. Normandy Square Associates Ltd. Partnership, 817 F.Supp. 899.

D.Kan. 1993. Dismissal of cause of action for failure to state claim upon which relief can be granted is appropriate only if it appears that plaintiff can prove no set of facts in support of claim which would entitle him to relief.

> Kelley Metal Trading Co. v. Al-Jon/United, Inc., 812 F.Supp. 185.

D.Kan. 1992. Court may not dismiss cause of action for failure to state claim unless it appears beyond doubt that plaintiff can prove no set of facts in support of theory of recovery that would entitle him or her to relief.

> Reeve v. Union Pacific R. Co., 790 F.Supp. 1074.

D.Kan. 1992. Court may not dismiss cause of action for failure to state claim unless it appears beyond doubt that plaintiff can prove

no set of facts to support theory of recovery that would entitle plaintiff to relief.

> Siefkes v. Nichols, 788 F.Supp. 477.

D.Kan. 1992. Court may not dismiss cause of action for failure to state a claim unless it appears beyond a doubt that plaintiffs can prove no set of facts in support of their theory of relief that would entitle them to recovery.

> Norton v. National Research Foundation, 141 F.R.D. 510.

D.Kan. 1991. Court may not dismiss cause of action for failure to state claim unless it appears beyond a doubt that plaintiff can prove no set of facts in support of theory of recovery that would entitle him to relief.

> Federal Deposit Ins. Corp. v. Thayer Ins. Agency, Inc., 780 F.Supp. 745.

D.Kan. 1991. Issue in reviewing sufficiency of complaint is not whether plaintiff will ultimately prevail, but whether plaintiff is entitled to offer evidence to support claims. Fed. Rules Civ.Proc.Rule 12(b)(6), 28 U.S.C.A.

> Covell v. Photo Images, Inc., 774 F.Supp. 1321.

D.Kan. 1991. Sufficiency of complaint for purposes of motion to dismiss is not assessed from whether plaintiffs may ultimately prevail but from whether plaintiffs are entitled to present evidence in support of their claims. Fed. Rules Civ.Proc.Rule 12(b)(6), 28 U.S.C.A.

> Adams v. Walker, 767 F.Supp. 1099.

D.Kan. 1991. Plaintiffs' alleged failure to comply with federal rule on format of complaint did not warrant dismissal of complaint, especially where defendants did not allege that they lacked understanding or were having difficulty in responding to complaint, but rather appeared to be merely pushing technical point. Fed. Rules Civ.Proc.Rule 10(b), 28 U.S.C.A.

> Kjorlie v. Lundin, 765 F.Supp. 671, reconsideration denied 1991 WL 290452.

D.Kan. 1991. Cause of action may not be dismissed for failure to state a claim unless it appears beyond a doubt that plaintiff can prove no set of facts in support of theory of recovery that would entitle her to relief. Fed.Rules Civ. Proc.Rule 12(b)(6), 28 U.S.C.A.

> Lawton v. Medevac Mid-America, Inc., 138 F.R.D. 586.

D.Kan. 1990. Motions to dismiss are disfavored; complaint should not be dismissed for failure to state claim unless it appears beyond doubt that plaintiff can prove no set of facts in support of its claim which would entitle it to relief.

> In re Department of Energy Stripper Well Exemption Litigation, 752 F.Supp. 1534.

D.Kan. 1990. Court may not dismiss cause of action for failure to state claim unless it appears beyond doubt that plaintiff can prove no set of facts in support of theory of recovery that would entitle him to relief; court must view all reasonable inferences in favor of plaintiff and pleadings must be liberally construed.

> Tersiner v. Union Pacific R. Co., 740 F.Supp. 1519, on reconsideration 743 F.Supp. 1463.

D.Kan. 1990. In deciding motion to dismiss complaint for failure to state cause of action, court must accept as true on their face well-pleaded factual allegations in complaint and draw all reasonable inferences in favor of plaintiffs, and dismissal is appropriate only if it appears beyond a reasonable doubt that plaintiff can prove no set of facts in support of claim that would entitle it to relief. Fed.Rules Civ.Proc. Rule 12(b)(6), 28 U.S.C.A.

> Pizza Management, Inc. v. Pizza Hut, Inc., 737 F.Supp. 1154, entered 1990 WL 112967.

D.Kan. 1986. Motions to dismiss for failure to state a claim are generally viewed with disfavor and are rarely granted. Fed.Rules Civ. Proc.Rule 12(b)(6), 28 U.S.C.A.

> Crow v. U.S., 634 F.Supp. 1085.

W.D.Ky. 1994. Dismissal of complaint for failure to state claim for which relief can be granted is proper when plaintiff can prove no set of facts in support of her claim that would entitle her to relief. Fed.Rules Civ.Proc.Rule 12(b)(6), 28 U.S.C.A.

> Wilson v. Webb, 869 F.Supp. 496.

E.D.La. 1997. Dismissal of complaint is proper if complaint lacks allegation regarding required element necessary to obtain relief. Fed.Rules Civ.Proc.Rule 12(b)(6), 28 U.S.C.A.

> Reyes v. Sazan, 981 F.Supp. 973.

Conclusory allegations or legal conclusions masquerading as factual conclusions will not suffice to prevent motion to dismiss complaint for failure to state claim. Fed.Rules Civ.Proc. Rule 12(b)(6), 28 U.S.C.A.

> Reyes v. Sazan, 981 F.Supp. 973.

E.D.La. 1996. Conclusory allegations or legal conclusions masquerading as facts will not suffice to prevent a motion to dismiss for failure to state claim. Fed.Rules Civ.Proc.Rule 12(b)(6), 28 U.S.C.A.

> Baustian v. State of La., 910 F.Supp. 274, reconsideration denied 929 F.Supp. 980.

E.D.La. 1994. Dismissal for failure to state claim is not appropriate unless it appears beyond doubt that plaintiff can prove no set of facts in support of his claim that would entitle him to relief. Fed.Rules Civ.Proc.Rule 12(b)(6), 28 U.S.C.A.

> Castano v. American Tobacco Co., 870 F.Supp. 1425, reconsideration denied.

E.D.La. 1994. In considering motion to dismiss for failure to state claim upon which relief can be granted, court must accept all material allegations of complaint as true and construe them in light most favorable to non-moving party; motion will succeed only if plaintiff can prove no set of facts which would entitle him to relief. Fed.Rules Civ.Proc.Rule 12(b)(6), 28 U.S.C.A.

> Robertson v. Burger King, Inc., 848 F.Supp. 78, reconsideration denied 155 F.R.D. 580.

M.D.La. 1995. Dismissal of plaintiffs' complaint is proper if plaintiffs are unable to establish facts in support of their claims entitling them to relief. Fed.Rules Civ.Proc.Rule 12(b)(6), 28 U.S.C.A.

> Payne v. Fontenot, 925 F.Supp. 414.

W.D.La. 1996. To overcome motion to dismiss for failure to state claim, plaintiff's complaint must set forth specific facts and not merely conclusory allegations or legal conclusions masquerading as factual conclusions. Fed.Rules Civ.Proc.Rule 12(b)(6), 28 U.S.C.A.

> Howard v. Town of Jonesville, 935 F.Supp. 855.

W.D.La. 1996. To withstand motion to dismiss for failure to state claim upon which relief can be granted, it is not required that complaint outline all elements of claim, but is sufficient if inferences may be drawn that those elements exist. Fed.Rules Civ.Proc., Rule 12(b)(6), 28 U.S.C.A.

> Hunt v. Steve Dement Bail Bonds, Inc., 914 F.Supp. 1390, affirmed 96 F.3d 1443.

W.D.La. 1995. Dismissal is proper for failure to state a claim if complaint lacks allegation regarding required element necessary to obtain relief. Fed.Rules Civ.Proc.Rule 12(b)(6), 28 U.S.C.A.

> Evangeline Telephone Co., Inc. v. AT & T Communications of South Central States, Inc., 916 F.Supp. 598.

W.D.La. 1995. For purposes of deciding motion to dismiss for failure to state a claim, court's inquiry is directed to whether allegations constitute statement of claim that includes short and plain statement of claim that gives defendants fair notice of what plaintiff's claim is and grounds upon which it rests. Fed.Rules Civ.Proc.Rule 12(b)(6), 28 U.S.C.A.

> Citrano v. Allen Correctional Center, 891 F.Supp. 312.

For purposes of deciding motion to dismiss for failure to state a claim, there is no requirement that plaintiff set out in detail facts upon which he bases his claim; court will presume that general allegations embrace those specific facts that are necessary to support the claim, but conclusory allegations concerning legal effect of events alleged do not have to be accepted by the court. Fed.Rules Civ.Proc.Rule 12(b)(6), 28 U.S.C.A.

> Citrano v. Allen Correctional Center, 891 F.Supp. 312.

D.Me. 1995. On a motion to dismiss, the plaintiff must set forth factual allegations, either direct or inferential, respecting each material element necessary to sustain recovery under some actionable legal theory; court need not accept bald assertions or unsubstantiated conclusions. Fed.Rule Civ.Proc.Rule 12(b)(6), 28 U.S.C.A.

> Carey v. Mt. Desert Island Hosp., 910 F.Supp. 7.

D.Me. 1993. To resolve motion to dismiss for failure to state claim, district court must accept as true all factual allegations in complaint, construe them in favor of plaintiff, and decide whether, as matter of law, plaintiff could prove no set of facts which would entitle him to relief. Fed.Rules Civ.Proc.Rule 12(b)(6), 28 U.S.C.A.

> Jackson v. Faber, 834 F.Supp. 471.

D.Me. 1993. To resolve motion to dismiss for failure to state claim, district court must accept as true all factual allegations in complaint, construe them in favor of plaintiff, and decide whether, as matter of law, plaintiff could prove no set of facts which would entitle her to relief. Fed.Rules Civ.Proc.Rule 12(b)(6), 28 U.S.C.A.

> Carlson v. Rice, 832 F.Supp. 17.

D.Me. 1993. Standard for dismissal of counterclaim for failure to state claim is whether counterclaimant can prove no set of facts in support of her claim which would entitle her to relief, and thus if trial court accepts counterclaimant's facts and can envision no reasonable application of law that would entitled her to relief, court may rightly dismiss case. Fed.Rules Civ.Proc.Rule 12(b)(6), 28 U.S.C.A.

> Eagle Snacks, Inc. v. Our Company, Inc., 831 F.Supp. 1.

D.Me. 1993. Complaint should not be dismissed unless it appears beyond doubt that plaintiffs can prove no set of facts which would entitle them to relief.

> F.D.I.C. v. S. Prawer & Co., 829 F.Supp. 439.

D.Me. 1993. In deciding motion to dismiss based on failure to plead fraud with sufficient particularity, district court must accept factual allegations set forth in complaint as true and must draw all reasonable inferences in favor of

plaintiffs; complaint should not be dismissed unless it appears beyond doubt that plaintiffs can prove no set of facts which would entitle them to relief.

> Wyman v. Prime Discount Securities, 819 F.Supp. 79.

D.Me. 1991. Court should not dismiss complaint if facts pled support any possible theory of relief.

> Inhabitants of City of Saco v. General Elec. Co., 779 F.Supp. 186.

D.Me. 1991. Sufficiency of pleading on motion to dismiss for failure to state claim must be considered in light of liberal notice pleading requirements. Fed.Rules Civ.Proc.Rule 12(b)(6), 28 U.S.C.A.

> Reid v. Gruntal & Co., Inc., 760 F.Supp. 945.

D.Md. 1997. A motion to dismiss will be granted if there is either lack of cognizable legal theory or absence of sufficient facts alleged under cognizable legal theory.

> Quraishi v. Shalala, 962 F.Supp. 55.

D.Md. 1993. Complaint should not be dismissed for failure to state claim on which relief can be transferred unless it appears beyond doubt that plaintiff can prove no set of facts to entitle him to relief. Fed.Rules Civ.Proc.Rule 12(b)(6), 28 U.S.C.A.; 42 U.S.C.A. § 1983.

> Blackwell v. Mayor and Com'rs of Delmar, 841 F.Supp. 151.

D.Md. 1992. Court may grant motion to dismiss only if it is clear that no relief could be granted under any set of facts that could be proved consistent with allegations.

> Duane v. Government Employees Ins. Co., 784 F.Supp. 1209, affirmed 37 F.3d 1036, certiorari granted 115 S.Ct. 1251, 513 U.S. 1189, 131 L.Ed.2d 132, certiorari dismissed 115 S.Ct. 2272, 515 U.S. 1101, 132 L.Ed.2d 253.

D.Md. 1991. Complaint should not be dismissed for insufficiency unless it appears a certainty that plaintiff is entitled to no relief under any state of facts which could be proved in support of claim.

> U.S. v. Fairchild Industries, Inc., 766 F.Supp. 405.

D.Md. 1990. Motion to dismiss for failure to state a claim may be granted if it appears beyond doubt that plaintiff can prove no set of facts in support of his or her claim which would entitle him or her to relief. Fed.Rules Civ.Proc. Rule 12(b)(6), 28 U.S.C.A.

> Herlihy v. Ply-Gem Industries, Inc., 752 F.Supp. 1282.

D.Md. 1989. Pro se action against 69 defendants was subject to dismissal for failure to comply with requirement that plaintiffs provide "a short and plain statement of * * * [their] claim"; because violation was so egregious and because inclusion of at least some of defendants was frivolous, dismissal, rather than granting plaintiff's leave to amend, was appropriate. Fed.Rules Civ.Proc.Rule 8(a), 28 U.S.C.A.

> Anderson v. University of Maryland School of Law, 130 F.R.D. 616, affirmed 900 F.2d 249.

D.Mass. 1997. Despite highly deferential reading courts accord complaint on motion to dismiss for failure to state a claim, courts need not credit bald assertions or unsubstantiated conclusions. Fed.Rules Civ.Proc.Rule 12(b)(6), 28 U.S.C.A.

> Raso v. Lago, 958 F.Supp. 686, affirmed 135 F.3d 11, certiorari denied 119 S.Ct. 44.

D.Mass. 1996. In order to maintain claim for relief, plaintiff needs only allege generalized statement of facts from which defendant will be able to frame responsive pleading; if claim is legally sufficient based on any viable theory, court must deny motion to dismiss. Fed.Rules Civ.Proc.Rule 12(b)(6), 28 U.S.C.A.

> Budnick v. Baybanks, Inc., 921 F.Supp. 30.

D.Mass. 1995. If complaint is sufficient to state cause of action in accordance with law under any theory, court must deny motion to dismiss. Fed.Rules Civ.Proc.Rule 12(b)(6), 28 U.S.C.A.

> Siniscalchi v. Shop-Rite Supermarkets, Inc., 903 F.Supp. 182.

D.Mass. 1995. On motion to dismiss for failure to state claim, complaint will be deemed insufficient if plaintiff relies upon bald assertions, unsupportable conclusions and opprobrious epithets. Fed.Rules Civ.Proc.Rule 12(b)(6), 28 U.S.C.A.

> McDonald v. Com. of Mass., 901 F.Supp. 471.

D.Mass. 1995. In deciding motion to dismiss for failure to state claim upon which relief can be granted, court must look only to allegations, and, if under any theory, they are sufficient to state cause of action in accordance with law, motion to dismiss must be denied. Fed. Rules Civ.Proc.Rule 12(b)(6), 28 U.S.C.A.

> General Elec. Co. v. Lyon, 894 F.Supp. 544.

D.Mass. 1995. On motion to dismiss for failure to state claim, court is required to look only to allegations of complaint and if under any theory they are sufficient to state cause of action in accordance with law, motion must be denied. Fed.Rules Civ.Proc.Rule 12(b)(6), 28 U.S.C.A.

> Dominique v. Weld, 880 F.Supp. 928, affirmed 73 F.3d 1156.

D.Mass. 1995. If under any theory complaint is sufficient to state cause of action in accordance with the law, motion to dismiss complaint for failure to state claim must be denied. Fed.Rules Civ.Proc.Rule 12(b)(6), 28 U.S.C.A.

> Vartanian v. Monsanto Co., 880 F.Supp. 63.

D.Mass. 1995. If under any theory complaint is sufficient to state a cause of action in accordance with the law, a motion to dismiss complaint must be denied. Fed.Rules Civ.Proc. Rule 12(b)(6), 28 U.S.C.A.

> Sarocco v. General Elec. Co., 879 F.Supp. 156.

D.Mass. 1995. On review of motion to dismiss complaint filed by pro se litigant, district court must look to allegations of complaint and deny motion to dismiss if allegations are sufficient under any theory to state cause of action in accordance with law.

> Gonyer v. McDonald, 874 F.Supp. 464.

D.Mass. 1994. Plaintiff's complaint may not be dismissed for failure to state claim unless it appears beyond doubt that plaintiff can prove no set of facts in support of its claim which would entitle it to relief.

> Talbott v. C.R. Bard, Inc., 865 F.Supp. 37, affirmed 63 F.3d 25, certiorari dismissed 116 S.Ct. 1892, 517 U.S. 1230, 135 L.Ed.2d 169.

D.Mass. 1994. While complaint need only set forth a generalized statement of facts to withstand motion to dismiss for failure to state a claim, plaintiff must provide enough information to outline the elements of the claim. Fed. Rules Civ.Proc.Rule 12(b)(6), 28 U.S.C.A.

> Abany v. Fridovich, 862 F.Supp. 615.

D.Mass. 1994. In assessing motion to dismiss for failure to state claim, court must accept as true all material allegations in complaint, drawing all reasonable inferences therefrom in plaintiff's favor; motion may only be granted if it appears beyond doubt that plaintiff can prove no set of facts that would entitle plaintiff to relief. Fed.Rules Civ.Proc.Rule 12(b)(6), 28 U.S.C.A.

> U.S. v. Rockland Trust Co., 860 F.Supp. 895.

D.Mass. 1994. In deciding motion to dismiss for failure to state claim, court must look only to allegations of complaint, and if under any theory they are sufficient to state cause of action in accordance with the law, motion to dismiss complaint must be denied. Fed.Rules Civ.Proc.Rule 12(b)(6), 28 U.S.C.A.

> Rodowicz v. Massachusetts Mut. Life Ins. Co., 857 F.Supp. 992, order vacated on reconsideration 915 F.Supp. 486.

D.Mass. 1994. In considering a motion to dismiss for failure to state claim upon which relief may be granted, court is required to look only to allegations of complaint and to deny motion under any theory if allegations are sufficient to state cause of action in accordance with the law. Fed.Rules Civ.Proc.Rule 12(b)(6), 28 U.S.C.A.

Pierce v. Runyon, 857 F.Supp. 129.

D.Mass. 1994. Trial court may dismiss complaint for failure to state claim only if no relief can be granted based on any set of facts that could be proved consistent with plaintiff's allegations. Fed.Rules Civ.Proc.Rule 12(b)(6), 28 U.S.C.A.

Massachusetts Candy & Tobacco Distributors, Inc. v. Golden Distributors, Ltd., 852 F.Supp. 63.

D.Mass. 1993. Complaint will be dismissed pursuant to motion to dismiss for failure to state claim only when it appears that plaintiff cannot recover on any viable theory. Fed.Rules Civ.Proc.Rule 12(b)(6), 28 U.S.C.A.

Sharpe v. Kelley, 835 F.Supp. 33.

D.Mass. 1993. Dismissal of complaint for failure to state claim on which relief may be granted is permissible only if it appears beyond doubt that plaintiff can prove no set of facts in support of her claim which would entitle her to relief. Fed.Rules Civ.Proc.Rule 12(b)(6), 28 U.S.C.A.

Spalding v. Reliance Standard Life Ins. Co., 835 F.Supp. 23.

D.Mass. 1993. When confronted with motion to dismiss, court must accept as true facts alleged by plaintiff in complaint and drawn all reasonable inferences in plaintiff's favor, and may not dismiss claim unless it appears beyond doubt that plaintiff can prove no set of facts in support of claim which would entitle him to relief. Fed.Rules Civ.Proc.Rule 12(b)(6), 28 U.S.C.A.

Devlin v. WSI Corp., 833 F.Supp. 69.

D.Mass. 1993. Plaintiff's complaints may not be dismissed for failure to state a claim unless it appears beyond doubt that plaintiff can prove no set of facts in support of his claim which would entitled him to relief.

Branch v. F.D.I.C., 825 F.Supp. 384.

D.Mass. 1993. Dismissal for failure to state a claim is generally inappropriate unless it appears beyond doubt that plaintiff can prove no set of facts in support of his claims which would entitle him to relief. Fed.Rules Civ.Proc. Rule 12(b)(6), 28 U.S.C.A.

Colby v. Hologic, Inc., 817 F.Supp. 204.

D.Mass. 1992. Court may dismiss plaintiff's claims only if complaint presents no set of facts that could support recovery.

Lennon v. Walsh, 798 F.Supp. 845.

D.Mass. 1992. Court may grant dismissal for failure to state a claim only if it clearly appears, according to facts alleged, that plaintiff cannot recover on any viable theory. Fed.Rules Civ.Proc.Rule 12(b)(6), 28 U.S.C.A.; M.G.L.A. c. 152, §§ 1 et seq., 15, 24.

Bergeson v. Franchi, 783 F.Supp. 713.

D.Mass. 1991. No count in complaint should be dismissed for failure to state claim unless it appears beyond doubt that plaintiff can prove no set of facts which would entitle him to relief. Fed.Rules Civ.Proc.Rule 12(b)(6), 28 U.S.C.A.

Cullen v. Darvin, 132 B.R. 211.

D.Mass. 1991. In reviewing motion to dismiss for failure to state cause of action, court must accept factual allegations in complaint as true and draw all reasonable inferences in favor of plaintiff, and complaint can be dismissed only if it appears beyond doubt that plaintiffs can prove no set of facts which would entitle them to relief. Fed.Rules Civ.Proc.Rule 12(b)(6), 28 U.S.C.A.

In re Healthco Intern., Inc. Securities Litigation, 777 F.Supp. 109.

D.Mass. 1991. Complaint should not be dismissed for failure to state claim upon which relief can be granted unless it appears beyond doubt that plaintiff can prove no set of facts that would entitle him to relief; in deciding motion, court must accept facts as set forth in complaint as true, and must draw all reasonable inferences in plaintiff's favor. Fed.Rules Civ.Proc. Rule 12(b)(6), 28 U.S.C.A.

Andujar v. City of Boston, 760 F.Supp. 238.

D.Mass. 1991. Motions to dismiss for failure to satisfy fraud pleading rule's particularity requirement may properly be characterized as motions to dismiss for failure to state claim, and thus, in deciding motion, district court must accept factual allegations set forth in complaint as true and draw all reasonable inferences in favor of plaintiff, and complaint should not be dismissed unless it appears beyond reasonable doubt that plaintiff can prove no set of facts which would entitle him to relief. Fed.Rules Civ.Proc.Rules 9(b), 12(b)(6), 28 U.S.C.A.

Driscoll v. Landmark Bank for Sav., 758 F.Supp. 48.

D.Mass. 1990. Complaint should not be dismissed unless it appears beyond doubt that plaintiffs can prove no set of facts which would entitle them to relief. Fed.Rules Civ.Proc.Rule 12(b)(6), 28 U.S.C.A.

Kuney Intern., S.A. v. DiIanni, 746 F.Supp. 234.

D.Mass. 1988. Court may dismiss derivative action because plaintiffs are inadequate representatives, but may not do so for failure to state a claim upon which relief may be granted on the ground that the plaintiffs do not allege that they are adequate representatives. Fed. Rules Civ.Proc.Rules 12(b)(6), 23.1, 28 U.S.C.A.

> Abeloff v. Barth, 119 F.R.D. 332.

E.D.Mich. 1998. In order to defeat motion to dismiss, opposing party must allege sufficient facts in complaint, as to each material element, so that decision in his favor is conceivable under legal theory he advances. Fed.Rules Civ. Proc.Rule 12(b)(6), 28 U.S.C.A.

> Lanni v. Engler, 994 F.Supp. 849.

E.D.Mich. 1996. Dismissal for failure to state claim upon which relief can be granted is appropriate if complaint fails to set forth allegation of required element of claim. Fed.Rules Civ.Proc.Rule 12(b)(6), 28 U.S.C.A.

> Niece v. Fitzner, 922 F.Supp. 1208.

E.D.Mich. 1995. Dismissal for failure to state claim should be granted as matter of law if it appears that, in light most favorable to plaintiff, and with every doubt resolved in his favor, complaint fails to state any valid claim for relief. Fed.Rules Civ.Proc.Rule 12(b), 28 U.S.C.A.

> Pittiglio v. Michigan Nat. Corp., 906 F.Supp. 1145.

E.D.Mich. 1995. If when all legal conclusions or unwarranted factual inferences are removed from pleadings remainder does not include direct or inferential allegations of fact respecting all of material elements of cause of action, then dismissal for failure to state cause of action is warranted. Fed.Rules Civ.Proc. Rule 12(b)(6), 28 U.S.C.A.

> Greenberg v. Compuware Corp., 889 F.Supp. 1012.

E.D.Mich. 1994. In order for complaint to be dismissed for failure to state claim upon which relief can be granted, court must conclude beyond doubt that plaintiff can prove no set of facts in support of his claim which would entitle him to relief. Fed.Rules Civ.Proc.Rule 12(b)(6), 28 U.S.C.A.

> U.S. ex rel. Moore v. University of Michigan, 860 F.Supp. 400.

E.D.Mich. 1994. Complaint should not be dismissed for failure to state a claim upon which relief may be granted unless it appears without doubt that plaintiff can prove no set of facts in support of his claim which would entitle him to relief. Fed.Rules Civ.Proc.Rule 12(b)(6), 28 U.S.C.A.

> Fishbach-Natkin, Inc. v. Shimizu America Corp., 854 F.Supp. 1294.

E.D.Mich. 1994. Motion to dismiss should not be granted unless it appears beyond doubt that plaintiff can prove no set of facts in support of his claim that would entitle him to relief. Fed.Rules Civ.Proc.Rule 12(b)(6), 28 U.S.C.A.

> Strout v. U.S. Parole Com'n, 842 F.Supp. 948, affirmed 40 F.3d 136.

E.D.Mich. 1994. Complaint will be dismissed only if it is clear that no relief could be granted under any set of facts that could be proven in support of claim. Fed.Rules Civ. Proc.Rule 12(b), 28 U.S.C.A.

> Doran v. McGinnis, 158 F.R.D. 383.

E.D.Mich. 1993. In order for complaint to be dismissed for failure to state claim upon which relief can be granted, court must conclude beyond doubt that plaintiff can prove no set of facts in support of claim which would entitle him to relief; in making decision, court must liberally construe pleadings in favor of nonmovant and accept as true all well-pleaded allegations. Fed.Rules Civ.Proc.Rule 12(b)(6), 28 U.S.C.A.

> Juide v. City of Ann Arbor, 839 F.Supp. 497, affirmed 107 F.3d 870.

E.D.Mich. 1993. Upon motion to dismiss for failure to state claim, complaint should not be dismissed unless it appears without doubt that plaintiff can prove no set of facts in support of its claim which would entitle it to relief. Fed.Rules Civ.Proc.Rule 12(b)(6), 28 U.S.C.A.

> County of Oakland by Kuhn v. Vista Disposal, Inc., 826 F.Supp. 218.

E.D.Mich. 1993. Complaint should not be dismissed on motion to dismiss for failure to state claim or motion for judgment on pleadings unless it appears without doubt that plaintiff can prove no set of facts in support of his claim which would entitle him to relief. Fed.Rules Civ.Proc.Rule 12(b)(6), (c), 28 U.S.C.A.

> Computer Leasco, Inc. v. Volvo White Truck Corp., 820 F.Supp. 326.

E.D.Mich. 1993. On motion to dismiss for failure to state a cause of action or motion for judgment on the pleadings, complaint should not be dismissed unless it appears without doubt that plaintiff can prove no set of facts in support of claim which would entitle him to relief. Fed.Rules Civ.Proc.Rule 12(b)(6), (c), 28 U.S.C.A.

> Greenan v. Romeo Village Police Dept., 819 F.Supp. 658.

E.D.Mich. 1992. In considering motion to dismiss complaint for failure to state claim upon which relief can be granted, district court must accept as true all factual allegations in complaint, and motion must be denied unless it appears beyond doubt that nonmoving party cannot prove set of facts which would permit

relief. Fed.Rules Civ.Proc.Rule 12(b)(6), 28 U.S.C.A.

Lindsey v. Jansante, 806 F.Supp. 651.

E.D.Mich. 1992. In ruling on motion to dismiss for failure to state claim upon which relief can be granted, district court must determine whether legally cognizable claims have been pled by accepting as true all factual allegations in complaint or countercomplaint, and motion must be denied unless it appears beyond doubt that nonmovant can prove no set of facts which would permit relief. Fed.Rules Civ.Proc. Rule 12(b)(6), 28 U.S.C.A.

Chartrand v. Chrysler Corp., 785 F.Supp. 666.

E.D.Mich. 1992. Complaint should not be dismissed unless it appears without doubt that plaintiff can prove no set of facts in support of claim which would entitle plaintiff to relief. Fed.Rules Civ.Proc.Rule 12(b)(6), (c), 28 U.S.C.A.

County of Oakland by Kuhn v. City of Detroit, 784 F.Supp. 1275.

E.D.Mich. 1990. Claim cannot be dismissed for failure to state claim upon which relief can be granted unless plaintiff fails to prove, beyond doubt, set of facts to support his claim for relief. Fed.Rules Civ.Proc.Rule 12(b)(6), 28 U.S.C.A.

Wilson v. Kiss, 751 F.Supp. 1249.

E.D.Mich. 1986. Legal sufficiency, rather than probability of success, is test to be applied in considering motion to dismiss for failure to state claim upon which relief could be granted. Fed.Rules Civ.Proc.Rule 12(b)(6), 28 U.S.C.A.

Ecclesiastical Order of Ism of Am, Inc. v. Chasin, 653 F.Supp. 1200, affirmed 845 F.2d 113.

W.D.Mich. 1997. Although complaint is to be liberally construed, it is still necessary that complaint contain more than bare assertions of legal conclusions to overcome motion to dismiss. Fed.Rules Civ.Proc.Rule 12(b)(6), 28 U.S.C.A.

Kearney v. Jandernoa, 979 F.Supp. 576.

W.D.Mich. 1997. Although complaint is to be liberally construed, it is still necessary that complaint contain more than bare assertions of legal conclusions in order to withstand motion to dismiss for failure to state a claim. Fed. Rules Civ.Proc.Rule 12(b)(6), 28 U.S.C.A.

Gibson v. Sain, 979 F.Supp. 557.

Dismissal of complaint for failure to state a claim is proper if complaint fails to allege element necessary for relief, or if an affirmative defense or other bar to relief appears on face of complaint, such as absolute immunity of defen-

dant. Fed.Rules Civ.Proc.Rule 12(b)(6), 28 U.S.C.A.

Gibson v. Sain, 979 F.Supp. 557.

W.D.Mich. 1996. Action may be dismissed if complaint fails to state claim upon which relief can be granted. Fed.Rules Civ.Proc.Rule 12(b)(6), 28 U.S.C.A.

Van Domelen v. Menominee County, 935 F.Supp. 918.

W.D.Mich. 1996. Dismissal of complaint is proper if complaint fails to allege element necessary for relief or if affirmative defense or other bar to relief is apparent from face of complaint, such as official immunity of defendant.

Emery v. U.S., 920 F.Supp. 788.

W.D.Mich. 1995. In ruling on motion to dismiss for failure to state claim, dismissal is proper if complaint fails to allege element necessary for relief, or affirmative defense or another matter precluding relief appears on face of complaint, including official immunity. Fed. Rules Civ.Proc.Rule 12(b)(6), 28 U.S.C.A.

Hilliard v. Shell Western E & P, Inc., 885 F.Supp. 169, reconsideration denied 1995 WL 549259.

W.D.Mich. 1994. Claim should not be dismissed unless it appears beyond doubt that plaintiff can prove no set of facts in support of claim that would entitle him to relief. Fed. Rules Civ.Proc.Rule 12(b)(6), 28 U.S.C.A.

Jones v. Stine, 843 F.Supp. 1186.

W.D.Mich. 1994. Dismissal for failure to state a claim is proper only if it is clear that no relief could be granted under any set of facts that could be proved consistent with allegations. Fed.Rules Civ.Proc.Rule 12(b)(6), 28 U.S.C.A.

Torrie By and Through Torrie v. Cwayna, 841 F.Supp. 1434.

W.D.Mich. 1993. Dismissal for failure to state claim is proper only if it is clear that no relief could be granted under any set of facts that could be proved consistent with the allegations. Fed.Rules Civ.Proc.Rule 12(b)(6), 28 U.S.C.A.

Hilliard v. Shell Western E & P, Inc., 836 F.Supp. 1365, reversed 149 F.3d 1183.

Dismissal for failure to state claim is proper if complaint fails to allege an element necessary for relief or if affirmative defense or other bar to relief is apparent from face of complaint, such as official immunity of defendant. Fed.Rules Civ.Proc.Rule 12(b)(6), 28 U.S.C.A.

Hilliard v. Shell Western E & P, Inc., 836 F.Supp. 1365, reversed 149 F.3d 1183.

W.D.Mich. 1993. In motion to dismiss for failure to state a claim, court's inquiry is limited to whether challenged pleadings set forth allegations sufficient to make out elements of right to relief. Fed.Rules Civ.Proc.Rules 9(b), 12(b)(6), 28 U.S.C.A.

> Sheldon Co. Profit Sharing Plan and Trust v. Smith, 828 F.Supp. 1262.

W.D.Mich. 1993. Court cannot dismiss plaintiff's complaint unless it appears beyond doubt plaintiff can prove no set of facts in support of its claim which would entitle it to relief. Fed.Rules Civ.Proc.Rule 12(b)(6), 28 U.S.C.A.

> Moore v. Johnson, 826 F.Supp. 1106.

W.D.Mich. 1993. Dismissal for failure to state claim on which relief can be granted is proper if it appears beyond doubt that plaintiff can prove no set of facts in support of claim that would entitle him to relief, if complaint fails to allege an element necessary for relief, or if affirmative defense or other bar to relief is apparent from face of complaint. Fed.Rules Civ.Proc.Rule 12(b)(6), 28 U.S.C.A.

> Theuerkauf v. United Vaccines Div. of Harlan Sprague Dawley, Inc., 821 F.Supp. 1238.

W.D.Mich. 1993. Claim should not be dismissed for failure to state claim unless it appears beyond doubt that plaintiff can prove no set of facts in support of claim which would entitle her to relief. Fed.Rules Civ.Proc.Rule 12(b)(6), 28 U.S.C.A.

> Coker on Behalf of Coker v. Henry, 813 F.Supp. 567, affirmed 25 F.3d 1047.

W.D.Mich. 1992. Dismissal for failure to state claim upon which relief can be granted is proper only if it appears beyond doubt that plaintiff can prove no set of facts in support of his claim which would entitle him to relief or if complaint fails to allege element necessary for relief, or if affirmative defense or other bar to relief is apparent from face of complaint. Fed. Rules Civ.Proc.Rule 12(b)(6), 28 U.S.C.A.

> Coplin and Associates, Inc. v. U.S., 814 F.Supp. 643, affirmed 27 F.3d 566.

W.D.Mich. 1991. In reviewing motion to dismiss for lack of subject matter jurisdiction, district court's inquiry is whether challenged pleading sets forth allegations sufficient to show that court has subject matter jurisdiction in the case; in making such determination, pleadings are to be taken as true and construed in light most favorable to party opposing the motion. Fed.Rules Civ.Proc.Rule 12(b)(1), 28 U.S.C.A.

> Cooper Industries, Inc. v. U.S. E.P.A., 775 F.Supp. 1027.

W.D.Mich. 1991. Court must deny motion to dismiss for failure to state claim unless it can be established beyond doubt that plaintiff can prove no set of facts in support of his claim which would entitle him to relief. Fed.Rules Civ.Proc.Rule 12(b)(6), 28 U.S.C.A.

> State of Mich. v. U.S., 773 F.Supp. 997, affirmed 994 F.2d 1197.

W.D.Mich. 1990. Court must deny motion to dismiss unless it can be established beyond doubt that plaintiff can prove no set of facts in support of his claim which would entitle him to relief. Fed.Rules Civ.Proc.Rule 12(b)(6), 28 U.S.C.A.

> White v. City of Muskegon, Mich., 749 F.Supp. 829.

W.D.Mich. 1989. Court cannot dismiss complaint unless it appears beyond doubt that plaintiff can prove no set of facts in support of its claim which would entitle it to relief. Fed. Rules Civ.Proc.Rule 12(b)(6), 28 U.S.C.A.

> Mercado v. Kingsley Area Schools/Traverse City Public Schools Adult Educ. Consortium, 727 F.Supp. 335.

W.D.Mich. 1982. Naph-Sol Refining Co. v. Murphy Oil Corp., 550 F.Supp. 297, affirmed in part, reversed in part Mobil Oil Corp. v. Department of Energy, 728 F.2d 1477, certiorari denied 104 S.Ct. 3545, 467 U.S. 1255, 82 L.Ed.2d 849, certiorari denied 104 S.Ct. 3545, 467 U.S. 1255, 82 L.Ed.2d 849.

D.Minn. 1996. Complaint should not be dismissed if it states claim on any legal theory. Vizenor v. Babbitt, 927 F.Supp. 1193.

D.Minn. 1994. Court will dismiss complaint only when it appears that plaintiff cannot prove any set of facts that supports claim.

> Ben Oehrleins and Sons and Daughter, Inc. v. Hennepin County, Minn., 867 F.Supp. 1430.

D.Minn. 1994. Court will dismiss complaint only when it appears that plaintiff cannot prove any set of facts that supports claim.

> Allstate Financial Corp. v. U.S., 860 F.Supp. 653.

D.Minn. 1994. Court will dismiss complaint only when it appears plaintiff cannot prove any set of facts that supports claim. Fed.Rules Civ.Proc.Rule 12, 28 U.S.C.A.

> Maxwell v. K Mart Corp., 851 F.Supp. 1343.

D.Minn. 1993. Because dismissal on pleadings is an extreme remedy, it is not favored by the courts and is employed only when it appears beyond a doubt that plaintiff can prove no set of facts in support of his claim which would entitle him to relief. Fed.Rules Civ.Proc.Rule 12(b)(6), 28 U.S.C.A.

> Slice v. Sons of Norway, 866 F.Supp. 397, affirmed 34 F.3d 630.

D.Minn. 1993. Court may dismiss complaint for failure to state a claim only if it is clear that no relief could be granted under any set of facts that could be proved consistent with the allegations. Fed.Rules Civ.Proc.Rule 12(b)(6), 28 U.S.C.A.

> Tonn v. U.S., 847 F.Supp. 711, affirmed 27 F.3d 1356, rehearing and suggestion for rehearing denied, certiorari denied 115 S.Ct. 1107, 513 U.S. 1153, 130 L.Ed.2d 1073, rehearing denied 115 S.Ct. 1726, 514 U.S. 1078, 131 L.Ed.2d 584.

D.Minn. 1993. Motion to dismiss will be granted only if it appears beyond doubt that plaintiff can prove no set of facts which would entitle him to relief.

> In re U.S. ex rel. Hall, 825 F.Supp. 1422, affirmed U.S. ex rel. Hall v. Creative Games Technology, Inc., 27 F.3d 572, certiorari denied 115 S.Ct. 1112, 513 U.S. 1155, 130 L.Ed.2d 1076.

D.Minn. 1991. Court may dismiss complaint only if it is clear that no relief could be granted under any set of facts that could be proved consistent with allegations, but court may not assume that plaintiffs can prove facts not alleged or that defendant violated laws in ways not alleged. Fed.Rules Civ.Proc.Rule 12(b), 28 U.S.C.A.

> Brennan v. Chestnut, 777 F.Supp. 1469, affirmed 973 F.2d 644.

N.D.Miss. 1998. To survive a motion to dismiss for failure to state a claim, a complaint must contain either direct allegations on every material point necessary to sustain a recovery or allegations from which an inference fairly may be drawn that evidence on these material points will be introduced at trial. Fed.Rules Civ.Proc.Rule 12(b)(6), 28 U.S.C.A.

> Myers v. Guardian Life Ins. Co. of America, Inc., 5 F.Supp.2d 423.

Conclusory allegations or legal conclusions masquerading as factual conclusions will not suffice to prevent dismissal for failure to state a claim. Fed.Rules Civ.Proc.Rule 12(b)(6), 28 U.S.C.A.

> Myers v. Guardian Life Ins. Co. of America, Inc., 5 F.Supp.2d 423.

Dismissal for failure to state a claim is never warranted because the court believes the plaintiff is unlikely to prevail on the merits. Fed.Rules Civ.Proc.Rule 12(b)(6), 28 U.S.C.A.

> Myers v. Guardian Life Ins. Co. of America, Inc., 5 F.Supp.2d 423.

Even if it appears almost a certainty that the facts alleged cannot be proved to support the claim, the complaint cannot be dismissed so long as it states a claim. Fed.Rules Civ.Proc. Rule 12(b)(6), 28 U.S.C.A.

> Myers v. Guardian Life Ins. Co. of America, Inc., 5 F.Supp.2d 423.

N.D.Miss. 1997. Dismissal for failure to state claim is never warranted because court believes plaintiff is unlikely to prevail on merits; even if it appears almost certainty that facts alleged cannot be proved to support claim, complaint cannot be dismissed as long as complaint states claim. Fed.Rules Civ.Proc.Rule 12(b)(6), 28 U.S.C.A.

> Moore v. Carroll County, Miss., 960 F.Supp. 1084.

N.D.Miss. 1993. Motion to dismiss should not be granted unless it appears beyond doubt that plaintiff can prove no set of facts in support of claim that would entitle him to relief.

> Prewitt v. Moore, 840 F.Supp. 436.

S.D.Miss. 1997. To survive motion to dismiss for failure to state claim, complaint must contain either direct allegations on every material point necessary to sustain recovery or contain allegations from which inference fairly may be drawn that evidence of those material points will be introduced at trial. Fed.Rules Civ.Proc. Rule 12(b)(6), 28 U.S.C.A.

> Columbia Gulf Transmission Co. v. U.S., 966 F.Supp. 1453.

S.D.Miss. 1994. Complaint should not be dismissed for failure to state a claim unless it appears beyond doubt that plaintiff can prove no set of facts in support of claims that would entitle him or her to relief. Fed.Rules Civ.Proc. Rule 12(b)(6), 28 U.S.C.A.

> Harper v. Forrest County, Mississippi, 859 F.Supp. 251, affirmed 55 F.3d 633.

S.D.Miss. 1994. Complaint should not be dismissed for failure to state claim unless it appears beyond doubt that plaintiff can prove no set of facts in support of his claims that would entitle him to relief. Fed.Rules Civ.Proc. Rule 12(b)(6), 28 U.S.C.A.

> California Union Ins. Co. v. City of Walnut Grove, Miss., 857 F.Supp. 515.

E.D.Mo. 1996. Court should not grant motion to dismiss for failure to state claim merely because complaint does not allege with precision each element of offense needed for recovery. Fed.Rules Civ.Proc.Rule 12(b)(6), 28 U.S.C.A.

> In re Ticketmaster Corp. Antitrust Litigation, 929 F.Supp. 1272, affirmed in part, vacated in part, reversed in part Campos v. Ticketmaster Corp., 140 F.3d 1166.

For purposes of motion to dismiss for failure to state claim, complaint is sufficient if it contains allegations from which inference may be drawn that evidence on material points will be introduced at trial.　Fed.Rules Civ.Proc.Rule 12(b)(6), 28 U.S.C.A.

> In re Ticketmaster Corp. Antitrust Litigation, 929 F.Supp. 1272, affirmed in part, vacated in part, reversed in part Campos v. Ticketmaster Corp., 140 F.3d 1166.

In ruling on motion to dismiss for failure to state claim, court must view complaint in light most favorable to plaintiffs and should not dismiss it merely because court doubts that plaintiffs will be able to prove all necessary allegations.　Fed.Rules Civ.Proc.Rule 12(b)(6), 28 U.S.C.A.

> In re Ticketmaster Corp. Antitrust Litigation, 929 F.Supp. 1272, affirmed in part, vacated in part, reversed in part Campos v. Ticketmaster Corp., 140 F.3d 1166.

E.D.Mo. 1996.　Motion to dismiss is likely to be granted only in the unusual case in which plaintiff includes allegations that show on face of the complaint that there is some insuperable bar to relief.

> Kelleher v. Aerospace Community Credit Union, 927 F.Supp. 361.

E.D.Mo. 1995.　Motion to dismiss for failure to state a claim is likely to be granted only in unusual case in which plaintiff includes allegations that show on face of complaint that there is some insuperable bar to relief.　Fed. Rules Civ.Proc.Rule 12(b)(6), 28 U.S.C.A.

> Hartman v. Smith & Davis Mfg. Co., 904 F.Supp. 983.

E.D.Mo. 1995.　Motion to dismiss for failure to state a claim will not be granted merely because complaint does not state every element necessary for recovery with precision.　Fed. Rules Civ.Proc.Rule 12(b)(6), 28 U.S.C.A.

> Mauzy v. Mexico School Dist. No. 59, 878 F.Supp. 153.

Complaint should not be dismissed for failure to state a claim unless it appears beyond a doubt that plaintiff can prove no set of facts in support of his claim which would entitle him to relief.　Fed.Rules Civ.Proc.Rule 12(b)(6), 28 U.S.C.A.

> Mauzy v. Mexico School Dist. No. 59, 878 F.Supp. 153.

E.D.Mo. 1994.　Cause of action should not be dismissed for failure to state claim upon which relief can be granted unless, from face of complaint, it appears beyond reasonable doubt that plaintiff can prove no set of facts in support of his claim which would entitle him to relief.　Fed.Rules Civ.Proc.Rule 12(b)(6), 28 U.S.C.A.

> Mathis v. American Group Life Ins. Co., 873 F.Supp. 1348.

E.D.Mo. 1994.　Cause of action should not be dismissed for failure to state a claim unless, from face of complaint, it appears beyond rea-

sonable doubt that plaintiff can prove no set of facts in support of his claim which would entitle him to relief.　Fed.Rules Civ.Proc.Rule 12(b)(6), 28 U.S.C.A.

> Wittmann v. U.S., 869 F.Supp. 726.

E.D.Mo. 1994.　Plaintiff's complaint should not be dismissed for failure to state claim unless it appears beyond doubt that plaintiff can prove no set of facts in support of claim which would entitle plaintiff to relief.　Fed. Rules Civ.Proc.Rule 12(b)(6), 28 U.S.C.A.

> Trans World Airlines, Inc. v. Berger, 864 F.Supp. 106.

E.D.Mo. 1993.　Court should not grant motion to dismiss merely because complaint does not state with precision every element of offense necessary for recovery.

> Russell v. City of Overland Police Dept., 838 F.Supp. 1350.

Pro se complaint is to be liberally construed and should not be dismissed unless plaintiff can prove no set of facts to support claim.

> Russell v. City of Overland Police Dept., 838 F.Supp. 1350.

E.D.Mo. 1993.　Cause of action should not be dismissed for failure to state claim unless, from face of complaint, it appears beyond reasonable doubt that plaintiff can prove no set of facts in support of his claim which would entitle him to relief.

> Resolution Trust Corp. v. Gershman, 829 F.Supp. 1095.

E.D.Mo. 1993.　Court should not grant motion to dismiss merely because complaint does not state with precision every element of offense necessary for recovery.

> Gruben v. Famous-Barr Co., 823 F.Supp. 664.

Complaint is sufficient if it contains allegations from which an inference can be drawn that evidence on these material points will be introduced at trial.

> Gruben v. Famous-Barr Co., 823 F.Supp. 664.

Court should not dismiss complaint unless it appears beyond reasonable doubt that plaintiff can prove no set of facts in support of his claim which would entitle him to relief.

> Gruben v. Famous-Barr Co., 823 F.Supp. 664.

Motion to dismiss is likely to be granted only in unusual case in which plaintiff includes allegations that show on face of complaint that there is some insuperable bar to relief.

> Gruben v. Famous-Barr Co., 823 F.Supp. 664.

E.D.Mo. 1992.　Court should not grant motion to dismiss merely because complaint does not state with precision every element of offense necessary for recovery, and complaint is sufficient if it contains allegations from which inference can be drawn that evidence on these material points will be introduced at trial. Fed. Rules Civ.Proc.Rule 12(b)(6), 28 U.S.C.A.

Travis v. Frank, 804 F.Supp. 1160.

Court should not dismiss complaint unless it appears beyond a reasonable doubt that plaintiff can prove no set of facts in support of claim which would entitle him to relief; thus, motion to dismiss is likely to be granted only in the unusual case in which plaintiff includes allegations that show on the face of the complaint that there is some insuperable bar to relief. Fed. Rules Civ.Proc.Rule 12(b)(6), 28 U.S.C.A.

Travis v. Frank, 804 F.Supp. 1160.

E.D.Mo. 1992. Pro se complaint is to be liberally construed and should not be dismissed unless plaintiff can prove no set of facts to support claims.

Logan v. U.S., 792 F.Supp. 663, affirmed 978 F.2d 1263.

E.D.Mo. 1992. Court should not grant motion to dismiss merely because complaint does not state with precision every element of the offense necessary for recovery.

Wright v. Caspari, 779 F.Supp. 1025.

E.D.Mo. 1991. Motion to dismiss is likely to be granted only in unusual case in which plaintiff includes allegations that show on face of complaint that there is some insuperable bar to relief.

O'Dell v. McSpadden, 780 F.Supp. 639, affirmed 994 F.2d 843, certiorari denied 114 S.Ct. 260, 510 U.S. 895, 126 L.Ed.2d 212.

E.D.Mo. 1991. Complaint is sufficient if it contains allegations from which inference can be drawn that evidence on material points will be introduced at trial. Fed.Rules Civ.Proc.Rule 12(b)(6), 28 U.S.C.A.

Cook v. Foster Forbes Glass, 776 F.Supp. 1391.

E.D.Mo. 1991. Motion to dismiss will not be granted merely because complaint does not state with precision every element necessary for recovery.

Sweeney v. Kroger Co., 773 F.Supp. 1266.

E.D.Mo. 1991. Court should not grant motion to dismiss merely because complaint does not state with precision every element of offense necessary for recovery; complaint is sufficient if it contains allegations from which inference can be drawn that evidence on these material points will be introduced at trial.

Waldermeyer v. ITT Consumer Financial Corp., 767 F.Supp. 989.

E.D.Mo. 1990. Motion to dismiss will not be granted merely because complaint does not state with precision every element necessary for recovery.

Fercom Aquaculture Corp. v. U.S., 740 F.Supp. 736.

Complaint should not be dismissed unless it appears beyond doubt that plaintiff can prove no set of facts in support of his or her claim which entitle him or her to relief.

Fercom Aquaculture Corp. v. U.S., 740 F.Supp. 736.

E.D.Mo. 1990. Dismissal is not warranted merely because complaint does not state with precision every element necessary for recovery.

Formanek v. Arment, 737 F.Supp. 72.

E.D.Mo. 1985. A motion to dismiss will not be granted merely because the complaint does not state every element necessary for recovery with precision.

Miener v. Special School Dist. of St. Louis County, Mo., 607 F.Supp. 1425, affirmed in part, reversed in part 800 F.2d 749.

E.D.Mo. 1983. Moessmer v. U.S., 569 F.Supp. 782, affirmed 760 F.2d 236, 79 A.L.R. Fed. 821.

W.D.Mo. 1995. As practical matter dismissal for failure to state cause of action is likely to be granted only in unusual case in which plaintiff includes allegations that show on face of complaint that there is some insuperable bar to relief. Fed.Rules Civ.Proc.Rule 12(b)(6), 28 U.S.C.A.

F.T.C. v. Freeman Hosp., 914 F.Supp. 331.

W.D.Mo. 1994. Motion to dismiss should not be granted unless it appears beyond doubt that plaintiff can prove no set of facts in support of claim which would entitle her to relief.

Osborn v. Professional Service Industries Inc., 872 F.Supp. 679.

W.D.Mo. 1993. In considering motion to dismiss, court liberally construes complaint in light most favorable to plaintiff and will draw all inferences which may be drawn from the facts alleged in favor of the plaintiffs; court will not dismiss complaint unless it appears complainant can prove no set of facts which would entitle him or her to relief.

Boyle v. City of Liberty, Mo., 833 F.Supp. 1436.

W.D.Mo. 1985. A complaint will not be dismissed merely because the court doubts that plaintiff will prevail on the action.

Honeywell v. Village of Lakeside, 604 F.Supp. 932.

W.D.Mo. 1984. Gale v. Moore, 587 F.Supp. 1491, affirmed as modified 763 F.2d 341.

D.Mont. 1991. Motion to dismiss for failure to state claim for relief is not to be granted unless it appears to certainty that plaintiff is entitled to no relief under any stated facts which could be proved in support of claim. Fed.Rules Civ.Proc.Rule 12(b)(6), 28 U.S.C.A.

　　Neumann v. Aid Ass'n for Lutherans, 775 F.Supp. 1350.

D.Mont. 1989. Dismissal of action is improper where material allegations of plaintiff's complaint, viewed in their most favorable light, are legally sufficient to establish claim. Fed. Rules Civ.Proc.Rule 12(b)(6), 28 U.S.C.A.

　　Sternhagen v. Dow Co., 711 F.Supp. 1027.

D.Neb. 1963. Rhodes v. Van Steenberg, 225 F.Supp. 113, affirmed 334 F.2d 709, certiorari denied 85 S.Ct. 263, 379 U.S. 915, 13 L.Ed.2d 186, motion denied 258 F.Supp. 546, affirmed 418 F.2d 1309, certiorari denied 90 S.Ct. 1382, 397 U.S. 1049, 25 L.Ed.2d 662.

D.Nev. 1995. Court may grant a motion to dismiss for failure to state a claim on which relief can be granted only if it appears beyond a doubt that plaintiff can prove no set of facts in support of claim which would entitle him to relief. Fed.Rules Civ.Proc.Rule 12(b)(6), 28 U.S.C.A.

　　Fox v. Sierra Development Co., 876 F.Supp. 1169.

D.Nev. 1994. District court may not grant motion to dismiss for failure to state claim unless it appears beyond doubt that plaintiff can prove no set of facts in support of claim which would entitle him to relief. Fed.Rules Civ.Proc. Rule 12(b)(6), 28 U.S.C.A.

　　Churchill v. Barach, 863 F.Supp. 1266.

D.Nev. 1994. Court may not grant motion to dismiss for failure to state claim unless it appears beyond doubt that plaintiff can prove no set of facts in support of his claim which would entitle him to relief.

　　Hallett v. U.S. Dept. of Navy, 850 F.Supp. 874.

D.Nev. 1992. Complaint may be dismissed for failure to state a claim if there is no set of facts within complaint's framework that would entitle complainant to relief. Fed.Rules Civ. Proc.Rule 12(b)(6), 28 U.S.C.A.

　　Hutchison v. KFC Corp., 809 F.Supp. 68.

D.Nev. 1992. Court may grant motion to dismiss for failure to state a claim on which relief can be granted only if it appears beyond doubt that plaintiff can prove no set of facts in support of claim which would entitle him to relief.

　　Tahoe Sierra Preservation Council, Inc. v. Tahoe Regional Planning Agency, 808 F.Supp. 1484, affirmed in part, reversed in part 34 F.3d 753, opinion amended 42

F.3d 1306, certiorari denied California v. Tahoe Sierra Preservation Council, 115 S.Ct. 1401, 514 U.S. 1036, 131 L.Ed.2d 288, certiorari denied 115 S.Ct. 1401, 514 U.S. 1036, 131 L.Ed.2d 288, on remand 992 F.Supp. 1218.

D.Nev. 1992. Court may grant motion to dismiss for failure to state a claim on which relief can be granted only if it appears beyond doubt that plaintiff can prove no set of facts in support of his claim which would entitled him to relief. Fed.Rules Civ.Proc.Rule 12(b)(6), 28 U.S.C.A.

　　Tahoe Sierra Preservation Council, Inc. v. Tahoe Regional Planning Agency, 808 F.Supp. 1474, affirmed in part, reversed in part 34 F.3d 753, opinion amended 42 F.3d 1306, certiorari denied California v. Tahoe Sierra Preservation Council, 115 S.Ct. 1401, 514 U.S. 1036, 131 L.Ed.2d 288, certiorari denied 115 S.Ct. 1401, 514 U.S. 1036, 131 L.Ed.2d 288, on remand 992 F.Supp. 1218.

D.Nev. 1985. Essential elements of claim asserted must be supplied by actual pleadings, or the claim will fall to motion to dismiss. Fed.Rules Civ.Proc.Rule 12(b)(6), 28 U.S.C.A.

　　Laxalt v. McClatchy, 622 F.Supp. 737.

D.N.H. 1995. Motion to dismiss for failure to state a claim focuses not on whether plaintiff will ultimately prevail but whether claimant is entitled to offer evidence to support claims. Fed.Rules Civ.Proc.Rule 12(b)(6), 28 U.S.C.A.

　　Gardner v. Blue Mountain Forest Ass'n, 902 F.Supp. 14.

D.N.H. 1995. Whether a motion to dismiss for failure to state a claim will be successful is not dependent upon likelihood of success on merits, but rather upon whether plaintiff is entitled to offer evidence to support his claim; thus, dismissal should be granted only if it clearly appears, according to facts alleged, that plaintiff cannot recover on any viable theory. Fed.Rules Civ.Proc.Rule 12(b)(6), 28 U.S.C.A.

　　Kopf v. Chloride Power Electronics, Inc., 882 F.Supp. 1183.

D.N.H. 1994. In ruling on defendant's motion to dismiss complaint, district court reviews allegations of complaint in light most favorable to plaintiff, accepts all material allegations as true, and dismisses plaintiff's claims only if no set of facts entitles him to relief. Fed.Rules Civ.Proc.Rule 12(b)(6), 28 U.S.C.A.

　　Grunbeck v. Dime Sav. Bank of New York, FSB, 848 F.Supp. 294, vacated 74 F.3d 331.

D.N.H. 1993. Court must deny motion to dismiss for failure to state claim unless it plainly appears that plaintiff can prove no set of facts thereunder which would entitle her to recover. Fed.Rules Civ.Proc.Rule 12(b)(6), 28 U.S.C.A.

> Pension Plan of Public Service Co. of New Hampshire v. KPMG Peat Marwick, 815 F.Supp. 52.

D.N.H. 1992. On a motion to dismiss for failure to state a claim, a plaintiff need not establish likelihood of success on merits, but only whether she is entitled to offer evidence to support her claim. Fed.Rules Civ.Proc.Rule 12(b)(6), 28 U.S.C.A.

> Godfrey v. Perkin-Elmer Corp., 794 F.Supp. 1179.

D.N.H. 1992. In deciding motion to dismiss for failure to state claim on which relief can be granted, court must accept factual allegations set forth in complaint as true, indulging every reasonable inference in plaintiff's favor, and complaint can be dismissed only if it appears beyond doubt that plaintiff can prove no set of facts which would entitle him to relief. Fed.Rules Civ.Proc.Rule 12(b)(6), 28 U.S.C.A.

> Greenberg v. Howtek, Inc., 790 F.Supp. 1181.

D.N.H. 1991. On motion to dismiss, trial court's consideration is limited to allegations contained in complaint and those allegations are to be construed in light most favorable to plaintiff and taken as admitted, with dismissal to be ordered only if plaintiff is not entitled to relief under any set of facts he could prove. Fed.Rules Civ.Proc.Rule 12, 28 U.S.C.A.

> Orono Karate, Inc. v. Fred Villari Studio of Self Defense, Inc., 776 F.Supp. 47.

D.N.H. 1990. In ruling on motion to dismiss for failure to state claim, district court follows well-established requirement that material facts alleged in complaint are to be construed in light most favorable to plaintiff and taken as admitted, with dismissal to be ordered only if plaintiff is not entitled to relief under any set of facts he could prove. Fed.Rules Civ.Proc. Rule 12(b)(6), 28 U.S.C.A.

> Save On Surplus Pension Plan v. United Saver's Bancorp, Inc., 760 F.Supp. 971, on reconsideration 1990 WL 264538.

D.N.H. 1987. Standard for granting motion to dismiss is not likelihood of success on merits, but is whether plaintiff is entitled to offer evidence to support his claim.

> Behre v. Thomas, 665 F.Supp. 89, affirmed 843 F.2d 1385.

D.N.J. 1997. Rule governing motion to dismiss for failure to state claim authorizes court to dismiss claim on basis of dispositive issue of law. Fed.Rules Civ.Proc.Rule 12(b)(6), 28 U.S.C.A.

> Crossroads Cogeneration Corp. v. Orange and Rockland Utilities, Inc., 969 F.Supp. 907.

D.N.J. 1996. Threshold to withstand motion to dismiss for lack of subject-matter jurisdiction is lower than that required for motion to dismiss for failure to state claim. Fed.Rules Civ.Proc.Rule 12(b)(1, 6), 28 U.S.C.A.

> Watts v. I.R.S., 925 F.Supp. 271.

D.N.J. 1995. Motion to dismiss for failure to state claim may be granted only if, accepting all well-pleaded allegations in complaint as true, and viewing them in light most favorable to plaintiff, plaintiff is not entitled to relief. Fed.Rules Civ.Proc.Rule 12(b)(6), 28 U.S.C.A.

> Stehney v. Perry, 907 F.Supp. 806, affirmed 101 F.3d 925.

For purposes of motion to dismiss for failure to state claim, party is required only to plead short plain statement of claim showing that pleader is entitled to relief in order to set forth valid claim. Fed.Rules Civ.Proc.Rules 8(a), 12(b)(6), 28 U.S.C.A.

> Stehney v. Perry, 907 F.Supp. 806, affirmed 101 F.3d 925.

D.N.J. 1995. In deciding motion to dismiss, district court must accept all factual allegations contained in complaint as true and draw all reasonable inferences therefrom in favor of plaintiff; test is whether, under any reasonable reading of the pleadings, plaintiff may be entitled to relief. Fed.Rules Civ.Proc. Rule 12(b)(6), 28 U.S.C.A.

> Presbytery of New Jersey of the Orthodox Presbyterian Church v. Florio, 902 F.Supp. 492, affirmed 99 F.3d 101, certiorari denied 117 S.Ct. 1334, 137 L.Ed.2d 494.

D.N.J. 1995. Motion to dismiss for failure to state claim upon which relief can be granted may be granted only if accepting all well-pleaded allegations in complaint as true, and viewing them in light most favorable to plaintiff, plaintiff is not entitled to relief. Fed.Rules Civ.Proc. Rule 12(b)(6), 28 U.S.C.A.

> Turner-Adeniji v. Accountants on Call, 892 F.Supp. 645.

D.N.J. 1995. Judge's disbelief of complaint's actual allegations is not sufficient to support dismissal for failure to state a claim. Fed.Rules Civ.Proc.Rule 12(b)(6), 28 U.S.C.A.

> Zucker v. Quasha, 891 F.Supp. 1010, affirmed 82 F.3d 408, certiorari denied 117 S.Ct. 85, 136 L.Ed.2d 42.

D.N.J. 1994. Court may not dismiss complaint for failure to state claim upon which relief can be granted unless it appears beyond doubt that plaintiff can prove no set of facts in support of claim which would entitle him or her to relief. Fed.Rules Civ.Proc.Rule 12(b)(6), 28 U.S.C.A.

> Hakimoglu v. Trump Taj Mahal Associates, 876 F.Supp. 625, affirmed 70 F.3d 291.

To withstand motion to dismiss complaint for failure to state claim upon which relief can be granted, it is not necessary for plaintiff to plead evidence, and it is not necessary to plead facts that serve as basis for claim. Fed.Rules Civ.Proc.Rule 12(b)(6), 28 U.S.C.A.

Hakimoglu v. Trump Taj Mahal Associates, 876 F.Supp. 625, affirmed 70 F.3d 291.

D.N.J. 1994. Complaint should not be dismissed for failure to state a claim if plaintiff can prove any set of facts in support of his claim that would entitle him to relief. Fed.Rules Civ.Proc.Rule 12(b)(6), 28 U.S.C.A.

Johnson v. State of N.J., 869 F.Supp. 289, reconsideration denied 1995 WL 46367.

D.N.J. 1994. It is not necessary for plaintiff to plead evidence, and it is not necessary to plead facts that serve as basis for a claim, in order to survive motion to dismiss for failure to state claim upon which relief may be granted. Fed.Rules Civ.Proc.Rule 12(b)(6), 28 U.S.C.A.

Morris v. Azzi, 866 F.Supp. 149.

D.N.J. 1994. Dismissal of claim for failure to state claim upon which relief can be granted should be granted only if it appears beyond doubt that plaintiff can prove no set of facts in support of claim which would entitle him to relief. Fed.Rules Civ.Proc.Rule 12(b)(6), 28 U.S.C.A.

Bishop v. Okidata, Inc., 864 F.Supp. 416.

D.N.J. 1994. Court may dismiss complaint for failure to state claim upon which relief may be granted when it appears beyond doubt that no relief could be granted under any set of facts which could be proved consistent with allegations, but complaint should not be dismissed for failure to state claim unless it appears beyond doubt that plaintiff can prove no set of facts in support of his claim which would entitle him to relief. Fed.Rules Civ.Proc.Rule 12(b)(6), 28 U.S.C.A.

Biase v. Kaplan, 852 F.Supp. 268.

D.N.J. 1994. Complaint should be dismissed for failure to state a claim only where plaintiff can prove no set of facts in support of her claim which would entitle her to relief. Fed.Rules Civ.Proc.Rule 12, 28 U.S.C.A.

Crawford v. West Jersey Health Systems (Voorhees Div.), 847 F.Supp. 1232.

D.N.J. 1994. Dismissals for failure to state a claim upon which relief can be granted are warranted only in cases in which it appears beyond doubt that plaintiff can prove no set of facts in support of his claim which would entitle him to relief. Fed.Rules Civ.Proc., Rule 12(b)(6), 28 U.S.C.A.; 18 U.S.C.A. § 1962(c, d).

O'Rourke v. Crosley, 847 F.Supp. 1208.

D.N.J. 1993. Plaintiff's complaint must be dismissed for failure to state claim if defendant demonstrates beyond doubt that plaintiff can prove no set of facts in support of his claim which would entitle him to relief. Fed.Rules Civ.Proc.Rule 12(b)(6), 28 U.S.C.A.

Rolo v. City Investing Co. Liquidating Trust, 845 F.Supp. 182, affirmed 43 F.3d 1462, vacated on rehearing 66 F.3d 312, on remand 897 F.Supp. 826, affirmed 155 F.3d 644, vacated 66 F.3d 312, on remand 897 F.Supp. 826, affirmed 155 F.3d 644.

D.N.J. 1993. Court may not dismiss complaint for failure to state claim upon which relief can be granted unless it appears beyond doubt that plaintiff can prove no set of facts in support of his claim which would entitle him to relief. Fed.Rules Civ.Proc.Rule 12(b)(6), 28 U.S.C.A.

Renz v. Schreiber, 832 F.Supp. 766.

D.N.J. 1992. Court may dismiss a complaint for failure to state a claim where it appears beyond doubt that no relief could be granted under any set of facts which could be proved consistent with allegations. Fed.Rules Civ.Proc.Rule 12(b)(6), 28 U.S.C.A.

Bermingham v. Sony Corp. of America, Inc., 820 F.Supp. 834, affirmed 37 F.3d 1485.

D.N.J. 1992. Court may dismiss case for failure to state a claim upon which relief can be granted if it appears beyond doubt that plaintiff can prove no set of facts in support of claim which would entitle him to relief. Fed.Rules Civ.Proc.Rule 12(b)(6), 28 U.S.C.A.

Westinghouse Elec. Corp. by Levit v. Franklin, 789 F.Supp. 1313, reversed 993 F.2d 349.

D.N.J. 1992. Complaint cannot be dismissed for failure to state claim unless court is certain that no set of facts can be proved that would entitle plaintiff to relief. Fed.Rules Civ. Proc.Rule 12(b)(6), 28 U.S.C.A.

Pelullo v. Patterson, 788 F.Supp. 234.

D.N.J. 1992. Court may dismiss complaint for failure to state claim where it appears beyond doubt that no relief could be granted under any set of facts which could be proved consistent with allegations. Fed.Rules Civ. Proc.Rule 12(b)(6), 28 U.S.C.A.

Casper v. Paine Webber Group, Inc., 787 F.Supp. 1480.

D.N.J. 1991. Complaint should not be dismissed for failure to state a claim unless it appears beyond a doubt that plaintiff can prove no set of facts in support of claim which would entitle him to relief.

Pygatt v. Painters' Local No. 277, Intern. Broth. of Painters & Allied Trades, 763 F.Supp. 1301.

Motions to dismiss should be granted sparingly and only where complaint discloses that plaintiff cannot possibly prove case entitling him to relief.

> Pygatt v. Painters' Local No. 277, Intern. Broth. of Painters & Allied Trades, 763 F.Supp. 1301.

D.N.J. 1990. In ruling on motion to dismiss for failure to state a claim, cause of action should not be dismissed unless it appears beyond doubt that plaintiff can prove no set of facts in support of his or her claim which would entitle him or her to relief. Fed.Rules Civ.Proc. Rule 12(b)(6), 28 U.S.C.A.

> Sandom v. Travelers Mortg. Services, Inc., 752 F.Supp. 1240, 30 Wage & Hour Cas. (BNA) 228.

D.N.J. 1990. A party seeking to dismiss on basis of failure to state a claim upon which relief could be granted must show that the plaintiff can prove no set of facts in support of its claim that would entitle it to relief by law, and judge must consider all facts alleged by plaintiff as true, and must draw all reasonable inferences in favor of plaintiff. Fed.Rules Civ. Proc.Rule 12(b)(6), 28 U.S.C.A.

> Connor v. U.S. E.E.O.C., 736 F.Supp. 570.

D.N.M. 1995. For purposes of motion to dismiss, material allegations of complaint must be accepted as true, court must construe pleadings liberally, and if any possibility of relief exists, claims should not be dismissed.

> La Compania Ocho, Inc. v. U.S. Forest Service, 874 F.Supp. 1242.

D.N.M. 1994. Dismissal for failure to state a claim upon which relief can be granted is appropriate when complaint raises an arguable question of law which district court ultimately finds is correctly resolved against plaintiff. Fed.Rules Civ.Proc.Rule 12(b)(6), 28 U.S.C.A.

> Valdez v. Albuquerque Public Schools, 875 F.Supp. 740.

D.N.M. 1994. Dismissal is appropriate only if it appears beyond a doubt that plaintiff can prove no set of facts in support of his claim which would entitle him to relief.

> Tafoya v. Bobroff, 865 F.Supp. 742, affirmed 74 F.3d 1250.

On motion to dismiss, District Court must construe pleadings liberally, and, if any possibility of relief exists, should not dismiss claim.

> Tafoya v. Bobroff, 865 F.Supp. 742, affirmed 74 F.3d 1250.

D.N.M. 1993. On motion to dismiss for failure to state claim, federal district court views facts in light most favorable to plaintiff, and grants motion to dismiss when plaintiff can establish no set of facts that entitle him to relief. Fed.Rules Civ.Proc.Rule 12, 28 U.S.C.A.

> Schwartzman, Inc. v. General Elec. Co., 848 F.Supp. 942.

D.N.M. 1993. For purposes of motion to dismiss, material allegations of complaint must be accepted as true; dismissal is appropriate only if it appears beyond doubt that plaintiff can prove no set of facts in support of his claim which would entitle him to relief. Fed.Rules Civ.Proc.Rule 12(b)(6), 28 U.S.C.A.

> Schwartzman, Inc. v. Atchison, Topeka & Santa Fe Ry. Co., 842 F.Supp. 475.

D.N.M. 1993. Complaint should not be dismissed unless it appears beyond doubt that plaintiff can prove no set of facts in support of his claim which would entitle him to relief.

> Ruiz v. Kepler, 832 F.Supp. 1444.

D.N.M. 1990. Complaint should not be dismissed unless it appears beyond reasonable doubt that plaintiff can prove no set of facts in support of claim which entitle him to relief; court must construe pleadings liberally, and if there is any possibility of relief, then case should not be dismissed.

> U.S. v. $31,000 in U.S. Currency, 740 F.Supp. 803.

D.N.M. 1987. While detailed listing of facts is not required, general legal conclusions will seldom satisfy pleader's duty to state grounds upon which claim rests, and will not survive motion to dismiss where no facts are alleged to support conclusions. Fed.Rules Civ. Proc.Rule 8(a)(2), 28 U.S.C.A.

> Romero v. Otero, 678 F.Supp. 1535.

E.D.N.Y. 1998. For purposes of a motion to dismiss for failure to state a claim, a plaintiff need not set out in detail the facts upon which his claim is based, so long as he states his claim in a manner to give the defendant fair notice of what his claim is and the grounds upon which it rests. Fed.Rules Civ.Proc.Rule 12(b)(6), 28 U.S.C.A.

> Great Atlantic & Pacific Tea Co., Inc. v. Town of East Hampton, 997 F.Supp. 340.

Where a complaint charges each element necessary to recover, dismissal of the case for failure to set out evidential facts can seldom be warranted. Fed.Rules Civ.Proc.Rule 12(b)(6), 28 U.S.C.A.

> Great Atlantic & Pacific Tea Co., Inc. v. Town of East Hampton, 997 F.Supp. 340.

E.D.N.Y. 1998. Where complaint is filed that charges each element necessary to recover, dismissal of case for failure to set out evidential facts can seldom be warranted. Fed.Rules Civ. Proc.Rule 12(b)(6), 28 U.S.C.A.

> Stordeur v. Computer Associates Intern., Inc., 995 F.Supp. 94.

E.D.N.Y. 1997. While liberal standard governs motions to dismiss for failure to state claim, bald assertions and conclusions of law will not suffice. Fed.Rules Civ.Proc.Rule 12(b)(6), 28 U.S.C.A.

Harary v. Allstate Ins. Co., 983 F.Supp. 95.

E.D.N.Y. 1996. Where complaint is filed that charges each element necessary to recover on claim, dismissal of case for failure to set out essential facts can seldom be warranted. Fed. Rules Civ.Proc.Rule 12(b)(6), 28 U.S.C.A.

Russell v. Northrop Grumman Corp., 921 F.Supp. 143.

Complaint whereby it is legally feasible that relief could be granted under any set of facts consistent with allegations will survive motion to dismiss. Fed.Rules Civ.Proc.Rule 12(b)(6), 28 U.S.C.A.

Russell v. Northrop Grumman Corp., 921 F.Supp. 143.

E.D.N.Y. 1996. If complaint charges each element necessary to recover, dismissal for failure to set out evidential facts can seldom be warranted; individual allegations, however, that are so baldly conclusory that they fail to give notice of basic events and circumstances of which plaintiff complains are meaningless and insufficient to state claim. Fed.Rules Civ.Proc. Rule 12(b)(6), 28 U.S.C.A.

Greenberg v. New York State, 919 F.Supp. 637.

Pro se party's general conclusions, completely unsupported by specific allegations of fact, are not sufficient to overcome motion to dismiss complaint for failure to state claim upon which relief can be granted. Fed.Rules Civ.Proc.Rule 12(b)(6), 28 U.S.C.A.

Greenberg v. New York State, 919 F.Supp. 637.

E.D.N.Y. 1995. If complaint is so confused, ambiguous, vague, or otherwise unintelligible that its true substance, if any, is well disguised, court may dismiss it. Fed.Rules Civ. Proc.Rule 8(a), 28 U.S.C.A.

Burke v. Dowling, 944 F.Supp. 1036.

E.D.N.Y. 1995. On motion to dismiss, defendants must demonstrate that plaintiffs' claims cannot succeed under any interpretation of facts.

Rini v. Zwirn, 886 F.Supp. 270.

E.D.N.Y. 1994. Motion to dismiss for failure to state claim should be granted only when it appears beyond doubt that plaintiff can prove no set of facts in support of his claim which would entitle him to relief. Fed.Rules Civ.Proc. Rule 12(b)(6), 28 U.S.C.A.

Williams v. Friedman, 866 F.Supp. 88.

E.D.N.Y. 1994. District court may grant motion to dismiss for failure to state claim only where it is beyond doubt that plaintiff cannot prove any set of facts supporting entitlement to relief. Fed.Rules Civ.Proc.Rule 12(b)(6), 28 U.S.C.A.

Schonholz v. Long Island Jewish Medical Center, 858 F.Supp. 350.

E.D.N.Y. 1994. Court may grant motion to dismiss for failure to state claim only when it is beyond doubt that plaintiff cannot prove any set of facts supporting entitlement to relief. Fed. Rules Civ.Proc.Rule 12(b)(6), 28 U.S.C.A.

Campo v. 1st Nationwide Bank, 857 F.Supp. 264.

E.D.N.Y. 1994. Court may grant motion to dismiss for failure to state a claim only where it is beyond doubt that plaintiff cannot prove any set of facts supporting entitlement to relief. Fed.Rules Civ.Proc.Rule 12(b)(6), 28 U.S.C.A.

Julian v. New York City Transit Authority, 857 F.Supp. 242, affirmed 52 F.3d 312.

E.D.N.Y. 1994. Complaint should not be dismissed for failure to state claim unless it appears beyond doubt that plaintiff can prove no set of facts in support of claim which would entitle him to relief, and pro se complaints are to be construed with even greater liberality. Fed.Rules Civ.Proc.Rule 12(b)(6), 28 U.S.C.A.

Levy v. Lerner, 853 F.Supp. 636, affirmed 52 F.3d 312.

E.D.N.Y. 1994. Admonition not to dismiss for failure to state claim unless it appears beyond doubt that plaintiff can prove no set of facts in support of his claim that would entitle him to relief assumes greater weight if complaint alleges violation of civil rights. Fed. Rules Civ.Proc.Rule 12(b)(6), 28 U.S.C.A.

Respass v. New York City Police Dept., 852 F.Supp. 173.

E.D.N.Y. 1994. Court should not dismiss complaint for failure to state a claim unless it appears beyond doubt that plaintiff can prove no set of facts in support of his claim which would entitle him to relief. Fed.Rules Civ.Proc. Rule 12(b)(6), 28 U.S.C.A.

Bezerra v. County of Nassau, 846 F.Supp. 214.

E.D.N.Y. 1994. On motion to dismiss for failure to state claim, court should not dismiss complaint unless it appears beyond doubt that plaintiff can prove no set of facts in support of his claim which would entitle him to relief. Fed.Rules Civ.Proc.Rule 12(b)(6), 28 U.S.C.A.

En Vogue v. UK Optical Ltd., 843 F.Supp. 838.

E.D.N.Y. 1994. Motion to dismiss must be denied, unless movant successfully persuades court beyond doubt that plaintiff can prove no set of facts in support of her claim which would entitle her to relief, and court must apply this standard with particular strictness where complaint alleges violation of plaintiff's civil rights. Fed.Rules Civ.Proc.Rule 12(b)(6), 28 U.S.C.A.; Civil Rights Act of 1964, § 701 et seq., 42 U.S.C.A. § 2000e et seq.; 42 U.S.C.A. § 1981; N.Y.McKinney's Executive Law § 296; New York City Administrative Code, § 8–101 et seq.

> Alie v. NYNEX Corp., 158 F.R.D. 239.

E.D.N.Y. 1993. On motion to dismiss, court must limit its analysis to four corners of complaint and may dismiss complaint only when it is clear that plaintiff can prove no set of facts upon which he would be entitled to relief. Fed.Rules Civ.Proc.Rule 12(b)(6), 28 U.S.C.A.

> Bharucha v. Reuters Holdings PLC, 810 F.Supp. 37.

E.D.N.Y. 1992. Complaint will be dismissed if plaintiffs can prove no set of facts supporting their claims.

> Bilick v. Eagle Elec. Mfg. Co., Inc., 807 F.Supp. 243.

E.D.N.Y. 1992. On motion to dismiss complaint for failure to state claim upon which relief can be granted, complaint is construed in light most favorable to plaintiff, i.e., read with great generosity, and should not be dismissed unless it appears beyond doubt that plaintiff can prove no set of facts in support of his claim that would entitle him to relief. Fed.Rules Civ.Proc. Rule 12(b)(6), 28 U.S.C.A.

> U.S. v. Private Sanitation Industry Ass'n of Nassau/Suffolk, Inc., 793 F.Supp. 1114.

E.D.N.Y. 1991. Court should not dismiss complaint for failure to state claim unless it appears beyond doubt that plaintiff can prove no set of facts in support of claim which would entitle him to relief. Fed.Rules Civ.Proc.Rule 12(b)(6), 28 U.S.C.A.

> Cruz v. Robert Abbey, Inc., 778 F.Supp. 605.

E.D.N.Y. 1991. A complaint cannot be dismissed for failure to state a claim unless it appears beyond a doubt that the plaintiff can prove no set of facts in support of his claim which would entitle him to relief.

> Plotkin v. Bearings Ltd., 777 F.Supp. 1105.

E.D.N.Y. 1991. Complaint cannot be dismissed for failure to state claim unless it appears beyond doubt that plaintiff can prove no set of facts in support of his or her claim which would entitle him or her to relief. Fed.Rules Civ.Proc.Rule 12(b)(6), 28 U.S.C.A.

> Fickling v. Com. of Australia, 775 F.Supp. 66.

E.D.N.Y. 1991. A complaint cannot be dismissed for failure to state a claim unless it appears, beyond a reasonable doubt, that the

plaintiff can prove no set of facts in support of a claim which could entitle him to relief.

> Clay v. ILC Data Device Corp., 771 F.Supp. 40.

E.D.N.Y. 1988. Complaint is not subject to dismissal for legal insufficiency unless complaint fails to state claim upon which some relief, not limited by request in complaint, may be granted. Fed.Rules Civ.Proc.Rule 54(c), 28 U.S.C.A.

> U.S. v. Bonanno Organized Crime Family of La Cosa Nostra, 683 F.Supp. 1411, affirmed 879 F.2d 20.

N.D.N.Y. 1997. Although federal court must construe a pro se plaintiff's inartful pleading liberally, complaint consisting of nothing more than naked assertions, and setting forth no facts upon which a court could find a violation, fails to state claim on which relief may be granted. Fed.Rules Civ.Proc.Rule 12(b)(6), 28 U.S.C.A.

> Anonymous v. Kaye, 987 F.Supp. 131.

N.D.N.Y. 1997. Motion to dismiss for failure to state a claim should be read in the context of the pleading requirements of rule requiring short and plain statement of claim, and though court reads pro se complaints as broadly as possible to find a valid claim, complaint, nonetheless, must satisfy the minimum pleading requirements of latter rule. Fed Rules Civ.Proc.Rules 8(a), 12(b)(6), 28 U.S.C.A.

> Wenger v. Canastota Cent. School Dist., 961 F.Supp. 416.

N.D.N.Y. 1995. Despite liberality of pleading requirement, naked allegations that are too conclusory cannot survive motion to dismiss. Fed.Rules Civ.Proc.Rule 12(b)(6), 28 U.S.C.A.

> Kraemer v. Elmira Auto Paint Supplies, Inc., 903 F.Supp. 315.

N.D.N.Y. 1995. Counts of complaint had to be dismissed against certain defendants when plaintiff made no allegations or claims against those defendants under those counts.

> Polite v. Casella, 901 F.Supp. 90.

N.D.N.Y. 1995. Court's inquiry on motion to dismiss for failure to state claim is merely directed to whether plaintiff's allegations constitute statement of claim under rule which calls for short and plain statement of claim showing that pleader is entitled to relief. Fed.Rules Civ.Proc.Rules 8(a), 12(b)(6), 28 U.S.C.A.

> Board of Trustees of Trucking Employees of North Jersey Welfare Fund, Incorporated--Pension Fund v. Canny, 900 F.Supp. 583.

N.D.N.Y. 1995. Complaint should not be dismissed for failure to state claim unless it appears, beyond doubt, that plaintiffs can prove no set of facts which would entitle them to

relief. Fed.Rules Civ.Proc.Rule 12(b)(6), 28 U.S.C.A.

> Board of Trustees of Trucking Employees of North Jersey Welfare Fund v. Canny, 876 F.Supp. 14.

N.D.N.Y. 1995. Complaint should not be dismissed for failure to state claim unless it appears, beyond doubt, that plaintiff can prove no set of facts which would entitle him to relief. Fed.Rules Civ.Proc.Rule 12(b)(6), 28 U.S.C.A.

> Craft v. McNulty, 875 F.Supp. 121.

N.D.N.Y. 1995. When complaint does not comply with rule governing pleadings, court may strike any portion of complaint that is redundant or immaterial; however, where complaint is so ambiguous and vague that its true substance, if any, is well disguised, dismissal is proper. Fed.Rules Civ.Proc.Rule 8, 28 U.S.C.A.

> Powell v. Marine Midland Bank, 162 F.R.D. 15.

N.D.N.Y. 1994. District court has discretion to dismiss pleadings which do not contain a short and plain statement of pleader's claim. Fed.Rules Civ.Proc.Rule 8(a), 28 U.S.C.A.

> Segarra v. Messina, 153 F.R.D. 22, on reconsideration 158 F.R.D. 230.

Complaint should not be dismissed for failure to state claim upon which relief can be granted unless it appears, beyond doubt, that plaintiff can prove no set of facts which would entitle him or her to relief. Fed.Rules Civ.Proc. Rule 12(b)(6), 28 U.S.C.A.

> Segarra v. Messina, 153 F.R.D. 22, on reconsideration 158 F.R.D. 230.

N.D.N.Y. 1993. Motion to dismiss for failure to state claim cannot be granted unless it appears from face of complaint that complaint cannot prove any set of facts in support of its claim that would entitle it to relief. Fed.Rules Civ.Proc.Rule 12(b)(6), 28 U.S.C.A.

> Gould v. Russi, 830 F.Supp. 139.

N.D.N.Y. 1993. If motion to dismiss is made prior to any discovery or filing of answer, district court is loath to dismiss complaint regardless of whether plaintiff is unlikely to prevail, unless defendant can demonstrate that plaintiff is unable to prove facts which would entitle him to relief. Fed.Rules Civ.Proc.Rule 12(b)(6), 28 U.S.C.A.

> Lawrence v. Cade & Saunders, P.C., 149 F.R.D. 14.

N.D.N.Y. 1990. Claim will be dismissed under rule concerning dismissal for failure to state a claim only if it appears beyond doubt that plaintiff can prove no set of facts supporting his or her legal claim which will entitle him

or her to relief. Fed.Rules Civ.Proc.Rule 12(b)(6), 28 U.S.C.A.

> Wanamaker v. Columbian Rope Co., 740 F.Supp. 127.

N.D.N.Y. 1990. Motion to dismiss for failure to state a claim will be granted only if it appears beyond doubt that plaintiff can prove no set of facts supporting his or her legal claim which will entitle him or her to relief. Fed. Rules Civ.Proc.Rule 12(b)(6), 28 U.S.C.A.

> Knight v. Storex Systems, Inc., 739 F.Supp. 739.

S.D.N.Y. 1998. The court may not grant the motion to dismiss for failure to state a claim merely because recovery seems remote or unlikely. Fed.Rules Civ.Proc.Rule 12(b)(6), 28 U.S.C.A.

> Laborers Local 17 Health & Ben. Fund v. Philip Morris, Inc., 7 F.Supp.2d 277.

A pleading will survive a motion to dismiss if it alleges a set of facts that would entitle the plaintiff to relief if proven.

> Laborers Local 17 Health & Ben. Fund v. Philip Morris, Inc., 7 F.Supp.2d 277.

S.D.N.Y. 1997. When complaint does not comply with federal rule requiring short and plain statement of claim, district court has authority to strike any immaterial portions or to dismiss complaint. Fed.Rules Civ.Proc.Rule 8, 28 U.S.C.A.

> Shuster v. Oppelman, 962 F.Supp. 394.

S.D.N.Y. 1996. Conclusory allegations are insufficient to withstand motion to dismiss.

> Northwestern Mut. Life Ins. Co. v. Wender, 940 F.Supp. 62.

S.D.N.Y. 1996. District court may grant motion to dismiss for failure to state a claim only if, assuming all facts alleged to be true, plaintiff still fails to plead the basic elements of a cause of action. Fed.Rules Civ.Proc.Rule 12(b)(6), 28 U.S.C.A.

> Corcoran v. New York Power Authority, 935 F.Supp. 376.

S.D.N.Y. 1996. As long as record yields view of evidence upon which jury could rationally find for plaintiff, he is entitled to have jury pass upon case, and complaint may not be dismissed.

> Kramer v. Showa Denko K.K., 929 F.Supp. 733.

S.D.N.Y. 1996. In ruling on motion to dismiss for failure to state claim, court must construe pleadings liberally, and mere vagueness or lack of detail is not sufficient ground for motion to dismiss. Fed.Rules Civ.Proc.Rule 12(b)(6), 28 U.S.C.A.

> Marisol A. by Forbes v. Giuliani, 929 F.Supp. 662, motion to certify allowed by 1996 WL 419887, affirmed 126 F.3d 372.

S.D.N.Y. 1996. On motion to dismiss for failure to state claim upon which relief can be granted, plaintiff need not come forward with proof of his allegations; rather, motion must be denied if plaintiff alleges facts which, taken as true, constitute a claim. Fed.Rules Civ.Proc. Rule 12(b)(6), 28 U.S.C.A.

> Detko v. Blimpies Restaurant, 924 F.Supp. 555.

Complaint containing only conclusory, vague or general allegations cannot survive motion to dismiss. Fed.Rules Civ.Proc.Rule 12(b)(6), 28 U.S.C.A.

> Detko v. Blimpies Restaurant, 924 F.Supp. 555.

S.D.N.Y. 1996. Complaint consisting of nothing more than naked assertions, and setting forth no facts upon which court could grant relief, fails to state claim upon which relief can be granted. Fed.Rules Civ.Proc.Rule 12(b)(6), 28 U.S.C.A.

> DeFalco v. Dirie, 923 F.Supp. 473.

S.D.N.Y. 1996. Claims based only on vague, conclusory or general allegations of wrongdoing cannot survive motion to dismiss. Fed.Rules Civ.Proc.Rule 12(b)(6), 28 U.S.C.A.

> King v. Pine Plains Cent. School Dist., 918 F.Supp. 772.

S.D.N.Y. 1996. Although district court, on motion to dismiss, must accept allegations in complaint as true and may not dismiss complaint unless it appears beyond doubt that plaintiff can prove no set of facts in support of claim that would entitle him to relief, complaint which contains only conclusory, vague or general allegations cannot survive motion to dismiss. Fed.Rules Civ.Proc.Rule 12(b)(6), 28 U.S.C.A.

> Yamen by Yamen v. Board of Educ. of Arlington Cent. School Dist., 909 F.Supp. 207.

S.D.N.Y. 1996. Mere conclusory allegation may not withstand motion to dismiss.

> Katzman v. Victoria's Secret Catalogue, 167 F.R.D. 649, reargument denied 939 F.Supp. 274, affirmed 113 F.3d 1229.

S.D.N.Y. 1995. Even on motion to dismiss, court cannot accept "naked assertions" in complaint that does not set forth supporting allegations of facts. Fed.Rules Civ.Proc.Rule 12(b)(6), 28 U.S.C.A.

> Odom v. Columbia University, 906 F.Supp. 188.

S.D.N.Y. 1995. To survive motion to dismiss for failure to state claim, plaintiff need not come forward with proof of its allegations; plaintiff must, however, allege facts that, taken as true, constitute claim. Fed.Rules Civ.Proc. Rule 12(b)(6), 28 U.S.C.A.

> HBP Associates v. Marsh, 893 F.Supp. 271.

S.D.N.Y. 1995. Complaint which states only conclusory legal claim with respect to alleged basis for recovery is not well-pleaded and cannot withstand motion to dismiss pursuant to Federal Rules of Civil Procedure. Fed. Rules Civ.Proc.Rule 12(b)(6), 28 U.S.C.A.

> Richman v. W.L. Gore & Associates, Inc., 881 F.Supp. 895, opinion modified 988 F.Supp. 753, motion to certify appeal denied 1998 WL 231015.

Inadequately pleaded factual allegations, for purposes of motion to dismiss complaint, include those that are purely conclusory. Fed. Rules Civ.Proc.Rule 12(b)(6), 28 U.S.C.A.

> Richman v. W.L. Gore & Associates, Inc., 881 F.Supp. 895, opinion modified 988 F.Supp. 753, motion to certify appeal denied 1998 WL 231015.

S.D.N.Y. 1995. Motion to dismiss for failure to state claim upon which relief can be granted should be granted only if it appears beyond doubt that plaintiffs can prove no set of facts in support of their claims which would entitle them to relief. Fed.Rules Civ.Proc.Rule 12(b)(6), 28 U.S.C.A.

> D'Orange v. Feely, 877 F.Supp. 152.

S.D.N.Y. 1995. When considering sufficiency of complaint on motion to dismiss for failure to state claim or for lack of jurisdiction over subject matter, court accepts as true all factual allegations in complaint and draws inferences from these allegations in light most favorable to plaintiff, and dismissal is warranted only if, under any set of facts that plaintiff can prove consistent with the allegations, it is clear that no relief can be granted. Fed.Rules Civ. Proc.Rule 12(b), 28 U.S.C.A.

> People by Vacco v. Mid Hudson Medical Group, P.C., 877 F.Supp. 143.

S.D.N.Y. 1995. If there exists any set of facts that could be construed so as to entitle plaintiff to relief, complaint should not be dismissed for failure to state a claim. Fed.Rules Civ.Proc.Rule 12(b)(6), 28 U.S.C.A.

> Lomaglio Associates Inc. v. LBK Marketing Corp., 876 F.Supp. 41.

S.D.N.Y. 1994. Motion to dismiss must be denied unless it appears beyond a doubt that plaintiff can prove no set of facts in support of his claim that would entitle him to relief.

> Virgin Atlantic Airways Ltd. v. British Airways PLC, 872 F.Supp. 52.

S.D.N.Y. 1994. Only if, assuming all facts as true, plaintiff still fails to plead the basic elements of a cause of action can court dismiss claim. Fed.Rules Civ.Proc.Rule 12(b)(6), 28 U.S.C.A.

Philippeaux v. North Central Bronx Hosp., 871 F.Supp. 640, affirmed 104 F.3d 353, certiorari denied 117 S.Ct. 1110, 137 L.Ed.2d 312.

S.D.N.Y. 1994. Motion to dismiss for failure to state claim on which relief can be granted will be denied unless it appears to a certainty that plaintiff can prove no set of facts entitling him to relief. Fed.Rules Civ.Proc.Rule 12(b)(6), 28 U.S.C.A.

Tribune Co. v. Purcigliotti, 869 F.Supp. 1076, affirmed 66 F.3d 12.

S.D.N.Y. 1994. Complaint should not be dismissed for failure to state a claim unless it appears beyond a doubt that plaintiff can prove no set of facts in support of claim which would entitle him to relief. Fed.Rules Civ.Proc.Rule 12(b)(6), 28 U.S.C.A.

Shub v. Hankin, 869 F.Supp. 213, affirmed 66 F.3d 308.

S.D.N.Y. 1994. Since dismissal of complaint for failure to state claim is drastic step, motion to dismiss on this basis must be denied unless it appears beyond doubt that plaintiff can prove no set of facts in support of its claim that would entitle it to relief. Fed.Rules Civ.Proc. Rule 12(b)(6), 28 U.S.C.A.

Reed Intern. Trading Corp. v. Donau Bank AG, 866 F.Supp. 750.

S.D.N.Y. 1994. In deciding a motion to dismiss, court must consider legal sufficiency of complaint, not weight of evidence which might be offered at trial, and in order to prevail, movant must demonstrate beyond doubt that plaintiff can prove no set of facts in support of claim which would entitle him to relief. Fed. Rules Civ.Proc.Rule 12(b)(6), 28 U.S.C.A.

Abbasi v. Herzfeld & Rubin, P.C., 863 F.Supp. 144.

Conclusory allegations that fail to give defendant notice of material elements of claim are insufficient as a matter of law to state a claim for purposes of motion to dismiss. Fed.Rules Civ.Proc.Rule 12(b)(6), 28 U.S.C.A.

Abbasi v. Herzfeld & Rubin, P.C., 863 F.Supp. 144.

S.D.N.Y. 1994. In deciding motion to dismiss, district court accepts plaintiff's allegations as true, construes all factual allegations in plaintiff's favor and may dismiss complaint only if it appears beyond doubt that plaintiff could prove no set of facts in support of its claim which would entitle it to relief.

Lopes v. U.S., 862 F.Supp. 1178.

S.D.N.Y. 1994. To dismiss complaint for failure to state claim upon which relief may be granted, it must appear beyond doubt that plaintiff can prove no set of facts in support of his claim which would entitle him to relief. Fed.Rules Civ.Proc.Rule 12(b)(6), 28 U.S.C.A.

New Alliance Party v. New York State Bd. of Elections, 861 F.Supp. 282.

S.D.N.Y. 1994. On motion to dismiss for failure to state claim on which relief can be granted, court may not dismiss complaint unless movant shows beyond doubt that plaintiff can prove no set of facts in support of claim which would entitle him to relief. Fed.Rules Civ.Proc.Rule 12(b)(6), 28 U.S.C.A.

Sazerac Co., Inc. v. Falk, 861 F.Supp. 253.

S.D.N.Y. 1994. Complaint should not be dismissed simply because claimant's allegations do not support legal theory it advances; court has duty to examine complaint to determine if allegations provide for relief on any possible theory.

Podell v. Citicorp Diners Club, Inc., 859 F.Supp. 701.

S.D.N.Y. 1994. Motion to dismiss a Racketeer Influenced Corrupt Organizations (RICO) claim should be granted only if it is clear that no relief could be granted under any set of facts that could be proved consistent with the allegations. 18 U.S.C.A. § 1962(c).

McCormack Intern. Corp. v. Vohra, 858 F.Supp. 415.

S.D.N.Y. 1994. Complaint should not be dismissed for failure to state claim unless it appears beyond doubt that plaintiff can prove no set of facts in support of his claim which would entitle him to relief. Fed.Rules Civ.Proc. Rule 12(b)(6), 28 U.S.C.A.

Ruderman v. Police Dept. of City of New York, 857 F.Supp. 326.

S.D.N.Y. 1994. Complaint should not be dismissed for failure to state claim unless, after viewing plaintiff's allegations in favorable light, it appears beyond doubt that plaintiff can prove no set of facts in support of his claim which would entitle him to relief. Fed.Rules Civ.Proc. Rule 12(b)(6), 28 U.S.C.A.

Marsden v. Federal Bureau of Prisons, 856 F.Supp. 832.

S.D.N.Y. 1994. Court may not dismiss complaint for failure to state claim on which relief can be granted unless movant demonstrates beyond doubt that plaintiff can prove no set of facts in support of claim which would entitle him to relief. Fed.Rules Civ.Proc.Rule 12(b)(6), 28 U.S.C.A.

Barnum v. Millbrook Care Ltd. Partnership, 850 F.Supp. 1227, affirmed 43 F.3d 1458.

S.D.N.Y. 1994. Motion to dismiss for failure to state a claim should be denied unless it appears to a certainty that plaintiff can prove no set of facts entitling him to relief. Fed.Rules Civ.Proc.Rule 12(b)(6), 28 U.S.C.A.

Moscowitz v. Brown, 850 F.Supp. 1185.

S.D.N.Y. 1994. Motion for failure to state claim upon which relief can be granted tests only sufficiency of complaint and should not be granted unless it appears beyond doubt that plaintiff can prove no set of facts in support of his claim which would entitle him to relief. Fed.Rules Civ.Proc.Rule 12(b)(6), 28 U.S.C.A.

Naso v. Park, 850 F.Supp. 264.

S.D.N.Y. 1994. For purposes of motion to dismiss for failure to state claim upon which relief may be granted, complaint may not be dismissed unless relief cannot be granted under any set of facts alleged, and, thus, district court must accept plaintiff's factual allegations as true, while reaching its own conclusions of law. Fed.Rules Civ.Proc.Rule 12(b)(6), 28 U.S.C.A.

Argenbright Sec. v. Ceskoslovenske Aeroline, 849 F.Supp. 276.

S.D.N.Y. 1994. Complaint should not be dismissed for failure to state claim unless it appears beyond doubt that plaintiff can prove no set of facts in support of claim which would entitle him to relief. Fed.Rules Civ.Proc.Rule 12(b)(6), 28 U.S.C.A.

Coliniatis v. Dimas, 848 F.Supp. 462.

S.D.N.Y. 1994. Complaint should not be dismissed for failure to state claim unless it appears beyond doubt that plaintiff can prove no set of facts in support of his claim which would entitle him to relief. Fed.Rules Civ.Proc.Rule 12(b)(6), 28 U.S.C.A.

Kahn v. Inspector General of U.S. Dept. of Health and Human Services, 848 F.Supp. 432.

S.D.N.Y. 1994. Party seeking dismissal will prevail only if plaintiff's allegations could not possibly constitute cause of action.

Gluckman v. American Airlines, Inc., 844 F.Supp. 151.

S.D.N.Y. 1993. Complaint should not be dismissed for failure to state claim unless it appears beyond doubt that plaintiff can prove no set of facts in support of its claim that would entitle it to relief. Fed.Rules Civ.Proc.Rule 12(b)(6), 28 U.S.C.A.

Luedke v. Delta Air Lines, Inc., 159 B.R. 385.

S.D.N.Y. 1993. Complaint should not be dismissed for failure to state claim unless it appears beyond doubt that plaintiff can prove no set of facts in support of his claim which

would entitle him to relief. Fed.Rules Civ.Proc. Rule 12(b)(6), 28 U.S.C.A.

Brower-Coad v. Fundamental Brokers, Inc., 856 F.Supp. 147.

S.D.N.Y. 1993. Complaint should not be dismissed for failure to state claim unless it appears beyond doubt that plaintiff can prove no set of facts in support of claim which would entitle him to relief. Fed.Rules Civ.Proc.Rule 12(b)(6), 28 U.S.C.A.

Gruby v. Brady, 838 F.Supp. 820.

S.D.N.Y. 1993. Complaint should not be dismissed for failure to state claim unless it appears beyond doubt that no relief can be granted under any set of facts plaintiff could prove in support of claim, accepting as true all of plaintiff's factual allegations, construing complaint in light most favorable to plaintiff, and drawing all permissible inferences in favor of plaintiff. Fed.Rules Civ.Proc.Rule 12(b)(6), 28 U.S.C.A.

Keenan v. D.H. Blair & Co., Inc., 838 F.Supp. 82.

S.D.N.Y. 1993. Court may not dismiss complaint unless movant demonstrates beyond doubt that plaintiff can prove no set of facts in support of his claim which would entitle him to relief. Fed.Rules Civ.Proc.Rule 12(b)(6), 28 U.S.C.A.

Morin v. Trupin, 835 F.Supp. 126.

S.D.N.Y. 1993. District court should grant motion to dismiss for failure to state claim only if it is clear that no relief could be granted under any set of facts that could be proved consistent with allegations. Fed.Rules Civ. Proc.Rule 12(b)(6), 28 U.S.C.A.

Posr v. City of New York, 835 F.Supp. 120, affirmed 22 F.3d 1091.

S.D.N.Y. 1993. Court may not dismiss complaint on Rule 12(b)(6) motion unless movant demonstrates beyond doubt that plaintiff can prove no set of facts in support of his claim which would entitle him to relief. Fed.Rules Civ.Proc.Rule 12(b)(6), 28 U.S.C.A.

Morin v. Trupin, 832 F.Supp. 93.

S.D.N.Y. 1993. Motion to dismiss for failure to state claim upon which relief can be granted will not be granted unless it appears beyond doubt that plaintiff can prove no set of facts in support of its claim which would entitle it to relief. Fed.Rules Civ.Proc.Rule 12(b)(6), 28 U.S.C.A.

U.S. v. All Right, Title and Interest in Five Parcels of Real Property and Appurtances Thereto Known as 64 Lovers Lane, 830 F.Supp. 750.

S.D.N.Y. 1993. Complaint cannot be dismissed unless it appears beyond doubt that plaintiff can prove no set of facts in support of its claim that would entitle it to relief. Fed. Rules Civ.Proc.Rule 12(b)(6), 28 U.S.C.A.

> K. Bell & Associates, Inc. v. Lloyd's Underwriters, 827 F.Supp. 985.

S.D.N.Y. 1993. On motion to dismiss, complaint cannot be dismissed unless it appears beyond a doubt that plaintiff can prove no set of facts in support of claim which would entitle him to relief.

> Yusuf v. Vassar College, 827 F.Supp. 952, affirmed in part, reversed in part 35 F.3d 709.

S.D.N.Y. 1993. Complaint should not be dismissed for failure to state claim upon which relief can be granted unless it appears beyond doubt that plaintiff can prove no set of facts in support of his or her claim that would entitle plaintiff to relief. Fed.Rules Civ.Proc.Rule 12(b)(6), 28 U.S.C.A.

> Liddy v. Cisneros, 823 F.Supp. 164.

S.D.N.Y. 1993. Motion to dismiss should be granted only if, after reviewing complaint, it appears beyond doubt that plaintiff can prove no set of facts in support of claim entitling plaintiff to relief. Fed.Rules Civ.Proc.Rule 12(b)(6), 28 U.S.C.A.

> Henschke v. New York Hospital-Cornell Medical Center, 821 F.Supp. 166.

S.D.N.Y. 1993. Court may not dismiss complaint for failure to state claim upon which relief can be granted unless movant demonstrates beyond doubt that plaintiff can prove no set of facts in support of his claim which would entitle him to relief. Fed.Rules Civ.Proc.Rule 12(b)(6), 28 U.S.C.A.

> Milam v. Herrlin, 819 F.Supp. 295.

S.D.N.Y. 1992. Court should dismiss complaint for failure to state claim only if it appears beyond doubt that plaintiff can prove no set of facts supporting its claim that entitles it to relief. Fed.Rules Civ.Proc.Rule 12(b)(6), 28 U.S.C.A.

> East Coast Novelty Co., Inc. v. City of New York, 809 F.Supp. 285.

S.D.N.Y. 1992. Defendant is entitled to dismissal for failure to state a claim upon which relief can be granted only when it appears beyond a reasonable doubt that plaintiff can prove no set of facts in support of his claim which would entitle him to relief. Fed.Rules Civ.Proc.Rule 12(b)(6), 28 U.S.C.A.

> Federal Ins. Co. v. May Dept. Stores Co., 808 F.Supp. 347.

S.D.N.Y. 1992. Motion to dismiss for failure to state a claim should be granted only if it appears beyond doubt that plaintiffs can prove no set of facts in support of their claims which

would entitle them to relief. Fed.Rules Civ. Proc.Rule 12(b)(6), 28 U.S.C.A.

> In re AnnTaylor Stores Securities Litigation, 807 F.Supp. 990.

S.D.N.Y. 1992. Claim will be dismissed for failure to state cognizable claim where it appears beyond doubt that plaintiff can prove no set of facts in support of his claim which would entitle him to relief. Fed.Rules Civ.Proc. Rule 12(b)(6), 28 U.S.C.A.

> Barrett v. U.S. Banknote Corp., 806 F.Supp. 1094.

S.D.N.Y. 1992. To dismiss complaint for failure to state claim upon which relief can be granted, court must accept plaintiff's allegations at face value, must construe allegations in complaint in plaintiff's favor, and must dismiss complaint only if it appears beyond doubt that plaintiff can prove no set of facts in support of his claim which would entitle him to relief. Fed.Rules Civ.Proc.Rule 12(b)(6), 28 U.S.C.A.

> Van Brunt v. Rauschenberg, 799 F.Supp. 1467.

S.D.N.Y. 1992. Court should dismiss complaint for failure to state a claim only if it appears beyond a doubt that plaintiff can prove no set of facts supporting its claim. Fed.Rules Civ.Proc.Rule 12(b)(6), 28 U.S.C.A.

> Wood v. Brosse U.S.A., Inc., 788 F.Supp. 772.

S.D.N.Y. 1992. Motion to dismiss for failure to state a claim may be granted only when it appears that plaintiff can prove no set of facts in support of his or her complaint that would entitle him or her to relief. Fed.Rules Civ.Proc. Rule 12(b)(6), 28 U.S.C.A.

> Glasford v. New York State Dept. of Social Services, 787 F.Supp. 384.

S.D.N.Y. 1992. In considering motion to dismiss for failure to state claim upon which relief may be granted, court is required to accept facts alleged in complaint as true, draw all reasonable inferences in favor of plaintiff, and dismiss only if it appears beyond doubt that plaintiff can prove no set of facts that would entitle plaintiff to relief. Fed.Rules Civ.Proc. Rule 12(b)(6), 28 U.S.C.A.

> Kendrick v. Sullivan, 784 F.Supp. 94.

S.D.N.Y. 1991. Motion to dismiss for failure to state claim upon which relief may be granted was not proper vehicle to dismiss allegations from complaint on grounds of irrelevancy. Fed.Rules Civ.Proc.Rule 12(b)(6), 28 U.S.C.A.

> In re Chateaugay Corp., 130 B.R. 690, opinion withdrawn and vacated 1993 WL 388809.

S.D.N.Y. 1991. Motion to dismiss must be denied unless it appears beyond doubt that plaintiff can prove no set of facts in support of his claim which would entitle him to relief. Fed.Rules Civ.Proc.Rule 12(b)(6), 28 U.S.C.A.

> Landy v. Heller, White & Co., 783 F.Supp. 125.

S.D.N.Y. 1991. Court should dismiss complaint for failure to state claim only if it appears beyond doubt that, construing complaint's allegations in light most favorable to plaintiff and accepting those allegations as true, plaintiff can prove no set of facts supporting its claim that entitles it to relief. Fed.Rules Civ.Proc.Rule 12(b)(6), 28 U.S.C.A.

> Music Deli & Groceries, Inc. v. I.R.S., Dist. of Manhattan, 781 F.Supp. 992.

S.D.N.Y. 1991. Dismissal for failure to state claim is warranted only if, taking complaint's claims at face value, it appears beyond doubt that plaintiff can prove no set of facts which would entitle plaintiff to relief. Fed. Rules Civ.Proc.Rule 12(b)(6), 28 U.S.C.A.

> Straube v. Florida Union Free School Dist., 778 F.Supp. 774.

S.D.N.Y. 1991. Complaint should not be dismissed unless, looking solely at complaint and its exhibits and taking supported allegations therein as true, it appears beyond doubt that plaintiffs can prove no set of facts in support of claim which would entitle them to relief. Fed. Rules Civ.Proc.Rules 10(c), 12(b)(6), 28 U.S.C.A.

> Church of Scientology Intern. v. Eli Lilly & Co., 778 F.Supp. 661, reargument denied 1992 WL 80709.

S.D.N.Y. 1991. In deciding motion to dismiss for failure to state a claim upon which relief may be granted, complaint must be read generously and every inference drawn in favor of plaintiff; complaint should be dismissed only if it appears beyond doubt that plaintiff can prove no set of facts in support of his or her claim which would entitle him or her to relief. Fed.Rules Civ.Proc.Rule 12(b)(6), 28 U.S.C.A.

> Drexel Burnham Lambert Inc. v. Saxony Heights Realty Associates, 777 F.Supp. 228.

S.D.N.Y. 1991. Complaint should be dismissed on the pleadings only if it appears beyond reasonable doubt that plaintiff can prove no set of facts in support of his claim which would entitle him to relief. Fed.Rules Civ.Proc. Rule 12(b)(6), 28 U.S.C.A.

> Parnes v. Mast Property Investors, Inc., 776 F.Supp. 792.

S.D.N.Y. 1991. In ruling on motion to dismiss for failure to state claim, courts view all facts and allegations in complaint in light most favorable to plaintiff; moreover, courts must liberally construe allegations in complaint and deny motion unless it appears beyond doubt that plaintiff can prove no set of facts in support

of her claim which would entitle her to relief. Fed.Rules Civ.Proc.Rule 12(b)(6), 28 U.S.C.A.

> Deleu v. Scaife, 775 F.Supp. 712.

S.D.N.Y. 1991. Motion to dismiss for failure to state a claim tests only sufficiency of complaint and should not be granted unless it appears beyond a doubt that plaintiff can prove no set of facts in support of claim which would entitle him to relief. Fed.Rules Civ.Proc.Rule 12(b)(6), 28 U.S.C.A.

> Amlon Metals, Inc. v. FMC Corp., 775 F.Supp. 668.

S.D.N.Y. 1991. Complaint should not be dismissed for failure to state a claim unless it appears beyond doubt that plaintiff can prove no set of facts in support of his claim that would entitle him to relief, and thus doubt as to plaintiff's ability to prove his case is not reason for dismissal of pleadings for failure to state a claim on which relief can be granted. Fed. Rules Civ.Proc.Rule 12(b)(6), 28 U.S.C.A.

> Drexel Burnham Lambert Group, Inc. v. Microgenesys, Inc., 775 F.Supp. 660.

S.D.N.Y. 1991. Although allegations of bad faith are not subject to strict pleading rules, but only to notice requirements, simply adding words "bad faith" to complaint will not withstand motion to dismiss. Fed.Rules Civ.Proc. Rules 8(a), 9(b), 28 U.S.C.A.

> Stoner v. Walsh, 772 F.Supp. 790.

S.D.N.Y. 1991. In dealing with motion to dismiss for failure to state claim, court must construe complaint's allegations in light most favorable to plaintiff and accept those allegations as true and should then dismiss complaint only if it appears beyond doubt that plaintiff can prove no set of facts supporting its claim that would entitle it to relief. Fed.Rules Civ.Proc. Rule 12(b)(6), 28 U.S.C.A.

> Citicorp Intern. Trading Co., Inc. v. Western Oil & Refining Co., Inc., 771 F.Supp. 600.

S.D.N.Y. 1991. Complaint should not be dismissed for failure to state a claim unless it appears beyond doubt that the plaintiff can prove no set of facts in support of his claim which would entitle him to relief.

> Macmillan, Inc. v. Federal Ins. Co., 764 F.Supp. 38.

S.D.N.Y. 1991. Claim will be dismissed only if its allegation would entitle claimant to relief on no possible theory, even though theory of party asserting claim was incorrect.

> Geler v. National Westminster Bank USA, 763 F.Supp. 722.

S.D.N.Y. 1991. Motion to dismiss for failure to state claim is properly granted only if it is clear that no relief can be granted under any set of facts that could be proved consistently with allegations of complaint. Fed.Rules Civ.Proc. Rule 12(b)(6), 28 U.S.C.A.

> Franklin Electronic Publishers, Inc. v. Unisonic Products Corp., 763 F.Supp. 1.

S.D.N.Y. 1991. If initial complaint does not comply with requirement that it be short and plain, court may on its own power dismiss complaint. Fed.Rules Civ.Proc.Rule 8(a), 28 U.S.C.A.

> Lasky v. Shearson Lehman Bros. Inc., 139 F.R.D. 597.

S.D.N.Y. 1991. Plaintiff's pro se action against the United States, various government agencies, various present and former government officials and assorted other entities and individuals failed to meet requirement of providing defendants with fair notice and was subject to dismissal; complaint provided only conclusory, vague, and general factual allegations. Fed.Rules Civ.Proc.Rule 8(a)(2), (e)(1), 28 U.S.C.A.

> Barsella v. U.S., 135 F.R.D. 64.

S.D.N.Y. 1990. Complaint should not be dismissed for failure to state claim unless it appears beyond doubt that plaintiff can prove no set of facts in support of its claim which would entitle it to relief; in making this determination, court accepts plaintiff's pleadings at face value and construes allegations in complaint in favor of plaintiff. Fed.Rules Civ.Proc. Rule 12(b)(6), 28 U.S.C.A.

> Macmillan, Inc. v. Federal Ins. Co., 741 F.Supp. 1079.

S.D.N.Y. 1990. Motion to dismiss for failure to state a claim tests only the sufficiency of a complaint and should not be granted unless it appears beyond a doubt that the plaintiff can prove no set of facts in support of his claim which would entitle him to relief.

> Borden, Inc. v. Spoor Behrins Campbell & Young, Inc., 735 F.Supp. 587.

S.D.N.Y. 1989. District court should dismiss complaint for failure to state claim upon which relief can be granted only if it appears beyond doubt that plaintiff can prove no set of facts supporting its claim that entitles it to relief. Fed.Rules Civ.Proc.Rule 12(b)(6), 28 U.S.C.A.

> Branko Intern., Inc. v. Saudi Arabian Airlines, 704 F.Supp. 386, affirmed Branko Intl v. Saudi Arabian Airlines, 880 F.2d 1318.

S.D.N.Y. 1988. Claim which asserted both fraud and breach of contract as theories of liability was required to be dismissed; however, plaintiff was entitled to leave to amend its complaint. Fed.Rules Civ.Proc.Rule 15(a), 28 U.S.C.A.

> East River Sav. Bank v. Secretary of Housing and Urban Development, 702 F.Supp. 448.

S.D.N.Y. 1988. Complaint should not be dismissed for insufficiency unless it appears to certainty that plaintiff is entitled to no relief under any state of facts which could be proved in support of claim made.

> Bruce v. Martin, 691 F.Supp. 716, reargument denied 702 F.Supp. 66, on reconsideration 712 F.Supp. 442, on reconsideration 712 F.Supp. 442.

S.D.N.Y. 1987. Under liberal notice theory of pleading, failure of complaint to state with precision all elements necessary to give rise to cognizable claim is not by itself grounds for dismissal for failure to state claim upon which relief can be granted.

> Raine v. Lorimar Productions, Inc., 71 B.R. 450.

S.D.N.Y. 1987. Issue upon motion to dismiss is not whether plaintiffs' account is plausible or implausible; rather, issue is whether complaint is legally sufficient.

> Bozsi Ltd. Partnership v. Lynott, 676 F.Supp. 505.

S.D.N.Y. 1987. A complaint should not be dismissed for failure to state a claim unless it appears beyond a doubt that the plaintiff can prove no set of facts in support of a claim that would entitle him to relief and, if plaintiff is filing pro se, court should construe complaint broadly, and not hold it to the same standards as complaint drafted by an attorney. Fed.Rules Civ.Proc.Rule 12(b)(6), 28 U.S.C.A.

> Young v. Calhoun, 656 F.Supp. 970.

S.D.N.Y. 1987. In considering defendant's motion to dismiss for failure to state a cause of action and failure to plead fraud with specificity, court is bound by general rule that for defendant to succeed it must demonstrate beyond doubt that plaintiff can prove no set of facts in support of claim which would entitle plaintiff to relief; factual allegations contained in complaints are accepted as true for purpose of deciding motion. Fed.Rules Civ.Proc.Rules 9(b), 12(b), 28 U.S.C.A.

> Moll v. US Life Title Ins. Co. of New York, 654 F.Supp. 1012, on reconsideration 700 F.Supp. 1284, reconsideration denied 1988 WL 142468.

S.D.N.Y. 1985. Complaint should not be dismissed unless it appears beyond doubt that plaintiff can prove no set of facts in support of his claim which would entitle him to relief.

> Equitable Life Assur. Soc. of U.S. v. Alexander Grant & Co., 627 F.Supp. 1023.

S.D.N.Y. 1985. Strength of complaint's allegations are not factors for court to consider when ruling on motion to dismiss for failure to state claim, but rather, office of motion to dismiss for failure to state claim is solely to determine legal feasibility of complaint. Fed. Rules Civ.Proc., Rule 12(b)(6), 28 U.S.C.A.

Lasky v. American Broadcasting Companies, Inc., 606 F.Supp. 934.

W.D.N.Y. 1996. Helpfulness is not the standard for sufficiency of pleadings and for motions to dismiss for failure to state claim. Fed.Rules Civ.Proc.Rule 12(b)(6), 28 U.S.C.A.

Spurlock v. NYNEX, 949 F.Supp. 1022.

W.D.N.Y. 1994. Complaint will be dismissed only if it appears beyond doubt that plaintiff can prove no set of facts which would entitle her to relief. Fed.Rules Civ.Proc.Rule 12, 28 U.S.C.A.

Hamilton v. New York State Dept. of Mental Hygiene, 876 F.Supp. 470.

W.D.N.Y. 1994. Complaint will be dismissed only if it appears beyond doubt that plaintiff can prove no set of facts which would entitle him to relief.

Koch v. Mirza, 869 F.Supp. 1031.

E.D.N.C. 1993. Motion to dismiss for failure to state claim should be denied unless it appears beyond doubt that plaintiff can prove no set of facts in support of claim which would entitle him to relief. Fed.Rules Civ.Proc.Rule 12(b)(6), 28 U.S.C.A.

Bass v. City of Wilson, 835 F.Supp. 255.

E.D.N.C. 1992. Dismissal of complaint for failure to state claim is appropriate when, as matter of law, no relief could be granted under any set of facts that could be proven consistent with plaintiff's allegations. Fed.Rules Civ.Proc. Rule 12(b)(6), 28 U.S.C.A.

Environmental Defense Fund v. Tidwell, 837 F.Supp. 1344.

E.D.N.C. 1991. Motion to dismiss for failure to state claim should be granted where it appears beyond doubt that plaintiff can prove no set of facts in support of her claim which would entitle her to relief. Fed.Rules Civ.Proc. Rule 12(b)(6), 28 U.S.C.A.

Bajkowski v. U.S., 787 F.Supp. 539.

M.D.N.C. 1996. In deciding whether claim has been stated, for purposes of motion to dismiss for failure to state claim, procedural rule setting forth general rules of pleading requires only notice pleading such that defendant receives fair notice from complaint of claim and grounds on which the claim rests. Fed.Rules Civ.Proc.Rules 8, 12(b)(6), 28 U.S.C.A.

Pardasani v. Rack Room Shoes Inc., 912 F.Supp. 187.

M.D.N.C. 1994. In ruling on motion to dismiss for failure to state a claim, court should accept as true all well-pleaded allegations and, viewing complaint in light most favorable to plaintiff, should not dismiss unless it appears certain that plaintiff can prove no set of facts which would entitle him to relief. Fed.Rules Civ.Proc.Rule 12(b)(6), 28 U.S.C.A.

Shanks v. Forsyth County Park Authority, Inc., 869 F.Supp. 1231.

W.D.N.C. 1996. Rule governing dismissal of actions authorizes dismissal based on dispositive issue of law. Fed.Rules Civ.Proc.Rule 12(b), 28 U.S.C.A.

Ryder v. Freeman, 918 F.Supp. 157, appeal dismissed, cause remanded 112 F.3d 510.

Nothing in rule governing dismissal for failure to state claim confines its sweep to claims of law which are obviously insupportable. Fed.Rules Civ.Proc.Rule 12(b)(6), 28 U.S.C.A.

Ryder v. Freeman, 918 F.Supp. 157, appeal dismissed, cause remanded 112 F.3d 510.

W.D.N.C. 1994. Party seeking dismissal for failure to state claim must demonstrate that nonmovant has stated no facts in its complaint which entitle it to relief. Fed.Rules Civ.Proc. Rule 12(b)(6), 28 U.S.C.A.

Kristufek v. Saxonburg Ceramics, Inc., 901 F.Supp. 1018, affirmed 60 F.3d 823.

W.D.N.C. 1993. Court may not dismiss allegations and complaint unless plaintiff can prove no set of facts entitling it to relief. Fed. Rules Civ.Proc.Rule 12(b), 28 U.S.C.A.

American Angus Ass'n v. Sysco Corp., 865 F.Supp. 1174.

W.D.N.C. 1990. Court should deny motion to dismiss for failure to state a claim unless it appears beyond doubt that plaintiff can prove no set of facts in support of his claim which would entitle him to relief. Fed.Rules Civ.Proc. Rule 12(b)(6), 28 U.S.C.A.

I R Const. Products Co., Inc. v. D.R. Allen & Son, Inc., 737 F.Supp. 895.

D.N.D. 1994. Motion to dismiss for failure to state claim should not be granted unless it appears beyond doubt that plaintiff can prove no set of facts which would entitle him to relief. Fed.Rules Civ.Proc.Rule 12(b)(6), 28 U.S.C.A.

Thomson v. Olson, 866 F.Supp. 1267, affirmed 56 F.3d 69.

N.D.Ohio 1994. Complaint is to be dismissed for failure to state claim only if it appears beyond doubt that plaintiff can prove no set of facts in support of his claim that would entitle him to relief. Fed.Rules Civ.Proc.Rule 12(b)(6), 28 U.S.C.A.

Heights Community Congress v. Smythe, Cramer Co., 862 F.Supp. 204.

N.D.Ohio 1994. Motion to dismiss for failure to state a claim upon which relief may be granted should be denied unless it can be established beyond doubt that plaintiff can prove no set of facts in support of his or her claim which would entitle plaintiff to relief. Fed.Rules Civ. Proc.Rule 12(b)(6), 28 U.S.C.A.

Resolution Trust Corp. v. Zimmerman, 853 F.Supp. 1016.

N.D.Ohio 1994. Complaint should not be dismissed for failure to state a claim unless it appears beyond doubt that plaintiff can prove no set of facts in support of claim which would entitle plaintiff to relief. Fed.Rules Civ.Proc. Rule 12(b)(6), 28 U.S.C.A.

Cione v. Gorr, 843 F.Supp. 1199.

N.D.Ohio 1993. District court is without authority to dismiss claims unless it can be demonstrated beyond doubt that plaintiff can prove no set of facts that would entitle it to relief. Fed.Rules Civ.Proc.Rule 12(b), 28 U.S.C.A.

City of Toledo v. Beazer Materials and Services, Inc., 833 F.Supp. 646.

N.D.Ohio 1992. Motion to dismiss for failure to state claim should be denied unless it can be established beyond a doubt that plaintiff can prove no set of facts in support of his or her claim which would entitle plaintiff to relief. Fed.Rules Civ.Proc.Rule 12(b)(6), 28 U.S.C.A.

Stychno v. Ohio Edison Co., 806 F.Supp. 663.

N.D.Ohio 1991. Complaint is to be dismissed for failure to state claim on which relief can be granted only if plaintiff can prove no set of facts in support of claim which entitles plaintiff to relief. Fed.Rules Civ.Proc.Rule 12(b)(6), 28 U.S.C.A.

Emser v. Curtis Industries, Inc., 774 F.Supp. 1076.

N.D.Ohio 1990. Motion to dismiss will be granted only if, treating all well-pled allegations as true, nonmovant will be unable to recover under pleadings in question.

Gould, Inc. v. Mitsui Min. & Smelting Co., Ltd., 750 F.Supp. 838.

S.D.Ohio 1997. Complaint will not be dismissed for failure to state claim on which relief can be granted unless there is no law to support claims made, facts alleged are insufficient to state a claim, or there is an unsurmountable bar on face of complaint. Fed.Rules Civ.Proc.Rule 12(b)(6), 28 U.S.C.A.

Tanksley & Associates v. Willard Industries, Inc., 961 F.Supp. 203.

S.D.Ohio 1996. Complaint will not be dismissed for failure to state claim upon which relief could be granted unless there is no law to support claims made, if facts alleged are insuffi-

cient to state claim, or if there is insurmountable bar on face of complaint. Fed.Rules Civ. Proc.Rule 12(b)(6), 28 U.S.C.A.

In re Dublin Securities, Inc., 197 B.R. 66, affirmed 133 F.3d 377, rehearing and suggestion for rehearing denied, certiorari denied Terlecky v. Hurd, 119 S.Ct. 45.

S.D.Ohio 1996. Motion to dismiss for failure to state claim will be granted if complaint is without merit due to absence of law to support claim of type made or of facts sufficient to make valid claim, or where face of complaint reveals that there is insurmountable bar to relief. Fed. Rules Civ.Proc.Rule 12(b)(6), 28 U.S.C.A.

Dorsey v. Tompkins, 917 F.Supp. 1195.

S.D.Ohio 1996. It is inappropriate to dismiss complaint based solely upon faulty prayer for relief.

Pickens v. Kanawha River Towing, 916 F.Supp. 702.

S.D.Ohio 1995. To survive motion to dismiss for failure to state claim upon which relief may be granted, complaint must contain either direct or inferential allegations respecting all material elements to sustain recovery under some viable legal theory. Fed.Rules Civ.Proc. Rule 12(b)(6), 28 U.S.C.A.

Klusty v. Taco Bell Corp., 909 F.Supp. 516.

S.D.Ohio 1994. Court may not dismiss complaint for failure to state claim upon which relief can be granted unless it appears beyond doubt that plaintiff can prove no set of facts which would entitle him or her to requested relief. Fed.Rules Civ.Proc.Rule 12(b)(6), 28 U.S.C.A.

Martinez v. Western Ohio Health Care Corp., 872 F.Supp. 469.

S.D.Ohio 1994. Court may grant motion to dismiss for failure to state claim only if it appears beyond doubt that plaintiffs can prove no set of facts in support of their claims which would entitle them to relief. Fed.Rules Civ. Proc.Rule 12(b)(6), 28 U.S.C.A.

Johnson v. University Surgical Group Associates of Cincinnati, 871 F.Supp. 979.

S.D.Ohio 1994. Court may grant motion to dismiss for failure to state claim only if it appears beyond doubt that plaintiffs can prove no set of facts in support of their claims which would entitle them to relief. Fed.Rules Civ. Proc.Rule 12(b)(6), 28 U.S.C.A.

Federspiel v. Ohio Republican Party State Cent. Committee, 867 F.Supp. 617, affirmed 85 F.3d 628.

S.D.Ohio 1994. District court may not dismiss claim for failure to state claim upon which relief can be granted unless it is apparent beyond a doubt to court that plaintiff can prove no set of facts to support claim that would entitle plaintiff to relief. Fed.Rules Civ.Proc.Rule 12(b)(6), 28 U.S.C.A.

>   Pappas v. Bethesda Hosp. Ass'n, 861 F.Supp. 616.

S.D.Ohio 1994. On motion to dismiss for failure to state claim, court must accept as true all allegations in well-pleaded complaint under attack and may grant motion only if it appears beyond doubt that plaintiff can prove no set of facts in support of their claims. Fed.Rules Civ.Proc.Rule 12(b)(6), 28 U.S.C.A.

>   State of Ohio ex rel. Fisher v. Louis Trauth Dairy, Inc., 856 F.Supp. 1229.

S.D.Ohio 1993. District court may not dismiss claim for failure to state a claim unless it is apparent beyond a doubt to the court that plaintiff can prove no set of facts to support a claim which would entitle him to relief. Fed. Rules Civ.Proc.Rule 12(b)(6), 28 U.S.C.A.

>   Martin v. Voinovich, 840 F.Supp. 1175.

S.D.Ohio 1993. When determining sufficiency of complaint in face of motion to dismiss, court will apply principle that complaint should not be dismissed for failure to state claim unless it appears beyond doubt that plaintiff can prove no set of facts in support of his claim which would entitle him to relief. Fed.Rules Civ.Proc. Rule 12(b)(6), 28 U.S.C.A.

>   City of Heath, Ohio v. Ashland Oil, Inc., 834 F.Supp. 971.

S.D.Ohio 1992. In ruling upon motion to dismiss, court must accept as true all well-pleaded allegations of complaint and may dismiss action only if it appears beyond doubt that plaintiff can prove no set of facts that would entitle him to relief. Fed.Rules Civ.Proc.Rule 12(b)(6), 28 U.S.C.A.

>   Operation Badlaw, Inc. v. Licking County General Health Dist. Bd. of Health, 866 F.Supp. 1059, affirmed 991 F.2d 796.

S.D.Ohio 1992. Motion to dismiss for failure to state claim upon which relief can be granted should not be granted unless it appears beyond doubt that plaintiff can prove no set of facts in support of claim which would entitle plaintiff to relief. Fed.Rules Civ.Proc.Rule 12(b)(6), 28 U.S.C.A.

>   Elliott v. New Miami Bd. of Educ., 799 F.Supp. 818.

S.D.Ohio 1990. Complaint will be dismissed for failure to state claim if there is no law to support claims made, if facts alleged are insufficient to state claim, or if insurmountable bar to relief appears on face of complaint. Fed.Rules Civ.Proc.Rule 12(b)(6), 28 U.S.C.A.

>   Firestone v. Galbreath, 747 F.Supp. 1556, affirmed in part 976 F.2d 279, rehearing denied, certified question answered 616 N.E.2d 202, 67 Ohio St.3d 87, answer to

certified question conformed to 25 F.3d 323, on remand 895 F.Supp. 917, affirmed in part, reversed in part 25 F.3d 323, on remand 895 F.Supp. 917.

S.D.Ohio 1989. Federal district court will grant defendant's motion for dismissal for failure to state claim upon which relief can be granted if complaint is without any merit due to absence of law to support claim of type made or of facts sufficient to make valid claim or, if on face of complaint, there is insurmountable bar to relief indicating that plaintiff does not have claim. Fed.Rules Civ.Proc.Rule 12(b)(6), 28 U.S.C.A.

>   Minatsis v. Brown, 713 F.Supp. 1056.

S.D.Ohio 1988. Complaint should not be dismissed for failure to state a claim unless its appears beyond doubt that plaintiff can prove no set of facts in support of his or her claim which would entitle him or her to relief. Fed. Rules Civ.Proc.Rule 12(b)(6), 28 U.S.C.A.

>   Stengel v. City of Columbus, Ohio, 737 F.Supp. 1457.

S.D.Ohio 1988. Complaint may not be dismissed for failure to state claim unless it appears beyond doubt that plaintiff can prove no set of facts to support claim which would entitle him to relief. Fed.Rules Civ.Proc.Rule 12(b)(6), 28 U.S.C.A.

>   S.E.C. v. Davis, 689 F.Supp. 767.

S.D.Ohio 1987. Standards for dismissal of complaint as frivolous under § 1915(d) and dismissal for failure to state claim upon which relief can be granted under Rule 12(b)(6) are identical; action is frivolous if it appears beyond doubt that plaintiff can prove no set of facts which would entitle him to relief. 28 U.S.C.A. § 1915(d); Fed.Rules Civ.Proc.Rule 12(b)(6), 28 U.S.C.A.

>   Lawler v. Marshall, 687 F.Supp. 1176, reversed 898 F.2d 1196.

S.D.Ohio 1983. Once court has jurisdictional power to hear case, it is separate matter whether complaint states claim upon which relief may be granted.

>   Haines v. General Motors Corp., 603 F.Supp. 471.

N.D.Okl. 1995. Complaint should not be dismissed unless it appears that plaintiff cannot prove facts entitling him to relief.

>   F.D.I.C. v. Hinch, 879 F.Supp. 1099.

W.D.Okl. 1995. A motion to dismiss for failure to state a claim upon which relief can be granted must overcome a strong presumption in favor of plaintiff, and court will not dismiss complaint unless it appears beyond doubt that plaintiff can prove no set of facts in support of his claim that would entitle him to relief. Fed. Rules Civ.Proc.Rule 12(b)(6), 28 U.S.C.A.

> Carter v. State Ins. Fund, 877 F.Supp. 575.

W.D.Okl. 1986. Complaint should not be dismissed merely because plaintiff's allegations do not support a stated legal theory, as court is obligated to determine whether allegations support relief on any possible theory. Fed.Rules Civ.Proc.Rule 12(b)(6), 28 U.S.C.A.

> Richey v. Westinghouse Credit Corp., 667 F.Supp. 752.

D.Or. 1995. Motion to dismiss for failure to state claim will only be granted if it appears beyond doubt that plaintiff can prove no set of facts in support of his claim which would entitle him to relief. Fed.Rules Civ.Proc.Rule 12(b)(6), 28 U.S.C.A.

> Rowley v. American Airlines, 875 F.Supp. 708.

D.Or. 1994. District court should not grant motion to dismiss for failure to state claim unless it appears beyond doubt that plaintiff can prove no facts in support of claim. Fed.Rules Civ.Proc.Rule 12, 28 U.S.C.A.

> Mittendorf v. Stone Lumber Co., 874 F.Supp. 292.

D.Or. 1994. Motion to dismiss for failure to state claim may only be granted if it appears beyond doubt that plaintiff can prove no set of facts in support of his claim which would entitle him to relief. Fed.Rules Civ.Proc.Rule 12(b)(6), 28 U.S.C.A.

> Steinke v. Washington County, 857 F.Supp. 55.

D.Or. 1993. Court should not dismiss complaint unless it appears beyond doubt that plaintiff cannot prove any facts in support of its claim which would allow it relief.

> Thomas Creek Lumber and Log Co. v. Madigan, 815 F.Supp. 355.

D.Or. 1993. District court will dismiss complaint for failing to state claim upon which relief can be granted only when it appears beyond doubt that plaintiff can prove no set of facts in support of claim which would entitle plaintiff to relief. Fed.Rules Civ.Proc.Rule 12(b)(6), 28 U.S.C.A.

> Johnson v. Con-Vey/Keystone, Inc., 814 F.Supp. 931.

D.Or. 1991. District court should dismiss complaint for failure to state claim only when it appears beyond reasonable doubt that plaintiff can prove no set of facts in support of claim which would entitle plaintiff to relief. Fed. Rules Civ.Proc.Rule 12(b)(6), 28 U.S.C.A.

> Showalter v. Rinard, 126 B.R. 596.

D.Or. 1991. Dismissal for failure to state a claim is proper only when it appears to certain-ty that plaintiffs can prove no set of facts in support of their claim that would entitle them to relief. Fed.Rules Civ.Proc.Rule 12(b)(6), 28 U.S.C.A.

> In re Sause Bros. Ocean Towing, 801 F.Supp. 378.

D.Or. 1991. Dismissal for failure to state claim is proper only if it appears to certainty that plaintiff can prove no set of facts in support of claim that would entitle him or her to relief.

> Jose v. M/V Fir Grove, 801 F.Supp. 349.

D.Or. 1991. Dismissal for failure to state a claim is proper only when it appears to a certainty that plaintiff can prove no set of facts in support of claim that would entitle him to relief.

> Jose v. M/V Fir Grove, 765 F.Supp. 1024.

D.Or. 1990. To warrant dismissal of case for failure to state cause of action, it must appear with certainty that nonmoving party is not entitled to relief under facts presented in pleadings; all allegations of material fact are taken as true and viewed in light most favorable to nonmoving party. Fed.Rules Civ.Proc.Rule 12(b)(6), 28 U.S.C.A.

> Pineros Y Campesinos Unidos del Noroeste v. Goldschmidt, 790 F.Supp. 216.

D.Or. 1990. Court should dismiss complaint for failure to state claim only if it appears beyond doubt that plaintiff can prove no set of facts in support of claim which would entitle plaintiff to relief. Fed.Rules Civ.Proc.Rule 12(b)(6), 28 U.S.C.A.

> Showalter v. Rinard, 752 F.Supp. 963, reconsideration denied 126 B.R. 596.

D.Or. 1990. Dismissal for failure to state claim is proper only when it appears to certainty that plaintiff can prove no set of facts in support of claim that would entitle him to relief.

> Snohomish County Public Utility Dist. No. 1 v. Pacificorp, 745 F.Supp. 1581.

E.D.Pa. 1996. Complaint may be dismissed for failure to state claim upon which relief may be granted if facts pled and reasonable inferences therefrom are legally insufficient to support the relief requested. Fed.Rules Civ. Proc.Rule 12(b)(6), 28 U.S.C.A.

> Adams v. U.S. E.E.O.C., 932 F.Supp. 660.

E.D.Pa. 1996. Complaint may be dismissed for failure to state claim when facts pled and reasonable inferences therefrom are legally insufficient to support relief sought. Fed.Rules Civ.Proc.Rule 12(b)(6), 28 U.S.C.A.

> Nelson v. Temple University, 920 F.Supp. 633.

E.D.Pa. 1996. Vague and conclusory allegations contained in complaint do not provide fair notice of plaintiff's claims and will not survive motion to dismiss. Fed.Rules Civ.Proc. Rules 8(a), 12(b)(6), 28 U.S.C.A.

> Slater v. Marshall, 915 F.Supp. 721.

E.D.Pa. 1996. To survive motion to dismiss for failure to state claim, plaintiff must set forth facts which state claim as matter of law. Fed.Rules Civ.Proc.Rule 12(b)(6), 28 U.S.C.A.

> Miller v. Group Voyagers, Inc., 912 F.Supp. 164.

E.D.Pa. 1995. In order to survive motion to dismiss for failure to state claim upon which relief can be granted, plaintiff must provide enough evidence to support his claim, but does not need to demonstrate that he will ultimately prevail on merits. Fed.Rules Civ.Proc.Rule 12(b)(6), (e), 28 U.S.C.A.

> Taylor v. Cox, 912 F.Supp. 140.

E.D.Pa. 1995. Vague and conclusory allegations do not provide fair notice and will not survive motion to dismiss. Fed.Rules Civ.Proc. Rule 8(a), 28 U.S.C.A.

> Slater v. Marshall, 906 F.Supp. 256.

E.D.Pa. 1995. To survive motion to dismiss for failure to state claim, plaintiff must set forth facts, and not mere conclusions, which state claim as matter of law. Fed.Rules Civ. Proc.Rule 12(b)(6), 28 U.S.C.A.

> Sterling v. Southeastern Pennsylvania Transp. Authority, 897 F.Supp. 893.

Plaintiff must set forth facts supporting his or her claim, and cannot rely exclusively on vague and conclusory allegations in opposing motion to dismiss for failure to state claim. Fed.Rules Civ.Proc.Rules 8(a)(2), 12(b)(6), 28 U.S.C.A.

> Sterling v. Southeastern Pennsylvania Transp. Authority, 897 F.Supp. 893.

E.D.Pa. 1995. District court will grant a motion to dismiss for failure to state a claim only if nonmoving party cannot prevail legally under set of facts alleged. Fed.Rules Civ.Proc. Rule 12(b)(6), 28 U.S.C.A.

> Frankel v. Warwick Hotel, 881 F.Supp. 183.

E.D.Pa. 1995. Complaint is properly dismissed for failure to state claim only if it appears certain that plaintiff cannot prove any set of facts in support of its claim which would entitle it to relief. Fed.Rules Civ.Proc.Rule 12(b)(6), 28 U.S.C.A.

> School Dist. of Philadelphia v. Pennsylvania Milk Marketing Bd., 877 F.Supp. 245.

E.D.Pa. 1994. Complaint is properly dismissed for failure to state a claim upon which relief can be granted if it appears certain that plaintiff cannot prove any set of facts in support

of its claim which would entitle it to relief. Fed.Rules Civ.Proc.Rule 12(b)(6), 28 U.S.C.A.

> Leach v. Quality Health Services, Inc., 869 F.Supp. 315.

E.D.Pa. 1994. Dismissal of complaint for failure to state claim is not appropriate unless it clearly appears that plaintiff can prove no set of facts in support of his claim which would entitle him to relief. Fed.Rules Civ.Proc.Rule 12(b)(6), 28 U.S.C.A.

> Builders Square, Inc. v. Saraco, 868 F.Supp. 748.

E.D.Pa. 1994. Complaint should not be dismissed for failure to state claim unless plaintiff alleges no set of facts in support of claim that would entitle him to relief. Fed.Rules Civ.Proc.Rule 12(b)(6), 28 U.S.C.A.

> Winterberg v. CNA Ins. Co., 868 F.Supp. 713, affirmed 72 F.3d 318.

E.D.Pa. 1994. Motion to dismiss for failure to state a claim should be granted only if there is no conceivable set of facts that could be proved that would entitle plaintiff to relief. Fed.Rules Civ.Proc.Rule 12(b)(6), 28 U.S.C.A.

> Pittman v. Correctional Healthcare Solutions, Inc., 868 F.Supp. 105.

E.D.Pa. 1994. In reviewing motion to dismiss for failure to state claim upon which relief can be granted, court must determine whether party making claim would be entitled to relief under any set of facts that could be established in support of his or her claim. Fed.Rules Civ. Proc.Rule 12(b)(6), 28 U.S.C.A.

> Mulgrew v. Sears Roebuck & Co., 868 F.Supp. 98.

E.D.Pa. 1994. Dismissal is allowed for failure to state a claim only in those instances where it is certain that no relief could be granted under any set of facts that could be proved. Fed.Rules Civ.Proc.Rule 12(b)(6), 28 U.S.C.A.

> Strange v. Nationwide Mut. Ins. Co., 867 F.Supp. 1209.

E.D.Pa. 1994. Complaint is properly dismissed on motion to dismiss for failure to state claim upon which relief can be granted only if it appears certain that plaintiff cannot prove any set of facts in support of its claim which would entitle it to relief. Fed.Rules Civ.Proc.Rule 12(b)(6), 28 U.S.C.A.

> Youse v. Carlucci, 867 F.Supp. 317.

E.D.Pa. 1994. Court will grant motion to dismiss for failure to state claim only if there is no set of facts under which nonmoving party can prevail. Fed.Rules Civ.Proc.Rule 12(b)(6), 28 U.S.C.A.

> Moser v. Bascelli, 865 F.Supp. 249.

E.D.Pa. 1994. Dismissal for failure to state claim upon which relief may be granted is appropriate only when plaintiff has alleged no set of facts which, if proved, would entitle plaintiff to relief. Fed.Rules Civ.Proc.Rule 12(b)(6), 28 U.S.C.A.

Philadelphia Reserve Supply Co. v. Nowalk & Associates, Inc., 864 F.Supp. 1456.

E.D.Pa. 1994. Court will grant motion to dismiss for failure to state claim only if there is no set of facts under which nonmoving party can prevail. Fed.Rules Civ.Proc.Rule 12(b)(6), 28 U.S.C.A.

Cohen v. Oasin, 863 F.Supp. 225.

E.D.Pa. 1994. Complaint shall be dismissed for failure to state a cause of action only if it is clear that no relief could be granted under any set of facts that could be proved consistent with the allegations. Fed.Rules Civ. Proc.Rule 12(b)(6), 28 U.S.C.A.

Piedmont Airlines, Inc. v. Air Line Pilots Ass'n, 863 F.Supp. 212.

E.D.Pa. 1994. Complaint should not be dismissed for failure to state claim unless it appears beyond doubt that plaintiff can prove no set of facts which would entitle her to relief. Fed.Rules Civ.Proc.Rule 12(b)(6), 28 U.S.C.A.

Verde v. City of Philadelphia, 862 F.Supp. 1329.

E.D.Pa. 1994. Complaint should be dismissed for failure to state claim upon which relief can be granted only when it is clear that no relief can be granted under any set of facts that can be proved consistent with allegations. Fed.Rules Civ.Proc.Rule 12(b)(6), 28 U.S.C.A.

Spring Garden Associates, L.P. v. Resolution Trust Corp., 860 F.Supp. 1070, reconsideration denied, affirmed 68 F.3d 457.

E.D.Pa. 1994. Motion to dismiss for failing to state claim for which relief can be granted may succeed only when it appears that claimant can prove no set of facts in support of his claim that would entitle him to relief. Fed. Rules Civ.Proc.Rule 12(b)(6), 28 U.S.C.A.

Total Care Systems, Inc. v. Coons, 860 F.Supp. 236.

E.D.Pa. 1994. Complaint must provide defendant with fair notice of plaintiff's claim and grounds in which it rests; vague and conclusory allegations do not provide fair notice and thus cannot survive motion to dismiss. Fed.Rules Civ.Proc.Rule 12(b)(6), 28 U.S.C.A.

Bieros v. Nicola, 860 F.Supp. 226.

E.D.Pa. 1994. Dismissal for failure to state cognizable claim is not appropriate unless it appears beyond doubt that plaintiff can prove no set of facts in support of claim which would

entitle plaintiff to relief. Fed.Rules Civ.Proc. Rule 12(b)(6), 28 U.S.C.A.

Kearney v. U.S. Healthcare, Inc., 859 F.Supp. 182.

Complaint may be dismissed when facts pled and reasonable inferences from the facts are legally insufficient to support relief sought. Fed.Rules Civ.Proc.Rule 12(b)(6), 28 U.S.C.A.

Kearney v. U.S. Healthcare, Inc., 859 F.Supp. 182.

E.D.Pa. 1994. A complaint should be dismissed for failure to state a claim only where it is clear that no relief could be granted under any set of facts that could be proved consistent with the allegations. Fed.Rules Civ.Proc.Rule 12(b)(6), 28 U.S.C.A.

Lutz Appellate Services, Inc. v. Curry, 859 F.Supp. 180.

E.D.Pa. 1994. On motion to dismiss for failure to state claim, complaint should be dismissed only if it is clear that no relief could be granted under any set of facts that could be proved consistent with allegations. Fed.Rules Civ.Proc.Rule 12(b)(6), 28 U.S.C.A.

Fox Fuel, a Div. of Keroscene, Inc. v. Delaware County Schools Joint Purchasing Bd., 856 F.Supp. 945.

E.D.Pa. 1994. Complaint is properly dismissed for failure to state claim upon which relief may be granted only if it appears certain that plaintiff cannot prove any set of facts in support of its claim which would entitle it to relief. Fed.Rules Civ.Proc.Rule 12(b)(6), 28 U.S.C.A.

U.S. v. Witco Corp., 853 F.Supp. 139.

E.D.Pa. 1994. Complaint is properly dismissed for failure to state a claim if it appears certain that plaintiff cannot prove any set of facts in support of claim that would entitle him to relief. Fed.Rules Civ.Proc.Rule 12(b)(6), 28 U.S.C.A.

Bieros v. Nicola, 851 F.Supp. 683.

E.D.Pa. 1994. Complaint may not be dismissed for failure to state claim upon which relief can be granted unless it appears beyond doubt that plaintiff can prove no set of facts in support of his claim which would entitle him to relief. Fed.Rules Civ.Proc.Rule 12(b)(6), 28 U.S.C.A.

Trinsey v. Mitchell, 851 F.Supp. 167.

E.D.Pa. 1994. Complaint is properly dismissed if it appears certain that plaintiff cannot prove any set of facts in support of his claim that would entitle him to relief. Fed.Rules Civ.Proc.Rule 12(b)(6), 28 U.S.C.A.

Brennan v. National Telephone Directory Corp., 850 F.Supp. 331.

E.D.Pa. 1994. Complaint is properly dismissed if it appears certain that plaintiff cannot prove any set of facts in support of his claim that would entitle him to relief. Fed.Rules Civ.Proc.Rule 12(b)(6), 28 U.S.C.A.

Raines v. Haverford College, 849 F.Supp. 1009.

E.D.Pa. 1994. Complaint is properly dismissed for failure to state claim upon which relief may be granted only if it appears certain that plaintiff cannot prove any set of facts in support of his claim which would entitle him to relief. Fed.Rules Civ.Proc.Rule 12(b)(6), 28 U.S.C.A.

Arber v. Equitable Beneficial Life Ins. Co., 848 F.Supp. 1204.

E.D.Pa. 1994. Complaint is properly dismissed for failure to state a claim if it appears certain that plaintiff cannot prove any set of facts in support of his claim that would entitle him to relief. Fed.Rules Civ.Proc.Rule 12(b)(6), 28 U.S.C.A.

Hunt v. U.S. Air Force, 848 F.Supp. 1190.

E.D.Pa. 1994. In considering motion to dismiss for failure to state claim, complaint's allegations are to be construed favorably to pleader and complaint should not be dismissed unless it appears beyond doubt that plaintiff can prove no set of facts in support of his claim which would entitle him to relief. Fed.Rules Civ.Proc.Rule 12(b)(6), 28 U.S.C.A.

Simmons v. Community Service Providers, Inc., 847 F.Supp. 351.

E.D.Pa. 1994. Complaint is properly dismissed, under rule governing motion to dismiss for failure to state claim upon which relief can be granted, if it appears certain that plaintiff cannot prove any set of facts in support of his claim that would entitle him to relief. Fed. Rules Civ.Proc.Rule 12(b)(6), 28 U.S.C.A.

Jones v. Hinton, 847 F.Supp. 41.

E.D.Pa. 1994. Complaint is to be dismissed for failure to state claim upon which relief may be granted only if it appears beyond doubt that plaintiff can prove no set of facts in support of his claim which would entitle him to relief. Fed.Rules Civ.Proc.Rule 12(b)(6), 28 U.S.C.A.

Interdigital Technology Corp. v. OKI America, Inc., 845 F.Supp. 276.

E.D.Pa. 1994. Court may grant motion to dismiss complaint for failure to state claim upon which relief can be granted only if it appears beyond doubt that plaintiff can prove no facts to support relief requested. Fed.Rules Civ.Proc.Rule 12(b)(6), 28 U.S.C.A.

Atlantic Paper Box Co. v. Whitman's Chocolates, 844 F.Supp. 1038.

E.D.Pa. 1994. In considering motion to dismiss for failing to state claim upon which relief may be granted, the complaints' allegations are to be construed favorably to the pleader and the complaint should not be dismissed unless it appears beyond a doubt that plaintiff can prove not set of facts in support of claim which would entitle plaintiff to relief. Fed. Rules Civ.Proc.Rule 12(b)(6), 28 U.S.C.A.

Johnson v. Resources for Human Development, Inc., 843 F.Supp. 974.

E.D.Pa. 1994. District court should not dismiss case for failure to state a claim unless it clearly appears that no relief can be granted under any set of facts that could be proved consistent with plaintiff's allegations. Fed. Rules Civ.Proc.Rule 12(b)(6), 28 U.S.C.A.

Confederation Life Ins. Co. v. Goodman, 842 F.Supp. 836.

E.D.Pa. 1994. On motion to dismiss for failure to state claim, court must determine whether party making claim would be entitled to relief under any set of facts that could be established in support of a claim. Fed.Rules Civ.Proc.Rule 12(b)(6), 28 U.S.C.A.

Boyce v. Nationwide Mut. Ins. Co., 842 F.Supp. 822.

E.D.Pa. 1994. Complaint is properly dismissed for failure to state a claim if it appears certain that plaintiff cannot prove any set of facts in support of claim that would entitle him to relief. Fed.Rules Civ.Proc.Rule 12(b)(6), 28 U.S.C.A.

Smith v. City of Chester, 842 F.Supp. 147, reconsideration denied 155 F.R.D. 95.

E.D.Pa. 1994. District court must grant motion to dismiss for failure to state claim upon which relief can be granted only if it appears beyond doubt that plaintiff can prove no set of facts in support of his claim which would entitle him to relief. Fed.Rules Civ.Proc.Rule 12(b)(6), 28 U.S.C.A.

Melendez v. Horizon Cellular Telephone Co., 841 F.Supp. 687.

E.D.Pa. 1994. Court may dismiss complaint for failure to state claim only if it appears beyond doubt that plaintiff can prove no set of facts which would justify relief. Fed.Rules Civ. Proc.Rule 12(b)(6), 28 U.S.C.A.

Brown v. Peoples Sec. Ins., 158 F.R.D. 350.

E.D.Pa. 1993. Complaint is properly dismissed for failure to state claim if it appears certain that plaintiff cannot prove any set of facts in support of his or her claim that would entitle him or her to relief. Fed.Rules Civ.Proc. Rule 12(b)(6), 28 U.S.C.A.

In re Fidelity Bank Trust Fee Litigation, 839 F.Supp. 318, affirmed Lewis v. Fidelity Bank, 43 F.3d 1461.

E.D.Pa. 1993. In deciding motion to dismiss for failure to state claim, court need not determine whether plaintiff will ultimately prevail, but rather whether plaintiff can prove any sets of facts to support claim that would entitle him to prevail. Fed.Rules Civ.Proc.Rule 12(b)(6), 28 U.S.C.A.

In re Corestates Trust Fee Litigation, 837 F.Supp. 104, affirmed 39 F.3d 61.

E.D.Pa. 1993. Test applied to determine legal sufficiency of claim is whether it appears beyond doubt that claimant can prove no facts which would support relief requested. Fed.Rules Civ.Proc.Rule 12(b)(6), 28 U.S.C.A.

Great West Life Assur. Co. v. Levithan, 834 F.Supp. 858.

E.D.Pa. 1993. Complaint can be dismissed only if plaintiff has alleged no set of facts upon which relief can be granted. Fed.Rules Civ. Proc.Rule 12(b)(6), 28 U.S.C.A.

Dibiase v. SmithKline Beecham Corp., 834 F.Supp. 143.

E.D.Pa. 1993. Complaint is properly dismissed only if it appears certain that plaintiff cannot prove any set of facts in support of claim that would entitle him to relief. Fed.Rules Civ.Proc.Rule 12(b)(6), 28 U.S.C.A.

Edwards v. U.S., 833 F.Supp. 521.

E.D.Pa. 1993. Dismissal for failure to state a claim is only appropriate if it appears beyond a doubt that plaintiff can prove no set of facts in support of claim that would entitle him or her to relief. Fed.Rules Civ.Proc.Rule 12(b)(6), 28 U.S.C.A.

U.S. v. Com. of Pa., 832 F.Supp. 122.

E.D.Pa. 1993. Complaint should not be dismissed unless it appears beyond doubt that plaintiff can prove no set of facts in support of claim that would entitle him to relief.

Sorge v. Wright's Knitwear Corp., 832 F.Supp. 118.

E.D.Pa. 1993. Complaint should be dismissed for failure to state claim only where, taking all allegations of complaint as true, and making all reasonable inferences in plaintiffs' favor, it appears beyond doubt that plaintiffs can prove no set of facts in support of their claims which would entitle them to relief; standard is same for RICO as for non-RICO claims. Fed.Rules Civ.Proc.Rule 12(b)(6), 28 U.S.C.A.; 18 U.S.C.A. § 1961 et seq.

Gurfein v. Sovereign Group, 826 F.Supp. 890.

E.D.Pa. 1993. In order to prevail on motion to dismiss for failure to state claim, defendant must establish that plaintiff can prove no set of facts which would entitle it to relief.

Institute of Pennsylvania Hosp. v. Travelers Ins. Co., 825 F.Supp. 727.

E.D.Pa. 1993. To prevail on motion to dismiss, defendant must establish that plaintiff can prove no set of facts which would entitle her to relief; however, where motion to dismiss is based on lack of jurisdiction, plaintiff has burden to prove that jurisdiction exists and must submit affidavits and other relevant evidence to resolve factual dispute concerning jurisdiction. Fed.Rules Civ.Proc.Rule 12(b)(1, 6), 28 U.S.C.A.

Lattanzio v. Security Nat. Bank, 825 F.Supp. 86.

E.D.Pa. 1993. In deciding motion to dismiss for failure to state a claim, court must accept as true all factual allegations contained in complaint and draw from them all reasonable inferences, and complaint should be dismissed only if it is clear that no relief can be granted under any set of facts which could be proved.

Greenwood v. Singel, 823 F.Supp. 1207.

E.D.Pa. 1993. Federal court may grant motion to dismiss for failure to state a claim if it appears beyond a doubt that plaintiff can prove no facts to support relief requested. Fed.Rules Civ.Proc.Rule 12(b)(6), 28 U.S.C.A.

Glaziers and Glassworkers Union Local 252 Annuity Fund v. Newbridge Securities, Inc., 823 F.Supp. 1191.

E.D.Pa. 1993. Case should not be dismissed for failure to state claim unless it appears certain that no relief can be granted under any set of facts that could be proved consistent with plaintiff's allegations.

Resolution Trust Corp. v. Farmer, 823 F.Supp. 302.

E.D.Pa. 1993. A complaint should not be dismissed for failure to state claim unless it appears beyond doubt that plaintiff can prove no set of facts in support of claim which would entitle plaintiff to relief.

In re One Meridian Plaza Fire Litigation, 820 F.Supp. 1492.

E.D.Pa. 1993. Court may grant motion to dismiss for failure to state claim on which relief can be granted if it appears beyond doubt that plaintiff can prove no facts to support requested relief. Fed.Rules Civ.Proc.Rule 12(b)(6), 28 U.S.C.A.

Le Grand v. Lincoln, 818 F.Supp. 112.

E.D.Pa. 1993. Complaint is properly dismissed for failure to state a claim only if it appears certain that plaintiff cannot prove any set of facts in support of her claim that would entitle her to relief. Fed.Rules Civ.Proc.Rules 8(a), 12(b)(6), 28 U.S.C.A.

Oshiver v. Levin, Fishbein, Sedran and Berman, 818 F.Supp. 104, affirmed in part, reversed in part 38 F.3d 1380, on remand 910 F.Supp. 225, affirmed 96 F.3d 1434.

E.D.Pa. 1993. Dismissal for failure to state claim upon which relief can be granted is limited to those instances where it is certain that no relief could be granted under any set of facts that could be proved; thus, if facts pled in complaint and reasonable inferences therefrom are legally insufficient, motion to dismiss may be granted. Fed.Rules Civ.Proc.Rule 12(b)(6), 28 U.S.C.A.

    Clark v. Sears Roebuck & Co., 816 F.Supp. 1064.

E.D.Pa. 1993. Dismissal for failure to state claim upon which relief may be granted is proper only if it appears beyond doubt that plaintiff can prove no set of facts in support of claim which would entitle plaintiff to relief. Fed.Rules Civ.Proc.Rule 12(b)(6), 28 U.S.C.A.

    Bolden v. Niagara Fire Ins. Co., 814 F.Supp. 444, affirmed 8 F.3d 810.

E.D.Pa. 1993. Complaint should not be dismissed for failure to state claim unless it appears beyond doubt that plaintiff can prove no set of facts in support of his claim which would entitle him to relief, taking all well-pleaded factual allegations in complaint as true, drawing all reasonable inferences from allegations, and viewing them in light most favorable to plaintiff. Fed.Rules Civ.Proc.Rule 12(b)(6), 28 U.S.C.A.

    Jones v. Philadelphia College of Osteopathic Medicine, 813 F.Supp. 1125.

E.D.Pa. 1993. District court may grant motion to dismiss for failure to state a claim upon which relief can be granted only if it appears beyond a doubt that plaintiff can prove no set of facts in support of claim which would entitle him to relief. Fed.Rules Civ.Proc.Rule 12(b)(6), 28 U.S.C.A.

    Johnson-Lloyd v. Vocational Rehabilitation Office, Pennsylvania Dept. of Labor and Industry, 813 F.Supp. 1120.

E.D.Pa. 1993. Court may dismiss complaint only where it appears beyond doubt that plaintiffs can prove no set of facts in support of their claim that would entitle them to relief.

    Seidman v. American Mobile Systems, Inc., 813 F.Supp. 323.

E.D.Pa. 1993. Dismissal for failure to state claim is not appropriate unless it clearly appears that plaintiff can prove no set of facts in support of his claim that would entitle him to relief. Fed.Rules Civ.Proc.Rule 12(b)(6), 28 U.S.C.A.

    Defeo v. Sill, 810 F.Supp. 648.

    Complaint may be dismissed for failure to state a claim when facts pled and reasonable inferences derived therefrom are legally insufficient to support relief sought. Fed.Rules Civ. Proc.Rule 12(b)(6), 28 U.S.C.A.

    Defeo v. Sill, 810 F.Supp. 648.

E.D.Pa. 1993. District court may grant motion to dismiss for failure to state a claim only if it appears beyond a doubt that plaintiff can prove no set of facts in support of claim which would entitle him to relief. Fed.Rules Civ.Proc.Rule 12(b)(6), 28 U.S.C.A.

    Barrett v. City of Allentown, 152 F.R.D. 50.

E.D.Pa. 1993. On motion to dismiss for failure to state a claim, court must determine whether party making claim would be entitled to relief under any set of facts that could be established in support of his or her claim. Fed. Rules Civ.Proc.Rule 12(b)(6), 28 U.S.C.A.

    Friedman v. Lansdale Parking Authority, 151 F.R.D. 42.

E.D.Pa. 1993. On motion to dismiss for failure to state a claim, complaint may be dismissed only if it appears that plaintiffs cannot prove any set of facts in support of their claim that would entitle them to relief. Fed.Rules Civ.Proc.Rule 12(b)(6), 28 U.S.C.A.

    Johnson v. U.S., 147 F.R.D. 91.

E.D.Pa. 1992. Court may grant motion to dismiss if it appears beyond doubt that plaintiff can prove no facts to support the relief requested. Fed.Rules Civ.Proc.Rule 12(b)(6), 28 U.S.C.A.

    Glaziers and Glassworkers Union Local 252 Annuity Fund v. Newbridge Securities, Inc., 823 F.Supp. 1185, on reconsideration in part 823 F.Supp. 1188.

E.D.Pa. 1992. Complaint should not be dismissed unless it appears beyond doubt that plaintiff can prove no set of facts in support of claim that would entitle him to relief. Fed. Rules Civ.Proc.Rule 12(b)(1), 28 U.S.C.A.

    Brossman Sales, Inc. v. Broderick, 808 F.Supp. 1209.

E.D.Pa. 1992. Claim should not be dismissed for failing to state claim unless it appears beyond doubt that nonmoving party can prove no set of facts in support of its allegations which would entitle it to relief after pleading is construed in light most favorable to a nonmoving party. Fed.Rules Civ.Proc.Rule 12(b)(6), 28 U.S.C.A.

    In re Sunrise Securities Litigation, 793 F.Supp. 1306.

E.D.Pa. 1992. Case should not be dismissed for failure to state a claim unless it clearly appears that no relief can be granted under any set of facts that could be proved consistent with plaintiff's allegations.

    Price v. Philadelphia Elec. Co., 790 F.Supp. 97, reconsideration denied 1992 WL 165580.

E.D.Pa. 1992. Case should not be dismissed for failure to state claim upon which relief can be granted, unless it clearly appears that no relief can be granted under any set of facts that could be proved consistent with plaintiff's allegations. Fed.Rules Civ.Proc.Rule 12(b)(6), 28 U.S.C.A.

Elliott v. State Farm Mut. Auto. Ins. Co., 786 F.Supp. 487.

E.D.Pa. 1992. Complaint may be dismissed for failure to state claim for which relief can be granted only if it reveals no set of facts that would entitle plaintiff to relief as matter of law. Fed.Rules Civ.Proc.Rule 12(b)(6), 28 U.S.C.A.

Fields v. Graff, 784 F.Supp. 224.

E.D.Pa. 1992. In ruling on motion to dismiss for failure to state claim, court must accept as true all factual allegations and all reasonable inferences that can be drawn therefrom, and must view them in light most favorable to plaintiff, i.e., nonmoving party; court may dismiss complaint only if it is clear that no relief could be granted under any set of facts that could be proved consistent with allegations. Fed.Rules Civ.Proc.Rule 12(b)(6), 28 U.S.C.A.

Warner Cable Communications Inc. v. Borough of Schuylkill Haven, 784 F.Supp. 203.

E.D.Pa. 1991. On a motion to dismiss for failure to state a valid claim, the question before the court is whether the plaintiff could prove any set of facts in support of his claim that would entitle the plaintiff to relief. Fed.Rules Civ.Proc.Rule 12(b)(6), 28 U.S.C.A.

U.S. Dept. of Housing and Urban Development ex rel. Givler v. Smith, 775 F.Supp. 172.

E.D.Pa. 1991. Question on motion to dismiss is not whether plaintiffs will ultimately prevail but, rather, whether they prove any sets of facts in support of their claims that would entitle them to relief. Fed.Rules Civ.Proc.Rule 12(b)(6), 28 U.S.C.A.

In re Meridian Securities Litigation, 772 F.Supp. 223.

E.D.Pa. 1991. If facts pled and reasonable inferences therefrom legally suffice to support relief requested, court will deny motion to dismiss; when reviewing motions to dismiss, district court assumes that all allegations in complaint are true and examines allegations in light most favorable to nonmoving party. Fed.Rules Civ.Proc.Rule 12(b); 28 U.S.C.A.

Action Air Freight, Inc. v. Pilot Air Freight Corp., 769 F.Supp. 899, appeal dismissed 961 F.2d 207.

E.D.Pa. 1991. Motion to dismiss tests legal sufficiency of complaint. Fed.Rules Civ. Proc.Rule 12, 28 U.S.C.A.

U.S. v. Kensington Hosp., 760 F.Supp. 1120.

Court may grant motion to dismiss for failure to state a claim upon which relief can be granted only if it appears beyond doubt that plaintiffs can prove no facts to support relief requested. Fed.Rules Civ.Proc.Rule 12(b)(6), 28 U.S.C.A.

U.S. v. Kensington Hosp., 760 F.Supp. 1120.

E.D.Pa. 1991. If facts pled in complaint and reasonable inferences therefrom are legally insufficient, motion to dismiss may be granted. Fed.Rules Civ.Proc.Rule 12(b)(6), 28 U.S.C.A.

McCoy v. U.S., 758 F.Supp. 299.

E.D.Pa. 1990. Complaint will not be dismissed for failure to state claim unless it appears beyond doubt that plaintiff can prove no set of facts that would entitle him to relief. Fed.Rules Civ.Proc.Rule 12(b)(6), 28 U.S.C.A.

Berkery v. U.S., 767 F.Supp. 660.

E.D.Pa. 1990. Complaint should not be dismissed unless it appears beyond doubt that plaintiff could prove no set of facts in support of claim which would entitle him to relief.

Federal Ins. Co. v. Ayers, 741 F.Supp. 1179, reconsideration denied 760 F.Supp. 1118.

E.D.Pa. 1990. On motion to dismiss for failure to state claim upon which relief can be granted, question before court is not whether plaintiff will ultimately prevail; rather, it is whether plaintiff could prove any set of facts in support of claim that would entitle plaintiff to relief. Fed.Rules Civ.Proc.Rule 12(b)(6), 28 U.S.C.A.

Coffman v. Wilson Police Dept., 739 F.Supp. 257.

E.D.Pa. 1988. Court may dismiss complaint for failure to state claim only if it appears to certainty that no relief could be granted under any set of facts which would be proved. Fed.Rules Civ.Proc.Rule 12(b)(6), 28 U.S.C.A.

Kronmuller v. West End Fire Co. No. 3 Fire Dept. of Borough of Phoenixville, 123 F.R.D. 170.

Even if court doubts that plaintiff would ultimately prevail, so long as plaintiff colorably states facts which, if proven, would entitle him to relief, motion to dismiss should not be granted. Fed.Rules Civ.Proc.Rule 12(b), 28 U.S.C.A.

Kronmuller v. West End Fire Co. No. 3 Fire Dept. of Borough of Phoenixville, 123 F.R.D. 170.

M.D.Pa. 1994. Complaint may be dismissed only if it appears that plaintiff cannot prove any set of facts in support of his claim that would entitled him to relief.

Simms v. Exeter Architectural Products, Inc., 868 F.Supp. 677.

Complaint should never be dismissed for failure to state a claim unless court is convinced beyond doubt that plaintiff can prove no set of facts to support claim which would permit recovery.

Simms v. Exeter Architectural Products, Inc., 868 F.Supp. 677.

M.D.Pa. 1994. Claim may not properly be dismissed for lack of jurisdiction merely because theories of recovery alleged probably are false. Fed.Rules Civ.Proc.Rule 12(b)(1), 28 U.S.C.A.

Nationwide Ins. Co. v. Agway Ins. Co., 845 F.Supp. 252, reversed 77 F.3d 463.

M.D.Pa. 1993. Complaint may be dismissed only if it appears that plaintiff cannot prove any set of facts in support of his claim that would entitle him to relief.

Hunter v. Carbondale Area School Dist., 829 F.Supp. 714, affirmed 5 F.3d 1489, certiorari denied 114 S.Ct. 903, 510 U.S. 1081, 127 L.Ed.2d 94.

Complaint should never be dismissed for failure to state claim unless court is convinced beyond doubt that plaintiff can prove no set of facts to support claim which would permit recovery.

Hunter v. Carbondale Area School Dist., 829 F.Supp. 714, affirmed 5 F.3d 1489, certiorari denied 114 S.Ct. 903, 510 U.S. 1081, 127 L.Ed.2d 94.

M.D.Pa. 1993. When court addresses motion to dismiss for failure to state claim upon which relief can be granted, it may dismiss the complaint only if it appears to a certainty that no relief could be granted under any set of facts which could be proven. Fed.Rules Civ.Proc. Rule 12(b)(6), 28 U.S.C.A.

Wexco Inc. v. IMC, Inc., 820 F.Supp. 194.

M.D.Pa. 1993. For purposes of motion to dismiss for failure to state claim upon which relief can be granted, court must accept as true all well-pleaded allegations of complaint and construe them favorably to plaintiff and cannot grant motion unless plaintiff can prove no set of facts in support of his claim which would entitle him to relief. Fed.Rules Civ.Proc.Rule 12(b)(6), 28 U.S.C.A.

Rogers v. Mount Union Borough by Zook, 816 F.Supp. 308.

M.D.Pa. 1992. Complaint should never be dismissed for failure to state claim unless court is convinced beyond a doubt that plaintiff cannot prove any set of facts to support claim that would permit recovery.

Veteto v. Miller, 829 F.Supp. 1486.

M.D.Pa. 1990. When considering motion to dismiss for failure to state claim upon which relief can be granted, reviewing court must accept all well-pleaded allegations in complaint as true and view them in light most favorable to plaintiff.

Ross v. Zavarella, 732 F.Supp. 1306, appeal dismissed 916 F.2d 898.

M.D.Pa. 1990. Complaint may be dismissed for failure to state claim only if it appears that plaintiffs cannot establish any set of facts in support of their claims which would entitle them to relief. Fed.Rules Civ.Proc.Rule 12(b)(6), 28 U.S.C.A.

Lutz v. Chromatex, Inc., 730 F.Supp. 1328.

W.D.Pa. 1998. In ruling on motion to dismiss for failure to state claim, court looks to whether sufficient facts are pleaded to determine that complaint is not frivolous, and to provide defendants with adequate notice to frame answer.

Aronson v. Creditrust Corp., 7 F.Supp.2d 589.

W.D.Pa. 1996. If no cause of action can be identified on motion to dismiss for failure to state claim, dismissal is proper. Fed.Rules Civ. Proc.Rule 12(b)(6), 28 U.S.C.A.

City of Erie v. Guaranty Nat. Ins. Co., 935 F.Supp. 610, affirmed 109 F.3d 156.

W.D.Pa. 1995. If no cause of action can be identified, dismissal for failure to state claim is proper. Fed.Rules Civ.Proc.Rule 12(b)(6), 28 U.S.C.A.

Saint Vincent Health Center v. Shalala, 937 F.Supp. 496, affirmed 96 F.3d 1434.

W.D.Pa. 1995. Motion to dismiss for failure to state claim tests legal sufficiency of complaint; motion does not attack merits of case. Fed.Rules Civ.Proc.Rule 12(b)(6), 28 U.S.C.A.

Ford v. Johnson, 899 F.Supp. 227.

W.D.Pa. 1995. On motion to dismiss, district court must consider whether relief could be granted under any set of facts that could be proved consistent with allegations in plaintiffs complaint; if no cause of action can be identified, dismissal is ordinarily proper. Fed.Rules Civ.Proc.Rule 12(b)(6), 28 U.S.C.A.

Metcalf v. PaineWebber Inc., 886 F.Supp. 503, affirmed 79 F.3d 1138.

W.D.Pa. 1994. On a motion to dismiss for failure to state a claim, question before district court is not whether plaintiff will ultimately prevail; rather, question is whether plaintiff can prove any set of facts in support of claim that will entitle plaintiff to relief. Fed.Rules Civ. Proc.Rule 12(b)(6), 28 U.S.C.A.

Dugan v. Bell Telephone of Pennsylvania, 876 F.Supp. 713.

W.D.Pa. 1994. Question before court on motion to dismiss is whether plaintiffs can prove any set of facts in support of their claims that will entitle them to relief, not whether they will ultimately prevail. Fed.Rules Civ.Proc. Rule 12, 28 U.S.C.A.

> Ferry v. Mutual Life Ins. Co. of New York, 868 F.Supp. 764.

W.D.Pa. 1994. To prevail on motion to dismiss for failure to state a claim, movant must establish that no relief could be granted under any set of facts that plaintiff could prove. Fed. Rules Civ.Proc.Rule 12(b)(6), 28 U.S.C.A.

> In re Chambers Development Securities Litigation, 848 F.Supp. 602.

W.D.Pa. 1994. Question before court on motion to dismiss is not whether plaintiffs will ultimately prevail, but whether plaintiffs can prove any set of facts in support of claims that will entitle them to relief. Fed.Rules Civ.Proc. Rule 12(b)(1, 6), 28 U.S.C.A.

> Laborers Combined Funds of Western Pennsylvania v. Ruscitto, 848 F.Supp. 598.

W.D.Pa. 1993. District court may dismiss complaint only if it appears beyond doubt that plaintiff can prove no set of facts in support of claims. Fed.Rules Civ.Proc.Rule 12, 28 U.S.C.A.

> In re Phar-Mor, Inc. Litigation, 848 F.Supp. 46.

W.D.Pa. 1993. Complaint should not be dismissed for failure to state a claim unless it appears beyond a doubt that plaintiff can prove no set of facts in support of his or her claim which would entitle him or her to relief. Fed. Rules Civ.Proc.Rule 12(b)(6), 28 U.S.C.A.

> Erie City Retirees Ass'n v. City of Erie, 838 F.Supp. 1048.

W.D.Pa. 1993. To prevail on motion to dismiss for failure to state claim, movant must establish that no relief could be granted under any set of facts that plaintiff could prove. Fed. Rules Civ.Proc.Rule 12(b)(6), 28 U.S.C.A.

> In re Westinghouse Securities Litigation, 832 F.Supp. 948, affirmed in part, reversed in part 90 F.3d 696, on remand 1998 WL 119554.

W.D.Pa. 1988. To merit dismissal of complaint, plaintiff's pleading must fail to meet liberal requirements for pleading claim set out in civil procedure rule which calls for short and plain statement of claim showing that pleader is entitled to relief. Fed.Rules Civ.Proc.Rules 8(a, b), 12(b)(6), 28 U.S.C.A.

> Cohen v. McAllister, 688 F.Supp. 1040.

D.Puerto Rico 1998. On motion to dismiss for failure to state claim, court must look leniently at allegations in complaint and determine if those allegations can reasonably admit of a claim. Fed.Rules Civ.Proc.Rules 12(b)(6), 28 U.S.C.A.

> Martinez Colon v. Santander Nat. Bank, 4 F.Supp.2d 53.

D.Puerto Rico 1995. To withstand motion to dismiss for failure to state claim upon which relief may be granted, complaint must set forth factual allegations, either direct or inferential, regarding each material element necessary to sustain recovery under some actionable legal theory, and failure to make sufficient allegations supporting claim warrants dismissal of complaint. Fed.Rules Civ.Proc.Rule 12(b)(6), 28 U.S.C.A.

> Rullan v. Council of Co-Owners of McKinley Court Condominium, 899 F.Supp. 857.

D.Puerto Rico 1994. Complaint should not be dismissed for failure to state a claim unless it appears beyond a doubt that plaintiff can prove no set of facts in support of claim which would entitle him to relief. Fed.Rules Civ.Proc.Rule 12(b)(6), 28 U.S.C.A.

> Flamand v. American Intern. Group, Inc., 876 F.Supp. 356.

D.Puerto Rico 1993. Complaint should not be dismissed for failure to state claim unless it appears beyond doubt that plaintiff can prove no set of facts in support of claim which would entitle him to relief. Fed.Rules Civ.Proc.Rule 12(b)(6), 28 U.S.C.A.

> Padilla Rodriguez v. Llorens Quinones, 813 F.Supp. 924.

D.Puerto Rico 1992. Motion to dismiss action for failure to state claim may not be granted unless it is certain that plaintiff would not be entitled to recover under any set of facts which could be proven at trial.

> In re San Juan Dupont Plaza Hotel Fire Litigation, 789 F.Supp. 1212.

D.Puerto Rico 1992. Only where plaintiffs' allegations are so inadequate that they render plaintiffs unable to prove any set of operative facts in support of their claim, may district court take extraordinary measure of dismissal for failure to state cause of action. Fed.Rules Civ.Proc.Rule 12(b)(6), 28 U.S.C.A.

> Satellite Broadcasting Cable, Inc. v. Telefonica de Espana, 786 F.Supp. 1089, opinion adhered to as modified on reconsideration 807 F.Supp. 210.

D.Puerto Rico 1991. Dismissal for failure to state claim upon which relief may be granted would be granted only as to claims for which pleading shows no set of facts that could entitle plaintiff to relief. Fed.Rules Civ.Proc.Rule 12(b), 28 U.S.C.A.

> Cooperativa de Ahorro y Credito Aguada v. Kidder, Peabody & Co., 758 F.Supp. 64.

D.R.I. 1996. Claim need only show faintest likelihood of validity to survive motion to dismiss for failure to state claim. Fed.Rules Civ.Proc.Rule 12(b)(6), 28 U.S.C.A.

Iacampo v. Hasbro, Inc., 929 F.Supp. 562.

If, under any theory, allegations in complaint are sufficient to state cause of action in accordance with law, court must deny motion to dismiss for failure to state claim. Fed.Rules Civ.Proc.Rule 12(b)(6), 28 U.S.C.A.

Iacampo v. Hasbro, Inc., 929 F.Supp. 562.

Question before court on motion to dismiss for failure to state claim is whether complaint, viewed in light most favorable to plaintiff and with all doubts resolved in her favor, states any valid claim for relief. Fed.Rules Civ.Proc.Rule 12(b)(6), 28 U.S.C.A.

Iacampo v. Hasbro, Inc., 929 F.Supp. 562.

D.R.I. 1995. Court may only grant motion to dismiss if plaintiff cannot prove any facts supporting its claim for relief. Fed.Rules Civ. Proc.Rule 12(b)(6), 28 U.S.C.A.

U.S. v. F.D.I.C., 899 F.Supp. 50.

In motion to dismiss, defendant must show that plaintiff's claim is insufficient as matter of law. Fed.Rules Civ.Proc.Rule 12(b)(6), 28 U.S.C.A.

U.S. v. F.D.I.C., 899 F.Supp. 50.

In considering motion to dismiss, court, viewing complaint in light most favorable to plaintiff and resolving every doubt in plaintiff's favor, must decide whether allegations set forth any valid claim for relief. Fed.Rules Civ.Proc. Rule 12(b)(6), 28 U.S.C.A.

U.S. v. F.D.I.C., 899 F.Supp. 50.

D.R.I. 1995. To be successful on motion to dismiss for failure to state claim, defendants had burden of showing that plaintiffs' claims were insufficient as matter of law; question before court, therefore, was whether complaint, viewed in light most favorable to plaintiffs and with every doubt resolved on their behalf, stated any valid claim for relief. Fed.Rules Civ.Proc. Rule 12(b)(6), 28 U.S.C.A.

National Educ. Association-Rhode Island by Scigulinsky v. Retirement Bd. of Rhode Island Employees' Retirement System, 890 F.Supp. 1143.

D.R.I. 1995. Court must deny motion to dismiss for failure to state claim if allegations of complaint permit relief to be granted on any theory, even one not expressly stated therein. Fed.Rules Civ.Proc.Rule 12(b)(6), 28 U.S.C.A.

Socha v. National Ass'n of Letter Carriers Branch No. 57 (Merged), 883 F.Supp. 790.

If, despite opportunity to fine tune complaint, especially at court's direction, a naked conclusion, unanchored in any meaningful set of factual averments is the asserted basis for relief, dismissal may follow.

Socha v. National Ass'n of Letter Carriers Branch No. 57 (Merged), 883 F.Supp. 790.

D.R.I. 1995. In deciding motion to dismiss for failure to state claim upon which relief can be granted, court must accept well-pleaded factual averments of the complaint as true, and construe these facts in the light most flattering to the plaintiff's cause, and court must deny motion to dismiss if allegations of the complaint permit relief to be granted on any theory, even one not expressly stated therein. Fed.Rules Civ.Proc.Rule 12(b)(6), 28 U.S.C.A.

Scully Signal Co. v. Joyal, 881 F.Supp. 727.

D.R.I. 1995. Complaint should not be dismissed for failure to state claim upon which relief can be granted unless it appears beyond doubt from pleadings that party opposing motion can prove no set of facts which would support claim for relief. Fed.Rules Civ.Proc. Rule 12(b)(6), 28 U.S.C.A.

Cok v. Forte, 877 F.Supp. 797, affirmed 69 F.3d 531.

D.R.I. 1992. Motion to dismiss based on failure to state claim upon which relief can be granted should not be granted unless it appears beyond doubt that plaintiff can prove no set of facts in support of his claim which would entitle him to relief. Fed.Rules Civ.Proc.Rule 12(b)(6), 28 U.S.C.A.

Morgan v. Ellerthorpe, 785 F.Supp. 295.

D.R.I. 1991. Complaint should not be dismissed for failure to state claim upon which relief can be granted unless it appears beyond doubt that plaintiff can prove no set of facts in support of his claim which could entitle him to relief. Fed.Rules Civ.Proc.Rule 12(b)(6), 28 U.S.C.A.

Fenner v. Moran, 772 F.Supp. 59.

Motion to dismiss for failure to state claim upon which relief may be granted must be denied if allegations of complaint permit relief to be granted on any theory, even one not expressly stated. Fed.Rules Civ.Proc.Rule 12(b)(6), 28 U.S.C.A.

Fenner v. Moran, 772 F.Supp. 59.

D.R.I. 1991. District court must deny motion to dismiss if allegations of complaint permit relief to be granted on any theory, even when not expressly stated therein. Fed.Rules Civ. Proc.Rule 12(b)(6), 28 U.S.C.A.

Sarit v. Drug Enforcement Admin., 759 F.Supp. 63.

D.R.I. 1990. Court must deny a motion to dismiss if allegations of complaint permit relief to be granted on any theory, even one not expressly stated therein. Fed.Rules Civ.Proc. Rule 12(b)(6), 28 U.S.C.A.

O'Neil v. Q.L.C.R.I., Inc., 750 F.Supp. 551.

D.S.C. 1994. In deciding motion to dismiss for failure to state claim, court should not dismiss complaint unless it appears beyond doubt that plaintiff can prove no set of facts in support of his claim which would entitle him to relief. Fed.Rules Civ.Proc.Rule 12(b)(6), 28 U.S.C.A.

Colleton Regional Hosp. v. MRS Medical Review Systems, Inc., 866 F.Supp. 896.

D.S.C. 1994. In deciding motion to dismiss for failure to state claim, court should not dismiss complaint unless it appears beyond doubt that plaintiff can prove no set of facts in support of his claim which would entitle him to relief. Fed.Rules Civ.Proc.Rule 12(b)(6), 28 U.S.C.A.

Colleton Regional Hosp. v. MRS Medical Review Systems, Inc., 866 F.Supp. 891.

D.S.D. 1993. Claim should not be dismissed for failure to state a claim unless it is patently clear that plaintiff can prove no set of facts in support of claim which would entitle it to relief, and for purposes of motion to dismiss for failure to state a claim, all well-pleaded factual allegations contained in complaint are taken as true. Fed.Rules Civ.Proc.Rule 12(b)(6), 28 U.S.C.A.

FGS Constructors, Inc. v. Carlow, 823 F.Supp. 1508.

Issue presented by motion to dismiss for failure to state a claim is whether, taking all well-pleaded factual allegations in complaint as true, plaintiff has succeeded in stating claim that would entitle plaintiff to relief against defendant under some set of facts. Fed.Rules Civ.Proc.Rule 12(b)(6), 28 U.S.C.A.

FGS Constructors, Inc. v. Carlow, 823 F.Supp. 1508.

D.S.D. 1992. When motion to dismiss for failure to state a claim is made, court must view all well-pleaded factual allegations in complaint as true and cannot dismiss complaint unless it appears beyond doubt that no set of facts can be proved which would entitle plaintiff to relief; all reasonable inferences arising from facts pleaded must also be construed most favorably to plaintiff. Fed.Rules Civ.Proc.Rule 12(b)(6), 28 U.S.C.A.

Mousseaux v. U.S. Com'r of Indian Affairs, 806 F.Supp. 1433, affirmed in part, remanded in part 28 F.3d 786.

E.D.Tenn. 1996. To survive motion to dismiss, complaint must articulate more than bare assertion of factual allegations; complaint must contain either direct or inferential allegations respecting all material elements to sustain re-

covery under some viable legal theory. Fed. Rules Civ.Proc.Rule 12(b)(6), 28 U.S.C.A.

Coffey v. Chattanooga-Hamilton County Hosp. Authority, 932 F.Supp. 1023.

E.D.Tenn. 1996. Complaint must articulate more than bare assertion of legal conclusions in order to survive motion to dismiss for failure to state claim upon which relief can be granted. Fed.Rules Civ.Proc.Rule 12(b)(6), 28 U.S.C.A.

Caldwell v. Rowland, 932 F.Supp. 1018.

Complaint must contain either direct or inferential allegations regarding all material elements necessary to sustain recovery under some viable legal theory in order to survive motion to dismiss for failure to state claim upon which relief can be granted. Fed.Rules Civ.Proc.Rule 12(b)(6), 28 U.S.C.A.

Caldwell v. Rowland, 932 F.Supp. 1018.

E.D.Tenn. 1996. In reviewing motion to dismiss for failure to state claim, court must liberally construe complaint in favor of party opposing motion; however, complaint must articulate more than bare assertion of legal conclusions. Fed.Rules Civ.Proc.Rule 12(b)(6), 28 U.S.C.A.

Ketron v. Chattanooga-Hamilton County Hosp. Authority, 919 F.Supp. 280.

To survive motion to dismiss for failure to state claim, complaint must contain either direct or inferential allegations respecting all material elements to sustain recovery under some viable legal theory. Fed.Rules Civ.Proc.Rule 12(b)(6), 28 U.S.C.A.

Ketron v. Chattanooga-Hamilton County Hosp. Authority, 919 F.Supp. 280.

E.D.Tenn. 1995. Court must liberally construe complaint in favor of party opposing motion to dismiss for failure to state claim upon which relief can be granted; however, complaint must articulate more than bare assertion of legal conclusions. Fed.Rules Civ.Proc.Rule 12(b)(6), 28 U.S.C.A.

Frizzell v. Southwest Motor Freight, Inc., 906 F.Supp. 441.

Complaint must contain either direct or inferential allegations respecting all material elements to sustain recovery under some viable legal theory when faced with motion to dismiss for failure to state a claim upon which relief can be granted. Fed.Rules Civ.Proc.Rule 12(b)(6), 28 U.S.C.A.

Frizzell v. Southwest Motor Freight, Inc., 906 F.Supp. 441.

E.D.Tenn. 1995. Court may not grant motion to dismiss for failure to state claim based on disbelief of complaint's factual allegations and while this standard is decidedly liberal, it requires more than bare assertion of legal conclusions. Fed.Rules Civ.Proc.Rule 12(b)(6), 28 U.S.C.A.

> Reynolds v. Massachusetts Cas. Ins. Co., 900 F.Supp. 915, reversed 113 F.3d 1450.

M.D.Tenn. 1991. In deciding motion to dismiss for failure to state a claim on which relief can be granted, court must assume all facts averred in complaint as true, and indulge all reasonable inferences in favor of plaintiff; court cannot grant such motion unless it appears beyond doubt that plaintiff can prove no set of facts in support of his claim which would entitle him to relief. Fed.Rules Civ.Proc.Rule 12(b)(6), 28 U.S.C.A.

> Hardy v. First American Bank, N.A., 774 F.Supp. 1078.

W.D.Tenn. 1997. Dismissal is proper on motion to dismiss for failure to state claim if complaint lacks allegation regarding required element necessary to obtain relief. Fed.Rules Civ.Proc.Rule 12(b)(6), 28 U.S.C.A.

> Kutner v. Sprint Communications Co. L.P., 971 F.Supp. 302.

W.D.Tenn. 1996. Complaint should not be dismissed for failure to state a claim because it does not state all elements giving rise to legal basis of recovery or because plaintiff misconceived proper theory or claim if plaintiff is entitled to relief under any other theory. Fed.Rules Civ.Proc.Rule 12(b)(6), 28 U.S.C.A.

> Burnett v. Tyco Corp., 932 F.Supp. 1039.

W.D.Tenn. 1995. When appraising sufficiency of complaint in context of motion to dismiss for failure to state claim, the accepted rule is that all a complaint need do is afford defendant fair notice of what plaintiff's claim is and the grounds upon which it rests. Fed.Rules Civ.Proc.Rule 12(b)(6), 28 U.S.C.A.

> Scarborough v. Brown Group, Inc., 935 F.Supp. 954.

Complaint should not be dismissed for failure to state claim because it does not state all the elements giving rise to a legal basis of recovery or because plaintiff misconceived the proper theory or claim if plaintiff is entitled to relief under any theory. Fed.Rules Civ.Proc.Rule 12(b)(6), 28 U.S.C.A.

> Scarborough v. Brown Group, Inc., 935 F.Supp. 954.

W.D.Tenn. 1993. Violation of pleading rule by asserting nothing but conclusory allegations that do not afford notice to court or to opposing parties of nature and basis of claim and general type of litigation involved calls for dismissal of complaint for failure to state legally cognizable claim; however, claim should not be dismissed unless it appears beyond doubt that plaintiff can prove no set of facts in support of

claim that would entitle him to relief. Fed. Rules Civ.Proc.Rules 8, 12(b)(6), 28 U.S.C.A.

> Tacker v. Wilson, 830 F.Supp. 422.

Complaint should not be dismissed for plaintiff's failure to state facts that defendants might meticulously have hidden from plaintiff and that only discovery process might reveal. Fed.Rules Civ.Proc.Rules 8, 8(a), 12(b)(6), 28 U.S.C.A.

> Tacker v. Wilson, 830 F.Supp. 422.

W.D.Tenn. 1992. On motion to dismiss for failure to state a claim, court must accept as true all factual allegations in complaint and resolve all reasonable inferences in favor of plaintiff, and dismissal is appropriate only if it appears beyond doubt that plaintiff can prove no set of facts in support of claim which would entitle him or her to relief. Fed.Rules Civ.Proc. Rule 12(b)(6), 28 U.S.C.A.

> People First of Tennessee v. Arlington Developmental Center, 878 F.Supp. 97.

E.D.Tex. 1996. Dismissal for failure to state claim is proper only if there is either (1) lack of cognizable legal theory, or (2) absence of sufficient facts alleged under cognizable legal theory. Fed.Rules Civ.Proc.Rule 12(b)(6), 28 U.S.C.A.

> Stewart Glass & Mirror, Inc. v. U.S.A. Glas, Inc., 940 F.Supp. 1026.

E.D.Tex. 1994. Unless pleadings on their face reveal beyond doubt that plaintiffs can prove no set of facts that would entitle them to relief, dismissal for failure to state claim upon which relief can be granted is inappropriate. Fed.Rules Civ.Proc.Rule 12(b)(6), 28 U.S.C.A.

> Sheppard v. Texas Dept. of Transp., 158 F.R.D. 592.

E.D.Tex. 1994. Complaint should not be dismissed for failure to state claim upon which relief can be granted unless it appears, beyond doubt, that plaintiff can prove no set of facts in support of his claim which would entitle him to relief. Fed.Rules Civ.Proc.Rule 12(b)(6), 28 U.S.C.A.

> F.D.I.C. v. Daniel, 158 F.R.D. 101.

E.D.Tex. 1993. District court will dismiss complaint for failure to state claim on which relief can be granted only if it is clear that no relief could be granted under any set of facts that could be proved consistent with allegations. Fed.Rules Civ.Proc.Rule 12(b)(6), 28 U.S.C.A.

> DeFrancis v. Bush, 839 F.Supp. 13.

N.D.Tex. 1993. Motion to dismiss complaint for failure to state claim should be granted only when it appears beyond doubt that plaintiffs can prove no set of facts in support of their claims that would entitle them to relief. Fed.Rules Civ.Proc.Rule 12(b)(6), 28 U.S.C.A.

Mills v. Injury Benefits Plan of Schepps-Foremost, Inc., 851 F.Supp. 804.

N.D.Tex. 1993. Complaint may not be dismissed for failure to state claim unless it appears beyond doubt that plaintiff can prove no set of facts in support of his claim which would entitle him to relief. Fed.Rules Civ.Proc.Rule 12(b), (b)(6), 28 U.S.C.A.

Tuchman v. DSC Communications Corp., 818 F.Supp. 971, affirmed 14 F.3d 1061, rehearing and rehearing denied 20 F.3d 1172.

N.D.Tex. 1992. Complaint should not be dismissed for failure to state claim unless it appears beyond doubt that plaintiff can prove no set of facts that would entitle him to relief. Fed.Rules Civ.Proc.Rule 12(b)(6), 28 U.S.C.A.

Electronic Data Systems Corp. v. Computer Associates Intern., Inc., 802 F.Supp. 1463.

S.D.Tex. 1998. Dismissal for failure to state a claim upon which relief may be granted can be based either on a lack of a cognizable legal theory or the absence of sufficient facts alleged under a cognizable legal theory. Fed. Rules Civ.Proc.Rule 12(b)(6), 28 U.S.C.A.

Frith v. Guardian Life Ins. Co. of America, 9 F.Supp.2d 734.

S.D.Tex. 1998. Dismissal of complaint for failure to state claim is proper if complaint lacks an allegation regarding any element of plaintiff's claims that is necessary to obtain relief. Fed.Rules Civ.Proc.Rule 12(b)(6), 28 U.S.C.A.

Matthews v. High Island Independent School Dist., 991 F.Supp. 840.

Conclusory allegations or legal conclusions masquerading as factual conclusions will not suffice to prevent motion to dismiss for failure to state a claim. Fed.Rules Civ.Proc.Rule 12(b)(6), 28 U.S.C.A.

Matthews v. High Island Independent School Dist., 991 F.Supp. 840.

S.D.Tex. 1995. To avoid dismissal for failure to state claim, plaintiff must plead specific facts, not mere conclusory allegations. Fed. Rules Civ.Proc.Rule 12(b)(6), 28 U.S.C.A.

Bonton v. Archer Chrysler Plymouth, Inc., 889 F.Supp. 995.

S.D.Tex. 1995. Dismissal for failure to state claim is only proper if allegations in pleadings show bar to relief. Fed.Rules Civ.Proc. Rule 12(b)(6), 28 U.S.C.A.

Mason v. F.D.I.C., 888 F.Supp. 799.

S.D.Tex. 1994. Motions to dismiss for failure to state claim are disfavored and may not be granted unless it appears to a certainty that plaintiff would not be entitled to recover under any state of facts which could be proved in support of its claim. Fed.Rules Civ.Proc.Rule 12, 28 U.S.C.A.

TCA Bldg. Co. v. Northwestern Resources Co., 861 F.Supp. 1366.

S.D.Tex. 1994. Dismissal for failure to state claim is proper if plaintiff fails to allege either cognizable legal injury or sufficient facts to support cognizable legal theory. Fed.Rules Civ.Proc.Rule 12(b)(6), 28 U.S.C.A.

Kjellvander v. Citicorp, 156 F.R.D. 138.

Claim should be dismissed or proposed amendment disallowed if plaintiff fails to plead facts that, if established, would entitle plaintiff to relief. Fed.Rules Civ.Proc.Rule 12(b)(6), 28 U.S.C.A.

Kjellvander v. Citicorp, 156 F.R.D. 138.

S.D.Tex. 1993. Complaint may not be dismissed for failure to state claim upon which relief can be granted unless it appears certain that plaintiffs cannot prove any set of facts in support of their claim that would entitle them to relief. Fed.Rules Civ.Proc.Rule 12(b)(6), 28 U.S.C.A.

In re Browning-Ferris Industries, Inc. Shareholder Derivative Litigation, 830 F.Supp. 361, 125 A.L.R. Fed. 743, affirmed Cohen v. Ruckelshaus, 20 F.3d 465.

S.D.Tex. 1993. Motion to dismiss must be denied unless court finds that plaintiff cannot prove any set of facts to support its claims for relief.

Resolution Trust Corp. v. Norris, 830 F.Supp. 351.

S.D.Tex. 1993. Motion to dismiss for failure to state claim upon which relief may be granted must be denied unless it appears to certainty that plaintiffs can prove no set of facts that would entitle them to relief. Fed.Rules Civ.Proc.Rule 12(b)(6), 28 U.S.C.A.

Askanase v. Fatjo, 828 F.Supp. 465.

S.D.Tex. 1993. Complaint should not be dismissed for failure to state a claim unless it appears beyond doubt that plaintiff can prove no set of facts in support of his claims which would entitle him to relief.

Maxwell v. Henry, 815 F.Supp. 213.

S.D.Tex. 1993. Dismissal for failure to state claim upon which relief may be granted is rare, and should only be granted where it appears beyond doubt that plaintiff can prove no set of facts in support of his claim that would entitle him to relief. Fed.Rules Civ.Proc.Rule 12(b)(6), 28 U.S.C.A.

Maritrend, Inc. v. Galveston Wharves, 152 F.R.D. 543.

S.D.Tex. 1993. Motion to dismiss for failure to state claim upon which relief can be granted tests only formal sufficiency of statements of claims for relief, and is not procedure for resolving contests about facts or merits of case. Fed.Rules Civ.Proc.Rule 12(b)(6), 28 U.S.C.A.

Askanase v. Fatjo, 148 F.R.D. 570.

S.D.Tex. 1992. Motion to dismiss must be denied unless court finds beyond all doubt that plaintiff cannot prove any facts to support its claims for relief.

F.D.I.C. v. Nathan, 804 F.Supp. 888.

S.D.Tex. 1992. Complaint should not be dismissed for failure to state claim upon which relief can be granted, unless it appears beyond doubt that plaintiff can prove no set of facts in support of his claim which would entitle him to relief. Fed.Rules Civ.Proc.Rule 12(b)(6), 28 U.S.C.A.

F.D.I.C. v. Howse, 802 F.Supp. 1554.

W.D.Tex. 1994. Complaint should not be dismissed for failure to state claim upon which relief can be granted unless it appears beyond doubt that plaintiff can prove no set of facts in support of claim which would entitle him to relief. Fed.Rules Civ.Proc.Rule 12, 28 U.S.C.A.

Bowers v. Baylor University, 862 F.Supp. 142.

W.D.Tex. 1991. Dismissal is proper for failure to state claim upon which relief can be granted if complaint lacks allegation regarding element necessary to obtain relief. Fed.Rules Civ.Proc.Rule 12(b)(6), 28 U.S.C.A.

Rheams v. Bankston, Wright & Greenhill, 756 F.Supp. 1004.

D.Utah 1994. Motion to dismiss complaint will not be granted unless it appears beyond doubt that plaintiff can prove no set of facts in support of his claim which would entitle him to relief.

Cooperative Communications, Inc. v. AT & T Corp., 867 F.Supp. 1511.

D.Utah 1994. Complaint does not warrant dismissal for failure to state claim unless it appears beyond doubt that plaintiff can prove no set of facts in support of his claim which would entitle him to relief. Fed.Rules Civ.Proc. Rule 12(b)(6), 28 U.S.C.A.

Oppenheimer v. Novell, Inc., 851 F.Supp. 412.

D.Utah 1993. Motion to dismiss for failure to state claim must be denied unless it appears beyond doubt that plaintiff can prove no set of facts in support of his claim which would entitle him to relief. Fed.Rules Civ.Proc.Rule 12(b)(6), 28 U.S.C.A.

Goodnight v. Shalala, 837 F.Supp. 1564.

D.Utah 1993. Motion to dismiss should be granted where it appears to a certainty that plaintiff would not be entitled to relief under any state of facts which could be proved in support of its claims. Fed.Rules Civ.Proc.Rule 12, 28 U.S.C.A.

Iadanza v. Mather, 820 F.Supp. 1371.

D.Vt. 1993. Dismissal of complaint for failure to state claim is reserved for those cases where it appears certain that plaintiff can prove no set of facts in support of claim which would entitled him to relief. Fed.Rules Civ.Proc.Rule 12(b)(6), 28 U.S.C.A.

Barquin v. Roman Catholic Diocese of Burlington, Vermont, Inc., 839 F.Supp. 275.

E.D.Va. 1996. Complaint should survive motion to dismiss for failure to state a claim if it sets out facts sufficient for court to infer that all of the required elements of the cause of action are present. Fed.Rules Civ.Proc.Rule 12(b)(6), 28 U.S.C.A.

Oram v. Dalton, 927 F.Supp. 180.

E.D.Va. 1996. Court should not dismiss complaint simply because it appears on face of pleadings that chance of recovery is remote and unlikely. Fed.Rules Civ.Proc.Rule 12(b)(6), 28 U.S.C.A.

Materson v. Stokes, 166 F.R.D. 368.

E.D.Va. 1995. While dismissal may be appropriate where complaint contains detailed description of underlying facts that fail to state viable claim, dismissal for failure to state claim is improper where complaint is broad. Fed. Rules Civ.Proc.Rule 12(b)(6), 28 U.S.C.A.

Treadwell v. Murray, 878 F.Supp. 49.

E.D.Va. 1994. Dismissal for failure to state a claim upon which relief can be granted is properly granted where, assuming facts in complaint are true, it is clear as matter of law that no relief could be granted under any set of facts that could be proved consistent with allegations. Fed.Rules Civ.Proc.Rule 12(b)(6), 28 U.S.C.A.

Weill v. Dominion Resources, Inc., 875 F.Supp. 331.

E.D.Va. 1994. Motion to dismiss for failure to state claim upon which relief may be granted should be granted only when it appears to certainty that plaintiff would not be entitled to relief under any set of facts which could be proven in support of his claim. Fed.Rules Civ. Proc.Rule 12(b)(6), 28 U.S.C.A.

Burcher v. McCauley, 871 F.Supp. 864.

E.D.Va. 1994. Complaint should not be dismissed for failure to state claim upon which relief can be granted unless it appears beyond doubt that plaintiff can prove no set of facts in support of his claim which would entitle him to relief; court should not dismiss complaint even if it appears on face of pleadings that chance of recovery is very remote. Fed.Rules Civ.Proc. Rule 12(b)(6), 28 U.S.C.A.

> Fratus v. U.S., 859 F.Supp. 991.

E.D.Va. 1994. District court should not grant motion to dismiss for failure to state claim upon which relief can be granted unless it appears beyond doubt that plaintiff can prove no set of facts in support of claim which would entitle him to relief. Fed.Rules Civ.Proc.Rule 12(b)(6), 28 U.S.C.A.

> Ocean Breeze Festival Park, Inc. v. Reich, 853 F.Supp. 906, affirmed Virginia Beach Policemen's Benev. Ass'n v. Reich, 96 F.3d 1440.

E.D.Va. 1994. Complaint should not be dismissed for failure to state claim upon which relief can be granted unless it appears beyond doubt that plaintiffs can prove no set of facts in support of their claim which would entitle them to relief. Fed.Rules Civ.Proc.Rule 12(b)(6), 28 U.S.C.A.

> Chisolm v. Charlie Falk Auto Wholesalers, Inc., 851 F.Supp. 739, vacated 95 F.3d 331.

Court should not dismiss complaint for failure to state claim upon which relief can be granted unless it appears beyond doubt that plaintiffs can prove no set of facts in support of their claim which would entitle them to relief, even if it appears on face of pleadings that chance of recovery is very remote. Fed.Rules Civ.Proc.Rule 12(b)(6), 28 U.S.C.A.

> Chisolm v. Charlie Falk Auto Wholesalers, Inc., 851 F.Supp. 739, vacated 95 F.3d 331.

E.D.Va. 1994. Complaint should not be dismissed unless it appears beyond doubt that plaintiffs can prove no set of facts in support of their claim which would entitle them to relief; court should not dismiss complaint even if it appears on face of pleadings that chance of recovery is very remote. Fed.Rules Civ.Proc. Rule 12(b)(6), 28 U.S.C.A.

> Higgins v. Medical College of Hampton Roads, 849 F.Supp. 1113.

E.D.Va. 1994. Complaint should not be dismissed for failure to state claim upon which relief can be granted unless it appears beyond doubt that plaintiffs can prove no set of facts in support of their claim which would entitle them to relief. Fed.Rules Civ.Proc.Rule 12(b)(6), 28 U.S.C.A.

> American Exp. Travel Related Services Co., Inc. v. Lominac, 158 F.R.D. 376.

Court should not dismiss complaint for failure to state claim upon which relief can be granted, even if it appears on face of pleadings

that chance of recovery is very remote. Fed. Rules Civ.Proc.Rule 12(b)(6), 28 U.S.C.A.

> American Exp. Travel Related Services Co., Inc. v. Lominac, 158 F.R.D. 376.

E.D.Va. 1994. Motion to dismiss should be granted only if it plainly appears from pleadings that there is no set of facts that plaintiff could plead in support of her claim that would entitle plaintiff to relief. Fed.Rules Civ.Proc.Rule 12(b)(1, 4), 28 U.S.C.A.

> Jacobi v. Blocker, 153 F.R.D. 84.

E.D.Va. 1993. Complaint should not be dismissed for failure to state a claim unless it appears beyond a doubt that plaintiffs can prove no set of facts in support of claim which would entitle them to relief. Fed.Rules Civ.Proc.Rule 12(b)(6), 28 U.S.C.A.

> B.M.H. by C.B. v. School Bd. of City of Chesapeake, Va., 833 F.Supp. 560.

E.D.Va. 1993. Only if it is beyond doubt that plaintiff can prove no set of facts in support of his claim should motion to dismiss be granted. Fed.Rules Civ.Proc.Rule 12(b), 28 U.S.C.A.

> U.S. for Use and Benefit of Owens v. Olympic Marine Services, Inc., 827 F.Supp. 1232.

E.D.Va. 1993. Pro se complaint, no matter how unartfully pleaded, must survive motion to dismiss for failure to state claim unless it appears beyond doubt that plaintiff can prove no set of facts in support of claim which would entitle him to relief. Fed.Rules Civ.Proc.Rule 12(b)(6), 28 U.S.C.A.

> Terry v. Bobb, 827 F.Supp. 366.

E.D.Va. 1993. Dismissal for failure to state a claim upon which relief can be granted is appropriate if it appears beyond doubt that plaintiff can prove no set of facts in support of his claim which would entitle him to relief. Fed.Rules Civ.Proc.Rule 12(b)(6), 28 U.S.C.A.

> McNeal v. Harper, 816 F.Supp. 421.

E.D.Va. 1992. Complaint, no matter how unartfully pleaded, must survive motion to dismiss for failure to state claim unless it appears beyond doubt that plaintiff can prove no set of facts in support of claim which would entitle plaintiff to relief. Fed.Rules Civ.Proc.Rule 12(b)(6), 28 U.S.C.A.

> Islam v. Jackson, 782 F.Supp. 1111.

E.D.Va. 1991. Motion to dismiss should not be granted unless it appears to certainty that nonmoving party would be entitled to no relief under any state of facts which could be proved in support of its claim if plaintiff's allegations in complaint are taken as true. Fed. Rules Civ.Proc.Rule 12(b)(6), 28 U.S.C.A.

> Maldonado v. Nutri/System, Inc., 776 F.Supp. 278.

E.D.Va. 1989. Dismissal is not warranted unless it appears to certainty that nonmoving party would be entitled to no relief under any state of facts which could be proven in support of its claim. Fed.Rules Civ.Proc.Rule 12(b)(6), 28 U.S.C.A.

> El-Amin v. State Bd. of Elections, Com. of Va., 721 F.Supp. 770.

W.D.Va. 1997. Court's conviction that plaintiff will not succeed on his claim does not justify dismissal for failure to state cause of action, if plaintiff has colorably stated allegations necessary to his cause of action. Fed. Rules Civ.Proc.Rule 12(b)(6), 28 U.S.C.A.

> Virginia Vermiculite, Ltd. v. W.R. Grace & Company- Conn., 965 F.Supp. 802, reversed Vermiculite v. W.R. Grace & Company - Connecticut, 156 F.3d 535.

W.D.Va. 1995. Complaint should not be dismissed unless it appears beyond doubt that plaintiff can prove no set of facts in support of his claim which would entitle him to relief. Fed.Rules Civ.Proc.Rule 12(b)(6), 28 U.S.C.A.

> Muhly v. Espy, 877 F.Supp. 294.

W.D.Va. 1995. Complaint should not be dismissed unless it appears beyond doubt that plaintiff can prove no set of facts in support of his claim which would entitle him to relief.

> Martin v. ITT Commercial Finance Corp., 876 F.Supp. 824.

W.D.Va. 1992. When ruling on motion to dismiss complaint for failure to state claim, question is whether, construing allegations in light most favorable to plaintiff, it is clear as matter of law that court could grant no relief under any set of facts that could be proved consistent with allegations.

> Lewis v. McDorman, 820 F.Supp. 1001, affirmed 28 F.3d 1210.

W.D.Va. 1992. If it appears to certainty that plaintiff would be entitled to no relief under any state of facts which could be proved in support of his claim, claim must be dismissed on motion without regard to whether it is based on outlandish legal theory or on close but ultimately unavailing one. Fed.Rules Civ.Proc. Rule 12(b)(6), 28 U.S.C.A.

> Stevens v. Jackson, 800 F.Supp. 344.

D.Virgin Islands 1997. Pleadings are not sufficient to withstand motion to dismiss for failure to state claim where plaintiff rests on subjective characterizations or unsubstantiated conclusions. Fed.Rules Civ.Proc.Rule 12(b)(6), 28 U.S.C.A.

> Government Guarantee Fund of Republic of Finland v. Hyatt Corp., 955 F.Supp. 441.

D.Virgin Islands 1996. Law of Third Circuit requires dismissal of even pro se complaints when such complaints contain only vague and conclusory allegations of unconstitutional conduct. Fed.Rules Civ.Proc.Rule 12(b)(6), 28 U.S.C.A.

> Julien v. Committee of Bar Examiners for Practice of Law, 923 F.Supp. 707.

D.Virgin Islands 1996. As motion to dismiss for failure to state claim tests sufficiency of allegation in complaint, plaintiff is required to set forth sufficient information to outline elements of his claim or to permit inferences to be drawn that those elements exist. Fed.Rules Civ.Proc.Rule 12(b)(6), 28 U.S.C.A.

> Government Guarantee Fund v. Hyatt Corp., 166 F.R.D. 321, affirmed 95 F.3d 291.

D.Virgin Islands 1987. Failure to include short and plain statement of jurisdictional basis of claim normally requires dismissal, unless defect can be corrected by amendment as of right or by leave of court. Fed.Rules Civ.Proc. Rule 8(a), 28 U.S.C.A.

> Fraser v. James, 655 F.Supp. 1073.

District court should allow plaintiff to amend complaint, and should not dismiss for failure to include statement of jurisdictional basis, whenever it appears that basis for federal jurisdiction exists, or may exist, and can be stated by plaintiff. Fed.Rules Civ.Proc.Rule 8(a), 28 U.S.C.A.

> Fraser v. James, 655 F.Supp. 1073.

E.D.Wash. 1993. Complaint should not be dismissed for lack of subject matter jurisdiction unless it appears beyond doubt that plaintiff can prove no set of facts in support of its claim which would entitle it to relief. Fed.Rules Civ. Proc.Rule 12(b)(1), 28 U.S.C.A.

> Hanford Downwinders Coalition, Inc. v. Dowdle, 841 F.Supp. 1050, affirmed 71 F.3d 1469, affirmed Columbia River United v. Dowdle, 76 F.3d 385.

E.D.Wash. 1991. For purposes of deciding motion to dismiss for failure to state claim upon which relief can be granted, court assumes truth of all plaintiffs' material allegations and motion may not be granted unless it appears beyond doubt that plaintiffs can prove no set of facts in support of their claim which would entitle them to relief. Fed.Rules Civ.Proc.Rule 12(b)(6), 28 U.S.C.A.

> Wegbreit v. Marley Orchards Corp., 793 F.Supp. 957, reinstatement granted by 793 F.Supp. 965.

W.D.Wash. 1994. Court may not grant motion to dismiss for failure to state claim unless it appears beyond doubt that plaintiffs can prove no set of facts in support of claim that would entitle them to relief. Fed.Rules Civ. Proc.Rule 12(b)(6), 28 U.S.C.A.

> In re New England Mut. Life Ins. Co. Litigation, 841 F.Supp. 345, affirmed 54 F.3d 786.

W.D.Wash. 1992. Complaint will be dismissed for failure to state claim only if there is no set of facts under which plaintiff can prove his claim. Fed.Rules Civ.Proc.Rule 12(b)(6), 28 U.S.C.A.

> Radical Products, Inc. v. Sundays Distributing, 821 F.Supp. 648.

N.D.W.Va. 1995. For purposes of motion to dismiss for failure to state claim, complaint is construed in light most favorable to party making the claim and essentially court's inquiry is directed to whether the allegations constitute a statement of a claim. Fed.Rules Civ.Proc.Rule 12(b)(6), 28 U.S.C.A.

> Booth v. Old Nat. Bank, 900 F.Supp. 836.

S.D.W.Va. 1996. In general, motion to dismiss for failure to state claim should not be granted unless it appears certain that plaintiff can prove no set of facts which would support its claim and would entitle it to relief. Fed. Rules Civ.Proc.Rule 12(b)(6), 28 U.S.C.A.

> McClenathan v. Rhone-Poulenc, Inc., 926 F.Supp. 1272.

S.D.W.Va. 1995. Federal district court should not grant motion to dismiss solely because of minor defects in pleading. Fed.Rules Civ.Proc.Rule 12(b)(6), 28 U.S.C.A.

> Pen Coal Corp. v. William H. McGee and Co., Inc., 903 F.Supp. 980.

S.D.W.Va. 1994. Complaint should not be dismissed for failure to state claim unless it appears beyond doubt that plaintiff can prove no set of facts in support of claim which would entitle plaintiff to relief. Fed.Rules Civ.Proc. Rule 12(b)(6), 28 U.S.C.A.

> Cromer v. Lounsbury Chiropractic Offices, Inc., 866 F.Supp. 960.

S.D.W.Va. 1994. Motion to dismiss for failure to state claim should generally not be granted unless it appears certain that plaintiff can prove no set of facts that would support claim and entitle plaintiff to relief. Fed.Rules Civ.Proc.Rule 12(b)(6), 28 U.S.C.A.

> Cook v. Espy, 856 F.Supp. 1095.

E.D.Wis. 1996. Court has authority to dismiss any claim based on indisputably meritless legal theory and any claim whose factual contentions are clearly baseless.

> Richmond v. Cagle, 920 F.Supp. 955.

E.D.Wis. 1995. In deciding motion to dismiss for failure to state claim upon which relief can be granted, district court must accept as true all well-pleaded factual allegations contained in plaintiff's complaint, viewing all reasonable inferences in light most favorable to plaintiff; plaintiff, however, must set forth factual allegations in complaint adequate to establish essential elements of his or her claim, and legal conclusions lacking adequate support should not be considered. Fed.Rules Civ.Proc. Rule 12(b)(6), 28 U.S.C.A.

> Mann v. Hanil Bank, 900 F.Supp. 1077.

E.D.Wis. 1995. Complaint should not be dismissed for failure to state claim unless it is clear that plaintiff would not be entitled to relief even if factual allegations were proven. Fed. Rules Civ.Proc.Rule 12(b)(6), 28 U.S.C.A.

> Zanella v. Principal Mut. Life Ins. Co., 878 F.Supp. 144.

E.D.Wis. 1995. Dismissal is appropriate only where it appears beyond doubt that plaintiffs can prove no set of facts in support of their claims which would entitle them to relief. Fed. Rules Civ.Proc.Rule 12(b)(6), 28 U.S.C.A.

> Kaufmann v. U.S., 876 F.Supp. 1044.

To avoid dismissal, plaintiffs must do more than attach bare legal conclusions to narrated facts. Fed.Rules Civ.Proc.Rule 12(b)(6), 28 U.S.C.A.

> Kaufmann v. U.S., 876 F.Supp. 1044.

E.D.Wis. 1994. Complaint should not be dismissed for failure to state claim unless it is clear that plaintiff would not be entitled to relief even if factual allegations were proven.

> Stefanski v. R.A. Zehetner & Associates, Inc., 855 F.Supp. 1030.

E.D.Wis. 1994. Court must deny motion to dismiss for failure to state claim upon which relief can be granted unless it appears beyond doubt that plaintiff is unable to prove any set of facts which would entitle him or her to relief. Fed.Rules Civ.Proc.Rule 12(b)(6), 28 U.S.C.A.

> McCulley v. U.S. Dept. of Veterans Affairs, 851 F.Supp. 1271.

E.D.Wis. 1994. Though complaint should not be dismissed for failure to state claim unless it appears beyond doubt that plaintiff can prove no set of facts in support of claim which would entitle him to relief, accepting as true the factual allegations of the complaint, nevertheless, plaintiff must allege sufficient facts to outline the cause of action, proof of which is essential to recovery. Fed.Rules Civ.Proc.Rule 12(b)(6), 28 U.S.C.A.

> Carney v. White, 843 F.Supp. 462, affirmed 60 F.3d 1273.

E.D.Wis. 1994. In context of motion to dismiss for failure to state a claim, complaint must set forth factual allegations adequate to establish essential elements of claim, and legal conclusions lacking adequate support should not be considered. Fed.Rules Civ.Proc.Rule 12(b)(6), 28 U.S.C.A.

Nunley v. Kloehn, 158 F.R.D. 614.

Court must deny motion to dismiss for failure to state a claim unless it appears beyond doubt that plaintiff is unable to prove any set of facts that would entitle him or her to relief. Fed.Rules Civ.Proc.Rule 12(b)(6), 28 U.S.C.A.

Nunley v. Kloehn, 158 F.R.D. 614.

E.D.Wis. 1990. Where plaintiff fails to allege essential element of claim, complaint must be dismissed for failure to state a claim upon which relief can be granted. Fed.Rules Civ. Proc.Rule 12(b)(6), 28 U.S.C.A.

Listenbee v. City of Milwaukee, 753 F.Supp. 780, affirmed 976 F.2d 348.

E.D.Wis. 1987. Complaint should not be dismissed for failure to state claim unless it appears beyond doubt that plaintiff could prove no set of facts in support of his claim.

Thomas v. U.S., 671 F.Supp. 15, affirmed 890 F.2d 18.

W.D.Wis. 1996. Plaintiff has responsibility to include allegations of fact sufficient to establish crucial elements of claim, and complaint that asserts legal conclusions without adequate factual allegations supporting them may be dismissed for failure to state claim on which relief may be granted. Fed.Rules Civ.Proc.Rule 12(b)(6), 28 U.S.C.A.

Menominee Indian Tribe of Wisconsin v. Thompson, 943 F.Supp. 999.

W.D.Wis. 1992. Complaint may only be dismissed for failure to state claim if it appears beyond doubt that plaintiff can prove no set of facts in support of his claim which would entitle him to relief. Fed.Rules Civ.Proc.Rule 12(b)(6), 28 U.S.C.A.

Heideman v. Wirsing, 840 F.Supp. 1285, affirmed 7 F.3d 659.

Vagueness or lack of detail are insufficient grounds to dismiss complaint for failure to state claim, but court should not draw inferences unless they are plainly apparent from face of complaint. Fed.Rules Civ.Proc.Rule 12(b)(6), 28 U.S.C.A.

Heideman v. Wirsing, 840 F.Supp. 1285, affirmed 7 F.3d 659.

D.Wyo. 1994. Court should not grant motion to dismiss for failure to state claim unless it appears beyond doubt that plaintiff could prove no set of facts supporting claim which would entitle plaintiff to relief. Fed.Rules Civ.Proc. Rule 12(b)(6), 28 U.S.C.A.

Duart v. FMC Wyoming Corp., 859 F.Supp. 1447, affirmed 72 F.3d 117.

D.Wyo. 1994. Courts should not grant motion to dismiss for failure to state claim unless it

appears beyond doubt that plaintiff could prove no set of facts supporting claim that would entitle plaintiff to relief. Fed.Rules Civ.Proc. Rule 12(b)(6), 28 U.S.C.A.

Bintner v. Burlington Northern, Inc., 857 F.Supp. 1484.

D.Wyo. 1993. Constitutional claim under § 1983 should not be dismissed on motion unless it appears beyond doubt that plaintiff could prove no set of facts in support of claim that would entitle him to relief. 42 U.S.C.A. § 1983.

Goss v. Sullivan, 839 F.Supp. 1532.

D.Wyo. 1993. Court must not dismiss complaint for failing to state cause of action, unless it appears beyond doubt that plaintiff can prove no set of facts supporting his claim which would entitle him to relief. Fed.Rules Civ.Proc. Rule 12(b)(6), 28 U.S.C.A.

Hirsch v. Copenhaver, 839 F.Supp. 1524, affirmed 46 F.3d 1151.

D.Wyo. 1993. Dismissal of case for failure to state claim requires legal determination that plaintiff can prove no set of facts in support of her claim to entitle her to relief. Fed.Rules Civ.Proc.Rule 12(b)(6), 28 U.S.C.A.

Gustafson v. Bridger Coal Co., 834 F.Supp. 352.

D.Wyo. 1993. Because dismissal is extremely harsh remedy, party cannot prevail on motion to dismiss unless it appears beyond doubt that opposing party can prove no set of facts entitling it to relief. Fed.Rules Civ.Proc. Rules 8(a)(2), 12(b)(6), 28 U.S.C.A.

Winders v. United Transp. Union, 833 F.Supp. 860.

D.Wyo. 1993. In order to grant dismissal for failure to state a claim, court must make legal determination that plaintiff can prove no set of facts in support of claim that would entitle her to relief and, in making that determination, court is required to view facts in light most favorable to the plaintiff, giving plaintiff the benefit of all reasonable inferences that can be drawn from the facts pled. Fed.Rules Civ. Proc.Rule 12(b)(6), 28 U.S.C.A.

White v. Continental General Ins. Co., 831 F.Supp. 1545.

D.Wyo. 1991. District court will not grant motion to dismiss unless it appears beyond doubt that plaintiff could prove no set of facts supporting its claim which would entitle it to relief.

Meredith v. Health Care Products, Inc., 777 F.Supp. 923.

Bkrtcy.E.D.Ark. 1992. Complaint should not be dismissed for failure to state claim upon which relief can be granted unless it appears beyond doubt that plaintiff can prove no set of facts in support of his claim which would entitle him to relief. Fed.Rules Civ.Proc.Rule 12(b)(6), 28 U.S.C.A.

In re Castle Industries, Inc., 147 B.R. 941.

Complaint may be dismissed for failure to state claim upon which relief can be granted where complaint clearly shows that plaintiff cannot recover under any circumstances. Fed. Rules Civ.Proc.Rule 12(b)(6), 28 U.S.C.A.

In re Castle Industries, Inc., 147 B.R. 941.

Bkrtcy.E.D.Ark. 1992. In deciding motion to dismiss, court must take all allegations of complaint as true, and dismissal is proper when complaint clearly shows plaintiff cannot recover under any circumstances.

In re Klober, 142 B.R. 297, motion to set aside judgment denied 142 B.R. 300.

Bkrtcy.E.D.Ark. 1988. Complaint should not be dismissed merely because plaintiff's allegations do not support particular legal theory he advances, because complaint does not state all elements that give rise to legal basis for recovery, or because court doubts that plaintiff will prevail in action. Fed.Rules Civ.Proc.Rule 12(b)(5), 28 U.S.C.A.

In re Hollis and Co., 86 B.R. 152.

Bkrtcy.E.D.Ark. 1988. Complaints should not be dismissed merely because plaintiff's allegations do not support particular legal theory he advances, for court is under duty to examine complaint to determine if allegations provide for relief on any possible theory; question is whether, in light most favorable to plaintiff, complaint states any valid claim for relief. Fed. Rules Civ.Proc.Rule 12(b)(6), 28 U.S.C.A.

In re Hollis & Co., 83 B.R. 588.

Bkrtcy.C.D.Cal. 1996. Motion to dismiss for failure to state a claim is viewed with disfavor and is rarely granted. Fed.Rules Civ. Proc.Rule 12(b)(6), 28 U.S.C.A.; Fed.Rules Bankr.Proc.Rule 7012, 11 U.S.C.A.

In re County of Orange, 191 B.R. 1005.

Party moving to dismiss complaint for failure to state a claim can prevail only if it appears beyond all doubt that plaintiffs can prove no set of facts in support of their claims that would entitle plaintiffs to relief. Fed.Rules Bankr. Proc.Rule 7012, 11 U.S.C.A.

In re County of Orange, 191 B.R. 1005.

Bkrtcy.C.D.Cal. 1993. On motion to dismiss, court must accept as true all factual allegations in light most favorable to plaintiff, and must deny request to dismiss unless it appears beyond doubt that plaintiff can prove no set of facts in support of his claim that would entitle him to relief. Fed.Rules Bankr.Proc. Rule 7012(b), 11 U.S.C.A.; Fed.Rules Civ.Proc. Rule 12(b)(6), 28 U.S.C.A.

In re NSB Film Corp., 160 B.R. 151.

Bkrtcy.D.Colo. 1995. Regardless of precise legal theory proffered in support of set of facts, if facts state some claim for relief, even if other than that framed by plaintiff, court may not dismiss complaint.

In re Hamilton, 186 B.R. 991.

Bkrtcy.D.Conn. 1990. Motion to dismiss for failure to state claim upon which relief can be granted should not be granted unless it appears beyond doubt that plaintiff can prove no set of facts in support of his claim which would entitle him to relief. Fed.Rules Civ.Proc. Rule 12(b)(6), 28 U.S.C.A.

In re Schiraldi, 116 B.R. 359.

Bkrtcy.D.Del. 1994. If plaintiff can prove any set of facts in support of his or her claim that would entitle him or her to relief, complaint should not be dismissed. Fed.Rules Civ. Proc.Rule 12(b)(6), 28 U.S.C.A.

In re McMahon Books, Inc., 173 B.R. 868.

Bkrtcy.M.D.Fla. 1995. Motions to dismiss for failure to state claim for which relief can be granted are generally denied unless movant can prove legal insufficiency of claim.

In re American Fabricators, Inc., 186 B.R. 526.

Bkrtcy.N.D.Ga. 1990. For motion to dismiss to succeed, it must clearly appear from complaint that plaintiff can prove no set of facts in support of its claims that would entitle it to relief, and court must consider both pleaded facts and reasonable inferences from pleaded facts in light most favorable to plaintiff.

Matter of Munford, Inc., 115 B.R. 390.

Bkrtcy.N.D.Ill. 1997. So long as fair notice has been given and court can glean actionable claim from complaint, court must entertain plaintiff's case and may not dismiss it for failure to state claim. Fed.Rules Civ.Proc.Rule 8(a), 28 U.S.C.A.; Fed.Rules Bankr.Proc.Rule 7008, 11 U.S.C.A.

In re Barr, 207 B.R. 168.

Bkrtcy.N.D.Ill. 1996. Under rule governing motions to dismiss, allegations in pleading are to be construed in favor of nonmovant, and motion should be granted only if movant clearly established that no material issue of fact remains to be resolved and that he or she is entitled to judgment as matter of law. Fed. Rules Civ.Proc.Rule 12(b), 28 U.S.C.A.

In re Lakeside Community Hosp., 191 B.R. 122.

Bkrtcy.N.D.Ill. 1994. For bankruptcy trustee to prevail on motion to dismiss counterclaims, it must clearly appear from pleadings that creditors can prove no set of facts in support of their claims which entitle them to relief. Fed.Rules Civ.Proc.Rule 12(b-h), 28

U.S.C.A.; Fed.Rules Bankr.Proc.Rule 7012(b), 11 U.S.C.A.

In re Midway Airlines, Inc., 175 B.R. 239.

For purposes of motion to dismiss, issue is not whether creditors will ultimately prevail on their counterclaims, but whether they have pleaded causes of action sufficient to entitle them to offer evidence in support of their claims. Fed.Rules Civ.Proc.Rule 12(b-h), 28 U.S.C.A.; Fed.Rules Bankr.Proc.Rule 7012(b), 11 U.S.C.A.

In re Midway Airlines, Inc., 175 B.R. 239.

Bkrtcy.N.D.Ill. 1994. Bankruptcy court should grant motion to dismiss for failure to state claim upon which relief can be granted only if it appears beyond question that plaintiff can prove no set of facts that would entitle plaintiff to relief. Fed.Rules Bankr.Proc.Rule 7012, 11 U.S.C.A.; Fed.Rules Civ.Proc.Rule 12(b)(6), 28 U.S.C.A.

In re Envirodyne Industries, Inc., 174 B.R. 986.

Bkrtcy.N.D.Ill. 1994. Complaint should be dismissed for failure to state claim if it appears beyond doubt that plaintiff can prove no set of facts that would entitle it to relief.

In re Luria Steel and Trading Corp., 168 B.R. 913.

Bkrtcy.N.D.Ill. 1994. Complaint should be dismissed for failure to state claim if it appears beyond doubt that plaintiff can prove no set of facts which would entitle him to relief.

In re Luria Steel and Trading Corp., 164 B.R. 293, opinion supplemented 168 B.R. 913, affirmed 189 B.R. 418.

Bkrtcy.N.D.Ill. 1993. For debtor to prevail on its motion to dismiss for failure to state claim, it must clearly appear from pleadings that lender, bringing nondischargeability complaint, can prove no set of facts in support of its claims which would entitle it to relief. Fed. Rules Civ.Proc.Rule 12, 28 U.S.C.A.; Fed.Rules Bankr.Proc.Rule 7012, 11 U.S.C.A.

In re Leigh, 165 B.R. 203.

Bkrtcy.N.D.Ill. 1993. Complaint may not be dismissed for failure to state cause of action upon which relief can be granted, unless it appears beyond doubt that plaintiff can prove no facts which would entitle plaintiff to relief. Fed.Rules Civ.Proc.Rule 12(b)(6), 28 U.S.C.A.

In re Papa's Market Cafe, Inc., 162 B.R. 519.

Bkrtcy.N.D.Ill. 1993. Dismissal of complaint is appropriate if complaint fails to state claim upon which relief can be granted and moving party is entitled to judgment as matter of law. Fed.Rules Civ.Proc.Rule 12(b), 28 U.S.C.A.

In re Germansen Decorating, Inc., 149 B.R. 522.

Bkrtcy.N.D.Ill. 1992. For defendants to prevail on motion to dismiss, it must appear beyond doubt from pleadings that plaintiff can prove no set of facts in support of its claims which would entitle it to relief.

In re Schraiber, 141 B.R. 1008.

Bkrtcy.N.D.Ill. 1991. Mere vagueness or lack of detail does not constitute sufficient basis for dismissal of complaint treated under principles of federal court notice pleading.

In re Pettibone Corp., 138 B.R. 210.

Bkrtcy.N.D.Ill. 1991. In order to prevail on motion to dismiss for failure to state claim upon which relief can be granted, it must appear beyond doubt from pleadings that no set of facts can be proven which would warrant relief on the claims stated. Fed.Rules Civ.Proc.Rule 12(b)(6), 28 U.S.C.A.

In re Aluminum Mills Corp., 132 B.R. 869.

Bkrtcy.N.D.Ill. 1990. In order for defendants to prevail on motions to dismiss, it must clearly appear from pleadings that plaintiff can prove no set of facts in support of its claims which would entitle it to relief; issue is not whether plaintiff will ultimately prevail, but whether plaintiff has pleaded cause of action sufficient to entitle it to offer evidence in support of its claims.

In re Churchfield Management & Inv. Corp., 122 B.R. 76.

Bkrtcy.N.D.Ill. 1990. For defendant to prevail on motion to dismiss for failure to state claim, it must clearly appear from pleadings that plaintiff can prove no set of facts in support of its claim which would entitle it to relief; issue is not whether plaintiff will ultimately prevail, but whether plaintiff has pleaded cause of action sufficient to entitle it to offer evidence in support of its claim.

In re Blumberg, 112 B.R. 236.

Bkrtcy.N.D.Ill. 1989. For movant to prevail on motion to dismiss for failure to state claim upon which relief could be granted, it would have to appear from pleading that plaintiff could prove no set of facts in support of its claims which would entitle it to relief; the issue was not whether plaintiff would ultimately prevail, but whether plaintiff had pleaded cause of action sufficient to entitle it to offer evidence in support of its claims.

In re Valley Liquors, Inc., 103 B.R. 961.

Bkrtcy.N.D.Ind. 1989. Under the Federal Rules, there is no requirement that complaint state facts sufficient to constitute cause of action, but only that there be short and plain statement of claim showing that pleader is entitled to relief, and pleader need not allege legal theory on which he relies; failure to plead facts showing theory of liability does not warrant dismissal. Fed.Rules Civ.Proc.Rule 12(b)(6), 28 U.S.C.A.

  In re Diaz, 120 B.R. 967.

Basic test on motion to dismiss for failure to state claim upon which relief can be granted is whether complaint, with all the well-pled material facts taken as true and construed in the light most favorable to the plaintiff, sets forth facts sufficient to state legal claim. Fed.Rules Civ.Proc.Rule 12(b)(6), 28 U.S.C.A.

  In re Diaz, 120 B.R. 967.

Accepted rule in appraising the sufficiency of the complaint is that it should not be dismissed for failure to state claim unless it appears beyond doubt that plaintiff can prove no set of facts in support of his claim which would entitle him to relief. Fed.Rules Civ.Proc.Rule 12(b)(6), 28 U.S.C.A.

  In re Diaz, 120 B.R. 967.

Mere vagueness or lack of detail does not constitute sufficient grounds to grant motion to dismiss for failure to state claim upon which relief can be granted. Fed.Rules Civ.Proc.Rule 12(b)(6), 28 U.S.C.A.

  In re Diaz, 120 B.R. 967.

Bkrtcy.D.Md. 1990. Motions to dismiss for failure to state claims should be granted only if there is no doubt, even if plaintiff is able to prove all facts necessary to support claim as alleged, plaintiff would not be entitled to relief sought. Fed.Rules Civ.Proc.Rule 12(b)(6), 28 U.S.C.A.

  In re Stereo Equipment Sales, Inc., 119 B.R. 70.

Bkrtcy.D.Md. 1990. Motions to dismiss for failure to state claim should only be granted if there is no doubt that, even if plaintiff is able to prove all facts necessary to support his claim as alleged, plaintiff would not be entitled to the relief sought. Fed.Rules Civ.Proc.Rule 12(b)(6), 28 U.S.C.A.; Bankruptcy Rule 7012(b), 11 U.S.C.A.

  In re Marino, 115 B.R. 863.

Bkrtcy.D.Mass. 1995. Great specificity is ordinarily not required to survive motion to dismiss for failure to state claim upon which relief can be granted; it is enough for plaintiff to sketch action claim by means of generalized statement of facts from which defendant will be able to frame responsive pleading. Fed.Rules Civ.Proc.Rule 12(b)(6), 28 U.S.C.A.

  In re Boston Investors Group, L.P., 182 B.R. 637.

Bkrtcy.D.Mass. 1994. Motion for summary judgment which attacks legal sufficiency of claim made and involves no factual assertions is more akin to motion to dismiss and should not be granted unless it clearly appears, according to facts alleged, that plaintiff cannot recover on any viable theory. Fed.Rules Bankr. Proc.Rule 7056, 11 U.S.C.A.; Fed.Rules Civ. Proc.Rules 12(b)(6), 56, 28 U.S.C.A.

  In re Myers, 175 B.R. 122.

Bkrtcy.D.Mass. 1993. Motion to dismiss must be denied unless it appears that plaintiff can prove no set of facts in support of its claim that would entitle it to relief sought.

  In re American Spring Bed Mfg. Co., 153 B.R. 365.

Bkrtcy.D.Mass. 1992. Motion to dismiss must be denied unless it appears that plaintiff could prove no set of facts in support of its claim that would entitle it to relief sought. Fed.Rules Civ.Proc.Rule 12(b)(6), 28 U.S.C.A.

  In re Demakes Enterprises, Inc., 143 B.R. 304.

Bkrtcy.D.Nev. 1986. Complaint is sufficient to avoid dismissal if, within framework of complaint, defendant is informed with reasonable particularity of legally cognizable claim against him; allegations that are conclusory and do not set forth sufficient material facts to support plaintiffs' claim are not sufficient. Fed. Rules Civ.Proc.Rule 12(b)(6), 28 U.S.C.A.

  In re Baker, 66 B.R. 652.

Bkrtcy.D.N.H. 1995. On motion to dismiss for failure to state claim upon which relief can be granted, court must accept allegations of complaint as true and, if allegations are sufficient to state cause of action in accordance with law under any theory, motion must be denied. Fed.Rules Civ.Proc.Rule 12(b)(6), 28 U.S.C.A.

  In re Mealey, 189 B.R. 20.

Bkrtcy.E.D.N.Y. 1998. To survive motion to dismiss for failure to state claim, complaint must be "well pleaded" and contain more than mere conclusory statements that plaintiff has valid claim of some type and is thus deserving of relief. Fed.Rules Bankr.Proc.Rule 7012(b), 11 U.S.C.A.; Fed.Rules Civ.Proc.Rule 12(b)(6), 28 U.S.C.A.

  In re John's Insulation, Inc., 221 B.R. 683.

Bkrtcy.E.D.N.Y. 1994. Complaint should not be dismissed for failure to state claim upon which relief can be granted, unless it appears beyond doubt that plaintiff can prove no set of facts in support of his claim which would entitle him to relief.

  In re Perez, 173 B.R. 284.

Bkrtcy.E.D.N.Y. 1994. Motion to dismiss for failure to state claim upon which relief may be granted goes to face of complaint, and should not be granted where material issues of fact remain unresolved. Fed.Rules Civ.Proc. Rule 12(b)(6), 28 U.S.C.A.

In re Wise, 173 B.R. 75.

Bkrtcy.E.D.N.Y. 1993. Complaint may be dismissed for failure to state claim upon which relief can be granted if it lacks allegation regarding required element necessary to obtain relief, or if it does not contain sufficient factual averments with respect to material element underlying claim. Fed.Rules Civ.Proc.Rule 12(b)(6), 28 U.S.C.A.

In re Gouiran Holdings, Inc., 158 B.R. 3, reversed 165 B.R. 104.

Bkrtcy.E.D.N.Y. 1993. Complaint should be dismissed for failing to state claim upon which relief can be granted only when it appears with certainty that no set of facts can be proven at trial that would entitle plaintiff to any relief. Fed.Rules Civ.Proc.Rule 12(b)(6), 28 U.S.C.A.

In re Rosen, 151 B.R. 648.

Bkrtcy.N.D.N.Y. 1992. Motion for dismissal based on failure to state claim should be granted only if, viewing complaint in light most favorable to plaintiff, it appears beyond doubt that plaintiff cannot prove any facts which would entitle it to relief. Fed.Rules Civ.Proc. Rule 12(b)(6), 28 U.S.C.A.

In re Bennett, 142 B.R. 616.

Bkrtcy.S.D.N.Y. 1996. If Chapter 11 debtor has not asserted in its complaint any facts which would entitle it to claim for which relief could be granted, bankruptcy court must grant creditor's motion for dismissal. Fed.Rules Civ. Proc.Rule 12(b)(6), 28 U.S.C.A.; Fed.Rules Bankr.Proc.Rule 7012, 11 U.S.C.A.

In re GNK Enterprises, Inc., 197 B.R. 444.

Bkrtcy.S.D.N.Y. 1994. Complaint may be dismissed for failure to state claim upon which relief can be granted only when plaintiff would not be entitled to any type of relief, even if plaintiff prevailed on merits of its factual allegations. Fed.Rules Civ.Proc.Rule 12(b)(6), 28 U.S.C.A.

In re 80 Nassau Associates, 169 B.R. 832.

Bkrtcy.S.D.N.Y. 1994. Motion to dismiss for failure to state claim may be granted only where it appears beyond reasonable doubt that no set of facts can be proven at trial that would entitle plaintiff to relief. Fed.Rules Civ.Proc. Rule 12(b)(6), 28 U.S.C.A.; Fed.Rules Bankr. Proc.Rule 7012, 11 U.S.C.A.

In re Leslie Fay Companies, Inc., 166 B.R. 802.

Bkrtcy.S.D.N.Y. 1993. In adversary proceeding, court should deny motion to dismiss for failure to state claim upon which relief can be granted unless it appears beyond doubt that nonmoving party can prove no set of facts in

support of claim which would entitle him to relief. Fed.Rules Bankr.Proc.Rule 7012(b), 11 U.S.C.A.; Fed.Rules Civ.Proc.Rule 12(b)(6), 28 U.S.C.A.

In re Kressner, 159 B.R. 428.

Bkrtcy.S.D.N.Y. 1993. Focus of court's inquiry on motion to dismiss for failure to state claim upon which relief can be granted is whether pleading is sufficient to entitle pleader to offer evidence in support of its claims; complaint should not be dismissed unless it appears beyond doubt that plaintiff can prove no set of facts in support of its claims which would entitle it to relief. Fed.Rules Civ.Proc.Rule 12(b)(6), 28 U.S.C.A.

In re Chateaugay Corp., 154 B.R. 843, as amended.

Bkrtcy.S.D.N.Y. 1993. Motion for dismissal for failure to state claim should be denied unless it appears beyond doubt that plaintiff can prove no set of facts in support of claim which would entitle plaintiff to relief. Fed.Rules Civ. Proc.Rule 12(b)(6), 28 U.S.C.A.; Fed.Rules Bankr.Proc.Rule 7012(b), 11 U.S.C.A.

In re Keppler, 152 B.R. 417.

Bkrtcy.S.D.N.Y. 1993. Dismissal of complaint for failure to state claim upon which relief can be granted is proper only if it is clear that no relief could be granted under any set of facts that could be proved consistent with the allegations. Fed.Rules Civ.Proc.Rule 12(b)(6), 28 U.S.C.A.

In re Chateaugay Corp., 150 B.R. 529, affirmed 170 B.R. 551.

Bkrtcy.S.D.N.Y. 1991. Motion to dismiss complaint for failure to state claim upon which relief can be granted must be granted when it appears with certainty that no set of facts could be proven at trial which would entitle plaintiff to any relief.

In re Grabowski, 126 B.R. 24.

Bkrtcy.S.D.N.Y. 1990. In construing complaint in context of motion to dismiss for failure to state claim upon which relief can be granted, court should deny motion unless plaintiff can prove no set of facts in support of claim which would entitle plaintiff to relief claimed. Fed. Rules Civ.Proc.Rule 12(b)(6), 28 U.S.C.A.

In re Grossinger's Associates, 115 B.R. 449.

Bkrtcy.W.D.N.Y. 1993. Motion to dismiss for failure to state claim must be granted when it appears with certainty that there is no set of facts that could be proven at trial that would entitle plaintiff to any relief. Fed.Rules Civ. Proc.Rule 12(b)(6), 28 U.S.C.A.

In re Metro Water and Coffee Services, Inc., 157 B.R. 742.

Bkrtcy.S.D.Ohio 1991. Case should be dismissed for failure to state cause of action upon which relief can be granted if complaint is without merit because of absence of law to support claim of type made, or of facts sufficient to make valid claim, or if on face of complaint there is insurmountable bar to relief indicating that plaintiff does not have claim. Fed.Rules Civ.Proc.Rule 12(b)(6), 28 U.S.C.A.

    In re Gitlitz, 127 B.R. 397.

Bkrtcy.S.D.Ohio 1991. Complaint may not be dismissed for failure to state claim unless it appears beyond doubt that no relief could be granted under any set of facts that could be proved consistent with allegations. Fed.Rules Civ.Proc.Rule 12(b)(6), 28 U.S.C.A.

    In re Statewide Pools, Inc., 126 B.R. 877.

Bkrtcy.S.D.Ohio 1990. Motion to dismiss is attack upon legal sufficiency of complaint, and court is restricted to the pleadings. Fed. Rules Civ.Proc., Rule 12(b)(6), 28 U.S.C.A.; Bankruptcy Rule 7012(b), 11 U.S.C.A.

    In re Schnippel, 121 B.R. 784.

Bkrtcy.E.D.Pa. 1994. Complaint should not be dismissed for failure to state claim upon which relief can be granted unless it is appears beyond doubt that plaintiff can prove no set of facts in support of his claim which would entitle him to relief. Fed.Rules Bankr.Proc.Rule 7012, 11 U.S.C.A.; Fed.Rules Civ.Proc.Rule 12(b)(6), 28 U.S.C.A.

    In re Harry Levin, Inc., 175 B.R. 560, leave to appeal denied 1995 WL 581431.

Bkrtcy.E.D.Pa. 1994. Court should deny motion to dismiss for failure to state claim upon which relief can be granted, unless it appears beyond doubt that plaintiff can prove no set of facts in support of claim which would entitle him to relief. Fed.Rules Civ.Proc.Rule 12(b)(6), 28 U.S.C.A.

    In re Downingtown Indus. & Agr. School, 172 B.R. 813.

Bkrtcy.E.D.Pa. 1985. Motion to dismiss a complaint for failure to state a claim upon which relief may be granted tests formal legal sufficiency of complaint as to whether plaintiff has conformed to "notice pleading" provisions of Federal Civil Rule 8(a)(2). Fed.Rules Civ. Proc.Rule 8(a)(2), 28 U.S.C.A.

    In re Stevenson, 49 B.R. 914.

Bkrtcy.W.D.Pa. 1993. Bankruptcy court must, when entertaining motion to dismiss for failure to state claim, take all factual allegations of complaint as true, construe them in light most favorable to plaintiff, and determine whether plaintiff might be entitled to relief under any reasonable reading of complaint; dismissal is warranted only when it is manifestly obvious that plaintiff cannot prove any set of facts which would entitle it to relief. Fed.Rules Civ.Proc.Rule 12(b)(6), 28 U.S.C.A.

    In re Biggs, Inc., 159 B.R. 737.

Bkrtcy.D.Vt. 1990. Bankruptcy court will deny motion to dismiss for failure to state claim upon which relief may be granted unless it appears to a certainty that plaintiff is entitled to no relief under any state of facts which could be proved consistent in support of allegations. Bankruptcy Rule 7012(b), 11 U.S.C.A.; Fed. Rules Civ.Proc.Rule 12(b)(6), 28 U.S.C.A.

    In re Kelton Motors Inc., 121 B.R. 166.

Mere conclusory allegations unsupported by factual assertions will not withstand motion to dismiss, and bankruptcy court is not bound to accept them as true. Bankruptcy Rule 7008, 11 U.S.C.A.; Fed.Rules Civ.Proc.Rule 8(a)(2), 28 U.S.C.A.

    In re Kelton Motors Inc., 121 B.R. 166.

Bkrtcy.E.D.Va. 1994. Complaint should not be dismissed for failure to state claim unless it appears beyond doubt that plaintiff can prove no set of facts which would entitle it to relief. Fed.Rules Civ.Proc.Rule 12(b)(6), 28 U.S.C.A.

    In re Richels, 163 B.R. 760.

Fed.Cl. 1993. Motion for failure to state a claim upon which relief can be granted is appropriate where plaintiff could assert no set of facts which would support his claim.

    Kane v. U.S., 28 Fed.Cl. 10, affirmed 43 F.3d 1446.

⊙━**1773. Clear or certain nature of insufficiency.**

Library references

    C.J.S. Federal Civil Procedure § 821.

C.A.D.C. 1998. Dismissal for failure to state a claim is appropriate only if it appears beyond doubt that the plaintiff can prove no set of facts in support of his claim which would entitle him to relief. Fed.Rules Civ.Proc.Rule 12(b)(6), 28 U.S.C.A.

    Chandler v. District of Columbia Dept. of Corrections, 145 F.3d 1355, 330 U.S.App. D.C. 285.

C.A.D.C. 1996. Complaint should not be dismissed for failure to state claim unless it appears beyond doubt that plaintiff can prove no set of facts in support of its claim which would entitle him to relief.

    Atchinson v. District of Columbia, 73 F.3d 418, 315 U.S.App.D.C. 318.

C.A.D.C. 1985. A complaint should not be dismissed for failure to state a claim unless it appears beyond doubt that plaintiff can prove no set of facts in support of his or her claim which would entitle him or her to relief.

    Doe v. U.S. Dept. of Justice, 753 F.2d 1092, 243 U.S.App.D.C. 354.

C.A.D.C. 1984. Complaint should not be dismissed for failure to state a claim unless it appears that plaintiff could prove no facts in

support of his claim which would entitle him to relief.
> District of Columbia v. Air Florida, Inc., 750 F.2d 1077, 243 U.S.App.D.C. 1.

C.A.D.C. 1984. Ramirez de Arellano v. Weinberger, 745 F.2d 1500, 240 U.S.App.D.C. 363, certiorari granted, vacated 105 S.Ct. 2353, 471 U.S. 1113, 86 L.Ed.2d 255, on remand 788 F.2d 762, 252 U.S.App.D.C. 137.

C.A.8 1985. Court should not dismiss complaint for failure to state claim unless it appears beyond doubt that plaintiff can prove no set of facts in support of his claim which would entitle him to relief.
> May v. C.I.R., 752 F.2d 1301.

C.A.9 1997. Dismissal for failure to state claim is improper unless it appears beyond doubt that plaintiff can prove no set of facts in support of his claim which would entitle him to relief. Fed.Rules Civ.Proc.Rule 12(b)(6), 28 U.S.C.A.
> In re Rogstad, 126 F.3d 1224.

C.A.Fed. 1998. Court may dismiss for failure to state claim upon which relief may be granted only when it is beyond doubt that plaintiff can prove no set of facts in support of his claim that would entitle him to relief.
> Southfork Systems, Inc. v. U.S., 141 F.3d 1124.

C.A.Fed. (Dist.Col.) 1997. Complaint should be dismissed for failure to state claim when it appears beyond doubt that plaintiff can prove no set of facts in support of his claim which would entitle him to relief.
> Consolidated Edison Co. of New York v. O'Leary, 117 F.3d 538, rehearing denied, in banc suggestion declined, certiorari denied 118 S.Ct. 1036, 140 L.Ed.2d 103.

C.A.5 (Ala.) 1980. Thompson v. Bass, 616 F.2d 1259, certiorari denied 101 S.Ct. 399, 449 U.S. 983, 66 L.Ed.2d 245.

C.A.9 (Ariz.) 1995. Complaint should not be dismissed for failure to state claim on which relief can be granted unless plaintiff could prove no set of facts in support of his claim that would entitle him to relief. Fed.Rules Civ.Proc.Rule 12(b)(6), 28 U.S.C.A.
> Parks School of Business, Inc. v. Symington, 51 F.3d 1480.

C.A.8 (Ark.) 1998. Complaint should not be dismissed for failure to state claim unless it appears beyond doubt that plaintiff can prove no set of facts in support of claim that would demonstrate entitlement to relief. Fed.Rules Civ.Proc.Rule 12(b)(6), 28 U.S.C.A.
> Springdale Educ. Ass'n v. Springdale School Dist., 133 F.3d 649.

C.A.8 (Ark.) 1996. In considering motion to dismiss, court must construe complaint liberally and assume all factual allegations to be true; dismissal should not be granted unless it appears beyond reasonable doubt that plaintiff can prove no set of facts that would entitle relief.
> Goss v. City of Little Rock, 90 F.3d 306, appeal after remand 151 F.3d 861, rehearing and suggestion for rehearing denied.

C.A.9 (Cal.) 1998. Dismissal for failure to state claim is warranted if it appears beyond doubt that plaintiff can prove no set of facts in support of his or her claims that would entitle him or her to relief. Fed.Rules Civ.Proc.Rule 12(b)(6), 28 U.S.C.A.
> Jensen v. City of Oxnard, 145 F.3d 1078.

C.A.9 (Cal.) 1998. Complaint should not be dismissed for failure to state a claim unless it appears beyond doubt that plaintiff can prove no set of facts in support of his claim which would entitle him to relief. Fed.Rules Civ.Proc. Rule 12(b)(6), 28 U.S.C.A.
> Steckman v. Hart Brewing, Inc., 143 F.3d 1293.

C.A.9 (Cal.) 1998. Complaint should not be dismissed for failure to state claim unless it appears beyond doubt that plaintiff can prove no set of facts in support of claim that would entitle plaintiff to relief.
> Tyler v. Cisneros, 136 F.3d 603.

C.A.9 (Cal.) 1998. Complaint should not be dismissed for failure to state claim upon which relief can be granted unless it appears beyond doubt that plaintiff can prove no set of facts in support of his claim which would entitle him to relief. Fed.Rules Civ.Proc.Rule 12(b)(6), 28 U.S.C.A.
> Wyler Summit Partnership v. Turner Broadcasting System, Inc., 135 F.3d 658.

C.A.9 (Cal.) 1997. On review of dismissal for failure to state claim upon which relief can be granted, all allegations of material fact are taken as true and construed in light most favorable to nonmoving party; complaint should not be dismissed unless it appears beyond doubt that plaintiff can prove no set of facts in support of his claim which would entitle him to relief. Fed.Rules Civ.Proc.Rule 12(b)(6), 28 U.S.C.A.
> Jacobellis v. State Farm Fire & Cas. Co., 120 F.3d 171.

C.A.9 (Cal.) 1996. Complaint should not be dismissed unless it appears beyond doubt that plaintiff can prove no set of facts in support of claim that would entitle her to relief.
> California CNG, Inc. v. Southern California Gas Co., 96 F.3d 1193, as amended.

For references to other topics, see Descriptive-Word Index

C.A.9 (Cal.) 1996. Complaint should not be dismissed for failure to state a claim unless it appears beyond doubt that plaintiff can prove no set of facts in support of his or her claim which would entitle plaintiff to relief.

Sabow v. U.S., 93 F.3d 1445, as amended.

C.A.9 (Cal.) 1996. Complaint should not be dismissed for failure to state claim unless it appears beyond doubt that plaintiff can prove no set of facts in support of his claim which would entitle him to relief. Fed.Rules Civ.Proc. Rule 12(b)(6), 28 U.S.C.A.

SmileCare Dental Group v. Delta Dental Plan of California, Inc., 88 F.3d 780, certiorari denied 117 S.Ct. 583, 136 L.Ed.2d 513.

C.A.9 (Cal.) 1996. Complaint should not be dismissed unless it appears beyond doubt that plaintiff can prove no set of facts in support of claim which would entitle plaintiff to relief. Fed.Rules Civ.Proc.Rule 12(b)(6), 28 U.S.C.A.

Lewis v. Telephone Employees Credit Union, 87 F.3d 1537.

C.A.9 (Cal.) 1996. Complaint should not be dismissed for failure to state claim unless it appears beyond doubt that plaintiff can prove no set of facts that would entitle her to relief. Fed.Rules Civ.Proc.Rule 12(b)(6), 28 U.S.C.A.

Smith v. Jackson, 84 F.3d 1213.

C.A.9 (Cal.) 1996. Complaint should not be dismissed for failure to state claim unless it appears beyond doubt that plaintiff can prove no set of facts in support of his claim which would entitle him to relief. Fed.Rules Civ.Proc. Rule 12(b)(6), 28 U.S.C.A.

Kimes v. Stone, 84 F.3d 1121.

C.A.9 (Cal.) 1996. Complaint should not be dismissed for failure to state claim unless plaintiff can prove no set of facts in support of claim that would entitle him to relief. Fed. Rules Civ.Proc.Rule 12(b)(6), 28 U.S.C.A.

Cahill v. Liberty Mut. Ins. Co., 80 F.3d 336.

C.A.9 (Cal.) 1996. Complaint should not be dismissed unless it appears beyond doubt that plaintiff can prove no set of facts in support of claim which would entitle plaintiff to relief. Fed.Rules Civ.Proc.Rule 12(b)(6), 28 U.S.C.A.

Strother v. Southern California Permanente Medical Group, 79 F.3d 859, as amended on denial of rehearing, and as amended on denial of rehearing.

C.A.9 (Cal.) 1995. Complaint should not be dismissed unless it appears beyond doubt that plaintiff can prove no set of facts in support of his or her claim which would entitle him or her to relief. Fed.Rules Civ.Proc.Rule 12(b)(6), 28 U.S.C.A.

Hydranautics v. FilmTec Corp., 70 F.3d 533, appeal after remand 100 F.3d 962.

C.A.9 (Cal.) 1995. Complaint should be dismissed for failure to state claim when it appears beyond doubt that plaintiff can prove no set of facts in support of claim which would entitle plaintiff to relief. Fed.Rules Civ.Proc. Rule 12(b)(6), 28 U.S.C.A.

Freeman v. Time, Inc., 68 F.3d 285.

C.A.9 (Cal.) 1986. Court of Appeals may affirm district court's dismissal of action for failure to state a claim upon which relief may be granted only if it appears to a certainty that plaintiff would be entitled to no relief under any state of facts that could be proved.

Fidelity Financial Corp. v. Federal Home Loan Bank of San Francisco, 792 F.2d 1432, certiorari denied 107 S.Ct. 949, 479 U.S. 1064, 93 L.Ed.2d 998.

C.A.9 (Cal.) 1986. Court of Appeals reviews de novo district court's denial of motion to dismiss for failure to state a claim upon which relief can be granted; Court must accept all material allegations in the complaint as true and construe them in light most favorable to plaintiff; dismissal is warranted only if it appears to a certainty that plaintiff would be entitled to no relief under any state of facts that could be proved.

NL Industries, Inc. v. Kaplan, 792 F.2d 896.

C.A.9 (Cal.) 1984. Litchfield v. Spielberg, 736 F.2d 1352, certiorari denied 105 S.Ct. 1753, 470 U.S. 1052, 84 L.Ed.2d 817.

C.A.9 (Cal.) 1977. Jacobson v. Tahoe Regional Planning Agency, 566 F.2d 1353, certiorari granted Lake Country Estates, Inc. v. Tahoe Regional Planning Agency, 98 S.Ct. 2843, 436 U.S. 943, 56 L.Ed.2d 784, affirmed in part, reversed in part 99 S.Ct. 1171, 440 U.S. 391, 59 L.Ed.2d 401, on remand 474 F.Supp. 901.

C.A.10 (Colo.) 1996. Motion to dismiss is appropriate when it appears beyond doubt that plaintiff could prove no set of facts entitling it to relief.

U.S. v. Colorado Supreme Court, 87 F.3d 1161, on remand 988 F.Supp. 1368.

C.A.10 (Colo.) 1995. Dismissal for failure to state claim is appropriate where plaintiff can prove no set of facts in support of claims that would entitle him to relief. Fed.Rules Civ.Proc. Rule 12(b)(6), 28 U.S.C.A.

Reynolds v. School Dist. No. 1, Denver, Colo., 69 F.3d 1523.

C.A.10 (Colo.) 1985. A complaint should not be dismissed for failure to state a claim unless it appears beyond a doubt that plaintiff can prove no set of facts in support of his claim which would entitle him to relief.

> Shoultz v. Monfort of Colorado, Inc., 754 F.2d 318, certiorari denied 106 S.Ct. 1259, 475 U.S. 1044, 89 L.Ed.2d 569.

C.A.10 (Colo.) 1984. When a complaint and action are dismissed for failure to state a claim upon which relief can be granted, it must appear beyond doubt that plaintiff can prove no set of facts that would entitle him to relief. Fed.Rules Civ.Proc.Rule 12(b)(6), 28 U.S.C.A.

> Swanson v. Bixler, 750 F.2d 810.

C.A.2 (Conn.) 1998. Granting a motion to dismiss for a plaintiff's failure to state a claim is only proper where the court has no doubt that the plaintiff can prove no set of facts to demonstrate that the plaintiff is entitled to relief. Fed.Rules Civ.Proc.Rule 12(b)(6), 28 U.S.C.A.

> McClellan v. Cablevision of Connecticut, Inc., 149 F.3d 161.

C.A.2 (Conn.) 1998. Dismissal for failure to state claim upon which relief may be granted is not appropriate unless it appears beyond doubt that the plaintiff can prove no set of facts in support of his claim which would entitle him to relief. Fed.Rules Civ.Proc.Rule 12(b)(6), 28 U.S.C.A.

> Chance v. Armstrong, 143 F.3d 698.

Rule that dismissal is inappropriate unless it appears beyond doubt that the plaintiff can prove no set of facts in support of his claim which would entitle him to relief applies with particular force when the plaintiff alleges civil rights violations or when the complaint is submitted pro se. Fed.Rules Civ.Proc.Rule 12(b)(6), 28 U.S.C.A.

> Chance v. Armstrong, 143 F.3d 698.

C.A.2 (Conn.) 1997. Complaint may be dismissed for failure to state claim only when it appears beyond doubt that plaintiff can prove no set of facts in support of his claim which would entitle him to relief. Fed.Rules Civ.Proc. Rule 12(b)(6), 28 U.S.C.A.

> Northrop v. Hoffman of Simsbury, Inc., 134 F.3d 41.

C.A.2 (Conn.) 1995. On motion to dismiss for failure to state a claim, complaint may be dismissed only where it appears beyond doubt that the plaintiff can prove no set of facts in support of his claim which would entitle him to relief. Fed.Rules Civ.Proc.Rule 12(b)(6), 28 U.S.C.A.

> Gant v. Wallingford Bd. of Educ., 69 F.3d 669.

C.A.2 (Conn.) 1995. Dismissal of action for failure to state claim on which relief may be granted is only appropriate where it appears beyond doubt that plaintiff can prove no set of

facts in support of claim which would entitle him to relief. Fed.Rules Civ.Proc.Rule 12(b)(6).

> Staron v. McDonald's Corp., 51 F.3d 353.

C.A.11 (Fla.) 1998. Complaint may not be dismissed for failure to state a claim unless it appears beyond doubt that the plaintiffs can prove no set of facts in support of their claim which would entitle them to relief. Fed.Rules Civ.Proc.Rule 12(b)(6), 28 U.S.C.A.

> Roberts v. Florida Power & Light Co., 146 F.3d 1305.

C.A.11 (Fla.) 1998. Court should not dismiss a suit on the pleadings alone unless it appears beyond doubt that the plaintiff can prove no set of facts in support of his or her claim. Fed.Rules Civ.Proc.Rule 12(b)(6), 28 U.S.C.A.

> Beck v. Deloitte & Touche, Deloitte, Haskins & Sells, Ernest & Young, L.L.P., 144 F.3d 732.

In seeking dismissal for failure to state a viable claim, a defendant bears the very high burden of showing that the plaintiff cannot conceivably prove any set of facts that would entitle him or her to relief. Fed.Rules Civ.Proc. Rule 12(b)(6), 28 U.S.C.A.

> Beck v. Deloitte & Touche, Deloitte, Haskins & Sells, Ernest & Young, L.L.P., 144 F.3d 732.

C.A.11 (Fla.) 1997. Complaint may not be dismissed for failure to state claim unless it appears beyond doubt that plaintiff can prove no set of facts in support of claim which would entitle him to relief. Fed.Rules Civ.Proc.Rule 12(b)(6), 28 U.S.C.A.

> Brown v. Budget Rent-A-Car Systems, Inc., 119 F.3d 922.

C.A.11 (Fla.) 1997. District court may not dismiss complaint unless it appears beyond doubt that plaintiff can prove no set of facts in support of the claim which would entitle him or her to relief.

> Villarreal v. Woodham, 113 F.3d 202.

C.A.11 (Fla.) 1996. Complaint should not be dismissed for failure to state claim unless it appears beyond doubt that plaintiff can prove no set of facts in support of his claim which would entitle him to relief. Fed.Rules Civ.Proc. Rule 12(b)(6), 28 U.S.C.A.

> In re Johannessen, 76 F.3d 347.

C.A.11 (Fla.) 1996. Complaint may not be dismissed for failure to state cause of action unless plaintiff can prove no set of facts which would entitle him to relief.

> Martinez v. American Airlines, Inc., 74 F.3d 247.

C.A.11 (Fla.) 1984. Dykes v. Hosemann, 743 F.2d 1488, on rehearing 776 F.2d 942, on remand 783 F.2d 1000, certiorari denied 107 S.Ct. 569, 479 U.S. 983, 93 L.Ed.2d 574.

C.A.11 (Ga.) 1996. Complaint should not be dismissed for failure to state claim unless it appears beyond doubt that plaintiff can prove no set of facts in support of his or her claim which would entitle him or her to relief. Fed. Rules Civ.Proc.Rule 12(b)(6), 28 U.S.C.A.

Harris v. Procter & Gamble Cellulose Co., 73 F.3d 321.

C.A.11 (Ga.) 1990. Dismissal of complaints on basis that complaints are frivolous under statute should only be ordered when the claims are factually inadequate, in that they are clearly baseless or are legally inadequate, in that they are indisputably meritless. 28 U.S.C.A. § 1915(d).

Prather v. Norman, 901 F.2d 915.

C.A.11 (Ga.) 1985. A complaint should not be dismissed for failure to state a claim unless it appears beyond doubt that plaintiff can prove no set of facts in support of his claims which would entitle him to relief. Fed.Rules Civ.Proc. Rule 12(b)(6), 28 U.S.C.A.

Friedlander v. Nims, 755 F.2d 810.

C.A.11 (Ga.) 1982. Bracewell v. Nicholson Air Services, Inc., 680 F.2d 103, appeal after remand 748 F.2d 1499, rehearing denied 755 F.2d 176.

C.A.9 (Hawai'i) 1997. Complaint should not be dismissed unless it appears beyond doubt that plaintiff can prove no set of facts in support of his or her claim that would entitle him or her to relief.

Yamaguchi v. U.S. Dept. of the Air Force, 109 F.3d 1475.

C.A.9 (Hawai'i) 1996. Complaint should not be dismissed for failure to state claim unless it appears beyond doubt that plaintiff can prove no set of facts in support of claim that would entitle plaintiff to relief. Fed.Rules Civ.Proc. Rule 12(b)(6), 28 U.S.C.A.

Jenkins v. Commonwealth Land Title Ins. Co., 95 F.3d 791.

C.A.9 (Idaho) 1996. Complaint should not be dismissed for failure to state claim unless it appears beyond doubt that plaintiff can prove no set of facts in support of his claim that would entitle him to relief. Fed.Rules Civ.Proc.Rule 12(b)(6), 28 U.S.C.A.

Santana v. Zilog, Inc., 95 F.3d 780.

C.A.7 (Ill.) 1998. Complaint should not be dismissed for failure to state a claim unless it appears beyond doubt that the plaintiff can prove no set of facts in support of his or her claim which would entitle him or her to relief. Fed.Rules Civ.Proc.Rule 12(b)(6), 28 U.S.C.A.

Herdrich v. Pegram, 154 F.3d 362.

C.A.7 (Ill.) 1998. Complaint may not be dismissed unless it is impossible to prevail under any set of facts that could be proved consistent with the allegations. Fed.Rules Civ.Proc. Rule 12(b)(6), 28 U.S.C.A.

Moriarty v. Larry G. Lewis Funeral Directors Ltd., 150 F.3d 773.

C.A.7 (Ill.) 1998. On motion to dismiss for failure to state claim, allegations in complaint must be accepted as true, and court must look to see whether there is any possible interpretation of the complaint under which it can state a claim. Fed.Rules Civ.Proc.Rule 12(b)(6), 28 U.S.C.A.

Martinez v. Hooper, 148 F.3d 856.

For complaint to be properly dismissed for failure to state claim, it must appear beyond doubt that plaintiff can prove no set of facts which would entitle him or her to relief. Fed. Rules Civ.Proc.Rule 12(b)(6), 28 U.S.C.A.

Martinez v. Hooper, 148 F.3d 856.

C.A.7 (Ill.) 1998. A complaint may not be dismissed unless no relief could be granted under any set of facts that could be proved consistent with the allegations.

Nance v. Vieregge, 147 F.3d 589.

C.A.7 (Ill.) 1998. A complaint should not be dismissed for failure to state a claim unless it appears beyond doubt that the plaintiff can prove no set of facts in support of his claim which would entitle him to relief. Fed.Rules Civ.Proc.Rule 12(b)(6), 28 U.S.C.A.

Eison v. McCoy, 146 F.3d 468, rehearing denied.

C.A.7 (Ill.) 1998. Motion to dismiss for failure to state claim may be granted only if it appears beyond doubt from pleadings that plaintiff is unable to prove any set of facts that would entitle her to relief. Fed.Rules Civ.Proc. Rule 12(b)(6), 28 U.S.C.A.

Doe v. University of Illinois, 138 F.3d 653.

C.A.7 (Ill.) 1998. Dismissal for failure to state claim is warranted only if plaintiff can prove no set of facts in support of his or her claims that would entitle him or her to relief. Fed.Rules Civ.Proc.Rule 12(b)(6), 28 U.S.C.A.

Kelley v. Crosfield Catalysts, 135 F.3d 1202.

C.A.7 (Ill.) 1997. Complaint is properly dismissed for failure to state claim when plaintiff can prove no set of facts in support of his or her claim that would entitle plaintiff to relief. Fed.Rules Civ.Proc.Rule 12(b)(6), 28 U.S.C.A.

Jang v. A.M. Miller and Associates, 122 F.3d 480.

C.A.7 (Ill.) 1997. Complaint need not allege all facts essential to recovery under plaintiff's legal theory; complaint may not be dismissed unless it is impossible to prevail under any set of facts that could be proved consistent with the allegations.

Albiero v. City of Kankakee, 122 F.3d 417.

C.A.7 (Ill.) 1996. Complaint should not be dismissed for failure to state claim unless it appears beyond doubt that plaintiff can prove no set of facts in support of his or her claim that would entitle him or her to relief.

Wilczynski v. Lumbermens Mut. Cas. Co., 93 F.3d 397, on remand 998 F.Supp. 931.

C.A.7 (Ill.) 1996. Claim should be dismissed only where it appears beyond doubt that plaintiff can prove no set of facts that would entitle her to relief. Fed.Rules Civ.Proc.Rule 12(b)(6), 28 U.S.C.A.

Homeyer v. Stanley Tulchin Associates, Inc., 91 F.3d 959.

C.A.7 (Ill.) 1996. On motion to dismiss for failure to state a claim, court accepts all factual allegations in complaint and draws all reasonable inferences from these facts in favor of plaintiff, and claim may be dismissed only if it appears beyond doubt that plaintiff can prove no set of facts in support of claim which would entitle him or her to relief. Fed.Rules Civ.Proc. Rule 12(b)(6), 28 U.S.C.A.

Antonelli v. Sheahan, 81 F.3d 1422.

C.A.7 (Ill.) 1996. Complaint should not be dismissed for failure to state claim unless it appears beyond doubt that plaintiff can prove no set of facts in support of claim that would entitle plaintiff to relief. Fed.Rules Civ.Proc. Rule 12(b)(6), 28 U.S.C.A.

Doherty v. City of Chicago, 75 F.3d 318, amended.

C.A.7 (Ill.) 1996. Motions to dismiss that test legal sufficiency of complaint are granted when plaintiff can prove no set of facts entitling it to relief.

In re HealthCare Compare Corp. Securities Litigation, 75 F.3d 276.

C.A.7 (Ill.) 1996. Dismissal for failure to state claim is appropriate only if it is clear that no relief could be granted under any set of facts that could be proved consistent with allegations. Fed.Rules Civ.Proc.Rule 12(b)(6), 28 U.S.C.A.

Panaras v. Liquid Carbonic Industries Corp., 74 F.3d 786, rehearing denied.

C.A.7 (Ill.) 1996. Dismissal for failure to state a claim is proper only where it appears beyond a doubt that plaintiff can prove no set of facts in support of its claims that would entitle it to relief. Fed.Rules Civ.Proc.Rule 12(b)(6), 28 U.S.C.A.

Travel All Over the World, Inc. v. Kingdom of Saudi Arabia, 73 F.3d 1423.

C.A.7 (Ill.) 1995. Complaint should not be dismissed for failure to state claim upon which

relief can be granted unless it appears beyond doubt that nonmoving party can prove no set of facts in support of his claim which would entitle him to relief. Fed.Rules Civ.Proc.Rule 12(b)(6), 28 U.S.C.A.

Williams v. Ramos, 71 F.3d 1246.

C.A.7 (Ill.) 1995. Complaint should not be dismissed unless it appears that plaintiff can prove no set of facts in support of its claim.

Baxter Healthcare Corp. v. O.R. Concepts, Inc., 69 F.3d 785, rehearing and suggestion for rehearing denied.

C.A.7 (Ill.) 1995. Complaint or counterclaim is subject to dismissal for failure to state claim upon which relief can be granted only if nonmoving party can prove no set of facts consistent with its complaint or counterclaim that would entitle it to relief. Fed.Rules Civ. Proc.Rule 12(b)(6), 28 U.S.C.A.

Northern Trust Co. v. Peters, 69 F.3d 123.

C.A.7 (Ill.) 1995. Motion to dismiss for failure to state claim should be granted only if plaintiff could prove no set of facts, consistent with his or her complaint and attachments, upon which defendant could be liable.

Siefken v. Village of Arlington Heights, 65 F.3d 664.

C.A.7 (Ill.) 1995. Dismissal for failure to state claim upon which relief can be granted is permitted only where it appears beyond doubt that plaintiff can prove no set of facts in support of his claim which would entitle him to relief. Fed.Rules Civ.Proc.Rule 12(b)(6), 28 U.S.C.A.

Chaney v. Suburban Bus Div. of Regional Transp. Authority, 52 F.3d 623.

C.A.7 (Ill.) 1984. Under simplified notice pleading, allegations of complaint should be liberally construed and complaint should not be dismissed for failure to state claim unless it appears beyond doubt that plaintiff can prove no set of facts in support of claim which would entitle him to relief. Fed.Rules Civ.Proc.Rule 12, 28 U.S.C.A.

Lewis v. Local Union No. 100 of Laborers' Intern. Union of North America, AFL-CIO, 750 F.2d 1368.

C.A.7 (Ill.) 1984. Altman v. Hurst, 734 F.2d 1240, certiorari denied 105 S.Ct. 385, 469 U.S. 982, 83 L.Ed.2d 320.

C.A.7 (Ill.) 1973. Hampton v. City of Chicago, Cook County, Ill., 484 F.2d 602, certiorari denied 94 S.Ct. 1413, 415 U.S. 917, 39 L.Ed.2d 471, certiorari denied Hanrahan v. Hampton, 94 S.Ct. 1414, 415 U.S. 917, 39 L.Ed.2d 471, appeal after remand 600 F.2d 600, certiorari granted in part, reversed in part 100 S.Ct. 1987, 446 U.S. 754, 64 L.Ed.2d 670, rehearing denied 101 S.Ct. 33, 448 U.S. 913, 65 L.Ed.2d 1176, rehearing denied Johnson v. Hampton, 101

S.Ct. 33, 448 U.S. 913, 65 L.Ed.2d 1177, on remand 499 F.Supp. 640, appeal dismissed 643 F.2d 478, on remand 522 F.Supp. 140.

C.A.7 (Ind.) 1996. Dismissal is appropriate only if it is clear that no relief could be granted under any set of facts that could be proved consistent with allegations in complaint. Fed.Rules Civ.Proc.Rule 12(b)(6), 28 U.S.C.A.
> Jones v. General Elec. Co., 87 F.3d 209, certiorari denied 117 S.Ct. 510, 136 L.Ed.2d 400.

C.A.7 (Ind.) 1984. Zapp v. United Transp. Union, 727 F.2d 617, appeal after remand 879 F.2d 1439, rehearing denied, certiorari denied 110 S.Ct. 722, 493 U.S. 1021, 107 L.Ed.2d 742.

C.A.8 (Iowa) 1985. Dismissal of pro se complaint is warranted only if the face of the complaint shows an insuperable bar to relief. Fed.Rules Civ.Proc.Rule 8(f), 28 U.S.C.A.
> Munz v. Parr, 758 F.2d 1254, on remand 1991 WL 365063, affirmed 972 F.2d 971.

C.A.6 (Ky.) 1997. For dismissal to be proper, it must appear beyond doubt that plaintiff would not be able to recover under any set of facts that could be presented consistent with allegations of complaint. Fed.Rules Civ.Proc. Rule 12(b)(6), 28 U.S.C.A.
> Mattei v. Mattei, 126 F.3d 794, rehearing and suggestion for rehearing denied, and rehearing denied, certiorari denied 118 S.Ct. 1799, 140 L.Ed.2d 939.

C.A.5 (La.) 1996. Motion to dismiss for failure to state claim may be granted only if it appears that no relief could be granted under any set of facts that could be proved consistent with allegations. Fed.Rules Civ.Proc.Rule 12(b)(6), 28 U.S.C.A.
> Morin v. Caire, 77 F.3d 116, 144 A.L.R. Fed. 719.

C.A.5 (La.) 1994. Dismissal for failure to state claim is disfavored in law and justified only if it appears beyond doubt that plaintiff can prove no set of facts in support of claim that would entitle him to relief. Fed.Rules Civ.Proc. Rule 12(b)(6), 28 U.S.C.A.
> Matter of U.S. Abatement Corp., 39 F.3d 556.

C.A.5 (La.) 1982. Carpenters Local Union No. 1846 of United Broth. of Carpenters and Joiners of America, AFL-CIO v. Pratt-Farnsworth, Inc., 690 F.2d 489, rehearing denied 696 F.2d 996, certiorari denied 104 S.Ct. 335, 464 U.S. 932, 78 L.Ed.2d 305, on remand 609 F.Supp. 1299, on remand 609 F.Supp. 1302.

C.A.5 (La.) 1962. Halliburton Co. v. Norton Drilling Co., 302 F.2d 431, rehearing en banc denied 313 F.2d 380, certiorari denied 83 S.Ct. 1870, 374 U.S. 829, 10 L.Ed.2d 1052.

C.A.8 (Minn.) 1998. A complaint shall be dismissed for failure to state a claim only if it is clear that no relief can be granted under any set of facts that could be proved consistent with the allegations.
> Enowmbitang v. Seagate Technology, Inc., 148 F.3d 970.

C.A.8 (Minn.) 1998. Dismissal for failure to state claim upon which relief may be granted is proper only when complaint on its face reveals some insuperable bar to relief. Fed.Rules Civ.Proc.Rule 12(b)(6), 28 U.S.C.A.
> Duffy v. Landberg, 133 F.3d 1120, rehearing denied, certiorari denied 119 S.Ct. 62.

C.A.8 (Mo.) 1997. Complaint should be dismissed for failure to state claim only if, construed most favorably to the nonmoving party, it is clear that no relief could be granted under any set of facts that could be proved consistent with the allegations. Fed.Rules Civ. Proc.Rule 12(b)(6), 28 U.S.C.A.
> Haberthur v. City of Raymore, Missouri, 119 F.3d 720.

C.A.8 (Mo.) 1997. Motion to dismiss for failure to state claim should be granted only if it is clear that no relief could be granted under any set of facts, construing allegations in complaint favorably to pleader. Fed.Rules Civ.Proc. Rule 12(b)(6), 28 U.S.C.A.
> County of St. Charles, Mo. v. Missouri Family Health Council, 107 F.3d 682, rehearing denied, certiorari denied 118 S.Ct. 160, 139 L.Ed.2d 105.

C.A.8 (Mo.) 1996. Dismissal for failure to state claim is inappropriate unless it appears beyond doubt that plaintiff can prove no set of facts in support of his claim which would entitle him to relief. Fed.Rules Civ.Proc.Rule 12(b)(6), 28 U.S.C.A.
> Hafley v. Lohman, 90 F.3d 264, rehearing and suggestion for rehearing denied, certiorari denied 117 S.Ct. 1081, 137 L.Ed.2d 216.

C.A.8 (Mo.) 1996. In considering motion to dismiss, court accepts as true all factual allegations in complaint, and motion will be granted only if no set of facts would entitle plaintiff to relief.
> McSherry v. Trans World Airlines, Inc., 81 F.3d 739.

C.A.8 (Mo.) 1995. Motion to dismiss for failure to state claim upon which relief can be granted should be granted as practical matter only in unusual case in which plaintiff includes allegations that show on face of complaint that there is some insuperable bar to relief. Fed. Rules Civ.Proc.Rule 12(b)(6), 28 U.S.C.A.
> Frey v. City of Herculaneum, 44 F.3d 667.

C.A.8 (Mo.) 1987. In evaluating motion to dismiss for failure to state a claim, pro se complaint must be liberally construed, and court should not dismiss complaint unless it appears beyond doubt that plaintiff can prove no set of facts in support of his claim which could entitle him to relief. Fed.Rules Civ.Proc. Rule 12(b)(6), 28 U.S.C.A.

Valiant-Bey v. Morris, 829 F.2d 1441.

C.A.8 (Mo.) 1983. Miner v. Brackney, 719 F.2d 954, certiorari denied 104 S.Ct. 3554, 467 U.S. 1259, 82 L.Ed.2d 856.

C.A.8 (Mo.) 1979. Thomas W. Garland, Inc. v. City of St. Louis, 596 F.2d 784, certiorari denied 100 S.Ct. 208, 444 U.S. 899, 62 L.Ed.2d 135, certiorari denied Manley Inv. Co. v. Thomas W. Garland, Inc., 100 S.Ct. 208, 444 U.S. 899, 62 L.Ed.2d 135, on remand 492 F.Supp. 402.

C.A.8 (Neb.) 1998. District court should not dismiss claim for failure to state claim upon which relief can be granted unless it appears beyond doubt that plaintiff can prove no set of facts in support of claim that would demonstrate entitlement to relief. Fed.Rules Civ.Proc. Rule 12(b)(6), 28 U.S.C.A.

Anderson v. Nissan Motor Co., Ltd., 139 F.3d 599.

C.A.8 (Neb.) 1996. Complaint should not be dismissed for failure to state claim unless it appears beyond doubt that plaintiff can prove no set of facts in support of his claim which would entitle him to relief. Fed.Rules Civ.Proc. Rule 12(b)(6), 28 U.S.C.A.

Atkinson v. Bohn, 91 F.3d 1127.

C.A.8 (Neb.) 1992. Dismissal for failure to state claim is inappropriate unless it appears beyond doubt that plaintiff can prove no set of facts in support of its claim which would entitle him to relief, and court must accept all well-pleaded allegations of complaint as true, and all reasonable inferences therefrom must be construed favorably to the pleader. Fed.Rules Civ. Proc.Rule 12(b)(6), 28 U.S.C.A.

McCormack v. Citibank, N.A., 979 F.2d 643, rehearing denied, appeal after remand 100 F.3d 532.

C.A.9 (Nev.) 1998. A complaint should not be dismissed for failure to state a claim upon which relief can be granted unless it appears beyond a reasonable doubt that the plaintiffs can prove no set of facts in support of their claim that would entitle them to relief. Fed. Rules Civ.Proc.Rule 12(b)(6), 28 U.S.C.A.

Butler v. Apfel, 144 F.3d 622.

C.A.9 (Nev.) 1997. Complaint should not be dismissed for failure to state claim unless it appears beyond doubt that plaintiff can prove no set of facts in support of his claim which would entitle him to relief.

Vignolo v. Miller, 120 F.3d 1075.

C.A.9 (Nev.) 1995. Complaint should not be dismissed unless it appears beyond doubt that plaintiff can prove no set of facts in support of his or her claim which would entitle him or her to relief. Fed.Rules Civ.Proc.Rule 12(b)(6), 28 U.S.C.A.

Hicks v. Small, 69 F.3d 967.

C.A.9 (Nev.) 1977. Jacobson v. Tahoe Regional Planning Agency, 566 F.2d 1353, certiorari granted Lake Country Estates, Inc. v. Tahoe Regional Planning Agency, 98 S.Ct. 2843, 436 U.S. 943, 56 L.Ed.2d 784, affirmed in part, reversed in part 99 S.Ct. 1171, 440 U.S. 391, 59 L.Ed.2d 401, on remand 474 F.Supp. 901.

C.A.3 (N.J.) 1998. Dismissal for failure to state a claim occurs only if plaintiff can prove no set of facts in support of his claim which would entitle him to relief. Fed.Rules Civ.Proc. Rule 12(b)(6), 28 U.S.C.A.

Ford v. Schering-Plough Corp., 145 F.3d 601.

C.A.3 (N.J.) 1998. A complaint should be dismissed only if, after accepting as true all of the facts alleged in the complaint, and drawing all reasonable inferences in the plaintiff's favor, no relief could be granted under any set of facts consistent with the allegations of the complaint. Fed.Rules Civ.Proc.Rule 12(b)(6), 28 U.S.C.A.

Trump Hotels & Casino Resorts, Inc. v. Mirage Resorts Inc., 140 F.3d 478.

C.A.3 (N.J.) 1996. In reviewing motion to dismiss for failure to state claim, court determines whether, under any reasonable reading of pleadings, plaintiffs may be entitled to relief, and court must accept as true factual allegations in complaint and all reasonable inferences that can be drawn therefrom. Fed.Rules Civ. Proc.Rule 12(b)(6), 28 U.S.C.A.

Nami v. Fauver, 82 F.3d 63.

C.A.10 (N.M.) 1996. District court should not dismiss complaint for failure to state claim upon which relief could be granted unless it appears beyond doubt that plaintiff could prove no set of facts in support of his claim that would entitle him to relief. Fed.Rules Civ.Proc.Rule 12(b)(6), 28 U.S.C.A.

Riddle v. Mondragon, 83 F.3d 1197.

C.A.10 (N.M.) 1995. Dismissal is only appropriate when plaintiff can prove no set of facts to support claim for relief. Fed.Rules Civ.Proc.Rule 12(b)(6), 28 U.S.C.A.

Jojola v. Chavez, 55 F.3d 488.

C.A.2 (N.Y.) 1998. A district court should deny a motion to dismiss for failure to state a claim upon which relief can be granted unless it appears to a certainty that a plaintiff can prove no set of facts entitling him to relief. Fed.Rules Civ.Proc.Rule 12(b)(6), 28 U.S.C.A.

>Grandon v. Merrill Lynch & Co., Inc., 147 F.3d 184.

C.A.2 (N.Y.) 1998. Standard precluding dismissal of complaint unless it appears beyond a reasonable doubt that plaintiff can prove no set of facts in support of claim which would entitle him to relief is applied with particular strictness when plaintiff complains of civil rights violation. Fed.Rules Civ.Proc.Rule 12(c), 28 U.S.C.A.

>Irish Lesbian and Gay Organization v. Giuliani, 143 F.3d 638.

C.A.2 (N.Y.) 1998. Dismissal for failure to state claim is proper only where it appears beyond doubt that plaintiff can prove no set of facts in support of claim which would entitle him to relief. Fed.Rules Civ.Proc.Rule 12(b)(6), 28 U.S.C.A.

>Scotto v. Almenas, 143 F.3d 105.

C.A.2 (N.Y.) 1997. Dismissal for failure to state claim is warranted only if it appears beyond doubt that plaintiff can prove no set of facts in support of his claim which would entitle him to relief, and, in ruling on defendant's motion, court must accept as true all factual allegations in complaint and must draw all reasonable inferences in favor of plaintiff. Fed. Rules Civ.Proc.Rule 12(b)(6), 28 U.S.C.A.

>Hamilton Chapter of Alpha Delta Phi, Inc. v. Hamilton College, 128 F.3d 59.

C.A.2 (N.Y.) 1997. Although less stringent standards apply where litigant is pro se, dismissal is nevertheless appropriate where it appears beyond doubt that plaintiff can prove no set of facts in support of his claim which would entitle him to relief.

>Rodriguez v. Weprin, 116 F.3d 62.

C.A.2 (N.Y.) 1996. Dismissal of complaint is warranted, for failure to state cause of action upon which relief may be granted, only if it plainly appears that plaintiff can prove no set of facts in support of his claim which would entitle him to relief.

>In re Maxwell Communication Corp. plc by Homan, 93 F.3d 1036.

C.A.2 (N.Y.) 1996. Dismissal for failure to state a claim is only proper when it appears beyond doubt that there are no set of facts in support of plaintiff's claim which would entitle plaintiff to relief. Fed.Rules Civ.Proc.Rule 12(b)(6), 28 U.S.C.A.

>Harsco Corp. v. Segui, 91 F.3d 337.

C.A.2 (N.Y.) 1996. Complaint may not be dismissed for failure to state claim unless it appears beyond doubt that plaintiff can prove no set of facts in support of his or her claim which would entitle him or her to relief. Fed. Rules Civ.Proc.Rule 12(b)(6), 28 U.S.C.A.

>Bernheim v. Litt, 79 F.3d 318.

Recovery may appear remote and unlikely on face of pleading, but that is not test for dismissal for failure to state claim. Fed.Rules Civ.Proc.Rule 12(b)(6), 28 U.S.C.A.

>Bernheim v. Litt, 79 F.3d 318.

C.A.2 (N.Y.) 1995. Dismissal of complaint for failure to state a claim is appropriate only where it appears beyond doubt that most of facts would forbid recovery on plaintiff's claims. Fed.Rules Civ.Proc.Rule 12(b)(6), 28 U.S.C.A.

>Baker v. Cuomo, 58 F.3d 814, rehearing denied, rehearing granted in part 67 F.3d 39, certiorari denied Pataki v. Baker, 116 S.Ct. 488, 516 U.S. 980, 133 L.Ed.2d 415, vacated in part on rehearing en banc 85 F.3d 919.

C.A.2 (N.Y.) 1995. District court should grant motion to dismiss for failure to state claim on which relief can be granted only if, after viewing plaintiff's allegations in most favorable light, it appears beyond doubt that plaintiff can prove no set of facts in support of his claim which would entitle him to relief. Fed.Rules Civ.Proc.Rule 12(b)(6), 28 U.S.C.A.

>Bolt Elec., Inc. v. City of New York, 53 F.3d 465.

C.A.2 (N.Y.) 1991. In ruling on motion to dismiss for failure to state claim upon which relief can be granted, court is required to accept material facts alleged in complaint as true, and not to dismiss unless it appears beyond doubt that plaintiff can prove no set of facts in support of claim which would entitle him to relief. Fed.Rules Civ.Proc.Rule 12(b)(6), 28 U.S.C.A.

>Easton v. Sundram, 947 F.2d 1011, certiorari denied 112 S.Ct. 1943, 504 U.S. 911, 118 L.Ed.2d 548.

Rule that court should not grant motion to dismiss for failure to state claim upon which relief can be granted unless it appears beyond doubt that plaintiff can prove no set of facts in support of his claim which would entitle him to relief applies with greater force where complaint is pro se or where plaintiff complains of civil rights violation. Fed.Rules Civ.Proc.Rule 12(b)(6), 28 U.S.C.A.

>Easton v. Sundram, 947 F.2d 1011, certiorari denied 112 S.Ct. 1943, 504 U.S. 911, 118 L.Ed.2d 548.

C.A.2 (N.Y.) 1985. A prisoner's pro se complaint under 42 U.S.C.A. § 1983 may be dismissed only if it appears that plaintiff can prove no set of facts in support of his claim that would entitle him to relief.

>Massop v. Coughlin, 770 F.2d 299.

C.A.2 (N.Y.) 1985. While plaintiff who has once taken advantage of opportunity to amend his complaint in light of defects to which his attention has been drawn should be able to achieve some clarity and precision, and may properly be denied yet another opportunity to amend, it is nevertheless the rule that court should not dismiss the complaint unless it appears beyond doubt that plaintiff can prove no set of facts in support of claim which would entitle him to relief. Fed.Rules Civ.Proc.Rule 12(b)(6), 28 U.S.C.A.

Goldman v. Belden, 754 F.2d 1059.

C.A.2 (N.Y.) 1984. District court should deny motion to dismiss unless it appears to certainty that plaintiff can prove no set of facts entitling him to relief; district court should not be swayed into granting the motion because the possibility of ultimate recovery is remote.

Ryder Energy Distribution Corp. v. Merrill Lynch Commodities Inc., 748 F.2d 774, on remand 684 F.Supp. 27, affirmed 865 F.2d 492.

C.A.2 (N.Y.) 1984. A complaint should not be dismissed for failure to state a claim unless it appears beyond doubt that plaintiff can prove no set of facts in support of claim which would entitle him to relief. Fed.Rules Civ.Proc.Rule 12(b)(6), 28 U.S.C.A.

Dahlberg v. Becker, 748 F.2d 85, certiorari denied 105 S.Ct. 1845, 470 U.S. 1084, 85 L.Ed.2d 144.

C.A.4 (N.C.) 1996. It is only in unusual case where complaint on its face reveals some insuperable bar to relief that dismissal for failure to state claim is warranted. Fed.Rules Civ.Proc.Rule 12(b)(6), 28 U.S.C.A.

Boring v. Buncombe County Bd. of Educ., 98 F.3d 1474, rehearing granted, opinion vacated, on rehearing 136 F.3d 364, certiorari denied 119 S.Ct. 47.

C.A.4 (N.C.) 1996. Dismissal for failure to state a claim is proper where it is clear that no relief could be granted under any set of facts that could be proved consistent with the allegations. Fed.Rules Civ.Proc.Rule 12(b)(6), 28 U.S.C.A.

Randall v. U.S., 95 F.3d 339, certiorari denied 117 S.Ct. 1085, 137 L.Ed.2d 219, rehearing denied 117 S.Ct. 1463, 137 L.Ed.2d 566.

C.A.4 (N.C.) 1996. Motion to dismiss for failure to state claim should not be granted unless it appears to a certainty that plaintiff would be entitled to no relief under any state of facts which could be proved in support of his claim. Fed.Rules Civ.Proc.Rule 12(b)(6), 28 U.S.C.A.

McNair v. Lend Lease Trucks, Inc., 95 F.3d 325.

C.A.4 (N.C.) 1995. Dismissal for failure to state claim upon which relief can be granted is proper where it is clear that no relief could be granted under any set of facts that could be proved consistent with allegations. Fed.Rules Civ.Proc.Rule 12(b)(6), 28 U.S.C.A.

Biggs v. Meadows, 66 F.3d 56.

C.A.6 (Ohio) 1998. Complaint should not be dismissed for failure to state claim unless it appears beyond doubt that plaintiff can prove no set of facts in support of his claim which would entitle him to relief. Fed.Rules Civ.Proc. Rule 12(b)(6), 28 U.S.C.A.

Lewis v. ACB Business Services, Inc., 135 F.3d 389.

C.A.6 (Ohio) 1997. In deciding motion to dismiss, court must construe complaint in light most favorable to plaintiff, accept all factual allegations as true, and determine whether plaintiff undoubtedly can prove no set of facts in support of his claims that would entitle him to relief. Fed.Rules Civ.Proc.Rule 12(b)(6), 28 U.S.C.A.

Andrews v. State of Ohio, 104 F.3d 803, rehearing and suggestion for rehearing denied.

C.A.6 (Ohio) 1996. Motion to dismiss may be granted only if it is clear that no relief could be granted under any set of facts that could be proved consistent with allegations. Fed.Rules Civ.Proc.Rule 12(b)(6), 28 U.S.C.A.

Sistrunk v. City of Strongsville, 99 F.3d 194, rehearing and suggestion for rehearing denied, certiorari denied 117 S.Ct. 2409, 138 L.Ed.2d 175.

C.A.6 (Ohio) 1995. In ruling on motion to dismiss complaint for failure to state claim, district court must construe complaint in light most favorable to plaintiff, accept all factual allegations as true, and determine whether plaintiff undoubtedly can prove no set of facts in support of his claims that would entitle him to relief. Fed.Rules Civ.Proc.Rule 12(b)(6), 28 U.S.C.A.

Columbia Natural Resources, Inc. v. Tatum, 58 F.3d 1101, rehearing and suggestion for rehearing denied, certiorari denied 116 S.Ct. 1041, 516 U.S. 1158, 134 L.Ed.2d 189, rehearing denied 116 S.Ct. 1560, 517 U.S. 1163, 134 L.Ed.2d 661.

C.A.6 (Ohio) 1995. In ruling on motion to dismiss for failure to state a claim, it is not function of court to weigh evidence or evaluate credibility of witnesses; instead, court should deny motion unless it is clear that plaintiff can prove no set of facts in support of his or her claim that would entitle him or her to relief. Fed.Rules Civ.Proc.Rule 12(b)(6), 28 U.S.C.A.

Miller v. Currie, 50 F.3d 373.

C.A.6 (Ohio) 1991. Motion to dismiss may only be granted if it appears beyond doubt that plaintiff can prove no set of facts in support of his claim which would entitle him to relief. Fed.Rules Civ.Proc.Rule 12(b), 28 U.S.C.A.

Ang v. Procter & Gamble Co., 932 F.2d 540.

C.A.6 (Ohio) 1984. Complaint should not be dismissed unless it appears beyond doubt that plaintiff can prove no set of facts in support of his claim which would entitle him to relief.

Lee v. Western Reserve Psychiatric Habilitation Center, 747 F.2d 1062.

C.A.10 (Okl.) 1998. Dismissal for failure to state a claim is proper only when it is clear beyond doubt that the complaint, viewed most favorably to the plaintiff, cannot be read to state a valid claim. Fed.Rules Civ.Proc.Rule 12(b)(6), 28 U.S.C.A.

Shaffer v. Saffle, 148 F.3d 1180.

C.A.10 (Okl.) 1997. Motion to dismiss for failure to state claim should not be granted unless it appears beyond doubt that plaintiff can prove no set of facts in support of his claim which would entitle him to relief. Fed.Rules Civ.Proc.Rule 12(b)(6), 28 U.S.C.A.

GFF Corp. v. Associated Wholesale Grocers, Inc., 130 F.3d 1381.

C.A.10 (Okl.) 1994. Dismissal is proper only if it appears beyond doubt that plaintiffs can prove no set of facts in support of claim which would entitle them to relief. Fed.Rules Civ.Proc.Rule 12(b)(6), 28 U.S.C.A.

Graham v. Independent School Dist. No. I-89, 22 F.3d 991.

C.A.9 (Or.) 1996. In appraising sufficiency of complaint, Court of Appeals follows accepted rule that complaint should not be dismissed for failure to state claim unless it appears beyond doubt that plaintiff can prove no set of facts in support of claim which would entitle him or her to relief. Fed.Rules Civ.Proc.Rule 12(b)(6), 28 U.S.C.A.

Walleri v. Federal Home Loan Bank of Seattle, 83 F.3d 1575, on remand 965 F.Supp. 1459.

C.A.3 (Pa.) 1997. Motion to dismiss for failure to state claim should be granted if it appears to certainty that no relief could be granted under any set of facts which could be proved, but court need not credit complaint's bald assertions or legal conclusions when deciding motion to dismiss. Fed.Rules Civ.Proc.Rule 12(b)(6), 28 U.S.C.A.

Morse v. Lower Merion School Dist., 132 F.3d 902.

C.A.3 (Pa.) 1977. Bogosian v. Gulf Oil Corp., 561 F.2d 434, certiorari denied 98 S.Ct. 1280, 434 U.S. 1086, 55 L.Ed.2d 791, on remand 596 F.Supp. 62.

C.A.1 (Puerto Rico) 1998. Dismissal of complaint for failure to state a cause of action is appropriate only if it clearly appears, according to the facts alleged, that the plaintiff cannot recover on any viable theory. Fed.Rules Civ. Proc.Rule 12(b)(6), 28 U.S.C.A.

Figueroa v. Rivera, 147 F.3d 77.

C.A.1 (R.I.) 1996. District court should not grant motion to dismiss for failure to state a claim unless it appears to a certainty that plaintiff would be unable to recover under any set of facts, and Court of Appeals reviews under the same standard. Fed.Rules Civ.Proc.Rule 12(b)(6), 28 U.S.C.A.

Roma Const. Co. v. aRusso, 96 F.3d 566, on remand 1998 WL 156708.

C.A.8 (S.D.) 1997. Complaint should not be dismissed for failure to state claim unless it appears beyond doubt that plaintiff can prove no set of facts in support of his claim which would entitle him to relief. Fed.Rules Civ.Proc. Rule 12(b)(6), 28 U.S.C.A.

Parnes v. Gateway 2000, Inc., 122 F.3d 539.

Complaint must be viewed in light most favorable to plaintiff and should not be dismissed merely because court doubts that plaintiff will be able to prove all necessary factual allegations. Fed.Rules Civ.Proc.Rule 12(b)(6), 28 U.S.C.A.

Parnes v. Gateway 2000, Inc., 122 F.3d 539.

Dismissal for failure to state claim is likely to be granted only in unusual case in which plaintiff includes allegations that show on face of complaint that there is some insuperable bar to relief. Fed.Rules Civ.Proc.Rule 12(b)(6), 28 U.S.C.A.

Parnes v. Gateway 2000, Inc., 122 F.3d 539.

C.A.6 (Tenn.) 1998. On motion to dismiss for failure to state a claim upon which relief can be granted, Court of Appeals must construe the complaint in the light most favorable to the plaintiff, accept the complaint's factual allegations as true, and determine whether it is beyond a doubt that the plaintiff can prove no set of facts in support of his claims that would entitle him to relief. Fed.Rules Civ.Proc.Rule 12(b)(6), 28 U.S.C.A.

Coger v. Board of Regents of State of Tenn., 154 F.3d 296.

C.A.6 (Tenn.) 1998. Motion to dismiss for failure to state claim requires court to construe complaint in light most favorable to plaintiff, accept all of complaint's factual allegations as true, and determine whether plaintiff undoubtedly can prove no set of facts in support of claims that would entitle relief. Fed.Rules Civ. Proc.Rule 12(b)(6), 28 U.S.C.A.

Grindstaff v. Green, 133 F.3d 416.

C.A.6 (Tenn.) 1997. Motion to dismiss is properly granted only if it appears that plaintiff can prove no set of facts which would entitle her to relief. Fed.Rules Civ.Proc.Rule 12, 28 U.S.C.A.

U.S. ex rel. McKenzie v. Bellsouth Telecommunications, Inc., 123 F.3d 935, certiorari denied 118 S.Ct. 855, 139 L.Ed.2d 755.

C.A.6 (Tenn.) 1996. In order for dismissal of complaint for failure to state claim to be proper, it must appear beyond doubt that plaintiff would not be able to recover under any set of facts that could be presented consistent with allegations of complaint. Fed.Rules Civ.Proc. Rule 12(b)(6), 28 U.S.C.A.

Bower v. Federal Exp. Corp., 96 F.3d 200.

C.A.6 (Tenn.) 1996. Dismissal is improper unless it is clear that plaintiffs can prove no set of facts that would support their claim. Fed. Rules Civ.Proc.Rule 12(b)(6), 28 U.S.C.A.

Brock v. McWherter, 94 F.3d 242.

C.A.6 (Tenn.) 1996. On motion to dismiss for failure to state a claim, court must construe complaint in light most favorable to plaintiff, accept all factual allegations as true, and determine whether plaintiff undoubtedly can prove no set of facts in support of his claims that would entitle him to relief.

Cline v. Rogers, 87 F.3d 176, certiorari denied 117 S.Ct. 510, 136 L.Ed.2d 400.

C.A.6 (Tenn.) 1996. Motion to dismiss for failure to state claim should not be granted unless it appears beyond doubt that plaintiff can prove no set of facts in support of claim which would entitle him or her to relief. Fed.Rules Civ.Proc.Rule 12(b)(6), 28 U.S.C.A.

Lillard v. Shelby County Bd. of Educ., 76 F.3d 716.

C.A.6 (Tenn.) 1983. Windsor v. The Tennessean, 719 F.2d 155, 69 A.L.R. Fed. 896, rehearing denied 726 F.2d 277, certiorari denied 105 S.Ct. 105, 469 U.S. 826, 83 L.Ed.2d 50.

C.A.5 (Tex.) 1998. Case or a portion thereof may not be dismissed for failure to state a claim unless it appears certain that the plaintiffs cannot prove any set of facts in support of their claim that would entitle them to relief. Fed. Rules Civ.Proc.Rule 12(b)(6), 28 U.S.C.A.

Doe on Behalf of Doe v. Dallas Independent School Dist., 153 F.3d 211.

C.A.5 (Tex.) 1998. Dismissal for failure to state a claim is appropriate only if there is no set of facts that could be proven consistent with the allegations in the complaint that would entitle the plaintiff to relief. Fed.Rules Civ. Proc.Rule 12(b)(6), 28 U.S.C.A.

Power Entertainment, Inc. v. National Football League Properties, Inc., 151 F.3d 247.

C.A.5 (Tex.) 1998. Dismissal for failure to state claim is appropriate only if it appears that no relief could be granted under any set of facts that could be proven consistent with the allegations. Fed.Rules Civ.Proc.Rule 12(b)(6), 28 U.S.C.A.

McConathy v. Dr. Pepper/Seven Up Corp., 131 F.3d 558.

C.A.5 (Tex.) 1997. District court may not dismiss complaint for failure to state claim unless it appears beyond doubt that plaintiff can prove no set of facts that would entitle him to relief. Fed.Rules Civ.Proc.Rule 12(b)(6), 28 U.S.C.A.

U.S. ex rel. Thompson v. Columbia/HCA Healthcare Corp., 125 F.3d 899, rehearing denied.

C.A.5 (Tex.) 1997. District court may not dismiss complaint for failure to state claim unless it appears beyond doubt that plaintiff can prove no set of facts in support of his claim which would entitle him to relief. Fed.Rules Civ.Proc.Rule 12(b)(6), 28 U.S.C.A.

Lowrey v. Texas A & M University System, 117 F.3d 242, on remand 11 F.Supp.2d 895.

C.A.5 (Tex.) 1996. Complaint may not be dismissed for failure to state claim upon which relief can be granted unless it appears certain that plaintiff cannot prove any set of facts in support of his claim that would entitle him to relief. Fed.Rules Civ.Proc.Rule 12(b)(6), 28 U.S.C.A.

Home Capital Collateral, Inc. v. F.D.I.C., 96 F.3d 760.

C.A.5 (Tex.) 1996. Dismissal is only proper when it appears certain that plaintiffs cannot prove any set of facts in support of their claim that would entitle them to relief.

McAllister v. F.D.I.C., 87 F.3d 762.

C.A.5 (Tex.) 1996. Motion to dismiss may be granted only if it appears that no relief could be granted under any set of facts that could be proven consistent with allegations. Fed.Rules Civ.Proc.Rule 12(b)(6), 28 U.S.C.A.

Meadowbriar Home for Children, Inc. v. Gunn, 81 F.3d 521.

C.A.5 (Tex.) 1996. District court must deny motion to dismiss for failure to state claim unless complaint fails to state any set of facts upon which relief could be granted; rule allowing such dismissal measures sufficiency of plaintiff's allegations, and when plaintiff has prevailed after full trial on merits, denial of motion to dismiss becomes moot since plaintiff has proved facts sufficient to support relief. Fed.Rules Civ.Proc.Rule 12(b)(6), 28 U.S.C.A.

> Bennett v. Pippin, 74 F.3d 578, rehearing denied, certiorari denied 117 S.Ct. 68, 136 L.Ed.2d 29, rehearing denied 117 S.Ct. 541, 136 L.Ed.2d 425.

C.A.5 (Tex.) 1996. Dismissal of complaint for failure to state claim is not proper unless it appears, based solely on the pleadings, that plaintiff can prove no set of facts in support of his claim which would entitle him to relief. Fed.Rules Civ.Proc.Rule 12(b)(6), 28 U.S.C.A.

> Eason v. Holt, 73 F.3d 600, appeal after remand 114 F.3d 1182.

C.A.5 (Tex.) 1995. Claim may not be dismissed unless it appears certain that plaintiff cannot prove any set of facts in support of her claim which would entitle her to relief.

> Rodriguez v. U.S., 66 F.3d 95, certiorari denied 116 S.Ct. 1058, 516 U.S. 1166, 134 L.Ed.2d 202.

C.A.5 (Tex.) 1995. Motion to dismiss for failure to state a claim may be granted only if it appears that no relief could be granted under any set of facts that could be proven consistent with allegations. Fed.Rules Civ.Proc.Rule 12(b)(6), 28 U.S.C.A.

> Bulger v. U.S. Bureau of Prisons, 65 F.3d 48.

C.A.5 (Tex.) 1991. Court should dismiss case only if affirmative defense or other bar to relief appears on face of complaint. Fed.Rules Civ.Proc.Rule 12(b)(6), 28 U.S.C.A.

> Garrett v. Commonwealth Mortg. Corp. of America, 938 F.2d 591.

C.A.5 (Tex.) 1980. Gay Student Services v. Texas A & M University, 612 F.2d 160, rehearing denied 620 F.2d 300, certiorari denied 101 S.Ct. 608, 449 U.S. 1034, 66 L.Ed.2d 495, appeal after remand 737 F.2d 1317, appeal dismissed, certiorari denied 105 S.Ct. 1860, 471 U.S. 1001, 85 L.Ed.2d 155, rehearing denied 105 S.Ct. 2369, 471 U.S. 1120, 86 L.Ed.2d 268.

C.A.5 (Tex.) 1972. Lipscomb v. Jonsson, 459 F.2d 335, on remand 399 F.Supp. 782, reversed 551 F.2d 1043, application granted Wise v. Lipscomb, 98 S.Ct. 15, 434 U.S. 1329, 54 L.Ed.2d 41, application denied 98 S.Ct. 424, 434 U.S. 935, 54 L.Ed.2d 295, certiorari granted 98 S.Ct. 716, 434 U.S. 1008, 54 L.Ed.2d 750, reversed 98 S.Ct. 2493, 437 U.S. 535, 57 L.Ed.2d 411, on remand 583 F.2d 212, appeal after remand 643 F.2d 319, 72 A.L.R. Fed. 410.

C.A.10 (Utah) 1996. Dismissal for failure to state a cause of action is inappropriate unless plaintiff can prove no set of facts in support of his claims to entitle him to relief. Fed.Rules Civ.Proc.Rule 12(b)(6), 28 U.S.C.A.

> Pelt v. State of Utah, 104 F.3d 1534.

C.A.10 (Utah) 1996. Court of Appeals reviews order granting motion to dismiss for failure to state a claim de novo; dismissal is inappropriate unless plaintiff can prove no set of facts in support of his claims to entitle him to relief, and court must accept as true all factual allegations in the complaint, construe them in a light most favorable to plaintiff, and resolve all reasonable inferences in plaintiff's favor. Fed.Rules Civ.Proc.Rule 12(b), 28 U.S.C.A.

> Seamons v. Snow, 84 F.3d 1226, 141 A.L.R. Fed. 713, on remand 15 F.Supp.2d 1150.

C.A.4 (Va.) 1996. Dismissal for failure to state claim is proper only if court can conclude that on claim as pleaded claimant could prove no set of facts that would entitle her or him to relief. Fed.Rules Civ.Proc.Rule 12(b)(6), 28 U.S.C.A.

> Bryan v. Rectors and Visitors of University of Virginia, 95 F.3d 349.

C.A.9 (Wash.) 1996. Plaintiff's complaint was not to be dismissed for failure to state claim unless it appeared beyond doubt that plaintiff could prove no set of facts in support of its claim which would entitle it to relief. Fed. Rules Civ.Proc.Rule 12(b)(6).

> Cost Management Services, Inc. v. Washington Natural Gas Co., 99 F.3d 937.

C.A.9 (Wash.) 1995. Dismissal for failure to state claim will not be approved unless it appears beyond doubt that plaintiff can prove no set of facts in support of his claim that would entitle him to relief. Fed.Rules Civ.Proc.Rule 12(b)(6), 28 U.S.C.A.

> Gotcher v. Wood, 66 F.3d 1097, certiorari granted, vacated 117 S.Ct. 1840, 137 L.Ed.2d 1045, on remand 122 F.3d 39.

C.A.7 (Wis.) 1998. A complaint should not be dismissed for failure to state a claim unless it appears beyond doubt that the plaintiff can prove no set of facts in support of his claim that would demonstrate an entitlement to relief. Fed.Rules Civ.Proc.Rule 12(b)(6), 28 U.S.C.A.

> Fries v. Helsper, 146 F.3d 452, rehearing and suggestion for rehearing denied.

C.A.7 (Wis.) 1997. Dismissal for failure to state claim is proper only where plaintiff can prove no set of facts that would entitle plaintiff to relief. Fed.Rules Civ.Proc.Rule 12(b)(6), 28 U.S.C.A.

> Mallett v. Wisconsin Div. of Vocational Rehabilitation, 130 F.3d 1245.

C.A.7 (Wis.) 1996. District court should not dismiss complaint for failure to state claim unless it appears beyond doubt that plaintiff can prove no set of facts in support of his claim which would entitle him to relief. Fed.Rules Civ.Proc.Rule 12(b)(6), 28 U.S.C.A.

> Hamlin v. Vaudenberg, 95 F.3d 580.

C.A.7 (Wis.) 1995. Federal district court should not dismiss complaint if plaintiff could prevail under any set of facts that could be proved consistent with the allegations.

> Luckett v. Rent-A-Center, Inc., 53 F.3d 871, rehearing denied, certiorari denied 116 S.Ct. 420, 516 U.S. 965, 133 L.Ed.2d 337, leave to file for rehearing denied 116 S.Ct. 804, 516 U.S. 1086, 133 L.Ed.2d 751.

M.D.Ala. 1996. On a motion to dismiss for failure to state a claim upon which relief may be granted, movant sustains very high burden as motion will be denied unless it appears beyond a doubt that plaintiff can prove no set of facts in support of its claims. Fed.Rules Civ.Proc.Rule 12(b)(6), 28 U.S.C.A.

> Mays v. U.S. Postal Service, 928 F.Supp. 1552, affirmed 122 F.3d 43.

M.D.Ala. 1996. Court may dismiss complaint if it is clear that no relief could be granted under any set of facts that could be proven consistent with allegations.

> Alfa Financial Corp. v. Key, 927 F.Supp. 423, affirmed 112 F.3d 1172.

M.D.Ala. 1996. Court may dismiss complaint for failure to state claim only if it is clear that no relief could be granted under any set of facts that could be proven consistent with allegations.

> Gaither v. Barron, 924 F.Supp. 134.

M.D.Ala. 1996. Court may dismiss complaint for failure to state claim only if it is clear that no relief could be granted under any set of facts that could be proven consistent with allegations in complaint. Fed.Rules Civ.Proc.Rule 12(b)(6), 28 U.S.C.A.

> Kelley v. Troy State University, 923 F.Supp. 1494.

M.D.Ala. 1995. In ruling on motion to dismiss, dismissal is warranted only if it is clear that no relief could be granted under any set of facts that could be proved consistent with allegations. Fed.Rules Civ.Proc.Rule 12(b)(6), 28 U.S.C.A.

> Florida Seed Co., Inc. v. Monsanto Co., 915 F.Supp. 1167, affirmed 105 F.3d 1372, certiorari denied 118 S.Ct. 296, 139 L.Ed.2d 228.

M.D.Ala. 1995. Motions to dismiss for failure to state claim should be denied unless it appears beyond doubt that plaintiff can prove no set of facts in support of its claims. Fed. Rules Civ.Proc.Rule 12(b)(6), 28 U.S.C.A.

> Missildine v. City of Montgomery, 907 F.Supp. 1501.

M.D.Ala. 1995. Motion to dismiss for failure to state claim should be denied unless it appears beyond doubt that plaintiff can prove no set of facts in support of its claim. Fed. Rules Civ.Proc.Rule 12(b)(6), 28 U.S.C.A.

> James By and Through Singleton v. Tallassee High School, 907 F.Supp. 364, affirmed 104 F.3d 372.

M.D.Ala. 1995. Court may dismiss complaint for failure to state a claim only if no relief could be granted under any set of facts that could be proved consistent with the allegations. Fed.Rules Civ.Proc.Rule 12(b)(6), 28 U.S.C.A.

> D.R. by Robinson v. Phyfer, 906 F.Supp. 637.

M.D.Ala. 1995. Complaint may be dismissed for failure to state claim only if it is clear that no relief could be granted under any set of facts that could be proved consistent with the allegations. Fed.Rules Civ.Proc.Rule 12(b)(6), 28 U.S.C.A.

> Shaw-Campbell v. Runyon, 888 F.Supp. 1111.

M.D.Ala. 1995. On motion to dismiss for failure to state a cause upon which relief may be granted, movant sustains a very high burden; such motions should be denied unless it appears beyond a doubt that plaintiff can prove no set of facts in support of his claims. Fed.Rules Civ. Proc.Rule 12(b)(6), 28 U.S.C.A.

> Lightner v. City of Ariton, Ala., 884 F.Supp. 468.

M.D.Ala. 1995. Court may dismiss complaint only if it is clear that no relief could be granted under any set of facts that could be proven consistent with the allegations.

> Harris v. James, 883 F.Supp. 1511, reversed 127 F.3d 993.

M.D.Ala. 1995. Assuming that facts are true, complaint may be dismissed for failure to state claim only if it is clear that no relief could be granted under any set of facts that could be proved consistent with allegations. Fed.Rules Civ.Proc.Rule 12(b)(6), 28 U.S.C.A.

> Browning v. City of Wedowee, Ala., 883 F.Supp. 618.

E.D.Ark. 1996. Complaint should not be dismissed unless it appears beyond doubt that plaintiff can prove no set of facts thereunder which would entitle her to relief. Fed.Rules Civ.Proc.Rule 12(b)(6), 28 U.S.C.A.

> Hicks v. Brown, 929 F.Supp. 1184.

E.D.Ark. 1995. District court may grant motion to dismiss complaint for failure to state claim only if, after viewing pleadings, it is patently clear that there is no set of facts that plaintiff could prove thereunder which would entitle him or her to relief. Fed.Rules Civ.Proc. Rule 12(b)(6), 28 U.S.C.A.

> Roy v. City of Little Rock, 902 F.Supp. 871.

E.D.Ark. 1995. Federal district court may grant defendants' motion to dismiss for failure to state claim only if, after viewing the pleadings, it is patently clear that there is no set of facts that plaintiff could prove thereunder which would entitle her to the relief sought in the complaint. Fed.Rules Civ.Proc.Rule 12(b)(6), 28 U.S.C.A.

> Grissom v. Waterloo Industries, Inc., 902 F.Supp. 867.

W.D.Ark. 1995. A complaint should not be dismissed for failure to state a claim unless it appears beyond doubt that plaintiff can prove no set of facts in support of his claim which would entitle him to relief. Fed.Rules Civ.Proc. Rule 12(b)(6), 28 U.S.C.A.

> Coatney v. Enterprise Rent-A-Car Co., 897 F.Supp. 1205.

C.D.Cal. 1997. Court may not dismiss complaint for failure to state claim unless it appears beyond doubt that plaintiff can prove no set of facts in support of his or her claim which would entitle him or her to relief. Fed. Rules Civ.Proc.Rule 12(b)(6), 28 U.S.C.A.

> National Coalition Government of Union of Burma v. Unocal, Inc., 176 F.R.D. 329.

C.D.Cal. 1996. Court must not dismiss complaint for failure to state claim unless it appears beyond doubt that plaintiff can prove no set of facts in support of his claim which would entitle him to relief. Fed.Rules Civ.Proc. Rule 12(b)(6), 28 U.S.C.A.

> Remington Investments, Inc. v. Kadenacy, 930 F.Supp. 446.

C.D.Cal. 1996. Court must not dismiss complaint for failure to state a claim unless it appears beyond doubt that plaintiff can prove no set of facts in support of his claim which would entitle him to relief. Fed.Rules Civ.Proc. Rules 8(a), 12(b)(6), 28 U.S.C.A.

> Gould v. Harris, 929 F.Supp. 353.

C.D.Cal. 1996. Motion to dismiss for failure to state claim should be granted when it is clear that plaintiff can prove no set of facts in support of claim that would entitle him to relief. Fed.Rules Civ.Proc.Rule 12(b)(6), 28 U.S.C.A.

> Brenizer v. Ray, 915 F.Supp. 176.

C.D.Cal. 1996. Motion to dismiss for lack of subject matter jurisdiction or for failure to state claim should be granted when it is clear that plaintiff can prove no set of facts in support of claim that would entitle him to relief. Fed. Rules Civ.Proc.Rule 12(b)(1, 6), 28 U.S.C.A.

> Cevallos v. City of Los Angeles, 914 F.Supp. 379.

C.D.Cal. 1995. Court may dismiss complaint for failure to state claim upon which relief can be granted only if it appears beyond doubt that plaintiff can prove no set of facts in support of claim which would entitle him to relief. Fed.Rules Civ.Proc.Rule 12(b)(6), 28 U.S.C.A.

> Grace v. Federal Emergency Management, 889 F.Supp. 394.

E.D.Cal. 1996. Court may not dismiss complaint for failure to state claim unless it appears beyond doubt that plaintiff can prove no set of facts in support of claim which would entitle him or her to relief. Fed.Rules Civ.Proc. Rule 12(b)(6), 28 U.S.C.A.

> Youngberg v. Bekins Co., 930 F.Supp. 1396.

E.D.Cal. 1995. Court may not dismiss complaint for failure to state claim unless it appears beyond reasonable doubt that plaintiff can prove no set of facts in support of claim which would entitle him or her to relief. Fed. Rules Civ.Proc.Rule 12(b)(6), 28 U.S.C.A.

> DePaoli v. Carlton, 878 F.Supp. 1351.

N.D.Cal. 1996. Even if face of pleadings suggests that chance of recovery is remote, trial court must ordinarily allow plaintiff to develop case at initial stage of proceedings by denying motion to dismiss for failure to state claim upon which relief can be granted. Fed.Rules Civ. Proc.Rule 12(b)(6), 28 U.S.C.A.

> Lilley v. Charren, 936 F.Supp. 708.

N.D.Cal. 1996. Motion to dismiss will be denied unless it appears that plaintiff can prove no set of facts which entitle him or her to relief.

> Roessert v. Health Net, 929 F.Supp. 343.

N.D.Cal. 1996. Motion to dismiss complaint for failure to state claim cannot be granted unless it appears beyond doubt that plaintiff can prove no set of facts in support of his claim that would entitle him to relief. Fed.Rules Civ.Proc.Rule 12(b)(6), 28 U.S.C.A.

> Informix Software, Inc. v. Oracle Corp., 927 F.Supp. 1283.

N.D.Cal. 1996. Motion to dismiss will be denied unless it appears that plaintiff can prove no set of facts which would entitle him or her to relief. Fed.Rules Civ.Proc.Rule 12(b)(6), 28 U.S.C.A.

> Bernstein v. U.S. Dept. of State, 922 F.Supp. 1426.

N.D.Cal. 1996. Complaint should only be dismissed where, assuming all allegations as true in light most favorable to plaintiff, it appears beyond doubt that no set of facts could support plaintiff's claim for relief.

> Ultrapure Systems, Inc. v. Ham-Let Group, 921 F.Supp. 659.

N.D.Cal. 1996. Motion to dismiss for failure to state claim should not be granted unless it appears beyond doubt that plaintiff can prove no set of facts in support of claim which would entitle plaintiff to relief. Fed.Rules Civ.Proc. Rules 12(b)(6), 28 U.S.C.A.

Holmes v. California Army Nat. Guard, 920 F.Supp. 1510, reversed 124 F.3d 1126, rehearing and suggestion for rehearing denied 155 F.3d 1049.

N.D.Cal. 1995. On motion to dismiss for failure to state a claim, even if face of pleading suggests chance of recovery is remote, district court must allow plaintiff to develop her case at this stage of proceedings. Fed.Rules Civ.Proc. Rule 12(b)(6), 28 U.S.C.A.

Himaka v. Buddhist Churches of America, 917 F.Supp. 698.

N.D.Cal. 1995. In ruling on motion to dismiss for failure to state claim, court must construe complaint liberally, and dismissal should not be granted unless it appears to a certainty that plaintiff can prove no set of facts in support of his claim that would entitle him to relief. Fed.Rules Civ.Proc.Rule 12(b)(6), 28 U.S.C.A.

Don King Productions/Kingvision v. Lovato, 911 F.Supp. 419.

N.D.Cal. 1995. Motion to dismiss for failure to state claim must be denied unless it appears that plaintiffs can prove no set of facts which would entitle them to relief.

Bates v. Jones, 904 F.Supp. 1080.

N.D.Cal. 1995. Under liberal federal pleading policies, plaintiff need only give defendant fair notice of the claims against it; claim should not be dismissed unless it is certain that law would not permit the requested relief even if all of the allegations in the complaint were proven true. Fed.Rules Civ.Proc.Rule 12(b)(6), 28 U.S.C.A.

Stack v. Lobo, 903 F.Supp. 1361.

N.D.Cal. 1995. Motion to dismiss complaint for failure to state claim should not be granted unless it appears beyond doubt that plaintiff can prove no set of facts in support of his claim which would entitle him to relief. Fed.Rules Civ.Proc.Rule 12(b)(6), 28 U.S.C.A.

Arbabian v. BP America, 898 F.Supp. 703.

N.D.Cal. 1994. Motion to dismiss, for failure to state cause of action upon which relief can be granted, tests the sufficiency of the complaint; dismissal of an action on this ground is appropriate only where it appears beyond doubt that the plaintiff can prove no set of facts in support of his claim which would entitle him to relief. Fed.Rules Civ.Proc.Rule 12(b)(6), 28 U.S.C.A.

In re Gupta Corp. Securities Litigation, 900 F.Supp. 1217.

N.D.Cal. 1984. Wickland Oil Terminals v. Asarco, Inc., 590 F.Supp. 72, reversed in part, appeal dismissed in part 792 F.2d 887, on remand 654 F.Supp. 955.

N.D.Cal. 1979. Mori v. International Broth. of Boilermakers, Iron Ship Builders, Blacksmiths, Forgers and Helpers, Local Lodge No. 6, 482 F.Supp. 838, reversed 653 F.2d 1279, stay granted 102 S.Ct. 1046, 454 U.S. 1301, 70 L.Ed.2d 370, certiorari denied 102 S.Ct. 1011, 454 U.S. 1147, 71 L.Ed.2d 301.

S.D.Cal. 1998. Dismissal is warranted where it appears beyond doubt that plaintiff can prove no set of facts which would entitle him to relief. Fed.Rules Civ.Proc.Rules 8(a), 12(b)(6), 28 U.S.C.A.

Ricotta v. State of Cal., 4 F.Supp.2d 961.

S.D.Cal. 1995. In reviewing complaint on motion to dismiss for failure to state claim, court should let claims stand unless it appears beyond doubt that plaintiff can prove no set of facts in support of claim which would entitle plaintiff to relief. Fed.Rules Civ.Proc.Rule 12(b)(6), 28 U.S.C.A.

Industrial Truck Ass'n, Inc. v. Henry, 909 F.Supp. 1368, reversed 125 F.3d 1305.

D.Colo. 1998. Complaint should not be dismissed for failure to state a claim unless it appears beyond doubt that the plaintiff can prove no set of facts in support of his claim which would entitle him to relief. Fed.Rules Civ.Proc.Rule 12(b)(6), 28 U.S.C.A.

Reeves v. Queen City Transp., 10 F.Supp.2d 1181.

D.Colo. 1997. Dismissal for failure to state a claim is appropriate only if plaintiff can prove no set of facts in support of his claims that would entitle him to relief. Fed.Rules Civ.Proc. Rule 12(b)(6), 28 U.S.C.A.

Jefferson County School Dist. No. R-1 v. Moody's Investor's Services, Inc., 988 F.Supp. 1341.

D.Colo. 1996. A case should not be dismissed for failure to state a claim unless district court determines beyond a doubt that plaintiff can prove no set of facts which entitle him to relief. Fed.Rules Civ.Proc.Rule 12(b)(6), 28 U.S.C.A.

Gerd v. United Parcel Service, Inc., 934 F.Supp. 357.

D.Colo. 1996. For purposes of motion to dismiss for failure to state claim, court accepts all factual allegations as true and resolves all reasonable inferences in favor of plaintiffs, and case should not be dismissed for failure to state claim unless court determines that plaintiff can prove no set of facts which would entitled it to

relief. Fed.Rules Civ.Proc.Rule 12(b)(6), 28 U.S.C.A.

> Beal Corp. Liquidating Trust v. Valleylab, Inc., 927 F.Supp. 1350.

D.Colo. 1996. In determining sufficiency of complaint, complaint should not be dismissed for failure to state a claim unless it appears beyond doubt that plaintiff can prove no set of facts in support of his claim which would entitle him to relief. Fed.Rules Civ.Proc.Rule 12(b)(6), 28 U.S.C.A.

> Bowe v. SMC Elec. Products, Inc., 916 F.Supp. 1066.

D.Colo. 1995. In ruling on motion to dismiss, trial court accepts all factual allegations as true, and resolves all reasonable inferences in favor of plaintiffs; case should not be dismissed for failure to state claim unless trial court determines beyond doubt that plaintiffs can prove no set of facts which entitle them to relief. Fed. Rules Civ.Proc.Rule 12(b)(6), 28 U.S.C.A.

> Yoder v. Honeywell Inc., 900 F.Supp. 240, affirmed 104 F.3d 1215, certiorari denied 118 S.Ct. 55, 139 L.Ed.2d 19.

D.Colo. 1995. Claim should not be dismissed for failure to state cause of action unless it appears beyond doubt that plaintiff can prove no set of facts which would entitle him to relief. Fed.Rules Civ.Proc.Rule 12(b)(6), 28 U.S.C.A.

> Johnson v. N.T.I., a Div. of Colorado Springs Circuits, 898 F.Supp. 762.

D.Colo. 1995. Claim should not be dismissed for failure to state claim unless it appears beyond doubt that plaintiff can prove no set of facts which would entitle him or her to relief. Fed.Rules Civ.Proc.Rule 12(b)(6), 28 U.S.C.A.

> Brooks v. Bank of Boulder, 891 F.Supp. 1469.

D.Colo. 1995. Court should not dismiss cause of action for failure to state a claim unless court determines that plaintiff can prove no set of facts that would entitle him to relief. Fed. Rules Civ.Proc.Rule 12(b)(6), 28 U.S.C.A.

> Arkansas-Platte & Gulf Partnership v. Dow Chemical Co., 886 F.Supp. 762.

Complaint should be dismissed for failure to state a claim only when it appears that plaintiff can prove no set of facts in support of claim that would entitle plaintiff to relief, even when all well-pleaded allegations in complaint are accepted as true and construed in light most favorable to plaintiff; so long as plaintiff offers evidence in support of legally recognized claim for relief, motion must be denied. Fed.Rules Civ.Proc.Rule 12(b)(6), 28 U.S.C.A.

> Arkansas-Platte & Gulf Partnership v. Dow Chemical Co., 886 F.Supp. 762.

D.Colo. 1984. For defendant to prevail on motion to dismiss for failure to state claim upon which relief can be granted, it must appear beyond doubt that plaintiff can prove no set of facts in support of his claim which would entitle him to relief; all facts must be construed in favor of plaintiff. Fed.Rules Civ.Proc.Rule 12(b)(6), 28 U.S.C.A.

> Hiatt v. Schreiber, 599 F.Supp. 1142.

D.Colo. 1982. Martinez v. Winner, 548 F.Supp. 278, affirmed in part, reversed in part and remanded 771 F.2d 424, opinion modified on denial of rehearing 778 F.2d 553, certiorari granted, vacated Tyus v. Martinez, 106 S.Ct. 1787, 475 U.S. 1138, 90 L.Ed.2d 333, on remand 800 F.2d 230.

D.Conn. 1998. Dismissal of a complaint for failure to state a claim is inappropriate unless it is clear that no relief could be granted under any set of facts that could be proved consistent with the allegations. Fed.Rules Civ. Proc.Rule 12(b)(6), 28 U.S.C.A.

> Feiner v. SS & C Technologies, 11 F.Supp.2d 204.

D.Conn. 1998. Court may dismiss the complaint for failure to state a claim only where it appears beyond doubt that plaintiff can prove no set of facts in support of his or her claim which would entitle him or her to relief. Fed. Rules Civ.Proc.Rule 12(b)(6), 28 U.S.C.A.

> McDonald v. Timex Corp., 9 F.Supp.2d 120.

D.Conn. 1996. Court may dismiss complaint only if it appears beyond a doubt that plaintiff can prove no set of facts in support of claims in complaint that would entitle him or her to relief.

> Harvey v. Harvey, 931 F.Supp. 127, affirmed 108 F.3d 329.

D.Conn. 1996. Court may dismiss complaint only where it appears beyond doubt that plaintiff can prove no set of facts in support of his claim which would entitle him to relief. Fed.Rules Civ.Proc.Rule 12(b)(6), 28 U.S.C.A.

> Williams v. Hoffman/New Yorker, Inc., 923 F.Supp. 350.

D.Conn. 1996. If full text of additional documents submitted by defendants on motion to dismiss for failure to state cause of action reveal that plaintiff cannot possibly prove a claim, claim will be dismissed. Fed.Rules Civ. Proc.Rule 12(b)(6), 28 U.S.C.A.

> In re Hunter Environmental Services, Inc. Securities Litigation, 921 F.Supp. 914.

D.Conn. 1996. Motion to dismiss for failure to state claim upon which relief can be granted should be granted only if it is clear that no relief could be granted under any set of facts that could be proved consistent with allegations. Fed.Rules Civ.Proc.Rule 12(b)(6), 28 U.S.C.A.

Messier v. Southbury Training School, 916 F.Supp. 133.

D.Conn. 1996. Motion to dismiss should be granted only when it appears beyond doubt that plaintiff fails to state any claim upon which relief may be granted. Fed.Rules Civ.Proc.Rule 12(b)(6), 28 U.S.C.A.

Meyers v. Arcudi, 915 F.Supp. 522.

D.Conn. 1996. Dismissal for failure to state claim on which relief can be granted is warranted only if, under any set of facts plaintiff can prove consistent with the allegations, it is clear that no relief can be granted, accepting all material facts alleged in complaint as true and drawing all reasonable inferences in favor of the pleader. Fed.Rules Civ.Proc.Rule 12(b)(6), 28 U.S.C.A.

Hyun v. South Kent School, 166 F.R.D. 272.

D.Conn. 1995. Complaint will not be dismissed unless it appears beyond doubt that plaintiff can prove no set of facts in support of his claim which would entitle him to relief.

Wilhelm v. Sunrise Northeast, Inc., 923 F.Supp. 330.

D.Conn. 1995. Dismissal for failure to state claim is warranted only if, under any set of facts that plaintiff can prove consistent with allegations, it is clear that no relief can be granted. Fed.Rules Civ.Proc.Rule 12(b)(6), 28 U.S.C.A.

Venclauskas v. State of Conn., Dept. of Public Safety, Div. of State Police, 921 F.Supp. 78.

D.Conn. 1995. In deciding motion to dismiss, court must accept material facts alleged in complaint as true and draw all reasonable inferences in favor of pleader to determine whether plaintiff has stated claim on which relief may be granted; dismissal is warranted only if it is clear that no relief can be granted under any set of facts that plaintiff can prove consistent with allegations. Fed.Rules Civ.Proc.Rule 12(b)(6), 28 U.S.C.A.

Gorman v. Hughes Danbury Optical Systems, 908 F.Supp. 107.

D.Conn. 1995. Dismissal is not warranted unless it appears beyond doubt that plaintiff can prove no set of facts in support of claim which would entitle plaintiff to relief. Fed.Rules Civ.Proc.Rule 12(b)(6), 28 U.S.C.A.

Velez v. City of New London, 903 F.Supp. 286.

Question on motion to dismiss for failure to state claim is whether or not it appears to certainty under existing laws that no relief can be granted under any set of facts that might be proved in support of claims. Fed.Rules Civ.Proc.Rule 12(b)(6), 28 U.S.C.A.

Velez v. City of New London, 903 F.Supp. 286.

D.Conn. 1995. Court may dismiss complaint for failure to state claim only where it appears beyond doubt that plaintiff can prove no set of facts in support of his claim which would entitle him to relief. Fed.Rules Civ.Proc. Rule 12(b)(6), 28 U.S.C.A.

Sitka v. U.S., 903 F.Supp. 282.

D.Conn. 1995. Complaint should not be dismissed for failure to state a claim unless it appears beyond doubt that plaintiff can prove no set of facts in support of his claim which would entitle him to relief. Fed.Rules Civ.Proc. Rule 12(b)(6), 28 U.S.C.A.

Mullins v. Pfizer, Inc., 899 F.Supp. 69.

D.Conn. 1995. Complaint will not be dismissed unless it appears beyond doubt that plaintiff can prove no set of facts in support of his claim which would entitle him to relief.

Seeman v. Arthur Andersen & Co., 896 F.Supp. 250.

D.Conn. 1995. Federal district court can dismiss for failure to state claim only it if appears beyond doubt that plaintiff can prove no set of facts in support of her claim which would entitle her to relief. Fed.Rules Civ.Proc. Rule 12(b)(6), 28 U.S.C.A.

Bennett v. Beiersdorf, Inc., 889 F.Supp. 46.

D.Conn. 1995. Motion to dismiss will be granted only if it is clear that plaintiff can prove no set of facts as grounds for relief.

F.D.I.C. v. Raffa, 882 F.Supp. 1236.

D.Conn. 1994. Dismissal of complaint for failure to state claim is warranted only if, under any set of facts that plaintiff can prove consistent with the allegations, it is clear that no relief can be granted. Fed.Rules Civ.Proc.Rule 12(b)(6), 28 U.S.C.A.

Gregory v. Southern New England Telephone Co., 896 F.Supp. 78.

D.Conn. 1994. A complaint should not be dismissed for failure to state a claim unless it appears beyond a doubt that plaintiff can prove no set of facts in support of claim which would entitle him to relief. Fed.Rules Civ.Proc.Rule 12(b)(6), 28 U.S.C.A.

GICC Capital Corp. v. Technology Finance Group, Inc., 891 F.Supp. 64, affirmed 67 F.3d 463, certiorari denied 116 S.Ct. 2547, 518 U.S. 1017, 135 L.Ed.2d 1067.

D.Conn. 1994. Complaint should only be dismissed for failure to state upon which relief can be granted where no set of facts consistent with allegations could be proven which would entitle plaintiff to relief. Fed.Rules Civ.Proc. Rule 12(b)(6), 28 U.S.C.A.

> Bailey-Gates v. Aetna Life Ins. Co., 890 F.Supp. 73.

D.Del. 1996. On motion to dismiss, court will dismiss complaint only if it appears beyond doubt that plaintiffs can prove no set of facts in support of their claim which would entitle them to relief. Fed.Rules Civ.Proc.Rule 12(b)(6), 28 U.S.C.A.

> Panhandle Eastern Pipe Line Co. v. Utilicorp United Inc., 928 F.Supp. 466.

D.Del. 1996. Court will dismiss complaint for failure to state claim only if it appears beyond doubt that plaintiffs can prove no set of facts in support of their claim that would entitle them to relief. Fed.Rules Civ.Proc.Rule 12(b)(6), 28 U.S.C.A.

> Johnson v. Cullen, 925 F.Supp. 244.

D.Del. 1996. Standard for deciding motion to dismiss for failure to state claim is whether, under any reasonable reading of the pleadings, plaintiff may be entitled to relief. Fed.Rules Civ.Proc.Rule 12(b)(6), 28 U.S.C.A.

> Falkenberg Capital Corp. v. Dakota Cellular, Inc., 925 F.Supp. 231.

D.Del. 1995. For purposes of motion to dismiss for failure to state claim, plaintiff need not prove merits of its case; only if it is beyond doubt that plaintiff can prove no set of facts to support its claim should defendants prevail. Fed.Rules Civ.Proc.Rule 12(b)(6), 28 U.S.C.A.

> Delaware Health Care, Inc. v. MCD Holding Co., 893 F.Supp. 1279.

D.Del. 1991. Under Federal Rules of Civil Procedure, count of complaint may be dismissed for failure to state claim only if, when accepting all factual allegations in complaint as true and drawing all reasonable inferences from those facts, no relief could be granted under any set of facts that could be proved. Fed.Rules Civ.Proc.Rule 12(b)(6), 28 U.S.C.A.

> Brug v. Enstar Group, Inc., 755 F.Supp. 1247.

D.D.C. 1996. In determining whether plaintiff has failed to state cause of action, court must limit its review to pleadings, and defendant must show beyond doubt that plaintiff can prove no set of facts in support of his claim which would entitle him to relief.

> Caudle v. Thomason, 942 F.Supp. 635.

D.D.C. 1996. Dismissal for failure to state claim is only appropriate if it appears beyond doubt that no set of facts proffered in support of claims would entitle plaintiffs to relief. Fed. Rules Civ.Proc.Rule 12(b)(6), 28 U.S.C.A.

> Bridges v. Blue Cross and Blue Shield Ass'n, 935 F.Supp. 37.

D.D.C. 1996. Claim must be dismissed if it appears beyond doubt that plaintiff can prove no set of facts in support of claim that would entitle plaintiff to relief. Fed.Rules Civ.Proc. Rule 12(b)(6), 28 U.S.C.A.

> Rendall-Speranza v. Nassim, 932 F.Supp. 19.

D.D.C. 1996. Dismissal for failure to state claim is appropriate only if it appears beyond doubt that no set of facts proffered in support of plaintiff's claim would entitle him to relief. Fed.Rules Civ.Proc.Rule 12(b)(6), 28 U.S.C.A.

> Gillet v. King, 931 F.Supp. 9, affirmed 132 F.3d 1481, 328 U.S.App.D.C. 135.

D.D.C. 1996. Court may not dismiss complaint unless it is clear that no relief can be granted under any set of facts that could be proved consistent with the allegations. Fed. Rules Civ.Proc.Rule 12(b), 28 U.S.C.A.

> Moore v. Aspin, 916 F.Supp. 32.

D.D.C. 1996. Complaint should not be dismissed for failure to state a claim unless it appears beyond a doubt that plaintiff can prove no set of facts in support of claim which would entitle her to relief. Fed.Rules Civ.Proc.Rule 12(b)(6), 28 U.S.C.A.

> Williams v. District of Columbia, 916 F.Supp. 1.

D.D.C. 1995. In considering motion to dismiss, court must assume truth of factual allegations of complaint and liberally construe them in favor of plaintiff; it may dismiss complaint for failure to state claim only if it appears that plaintiff can prove no set of facts in support of its claim that would entitle plaintiff to relief. Fed.Rules Civ.Proc.Rule 12(b)(6), 28 U.S.C.A.

> Mobile Exploration & Producing U.S., Inc. v. Babbitt, 913 F.Supp. 5.

D.D.C. 1995. Court may dismiss complaint for failure to state claim on which relief can be granted only if it appears beyond doubt that plaintiff can prove no set of facts in support of his claim which would entitle him to relief. Fed.Rules Civ.Proc.Rule 12(b)(6), 28 U.S.C.A.

> de Los Rios v. NationsBank, N.A., 911 F.Supp. 8.

D.D.C. 1995. Motion to dismiss for failure to state claim should not be granted unless it appears that plaintiff can prove no set of facts entitling her to the relief sought in complaint. Fed.Rules Civ.Proc.Rule 12(b)(6), 28 U.S.C.A.

> Taye v. Amundson, 908 F.Supp. 21.

D.D.C. 1995. Court will not dismiss plaintiff's complaint for failure to state claim unless it appears beyond doubt that plaintiff can prove no set of facts in support of his claim that would entitle him to relief. Fed.Rules Civ.Proc.Rule 12(b)(6), 28 U.S.C.A.

Transworld Products Co., Inc. v. Canteen Corp., 908 F.Supp. 1.

D.D.C. 1995. Motion to dismiss should not be granted unless it appears beyond doubt that the plaintiff can prove no set of facts in support of its claim which would entitle it to relief. Fed.Rules Civ.Proc.Rule 12(b)(6), 28 U.S.C.A.

Federation for American Immigration Reform, Inc. v. Reno, 897 F.Supp. 595, affirmed 93 F.3d 897, 320 U.S.App.D.C. 234, certiorari denied 117 S.Ct. 2510, 138 L.Ed.2d 1013.

D.D.C. 1995. Pro se complaint should not be dismissed for failure to state claim unless it appears beyond doubt that plaintiff can prove no set of facts in support of his claim which would entitle him to relief.

Pryor-El v. Kelly, 892 F.Supp. 261.

D.D.C. 1995. Dismissal for failure to state a claim is warranted only where it appears beyond doubt that plaintiff can prove no set of facts in support of her claim entitling her to relief. Fed.Rules Civ.Proc.Rule 12(b)(6), 28 U.S.C.A.

Whitaker v. Washington Metropolitan Area Transit Authority, 889 F.Supp. 505.

D.D.C. 1995. Federal district court may dismiss complaint for failure to state claim only if it appears that plaintiff can prove no set of facts in support of her claim that would entitle her to relief. Fed.Rules Civ.Proc.Rule 12(b)(6), 28 U.S.C.A.

Thomas v. District of Columbia, 887 F.Supp. 1.

D.D.C. 1995. Dismissal for failure to state claim is warranted only when it appears that plaintiff can prove no set of facts in support of his claim which would entitle him to relief. Fed.Rules Civ.Proc.Rule 12(b)(6), 28 U.S.C.A.

Anderson v. Local 201 Reinforcing Rodmen, 886 F.Supp. 94.

D.D.C. 1995. Court may dismiss complaint for failure to state claim upon which relief can be granted only if it appears that plaintiff can prove no set of facts in support of his or her claim that would entitle him or her to relief. Fed.Rules Civ.Proc.Rule 12(b)(6), 28 U.S.C.A.

Nicastro v. Clinton, 882 F.Supp. 1128, affirmed 84 F.3d 1446, 318 U.S.App.D.C. 72.

D.D.C. 1995. Court should not grant motion to dismiss for failure to state claim upon which relief may be granted unless it appears that plaintiff can prove no set of facts entitling

plaintiff to relief sought in complaint. Fed. Rules Civ.Proc.Rule 12(b)(6), 28 U.S.C.A.

Caliendo v. Bentsen, 881 F.Supp. 44.

D.D.C. 1995. In ruling on motion to dismiss for failure to state a claim upon which relief may be granted, district court must accept as true each of the allegations in complaint; motion should not be granted unless it appears that plaintiff can prove no set of facts entitling him or her to relief sought in complaint. Fed. Rules Civ.Proc.Rule 12(b)(6), 28 U.S.C.A.

Campbell-El v. District of Columbia, 881 F.Supp. 42.

D.D.C. 1995. Dismissal is only appropriate if it appears beyond a doubt that no set of facts proffered in support of plaintiffs' claim would entitle them to relief. Fed.Rules Civ. Proc.Rule 12(b), 28 U.S.C.A.

Judicial Watch, Inc. v. Clinton, 880 F.Supp. 1, affirmed 76 F.3d 1232, 316 U.S.App. D.C. 179.

D.D.C. 1995. When assessing motion to dismiss for failure to state claim, complaint should be dismissed only if it appears beyond doubt that no set of facts proffered in support of plaintiff's claim would entitle him to relief. Fed.Rules Civ.Proc.Rule 12(b)(6), 28 U.S.C.A.

Dominion Cogen, D.C., Inc. v. District of Columbia, 878 F.Supp. 258.

D.D.C. 1993. Complaint should not be dismissed for failure to state claim upon which relief can be granted unless it appears beyond doubt that plaintiff can prove no set of facts in support of his claim which would entitle him to relief. Fed.Rules Civ.Proc.Rule 12(b), 28 U.S.C.A.

Board of Directors of Chestnut Grove Condominium Unit Owners' Ass'n v. Resolution Trust Corp., 161 B.R. 860.

D.D.C. 1985. A motion to dismiss may be granted only if it appears beyond doubt that plaintiff can prove no set of facts in support of claim which would entitle him to relief.

Powell v. Nigro, 601 F.Supp. 144.

M.D.Fla. 1998. Pro se plaintiff's complaint would not be dismissed for failure to state a claim unless it appeared beyond doubt that the plaintiff could prove no set of facts in support of claim that would entitle her to relief. Fed.Rules Civ.Proc.Rule 12(b)(6), 28 U.S.C.A.

Woods v. Commissioner, I.R.S., 8 F.Supp.2d 1357.

M.D.Fla. 1998. Complaint should not be dismissed for failure to state claim unless it appears beyond doubt that plaintiffs can prove no set of facts that would entitle them to relief. Fed.Rules Civ.Proc.Rule 12(b)(6), 28 U.S.C.A.

    American Charities for Reasonable Fundraising Regulation, Inc. v. Pinellas County, 997 F.Supp. 1481.

M.D.Fla. 1997. Dismissal is proper only when no construction of complaint's factual allegations supports cause of action.

    Chumbley v. Gashinski, 983 F.Supp. 1406.

M.D.Fla. 1997. District Court can only dismiss count for failure to state a claim if it appears beyond a doubt that plaintiff can prove no set of facts in support of claim that would entitle him to relief, and court cannot dismiss count merely because plaintiff's allegations do not support the theory he intends to proceed on, as court is under duty to examine complaint to determine if allegations provide for relief under any possible theory. Fed.Rules Civ.Proc.Rule 12(b)(6), 28 U.S.C.A.

    Unkel v. Liggett Group Inc., 172 F.R.D. 474.

M.D.Fla. 1996. Complaint should not be dismissed for failure to state claim upon which relief can be granted unless it appears beyond doubt that plaintiff can prove no set of facts in support of his claim which would entitle him to relief. Fed.Rules Civ.Proc.Rule 12(b)(6), 28 U.S.C.A.

    Battista v. Cannon, 934 F.Supp. 400.

M.D.Fla. 1996. Complaint should not be dismissed for failure to state claim unless it appears beyond doubt that plaintiff can prove no set of facts that would entitle plaintiff to relief.

    Jackson v. Motel 6 Multipurpose, Inc., 931 F.Supp. 825.

M.D.Fla. 1996. Complaint should not be dismissed for failure to state cause of action unless it appears beyond doubt that plaintiff can prove no set of facts in support of his claim which would entitle him to relief. Fed.Rules Civ.Proc.Rule 12(b)(6), 28 U.S.C.A.

    Kritzman v. UNUM Life Ins. Co. of America, 928 F.Supp. 1165.

M.D.Fla. 1996. District court should not dismiss complaint for failure to state claim unless it appears beyond doubt that plaintiff can prove no set of facts that would entitle plaintiff to relief.

    Veltmann v. Walpole Pharmacy, Inc., 928 F.Supp. 1161.

M.D.Fla. 1996. Complaint should not be dismissed for failure to state claim unless it appears beyond doubt that plaintiff can prove

no set of facts that would entitle him to relief. Fed.Rules Civ.Proc.Rule 12(b)(6), 28 U.S.C.A.

    White v. Florida Highway Patrol, Div. of Florida Dept. of Highway Safety & Motor Vehicles, 928 F.Supp. 1153.

M.D.Fla. 1996. Complaint should not be dismissed for failure to state claim unless it appears beyond doubt that plaintiff can prove no set of facts that would entitle plaintiff to relief. Fed.Rules Civ.Proc.Rule 12(b)(6), 28 U.S.C.A.

    Hammer v. Hillsborough County Through Bd. of County Com'rs, 927 F.Supp. 1540.

M.D.Fla. 1996. Complaint should not be dismissed for failure to state claim unless it appears beyond doubt that plaintiff can prove no set of facts in support of his claim which would entitle him to relief. Fed.Rules Civ.Proc. Rule 12(b)(6), 28 U.S.C.A.

    Harris v. Iorio, 922 F.Supp. 588, affirmed 136 F.3d 139.

M.D.Fla. 1996. Court should not dismiss complaint for failure to state a claim unless it appears beyond doubt that plaintiff can prove no set of facts in support of his claim which would entitle him to relief. Fed.Rules Civ.Proc. Rule 12(b)(6), 28 U.S.C.A.

    Mangin v. Westco Sec. Systems, Inc., 922 F.Supp. 563.

M.D.Fla. 1995. Complaint should not be dismissed for failure to state claim unless it appears beyond doubt that plaintiff can prove no set of facts that would entitle him to relief. Fed.Rules Civ.Proc.Rule 12(b)(6), 28 U.S.C.A.

    Fuller v. Johannessen, 180 B.R. 682, vacated In re Johannessen, 76 F.3d 347.

M.D.Fla. 1995. Complaint should not be dismissed for failure to state claim unless it appears beyond doubt that plaintiff can prove no set of facts that would entitle him or her to relief. Fed.Rules Civ.Proc.Rule 12(b)(6), 28 U.S.C.A.

    Eidson v. Arenas, 910 F.Supp. 609.

M.D.Fla. 1995. Complaint should not be dismissed for failure to state claim unless it appears beyond doubt that plaintiff can prove no set of facts that would entitle plaintiff to relief. Fed.Rules Civ.Proc.Rule 12(b)(6), 28 U.S.C.A.

    Howry v. Nisus, Inc., 910 F.Supp. 576.

M.D.Fla. 1995. Complaint should not be dismissed for failure to state a claim unless it appears beyond doubt that plaintiff can prove no set of facts that would entitle him to relief.

    Italiano v. Jones Chemicals, Inc., 908 F.Supp. 904.

M.D.Fla. 1995. Court should not grant motion to dismiss for failure to state claim

unless plaintiff can prove no set of facts in support of claim entitling plaintiff to relief.
> Harding v. Winn-Dixie Stores, Inc., 907 F.Supp. 386.

M.D.Fla. 1995. Complaint should not be dismissed for failure to state claim upon which relief can be granted unless it appears beyond doubt that plaintiff can prove no set of facts in support of his claim which would entitle him to relief. Fed.Rules Civ.Proc.Rule 12(b)(6), 28 U.S.C.A.
> Medina v. Minerva, 907 F.Supp. 379.

M.D.Fla. 1995. Complaint should not be dismissed for failure to state claim unless it appears beyond doubt that plaintiff can prove no set of facts that would entitle him to relief. Fed.Rules Civ.Proc.Rule 12(b), 28 U.S.C.A.
> Hicks v. Lewis, 904 F.Supp. 1368.

M.D.Fla. 1995. To dismiss claim for failure to state claim upon which relief can be granted, defendant must demonstrate that plaintiff can prove no set of facts which would entitle it to relief.
> Dominican Energy Ltd., Inc. v. Dominican Republic, 903 F.Supp. 1507.

M.D.Fla. 1995. Complaint should not be dismissed for failure to state claim unless it appears beyond a doubt that plaintiff can prove no set of facts that support claim for relief.
> Rickman v. Precisionaire, Inc., 902 F.Supp. 232.

M.D.Fla. 1995. Complaint should not be dismissed for failure to state claim unless it appears beyond doubt that plaintiff can prove no set of facts that would entitle him to relief. Fed.Rules Civ.Proc.Rule 12(b)(6), 28 U.S.C.A.
> Harris v. McDonald's Corp., 901 F.Supp. 1552.

M.D.Fla. 1995. Complaint should not be dismissed for failure to state claim unless it appears beyond doubt that plaintiff can prove no set of facts that support claim for relief.
> Krehling v. Baron, 900 F.Supp. 1578.

M.D.Fla. 1995. Complaint should not be dismissed for failure to state claim unless it appears beyond doubt that plaintiff can prove no set of facts that would entitle him to relief. Fed.Rules Civ.Proc.Rule 12(b)(6), 28 U.S.C.A.
> Krehling v. Baron, 900 F.Supp. 1574.

M.D.Fla. 1995. Defendant to be entitled to grant of motion to dismiss must demonstrate that plaintiff can prove no set of facts consistent with pleadings which would entitle it to relief.
> Sullivan Properties, Inc. v. City of Winter Springs, 899 F.Supp. 587.

M.D.Fla. 1995. Motion to dismiss for failure to state claim on which relief can be granted will be denied unless it appears beyond all

doubt that plaintiff can prove no set of facts in support of his claims that would entitle him to relief. Fed.Rules Civ.Proc.Rule 12(b)(6), 28 U.S.C.A.
> Vaughn v. Kerley, 897 F.Supp. 1413.

M.D.Fla. 1995. Courts should not dismiss complaint for failure to state claim unless it appears beyond doubt that plaintiff can prove no set of facts that would entitle him to relief. Fed.Rules Civ.Proc.Rule 12(b)(6), 28 U.S.C.A.
> Harmony Homes, Inc. v. U.S. on Behalf of Small Business Admin., 890 F.Supp. 1032.

M.D.Fla. 1995. Complaint should not be dismissed for failure to state a claim unless it appears beyond a doubt that plaintiff can prove no set of facts that would entitle him to relief.
> Parsons v. Nationwide Mut. Ins. Co., 889 F.Supp. 465.

M.D.Fla. 1995. Motion to dismiss for failure to state claim on which relief can be granted will be denied unless it appears beyond all doubt that plaintiff can prove no set of facts in support of his claims that would entitle him to relief. Fed.Rules Civ.Proc.Rule 12(b)(6), 28 U.S.C.A.
> Gangloff v. Poccia, 888 F.Supp. 1549.

M.D.Fla. 1995. Complaint should not be dismissed for failure to state claim unless it appears beyond doubt that plaintiff can prove no set of facts that would entitle plaintiff to relief. Fed.Rules Civ.Proc.Rule 12(b)(6), 28 U.S.C.A.
> Lajos v. duPont Pub., Inc., 888 F.Supp. 143.

M.D.Fla. 1995. Motion to dismiss for failure to state claim should not be granted unless it appears to certainty that plaintiff would not be entitled to recover under any state of facts which could be proved in support of claim. Fed.Rules Civ.Proc.Rule 12, 28 U.S.C.A.
> Cramer v. State of Fla., 885 F.Supp. 1545, affirmed 117 F.3d 1258.

M.D.Fla. 1995. Motion to dismiss should be granted only where plaintiff can prove no set of facts upon which relief could be granted.
> Anthony Distributors, Inc. v. Miller Brewing Co., 882 F.Supp. 1024, reconsideration denied 162 F.R.D. 169.

M.D.Fla. 1991. Complaint should not be dismissed for failure to state claim unless it appears beyond reasonable doubt that plaintiff can prove no set of facts that would entitle him to relief.
> Draughon v. City of Oldsmar, 767 F.Supp. 1144.

M.D.Fla. 1989. Complaint should not be dismissed for failure to state a claim unless it appears beyond doubt that plaintiff can prove no set of facts that would entitle him to relief and, in ruling on the motion to dismiss, court is required to view the complaint in light most favorable to the plaintiff.

> Everdell v. Preston, 717 F.Supp. 1498.

N.D.Fla. 1995. Motion to dismiss for failure to state claim cannot be granted unless complaint alleges no set of facts, which, if proved, would entitle plaintiff to relief. Fed. Rules Civ.Proc.Rule 12(b)(6), 28 U.S.C.A.

> Foster v. Jackson County, Fla., 895 F.Supp. 301.

N.D.Fla. 1995. Motion to dismiss for failure to state claim on which relief can be granted cannot be granted unless complaint alleges no set of facts, which, if proved, would entitle plaintiff to relief.

> CSX Transp., Inc. v. City of Pensacola, Fla., 887 F.Supp. 275, reconsideration denied 936 F.Supp. 885.

N.D.Fla. 1995. Motion to dismiss for failure to state claim cannot be granted unless complaint alleges no set of facts which, if proved, would entitle plaintiff to relief. Fed. Rules Civ.Proc.Rule 12(b)(6), 28 U.S.C.A.

> T.W.M. v. American Medical Systems, Inc., 886 F.Supp. 842.

S.D.Fla. 1998. Complaint should not be dismissed for failure to state a claim unless it appears beyond doubt that the plaintiff can prove no set of facts in support of his claim which would entitle him to relief. Fed.Rules Civ.Proc.Rule 8(a), 28 U.S.C.A.

> Rowe v. City of Fort Lauderdale, 8 F.Supp.2d 1369.

S.D.Fla. 1998. Dismissal of a complaint for failure to state a claim is appropriate only if it is clear that no relief could be granted under any set of facts that could be proved consistent with the allegations. Fed.Rules Civ.Proc.Rule 12(b)(6), 28 U.S.C.A.

> Nautica Intern., Inc. v. Intermarine USA, L.P., 5 F.Supp.2d 1333.

Complaint should not be dismissed for failure to state a claim upon which relief can be granted unless it appears beyond doubt that the plaintiff can prove no set of facts in support of his or her claim which would entitle him or her to relief, but the plaintiff may not merely "label" his or her claims. Fed.Rules Civ.Proc.Rule 12(b)(6), 28 U.S.C.A.

> Nautica Intern., Inc. v. Intermarine USA, L.P., 5 F.Supp.2d 1333.

Dismissal of a complaint is appropriate when, on the basis of a dispositive issue of law, no construction of the factual allegations of a complaint will support the cause of action. Fed.Rules Civ.Proc.Rule 12(b)(6), 28 U.S.C.A.

> Nautica Intern., Inc. v. Intermarine USA, L.P., 5 F.Supp.2d 1333.

S.D.Fla. 1996. In appraising sufficiency of complaint, complaint should not be dismissed for failure to state claim unless it appears beyond doubt that plaintiff can prove no set of facts in support of his claim which would entitle him to relief. Fed.Rules Civ.Proc.Rules 8(a), 12(b)(6), 28 U.S.C.A.

> Ferreiro v. U.S., 934 F.Supp. 1375, reversed 128 F.3d 732.

S.D.Fla. 1996. Complaint should not be dismissed for failure to state claim unless it appears beyond doubt that plaintiff can prove no set of facts in support of his claim which would entitle him to relief. Fed.Rules Civ.Proc. Rule 12(b)(6), 28 U.S.C.A.

> Blount v. Sterling Healthcare Group, Inc., 934 F.Supp. 1365.

S.D.Fla. 1996. A complaint should not be dismissed for failure to state a claim unless it is beyond a doubt that claimant can prove no set of facts that would entitle him to relief. Fed. Rules Civ.Proc.Rule 12(b)(6), 28 U.S.C.A.

> Fernandez v. Community Asphalt, Inc., 934 F.Supp. 418.

S.D.Fla. 1996. Court will not grant motion to dismiss for failure to state claim upon which relief can be granted, unless plaintiff fails to prove any facts that would entitle him to relief. Fed.Rules Civ.Proc.Rule 12(b)(6), 28 U.S.C.A.

> Lopez v. First Union Nat. Bank, 931 F.Supp. 860, reversed 129 F.3d 1186, rehearing and suggestion for rehearing denied Coronado v. Bankatlantic Bancorp, Inc., 141 F.3d 1191.

S.D.Fla. 1996. Motion to dismiss will be granted where it is clear that no relief could be granted under any set of facts that could be proven consistent with the allegations.

> Betancourt v. Marine Cargo Management, Inc., 930 F.Supp. 606.

Dismissal is justified only when allegations of the complaint itself clearly demonstrate that plaintiff does not have a claim.

> Betancourt v. Marine Cargo Management, Inc., 930 F.Supp. 606.

S.D.Fla. 1996. Motion to dismiss should not be granted unless it appears beyond doubt that plaintiff can prove no set of facts in support of claim which would entitle plaintiff to relief.

> Rendon v. State of Fla., 930 F.Supp. 601.

S.D.Fla. 1996. Motion to dismiss for failure to state claim will be granted where it is clear that no relief could be granted under any set of facts that could be proven consistent with allegations.

> Sonnenreich v. Philip Morris Inc., 929 F.Supp. 416.

S.D.Fla. 1995. Complaint should not be dismissed for failure to state a claim unless it appears beyond doubt that plaintiff can prove no such facts that would entitle him to relief. Fed.Rules Civ.Proc.Rule 12(b)(6), 28 U.S.C.A.

> Harvey M. Jasper Retirement Trust v. Ivax Corp., 920 F.Supp. 1260.

S.D.Fla. 1995. Complaint should not be dismissed unless plaintiffs can prove no set of facts in support of their claims which would entitle them to relief.

> Nussbaum v. Mortgage Service America Co., 913 F.Supp. 1548.

Court may dismiss complaint when, on dispositive issue of law, no construction of factual allegations will support cause of action.

> Nussbaum v. Mortgage Service America Co., 913 F.Supp. 1548.

S.D.Fla. 1995. Claim may be dismissed for failure to state cause of action only if it is clear that no relief could be granted under any set of facts consistent with allegations. Fed. Rules Civ.Proc.Rule 12(b)(6), 28 U.S.C.A.

> In re Cascade Intern. Securities Litigation, 894 F.Supp. 437.

S.D.Fla. 1995. Motion to dismiss will be granted where it is clear that no relief could be granted under any set of facts that could be proven consistent with the allegations. Fed. Rules Civ.Proc.Rule 12(c), 28 U.S.C.A.

> Canon v. Clark, 883 F.Supp. 718.

S.D.Fla. 1995. Pleadings must show that plaintiffs have no claim before motion to dismiss for failure to state claim may be granted. Fed.Rules Civ.Proc.Rule 12(b)(6), 28 U.S.C.A.

> Trustees of Hotel Industry Pension Fund v. Carol Management Corp., 880 F.Supp. 1548.

S.D.Fla. 1994. Accepted rule for appraising sufficiency of complaint is that complaint should not be dismissed for failure to state a claim unless it appears beyond doubt that plaintiff can prove no set of facts in support of his claim which would entitle him to relief. Fed. Rules Civ.Proc.Rules 8(a), 12(b)(6), 28 U.S.C.A.

> Tamiami Partners, Ltd. By and Through Tamiami Development Corp. v. Miccosukee Tribe of Indians of Florida, 898 F.Supp. 1549, affirmed in part, appeal dismissed in part 63 F.3d 1030.

S.D.Fla. 1994. Accepted rule for appraising sufficiency of a complaint is that complaint should not be dismissed for failure to state a claim unless it appears beyond all doubt that plaintiff can prove no set of facts in support of his claim which would entitle him to relief. Fed.Rules Civ.Proc.Rule 12(b)(6), 28 U.S.C.A.

> Burnett v. A. Bottacchi S.A. de Navegacion, 882 F.Supp. 1050.

S.D.Fla. 1994. Motion to dismiss should not be granted unless plaintiff can prove no set of facts in support of his claim entitling him to relief.

> Bunger v. Hartman, 851 F.Supp. 461.

S.D.Fla. 1993. Court may not dismiss suit for failure to state claim on which relief may be granted unless it is clear that no relief could be granted under any set of facts that could be proved consistent with complaint. Fed.Rules Civ.Proc.Rule 12(b)(6), 28 U.S.C.A.

> Joaquim v. Royal Caribbean Cruises, Ltd., 899 F.Supp. 600, reversed in part, vacated in part 52 F.3d 1071.

S.D.Fla. 1986. In ruling on a motion to dismiss under the Federal Rules of Civil Procedure the district court is required to accept the pleaded facts as true and resolve any factual issues in a manner favorable to the plaintiff and such motions to dismiss should not be granted unless the plaintiff can prove no set of facts in support of his claim which would entitle him to relief. Fed.Rules Civ.Proc.Rule 12(b)(6), 28 U.S.C.A.

> Quinones v. Durkis, 638 F.Supp. 856.

N.D.Ga. 1996. Complaint may be dismissed for failure to state cause of action upon which relief can be granted if it appears that plaintiff cannot possibly prove any set of facts consistent with allegations in complaint upon which he would be entitled to relief. Fed.Rules Civ.Proc.Rule 12(b)(6), 28 U.S.C.A.

> Marshall v. City of Atlanta, 195 B.R. 156.

N.D.Ga. 1996. On motion to dismiss for failure to state claim upon which relief can be granted, court must ascertain whether, under any set of facts which may be proven from complaint, claims made are so insufficient as to never succeed in court. Fed.Rules Civ.Proc. Rule 12(b)(6), 28 U.S.C.A.

> District 65 Retirement Trust for Members of Bureau of Wholesale Sales Representatives v. Prudential Securities, Inc., 925 F.Supp. 1551.

N.D.Ga. 1995. Complaint may not be dismissed for failure to state claim unless it appears beyond doubt that plaintiff can prove no set of facts in support of its claim which would entitle it to relief. Fed.Rules Civ.Proc.Rule 12(b)(6), 28 U.S.C.A.

> Tee v. UAL Corp., 902 F.Supp. 1572, affirmed 91 F.3d 163, certiorari denied 117 S.Ct. 2432, 138 L.Ed.2d 194.

N.D.Ga. 1995. Motion to dismiss must be denied unless it is clear from complaint and allegations that plaintiff can prove no set of facts which would entitle plaintiff to relief and all inferences that can be drawn from allegations in complaint are to be construed in favor of plaintiff.

> Childree v. UAP/GA AG Chem, Inc., 892 F.Supp. 1554, affirmed in part, vacated in part, reversed in part 92 F.3d 1140, certiorari denied 117 S.Ct. 1080, 137 L.Ed.2d 216.

N.D.Ga. 1983. Stone Mountain Game Ranch, Inc. v. Hunt, 570 F.Supp. 238, affirmed 746 F.2d 761.

S.D.Ga. 1996. District court should grant motion to dismiss only if it appears beyond doubt that plaintiff can prove no set of facts in support of its claim. Fed.Rules Civ.Proc.Rule 12(b)(6), 28 U.S.C.A.

> Powell v. Department of Human Resources of State of Ga., 918 F.Supp. 1575, affirmed 114 F.3d 1074.

S.D.Ga. 1995. Court should not dismiss a complaint for failure to state a claim unless it is clear that plaintiff can prove no set of facts in support of his claim which would entitle him to relief. Fed.Rules Civ.Proc.Rule 12(b)(6), 28 U.S.C.A.

> McCoy v. Johnson Controls World Services, Inc., 878 F.Supp. 229.

D.Hawai'i 1997. In deciding whether complaint should be dismissed for failure to state claim, district court must determine whether it appears to a certainty under existing law that no relief can be granted under any set of facts that might be proved in support of plaintiffs' claims. Fed.Rules Civ.Proc.Rule 12(b)(6), 28 U.S.C.A.

> Burns-Vidlak by Burns v. Chandler, 980 F.Supp. 1144.

D.Hawai'i 1996. Complaint should not be dismissed for failure to state claim unless it appears beyond doubt that plaintiff can prove no set of facts in support of her claim which would entitle her to relief. Fed.Rules Civ.Proc. Rule 12(b)(6), 28 U.S.C.A.

> Water Com'n of County of Hawai'i v. National American Ins. Co., 930 F.Supp. 1411.

D.Hawai'i 1996. Complaint should not be dismissed for failure to state claim unless it appears beyond doubt that plaintiff can prove no set of facts in support of her claim which would entitle her to relief. Fed.Rules Civ.Proc. Rule 12(b)(6), 28 U.S.C.A.

> Otani v. State Farm Fire & Cas. Co., 927 F.Supp. 1330.

D.Hawai'i 1996. Complaint should not be dismissed for failure to state claim unless it appears beyond doubt that plaintiff can prove no set of facts in support of her claim which would entitle her to relief. Fed.Rules Civ.Proc. Rule 12(b)(6), 28 U.S.C.A.

> Ho v. State Farm Mut. Auto. Ins. Co., 926 F.Supp. 964, reversed in part 117 F.3d 1425.

D.Hawai'i 1995. On motion to dismiss for failure to state claim, issue is not whether plaintiff's success on merits is likely, but rather whether plaintiff is entitled to proceed beyond threshold in attempting to establish his claims; court must determine whether it appears to a certainty under existing law that no relief can be granted under any set of facts that might be proved in support of plaintiff's claims. Fed. Rules Civ.Proc.Rule 12(b)(6), 28 U.S.C.A.

> Moore v. Kamikawa, 940 F.Supp. 260, affirmed 82 F.3d 423.

D.Hawai'i 1995. Complaint should not be dismissed for failure to state claim unless it appears beyond doubt that plaintiff can prove no set of facts in support of claim which would entitle him to relief. Fed.Rules Civ.Proc.Rule 12(b)(6), 28 U.S.C.A.

> Fasi v. Gannett Co., Inc., 930 F.Supp. 1403, affirmed 114 F.3d 1194, certiorari denied 118 S.Ct. 302, 139 L.Ed.2d 233.

D.Hawai'i 1995. Complaint should not be dismissed for failure to state claim unless it appears beyond doubt that plaintiff can prove no set of facts in support of his claim which would entitle him to relief. Fed.Rules Civ.Proc. Rule 12(b)(6), 28 U.S.C.A.

> Stone v. Continental Airlines, Inc., 905 F.Supp. 823.

D.Hawai'i 1995. In determining whether to grant motion to dismiss for failure to state claim upon which relief can be granted, district court must accept as true plaintiff's allegations contained in complaint and view them in light most favorable to plaintiff, and thus complaint must stand unless it appears beyond doubt that plaintiff has alleged no facts that would entitle him to relief. Fed.Rules Civ.Proc.Rule 12(b)(6), 28 U.S.C.A.

> Forsyth v. Eli Lilly and Co., 904 F.Supp. 1153.

On motion to dismiss for failure to state claim upon which relief can be granted, district court must determine whether or not it appears to certainty under existing law that no relief can be granted under any set of facts that might be proved in support of plaintiffs' claims. Fed. Rules Civ.Proc.Rule 12(b)(6), 28 U.S.C.A.

> Forsyth v. Eli Lilly and Co., 904 F.Supp. 1153.

D.Idaho 1996. Motion to dismiss for failure to state claim should not be granted unless it appears beyond doubt that plaintiff can prove no set of facts in support of claim that would entitle plaintiff to relief; all allegations of material fact in complaint are taken as true and construed in light most favorable to nonmoving party. Fed.Rules Civ.Proc.Rule 12(b)(6), 28 U.S.C.A.

> Harris v. Roderick, 933 F.Supp. 977, affirmed 126 F.3d 1189, certiorari denied Smith v. Harris, 118 S.Ct. 1051, 140 L.Ed.2d 114.

D.Idaho 1995. Complaint need not be dismissed for failure to state a claim unless it appears beyond doubt that plaintiff can prove no set of facts in support of claim which would entitle plaintiff to relief. Fed.Rules Civ.Proc. Rule 12(b)(6), 28 U.S.C.A.

> Santana v. Zilog, Inc., 878 F.Supp. 1373, affirmed 95 F.3d 780.

D.Idaho 1995. Complaint should not be dismissed for failure to state claim unless it appears beyond doubt that plaintiff can prove no set of facts in support of claim which would entitle plaintiff to relief. Fed.Rules Civ.Proc. Rule 12(b)(6), 28 U.S.C.A.

> Erickson v. Luke, 878 F.Supp. 1364.

Complaint cannot be dismissed for failure to state claim unless it appears beyond doubt that plaintiff can prove no set of facts in support of claim which would entitle plaintiff to relief. Fed.Rules Civ.Proc.Rule 12(b)(6), 28 U.S.C.A.

> Erickson v. Luke, 878 F.Supp. 1364.

C.D.Ill. 1998. Pro se complaints are to be liberally construed and may be dismissed for failure to state a claim only if it appears beyond doubt that the plaintiff can prove no set of facts in support of his claim which entitle him to relief. Fed.Rules Civ.Proc.Rule 12(b)(6), 28 U.S.C.A.

> Jones v. Edgar, 3 F.Supp.2d 979.

C.D.Ill. 1997. Dismissal should not be granted unless it appears beyond doubt that plaintiff can prove no set of facts in support of his claim that would entitle him to relief. Fed. Rules Civ.Proc.Rule 12(b)(6), 28 U.S.C.A.

> Harrell v. City of Jacksonville, 976 F.Supp. 777.

C.D.Ill. 1997. Pro se complaint can be dismissed for failure to state claim only if it appears beyond doubt that plaintiff can prove no set of facts in support of his claim which would entitle him to relief.

> Walton v. Lyons, 962 F.Supp. 126.

C.D.Ill. 1996. In ruling on motion to dismiss, court considers whether relief is possible under any set of facts that could be established consistent with allegations in complaint, and will dismiss claim only if it is beyond doubt that no set of facts would entitle plaintiff to relief. Fed.Rules Civ.Proc.Rule 12(b)(6), 28 U.S.C.A.

> Tobin v. City of Peoria, Ill., 939 F.Supp. 628.

C.D.Ill. 1996. Dismissal is not granted unless it appears beyond doubt that the plaintiff can prove no set of facts in support of his claim that would entitle him to relief. Fed.Rules Civ.Proc.Rule 12, 28 U.S.C.A.

> Stevens v. Umsted, 921 F.Supp. 530, affirmed 131 F.3d 697.

C.D.Ill. 1996. Motion to dismiss for failure to state claim will only be granted where it appears beyond doubt that plaintiff can prove no set of facts in support of his claim which would entitle him to relief. Fed.Rules Civ.Proc. Rule 12(b)(6), 28 U.S.C.A.

> Resolution Trust Corp. v. S & K Chevrolet Co., 918 F.Supp. 1235, opinion vacated in part on reconsideration 923 F.Supp. 135.

C.D.Ill. 1995. In deciding whether allegations in plaintiff's complaint are sufficient to state claim upon which relief might be granted, court should not ask whether complaint points to appropriate statute or legal theory, but should instead inquire whether relief is possible under any set of facts that could be established consistent with plaintiff's allegations.

> Diehl v. ACRI Co., 910 F.Supp. 439.

C.D.Ill. 1995. Dismissal for failure to state claim is not granted unless it appears beyond doubt that plaintiff can prove no set of facts in support of his claim that would entitle him to relief.

> Management Services of Illinois, Inc. v. Health Management Systems, Inc., 907 F.Supp. 289.

C.D.Ill. 1995. Dismissal of complaint is not granted unless it appears beyond doubt that plaintiff can prove no set of facts in support of his claim which would entitle him to relief.

> Resolution Trust Corp. v. Chapman, 895 F.Supp. 1072.

C.D.Ill. 1995. A motion to dismiss for failure to state a claim will only be granted if appears beyond a doubt that plaintiff can prove no set of facts in support of claim which would entitle him to relief. Fed.Rules Civ.Proc.Rule 12(b)(6), 28 U.S.C.A.

> Griffith v. Keystone Steel and Wire, Div. of Keystone Consol. Industries, Inc., 887 F.Supp. 1133.

C.D.Ill. 1995. Motion to dismiss will only be granted if it appears beyond doubt that plaintiff can prove no set of facts in support of his claim which would entitle him to relief. Fed.Rules Civ.Proc.Rule 12(b), 28 U.S.C.A.

> Piquard v. City of East Peoria, 887 F.Supp. 1106.

N.D.Ill. 1998. Complaint should not be dismissed for failure to state a claim unless it appears beyond a reasonable doubt that the plaintiff can prove no set of facts in support of his claim which would entitle him to relief. Fed.Rules Civ.Proc.Rule 12(b)(6), 28 U.S.C.A.

> Cunningham v. Eyman, 11 F.Supp.2d 969.

N.D.Ill. 1998. Motion to dismiss for failure to state claim should not be granted unless it appears beyond doubt that plaintiff can prove no set of facts in support of his claim which would entitle him to relief. Fed.Rules Civ.Proc. Rule 12(b)(6), 28 U.S.C.A.

> Warren v. Sakuri, 9 F.Supp.2d 991.

N.D.Ill. 1998. A complaint will not be dismissed for failure to state a claim unless it appears beyond doubt that the plaintiff can prove no set of facts warranting relief. Fed. Rules Civ.Proc.Rule 12(b)(6), 28 U.S.C.A.

> Native American Arts, Inc. v. J.C. Penney Co., Inc., 5 F.Supp.2d 599.

N.D.Ill. 1998. District court may dismiss complaint, as failing to state claim upon which relief can be granted, only if it appears beyond doubt that plaintiff can prove no set of facts in support of his claim that would entitle him to relief. Fed.Rules Civ.Proc.Rule 12(b)(6), 28 U.S.C.A.

> McLaughlin v. Cook County Dept. of Corrections, 993 F.Supp. 661.

N.D.Ill. 1997. Complaint should not be dismissed for failure to state claim unless it appears beyond reasonable doubt that plaintiff can prove no set of facts in support of his claim which would entitle him to relief. Fed.Rules Civ.Proc.Rule 12(b)(6), 28 U.S.C.A.

> Cemail v. Viking Dodge, Inc., 982 F.Supp. 1296.

N.D.Ill. 1997. Complaint will not be dismissed for failure to state claim unless it appears beyond doubt that plaintiff can prove no set of facts warranting relief. Fed.Rules Civ. Proc.Rule 12(b)(6), 28 U.S.C.A.

> Ozkaya v. Telecheck Services, Inc., 982 F.Supp. 578.

N.D.Ill. 1997. Dismissal for failure to state claim is proper only if it appears beyond doubt that plaintiff can prove no set of facts in support of his claim that would entitle him to relief. Fed.Rules Civ.Proc.Rule 12(b)(6), 28 U.S.C.A.

> Pelfresne v. Village of Rosemont, 952 F.Supp. 589, rehearing denied 174 F.R.D. 72.

N.D.Ill. 1996. In determining under the Prison Litigation Reform Act (PRLA), whether to dismiss, for failure to state a claim, prisoner complaint against government officials or employees, court must accept as true allegations of complaint and inferences that may be reasonably drawn from them, allegations of pro se complaint are to be liberally construed, and motion to dismiss may be granted only if court concludes that no relief could be granted under any set of facts that could be proved consistent with the allegations. 28 U.S.C.A. § 1915A.

> Jones v. Russell, 950 F.Supp. 855.

N.D.Ill. 1996. Because federal courts only require notice pleading, pleadings must be liberally construed in connection with motion to dismiss for failure to state claim, and mere vagueness or lack of detail alone cannot be sufficient grounds for dismissal; test is whether it appears beyond doubt that nonmovant can prove no set of facts in support of his claim which would entitle him to relief. Fed.Rules Civ.Proc.Rule 12(b)(6), 28 U.S.C.A.

> Stepan Co. v. Winter Panel Corp., 948 F.Supp. 802.

N.D.Ill. 1996. Test for motion to dismiss for failure to state claim is whether it appears beyond doubt that plaintiff can prove no set of facts in support of claim which would entitle him to relief. Fed.Rules Civ.Proc.Rule 12(b)(6), 28 U.S.C.A.

> Schoiber v. Emro Marketing Co., 941 F.Supp. 730.

N.D.Ill. 1996. Since dismissal is a drastic measure, complaint should be dismissed only if it appears beyond doubt that plaintiff can prove no set of facts in support of his claim which would entitle him to relief. Fed.Rules Civ.Proc. Rule 12(b)(6), 28 U.S.C.A.

> Gallagher Corp. v. Massachusetts Mut. Life Ins. Co., 940 F.Supp. 176.

N.D.Ill. 1996. Dismissal for failure to state a claim is not granted unless it appears beyond a doubt that plaintiff can prove no set of facts in support of his claim which would entitle him to relief. Fed.Rules Civ.Proc.Rule 12(b), 28 U.S.C.A.

> Training Institute, Inc. v. City of Chicago, 937 F.Supp. 743.

N.D.Ill. 1996. Court may dismiss complaint only if it appears beyond doubt that plaintiff can prove no set of facts in support of his claims that would entitle him to relief. Fed.Rules Civ.Proc.Rule 12(b)(6), 28 U.S.C.A.

> Cooper v. Smith, 936 F.Supp. 515.

N.D.Ill. 1996. Strict standard applies when court evaluates legal sufficiency of plaintiff's factual allegations; court may grant a motion to dismiss only if it appears beyond doubt that plaintiff can prove no set of facts in

support of his claim which would entitle him to relief. Fed.Rules Civ.Proc.Rule 12(b)(6), 28 U.S.C.A.

Compton v. Chinn Enterprises, Inc., 936 F.Supp. 480, reconsideration denied 957 F.Supp. 139.

N.D.Ill. 1996. Motion to dismiss should not be granted unless it appears beyond doubt that plaintiff can prove no set of facts in support of his claim which would entitle him to relief.

Venzor v. Gonzalez, 936 F.Supp. 445.

N.D.Ill. 1996. For purposes of motion to dismiss complaint, dismissal was appropriate only if it appeared beyond doubt that plaintiff could prove no set of facts, consistent with complaint's allegations, that would entitle plaintiff to relief. Fed.Rules Civ.Proc.Rule 12(b)(6), 28 U.S.C.A.

Carl A. Haas Auto. Imports, Inc. v. Lola Cars Ltd., 933 F.Supp. 1381.

N.D.Ill. 1996. Allegations of complaint should not be dismissed for failure to state claim unless it appears beyond doubt that plaintiff can prove no set of facts in support of his claim which would entitle him to relief. Fed. Rules Civ.Proc.Rule 12(b)(6), 28 U.S.C.A.

Alexander v. Continental Motor Werks, Inc., 933 F.Supp. 715, reconsideration denied 1996 WL 529347.

N.D.Ill. 1996. If, when viewed in light most favorable to plaintiff, complaint fails to state a claim upon which relief can be granted, court must dismiss case; however, court may dismiss complaint only if it appears beyond a doubt that plaintiff can prove no set of facts in support of his claims that would entitle him to relief. Fed.Rules Civ.Proc.Rule 12(b)(6), 28 U.S.C.A.

Lewis v. Cotton, 932 F.Supp. 1116.

N.D.Ill. 1996. Court may dismiss complaint for failure to state claim only if it appears beyond doubt that plaintiff can prove no set of facts in support of his claims that would entitle him to relief. Fed.Rules Civ.Proc.Rule 12(b)(6), 28 U.S.C.A.

Vitello v. Liturgy Training Publications, 932 F.Supp. 1093.

N.D.Ill. 1996. Complaint should not be dismissed for failure to state claim upon which relief can be granted if relief could be granted under any set of facts consistent with complaint's allegations. Fed.Rules Civ.Proc.Rule 12(b)(6), 28 U.S.C.A.

Taylor v. Quality Hyundai, Inc., 932 F.Supp. 218, affirmed in part, reversed in part 150 F.3d 689, rehearing denied.

N.D.Ill. 1996. Motion to dismiss should not be granted unless it appears beyond doubt

that plaintiff can prove no set of facts in support of his claim which would entitle him to relief.

Grand Park Surgical Center, Inc. v. Inland Steel Co., 930 F.Supp. 1214.

N.D.Ill. 1996. Motion to dismiss for failure to state a claim should not be granted unless it appears beyond a doubt that plaintiff can prove no set of facts in support of claims that would entitle him to relief; all factual allegations contained in complaint are taken as true and all reasonable inferences therefrom are construed in the plaintiff's favor. Fed.Rules Civ.Proc.Rule 12(b)(6), 28 U.S.C.A.

Abdoh v. City of Chicago, 930 F.Supp. 311.

N.D.Ill. 1996. Court may dismiss complaint for failure to state claim only if it appears beyond doubt that plaintiff can prove no set of facts in support of his claims that would entitle him to relief. Fed.Rules Civ.Proc.Rule 12(b)(6), 28 U.S.C.A.

Moore v. Allstate Ins. Co., 928 F.Supp. 744.

N.D.Ill. 1996. On motion to dismiss for failure to state claim, court will dismiss complaint only when it appears beyond doubt that plaintiff can prove no consistent set of facts entitling him or her to relief. Fed.Rules Civ. Proc.Rule 12(b)(6), 28 U.S.C.A.

McMurry v. Sheahan, 927 F.Supp. 1082.

N.D.Ill. 1996. Complaint should not be dismissed for failure to state claim if there is any set of facts that would support claim entitling plaintiff to relief; complaint need not identify a legal theory, and even specifying an incorrect inquiry is not fatal. Fed.Rules Civ.Proc. Rule 12(b)(6), 28 U.S.C.A.

Milazzo v. O'Connell, 925 F.Supp. 1331, affirmed 108 F.3d 129, rehearing and suggestion for rehearing denied.

On motion to dismiss for failure to state claim, the only question is whether relief is possible under any set of facts that could be established consistent with the allegations. Fed.Rules Civ.Proc.Rule 12(b)(6), 28 U.S.C.A.

Milazzo v. O'Connell, 925 F.Supp. 1331, affirmed 108 F.3d 129, rehearing and suggestion for rehearing denied.

N.D.Ill. 1996. Court may dismiss complaint only if it appears beyond doubt that plaintiff can prove no set of facts in support of his claims that would entitle him to relief. Fed.Rules Civ.Proc.Rule 12(b)(6), 28 U.S.C.A.

Horton v. Marovich, 925 F.Supp. 540.

N.D.Ill. 1996. Court may dismiss complaint for failure to state claim only if it appears beyond doubt that plaintiff can prove no set of facts in support of his claims that would entitle him to relief. Fed.Rules Civ.Proc.Rule 12(b)(6), 28 U.S.C.A.

Horton v. Marovich, 925 F.Supp. 532.

N.D.Ill. 1996. Court may grant motion to dismiss complaint only if it appears beyond doubt that plaintiff can prove no set of facts in support of his claims that would entitle him to relief. Fed.Rules Civ.Proc.Rule 12(b)(6), 28 U.S.C.A.

Levine v. Kling, 922 F.Supp. 127, affirmed 123 F.3d 580.

N.D.Ill. 1996. Complaint should not be dismissed for failure to state claim unless it appears beyond doubt that plaintiff can prove no set of facts in support of claim which would entitle plaintiff to relief. Fed.Rules Civ.Proc. Rule 12(b)(6), 28 U.S.C.A.

Bricklayers Union Local 21 v. Edgar, 922 F.Supp. 100.

N.D.Ill. 1996. Court may dismiss complaint for failure to state claim only if it appears beyond doubt that plaintiff can prove no set of facts in support of his claims that would entitle him to relief. Fed.Rules Civ.Proc.Rule 12(b)(6), 28 U.S.C.A.

Glass v. Kemper Corp., 920 F.Supp. 928, affirmed 133 F.3d 999, rehearing denied.

N.D.Ill. 1996. Motion to dismiss complaint for failure to state claim will be denied unless it appears beyond doubt that plaintiff can prove no facts that would entitle him or her to relief.

Spiegel v. City of Chicago, 920 F.Supp. 891.

N.D.Ill. 1996. District court may dismiss complaint for failure to state a claim only if it appears beyond doubt that plaintiff can prove no set of facts in support of his claim which would entitle him to relief. Fed.Rules Civ.Proc. Rule 12(b)(6), 28 U.S.C.A.

Thomas v. Chicago Housing Authority, 919 F.Supp. 1159.

N.D.Ill. 1996. Defendant's motion to dismiss is to be granted only if it is clear that no relief could be granted under any set of facts that could be proved consistent with allegations.

Yellow Cab Co. v. City of Chicago, 919 F.Supp. 1133.

N.D.Ill. 1996. Motion to dismiss for failure to state a claim should not be granted unless it appears beyond doubt that plaintiff can prove no set of facts in support of his claim which would entitle him to relief. Fed.Rules Civ.Proc.Rule 12(b)(6), 28 U.S.C.A.

Tarver v. North American Co. for Life and Health Ins., 919 F.Supp. 1128.

N.D.Ill. 1996. Dismissal for failure to state claim should not be granted unless it appears beyond doubt that plaintiff can prove no set of facts in support of his claims which would entitle him to relief. Fed.Rules Civ.Proc.Rule 12(b)(6), 28 U.S.C.A.

Fernandez v. Wolff, 919 F.Supp. 1120.

N.D.Ill. 1996. Motion to dismiss for failure to state a claim is granted only where it is beyond doubt that plaintiff is unable to prove any set of facts that would entitle him to relief. Fed.Rules Civ.Proc.Rule 12(b)(6), 28 U.S.C.A.

Sumpter v. Mack Chicago Corp., 918 F.Supp. 256.

N.D.Ill. 1996. District court will dismiss claim only where it appears beyond doubt that plaintiff can prove no set of facts in support of his claim which would entitle him to relief. Fed.Rules Civ.Proc.Rule 12(b)(6), 28 U.S.C.A.

Allied Vision Group, Inc. v. RLI Professional Technologies, Inc., 916 F.Supp. 778.

N.D.Ill. 1996. Complaint should be dismissed for failure to state claim only if it appears beyond doubt that plaintiff is unable to prove any set of facts that would entitle him to relief; while plaintiff need not set out in detail all facts upon which claim is based, he must allege sufficient facts to outline cause of action. Fed.Rules Civ.Proc.Rule 12(b)(6), 28 U.S.C.A.

Credit General Ins. Co. v. Midwest Indem. Corp., 916 F.Supp. 766.

N.D.Ill. 1996. Dismissal of complaint for failure to state claim upon which relief may be granted is appropriate only if it appears beyond doubt that plaintiff can prove no set of facts consistent with complaint's allegations that would entitle plaintiff to relief. Fed.Rules Civ. Proc.Rule 12(b)(6), 28 U.S.C.A.

Hernandez v. Vidmar Buick Co., 910 F.Supp. 422, reversed Gibson v. Bob Watson Chevrolet-Geo, Inc., 112 F.3d 283.

N.D.Ill. 1995. Court should only dismiss complaint for failure to state claim if it appears beyond a doubt that plaintiff cannot establish any set of facts that would entitle it to relief requested. Fed.Rules Civ.Proc.Rule 12(b)(6), 28 U.S.C.A.

Abbott Laboratories v. Zenith Laboratories, Inc., 934 F.Supp. 925, dismissed 78 F.3d 603.

N.D.Ill. 1995. Motion to dismiss for failure to state claim should not be granted unless it appears beyond doubt that plaintiff can prove no set of facts in support of his claims which would entitle him to relief. Fed.Rules Civ.Proc. Rule 12(b)(6), 28 U.S.C.A.

Foster v. Unknown Cook County Deputy Sheriff, 914 F.Supp. 221.

N.D.Ill. 1995. Motion to dismiss for failure to state claim should not be granted unless it appears beyond doubt that plaintiff can prove no set of facts in support of his claims that would entitle him to relief. Fed.Rules Civ.Proc. Rule 12(b)(6), 28 U.S.C.A.

TLMS Motor Corp. v. Toyota Motor Distributors, Inc., 912 F.Supp. 329.

N.D.Ill. 1995. Dismissal is only proper if it appears beyond any doubt that plaintiffs can prove no set of facts in support of their claim which would entitle them to relief. Fed.Rules Civ.Proc.Rule 12(b), 28 U.S.C.A.

Dertz v. City of Chicago, 912 F.Supp. 319, on reconsideration in part 1997 WL 85169.

N.D.Ill. 1995. Only question in motion to dismiss for failure to state a claim is whether relief is possible under any set of facts that could be established consistent with allegations. Fed.Rules Civ.Proc.Rule 12(b)(6), 28 U.S.C.A.

Montgomery Ward & Co., Inc. v. Warehouse, Mail Order, Office, Technical and Professional Employees Union, 911 F.Supp. 1094.

Motion to dismiss for failure to state a claim will only be granted if it is beyond doubt that nonmovant can plead no facts that would support his claim for relief. Fed.Rules Civ. Proc.Rule 12(b)(6), 28 U.S.C.A.

Montgomery Ward & Co., Inc. v. Warehouse, Mail Order, Office, Technical and Professional Employees Union, 911 F.Supp. 1094.

N.D.Ill. 1995. Court may grant motion to dismiss for failure to state claim only if it appears beyond doubt that plaintiff can prove no set of facts in support of his or her claim which would entitle him or her to relief. Fed. Rules Civ.Proc.Rule 12(b)(6), 28 U.S.C.A.

Erickson v. Board of Governors of State Colleges and Universities for Northeastern Illinois University, 911 F.Supp. 316.

N.D.Ill. 1995. Plaintiff's claim may only be dismissed if it appears beyond doubt that he can prove no set of facts in support of his claim which would entitle him to relief. Fed.Rules Civ.Proc.Rules 8(a), 12(b)(6), 28 U.S.C.A.

Allied Metal Co. v. Edgerton Metal Products, Inc., 908 F.Supp. 576.

N.D.Ill. 1995. In ruling on motion to dismiss, unless it appears beyond doubt that plaintiff can prove no facts which would entitle them to relief, trial court must deny motion. Fed. Rules Civ.Proc.Rule 12(b)(6), 28 U.S.C.A.

Lindgren v. Moore, 907 F.Supp. 1183.

N.D.Ill. 1995. Complaint can be dismissed for failure to state a claim only if plaintiff cannot prove any set of facts upon which relief may be granted. Fed.Rules Civ.Proc.Rule 12(b)(6), 28 U.S.C.A.

Little v. State of Ill. Dept. of Revenue, Bureau of Criminal Investigation, 907 F.Supp. 280.

N.D.Ill. 1995. Complaint will not be dismissed unless it is clear that no relief could be granted under any set of facts that could be proved consistent with allegations.

Johnson v. Baxter Healthcare Corp., 907 F.Supp. 271.

N.D.Ill. 1995. Motion to dismiss for failure to state claim will only be granted if it is beyond doubt that nonmovant can plead no facts that would support his claim for relief. U.S. v. Brickman, 906 F.Supp. 1164.

N.D.Ill. 1995. Complaint should not be dismissed for failure to state a claim unless it appears beyond doubt that plaintiff can prove no set of facts in support of his claim that would entitle him to relief. Fed.Rules Civ.Proc.Rule 12(b)(6), 28 U.S.C.A.

Graves v. Tru-Link Fence Co., 905 F.Supp. 515.

N.D.Ill. 1995. If, when viewed in light most favorable to plaintiff, complaint fails to state claim upon which relief can be granted, court must dismiss case; however, court may dismiss complaint only if it appears beyond doubt that plaintiff can prove no set of facts in support of its claim that would entitle it to relief. Fed.Rules Civ.Proc.Rule 12(b)(6), 28 U.S.C.A.

Servpro Industries, Inc. v. Schmidt, 905 F.Supp. 475.

N.D.Ill. 1995. Motion to dismiss for failure to state claim upon which relief can be granted should not be granted unless it appears beyond doubt that plaintiff can prove no set of facts in support of his claims which would entitle him to relief. Fed.Rules Civ.Proc.Rule 12(b)(6), 28 U.S.C.A.

Gilbert v. First Alert, Inc., 904 F.Supp. 714, opinion amended 165 F.R.D. 81.

N.D.Ill. 1995. Motion to dismiss for failure to state claim upon which relief can be granted should not be granted unless it appears beyond a doubt that plaintiff can prove no set of facts in support of his claims which would entitle him to relief. Fed.Rules Civ.Proc.Rule 12(b)(6), 28 U.S.C.A.

Industrial Specialty Chemicals, Inc. v. Cummins Engine Co., Inc., 902 F.Supp. 805.

N.D.Ill. 1995. In considering motion for dismissal based on failure to state a claim on which relief can be granted, district court accepts as true a complaint's well-pleaded factual allegations, together with all reasonable inferences in the plaintiff's favor; dismissal is appropriate only if it appears beyond doubt that plaintiff can prove no set of facts consistent with complaint's allegations that would entitle plaintiff to relief. Fed.Rules Civ.Proc.Rule 12(b)(6), 28 U.S.C.A.

Viero v. Bufano, 901 F.Supp. 1387.

N.D.Ill. 1995. Only if allegations of the complaint, and all reasonable inferences drawn therefrom, could not support any cause of action may district court grant motion to dismiss for failure to state claim upon which relief could be granted. Fed.Rules Civ.Proc.Rule 12(b)(6), 28 U.S.C.A.

Marks v. CDW Computer Centers, Inc., 901 F.Supp. 1302.

N.D.Ill. 1995. Court may dismiss complaint pursuant to motion for failure to state a claim on which relief can be granted only if it is clear that no relief could be granted under any set of facts that could be proved consistent with allegations. Fed.Rules Civ.Proc.Rule 12(b)(6), 28 U.S.C.A.

Patterson v. Xerox Corp., 901 F.Supp. 274.

N.D.Ill. 1995. Motion to dismiss should not be granted unless it appears beyond doubt that plaintiff can prove no set of facts in support of claims which would entitle him to relief. Fed.Rules Civ.Proc.Rule 12, 28 U.S.C.A.

Chaney v. City of Chicago, 901 F.Supp. 266.

N.D.Ill. 1995. Dismissal of complaint is proper only if it appears beyond doubt that plaintiff can prove no set of facts in support of claim which would entitle him to relief. Fed.Rules Civ.Proc. Rule 12, 28 U.S.C.A.

Maas v. U.S., 897 F.Supp. 1098, affirmed 94 F.3d 291.

N.D.Ill. 1995. In ruling on motion to dismiss for failure to state claim upon which relief may be granted, facts as alleged are viewed in light most favorable to plaintiffs and, unless it appears beyond doubt that plaintiffs can prove no set of facts that would entitle them to relief, court must deny motion; however, court need not strain to find inferences favorable to plaintiffs that are not apparent on face of complaint, and court is not required to accept legal conclusions either alleged or inferred from pleaded facts. Fed.Rules Civ.Proc.Rule 12(b)(6), 28 U.S.C.A.

National Organization for Women, Inc. v. Scheidler, 897 F.Supp. 1047.

N.D.Ill. 1995. Motion to dismiss for failure to state claim on which relief can be granted will be granted only if it is beyond doubt that plaintiff is unable to prove any facts that would entitle him to relief. Fed.Rules Civ.Proc.Rule 12(b)(6), 28 U.S.C.A.

Angara v. City of Chicago, 897 F.Supp. 355.

N.D.Ill. 1995. Motion to dismiss for failure to state claim should be granted only if court is certain that plaintiff cannot prove any set of facts which would entitle him to relief. Fed.Rules Civ.Proc.Rule 12(b)(6), 28 U.S.C.A.

Lowe v. Brown, 896 F.Supp. 793.

In order for motion to dismiss for failure to state claim to be granted, it must be impossible for plaintiff to succeed. Fed.Rules Civ.Proc. Rule 12(b)(6), 28 U.S.C.A.

Lowe v. Brown, 896 F.Supp. 793.

N.D.Ill. 1995. Defendant's motion to dismiss may be granted only if it is indisputably clear that plaintiff is not entitled to relief based on the allegations in plaintiff's complaint.

Banks v. Chicago Bd. of Educ., 895 F.Supp. 206.

N.D.Ill. 1995. Motion to dismiss for failure to state a claim should not be granted unless it appears beyond doubt that plaintiff can prove no set of facts in support of his claim that would entitle him to relief. Fed.Rules Civ.Proc. Rule 12(b)(6), 28 U.S.C.A.

Hamros v. Bethany Homes and Methodist Hosp. of Chicago, 894 F.Supp. 1176.

N.D.Ill. 1995. Dismissal for failure to state claim is permitted only where it appears beyond doubt that plaintiff can prove no set of facts in support of her claim which would entitle her to relief. Fed.Rules Civ.Proc.Rule 12(b)(6), 28 U.S.C.A.

Howard v. Board of Educ. of Sycamore Community Unit School Dist. No. 427, 893 F.Supp. 808.

N.D.Ill. 1995. Action can only be dismissed for failure to state claim if it appears beyond doubt that plaintiff can prove no set of facts in support of his action which would entitle him to relief. Fed.Rules Civ.Proc.Rule 12(b)(6), 28 U.S.C.A.

Daulo v. Commonwealth Edison, 892 F.Supp. 1088.

N.D.Ill. 1995. Motion to dismiss for failure to state a claim on which relief can be granted should not be granted unless it appears beyond doubt that plaintiff can prove no set of effects in support of claims which entitle him to relief. Fed Rules Civ.Proc.Rule 12(b)(6), 28 U.S.C.A.

Robinson v. Illinois State Correctional Center (Stateville) Warden, 890 F.Supp. 715.

N.D.Ill. 1995. Only question on motion to dismiss for failure to state claim upon which relief can be granted is whether relief is possible under any set of facts that could be established consistent with the allegations. Fed.Rules Civ. Proc.Rule 12(b)(6), 28 U.S.C.A.

Egan v. Palos Community Hosp., 889 F.Supp. 331.

N.D.Ill. 1995. Motion to dismiss should not be granted unless it appears beyond doubt that plaintiff can prove no set of facts in support of his claims which would entitle him to relief.

Terrell v. Childers, 889 F.Supp. 311.

N.D.Ill. 1995. Motion to dismiss for failure to state actionable claim will not be granted unless it appears beyond doubt that plaintiff can prove no set of facts in support of his claims which would entitle him to relief. Fed.Rules Civ.Proc.Rule 12(b)(6), 28 U.S.C.A.

> Gonzalez v. City of Chicago, 888 F.Supp. 887.

N.D.Ill. 1995. Motion to dismiss for failure to state a claim is granted only where it is beyond doubt that plaintiff is unable to prove any set of facts that would entitle her to relief. Fed.Rules Civ.Proc.Rule 12(b)(6), 28 U.S.C.A.

> Rojicek v. Community Consol. School Dist. 15, 888 F.Supp. 878, on reconsideration in part.

N.D.Ill. 1995. Motion to dismiss should not be granted unless it appears beyond doubt that plaintiff can prove no set of facts in support of his claims which would entitle him to relief.

> Jablonski v. Chas. Levy Circulating Co., 888 F.Supp. 84.

N.D.Ill. 1995. Dismissal is proper only if it appears beyond doubt that plaintiff can prove no set of facts in support of his claim that would entitle him to relief. Fed.Rules Civ.Proc.Rule 12(b)(6), 28 U.S.C.A.

> Curcio v. Chinn Enterprises, Inc., 887 F.Supp. 190.

N.D.Ill. 1995. Plaintiff is required to set forth a short and plain statement of claim, showing that he is entitled to relief; and plaintiff's claim may only be dismissed if it appears beyond doubt that he can prove no set of facts in support of his claim which would entitle him to relief. Fed.Rules Civ.Proc.Rule 12(b)(6), 28 U.S.C.A.

> Caplan v. International Fidelity Ins. Co., 885 F.Supp. 175.

N.D.Ill. 1995. In deciding motion to dismiss, court must accept as true facts presented in complaint, and any inferences which may be drawn from them must be viewed in light most favorable to nonmoving party; dismissal is appropriate only if nonmoving party can prove no set of facts which would entitle him to relief.

> Offutt v. Kaplan, 884 F.Supp. 1179.

N.D.Ill. 1995. Motion to dismiss for failure to state claim should be granted only if court is certain that plaintiff cannot prove any set of facts which would entitle plaintiff to relief. Fed.Rules Civ.Proc.Rule 12(b)(6), 28 U.S.C.A.

> Shipbaugh v. Boys & Girls Clubs of America, 883 F.Supp. 295.

N.D.Ill. 1995. Motion to dismiss for failure to state claim upon which relief can be granted should not be granted unless it appears beyond doubt that plaintiff can prove no set of facts in support of his claims which would entitle him to relief. Fed.Rules Civ.Proc.Rule 12(b)(6), 28 U.S.C.A.

> Jackson Nat. Life Ins. Co. v. Gofen & Glossberg, Inc., 882 F.Supp. 713.

N.D.Ill. 1995. Motion to dismiss for failure to state a claim is granted only where it is beyond a doubt that plaintiff is unable to prove any set of facts that would entitle him to relief. Fed.Rules Civ.Proc.Rule 12(b)(6), 28 U.S.C.A.

> Abeja-Ortiz v. Cisneros, 882 F.Supp. 124.

N.D.Ill. 1995. Court should not dismiss complaint unless it appears beyond doubt that plaintiff can prove no set of facts in support of his claim which would entitle him to relief.

> Pena v. Mattox, 880 F.Supp. 567, affirmed 84 F.3d 894.

N.D.Ill. 1995. When court rules upon motion to dismiss, it searches complaint to determine whether plaintiff may allege any set of facts which might entitle it to relief.

> Ziemack v. Centel Corp., 163 F.R.D. 530.

N.D.Ill. 1995. Motion to dismiss for failure to state claim should not be granted unless it appears beyond doubt that plaintiff can prove no set of facts in support of his claims which would entitle him to relief. Fed.Rules Civ.Proc. Rule 12(b)(6), 28 U.S.C.A.

> Hoban v. USLIFE Credit Life Ins. Co., 163 F.R.D. 509.

N.D.Ill. 1995. On motion to dismiss for failure to state claim, only question is whether relief is possible under any set of facts that could be established consistent with allegations. Fed.Rules Civ.Proc.Rule 12(b)(6), 28 U.S.C.A.

> Chandler v. Southwest Jeep-Eagle, Inc., 162 F.R.D. 302.

N.D.Ill. 1994. In ruling on motion to dismiss, court considers whether relief is possible under any set of facts that could be established consistent with allegations of complaint. Fed. Rules Civ.Proc.Rule 12, 28 U.S.C.A.

> Doe v. City of Chicago, 883 F.Supp. 1126.

Claim may be dismissed only if it is beyond doubt that under no set of facts would plaintiffs' allegations entitle them to relief. Fed.Rules Civ.Proc.Rule 12, 28 U.S.C.A.

> Doe v. City of Chicago, 883 F.Supp. 1126.

N.D.Ill. 1994. Motion to dismiss for failure to state a claim may be granted only if it appears beyond a doubt that plaintiff can prove no set of facts in support of claim which would entitle him to relief. Fed.Rules Civ.Proc.Rule 12(b)(6), 28 U.S.C.A.

> Mollfulleda v. Phillips, 882 F.Supp. 689, on reconsideration in part 882 F.Supp. 698.

N.D.Ill. 1993. Motion to dismiss for failure to state a claim may be granted if it is beyond a doubt that plaintiff is unable to prove any set of facts that would entitle it to relief. Fed.Rules Civ.Proc.Rule 12(b)(6), 28 U.S.C.A.

> AM Intern., Inc. v. Graphic Management Associates, Inc., 836 F.Supp. 487, affirmed 44 F.3d 572.

N.D.Ill. 1991. Motion to dismiss should not be granted unless it appears beyond doubt that plaintiff can prove no set of facts in support of his claims which would entitle him to relief. Fed.Rules Civ.Proc.Rule 12(b)(6), 28 U.S.C.A.

> Doran v. Corn Products-U.S., a Div. of CPC, Intern., Inc., 776 F.Supp. 368.

N.D.Ill. 1990. Dismissal is proper if it appears beyond doubt that plaintiffs can prove no set of facts in support of their claims that would entitle them to relief requested.

> In re VMS Securities Litigation, 752 F.Supp. 1373.

N.D.Ill. 1988. Showing beyond doubt that plaintiff can prove no set of facts in support of claim that would entitle him to relief is required to obtain dismissal for failure to state claim upon which relief can be granted. Fed.Rules Civ.Proc.Rule 12(b)(6), 28 U.S.C.A.

> Capalbo v. PaineWebber, Inc., 694 F.Supp. 1315.

N.D.Ill. 1985. Complaint should not be dismissed unless it appears beyond doubt that plaintiff could prove no set of facts which would entitle him to relief.

> Lehpamer v. Troyer, 601 F.Supp. 1466, affirmed 787 F.2d 595.

N.D.Ill. 1985. For purposes of motion to dismiss, court assumes facts alleged in complaint are true and cannot grant motion unless it appears beyond doubt that plaintiff can recover on no set of facts consistent with his allegations.

> Bilka v. Pepe's Inc., 601 F.Supp. 1254.

N.D.Ill. 1984. Motion to dismiss for failure to state claim cannot be granted unless it appears beyond doubt, assuming that all allegations in complaint are true, that plaintiff can prove no set of facts in support of claim which would entitle him to relief. Fed.Rules Civ.Proc. Rule 12(b)(6), 28 U.S.C.A.

> Gibson v. Babcock, 601 F.Supp. 1156.

N.D.Ill. 1984. Under Federal Rules of Civil Procedure, court should not dismiss complaint unless it is clear that no relief could be granted under any set of facts that could be proved consistent with allegation. Fed.Rules Civ.Proc.Rule 8(a)(2), 28 U.S.C.A.

> Ross v. Ross, 104 F.R.D. 439.

N.D.Ill. 1983. Brunswick Corp. v. Riegel Textile Corp., 578 F.Supp. 893, affirmed 752 F.2d 261, certiorari denied 105 S.Ct. 3480, 472 U.S. 1018, 87 L.Ed.2d 615.

N.D.Ill. 1983. Chicago Heights Venture v. Dynamit Nobel of America, Inc., 575 F.Supp. 214, affirmed 782 F.2d 723.

N.D.Ill. 1983. Angulo v. The Levy Co., 568 F.Supp. 1209, 26 Wage & Hour Cas. (BNA) 619, affirmed Flores v. Levy Co., 757 F.2d 806.

N.D.Ill. 1962. R. I. T. A. Chemical Corp. v. Malmstrom Chemical Corp., 200 F.Supp. 954, motion denied 31 F.R.D. 213.

N.D.Ind. 1998. Complaint states no actionable claim when it appears beyond doubt that plaintiff can prove no set of facts consistent with his complaint that would entitle him to relief. 28 U.S.C.A. § 1950A; Fed.Rules Civ. Proc.Rule 15(a), 28 U.S.C.A.

> Zimmerman v. Hoard, 5 F.Supp.2d 633.

N.D.Ind. 1996. Court should not dismiss complaint for failure to state cause of action unless it appears beyond doubt that plaintiff can prove no set of facts in support of his claim that would entitle him to relief. Fed.Rules Civ.Proc. Rule 12(b)(6), 28 U.S.C.A.

> Ninth Ave. Remedial Group v. Allis-Chalmers Corp., 195 B.R. 716.

N.D.Ind. 1996. Motion to dismiss will not be granted unless it appears beyond doubt that plaintiff can prove no set of facts in support of his claim which would entitle him to relief. Fed.Rules Civ.Proc.Rule 12(b), 28 U.S.C.A.

> Crawford v. Indiana Dept. of Correction, 937 F.Supp. 785, reversed 115 F.3d 481.

N.D.Ind. 1996. Complaint states no actionable claim where it appears beyond doubt that plaintiff can prove no set of facts in support of claim which would entitle plaintiff to relief. Fed.Rules Civ.Proc.Rule 12(b)(6), 28 U.S.C.A.

> Brown v. McBride, 929 F.Supp. 1132.

N.D.Ind. 1996. Complaint may be dismissed for failure to state claim upon which relief can be granted if it appears beyond doubt that plaintiff can prove no set of facts in support of his claim which would entitle him to relief. Fed.Rules Civ.Proc.Rule 12(b)(6), 28 U.S.C.A.

> Lerch v. Boyer, 929 F.Supp. 319.

N.D.Ind. 1995. If relief under some legal theory would be appropriate upon any set of facts consistent with complaint's allegations, complaint should not be dismissed.

> Eichhorn, Eichhorn & Link v. Travelers Ins. Co., 896 F.Supp. 812.

N.D.Ind. 1995. District court may not dismiss complaint unless it appears beyond doubt that plaintiff can prove no set of facts in support of his claim which would entitle him to relief. Fed.Rules Civ.Proc.Rule 12(b)(1), 28 U.S.C.A.

TJ's South, Inc. v. Town of Lowell, 895 F.Supp. 1116, opinion amended 924 F.Supp. 92.

N.D.Ind. 1995. Dismissal for failure to state a claim is improper unless it appears beyond a doubt that plaintiff can prove no set of facts in support of his claim which would entitle him to relief. Fed.Rules Civ.Proc.Rule 12(b)(6), 28 U.S.C.A.

Nielsen v. International Ass'n of Machinists & Aerospace Workers, Local Lodge 2569, 895 F.Supp. 1093, affirmed 94 F.3d 1107, rehearing and suggestion for rehearing denied, certiorari denied 117 S.Ct. 1426, 137 L.Ed.2d 536.

N.D.Ind. 1994. Dismissal of complaint is appropriate if it appears beyond doubt that plaintiff can prove no set of facts in support of his claim which would entitle him to relief. Fed.Rules Civ.Proc.Rule 12(b)(6), 28 U.S.C.A.

Graham v. Henderson, 897 F.Supp. 1157, affirmed 59 F.3d 173, rehearing and suggestion for rehearing denied, certiorari denied 116 S.Ct. 535, 516 U.S. 997, 133 L.Ed.2d 440.

S.D.Ind. 1996. Complaint fails to state claim for which relief may be granted if, viewing facts in light most favorable to plaintiff and assuming them to be true, it appears beyond doubt that plaintiff can prove no set of facts in support of claim that would entitle him to relief.

Douglas v. DeBruyn, 936 F.Supp. 572.

Pro se complaint will be dismissed only if it is beyond doubt that there is no set of facts under which plaintiff could obtain relief.

Douglas v. DeBruyn, 936 F.Supp. 572.

S.D.Ind. 1996. Only question on motion to dismiss for failure to state claim is whether relief is possible under any set of facts that could be established consistent with allegations. Fed.Rules Civ.Proc.Rule 12(b)(6), 28 U.S.C.A.

Love v. Bolinger, 927 F.Supp. 1131.

S.D.Ind. 1996. Dismissal for failure to state claim upon which relief may be granted is appropriate only if it appears beyond doubt that plaintiffs can prove no set of facts consistent with allegations in complaint that would entitle them to relief. Fed.Rules Civ.Proc.Rule 12(b)(6), 28 U.S.C.A.

Bradley v. Work, 916 F.Supp. 1446, affirmed 154 F.3d 704.

S.D.Ind. 1995. Dismissal of a complaint for failure to state a claim is appropriate only if it appears to a certainty that plaintiffs cannot establish any set of facts which would entitle

them to relief they seek. Fed.Rules Civ.Proc. Rule 12(b)(6), 28 U.S.C.A.

Buck Creek Coal, Inc. v. United Workers of America, 917 F.Supp. 601.

S.D.Ind. 1995. In deciding motion to dismiss for failure to state claim upon which relief may be granted, Court must accept as true all facts alleged, together with all reasonable inferences which may be derived from those facts; dismissal is proper only if it appears beyond doubt that plaintiff can prove no set of facts that would entitle it to the requested relief. Fed. Rules Civ.Proc.Rule 12(b)(6), 28 U.S.C.A.

Enviroplan, Inc. v. Western Farmers Elec. Co-op., 900 F.Supp. 1055.

S.D.Ind. 1994. Dismissal for failure to state claim is proper only if it appears beyond doubt that plaintiff can prove no set of facts in support of his claim that would entitle him to relief requested.

Scariano v. Justices of Supreme Court of State of Ind., 852 F.Supp. 708, affirmed 38 F.3d 920, rehearing and suggestion for rehearing denied 47 F.3d 173, certiorari denied 115 S.Ct. 2582, 515 U.S. 1144, 132 L.Ed.2d 831.

N.D.Iowa 1997. Motion to dismiss complaint for failure to state claim should be granted as a practical matter only in unusual case in which plaintiff includes allegations that show on face of complaint that there is some insuperable bar to relief. Fed.Rules Civ.Proc.Rule 12(b)(6), 28 U.S.C.A.

Doe v. Hartz, 970 F.Supp. 1375, reversed in part, vacated in part 134 F.3d 1339.

N.D.Iowa 1995. Complaint should not be dismissed for failure to state claim unless it appears beyond doubt that plaintiff can prove no set of facts in support of his claim which would entitle him to relief. Fed.Rules Civ.Proc. Rule 12(b)(6), 28 U.S.C.A.

Powell v. Tordoff, 911 F.Supp. 1184.

N.D.Iowa 1995. It is only in the unusual case where complaint on its face reveals some insuperable bar to relief that dismissal for failure to state claim is warranted. Fed.Rules Civ.Proc.Rule 12(b)(6), 28 U.S.C.A.

Quality Refrigerated Services, Inc. v. City of Spencer, 908 F.Supp. 1471.

N.D.Iowa 1995. It is only in "unusual case" where complaint on its face reveals some insuperable bar to relief such that dismissal for failure to state claim is warranted. Fed.Rules Civ.Proc.Rule 12(b)(6), 28 U.S.C.A.

Dahl v. Kanawha Inv. Holding Co., 161 F.R.D. 673.

S.D.Iowa 1986. Court will not determine plaintiff's claim to be frivolous unless it appears beyond doubt that plaintiff can prove no set of facts that would entitle him to relief. 28 U.S.C.A. § 1915(d).

> Stewart v. McManus, 647 F.Supp. 1024.

D.Kan. 1998. Court may not dismiss a cause of action for failure to state a claim unless it appears beyond doubt that the claimant can prove no set of facts supporting the claim which would entitle the claimant to relief. Fed.Rules Civ.Proc.Rule 12(b)(6), 28 U.S.C.A.

> Ortega v. Nguyen, 7 F.Supp.2d 1178.

D.Kan. 1997. Dismissal for failure to state claim is appropriate only if it is clear that no relief could be granted under any set of facts that could be proved consistent with allegations. Fed.Rules Civ.Proc.Rule 12(b)(6), 28 U.S.C.A.

> Whayne v. State of Kan., 980 F.Supp. 387.

D.Kan. 1996. Motions to dismiss are disfavored, and court may not dismiss case for failure to state a claim unless it appears beyond doubt that plaintiff can prove no set of facts which would entitle him to relief.

> Patrick v. City of Overland Park, Kan., 937 F.Supp. 1491.

D.Kan. 1996. In reviewing sufficiency of complaint, court should read complaint in light most favorable to plaintiff with all doubts resolved in his favor; all well-pleaded facts and allegations in complaint must be taken as true and complaint should not be dismissed for failure to state claim unless it appears beyond doubt that plaintiff can prove no set of facts in support of his claim which would entitle him to relief. Fed.Rules Civ.Proc.Rule 12(b)(6), 28 U.S.C.A.

> S.A.I., Inc. v. General Elec. Railcar Services Corp., 935 F.Supp. 1150.

D.Kan. 1996. Dismissal of cause of action for failure to state claim is appropriate only where it appears beyond doubt that plaintiff can prove no set of facts in support of theory of recovery that would entitle him or her to relief or where issue of law is dispositive. Fed.Rules Civ.Proc.Rule 12(b)(6), 28 U.S.C.A.

> Fusion, Inc. v. Nebraska Aluminum Castings, Inc., 934 F.Supp. 1270.

D.Kan. 1996. Court may not dismiss cause of action for failure to state claim unless it appears beyond doubt that plaintiff can prove no set of facts in support of theory of recovery that would entitle him or her to relief. Fed. Rules Civ.Proc.Rule 12(b)(6), 28 U.S.C.A.

> Aguirre v. McCaw RCC Communications, Inc., 923 F.Supp. 1431.

D.Kan. 1996. Court should not consider matters beyond pleadings as basis for granting dispositive motion to dismiss, but party opposing motion is not so limited, and motion should be granted only if it appears beyond reasonable doubt that plaintiff can prove no set of facts in

support of his claim which would entitle him to relief. Fed.Rules Civ.Proc.Rule 12(b)(6), 28 U.S.C.A.

> Raytheon Aircraft Credit Corp. v. Pal Air Intern., Inc., 923 F.Supp. 1408.

D.Kan. 1996. Dismissal of complaint for failure to state claim upon which relief may be granted is appropriate only if it is clear that no relief could be granted under any set of facts that could be proved consistent with allegations therein; purpose of applicable Rule· of Civil Procedure is to allow defendant to test whether, as matter of law, plaintiff is entitled to legal relief even if everything alleged in complaint is true. Fed.Rules Civ.Proc.Rule 12(b)(6), 28 U.S.C.A.

> Mounkes v. Conklin, 922 F.Supp. 1501.

D.Kan. 1996. Dismissal for failure to state claim is appropriate only if it is clear that no relief could be granted under any set of facts that could be proved consistent with the allegations. Fed.Rules Civ.Proc.Rule 12(b)(6), 28 U.S.C.A.

> Boyer v. Board of County Com'rs of County of Johnson County, 922 F.Supp. 476, affirmed 108 F.3d 1388.

D.Kan. 1996. Dismissal for failure to state claim is appropriate only if it is clear that no relief could be granted under any set of facts that could be proved consistent with allegations. Fed.Rules Civ.Proc.Rule 12(b)(6), 28 U.S.C.A.

> Gudenkauf v. Stauffer Communications, Inc., 922 F.Supp. 461.

D.Kan. 1996. Court may not dismiss case for failure to state claim unless it appears beyond doubt that plaintiff can prove no set of facts in support of his claims which would entitle him to relief. Fed.Rules Civ.Proc.Rule 12(b)(6), 28 U.S.C.A.

> Shroff v. Bernardo, 920 F.Supp. 156.

D.Kan. 1996. Court may not dismiss case for failure to state claim unless it appears beyond doubt that plaintiff can prove no set of facts in support of claims which would entitle plaintiff to relief. Fed.Rules Civ.Proc.Rule 12(b)(6), 28 U.S.C.A.

> Spillman v. Carter, 918 F.Supp. 336.

D.Kan. 1996. Court may not dismiss cause of action for failure to state claim unless it appears beyond doubt that plaintiff can prove no set of facts in support of theory of recovery that would entitle him or her to relief.

> Burton v. R.J. Reynolds Tobacco Co., 916 F.Supp. 1102.

D.Kan. 1996. Complaint should not be dismissed for failure to state claim unless it appears beyond doubt that plaintiff can prove no set of facts in support of his claim which

would entitle him to relief. Fed.Rules Civ.Proc. Rule 12(b)(6), 28 U.S.C.A.

> Houck v. City of Prairie Village, Kan., 912 F.Supp. 1438, on reconsideration in part 924 F.Supp. 120.

D.Kan. 1996. Complaint should not be dismissed for failure to state claim unless it appears beyond doubt that plaintiff can prove no set of facts in support of claim which would entitle him or her to relief. Fed.Rules Civ.Proc. Rule 12(b)(6), 28 U.S.C.A.

> Houck v. City of Prairie Village, Kan., 912 F.Supp. 1428, on reconsideration 942 F.Supp. 493, reconsideration denied 950 F.Supp. 312.

D.Kan. 1996. Dismissal of cause of action for failure to state claim is appropriate only when it appears beyond doubt that plaintiff can prove no set of facts in support of theory of recovery that would entitle plaintiff to relief, or when issue of law is dispositive.

> Henry v. F.D.I.C., 168 F.R.D. 55.

D.Kan. 1996. Motions to dismiss are disfavored: complaint should not be dismissed for failure to state a claim unless it appears beyond a doubt that the plaintiff can prove no set of facts in support of his or her claim which would entitle him or her to relief.

> Obbards v. Horton Community Hosp., Inc., 164 F.R.D. 553.

D.Kan. 1995. Court may not dismiss cause of action for failure to state a claim unless it appears beyond doubt that plaintiff can prove no set of facts in support of theory of recovery that would entitle him or her to relief. Fed. Rules Civ.Proc.Rule 12(b)(6), 28 U.S.C.A.

> Old Colony Ventures I, Inc. v. SMWNPF Holdings, Inc., 910 F.Supp. 543.

D.Kan. 1995. Court may not dismiss case for failure to state claim unless it appears beyond doubt that plaintiff can prove no set of facts in support of his claims which would entitle him to relief.

> Butler v. Capitol Federal Sav., 904 F.Supp. 1230.

D.Kan. 1995. Court may dismiss complaint only if it is clear that no relief could be granted under any set of facts that could be proven consistent with allegations.

> Asselin v. Shawnee Mission Medical Center, Inc., 903 F.Supp. 1454.

D.Kan. 1995. Complaint may not be dismissed for failure to state a claim upon which relief may be granted unless it appears beyond doubt that plaintiff can prove no set of facts in support of theory of recovery that would entitle him to relief. Fed.Rules Civ.Proc.Rule 12(b)(6), 28 U.S.C.A.

> Lyman v. Nabil's Inc., 903 F.Supp. 1443.

D.Kan. 1995. Dismissal of a complaint for failing to state a claim is appropriate only if it is clear that no relief could be granted under any set of facts that could be proved consistent with allegations. Fed.Rules Civ.Proc.Rule 12(b)(6), 28 U.S.C.A.

> Gudenkauf v. Stauffer Communications, Inc., 896 F.Supp. 1082.

D.Kan. 1995. Court may not dismiss cause of action for failure to state a claim unless it appears beyond doubt that plaintiff can prove no set of facts in support of theory of recovery that would entitle him or her to relief. Fed. Rules Civ.Proc.Rule 12(b)(6), 28 U.S.C.A.

> Garland Co. Inc. v. Ecology Roof Systems Corp., 895 F.Supp. 274.

D.Kan. 1995. Dismissal for failure to state claim is appropriate only if it is clear that no relief could be granted under any set of facts that could be proved consistent with allegations. Fed.Rules Civ.Proc.Rule 12(b)(6), 28 U.S.C.A.

> Olds v. Alamo Group (KS), Inc., 889 F.Supp. 447.

D.Kan. 1995. Dismissal of complaint for failure to state a claim is proper only where it is clear that plaintiff can prove no set of facts in support of claim to entitle him to relief. Fed. Rules Civ.Proc.Rule 12(b)(6), 28 U.S.C.A.

> Smith v. Harvey County Jail, 889 F.Supp. 426.

D.Kan. 1995. Dismissal for failure to state claim is appropriate only if it is clear that no relief could be granted under any set of facts that could be proved consistent with allegations of complaint. Fed.Rules Civ.Proc.Rule 12(b)(6), 28 U.S.C.A.

> Davis v. Olin, 886 F.Supp. 804.

D.Kan. 1995. Court may not dismiss cause of action for failure to state a claim unless it appears beyond doubt that plaintiff can prove no set of facts in support of theory of recovery that would entitle him or her to relief. Fed. Rules Civ.Proc.Rule 12(b)(6), 28 U.S.C.A.

> Burton v. R.J. Reynolds Tobacco Co., 884 F.Supp. 1515.

D.Kan. 1995. Court may not dismiss cause of action for failure to state claim unless it appears beyond doubt that plaintiff can prove no set of facts in support of the theory of recovery that would entitle him to relief. Fed. Rules Civ.Proc.Rule 12(b)(6), 28 U.S.C.A.

> Witt v. Roadway Exp., 880 F.Supp. 1455, affirmed in part, reversed in part 136 F.3d 1424, certiorari denied 119 S.Ct. 188.

D.Kan. 1984. Beck v. Kansas University Psychiatry Foundation, 580 F.Supp. 527, reconsideration denied 671 F.Supp. 1552.

E.D.Ky. 1996. District court's grant of motion to dismiss is proper when there is no set of facts that would allow plaintiff to recover.

Jessie v. Carter Health Care Center, Inc., 926 F.Supp. 613.

W.D.Ky. 1995. In deciding a motion to dismiss for failure to state claim upon which relief can be granted, complaint must be liberally construed and viewed in light most favorable to plaintiff and complaint may not be dismissed unless it appears beyond a doubt that plaintiff can prove no set of facts in support of his claim that would entitle him to relief. Fed.Rules Civ.Proc.Rule 12(b)(6), 28 U.S.C.A.

Barmet Aluminum Corp. v. Doug Brantley & Sons, Inc., 914 F.Supp. 159.

W.D.Ky. 1995. When considering motion for dismissal, district court must determine if reasonable jury could find for plaintiff under any set of facts; court must also accept allegations of complaint as true and should dismiss claim only if it appears that record as whole could not lead rational trier of fact to give plaintiff requested relief.

Cheatham v. Paisano Publications, Inc., 891 F.Supp. 381.

E.D.La. 1997. Dismissal of complaint for failure to state claim is inappropriate unless pleadings on their face reveal beyond doubt that plaintiffs can prove no set of facts that would entitle them to relief, or if an affirmative defense or other bar to relief appears on face of complaint. Fed.Rules Civ.Proc.Rule 12(b)(6), 28 U.S.C.A.

Reyes v. Sazan, 981 F.Supp. 973.

E.D.La. 1996. Complaint should not be dismissed for failure to state claim unless it appears beyond doubt that plaintiff cannot prove any set of facts in support of her claim that would entitle her to relief; however, conclusory allegations or legal conclusions masquerading as factual conclusions will not suffice to prevent motion to dismiss. Fed.Rules Civ.Proc.Rule 12(b)(6), 28 U.S.C.A.

Jefferson v. Lead Industries Ass'n, Inc., 930 F.Supp. 241, affirmed 106 F.3d 1245.

E.D.La. 1996. Motion to dismiss for failure to state claim should only be granted if it appears that no relief could be granted under any set of facts that could be proved consistent with allegations. Fed.Rules Civ.Proc.Rule 12(b)(6), 28 U.S.C.A.

Baustian v. State of La., 910 F.Supp. 274, reconsideration denied 929 F.Supp. 980.

E.D.La. 1995. In reviewing motion to dismiss, court accepts as true all well pleaded allegations and views them in light most favorable to plaintiff; dismissal is proper only if no relief could be granted under any set of facts

consistent with allegations. Fed.Rules Civ. Proc.Rule 12(b)(6), 28 U.S.C.A.

Laspopoulos v. F.B.I., 884 F.Supp. 214.

M.D.La. 1995. On motion to dismiss for failure to state claim, district court must accept all well-pleaded facts as true and review them in light most favorable to plaintiff; motion must be denied unless it appears certain that plaintiff cannot prove any set of facts in support of his claim that would entitle him to relief.

Knight v. McKeithen, 903 F.Supp. 999, on subsequent appeal Lucas v. McKeithen, 102 F.3d 171.

W.D.La. 1996. Complaint may not be dismissed for failure to state claim unless it appears certain that plaintiff cannot prove any set of facts that would entitle him to relief. Fed. Rules Civ.Proc.Rule 12(b)(6), 28 U.S.C.A.

Howard v. Town of Jonesville, 935 F.Supp. 855.

W.D.La. 1996. Unless it appears beyond doubt that plaintiff can prove no set of facts in support of his claim which would entitle him to relief, complaint should not be dismissed for failure to state claim, and leave to amend should be liberally granted.

Todd v. Brown & Williamson Tobacco Corp., 924 F.Supp. 59.

W.D.La. 1996. When defendant moves for dismissal for failure to state claim upon which relief can be granted, court must accept all well-pleaded facts as true, consider allegations of complaint in light most favorable to plaintiff, and refuse to grant dismissal unless allegations do not support relief on any possible theory. Fed.Rules Civ.Proc., Rule 12(b)(6), 28 U.S.C.A.

Hunt v. Steve Dement Bail Bonds, Inc., 914 F.Supp. 1390, affirmed 96 F.3d 1443.

W.D.La. 1995. When considering motion to dismiss for failure to state a claim, court is to accept plaintiff's factual allegations as true and determine if it appears beyond doubt that plaintiff can prove no set of facts in support of his claim which would entitle him to relief. Fed. Rules Civ.Proc.Rule 12(b)(6), 28 U.S.C.A.

Evangeline Telephone Co., Inc. v. AT & T Communications of South Central States, Inc., 916 F.Supp. 598.

W.D.La. 1995. Motion to dismiss for failure to state a claim will be denied if allegations support relief on any possible theory. Fed. Rules Civ.Proc.Rule 12(b)(6), 28 U.S.C.A.

Citrano v. Allen Correctional Center, 891 F.Supp. 312.

Court will bend over backwards to avoid granting motion to dismiss for failure to state a claim. Fed.Rules Civ.Proc.Rule 12(b)(6), 28 U.S.C.A.

> Citrano v. Allen Correctional Center, 891 F.Supp. 312.

W.D.La. 1995. For purposes of motion to dismiss for failure to state claim, complaint is construed in light most favorable to plaintiff and its allegations are taken as true; complaint will not be dismissed unless it appears beyond doubt that plaintiff can prove no set of facts in support of his claim which would entitle him to relief.

> Thompson v. Safety Council of Southwest Louisiana, 891 F.Supp. 306.

D.Me. 1996. Complaint should not be dismissed on motion to dismiss unless it appears beyond doubt that plaintiffs can prove no set of facts which would entitle them to relief.

> Bohrmann v. Maine Yankee Atomic Power Co., 926 F.Supp. 211.

D.Me. 1984. In re All Maine Asbestos Litigation, 581 F.Supp. 963, on reconsideration 651 F.Supp. 913, opinion supplemented on denial of reconsideration 655 F.Supp. 1169, affirmed 854 F.2d 1328.

D.Md. 1998. Court should not dismiss complaint for failure to state claim unless it appears beyond doubt that plaintiff can prove no set of facts which would entitle him to relief. Fed.Rules Civ.Proc.Rule 12(b)(6), 28 U.S.C.A.

> Jersey Heights Neighborhood Ass'n v. Glendening, 2 F.Supp.2d 772.

D.Md. 1996. At pleadings stage, plaintiffs are not required to determine fact of injury and, to survive motion to dismiss, they need only show that there is at least one set of facts consistent with their allegations that would entitle them to relief.

> In re American Honda Motor Co., Inc. Dealerships Relations Litigation, 941 F.Supp. 528.

D.Md. 1996. Motion to dismiss for failure to state claim must be denied unless it appears beyond doubt that plaintiff can prove no set of facts in support of its claim which would entitle it to relief. Fed.Rules Civ.Proc.Rule 12(b)(6), 28 U.S.C.A.

> All Risks, Ltd. v. Equitable Life Assur. Soc. of U.S., 931 F.Supp. 409.

D.Md. 1996. Motion to dismiss for failure to state claim must be denied unless it appears beyond doubt that plaintiff can prove no set of facts in support of his claim which would entitle him to relief. Fed.Rules Civ.Proc.Rule 12(b)(6), 28 U.S.C.A.

> Keeler v. Mayor & City Council of Cumberland, 928 F.Supp. 591, motion denied 951 F.Supp. 83.

Court may dismiss complaint for failure to state claim only if it appears, as matter of law, that no set of facts plaintiffs might prove would entitle them to relief under any legal theory. Fed.Rules Civ.Proc.Rule 12(b)(6), 28 U.S.C.A.

> Keeler v. Mayor & City Council of Cumberland, 928 F.Supp. 591, motion denied 951 F.Supp. 83.

D.Md. 1996. Motion to dismiss for failure to state claim should be denied unless it appears beyond doubt that plaintiff can prove no set of facts in support of his claim which would entitle him to relief. Fed.Rules Civ.Proc.Rule 12(b)(6), 28 U.S.C.A.

> Thompson v. Memorial Hosp. at Easton, Maryland, Inc., 925 F.Supp. 400.

D.Md. 1995. In assessing a motion to dismiss, district court must accept all well-pleaded factual allegations in complaint as true and cannot dismiss unless it appears that plaintiff can prove no set of facts that would entitle him to relief.

> Lipscomb v. Clearmont Const. and Development Co., Inc., 930 F.Supp. 1105, affirmed 91 F.3d 131.

D.Md. 1995. In ruling on motion to dismiss, complaint should not be dismissed unless it appears beyond doubt that plaintiff can prove no set of facts that would entitle him to relief. Fed.Rules Civ.Proc.Rule 12(b)(6), 28 U.S.C.A.

> Ginsburg v. Agora, Inc., 915 F.Supp. 733.

D.Md. 1995. Motion to dismiss for failure to state claim ought not be granted unless it appears beyond doubt that plaintiff can prove no set of facts in support of claim which would entitle plaintiff to relief. Fed.Rules Civ.Proc. Rule 12(b)(6), 28 U.S.C.A.

> Kohler v. Shenasky, 914 F.Supp. 1206.

D.Md. 1995. Court should not dismiss complaint unless it appears beyond doubt that plaintiff can prove no set of facts entitling him to relief. Fed.Rules Civ.Proc.Rule 12(b)(6), 28 U.S.C.A.

> Orci v. Insituform East, Inc., 901 F.Supp. 978.

D.Md. 1995. Motion to dismiss for failure to state claim ought not to be granted unless it appears beyond doubt that plaintiff can prove no set of facts in support of his claim which would entitle him to relief. Fed.Rules Civ.Proc. Rule 12(b)(6), 28 U.S.C.A.

> U.S. ex rel. Mayman v. Martin Marietta Corp., 894 F.Supp. 218.

D.Md. 1995. Court should not dismiss complaint unless it appears beyond doubt that plaintiff can prove no set of facts entitling him to relief.

> Fornshill v. Ruddy, 891 F.Supp. 1062, affirmed 89 F.3d 828.

D.Md. 1995. Dismissal for failure to state claim is only appropriate if it appears beyond doubt that plaintiff can prove no set of facts in support of claim which would entitle him to relief. Fed.Rules Civ.Proc.Rule 12(b)(6), 28 U.S.C.A.

> Carlson v. U.S. Dept. of Health and Human Services, 879 F.Supp. 545.

D.Md. 1994. Court should not dismiss claim unless it appears beyond doubt that plaintiff can prove no set of facts in support of claim which would entitle him to relief. Fed.Rules Civ.Proc.Rule 12(b), 28 U.S.C.A.

> Ammer v. U.S., 881 F.Supp. 1007, affirmed 56 F.3d 60.

D.Md. 1994. Motion to dismiss should be denied unless it appears beyond doubt that plaintiff can prove no set of facts in support of its claim which would entitle it to relief. Fed. Rules Civ.Proc.Rule 12(b)(6), 28 U.S.C.A.

> Lust v. Burke, 876 F.Supp. 1474.

D.Md. 1984. Levey v. E. Stewart Mitchell, Inc., 585 F.Supp. 1030, affirmed 762 F.2d 998.

D.Md. 1983. Vaughns v. Board of Educ. of Prince George's County, 574 F.Supp. 1280, affirmed in part, reversed in part 758 F.2d 983.

D.Mass. 1996. It is not proper to dismiss complaint for failure to state claim unless it is clear that no relief could be granted under any set of facts that could be proved consistent with the allegations. Fed.Rules Civ.Proc.Rule 12(b)(6), 28 U.S.C.A.

> American Management Services, Inc. v. George S. May Intern. Co., 933 F.Supp. 64.

D.Mass. 1996. Complaint should not be dismissed unless it appears beyond doubt that plaintiff can prove no set of facts in support of his claim which would entitle him to relief. Canney v. City of Chelsea, 925 F.Supp. 58.

If complaint is sufficient to state cause of action in accordance with law under any theory, district court must deny motion to dismiss. Canney v. City of Chelsea, 925 F.Supp. 58.

D.Mass. 1996. Claim cannot be dismissed for failure to state claim unless it appears beyond doubt that plaintiff can prove no set of facts which would entitle it to relief. Fed.Rules Civ.Proc.Rule 12(b)(6), 28 U.S.C.A.

> Milford Power Ltd. Partnership by Milford Power Associates Inc. v. New England Power Co., 918 F.Supp. 471.

D.Mass. 1996. If allegations in complaint are sufficient to state cause of action in accordance with law under any theory, court must deny motion to dismiss for failure to state claim. Fed.Rules Civ.Proc.Rule 12(b)(6), 28 U.S.C.A.

> Day v. Fallon Community Health Plan, Inc., 917 F.Supp. 72.

D.Mass. 1996. Complaint should only be dismissed when it appears that plaintiff can prove no set of facts in support of his claim which would entitle him to relief. Fed.Rules Civ.Proc.Rule 12(b)(6), 28 U.S.C.A.

> Choroszy v. Wentworth Institute of Technology, 915 F.Supp. 446.

D.Mass. 1995. Motion to dismiss for failure to state claim upon which relief may be granted should only be granted when, taking allegations in complaint as true, it appears beyond doubt that plaintiff cannot prove any set of facts in support of its claim which would entitle it to relief. Fed.Rules Civ.Proc.Rule 12(b)(6), 28 U.S.C.A.

> Herb Chambers I-93, Inc. v. Mercedes-Benz of North America, 911 F.Supp. 34.

D.Mass. 1995. Dismissal of a complaint is appropriate for failure to state a claim if, accepting truth of factual allegations and drawing all reasonable inferences in plaintiff's favor, plaintiff cannot recover on any viable theory. Fed.Rules Civ.Proc.Rule 12(b)(6), 28 U.S.C.A.

> Lowden v. William M. Mercer, Inc., 903 F.Supp. 212.

D.Mass. 1995. It is not proper to dismiss complaint for failure to state a claim unless it is clear that no relief could be granted under any set of facts that could be proved consistent with the allegations. Fed.Rules Civ.Proc.Rule 12(b)(6), 28 U.S.C.A.

> Britton v. Maloney, 901 F.Supp. 444.

D.Mass. 1995. If, under any theory, complaint is sufficient to state cause of action in accordance with law, motion to dismiss complaint must be denied. Fed.Rules Civ.Proc.Rule 12(b)(1, 6), 28 U.S.C.A.

> Duncan v. Santaniello, 900 F.Supp. 547.

If complaint is sufficient to state cause of action in accordance with law, under any theory, court must deny motion to dismiss. Fed. Rules Civ.Proc.Rule 12(b)(6), 28 U.S.C.A.

> Duncan v. Santaniello, 900 F.Supp. 547.

D.Mass. 1995. If under any theory complaint is sufficient to state cause of action in accordance with law, motion to dismiss complaint must be denied. Fed.Rules Civ.Proc.Rule 12, 28 U.S.C.A.

> Zawrotny v. F.D.I.C., 895 F.Supp. 16.

D.Mass. 1995. Motion to dismiss should be granted only if plaintiff can prove no set of facts that would entitle him to relief on any of his claims. Fed.Rules Civ.Proc.Rule 12(b)(6), 28 U.S.C.A.

> Whelan v. Intergraph Corp., 889 F.Supp. 15.

D.Mass. 1995. In considering motion to dismiss, complaint will be dismissed only if it is clear that no relief could be granted under any set of facts that could be proved consistent with allegations. Fed.Rules Civ.Proc.Rule 12(b)(6), 28 U.S.C.A.

> American Tel. & Tel. Co. v. IMR Capital Corp., 888 F.Supp. 221.

D.Mass. 1995. In considering motion to dismiss, court assumes that all material allegations set forth in complaint are true; averments of complaint, as well as proper inferences arising therefrom, are liberally construed in favor of plaintiff, and claim will not be dismissed unless it appears beyond doubt that plaintiff can provide no set of facts in support of claim which would entitle plaintiff to relief.

> Mulloy v. U.S., 884 F.Supp. 622.

D.Mass. 1995. Dismissal of an action for failure to state a claim is proper if plaintiff cannot recover under any viable theory. Fed. Rules Civ.Proc.Rule 12(b)(6), 28 U.S.C.A.

> Masso v. United Parcel Service of America, Inc., 884 F.Supp. 610.

D.Mass. 1995. When ruling on motion to dismiss for failure to state a claim, district court must take factual averments of complaint and factual allegations of proposed amendment to complaint as true and indulge every reasonable inference in plaintiff's favor; court may dismiss claim for failure to state a claim only if it clearly appears according to facts alleged that plaintiff cannot recover on any viable theory. Fed.Rules Civ.Proc.Rule 12(b)(6), 28 U.S.C.A.

> Geo. P. Reintjes Co., Inc. v. Riley Stoker Corp., 161 F.R.D. 2, affirmed 71 F.3d 44.

E.D.Mich. 1998. Dismissal for failure to state a claim is disfavored; complaint should not be dismissed for failure to state a claim unless it appears beyond doubt that plaintiff can prove no set of facts in support of his claim which would entitle him to relief. Fed.Rules Civ.Proc. Rule 12(b)(6), 28 U.S.C.A.

> Teamsters Local 372 v. Detroit Newspapers, 993 F.Supp. 1052.

E.D.Mich. 1996. Complaint should be dismissed for failure to state claim only if it appears that plaintiff can prove no set of facts in support of his claim which would entitle him to relief. Fed.Rules Civ.Proc.Rule 12(b)(6), 28 U.S.C.A.

> Tidik v. Ritsema, 938 F.Supp. 416.

E.D.Mich. 1996. Complaint should be dismissed for failure to state claim only where it appears that plaintiff can prove no set of facts in support of her claim which would entitle her to relief. Fed.Rules Civ.Proc.Rule 12(b)(6), 28 U.S.C.A.

> Willing v. Lake Orion Community Schools Bd. of Trustees, 924 F.Supp. 815.

E.D.Mich. 1996. In order for court to dismiss complaint for failure to state claim, it must appear beyond doubt that plaintiff can prove no set of facts supporting his claim that would entitle him to relief. Fed.Rules Civ.Proc.Rule 12(b)(6), 28 U.S.C.A.

> Niece v. Fitzner, 922 F.Supp. 1208.

E.D.Mich. 1996. Complaint will not be dismissed for failure to state claim unless it appears beyond doubt that plaintiff can prove no set of facts in support of his claim which would entitle him to relief. Fed.Rules Civ.Proc. Rule 12(b)(6), 28 U.S.C.A.

> Guzinski v. Hasselbach, 920 F.Supp. 762.

E.D.Mich. 1995. Complaint should not be dismissed unless it appears beyond doubt that plaintiff can prove no set of facts in support of his claim which could entitle him to relief. Fed.Rules Civ.Proc.Rule 12(b), 28 U.S.C.A.

> Pittiglio v. Michigan Nat. Corp., 906 F.Supp. 1145.

E.D.Mich. 1995. Complaint will not be dismissed for failure to state claim unless it appears beyond doubt that plaintiff can prove no set of facts in support of claim which would entitle him to relief.

> Riley v. Kurtz, 893 F.Supp. 709.

E.D.Mich. 1995. Court's inquiry on motion to dismiss or for judgment on the pleadings is limited to whether challenged pleadings set forth allegations sufficient to make out elements of right to relief; complaint should not be dismissed unless it appears without doubt that plaintiff can prove no set of facts in support of his claim that would entitle him to relief. Fed. Rules Civ.Proc.Rule 12(b)(6), (c), 28 U.S.C.A.

> Branch Intern. Services, Inc. v. Budde, 890 F.Supp. 659, affirmed 89 F.3d 832.

E.D.Mich. 1995. Although pleadings by pro se litigants are held to less stringent standards than formal pleading drafted by lawyers, court may use its discretion to dismiss pleading if it appears beyond doubt that plaintiff can prove no set of facts in support of his claim which would entitle him to relief. Fed.Rules Civ.Proc.Rules 8(a), 12(b)(1, 6), 28 U.S.C.A.

> Anderson v. Office of Atty. Gen., Dept. of Justice, 890 F.Supp. 648.

E.D.Mich. 1988. When dismissal for failure to state claim is sought, complaint should not be dismissed unless it appears beyond doubt that plaintiff can prove no set of facts in support of his claim which would entitle him to relief. Fed.Rules Civ.Proc.Rule 12(b)(6), 28 U.S.C.A.

> Gene Cope & Associates, Inc. v. Aura Promotions, Ltd., 692 F.Supp. 724.

W.D.Mich. 1995. In ruling on motion to dismiss for failure to state claim, dismissal is proper only if it is clear that no relief could be granted under any set of facts that could be proved consistent with allegations. Fed.Rules Civ.Proc.Rule 12(b)(6), 28 U.S.C.A.

> Hilliard v. Shell Western E & P, Inc., 885 F.Supp. 169, reconsideration denied 1995 WL 549259.

W.D.Mich. 1995. On motion to dismiss for failure to state a claim, a claim should not be dismissed unless it appears beyond a doubt that plaintiff can prove no set of facts in support of claim which would entitle him to relief. Fed. Rules Civ.Proc.Rule 12(b)(6), 28 U.S.C.A.

> McCready v. Michigan State Bar, 881 F.Supp. 300.

D.Minn. 1998. Motion to dismiss should be granted as practical matter only in the unusual case in which plaintiff includes allegations that show on face of complaint that there is some insuperable bar to relief. Fed.Rules Civ. Proc.Rule 12(b)(6), 28 U.S.C.A.

> U.S. ex rel. Zissler v. Regents of the University of Minnesota, 992 F.Supp. 1097, reversed 154 F.3d 870.

D.Minn. 1996. Complaint should not be dismissed for failure to state claim unless it appears beyond doubt that plaintiff can prove no set of facts in support of his claim which would entitle him to relief. Fed.Rules Civ.Proc. Rule 12(b)(6), 28 U.S.C.A.

> Grillo v. John Alden Life Ins. Co., 939 F.Supp. 685.

D.Minn. 1996. Court will grant motion to dismiss if it appears beyond doubt that plaintiff can prove no set of facts that would entitle him to relief.

> Thompson By and Through Buchanon v. Board of Special School Dist. No. 1, 936 F.Supp. 644, affirmed Thompson By and Through Buckhanon v. Board of Special School Dist. No. 1 (Minneapolis), 144 F.3d 574.

D.Minn. 1996. On motion to dismiss, district court must resolve any ambiguities concerning sufficiency of claims in favor of plaintiffs, giving them benefit of every reasonable inference drawn from well pleaded facts and allegations in complaints, and may only dismiss counts of complaint if it is clear that no relief could be granted under any set of facts that could be proved consistent with allegations. Fed.Rules Civ.Proc.Rule 12(b)(6), 28 U.S.C.A.

> Vizenor v. Babbitt, 927 F.Supp. 1193.

D.Minn. 1996. Complaint may be dismissed for failure to state claim upon which relief can be granted only if it appears beyond doubt that plaintiff can prove no set of facts which would entitle him to relief. Fed.Rules Civ.Proc.Rule 12(b)(6), 28 U.S.C.A.

> Krambeer v. Eisenberg, 923 F.Supp. 1170.

D.Minn. 1996. Motion to dismiss will be granted only if it appears beyond doubt that plaintiff can prove no set of facts which would entitle him to relief. Fed.Rules Civ.Proc.Rule 12, 28 U.S.C.A.

> Gonzales v. West End Iron and Metal Corp., 915 F.Supp. 1031.

D.Minn. 1995. Frequently stated requirement that complaint may not be dismissed for failure to state claim unless plaintiff can prove "no set of facts in support" of claim is not applied literally; however, standard for dismissal for failure to state claim is very high one. Fed.Rules Civ.Proc.Rule 12(b)(6), 28 U.S.C.A.

> Doe v. Norwest Bank Minnesota, N.A., 909 F.Supp. 668, affirmed 107 F.3d 1297, rehearing and suggestion for rehearing denied.

D.Minn. 1995. Court will dismiss complaint for failure to state claim only when it appears plaintiff cannot prove any set of facts that supports claim. Fed.Rules Civ.Proc.Rule 12(b)(6), 28 U.S.C.A.

> Bebo v. Minntech Corp., 909 F.Supp. 662.

N.D.Miss. 1998. To qualify for dismissal for failure to state a claim, a complaint must on its face show a bar to relief. Fed.Rules Civ. Proc.Rule 12(b)(6), 28 U.S.C.A.

> Myers v. Guardian Life Ins. Co. of America, Inc., 5 F.Supp.2d 423.

N.D.Miss. 1997. Dismissal for failure to state claim on which relief can be granted is not appropriate unless it appears beyond doubt that plaintiff can prove no set of facts in support of claim which would entitle him to relief. Fed. Rules Civ.Proc.Rule 12(b)(6), 28 U.S.C.A.

> Killebrew v. City of Greenwood, Miss., 988 F.Supp. 1010.

N.D.Miss. 1995. Purpose of motion to dismiss for failure to state a claim is to test the statement of the claim for relief as set out in complaint; motion may be granted only if it appears that no relief can be granted under any set of facts that could be proved consistent with the allegation. Fed.Rules Civ.Proc.Rule 12(b)(6), 28 U.S.C.A.

> Harris v. Mississippi Valley State University, 899 F.Supp. 1561.

N.D.Miss. 1995. Even if it appears an almost certainty that facts alleged in complaint cannot be proved to support claim, complaint cannot be dismissed so long as it states claim. Fed.Rules Civ.Proc.Rule 12(b)(6), 28 U.S.C.A.

> Cunningham v. Dun & Bradstreet Plan Services, Inc., 889 F.Supp. 932, affirmed 105 F.3d 655.

Dismissal for failure to state claim is appropriate only when court accepts as true all well-pled allegations of fact, and it appears beyond doubt that plaintiff can prove no set of facts in support of claim which would entitle plaintiff to relief. Fed.Rules Civ.Proc.Rule 12(b)(6), 28 U.S.C.A.

> Cunningham v. Dun & Bradstreet Plan Services, Inc., 889 F.Supp. 932, affirmed 105 F.3d 655.

S.D.Miss. 1996. Dismissal for failure to state claim is not appropriate unless it appears to a certainty that plaintiff would not be entitled to relief under any set of facts that could be proven, consistent with allegation. Fed.Rules Civ.Proc.Rule 12(b)(6), 28 U.S.C.A.

> Vance v. Boyd Mississippi, Inc., 923 F.Supp. 905.

S.D.Miss. 1996. Complaint should not be dismissed for failure to state claim unless it appears beyond doubt that plaintiff can prove no set of facts in support of his claims which would entitle him to relief. Fed.Rules Civ.Proc. Rule 12(b)(6), 28 U.S.C.A.

> Citizens' Right to Vote v. Morgan, 916 F.Supp. 601.

S.D.Miss. 1992. Complaint should not be dismissed for failure to state claim unless it appears beyond doubt that plaintiff can prove no set of facts in support of claim which would entitle plaintiff to relief. Fed.Rules Civ.Proc. Rule 12(b)(6), 28 U.S.C.A.

> Richardson, By and Through Rogers v. Southwest Mississippi Regional Medical Center, 794 F.Supp. 198.

E.D.Mo. 1997. Motion to dismiss is likely to be granted only in unusual case in which plaintiff includes allegations that show on face of complaint that there is some insuperable bar to relief.

> Doan v. I.N.S., 990 F.Supp. 744.

E.D.Mo. 1996. Court should not dismiss complaint for failure to state claim unless it appears beyond reasonable doubt that plaintiff can prove no set of facts in support of his claim that would entitle him to relief. Fed.Rules Civ.Proc.Rule 12(b)(6), 28 U.S.C.A.

> In re Ticketmaster Corp. Antitrust Litigation, 929 F.Supp. 1272, affirmed in part, vacated in part, reversed in part Campos v. Ticketmaster Corp., 140 F.3d 1166.

Motion to dismiss for failure to state claim is likely to be granted only in unusual case in which plaintiff includes allegations that show on face of complaint that there is some insuperable bar to relief. Fed.Rules Civ.Proc.Rule 12(b)(6), 28 U.S.C.A.

> In re Ticketmaster Corp. Antitrust Litigation, 929 F.Supp. 1272, affirmed in part, vacated in part, reversed in part Campos v. Ticketmaster Corp., 140 F.3d 1166.

E.D.Mo. 1996. Cause of action should not be dismissed for failure to state claim unless, from face of complaint, it appears beyond reasonable doubt that plaintiff can prove no set of facts in support of his claim which would entitle him to relief. Fed.Rules Civ.Proc.Rule 12(b)(6), 28 U.S.C.A.

> Kelleher v. Aerospace Community Credit Union, 927 F.Supp. 361.

E.D.Mo. 1996. Motion to dismiss complaint should not be granted unless it appears beyond doubt that plaintiff can prove no set of facts which would entitle him to relief. Fed. Rules Civ.Proc.Rule 12(b)(6), 28 U.S.C.A.

> Vankempen v. McDonnell Douglas Corp., 923 F.Supp. 146.

E.D.Mo. 1996. Complaint should not be dismissed for failure to state claim upon which relief can be granted unless it appears beyond doubt that plaintiff can prove no set of facts which would entitle him or her to relief. Fed. Rules Civ.Proc.Rule 12(b)(6), 28 U.S.C.A.

> Lilley v. State of Mo., 920 F.Supp. 1035, affirmed 111 F.3d 135.

E.D.Mo. 1996. Motion to dismiss complaint should not be granted unless it appears beyond doubt that plaintiff can prove no set of facts that would entitle him to relief.

> Baucom v. DePaul Health Center, 918 F.Supp. 288.

E.D.Mo. 1996. Motion to dismiss is likely to be granted only in unusual case in which plaintiff includes allegations that show on face of complaint that there is some insuperable bar to relief.

> Walker Management, Inc. v. Affordable Communities of Missouri, 912 F.Supp. 455.

E.D.Mo. 1996. Motion to dismiss complaint should not be granted unless it appears beyond doubt that plaintiff can prove no set of facts that would entitle him or her to relief. Fed.Rules Civ.Proc.Rule 12(b)(6), 28 U.S.C.A.

> Mann v. Duke Mfg. Co., 166 F.R.D. 415.

E.D.Mo. 1995. Complaint shall not be dismissed for failure to state claim for which relief can be granted unless it appears beyond doubt that plaintiff can prove no set of facts in support of claim entitling him or her to relief. Fed. Rules Civ.Proc.Rule 12(b)(6), 28 U.S.C.A.

> Swartzbaugh v. State Farm Ins. Companies, 924 F.Supp. 932.

On motion to dismiss for failure to state claim, if as matter of law it is clear that no relief could be granted under any set of facts that could be proved consistent with allegations, claim must be dismissed, without regard to whether it is based on outlandish legal theory or on close but ultimately unavailing one. Fed. Rules Civ.Proc.Rule 12(b)(6), 28 U.S.C.A.

Swartzbaugh v. State Farm Ins. Companies, 924 F.Supp. 932.

E.D.Mo. 1995. Cause of action should not be dismissed for failure to state a claim unless, from face of complaint, it appears beyond a reasonable doubt that plaintiff can prove no set of facts in support of claim which would entitle him to relief. Fed.Rules Civ.Proc.Rule 12(b)(6), 28 U.S.C.A.

Hartman v. Smith & Davis Mfg. Co., 904 F.Supp. 983.

E.D.Mo. 1995. Motion to dismiss complaint should not be granted unless it appears beyond doubt that plaintiff can prove no set of facts which would entitle him to relief.

Carter v. Lutheran Medical Center, 879 F.Supp. 94, appeal dismissed 87 F.3d 1025.

E.D.Mo. 1985. A complaint should not be dismissed unless it appears beyond doubt that plaintiff can prove no set of facts in support of his claim which would entitle him to relief.

Miener v. Special School Dist. of St. Louis County, Mo., 607 F.Supp. 1425, affirmed in part, reversed in part 800 F.2d 749.

E.D.Mo. 1984. Pro se civil rights complaint is held to less stringent standards than those required of complaints drafted by attorney, and can be dismissed for failure to state a claim only if it appears beyond doubt that plaintiff could prove no set of facts supporting claim for relief.

Harvey v. Three Doctors from India, 598 F.Supp. 739.

E.D.Mo. 1984. With regard to statute providing that action is frivolous and may be dismissed if it fails to state claim upon which relief can be granted, pro se civil rights complaint is held to less stringent standards than those required of complaint drafted by attorney, and can be dismissed for failure to state claim only if it appears beyond doubt that plaintiff could prove no set of facts supporting claim for relief. 28 U.S.C.A. §§ 1915, 1915(d); 42 U.S.C.A. § 1983.

Love v. Black, 597 F.Supp. 1092.

E.D.Mo. 1983. Missouri Pacific Employes' Hosp. Ass'n v. Donovan, 576 F.Supp. 208, affirmed 745 F.2d 1174.

D.Mont. 1983. Intake Water Co. v. Yellowstone River Compact Com'n, 590 F.Supp. 293, appeal dismissed 105 S.Ct. 316, 469 U.S. 925, 83 L.Ed.2d 254, affirmed 769 F.2d 568, certiorari denied 106 S.Ct. 2288, 476 U.S. 1163, 90 L.Ed.2d 729.

D.Neb. 1997. Pleader need not be given opportunity to be heard where facial defect in complaint is clearly irremediable.

Slangal v. Cassel, 962 F.Supp. 1214.

D.Neb. 1996. On motion to dismiss for failure to state claim, the question is whether, in the light most favorable to plaintiff, complaint states any valid claim for relief. Fed.Rules Civ.Proc.Rule 12(b)(6), 28 U.S.C.A.

Karstens v. International Gamco, Inc., 939 F.Supp. 1430.

D.Neb. 1996. Complaint must not be dismissed for failure to state a claim unless it appears beyond a doubt that plaintiff can prove no set of facts in support of claim which would entitle him to relief. Fed.Rules Civ.Proc.Rule 12(b)(6), 28 U.S.C.A.

Christianson v. Clarke, 932 F.Supp. 1178.

D.Neb. 1984. Complaint is not to be dismissed unless it appears beyond doubt that plaintiff can prove no set of facts in support of his claim which would entitle him to relief.

U.S. v. Articles of Drug, 601 F.Supp. 392.

D.Nev. 1997. Court may not grant motion to dismiss for failure to state claim unless it appears beyond doubt that plaintiff can prove no set of facts in support of his claim which would entitle him to relief. Fed.Rules Civ.Proc. Rule 12(b)(6), 28 U.S.C.A.

Martin v. State Farm Mut. Auto. Ins. Co., 960 F.Supp. 233.

D.Nev. 1996. Motion to dismiss for failure to state claim will only be granted if it appears beyond doubt that plaintiff can prove no set of facts in support of his claim which would entitle him to relief. Fed.Rules Civ.Proc.Rule 12(b)(6), 28 U.S.C.A.

Tanner v. Prima Donna Resorts, Inc., 919 F.Supp. 351.

D.Nev. 1995. Court may grant motion to dismiss for failure to state claim only if it appears beyond doubt that plaintiff can prove no set of facts in support of claim which would entitle plaintiff to relief.

Alexander v. Espy, 898 F.Supp. 716, reversed 139 F.3d 733.

D.Nev. 1995. Claim may be dismissed for failure to state claim upon which relief can be granted only if it appears beyond doubt that plaintiff can prove no set of facts in support of claim which would entitle plaintiff to relief. Fed.Rules Civ.Proc.Rule 12(b)(6), 28 U.S.C.A.

Conkey v. Reno, 885 F.Supp. 1389.

D.Nev. 1995. On motion to dismiss, issue is not whether plaintiff will ultimately prevail, but whether he is entitled to offer evidence in support of his claims, and thus court may not grant motion to dismiss for failure to state claim unless it appears beyond doubt that plaintiff can prove no set of facts in support of his claim which would entitle him to relief. Fed.Rules Civ.Proc.Rule 12, 28 U.S.C.A.

> Paradise v. Robinson and Hoover, 883 F.Supp. 521.

D.N.H. 1996. In considering motion to dismiss for failure to state claim, material facts alleged in complaint are to be construed in light most favorable to plaintiff and taken as admitted, with dismissal to be ordered only if plaintiff is not entitled to relief under any set of facts he could prove. Fed.Rules Civ.Proc.Rule 12(b)(6), 28 U.S.C.A.

> Minion Inc. v. Burdin, 929 F.Supp. 521.

D.N.H. 1995. Court may grant motion to dismiss for failure to state claim only if it clearly appears, according to facts alleged, that plaintiff cannot recover on any viable theory. Fed.Rules Civ.Proc.Rule 12(b)(6), 28 U.S.C.A.

> Optical Alignment Systems and Inspection Services, Inc. v. Alignment Services of North America, Inc., 909 F.Supp. 58.

D.N.H. 1995. Dismissal for failure to state claim is appropriate only if it clearly appears, according to facts alleged, that plaintiff cannot recover on any viable theory. Fed.Rules Civ. Proc.Rule 12(b)(6), 28 U.S.C.A.

> Miller v. CBC Companies, Inc., 908 F.Supp. 1054.

D.N.H. 1995. In considering motion to dismiss for failure to state a claim, material facts alleged in complaint are to be construed in light most favorable to plaintiff and taken as admitted, with dismissal to be ordered only if plaintiff is not entitled to relief under any set of facts he could prove. Fed.Rules Civ.Proc.Rule 12(b)(6), 28 U.S.C.A.

> Gardner v. Blue Mountain Forest Ass'n, 902 F.Supp. 14.

D.N.H. 1993. Court may grant motion to dismiss for failure to state claim only if it clearly appears, according to facts alleged, that plaintiff cannot recover on any viable theory. Fed.Rules Civ.Proc.Rule 12(b)(6), 28 U.S.C.A.

> Gilbert v. Essex Group, Inc., 930 F.Supp. 683.

D.N.H. 1983. Chasan v. Village Dist. of Eastman, 572 F.Supp. 578, affirmed 745 F.2d 43.

D.N.J. 1997. Nothing in rule governing motion to dismiss for failure to state claim confines its sweep to claims of law which are obviously insupportable; on the contrary, if, as a matter of law, it is clear that no relief could be granted under any set of facts that could be proved consistent with allegations, claim must be dismissed without regard to whether it is based on outlandish legal theory or on close but ultimately unavailing one. Fed.Rules Civ.Proc. Rule 12(b)(6), 28 U.S.C.A.

> Crossroads Cogeneration Corp. v. Orange and Rockland Utilities, Inc., 969 F.Supp. 907.

D.N.J. 1996. Federal district court may not dismiss complaint for failure to state claim unless plaintiff can prove no set of facts which would entitle him or her to relief. Fed.Rules Civ.Proc.Rule 12(b)(6), 28 U.S.C.A.

> Tennsco Corp. v. Estey Metal Products, Inc., 200 B.R. 542.

D.N.J. 1996. Court may dismiss complaint for failure to state claim only if it is clear that no relief could be granted under any set of facts that could be proved consistent with the allegations. Fed.Rules Civ.Proc.Rule 12(b)(6), 28 U.S.C.A.

> DeJoy v. Comcast Cable Communications Inc., 941 F.Supp. 468.

D.N.J. 1996. Motion to dismiss for failure to state claim may be granted only if, accepting all well-pleaded allegations in complaint as true, and viewing them in light most favorable to plaintiff, plaintiff is not entitled to relief; court may not dismiss complaint unless plaintiff can prove no set of facts which would entitle him to relief. Fed.Rules Civ.Proc.Rule 12(b)(6), 28 U.S.C.A.

> SC Holdings, Inc. v. A.A.A. Realty Co., 935 F.Supp. 1354.

D.N.J. 1996. Court may not dismiss complaint for failure to state claim upon which relief can be granted unless it appears beyond doubt that plaintiff can prove no set of facts in support of claim which would entitle plaintiff to relief. Fed.Rules Civ.Proc.Rule 12(b)(6), 28 U.S.C.A.

> Schanzer v. Rutgers University, 934 F.Supp. 669.

D.N.J. 1996. Dismissal of complaint for failure to state claim is proper when it appears beyond doubt that no relief could be granted under any set of facts which could be proved consistent with allegations of the complaint. Fed.Rules Civ.Proc.Rule 12(b)(6), 28 U.S.C.A.

> Robinson v. Fauver, 932 F.Supp. 639.

D.N.J. 1996. Court may dismiss complaint for failure to state claim where it appears beyond doubt that no relief could be granted under set of facts which could be proved consistent with the allegations. Fed.Rules Civ.Proc. Rule 12(b)(6), 28 U.S.C.A.

> Weiner v. Quaker Oats Co., 928 F.Supp. 1372, reversed 129 F.3d 310.

D.N.J. 1996. Court may dismiss complaint for failure to state claim where it appears beyond doubt that no relief could be granted under any set of facts which could be proved consistent with allegations; issue is not whether plaintiff will ultimately prevail but whether plaintiff is entitled to offer evidence to support claims. Fed.Rules Civ.Proc.Rule 12(b)(6), 28 U.S.C.A.

    Interfaith Community Organization v. AlliedSignal, Inc., 928 F.Supp. 1339.

D.N.J. 1996. Complaint cannot be dismissed unless court is certain that no set of facts can be proved that would entitle plaintiff to relief. Fed.Rules Civ.Proc.Rule 12(b)(6), 28 U.S.C.A.

    Kelly v. Borough of Sayreville, 927 F.Supp. 797, affirmed 107 F.3d 1073.

D.N.J. 1996. In deciding motion to dismiss for failure to state claim, pro se complaint should be dismissed if, accepting as true all of plaintiff's allegations and reasonable inferences to be drawn therefrom, no relief could be granted under any set of facts consistent with allegations of complaint. Fed.Rules Civ.Proc.Rule 12(b)(6), 28 U.S.C.A.

    Watts v. I.R.S., 925 F.Supp. 271.

D.N.J. 1996. When reviewing motion to dismiss for failure to state claim, federal district court will accept plaintiffs' contentions as true, view them liberally so as to give plaintiffs the benefit of all inferences which may be drawn therefrom, and determine whether it appears beyond doubt that plaintiffs can prove no set of facts in support of their claim which would entitle them to relief. Fed.Rules Civ.Proc.Rule 12(b)(6), 28 U.S.C.A.

    Sperling v. Hoffmann-La Roche, Inc., 924 F.Supp. 1396.

D.N.J. 1995. Court must deny motion to dismiss for failure to state claim for relief unless it appears beyond doubt that plaintiff can prove no set of facts in support of his claim which would entitle him to relief. Fed.Rules Civ.Proc. Rule 12(b)(6), 28 U.S.C.A.

    U.S. v. Jones, 916 F.Supp. 383.

D.N.J. 1995. Court must dismiss for failure to state a claim if, as matter of law, it is clear that no relief could be granted under any set of facts that could be proved consistent with the allegation. Fed.Rules Civ.Proc.Rule 12(b)(6), 28 U.S.C.A.

    Woods Corporate Associates v. Signet Star Holdings, Inc., 910 F.Supp. 1019.

D.N.J. 1995. When, after viewing allegations in complaint in light most favorable to nonmovant, it appears beyond doubt that no relief could be granted under any set of facts which could prove consistent with allegations, court shall dismiss complaint for failure to state a claim. Fed.Rules Civ.Proc.Rule 12(b)(6), 28 U.S.C.A.

    King v. Port Authority of New York and New Jersey, 909 F.Supp. 938, affirmed 106 F.3d 385.

D.N.J. 1995. Court may not dismiss complaint for failure to state claim unless plaintiff can prove no set of facts which would entitle him or her to relief. Fed.Rules Civ.Proc.Rule 12(b)(6), 28 U.S.C.A.

    Stehney v. Perry, 907 F.Supp. 806, affirmed 101 F.3d 925.

D.N.J. 1995. Motion to dismiss complaint will be granted when, taking allegations in complaint and all reasonable inferences therefrom as true, plaintiff can prove no set of facts that would entitle him to relief; however, evaluation of pro se litigant's complaint is less exacting than that of complaints submitted by attorneys and for court to dismiss pro se complaint, it must find beyond doubt that plaintiff can prove no facts in support of claims which would entitle him to relief. Fed.Rules Civ.Proc.Rule 12(b)(6), 28 U.S.C.A.

    Weinstein v. Township of Franklin, N.J., 898 F.Supp. 271.

D.N.J. 1995. Plaintiff's complaint must be dismissed for failure to state claim if defendant demonstrates beyond a doubt that plaintiff can prove no set of facts in support of his claim which would entitle him to relief. Fed.Rules Civ.Proc.Rule 12(b)(6), 28 U.S.C.A.

    Town of Secaucus v. U.S. Dept. of Transp., 889 F.Supp. 779, affirmed 79 F.3d 1139.

D.N.J. 1995. In appraising sufficiency of complaint on motion to dismiss for failing to state claim, critical inquiry is whether, taking allegations of complaint as true and viewing them liberally, giving plaintiff benefit of all inferences which fairly may be drawn from them, it appears beyond doubt that plaintiff can prove no set of facts in support of claim that would entitle him to relief. Fed.Rules Civ.Proc. Rule 12(b)(6), 28 U.S.C.A.

    Stanziale v. County of Monmouth, 884 F.Supp. 140.

D.N.J. 1995. District court considering motion to dismiss complaint for failure to state claim upon which relief can be granted may not grant motion unless it appears beyond doubt that plaintiff can prove no set of facts in support of his claim which would entitle him to relief. Fed.Rules Civ.Proc.Rule 12(b)(6), 28 U.S.C.A.

    Jordan v. New Jersey Dept. of Corrections, 881 F.Supp. 947.

D.N.J. 1995. Claim embodied in complaint or counterclaim must be dismissed for failure to state claim if opposing party demonstrates beyond a doubt that claimant can prove no set of facts in support of his claim which

would entitle him to relief. Fed.Rules Civ.Proc. Rule 12(b)(6), 28 U.S.C.A.

> MCI Telecommunications Corp. v. Graphnet, Inc., 881 F.Supp. 126.

D.N.J. 1991. Complaint cannot be dismissed for failure to state a claim unless district court is certain that no set of facts can be proved that would entitle plaintiff to relief. Fed.Rules Civ.Proc.Rule 12(b)(6), 28 U.S.C.A.

> Riveredge Associates v. Metropolitan Life Ins. Co., 774 F.Supp. 897.

D.N.J. 1991. District court may dismiss complaint for failure to state a claim where it appears beyond a doubt that no relief could be granted under any set of facts which could be proved consistent with allegations. Fed.Rules Civ.Proc.Rule 12(b)(6), 28 U.S.C.A.

> Glenside West Corp. v. Exxon Co., U.S.A., a Div. of Exxon Corp., 761 F.Supp. 1100.

D.N.J. 1989. Test to be applied in deciding motion to dismiss for failure to state a claim requires court to accept as true factual allegations in complaint and all reasonable inferences that can be drawn from them and to refrain from granting dismissal unless it is certain that no relief could be granted under any set of facts which could be proved. Fed.Rules Civ.Proc. Rule 12(b)(6), 28 U.S.C.A.

> Harmon v. Holmes, 712 F.Supp. 451.

D.N.M. 1997. Complaint may be dismissed for failure to state claim only if plaintiff can prove no set of facts to support claim. Fed.Rules Civ.Proc.Rule 12(b)(6), 28 U.S.C.A.

> New Memorial Associates v. Credit Gen. Ins. Corp., 973 F.Supp. 1027.

D.N.M. 1996. Pro se plaintiff is held to less stringent pleading standards than are attorneys, and constitutional claim under § 1983 should not be dismissed unless it appears beyond doubt that plaintiff can prove no set of facts in support of his or her claim that would entitle him or her to relief; nonetheless, when pro se plaintiff presents nothing more than conclusory allegations of constitutional violation, his or her claim may properly be dismissed. 42 U.S.C.A. § 1983.

> Nagol v. State of N.M., 923 F.Supp. 190.

D.N.M. 1996. Court may not grant a motion to dismiss for failure to state a claim unless it appears that plaintiff can prove no set of facts in support of claims that would entitle plaintiff to relief. Fed.Rules Civ.Proc.Rule 12(b)(6), 28 U.S.C.A.

> Newsome v. County of Santa Fe, 922 F.Supp. 519.

D.N.M. 1996. Court may dismiss complaint for failure to state a claim if it appears to a certainty that the plaintiff can prove no set of facts in support of her claim which would entitle her to relief. Fed.Rules Civ.Proc.Rule 12(b)(6), 28 U.S.C.A.

> Sutton v. New Mexico Dept. of Children, Youth and Families, 922 F.Supp. 516.

D.N.M. 1995. Dismissal for failure to state claim is appropriate only if plaintiff can establish no set of facts in support of her claim that would entitle her to relief. Fed.Rules Civ.Proc. Rule 12(b)(6), 28 U.S.C.A.

> City of Las Cruces v. El Paso Elec. Co., 904 F.Supp. 1238, reconsideration denied 1996 WL 33125, certification dismissed 954 P.2d 72, 124 N.M. 640.

E.D.N.Y. 1998. Court will dismiss complaint where it appears beyond doubt, even when complaint is liberally construed, that plaintiff can prove no set of facts which would entitle him to relief; same standard applies to denial of motion to amend pleading based on futility of amendment.

> Wilson v. Westmoreland Farm, Inc., 989 F.Supp. 451.

E.D.N.Y. 1997. Complaint should not be dismissed for failure to state claim unless it appears beyond doubt that plaintiff can prove no set of facts in support of his claim which would entitle him to relief. Fed.Rules Civ.Proc. Rule 12(b)(6), 28 U.S.C.A.

> Allstate Ins. Co. v. American Transit Ins. Co., 977 F.Supp. 197.

E.D.N.Y. 1996. Motion to dismiss for failure to state claim should not be granted unless it appears beyond doubt that plaintiff can prove no set of facts in support of claim which would entitle him or her to relief. Fed.Rules Civ.Proc. Rule 12(b)(6), 28 U.S.C.A.

> Campbell v. Grayline Air Shuttle, Inc., 930 F.Supp. 794.

E.D.N.Y. 1996. Complaint should not be dismissed unless it appears beyond doubt that plaintiff can prove no set of facts in support of his claims which would entitle him to relief.

> Kenna v. U.S., 927 F.Supp. 62.

E.D.N.Y. 1996. On motion to dismiss for failure to state a claim, court should not dismiss complaint unless it appears beyond doubt that plaintiff can prove no set of facts in support of his claim which would entitle him to relief. Fed.Rules Civ.Proc.Rule 12(b)(6), 28 U.S.C.A.

> Protter v. Nathan's Famous Systems, Inc., 925 F.Supp. 947.

E.D.N.Y. 1996. District court should grant motion to dismiss for failure to state claim only if it is clear that no relief could be granted under any set of facts that could be proved consistent with allegations. Fed.Rules Civ. Proc.Rule 12(b)(6), 28 U.S.C.A.

> Roucchio v. Coughlin, 923 F.Supp. 360.

E.D.N.Y. 1996. District court should grant motion to dismiss under Rule 12(b) only if it is clear that no relief could be granted under any set of facts that could be proved consistent with the allegations, reading the facts alleged in the compliant in the light most favorable to plaintiff, and accepting those allegations as true. Fed.Rules Civ.Proc.Rule 12(b), 28 U.S.C.A.

> Berkowitz By Berkowitz v. New York City Bd. of Educ., 921 F.Supp. 963.

E.D.N.Y. 1996. District court should grant motion to dismiss for failure to state claim only if it is clear that no relief could be granted under any set of facts that could be proved consistent with allegations. Fed.Rules Civ. Proc.Rule 12(b)(6), 28 U.S.C.A.

> Russell v. Northrop Grumman Corp., 921 F.Supp. 143.

E.D.N.Y. 1996. District court should grant motion to dismiss for failure to state claim only if it is clear that no relief could be granted under any set of circumstances that could be proved consistent with allegations. Fed.Rules Civ.Proc.Rule 12(b)(6), 28 U.S.C.A.

> Greenberg v. New York State, 919 F.Supp. 637.

E.D.N.Y. 1996. Standard necessary to survive motion to dismiss is whether there is any set of facts that, if proved, would entitle plaintiffs to relief.

> Walls v. Giuliani, 916 F.Supp. 214.

E.D.N.Y. 1996. District court should grant motion to dismiss only if it is clear that no relief could be granted under any set of facts that could be proved consistent with the allegations. Fed.Rules Civ.Proc.Rule 12(b)(6), 28 U.S.C.A.

> Walker v. Mahoney, 915 F.Supp. 548.

E.D.N.Y. 1995. Motion to dismiss for failure to state claim should be granted only when it appears beyond doubt that plaintiff can prove no set of facts in support of his claim which would entitle him to relief. Fed.Rules Civ.Proc. Rule 12(b)(6), 28 U.S.C.A.

> Salomon v. Roche Compuchem Laboratories, Inc., 909 F.Supp. 126.

E.D.N.Y. 1995. Complaint will be dismissed for failure to state claim if it appears beyond doubt that plaintiff can prove no set of facts in support of his or her claim which would entitle him or her to relief. Fed.Rules Civ.Proc. Rule 12(b)(6), 28 U.S.C.A.

> Taylor v. Brentwood Union Free School Dist., 908 F.Supp. 1165.

Complaint alleging § 1983 claims should not be dismissed unless it appears beyond doubt that plaintiff can prove no set of facts in support of his or her claims which would entitle him or her to relief. 42 U.S.C.A. § 1983.

> Taylor v. Brentwood Union Free School Dist., 908 F.Supp. 1165.

E.D.N.Y. 1995. Complaint will be dismissed for failure to state a claim if it appears beyond doubt that the plaintiff can prove no set of facts in support of his claim that would entitle him to relief. Fed.Rules Civ.Proc.Rule 12(b)(6), 28 U.S.C.A.

> Gerzog v. London Fog Corp., 907 F.Supp. 590.

E.D.N.Y. 1995. On motion to dismiss for failure to state a claim, court should not dismiss unless it appears beyond doubt that plaintiff can prove no set of facts in support of his claim that would entitle him to relief. Fed.Rules Civ.Proc. Rule 12(b)(6), 28 U.S.C.A.

> Nowosad v. English, 903 F.Supp. 377.

E.D.N.Y. 1995. Complaint should not be dismissed for failure to state claim, unless it appears beyond doubt that plaintiff can prove no set of facts in support of his claim which would entitle him to relief.

> Audell Petroleum Corp. v. Suburban Paraco Corp., 903 F.Supp. 364.

Complaint should be summarily dismissed for failure to state a claim only if it is clear that no relief could be granted under any set of facts that could be proved consistent with the allegations. Fed.Rules Civ.Proc.Rule 12(b)(6), 28 U.S.C.A.

> Audell Petroleum Corp. v. Suburban Paraco Corp., 903 F.Supp. 364.

E.D.N.Y. 1995. On motion to dismiss for failure to state claim, court should not dismiss complaint unless it appears beyond doubt that plaintiff can prove no set of facts in support of claim which would entitle plaintiff to relief. Fed.Rules Civ.Proc.Rule 12(b)(6), 28 U.S.C.A.

> PdP Parfums de Paris, S.A. v. International Designer Fragrances, Inc., 901 F.Supp. 581.

E.D.N.Y. 1995. District court should grant motion to dismiss for failure to state claim only if it is clear that no relief could be granted under any set of facts that could be proved consistent with allegations in complaint. Fed. Rules Civ.Proc.Rule 12(b), 28 U.S.C.A.

> Hollingsworth v. Robinson, 901 F.Supp. 565.

E.D.N.Y. 1995. Motion to dismiss for failure to state claim upon which relief can be granted should be granted only when it appears beyond doubt that plaintiff can prove no set of facts in support of his claim which would entitle him to relief. Fed.Rules Civ.Proc.Rule 12(b)(6), 28 U.S.C.A.

> Liberty Life Assur. Co. of Boston v. Toys R Us, Inc., 901 F.Supp. 556.

E.D.N.Y. 1995. Court should not dismiss complaint for failure to state claim upon which relief can be granted unless it appears beyond doubt that plaintiff can prove no set of facts in support of claim which would entitle him to relief. Fed.Rules Civ.Proc.Rule 12(b)(6), 28 U.S.C.A.

> Leykis v. NYP Holdings, Inc., 899 F.Supp. 986.

E.D.N.Y. 1995. Generally, complaint should not be dismissed for failure to state cause of action unless it appears that plaintiff can prove no set of facts that would entitle him to relief. Fed.Rules Civ.Proc.Rule 12(b)(6), 28 U.S.C.A.

> Tsenes v. Trans-Continental Credit and Collection Corp., 892 F.Supp. 461.

E.D.N.Y. 1995. Dismissal of complaint for failure to state a claim is proper only where it appears beyond doubt that plaintiff can prove no set of facts in support of his claim which would entitle him to relief. Fed.Rules Civ.Proc.Rule 12(b)(6), 28 U.S.C.A.

> Clarry v. U.S., 891 F.Supp. 105, affirmed 85 F.3d 1041.

E.D.N.Y. 1995. Motion to dismiss should be granted only if it is clear that no relief could be granted under any set of facts that could be proved consistent with allegations. Fed.Rules Civ.Proc.Rule 12(b)(6), 28 U.S.C.A.

> Lavian v. Haghnazari, 884 F.Supp. 670.

E.D.N.Y. 1995. Motion to dismiss for failure to state claim on which relief can be granted should be granted only if it appears beyond doubt that plaintiff can prove no set of facts in support of his claim which would entitle him to relief. Fed.Rules Civ.Proc.Rule 12(b)(6), 28 U.S.C.A.

> U.S. for Use and Benefit of Dragone Bros. Inc. v. Moniaros Contracting Corp., 882 F.Supp. 1267.

E.D.N.Y. 1984. Complaint should not be dismissed unless it appears beyond doubt that plaintiff can prove no set of facts in support of his claim which would entitle him to relief.

> Barrett v. Suffolk Transp. Services, Inc., 600 F.Supp. 81.

N.D.N.Y. 1998. Complaint will be dismissed for failure to state a claim only if it appears beyond doubt that plaintiff can prove no set of facts in support of its claim that would entitle it to relief. Fed.Rules Civ.Proc.Rule 12(b)(6), 28 U.S.C.A.

> Cetenich v. Alden, 11 F.Supp.2d 238.

N.D.N.Y. 1998. Where motion to dismiss is made prior to any discovery or filing of an answer, court is loath to dismiss complaint, regardless of whether plaintiff is unlikely to prevail, unless defendant can demonstrate that plaintiff is unable to prove facts which would entitle him to relief; this caution against dismissal applies with even greater force where the complaint is pro se, or where the plaintiff complains of a civil rights violation. Fed.Rules Civ.Proc.Rule 12(b)(6), 28 U.S.C.A.

> Proctor v. Vadlamudi, 992 F.Supp. 156.

N.D.N.Y. 1996. Complaint should not be dismissed for failure to state claim unless it appears beyond a reasonable doubt that plaintiff cannot establish set of facts to sustain claim which would permit relief. Fed.Rules Civ.Proc.Rule 12(b)(6), 28 U.S.C.A.

> Mann by Parent v. Meachem, 929 F.Supp. 622.

N.D.N.Y. 1996. Complaint should not be dismissed for failure to state a claim unless it appears beyond a reasonable doubt that plaintiff cannot in any way establish a set of facts to sustain her claim which would permit relief. Fed.Rules Civ.Proc.Rule 12(b)(6), 28 U.S.C.A.

> Lyng Motors & Service, Inc. v. U.S., 923 F.Supp. 356.

N.D.N.Y. 1996. District court should not dismiss complaint for failure to state a claim unless it appears beyond a doubt that plaintiff can prove no set of facts in support of claim which would entitle him to relief. Fed.Rules Civ.Proc.Rule 12(b)(6), 28 U.S.C.A.

> Clarke v. TRW, Inc., 921 F.Supp. 927.

N.D.N.Y. 1996. District court will only grant motion to dismiss for failure to state claim upon which relief can be granted if it appears beyond doubt that plaintiff can prove no set of facts in support of his claim which would entitle him to relief. Fed.Rules Civ.Proc.Rule 12(b)(6), 28 U.S.C.A.

> Ellis v. Civil Service Employees Ass'n, Inc., Local 1000, AFSCME, AFL-CIO, 913 F.Supp. 684.

N.D.N.Y. 1996. Complaint should not be dismissed for failure to state claim unless it appears, beyond doubt, that plaintiff can prove no set of facts that would entitle him to relief. Fed.Rules Civ.Proc.Rule 12(b)(6), 28 U.S.C.A.

> Greene v. Hawes, 913 F.Supp. 136.

N.D.N.Y. 1996. Complaint should not be dismissed unless it appears beyond reasonable doubt that plaintiff cannot in any way establish set of facts to sustain her claim which would permit relief. Fed.Rules Civ.Proc.Rule 12(b)(6), 28 U.S.C.A.

> Brown v. City of Oneonta, 911 F.Supp. 580, on reconsideration in part 916 F.Supp. 176, reversed in part, appeal dismissed in part 106 F.3d 1125.

N.D.N.Y. 1995. Court should not dismiss for failure to state claim unless it is clear that plaintiffs in no way can establish set of facts to sustain their claim that would permit relief. Fed.Rules Civ.Proc.Rule 12(b)(6), 28 U.S.C.A.

> Walker v. Reno, 925 F.Supp. 124.

N.D.N.Y. 1995. Complaint should not be dismissed unless it appears beyond a reasonable doubt that plaintiff cannot in any way establish set of facts to sustain her claim that would permit relief. Fed.Rules Civ.Proc.Rule 12(b)(6), 28 U.S.C.A.

> Barney v. U.S., 903 F.Supp. 324.

N.D.N.Y. 1995. Complaint should not be dismissed for failure to state claim unless it appears, beyond doubt, that plaintiff can prove no set of facts that would entitle him or her to relief. Fed.Rules Civ.Proc.Rule 12(b)(6), 28 U.S.C.A.

> Polite v. Casella, 901 F.Supp. 90.

N.D.N.Y. 1995. Complaint should not be dismissed for failure to state claim unless it appears, beyond doubt, that plaintiff can prove no set of facts that would entitle plaintiff to relief. Fed.Rules Civ.Proc.Rule 12(b)(6), 28 U.S.C.A.

> Board of Trustees of Trucking Employees of North Jersey Welfare Fund, Incorporated--Pension Fund v. Canny, 900 F.Supp. 583.

N.D.N.Y. 1995. Court should not grant motion to dismiss for failure to state claim unless it appears clear that plaintiff cannot in any way establish set of facts to sustain his claim which would permit relief. Fed.Rules Civ.Proc.Rule 12(b)(6), 28 U.S.C.A.

> Garg v. Albany Indus. Development Agency, 899 F.Supp. 961, affirmed 104 F.3d 351.

N.D.N.Y. 1995. For purposes of a motion to dismiss for failure to state claim on which relief can be granted, court construes complaint in light most favorable to plaintiffs and will grant motion only if it appears beyond doubt that plaintiffs can prove no set of facts in support of claim which would entitle him to relief. Fed.Rules Civ.Proc.Rule 12(b)(6), 28 U.S.C.A.

> Cox v. Commissioners of Election of Delaware County (New York), 899 F.Supp. 111.

N.D.N.Y. 1995. Courts should construe complaints filed by pro se plaintiffs liberally, granting motion to dismiss only where it ap-

pears beyond doubt that plaintiff can prove no set of facts in support of his claim which would entitle him to relief. Fed.Rules Civ.Proc.Rule 12(b)(6), 28 U.S.C.A.

> Vargas v. Pataki, 899 F.Supp. 96.

N.D.N.Y. 1995. In reviewing motion to dismiss for failure to state claim upon which relief may be granted, court should deny motion unless it appears to a certainty that plaintiff can prove no set of facts entitling him to relief. Fed.Rules Civ.Proc.Rule 12(b)(6), 28 U.S.C.A.

> Martin v. Coughlin, 895 F.Supp. 39.

N.D.N.Y. 1995. Complaints should not be dismissed for failure to state claim unless it appears beyond doubt that plaintiff can prove no set of facts in support of his claim which would entitle him to relief. Fed.Rules Civ.Proc. Rule 12(b)(6), 28 U.S.C.A.

> Beeman v. Lacy, Katzen, Ryen & Mittleman, 892 F.Supp. 405.

N.D.N.Y. 1995. Complaint should not be dismissed for failure to state a claim unless is appears beyond a reasonable doubt that plaintiff cannot in any way establish a set of facts to sustain her claim which would permit relief. Fed.Rules Civ.Proc.Rule 12(b)(6), 28 U.S.C.A.

> Romand v. Zimmerman, 881 F.Supp. 806.

N.D.N.Y. 1994. Court should not dismiss plaintiff's complaint for failure to state claim on which relief can be granted unless it appears beyond doubt that plaintiff can prove no set of facts in support of its claim which would entitle it to relief. Fed.Rules Civ.Proc.Rule 12(b)(6), 28 U.S.C.A.

> Doolittle v. Ruffo, 882 F.Supp. 1247.

N.D.N.Y. 1984. Dahlberg v. Becker, 581 F.Supp. 855, affirmed 748 F.2d 85, certiorari denied 105 S.Ct. 1845, 470 U.S. 1084, 85 L.Ed.2d 144.

N.D.N.Y. 1981. Oneida Indian Nation of New York v. State of N. Y., 520 F.Supp. 1278, 65 A.L.R. Fed. 606, affirmed in part, reversed in part 691 F.2d 1070, on subsequent appeal Oneida Indian Nation of Wisconsin v. State of N.Y., 732 F.2d 259, on remand 102 F.R.D. 450, cause remanded Oneida of Thames Band v. State of N.Y., 757 F.2d 19, motion to recall mandate denied 771 F.2d 51, certiorari denied 106 S.Ct. 78, 474 U.S. 823, 88 L.Ed.2d 64, on remand 649 F.Supp. 420, affirmed 860 F.2d 1145, certiorari denied 110 S.Ct. 200, 493 U.S. 871, 107 L.Ed.2d 154, certiorari denied 110 S.Ct. 200, 493 U.S. 871, 107 L.Ed.2d 154.

S.D.N.Y. 1997. Motion to dismiss for failure to state claim cannot be granted simply because recovery appears remote or unlikely on face of complaint. Fed.Rules Civ.Proc.Rule 12(b)(6), 28 U.S.C.A.

> Rogers v. New York City Bd. of Elections, 988 F.Supp. 409.

S.D.N.Y. 1997. Where it is clear that plaintiff can prove no set of facts in support of his or her claim that would warrant relief, motion to dismiss must be granted. Fed.Rules Civ.Proc.Rule 12(b)(6), 28 U.S.C.A.

> Madison Restoration Corp. v. Smithsonian Institute, 985 F.Supp. 434.

S.D.N.Y. 1997. Pleadings are not subject to dismissal for failure to state claim unless it appears to certainty that party cannot possibly be entitled to relief under any set of facts which could be proven in support of claim. Fed.Rules Civ.Proc.Rule 12(b)(6), 28 U.S.C.A.

> E.E.O.C. v. Kidder, Peabody & Co. Inc., 979 F.Supp. 245, affirmed 156 F.3d 298.

S.D.N.Y. 1996. Dismissal for failure to state claim is warranted only where it appears beyond doubt that plaintiff can prove no set of facts in support of his claim which would entitle him to relief. Fed.Rules Civ.Proc.Rule 12(b)(6), 28 U.S.C.A.

> In re St. Johnsbury Trucking Co., Inc., 199 B.R. 84.

S.D.N.Y. 1996. Merely because recovery appears remote and unlikely on face of complaint is not sufficient reason to dismiss for failure to state claim upon which relief can be granted; issue is not whether plaintiff will ultimately prevail but whether claimant is entitled to offer evidence to support claims. Fed.Rules Civ.Proc.Rule 12(b)(6), 28 U.S.C.A.

> In re TCW/DW North American Government Income Trust Securities Litigation, 941 F.Supp. 326, reconsideration denied.

S.D.N.Y. 1996. Court should grant motion to dismiss for failure to state claim only if, after viewing pleader's allegations in favorable light, it appears beyond doubt that pleader can prove no set of facts in support of his claim which would entitle him to relief. Fed.Rules Civ.Proc. Rule 12(b)(6), 28 U.S.C.A.

> Northwestern Mut. Life Ins. Co. v. Wender, 940 F.Supp. 62.

S.D.N.Y. 1996. Complaint will not be dismissed for failure to state claim unless it appears that plaintiff can prove no set of facts in support of claim that would entitle him or her to relief requested. Fed.Rules Civ.Proc.Rule 12(b)(6), 28 U.S.C.A.

> Erbacci, Cerone, and Moriarty, Ltd. v. U.S., 939 F.Supp. 1045.

S.D.N.Y. 1996. Court in judging legal sufficiency of complaint against motion to dismiss for failure to state claim must accept all factual allegations in complaint as true, and may only

dismiss action where it appears beyond doubt that plaintiff can prove no set of facts in support of his claim for relief. Fed.Rules Civ.Proc.Rule 12(b)(6), 28 U.S.C.A.

> Estate of Lennon by Lennon v. Screen Creations, Ltd., 939 F.Supp. 287.

S.D.N.Y. 1996. Complaint should not be dismissed for failure to state claim unless it appears beyond doubt that plaintiff can prove no set of facts in support of her claim which would entitle her to relief. Fed.Rules Civ.Proc. Rule 12(b)(6), 28 U.S.C.A.

> Wolff v. City of New York Financial Services Agency (FISA), 939 F.Supp. 258.

S.D.N.Y. 1996. Dismissal of complaint for failure to state claim is inappropriate unless it appears beyond doubt that plaintiff can prove no set of facts that would entitle it to relief. Fed.Rules Civ.Proc.Rule 12(b)(6), 28 U.S.C.A.

> Sage Realty Corp. v. ISS Cleaning Services Group, Inc., 936 F.Supp. 130.

S.D.N.Y. 1996. To prevail on motion to dismiss for failure to state claim, moving party must demonstrate beyond doubt that plaintiff can prove no set of facts in support of his claim which would entitle him to relief. Fed.Rules Civ.Proc.Rule 12(b)(6), 28 U.S.C.A.

> Green v. Kadilac Mortg. Bankers, Ltd., 936 F.Supp. 108.

S.D.N.Y. 1996. District court may grant motion to dismiss for failure to state a claim only if it appears beyond doubt that plaintiff can prove no set of facts in support of his claim which would entitle him to relief. Fed.Rules Civ.Proc.Rule 12(b)(6), 28 U.S.C.A.

> Corcoran v. New York Power Authority, 935 F.Supp. 376.

S.D.N.Y. 1996. Complaint should not be dismissed for failure to state claim unless it appears beyond doubt that plaintiff can prove no set of facts in support of his claim which would entitle him to relief.

> Johnson v. A.P. Products, Ltd., 934 F.Supp. 625.

S.D.N.Y. 1996. District court may only grant motion to dismiss if, after viewing complaint in light most favorable to plaintiff, it is clear beyond doubt that plaintiff can prove no set of facts in support of his claim.

> Argento v. Airborne Freight Corp., 933 F.Supp. 373.

S.D.N.Y. 1996. Motion to dismiss must be denied unless it appears beyond doubt that plaintiff can prove no set of facts in support of his claim which would entitle him to relief. Fed.Rules Civ.Proc.Rule 12(b)(6), 28 U.S.C.A.

> Zheng v. I.N.S., 933 F.Supp. 338.

S.D.N.Y. 1996. Dismissal for failure to state a claim is warranted only where it appears beyond doubt that plaintiff can prove no set of facts in support of his claim which would entitle him to relief. Fed.Rules Civ.Proc.Rule 12(b)(6), 28 U.S.C.A.

    Levitin v. Homburger, 932 F.Supp. 508, affirmed 107 F.3d 3.

S.D.N.Y. 1996. Complaint should be dismissed for failure to state claim only if it appears beyond doubt that plaintiff can prove no set of facts in support of his claim which would entitle him to relief. Fed.Rules Civ.Proc.Rule 12(b)(6), 28 U.S.C.A.

    Lehman v. USAIR Group, Inc., 930 F.Supp. 912.

S.D.N.Y. 1996. Court may dismiss complaint for failure to state claim only if it is clear that no relief could be granted under any set of facts that could be proven consistent with allegations. Fed.Rules Civ.Proc.Rule 12(b)(6), 28 U.S.C.A.

    Marisol A. by Forbes v. Giuliani, 929 F.Supp. 662, motion to certify allowed by 1996 WL 419887, affirmed 126 F.3d 372.

S.D.N.Y. 1996. Court should dismiss complaint for failure to state claim only if it appears beyond doubt that plaintiff can prove no set of facts in support of claim which would entitle him or her to relief. Fed.Rules Civ.Proc.Rule 12(b)(6), 28 U.S.C.A.

    Cohen v. Davis, 926 F.Supp. 399.

S.D.N.Y. 1996. Motion to dismiss should not be granted unless, after accepting all allegations contained in complaint as true and drawing all reasonable inferences in favor of non-movant, it appears beyond doubt that plaintiff can prove no set of facts in support of his claim which would entitle him to relief.

    Resolution Trust Corp. v. Young, 925 F.Supp. 164.

S.D.N.Y. 1996. When deciding motion to dismiss for failure to state claim, court may dismiss complaint only if it appears beyond doubt that plaintiff can prove no set of facts in support of claim which would entitle plaintiff to relief. Fed.Rules Civ.Proc.Rule 12(b)(6), 28 U.S.C.A.

    Wray v. Edward Blank Associates, Inc., 924 F.Supp. 498.

S.D.N.Y. 1996. Only if it appears beyond a doubt that plaintiff can prove no set of facts in support of claim which would entitle him to relief should district court grant motion to dismiss for failure to state a claim. Fed.Rules Civ.Proc.Rule 12(b)(6), 28 U.S.C.A.

    Robins v. Max Mara, U.S.A., Inc., 923 F.Supp. 460, reconsideration denied 1996 WL 88565.

S.D.N.Y. 1996. Motion to dismiss for failure to state claim should be granted only if it appears beyond doubt that plaintiff can prove no set of facts that would entitle it to relief. Fed.Rules Civ.Proc.Rule 12(b)(6), 28 U.S.C.A.

    Papa's-June Music, Inc. v. McLean, 921 F.Supp. 1154.

S.D.N.Y. 1996. On motion to dismiss, court should read complaint generously and should not dismiss complaint unless it appears beyond doubt that plaintiff can prove no set of facts in support of his claim which would entitle him to relief. Fed.Rules Civ.Proc.Rule 12(b)(6), 28 U.S.C.A.

    Tagare v. NYNEX Network Systems Co., 921 F.Supp. 1146.

S.D.N.Y. 1996. Action cannot be dismissed for failure to state claim upon which relief can be granted unless it appears that plaintiff can prove no set of facts in support of his claim which would entitle him to relief. Fed.Rules Civ.Proc.Rule 12(b)(6), 28 U.S.C.A.

    New York City Dept. of Finance v. Twin Rivers, Inc., 920 F.Supp. 50, on reargument 929 F.Supp. 172.

S.D.N.Y. 1996. Motion to dismiss for failure to state claim should be granted only if it appears beyond doubt that plaintiffs can prove no set of facts entitling them to relief. Fed. Rules Civ.Proc.Rule 12(b)(6), 28 U.S.C.A.

    Adams v. New Rochelle Hosp. Medical Center, 919 F.Supp. 711.

S.D.N.Y. 1996. Complaint should not be dismissed for failure to state claim unless it appears beyond doubt that plaintiff can prove no set of facts in support of claim which would entitle plaintiff to relief. Fed.Rules Civ.Proc. Rule 12(b)(6), 28 U.S.C.A.

    Storr v. Anderson School, 919 F.Supp. 144.

S.D.N.Y. 1996. In order to prevail on motion to dismiss for failure to state claim, moving party must demonstrate beyond doubt that plaintiff can prove no set of facts in support of his claim which would entitle him to relief. Fed.Rules Civ.Proc.Rule 12(b)(6), 28 U.S.C.A.

    King v. Pine Plains Cent. School Dist., 918 F.Supp. 772.

S.D.N.Y. 1996. In evaluating motion to dismiss for failure to state claim, court must accept material facts alleged in complaint as true, and must not dismiss action unless it appears beyond doubt that plaintiff can prove no set of facts in support of its claim that would entitle it to relief. Fed.Rules Civ.Proc.Rule 12(b)(6), 28 U.S.C.A.

    Walsh v. McGee, 918 F.Supp. 107.

S.D.N.Y. 1996. Motion to dismiss for failure to state a claim should be granted only where it appears beyond doubt that plaintiff can prove no set of facts in support of his claim which would entitle him to relief. Fed.Rules Civ.Proc.Rule 12(b)(6), 28 U.S.C.A.

McCarthy v. Sturm, Ruger and Co., Inc., 916 F.Supp. 366, affirmed 119 F.3d 148.

S.D.N.Y. 1996. Court can dismiss action for failure to state claim upon which relief can be granted only if it appears beyond doubt that plaintiff can prove no set of facts in support of his claim which would entitle him to relief. Fed.Rules Civ.Proc.Rule 12(b)(6), 28 U.S.C.A.

Bonner v. Guccione, 916 F.Supp. 271.

S.D.N.Y. 1996. Complaint may be dismissed for failure to state a claim only if plaintiff can prove no set of facts that would entitle him to relief; consequently, for purposes of motion to dismiss, all allegations in complaint must be presumed true. Fed.Rules Civ.Proc. Rule 12(b)(6), 28 U.S.C.A.

Shannon v. MTA Metro-North R.R., 915 F.Supp. 591.

S.D.N.Y. 1996. District court may grant motion to dismiss only if plaintiff can prove no set of facts that would entitle it to relief.

Resolution Trust Corp. v. Coopers & Lybrand, 915 F.Supp. 584.

S.D.N.Y. 1996. Complaint must be dismissed for failure to state claim only if it appears beyond reasonable doubt that plaintiff can prove no set of facts in support of his claim that would entitle him to relief. Fed.Rules Civ.Proc. Rule 12(b)(6), 28 U.S.C.A.

Hernandez v. Cunningham, 914 F.Supp. 72.

Trial court should grant motion to dismiss for failure to state claim only if it is clear that no relief could be granted under any set of facts that could be proved consistent with the allegations. Fed.Rules Civ.Proc.Rule 12(b)(6), 28 U.S.C.A.

Hernandez v. Cunningham, 914 F.Supp. 72.

S.D.N.Y. 1996. Complaint should not be dismissed for failure to state claim unless it appears that plaintiff could prove no set of facts in support of his claim that would entitle him to relief. Fed.Rules Civ.Proc.Rule 12(b)(6), 28 U.S.C.A.

Arce v. Banks, 913 F.Supp. 307, as amended.

S.D.N.Y. 1996. On motion to dismiss for failure to state cause of action, factual allegations of complaint are presumed to be true and all factual inferences must be drawn in plaintiffs' favor, and against defendants, and court may not dismiss complaint unless movant demonstrates beyond doubt that plaintiff can prove no set of facts in support of claim which would

entitle him to relief. Fed.Rules Civ.Proc.Rule 12(b)(6), 28 U.S.C.A.

Siben v. American Airlines, Inc., 913 F.Supp. 271.

S.D.N.Y. 1996. Cause of action may not be dismissed unless it appears beyond doubt that plaintiff can prove no set of facts in support of his claim which would entitle him to relief. Fed.Rules Civ.Proc.Rule 12(b)(6), 28 U.S.C.A.

Langner v. Brown, 913 F.Supp. 260.

S.D.N.Y. 1996. District court will only dismiss complaint for failure to state claim when court finds beyond reasonable doubt that plaintiff can prove no set of facts to support claim that plaintiff is entitled to relief. Fed.Rules Civ.Proc.Rule 12(b)(6), 28 U.S.C.A.

Centre-Point Merchant Bank Ltd. v. American Exp. Bank Ltd., 913 F.Supp. 202.

S.D.N.Y. 1996. On motion to dismiss for failure to state claim, district court must accept allegations in complaint as true and may not dismiss complaint unless it appears beyond doubt that plaintiff can prove no set of facts in support of his claim which would entitle him to relief. Fed.Rules Civ.Proc.Rule 12(b)(6), 28 U.S.C.A.

Yamen by Yamen v. Board of Educ. of Arlington Cent. School Dist., 909 F.Supp. 207.

S.D.N.Y. 1996. Complaint must be dismissed for failure of pleading to state claim upon which relief can be granted if it appears beyond reasonable doubt that plaintiff can prove no set of facts in support of claim that would entitle him to relief; motion should be granted if it is clear that no relief could be granted under any set of facts that could be proved consistent with allegations. Fed.Rules Civ.Proc.Rule 12(b)(6), 28 U.S.C.A.

Szoke v. Carter, 165 F.R.D. 34.

S.D.N.Y. 1995. District court should grant motion to dismiss for failure to state claim for relief only if it is clear that no relief could be granted under any set of facts that could be proved consistent with allegations. Fed.Rules Civ.Proc.Rule 12(b)(6), 28 U.S.C.A.

Matter of Mediators, Inc., 190 B.R. 515, affirmed 105 F.3d 822.

S.D.N.Y. 1995. Motion to dismiss for failure to state claim must be denied unless it appears beyond doubt that plaintiff can prove no set of facts in support of claim which would entitle plaintiff to relief. Fed.Rules Civ.Proc. Rule 12(b)(6), 28 U.S.C.A.

B.V. Optische Industrie De Oude Delft v. Hologic, Inc., 909 F.Supp. 162, reconsideration denied 925 F.Supp. 162.

S.D.N.Y. 1995. Action cannot be dismissed unless it appears beyond doubt that plaintiff can prove no set of facts in support of claim which would entitle plaintiff to relief. Fed.Rules Civ.Proc.Rule 12(b)(6), 28 U.S.C.A.

> State Wide Photocopy, Corp. v. Tokai Financial Services, Inc., 909 F.Supp. 137.

S.D.N.Y. 1995. Court may not dismiss complaint for failure to state a claim unless movant demonstrates beyond doubt that plaintiff can prove no set of facts in support of his claim which would entitle him to relief. Fed. Rules Civ.Proc.Rule 12(b)(6), 28 U.S.C.A.

> Red Ball Interior Demolition Corp. v. Palmadessa, 908 F.Supp. 1226.

S.D.N.Y. 1995. On motion to dismiss, court is required to accept allegations in complaint as true and may not dismiss complaint unless it appears beyond doubt that plaintiff can prove no set of facts in support of his claim that would entitle him to relief. Fed.Rules Civ.Proc. Rule 12(b)(6), 28 U.S.C.A.

> Buckley v. Consolidated Edison Co. of New York, Inc., 908 F.Supp. 217, subsequent determination 934 F.Supp. 104, vacated 127 F.3d 270, on reconsideration 155 F.3d 150, affirmed 155 F.3d 150.

S.D.N.Y. 1995. Motion to dismiss for failure to state a claim must be denied unless it appears beyond doubt that plaintiff can prove no set of facts in support of claim which would entitle him to relief. Fed.Rules Civ.Proc.Rule 12(b)(6), 28 U.S.C.A.

> PI, Inc. v. Quality Products, Inc., 907 F.Supp. 752, reargument denied 916 F.Supp. 332.

S.D.N.Y. 1995. Court should grant motion to dismiss for failure to state claim only if it appears beyond doubt that plaintiffs can prove no set of facts in support of claim which would entitle them to relief. Fed.Rules Civ.Proc.Rule 12(b)(6), 28 U.S.C.A.

> Pier Connection, Inc. v. Lakhani, 907 F.Supp. 72.

S.D.N.Y. 1995. Motion to dismiss should not be granted unless it appears beyond doubt that plaintiff can prove no set of facts in support of his claim which would entitle him to relief. Fed.Rules Civ.Proc.Rule 12(b)(6), 28 U.S.C.A.

> Odom v. Columbia University, 906 F.Supp. 188.

S.D.N.Y. 1995. Dismissal of complaint for failure to state a claim is inappropriate unless it appears beyond doubt that plaintiff can prove no set of facts that would entitle him to relief. Fed.Rules Civ.Proc.Rule 12(b)(6), 28 U.S.C.A.

> Schmelzer v. Norfleet, 903 F.Supp. 632.

S.D.N.Y. 1995. Complaint may be dismissed for failure to state cause of action only if it appears beyond doubt that plaintiff can prove no set of facts in support of his claim which would entitle him to relief. Fed.Rules Civ.Proc. Rule 12(b)(6), 28 U.S.C.A.

> Prisco v. State of N.Y., 902 F.Supp. 400.

S.D.N.Y. 1995. Pro se complaint is to be liberally construed, held to less stringent standards than formal pleadings drafted by lawyers, and can only be dismissed for failure to state a claim if it appears beyond a doubt that plaintiff can prove no set of facts in support of claim which would entitle him to relief.

> Malsh v. Austin, 901 F.Supp. 757.

S.D.N.Y. 1995. Motion to dismiss for failure to state a claim can be granted where it appears beyond doubt that plaintiff can prove no set of facts in support of his claim which would entitle him to relief. Fed.Rules Civ.Proc. Rule 12(b)(6), 28 U.S.C.A.

> Smith v. O'Connor, 901 F.Supp. 644.

S.D.N.Y. 1995. Dismissal of complaint for failure to state claim upon which relief can be granted is warranted only where it appears beyond doubt that plaintiff can prove no set of facts in support of his claim which would entitle him to relief. Fed.Rules Civ.Proc.Rule 12(b)(6), 28 U.S.C.A.

> Gershon v. Wal-Mart Stores, Inc., 901 F.Supp. 128.

S.D.N.Y. 1995. District court should grant motion to dismiss for failure to state a claim only if, after viewing plaintiff's allegations in favorable light, it appears beyond doubt that plaintiff can prove no set of facts in support of his claim which would entitle him to relief. Fed.Rules Civ.Proc.Rule 12(b)(6), 28 U.S.C.A.

> Kemer v. Johnson, 900 F.Supp. 677, affirmed 101 F.3d 683, certiorari denied 117 S.Ct. 441, 136 L.Ed.2d 338.

In order to justify dismissal of pro se complaint, it must be beyond doubt that plaintiff can prove no set of facts in support of his claim which would entitle him to relief. Fed.Rules Civ.Proc.Rule 12(b)(6), 28 U.S.C.A.

> Kemer v. Johnson, 900 F.Supp. 677, affirmed 101 F.3d 683, certiorari denied 117 S.Ct. 441, 136 L.Ed.2d 338.

S.D.N.Y. 1995. Complaint must be dismissed for failure to state claim upon which relief can be granted only if it appears beyond reasonable doubt that plaintiff can prove no set of facts in support of claim that would entitle him to relief. Fed.Rules Civ.Proc.Rule 12(b)(6), 28 U.S.C.A.

> Christopher v. Laidlaw Transit Inc., 899 F.Supp. 1224.

Trial court should grant motion to dismiss for failure to state claim upon which relief can be granted only if it is clear that no relief could be granted under any set of facts that could be proved consistent with allegations. Fed.Rules Civ.Proc.Rule 12(b)(6), 28 U.S.C.A.

> Christopher v. Laidlaw Transit Inc., 899 F.Supp. 1224.

S.D.N.Y. 1995. Complaint must be dismissed for failure to state claim upon which relief can be granted only if it appears beyond reasonable doubt that plaintiff can prove no set of facts in support of her claim that would entitle her to relief. Fed.Rules Civ.Proc.Rule 12(b)(6), 28 U.S.C.A.

> Saunderson v. Gary Goldberg & Co., Inc., 899 F.Supp. 177.

Trial court should grant dismissal of complaint for failure to state cause of action upon which relief may be granted only if it is clear that no relief could be granted under any set of facts that could be proved consistent with allegations. Fed.Rules Civ.Proc.Rule 12(b)(6), 28 U.S.C.A.

> Saunderson v. Gary Goldberg & Co., Inc., 899 F.Supp. 177.

S.D.N.Y. 1995. On motion to dismiss, district court accepts as true all factual allegations of complaint and grants motion only if it appears beyond doubt that plaintiff can prove no set of facts in support of his claim that would entitle him to relief. Fed.Rules Civ.Proc.Rule 12(b)(6), 28 U.S.C.A.

> Fighting Finest, Inc. v. Bratton, 898 F.Supp. 192, affirmed 95 F.3d 224.

S.D.N.Y. 1995. Dismissal of complaint for failure to state claim is inappropriate unless it appears beyond doubt that plaintiff can prove no set of facts that would entitle him to relief. Fed.Rules Civ.Proc.Rule 12(b)(6), 28 U.S.C.A.

> Tarafa v. Manigo, 897 F.Supp. 172.

S.D.N.Y. 1995. Complaint will be dismissed for failure to state a claim only where it appears beyond doubt that plaintiff can prove no facts supporting his claim that entitle him to relief, construing the complaint in the light most favorable to the plaintiff. Fed.Rules Civ. Proc.Rule 12(b)(6), 28 U.S.C.A.

> Orraca v. City of New York, 897 F.Supp. 148.

S.D.N.Y. 1995. Dismissal of complaint for failure to state claim is appropriate only if it appears beyond doubt that plaintiff can prove no set of facts in support of his claim which would entitle him to relief. Fed.Rules Civ.Proc. Rule 12(b)(6), 28 U.S.C.A.

> McIlwain v. Korbean Intern. Inv. Corp., 896 F.Supp. 1373.

S.D.N.Y. 1995. Motion to dismiss complaint for failure to state claim should be granted only if it appears beyond doubt that plaintiffs can prove no set of facts in support of their claims which would entitle them to relief. Fed. Rules Civ.Proc.Rule 12(b)(6), 28 U.S.C.A.

> Trustees of Plumbers and Pipefitters Nat. Pension Fund v. De-Con Mechanical Contractors, Inc., 896 F.Supp. 342.

S.D.N.Y. 1995. Court may not dismiss complaint unless movant demonstrates beyond doubt that plaintiff can prove no set of facts in support of his claim which would entitle him to relief. Fed.Rules Civ.Proc.Rule 12(b), 28 U.S.C.A.

> In re Nasdaq Market-Makers Antitrust Litigation, 894 F.Supp. 703.

S.D.N.Y. 1995. Motion to dismiss for failure to state claim must be denied unless it appears beyond doubt that plaintiffs can prove no set of facts in support of their claim which would entitle them to relief. Fed.Rules Civ. Proc.Rule 12(b)(6), 28 U.S.C.A.

> International Customs Associates, Inc. v. Ford Motor Co., 893 F.Supp. 1251.

S.D.N.Y. 1995. Complaint may be dismissed for failure to state claim upon which relief can be granted only if it appears beyond doubt that plaintiff can prove no set of facts in support of its claim that would entitle him to relief. Fed.Rules Civ.Proc.Rule 12(b)(6), 28 U.S.C.A.

> Foxley v. Sotheby's Inc., 893 F.Supp. 1224, reargument denied.

S.D.N.Y. 1995. Rule, which is particularly applicable in pro se civil rights actions, is that complaint should not be dismissed unless it appears beyond doubt that plaintiff can prove no set of facts in support of her claim which would entitle her to relief.

> Glendora v. Cablevision Systems Corp, 893 F.Supp. 264.

S.D.N.Y. 1995. When considering sufficiency of complaint under motion to dismiss for failure to state claim, court accepts as true all factual allegations in complaint and draws inferences from allegations in light most favorable to plaintiff; dismissal is warranted only if, under any set of facts that plaintiff can prove consistent with allegations, it is clear that no relief can be granted. Fed.Rules Civ.Proc.Rule 12(b)(6), 28 U.S.C.A.

> Kramer v. Pollock-Krasner Foundation, 890 F.Supp. 250.

S.D.N.Y. 1995. Dismissal for failure to state a claim is appropriate only where it appears beyond a doubt that plaintiff can prove no set of facts in support of claim which would entitle him to relief. Fed.Rules Civ.Proc.Rule 12(b)(6), 28 U.S.C.A.

> Heredia v. U.S., 887 F.Supp. 77.

S.D.N.Y. 1995. Motion to dismiss for failure to state claim should be granted only if it appears beyond doubt that plaintiff can prove no set of facts in support of claims which would entitle plaintiff to relief. Fed.Rules Civ.Proc. Rule 12(b)(6), 28 U.S.C.A.

> Bio-Technology General Corp. v. Genentech, Inc., 886 F.Supp. 377, appeal dismissed 66 F.3d 344.

S.D.N.Y. 1995. Motion to dismiss on the pleadings may be granted only if it appears certain that no relief could be granted under any set of facts that could be proved consistent with the allegations. Fed.Rules Civ.Proc.Rule 12(c), 28 U.S.C.A.

> AD/SAT, a Div. of Skylight, Inc. v. Associated Press, 885 F.Supp. 511, reconsideration denied 920 F.Supp. 1287.

S.D.N.Y. 1995. Dismissal for failure to state claim is warranted only if, under any set of facts that plaintiff can prove consistent with allegations, it is clear that no relief can be granted. Fed.Rules Civ.Proc.Rule 12(b), 28 U.S.C.A.

> Rahman v. McElroy, 884 F.Supp. 782.

S.D.N.Y. 1995. Rule which allows dismissal for failure to state claim imposes substantial burden of proof upon moving party; court may not dismiss complaint unless movant demonstrates beyond doubt that plaintiff can prove no set of facts in support of claim which would entitle plaintiff to relief. Fed.Rules Civ. Proc.Rule 12(b)(6), 28 U.S.C.A.

> Hubbell Inc. v. Pass & Seymour, Inc., 883 F.Supp. 955, motion to certify denied 1995 WL 464906.

S.D.N.Y. 1995. In order to prevail on motion to dismiss for failure to state a claim, moving party must demonstrate beyond doubt that plaintiff can prove no set of facts in support of his claim which would entitle him to relief. Fed.Rules Civ.Proc.Rule 12(b)(6), 28 U.S.C.A.

> McCoy v. Goldberg, 883 F.Supp. 927.

S.D.N.Y. 1995. Dismissal for failure to state claim is warranted only if, under any set of facts that plaintiff can prove consistent with allegations, it is clear that no relief can be granted. Fed.Rules Civ.Proc.Rule 12(b)(6), 28 U.S.C.A.

> Guice-Mills v. Brown, 882 F.Supp. 1427.

S.D.N.Y. 1995. District court should dismiss complaint for failure to state a claim only if it appears beyond doubt that plaintiff can prove no set of facts in support of her claim which would entitle her to relief. Fed.Rules Civ.Proc.Rule 12(b)(6), 28 U.S.C.A.

> Bent v. Mount Sinai Medical Center, 882 F.Supp. 353.

S.D.N.Y. 1992. Complaint must be dismissed under Federal Rules of Civil Procedure only if it appears beyond reasonable doubt that plaintiff can prove no set of facts in support of his claim which would entitle him to relief. Fed.Rules Civ.Proc.Rule 12(b)(1, 6), 28 U.S.C.A.

> Ackerman v. National Property Analysts, Inc., 887 F.Supp. 494.

Trial court should grant motion to dismiss for failure to state a claim only if it is clear that no relief could be granted under any set of facts that could be proved consistent with the allegations. Fed.Rules Civ.Proc.Rule 12(b)(6), 28 U.S.C.A.

> Ackerman v. National Property Analysts, Inc., 887 F.Supp. 494.

S.D.N.Y. 1990. Motion to dismiss for failure to state claim should not be granted simply because possibility of ultimate recovery is remote. Fed.Rules Civ.Proc.Rule 12(b)(6), 28 U.S.C.A.

> Citibank, N.A. v. K-H Corp., 745 F.Supp. 899.

S.D.N.Y. 1989. Generally, complaint may be dismissed for failure to state claim only if claims are unquestionably insufficient to entitle plaintiff to relief regardless of supporting facts that may be proved at trial; accordingly, doubt as to party's ability to prove his case, no matter how unlikely it seems he will be able to prove it, is no reason for dismissing pleading for failure to state claim upon which relief may be granted.

> In re Lady Madonna Industries, Inc., 99 B.R. 536.

S.D.N.Y. 1987. Doubt as to party's ability to prove his case is no reason for dismissing pleadings for failure to state claim upon which relief can be granted, no matter how unlikely it seems party will be unable to prove his case.

> Raine v. Lorimar Productions, Inc., 71 B.R. 450.

S.D.N.Y. 1969. Seidenberg v. McSorleys' Old Ale House, Inc., 308 F.Supp. 1253, subsequent determination 317 F.Supp. 593.

W.D.N.Y. 1996. Motion to dismiss for failure to state claim may be granted only where it appears beyond doubt that plaintiff can prove no set of facts in support of his claim which would entitle him to relief. Fed.Rules Civ.Proc. Rule 12(b)(6), 28 U.S.C.A.

> Stadt v. University of Rochester, 921 F.Supp. 1023.

W.D.N.Y. 1996. Complaint should not be dismissed for failure to state claim unless it appears beyond doubt that plaintiff can prove no set of facts in support of his claim which would entitle him to relief. Fed.Rules Civ.Proc. Rule 12(b)(6), 28 U.S.C.A.

> Amaker v. Hakes, 919 F.Supp. 127.

W.D.N.Y. 1996. Court should grant motion to dismiss for failure to state claim only if, after viewing plaintiff's allegations in favorable light, it appears beyond doubt that plaintiff can prove no set of facts in support of his claim which would entitle him to relief. Fed.Rules Civ.Proc.Rule 12(b)(6), 28 U.S.C.A.

> McCarthy v. Board of Trustees of Erie Community College, 914 F.Supp. 937.

W.D.N.Y. 1995. Complaint should not be dismissed for failure to state claim unless it appears beyond doubt that plaintiff can prove no set of facts in support of claims which would entitle him or her to relief. Fed.Rules Civ.Proc. Rule 12(b)(6), 28 U.S.C.A.

> National Elec. Ben. Fund v. Heary Bros. Lightning Protection Co., Inc., 931 F.Supp. 169.

W.D.N.Y. 1995. Complaint should not be dismissed for failure to state claim unless it appears beyond doubt that plaintiff can prove no set of facts in support of his or her claims which would entitle him or her to relief. Fed. Rules Civ.Proc.Rule 12(b)(6), 28 U.S.C.A.

> Tout v. Erie Community College, 923 F.Supp. 13.

W.D.N.Y. 1995. In order for court to dismiss complaint under Rule 12, it must appear beyond doubt that plaintiff could prove no set of facts entitling him to relief. Fed.Rules Civ. Proc.Rule 12, 28 U.S.C.A.

> Roeder v. General Signal Corp., 901 F.Supp. 124.

Dismissal is proper only when it appears beyond doubt that plaintiff can prove no set of facts in support of his claim which would entitle him to relief. Fed.Rules Civ.Proc.Rule 12, 28 U.S.C.A.

> Roeder v. General Signal Corp., 901 F.Supp. 124.

W.D.N.Y. 1995. Complaint should not be dismissed for failure to state a claim unless it appears beyond doubt that plaintiff can prove no set of facts in support of his claims which would entitle him to relief. Fed.Rules Civ.Proc. Rule 12(b)(6), 28 U.S.C.A.

> Chrzanowski v. Lichtman, 884 F.Supp. 751.

E.D.N.C. 1998. As a practical matter, a dismissal for failure to state a claim is likely to be granted only in the unusual case in which a plaintiff includes allegations that show on the face of the complaint that there is some insuperable bar to relief. Fed.Rules Civ.Proc.Rule 12(b)(6), 28 U.S.C.A.

> Eirschele By and Through Eirschele v. Craven County Bd. of Educ., 7 F.Supp.2d 655.

E.D.N.C. 1998. Motion to dismiss for failure to state a claim should only be granted where the plaintiff can prove no set of facts which would entitle him to relief. Fed.Rules Civ.Proc.Rule 12(b)(6), 28 U.S.C.A.

> Willis v. MCI Telecommunications, 3 F.Supp.2d 673.

M.D.N.C. 1995. In ruling on motion to dismiss, Court should accept as true all well-pleaded allegations, and, viewing complaint in light most favorable to plaintiff, should not dismiss case unless it appears certain that plaintiff can prove no set of facts which would entitle it to relief. Fed.Rules Civ.Proc.Rule 12(b)(6), 28 U.S.C.A.

> Food Lion, Inc. v. Capital Cities/ABC, Inc., 887 F.Supp. 811.

M.D.N.C. 1994. Motion to dismiss for failure to state claim for relief should not be granted unless it appears to a certainty that plaintiff would be entitled to no relief any state of facts which could be proved in support of his claim. Fed.Rules Civ.Proc.Rule 12(b)(6), 28 U.S.C.A.

> Liner v. DiCresce, 905 F.Supp. 280.

M.D.N.C. 1985. On a motion to dismiss a pro se complaint, court must be able to conclude with assurance that, under allegations of the complaint, it appears beyond a reasonable doubt plaintiff can prove no set of facts in support of his claim which would entitle him to relief.

> Waller v. Butkovich, 605 F.Supp. 1137.

W.D.N.C. 1996. Complaint should not be dismissed for failure to state claim unless it appears beyond doubt that plaintiff can prove no set of facts in support of his claim which would entitle him to relief. Fed.Rules Civ.Proc. Rule 12(b)(6), 28 U.S.C.A.

> TIG Ins. Co. v. Deaton, Inc., 932 F.Supp. 132.

W.D.N.C. 1996. If as matter of law it is clear that no relief could be granted under any set of facts, claim must be dismissed, without regard to whether it is based on outlandish legal theory. Fed.Rules Civ.Proc.Rule 12(b)(6), 28 U.S.C.A.

> Ryder v. Freeman, 918 F.Supp. 157, appeal dismissed, cause remanded 112 F.3d 510.

W.D.N.C. 1994. Complaint should not be dismissed for failure to state claim unless it appears beyond doubt that plaintiff can prove no set of facts in support of his claim which would entitle him to relief. Fed.Rules Civ.Proc. Rule 12(b)(6), 28 U.S.C.A.

> Kristufek v. Saxonburg Ceramics, Inc., 901 F.Supp. 1018, affirmed 60 F.3d 823.

D.N.D. 1994. Only when complaint on its face reveals some insuperable bar to relief should dismissal for failure to state claim be ordered. Fed.Rules Civ.Proc.Rule 12(b)(6), 28 U.S.C.A.

> Thomson v. Olson, 866 F.Supp. 1267, affirmed 56 F.3d 69.

N.D.Ohio 1996. Court will not dismiss complaint for failure to state a claim unless it appears beyond doubt that plaintiff can prove no set of facts in support of claim which would entitle him to relief; court must determine whether plaintiff is entitled to offer evidence to support claims made in complaint. Fed.Rules Civ.Proc.Rule 12(b)(6), 28 U.S.C.A.

> Davis v. Kent State University, 928 F.Supp. 729.

N.D.Ohio 1996. Court is to dismiss complaint for failure to state claim only if it is clear that no relief could be granted under any set of facts that could be proved consistent with allegations. Fed.Rules Civ.Proc.Rule 12(b)(6), 28 U.S.C.A.

> Gausmann v. City of Ashland, 926 F.Supp. 635.

N.D.Ohio 1996. District court will not dismiss complaint for failure to state a claim unless it appears beyond doubt that plaintiff can prove no set of facts in support of his claim which would entitle him to relief. Fed.Rules Civ.Proc.Rule 12(b)(6), 28 U.S.C.A.

> Czupih v. Card Pak Inc., 916 F.Supp. 687.

N.D.Ohio 1995. Complaint does not state claim upon which relief can be granted if it appears beyond doubt that plaintiff can prove no set of facts in support of his claim which would entitle him to relief. Fed.Rules Civ.Proc. Rule 12(b)(6), 28 U.S.C.A.

> Schott v. Secretary of Treasury, 909 F.Supp. 506.

N.D.Ohio 1995. In deciding motion to dismiss for failure to state claim, court is to dismiss complaint only if it is clear that no relief could be granted under any set of facts that could be proved consistent with allegations. Fed.Rules Civ.Proc.Rule 12(b)(6), 28 U.S.C.A.

> I-Star Communications Corp. v. City of East Cleveland, 885 F.Supp. 1035.

N.D.Ohio 1995. When considering motion to dismiss for failure to state a claim, court is constrained to accept all allegations of the complaint, and motion should be denied unless it can be established beyond a doubt that plaintiff can prove no set of facts in support of the claim that would entitle plaintiff to relief. Fed.Rules Civ.Proc.Rule 12(b)(6), 28 U.S.C.A.

> U.S. on Behalf of Woodruff v. Fairways Villas Condominium Ass'n, 879 F.Supp. 798, vacated 920 F.Supp. 115.

N.D.Ohio 1976. Alloy Cast Steel Co. v. United Steel Workers of America, 70 F.R.D. 687, supplemented 429 F.Supp. 445.

S.D.Ohio 1996. Motion to dismiss for failure to state claim upon which relief could be granted should not be granted unless it appears beyond a doubt that plaintiff can prove no set of facts in support of his claim that would entitle him to relief. Fed.Rules Civ.Proc.Rule 12(b)(6), 28 U.S.C.A.

> In re Dublin Securities, Inc., 197 B.R. 66, affirmed 133 F.3d 377, rehearing and suggestion for rehearing denied, certiorari denied Terlecky v. Hurd, 119 S.Ct. 45.

S.D.Ohio 1996. Denial of motion to dismiss for failure to state claim upon which relief can be granted is proper unless it can be established beyond doubt that plaintiff can prove no set of facts in support of his claim which would entitle him to relief. Fed.Rules Civ.Proc.Rule 12(b)(6), 28 U.S.C.A.

> Dicks v. Capital Cities/ABC, Inc., 933 F.Supp. 694.

S.D.Ohio 1996. Complaint may not be dismissed for failure to state claim unless it appears beyond doubt that plaintiff can prove no set of facts in support of his claim which would entitle him to relief. Fed.Rules Civ.Proc.Rule 12(b)(6), 28 U.S.C.A.

> Dorsey v. Tompkins, 917 F.Supp. 1195.

S.D.Ohio 1995. On motion to dismiss for failure to state claim upon which relief can be granted, district court must determine whether plaintiff undoubtedly can prove no set of facts in support of his claims that would entitle him to relief. Fed.Rules Civ.Proc.Rule 12(b)(6), 28 U.S.C.A.

> Barney v. Holzer Clinic, Ltd., 902 F.Supp. 139, affirmed as modified 110 F.3d 1207.

Complaint must be dismissed for failure to state claim upon which relief can be granted if, using any admissible facts, plaintiff cannot recover under viable legal theory. Fed.Rules Civ. Proc.Rule 12(b)(6), 28 U.S.C.A.

> Barney v. Holzer Clinic, Ltd., 902 F.Supp. 139, affirmed as modified 110 F.3d 1207.

S.D.Ohio 1995. On motion to dismiss for failure to state claim upon which relief can be granted, district court accepts as true all factual allegations in plaintiff's pleadings, and determines whether it appears beyond doubt that plaintiff can prove no set of facts in support of its claim which would entitle plaintiff to relief. Fed.Rules Civ.Proc.Rule 12(b)(6), 28 U.S.C.A.

> U.S. v. Tuente Livestock, 888 F.Supp. 1416.

S.D.Ohio 1994. Motion to dismiss for failure to state claim upon which relief can be granted must be denied unless it appears beyond doubt that plaintiff can prove no set of facts in support of claim which would entitle her to relief. Fed.Rules Civ.Proc.Rule 12(b)(6), 28 U.S.C.A.

> Misch v. Community Mut. Ins. Co., 896 F.Supp. 734.

S.D.Ohio 1991. Motion to dismiss for failure to state claim will be granted only if it appears to legal certainty that no relief could be granted under any set of facts that could be proven. Fed.Rules Civ.Proc.Rule 12, 28 U.S.C.A.; Ohio R.C. § 2307.31 et seq.

> U.S. v. Pretty Products, Inc., 780 F.Supp. 1488.

S.D.Ohio 1986. When affirmative defense is raised on Rule 12(b) motion to dismiss, test is whether complaint includes allegations of fact that effectively vitiate ability to recover; motion can only be granted where defense appears clearly on face of complaint. Fed.Rules Civ. Proc.Rule 12(b)(6), 28 U.S.C.A.

> Cincinnati Gas & Elec. Co. v. General Elec. Co., 656 F.Supp. 49.

S.D.Ohio 1984. When passing on a motion to dismiss the court must determine whether it appears beyond doubt that plaintiffs can prove no set of facts in support of their claim which would entitle them to relief. Fed.Rules Civ.Proc.Rule 12(b), 28 U.S.C.A.

> Banks v. City of Forest Park, 599 F.Supp. 465, appeal dismissed 754 F.2d 372.

N.D.Okl. 1996. To prevail on motion to dismiss, defendant must establish that there is no set of circumstances upon which plaintiff would be entitled to relief; for purposes of this analysis, court accepts as true all material allegations in complaint. Fed.Rules Civ.Proc.Rule 12(b)(6), 28 U.S.C.A.

> Whatley v. City of Bartlesville, Okl., 932 F.Supp. 1300.

N.D.Okl. 1995. To prevail on motion to dismiss, defendant must establish that there would be no set of circumstances upon which plaintiff would be entitled to relief.

> Ladd v. Sertoma Handicapped Opportunity Program, Inc., 917 F.Supp. 766.

D.Or. 1996. Motion to dismiss for failure to state a claim can be granted only if it appears beyond doubt that plaintiff can prove no set of facts in support of its claim which would entitle it to relief. Fed.Rules Civ.Proc.Rule 12(b)(6), 28 U.S.C.A.

> Freedman v. Louisiana-Pacific Corp., 922 F.Supp. 377.

D.Or. 1996. Dismissal for failure to state claim is proper only when it appears to certainty that plaintiff can prove no set of facts in support of his claim that would entitle him to relief.

> Decker v. Richardson, 920 F.Supp. 141.

D.Or. 1996. Dismissal for failure to state claim is proper only when it appears to certainty that plaintiff can prove no set of facts in support of his claim that would entitle him to relief.

> Kolander v. Weeks, 916 F.Supp. 1042.

D.Or. 1996. Motion to dismiss for failure to state claim will only be granted if it appears beyond doubt that plaintiff can prove no set of facts in support of his claim which would entitle him to relief. Fed.Rules Civ.Proc.Rule 12(b)(6), 28 U.S.C.A.

> Snead v. Metropolitan Property and Cas. Ins. Co., 909 F.Supp. 775.

D.Or. 1995. Motion to dismiss for failure to state claim can be granted only if it appears beyond doubt that plaintiff can prove no set of facts in support of its claim which would entitle it to relief. Fed.Rules Civ.Proc.Rule 12(b)(6), 28 U.S.C.A.

> Catellus Development Corp. v. L.D. McFarland Co., 910 F.Supp. 1509.

D.Or. 1995. A motion to dismiss for failure to state a claim should not be granted unless it appears beyond a doubt that plaintiff can prove no set of facts in support of claim which would entitle him to relief. Fed.Rules Civ.Proc.Rule 12(b)(6), 28 U.S.C.A.

> Hardwick v. Curtis Trailers Inc., 896 F.Supp. 1037.

D.Or. 1995. Motion to dismiss for failure to state claim should not be granted unless it appears beyond doubt that plaintiff can prove no set of facts in support of his claim which would entitle him to relief. Fed.Rules Civ.Proc. Rule 12(b)(6), 28 U.S.C.A.

> Price v. Taco Bell Corp., 896 F.Supp. 1022.

D.Or. 1995. Motion to dismiss for failure to state a claim will only be granted if it appears beyond doubt that plaintiff can prove no set of facts in support of his claim which would entitle him to relief. Fed.Rules Civ.Proc.Rule 12(b)(6), 28 U.S.C.A.

> Stevens v. City of Cannon Beach, 893 F.Supp. 944, affirmed 106 F.3d 409, certiorari denied 117 S.Ct. 2515, 138 L.Ed.2d 1017.

D.Or. 1994. Motion to dismiss for failure to state claim on which relief could be granted should not be granted unless it appears beyond doubt that plaintiff can prove no set of facts in support of its claim which would entitle it to relief. Fed.Rules Civ.Proc.Rule 12(b)(6).

> Sorenson v. Concannon, 893 F.Supp. 1469.

D.Or. 1992. Dismissal for failure to state claim is proper only when it appears to certainty that plaintiff can prove no set of facts in support of claim that would entitle plaintiff to relief.

Newman v. Comprehensive Care Corp., 794 F.Supp. 1513.

D.Or. 1990. Court should dismiss complaint for failure to state claim only when it appears beyond doubt that plaintiff can prove no set of facts in support of claim which would entitle plaintiff to relief. Fed.Rules Civ.Proc. Rule 12(b)(6), 28 U.S.C.A.

Rolex Employees Retirement Trust v. Mentor Graphics Corp., 749 F.Supp. 1042.

E.D.Pa. 1997. Dismissal of complaint for failure to state claim is limited to those instances where it is certain that no relief could be granted under any set of facts that could be proved. Fed.Rules Civ.Proc.Rule 12(b)(6), 28 U.S.C.A.

Joe Hand Promotions, Inc. v. Rennard Street Enterprises, Inc., 954 F.Supp. 1046.

E.D.Pa. 1996. Claim may be dismissed for failure to state claim only if plaintiff can prove no set of facts in support of claim that would entitle him or her to relief. Fed.Rules Civ.Proc. Rule 12(b)(6), 28 U.S.C.A.

Death Row Prisoners of Pennsylvania v. Ridge, 948 F.Supp. 1258.

E.D.Pa. 1996. Court will grant motion to dismiss for failure to state claim only if facts and reasonable inferences therefrom are legally insufficient and it is clear that plaintiff cannot prove any facts upon which relief could be granted. Fed.Rules Civ.Proc.Rule 12(b)(6), 28 U.S.C.A.

Fair Housing Council of Suburban Philadelphia v. Boyertown Area Times, 945 F.Supp. 826.

E.D.Pa. 1996. Court will grant motion to dismiss for failure to state claim only if facts and reasonable inferences therefrom are legally insufficient and it is clear that plaintiff cannot prove any facts upon which relief could be granted. Fed.Rules Civ.Proc.Rule 12(b)(6), 28 U.S.C.A.

Irvin v. Borough of Darby, 937 F.Supp. 446.

E.D.Pa. 1996. In deciding motion to dismiss for failure to state claim upon which relief could be granted, court must take all well-pleaded factual allegations in complaint as true; dismissal is only appropriate if plaintiff could prove no set of facts that would entitle him to relief requested. Fed.Rules Civ.Proc.Rule 12(b)(6), 28 U.S.C.A.

Doe v. Provident Life and Acc. Ins. Co., 936 F.Supp. 302.

E.D.Pa. 1996. Dismissal of complaint for failure to state claim is appropriate only if plaintiff could prove no set of facts that would entitle him to relief requested. Fed.Rules Civ. Proc.Rule 12(b)(6), 28 U.S.C.A.

Cuffeld v. Supreme Court of Pennsylvania, 936 F.Supp. 266.

E.D.Pa. 1996. Claim may be dismissed for failure to state a claim only if plaintiff can prove no set of facts in support of claim that would entitle her to relief. Fed.Rules Civ.Proc.Rule 12(b)(6), 28 U.S.C.A.

Corbett v. Morgenstern, 934 F.Supp. 680.

E.D.Pa. 1996. Complaint is properly dismissed for failure to state claim upon which relief can be granted only if it appears certain that plaintiff cannot prove any set of facts in support of his claim which would entitle him to relief. Fed.Rules Civ.Proc.Rule 12(b)(6), 28 U.S.C.A.

Rashid v. Kite, 934 F.Supp. 144.

E.D.Pa. 1996. Complaint is properly dismissed for failure to state claim only if it appears certain that plaintiff cannot prove any set of facts in support of its claim which would entitle it to relief. Fed.Rules Civ.Proc.Rule 12(b)(6), 28 U.S.C.A.

Bryan v. Acorn Hotel, Inc., 931 F.Supp. 394.

E.D.Pa. 1996. Complaint should be dismissed for failure to state claim only where it is clear that no relief could be granted under any set of facts that could be proved consistent with the allegations. Fed.Rules Civ.Proc.Rule 12(b)(6), 28 U.S.C.A.

Colbert v. City of Philadelphia, 931 F.Supp. 389.

E.D.Pa. 1996. Complaint is properly dismissed only if appears certain that plaintiff can prove no set of facts in support of his claim which would entitle him to relief. Fed.Rules Civ.Proc.Rule 12(b)(6), 28 U.S.C.A.

Dolla v. Unicast Co., 930 F.Supp. 202.

E.D.Pa. 1996. In ruling on motion to dismiss for failure to state claim, court must accept as true all allegations in pleadings and must give plaintiff benefit of every favorable inference that can be drawn from those allegations; complaint is properly dismissed only if it appears certain that plaintiff cannot prove any set of facts in support of his claim that would entitle him to relief. Fed.Rules Civ.Proc.Rule 12(b)(6), 28 U.S.C.A.

Barber v. Grow, 929 F.Supp. 820.

E.D.Pa. 1996. Claims may only be dismissed for failure to state claim if plaintiff cannot demonstrate any set of facts which would entitle it to relief. Fed.Rules Civ.Proc. Rule 12(b)(6), 28 U.S.C.A.

Barnes Foundation v. Township of Lower Merion, 927 F.Supp. 874.

E.D.Pa. 1996. Complaint is properly dismissed only if it appears certain that plaintiff cannot prove any set of facts in support of its claim which would entitle it to relief. Fed. Rules Civ.Proc.Rule 12(b)(6), 28 U.S.C.A.

Williams v. Discovery Day School, 924 F.Supp. 41.

E.D.Pa. 1996. Complaint is properly dismissed only if it appears certain that plaintiff cannot prove any set of facts in support of claim which would entitle it to relief. Fed.Rules Civ. Proc.Rule 12(b)(6), 28 U.S.C.A.

Williams v. Stone, 923 F.Supp. 689, affirmed 109 F.3d 890, certiorari denied 118 S.Ct. 383, 139 L.Ed.2d 299.

E.D.Pa. 1996. Complaint is properly dismissed only if it appears certain that plaintiff cannot prove any set of facts in support of his claim which would entitle him to relief.

Queen City Pizza, Inc. v. Domino's Pizza, Inc., 922 F.Supp. 1055, affirmed 124 F.3d 430, rehearing and rehearing denied 129 F.3d 724, certiorari denied Baughans, Inc. v. Domino's Pizza, Inc., 118 S.Ct. 1385, 140 L.Ed.2d 645.

E.D.Pa. 1996. In considering motion to dismiss for failure to state claim, court must accept as true all of allegations in pleadings and must give plaintiff benefit of every favorable inference that can be drawn from those allegations; complaint is properly dismissed only if it appears certain that plaintiff cannot prove any set of facts in support of its claim which would entitle it to relief. Fed.Rules Civ.Proc.Rule 12(b)(6), 28 U.S.C.A.

Logue v. Logano Trucking Co., 921 F.Supp. 1425.

E.D.Pa. 1996. Dismissal for failure to state claim is not appropriate unless it is clear that no relief could be granted under any set of facts that could be proved consistent with allegations. Fed.Rules Civ.Proc.Rule 12(b)(6), 28 U.S.C.A.

Nelson v. Temple University, 920 F.Supp. 633.

E.D.Pa. 1996. Complaint is properly dismissed for failure to state a claim only if it appears certain that plaintiff cannot prove any set of facts in support of its claim which would entitle it to relief. Fed.Rules Civ.Proc.Rule 12(b)(6), 28 U.S.C.A.

Esfahani v. Medical College of Pennsylvania, 919 F.Supp. 832.

E.D.Pa. 1996. Issue before court in motion to dismiss for failure to state claim, is not whether plaintiff will ultimately prevail, but, rather, whether he would be entitled to relief under any set of facts he could prove consistent with allegations set forth in complaint. Fed. Rules Civ.Proc.Rule 12(b)(6), 28 U.S.C.A.

Stone v. Pennsylvania Merchant Group, Ltd., 915 F.Supp. 727.

Purpose of motion to dismiss for failure to state claim, is to test sufficiency of complaint, and complaint should not be dismissed for failure to state a claim unless it appears beyond doubt that plaintiff can prove no set of facts in support of his claim which would entitle him to relief. Fed.Rules Civ.Proc.Rule 12(b)(6), 28 U.S.C.A.

Stone v. Pennsylvania Merchant Group, Ltd., 915 F.Supp. 727.

E.D.Pa. 1996. Complaint is properly dismissed for failure to state claim only if it appears certain that plaintiff cannot prove any set of facts in support of its claim which would entitle it to relief. Fed.Rules Civ.Proc.Rule 12(b)(6), 28 U.S.C.A.

Slater v. Marshall, 915 F.Supp. 721.

E.D.Pa. 1996. A claim may be dismissed for failure to state a claim only if plaintiff can prove no set of facts in support of claim that would entitle him to relief. Fed.Rules Civ.Proc. Rule 12(b)(6), 28 U.S.C.A.

Smyth v. Pillsbury Co., 914 F.Supp. 97.

E.D.Pa. 1996. Complaint is properly dismissed for failure to state claim only if it appears certain that plaintiff cannot prove any set of facts in support of his or her claim which would entitle him or her to relief. Fed.Rules Civ.Proc.Rule 12(b)(6), 28 U.S.C.A.

Miller v. Group Voyagers, Inc., 912 F.Supp. 164.

E.D.Pa. 1996. Complaint is properly dismissed for failure to state a claim only if it appears certain that plaintiff cannot prove any set of facts in support of its claim which would entitle it to relief. Fed.Rules Civ.Proc.Rule 12(b)(6), 28 U.S.C.A.

Johnson v. Hill, 910 F.Supp. 218.

E.D.Pa. 1995. Claim may only be dismissed on grounds of failure to state claim upon which relief can be granted if plaintiff cannot demonstrate any set of facts in support of claim that would entitle him to relief. Fed.Rules Civ.Proc.Rule 12(b)(6), 28 U.S.C.A.

Taylor v. Cox, 912 F.Supp. 140.

E.D.Pa. 1995. Court should dismiss claim for failure to state cause of action only if it appears to a certainty that no relief could be granted under any set of facts which could be proved. Fed.Rules Civ.Proc.Rule 12(b)(6), 28 U.S.C.A.

King v. M.R. Brown, Inc., 911 F.Supp. 161.

Because granting motion to dismiss for failure to state claim results in determination on merits at such an early stage of plaintiff's case, district court must take all well pleaded allegations as true, construe the complaint in light most favorable to plaintiff, and determine whether, under any reasonable reading of pleadings, plaintiff may be entitled to relief. Fed.Rules Civ.Proc.Rule 12(b)(6), 28 U.S.C.A.

> King v. M.R. Brown, Inc., 911 F.Supp. 161.

E.D.Pa. 1995. Complaint is properly dismissed for failure to state claim upon which relief can be granted only if it appears certain that plaintiff cannot prove any set of facts in support of its claim which would entitle it to relief. Fed.Rules Civ.Proc.Rule 12(b)(6), 28 U.S.C.A.

> Hewlett-Packard Co. v. Arch Associates Corp., 908 F.Supp. 265.

E.D.Pa. 1995. Complaint should be dismissed for failure to state a claim only where it is clear that no relief could be granted under any set of facts that could be proved consistent with the allegations. Fed.Rules Civ.Proc.Rule 12(b)(6), 28 U.S.C.A.

> Consolidated Rail Corp. v. United Transp. Union General Committee of Adjustment (PRR), 908 F.Supp. 258.

E.D.Pa. 1995. Complaint is properly dismissed only if it appears certain that plaintiff cannot prove any set of facts in support of its claim which would entitle it to relief. Fed. Rules Civ.Proc.Rule 12(b)(6), 28 U.S.C.A.

> Clarke v. Whitney, 907 F.Supp. 893.

E.D.Pa. 1995. In deciding motion to dismiss, factual allegations of complaint are to be accepted as true, reasonable factual inferences must be drawn in favor of nonmovant, and complaint should be dismissed only if it appears to certainty that no relief could be granted under any set of facts that could be proved.

> Trauma Service Group v. Keating, 907 F.Supp. 110.

E.D.Pa. 1995. Complaint is properly dismissed for failure to state claim only if it appears certain that plaintiff cannot prove any set of facts in support of claim which would entitle it to relief. Fed.Rules Civ.Proc.Rule 12(b)(6), 28 U.S.C.A.

> Slater v. Marshall, 906 F.Supp. 256.

E.D.Pa. 1995. Complaint may be dismissed for failure to state claim if it appears beyond doubt that plaintiff can prove no set of facts in support of his claim which would entitle him to relief. Fed.Rules Civ.Proc.Rule 12(b)(6), 28 U.S.C.A.

> Burks v. City of Philadelphia, 904 F.Supp. 421.

E.D.Pa. 1995. Motion to dismiss should be denied unless it appears beyond doubt that plaintiff can prove no set of facts in support of his claims which would entitle him to relief.

> Behr v. Snider, 900 F.Supp. 719.

E.D.Pa. 1995. Complaint is properly dismissed for failure to state claim only if it appears certain that plaintiff cannot prove any set of facts in support of claim which would entitle plaintiff to relief. Fed.Rules Civ.Proc.Rule 12(b)(6), 28 U.S.C.A.

> Sterling v. Southeastern Pennsylvania Transp. Authority, 897 F.Supp. 893.

E.D.Pa. 1995. On motion to dismiss under Rule 12(b)(6), defendants must show that under no set of facts will plaintiffs be able to establish alleged misrepresentations and omissions or material. Fed.Rules Civ.Proc.Rule 12(b)(6), 28 U.S.C.A.

> In re ValueVision Intern. Inc. Securities Litigation, 896 F.Supp. 434.

E.D.Pa. 1995. Complaint is properly dismissed pursuant to motion to dismiss only if it appears certain that plaintiff cannot prove any set of facts in support of its claim which would entitle it to relief. Fed.Rules Civ.Proc.Rule 12(b)(6), 28 U.S.C.A.

> Slater v. Marshall, 895 F.Supp. 93.

E.D.Pa. 1995. Complaint is properly dismissed only if it appears certain that plaintiff cannot prove any set of facts in support of its claim which would entitle it to relief. Fed. Rules Civ.Proc.Rule 12(b)(6), 28 U.S.C.A.

> Frederick v. Southeastern Pennsylvania Transp. Authority, 892 F.Supp. 122.

E.D.Pa. 1995. Claim should be dismissed for failure to state claim only where it is clear that no relief could be granted under any set of facts that could be proved consistent with the allegations. Fed.Rules Civ.Proc.Rule 12(b)(6), 28 U.S.C.A.

> Slabik v. Sorrentino, 891 F.Supp. 235, affirmed 82 F.3d 406.

E.D.Pa. 1995. Complaint is properly dismissed for failure to state claim only if it appears certain that plaintiff cannot prove any set of facts in support of its claim which would entitle it to relief. Fed.Rules Civ.Proc.Rule 12(b)(6), 28 U.S.C.A.

> Bennett v. State Farm Fire & Cas. Ins. Co., 890 F.Supp. 440.

E.D.Pa. 1995. Complaint is properly dismissed for failure to state claim only if it appears certain that plaintiff cannot prove any set of facts in support of its claim which would entitle it to relief. Fed.Rules Civ.Proc.Rule 12(b)(6), 28 U.S.C.A.

> Arber v. Equitable Beneficial Life Ins. Co., 889 F.Supp. 194.

E.D.Pa. 1995. Complaint is properly dismissed for failure to state claim only if it appears certain that plaintiff cannot prove any set of facts in support of its claim which would entitle it to relief. Fed.Rules Civ.Proc.Rule 12(b)(6), 28 U.S.C.A.

Allied Fire & Safety Equipment Co. v. Dick Enterprises, Inc., 886 F.Supp. 491.

E.D.Pa. 1995. Complaint is properly dismissed for failure to state claim upon which relief can be granted only if it appears certain that plaintiff cannot prove any set of facts in support of its claim which would entitle it to relief. Fed.Rules Civ.Proc.Rule 12(b)(6), 28 U.S.C.A.

Pierce v. Montgomery County Opportunity Bd., Inc., 884 F.Supp. 965.

E.D.Pa. 1995. Complaint is properly dismissed for failure to state claim only if it appears certain that plaintiff cannot prove any set of facts in support of its claim which would entitle it to relief. Fed.Rules Civ.Proc.Rule 12(b)(6), 28 U.S.C.A.

Caplan v. Fellheimer Eichen Braverman & Kaskey, 882 F.Supp. 1529.

E.D.Pa. 1995. District court may dismiss complaint only if it appears beyond doubt that plaintiff can prove no facts which would justify relief. Fed.Rules Civ.Proc.Rule 12(b)(6), 28 U.S.C.A.

Crighton v. Schuylkill County, 882 F.Supp. 411.

E.D.Pa. 1993. Dismissal for legal insufficiency is proper only when claim clearly appears to be immaterial and solely for purpose of obtaining jurisdiction, or is wholly and substantially frivolous. Fed.Rules Civ.Proc.Rule 12(b)(1), 28 U.S.C.A.

C. Jack Friedman, Ph.D. & Associates, P.C. v. Pennsylvania Blue Shield, 836 F.Supp. 263, affirmed 30 F.3d 1486.

E.D.Pa. 1992. Claim will be dismissed for failure to state claim only where it appears that plaintiff has alleged no set of facts in support of claim which would entitle him to relief. Fed. Rules Civ.Proc.Rule 12(b)(6), 28 U.S.C.A.

Tersco, Inc. v. E.I. DuPont de Nemours and Co., 879 F.Supp. 445.

E.D.Pa. 1992. Case should not be dismissed for failure to state a claim unless it clearly appears that no relief can be granted under any set of facts that could be proved consistent with plaintiff's allegations.

Freeman v. McKellar, 795 F.Supp. 733.

E.D.Pa. 1984. When presented with motion to dismiss, court must view pleadings in light most favorable to nonmoving party, and complaint should never be dismissed for failure to state claim unless it appears beyond doubt that plaintiff can prove no set of facts to support claim which would afford her relief.

Hooten v. Pennsylvania College of Optometry, 601 F.Supp. 1151.

M.D.Pa. 1997. Complaint should never be dismissed for failure to state a claim unless court is convinced beyond a doubt that plaintiff can prove no set of facts to support claim which would permit recovery. Fed.Rules Civ.Proc. Rule 12(b)(6), 28 U.S.C.A.

Reilly v. Gould, Inc., 965 F.Supp. 588.

M.D.Pa. 1996. Dismissal for failure to state claim is not appropriate unless it clearly appears that no relief can be granted under any set of facts that could be proved consistently with plaintiff's allegations. Fed.Rules Civ.Proc. Rule 12(b)(6), 28 U.S.C.A.

McCoy v. Pennsylvania Power and Light Co., 933 F.Supp. 438.

M.D.Pa. 1995. In determining whether claim should be dismissed for failure to state claim upon which relief may be granted, court looks only to facts alleged in complaint and its attachments without reference to other parts of record; dismissal was not appropriate unless it clearly appears that no relief can be granted under any set of facts that could be proved consistently with plaintiff's allegations. Fed. Rules Civ.Proc.Rule 12(b)(6), 28 U.S.C.A.

Sharrow v. Bailey, 910 F.Supp. 187.

M.D.Pa. 1995. Complaint should not be dismissed for failure to state claim unless it appears beyond doubt that plaintiff can prove no set of facts in support of his claim which would entitle him to relief. Fed.Rules Civ.Proc. Rule 12(b)(6), 28 U.S.C.A.

Hetzel v. Swartz, 909 F.Supp. 261.

Test for reviewing motion to dismiss for failure to state claim is whether under any reasonable reading of pleadings, plaintiff may be entitled to relief; however, court is not required to accept legal conclusions either alleged or inferred from pleaded facts. Fed.Rules Civ.Proc.Rule 12(b)(6), 28 U.S.C.A.

Hetzel v. Swartz, 909 F.Supp. 261.

M.D.Pa. 1995. Motion to dismiss for failure to state claim must be denied unless plaintiff cannot prove any facts in support of claim which would entitle him to relief. Fed.Rules Civ.Proc.Rule 12(b)(6), 28 U.S.C.A.

Seneca Ins. Co. v. Commercial Transp., Inc., 906 F.Supp. 239.

M.D.Pa. 1995. Dismissal for failure to state claim is not appropriate unless it clearly appears that no relief can be granted under any set of facts that could be proved consistently with plaintiff's allegations. Fed.Rules Civ.Proc. Rule 12(b)(6), 28 U.S.C.A.

> Shoemaker v. City of Lock Haven, 906 F.Supp. 230.

M.D.Pa. 1995. Motion to dismiss for failure to state claim upon which relief can be granted must be denied unless plaintiff cannot prove any facts in support of claim which would entitle her to relief. Fed.Rules Civ.Proc.Rule 12(b)(6), 28 U.S.C.A.

> Verney v. Pennsylvania Turnpike Com'n, 881 F.Supp. 145.

M.D.Pa. 1995. Dismissal of action for failure to state a claim is not appropriate unless it clearly appears that no relief can be granted under any set of facts that could be proved consistently with plaintiff's allegations. Fed. Rules Civ.Proc.Rule 12(b)(6), 28 U.S.C.A.

> Teamsters, Chauffeurs, Warehousemen and Helpers, Local 764 v. Greenawalt, 880 F.Supp. 1076.

M.D.Pa. 1985. For purposes of motion to dismiss, all material allegations of complaint must be accepted as true and construed in light most favorable to party opposing that motion; complaint may be dismissed only if it appears that plaintiff cannot establish any set of facts in support of claim that would entitle him to relief.

> Truhe v. Rupell, 641 F.Supp. 57.

W.D.Pa. 1997. Defective complaint will not be dismissed for failure to state claim unless it appears to certainty that defect in complaint cannot be cured by amendment. Fed.Rules Civ.Proc.Rule 12(b)(6), 28 U.S.C.A.

> Andrea L. by Judith B. v. Children and Youth Services of Lawrence County, 987 F.Supp. 418.

W.D.Pa. 1997. Court must construe pro se complaint more liberally than complaint drafted by attorney, and may grant dismissal thereof only if it appears beyond doubt that plaintiff can prove no set of facts in support of his or her claim that would entitle him or her to relief.

> Smith v. National Collegiate Athletic Ass'n, 978 F.Supp. 213, affirmed in part, vacated in part 139 F.3d 180, certiorari granted 119 S.Ct. 31, certiorari denied 119 S.Ct. 170.

W.D.Pa. 1996. Proper inquiry on motion to dismiss for failure to state a claim is whether relief could be granted under any set of facts that could be proved consistent with allegations. Fed.Rules Civ.Proc.Rule 12(b)(6), 28 U.S.C.A.

> Thomeier v. Rhone-Poulenc, Inc., 928 F.Supp. 548.

W.D.Pa. 1995. Proper inquiry on motion to dismiss for failure to state claim is whether relief could be granted under any set of facts

that could be proved consistent with allegations. Fed.Rules Civ.Proc.Rule 12(b)(6), 28 U.S.C.A.

> Saint Vincent Health Center v. Shalala, 937 F.Supp. 496, affirmed 96 F.3d 1434.

W.D.Pa. 1995. Court should not dismiss complaint, especially in civil rights action, unless it appears beyond doubt that plaintiff can prove no set of facts in support of her claims which would entitle her to relief.

> Ford v. Johnson, 899 F.Supp. 227.

W.D.Pa. 1995. Court cannot dismiss for failure to state claim unless it clearly appears that no relief can be granted under any set of facts that could be proved consistent with allegations in complaint. Fed.Rules Civ.Proc.Rule 12(b)(6), 28 U.S.C.A.

> Forbes v. Reno, 893 F.Supp. 476, affirmed 91 F.3d 123.

W.D.Pa. 1994. District Court cannot grant a motion to dismiss for failure to state cause of action upon which relief can be granted, unless it appears beyond doubt that plaintiff can prove no set of facts in support of his claim which would entitle him to relief. Fed.Rules Civ.Proc. Rule 12(b)(6), 28 U.S.C.A.

> In re Phar-Mor, Inc. Securities Litigation, 900 F.Supp. 777.

W.D.Pa. 1985. A complaint should not be dismissed unless it appears that plaintiff could prove no set of facts in support of his claim which would entitle him to relief.

> Means v. Maharowski, 602 F.Supp. 71, vacated 780 F.2d 1015.

D.Puerto Rico 1996. Complaint of plaintiff who was appearing pro se would be read generously by district court, and dismissal would not be appropriate unless it could be said with assurance that under allegations of complaint, which would be held to less stringent standards than formal pleadings drafted by lawyers, it appeared beyond doubt that plaintiff could prove no set of facts in support of his claim that would entitle him to relief. 28 U.S.C.A. § 1915(d).

> Santini v. Gierbolini, 937 F.Supp. 130, affirmed 114 F.3d 1169.

D.Puerto Rico 1996. Motion to dismiss for failure to state claim upon which relief can be granted requires determination whether plaintiff can prove no set of facts in support of her claim which would entitle her to recovery. Fed. Rules Civ.Proc.Rule 12(b)(6), 28 U.S.C.A.

> Marrero Artache v. Autoridad de Energia Electrica, 924 F.Supp. 346.

D.Puerto Rico 1996. Although court will not credit bald assertions or mere specious allegations, it will not dismiss complaint for failure to state claim unless it appears beyond doubt that plaintiff can prove no set of facts in

support of his claim which would entitle him to relief. Fed.Rules Civ.Proc.Rule 12(b)(6), 28 U.S.C.A.

> Figueroa v. Fernandez, 921 F.Supp. 889.

D.Puerto Rico 1995. Complaint should not be dismissed for failure to state claim unless it appears beyond doubt that plaintiff can prove no set of facts in support of his claim which would entitle him to relief. Fed.Rules Civ.Proc. Rule 12(b)(6), 28 U.S.C.A.

> Bonilla v. Trebol Motors Corp., 913 F.Supp. 655.

D.R.I. 1998. Dismissal on ground that plaintiff failed to state claim upon which relief could be granted is appropriate only if it appears beyond doubt that plaintiff can prove no set of facts in support of his or her claim which would entitle him or her to relief. Fed.Rules Civ.Proc.Rule 12(b)(6), 28 U.S.C.A.

> Zahn v. Yucaipa Capital Fund, 218 B.R. 656.

D.R.I. 1995. Civil complaint seeking money damages should not be dismissed for failure to state actionable claim unless it plainly appears that plaintiffs can prove no set of facts that would entitle them to recover; question must be resolved in light most favorable to plaintiffs with any doubt resolved on their behalf. Fed.Rules Civ.Proc.Rule 12(b)(6), 28 U.S.C.A.

> Roma Const. Co., Inc. v. aRusso, 906 F.Supp. 78, reversed 96 F.3d 566, on remand 1998 WL 156708.

D.R.I. 1995. Motion to dismiss should not be granted unless it appears beyond doubt that plaintiff can prove no set of facts in support of his claim which would entitle him to relief. Fed.Rules Civ.Proc.Rule 12(b)(6), 28 U.S.C.A.

> Nguyen v. Lewis/Boyle, Inc., 899 F.Supp. 58.

D.R.I. 1995. Court should grant motion to dismiss for failure to state claim only if plaintiff cannot prove any set of facts in support of its claim that would entitle it to relief. Fed.Rules Civ.Proc.Rule 12(b)(6), 28 U.S.C.A.

> National Educ. Association-Rhode Island by Scigulinsky v. Retirement Bd. of Rhode Island Employees' Retirement System, 890 F.Supp. 1143.

D.R.I. 1995. Complaint should not be dismissed for failure to state claim unless it appears beyond doubt that plaintiff can prove no set of facts in support of his claim which would entitle him to relief. Fed.Rules Civ.Proc.Rule 12(b)(6), 28 U.S.C.A.

> Lieberman-Sack v. Harvard Community Health Plan of New England, Inc., 882 F.Supp. 249.

D.R.I. 1986. In ruling on a motion to dismiss for failure to state a claim upon which relief may be granted, the complaint should not be dismissed merely because plaintiff's allegations did not support the legal theory plaintiff intends to proceed on, in view of the fact that the court is under a duty to examine the complaint to determine if the allegations provide for relief on any possible theory. Fed.Rules Civ. Proc.Rule 8(a), (e)(1), 12(b)(1), 28 U.S.C.A.

> Patriarca v. F.B.I., 639 F.Supp. 1193.

E.D.Tenn. 1996. Motion to dismiss for failure to state claim upon which relief can be granted requires court to construe complaint in light most favorable to plaintiff, accept all of complaint's factual allegations as true, and determine whether plaintiff undoubtedly can prove no set of facts in support of claims that would entitle her to relief. Fed.Rules Civ.Proc. Rule 12(b)(6), 28 U.S.C.A.

> Caldwell v. Rowland, 932 F.Supp. 1018.

E.D.Tenn. 1996. Motion to dismiss for failure to state claim requires court to construe complaint in light most favorable to plaintiff, accept all complaint's factual allegations as true, and determine whether plaintiff undoubtedly can prove no set of facts in support of claims that would entitle relief. Fed.Rules Civ. Proc.Rule 12(b)(6), 28 U.S.C.A.

> Ketron v. Chattanooga-Hamilton County Hosp. Authority, 919 F.Supp. 280.

E.D.Tenn. 1996. Motion to dismiss for failure to state claim upon which relief can be granted requires court to construe complaint in light most favorable to plaintiff, accept all complaint's factual allegations as true, and determine whether plaintiff undoubtedly can prove no set of facts in support of claims that would entitle relief. Fed.Rules Civ.Proc.Rule 12(b)(6), 28 U.S.C.A.

> Sharp v. Rainey, 910 F.Supp. 394.

E.D.Tenn. 1995. Motion to dismiss requires trial court to construe complaint in light most favorable to plaintiff, accept all of complaint's factual allegations as true, and to determine whether plaintiff undoubtedly can prove no set of facts in support of claims that would entitle relief. Fed.Rules Civ.Proc.Rule 12(b)(6), 28 U.S.C.A.

> Smith v. Grumman-Olsen Corp., 913 F.Supp. 1077.

E.D.Tenn. 1995. Motion to dismiss for failure to state a claim upon which relief can be granted requires court to construe complaint in light most favorable to plaintiff, accept all complaint's factual allegations as true, and determine whether plaintiff undoubtedly can prove no set of facts in support of claims that would entitle relief. Fed.Rules Civ.Proc.Rule 12(b)(6), 28 U.S.C.A.

> Frizzell v. Southwest Motor Freight, Inc., 906 F.Supp. 441.

E.D.Tenn. 1995. Motion to dismiss for failure to state claim requires court to construe complaint in light most favorable to plaintiff, accept all factual allegations as true, and determine whether plaintiff undoubtedly can prove no set of facts in support of his claims that would entitle him to relief. Fed.Rules Civ.Proc. Rule 12(b)(6), 28 U.S.C.A.

> Reynolds v. Massachusetts Cas. Ins. Co., 900 F.Supp. 915, reversed 113 F.3d 1450.

M.D.Tenn. 1997. District court is without authority to dismiss claims unless it can be demonstrated beyond doubt that plaintiff can prove no set of facts that would entitle him to relief.

> Southwest Williamson County Community Ass'n v. Slater, 976 F.Supp. 1119.

M.D.Tenn. 1996. Standard for reviewing motion to dismiss for failure to state claim is that factual allegations in complaint must be regarded as true, and claim should not be dismissed unless it appears beyond doubt that plaintiff can prove no set of facts in support of his claim which would entitle him to relief. Fed.Rules Civ.Proc.Rule 12(b)(6), 28 U.S.C.A.

> Craft v. Vanderbilt University, 940 F.Supp. 1185.

M.D.Tenn. 1996. On motion to dismiss, district court must construe complaint in light most favorable to plaintiff, accept all factual allegations as true, and determine whether plaintiff undoubtedly can prove no set of facts in support of claims that would entitle him or her to relief. Fed.Rules Civ.Proc.Rule 12(b)(6), 28 U.S.C.A.

> Rawls v. Sundquist, 929 F.Supp. 284, affirmed 113 F.3d 1235.

W.D.Tenn. 1996. Motion to dismiss for failure to state a claim upon which relief can be granted is appropriate only if it is clear that no relief could be granted under any set of facts that could be proved consistent with allegations. Fed.Rules Civ.Proc.Rule 12(b)(6), 28 U.S.C.A.

> Burnett v. Tyco Corp., 932 F.Supp. 1039.

W.D.Tenn. 1995. Motion to dismiss for failure to state claim is appropriate only if it is clear that no relief could be granted under any set of facts that could be proved consistent with the allegations. Fed.Rules Civ.Proc.Rule 12(b)(6), 28 U.S.C.A.

> Scarborough v. Brown Group, Inc., 935 F.Supp. 954.

W.D.Tenn. 1995. When plaintiff completely fails to allege any action by defendant, it necessarily appears beyond doubt that plaintiff

can prove no set of facts which would entitle him or her to relief.

> McKinney v. Compton, 888 F.Supp. 75.

E.D.Tex. 1998. Complaint may be dismissed for failure to state a claim if it appears beyond doubt that a plaintiff can prove no set of facts in support of his claim that would entitle him to relief. Fed.Rules Civ.Proc.Rule 12(b)(6), 28 U.S.C.A.

> Spicer v. Collins, 9 F.Supp.2d 673.

E.D.Tex. 1995. Complaint should not be dismissed for failure to state claim unless it appears beyond doubt that plaintiff can prove no set of facts in support of his claim that would entitle him to relief. Fed.Rules Civ.Proc.Rule 12(b)(6), 28 U.S.C.A.

> Cowen v. Mobil Oil Corp., 901 F.Supp. 1204.

E.D.Tex. 1995. Court considering motion to dismiss complaint for failure to state claim must focus on two central principles: first is that complaint should be liberally construed in favor of plaintiff with all well-pleaded facts in complaint taken as true, and second is that complaint should not be dismissed for failure to state claim unless it appears beyond doubt that plaintiff can prove no set of facts in support of his claim that would entitle him to relief. Fed. Rules Civ.Proc.Rule 12(b)(6), 28 U.S.C.A.

> U.S. v. American Petrofina Pipeline Co., 897 F.Supp. 304.

E.D.Tex. 1995. Complaint should not be dismissed for failure to state a claim unless it appears beyond a doubt that plaintiffs can prove no set of facts in support of claims which would entitle them to relief. Fed.Rules Civ.Proc.Rule 12(b)(6), 28 U.S.C.A.

> Murphy v. Wal-Mart Associates' Group Health Plan, 882 F.Supp. 95.

N.D.Tex. 1998. Dismissal for failure to state a claim is not appropriate unless it appears beyond a doubt that the plaintiff can prove no set of facts in support of his claim which would entitle him to relief. Fed.Rules Civ.Proc.Rule 12(b)(6), 28 U.S.C.A.

> Burlington Northern & Santa Fe Ry. Co. v. Consolidated Fibers, Inc., 7 F.Supp.2d 822.

N.D.Tex. 1996. Complaint cannot be dismissed for failure to state claim unless it appears beyond doubt that plaintiff can prove no set of facts in support of his claim which would entitle him to relief.

> Jewel Recovery, L.P. v. Gordon, 196 B.R. 348.

N.D.Tex. 1996. Complaint should not be dismissed for failure to state claim unless it appears beyond doubt that plaintiff can prove no set of facts that would entitle it to relief. Fed.Rules Civ.Proc.Rule 12(b)(6), 28 U.S.C.A.

> Roberts v. Dayton Hudson Corp., 914 F.Supp. 1421.

N.D.Tex. 1995. Motion to dismiss for failure to state claim should be granted only if it appears beyond doubt that plaintiff could prove no set of facts in support of his claim that would entitle him to relief. Fed.Rules Civ.Proc.Rule 12(b)(6), 28 U.S.C.A.

> Fuller v. Rich, 925 F.Supp. 459, affirmed in part 91 F.3d 138.

N.D.Tex. 1995. On motion to dismiss for failure to state a claim, district court must decide whether material facts alleged would entitle plaintiff to offer evidence regarding legal remedy it requests; unless answer is unequivocally no, motion must be denied. Fed.Rules Civ.Proc.Rule 12(b)(6), 28 U.S.C.A.

> Cook v. Fidelity Investments, 908 F.Supp. 438.

Complaint should not be dismissed for failure to state a claim unless it appears beyond doubt that plaintiff can prove no set of facts that would entitle it to relief. Fed.Rules Civ.Proc. Rule 12(b)(6), 28 U.S.C.A.

> Cook v. Fidelity Investments, 908 F.Supp. 438.

N.D.Tex. 1995. Motion to dismiss for failure to state claim upon which relief can be granted should only be granted when plaintiff could not prove any set of facts, under any reasonable reading of complaint, which would entitle him to relief. Fed.Rules Civ.Proc.Rule 12(b)(6), 28 U.S.C.A.

> U.S. v. Bantau, 907 F.Supp. 988.

N.D.Tex. 1983. U.S. v. American Airlines, Inc., 570 F.Supp. 654, reversed 743 F.2d 1114, rehearing denied 756 F.2d 882, certiorari dismissed 106 S.Ct. 420, 474 U.S. 1001, 88 L.Ed.2d 370.

S.D.Tex. 1997. Complaint cannot be dismissed for failure to state a claim unless it appears certain that plaintiff cannot prove any set of facts in support of its claim that would entitle it to relief. Fed.Rules Civ.Proc.Rule 12(b)(6), 28 U.S.C.A.

> Noorian v. Pie Mut. Ins. Co., 978 F.Supp. 690.

S.D.Tex. 1996. Claim should not be dismissed unless it appears beyond doubt that plaintiff can prove no set of facts in support of his claim which would entitle him to relief. Fed.Rules Civ.Proc.Rule 12(b)(6), 28 U.S.C.A.

> U.S. ex rel. James M. Thompson v. Columbia/HCA Healthcare Corp., 938 F.Supp. 399, affirmed in part, vacated in part 125 F.3d 899, rehearing denied.

S.D.Tex. 1996. On motion to dismiss for failure to state a claim upon which relief can be granted, court may not look beyond four corners of plaintiff's pleadings and, thus, motion must be denied unless it appears to a certainty that plaintiff can prove no set of facts in support of his claim that would entitle him to relief. Fed.Rules Civ.Proc.Rule 12(b)(6), 28 U.S.C.A.

> Jenkins v. Board of Educ. of Houston Independent School Dist., 937 F.Supp. 608.

S.D.Tex. 1996. Motion to dismiss for failure to state claim should not be granted unless it appears beyond doubt that plaintiff can prove no set of facts in support of his claim which would entitle him to relief. Fed.Rules Civ.Proc. Rule 12(b)(6), 28 U.S.C.A.

> Callis v. Sellars, 931 F.Supp. 504.

S.D.Tex. 1996. If district court considers pleadings exclusively on motion to dismiss for failure to state claim upon which relief can be granted, motion is granted only if it appears that no state of facts could be proven to support cause of action. Fed.Rules Civ.Proc.Rule 12(b)(6), 28 U.S.C.A.

> Amoco Chemical Co. v. Tex Tin Corp., 925 F.Supp. 1192.

S.D.Tex. 1996. Motion to dismiss for failure to state claim must be denied unless it appears to a certainty that plaintiff can prove no set of facts in support of his claim that would entitle him to relief. Fed.Rules Civ.Proc.Rule 12(b)(6), 28 U.S.C.A.

> Jolly v. Klein, 923 F.Supp. 931.

S.D.Tex. 1996. Motion to dismiss for failure to state claim should be granted only when it appears without doubt that plaintiff can prove no set of facts in support of his or her claims that would entitle him or her to relief. Fed. Rules Civ.Proc.Rule 12(b)(6), 28 U.S.C.A.

> Youngblood v. City of Galveston, Tex., 920 F.Supp. 103.

S.D.Tex. 1995. Motion to dismiss for failure to state claim must be denied unless it appears to a certainty that plaintiff can prove no set of facts in support of her claim that would entitle her to relief. Fed.Rules Civ.Proc.Rule 12(b)(6), 28 U.S.C.A.

> Patton v. United Parcel Service, Inc., 910 F.Supp. 1250.

S.D.Tex. 1995. Motion to dismiss must be denied unless it appears to certainty that plaintiff can prove no set of facts that would entitle her to relief. Fed.Rules Civ.Proc.Rule 12(b)(6), 28 U.S.C.A.

> Bonton v. Archer Chrysler Plymouth, Inc., 889 F.Supp. 995.

S.D.Tex. 1995. Motion to dismiss for failure to state claim on which relief may be granted will be granted only if it appears that plaintiff would not be entitled to relief under any set of facts that could be proven consistent will allegations. Fed.Rules Civ.Proc.Rule 12(b)(6), 28 U.S.C.A.

Matta v. May, 888 F.Supp. 808.

D.Utah 1996. If as matter of law it is clear that no relief could be granted under any set of facts that could be proved consistent with the allegations, claim must be dismissed, without regard to whether it is based on outlandish legal theory or on close but ultimately unavailable one. Fed.Rules Civ.Proc.Rule 12(b)(6), 28 U.S.C.A.

Tremelling v. Ogio Intern., Inc., 919 F.Supp. 392.

D.Utah 1996. Dismissal of a complaint for failure to state a claim is proper if it is clear that plaintiff can prove no set of facts that would entitle it to relief. Fed.Rules Civ.Proc. Rule 12(b)(6), 28 U.S.C.A.

Gossner Foods, Inc. v. Environmental Protection Agency, 918 F.Supp. 359.

D.Utah 1995. When motion to dismiss is filed, burden is on movant to show that non-movant can prove no set of facts in support of his claim which would entitle him to relief. Fed.Rules Civ.Proc.Rule 12(b), 28 U.S.C.A.

Lambertsen v. Utah Dept. of Corrections, 922 F.Supp. 533, affirmed 79 F.3d 1024.

D.Vt. 1996. Complaint must not be dismissed for failure to state claim unless it appears beyond doubt that plaintiff can prove no set of facts in support of his claim which would entitle him to relief. Fed.Rules Civ.Proc.Rule 12(b)(6), 28 U.S.C.A.

Bentley v. Northshore Development, Inc., 935 F.Supp. 500.

D.Vt. 1995. Standard for dismissal for failure to state claim requires that it be apparent that plaintiff is unable to prove any set of facts which would entitle her to relief. Fed. Rules Civ.Proc. Rule 12(b)(6), 28 U.S.C.A.

Goodstein v. Bombardier Capital, Inc., 889 F.Supp. 760, on reconsideration 167 F.R.D. 662.

E.D.Va. 1997. Action should not be dismissed for failure to state claim, unless it appears to a certainty that plaintiff can prove no facts in support of his claim which would entitle him to relief. Fed.Rules Civ.Proc.Rule 12(b)(6), 28 U.S.C.A..

Huntingdon Life Sciences, Inc. v. Rokke, 986 F.Supp. 982.

E.D.Va. 1997. Pro se complaint must survive motion to dismiss for failure to state claim unless it appears beyond doubt that plaintiff can prove no set of facts in support of his or her

claim which would entitle him or her to relief. Fed.Rules Civ.Proc.Rule 12(b)(6), 28 U.S.C.A.

Laremont-Lopez v. Southeastern Tidewater Opportunity Center, 968 F.Supp. 1075.

E.D.Va. 1997. Pro se complaint, no matter how unartfully pleaded, must survive motion to dismiss for failure to state a claim unless it appears beyond doubt that plaintiff can prove no set of facts in support of his claim which would entitle him to relief. Fed.Rules Civ.Proc. Rule 12(b)(6), 28 U.S.C.A.

Sculthorpe v. Virginia Retirement System, 952 F.Supp. 307.

E.D.Va. 1996. Motion to dismiss for failure to state claim should only be granted if it appears beyond doubt that plaintiff can prove no set of facts in support of his or her claim which would entitle him or her to relief. Fed. Rules Civ.Proc.Rule 12(b)(6), 28 U.S.C.A.

Sutter v. First Union Nat. Bank of Virginia, Inc., 932 F.Supp. 753.

E.D.Va. 1996. Motion to dismiss for failure to state claim should only be granted if it appears beyond doubt that plaintiff can prove no set of facts in support of his claim which would entitle him to relief. Fed.Rules Civ.Proc. Rule 12(b)(6), 28 U.S.C.A.

Reynolds and Reynolds Co. v. Hardee, 932 F.Supp. 149, affirmed 133 F.3d 916.

E.D.Va. 1996. Complaint should not be dismissed on motion to dismiss for failure to state claim upon which relief can be granted unless it appears beyond doubt that plaintiffs can prove no set of facts that would entitle them to relief. Fed.Rules Civ.Proc.Rule 12(b)(6), 28 U.S.C.A.

Mazur v. Woodson, 932 F.Supp. 144.

Court should not dismiss complaint on motion to dismiss for failure to state claim upon which relief can be granted even if chance of recovery on basis of pleadings appears remote. Fed.Rules Civ.Proc.Rule 12(b)(6), 28 U.S.C.A.

Mazur v. Woodson, 932 F.Supp. 144.

E.D.Va. 1996. Complaint should not be dismissed for failure to state a claim unless it appears beyond doubt that plaintiff can prove no set of facts that would entitle it to relief. Fed.Rules Civ.Proc.Rule 12(b)(6), 28 U.S.C.A.

Kentwood Ltd. v. U.S., 930 F.Supp. 227, vacated 957 F.Supp. 799.

Court should not dismiss complaint for failure to state a claim even if chance of recovery on basis of pleadings appears remote. Fed. Rules Civ.Proc.Rule 12(b)(6), 28 U.S.C.A.

Kentwood Ltd. v. U.S., 930 F.Supp. 227, vacated 957 F.Supp. 799.

E.D.Va. 1996. Motion to dismiss complaint for failure to state a claim should be denied unless it appears beyond doubt that plaintiff can prove no set of facts in support of his claim that would entitle him to relief. Fed. Rules Civ.Proc.Rule 12(b)(6), 28 U.S.C.A.

Oram v. Dalton, 927 F.Supp. 180.

E.D.Va. 1996. Claim should not be dismissed for failure to state a claim unless it appears to a certainty that plaintiff can prove no facts in support of claims that would entitle plaintiff to relief. Fed.Rules Civ.Proc.Rule 12(b)(6), 28 U.S.C.A.

International Longshoremen's Ass'n, S.S. Clerks Local 1624, AFL-CIO v. Virginia Intern. Terminals, Inc., 914 F.Supp. 1335.

Court should not dismiss complaint for failure to state a claim even if it appears on face of pleadings that chance of recovery is remote and unlikely. Fed.Rules Civ.Proc.Rule 12(b)(6), 28 U.S.C.A.

International Longshoremen's Ass'n, S.S. Clerks Local 1624, AFL-CIO v. Virginia Intern. Terminals, Inc., 914 F.Supp. 1335.

E.D.Va. 1996. Motion to dismiss for failure to state claim for relief should not be granted unless it appears to a certainty that plaintiff would be entitled to no relief under any state of facts that could be proved in support of his claim. Fed.Rules Civ.Proc.Rule 12(b)(6), 28 U.S.C.A.

Lewin v. Medical College of Hampton Roads, 910 F.Supp. 1161, affirmed 131 F.3d 135.

E.D.Va. 1996. Case should not be dismissed for failure to state claim unless it appears to a certainty that plaintiff can prove no set of facts in support of claims which would entitle him to relief. Fed.Rules Civ.Proc.Rule 12(b)(6), 28 U.S.C.A.

Materson v. Stokes, 166 F.R.D. 368.

E.D.Va. 1995. Motions to dismiss are to be granted sparingly and should be denied unless plaintiff can prove no set of facts to support claim and entitle plaintiff to relief. Fed.Rules Civ.Proc.Rule 12(b)(6), 28 U.S.C.A.

Williams v. Enterprise Leasing Co. of Norfolk/Richmond, 911 F.Supp. 988.

E.D.Va. 1995. Motion to dismiss for failure to state claim for relief should not be granted unless it appears to a certainty that plaintiff would be entitled to no relief under any state of facts which could be proved in support of his claim. Fed.Rules Civ.Proc.Rule 12(b)(6), 28 U.S.C.A.

Samuel v. Rose's Stores, Inc., 907 F.Supp. 159.

E.D.Va. 1995. District court will not dismiss any complaint for failure to state a claim

unless it appears beyond a doubt that plaintiff could not recover under any set of facts which could be proven. Fed.Rules Civ.Proc.Rule 12(b)(6), 28 U.S.C.A.

Keegan v. Dalton, 899 F.Supp. 1503.

E.D.Va. 1995. Court should not dismiss claim for failure to state claim upon which relief can be granted unless it appears to certainty that plaintiff can prove no set of facts in support of his claim which would entitle him to relief. Fed.Rules Civ.Proc.Rule 12(b)(6), 28 U.S.C.A.

Davis v. Hudgins, 896 F.Supp. 561, affirmed 87 F.3d 1308, certiorari denied 117 S.Ct. 1440, 137 L.Ed.2d 546.

E.D.Va. 1995. Claim should not be dismissed for failing to state claim upon which relief may be granted unless it appears to certainty that plaintiff can prove no set of facts in support of claim which would entitle plaintiff to relief. Fed.Rules Civ.Proc.Rule 12(b)(6), 28 U.S.C.A.

Kline v. Nationsbank of Virginia, N.A., 886 F.Supp. 1285.

E.D.Va. 1995. On motion to dismiss for failure to state claim on which relief can be granted, allegations of complaint are to be liberally construed and motion granted only if it appears beyond doubt that plaintiff can prove no set of facts in support of claim which would entitle him to relief. Fed.Rules Civ.Proc.Rule 12(b)(6), 28 U.S.C.A.

Westmoreland v. Brown, 883 F.Supp. 67.

E.D.Va. 1995. On motion to dismiss for failure to state a claim, claim should not be dismissed unless it appears to a certainty that plaintiff can prove no facts in support of claims which would entitle him to relief. Fed.Rules Civ.Proc.Rule 12(b)(6), 28 U.S.C.A.

Lane v. David P. Jacobson & Co., Ltd., 880 F.Supp. 1091.

E.D.Va. 1995. Standard approach to motion to dismiss requires court to presume that all factual allegations in complaint are true, to make all reasonable inferences in favor of nonmoving party, and not to dismiss any count unless it appears beyond doubt that recovery would be impossible under any set of facts which could be proven. Fed.Rules Civ.Proc. Rule 12(b)(6), 28 U.S.C.A.

Gasner v. County of Dinwiddie, 162 F.R.D. 280.

W.D.Va. 1996. Dismissals for failure to state a claim are generally disfavored and are granted only when it appears beyond doubt that plaintiff can prove no set of facts in support of claim which would entitle plaintiff to relief. Fed.Rules Civ.Proc.Rule 12(b)(6), 28 U.S.C.A.

> Brzonkala v. Virginia Polytechnic and State University, 935 F.Supp. 779, reversed 132 F.3d 949, rehearing granted, opinion vacated.

W.D.Va. 1996. Motion to dismiss for failure to state claim upon which relief may be granted should be denied unless it is clear as matter of law that, after accepting facts alleged in complaint to be true and construing allegations in light most favorable to plaintiff, court should not grant relief under any set of facts that petitioner could prove consistent with his allegations. Fed.Rules Civ.Proc.Rule 12(b)(6), 28 U.S.C.A.

> McAlpin v. Leeds & Northrup, Co., 912 F.Supp. 207.

W.D.Va. 1995. Complaint should not be dismissed unless it appears beyond doubt that plaintiff can prove no set of facts in support of his claim which would entitle him to relief.

> Federal Election Com'n v. Christian Action Network, 894 F.Supp. 946, affirmed 92 F.3d 1178.

N.D.W.Va. 1997. Court reviewing motion to dismiss for failure to state claim must accept plaintiff's factual allegations as true and should grant motion only when these allegations clearly demonstrate that plaintiff does not have claim. Fed.Rules Civ.Proc.Rule 12(b)(6), 28 U.S.C.A.

> Henegar v. Sears, Roebuck and Co., 965 F.Supp. 833.

N.D.W.Va. 1996. In considering motion to dismiss, court must accept as true all well pleaded factual allegations in complaint and must draw all reasonable inferences in favor of plaintiff; complaint should not be dismissed unless it appears to a certainty that there is no set of facts which could be proved to support claim or which would entitle plaintiff to relief. Fed.Rules Civ.Proc.Rule 12(b)(6), 28 U.S.C.A.

> Roe v. County Com'n of Monongalia County, 926 F.Supp. 74.

N.D.W.Va. 1996. Dismissal for failure to state claim upon which relief may be granted is proper when, assuming facts alleged in complaint are true and construing allegations in light most favorable to plaintiff, it is clear as matter of law that no relief can be granted under any set of facts that could be proved consistent with allegations of complaint. Fed. Rules Civ.Proc.Rule 12(b)(6), 28 U.S.C.A.

> Norris v. Detrick, 918 F.Supp. 977, affirmed 108 F.3d 1373.

Unartfully pled allegations will not be dismissed for failure to state claim on which relief may be granted unless it is beyond doubt that plaintiff can prove no set of facts entitling plaintiff to relief. Fed.Rules Civ.Proc.Rule 12(b)(6), 28 U.S.C.A.

> Norris v. Detrick, 918 F.Supp. 977, affirmed 108 F.3d 1373.

N.D.W.Va. 1995. Dismissal of complaint for failure to state claim is appropriate only if it appears to be a certainty that plaintiff would be entitled to no relief under any state of facts which could be proven in support of its claim. Fed.Rules Civ.Proc.Rule 12(b)(6), 28 U.S.C.A.

> Booth v. Old Nat. Bank, 900 F.Supp. 836.

Dismissal for failure to state claim is granted only in cases in which allegations raised in the complaint clearly demonstrate that plaintiff does not have claim and that no set of facts would support plaintiff's claim. Fed.Rules Civ. Proc.Rule 12(b)(6), 28 U.S.C.A.

> Booth v. Old Nat. Bank, 900 F.Supp. 836.

S.D.W.Va. 1995. In general, motion to dismiss for failure to state claim should not be granted unless it appears certain that plaintiff can prove no set of facts which would support its claim and would entitle it to relief. Fed. Rules Civ.Proc.Rule 12(b)(6), 28 U.S.C.A.

> Hurt v. U.S. (C.I.R.), 889 F.Supp. 248.

E.D.Wis. 1996. Complaint should be dismissed for failure to state claim upon which relief can be granted only if it appears beyond doubt that plaintiff could prove no set of facts entitling him to relief. Fed.Rules Civ.Proc.Rule 12(b)(6), 28 U.S.C.A.

> Metal Processing Co., Inc. v. Amoco Oil Co., 926 F.Supp. 828.

E.D.Wis. 1995. District court must deny motion to dismiss for failure to state claim upon which relief can be granted unless it appears beyond doubt that plaintiff is unable to prove any set of facts which would entitle him or her to relief. Fed.Rules Civ.Proc.Rule 12(b)(6), 28 U.S.C.A.

> Mann v. Hanil Bank, 900 F.Supp. 1077.

E.D.Wis. 1995. Complaint should not be dismissed for failure to state claim upon which relief can be granted unless it is beyond doubt that plaintiff can prove no set of facts to support claim. Fed.Rules Civ.Proc.Rule 12(b)(6), 28 U.S.C.A.

> Oak Ridge Care Center, Inc. v. Racine County, Wis., 896 F.Supp. 867.

E.D.Wis. 1995. Court will grant motion to dismiss for failure to state claim upon which relief can be granted if it is clear that plaintiff would not be entitled to relief even if complaint's factual allegations were proven. Fed. Rules Civ.Proc.Rule 12(b)(6), 28 U.S.C.A.

> O'Patka v. Menasha Corp., 878 F.Supp. 1202.

E.D.Wis. 1994. District court grants motion to dismiss for failure to state claim only if it is clear that plaintiff would not be entitled to relief even if complaint's factual allegations, and any facts consistent with and reasonably inferred from pleadings, were true. Fed.Rules Civ.Proc.Rule 12(b)(6), 28 U.S.C.A.

General Motors Corp. v. Johnson Matthey Inc., 855 F.Supp. 1005.

D.Wyo. 1996. Dismissal on motion to dismiss for failure to state a claim, is appropriate only if it appears beyond doubt that the plaintiff can prove no set of facts in support of his claim which would entitle him to relief. Fed.Rules Civ.Proc.Rule 12(b)(6), 28 U.S.C.A.

Marshall v. Board of County Com'rs for Johnson County, Wyo., 912 F.Supp. 1456.

D.Wyo. 1994. Dismissal for failure to state claim is appropriate only if plaintiff can prove no set of facts that would entitle him or her to relief. Fed.Rules Civ.Proc.Rule 12(b)(6), 28 U.S.C.A.

Gressley v. Deutsch, 890 F.Supp. 1474.

9th Cir.BAP (Cal.) 1994. Complaint should not be dismissed for failure to state claim upon which relief may be granted unless it appears beyond doubt that plaintiff can prove no set of facts in support of his claim which would entitle him to relief.

In re Aboukhater, 165 B.R. 904.

Bkrtcy.D.Colo. 1995. Dismissal is inappropriate unless plaintiff can prove no set of facts in support of his claims to entitle him to relief.

In re Hamilton, 186 B.R. 991.

Bkrtcy.D.Conn. 1995. Court should dismiss for failure to state claim upon which relief can be granted only if it appears beyond doubt that plaintiff can prove no set of facts in support of its claim that would entitle it to relief. Fed. Rules Civ.Proc.Rule 12(b)(6), 28 U.S.C.A.; Fed. Rules Bankr.Proc.Rule 7012, 11 U.S.C.A.

In re Carter Hill Associates, 188 B.R. 5.

Bkrtcy.D.Conn. 1995. Pleading should not be dismissed for failure to state claim upon which relief can be granted unless it appears beyond doubt that pleader can prove no set of facts in support of his or her claim which would entitle him or her to relief. Fed.Rules Bankr. Proc.Rule 7012(b), 11 U.S.C.A.; Fed.Rules Civ. Proc.Rule 12(b)(6), 28 U.S.C.A.

In re Thirteen Chapter 7 Cases of Former Trustee Germain, 182 B.R. 375.

Bkrtcy.D.Conn. 1995. Motion to dismiss standard requires court to accept material facts alleged in complaint as true, not to dismiss unless it appears beyond doubt that plaintiff can prove no set of facts in support of claim which would entitle plaintiff to relief, and to draw all inferences in light most favorable to plaintiff. Fed.Rules Civ.Proc.Rule 12(b)(6), 28 U.S.C.A.

In re Austin Driveway Services, Inc., 179 B.R. 390.

Bkrtcy.M.D.Fla. 1996. Ordinarily, complaint should not be dismissed with prejudice unless it is abundantly clear that defect in pleading is not curable and that plaintiff cannot, under any theory of law, sustain viable claim for which relief can be granted.

In re Hillsborough Holdings Corp., 203 B.R. 1000.

Bkrtcy.M.D.Fla. 1996. Complaint should not be dismissed unless it is beyond peradventure that under no circumstances can plaintiff prevail, even if all facts pled are established with requisite degree of proof.

In re Hollingsworth, 198 B.R. 832.

Bkrtcy.M.D.Fla. 1995. Motion to dismiss for failure to state claim upon which relief can be granted should be denied, unless it appears without doubt that plaintiff cannot prove set of facts in support of claim for which relief could be granted. Fed.Rules Civ.Proc.Rule 12(b)(6), 28 U.S.C.A.

In re Ricketson, 190 B.R. 684.

Bkrtcy.N.D.Ga. 1995. Complaint of pro se litigant will warrant dismissal whenever it is clear that litigant could not recover under any conceivable version of facts.

Matter of Swift, 185 B.R. 963.

Bkrtcy.N.D.Ill. 1996. To prevail on motion to dismiss, it must appear from pleadings that plaintiff can prove no set of facts that would entitle plaintiff to relief. Fed.Rules Civ. Proc.Rule 12(b), 28 U.S.C.A.

In re Lakeside Community Hosp., 191 B.R. 122.

Bkrtcy.N.D.Ill. 1996. For defendant to prevail on motion to dismiss for failure to state claim, it must appear from the pleadings that plaintiff can prove no set of facts in support of its claims which would entitle it to relief. Fed. Rules Civ.Proc.Rule 12(b)(6), 28 U.S.C.A.

In re Spiers Graff Spiers, 190 B.R. 1001.

Bkrtcy.N.D.Ill. 1984. If it appears beyond doubt that plaintiff can prove no set of facts in support of his claim, motion to dismiss for failure to state a claim must be granted.

In re Nantz, 44 B.R. 543.

Bkrtcy.N.D.Ill. 1984. In re Martin Grinding & Mach. Works, Inc., 42 B.R. 888, appeal decided 793 F.2d 592.

Bkrtcy.S.D.Ill. 1995. Motion to dismiss for failure to state claim can be granted only if it appears beyond doubt that plaintiff can prove no set of facts entitling him to relief. Fed.Rules Civ.Proc.Rule 12(b)(6), 28 U.S.C.A.

In re Knapp, 179 B.R. 106.

Bkrtcy.D.Kan. 1995. To prevail on motion to dismiss for failure to state claim, movant must demonstrate beyond doubt that there is no set of facts in support of plaintiff's theory of recovery that would entitle plaintiff to relief. Fed.Rules Civ.Proc.Rule 12(b)(6), 28 U.S.C.A.

In re American Freight System, Inc., 179 B.R. 952.

Bkrtcy.D.Mass. 1995. On motion to dismiss for failure to state claim upon which relief can be granted, plaintiff must be given the benefit of all reasonable inferences, and motion must be denied unless it appears that plaintiff can prove no set of facts in support of his claims that would entitle him to relief sought. Fed. Rules Civ.Proc.Rule 12(b)(6), 28 U.S.C.A.

In re Boston Investors Group, L.P., 182 B.R. 637.

Bkrtcy.D.N.H. 1996. In deciding motion to dismiss, bankruptcy court must accept allegations of complaint as true, and if, under any theory, allegations are sufficient to state cause of action in accordance with law, motion must be denied. Fed.Rules Civ.Proc.Rule 12(b)(6), 28 U.S.C.A.; Fed.Rules Bankr.Proc.Rule 7012(b), 11 U.S.C.A.

In re Dynaco Corp., 200 B.R. 750.

Bkrtcy.D.N.H. 1995. To grant motion for failure to state claim upon which relief can be granted, court must accept the allegations of the complaint as true and if, under any theory, the allegations are sufficient to state cause of action in accordance with the law, court must deny the motion to dismiss. Fed.Rules Civ.Proc.Rule 12(b)(6), 28 U.S.C.A.

In re Smith, 189 B.R. 240.

Bkrtcy.D.N.J. 1995. Test for determining when to dismiss for failure to state claim is whether, under any reasonable reading of pleadings, plaintiff may be entitled to relief. Fed.Rules Civ.Proc.Rule 12(b)(6), 28 U.S.C.A.

In re MacGregor Sporting Goods, Inc., 199 B.R. 502.

Movants are entitled to dismissal of complaint for failure to state claim if plaintiff can prove no set of facts in support of their claim that would entitle them to relief. Fed.Rules Civ.Proc.Rule 12(b)(6), 28 U.S.C.A.

In re MacGregor Sporting Goods, Inc., 199 B.R. 502.

Bkrtcy.E.D.N.Y. 1995. Court should deny motion to dismiss for failure to state claim unless it appears beyond doubt that plaintiff can prove no set of facts in support of his claim which would entitle him to relief. Fed.Rules Civ.Proc.Rule 12(b)(6), 28 U.S.C.A.

In re Jennings, 188 B.R. 110.

Complaint may be dismissed for failure to state cause of action only when plaintiff would not be entitled to any type of relief, even if he were to prevail on merits of his factual contentions. Fed.Rules Civ.Proc.Rule 12(b)(6), 28 U.S.C.A.

In re Jennings, 188 B.R. 110.

Bkrtcy.S.D.N.Y. 1996. Motion to dismiss for failure to state claim can be granted only where it appears certain that no set of facts could be proven at trial which would entitle plaintiff to relief. Fed.Rules Civ.Proc.Rule 12(b)(6), 28 U.S.C.A.

In re Bradlees Stores, Inc., 194 B.R. 555, appeal dismissed 210 B.R. 506.

Bkrtcy.S.D.N.Y. 1996. Motion to dismiss for failure to state claim can be granted only where it appears certain that no set of facts could be proven at trial which would entitle plaintiff to relief. Fed.Rules Civ.Proc.Rule 12(b)(6), 28 U.S.C.A.

In re 455 CPW Associates, 192 B.R. 85.

Bkrtcy.S.D.N.Y. 1996. Motion to dismiss for failure to state claim is granted only if no set of facts can be established to entitle plaintiff to relief. Rules Bankr.Proc.Rule 7012(b), 11 U.S.C.A.; Fed.Rules Civ.Proc.Rule 12(b)(6), 28 U.S.C.A.

In re 19 Court Street Associates, LLC, 190 B.R. 983.

Bkrtcy.S.D.N.Y. 1995. Court should not dismiss for failure to state claim on which relief can be granted unless it appears beyond doubt that plaintiff can prove no set of facts in support of his claim which would entitle him to relief. Fed.Rules Civ.Proc.Rule 12(b)(6), 28 U.S.C.A.

In re Mosello, 190 B.R. 165, affirmed 193 B.R. 147, affirmed 104 F.3d 352.

Bkrtcy.S.D.N.Y. 1995. Motion to dismiss for failure to state claim should not be granted unless it appears with certainty that no set of facts could be established at trial that would entitle plaintiff to any relief. Fed.Rules Civ. Proc.Rule 12(b)(6), 28 U.S.C.A.

In re Houbigant, Inc., 188 B.R. 347, corrected, reargument denied 190 B.R. 185, as amended.

Bkrtcy.S.D.N.Y. 1995. Motion to dismiss for failure to state a claim must be granted when it appears with certainty that no set of facts could be established at trial which would entitle plaintiff to any relief. Fed.Rules Civ. Proc.Rule 12(b)(6), 28 U.S.C.A.

In re Casey, 181 B.R. 763.

Bkrtcy.S.D.N.Y. 1995. Motion to dismiss for failure to state claim should be granted only if it appears with certainty that no set of facts can be established at trial which would entitle plaintiff to any relief. Fed.Rules Civ.Proc.Rule 12(b)(6), 28 U.S.C.A.

In re Commodore Business Machines, Inc., 180 B.R. 72.

Bkrtcy.S.D.Ohio 1995. Complaint should not be dismissed for failure to state claim upon which relief can be granted unless it appears beyond doubt that plaintiff can prove no set of facts in support of his claim which would entitle him to relief. Fed.Rules Civ.Proc.Rule 12(b)(6), 28 U.S.C.A.

In re Douglas, 190 B.R. 831.

Bkrtcy.E.D.Pa. 1996. Motions to dismiss for failure to state claim are generally viewed with disfavor and are to be granted only in the unusual case in which plaintiff alleges facts that show on face of complaint that there is some insuperable bar to relief requested. Fed.Rules Civ.Proc.Rule 12(b)(6), 28 U.S.C.A.

In re DuFrayne, 194 B.R. 354.

Motion to dismiss for failure to state claim may only be granted if it appears beyond reasonable doubt that plaintiff can prove no set of facts in support of its claim that would entitle it to relief, and burden of establishing that no claim has been stated is on movant. Fed.Rules Civ.Proc.Rule 12(b)(6), 28 U.S.C.A.

In re DuFrayne, 194 B.R. 354.

Bkrtcy.E.D.Pa. 1995. Court may not grant motion to dismiss for failure to state claim unless, accepting all allegations in complaint, and all reasonable inferences that can be drawn therefrom, as true, and viewing them in light most favorable to nonmovant, it appears beyond all reasonable doubt that plaintiff can prove no set of facts in support of claim that would entitle plaintiff to relief. Fed.Rules Civ.Proc.Rule 12(b)(6), 28 U.S.C.A.

In re Sacred Heart Hosp. of Norristown, 181 B.R. 195.

Bkrtcy.E.D.Pa. 1995. Complaint must not be dismissed for failing to state a claim unless it appears beyond reasonable doubt that plaintiffs can prove no set of facts in support of their claim that would entitle them to relief. Fed. Rules Civ.Proc.Rule 12(b)(6), 28 U.S.C.A.

In re Sverica Acquisition Corp., Inc., 179 B.R. 457.

Bkrtcy.E.D.Pa. 1985. For purposes of ruling on motion to dismiss, factual allegations of complaint must be viewed in light most favorable to plaintiff, and motion may be granted only if it appears certain that plaintiff is entitled to no relief under any statement of facts which could be proved in support of the claim.

In re Stevenson, 49 B.R. 914.

Bkrtcy.E.D.Pa. 1985. On motion to dismiss trustee's complaint after trustee's presentation of his case, bankruptcy court's role is to make all necessary credibility judgments and weigh all evidence to determine whether trustee is entitled to relief based on preponderance of evidence; resolution of such motion differs from determination of motion for dismissal made prior to trustee's presentation of his case, in which event court may grant dismissal only if it appears certain that trustee is entitled to no relief under any statement of facts which could be proved in support of his claim. Fed.Rules Civ.Proc.Rule 41(b), 28 U.S.C.A.

In re Ludwig Honold Mfg. Co., Inc., 46 B.R. 125.

Bkrtcy.M.D.Pa. 1996. Motion to dismiss for failure to state claim will be granted only if it appears beyond doubt that plaintiff can prove no set of facts in support of his claim which would entitle him to relief. Fed.Rules Civ.Proc. Rule 12(b)(6), 28 U.S.C.A.

In re Taylor, 195 B.R. 624.

Bkrtcy.W.D.Pa. 1995. In deciding motion to dismiss for failure to state claim, bankruptcy court must take all factual allegations of complaint as true, construe them in light most favorable to plaintiff, and determine whether plaintiff might be entitled to relief under any reasonable reading of complaint. Fed.Rules Bankr.Proc. Rule 7012, 11 U.S.C.A.; Fed.Rules Civ.Proc. Rule 12(b)(6), 28 U.S.C.A.

In re Ambulatory Medical & Surgical Health Care, Inc., 187 B.R. 888.

Dismissal for failure to state claim is warranted only when it is manifestly obvious that plaintiff cannot prove any set of facts which would entitle it to relief. Fed.Rules Bankr.Proc. Rule 7012, 11 U.S.C.A.; Fed.Rules Civ.Proc. Rule 12(b)(6), 28 U.S.C.A.

In re Ambulatory Medical & Surgical Health Care, Inc., 187 B.R. 888.

Bkrtcy.D.S.C. 1995. Motion to dismiss for failure to state claim may be granted when no set of facts could be proven at trial that would entitle plaintiff to relief. Fed.Rules Civ.Proc. Rule 12(b)(6), 28 U.S.C.A.; Fed.Rules Bankr. Proc.Rule 7012, 11 U.S.C.A.

In re Dunes Hotel Associates, 194 B.R. 967, appeal decided 153 F.3d 719.

Bkrtcy.N.D.Tex. 1996. Complaint may not be dismissed for failure to state claim upon which relief may be granted unless it appears beyond a doubt that plaintiff can prove no set of facts in support of his or her claim that would entitle plaintiff to relief. Fed.Rules Civ.Proc. Rule 12(b)(6), 28 U.S.C.A.; Fed.Rules Bankr. Proc.Rule 7012(b), 11 U.S.C.A.

In re Kelso, 196 B.R. 363.

⚷1774. Counterclaim.

Library references

C.J.S. Federal Civil Procedure § 823.

C.A.D.C. 1987. After dismissal of New Mexico's action challenging regulations promulgated by Secretary of Interior under Surface Mining Act as to exclusive regulatory authority of Office of Surface Mining Reclamation and Enforcement over "Indian lands," due to settlement agreement reached by New Mexico and Department of Interior, to which all parties except intervenor-Navajo Tribe of Indians had stipulated, district court erred in dismissing Tribe's counterclaim rather than transferring counterclaim to New Mexico federal court; although problems requiring New Mexico's bringing complaint in District of Columbia district court had been resolved, and although aspect of counterclaim relating to Surface Mining Act established appropriate venue in New Mexico, district court had authority to transfer rather than dismiss counterclaim, and best interests of parties and courts would be to have transfer effected rather than to force parties and another court to begin litigation on counterclaim anew. 28 U.S.C.A. §§ 1331, 1362; Surface Mining Control and Reclamation Act of 1979, § 520(c)(1), 30 U.S.C.A. § 1270(c)(1).

New Mexico ex rel. Energy and Minerals Dept., Min. and Minerals Div. v. U.S. Dept. of Interior, 820 F.2d 441, 261 U.S.App.D.C. 33.

C.A.7 (Ill.) 1974. Clark v. Universal Builders, Inc., 501 F.2d 324, certiorari denied 95 S.Ct. 657, 419 U.S. 1070, 42 L.Ed.2d 666, appeal after remand 706 F.2d 204.

C.A.2 (N.Y.) 1991. Compulsory counterclaims may be dismissed where initial claim giving rise to federal jurisdiction is dismissed. Fed.Rules Civ.Proc.Rule 13(a), 28 U.S.C.A.

Scott v. Long Island Sav. Bank, F.S.B., 937 F.2d 738.

D.Del. 1987. Permissive counterclaims require independent basis of jurisdiction to withstand dismissal. Fed.Rules Civ.Proc.Rule 13(a), 28 U.S.C.A.

Akzona Inc. v. E.I. du Pont de Nemours & Co., 662 F.Supp. 603.

D.D.C. 1995. In considering plaintiffs' motions to dismiss defendant's counterclaims, district court could dismiss counterclaim for failure to state claim only if it appeared that no set of facts could be proved in support of counterclaim that would entitle defendant to relief.

Barnstead Broadcasting Corp. v. Offshore Broadcasting Corp., 886 F.Supp. 874.

In considering motion to dismiss counterclaim, summary dismissal is only appropriate if it appears beyond a reasonable doubt that no set of facts proffered in support of counterclaim would entitle claimant to relief.

Barnstead Broadcasting Corp. v. Offshore Broadcasting Corp., 886 F.Supp. 874.

N.D.Ill. 1995. Counterdefendants who were included in caption of case but who were not named in any of counts set forth in counterclaim would be dismissed from case inasmuch as counterclaim thus stated no cause of action against them.

Servpro Industries, Inc. v. Schmidt, 905 F.Supp. 475.

N.D.Ill. 1994. Motion to dismiss tests sufficiency of counterclaim and does not decide merits of case. Fed.Rules Civ.Proc.Rule 12(b)(6), 28 U.S.C.A.

Whirlpool Financial Corp. v. Sevaux, 866 F.Supp. 1097.

N.D.Ill. 1994. Motion to dismiss counterclaim tested sufficiency, not merits, and would be granted only if it appeared beyond doubt that under no set of facts would defendant be entitled to relief on counterclaim, accepting all its allegations and drawing all inferences in favor of defendant. Fed.Rules Civ.Proc.Rule 12(b)(6), 28 U.S.C.A.

KRW Sales, Inc. v. Kristel Corp., 154 F.R.D. 186.

N.D.Ill. 1987. Defects in insurers' counterclaim for indemnification from corporation and individual insureds, for amounts insurers may have to pay as result of directors' and officers' liability policies issued to corporation and its subsidiary, were sufficient to call for dismissal of counterclaim; insurers' wholesale incorporation of voluminous allegations from their earlier pleadings made it difficult to say that insurers provided their adversaries and the court with either "short" or "plain" statement of their claim, and at least one of the essential elements was not fully stated in the counterclaim's own allegations, but was buried in incorporated allegations. Fed.Rules Civ.Proc. Rules 8, 9(b), 12(b)(6), 14, 28 U.S.C.A.

National Union Fire Ins. Co. of Pittsburgh, Pa. v. Continental Illinois Corp., 658 F.Supp. 775.

N.D.Ill. 1973. Calvin v. Conlisk, 367 F.Supp. 476, affirmed in part, reversed in part 520 F.2d 1, certiorari granted, vacated 96 S.Ct. 1093, 424 U.S. 902, 47 L.Ed.2d 307, on remand 534 F.2d 1251, certiorari denied Afro American Patrolmen's League, Inc. v. Conlisk, 96 S.Ct. 1109, 424 U.S. 912, 47 L.Ed.2d 316.

D.Kan. 1988. CERCLA counterclaims of buyers of corporation which operated industrial waste disposal facility were irrelevant, and thus required dismissal, in sellers' action to enforce terms of promissory notes given in consideration for purchase of corporation, as award would simply serve to indemnify buyers against sellers, given sellers' causative involvement, due to fact that, at time case was taken up, state had already moved in and had already put in place all that CERCLA remedies provided. Comprehensive Environmental Response, Compensation, and Liability Act of 1980, §§ 101 et seq., 107, 42 U.S.C.A. §§ 9601 et seq., 9607.

> Nunn v. Chemical Waste Management, Inc., 699 F.Supp. 1478, affirmed in part, reversed in part 856 F.2d 1464, rehearing denied.

D.Kan. 1988. In determining whether counterclaim should be dismissed, court applies same standards that are applied when considering motion to dismiss complaint for failure to state claim on which relief may be granted. Fed.Rules Civ.Proc.Rules 12(b)(6), 13, 28 U.S.C.A.

> Federal Deposit Ins. Corp. v. Renda, 692 F.Supp. 128.

Trial court's inquiry in reviewing sufficiency of counterclaims is not whether defendants will ultimately prevail, but whether they are entitled to offer evidence to support counterclaims. Fed.Rules Civ.Proc.Rules 12(b)(6), 13, 28 U.S.C.A.

> Federal Deposit Ins. Corp. v. Renda, 692 F.Supp. 128.

D.Mass. 1998. Motion to dismiss counterclaim for failure to state claim will be granted only if it appears, beyond doubt, that counterclaimant can prove no facts in support of its claim that entitles it to relief.

> Honeywell Consumer Products, Inc. v. Windmere Corp., 993 F.Supp..22.

Court is required to look only to allegations of counterclaim and if under any theory they are sufficient to state cause of action, motion to dismiss counterclaim must be denied.

> Honeywell Consumer Products, Inc. v. Windmere Corp., 993 F.Supp. 22.

D.Mass. 1996. In ruling on motion to dismiss counterclaim for failure to state claim, if, under any theory, allegations by counterclaimant were sufficient to state cause of action in accordance with applicable law, district court had to deny motion. Fed.Rules Civ.Proc.Rule 12(b)(6), 28 U.S.C.A.

> Milford Power Ltd. Partnership by Milford Power Associates Inc. v. New England Power Co., 918 F.Supp. 471.

E.D.Mich. 1992. In case of parallel state and federal litigation, dismissal of counterclaims in federal suit in deference to Michigan's compulsory joinder rule was inappropriate, where counterclaims were validly asserted within framework of federal compulsory counter-

claim. MCR 2.203(A); Fed.Rules Civ.Proc. Rules 13, 13(a), 28 U.S.C.A.

> Karakas v. McKeown, 783 F.Supp. 1028.

E.D.Mo. 1996. Motion to dismiss should not be granted merely because counterclaim does not state with precision every element of offense necessary for recovery; motion to dismiss should not be granted unless it appears beyond doubt that counterclaim plaintiff can prove no set of facts which would entitle it to relief.

> McDonnell Douglas Corp. v. SCI Technology, Inc., 933 F.Supp. 822.

D.Nev. 1987. Motion to dismiss counterclaim for failure to state claim should not be granted unless it appears to certainty that counterclaimants can prove no set of facts in support of their claims that would entitle them to relief.; counterclaims are construed and all doubts resolved in favor of pleaders, with facts alleged taken as true. Fed.Rules Civ.Proc.Rule 12(b)(6), 28 U.S.C.A.

> Safeco Ins. Co. of America v. Mirczak, 662 F.Supp. 1155.

E.D.N.Y. 1997. To prevail on its motion to dismiss defendant's counterclaims for failure to state claim, plaintiff had to establish that there existed no set of facts arguably supporting any of defendant's counterclaims. Fed.Rules Civ. Proc.Rule 12(b)(6), 28 U.S.C.A.

> Fox News Network, L.L.C. v. Time Warner Inc., 962 F.Supp. 339.

E.D.N.Y. 1995. Principles that complaint should not be dismissed unless it appears beyond doubt that plaintiff can prove no set of facts in support of claims which would entitle him to relief and that in considering motion to dismiss all factual allegations of complaint must be accepted as true and construed favorably to plaintiff apply equally to defendant's pleading asserting counterclaims. Fed.Rules Civ.Proc. Rule 12(b)(6), 28 U.S.C.A.

> D.S. America (East), Inc. v. Chromagrafx Imaging Systems, Inc., 873 F.Supp. 786.

S.D.N.Y. 1991. Rule that motion to dismiss for failure to state claim tests only sufficiency of complaint and should not be granted unless it appears beyond doubt that plaintiff can prove no set of facts in support of his claim which would entitle him to relief is equally applicable to motion to dismiss a counterclaim for failure to state claim. Fed.Rules Civ.Proc. Rule 12(b)(6), 28 U.S.C.A.

> Schatt v. Curtis Management Group, Inc., 764 F.Supp. 902.

In ruling on plaintiff's motion to dismiss defendants' counterclaim for failure to state claim, likelihood that defendants would prevail was immaterial, as was question of whether requested relief was appropriate or whether legal theories had been miscategorized. Fed. Rules Civ.Proc.Rule 12(b)(6), 28 U.S.C.A.

> Schatt v. Curtis Management Group, Inc., 764 F.Supp. 902.

M.D.N.C. 1995. Legal standard for dismissal of counterclaim is same as that for dismissal of complaint.

> Crown Cork & Seal Co., Inc. v. Dockery, 907 F.Supp. 147.

M.D.N.C. 1985. That pro se defendants expressed a "desire to assert an appropriate counterclaim" upon obtaining assistance of counsel was no basis for dismissing the counterclaims.

> Waller v. Butkovich, 605 F.Supp. 1137.

S.D.Ohio 1990. Counterclaim cannot be dismissed simply because plaintiff has failed to state precisely all elements that give rise to alleged legal basis for recovery. Fed.Rules Civ. Proc.Rules 8(a)(2), 9(b), 12(b)(6), 28 U.S.C.A.

> General Acquisition, Inc. v. GenCorp Inc., 766 F.Supp. 1460.

E.D.Pa. 1994. In determining motion to dismiss counterclaim for failure to state a claim, all assertions in pleading would be assumed to be true, all reasonable inferences would be drawn from pleading in favor of counterclaim plaintiff, and counterclaim would only be dismissed if counterclaim plaintiff had alleged no set of facts under which claim could be stated. Fed.Rules Civ.Proc.Rule 12(b)(6), 28 U.S.C.A.

> Centennial School Dist. v. Independence Blue Cross, 885 F.Supp. 683.

E.D.Pa. 1994. Standard for dismissal of counterclaim is same as standard for dismissal of complaint. Fed.Rules Civ.Proc.Rule 12(b)(6), 28 U.S.C.A.

> Johnson v. Resources for Human Development, Inc., 860 F.Supp. 218.

M.D.Pa. 1992. Failure to seek leave of court before filing counterclaim is procedural deficiency which, alone, will not constitute grounds for dismissal, particularly where deficiency is remedied by filing for leave to intervene. Fed.Rules Civ.Proc.Rules 13(f), 15(a), 28 U.S.C.A.

> United Services Auto. Ass'n v. Foster, 783 F.Supp. 916.

E.D.Va. 1987. Defendant's "counterclaim preservation" count, in which he alleged that he reasonably believed there were other and further breaches, violations, losses, liabilities, and causes of action which might be asserted against plaintiff and related party, flew in face of letter and spirit of federal rules, which required pleader to give his adversary fair notice; thus, count would be dismissed.

> Prudential-Bache Securities, Inc. v. Cullather, 678 F.Supp. 601.

Bkrtcy.N.D.Ill. 1996. Counterclaim may be dismissed only if it is clear from pleadings that defendant can prove no set of facts in support of its claim which would entitle it to relief.

> In re S.N.A. Nut Co., 191 B.R. 117.

Bkrtcy.S.D.N.Y. 1993. Party may move to dismiss counterclaim in adversary proceeding on ground that it fails to state claim upon which relief can be granted. Fed.Rules Bankr.Proc. Rule 7012(b), 11 U.S.C.A.; Fed.Rules Civ.Proc. Rule 12(b)(6), 28 U.S.C.A.

> In re Kressner, 159 B.R. 428.

Bkrtcy.S.D.N.Y. 1993. Chapter 11 debtor was entitled to dismissal of attempted purchaser's counterclaim for lost profits and consequential damages, which was remedy rather than claim upon which relief could be granted.

> In re Chateaugay Corp., 155 B.R. 636, affirmed, appeal dismissed 198 B.R. 848, affirmed 108 F.3d 1369.

⊂⇒**1775. Prayer.**

Library references

> C.J.S. Federal Civil Procedure § 824.

C.A.D.C. 1985. A district court should not grant a motion to dismiss for failure to state a claim for failure to seek technically appropriate remedy when availability of some relief is readily apparent on face of complaint. Fed.Rules Civ.Proc.Rule 12(b)(6), 28 U.S.C.A.

> Doe v. U.S. Dept. of Justice, 753 F.2d 1092, 243 U.S.App.D.C. 354.

C.A.5 (Miss.) 1987. Demand of improper remedy is not fatal to party's pleading, if statement of claim is otherwise sufficient to show entitlement to different form of relief. Fed. Rules Civ.Proc.Rule 12(b)(6), 28 U.S.C.A.

> Doss v. South Cent. Bell Telephone Co., 834 F.2d 421, rehearing denied 837 F.2d 1090.

C.D.Cal. 1996. Motion to dismiss complaint for failure to state claim will not be granted merely because plaintiff requests remedy to which he or she is not entitled; it need not appear that plaintiff can obtain specific relief demanded as long as court can ascertain from face of complaint that some relief can be granted. Fed.Rules Civ.Proc.Rule 12(b)(6), 28 U.S.C.A.

> Summit Technology, Inc. v. High-Line Medical Instruments, Co., 933 F.Supp. 918.

D.Colo. 1998. On motion to dismiss for failure to state claim, test of complaint lies in claim, not in prayer for relief. Fed.Rules Civ. Proc.Rule 12(b)(6), 28 U.S.C.A.

> Cassidy v. Millers Cas. Ins. Co. of Texas, 1 F.Supp.2d 1200.

Only issue on motion to dismiss is whether claim as stated would give plaintiff right to any relief, rather than particular relief demanded. Fed.Rules Civ.Proc.Rule 12(b)(6), 28 U.S.C.A.

> Cassidy v. Millers Cas. Ins. Co. of Texas, 1 F.Supp.2d 1200.

D.Colo. 1991. Prayers for punitive damages and court-ordered affirmative action program, which were asserted by employee claiming racial discrimination in employment, were not separate claims for relief and, thus, were not subject to dismissal on employer's motion.

> Smith v. Denver Public School Bd., 758 F.Supp. 1421.

S.D.N.Y. 1990. If complaint states case justifying any relief within court's power to grant, prayer for relief must be disregarded and action must not be dismissed for failure to state claim. Fed.Rules Civ.Proc.Rule 12(b)(6), 28 U.S.C.A.

> Babcock v. Frank, 729 F.Supp. 279.

E.D.N.C. 1991. Question of whether party may be able to recover punitive damages goes to issue of relief ultimately available, but has no bearing on validity of cause of action set forth in complaint. Fed.Rules Civ.Proc.Rule 12(b)(6), 28 U.S.C.A.

> Jones v. Wake County Hosp. System, Inc., 786 F.Supp. 538.

N.D.Ohio 1987. Inclusion in a complaint of an improper remedy does not require dismissal of a meritorious claim.

> Nicoletti v. Brown, 740 F.Supp. 1268.

E.D.Va. 1987. Motion to dismiss for failure to state claim upon which relief can be granted should not be granted for failure to seek technically appropriate remedy when availability of some relief is readily apparent on face of pleadings. Fed.Rules Civ.Proc.Rule 12(b)(6), 28 U.S.C.A.

> Prudential-Bache Securities, Inc. v. Cullather, 678 F.Supp. 601.

E.D.Va. 1987. Count in complaint seeking award of costs of suit, including reasonable attorney fees, would be dismissed to extent it attempted to state cause of action, but the language would be retained and construed as part of prayer for relief.

> Haigh v. Matsushita Elec. Corp. of America, 676 F.Supp. 1332.

W.D.Wis. 1985. Under Wisconsin law, a claim for punitive damages should be dismissed only if it is clear that the complaint fails to allege facts sufficient to state a claim for punitive damages.

> Elbe v. Wausau Hosp. Center, 606 F.Supp. 1491.

4. PARTICULAR ACTIONS, INSUFFICIENCY OF PLEADINGS IN.

⚷1781. In general.

Library references

> C.J.S. Federal Civil Procedure §§ 825, 839.

U.S.Or. 1989. Failure to comply with 60-day notice requirement of Resource Conservation and Recovery Act's citizen suit provision required dismissal of suit. Solid Waste Disposal Act, § 7002(b), as amended, 42 U.S.C.A. § 6972(b).

> Hallstrom v. Tillamook County, 110 S.Ct. 304, 493 U.S. 20, 107 L.Ed.2d 237, rehearing denied 110 S.Ct. 761, 493 U.S. 1037, 107 L.Ed.2d 777.

C.A.D.C. 1993. Sufficiency of complaint claiming that Secretary of Health and Human Services acted arbitrarily and capriciously in limiting hospitals' Medicare reimbursement rates was question on merits, and there was no real distinction between questions presented on motion to dismiss for failure to state claim and motion for summary judgment, and, thus, district court did not exceed its latitude in ruling on motion to dismiss when it looked beyond to Secretary's published responses to comments in rule-making proceeding and decided merits; record was not used to test any factual allegations in complaint. Fed.Rules Civ.Proc.Rules 12(b)(6), 56, 28 U.S.C.A.

> Marshall County Health Care Authority v. Shalala, 988 F.2d 1221, 300 U.S.App.D.C. 263.

C.A.5 (Ala.) 1981. Lynch v. Baxley, 651 F.2d 387, appeal after remand 744 F.2d 1452.

C.A.9 (Cal.) 1989. Summary judgment was inappropriate disposition after district court determined that it lacked subject matter jurisdiction over challenge to license for construction and operation of hydroelectric power facility in national forest; appropriate disposition would have been to dismiss the action. Federal Power Act, §§ 1 et seq., 313(b), as amended, 16 U.S.C.A. §§ 792 et seq., 825l(b).

> California Save Our Streams Council, Inc. v. Yeutter, 887 F.2d 908.

C.A.9 (Cal.) 1989. Motions to dismiss for failure to state claim must be viewed with particular skepticism in cases involving claims of inverse condemnation. Fed.Rules Civ.Proc. Rule 12(b)(6), 28 U.S.C.A.

> Moore v. City of Costa Mesa, 886 F.2d 260, certiorari denied 110 S.Ct. 2588, 496 U.S. 906, 110 L.Ed.2d 269.

C.A.9 (Cal.) 1986. Leave to amend complaint, rather than dismissal, was appropriate course of action, where opposition to motion to dismiss fairly advised defendant in district court as to nature of claim.

> Hall v. City of Santa Barbara, 833 F.2d 1270, certiorari denied 108 S.Ct. 1120, 485 U.S. 940, 99 L.Ed.2d 281.

C.A.10 (Colo.) 1989. Complaint's allegation of RICO violations by federal officials would be dismissed, where basis of RICO claim could not be discerned from complaint, plaintiff organization made no attempt to further define RICO claim in appeal, and plaintiff organization had provided no authority that such a claim would lie against group of federal officials on account of their misconduct. 18 U.S.C.A. §§ 1961, 1962.

> National Commodity and Barter Ass'n, National Commodity Exchange v. Gibbs, 886 F.2d 1240, on remand 790 F.Supp. 233, affirmed in part, reversed in part National Commodity and Barter Ass'n v. Archer, 31 F.3d 1521.

C.A.11 (Fla.) 1990. When district court granted in forma pauperis motion and required payment of partial filing fee, court must issue summons, and could not sua sponte dismiss complaint as frivolous. 28 U.S.C.A. § 1915; Fed.Rules Civ.Proc.Rule 4(a), 28 U.S.C.A.

> Herrick v. Collins, 914 F.2d 228.

Where defendants have not responded to complaint of in forma pauperis plaintiff, district court should first permit plaintiff to amend complaint to overcome its deficiencies; if court then determines that complaint is frivolous and that dismissal is warranted, district court should dismiss complaint without requiring plaintiff to pay any filing fee. 28 U.S.C.A. § 1915(d); Fed.Rules Civ.Proc.Rule 15(a), 28 U.S.C.A.

> Herrick v. Collins, 914 F.2d 228.

C.A.11 (Fla.) 1985. Where it was clear from face of complaint that plaintiff could prove no set of facts that would entitle him to relief, complaint should have been dismissed under rule for failure to state claim upon which relief could be granted, and district court erred in granting summary judgment for defendants. Fed.Rules Civ.Proc.Rule 12(b)(6), 28 U.S.C.A.

> Madison v. U.S., 752 F.2d 607, rehearing denied 758 F.2d 573.

C.A.7 (Ill.) 1993. Fact that plaintiff, in bringing Rule 10b-5 suit, fails to plead in complaint facts demonstrating timeliness of suit, does not entitle defendant to dismissal of suit; rationale that pleading such facts would allow judges to dispose of untimely statute claims efficiently is no longer applicable, since, if complaint does not reveal date at which statutory period of limitations began to run, defendant can simply supply that fact in affidavit attached to motion to dismiss, which will then be treated as motion for summary judgment. Fed.Rules Civ.Proc.Rules 12(b), 56, 28 U.S.C.A.; Securities Exchange Act of 1934, § 10(b), 15 U.S.C.A. § 78j(b).

> Tregenza v. Great American Communications Co., 12 F.3d 717, certiorari denied 114 S.Ct. 1837, 511 U.S. 1085, 128 L.Ed.2d 465.

C.A.8 (Iowa) 1985. Dismissal of a "John Doe" pleading is proper only when it appears that the true identity of the defendant cannot be learned through discovery or the court's intervention.

> Munz v. Parr, 758 F.2d 1254, on remand 1991 WL 365063, affirmed 972 F.2d 971.

C.A.6 (Ky.) 1994. Unavailability of evidence due to plaintiff's prelitigation destruction of evidence, and corresponding negative inferences, do not necessarily mandate dismissing case or granting summary judgment; nevertheless, summary judgment may be granted or verdict directed if district court determines that defendant is entitled to judgment as matter of law because plaintiff is unable, due to unavailability of evidence and negative inferences, to offer evidence sufficient to support its case. Fed.Rules Civ.Proc.Rules 50, 56, 28 U.S.C.A.

> Beil v. Lakewood Engineering and Mfg. Co., 15 F.3d 546.

C.A.8 (Neb.) 1993. Bankruptcy court did not clearly err in dismissing buyer's conversion and Uniform Commercial Code (UCC) claims against debtor bean seller's lender based on determination that no beans were identified to debtor's prepaid contracts with buyer. Neb. Rev.St. §§ 90–2722, 90–9307; U.C.C. §§ 2–722, 9–307, 9–318.

> In re Quality Processing, Inc., 9 F.3d 1360.

C.A.1 (N.H.) 1993. District court's dismissal of borrower's amended lender liability action complaint for failure to comply with concise pleading requirements of Federal Rules of Civil Procedure was not abuse of discretion, where court ordered borrowers to amend complaint in order to conform to concise pleading requirement, and indicated that number of defendants should be reduced, but borrowers filed 43–page, 358–paragraph amended complaint, adding two more defendants. Fed.Rules Civ. Proc.Rule 8(a), 28 U.S.C.A.

> Kuehl v. F.D.I.C., 8 F.3d 905, rehearing denied, certiorari denied 114 S.Ct. 1545, 511 U.S. 1034, 128 L.Ed.2d 196.

C.A.3 (N.J.) 1994. Under New Jersey and North Carolina Uniform Commercial Code (UCC) statute of frauds for securities transactions, plaintiff has right to ask defendant in breach of contract suit to admit fact that oral contract was made, thus precluding granting of motion to dismiss for failure to state claim on statute of frauds grounds in most cases, as such dismissal would deprive plaintiff of any opportunity to give such admission. N.J.S.A. 12A:8–319(d); N.C.G.S. § 25–8–319(d); Fed.Rules Civ. Proc.Rule 12(b)(6), 28 U.S.C.A.

ALA, Inc. v. CCAIR, Inc., 29 F.3d 855.

C.A.2 (N.Y.) 1991. Plaintiff may not evade properly argued motion to dismiss securities claims based upon contents of prospectus simply because plaintiff has chosen not to attach prospectus to complaint or to incorporate it by reference.

I. Meyer Pincus & Associates, P.C. v. Oppenheimer & Co., Inc., 936 F.2d 759.

C.A.2 (N.Y.) 1982. Oneida Indian Nation of New York v. State of N.Y., 691 F.2d 1070, on subsequent appeal Oneida Indian Nation of Wisconsin v. State of N.Y., 732 F.2d 259, on remand 102 F.R.D. 450, cause remanded Oneida of Thames Band v. State of N.Y., 757 F.2d 19, motion to recall mandate denied 771 F.2d 51, certiorari denied 106 S.Ct. 78, 474 U.S. 823, 88 L.Ed.2d 64, on remand 649 F.Supp. 420, affirmed 860 F.2d 1145, certiorari denied 110 S.Ct. 200, 493 U.S. 871, 107 L.Ed.2d 154, certiorari denied 110 S.Ct. 200, 493 U.S. 871, 107 L.Ed.2d 154.

C.A.6 (Ohio) 1996. Although naming individual defendant in complaint as employee of corporate defendant, plaintiffs failed to link him to any of conduct at issue, and thus claim against individual defendant was properly dismissed.

Vector Research, Inc. v. Howard & Howard Attorneys P.C., 76 F.3d 692, rehearing and suggestion for rehearing denied.

C.A.5 (Tex.) 1991. District court applied incorrect standard when it dismissed citizen's suit brought under the Clean Water Act against cattle feedlot after trial for lack of standing; though trial court's finding that reasonable trier of fact could find likelihood of recurrence and intermittent or sporadic discharges from feedlot would have been correct had feedlot challenged standing on motion for summary judgment, after matter proceeded to trial, question was what district court, as trier of fact, actually found. Federal Water Pollution Control Act Amendments of 1972, § 101 et seq., 33 U.S.C.A. § 1251 et seq.

Carr v. Alta Verde Industries, Inc., 931 F.2d 1055, rehearing denied.

Citizen suit under the Clean Water Act may be dismissed because defendant complies with Act subsequent to complaint if defendant's compliance moots action; in order to prove mootness, defendant must adduce evidence from which it is absolutely clear that allegedly wrongful behavior could not reasonably be expected to recur. Federal Water Pollution Control Act

Amendments of 1972, § 101 et seq., 33 U.S.C.A. § 1251 et seq.

Carr v. Alta Verde Industries, Inc., 931 F.2d 1055, rehearing denied.

C.D.Cal. 1994. For purposes of a motion to dismiss for failure to state a claim, allegation of appearance of impropriety by special master was sufficient to survive limited pleading requirements of general pleading rule, based on violation of due process right to impartial tribunal. U.S.C.A. Const.Amend. 5; Fed.Rules Civ. Proc.Rules 8, 12(b)(6), 28 U.S.C.A.

Church of Scientology Intern. v. Kolts, 846 F.Supp. 873.

C.D.Cal. 1989. Determination of whether vessel owner is entitled to limitation of liability would not be appropriate for dismissal motion. 46 U.S.C.A.App. § 183.

Complaint of Ingoglia, 723 F.Supp. 512.

N.D.Cal. 1989. Lumping all defendants together in professional negligence claims against attorney and law firms and failing to allege with specificity duty breached by any of defendants warranted dismissal of claims.

Levine v. Diamanthuset, Inc., 722 F.Supp. 579, reversed 950 F.2d 1478.

S.D.Cal. 1998. Court would dismiss with prejudice a federal racketeering action against a defendant even though he had not yet answered the complaint, where he was in an identical position to the other defendants, who had established via a motion to dismiss that plaintiff could not show a pattern of racketeering activity, and where the claims against him were integrally related to the claims against the moving defendants, in that plaintiff alleged that they were all involved in a conspiracy. 18 U.S.C.A. §§ 1861 et seq., 1862(c); Fed.Rules Civ.Proc. Rule 12(b)(6), 28 U.S.C.A.

Ricotta v. State of Cal., 4 F.Supp.2d 961.

D.Conn. 1994. Pleading private cost recovery action to recover response costs incurred or to be incurred in relation to hazardous waste cleanup of public landfill site together with action for contribution under CERCLA was not unnecessarily confusing, so as to require dismissal of claims; concern about procedural awkwardness was not alone basis to dismiss either of claims. Comprehensive Environmental Response, Compensation, and Liability Act of 1980, §§ 107(a)(4), 113(f), as amended, 42 U.S.C.A. §§ 9607(a)(4), 9613(f).

Companies for Fair Allocation v. Axil Corp., 853 F.Supp. 575.

D.Conn. 1993. On motion to dismiss, where court had no factual record before it, resolution of issue of whether defendants were entitled to qualified immunity was not appropriate.

Johnson v. Meachum, 839 F.Supp. 953.

D.D.C. 1996. Banks who brought action against multiple defendants, including estate of former ruler of Emirate of Dubai and company which was allegedly personal holding company and alter ego of ruler, in which civil Racketeer Influenced and Corrupt Organizations Act (RICO) and other claims were asserted based on alleged attempt to illegally and secretly take over banks, had alleged sufficient facts to survive motion to dismiss by estate and company, and were entitled to conduct discovery to determine entities or persons who had assumed legal obligations of company and ruler after his death.

First American Corp. v. Al-Nahyan, 948 F.Supp. 1107.

S.D.Fla. 1994. Chapter 7 trustee's second amended complaint against corporate debtor's former officers and directors did not comply with prior district court order requiring trustee to allege with "greatest specificity" those acts of defendants for which trustee claimed that defendants were liable, and, thus, proceeding would be dismissed as to those defendants, where trustee responded to order merely by attaching to complaint four charts that purported to show terms of service of each defendant with respect to particular allegations made in complaint.

In re Southeast Banking Corp., 855 F.Supp. 353, affirmed 69 F.3d 1539.

S.D.Fla. 1993. Decision whether omissions were material or part of total mix of information in market should not be made on motion to dismiss securities fraud claim. Securities Exchange Act of 1934, § 10(b), 15 U.S.C.A. § 78j(b).

In re Cascade Intern. Securities Litigation, 840 F.Supp. 1558, on reconsideration 894 F.Supp. 437.

S.D.Fla. 1993. Stockholder alleged fraud under federal and Florida securities law sufficiently to overcome motion to dismiss, even absent claim of manipulation or misrepresentation of stock value, where stockholder did allege that he sold stock based on buyer's misrepresentations; signed agreement for sale included buyer's allegedly false promise of highly paid consulting position, cash, and stock options and compensation. Securities Exchange Act of 1934, § 10(b), 15 U.S.C.A. § 78j(b).

Leisure Founders, Inc. v. CUC Intern., Inc., 833 F.Supp. 1562.

S.D.Fla. 1987. Summary disposition of issue of limitation of vessel owner's liability on motion to dismiss is inappropriate where factual development on issue of fault and issue of ownership of vessel is required to resolve question of entitlement to limitation. 46 U.S.C.A. § 185.

Rodriguez Morira v. Lemay, 659 F.Supp. 89.

S.D.Fla. 1985. Action against contractor defendants, which sought recovery of contributions and other monies allegedly owed by subcontractor pursuant to collective bargaining agreement, on basis that contractor facilitated obtaining subcontracts on project required dismissal, as federal court had no subject matter jurisdiction over contractor under ERISA, as it was not alleged that these defendants were employers or that they had any direct or indirect control of any operations, finances or business operations of employer, and parties lacked diversity. Employee Retirement Income Security Act of 1974, §§ 3(5), 502(a)(3), as amended, 29 U.S.C.A. §§ 1002(5), 1132(a)(3); West's F.S.A. § 255.05.

Giardiello v. Balboa Ins. Co., 661 F.Supp. 644, affirmed in part, reversed in part 837 F.2d 1566.

D.Hawai'i 1991. Plaintiff seeking tort damages for breach of contract was not required to allege in complaint what constituted defendant's wanton and reckless conduct, in order to withstand motion to dismiss for failure to state cause of action; because court drew all reasonable inferences in favor of nonmoving party, it was enough that complaint alleged defendant's wanton and reckless conduct. Fed. Rules Civ.Proc.Rule 12(b)(6), 28 U.S.C.A.

Paulson, Inc. v. Bromar, Inc., 775 F.Supp. 1329.

D.Hawai'i 1988. Failure of contractor RICO plaintiff to identify enterprise affected by defendant's racketeering activities resulted in dismissal with leave to file motion to amend.

C & W Const. Co. v. Brotherhood of Carpenters and Joiners of America, Local 745, AFL-CIO, 687 F.Supp. 1453.

C.D.Ill. 1992. In assessing sufficiency with which plaintiffs made their allegations of securities fraud in light of defendants' motion to dismiss for failure to state claim, district court would analyze identified affirmative statements individually and collectively in context in which they were made, but would not render any decision as to whether particular statement was rendered misleading by particular omission; it would merely determine whether plaintiffs sufficiently alleged circumstances under which they could conceivable prove claim of fraudulent misrepresentation under any set of facts at trial, or if alleged material omission clearly would not render any identified affirmative statement or statements made misleading under any set of facts. Fed.Rules Civ.Proc.Rule 12(b)(6), 28 U.S.C.A.; Securities Exchange Act of 1934, § 10(b), 15 U.S.C.A. § 78j(b).

Kas v. Caterpillar, Inc., 815 F.Supp. 1158.

N.D.Ill. 1995. Dismissal of Racketeer Influenced and Corrupt Organizations Act (RICO) complaint against creditor-bank was warranted since pattern of racketeering activity was not established. 18 U.S.C.A. § 1961 et seq.

> Travis v. Boulevard Bank N.A., 880 F.Supp. 1226.

N.D.Ill. 1991. Although taxpayers had standing to bring action to recover interest state allegedly lost when former state treasurer deposited excessive state funds in noninterest-bearing accounts, their attempt to shift basis of liability to meet challenges of defendants warranted granting of motion to dismiss without prejudice; at one point, taxpayers claimed that defendants were involved in fraudulent tying arrangements, and when challenged on having insufficiently pled their fraud claim, they claimed that bank fraud does not have same pleading requirements as common-law fraud.

> Ryan v. Cosentino, 776 F.Supp. 386.

N.D.Ill. 1991. It would be inappropriate on record to dismiss common carrier from action to recover for missing goods on ground that carrier was not subject to Interstate Commerce Commission (ICC) jurisdiction by virtue of present transaction, in which carrier contracted with interstate carrier to provide intrastate transportation, where, according to complaint, transported goods remained in commerce, that is they had not reached their final destination, during intrastate leg for which carrier was hired; at present stage of litigation it would be premature to find that carrier could not be liable under any reasonable set of facts. 49 U.S.C.A. § 10101 et seq.

> Tokio Marine and Fire Ins. Co., Ltd. v. Amato Motors, Inc., 764 F.Supp. 115, reversed 996 F.2d 874, rehearing denied.

N.D.Ill. 1989. Whether metropolitan sanitary district asserted claim for civil penalties under federal law, for which government would not be immune from suit under Clean Water Act, could not be determined from district's complaint against Department of Navy alleging that naval station failed to comply with permit to discharge into district's sewer system and thus motion to dismiss would be denied.

> Metropolitan Sanitary Dist. of Greater Chicago v. U.S. Dept. of Navy, 722 F.Supp. 1565, on reconsideration in part 737 F.Supp. 51.

N.D.Ind. 1993. Employee benefit plan's claim against securities broker/dealer for breach of fiduciary duty would not be dismissed since broker was in position of superior knowledge and understanding when he recommended to plan administrator that he invest in secured demand note for benefit of plan and existence of fiduciary duty between broker and administrator was question of fact to be determined by trier of fact.

> Schwartz v. Oberweis, 826 F.Supp. 280.

Employee benefit plan's breach of contract claim against securities broker/dealer would not be dismissed on ground that requirement of contractual privity applied to actions based on or sounding in contract under Indiana law.

> Schwartz v. Oberweis, 826 F.Supp. 280.

N.D.Iowa 1995. Dismissal for failure to state claim was appropriate as to defendants against whom plaintiffs failed to effect proper service of process, and against whom plaintiffs failed to state any factual allegations; however, plaintiffs were entitled to opportunity to cure defects in service as to six defendants against whom plaintiffs did make factual allegations. Fed.Rules Civ.Proc.Rule 12(b)(6), 28 U.S.C.A.

> Dahl v. Kanawha Inv. Holding Co., 161 F.R.D. 673.

D.Kan. 1997. Plaintiffs' claim for attorney fees in their complaint failed to state independent claim for relief and would be dismissed to that extent. Fed.Rules Civ.Proc.Rule 12(b)(6), 28 U.S.C.A.

> Classic Communications, Inc. v. Rural Telephone Service Co., Inc., 956 F.Supp. 910, reconsideration denied 1997 WL 231087.

D.Kan. 1993. Claim for punitive damages would not be dismissed for plaintiff's failure to comply with Kansas procedural requirements absent any indication as to what procedural requirements were overlooked. K.S.A. 60–3701 et seq.

> Clark v. Associates Commercial Corp., 149 F.R.D. 629.

W.D.Ky. 1993. Fact that Kentucky was no longer receiving Juvenile Justice and Delinquency Prevention Act funds did not warrant dismissal of action alleging violations by the state of the Act where state officials were appealing suspension of funding under JJDPA. 42 U.S.C.A. § 1983; Juvenile Justice and Delinquency Prevention Act of 1974, § 101 et seq., 42 U.S.C.A. § 5601 et seq.

> James v. Jones, 148 F.R.D. 196.

W.D.La. 1992. Area residents stated claim under Louisiana law sufficient to withstand motion to dismiss as matter of law, based on storage of industrial waste in open pits, against independent contractor which disposed of waste, on theory of absolute liability for ultrahazardous activity, and against contractor's principal, on theory of vicarious responsibility for such contractor's liability, regardless of whether principal could be considered a "proprietor" under section of the Civil Code imposing strict liability for acts of proprietor causing damage to his neighbor. LSA-C.C. art. 667; Fed.Rules Civ.Proc.Rule 12(b), 28 U.S.C.A.

> Updike v. Browning-Ferris, Inc., 808 F.Supp. 538.

W.D.La. 1986. Interstate commerce claim, asserted by nontenant rental car business against airport authority, could not be dismissed for failure to state a claim on basis of affirmative defense that authority, which imposed charge on entities which did not have contracts with authority but which nevertheless used airport facilities in furtherance of commercial enterprises, was acting as a market participant where airport authority did not allege affirmative defense in its pleading. Fed.Rules Civ.Proc.Rule 12(b)(6), 28 U.S.C.A.; U.S.C.A. Const. Art. 1, § 8, cl. 3.

    Airline Car Rental, Inc. v. Shreveport Airport Authority, 667 F.Supp. 293.

D.Me. 1995. When evaluating motion to dismiss equal protection claim, federal district court is required to surmise whether any state of facts could support plaintiffs' claim that their constitutional guaranty to equal protection of the laws has been violated; plaintiffs must plead minimal facts which permit reasonable inference of discrimination. U.S.C.A. Const.Amend. 14; Fed.Rules Civ.Proc.Rule 12, 28 U.S.C.A.

    Parker v. Wakelin, 882 F.Supp. 1131.

D.Md. 1988. Conclusory allegations against "defendants" were insufficiently specific to state claims against Administrator of Veterans Administration and head nurse to recover for breach of employment contract, intentional infliction of emotional distress, violation of constitutional rights, conspiracy to violate constitutional rights, and violation of civil rights under Maryland's guarantee of religious freedom; names of Administrator and head nurse did not appear in fact section of complaint. Md.Const.Declaration of Rights, Art. 36; Fed. Rules Civ.Proc.Rule 12(b)(6), 28 U.S.C.A.

    Baird v. Haith, 724 F.Supp. 367.

D.Md. 1974. Equal Employment Opportunity Commission v. Raymond Metal Products Co., 385 F.Supp. 907, stay granted E.E.O.C. v. Raymond Metal Products Co., Subsidiary of Raymond Intern., Inc., 1974 WL 10566, affirmed in part, reversed in part 530 F.2d 590, on remand 1978 WL 22437.

D.Mass. 1993. To survive motion for dismissal, complaint mounted upon Rule 10b–5 must contain, at minimum, factual allegations that would support reasonable inference that circumstances adverse to defendant's statements were known and deliberately or recklessly disregarded at time statements were made.

    Colby v. Hologic, Inc., 817 F.Supp. 204.

D.Mass. 1990. Where issue of whether Environmental Protection Agency's (EPA's) imposition of lien under Comprehensive Environmental Response, Compensation, and Liability Act (CERCLA) amounted to deprivation of significant property interest protected by due process clause was pending before First Circuit, EPA's motion to dismiss complaint alleging due process violation would be denied without prejudice to review following issuance of opinion by First Circuit. U.S.C.A. Const.Amends. 5, 14; Comprehensive Environmental Response, Compensation, and Liability Act of 1980, § 107(*l*), as amended, 42 U.S.C.A. § 9607(*l*).

    Juniper Development Group v. U.S., 774 F.Supp. 56.

D.C.Mass. 1985. Technical error in citation of statute on which claim was based would not support motion to dismiss for failure to state a claim or motion for summary judgment, where sufficient notice of factual basis of claim had been stated.

    Walters v. President and Fellows of Harvard College, 616 F.Supp. 471.

W.D.Mich. 1993. District court could dismiss civil Racketeer Influenced and Corrupt Organizations Act (RICO) claim, in addition to state law claims over which it declined to exercise supplemental jurisdiction, given that state law issues clearly predominated as 28 of the 29 counts in complaint were state law claims and state courts had concurrent jurisdiction to hear RICO claims. 18 U.S.C.A. § 1961 et seq.; 28 U.S.C.A. § 1367.

    Bodenner v. Graves, 828 F.Supp. 516.

D.Minn. 1989. Insurance subagent's failure to amend deficiently pled deceptive trade practices claim within 30 days allowed by court for amendment warranted dismissal of the claim. M.S.A. § 325D.44, subd. 1(1–12).

    James M. King and Associates, Inc. v. G.D. Van Wagenen Co., 717 F.Supp. 667.

D.Nev. 1975. Western Intern. Hotels v. Tahoe Regional Planning Agency, 387 F.Supp. 429, affirmed in part, vacated in part, reversed in part Jacobson v. Tahoe Regional Planning Agency, 558 F.2d 928, opinion withdrawn and superseded on denial of rehearing 566 F.2d 1353, certiorari granted Lake Country Estates, Inc. v. Tahoe Regional Planning Agency, 98 S.Ct. 2843, 436 U.S. 943, 56 L.Ed.2d 784, affirmed in part, reversed in part 99 S.Ct. 1171, 440 U.S. 391, 59 L.Ed.2d 401, on remand 474 F.Supp. 901.

D.N.J. 1994. Possibility that plaintiff might be able to establish threat of continuing racketeering activity is sufficient for plaintiff to survive motion to dismiss on grounds on failure to establish "pattern of racketeering activity" in Racketeer Influenced and Corrupt Organizations Act (RICO) action. 18 U.S.C.A. § 1962(c).

    O'Rourke v. Crosley, 847 F.Supp. 1208.

D.N.J. 1992. Allegations that securities fraud defendants failed to disclose illegal and deceptive practices will survive a motion to dismiss. Securities Exchange Act of 1934, § 1 et seq., 15 U.S.C.A. § 78a et seq.

Westinghouse Elec. Corp. by Levit v. Franklin, 789 F.Supp. 1313, reversed 993 F.2d 349.

D.N.J. 1990. Counts of complaint by plaintiff in securities fraud case, under various sections of federal securities laws, that defendants had fraudulently induced shareholders of corporation to guarantee its bond, were not so absolutely devoid of merit or frivolous as to warrant dismissal for lack of subject matter jurisdiction. 28 U.S.C.A. § 1332.

VT Investors v. R & D Funding Corp., 733 F.Supp. 823.

D.N.J. 1989. Inconsistency between nuclear power plant owner's answer to claims by co-owners and its counterclaim against those co-owners with respect to another nuclear power plant did not justify dismissal of counterclaims. Fed.Rules Civ.Proc.Rule 8(e)(2), 28 U.S.C.A.

Public Service Enterprise Group, Inc. v. Philadelphia Elec. Co., 722 F.Supp. 184.

Nuclear power plant owner's position that negligent conduct by operating owner of Pennsylvania plant did not breach owners' agreement did not warrant dismissal of operating owner's contingent counterclaim alleging owner's mismanagement as managing owner of New Jersey plant, where two other owners alleged negligent performance of contract by operating owner, and where managing owner's own complaint explicitly pleaded gross negligence.

Public Service Enterprise Group, Inc. v. Philadelphia Elec. Co., 722 F.Supp. 184.

E.D.N.Y. 1995. To survive motion to dismiss for failure to state claim, plaintiffs seeking to recover under Racketeer Influenced and Corrupt Organizations Act (RICO) need not establish that they can obtain precise relief they seek, so long as they can demonstrate that they are entitled to some relief. 18 U.S.C.A. §§ 1962, 1964(c).

Burke v. Dowling, 944 F.Supp. 1036.

E.D.N.Y. 1994. Motion to dismiss on immunity grounds was properly brought as motion to dismiss for failure to state a claim. Fed. Rules Civ.Proc.Rule 12(b)(6), 28 U.S.C.A.

Eisenberg v. District Attorney of County of Kings, 847 F.Supp. 1029.

E.D.N.Y. 1990. Standard of reviewing complaint to determine whether it states claim for relief does not distinguish between Racketeer Influenced and Corrupt Organizations Act claims and non-RICO claims. 18 U.S.C.A. § 1961 et seq.; Fed.Rules Civ.Proc.Rule 12(b)(6), 28 U.S.C.A.

Ruby Development Corp. v. Charrim Development Corp., 742 F.Supp. 1213.

E.D.N.Y. 1986. Lacking any evidence on whether alleged violations of Education for All Handicapped Children Act rose to the level of a bad-faith and egregious failure to meet the Act's requirement, and lacking a body of undisputed facts, the district court was required, for the purposes of motion to dismiss, to construe allegations in the light most favorable to the plaintiff and thus defendant's motion to dismiss claims for damages under the Act would be denied. Education of the Handicapped Act, § 615(b), as amended, 20 U.S.C.A. § 1415(b); Fed.Rules Civ.Proc.Rule 12(b)(6), 28 U.S.C.A.

Gerasimou by Gerasimou v. Ambach, 636 F.Supp. 1504.

E.D.N.Y. 1984. Pro se complaint against state court system, Supreme Court, judge and file clerk, which was unintelligible and contained no allegation that any defendant had caused or threatened to cause plaintiff any injury, and which did not indicate relief sought, would be dismissed for failure to state claim upon which relief could be granted. Fed.Rules Civ.Proc. Rule 12(b), 28 U.S.C.A.

Browne v. N.Y.S. Court System, 599 F.Supp. 36.

N.D.N.Y. 1998. Pro se plaintiff's failure to file amended complaint in accordance with terms of report and recommendation of United States Magistrate Judge directing that plaintiff should submit amended complaint which is typewritten and double spaced warranted dismissal, where plaintiff's original and second amended complaints were single spaced and handwritten in form that was largely illegible making it impossible for court to ascertain allegations of complaint.

Mercer v. Acting Com'r of Dept. of Corrections, 992 F.Supp. 519.

N.D.N.Y. 1995. Collection letter's language instructing debtors to contact debt collector immediately contradicted letter's validation notice, which was required by Fair Debt Collection Practices Act (FDCPA) and which informed debtors that they had 30 days to dispute the debt in writing; thus, both debt collector and debtors would be entitled to present expert proof to jury regarding effect of letter on least sophisticated consumer, and neither party was entitled to summary judgment or to dismissal for failure to state a claim. Truth in Lending Act, § 809(a), as amended, 15 U.S.C.A. § 1692g(a); Fed.Rules Civ.Proc., Rule 12(b)(6), 28 U.S.C.A.

Beeman v. Lacy, Katzen, Ryen & Mittleman, 892 F.Supp. 405.

N.D.N.Y. 1995. Plaintiff's complaint violated requirements of rule governing pleading and was dismissed without prejudice where complaint gave no indication of laws allegedly violated by defendant or source of court's jurisdiction over suit, and did not provide adequate description of particular acts by defendant which led to suit or explanation of how acts were illegal. Fed.Rules Civ.Proc.Rule 8, 28 U.S.C.A.

> Powell v. Marine Midland Bank, 162 F.R.D. 15.

S.D.N.Y. 1997. Failure to adequately allege cognizable Racketeer Influenced and Corrupt Organizations (RICO) Act injury is ground for dismissal at pleading stage. 18 U.S.C.A. § 1961 et seq.

> Aramony v. United Way of America, 969 F.Supp. 226.

S.D.N.Y. 1995. In absence of federal authority requiring dismissal of Racketeer Influenced and Corrupt Organizations Act (RICO) claims prior to accounting, RICO claim would not be dismissed. 18 U.S.C.A. § 1962.

> Stratavest Ltd. v. Rogers, 888 F.Supp. 35.

S.D.N.Y. 1993. While a court, generally, should not look beyond pleadings in deciding motion to dismiss, district court may review and consider, in securities fraud case, public disclosure documents required by law to be and which actually have been filed with Securities and Exchange Commission (SEC), particularly where plaintiff has been put on notice by defendant's proffer of public documents. Securities Exchange Act of 1934, § 10(b), 15 U.S.C.A. § 78j(b).

> Nivram Corp. v. Harcourt Brace Jovanovich, Inc., 840 F.Supp. 243.

S.D.N.Y. 1993. All of complaints in plaintiff's consolidated actions were subject to dismissal as frivolous and vexatious litigation, particularly as plaintiff would not be allowed to circumvent prior order and injunction, requiring prior leave of court before filing actions or motions in federal court, by filing in state court and entering federal court through removal process; plaintiff was essentially engaged in bad-faith attempt to relitigate adjudicated matters by adding names of judges, officials and private individuals who had been involved in numerous past decisions rejecting his claims.

> Sassower v. Abrams, 833 F.Supp. 253.

S.D.N.Y. 1993. Minimization inquiry under New York law with respect to wiretap warrant was inappropriate for motion to dismiss for failure to state claim upon which relief could be granted; question of how officers conducted wiretap, especially spot monitoring of potentially nonpertinent conversations, and nature of periodic reports were inherently factual and something which district court would not attempt to resolve on motion to dismiss.

N.Y.McKinney's CPL § 700.30, subd. 7; Fed. Rules Civ.Proc.Rule 12(b)(6), 28 U.S.C.A.

> U.S. v. All Right, Title and Interest in Five Parcels of Real Property and Appurtances Thereto Known as 64 Lovers Lane, 830 F.Supp. 750.

Resolving whether procedures used by government satisfied purpose of sealing requirement for electronic surveillance tapes was beyond purview of motion to dismiss. Fed.Rules Civ.Proc.Rule 12(b)(6), 28 U.S.C.A.

> U.S. v. All Right, Title and Interest in Five Parcels of Real Property and Appurtances Thereto Known as 64 Lovers Lane, 830 F.Supp. 750.

S.D.N.Y. 1993. Upon motion to dismiss in securities fraud action, district court may only rule on materiality of omission when reasonable minds could not differ on importance of information to reasonable investor. Fed.Rules Civ. Proc.Rule 12(b)(6), 28 U.S.C.A.; Securities Act of 1933, §§ 11, 12(2), 15 U.S.C.A. §§ 77k, 77l (2); Securities Exchange Act of 1934, § 10(b), 15 U.S.C.A. § 78j(b).

> In re AES Corp. Securities Litigation, 825 F.Supp. 578.

S.D.N.Y. 1993. Accountant's concession that two of 18 alleged securities purchases did in fact involve "securities" precluded dismissal of § 10(b) claim on ground that purchases were in fact merely "loans," not "securities." Securities Exchange Act of 1934, § 10(b), 15 U.S.C.A. § 78j(b).

> CMNY Capital, L.P. v. Deloitte & Touche, 821 F.Supp. 152, reargument denied.

S.D.N.Y. 1993. To extent that plaintiff can allege more compelling facts to demonstrate fraudulent intent, courts give less weight to warnings about disclosure and require that warnings be broadly worded to survive motion to dismiss securities fraud complaint. Securities Exchange Act of 1934, § 10(b), 15 U.S.C.A. § 78j(b).

> Sable v. Southmark/Envicon Capital Corp., 819 F.Supp. 324.

S.D.N.Y. 1993. Allegation by investors in limited partnership interests in real estate tax shelters that private placement memorandum (PPM) falsely asserted that properties which partnerships purchased had sufficient rental revenues to cover current operating expenses and primary debt service was sufficient to withstand motion to dismiss in securities fraud action, notwithstanding defendants' contention that statements were not materially false or misleading because investors' calculations failed to account for lump sum interest payments and repair expenses which other section of PPM assumed would be paid out of receipts of offer; defendant's own calculations showed a deficit in one of the properties, and complaint which alleged that there were material misstatements in 41 PPMs could not be dismissed on defendants' analysis of only three.

Adler v. Berg Harmon Associates, 816 F.Supp. 919.

S.D.N.Y. 1993. In Second Circuit, test for determining whether securities fraud plaintiff was placed on inquiry notice of alleged fraud is objective and mandates dismissal of or summary judgment on securities fraud claim, where pleadings disclose facts sufficient to have suggested to person of ordinary intelligence the probability that he has been defrauded; to satisfy this test, knowledge of the alleged fraud imputed to plaintiff must rise to level of the probable and not merely of the possible. Securities Exchange Act of 1934, §§ 10(b), 27, as amended, 15 U.S.C.A. §§ 78j(b), 78aa.

In re Integrated Resources Real Estate Ltd. Partnerships Securities Litigation, 815 F.Supp. 620.

Although investors' consistent failure to specify dates they purchased interests in partnerships would ordinarily have required dismissal of securities fraud claims against partnerships, dismissal was not required, where defendant partnerships provided comprehensive schedule setting forth purchase dates. Securities Exchange Act of 1934, §§ 10(b), 27, as amended, 15 U.S.C.A. §§ 78j(b), 78aa.

In re Integrated Resources Real Estate Ltd. Partnerships Securities Litigation, 815 F.Supp. 620.

S.D.N.Y. 1992. Whether operators of adult rest home received federal financial assistance and whether nondisabled residents received better treatment than disabled residents were fact questions precluding dismissal of suit alleging substandard care by residents under Rehabilitation Act. Rehabilitation Act of 1973, §§ 504, 504(a), 29 U.S.C.A. §§ 794, 794(a); Fed.Rules Civ.Proc.Rule 12(b)(6), 28 U.S.C.A.

Trautz v. Weisman, 809 F.Supp. 239.

S.D.N.Y. 1992. In securities fraud action, materiality of omitted or misrepresented fact is resolvable on motion to dismiss only if underlying facts are free of controversy and fact is so obviously unimportant that no reasonable shareholder could have viewed it as significantly altering total mix of information made available to plaintiffs. Securities Exchange Act of 1934, § 1 et seq., 15 U.S.C.A. § 78a et seq.; Securities Act of 1933, § 1 et seq., 15 U.S.C.A. § 77a et seq.; Fed.Rules Civ.Proc.Rule 12(b)(6), 28 U.S.C.A.

Maywalt v. Parker & Parsley Petroleum Co., 808 F.Supp. 1037.

S.D.N.Y. 1992. Allegations in investors' complaint regarding misrepresentations as to value of partnership units raised sufficient questions as to when investors should, with reasonable diligence, have discovered fraud and precluded dismissal, on limitations grounds, of investors' securities fraud claims against appraisers who valued partnership's assets in connection with offering of units. Securities Exchange of Act of 1934, § 10(b), as amended, 15 U.S.C.A. § 78j(b).

In re First American Center Securities Litigation, 807 F.Supp. 326.

S.D.N.Y. 1991. Shareholders' letters to corporation containing not only general allegations of reckless and negligent business practices carried out by corporation officers but also specifying purportedly wrongful acts, even if not meeting New York law requirements for specificity of demand, would not be dismissed for failure to comply with demand requirement where corporate officers did not challenge adequacy of demand. Fed.Rules Civ.Proc.Rule 23.1, 28 U.S.C.A.

Stoner v. Walsh, 772 F.Supp. 790.

Shareholder's conclusory allegations of "bad faith" on part of corporation directors will not survive directors' motion to dismiss, unless complaint states some set of facts from which it may be inferred that directors' actions might have been motivated by improper purpose; epithets such as "bad faith," "sham," "coverup" and the like are not evidence.

Stoner v. Walsh, 772 F.Supp. 790.

S.D.N.Y. 1991. Counterclaims asserted by pro se defendants would not be dismissed for violations of rule requiring pleadings to contain short and plain statement of claim, although many of the allegations contained in 220 paragraphs alleging 13 causes of action were repetitive, pleading was not model of clarity, and at least some of the later claims repeated allegations of earlier claims which had been found not to provide basis for relief. Fed.Rules Civ. Proc.Rule 8(a), 28 U.S.C.A.

Citicorp Intern. Trading Co., Inc. v. Western Oil & Refining Co., Inc., 771 F.Supp. 600.

Underlying claim that signature of note by shareholders was fraudulently induced by concealing earlier breach of contract with corporation was the same as another counterclaim, so later counterclaim would be dismissed as redundant, and shareholders would be permitted to assert damages resulting from impairment of their interest in property as damages on earlier counterclaim.

Citicorp Intern. Trading Co., Inc. v. Western Oil & Refining Co., Inc., 771 F.Supp. 600.

S.D.N.Y. 1991. Racketeer Influenced and Corrupt Organizations Act (RICO) claim, predicated on acts of securities fraud, mail fraud, and wire fraud was subject to dismissal, where securities fraud violations were not adequately alleged and allegations of predicate acts of mail and wire fraud were not pled with sufficient particularity. 18 U.S.C.A. § 1962(b, c); Fed. Rules Civ.Proc.Rules 9(b), 12(b)(6), 28 U.S.C.A.

> Connolly v. Havens, 763 F.Supp. 6.

S.D.N.Y. 1991. Because defendants are generally in best position to answer types of questions that may be posed in motion to dismiss for failure to plead fraud with particularity, churning claim should not be dismissed until after discovery so long as complaint meets threshold test of pleading sufficient facts from which churning may be inferred. Fed.Rules Civ.Proc.Rule 9(b), 28 U.S.C.A.

> Nilsen v. Prudential-Bache Securities, 761 F.Supp. 279.

S.D.N.Y. 1991. Court must dismiss complaint founded on allegations of securities fraud if allegedly omitted or misrepresented information was in fact appropriately disclosed.

> White v. Melton, 757 F.Supp. 267.

S.D.N.Y. 1989. Factual inquiry was required to weigh New York's interest in fair and truthful advertising against degree of interference with interstate commerce from regulation of airline advertising; thus, airline's claim for interference with interstate commerce would not be dismissed. U.S.C.A. Const. Art. 1, § 8, cl. 3; N.Y.McKinney's Executive Law § 63, subd. 12; N.Y.McKinney's General Business Law § 350.

> People of State of N.Y. by Abrams v. Trans World Airlines, Inc., 728 F.Supp. 162, on remand 556 N.Y.S.2d 803, 147 Misc.2d 697, affirmed in part 575 N.Y.S.2d 1, 171 A.D.2d 76.

S.D.N.Y. 1989. Neither allegation in pleadings that commodity exchange participated in fraud scheme nor conclusory allegation of exchange's bad faith preserved traders' fraud action from dismissal for failure to state cause of action. Fed.Rules Civ.Proc.Rule 12(b)(6), 28 U.S.C.A.; Commodity Exchange Act, § 22(b), as amended, 7 U.S.C.A. § 25(b).

> Grossman v. Citrus Associates of New York Cotton Exchange, Inc., 706 F.Supp. 221, reconsideration denied 1989 WL 51825.

Since it was unclear whether commodity traders intended to include "Doe" defendants in their fraud trading claim under Commodity Exchange Act, that action was dismissed for failure to state cause of action. Fed.Rules Civ. Proc.Rule 12(b)(6), 28 U.S.C.A.

> Grossman v. Citrus Associates of New York Cotton Exchange, Inc., 706 F.Supp. 221, reconsideration denied 1989 WL 51825.

S.D.N.Y. 1988. Pro se plaintiff's RICO claims would be dismissed, where plaintiff had failed to plead substantive elements of his RICO claim with any degree of particularity, and complaint with its attachment described only one allegedly fraudulent transaction, and thus did not satisfy statute's requirement of "pattern" of racketeering activity. 18 U.S.C.A. § 1961 et seq.

> Cornett v. Manufacturers Hanover Trust Co., 684 F.Supp. 78, affirmed 902 F.2d 1556, certiorari denied 111 S.Ct. 754, 498 U.S. 1047, 112 L.Ed.2d 774.

S.D.N.Y. 1986. Claim that some relief sought by Government in civil action under Racketeer Influenced and Corrupt Organizations Act action might be unavailable did not mandate dismissal of action for failure to state claim upon which relief could be granted. 18 U.S.C.A. §§ 1961 et seq., 1964; Fed.Rules Civ. Proc.Rule 12(b)(6), 28 U.S.C.A.

> U.S. v. Ianniello, 646 F.Supp. 1289, affirmed 824 F.2d 203.

S.D.N.Y. 1986. Dismissal of amended complaint was not warranted on basis of repetition of dismissed claims, but defendants would not be required to answer those portions of the amended complaint which had already been dismissed.

> Mechigian v. Art Capital Corp., 639 F.Supp. 702.

S.D.N.Y. 1977. Redington v. Touche Ross & Co., 428 F.Supp. 483, reversed 592 F.2d 617, certiorari granted 99 S.Ct. 563, 439 U.S. 979, 58 L.Ed.2d 649, reversed 99 S.Ct. 2479, 442 U.S. 560, 61 L.Ed.2d 82, on remand 612 F.2d 68, certiorari denied 99 S.Ct. 3095, 443 U.S. 904, 61 L.Ed.2d 872, certiorari denied Securities Investor Protection Corporation v. Touche Ross & Co., 99 S.Ct. 3096, 443 U.S. 904, 61 L.Ed.2d 872.

D.N.D. 1994. Complaint was subject to dismissal for violation of rule requiring short and plain statement of claim showing that plaintiff was entitled to relief, even though plaintiff was proceeding pro se; complaint, including attachments, exceeded 150 pages and contained surfeit of information, some of complaint was incomprehensible, and plaintiff had completed at least two years of law school and possessed capacity to set forth relevant facts and applicable law. Fed.Rules Civ.Proc.Rule 8(a)(2), 28 U.S.C.A.

> Thomson v. Olson, 866 F.Supp. 1267, affirmed 56 F.3d 69.

E.D.Pa. 1997. District court would dismiss all of closed-circuit television boxing match distributor's claims against remaining defendants after dismissing same claims against bar owners on owners' motion to dismiss complaint for failure to state claim, in distributor's action, alleging that defendants exhibited boxing match without paying required subscription fee, and asserting claims under Communications Act section governing unauthorized publication or use of communications and for conversion and interference with prospective economic advantage; however, in the interest of justice, court would allow distributor 20 days to amend its complaint. 28 U.S.C.A. § 1367(c); Communications Act of 1934, §§ 633, 705, as amended, 47 U.S.C.A. §§ 553, 605; Fed.Rules Civ.Proc.Rules 12(b)(6), 15(a), 28 U.S.C.A.

> Joe Hand Promotions, Inc. v. Rennard Street Enterprises, Inc., 954 F.Supp. 1046.

E.D.Pa. 1994. In light of the liberal pleading standards, plaintiffs' pro se complaint provided fair notice to defendant of nature and basis of the asserted claims and general indication of the type of litigation involved so as to survive motion to dismiss for failure to state claim upon which relief can be granted. Fed. Rules Civ.Proc.Rule 12(b)(6), 28 U.S.C.A.

> Brown v. Peoples Sec. Ins., 158 F.R.D. 350.

Although one of the plaintiffs was not named as party in caption of the plaintiffs' pro se complaint, claim of this plaintiff would not be dismissed for failure to comply with technical requirements of rule providing that in the complaint the title of the action shall include names of all the parties because caption is usually not considered part of pleader's statement of claim and is not determinative as to the parties to the action. Fed.Rules Civ.Proc.Rule 10, 28 U.S.C.A.

> Brown v. Peoples Sec. Ins., 158 F.R.D. 350.

E.D.Pa. 1992. Although complaint may state prima facie case for securities fraud, complaint must be dismissed if it fails to provide sufficient factual basis to substantiate its claims. Securities Exchange Act of 1934, § 10(b), 15 U.S.C.A. § 78j(b); Fed.Rules Civ.Proc.Rule 9(b), 28 U.S.C.A.

> In re American Travellers Corp. Securities Litigation, 806 F.Supp. 547.

E.D.Pa. 1990. Even though plaintiff need not plead elements necessary to prove Racketeer Influenced and Corrupt Organizations Act (RICO) enterprise, if allegations in complaint preclude existence of one or more required elements, then dismissal of complaint is appropriate. 18 U.S.C.A. §§ 1962, 1962(c).

> Federal Ins. Co. v. Ayers, 741 F.Supp. 1179, reconsideration denied 760 F.Supp. 1118.

M.D.Pa. 1998. Landowner's complaint alleging that various individual defendants cut and stole timber from her property in violation of Racketeer Influenced and Corrupt Or-

ganizations Act (RICO) was sufficient to survive motion to dismiss for lack of subject matter jurisdiction, though complaint did not allege a pattern of racketeering activity, as required by the Act; analysis of the claim's merits was not appropriate on motion to dismiss for lack of jurisdiction. 18 U.S.C.A. § 1961 et seq.; Fed.Rules Civ.Proc.Rule 12(b)(1), 28 U.S.C.A.

> McCreary v. Wilt, 11 F.Supp.2d 731.

W.D.Pa. 1994. Even if security fraud complaint was lacking in specifics regarding scienter of corporation and its officers and directors, complaint would survive motion to dismiss for lack of particularity given allegations of investors that they had thoroughly investigated all possible sources of information, including but not limited to all publicly available relevant information, before filing complaint and necessary information thus could have been within corporate defendants' exclusive control. Fed. Rules Civ.Proc.Rule 9(b), 28 U.S.C.A.; Securities Exchange Act of 1934, § 10(b), 15 U.S.C.A. § 78j(b).

> In re Chambers Development Securities Litigation, 848 F.Supp. 602.

W.D.Pa. 1985. In light of Court of Appeals' direction that courts adopt a liberal approach to Racketeer Influenced and Corrupt Organizations Act pleadings at motion to dismiss stage, account executive was not entitled to dismissal of securities customer's RICO claim because he had not been convicted of the predicate criminal acts. 18 U.S.C.A. §§ 1961 et seq., 1962(c).

> Witt v. Merrill Lynch, Pierce, Fenner & Smith, Inc., 602 F.Supp. 867.

D.Puerto Rico 1991. District court would dismiss travelers' claims that defendants violated Federal Aviation Administration regulations and federal tariffs in connection with seizure at airport of certain large, unmarked boxes that travelers were attempting to bring into Puerto Rico, inasmuch as travelers never identified what tariffs or regulations they contended were violated despite several opportunities to clarify issue.

> Salas Garcia v. Cesar Perez, 777 F.Supp. 137.

D.R.I. 1990. Claim by National Credit Union Administration Board, as conservator of credit union, that scheme existed to defraud union by purchasing real estate from union at less than fair market value, concealing interest of officer and director in transaction and then using real estate to obtain loan in amount exceeding purchase price of the land would not be dismissed for failure to specify specific acts of mail or wire fraud until conservator was allowed discovery on issue, even though it was possible that alleged fraud could have been carried out without use of mails or interstate wires; all defendants were business associates with offices at same location and all resided in same state. 18 U.S.C.A. §§ 657, 666, 1341, 1343, 1344, 1956(a), 1961(1)(B), 2113(b).

National Credit Union Admin. Bd. v. Regine, 749 F.Supp. 401.

D.R.I. 1990. Whether investment company's officers, directors and controlling shareholders had duty to disclose asset evaluation information in proxy concerning proposed sale of company's assets under Securities Exchange Act of 1934 required consideration of factual issues that could not be properly resolved in context of motion to dismiss. Securities Exchange Act of 1934, §§ 10(b), 14(a), 15 U.S.C.A. §§ 78j(b), 78n(a); Fed.Rules Civ.Proc.Rule 12(b)(6), 28 U.S.C.A.

Dowling v. Narragansett Capital Corp., 735 F.Supp. 1105.

Issue of materiality of alleged misrepresentations as to value of investment company's assets and nondisclosure of limitations on information underlying investment banking firm's fairness opinion in connection with proposed sale of company's assets could not be resolved on motion to dismiss in action under proxy and antifraud provisions of Securities Exchange Act of 1934. Securities Exchange Act of 1934, §§ 10(b), 14(a), 15 U.S.C.A. §§ 78j(b), 78n(a); Fed.Rules Civ.Proc.Rule 12(b)(6), 28 U.S.C.A.

Dowling v. Narragansett Capital Corp., 735 F.Supp. 1105.

Investment company's shareholders' allegations that same individuals controlled both investment company and holding company that purchased investment company's assets at inadequate price created fact issue as to whether "purchase" of investment company's shares had occurred within meaning of Securities Exchange Act provision prohibiting investment company from purchasing its own shares, precluding dismissal. Securities Exchange Act of 1934, § 13(e), 15 U.S.C.A. § 78m(e); Fed.Rules Civ.Proc.Rule 12(b)(6), 28 U.S.C.A.

Dowling v. Narragansett Capital Corp., 735 F.Supp. 1105.

D.R.I. 1986. Plaintiff's complaint which alleged violations of the Fourth Amendment to the United States Constitution, Freedom of Information Act, the Privacy Act, and the Omnibus Crime Control and Safe Streets Act met his burden of showing that he was alleging nonfrivolous federal questions despite the fact that there was substantial question concerning the applicability of the statutes to plaintiff's action. 5 U.S.C.A. §§ 552, 552a, 552a(g)(1); 18 U.S.C.A. §§ 2510–2520; 28 U.S.C.A. § 1331; Fed.Rules Civ.Proc.Rule 12(b)(1), 28 U.S.C.A; U.S.C.A. Const.Amend. 4.

Patriarca v. F.B.I., 639 F.Supp. 1193.

D.Utah 1994. Complaint alleging violations of Racketeer Influenced and Corrupt Organizations Act (RICO), securities law and various pendent state claims, would be dismissed for failure to comply with Civil Procedure Rule 8 requiring that pleadings contain short and plain statement of claim and that averments be simple, concise and direct; despite warning issued in rejection of earlier complaints, claimants continued to advance irrelevant and redundant allegations and consistently make repetitive legal conclusions unsupported by relevant facts, and to utilize sentences with passive verbs and awkward sentence construction making it difficult to read and identify wrongs complained of, perpetrators and victims. Fed.Rules Civ. Proc.Rule 8, 28 U.S.C.A.

Arena Land & Inv. Co., Inc. v. Petty, 906 F.Supp. 1470, affirmed 69 F.3d 547.

D.Vt. 1992. Whether bank's stock in fact traded in market sufficiently well developed to support presumption of reliance in securities fraud action under Securities and Exchange Commission (SEC) rule premised on theory of fraud on the market was not an issue that could be decided on motion to dismiss.

Walsh v. Chittenden Corp., 798 F.Supp. 1043.

D.Virgin Islands 1993. Allegations by owners of contaminated wells regarding purported failure to observe corporate formality between parent and subsidiary corporations and that subsidiaries acted as extensions of parent with regard to environmental policies and program were insufficient to warrant disregard of corporate separateness and to hold parent corporation liable for conduct of subsidiaries, under Virgin Islands law, but it did not appear beyond doubt that owners could prove no set of facts in support of their claims; therefore, claims against parent would not be dismissed, and owners would be given time to engage in necessary discovery to supplement their pleadings. Fed.Rules Civ.Proc.Rules 12(b)(6), 56, 28 U.S.C.A.

In re Tutu Wells Contamination Litigation, 846 F.Supp. 1243.

E.D.Wash. 1985. While count of federal complaint alleging violation of the Racketeer Influenced and Corrupt Organizations Act was facially within district court's subject matter jurisdiction, it could not survive a motion to dismiss for failure to state a claim in its present form. 18 U.S.C.A. § 1961 et seq.

Kinsey v. Nestor Exploration Ltd. - 1981A, 604 F.Supp. 1365.

E.D.Wis. 1993. Absolute immunity may properly be raised in support of motion to dismiss for failure to state claim. Fed.Rules Civ.Proc.Rule 12(b)(6), 28 U.S.C.A.

Kaufmann v. U.S., 840 F.Supp. 641.

Raising qualified immunity in motion to dismiss is permissible, although typically such defense is presented in summary judgment motion after benefits of additional factual development; thus, court may refrain from ruling on qualified immunity until further development of facts. Fed.Rules Civ.Proc.Rule 12(b), 28 U.S.C.A.

Kaufmann v. U.S., 840 F.Supp. 641.

Bkrtcy.N.D.Ill. 1991. Issue of shareholder ratification, as question of fact, could not be reached on motion to dismiss breach of fiduciary duty claims against Chapter 11 debtor's officers and directors in connection with prepetition leveraged buyout transaction wherein debtor acquired assets and liabilities of aluminum corporation.

In re Aluminum Mills Corp., 132 B.R. 869.

Bkrtcy.E.D.Va. 1994. Decision to pierce corporate veil depends largely on resolving questions of fact precluding resolution of issue on motion to dismiss.

In re Richels, 163 B.R. 760.

⚷1782. Accounting, actions for.

Library references

C.J.S. Federal Civil Procedure § 839.

⚷1783. Agency or brokerage, actions involving.

Library references

C.J.S. Federal Civil Procedure § 839.

D.Del. 1992. Plaintiff's allegations that defendant acted, not as mere employee, but as plaintiff's agent when he dealt with outside companies precluded dismissal of plaintiff's claim for breach of fiduciary duty under Delaware law.

Standard Chlorine of Delaware, Inc. v. Sinibaldi, 821 F.Supp. 232.

N.D.Ill. 1993. Allegation of broker-customer or investment advisor-customer relationship in claim under Illinois law for breach of fiduciary duty is sufficient to withstand motion to dismiss.

Caraluzzi v. Prudential Securities, Inc., 824 F.Supp. 1206.

W.D.Mich. 1985. Fact that customer, in stating a claim against brokerage firm under the Racketeering Influenced and Corrupt Organizations Act, set forth several allegations of securities fraud as a predicate act to support claim was insufficient to warrant dismissal of complaint as terminally repetitive or verbose. 18 U.S.C.A. § 1962(c).

Smith v. Oppenheimer and Co., Inc., 635 F.Supp. 936.

S.D.N.Y. 1987. Investor's breach of contract claim against brokerage firm, for losses he suffered when his metal futures account was liquidated, would be dismissed with prejudice; factual allegations underlying claim either related exclusively to events surrounding issuance of margin calls and liquidation of his count that had already been deemed to be res judicata, or failed to provide support for cause of action for breach of contract.

Michelson v. Merrill Lynch, Pierce, Fenner & Smith, Inc., 669 F.Supp. 1244.

After investor's claim under Commodity Exchange Act, as it related to brokerage firm's liquidation of his metal futures account, had been determined to be barred by res judicata, his subsequent failure to amend his claim under Act to allege conduct other than that related to account liquidation warranted dismissal of claim with prejudice. Commodity Exchange Act, § 4c, as amended, 7 U.S.C.A. § 6c.

Michelson v. Merrill Lynch, Pierce, Fenner & Smith, Inc., 669 F.Supp. 1244.

After investor's claim against nonexchange defendant under Commodity Exchange Act had been determined to allege insufficient facts, amended claim would be dismissed with prejudice due to investor's failure to remedy prior defect. Commodity Exchange Act, § 4b, as amended, 7 U.S.C.A. § 6b.

Michelson v. Merrill Lynch, Pierce, Fenner & Smith, Inc., 669 F.Supp. 1244.

⚷1784. Antitrust and price discrimination actions.

Library references

C.J.S. Federal Civil Procedure § 826.

C.A.8 (Mo.) 1989. Same interstate commerce analysis applies whether complaint alleging antitrust violation is dismissed for lack of subject matter jurisdiction or for failure to state claim upon which relief can be granted; district court must determine whether complaint adequately alleges nexus between defendant's conduct and interstate commerce. Sherman Anti-Trust Act, §§ 1, 2, 15 U.S.C.A. §§ 1, 2.

Huelsman v. Civic Center Corp., 873 F.2d 1171.

C.A.2 (N.Y.) 1983. Wickham Contracting Co., Inc. v. Board of Educ. of City of New York, 715 F.2d 21, on remand 1991 WL 84595, affirmed 955 F.2d 831, certiorari denied Local Union No. 3, Intern. Broth. of Elec. Workers, American Federation of Labor and Congress of Indus. Organizations v. Wickham Contracting Co., Inc., 113 S.Ct. 394, 506 U.S. 946, 121 L.Ed.2d 302.

C.A.4 (N.C.) 1975. Hospital Bldg. Co. v. Trustees of Rex Hosp., 511 F.2d 678, certiorari granted 96 S.Ct. 33, 423 U.S. 820, 46 L.Ed.2d 37, reversed 96 S.Ct. 1848, 425 U.S. 738, 48 L.Ed.2d 338, appeal after remand 691 F.2d 678,

71 A.L.R. Fed. 704, certiorari denied 104 S.Ct. 231, 464 U.S. 890, 78 L.Ed.2d 224, certiorari denied 104 S.Ct. 259, 464 U.S. 904, 78 L.Ed.2d 244, rehearing denied 104 S.Ct. 512, 464 U.S. 1003, 78 L.Ed.2d 700, appeal after remand 791 F.2d 288.

C.A.3 (Pa.) 1991. Allegation in antitrust complaint which raised possibility of competing inferences as to why plaintiff cardiologist's hospital staff privileges were terminated did not alone permit dismissal of amended complaint for failure to state a claim.

> Fuentes v. South Hills Cardiology, 946 F.2d 196.

C.D.Cal. 1994. Summary dismissals of antitrust actions are disfavored. Fed.Rules Civ. Proc.Rule 12(b)(6), 28 U.S.C.A.

> Smilecare Dental Group v. Delta Dental Plan of California, 858 F.Supp. 1035, affirmed 88 F.3d 780, certiorari denied 117 S.Ct. 583, 136 L.Ed.2d 513.

D.Colo. 1987. Standard to be applied on motion to dismiss for failure to state claim is even more stringent in evaluation of antitrust claims, where proof is in hands of alleged conspirators, and dismissals prior to giving plaintiff ample opportunity for discovery should be granted very sparingly. Fed.Rules Civ.Proc. Rule 12(b)(6), 28 U.S.C.A.

> H.R.M., Inc. v. Tele-Communications, Inc., 653 F.Supp. 645.

Conclusory allegations which merely recite litany of antitrust will not suffice to withstand motion to dismiss for failure to state claim. Fed.Rules Civ.Proc.Rule 12(b)(6), 28 U.S.C.A.

> H.R.M., Inc. v. Tele-Communications, Inc., 653 F.Supp. 645.

D.D.C. 1995. On motion to dismiss or for judgment on the pleadings in antitrust case, plaintiff must do more than simply paraphrase language of federal antitrust law or state in conclusory terms that defendant has violated those laws. Sherman Act, § 1 et seq., as amended, 15 U.S.C.A. § 1 et seq.

> Dial A Car, Inc. v. Transportation, Inc., 884 F.Supp. 584, affirmed 82 F.3d 484, 317 U.S.App.D.C. 240, rehearing and suggestion for rehearing denied.

M.D.Fla. 1989. That plaintiff filed antitrust action seeking treble damages did not warrant heightened scrutiny of plaintiff's complaint on motion to dismiss for failure to state cause of action.

> GTE Data Services, Inc. v. Electronic Data Systems Corp., 717 F.Supp. 1487.

D.Kan. 1996. Motions to dismiss antitrust claims for failure to state a claim are no more disfavored than motions to dismiss other types

of claims. Fed.Rules Civ.Proc.Rule 12(b)(6), 28 U.S.C.A.

> Classic Communications, Inc. v. Rural Telephone Service Co., Inc., 956 F.Supp. 896.

W.D.La. 1986. Sherman Act claims asserted by nontenant rental car business against airport authority, which imposed charges on entities which did not have contracts with authority but which nevertheless used airport facilities in furtherance of commercial enterprises, could not be dismissed for failure to state a claim, although authority claimed affirmative defense that it was exempt from antitrust liability under *Parker* doctrine, where authority did not allege affirmative defense in its pleading. Fed.Rules Civ.Proc.Rule 12(b)(6), 28 U.S.C.A.; Sherman Anti-Trust Act, § 1 et seq., 15 U.S.C.A. § 1 et seq.

> Airline Car Rental, Inc. v. Shreveport Airport Authority, 667 F.Supp. 293.

D.Md. 1981. In re Mid-Atlantic Toyota Antitrust Litigation, 525 F.Supp. 1265, opinion modified 541 F.Supp. 62, affirmed Com. of Pa. v. Mid-Atlantic Toyota Distributors, Inc., 704 F.2d 125.

D.Mass. 1992. Whether professional football league rule prohibiting sale of shares of an interest in any league franchise to any company not engaged in the business of professional football could be viewed as a restraint of trade in violation of federal antitrust law presented triable issues of fact, and precluded a decision based on complex financial and economic factors as a matter of law on a motion to dismiss. Sherman Anti-Trust Act, §§ 1, 2, 15 U.S.C.A. §§ 1, 2.

> Sullivan v. Tagliabue, 795 F.Supp. 56.

D.Nev. 1987. Failure of plaintiff to show required nexus between defendants' activities and interstate commerce so as to support its federal antitrust claims after defendants contested nexus to interstate commerce required dismissal of complaint for lack of subject matter jurisdiction.

> Parrish v. City of Reno, Nev., 118 F.R.D. 129.

N.D.N.Y. 1989. In order to sustain a motion to dismiss for failure to state a claim in an antitrust case, defendant must meet a more stringent standard than in other cases because proof is often in the hands of the alleged conspirators and plaintiff may need an opportunity to discover the facts necessary to withstand the motion. Fed.Rules Civ.Proc.Rule 12(b)(6), 28 U.S.C.A.

> Capital Imaging Associates, P.C. v. Mohawk Valley Medical Associates, Inc., 725 F.Supp. 669.

S.D.N.Y. 1990. Antitrust plaintiff's conclusory allegation that "labor organization" with which defendant union cooperated in its efforts to represent crew of ship was also employer and thus a nonlabor entity was insufficient to withstand motion to dismiss claim against union pursuant to labor dispute exemption to antitrust liability. Clayton Act, § 6, 15 U.S.C.A. § 17; Norris-LaGuardia Act, § 1, 29 U.S.C.A. § 101.

> Perry v. International Transport Workers' Federation, 750 F.Supp. 1189.

S.D.N.Y. 1985. Liberal pleading requirement applicable to motions to dismiss apply with full force to Sherman Act antitrust claims. Fed.Rules Civ.Proc.Rule 8(f), 28 U.S.C.A.; Sherman Anti-Trust Act, § 1 et seq., 15 U.S.C.A. § 1 et seq.

> CBS, Inc. v. Ahern, 108 F.R.D. 14.

S.D.N.Y. 1981. Solargen Elec. Motor Car Corp. v. American Motors Corp., 530 F.Supp. 22, affirmed 697 F.2d 297, certiorari denied Solargen Electric Motor Car Corp. v. General Motors Corp., 103 S.Ct. 217, 459 U.S. 910, 74 L.Ed.2d 172.

N.D.Ohio 1980. United Steel Workers of America, Local No. 1330 v. U. S. Steel Corp., 492 F.Supp. 1, affirmed in part, vacated in part 631 F.2d 1264.

D.Puerto Rico 1993. Complaint alleging violations of provisions of the Robinson-Patman Price Discrimination Act which merely quoted or paraphrased statutory language without any factual support failed to state claim upon which relief could be granted. Clayton Act, § 2(c-e), as amended by Robinson-Patman Price Discrimination Act, 15 U.S.C.A. § 13(c-e); Fed. Rules Civ.Proc.Rule 12(b)(6), 28 U.S.C.A.

> Caribe BMW, Inc. v. Bayerische Motoren Werke Aktiengesellschaft, 821 F.Supp. 802, vacated 19 F.3d 745.

Mere incantation of antitrust "buzz words" cannot substitute for necessary factual allegations establishing valid claim for recovery, for which relief can be granted. Fed.Rules Civ. Proc.Rule 12(b)(6), 28 U.S.C.A.

> Caribe BMW, Inc. v. Bayerische Motoren Werke Aktiengesellschaft, 821 F.Supp. 802, vacated 19 F.3d 745.

S.D.Tex. 1994. On their motion to dismiss claims in landowner's action against them for conspiracy to keep landowner from mining lignite from its property in violation of Sherman Antitrust Act, mining company and electric utilities were not entitled to heightened pleading standard akin to that in civil rights cases. Fed. Rules Civ.Proc.Rules 8(a), (e)(1), (f), 12(b)(6), 28 U.S.C.A.

> TCA Bldg. Co. v. Northwestern Resources Co., 861 F.Supp. 1366.

E.D.Va. 1987. Dismissals for failure to state claim, particularly in antitrust actions, should be granted very sparingly and only if it appears that plaintiff can prove no set of facts in support of his claim which would entitle him to relief; nevertheless, courts will require some reasonable particularity in pleading violations of federal antitrust laws.

> Reynolds Metals Co. v. Columbia Gas System, Inc., 669 F.Supp. 744.

⚷**1785. Assignments, actions involving.**

Library references

> C.J.S. Federal Civil Procedure §§ 829, 839.

N.D.Ill. 1989. Validity of assignment to hospital of health insurance benefits under Illinois law presented a question of intent not properly dealt with on motion to dismiss for failure to state a claim. Fed.Rules Civ.Proc. Rule 12(b)(6), 28 U.S.C.A.

> Columbus, Cuneo, Cabrini Medical Center v. Travelers Ins. Co., 725 F.Supp. 396.

⚷**1786. Automobile cases.**

Library references

> C.J.S. Federal Civil Procedure § 836.

⚷**1787. Bankruptcy trustees, actions by and against.**

Library references

> C.J.S. Federal Civil Procedure § 839.

D.Del. 1994. Claims brought by Chapter 11 debtors' creditors committees relating to alleged breaches of indentures had to be dismissed where, inter alia, they were duplicative of tortious interference claims asserted in same complaint. Fed.Rules Civ.Proc.Rule 12(b)(6), 28 U.S.C.A.

> In re Buckhead America Corp., 178 B.R. 956.

S.D.Fla. 1990. Improper mixing of claims of corporate debtors and individual creditors rendered trustee's complaint subject to dismissal. Fed.Rules Civ.Proc.Rules 8(e), 9(b), 28 U.S.C.A.

> Feltman v. Prudential Bache Securities, 122 B.R. 466.

S.D.N.Y. 1993. Creditor's fraud suit against Chapter 11 trustees and surety would be dismissed for failure to specify fraud with sufficient particularity; pleading alleged trustee's oral promise to close bankruptcy case by certain date, but did not allege when statement was made or in what context. Fed.Rules Civ.Proc. Rule 9(b), 28 U.S.C.A.

> Titsch v. Arnason, 150 B.R. 311.

S.D.Ohio 1990. Adversary proceeding brought against lessor for breach of alleged oral agreement permitting debtor-lessee to assign rights in written coal lease did not have to be dismissed for lack of cause of action; record contained facts which, if proven, could substantiate claims asserted by debtor's trustee, and facts had to be viewed in light most favorable to the trustee.

In re Sonnyco Coal, Inc., 131 B.R. 799.

Bkrtcy.E.D.Ark. 1995. Allegation that bankruptcy estate had continuing obligations to perform under lease of real property, and that trustee failed to perform under lease, was sufficiently clear to allege claim against the bankruptcy estate; thus, motion to dismiss for failure to state a claim had to be denied. Fed. Rules Civ.Proc.Rule 12(b)(6), 28 U.S.C.A.

In re Baldwin, 184 B.R. 558.

Buyers of Chapter 7 debtor's real property did not state claim against bankruptcy trustee for tortious interference with contract by alleging that trustee, after agreeing to sell real property to buyers, was furnished higher offer from another party, who was alleged competitor of buyers; claim did not allege tortious act by third party because trustee was not third party but was successor in interest to the debtors, and, thus, motion to dismiss for failure to state claim had to be granted. Fed.Rules Civ.Proc. Rule 12(b)(6), 28 U.S.C.A.

In re Baldwin, 184 B.R. 558.

Bkrtcy.E.D.Ark. 1988. Fact that complaint only named defendant in bankruptcy adversary proceeding in caption and thereafter referred only to defendant, without specifically naming party in body of complaint, did not entitle the party to dismissal; there was only one defendant, and there could be no doubt as to the party referred to in the allegations.

In re Hollis & Co., 83 B.R. 586.

Bkrtcy.N.D.Ill. 1993. Creditor sufficiently set forth Chapter 7 debtor's alleged fraud to survive debtor's motion to dismiss for failure to state claim, and to meet general rules of pleading, where creditor alleged that bank utilized funds obtained from creditor for debtor's corporation as though they were his own funds. Fed.Rules Civ.Proc.Rules 8, 9(b), 28 U.S.C.A.

In re Leigh, 165 B.R. 203.

Bkrtcy.N.D.Ill. 1991. On motion to dismiss fraudulent conveyance, equitable subordination, preference, and breach of fiduciary duty claims for failure to state claim upon which relief can be granted, issue was not whether official committee of unsecured creditors would ultimately prevail; rather, issue was whether committee had pleaded cause of action sufficient to entitle it to offer evidence in support of its claims. Fed.Rules Civ.Proc.Rule 12(b)(6), 28 U.S.C.A.; Fed.Rules Bankr.Proc.Rule 7012, 11 U.S.C.A.

In re Aluminum Mills Corp., 132 B.R. 869.

Fraudulent conveyance complaint against leveraged buyout lenders and controlling shareholder sufficiently pled actual intent to hinder, delay or defaud creditors under the Bankruptcy Code and under the applicable version of Illinois Uniform Fraudulent Conveyance Act to survive motion to dismiss for failure to state claim upon which relief can be granted; complaint alleged that leveraged buyout lenders and controlling shareholder knew or should have known that the leveraged buyout was structured so that debtor would not retain any of the loan proceeds, but would assume all obligations to repay those loans and that the leveraged buyout lenders and the controlling shareholder knew or should have known prior to the leveraged buyout that the leveraged buyout would render the debtor insolvent, severely undercapitalized, and unable to meets its obligations as they became due. Bankr.Code, 11 U.S.C.A. § 548(a)(1); Ill. Rev.Stat.1987, ch. 59, ¶ 4.

In re Aluminum Mills Corp., 132 B.R. 869.

Breach of fiduciary duty complaint asserted against officers and directors of Chapter 11 debtor in connection with prepetition leveraged buyout transaction wherein debtor acquired assets and liabilities of aluminum corporation was sufficient to withstand motion to dismiss for failure to state claim upon which relief can be granted; court could reasonably infer from complaint allegations that officers and directors acted in their own interest in approving leveraged buyout even though they knew that leveraged buyout would result in harm to both debtor and its creditors. Fed.Rules Civ.Proc.Rule 12(b)(6), 28 U.S.C.A.

In re Aluminum Mills Corp., 132 B.R. 869.

Count charging leveraged buyout lender with inducement of breach of fiduciary duty in connection with release of debtor's claims against lender was sufficient to withstand motion to dismiss for failure to state claim upon which relief can be granted. Fed.Rules Civ. Proc.Rule 12(b)(6), 28 U.S.C.A.

In re Aluminum Mills Corp., 132 B.R. 869.

Preferential transfer complaint asserted in connection with prepetition leveraged buyout transaction wherein Chapter 11 debtor acquired assets and liabilities of aluminum corporation was sufficient to withstand motion to dismiss for failure to state claim upon which relief can be granted; complaint alleged that preferential transfers were made within 90 days of the Chapter 11 filing while debtor was insolvent, and that transfers enabled leveraged buyout lender and shareholder to receive more than they would have received had debtor filed petition under Chapter 7. Bankr.Code, 11 U.S.C.A. § 547(b)(5); Fed.Rules Civ.Proc.Rule 12(b)(6), 28 U.S.C.A.; Fed.Rules Bankr.Proc.Rule 7012, 11 U.S.C.A.

In re Aluminum Mills Corp., 132 B.R. 869.

Equitable subordination claim against leveraged buyout lender in connection with pre-petition transaction wherein Chapter 11 debtor acquired assets and liabilities of aluminum corporation was sufficient to survive motion to dismiss for failure to state claim upon which relief can be granted; complaint alleged that lender had been party to fraudulent act which had potentially injured other creditors and that creditor had induced shareholders to breach their fiduciary duties to debtor in order to benefit leveraged buyout lender. Bankr.Code, 11 U.S.C.A. § 510(c); Fed.Rules Civ.Proc.Rule 12(b)(6), 28 U.S.C.A.

In re Aluminum Mills Corp., 132 B.R. 869.

Bkrtcy.D.Minn. 1987. Chapter 7 debtor's malicious prosecution or abuse of process claim against creditor for prepetition collection activities was essentially a counterclaim as to creditor's objection to discharge that should have been initially joined in debtor's answer and made fully subject to discovery during course of adversary proceeding, and debtor's failure to present claim until filing of cross motions for dismissal warranted denial. Fed.Rules Civ. Proc.Rule 13(a, b), 28 U.S.C.A.; Bankr.Code, 11 U.S.C.A. §§ 701 et seq., 727(a); Rules Bankr. Proc.Rule 7013, 11 U.S.C.A.

In re Drenckhahn, 77 B.R. 697.

Bkrtcy.W.D.Mo. 1989. Bankruptcy court will not dismiss complaint for failure to state claim upon which relief can be granted unless, viewing complaint in light most favorable to plaintiff, it appears beyond doubt that plaintiff can prove no set of facts which would entitle him/her to relief. Rules Bankr.Proc.Rule 7012(b), 11 U.S.C.A.; Fed.Rules Civ.Proc.Rule 12(b)(6), 28 U.S.C.A.

In re Kelpe, 98 B.R. 479.

Bkrtcy.D.Neb. 1989. Warrant holders and warrant holder creditors' committee had sufficiently pled conversion by political subdivision of state that was Chapter 9 debtor based on payment of operating expenses and professional fees on bond fund to withstand motion to dismiss, under Nebraska law, although immediate right to possession of money and bond fund had not been pled.

Matter of Sanitary and Imp. Dist. No. 7 of Lancaster County, Neb., 96 B.R. 967.

Bkrtcy.E.D.N.Y. 1993. Even if bankruptcy trustee misstated or otherwise mislabeled his claims for relief, such would not be sufficient to warrant dismissal of complaint, if facts alleged entitled him to relief of any kind.

In re Harvard Knitwear, Inc., 153 B.R. 617.

Pleading stage was inappropriate time to attempt to evaluate possible evidence or to determine whether bankruptcy trustee would ultimately succeed in supporting his alter ego

allegations against defendant so as to make defendant personally liable for transfers of debtors' monies to defendant's corporation.

In re Harvard Knitwear, Inc., 153 B.R. 617.

Bkrtcy.S.D.N.Y. 1991. Adversary proceeding seeking finding of personal liability of individual debtor and judgment against debtor would be dismissed, notwithstanding federal rule providing that leave to amend shall be freely given when justice so requires, in light of total deficiencies of complaint; complaint did not set forth statute or code section upon which cause of action was based, complaint did not allege fraudulent inducements with sufficient particularity to plead common-law fraud satisfactorily, and facts alleged did not provide defendant debtor with enough information to formulate and file answer. Fed.Rules Civ.Proc. Rule 15(a), 28 U.S.C.A.

In re Marceca, 127 B.R. 328.

Bkrtcy.S.D.N.Y. 1991. Nondischargeability complaint which repeated in 18 separate counts same claim that debtors intentionally engaged in willful and malicious conduct violated spirit of pleading rule requiring short and plain statement of claim requiring dismissal subject to being repleaded. Fed.Rules Civ.Proc. Rule 8(a), 28 U.S.C.A.; Bankruptcy Rule 7008, 11 U.S.C.A.; Bankr.Code, 11 U.S.C.A. § 523(a)(6).

In re Neely, 125 B.R. 392.

Bkrtcy.S.D.N.Y. 1989. Amendment, rather than dismissal, of actual fraud claims for relief asserted by bankruptcy trustee under federal and state law was warranted based on failure to allege that transfers were made with intent to hinder, delay, or defraud existing or future creditors, where facts constituting fraudulent scheme had been laid out in sufficient detail to fairly apprise defendant persons of nature of conduct, transactions, and occurrences of which trustee complained, and trustee alleged that transfers forced debtor into insolvency and that defendant persons acted in bad faith and seriously injured corporate debtor. Bankr. Code, 11 U.S.C.A. § 548; N.Y.McKinney's Debtor and Creditor Law § 270.

In re Ahead by a Length, Inc., 100 B.R. 157.

Bkrtcy.S.D.Ohio 1991. Dispute as to applicable statute of limitations precluded dismissal of Chapter 7 trustee's action to claim prepetition account receivable for failure to state cause of action. Fed.Rules Civ.Proc.Rule 12(b)(6), 28 U.S.C.A.

In re Statewide Pools, Inc., 126 B.R. 877.

Bkrtcy.E.D.Va. 1988. Bankruptcy court could not assume as true bankruptcy trustee's allegations in complaint of individual bankruptcy debtor's status as party to agreement, for purposes of motion to dismiss, where agreements attached as exhibits to complaint showed that individual debtor was not named as party in any of the agreements.

> In re Wilson, 90 B.R. 208.

Bkrtcy.E.D.Wis. 1988. Absence of allegations of intentional conduct by bank and financial corporation, which were defendants on bankruptcy trustee's claim alleging inequitable conduct encompassing fraud, was alone sufficient cause to grant motion to dismiss as to claim in adversary complaint.

> Matter of Universal Foundry Co., 88 B.R. 891, affirmed 163 B.R. 528, affirmed 30 F.3d 137.

Claim of adversary complaint of bankruptcy trustee alleging inequitable conduct encompassing fraud by bank and financial corporation was deficient and would accordingly be dismissed; complaint failed to particularize or give detailed description of each defendant's involvement in alleged fraud, it failed to state factual basis for believing there was fraudulent conspiracy, it failed to identify persons presenting or relying on any misrepresentation or omission, it failed to indicate whether alleged misrepresentations or omissions were communicated orally or in writing, two different time frames were used in discussing period when fraudulent conspiracy was in operation, and complaint failed to allege manner and extent to which defendants had "enhanced" their positions as result of fraudulent conduct.

> Matter of Universal Foundry Co., 88 B.R. 891, affirmed 163 B.R. 528, affirmed 30 F.3d 137.

⚬⇒**1788. Banks, actions involving.**

Library references

C.J.S. Federal Civil Procedure § 839.

C.A.8 (Neb.) 1992. In action asserting subrogated rights of corporation not only against bank which had secured letter of credit for corporation but against other banks in chain which had been successively contacted to provide the letter of credit, dismissal based on failure to state a claim, on theory of lack of privity with subsequent banks in the chain, was premature where relationships among the corporation and the various banks in the letter of credit transaction were far from clear and complaint sufficiently alleged that there were connections among all of the litigants. Fed.Rules Civ.Proc.Rule 12(b)(6), 28 U.S.C.A.

> McCormack v. Citibank, N.A., 979 F.2d 643, rehearing denied, appeal after remand 100 F.3d 532.

C.A.2 (N.Y.) 1987. Claims under New York Business Corporation Law sections creating cause of action solely against members of board of directors of corporation were properly dismissed as to judgment debtor's bank, since there was no allegation that bank had served as member of debtor's board of directors. N.Y.McKinney's Business Corporation Law §§ 510, 719.

> Atlanta Shipping Corp., Inc. v. Chemical Bank, 818 F.2d 240.

C.A.5 (Tex.) 1991. *D'Oench* doctrine justifies dismissal only if complaint alleges secret agreement or if complaint shows that plaintiffs lent themselves to scheme likely to mislead banking authorities. Fed.Rules Civ.Proc.Rule 12(b)(6), 28 U.S.C.A.; Federal Deposit Insurance Act, § 2[13](e), as amended, 12 U.S.C.A. § 1823(e).

> Garrett v. Commonwealth Mortg. Corp. of America, 938 F.2d 591.

D.Ariz. 1994. Whether Resolution Trust Corporation's (RTC) action against sole stockholder of failed savings and loan association for alleged improper payment of dividends was barred by limitations would be resolved on motion for summary judgment, rather than on motion to dismiss. Federal Deposit Insurance Act, § 2[11](d)(14), 12 U.S.C.A. § 1821(d)(14); A.R.S. § 10–048, subds. D, F. F.

> Resolution Trust Corp. v. Dean, 854 F.Supp. 626.

E.D.Ark. 1992. Court could not determine on motion to dismiss claim against accountants that savings and loan association was at least as much at fault for its losses as the accountants so that there could be no recovery under Arkansas comparative fault law. Fed.Rules Civ.Proc.Rule 12(b)(6), 28 U.S.C.A.

> F.D.I.C. v. Deloitte & Touche, 834 F.Supp. 1129.

D.D.C. 1992. Factual issues existed, precluding dismissal under three-year District of Columbia statute of limitations, on whether continuing tort doctrine applied in action against attorney for allegedly receiving improper payments from savings and loan association; it was not clear whether separate payments were discrete events or continuous stream of improper conduct. D.C.Code 1981, § 12–301(8).

> Resolution Trust Corp. v. Gardner, 788 F.Supp. 26.

Factual issues existed on whether circumstances warranted equitable tolling of three-year District of Columbia statute of limitations on action against attorney who allegedly received improper payments from savings and loan association and its subsidiary and, therefore, dismissal would be premature. D.C.Code 1981, § 12–301(8).

> Resolution Trust Corp. v. Gardner, 788 F.Supp. 26.

Resolution Trust Corporation (RTC) in its corporate capacity alleged sufficient facts to withstand motion to dismiss claim that savings and loan association's attorney breached disciplinary rule by receiving payments from association and its subsidiary for which savings and loan and subsidiary receive little or no benefit; there were sufficient allegations of pecuniary loss to client and financial gain to attorney to state claim for alleged breach of fiduciary duty. D.C.Code of Prof.Resp., DR 2–106(A); Federal Home Loan Bank Act, § 21A(*l*)(1), as amended, 12 U.S.C.A. § 1441a(*l*)(1).

> Resolution Trust Corp. v. Gardner, 788 F.Supp. 26.

S.D.Fla. 1993. Federal Deposit Insurance Corporation's (FDIC) complaint against former officers and directors of failed thrift would not be dismissed on grounds of vagueness, and FDIC would not be required to make more definite statement, where complaint adequately put every defendant on notice of period during which challenged loans were made, and conduct alleged to be tortious. Fed.Rules Civ.Proc. Rules 8(a), 9(e), 12(b)(6), 28 U.S.C.A.

> F.D.I.C. v. Gonzalez-Gorrondona, 833 F.Supp. 1545.

N.D.Ill. 1994. Record properly before court on bank's motion to dismiss borrowers' claims under Racketeer Influenced and Corrupt Organizations Act's (RICO) civil enforcement provision for obtaining and charging borrowers for unauthorized force-placed insurance did not permit parcelling of bank's charges to borrowers for force-placed insurance premiums into authorized and unauthorized components, and it could be reasonably inferred from complaint that unitary charges were added to borrowers' balances for costs of force-placed insurance and borrowers were entitled to opportunity to establish that there was no mechanism available to them by which to parcel charges into authorized and unauthorized components. 18 U.S.C.A. § 1964(c).

> Bermudez v. First of America Bank Champion, N.A., 860 F.Supp. 580, withdrawn pursuant to settlement 886 F.Supp. 643.

N.D.Ill. 1993. Complaint against collecting bank, for failing to exercise proper care in forwarding, for presentment, checks which lacked necessary endorsement, would be dismissed with leave to replead, where complaint failed to specify which of the plaintiffs, the drawer or drawee bank, had suffered loss as result of collecting bank's actions.

> Great Lakes Higher Educ. Corp. v. Austin Bank of Chicago, 837 F.Supp. 892.

N.D.Ill. 1991. Claims of purchasers of interests in real estate investments against investment advisor for violation of ERISA, common-law fraud, violation of Illinois Securities Law, violation of Illinois Consumer Fraud and Deceptive Business Practices Act, breach of fiduciary duty, and negligent misrepresentation would be dismissed for failure to allege loss causation, even though no authority was asserted that loss causation was essential element of any of those claims, where purchasers had effectively conceded such requirement. Employee Retirement Income Security Act of 1974, § 2 et seq., 29 U.S.C.A. § 1001 et seq.; Ill.S.H.A. ch. 121½, ¶¶ 137.1 et seq., 261 et seq.

> Lewis v. Hermann, 775 F.Supp. 1137, reconsideration denied 783 F.Supp. 1131, reinstatement denied 1992 WL 57939.

D.Minn. 1991. In action brought by Federal Deposit Insurance Corporation (FDIC), as receiver for bank, to recover under fidelity bonds issued to bank, issuer's counterclaim seeking declaration that FDIC was not entitled to indemnity from issuer pursuant to bonds was redundant and would be dismissed without prejudice; counterclaim sought same result as issuer's denials and affirmative defenses.

> Federal Deposit Ins. Corp. v. Bancinsure, Inc., 770 F.Supp. 496.

D.Mont. 1987. Farmers could not assert private cause of action against individuals in farm credit system under Farm Credit Act or its regulations; therefore, claims based on violations of Farm Credit Act required dismissal for failure to state claim upon which relief could be granted. Farm Credit Act of 1971, § 1.1 et seq., 12 U.S.C.A. § 2001 et seq.; Fed.Rules Civ.Proc. Rule 12(b)(6), 28 U.S.C.A.

> Brekke v. Volcker, 652 F.Supp. 651.

W.D.N.C. 1986. Assertion that good-faith reliance on advice of counsel precluded liability for involvement in allegedly fraudulent sale of assets of corporation with stock pledged to bank being liquidated was not ripe for consideration on motions to dismiss complaint of Federal Deposit Insurance Corporation for failure to state claim. Fed.Rules Civ.Proc.Rules 11, 12(b)(6), 28 U.S.C.A.

> Federal Deposit Ins. Corp. v. Kerr, 637 F.Supp. 828.

E.D.Pa. 1992. Whether outside directors and accountants justifiably relied on statements by law firm for failed savings and loan association, as needed to prevail on fraud claim under Florida common law, was fact question which could not be decided on motion to dismiss. Fed.Rules Civ.Proc.Rule 12(b)(6), 28 U.S.C.A.

> In re Sunrise Securities Litigation, 793 F.Supp. 1306.

N.D.Tex. 1990. Federal Deposit Insurance Corporation's (FDIC) contention that limited guaranties issued by subsidiary banks were "safe and sound" banking practice within meaning of Federal Reserve Act did not mandate dismissal of bank creditors' claims that issuance of guaranties violated general rule that national banks were not authorized to enter into guaranties. Federal Reserve Act, § 23A(a)(4), 12 U.S.C.A. § 371c(a)(4).

> Senior Unsecured Creditors' Committee of First RepublicBank Corp. v. Federal Deposit Ins. Corp., 749 F.Supp. 758.

☞1788.5. Civil rights actions.

Library references

C.J.S. Federal Civil Procedure § 839.

☞1788.6. —— In general.

C.A.D.C. 1991. Complete failure to allege facts that would permit conclusion that private parties acted under color of law was not type of procedural misstep that could have been overlooked in ruling on motion to dismiss civil rights action. 42 U.S.C.A. § 1983.

> Hoai v. Vo, 935 F.2d 308, 290 U.S.App.D.C. 142, rehearing denied, and rehearing denied, certiorari denied 112 S.Ct. 1578, 503 U.S. 967, 118 L.Ed.2d 220, rehearing denied 112 S.Ct. 2007, 504 U.S. 936, 118 L.Ed.2d 602.

C.A.9 (Ariz.) 1992. Dismissal of pro se litigant's civil rights complaint as sanction for litigant's failure to amend his complaint to remove words "et al" from caption and to identify additional defendants was not abuse of discretion. Fed.Rules Civ.Proc.Rule 10(a), 28 U.S.C.A.

> Ferdik v. Bonzelet, 963 F.2d 1258, as amended, certiorari denied 113 S.Ct. 321, 506 U.S. 915, 121 L.Ed.2d 242.

C.A.8 (Ark.) 1989. Pro se inmate's civil rights complaint was properly dismissed without prejudice for failing to comply with local rule providing for dismissal without prejudice of pro se complaints for failure of plaintiff to respond to court communications within 30 days. U.S.Dist.Ct.Rules D. Ark., Rule 3(c)(2).

> Settlemire v. Watson, 877 F.2d 13, rehearing denied.

C.A.9 (Cal.) 1995. When civil rights complaint is defective and appears to assert claims for which the exclusive remedy is habeas corpus, district court should state that the claims must be addressed in habeas petition and should dismiss the civil rights claims without prejudice. 42 U.S.C.A. § 1983.

> Trimble v. City of Santa Rosa, 49 F.3d 583.

C.A.9 (Cal.) 1989. Questions whether roadblock causing death of auto theft suspect was necessary to prevent escape and whether reasonable nondeadly alternative existed for apprehending suspect were issues of fact that could not be decided on motion to dismiss for failure to state § 1983 claim. 42 U.S.C.A. § 1983; U.S.C.A. Const.Amend. 4.

> Brower v. County of Inyo, 884 F.2d 1316.

C.A.10 (Colo.) 1992. Question of qualified immunity in civil rights suit is a purely legal question which requires determination of whether actions defendants allegedly took were actions that reasonable person could have believed were lawful, and if the actions were such, the defendants are entitled to dismissal before discovery, but if the actions are not those that reasonable person could have believed were lawful, then discovery may be necessary before motion for summary judgment on qualified immunity grounds can be resolved, but any such discovery must be tailored specifically to the immunity question.

> Workman v. Jordan, 958 F.2d 332, appeal after remand 32 F.3d 475, rehearing denied, certiorari denied 115 S.Ct. 1357, 514 U.S. 1015, 131 L.Ed.2d 215.

C.A.2 (Conn.) 1995. Question as to whether plaintiffs who sought smoking ban on fast-food restaurants, under ADA, would ever visit particular restaurants did not justify dismissal of complaints where plaintiffs alleged cognizable claims at least with respect to restaurants they did expect to visit. Americans with Disabilities Act of 1990, § 302, 42 U.S.C.A. § 12182.

> Staron v. McDonald's Corp., 51 F.3d 353.

C.A.11 (Fla.) 1988. Government officials who are potentially entitled to absolute immunity may seek to establish it by moving to dismiss the complaint, for failure to state a cause of action upon which relief can be granted, or admitting the facts and moving for judgment on the pleadings. 42 U.S.C.A. § 1983; Fed.Rules Civ.Proc.Rule 12(b)(6), (c), 28 U.S.C.A.

> Marx v. Gumbinner, 855 F.2d 783.

C.A.5 (Fla.) 1980. Crawford v. Western Elec. Co., Inc., 614 F.2d 1300, rehearing denied 620 F.2d 300, on remand 1982 WL 394, affirmed in part, reversed in part 745 F.2d 1373, rehearing denied 751 F.2d 394.

C.A.7 (Ill.) 1995. It was error to dismiss complaint challenging refusal of airport advertising company to accept advertisement from union on the basis that displays in the airport had not contained political advertising in the past where union alleged that display cases had contained political advertising in the past.

> Air Line Pilots Ass'n, Intern. v. Department of Aviation of City of Chicago, 45 F.3d 1144.

C.A.7 (Ill.) 1993. In qualified immunity cases, there is no special pleading standard that need be satisfied to survive motion to dismiss. Fed.Rules Civ.Proc.Rules 8, 9(b), 28 U.S.C.A.; 42 U.S.C.A. § 1983.

> Triad Associates, Inc. v. Robinson, 10 F.3d 492.

C.A.7 (Ill.) 1993. Trial court did not abuse its discretion in dismissing age discrimination suit as duplicative of suit already pending in same court; although plaintiff argued that first complaint contained claims for both intentional and unintentional violations of Age Discrimination in Employment Act (ADEA) while second complaint only contained claims for intentional violations, both complaints stated that constructive discharge was motivated solely by intent to discriminate, and no aspect of first complaint was grounded in disparate impact theory which is only theory capable of supporting unintentional discrimination claim under ADEA. Age Discrimination in Employment Act of 1967, § 2 et seq., 29 U.S.C.A. § 621 et seq.

Serlin v. Arthur Andersen & Co., 3 F.3d 221.

C.A.7 (Ill.) 1985. Where civil rights plaintiff had full opportunity to seek amendment of complaint, but failed to do so, John Doe police officer named in complaint was never served with summons and copy of complaint, so that district court lacked jurisdiction over him, and civil rights action against city failed to state claim for deprivation of civil rights, dismissal of both city and John Doe police officer was proper.

Strauss v. City of Chicago, 760 F.2d 765.

C.A.7 (Ill.) 1981. Briscoe v. LaHue, 663 F.2d 713, certiorari granted 102 S.Ct. 1708, 455 U.S. 1016, 72 L.Ed.2d 132, affirmed 103 S.Ct. 1108, 460 U.S. 325, 75 L.Ed.2d 96, certiorari denied Talley v. Crosson, 103 S.Ct. 1426, 460 U.S. 1037, 75 L.Ed.2d 787.

C.A.7 (Ind.) 1992. Issue of qualified immunity may be raised in motion to dismiss civil rights claim.

McMath v. City of Gary, Ind., 976 F.2d 1026, rehearing denied.

C.A.7 (Ind.) 1986. Where basis of civil rights suit against private defendants was state action via joint action with public defendants, so that challenge to district court's jurisdiction for lack of state action was also a challenge to existence of federal cause of action, jurisdiction could not be defeated by possibility that cause of action was not stated, but could be dismissed for lack of jurisdiction only if claim clearly appeared to be immaterial and made solely for purpose of obtaining jurisdiction or where such claim was wholly insubstantial and frivolous. 42 U.S.C.A. § 1983; Fed.Rules Civ.Proc.Rule 12(b), (b)(1, 6), 28 U.S.C.A.

Malak v. Associated Physicians, Inc., 784 F.2d 277.

C.A.7 (Ind.) 1983. Ekanem v. Health and Hosp. Corp. of Marion County, Ind., 724 F.2d 563, certiorari denied 105 S.Ct. 93, 469 U.S.

821, 83 L.Ed.2d 40, appeal after remand 778 F.2d 1254.

C.A.7 (Ind.) 1981. Briscoe v. LaHue, 663 F.2d 713, certiorari granted 102 S.Ct. 1708, 455 U.S. 1016, 72 L.Ed.2d 132, affirmed 103 S.Ct. 1108, 460 U.S. 325, 75 L.Ed.2d 96, certiorari denied Talley v. Crosson, 103 S.Ct. 1426, 460 U.S. 1037, 75 L.Ed.2d 787.

C.A.5 (La.) 1982. Smith v. Gonzales, 670 F.2d 522, rehearing denied 677 F.2d 113, certiorari denied 103 S.Ct. 361, 459 U.S. 1005, 74 L.Ed.2d 397, motion granted Arizona v. California, 103 S.Ct. 249, 459 U.S. 940, 74 L.Ed.2d 196, rehearing denied 103 S.Ct. 772, 459 U.S. 1137, 74 L.Ed.2d 984.

C.A.4 (Md.) 1993. If plaintiff asserting § 1983 claim fails to establish constitutional violation, defendant who has asserted qualified immunity is entitled to dismissal on basis of qualified immunity or under Rule 12(b)(6). Fed.Rules Civ.Proc.Rule 12(b)(6), 28 U.S.C.A.

American Civil Liberties Union of Maryland, Inc. v. Wicomico County, Md., 999 F.2d 780.

C.A.5 (Miss.) 1995. Where civil rights plaintiff has filed only one pleading, immediate dismissal ordinarily is not justified when plaintiff fails to meet heightened pleading required to overcome motion to dismiss based on qualified immunity, but rather plaintiff should be given opportunity to plead case properly before dismissal is considered. 42 U.S.C.A. § 1983.

Wicks v. Mississippi State Employment Services, 41 F.3d 991, certiorari denied 115 S.Ct. 2555, 515 U.S. 1131, 132 L.Ed.2d 809.

C.A.5 (Miss.) 1987. Former employee's request for compensatory and punitive damages under Title VII, rather than equitable relief, was not fatal to sex discrimination and retaliation claims. Civil Rights Act of 1964, § 701 et seq., 42 U.S.C.A. § 2000e et seq.

Doss v. South Cent. Bell Telephone Co., 834 F.2d 421, rehearing denied 837 F.2d 1090.

C.A.8 (Mo.) 1995. Civil rights pleadings should be construed liberally in connection with motions to dismiss for failure to state claim upon which relief can be granted. Fed.Rules Civ.Proc.Rule 12(b)(6), 28 U.S.C.A.

Frey v. City of Herculaneum, 44 F.3d 667.

In order to survive motion to dismiss for failure to state claim upon which relief can be granted, civil rights complaint must contain facts which state claim as matter of law and must not be conclusory. Fed.Rules Civ.Proc. Rule 12(b)(6), 28 U.S.C.A.

Frey v. City of Herculaneum, 44 F.3d 667.

C.A.8 (Mo.) 1992. When plaintiff in § 1983 action fails to allege violation of clearly established law, defendant pleading qualified immunity is entitled to dismissal before commencement of discovery. 42 U.S.C.A. § 1983.

Taylor v. Bowers, 966 F.2d 417, opinion modified on rehearing, certiorari denied 113 S.Ct. 394, 506 U.S. 946, 121 L.Ed.2d 302.

C.A.2 (N.Y.) 1996. Standard governing motions to dismiss for failure to state claim is applied with even greater force where plaintiff alleges civil rights violations. Fed.Rules Civ. Proc.Rule 12(b)(6), 28 U.S.C.A.

Bernheim v. Litt, 79 F.3d 318.

C.A.2 (N.Y.) 1995. Rule, that complaint should not be dismissed unless it appears beyond doubt that plaintiff can prove no set of facts in support of her claim which would entitle her to relief, is particularly applicable in pro se civil rights actions. Fed.Rules Civ.Proc. Rule 12(b)(6), 28 U.S.C.A.

Glendora v. Cablevision Systems Corp., 45 F.3d 36, on remand 893 F.Supp. 264.

District court could not summarily dismiss pro se civil rights complaint of "public access" cable television programmer against cable television company and its employees, arising from cancellation of cable television program, alleging First and Fourteenth Amendment violations, negligence, and state claims for emotional and reputational injuries, without determining whether private federal cause of action could be implied from provisions of Cable Communications Policy Act and Cable Television Consumer Protection and Competition Act, and action would be remanded for consideration of applicable state and federal cable television statutes, despite fact that potentially applicable statutes were not mentioned in complaint. 42 U.S.C.A. § 1983; Communications Act of 1934, §§ 1 et seq., 611(e), as amended, 47 U.S.C.A. §§ 521 et seq., 531(e); § 602(13), as amended, 42 U.S.C.(1988 Ed.) § 522(13); Fed.Rules Civ. Proc.Rule 12(b)(6), 28 U.S.C.A.; N.Y.McKinney's Executive Law §§ 811–831.

Glendora v. Cablevision Systems Corp., 45 F.3d 36, on remand 893 F.Supp. 264.

C.A.2 (N.Y.) 1994. While bald and uncorroborated allegation of retaliation for exercising First Amendment rights might prove inadequate to withstand motion to dismiss, alleging facts from which retaliatory intent on part of defendants reasonably may be inferred is sufficient. Fed.Rules Civ.Proc.Rule 9(b), 28 U.S.C.A.; U.S.C.A. Const.Amend. 1.

Gagliardi v. Village of Pawling, 18 F.3d 188.

C.A.2 (N.Y.) 1994. Standard for dismissing complaint for failure to state claim, whereby complaint may be dismissed only where it appears beyond doubt that plaintiff can prove no set of facts in support of his claim which would entitle him to relief, is applied with even greater force where plaintiff alleges civil rights violations or where complaint is submitted pro se. Fed.Rules Civ.Proc.Rule 12(b)(6), 28 U.S.C.A.

Hernandez v. Coughlin, 18 F.3d 133, certiorari denied 115 S.Ct. 117, 513 U.S. 836, 130 L.Ed.2d 63.

C.A.2 (N.Y.) 1993. In deciding motion to dismiss for failure to state claim, district court must construe any well-pleaded factual allegations in complaint in favor of plaintiff and may dismiss only where it appears beyond doubt that plaintiff can prove no set of facts in support of claim which would entitle him to relief; that caution applies with greater force where complaint is submitted pro se or plaintiff alleges civil rights violations. Fed.Rules Civ.Proc.Rule 12(b)(6), 28 U.S.C.A.

Sykes v. James, 13 F.3d 515, certiorari denied 114 S.Ct. 2749, 512 U.S. 1240, 129 L.Ed.2d 867.

C.A.2 (N.Y.) 1993. Insofar as § 1985 conspiracy claims asserted by purported property owners against private parties and government officials were viable claims, they were merely duplicative of conspiracy claims under § 1983 and were therefore unnecessary and would be dismissed. 42 U.S.C.A. §§ 1983, 1985.

Ferran v. Town of Nassau, 11 F.3d 21, certiorari denied 115 S.Ct. 572, 513 U.S. 1014, 130 L.Ed.2d 489, rehearing denied 115 S.Ct. 925, 513 U.S. 1121, 130 L.Ed.2d 804.

C.A.2 (N.Y.) 1993. Dismissal of § 1981 promotion discrimination claim was improper where determination as to whether promotion effectively created new contract between employer and employee could not be made simply by examining complaint; employee alleged denials of promotion from computer system manager on one occasion to deputy commissioner of office of management and administration and on two occasions to director of systems architecture. 42 U.S.C.A. § 1981.

Butts v. City of New York Dept. of Housing Preservation and Development, 990 F.2d 1397, on remand 1998 WL 13851.

C.A.2 (N.Y.) 1991. Rule that complaint should not be dismissed unless it appears beyond reasonable doubt that plaintiff can prove no set of facts in support of his claim which would entitle him to relief is to be applied with particular strictness when plaintiff complains of civil rights violation, or where plaintiff is appearing pro se. Fed.Rules Civ.Proc.Rule 12(b)(6), 28 U.S.C.A.

Branum v. Clark, 927 F.2d 698.

C.A.10 (Okl.) 1993. Where question whether court had subject matter jurisdiction was intertwined with merits of civil rights case, district court should have ruled on the merits rather than dismissing for lack of jurisdiction.

> Tilton v. Richardson, 6 F.3d 683, certiorari denied 114 S.Ct. 925, 510 U.S. 1093, 127 L.Ed.2d 218.

C.A.10 (Okl.) 1991. Irrespective of whether Equal Employment Opportunity Commission (EEOC) employees could be subject to suit for damages for improper conduct in connection with processing of discrimination charge, district court properly dismissed individual EEOC defendants, as not one allegation in complaint so much as mentioned them.

> Scheerer v. Rose State College, 950 F.2d 661, certiorari denied 112 S.Ct. 2995, 505 U.S. 1205, 120 L.Ed.2d 872.

C.A.10 (Okl.) 1989. Constitutional claim under § 1983 should not be dismissed unless it appears beyond a doubt that plaintiff could prove no set of facts in support of his claim that would entitle him to relief. 42 U.S.C.A. § 1983.

> Dunn v. White, 880 F.2d 1188, certiorari denied 110 S.Ct. 871, 493 U.S. 1059, 107 L.Ed.2d 954.

C.A.10 (Okl.) 1988. Constitutional claim under § 1983 should not be dismissed unless it appears beyond doubt that the plaintiff could prove no set of facts in support of his claim that would entitle him to relief. 42 U.S.C.A. § 1983.

> Meade v. Grubbs, 841 F.2d 1512.

Qualified immunity issue raised by members of Oklahoma Council on Law Enforcement Education and Training and Commissioner of Oklahoma Department of Health involved factual questions concerning defense so as to prevent ruling on whether defendants were entitled to qualified immunity defense on motion to dismiss claim for denial of medical care to pretrial detainee. 42 U.S.C.A. § 1983.

> Meade v. Grubbs, 841 F.2d 1512.

C.A.3 (Pa.) 1993. Section 1983 challenge to conditions of confinement brought by federal pretrial detainees should not have been dismissed on ground that issues were previously addressed in context of previous class action suit; it was not clear that all allegations raised were already addressed in earlier litigation and it was possible that only through complaints such as present one would district court become apprised of any failure to comply with prior court orders on conditions that actually had been addressed in prior litigation. Fed.Rules Civ.Proc.Rule 12(b)(6), 28 U.S.C.A.; 42 U.S.C.A. § 1983.

> Kost v. Kozakiewicz, 1 F.3d 176.

C.A.3 (Pa.) 1991. Where motion to dismiss federal civil rights action is based on lack of state action, dismissal is proper only for failure to state a claim, not for lack of jurisdiction. 28 U.S.C.A. §§ 1331, 1343(a)(3, 4); 42 U.S.C.A. § 1983; Fed.Rules Civ.Proc.Rule 12(b)(1, 6), 28 U.S.C.A.

> Boyle v. Governor's Veterans Outreach & Assistance Center, 925 F.2d 71.

C.A.3 (Pa.) 1988. Heightened specificity requirement for § 1983 claims does not alter general standard for ruling on motions to dismiss for failure to state a claim; complaints comply with this standard if they allege specific conduct violating plaintiff's rights, time and place of that conduct, and identity of responsible officials. Fed.Rules Civ.Proc.Rule 12(b)(6), 28 U.S.C.A.; 42 U.S.C.A. § 1983.

> Colburn v. Upper Darby Tp., 838 F.2d 663, certiorari denied 109 S.Ct. 1338, 489 U.S. 1065, 103 L.Ed.2d 808, on remand 1990 WL 74200, affirmed 946 F.2d 1017.

C.A.1 (R.I.) 1992. Unless plaintiff's allegations state claim of violation of clearly established law, defendant pleading qualified immunity is entitled to dismissal before commencement of discovery; qualified immunity is immunity from suit rather than mere defense to liability.

> Hoffman v. Reali, 973 F.2d 980.

C.A.6 (Tenn.) 1991. Defendant pleading qualified immunity is entitled to dismissal before commencement of discovery if plaintiff fails to state claim of violation of clearly established law.

> Daugherty v. Campbell, 935 F.2d 780, rehearing denied, certiorari denied 112 S.Ct. 939, 502 U.S. 1060, 117 L.Ed.2d 110.

C.A.5 (Tex.) 1996. Trial court erred in dismissing § 1983 complaint for failure to state claim where court failed to accept as true allegations plaintiffs made in complaint and trial court adopted portion of defendants' claims as fact without acknowledging any contradiction with complaint. 42 U.S.C.A. § 1983; Fed.Rules Civ.Proc.Rule 12(b)(6), 28 U.S.C.A.

> Baker v. Putnal, 75 F.3d 190.

C.A.5 (Tex.) 1995. In analyzing claim of qualified immunity in § 1983 action, defendant is entitled to dismissal if it becomes evident that plaintiff has failed to state or otherwise establish claim. 42 U.S.C.A. § 1983.

> Wells v. Bonner, 45 F.3d 90.

C.A.5 (Tex.) 1992. Mere conclusory allegations of deprivation of civil rights are insufficient to withstand motion to dismiss. 42 U.S.C.A. § 1983.

> Dillard v. Merrill Lynch, Pierce, Fenner & Smith, Inc., 961 F.2d 1148, certiorari denied 113 S.Ct. 1046, 506 U.S. 1079, 122 L.Ed.2d 355.

C.A.5 (Tex.) 1972. Lipscomb v. Jonsson, 459 F.2d 335, on remand 399 F.Supp. 782, reversed 551 F.2d 1043, application granted Wise v. Lipscomb, 98 S.Ct. 15, 434 U.S. 1329, 54 L.Ed.2d 41, application denied 98 S.Ct. 424, 434 U.S. 935, 54 L.Ed.2d 295, certiorari granted 98 S.Ct. 716, 434 U.S. 1008, 54 L.Ed.2d 750, reversed 98 S.Ct. 2493, 437 U.S. 535, 57 L.Ed.2d 411, on remand 583 F.2d 212, appeal after remand 643 F.2d 319, 72 A.L.R. Fed. 410.

C.A.9 (Wash.) 1993. Challenge to specificity of § 1983 complaint is properly raised only in motion to dismiss. 42 U.S.C.A. § 1983.
    Palmer v. Sanderson, 9 F.3d 1433.

C.A.9 (Wash.) 1987. District court did not err in dismissing plaintiff's claim for damages under § 1985 against foster mother of plaintiff's child, on ground that record contained no evidence that foster mother acted with a racial or class-based invidiously discriminatory animus, notwithstanding that foster mother's motion for summary judgment was not accompanied by any supporting materials. 42 U.S.C.A. § 1985.
    Coverdell v. Department of Social and Health Services, State of Wash., 834 F.2d 758.

C.A.7 (Wis.) 1987. Trial court's dismissal of employee's civil rights action based upon statute governing equal rights under the law could not be upheld on ground dismissal was exercise of court's discretion not to accept amendment to complaint on eve of trial, where only two months had elapsed between time district court dismissed original complaint and time plaintiff filed his amended complaint, and district court had several opportunities to state explicitly that it believed amended complaint was not timely filed, but in each instance, return to its view of statute as basis for its dismissal decision. 42 U.S.C.A. § 1981.
    Hussein v. Oshkosh Motor Truck Co., 816 F.2d 348.

M.D.Ala. 1996. Generally, to remedy deficient pleadings in § 1983 actions, courts grant plaintiff leave to amend complaint to allege more specific facts rather than dismissing cause of action. 42 U.S.C.A. § 1983.
    LaFleur v. Wallace State Community College, 955 F.Supp. 1406.

M.D.Ala. 1995. Just remedy where plaintiffs in civil rights under § 1983 failed to plead constitutional violations with sufficient particularity was to grant leave to amend rather than dismiss. 42 U.S.C.A. § 1983.
    Ross v. State of Ala., 893 F.Supp. 1545.

M.D.Ala. 1994. Fundamental rights and important questions of public policy are involved in actions under civil rights statutes, and court should not dismiss complaint unless it is frivolous or fails to state claim for relief. 42 U.S.C.A. § 1983.
    Malone v. Chambers County Bd. of Com'rs, 875 F.Supp. 773, reconsideration denied.

M.D.Ala. 1993. Court may grant motion for involuntary dismissal if defendant in Title VII case produces legitimate reason for allegedly discriminatory action during plaintiff's case, and court determines that plaintiff had opportunity to satisfy resulting burden to prove that proffered reason was pretextual or that discriminatory motive more likely than not lead to adverse decision before resting plaintiff's case, but that plaintiff failed to do so. Civil Rights Act of 1964, § 701 et seq., 42 U.S.C.A. § 2000e et seq.
    Williams v. Mead Coated Bd., Inc., 836 F.Supp. 1552, affirmed 41 F.3d 668.

M.D.Ala. 1992. Question whether police chief was member of elected official's personal staff and was not employee within meaning of Title VII was highly factual and could not be resolved based solely on pleadings. Civil Rights Act of 1964, § 701(f), as amended, 42 U.S.C.A. § 2000e(f).
    Patrick v. City of Florala, 793 F.Supp. 301.

S.D.Ala. 1990. Civil rights plaintiff's filing of Title VII suit before plaintiff had received right-to-sue notice from Equal Employment Opportunity Commission did not warrant dismissal, but rather plaintiff would be allowed to amend complaint to reflect that she received right-to-sue notice; defendants did not claim they were prejudiced by premature filing, dismissal would result in needless delay and expense, and footnote in complaint stated that plaintiff would amend complaint when she received right-to-sue notice. Civil Rights Act of 1964, § 701 et seq., 42 U.S.C.A. § 2000e et seq.
    Rolin v. Escambia County Bd. of Educ., 752 F.Supp. 1020.

D.Colo. 1988. Section 1983 claim should not be dismissed unless it clearly appears plaintiff can prove no set of facts in support of his claim which would entitle him to relief. 42 U.S.C.A. § 1983.
    Garcia v. Jefferson County, Colo., 687 F.Supp. 1498.

D.Colo. 1987. Plaintiffs' failure to amend their § 1985 claims, as ordered by district court, to allege class-based, discriminatory animus, and to provide factual basis for such allegations required dismissal of claims with prejudice. 42 U.S.C.A. § 1985.
    Trejo v. Wattles, 654 F.Supp. 1143.

D.Colo. 1982. Martinez v. Winner, 548 F.Supp. 278, affirmed in part, reversed in part and remanded 771 F.2d 424, opinion modified on denial of rehearing 778 F.2d 553, certiorari granted, vacated Tyus v. Martinez, 106 S.Ct.

1787, 475 U.S. 1138, 90 L.Ed.2d 333, on remand 800 F.2d 230.

D.Conn. 1996. Standard for dismissing complaint for failure to state claim is applied with even greater force where plaintiff alleges civil rights violations. Fed.Rules Civ.Proc.Rule 12(b)(6), 28 U.S.C.A.

> Morgan v. City of Milford, 914 F.Supp. 21.

D.Conn. 1988. Rule that complaint should not be dismissed for failure to state claim unless it appears beyond doubt that plaintiff can prove no set of facts in support of his claim which would entitle him to relief is applied with particular strictness when plaintiff contends there has been violation of his civil rights. Fed.Rules Civ.Proc.Rule 12(b)(6), 28 U.S.C.A.

> Herbst v. Daukas, 701 F.Supp. 964.

D.Conn. 1987. Motions to dismiss are disfavored in civil rights litigation. Fed.Rules Civ. Proc.Rule 12(b)(6), 28 U.S.C.A.

> Mahoney v. National Organization for Women, 681 F.Supp. 129.

D.Del. 1990. Claims that case involved sensitive state matters so that court should abstain, that defendants were entitled to official immunity, and that there was no federal constitutional issue provided bases for dismissal for failure to state a claim, but not for lack of jurisdiction. Fed.Rules Civ.Proc.Rule 12(b)(1, 6), 28 U.S.C.A.

> MacNamara v. County Council of Sussex County, 738 F.Supp. 134, affirmed 922 F.2d 832.

D.Del. 1977. National Ass'n for Advancement of Colored People v. Wilmington Medical Center, Inc., 426 F.Supp. 919, case remanded 599 F.2d 1247, on remand 491 F.Supp. 290, affirmed 657 F.2d 1322, 69 A.L.R. Fed. 539.

M.D.Fla. 1994. Civil rights action by lessee arising from eviction proceedings against him must be dismissed for failure to state claim, where lessee failed to establish causal connection between institution of eviction proceedings and his injuries, and proceedings were commenced by private litigants, who did not act under color of state law. 42 U.S.C.A. § 1983.

> Eidson v. Arenas, 155 F.R.D. 215.

M.D.Fla. 1993. In civil rights actions, conclusory allegations are insufficient to withstand motion to dismiss absent specific factual allegations. 42 U.S.C.A. § 1983.

> L.S.T. Inc. v. Crow, 834 F.Supp. 1355, reversed 49 F.3d 679.

M.D.Fla. 1993. District court would not dismiss with prejudice former employee's third civil rights complaint against city, for alleged refusal to provide sufficient pleadings, in light of employee's pro se status which invoked less stringent standards than if pleadings had been drafted by attorney, but district court warned that reasonable limits would be placed on number of amendments allowed.

> Middleton v. City of Lakeland, 830 F.Supp. 1449.

M.D.Fla. 1988. Court would not dismiss employment discrimination complaint for lack of specificity of the phrase "unequal terms and conditions of employment" where suit had been underway for two years before language was challenged as vague.

> E.E.O.C. v. Jacksonville Shipyards, Inc., 696 F.Supp. 1438.

S.D.Fla. 1992. Failure of second amended complaint to comply with pleading requirements previously set out by trial judge did not amount to clear record of delay or willful contempt that required involuntary dismissal. Fed. Rules Civ.Proc.Rule 41(b), 28 U.S.C.A.

> Lake Lucerne Civic Ass'n, Inc. v. Dolphin Stadium Corp., 801 F.Supp. 684.

S.D.Fla. 1988. Female employee's failure to allege that she had filed claim with county fair housing and appeals board did not require dismissal of employment discrimination action for lack of subject matter jurisdiction, where employee attached as exhibit copy of her charge of discrimination that had been filed with board and where there was no dispute as to authenticity of exhibit. Civil Rights Act of 1964, § 706(b, d), as amended, 42 U.S.C.A. § 2000e–5(c, e).

> Brown v. City of Miami Beach, 684 F.Supp. 1081.

C.D.Ill. 1990. Pro se civil rights complaint was frivolous so as to be subject to sua sponte dismissal where defendants were either judicial officers who were performing judicial functions and were therefore absolutely immune from suit or were private persons not acting under color of state law, and where it was impossible to divine what constitutional right plaintiff allegedly had lost at the hands of defendants.

> Sakovich v. City of Kankakee, 130 F.R.D. 394.

N.D.Ill. 1995. Complaint in parent's § 1983 civil rights action arising out of son's suicide while in custody of Illinois Department of Corrections would not be dismissed on ground that complaint as drafted appeared to seek damages against probation officer and department employee in their official capacities in violation of Eleventh Amendment, where plaintiff asserted that complaint, originally filed in state court under state pleading rules, was intended as an individual action; appropriate course was to let complaint stand on condition that plaintiff amend it to confirm its status as an individual action. U.S.C.A. Const.Amend. 11; 42 U.S.C.A. § 1983.

> Viero v. Bufano, 901 F.Supp. 1387.

N.D.Ill. 1995. Any confusion engendered by breadth, or lack thereof, of plaintiff's civil rights complaint was cured in plaintiff's response to defendant's motion to dismiss. Fed. Rules Civ.Proc.Rules 8, 12, 28 U.S.C.A.

> Chaney v. City of Chicago, 901 F.Supp. 266.

N.D.Ill. 1994. In motion to dismiss racial discrimination claim under equal protection clause, federal district court requires no more from plaintiffs' allegations of intent than what would satisfy notice pleading minimum under Civil Rule 8 and requirement under Civil Rule 9(b) that motive and intent be pleaded generally. U.S.C.A. Const.Amend. 14; Fed.Rules Civ. Proc.Rules 8, 9(b), 28 U.S.C.A.

> Hodges by Hodges v. Public Bldg. Com'n of Chicago, 864 F.Supp. 1493, reconsideration denied 873 F.Supp. 128.

N.D.Ill. 1994. There was triable issue, sufficient to defeat motion to dismiss, as to whether city park commissioners applied ostensibly neutral criteria in discriminatory manner in rejecting proposal for statue to be erected in city park; claim alleged that commissioners did not adhere to facially neutral guidelines and rejected statue even though it met all relevant criteria. U.S.C.A. Const.Amend. 1.

> Comite Pro-Celebracion v. Claypool, 863 F.Supp. 682.

N.D.Ill. 1994. There might have been facts that, if alleged and proved, would have tolled statute of limitations and allowed Equal Employment Opportunity Commission's (EEOC's) ADEA claim against city and public library to survive and, thus, city and public library were not entitled to dismissal of complaint as time barred. Age Discrimination in Employment Act of 1967, § 7(e)(2), as amended, 29 U.S.C.A. § 626(e)(2).

> E.E.O.C. v. Park Ridge Public Library, 856 F.Supp. 477.

N.D.Ill. 1994. Motions to dismiss in civil rights context are scrutinized with special care, and are disfavored. Fed.Rules Civ.Proc.Rule 12(b)(1), 28 U.S.C.A.

> U.S. v. Beethoven Associates Ltd. Partnership, 843 F.Supp. 1257.

N.D.Ill. 1993. Section 1983 plaintiffs' allegations that jury commissioners had systematically excluded certain groups from county jury pool were not impermissibly argumentative or conclusory so as to warrant dismissal of complaint, despite plaintiffs' inability to explain means by which commissioners allegedly excluded groups from pool, which was information presumably accessible only through discovery process. Fed.Rules Civ.Proc.Rule 8(a)(2), 28 U.S.C.A.; 42 U.S.C.A. § 1983.

> Ryan v. DuPage County Jury Com'n, 837 F.Supp. 898.

N.D.Ill. 1993. Although qualified immunity is affirmative defense, it is one that may, in some circumstances, be raised and decided on motion to dismiss before parties have commenced discovery. 42 U.S.C.A. § 1983.

> Connor v. Foster, 833 F.Supp. 727.

N.D.Ill. 1993. Pro se complaints are to be liberally construed, and pro se civil rights complaints may be dismissed only if it is beyond doubt that there is no set of facts under which plaintiff could obtain relief.

> Sampson v. Village Discount Outlet, Inc., 832 F.Supp. 1163, affirmed 43 F.3d 1474, rehearing denied.

N.D.Ill. 1993. Pro se civil rights complaints may not be dismissed unless it is beyond doubt that there is no set of facts under which plaintiff could obtain relief.

> Diaz v. Edgar, 831 F.Supp. 621.

N.D.Ill. 1993. Fact that there were questions regarding application of Illinois Tort Immunity Act to police chief who was being sued by police department personnel in § 1983 action arising out of city's interception of telephone communications over police department's private line did not require dismissal of complaint against police chief for failure to state a claim. S.H.A. 745 ILCS 10/2–201; Fed. Rules Civ.Proc.Rule 12(b)(6), 28 U.S.C.A.

> Amati v. City of Woodstock, Ill., 829 F.Supp. 998.

N.D.Ill. 1993. Motions to dismiss in civil rights context are scrutinized with special care, and are disfavored. Fed.Rules Civ.Proc.Rule 12(b)(1), 28 U.S.C.A.

> U.S. v. Aspen Square Management Co., Inc., 817 F.Supp. 707, vacated 1993 WL 268352.

N.D.Ill. 1993. Merits of civil rights plaintiffs' claim that, under Illinois law, delay in instituting postdeprivation forfeiture proceeding to determine probable cause violated due process could not be resolved within context of defendants' motion to dismiss; whether delay violated due process had to be made on ad hoc basis with court considering length of delay, reason for delay, and prejudice to claimant and proper consideration of these factors involved facts outside of complaint. U.S.C.A. Const. Amends. 5, 14; 42 U.S.C.A. § 1983.

> Jones v. Takaki, 153 F.R.D. 609.

N.D.Ill. 1992. Pro se complaints are to be liberally construed, and pro se civil rights complaints may be dismissed only if it is beyond doubt that there is no set of facts under which plaintiff could obtain relief.

> Coleman v. O'Grady, 803 F.Supp. 226, affirmed 19 F.3d 21.

N.D.Ill. 1990. Pro se complaints are to be liberally construed and pro se civil rights complaints may be dismissed only if it is beyond doubt that there is no set of facts under which plaintiff could obtain relief.

> Kness v. Grimm, 761 F.Supp. 513.

N.D.Ill. 1990. Assertions of equal protection and due process violations in amended civil rights complaint would be dismissed, where district court previously found that equal protection and due process claims were not adequately set forth in original complaint, and amended complaint set out no new allegations to support such claims. U.S.C.A. Const. Amends. 5, 14; 42 U.S.C.A. § 1983.

> Bennett v. Village of Oak Park, 748 F.Supp. 1329.

N.D.Ill. 1989. Dismissal of federal civil rights action brought by discharged police chief against mayor was proper, where complaint did not establish "stigma" component essential for police chief to establish violation of liberty interest. U.S.C.A. Const.Amend. 14; 42 U.S.C.A. § 1983.

> Harris v. Johnson, 731 F.Supp. 846.

N.D.Ill. 1989. Issue of whether school officials were entitled to qualified immunity in action challenging Illinois statute requiring elementary school students to recite Pledge of Allegiance would be determined on motion for summary judgment, rather than on motion to dismiss. Fed.Rules Civ.Proc.Rule 12(b)(6), 28 U.S.C.A.; Ill.S.H.A. ch. 122, ¶ 27–3.

> Sherman v. Community Consol. School Dist. 21 of Wheeling Tp., 714 F.Supp. 932.

N.D.Ill. 1986. Issue of whether specific program that receives federal funds has discriminated against handicapped person so as to support claim under Rehabilitation Act cannot be properly analyzed in abstract; thus, as long as some federal funding is alleged, program specificity issue is more properly subject of summary judgment motion than motion to dismiss. Rehabilitation Act of 1973, § 504, as amended, 29 U.S.C.A. § 794.

> Byers v. Rockford Mass Transit Dist., 635 F.Supp. 1387.

N.D.Ill. 1981. Yakin v. University of Illinois, Chicago Circle Campus, 508 F.Supp. 848, affirmed 760 F.2d 270.

N.D.Ill. 1978. Plummer v. Chicago Journeyman Plumbers' Local Union No. 130, U. A., 452 F.Supp. 1127, reversed Eggleston v. Chicago Journeymen Plumbers' Local Union No. 130, U. A., 657 F.2d 890, certiorari denied Joint Apprenticeship Committee Local No. 130, U.A. v. Eggleston, 102 S.Ct. 1710, 455 U.S. 1017, 72 L.Ed.2d 134, certiorari denied Plumbing Contractors Ass'n of Chicago & Cook County v. Plummer, 102 S.Ct. 1710, 455 U.S. 1017, 72 L.Ed.2d 134, certiorari denied 102 S.Ct. 1710, 455 U.S. 1017, 72 L.Ed.2d 134.

N.D.Ind. 1993. Although pled in conclusory language, allegations in poultry farm employee's sexual harassment and discrimination complaint, that employee was victim to continuous, repetitive, and degenerate cycle and pattern of sexual harassment and discrimination by her co-workers and supervisors, that she was wrongfully transferred and demoted in retaliation, and that employer was aware of, condoned, and ratified discriminatory conduct, were sufficient to survive motion to dismiss for failure to state claim on vagueness grounds. Fed.Rules Civ.Proc.Rules 8(a), 12(b)(6), 28 U.S.C.A.; Civil Rights Act of 1964, § 701 et seq., as amended, 42 U.S.C.A. § 2000e et seq.

> Garus v. Rose Acre Farms, Inc., 839 F.Supp. 563.

N.D.Ind. 1993. Court would not determine whether police had qualified immunity from § 1983 claim on motion to dismiss for failure to state claim, but rather, would wait until after being more fully apprised of details of case. 42 U.S.C.A. § 1983.

> Tracy For and on Behalf of Estate of Tracy v. Bittles, 820 F.Supp. 396.

N.D.Ind. 1985. National origin aspect of employment discrimination claim under section 1981 was dismissed. 42 U.S.C.A. § 1981.

> Abdulrahim v. Gene B. Glick Co., Inc., 612 F.Supp. 256.

D.Kan. 1997. Possibility that delay in responding to civil rights complainant's request for copy of her statement regarding her treatment by automobile dealership and reluctance to file criminal charges on her behalf violated equal protection if it was racially motivated precluded dismissal of civil rights claim against police and other city defendants. U.S.C.A. Const.Amend. 14; 42 U.S.C.A. § 1983.

> Wesley v. Don Stein Buick, Inc., 985 F.Supp. 1288, vacated in part 996 F.Supp. 1299.

D.Kan. 1992. Section 1983 action against correctional facility administrator would be dismissed as plaintiff failed to show that his claims were different than those asserted in pending class action in which he had standing as class member, and administrator had no liability for claims arising from conditions of confinement in other facilities named in complaint. 42 U.S.C.A. § 1983.

> Johnson v. KSIR Principal Adm'r and Staff, 804 F.Supp. 173.

D.Mass. 1996. Under Massachusetts civil rights statute, claim of son-in-law of public official against official and law enforcement officers, alleging intimidation designed to prevent son-in-law from testifying against official, would not be dismissed for failure to state claim, where defendants' only response to claim was to challenge ability of son-in-law to prove factual allegations. M.G.L.A. c. 12 § 11I; Fed. Rules Civ.Proc.Rule 12(b)(6), 28 U.S.C.A.

> Gerakaris v. Champagne, 913 F.Supp. 646.

D.Mass. 1995. On motion to dismiss for failure to state claim, civil rights claims are subject only to normal standards of pleading. Fed.Rules Civ.Proc.Rule 12(b)(6), 28 U.S.C.A.

> Dominique v. Weld, 880 F.Supp. 928, affirmed 73 F.3d 1156.

D.Mass. 1994. On motion to dismiss, civil rights claims are subject only to normal standards of pleading, i.e., complaint, accepted as true, may not be dismissed if it shows any set of facts that would entitle plaintiff to relief. Fed. Rules Civ.Proc.Rule 12(b)(6), 28 U.S.C.A.

> McGrath v. MacDonald, 853 F.Supp. 1.

D.Mass. 1994. District court may, in appropriate circumstances, note inadequacy of civil rights complaint and, on its own initiative, dismiss complaint, but it may not do so without at least giving plaintiffs notice of proposed action and affording them opportunity to address issues. 42 U.S.C.A. § 1983.

> Feliciano v. DuBois, 846 F.Supp. 1033.

D.Mass. 1986. Motion to dismiss brought in action under Civil Rights Act of 1964, § 701 et seq., as amended, 42 U.S.C.A. § 2000e et seq. must be scrutinized with special care. Fed. Rules Civ.Proc.Rule 12(b)(1, 6), 28 U.S.C.A.

> Baranek v. Kelly, 630 F.Supp. 1107.

E.D.Mich. 1994. In determining whether to grant motion to dismiss for failure to state claim, particularly where civil rights are involved, pro se plaintiffs are held to less stringent standard of review, and their pleadings are liberally construed. Fed.Rules Civ.Proc.Rule 12(b)(6), 28 U.S.C.A.; 42 U.S.C.A. § 1983.

> Middleton v. McGinnis, 860 F.Supp. 391.

E.D.Mich. 1994. Dismissal of complaints under civil rights statutes are scrutinized with special care, and pro se complaints are held to less stringent standards than those drafted by attorneys. Fed.Rules Civ.Proc.Rule 12(b)(6), 28 U.S.C.A.

> Strout v. U.S. Parole Com'n, 842 F.Supp. 948, affirmed 40 F.3d 136.

E.D.Mich. 1989. Complaint of parents who chose to educate their children at home, did not give notice to defendant school officials that parents alleged violation of state-created due process right, entitlement to neutral decision maker, or improper requirement of instruction only from certified teachers; thus, latter claims were required to be dismissed, as no proper amendment had been presented to court. Fed.Rules Civ.Proc.Rule 8, 28 U.S.C.A.

> Clonlara, Inc. v. Runkel, 722 F.Supp. 1442.

E.D.Mich. 1986. When considering dismissal on the pleadings, federal district courts must scrutinize plaintiff's civil rights claims with special care.

> Davey v. Tomlinson, 627 F.Supp. 1458.

E.D.Mich. 1982. Wygant v. Jackson Bd. of Educ., 546 F.Supp. 1195, affirmed 746 F.2d 1152, certiorari granted 105 S.Ct. 2015, 471 U.S. 1014, 85 L.Ed.2d 298, reversed 106 S.Ct. 1842, 476 U.S. 267, 90 L.Ed.2d 260, rehearing denied 106 S.Ct. 3320, 478 U.S. 1014, 92 L.Ed.2d 728.

W.D.Mich. 1997. Dismissals of complaints filed under civil rights statutes are scrutinized with special care.

> Winburn v. Bologna, 979 F.Supp. 531.

W.D.Mich. 1989. Dismissals of complaints filed under civil rights statutes are scrutinized with special care. Fed.Rules Civ.Proc.Rule 12(b)(6), 28 U.S.C.A.

> Mercado v. Kingsley Area Schools/Traverse City Public Schools Adult Educ. Consortium, 727 F.Supp. 335.

W.D.Mich. 1976. Thompson v. Board of Ed. of Romeo Community Schools, 71 F.R.D. 398, adhered to 519 F.Supp. 1373, reversed 709 F.2d 1200.

D.Minn. 1992. Where former prison inmate's Fifth Amendment claim contained bare allegations of race discrimination without any supporting facts, assertion that he would fill in details of complaint with additional discovery was inappropriate and insufficient to withstand motion to dismiss for failure to state a claim. Fed.Rules Civ.Proc.Rule 12(b)(6), 28 U.S.C.A.; U.S.C.A. Const.Amend. 5.

> Bellecourt v. U.S., 784 F.Supp. 623, affirmed in part, appeal dismissed in part 994 F.2d 427, rehearing denied (#92-1818), certiorari denied 114 S.Ct. 1049, 510 U.S. 1109, 127 L.Ed.2d 371.

E.D.Mo. 1983. McClure v. Esparza, 556 F.Supp. 569, affirmed 732 F.2d 162, certiorari denied 105 S.Ct. 2111, 471 U.S. 1052, 85 L.Ed.2d 477.

E.D.Mo. 1979. Vorbeck v. Whaley, 478 F.Supp. 1117, affirmed 620 F.2d 191.

D.Neb. 1992. Handicapped students' allegations of physical, sexual and emotional abuse while attending school were sufficient to satisfy heightened-pleading standard in § 1983 actions and overcome motion to dismiss for failure to state a claim by putting school on notice of nature of civil rights claims alleged and by enabling school to prepare response. Fed.Rules Civ.Proc.Rule 12(b)(6), 28 U.S.C.A.; 42 U.S.C.A. § 1983.

Geir By and Through Geir v. Educational Service Unit No. 16, 144 F.R.D. 680.

D.Neb. 1963. Rhodes v. Van Steenberg, 225 F.Supp. 113, affirmed 334 F.2d 709, certiorari denied 85 S.Ct. 263, 379 U.S. 915, 13 L.Ed.2d 186, motion denied 258 F.Supp. 546, affirmed 418 F.2d 1309, certiorari denied 90 S.Ct. 1382, 397 U.S. 1049, 25 L.Ed.2d 662.

D.Nev. 1989. Complaint against deputy district attorney for unconstitutional deprivation of property had to be dismissed, where plaintiff's allegations against her only concerned actions taken within her authority and role as prosecutor, and thus was barred by doctrine of prosecutorial immunity, and plaintiff had previously been given chance to amend his complaint to correct such deficiencies but failed to do so.

Johnson v. Reno Police Chief, 718 F.Supp. 36.

D.N.H. 1992. Dismissal of pro se civil rights complaint is appropriate only if plaintiff is not entitled to relief under any set of facts he or she could prove. 42 U.S.C.A. § 1983; Fed. Rules Civ.Proc.Rule 12(b)(6), 28 U.S.C.A.

Avery v. Powell, 806 F.Supp. 7.

D.N.J. 1995. Where action derives from pro se civil rights complaint, court must not dismiss action unless it appears beyond clear doubt that plaintiff can prove no set of facts which would entitle him or her to relief. Fed. Rules Civ.Proc.Rule 12(b)(6), 28 U.S.C.A.

Arons v. Donovan, 882 F.Supp. 379.

District court would dismiss independent gubernatorial candidate's claim that New Jersey statute permitting "qualified" candidates who have expended $150,000 and applied for matching funds to appear in interactive television debates was unconstitutional, where question of statute's constitutionality had not been adequately addressed by either side, and candidate had failed to make particularized arguments that statute was unconstitutional and failed to provide state with sufficiently clear notice of such claim. N.J.S.A. 19:44A–45.

Arons v. Donovan, 882 F.Supp. 379.

D.N.J. 1988. Dismissal of student's federal civil rights claims against school officials was required following dismissal of student's federal constitutional claims. 42 U.S.C.A. § 1983.

Palmer v. Merluzzi, 689 F.Supp. 400, affirmed 868 F.2d 90.

D.N.J. 1988. Pro se inmate's failure in § 1983 complaint to state which federal right was violated did not necessitate dismissal of complaint, in that liberality allowed in modern pleading precluded dismissal as long as pleading would permit recovery under any theory of law. Fed.Rules Civ.Proc.Rule 12(b)(6), 28 U.S.C.A.; 42 U.S.C.A. § 1983.

Douglas v. Marino, 684 F.Supp. 395.

E.D.N.Y. 1995. Complaint under ADEA against owner of employer in individual capacity was subject to dismissal, with former employees having 30 days to amend complaint to allege representative liability and not being foreclosed from later seeking leave to amend complaint to allege alter ego liability; ADEA does not allow for individual liability, but individuals may be named as defendants in their representative or official capacities for purposes of respondeat superior liability, and plaintiffs failed to adequately allege alter ego theory or any supporting facts for such liability. Age Discrimination in Employment Act of 1967, § 11(a, b), 29 U.S.C.A. § 630(a, b).

Leykis v. NYP Holdings, Inc., 899 F.Supp. 986.

Complaint under state Human Rights Law (HRL) against owner of employer in individual capacity was subject to dismissal, with former employees having opportunity to amend complaint to allege sufficient facts regarding owner's individual liability under HRL; they failed to plead facts regarding owner's involvement in creation, design or implementation of allegedly discriminatory plan, and failed to plead facts upon which court could infer owner's alleged intent to discriminate or involvement in allegedly discriminatory scheme. McKinney's Executive Law § 297, subd. 9; Fed.Rules Civ.Proc. Rule 12(b)(6), 28 U.S.C.A.

Leykis v. NYP Holdings, Inc., 899 F.Supp. 986.

E.D.N.Y. 1994. Motion to dismiss civil rights claim alleging excessive force by police officers for failure to state claim is appropriate if, accepting all allegations as true, it is clear that force used by officers in effecting arrest was objectively reasonable under circumstances. 42 U.S.C.A. § 1983; Fed.Rules Civ. Proc.Rule 12(b)(6), 28 U.S.C.A.; U.S.C.A. Const. Amend. 4.

Messina v. Mazzeo, 854 F.Supp. 116.

Motion to dismiss excessive force claim is only appropriate when it is clear that violence at issue is isolated incident which, when taking into account all of circumstances, establishes that excessive force was not used. Fed.Rules Civ.Proc.Rule 12(b)(6), 28 U.S.C.A.; U.S.C.A. Const.Amend. 4; 42 U.S.C.A. § 1983.

> Messina v. Mazzeo, 854 F.Supp. 116.

Mere fact that arrestee did not plead any serious injury resulting from alleged use of excessive force in effecting his arrest did not render civil rights complaint for excessive force dismissible as matter of law. Fed.Rules Civ. Proc.Rule 12(b)(6), 28 U.S.C.A.; U.S.C.A. Const. Amend. 4; 42 U.S.C.A. § 1983.

> Messina v. Mazzeo, 854 F.Supp. 116.

E.D.N.Y. 1994. Motion to dismiss must be denied, unless movant successfully persuades court beyond doubt that plaintiff can prove no set of facts in support of her claim which would entitle her to relief, and court must apply this standard with particular strictness where complaint alleges violation of plaintiff's civil rights. Fed.Rules Civ.Proc.Rule 12(b)(6), 28 U.S.C.A.; Civil Rights Act of 1964, § 701 et seq., 42 U.S.C.A. § 2000e et seq.; 42 U.S.C.A. § 1981; N.Y.McKinney's Executive Law § 296; New York City Administrative Code, § 8–101 et seq.

> Alie v. NYNEX Corp., 158 F.R.D. 239.

In order to survive motion to dismiss, complaint asserting civil rights violation must make specific factual allegations indicating deprivation of rights. Fed.Rules Civ.Proc.Rule 12(b)(6), 28 U.S.C.A.; Civil Rights Act of 1964, § 701 et seq., 42 U.S.C.A. § 2000e et seq.

> Alie v. NYNEX Corp., 158 F.R.D. 239.

Complaint consisting of nothing more than naked assertions, and setting forth no facts upon which court could find violation of civil rights acts, fails to state claim upon which relief may be granted. Fed.Rules Civ.Proc.Rule 12(b)(6), 28 U.S.C.A.; Civil Rights Act of 1964, § 701 et seq., 42 U.S.C.A. § 2000e et seq.; 42 U.S.C.A. § 1981; N.Y.McKinney's Executive Law § 296; New York City Administrative Code, § 8–101 et seq.

> Alie v. NYNEX Corp., 158 F.R.D. 239.

E.D.N.Y. 1987. Issues of material fact were present regarding whether Port Authority police employee's memorandum which was critical of Authority's ability to prevent or handle terrorist incidents constituted personal attack on supervisor which caused dissension and disharmony, undermined discipline, and interfered with operation of Authority police, thus precluding grant of Authority's motion to dismiss in action brought by employee alleging First Amendment violations. U.S.C.A. Const.Amend. 1.

> Brown v. Port Authority of New York and New Jersey, 656 F.Supp. 517, affirmed 867 F.2d 1423.

N.D.N.Y. 1996. Standard for motion for judgment on the pleadings and motion to dismiss for failure to state a claim is applied with particular strictness where plaintiff complains of civil rights violations. Fed.Rules Civ.Proc. Rule 12(b)(6), (c), 28 U.S.C.A.

> Volberg v. Pataki, 917 F.Supp. 909, affirmed 112 F.3d 507, certiorari denied 117 S.Ct. 1252, 137 L.Ed.2d 333.

N.D.N.Y. 1996. In civil rights action brought against city, university officials and various law enforcement officials for alleged racially discriminatory conduct in criminal investigation, Fourth Amendment claim against particular law enforcement official was to be dismissed with prejudice, where such official stated that he did not interview plaintiffs or any individuals on streets of city and that he did not wear police uniform when working, and plaintiffs made no allegations contradicting the official's statements. U.S.C.A. Const.Amend. 4.

> Brown v. City of Oneonta, 916 F.Supp. 176.

N.D.N.Y. 1995. In civil rights action in which only injury alleged by plaintiff was his wrongful conviction and incarceration as result of conduct of state police officers, it would be inappropriate to go forward due to pendency of federal habeas proceeding attacking state conviction, particularly in view of potential for collateral estoppel on habeas petition; however, rather than dismiss action, even without prejudice, court would stay all proceedings pending final resolution of habeas proceeding in order to avoid waste of judicial and other resources.

> Chamberlain v. Lishansky, 899 F.Supp. 108.

N.D.N.Y. 1994. An action, especially under the Civil Rights Act, should not be dismissed unless it appears to a certainty that plaintiff is not entitled to relief under any set of facts which could be proved in support of her claims. 42 U.S.C.A. § 1983.

> Bowman v. Campbell, 850 F.Supp. 144.

N.D.N.Y. 1993. District court's initial inquiry on motion to dismiss § 1983 action is to merely direct it to whether allegations constituted statement of claim, a short and plain statement of claim showing that pleader is entitled to relief. Fed.Rules Civ.Proc.Rules 8(a), 12(b)(6), 28 U.S.C.A.; 42 U.S.C.A. § 1983.

> Hall v. Dworkin, 829 F.Supp. 1403.

N.D.N.Y. 1978. Silver v. Mohasco Corp., 497 F.Supp. 1, reversed 602 F.2d 1083, certiorari granted 100 S.Ct. 519, 444 U.S. 990, 62 L.Ed.2d 418, reversed 100 S.Ct. 2486, 447 U.S. 807, 65 L.Ed.2d 532, on remand 103 F.R.D. 614, affirmed 647 F.2d 162.

S.D.N.Y. 1995. Under New York law, employer's motion to dismiss Human Rights Law claim would be subjected to same analysis as motion to dismiss ADA claim. Americans with Disabilities Act of 1990, § 2 et seq., 42 U.S.C.A.

§ 12101 et seq.; N.Y.McKinney's Executive Law § 290 et seq.

> Mohamed v. Marriott Intern., Inc., 905 F.Supp. 141.

S.D.N.Y. 1995. Independent contractor's counterclaim against manufacturer alleging that termination of distribution agreement was due to gender discrimination in violation of New York law failed to provide sufficient information to allege violation of statute, and, thus, counterclaim would be dismissed without prejudice to filing amendment within 30 days, where there was no indication as to what kind of factual basis existed for alleged violation, and information concerning nature of allegedly illegal conduct was required to evaluate whether "boycott" was essential to finding of violation by corporate entity, and, if so, what scope of refusals to deal were necessary to constitute boycott. N.Y.McKinney's Executive Law § 296, subd. 13; Fed.Rules Civ.Proc.Rule 12(b)(6), 28 U.S.C.A.

> International Business Machines Corp. v. Jennifer-Ashley Co., Inc., 872 F.Supp. 1256.

S.D.N.Y. 1994. No case or controversy appeared to exist under Article III, and, thus, dismissal on grounds of mootness was warranted in parent's action challenging impartiality of hearing officers reviewing school district decisions in relation to educational planning for handicapped children, inasmuch as parent stated that objectives of litigation had been achieved following alteration of New York's hearing officer system. N.Y.McKinney's Education Law § 4404; U.S.C.A. Const. Art. 3, § 2, cl. 1.

> Heldman on Behalf of T.H. v. Sobol, 846 F.Supp. 285.

S.D.N.Y. 1994. Qualified immunity question should be resolved at earliest possible stage of litigation, either in motion to dismiss, or, after discovery on limited question of objective reasonableness of challenged action, in motion for summary judgment. Fed.Rules Civ.Proc. Rules 12(b)(1, 6), (c), 56, 28 U.S.C.A.

> Chayo v. Kaladjian, 844 F.Supp. 163.

S.D.N.Y. 1993. Unlike absolute immunity, qualified immunity is measured by standard of objective reasonableness, and therefore cannot ordinarily support dismissal for failure to state claim. Fed.Rules Civ.Proc.Rule 12(b)(6), 28 U.S.C.A.

> Sassower v. Abrams, 833 F.Supp. 253.

S.D.N.Y. 1993. Plaintiff's civil rights claim against various government bodies, agencies and persons regarding child custody and abuse proceedings would be dismissed, as plaintiff's complaint failed to set forth short and plain statement of claim showing that he was entitled to relief; complaint was virtually incomprehen-

sible document accompanied by numerous "exhibits," and contained only conclusory, vague, and general factual allegations and thus provided court with no adequate basis to discern nature of plaintiff's claims. Fed.Rules Civ.Proc. Rule 8(a)(2), 28 U.S.C.A.; 42 U.S.C.A. § 1983.

> Levine v. County of Westchester, 828 F.Supp. 238, affirmed 22 F.3d 1090.

Plaintiff's civil rights claim against various states would be dismissed, as states are protected from suit by Eleventh Amendment, which bars suit against state in federal court unless it consents to be sued or Congress enacts legislation overriding state's Eleventh Amendment immunity. U.S.C.A. Const.Amend. 11; 42 U.S.C.A. § 1983.

> Levine v. County of Westchester, 828 F.Supp. 238, affirmed 22 F.3d 1090.

Plaintiff's civil rights claim against state Attorney General would be dismissed, as district court lacked subject matter jurisdiction over claims for injunctive relief based on state law. 42 U.S.C.A. § 1983.

> Levine v. County of Westchester, 828 F.Supp. 238, affirmed 22 F.3d 1090.

S.D.N.Y. 1993. City police officers' claims against county district attorney and district attorney's office (DAO) under § 1983 alleging that state criminal indictment against officers was improperly derived from immunized testimony due to failure to train or supervise would be dismissed due to relative infrequency of possible prosecutorial misconduct involving use immunity concerns arising from patrol guide testimony.

> Feerick v. Sudolnik, 816 F.Supp. 879, affirmed 2 F.3d 403.

S.D.N.Y. 1992. Court which determined that state prisoner whose civil rights claims for damages were dependent upon resolution of validity of the duration of his claim was required to first exhaust his state remedies as required by the federal habeas corpus statute would stay action pending exhaustion rather than dismissing it. 28 U.S.C.A. § 2254(b); 42 U.S.C.A. § 1983.

> Martorell v. McElwee, 794 F.Supp. 123.

S.D.N.Y. 1990. District court could not determine, on motion to dismiss, whether actions of town board in amending town code to require prior site plan approvals only for non-residential properties located in residential areas were solely legislative, and thus whether members were entitled to absolute immunity in civil rights action alleging First and Fourteenth Amendment violations, assuming applicability of absolute immunity to members of local town board; members could lose their immunity if their actions would only affect certain religious organization notwithstanding the arguably neutral language of statute, if only considerations before adopting amendment were whether members could stop practices of religious organization, or if members engaged in enforcement efforts in conjunction with town attorney and building inspector. Fed.Rules Civ.Proc.Rule 12(b)(6), 28 U.S.C.A.; U.S.C.A. Const.Amends. 1, 14; 42 U.S.C.A. § 1983.

> Moore v. Trippe, 743 F.Supp. 201.

District court could not determine, on motion to dismiss, whether members of town board were entitled to qualified immunity on claim in civil rights actions that they interfered with religious practices by amending town code to require prior site plan approval only for nonresidential properties located in residential areas; questions of qualified immunity are inherently fact-specific. Fed.Rules Civ.Proc.Rule 12(b)(6), 28 U.S.C.A.; U.S.C.A. Const.Amends. 1, 14; 42 U.S.C.A. § 1983.

> Moore v. Trippe, 743 F.Supp. 201.

Whether town attorney and town board members were entitled to qualified immunity in civil rights actions with respect to claims of Zen Buddhists and not-for-profit religious corporation that attorney and board members acted outside their authority when sending building inspector to find violations on property could not be resolved on motion to dismiss, since such inquiry was inherently fact-specific. 42 U.S.C.A. § 1983; Fed.Rules Civ.Proc.Rule 12(b)(6), 28 U.S.C.A.

> Moore v. Trippe, 743 F.Supp. 201.

S.D.N.Y. 1975. Gonzalez v. Shanker, 399 F.Supp. 858, certified question answered 533 F.2d 832.

W.D.N.Y. 1996. Claims would not be dismissed on motion for alleged failure to state a claim made two weeks before trial where defendants had been on notice from at least time that first amended complaint was filed over seven and a half years previously that plaintiff was seeking to pursue such claims, and had ample time for discovery, but brought no motion for summary judgment. Fed.Rules Civ.Proc.Rule 12(b)(6), 28 U.S.C.A.

> Jungels v. State University College of New York, 922 F.Supp. 779, affirmed 112 F.3d 504.

W.D.N.Y. 1994. Civil rights complaint against public employee would be dismissed sua sponte for failure to state claim upon which relief can be granted, even though motion to dismiss was not brought on his behalf; he was employed by state along with other defendants who brought motion, complaint failed to state claim against him, and he had not yet been served with summons and complaint at time motion was filed. 42 U.S.C.A. §§ 1983, 1985,

1986; Fed.Rules Civ.Proc.Rule 12(b)(6), 28 U.S.C.A.

> Koch v. Mirza, 869 F.Supp. 1031.

E.D.N.C. 1987. Although adverse impact discrimination cases generally are not resolved on motions for involuntary dismissal, Title VII and liberality with which it must correctly be construed does not override or preempt procedural requirements of federal rules. Civil Rights Act of 1964, § 701 et seq., as amended, 42 U.S.C.A. § 2000e et seq.; Fed.Rules Civ. Proc.Rule 41(b), 28 U.S.C.A.

> Harris v. Marsh, 679 F.Supp. 1204, opinion vacated in part on reconsideration 123 F.R.D. 204, affirmed in part, reversed in part Blue v. U.S. Dept. of Army, 914 F.2d 525, certiorari denied Chambers v. U.S. Dept. of Army, 111 S.Ct. 1580, 499 U.S. 959, 113 L.Ed.2d 645, affirmed in part, reversed in part 914 F.2d 525, certiorari denied 111 S.Ct. 1580, 499 U.S. 959, 113 L.Ed.2d 645.

E.D.N.C. 1987. Civil rights plaintiff's failure to comply with court order that he make "short and plain" statement of fact that would support what he believed to be his legal claim for deprivation of civil rights, justified dismissal of complaint; "supplemental complaint" simply added length without substance. 42 U.S.C.A. § 1983; Fed.Rules Civ.Proc.Rule 8, 28 U.S.C.A.

> Spencer v. Rhodes, 656 F.Supp. 458, affirmed 826 F.2d 1061, affirmed 826 F.2d 1061.

M.D.N.C. 1994. Court can dismiss for failure to state a claim on which relief can be granted in equal protection case requiring rational basis review; to survive motion to dismiss, plaintiff must allege facts sufficient to overcome presumption of rationality that applies to governmental classifications. U.S.C.A. Const.Amend. 14; Fed.Rules Civ.Proc.Rule 12(b)(6), 28 U.S.C.A.

> Shanks v. Forsyth County Park Authority, Inc., 869 F.Supp. 1231.

N.D.Ohio 1993. Police officer's argument that no federal claim had been stated by motorists arrested for exceeding posted speed limit did not require dismissal of motorists' § 1983 complaint on ground of qualified immunity. 42 U.S.C.A. § 1983.

> Rose v. Village of Peninsula, 839 F.Supp. 517.

N.D.Ohio 1991. Despite its sketchiness, § 1981 plaintiff's complaint alleged retaliatory failure to hire within two-year limitations period, precluding dismissal on limitations grounds. 42 U.S.C.A. § 1981.

> Robinson v. N & C Const. Co., 767 F.Supp. 843.

N.D.Ohio 1988. If plaintiff in § 1983 action fails to allege sufficient allegations to withstand qualified immunity defense, court may grant motion to dismiss complaint. 42 U.S.C.A. § 1983.

Martin v. City of Eastlake, 686 F.Supp. 620.

N.D.Ohio 1982. Meyers v. Ace Hardware, Inc., 95 F.R.D. 145, reconsideration denied 1982 WL 31058, appeal dismissed 812 F.2d 1407.

S.D.Ohio 1995. Before commencement of discovery in § 1983 action, defendant asserting qualified immunity is entitled to dismissal if plaintiff fails to state claim alleging violation of clearly established law; district court has duty to determine currently applicable law and whether that law was clearly established at time of alleged conduct and, if law was clearly established, district court cannot find that defendant knew that law forbade his or her conduct. 42 U.S.C.A. § 1983.

In re Cincinnati Radiation Litigation, 874 F.Supp. 796.

S.D.Ohio 1981. Morrow v. Bassman, 515 F.Supp. 587, affirmed 785 F.2d 309.

E.D.Pa. 1994. Complaint may be dismissed for failure to state claim where defendant contends that under facts alleged he is entitled to immunity, even though immunity is generally characterized as affirmative defense. Fed.Rules Civ.Proc.Rule 12(b)(6), 28 U.S.C.A.

Moser v. Bascelli, 865 F.Supp. 249.

E.D.Pa. 1992. General standard for motions to dismiss for failure to state claim upon which relief can be granted is modified in case of civil rights claims brought under § 1983 by adding requirement that complaint contain modicum of factual specificity, identifying particular conduct of defendants that is alleged to have harmed plaintiff. Fed.Rules Civ.Proc.Rule 12(b)(6), 28 U.S.C.A.; 42 U.S.C.A. § 1983.

Gilbert v. Feld, 788 F.Supp. 854.

County detective's assertion that he was entitled to qualified immunity on civil rights claim could not properly be raised on motion to dismiss absent showing that complaint itself established circumstances required for finding of qualified immunity. 42 U.S.C.A. § 1983; Fed.Rules Civ.Proc.Rule 12(b)(6), 28 U.S.C.A.

Gilbert v. Feld, 788 F.Supp. 854.

E.D.Pa. 1992. When defendant in civil rights action claims that he is entitled to qualified immunity, he may proceed by way of motion to dismiss, even though immunity is generally characterized as affirmative defense. Fed.

Rules Civ.Proc.Rules 8(c), 12(b), 28 U.S.C.A.; 42 U.S.C.A. § 1983.

Jordan v. Fox, Rothschild, O'Brien & Frankel, 787 F.Supp. 471, reconsideration denied 792 F.Supp. 393, affirmed and remanded 20 F.3d 1250, on remand 1995 WL 141465, vacated 20 F.3d 1250, on remand 1995 WL 141465.

E.D.Pa. 1991. Triable factual issues existed, sufficient to withstand motion to dismiss civil rights action, on whether police department and its medical employee could have had sufficient suspicion to warrant full body cavity search of police officer who sought to return to duty after disability leave. 42 U.S.C.A. § 1983; U.S.C.A. Const.Amend. 4.

McKenna v. City of Philadelphia, 771 F.Supp. 124.

E.D.Pa. 1991. Civil rights complaint by person whose name was used by police to identify criminal suspect would not be dismissed for his failure to identify responsible officers and detectives, where it appeared that names of officers and detectives involved could be obtained through discovery; however, denial of motion to dismiss was without prejudice to postdiscovery reassertion of position that defendant officers and detectives remained unidentified. Fed.Rules Civ.Proc.Rule 12(b)(6), 28 U.S.C.A.; 42 U.S.C.A. § 1983.

Sergio v. Doe, 769 F.Supp. 164.

E.D.Pa. 1990. Alleged superfluity in suing both police department and borough in § 1983 action could not properly be challenged on motion to dismiss for failure to state claim upon which relief can be granted; motion to dismiss for failure to state claim upon which relief can be granted questions validity of claims, not redundancy of claims. Fed.Rules Civ.Proc.Rule 12(b)(6), 28 U.S.C.A.

Coffman v. Wilson Police Dept., 739 F.Supp. 257.

E.D.Pa. 1973. Ammlung v. City of Chester, 355 F.Supp. 1300, affirmed 494 F.2d 811.

M.D.Pa. 1990. Heightened specificity requirement for § 1983 claims does not alter general standards for ruling on motions to dismiss for failure to state a claim. 42 U.S.C.A. § 1983; Fed.Rules Civ.Proc.Rule 12(b)(6), 28 U.S.C.A.

Associated Pennsylvania Constructors v. Jannetta, 738 F.Supp. 891.

M.D.Pa. 1986. Alleged failure of discharged employee to mitigate his damages did not warrant dismissal of complaint brought under Age Discrimination in Employment Act. Age Discrimination in Employment Act of 1967, § 2 et seq., 29 U.S.C.A. § 621 et seq.

Gabrielle v. Barrett, Haentjens & Co., 663 F.Supp. 1184.

M.D.Pa. 1985. Even though civil rights statute 42 U.S.C.A. § 1983 might be proper vehicle for vindication of First Amendment rights of employee attorney who was allegedly terminated for acting on behalf of another employee against county commissioners, court would not dismiss claims asserted against county, county officials and agencies directly under the Fourteenth Amendment on motion to dismiss. U.S.C.A. Const.Amends. 1, 14.

Kuchka v. Kile, 634 F.Supp. 502.

W.D.Pa. 1995. Court should not dismiss complaint, especially in civil rights action, unless it appears beyond doubt that plaintiff can prove no set of facts in support of her claims which would entitle her to relief.

Ford v. Johnson, 899 F.Supp. 227.

W.D.Pa. 1981. Al-Khazraji v. Saint Francis College, 523 F.Supp. 386, affirmed 784 F.2d 505, certiorari granted in part 107 S.Ct. 62, 479 U.S. 812, 93 L.Ed.2d 21, affirmed 107 S.Ct. 2022, 481 U.S. 604, 95 L.Ed.2d 582, rehearing denied 107 S.Ct. 3244, 483 U.S. 1011, 97 L.Ed.2d 749.

W.D.Pa. 1975. Wilson v. Sharon Steel Corp., 399 F.Supp. 403, vacated 549 F.2d 276, on remand 442 F.Supp. 231.

N.D.Tex. 1996. Because factual findings regarding subject matter jurisdiction are intertwined with merits of Title VII claim, court should not dismiss action unless plaintiff's alleged claim is immaterial or wholly insubstantial and frivolous. Civil Rights Act of 1964, § 701 et seq., 42 U.S.C.A. § 2000e et seq.

St. Germain v. Simmons Airline, 930 F.Supp. 1144.

N.D.Tex. 1994. District court would stay proceedings to allow exhaustion of Equal Employment Opportunity Commission (EEOC) conciliation requirement for bringing action against employer under ADEA on claims of "other similarly situated persons," rather than dismiss action, as dismissal would unfairly penalize allegedly injured applicants by conditioning their right to relief on events beyond their control, where EEOC failed to make conciliation efforts respecting such claims. Age Discrimination in Employment Act of 1967, § 7(b), 29 U.S.C.(1988 Ed.) § 626(b).

E.E.O.C. v. General Dynamics Corp., 849 F.Supp. 1158.

N.D.Tex. 1993. Because factual findings regarding subject-matter jurisdiction are intertwined with merits of Title VII case, district court will not dismiss case for lack of subject-matter jurisdiction unless plaintiff's claim to be "employee" of defendant is wholly insubstantial, i.e., obviously without merit or foreclosed by prior decisions, and frivolous. Fed.Rules Civ.Proc.Rule 12(b)(1), 28 U.S.C.A.; 42 U.S.C.A.

§ 1981; Civil Rights Act of 1964, § 701(f), as amended, 42 U.S.C.A. § 2000e(f).

Barnes v. Colonial Life and Acc. Ins. Co., 818 F.Supp. 978.

S.D.Tex. 1994. When considering motion to dismiss claim on ground that government official is entitled to qualified immunity, court must ascertain whether plaintiffs' allegations, if accepted as true, state claim for violation of any rights secured under Constitution. 42 U.S.C.A. § 1983.

Baker v. Putnal, 865 F.Supp. 389, affirmed in part, reversed in part 75 F.3d 190.

D.Utah 1995. Unless complaint states compensable claim for relief under Federal Constitution, damage suits concerning constitutional violations should not survive motion to dismiss.

Bourret v. Cisneros, 896 F.Supp. 1104.

E.D.Va. 1997. Pro se complaint involving civil rights issues should be liberally construed; dismissal may be appropriate where complaint contains detailed description of underlying facts which fail to state viable claim, but where complaint is broad, dismissal for failure to state a claim is improper. 42 U.S.C.A. § 1983; Fed. Rules Civ.Proc.Rule 12(b)(6), 28 U.S.C.A.

Sculthorpe v. Virginia Retirement System, 952 F.Supp. 307.

W.D.Va. 1997. Standard governing motion to dismiss for failure to state a claim is applied more strictly than normal when plaintiff alleges civil rights violations. Fed.Rules Civ. Proc.Rule 12(b)(1), 28 U.S.C.A.

Alston v. Virginia High School League, Inc., 176 F.R.D. 220.

W.D.Va. 1992. Court could dismiss civil rights action against state policeman who allegedly caused driver's death in automobile accident only if, taking allegations of complaint in light most favorable to plaintiff, it concludes that plaintiff could prove no set of facts entitling her to relief for injuries caused by excessive use of force during seizure. Fed.Rules Civ.Proc. Rules 12(b)(6), 56, 28 U.S.C.A.; 42 U.S.C.A. § 1983; U.S.C.A. Const.Amend. 4.

Hicks v. Leake, 821 F.Supp. 419.

E.D.Wis. 1993. To avoid dismissal of complaint for failure to state claim based on qualified immunity, plaintiffs must allege facts in their complaint that, taken as true, assert that individual defendants violated clearly established constitutional rights of which reasonable person would have known.

Kaufmann v. U.S., 840 F.Supp. 641.

W.D.Wis. 1993. There were not enough facts in record to determine whether arresting officer's search of motorist's vehicle, allegedly without motorist's consent, was constitutional, precluding dismissal of motorist's civil rights claim. U.S.C.A. Const.Amend. 4.

> U.S. ex rel. Verdone v. Circuit Court for Taylor County, 851 F.Supp. 345.

W.D.Wis. 1992. When considering motion to dismiss for failure to state § 1983 civil rights claim, court must decide whether moving party has shown that plaintiff has failed to allege facts that, if believed, would show that federal right was actually violated. Fed.Rules Civ.Proc.Rule 12(b)(6), 28 U.S.C.A.; 42 U.S.C.A. § 1983.

> Canedy v. Boardman, 801 F.Supp. 254, reversed 16 F.3d 183, appeal after remand 91 F.3d 30.

Bkrtcy.E.D.Pa. 1995. Plaintiff was not required, for purposes of avoiding dismissal of complaint as failing to state claim upon which relief could be granted, to plead facts underlying its due process allegations in evidential detail. U.S.C.A. Const.Amend. 14; Fed.Rules Civ.Proc.Rule 12(b)(6), 28 U.S.C.A.

> In re PVI Associates, 181 B.R. 210.

Civil rights complaint would not be dismissed for failing to state substantive due process claim upon which relief could be granted, merely because plaintiff failed to utilize "buzz words" or textbook definitions. U.S.C.A. Const. Amend. 14; Fed.Rules Civ.Proc.Rule 12(b)(6), 28 U.S.C.A.

> In re PVI Associates, 181 B.R. 210.

⚷**1788.10. —— Prisoners' actions.**

C.A.9 (Cal.) 1988. In civil rights cases where plaintiff appears pro se, court must construe pleadings liberally and must afford plaintiff benefit of any doubt; moreover, before dismissing pro se civil rights complaint for failure to state claim, district court must give plaintiff statement of complaint's deficiencies. Fed. Rules Civ.Proc.Rule 12(b)(6), 28 U.S.C.A.; 42 U.S.C.A. § 1983.

> Karim-Panahi v. Los Angeles Police Dept., 839 F.2d 621.

C.A.10 (Colo.) 1992. District court improperly dismissed claim that guard at jail told other inmates that plaintiff inmate was "snitch" and that as result plaintiff was severely beaten by groups of inmates by concluding that allegations were false based on testimony of defendant in telephonic evidentiary hearing and failing to consider any potential legal issues arising from allegations. U.S.C.A. Const.Amend. 8; Fed.Rules Civ.Proc.Rule 12(b)(6), 28 U.S.C.A.

> Northington v. Jackson, 973 F.2d 1518, appeal after remand 102 F.3d 1564.

C.A.10 (Colo.) 1989. Civil rights claims of prison inmate which were part of the subject matter of a class action to which inmate was a party by reason of being an inmate were properly dismissed without prejudice, allowing inmate to seek redress through the class action. 42 U.S.C.A. § 1983.

> Durre v. Dempsey, 869 F.2d 543.

C.A.5 (Fla.) 1979. Shabazz v. Barnauskas, 598 F.2d 345, on remand 600 F.Supp. 712, affirmed 790 F.2d 1536, certiorari denied 107 S.Ct. 655, 479 U.S. 1011, 93 L.Ed.2d 709.

C.A.11 (Ga.) 1993. District court should not erect unnecessary procedural barriers which many pro se litigants will have difficulty surmounting, unless court is willing to guide pro se litigants through obstacle course it has set up, or to allow them to skip some of less substantive obstacles.

> Kilgo v. Ricks, 983 F.2d 189.

District court did not abuse its discretion in dismissing as frivolous inmate's § 1983 claim against Commissioner of Georgia Department of Corrections, absent allegation that Department had policy of refusing to provide inmates with medical treatment or allegation that Commissioner participated in challenged conduct. 42 U.S.C.A. § 1983.

> Kilgo v. Ricks, 983 F.2d 189.

C.A.9 (Hawai'i) 1987. Prisoners' pro se complaint is held to less strict standard than standard applied to complaints drafted by lawyers; thus, it is appropriate to dismiss prisoners' action only if it is beyond doubt that prisoners can prove no set of facts in support of their claim which would entitle them to relief.

> Akao v. Shimoda, 832 F.2d 119, certiorari denied 108 S.Ct. 1301, 485 U.S. 993, 99 L.Ed.2d 511.

Prisoners' pro se action, alleging that prison overcrowding violated their right to be free from cruel and unusual punishment, should not have been dismissed without permitting prisoners opportunity to file amendment; although prisoners' allegations were not sufficiently specific and did not allege that prisoners personally had suffered cruel or inhuman punishment, it was not beyond doubt that prisoners would be unable to state claim for relief, where prisoners had alleged that due to population increase there was increase in stress, tension, communicable diseases, and confrontations between inmates. U.S.C.A. Const.Amend. 8.

> Akao v. Shimoda, 832 F.2d 119, certiorari denied 108 S.Ct. 1301, 485 U.S. 993, 99 L.Ed.2d 511.

C.A.7 (Ill.) 1987. Sua sponte dismissal, for failure to state claim and lack of subject matter jurisdiction, of inmate's suit for cruel and unusual punishment was improper where district court did not provide inmate with notice or hearing. Fed.Rules Civ.Proc.Rules 12(b)(1), 12(b)(6), 28 U.S.C.A.

> Shockley v. Jones, 823 F.2d 1068.

C.A.7 (Ind.) 1995. Prison inmate's claim for damages under § 1983 against police officers alleging that police officers conspired to procure his conviction for child molestation through variety of improper actions, including perjury, falsifying evidence, and withholding of exculpatory evidence were not cognizable under § 1983 because claims, if proven, would necessarily invalidate his conviction and defendant had not yet successfully challenged his conviction; however, because defendant could renew claims if he ever succeeded in overturning his conviction, dismissal without prejudice was appropriate. 42 U.S.C.A. § 1983.
Perez v. Sifel, 57 F.3d 503.

Prison inmate's § 1983 claims against police officers alleging illegal search and improper arrest leading to his conviction for child molestation had to be dismissed without prejudice, subject to defendant's renewal of claims if he ever succeeded in overturning his conviction, if district court determined on remand that result favorable to defendant on claims would necessarily call validity of his conviction into question. 42 U.S.C.A. § 1983.
Perez v. Sifel, 57 F.3d 503.

C.A.7 (Ind.) 1993. District court properly dismissed, rather than stayed, inmate's § 1983 action, alleging that his state murder conviction was "engineered" in violation of his constitutional rights, for his failure to exhaust state remedies; if, after exhaustion, inmate refiled his § 1983 action and was met by statute of limitations defense, he could raise doctrine of equitable tolling. 42 U.S.C.A. § 1983.
Heck v. Humphrey, 997 F.2d 355, certiorari granted 114 S.Ct. 751, 510 U.S. 1068, 127 L.Ed.2d 69, affirmed 114 S.Ct. 2364, 512 U.S. 477, 129 L.Ed.2d 383.

C.A.7 (Ind.) 1988. Section 1983 claims of prisoner who was proceeding pro se were improperly dismissed on the basis of an unclear complaint and his affirmative answer to judge's single, somewhat suggestive question as to whether inmate had claims for money damages against prison officials in their official capacities. 42 U.S.C.A. § 1983.
Abdul-Wadood v. Duckworth, 860 F.2d 280, rehearing denied.

C.A.7 (Ind.) 1988. Allegations in prisoner's complaint, that certain unidentified prison officials had violated Eighth Amendment rights by placing him in same cell with psychopathic inmate, were sufficient to survive dismissal on grounds of frivolousness. 28 U.S.C.A. § 1915(d).
Smith-Bey v. Hospital Adm'r, 841 F.2d 751.

Allegations in prisoner's complaint regarding assaults by fellow inmates, which did not indicate any personal involvement by prison staff, were not sufficient to state Eighth Amendment claim against staff sufficient to survive dismissal on grounds of frivolousness. 28 U.S.C.A. § 1915(d).
Smith-Bey v. Hospital Adm'r, 841 F.2d 751.

Allegations in prisoner's complaint, that prison staff had attempted to treat wound which required stitches by giving him ice pack, raised sufficient question regarding staff's alleged deliberate indifference to his serious medical needs to survive dismissal on grounds of frivolousness. 28 U.S.C.A. § 1915(d).
Smith-Bey v. Hospital Adm'r, 841 F.2d 751.

C.A.4 (Md.) 1989. Dismissing former federal prisoner's civil rights action against prison officials and staff of community treatment center based on his failure to obey court order requiring him to clarify charges against several defendants was not abuse of discretion, where magistrate had warned former prisoner that recommendation of dismissal would result from failure to obey order. Fed.Rules Civ.Proc.Rule 41(b), 28 U.S.C.A.; 42 U.S.C.A. § 1983.
Ballard v. Carlson, 882 F.2d 93, certiorari denied 110 S.Ct. 1145, 493 U.S. 1084, 107 L.Ed.2d 1049.

C.A.5 (Miss.) 1982. Green v. Ferrell, 664 F.2d 1292, rehearing denied 670 F.2d 181, rehearing denied Belton v. Ferrell, 670 F.2d 181, appeal after remand 801 F.2d 765, rehearing denied 807 F.2d 995, rehearing denied 807 F.2d 995, rehearing denied 808 F.2d 56, rehearing denied 808 F.2d 56.

C.A.8 (Mo.) 1995. Although liberal reading of inmate's pro se § 1983 complaint revealed facts which if proved would support claim that he was denied medical treatment, dismissal without prejudice was appropriate based on inmate's failure to comply with district court's order requiring him to specifically plead how each defendant violated his rights; district court's order was consistent with heightened standard of pleading required of complaints seeking damages from government officials, and, because dismissal was without prejudice, inmate was free to remedy deficiencies noted in court's order and refile complaint. 42 U.S.C.A. § 1983.
Edgington v. Missouri Dept. of Corrections, 52 F.3d 777.

C.A.2 (N.Y.) 1995. Prisoner's pro se § 1983 complaint should not have been dismissed for failure to comply with pleading requirements of Federal Rules of Civil Procedure, as amended complaint gave defendants fair notice of claims asserted, complaint could not properly have been dismissed for failure to state claim upon which relief can be granted, and defendants did not suggest that amended complaint did not give them notice of substance of claims or was otherwise unintelligible. Fed. Rules Civ.Proc.Rules 8, 12(b)(6), 28 U.S.C.A.

Simmons v. Abruzzo, 49 F.3d 83, on remand 1996 WL 79321, affirmed 104 F.3d 350.

C.A.2 (N.Y.) 1990. District court prematurely dismissed inmate's free exercise claim before determining whether his faith constituted religion and whether prison officials were depriving adherents of their free exercise rights. U.S.C.A. Const.Amend. 1; Fed.Rules Civ.Proc. Rule 12(c), 28 U.S.C.A.

Theriault v. A Religious Office in the Structure of the Government Requiring a Religious Test as a Qualification, 895 F.2d 104.

C.A.4 (N.C.) 1975. Where prisoner alleged that defendant sheriff had inflicted physical damage upon him, had discriminated against him, had subjected him to severe mental cruelty, had refused him mattress during confinement and had refused him toilet paper during entire period of his confinement, charges were not frivolous though allegations were vague and general and lacking in particularized background facts; district court accordingly erred in dismissing without evidentiary hearing. 42 U.S.C.A. § 1983; Fed.Rules Civ.Proc. rules 12(b)(6), 56, 56(e), 28 U.S.C.A.

Wooten v. Shook, 527 F.2d 976.

C.A.9 (Or.) 1981. Franklin v. State of Or., State Welfare Division, 662 F.2d 1337, on remand 563 F.Supp. 1310, affirmed in part, reversed in part 745 F.2d 1221.

C.A.5 (Tex.) 1995. District court did not abuse its discretion by dismissing, as frivolous, indigent Texas prisoner's civil rights claim under § 1983 that he was entitled to annual parole hearings; Texas law did not create any liberty interest in parole, for due process purposes, and change in parole rules did not implicate ex post facto prohibition. U.S.C.A. Const. Art. 1, § 10, cl. 1; Amend. 14; 28 U.S.C.A. § 1915(d); 42 U.S.C.A. § 1983.

Allison v. Kyle, 66 F.3d 71.

C.A.5 (Tex.) 1995. Inmate's claim was frivolous to the extent it sought damages for fact that his confinement in county jail was more disagreeable than it would have been had inmate been transferred immediately after conviction to Texas Department of Criminal Justice (TDCJ); inmate failed to show liberty interest created by state law proscribing his temporary confinement in county jail. U.S.C.A. Const. Amend. 14; 42 U.S.C.A. § 1983.

Biliski v. Harborth, 55 F.3d 160, rehearing denied.

Dismissal of inmate's civil rights claim on grounds of frivolousness was not abuse of discretion as to claims that jail officials interfered with right of access to courts or First Amendment rights by destroying or denying mail and claims regarding medical and dental care, where those claims were not included in complaint and were either conclusory or were not supported by adequate allegation of resulting prejudice. U.S.C.A. Const.Amend. 1; 28 U.S.C.A. § 1915(d); 42 U.S.C.A. § 1983.

Biliski v. Harborth, 55 F.3d 160, rehearing denied.

C.A.5 (Tex.) 1993. Trial court erred by dismissing as frivolous claim of prison inmate, that he suffered emotional distress by allegedly witnessing prison guard commit battery on another prisoner, on grounds that claimant was asserting constitutional rights of battered prisoner rather than his own, without considering argument that Eighth Amendment covered psychological harms sustained by prisoners. U.S.C.A. Const.Amend. 8; 28 U.S.C.A. § 1915(d); 42 U.S.C.A. § 1983.

Smith v. Aldingers, 999 F.2d 109.

C.A.2 (Vt.) 1991. District court should not have dismissed former pretrial detainee's § 1983 claims regarding his placement in administrative segregation for nine months without reviewing state law to determine whether statute or regulation prescribed mandatory procedures governing administrative as opposed to punitive segregation so as to create liberty interest in remaining in general population, and without analyzing possible punitive aspects of such lengthy segregation. 42 U.S.C.A. § 1983; U.S.C.A. Const.Amend. 14.

Covino v. Vermont Dept. of Corrections, 933 F.2d 128.

C.A.4 (Va.) 1975. Where prisoner alleged that defendant sheriff had inflicted physical damage upon him, had discriminated against him, had subjected him to severe mental cruelty, had refused him mattress during confinement and had refused him toilet paper during entire period of his confinement, charges were not frivolous though allegations were vague and general and lacking in particularized background facts; district court accordingly erred in dismissing without evidentiary hearing. 42 U.S.C.A. § 1983; Fed.Rules Civ.Proc. rules 12(b)(6), 56, 56(e), 28 U.S.C.A.

Wooten v. Shook, 527 F.2d 976.

C.A.9 (Wash.) 1995. Material issue of fact as to whether inmate had protectable liberty interest in remaining free of disciplinary segregation in state prison precluded dismissal of inmate's civil rights action for failure to state claim; record was insufficient to determine if disciplinary segregation at issue imposed atypical and significant hardship on inmate in relation to ordinary incidents of prison life.

U.S.C.A. Const.Amend. 14; 42 U.S.C.A. § 1983; Fed.Rules Civ.Proc.Rule 12(b)(6), 28 U.S.C.A.

 Gotcher v. Wood, 66 F.3d 1097, certiorari granted, vacated 117 S.Ct. 1840, 137 L.Ed.2d 1045, on remand 122 F.3d 39.

C.A.9 (Wash.) 1992. District court improperly supplied essential elements of pro se inmate's civil rights claim that were not initially pled by considering facts presented in another related case challenging same practice of prison officials in ruling on motion to dismiss present complaint. 42 U.S.C.A. § 1983; U.S.C.A. Const.Amend. 11; Fed.Rules Civ.Proc.Rule 12(b)(6), 28 U.S.C.A.

 Pena v. Gardner, 976 F.2d 469, as amended.

C.A.9 (Wash.) 1988. Pro se prison litigant's substantive due process claim arising from stabbing by fellow inmate, allegedly on guard's instructions, claimed more than negligence and thus should not have been summarily dismissed. U.S.C.A. Const.Amend. 14; 42 U.S.C.A. § 1983.

 Klingele v. Eikenberry, 849 F.2d 409.

D.Ariz. 1995. Inmates' concession that issues raised in their complaint concerning constitutionality of proposed prison policy on pornographic mail would have been more properly presented in separate class action addressing same prison policy supported grant of state's motion to dismiss.

 Wilson v. State of Ariz., 879 F.Supp. 1025.

D.Colo. 1991. It was improper to dismiss pro se prisoner's civil rights complaint based on prisoner's placement in segregation unit of medium security facility before correctional officials had answered where prisoner alleged that segregation served no valid administrative purpose and record failed to disclose whether prisoner was placed in segregation for administrative or supervisory reasons. 42 U.S.C.A. § 1983; U.S.C.A. Const.Amends. 5, 14.

 Klein v. Pyle, 767 F.Supp. 215.

D.D.C. 1993. Ongoing pattern of arbitrary exclusion from prison law library and pattern of harassment by chief librarian alleged by inmate was sufficient to state meaningful access to the courts claim for purposes of surviving Rule 12(b)(6) motion. Fed.Rules Civ.Proc.Rule 12(b)(6), 28 U.S.C.A.

 Martin v. Ezeagu, 816 F.Supp. 20.

Inmate's complaint which alleged ongoing pattern, and not isolated episode, of interference with his right to access to prison law library and which specifically stated how litigation he was pursuing was hampered and delayed by actions of chief librarian was sufficient to survive Rule 12(b)(6) motion; complaint stated that inmate was prevented from filing sentencing memorandum, motion for new trial and

motion to dismiss indictment before his sentencing hearing due to alleged actions by chief librarian. Fed.Rules Civ.Proc.Rule 12(b)(6), 28 U.S.C.A.

 Martin v. Ezeagu, 816 F.Supp. 20.

N.D.Ill. 1987. Prison officials' assertion that they were not involved in decision to approve whether individual would be allowed visitation privileges was insufficient basis to warrant dismissal of complaint, where inmate alleged that he wrote to prison officials requesting family visit, that prison official granted request, and that inmate was not permitted to visit with his family. Fed.Rules Civ.Proc. Rule 12(b)(6), 28 U.S.C.A.; Ill.S.H.A. ch. 38, ¶ 1003–7–2(f).

 U.S. ex rel. Adams v. O'Leary, 659 F.Supp. 736.

W.D.La. 1996. Pro se prisoner civil rights complaints must be read in liberal fashion and should not be dismissed unless it appears beyond all doubt that prisoner could prove no set of facts under which he would be entitled to relief.

 Hutchinson v. Belt, 957 F.Supp. 97.

D.Md. 1977. Cavey v. Levine, 435 F.Supp. 475, affirmed 580 F.2d 1047.

E.D.Mich. 1987. A prisoner's pro se complaint is held to less stringent standards than formal pleadings drafted by lawyers, and can only be dismissed for failure to state a claim if it appears beyond a doubt that prisoner can prove no set of facts in support of claim that would entitle him to relief.

 Pillette v. Detroit Police Dept., 661 F.Supp. 1145, affirmed 852 F.2d 1288.

S.D.N.Y. 1994. County jail inmate failed to state claim against county jail's medical director, arising from alleged inadequate or improper medical treatment, where inmate did not allege director's personal involvement in alleged wrongdoing. Fed.Rules Civ.Proc.Rule 12(b)(6), 28 U.S.C.A.

 Marsden v. Federal Bureau of Prisons, 856 F.Supp. 832.

S.D.N.Y. 1985. Where no damage is shown from interference with a prisoner's mailing privileges, dismissal or summary judgment of prisoner's suit challenging interference is properly granted.

 Gilliam v. Quinlan, 608 F.Supp. 823.

W.D.N.Y. 1996. In civil rights action by prisoner claiming that prison superintendent learned of allegedly unconstitutional conduct toward prisoner by means of inmate grievance program and yet failed to remedy conduct, superintendent did not submit any documented allegation of fact to indicate that he did not learn of prisoner's allegations through grievance appeals procedure or that he took action, and thus claim that superintendent was liable for damages under § 1983 was not subject to dismissal for failure to state claim. 42 U.S.C.A. § 1983; Fed.Rules Civ.Proc.Rule 12(b)(6), 28 U.S.C.A.

Amaker v. Hakes, 919 F.Supp. 127.

W.D.N.Y. 1987. Unsworn memorandum of attorney was insufficient, for purposes of prison officials' motion to dismiss, to establish that prison rule prohibiting inmates from talking while moving in line was necessary to maintain prison discipline despite claims of inmates that it violated their First Amendment Rights to speech and to practice their Islamic faith by giving salutations. U.S.C.A. Const.Amend. 1.

Montgomery v. Kelly, 661 F.Supp. 1051.

E.D.Pa. 1995. Prison employees' § 1983 claim against county would not be dismissed on ground that it sought to hold county liable for claims based entirely upon conduct of prison supervisor who had no policymaking authority; employees stated that they did not advance such theory of liability in their complaint. 42 U.S.C.A. § 1983.

Crighton v. Schuylkill County, 882 F.Supp. 411.

E.D.Pa. 1993. Civil rights claim by inmate in county prison that he should be transferred from administrative segregation to minimum security status would be dismissed as frivolous; inmate had no right under the United States Constitution to any specific custody status, and he did not identify any Pennsylvania regulation that could be said to create such an interest.

Williams v. Frame, 821 F.Supp. 1093.

Inmate's § 1983 claim that prison authorities delayed delivery of his legal mail would be dismissed as frivolous; although inmate alleged that one of his motions was dismissed by state court, dismissal was not apparently connected to any specific instance of mail delay; thus, to extent that inmate could be deemed to be alleging interference with his right to access to the courts, he failed to show that interference resulted in injury. 42 U.S.C.A. § 1983.

Williams v. Frame, 821 F.Supp. 1093.

Inmate's § 1983 claim based on assertion that counselors, guards, and another inmate read personal correspondence between himself and third inmate would be dismissed as frivolous, where inmate failed to allege he was even authorized to correspond with another inmate, as was required under applicable prison regulations; moreover, inmate's conclusion that his correspondence was actually opened and read by others appeared to be mere speculation inspired by conspiracy theory. 42 U.S.C.A. § 1983.

Williams v. Frame, 821 F.Supp. 1093.

Inmate's § 1983 claim based on allegation that some of his outgoing mail to news media and a religious group was lost would be dismissed as legally frivolous; inmate failed to even allege how his mail was lost, and claim appeared to be nothing more than a negligence claim, which is not actionable under § 1983. 42 U.S.C.A. § 1983.

Williams v. Frame, 821 F.Supp. 1093.

Inmate's allegation that cost of legal supplies and photocoying at prison was excessive, thereby violating his First Amendment rights as an indigent prisoner, would be dismissed as legally frivolous; inmate failed to show requisite actual injury, and volume of written material inmate had submitted in connection with actions filed in district court was proof positive that his right to free speech and access to the courts was not impeded by cost of legal supplies and photocopying. 42 U.S.C.A. § 1983; U.S.C.A. Const.Amend. 1.

Williams v. Frame, 821 F.Supp. 1093.

Inmate's § 1983 claim based on allegation that he was denied forms with which to file administrative grievances would be dismissed as frivolous; inmate referred to letters he had written to prison officials addressing his administrative complaints, and thus he did not demonstrate that alleged failure to provide him grievance forms denied him use of prison grievance process. 42 U.S.C.A. § 1983.

Williams v. Frame, 821 F.Supp. 1093.

N.D.Tex. 1992. Civil rights plaintiff, claiming deprivation of medical care by state official while detained in county jail, failed to state claim upon which relief could be granted where there was no evidence of prayer for monetary damages in complaint and granting injunctive relief would have served no purpose as plaintiff was no longer incarcerated in jail and no longer subject to repetition of alleged wrongs. Fed. Rules Civ.Proc.Rule 12(b)(6), 28 U.S.C.A.

Dupree v. Lubbock County Jail, 805 F.Supp. 20.

E.D.Va. 1990. A federal prisoner's *Bivens* action attacking his conviction and seeking damages and general remedies would be stayed, rather than dismissed, where dismissal of action would preclude prisoner from reasserting his claims following exhaustion of habeas corpus remedies.

Mosteller v. Smith, 751 F.Supp. 1200.

⬤═**1789. Conspiracy and fraud, actions involving.**

Library references

C.J.S. Federal Civil Procedure § 828.

C.A.2 (Conn.) 1993. General rule that district court should deny motion to dismiss unless it appears to certainty that plaintiff can prove no set of facts entitling him to relief applies even when fraud is pleaded. Fed.Rules Civ. Proc.Rule 9(b), 28 U.S.C.A.

> IUE AFL-CIO Pension Fund v. Herrmann, 9 F.3d 1049, certiorari denied 115 S.Ct. 86, 513 U.S. 822, 130 L.Ed.2d 38.

C.A.11 (Fla.) 1987. District court abused its discretion in dismissing Racketeer Influenced and Corrupt Organizations Act complaint with prejudice, even though plaintiff failed to distinguish between injuries sustained by him personally and those suffered derivatively as stockholder in corporation adversely affected by collapse of government securities corporation, where plaintiff appeared to allege some injuries that could not properly be characterized as deriving solely from his status as shareholder in customer of failed corporation. Fed.Rules Civ. Proc.Rule 15(a), 28 U.S.C.A.; 18 U.S.C.A. §§ 1961–1968.

> Warner v. Alexander Grant & Co., 828 F.2d 1528.

C.A.4 (Md.) 1988. Civil complaint filed under the Racketeer Influenced and Corrupt Organizations Act is vulnerable to motion to dismiss if it fails to allege either adequate injury to business or property or adequate causal nexus between injury and predicate acts of racketeering activity alleged. 18 U.S.C.A. §§ 1961–1968.

> Brandenburg v. Seidel, 859 F.2d 1179.

C.A.1 (Mass.) 1991. Racketeer Influenced and Corrupt Organizations Act (RICO) plaintiffs who initiated no discovery, did not request district court to stay ruling on motion to dismiss pending opportunity for discovery, and did not seek leave to amend complaint or suggest that by amending infirmities infecting RICO claim could be cured were not entitled to additional period of discovery or right to amend before dismissal. Fed.Rules Civ.Proc.Rule 9(b), 28 U.S.C.A.

> Feinstein v. Resolution Trust Corp., 942 F.2d 34.

In Racketeer Influenced and Corrupt Organizations Act (RICO) suit in which fraud has not been pleaded against given defendant with requisite specificity, dismissal should follow as to that defendant unless plaintiff at a bare minimum suggests to district court in timely manner that limited period of discovery will likely allow plaintiff to plug holes in complaint and requests leave to conduct discovery for that limited purpose and thereafter to amend complaint. 18 U.S.C.A. §§ 1961–1968; Fed.Rules Civ.Proc. Rule 9(b), 28 U.S.C.A.

> Feinstein v. Resolution Trust Corp., 942 F.2d 34.

C.A.1 (Mass.) 1985. Dismissal of fraud counts after plaintiffs had two opportunities to amend their complaint was well within discretion of district court, where plaintiffs were notified before amending second time that allegations of fraud in their complaint failed to meet particularity requirements of Fed.Rules Civ. Proc.Rule 9(b), 28 U.S.C.A. which governs pleading of fraud.

> Hayduk v. Lanna, 775 F.2d 441.

C.A.8 (Minn.) 1995. Failure to allege elements of mail and wire fraud with sufficient particularity required dismissal of Racketeer Influenced and Corrupt Organizations Act (RICO) claim. 18 U.S.C.A. §§ 1341, 1343, 1961–1968; Fed.Rules Civ.Proc.Rule 9(b), 28 U.S.C.A.

> Murr Plumbing, Inc. v. Scherer Bros. Financial Services Co., 48 F.3d 1066, rehearing denied.

C.A.2 (N.Y.) 1995. Former CEO and Chairman of the Board of corporation, who alleged that acquiring corporation violated Racketeer Influenced and Corrupt Organizations Act (RICO) in gaining control of corporation, contained sufficient allegations of "conscious behavior" beyond mere non-performance of contract, to raise an inference of intent to defraud, and survive motion to dismiss for failure to state claim upon which relief could be granted, even though complaint did not allege that acquiring corporation either achieved alleged goal of obtaining control of target corporation or broke its promises, and acquiring corporation's holdings after alleged scheme did not exceed share anticipated in original agreements, where former CEO of target corporation alleged that fraudulent conduct substantially diluted CEO's and other minority shareholders' share of target company, acquiring corporation joined forces with other major shareholder to command six of eight votes of board of directors, acquiring corporation took measures to effectuate CEO's removal and gain control of target company soon after entering agreements manifesting acquiring corporation's benign intentions and lack of design to take over control of CEO's corporation. 18 U.S.C.A. §§ 1341, 1343, 1961 et seq.; Fed.Rules Civ.Proc.Rule 12(b)(6), 28 U.S.C.A.

> Powers v. British Vita, P.L.C., 57 F.3d 176.

C.A.1 (R.I.) 1987. Dismissal should not be automatic once lower court determines that rule requiring party to plead fraud with particularity was not satisfied in connection with Racketeer Influenced and Corrupt Organizations Act predicate acts of mail and wire fraud; if, for example, specific allegations make it likely that defendant used interstate mail or telecommunications facilities and specific information as to use is likely in exclusive control of defendant, court should make second determination as to whether claim as presented warrants allowance of discovery and, if so, thereafter provide opportunity to amend defective complaint. 18 U.S.C.A. §§ 1341, 1343, 1961(1)(B), 1962(b-d), 1964(c); Fed.Rules Civ.Proc.Rule 9(b), 28 U.S.C.A.

> New England Data Services, Inc. v. Becher, 829 F.2d 286.

District court should not have dismissed, without further discovery, civil action under Racketeer Influenced and Corrupt Organizations Act alleging mail fraud and wire fraud where plaintiff provided outline of general scheme to defraud and established inference that mail or wire was used to transact scheme; requiring plaintiff to plead time, place and contents of communication between defendants, without allowing some discovery in addition to interrogatories, was unreasonable. 18 U.S.C.A. §§ 1341, 1343, 1961(1)(B), 1962(b-d), 1964(c); Fed.Rules Civ.Proc.Rule 9(b), 28 U.S.C.A.

> New England Data Services, Inc. v. Becher, 829 F.2d 286.

District court should have permitted further discovery before dismissal of civil Racketeer Influenced and Corrupt Organizations Act action alleging mail and wire fraud, even though plaintiff's original complaint did not plead fraud with particularity and even though plaintiff was given opportunity to serve interrogatories on defendants on issue of use of wires and mail, where defendants' response to interrogatories was that "to the best of [their] recollection," they had not used wires and mails and where plaintiff submitted affidavit contending that interrogatory answers were evasive and untruthful. 18 U.S.C.A. §§ 1341, 1343, 1961(1)(B), 1962(b-d), 1964(c); Fed.Rules Civ.Proc.Rule 9(b), 28 U.S.C.A.

> New England Data Services, Inc. v. Becher, 829 F.2d 286.

"Token" interrogatory on whether defendants had used wires and mails was not meaningful opportunity for plaintiff to discover if defendants had used mails or wires, which was information peculiarly within defendants' control in civil Racketeer Influenced and Corrupt Organizations Act action alleging mail and wire fraud; further discovery should have been permitted before complaint was dismissed for failure to plead fraud with particularity. 18 U.S.C.A. §§ 1341, 1343, 1961(1)(B), 1962(b-d), 1964(c); Fed.Rules Civ.Proc.Rule 9(b), 28 U.S.C.A.

> New England Data Services, Inc. v. Becher, 829 F.2d 286.

C.A.5 (Tex.) 1997. Dismissal for failure to plead fraud with particularity is treated as dismissal for failure to state claim. Fed.Rules Civ.Proc.Rules 9(b), 12(b)(6), 28 U.S.C.A.

> U.S. ex rel. Thompson v. Columbia/HCA Healthcare Corp., 125 F.3d 899, rehearing denied.

N.D.Cal. 1987. For purposes of motions to dismiss for failure to state claim, allegations that individual defendants were "persons" under Racketeer Influenced and Corrupt Organizations Act, and that certain combinations of such defendants were "associations in fact" that constituted RICO "enterprises" sufficiently distinguished between liable "persons" and "enterprises"; single defendant could be part of individuals that made up RICO enterprise. 18 U.S.C.A. §§ 1961 et seq., 1962(c); Fed.Rules Civ.Proc.Rule 12(b)(6), 28 U.S.C.A.

> Washington v. Baenziger, 673 F.Supp. 1478.

D.Colo. 1996. Dismissal of claim for failure to plead fraud with requisite particularity is treated as dismissal for failure to state claim upon which relief may be granted. Fed.Rules Civ.Proc.Rules 9(b), 12(b)(6), 28 U.S.C.A.

> Brooks v. Bank of Boulder, 911 F.Supp. 470.

D.Colo. 1995. Dismissal of fraud claim for failing to plead with sufficient particularity is treated as dismissal for failure to state claim upon which relief may be granted. Fed.Rules Civ.Proc.Rules 9(b), 12(b)(6), 28 U.S.C.A.

> Brooks v. Bank of Boulder, 891 F.Supp. 1469.

D.Conn. 1988. Complaint of plaintiff alleging RICO violation predicated on mail and wire fraud would not be dismissed for failure to comply with rule concerning pleading of fraud with particularity, and plaintiff would be granted 20 days in which to amend to add allegations of specificity, where arrangements described in complaint supported inference of facts that would satisfy elements of fraud. 18 U.S.C.A. §§ 1341, 1343, 1961 et seq.; Fed.Rules Civ. Proc.Rule 9(b), 28 U.S.C.A.

> Federal Paper Bd. Co., Inc. v. Amata, 693 F.Supp. 1376.

D.D.C. 1996. Dismissal of plaintiff's fraud, misrepresentation, and conspiracy complaint for failure to state claim was warranted, where claim rested on contention that prior landlord-tenant proceedings in District of Columbia Superior Court were illegal because defendant appeared before superior court without approval of bankruptcy court, which was in charge of owner's Chapter 11 case; automatic stay did not prevent Chapter 11 debtor-owner from bringing actions that would inure to benefit of bankruptcy estate. Bankr.Code, 11 U.S.C.A. § 362(a)(1); Fed.Rules Civ.Proc.Rule 12(b)(6), 28 U.S.C.A.

> El Bey v. Quantum Property Management Corp., 201 B.R. 324.

D.D.C. 1996. Failure to plead fraud with particularity is to be treated as a ground for dismissal for failure to state a claim upon which relief can be granted. Fed.Rules Civ.Proc.Rules 9(b), 12(b)(6), 28 U.S.C.A.

> U.S. ex rel. Alexander v. Dyncorp, Inc., 924 F.Supp. 292.

D.D.C. 1987. In view of fact that plaintiff set forth necessary elements of fraud claim pertaining to a series of note transactions and a personal loan guarantee for $150,000 line of credit, dismissal of claim due to insufficient specificity as to time, place, and contents of alleged misrepresentations was not warranted, and plaintiff would be allowed to amend his complaint to supply necessary detail. Fed. Rules Civ.Proc.Rules 8, 9(b), 12(b)(6), 28 U.S.C.A.

> Johnson v. Computer Technology Services, Inc., 670 F.Supp. 1036.

D.Idaho 1987. Review of pleadings filed by contractor, which pleadings were based on alleged negligence of United States in administering construction contracts between contractor and tribal housing authority, indicated that contractors could not cure failure to state claim under RICO, and thus, dismissal of complaint would be with prejudice. 18 U.S.C.A. §§ 1341, 1343, 1962; Fed.Rules Civ.Proc.Rule 9(b), 28 U.S.C.A.

> Snowbird Const. Co., Inc. v. U.S., 666 F.Supp. 1437.

N.D.Ill. 1997. Even if agreement between commercial rate natural gas customers and independent third-party supplier, under which supplier was to receive and review customers' monthly invoices from local distribution companies for accuracy and to inform customers of any discrepancies while attempting to resolve them, did not give rise as matter of law to fiduciary relationship under Illinois and Texas law, dismissal of customers' breach of fiduciary duty claims was not warranted for failure to plead breach with sufficient particularity, and customers were entitled to an opportunity to present proof to support informal fiduciary relationship theory. Fed.Rules Civ.Proc.Rule 9(b), 28 U.S.C.A.

> Petri v. Gatlin, 997 F.Supp. 956.

Court would not assume, for purposes of motion to dismiss natural gas customers' Racketeer Influenced and Corrupt Organizations Act (RICO) claims based on supplier's alleged scheme to defraud consumers, that supplier used mails to distribute allegedly fraudulent promotional brochures to prospective customers, even though assumption was consistent with customers' existing allegations; obvious relevance of assumed mailing made it almost unfathomable that customers would have accidentally omitted it and court was not empowered to hypothesize consistent facts for claims subject to rule requiring that fraud be averred with particularity. Fed.Rules Civ.Proc.Rules 9(b), 12(b)(6), 28 U.S.C.A.; 18 U.S.C.A. §§ 1341, 1962(c).

> Petri v. Gatlin, 997 F.Supp. 956.

N.D.Ill. 1993. Whether state employee's retirement amounted to withdrawal from conspiracy, for purpose of two-year limitation period for civil rights conspiracy claim under Illinois statute of limitations, was question of fact that had no bearing on motion to dismiss for failure to state claim. S.H.A. 735 ILCS 5/13–202; 42 U.S.C.A. § 1985.

> Wolf v. City of Chicago Heights, 828 F.Supp. 520.

N.D.Ill. 1989. Complaint count alleging conspiracy to violate female former employee's right to equal protection would not be dismissed, although the employee conceded the count failed to state claim, where the concession appeared to be predicated on failure to discover limited reading that had been given to judicial decision, employee had indicated she planned to amend her claim to plead around that decision, and court found complaint sufficient to state claim. U.S.C.A. Const.Amend. 14.

> Bertoncini v. Schrimpf, 712 F.Supp. 1336.

N.D.Ill. 1987. Investor's complaint under Illinois Consumer Fraud and Deceptive Practices Act against actor and advertising agency involved in promotion of first mortgage notes was deficient in that it failed to state circumstances constituting fraud with particularity, but would not be dismissed before discovery production by defendants; though investor would have to provide information regarding medium in which each advertisement appeared as well as approximate time and place and substance thereof, her ability to do so depended on that production. Ill.S.H.A. ch. 121½, ¶¶ 261–313; Fed.Rules Civ.Proc.Rule 9(b), 28 U.S.C.A.

> Ramson v. Layne, 668 F.Supp. 1162.

N.D.Ill. 1987. While it is preferable for Racketeer Influenced and Corrupt Organizations Act plaintiff to specify which subsection of Act was allegedly violated, failure to do so does not automatically constitute grounds for dismissal. 18 U.S.C.A. § 1962; Fed.Rules Civ. Proc.Rule 12(b)(6), 28 U.S.C.A.

> H.G. Gallimore, Inc. v. Abdula, 652 F.Supp. 437.

D.Kan. 1995. Claim asserted against cigarette manufacturer under Kansas Consumer Protection Act (KCPA) based on fraudulent concealment was dismissed for failure to comply with particularity requirements for pleadings in actions based on fraud; however, smoker was granted leave to amend complaint to allege violations of KCPA with particularity. K.S.A.

50–623 et seq.; Fed.Rules Civ.Proc.Rule 9(b), 28 U.S.C.A.

> Burton v. R.J. Reynolds Tobacco Co., 884 F.Supp. 1515.

D.Md. 1994. Allegations that each defendant committed predicate act within four years prior to filing of complaint under Racketeer Influenced and Corrupt Organizations Act (RICO), and that defendant's fraudulent concealment tolled applicable statute of limitations, was sufficient, at early stages of litigation, to withstand motion to dismiss on limitations grounds, but defendant could again address issue at later date by way of motion for partial summary judgment, if discovery indicated that any particular claim was barred by limitations. 18 U.S.C.A. § 1962 et seq.; Fed.Rules Civ.Proc. Rule 12(b)(6), 28 U.S.C.A.

> Lust v. Burke, 876 F.Supp. 1474.

D.Md. 1982. Adler v. American Standard Corp., 538 F.Supp. 572, on subsequent appeal 830 F.2d 1303.

D.Mass. 1995. Dismissal with prejudice was appropriate for failure to plead fraudulent misrepresentation claim with particularity; plaintiff made no request for leave to amend, and there was no indication by plaintiff that he could cure particularity deficiency. Fed.Rules Civ.Proc.Rule 9(b), 28 U.S.C.A.

> Whelan v. Intergraph Corp., 889 F.Supp. 15.

E.D.Mich. 1994. Failure to state fraud claim with particularity constitutes failure to state a claim; thus, complaint or any relevant part thereof, may be dismissed for failure to state a claim if particularity requirement is not met in pleading fraud. Fed.Rules Civ.Proc.Rule 9(b), 28 U.S.C.A.

> FFOC Co. v. Invent A.G., 882 F.Supp. 642.

W.D.Mich. 1995. For purposes of motion to dismiss for failure to state claim on which relief can be granted, where motion is filed before discovery, courts must be sensitive to fact that application of rule prior to discovery may permit sophisticated defrauders to conceal details of fraud successfully. Fed.Rules Civ.Proc. Rules 9(b), 12(b)(6), 28 U.S.C.A.

> State of Mich. ex rel. Kelley v. McDonald Dairy Co., 905 F.Supp. 447.

W.D.Mich. 1993. Although third-party plaintiff's fraudulent misrepresentation claim was vague, it was not appropriate to dismiss it for this shortcoming, and federal district court would treat third-party defendant's motion to dismiss for failure to allege misrepresentation with sufficient particularity as motion for more definite statement.

> Allendale Mut. Ins. Co. v. Triple-S Technologies, Inc., 851 F.Supp. 277.

D.N.J. 1987. Determinations that pleadings failed to allege facts to establish pattern of racketeering activity, for purposes of federal and state racketeering laws, and that claims were barred by act of state doctrine applied even to those defendants who had not moved to dismiss or had not yet been served or answered complaint. Fed.Rules Civ.Proc.Rule 12(b)(6), 28 U.S.C.A.; N.J.S.A. 2C:41–2 et seq.; 18 U.S.C.A. § 1962 et seq.

> Environmental Tectonics Corp., Intern. v. W.S. Kirkpatrick & Co., Inc., 659 F.Supp. 1381, affirmed in part, reversed in part 847 F.2d 1052, certiorari granted in part 109 S.Ct. 3213, 492 U.S. 905, 106 L.Ed.2d 563, affirmed 110 S.Ct. 701, 493 U.S. 400, 107 L.Ed.2d 816.

E.D.N.Y. 1995. Failure to state correct measure of damages in fraud action under New York law does not entitle defendant to dismissal for insufficiency. Fed.Rules Civ.Proc.Rule 9(b, g), 28 U.S.C.A.

> PdP Parfums de Paris, S.A. v. International Designer Fragrances, Inc., 901 F.Supp. 581.

E.D.N.Y. 1987. In light of pending criminal indictments and general allegations of civil securities fraud, Racketeer Influenced and Corrupt Organizations Act violation and state law fraud suit, district court was unprepared to rule on motion to dismiss that, as matter of law, officers' alleged conduct failed to satisfy state law standards for imposing exemplary damages. 18 U.S.C.A. § 1961 et seq.

> Greenfield v. Professional Care, Inc., 677 F.Supp. 110.

E.D.N.Y. 1987. Allegations that attorney knew, or in the alternative, was reckless if he did not know, of material omissions and affirmative misrepresentations contained in offering materials and that attorney participated and assisted in formation of partnership, sale of partnership interest to plaintiff and partnership's purchase of land and restaurant from one of attorney's clients were sufficient, for purposes of motion to dismiss for failure to plead with particularity, to state claim against attorney for aiding and abetting other partners and accountants in securities fraud in connection with offer and sale of partnership interest. Fed. Rules Civ.Proc.Rule 9(b), 28 U.S.C.A.

> Cohen v. Goodfriend, 665 F.Supp. 152.

S.D.N.Y. 1997. Dismissal of breach of fiduciary duty claim brought by purchaser of corporation against accounting firm that determined book value and purchase price of corporation was warranted, though complaint sufficiently alleged that purchaser was client of firm, where all fraud claims alleged against firm were dismissed.

ICD Holdings S.A. v. Frankel, 976 F.Supp. 234.

S.D.N.Y. 1996. Dismissal of complaint for failure to plead fraud with particularity was not warranted, even though complaint failed to state precisely all misstatements to which plaintiff referred and identity of speaker of any of misstatements, where plaintiff filed responsive pleading, and document discovery and testimony in affidavit fleshed out plaintiff's allegations. Fed.Rules Civ.Proc.Rule 9(b), 28 U.S.C.A.

Joseph Victori Wines, Inc. v. Vina Santa Carolina S.A., 933 F.Supp. 347.

S.D.N.Y. 1995. In ruling on motion to dismiss complaint for failure to plead fraud with particularity, court must read the complaint generously and draw all inferences in favor of the pleader and court must deny motion to dismiss as long as some of the allegations of fraud are adequate. Fed.Rules Civ.Proc.Rule 9(b), 28 U.S.C.A.

Trustees of Plumbers and Pipefitters Nat. Pension Fund v. De-Con Mechanical Contractors, Inc., 896 F.Supp. 342.

Claim for common-law fraud would be dismissed for failure to satisfy federal rule requiring that fraud be pled with particularity; complaint lacked any particulars as to specific instances of fraud, plaintiffs made only conclusory allegations that codefendant was alter ego of corporate defendant, and even if codefendant were the alter ego of defendant, this was not sufficient standing alone to support allegation of fraud. Fed.Rules Civ.Proc.Rule 9(b), 28 U.S.C.A.

Trustees of Plumbers and Pipefitters Nat. Pension Fund v. De-Con Mechanical Contractors, Inc., 896 F.Supp. 342.

S.D.N.Y. 1995. Investor's claims that general partner abused position and diverted money from various limited partnerships and corporations for his personal use were deficient and would be dismissed where all fraud allegations were made on information and belief. Fed.Rules Civ.Proc.Rule 9(b), 28 U.S.C.A.

Spira v. Nick, 876 F.Supp. 553.

While partnership, corporations, and groups involved in alleged mail and wire fraud could have been Racketeer Influenced and Corrupt Organizations Act (RICO) enterprises, failure to specify which entity was RICO "enterprise" would not automatically require dismissal where allegations would permit proof that defendants acted or conspired to act in prohibited manner with respect to entities capable of being RICO enterprises. 18 U.S.C.A. § 1961(1).

Spira v. Nick, 876 F.Supp. 553.

S.D.N.Y. 1992. To survive motion to dismiss for failure to state fraud claim with particularity, plaintiff claiming fraud must apprise each defendant of the scope of his or her participation in the alleged fraud. Fed.Rules Civ.Proc.Rule 9(b), 28 U.S.C.A.

Ackerman v. National Property Analysts, Inc., 887 F.Supp. 494.

For fraud complaint which alleges particular facts demonstrating knowledge of the defendants at the time that statements were false, plaintiffs' complaint may withstand motion to dismiss for failure to state fraud with particularity, where plaintiff alleges that offering memorandum was fraudulent and that defendants conspired together to mislead the plaintiff; but exception to requirement that plaintiff claiming fraud must apprise each defendant of scope of his or her participation in alleged fraud does not relieve plaintiff from properly pleading allegations which demonstrate that each defendant knew or had reason to know of the false statements and material omissions in offering material. Fed.Rules Civ.Proc.Rule 9(b), 28 U.S.C.A.

Ackerman v. National Property Analysts, Inc., 887 F.Supp. 494.

Plaintiffs' allegations of fraud were sufficient to withstand motion to dismiss for failure to state alleged fraud with particularity, as plaintiffs' allegations indicated sufficiently strong inference of scienter and causation, where plaintiffs charged that representations in private placement memoranda regarding management system for shopping centers to be operated by limited partnerships were intended to mislead plaintiffs into believing there would be a centralized management system to reduce costs, but system was merely scheme devised to obtain additional revenue for real estate management corporation, with no benefit to partnerships, and alleged that employee of real estate management corporation calculated amount of cash which was needed on monthly basis to meet each partnership's debt obligations and then projected rentals to these amounts, rental projections were off by at least 35%, and thus majority owners of real estate management corporation knew or should have known that projected rental income for shopping centers did not portray honest projection, and surety for investor plaintiffs entered into undisclosed indemnity agreement with real estate management corporation.

Ackerman v. National Property Analysts, Inc., 887 F.Supp. 494.

S.D.N.Y. 1990. Although stock purchaser's securities fraud complaint was technically defective in that purchaser did not state that certain information was so peculiarly within defendants' knowledge that purchaser could not be expected to plead other than upon information and belief, defect did not warrant dismissal;

defendants could move for Rule 11 sanctions if purchaser's allegations proved to have no reasonable basis. Fed.Rules Civ.Proc.Rule 9(b), 28 U.S.C.A.; Securities Exchange Act of 1934, § 10(b), 15 U.S.C.A. § 78j(b).

> Farley v. Baird, Patrick & Co., Inc., 750 F.Supp. 1209.

S.D.N.Y. 1990. Although investor's allegations satisfied pleading requirements as to identification of time, place and content of alleged misrepresentations, securities fraud claims would be dismissed where investor had not pleaded a single fact through which an inference of scienter could be made. Securities Exchange Act of 1934, § 10(b), 15 U.S.C.A. § 78j(b); Fed.Rules Civ.Proc.Rule 9(b), 28 U.S.C.A.; Securities Act of 1933, § 17(a), 15 U.S.C.A. § 77q(a); N.Y.McKinney's General Business Law § 352–e.

> Ruff v. Genesis Holding Corp., 728 F.Supp. 225.

S.D.N.Y. 1987. Allegations of conspiracy by film trust agreement against holder of film library and transferee of films were sufficiently detailed to put holder of film library and transferee on notice of specific nature of charges against them and withstand motion to dismiss for failure to state claim; allegations that holder of film library and transferee shared office space and personnel and that transferee paid well below fair market value for film library and obtained it free of royalty obligations were sufficient to establish claim of agreement to defraud trust agreement, and allegedly fraudulent stipulation promising advance notice of any film transfer and transfer of film library furnished necessary overt acts. Rules Bankr.Proc.Rules 7009, 7012, 11 U.S.C.A.; Fed.Rules Civ.Proc. Rules 9(b), 12, 28 U.S.C.A.

> Raine v. Lorimar Productions, Inc., 71 B.R. 450.

S.D.N.Y. 1987. Purchasers of limited partnership interests in corporation which was converted to limited partnership stated claims adequate to overcome motion to dismiss, under federal securities law and common law, which arose out of purchases, against various defendants who were alleged to have played role in offering and sale of assets; purchasers alleged they were misled into purchasing or investing by defendants' conduct in and failure to disclose unlawful insider trading. Fed.Rules Civ.Proc. Rules 8(a, e), 9(b), 12(b)(6), 28 U.S.C.A.; Securities Exchange Act of 1934, § 10(b), 15 U.S.C.A. § 78j(b); Securities Act of 1933, §§ 5, 12, 15 U.S.C.A. §§ 77e, 77*l*.

> Arden Way Associates v. Boesky, 664 F.Supp. 855.

S.D.N.Y. 1987. RICO claims against representatives and officer of brokerage firm were dismissed because trustees of retirement and pension plans failed to allege predicate acts of fraud with sufficient particularity. Fed.Rules Civ.Proc.Rule 9(b), 28 U.S.C.A.; 18 U.S.C.A. § 1962(c).

> Metzner v. D.H. Blair & Co., Inc., 663 F.Supp. 716.

D.S.C. 1996. Purported novelty of issues raised in farmers' state law fraud claims against seed company could not prevent dismissal under federal rules for failure to state a claim, since discovery would not change clear fatal defect in their fraud claims. Fed.Rules Civ. Proc.Rule 12(b)(6), 28 U.S.C.A.

> Gray v. Petoseed Co., Inc., 985 F.Supp. 625, affirmed 129 F.3d 1259.

N.D.Tex. 1993. Allegation in conspiracy complaint that one defendant was attorney representing the defendants in another action was sufficient to assert claim against that defendant for purposes of motion to dismiss for failure to state a claim. Fed.Rules Civ.Proc.Rule 12(b)(6), 28 U.S.C.A.

> Chevalier v. Animal Rehabilitation Center, Inc., 839 F.Supp. 1224.

S.D.Tex. 1996. Dismissal for failure to plead fraud with particularity is considered dismissal for failure to state claim upon which relief can be granted. Fed.Rules Civ.Proc.Rules 9(b), 12(b)(6), 28 U.S.C.A.

> U.S. ex rel. James M. Thompson v. Columbia/HCA Healthcare Corp., 938 F.Supp. 399, affirmed in part, vacated in part 125 F.3d 899, rehearing denied.

E.D.Va. 1987. Allegations of pattern of racketeering activity were sufficient to raise fact question as to claimed violation of Racketeer Influenced and Corrupt Organizations Act and thus to avoid motion to dismiss. 18 U.S.C.A. § 1962(c, d); Fed.Rules Civ.Proc.Rule 12(b)(6), 28 U.S.C.A.

> John C. Holland Enterprises, Inc. v. J.P. Mascaro & Sons, Inc., 653 F.Supp. 1242, affirmed 829 F.2d 1120.

Bkrtcy.E.D.N.Y. 1993. Plaintiff should be allowed to resort to discovery process and not easily be subject to dismissal of his complaint alleging conspiracy given fact that nature of conspiracies often make it impossible to provide details at pleading stage. Fed.Rules Civ.Proc. Rule 8, 28 U.S.C.A.

> In re Harvard Knitwear, Inc., 153 B.R. 617.

Even under liberal pleading requirements of federal rules, some minimum allegations must be made to sustain conspiracy charge. Fed.Rules Civ.Proc.Rule 8, 28 U.S.C.A.

> In re Harvard Knitwear, Inc., 153 B.R. 617.

⊙═1790. Contracts, actions involving in general.

Library references

C.J.S. Federal Civil Procedure § 829.

C.A.7 (Ill.) 1997. If contract is unambiguous, breach of contract claim is susceptible to dismissal for failure to state claim under Illinois law.

Echo, Inc. v. Whitson Co., Inc., 121 F.3d 1099.

C.A.7 (Ill.) 1995. Where plaintiff's cause of action arises out of contract which is attached to complaint as exhibit, and such attachment shows unambiguously on its face that relief prayed for is not merited, dismissal is both justified and appropriate.

Palda v. General Dynamics Corp., 47 F.3d 872, rehearing and suggestion for rehearing denied.

C.A.7 (Ill.) 1992. In context of parties' prior dealings and discussions, language of letter from automobile franchiser to dealer, stating that franchiser's plan was to exercise remaining lease options on building leased by dealer, and to increase rent maximum of three percent for each option, was sufficiently ambiguous as to franchiser's intent to make binding offer, so as to preclude dismissal of breach of contract action for failure to state a claim. Fed.Rules Civ.Proc.Rule 12(b)(6), 28 U.S.C.A.

Dawson v. General Motors Corp., 977 F.2d 369.

Language of letter purporting to accept alleged offer from automobile franchiser to dealer concerning building lease terms was sufficiently ambiguous to raise fact issue as to validity of acceptance, precluding dismissal of breach of contract action for failure to state a claim. Fed.Rules Civ.Proc.Rule 12(b)(6), 28 U.S.C.A.

Dawson v. General Motors Corp., 977 F.2d 369.

C.A.4 (Md.) 1992. Construction of ambiguous contract provisions is factual determination that precludes dismissal on motion for failure to state a claim. Fed.Rules Civ.Proc. Rule 12(b)(6), 28 U.S.C.A.

Martin Marietta Corp. v. International Telecommunications Satellite Organization, 991 F.2d 94.

Contract for provision of satellite launch services was ambiguous, precluding dismissal of satellite owner's breach of contract action against provider for failure to state a claim; contract was unclear as to whether failure of satellite to reach proper orbit was a "mission failure" that limited owner's remedy to another launch and whether "limitation of liability" provision barred any contract claim other than

replacement launch remedy. Fed.Rules Civ. Proc.Rule 12(b)(6), 28 U.S.C.A.

Martin Marietta Corp. v. International Telecommunications Satellite Organization, 991 F.2d 94.

C.A.1 (Mass.) 1988. Dismissal of gasoline service station franchisee's action against franchisor alleging breach of contract, violation of Petroleum Marketing Practices Act, and violation of Massachusetts Consumer Protection Act was proper; franchisee pleaded no facts adequate to entitle him to offer evidence in support of his entirely conclusory assertions, and papers in case made it clear there was no breach of contract. Fed.Rules Civ.Proc.Rule 12(b)(6), 28 U.S.C.A.

Gooley v. Mobil Oil Corp., 851 F.2d 513.

C.A.2 (N.Y.) 1990. Student's claims against university and board of trustees for breach of promise, abuse of power, malfeasance, breach of trust and fiduciary duty and breach of quasi contract, raised issues that were most properly and fully addressed in breach of contract claim and were appropriately dismissed.

Bobal v. Rensselaer Polytechnic Institute, 916 F.2d 759, certiorari denied 111 S.Ct. 1404, 499 U.S. 943, 113 L.Ed.2d 459.

D.Conn. 1990. Computer buyer's motion to dismiss seller's breach of contract complaint could not be denied on grounds that buyer waived contractual delivery requirement or that installment contract existed where seller failed to allege in the complaint waiver or that contract was installment contract.

D.P. Technology Corp. v. Sherwood Tool, Inc., 751 F.Supp. 1038.

S.D.Fla. 1992. While it did not appear that franchisees' claim against franchisor for negligent misrepresentation of certain material facts would support punitive damages claim under Florida law, court could not conclusively state that claim did not involve type of "gross negligence" required for punitive damages claim and, thus, claim would not be dismissed.

Burger King Corp. v. Austin, 805 F.Supp. 1007.

N.D.Ga. 1993. Under Georgia law, if contract is attached to complaint as exhibit, dismissal is appropriate if court finds that no possible relief can be granted under any construction of contract sued upon.

Breckenridge Creste Apartments, Ltd. v. Citicorp Mortg., Inc., 826 F.Supp. 460, affirmed 21 F.3d 1126.

N.D.Ill. 1995. Dismissal of debtors' breach of contract claim against creditor-bank for purchasing insurance in addition to that authorized under contract and charging it to debtors was not warranted under theory that debtors failed to perform under contract; debtors' claim was not based on failure by creditor to perform its duties under contract, but rather, debtors claimed that creditor violated contractual specification of remedies.

> Travis v. Boulevard Bank N.A., 880 F.Supp. 1226.

N.D.Ill. 1994. Legal point that choice of law principles applicable to Illinois breach of marriage promise action required application of Florida law, under which breach of such promises is not actionable, since parties became engaged in Florida, should have been raised via motion to dismiss or for summary judgment, and motion to set aside jury verdict on choice of law grounds amounted to untimely motion to dismiss and could not be granted as motion for judgment as a matter of law or as motion for new trial. West's F.S.A. § 771.01; Fed.Rules Civ.Proc.Rules 50, 59, 28 U.S.C.A.

> Wildey v. Springs, 840 F.Supp. 1259, affirmed in part, reversed in part 47 F.3d 1475, rehearing and suggestion for rehearing denied.

N.D.Ill. 1992. Determination of whether oral assurance is clear or specific enough to give rise to contract may be made on motion to dismiss. Fed.Rules Civ.Proc.Rule 12(b)(6), 28 U.S.C.A.

> Rand v. CF Industries, Inc., 797 F.Supp. 643.

N.D.Ill. 1987. Case should not be dismissed on mere ground that plaintiff has sought equitable relief when action is legal in nature; as long as plaintiff sets forth sufficient allegations to support contract action for damages, appropriateness of accounting or mandatory injunction request cannot justify dismissal, even if plaintiff does not specifically request damages.

> Cleland v. Stadt, 670 F.Supp. 814.

S.D.Ind. 1995. Defendant in breach of contract action was not entitled to dismissal of plaintiff's complaint, as dispute necessitated too great a factual inquiry to be determinable as matter of law, where defendant alleged that it did not owe plaintiff any payment under the terms of the contract because the invoices pursuant to which plaintiff sought to collect were not approved for payment as required under the contract; plaintiff alleged that emissions control and monitoring equipment called for in contract was properly installed at defendant's plant and certified in accordance with EPA standards, and that defendant inspected, accepted, and began using the equipment provided under the contract. Fed.Rules Civ.Proc.Rule 12(b)(6), 28 U.S.C.A.

> Enviroplan, Inc. v. Western Farmers Elec. Co-op., 900 F.Supp. 1055.

E.D.Mich. 1994. Complaint of subcontractor, seeking indemnity and contribution from general contractor under Michigan law for any liability found in underlying action against subcontractor, would not be dismissed for failure to state a claim upon which relief may be granted on ground that underlying claim was settled with no admission of liability by subcontractor; subcontractor would be ordered to amend complaint to reflect new factual circumstances. Fed.Rules Civ.Proc.Rule 12(b)(6), 28 U.S.C.A.

> Fishbach-Natkin, Inc. v. Shimizu America Corp., 854 F.Supp. 1294.

E.D.Mo. 1986. Contractor's claimed loss of profits was not so speculative as to require dismissal; contractor was entitled to recover consequential damages for breach of implied warranty. V.A.M.S. §§ 400.2–714, 400.2–715.

> Collegiate Enterprises, Inc. v. Otis Elevator Co., 650 F.Supp. 116.

E.D.N.Y. 1990. Motion to dismiss was inappropriate where plaintiff had stated claim for breach of contract, defendants asserted statute of frauds as affirmative defense, and both parties had submitted evidence in support of claim or defense; rather, appropriate motion was one for summary judgment. Fed.Rules Civ.Proc. Rules 12(b), 56, 28 U.S.C.A.; N.Y.McKinney's General Obligations Law § 5–701, subd. a, par. 1.

> Dickerson v. Kaplan, 763 F.Supp. 694, affirmed 963 F.2d 1522.

S.D.N.Y. 1990. To extent that complaint attempted to allege breach of contract claim, it was required to be dismissed; it could not be discerned from complaint the parties to alleged contract, where contract was made, substance of contract, or how contract was breached.

> Hardin v. DuPont Scandinavia (ARA-JET), 731 F.Supp. 1202.

S.D.N.Y. 1987. Whether shipper and shipping line had agreement regarding avoidance of equipment charges presented factual question precluding dismissal of shipper's counterclaim seeking indemnification from shipping line in event that it was deemed liable for freight forwarder for equipment charges in dispute.

> C.A. Venezolana de Navegacion v. Joseph Vinal Container Corp., 668 F.Supp. 335.

E.D.Pa. 1995. Subcontractor's allegations that it performed work for prime contractor in excess of the express contract and subcontractor's pleading that the express contract was breached by contractor were sufficient to show claims upon which relief could be granted and therefore, subcontractor's quasi contract claim would not be dismissed.

> Allied Fire & Safety Equipment Co. v. Dick Enterprises, Inc., 886 F.Supp. 491.

Under Pennsylvania law, subcontractor stated claims for negligent breach of contract and loss of bonding capacity against prime contractor and its sureties so as to preclude dismissal, given the substantial Pennsylvania case law subjecting party to tort liability for improperly performing its contractual duties.

Allied Fire & Safety Equipment Co. v. Dick Enterprises, Inc., 886 F.Supp. 491.

Subcontractor's claims that it was entitled to final payment under terms of the subcontract because it had completed its work and that it was entitled to payment for extra work it performed would be dismissed because these claims asserted rights to relief and were not independent causes of action.

Allied Fire & Safety Equipment Co. v. Dick Enterprises, Inc., 886 F.Supp. 491.

E.D.Pa. 1992. Seller's motion to dismiss buyer's breach of contract action would be denied, though seller was authorized by contract to terminate agreement by giving at least 90-day notice, where termination would become effective only at end of year in which notice was given.

Tersco, Inc. v. E.I. DuPont de Nemours and Co., 879 F.Supp. 445.

Buyer's claims against seller for breach of express warranty would be dismissed without prejudice, though seller agreed to express warranty that its products would meet its own standard specifications, where buyer did not allege in its complaint that products supplied by seller failed to satisfy its own specifications or any other specifications expressly agreed upon.

Tersco, Inc. v. E.I. DuPont de Nemours and Co., 879 F.Supp. 445.

E.D.Va. 1993. Fact that subcontractor bringing Miller Act action against general contractor erroneously called bond "performance bond" instead of "payment bond" would not alone support motion to dismiss; it was clear from complaint that subcontractor was alleging existence of bond which was given in order to protect suppliers and laborers and not one given to protect government. Miller Act, § 1(a)(1, 2), 40 U.S.C.A. § 270a(a)(1, 2); Fed.Rules Civ. Proc.Rule 12(b), 28 U.S.C.A.

U.S. for Use and Benefit of Owens v. Olympic Marine Services, Inc., 827 F.Supp. 1232.

S.D.W.Va. 1995. In suit by insured against agent and insurer, tort and contract claims against agent would not be dismissed for failure to state claim where agent's role in denial of insurance coverage was unclear and insurer's denial of insurance claim appeared upon agent's stationery and agent's name was listed directly below insurer's name on policy.

Pen Coal Corp. v. William H. McGee and Co., Inc., 903 F.Supp. 980.

⚷**1791. Copyright, trademark, patent and unfair competition actions.**

Library references

C.J.S. Federal Civil Procedure § 839.

D.Conn. 1991. Government's successful invocation of state secrets privilege in patent holder's action under Invention Secrecy Act alleging that government used, in exact or similar form, patented cryptographic encoding device warranted dismissal of action; maintenance of plaintiff's claim would require disclosure of state secrets to unauthorized persons, even during in camera proceeding, and would require detailed examination of entire range of government's cryptographic technology. 35 U.S.C.A. §§ 181, 183; 18 U.S.C.A. § 798.

Clift v. U.S., 808 F.Supp. 101.

D.D.C. 1988. Complaint apparently seeking relief from Trademark Trial and Appeals Board decision rejecting plaintiffs' application to register trademark had to be dismissed; plaintiffs failed to set forth principled, clear statement of claims, as required by Federal Rules of Civil Procedure, and it appeared that plaintiffs had not made good-faith effort to verify their allegations before filing complaint as required by Rule 11. Fed.Rules Civ.Proc.Rules 8, 11, 28 U.S.C.A.

Flying Tigers Oil Co., Inc. v. Flying Tigers Line, Inc., 118 F.R.D. 263.

D.Mass. 1986. Failure of complaint to allege compliance with copyright registration requirements was reason to grant motion to dismiss copyright infringement claim; however, since there was no showing that correction of defect would prejudice defendants, dismissal was without prejudice to filing of amended or supplemental complaint. 17 U.S.C.A. §§ 205(d), 411(a, b).

Quincy Cablesystems, Inc. v. Sully's Bar, Inc., 650 F.Supp. 838.

E.D.N.Y. 1987. Copyright infringement action could not be dismissed on ground that registered ads were derivative rather than original works, and therefore, material alleged to have been infringed upon was not protectable; classification of works was factual allegation of complaint, which was accepted as true for purposes of motion to dismiss.

Raffoler, Ltd. v. Peabody & Wright, Ltd., 671 F.Supp. 947.

S.D.N.Y. 1996. Patent licensor's failure to allege that it had performed its obligations under licensing agreement supported striking of its breach of contract allegation asserted in its counterclaim seeking accounting, rather than dismissal of counterclaim. Fed.Rules Civ.Proc. Rules 8(f), 12(f), 28 U.S.C.A.

> Reuben H. Donnelley Corp. v. Mark I Marketing Corp., 925 F.Supp. 203.

S.D.N.Y. 1992. Composer's claim for conspiracy against publishing company would be dismissed pursuant to rule requiring complaint to contain short and plain statement of claim showing that pleader is entitled to relief, even though composer stated claim for conspiracy, where composer failed to support claim with any facts. Fed.Rules Civ.Proc.Rule 8, 28 U.S.C.A.

> Kelly v. L.L. Cool J., 145 F.R.D. 32, affirmed 23 F.3d 398, certiorari denied 115 S.Ct. 365, 513 U.S. 950, 130 L.Ed.2d 318.

S.D.N.Y. 1991. Claim of German manufacturer of model railroad equipment that sales representative for former exclusive importer breached its fiduciary duty to manufacturer by selling Korean-made imitative track would not be dismissed for failure to state a claim where claim was not without some plausibility. Fed. Rules Civ.Proc.Rule 12(b)(6), 28 U.S.C.A.

> E.P. Lehmann Co. v. Polk's Modelcraft Hobbies, Inc., 770 F.Supp. 202.

Claim of German manufacturer of model railroad tracks for trade dress infringement by sales representative for former exclusive importer, involving claim of functionality, raised issues of fact and could not be dismissed for failure to state a claim. Lanham Trade-Mark Act, §§ 32(1), 43(a), 15 U.S.C.A. §§ 1114(1), 1143(a); Fed.Rules Civ.Proc.Rule 12(b)(6), 28 U.S.C.A.

> E.P. Lehmann Co. v. Polk's Modelcraft Hobbies, Inc., 770 F.Supp. 202.

S.D.N.Y. 1985. Whether sales representatives of products which allegedly infringed copyrights had actual or constructive knowledge of alleged infringement, whether they played sufficient role in furthering infringement to be held jointly and severally liable with manufacturer and distributor of products, and whether employee of sales representative engaged in solicitation efforts solely in her capacity as employee so as not to be individually liable were questions of fact which could not be resolved on motion to dismiss.

> Wales Indus. Inc. v. Hasbro Bradley, Inc., 612 F.Supp. 510.

Whether importer and distributor of convertible robot toys was "innocent infringer" who acted upon good-faith belief that toys were in public domain so as to be entitled to involuntary license was fact issue to be resolved at trial, in light of evidence that importer and distributor of toys did not enter into its initial contract

with manufacturer until after it had received formal notification of owner's copyright claim.

> Wales Indus. Inc. v. Hasbro Bradley, Inc., 612 F.Supp. 510.

W.D.N.Y. 1991. Argument by counsel for patent assignee, that "undisputed facts" showed that assignee could not prove requisite reliance element of affirmative defenses of fraud in assignor's action for royalties was inappropriate on motion to dismiss assignee's legal malpractice claim against counsel for negligent failure to preserve those affirmative defenses. Fed. Rules Civ.Proc.Rule 12(b)(6), 28 U.S.C.A.

> Sybron Transition Corp. v. Nixon, Hargrave, Devans & Doyle, 770 F.Supp. 803.

E.D.N.C. 1993. Whether allegedly infringing product is so confusingly similar as to cause likelihood of confusion regarding its origin within meaning of Lanham Act is question of fact, ill-suited for summary disposition on motion to dismiss for failure to state claim upon which relief can be granted. Lanham Trade-Mark Act, § 43(a), 15 U.S.C.A. § 1125(a); Fed. Rules Civ.Proc.Rule 12(b)(6), 28 U.S.C.A.

> Croydon Co., Inc. v. Unique Furnishings, Ltd., 831 F.Supp. 480.

E.D.Pa. 1994. Motion to dismiss code division multiple access (CDMA) cellular telephone technology portion of patent infringement action for lack of subject matter jurisdiction, based on allegation that patent holder sought impermissible advisory opinion, challenged sufficiency of pleading, and thus allegations in complaint had to be taken as true and complaint viewed liberally in favor of patent holder. Fed.Rules Civ.Proc.Rule 12(b)(1), 28 U.S.C.A.

> Interdigital Technology Corp. v. OKI America, Inc., 845 F.Supp. 276.

🗝**1792–1793.** *For other cases see earlier editions of this digest, the Decennial Digests, and WESTLAW.*

Library references

> C.J.S. Federal Civil Procedure.

🗝**1793. Employees and employment discrimination, actions involving.**

🗝**1793.1. —— In general.**

C.A.9 (Cal.) 1987. District court correctly dismissed § 1981 claims of employee who failed to put forth genuine issues of fact regarding disparate treatment or retaliation under Title VII. Civil Rights Act of 1964, §§ 701–718, 42 U.S.C.A. §§ 2000e to 2000e–17; 42 U.S.C.A. § 1981.

> Jurado v. Eleven-Fifty Corp., 813 F.2d 1406.

C.A.7 (Ill.) 1993. Trial court did not abuse its discretion in determining that no special factors outweighed court's interest in dismissing age discrimination suit which was duplicative of suit already pending in same court; although plaintiff, who filed second suit when it became apparent that he would be unable to refile first suit due to statute of limitations if motion to dismiss first suit were granted after statute of limitations had run, argued that he would be out of court if both suits were dismissed, that result would be plaintiff's fault for failing to follow rule requiring him to serve first complaint in timely manner. Fed.Rules Civ.Proc. Rule 4(j), 28 U.S.C.A; U.S.Dist.Ct.Rules N.D.Ill., General Rule 12(r).

> Serlin v. Arthur Andersen & Co., 3 F.3d 221.

C.A.7 (Ill.) 1992. Untimely filing of Title VII complaint by named plaintiff required dismissal of entire class action, where no one except plaintiff filed claim with Equal Employment Opportunity Commission (EEOC). Civil Rights Act of 1964, § 701 et seq., as amended, 42 U.S.C.A. § 2000e et seq.

> Banas v. American Airlines, 969 F.2d 477, rehearing denied.

C.A.7 (Ill.) 1988. Amended complaint under Federal Employers' Liability Act, which among other things, accused employer of failing to provide worker with reasonably safe place to work free of intentional supervisory harassment and deliberately inflicting emotional distress on worker, although not frivolous, was clearly dismissable where it concerned only harms brought about by acts that lacked any physical contact or threat of physical contact. Federal Employers' Liability Act, §§ 1–10, as amended, 45 U.S.C.A. §§ 51–60.

> Hammond v. Terminal R.R. Ass'n of St. Louis, 848 F.2d 95, certiorari denied 109 S.Ct. 1170, 489 U.S. 1032, 103 L.Ed.2d 229.

C.A.7 (Ill.) 1970. Waters v. Wisconsin Steel Works of International Harvester Co., 427 F.2d 476, certiorari denied United Order of American Bricklayers and Stone Masons, Local 21 v. Waters, 91 S.Ct. 137, 400 U.S. 911, 27 L.Ed.2d 151, certiorari denied 91 S.Ct. 137, 400 U.S. 911, 27 L.Ed.2d 151, on remand 1973 WL 11545, affirmed in part, reversed in part 502 F.2d 1309, certiorari denied 96 S.Ct. 2214, 425 U.S. 997, 48 L.Ed.2d 823, certiorari denied 96 S.Ct. 2214, 425 U.S. 997, 48 L.Ed.2d 823.

C.A.7 (Ind.) 1990. Trial court was not required to dismiss employee's sexual harassment claim prior to trial, and also dismiss pendent state claims, even though pleadings did not indicate any basis for award of monetary damages under Title VII and common-law damages and attorney fees were not available; employee had sought injunctive relief, in form of an order requiring employer to fire harassing employee and establish a mechanism for preventing further harassment. Civil Rights Act of 1964, § 701 et seq., 42 U.S.C.A. § 2000e et seq.

> Guess v. Bethlehem Steel Corp., 913 F.2d 463, rehearing denied.

C.A.8 (Iowa) 1989. Removed state court action by employee against employer, alleging emotional injury suffered during course of employment, should have been stayed during pendency of related workers' compensation proceedings rather than dismissed, as it was reasonably arguable under express language of Iowa Workers' Compensation Act that if benefits for emotional injury were not recoverable under Act they could be obtained through conventional tort action without being barred by exclusive remedy provision of Act. I.C.A. § 85.20.

> Dunlavey v. Economy Fire and Cas. Co., 887 F.2d 893.

C.A.8 (Minn.) 1995. Since black employee was fired before amendment adding section specifying that all phases of any contractual relationship, not just its initiation, are covered by civil rights statute guaranteeing equal rights under the law, employee's racial harassment and discriminatory discharge claims under that statute would be dismissed. 42 U.S.C.A. § 1981(a, b).

> Jeffries v. Metro-Mark, Inc., 45 F.3d 258, rehearing and suggestion for rehearing denied, certiorari denied 116 S.Ct. 102, 516 U.S. 830, 133 L.Ed.2d 56, rehearing denied 116 S.Ct. 584, 516 U.S. 1018, 133 L.Ed.2d 506.

C.A.2 (N.Y.) 1987. The district court was wholly justified in dismissing age discrimination complaint; despite nearly three years of discovery and repeated directions to file short and plain statement of the facts supporting age discrimination allegation, plaintiff failed to supply any facts supporting his allegation of age discrimination. Age Discrimination in Employment Act of 1967, § 2 et seq., 29 U.S.C.A. § 621 et seq.

> Becker v. Adams Drug Co., Inc., 819 F.2d 32, certiorari denied 108 S.Ct. 719, 484 U.S. 1015, 98 L.Ed.2d 669, rehearing denied 108 S.Ct. 1101, 485 U.S. 930, 99 L.Ed.2d 263.

C.A.3 (Pa.) 1993. At stage of determining whether city employee's complaint stated claim for retaliatory discharge, it could not be said that employee's letter to editor to criticize recent decision of city council to retain ordinance requiring city employees to reside in city interfered with interest of city in promoting services or that employee used public forum to resolve essentially private dispute. U.S.C.A. Const. Amend. 1.

> Holder v. City of Allentown, 987 F.2d 188, on remand 151 F.R.D. 552.

C.A.3 (Pa.) 1978. Novotny v. Great American Federal Sav. and Loan Ass'n, 584 F.2d 1235, certiorari granted 99 S.Ct. 830, 439 U.S. 1066, 59 L.Ed.2d 30, vacated 99 S.Ct. 2345, 442 U.S. 366, 60 L.Ed.2d 957, on remand 1980 WL 18553.

C.A.3 (Pa.) 1977. Nedd v. United Mine Workers of America, 556 F.2d 190, certiorari denied 98 S.Ct. 727, 434 U.S. 1013, 54 L.Ed.2d 757, on remand 488 F.Supp. 1208, affirmed Ambromovage v. United Mine Workers of America, 726 F.2d 972, on remand 506 F.Supp. 891.

C.A.6 (Tenn.) 1982. Kraft, Inc. v. Local Union 327, Teamsters, Chauffeurs, Helpers and Taxicab Drivers, 683 F.2d 131, on remand Central States Southeast and Southwest Areas Pension Fund v. Kraftco, Inc., 589 F.Supp. 1061, reversed 799 F.2d 1098, certiorari denied 107 S.Ct. 1291, 479 U.S. 1086, 94 L.Ed.2d 147.

C.A.5 (Tex.) 1978. Satterwhite v. City of Greenville, Tex., 578 F.2d 987, certiorari granted, vacated 100 S.Ct. 1334, 445 U.S. 940, 63 L.Ed.2d 773, on remand 634 F.2d 231.

M.D.Ala. 1995. Title VII plaintiff's allegations that, after being told that there were no positions available at restaurant, plaintiff had his wife telephone store to seek employment, that she did so, and that she was offered job without even an interview, were sufficient to rebut defendant's proffered legitimate reason for not hiring plaintiff, as required to preclude dismissal of Title VII failure to hire claim based on national origin. Civil Rights Act of 1964, § 701 et seq., as amended, 42 U.S.C.A. § 2000e et seq.

> Bahadirli v. Domino's Pizza, 873 F.Supp. 1528.

Even if pizza delivery franchisee made job offer to delivery driver applicant that would cut off liability for national origin discrimination, offer would not warrant dismissal of Title VII suit based on failure to mitigate damages, since offer would only cut off recovery from time of offer, but would not affect plaintiff's right to recover for time between alleged discrimination and date of offer. Civil Rights Act of 1964, § 701 et seq., as amended, 42 U.S.C.A. § 2000e et seq.

> Bahadirli v. Domino's Pizza, 873 F.Supp. 1528.

N.D.Cal. 1993. Claim by attorney that law firm had terminated her in retaliation for her complaints regarding firm's failure to provide smoke-free environment, in compliance with municipal antismoking ordinance would not be dismissed; while firm had argued generally that claims involving antismoking ordinance should be dismissed, firm had not responded to particular claim made by terminated attorney.

> Smedley v. Capps, Staples, Ward, Hastings and Dodson, 820 F.Supp. 1227.

N.D.Cal. 1990. At pleading stage, court may dismiss state law claims for failure to state claim where they are preempted by ERISA. Employee Retirement Income Security Act of 1974, § 2 et seq., 29 U.S.C.A. § 1001 et seq.

> Cox v. Eichler, 765 F.Supp. 601.

D.Colo. 1995. Former employer was not entitled to dismissal of employment discrimination, breach of contract, and promissory estoppel complaint for failure to state claim upon which relief can be granted; it was not beyond doubt that former employee could prove no set of facts which would entitle him to relief. Fed. Rules Civ.Proc.Rule 12(b)(6), 28 U.S.C.A.

> Johnson v. N.T.I., a Div. of Colorado Springs Circuits, 898 F.Supp. 762.

D.Colo. 1991. Question as to whether workplace harassment allegedly suffered by former employee arose out of employment precluded dismissal based on exclusivity provisions of Workmen's Compensation Act. West's C.R.S.A. § 8–43–104 (Repealed).

> Smith v. Colorado Interstate Gas Co., 777 F.Supp. 854.

Assuming that former employer's posttermination conduct, in informing prospective employer that former employee had not been laid off, was insufficient to establish triable case of intentional infliction of emotional harm, motion to dismiss was nonetheless not required to be granted; posttermination behavior was not to be considered alone but as part of former employer's pattern of conduct, and former employer had not argued that entire pattern of conduct failed to state cause of action.

> Smith v. Colorado Interstate Gas Co., 777 F.Supp. 854.

M.D.Fla. 1995. Difficulty in determining whether plaintiffs are qualified individuals with disabilities is one factor to be considered in ultimate rulings on motions to dismiss disability discrimination claims. Americans with Disabilities Act of 1990, § 2 et seq., 42 U.S.C.A. § 12101 et seq.

> Cramer v. State of Fla., 885 F.Supp. 1545, affirmed 117 F.3d 1258.

M.D.Fla. 1995. At motion to dismiss stage of Equal Pay Act litigation, it was impossible to determine whether sheriff's department employees sued by female employee had sufficient power over her to be declared her employer in economic reality, and thus court would not dismiss individual employees as defendants, in view of broad definition of "employer" under

Act. Fair Labor Standards Act of 1938, § 3(d), as amended, 29 U.S.C.A. § 203(d).

    Marshall v. Miller, 873 F.Supp. 628.

N.D.Ill. 1996. Whether employee's disability substantially limits one or more major life activities, as required to support ADA claim, is fact based inquiry which is not generally motion to dismiss territory. Americans with Disabilities Act of 1990, §§ 2 et seq., 3(2), 42 U.S.C.A. §§ 12101 et seq., 12102(2); Fed.Rules Civ.Proc. Rule 12(b)(6), 28 U.S.C.A.

    Banks v. Hit or Miss, Inc., 946 F.Supp. 569.

N.D.Ill. 1996. Although it is difficult, in context of motion to dismiss, for public employer to carry its burden of establishing that employee who was terminated based on political affiliation occupied policy-making or confidential position, such that employer had compelling interest justifying infringement on employee's First Amendment rights, it is possible that employee may plead particulars that show that employee has no claim, and in that case, employee pleads himself or herself out of court. U.S.C.A. Const.Amend. 1; Fed.Rules Civ.Proc. Rule 12(b)(6), 28 U.S.C.A.

    Milazzo v. O'Connell, 925 F.Supp. 1331, affirmed 108 F.3d 129, rehearing and suggestion for rehearing denied.

N.D.Ill. 1995. According to employee's allegations, intentional tort exception to exclusivity provision of Illinois Workers' Compensation Act might apply, such that motion to dismiss employee's intentional infliction of emotional distress claim against employer was premature. Fed.Rules Civ.Proc.Rule 12(b)(6), 28 U.S.C.A.; S.H.A. 820 ILCS 305/1 et seq.

    Daulo v. Commonwealth Edison, 892 F.Supp. 1088.

N.D.Ill. 1994. Trial court would not dismiss count of employee's §§ 1981 and 1983 complaint against city, even though plaintiff failed to identify what federal law or constitutional right was violated, as taking all reasonable inferences in her favor, plaintiff adequately pleaded that city violated Fourteenth Amendment guarantee of equal protection, where plaintiff sued city for racial discrimination following incident in which employee was assaulted by co-worker and subsequently was not promoted and was transferred to different branch of library, and library allegedly did not investigate assault incident as it indicated it would. U.S.C.A. Const.Amend. 14; 42 U.S.C.A. §§ 1981, 1983.

    Simmons v. Chicago Public Library, 860 F.Supp. 490.

N.D.Ill. 1994. Equal Employment Opportunity Commission's (EEOC) complaint's conclusory allegation that employer engaged in unlawful conduct by conditioning severance benefits on allegedly invalid release of employees' Age Discrimination in Employment Act (ADEA) rights and claims was insufficient to state claim under ADEA section making it unlawful for employer to discriminate against employee because employee has opposed unlawful practices and fact that EEOC supplied operative facts in its memorandum in opposition to employer's motion to dismiss for failure to state claim did not cure the deficiency because only allegations in complaint could be considered on motion to dismiss; however, because this pleading deficiency could be cured by importing factual allegations in the responsive brief into the complaint, judicial economy would be best served if district court considered whether amended complaint would state claim under this ADEA section. Fed.Rules Civ.Proc.Rule 12(b)(6), 28 U.S.C.A.; Age Discrimination in Employment Act of 1967, § 4(d), as amended, 29 U.S.C.A. § 623(d).

    E.E.O.C. v. Sears, Roebuck and Co., 857 F.Supp. 1233, opinion modified 883 F.Supp. 211.

N.D.Ill. 1993. Dismissal of retaliatory discharge action under Labor-Management Reporting and Disclosure Act would not be granted based upon failure to submit complaint signed by attorney; defendants had failed to show any prejudice arising from technical defect. Fed.Rules Civ.Proc.Rule 11, 28 U.S.C.A.; Labor-Management Reporting and Disclosure Act of 1959, §§ 101, 102, 29 U.S.C.A. §§ 411, 412.

    Stroud v. Senese, 832 F.Supp. 1206.

N.D.Ill. 1992. To extent that employee in retaliatory discharge action against her employer could defeat motion to dismiss by affidavit after failing to include in her complaint any facts regarding essential element of cause of action, employee could switch her theory of retaliation in responsive brief when such theory was supported by facts as alleged in her complaint. Fed.Rules Civ.Proc.Rule 12(b), 28 U.S.C.A.

    Bailey v. Policy Management Systems Corp. ("PMSC"), 814 F.Supp. 37.

N.D.Ill. 1991. Claims of purchasers of interests in real estate investments against investment advisor for violation of ERISA, common-law fraud, violation of Illinois Securities Law, violation of Illinois Consumer Fraud and Deceptive Business Practices Act, breach of fiduciary duty, and negligent misrepresentation would be dismissed for failure to allege loss causation, even though no authority was asserted that loss causation was essential element of any of those claims, where purchasers had effectively conceded such requirement. Employee Retirement Income Security Act of 1974, § 2 et seq., 29

U.S.C.A. § 1001 et seq.; Ill.S.H.A. ch. 121½, ¶¶ 137.1 et seq., 261 et seq.

> Lewis v. Hermann, 775 F.Supp. 1137, reconsideration denied 783 F.Supp. 1131, reinstatement denied 1992 WL 57939.

N.D.Ill. 1989. For purposes of motion to dismiss, sales agent for manufacturer sufficiently alleged breach of employment contract even though manufacturer argued that parties never reached agreement on contract's essential terms; argument that there was no mutuality of agreement and therefore no enforceable contract was issue of fact to be resolved at trial. Fed.Rules Civ.Proc.Rule 8(a), 28 U.S.C.A.

> Skinner v. Shirley of Hollywood, a Div. of Nat. Corset Supply House, 723 F.Supp. 50.

N.D.Ill. 1987. General contractor, subcontractors, and individual employees' complaint alleging due process violation from termination without hearing of those employees by Illinois Department of Labor officials on ground they were not Illinois laborers would not be dismissed; individuals had substantial interest in their continued employment, and there was no factual record on which to determine whether they received whatever process was due. U.S.C.A. Const.Amends. 5, 14; Ill.S.H.A. ch. 48, ¶¶ 2201, 2203.

> E & E Const. Co. v. State of Ill., 674 F.Supp. 269.

N.D.Ill. 1986. Whether civil rights plaintiff was "employee" under Title VII is fact-bound question and cannot be determined from face of the complaint, unless complaint happens to allege facts which clearly preclude such possibility. Civil Rights Act of 1964, § 601 et seq., as amended, 42 U.S.C.A. § 2000e et seq.

> Miller v. Advanced Studies, Inc., 635 F.Supp. 1196.

N.D.Ind. 1991. Expiration of collective bargaining agreements did not require that claims under LMRA for breach of collective bargaining agreements be dismissed for lack of jurisdiction or for failure to state claims; determination of parties' intent as to duration of collective bargaining agreements' terms was more properly made in summary judgment motion than in motion to dismiss. Fed.Rules Civ. Proc.Rule 12(b)(1, 6), 28 U.S.C.A.; Labor Management Relations Act, 1947, § 301(a), 29 U.S.C.A. § 185(a).

> Arndt v. Wheelabrator Corp., 763 F.Supp. 396, reversed Bidlack v. Wheelabrator Corp., 993 F.2d 603, certiorari denied 114 S.Ct. 291, 510 U.S. 909, 126 L.Ed.2d 240.

D.Kan. 1995. To extent that former police officer was attempting to assert substantive due process claim under § 1983 against city and its officials paralleling his claim that his discharge violated First Amendment, his substantive due process claim would be dismissed; where particular amendment provides explicit textual source of constitutional protection, that amendment, not generalized notion of substantive due process must be guide for analyzing claim. U.S.C.A. Const.Amends. 1, 14; 42 U.S.C.A. § 1983.

> Davis v. Olin, 886 F.Supp. 804.

D.Kan. 1994. It did not appear beyond a doubt that sex discrimination plaintiffs could prove no set of facts in support of their theory of recovery, although plaintiffs failed to specifically list two defendants in their Equal Employment Opportunity Commission (EEOC) complaints and, thus, plaintiffs were entitled to offer evidence on their theory of relief under Title VII and their complaint would not be dismissed for failure to state a claim inasmuch as there were fact issues existing precluding the court from determining whether failure to specifically list those two defendants mandated dismissal. Civil Rights Act of 1964, § 701 et seq., 42 U.S.C.A. § 2000e et seq.; Fed.Rules Civ.Proc.Rule 12(b)(6), 28 U.S.C.A.

> Gilmore v. List & Clark Const. Co., 862 F.Supp. 294.

To assess whether three companies named as defendants in sex discrimination action could be considered a "single employer" for purposes of Title VII, facts outside the pleadings were required; accordingly, because discovery had barely begun, it was premature to fully evaluate issue of whether all three companies were plaintiffs' employer for purposes of Title VII liability, and it was improper to dismiss the claims for failure to state a cause of action. Civil Rights Act of 1964, § 703, 42 U.S.C.A. § 2000e–2; Fed.Rules Civ.Proc.Rule 12(b)(6), 28 U.S.C.A.

> Gilmore v. List & Clark Const. Co., 862 F.Supp. 294.

E.D.Ky. 1957. Edmonds v. Fehler & Feinauer Const. Co., 149 F.Supp. 396, order set aside 252 F.2d 639.

D.Me. 1995. Claim of certain nonretired public school teachers who were members of Maine State Retirement System (MSRS) on certain date and all retired teachers who had retired after certain date that amendments to Maine State Retirement System (MSRS) unconstitutionally impaired their contractual rights as members of MSRS would not be dismissed for failure of statute to create any contractual rights; allegedly "dispositive" state court decision was decided under excessively narrow and literal standard which precluded full analysis of potential existence of contract, and thus was of greatly diminished persuasive authority, and more developed record than that presented at initial stage of proceedings and considered by state court in allegedly dispositive case was needed. U.S.C.A. Const. Art. 1, § 10, cl. 1; 5 M.R.S.A. §§ 17001, 17701–B, 17806, 17851, 17852; Fed.Rules Civ.Proc.Rule 12, 28 U.S.C.A.

> Parker v. Wakelin, 882 F.Supp. 1131.

D.Md. 1991. Whether employee's breach of contract claim against employer for failing to afford employee opportunity to participate in "rehabilitation employment" program was preempted by ERISA could not be determined in context of motion to dismiss, as it could not be determined from record whether program was part of ERISA-governed disability plan. Employee Retirement Income Security Act of 1974, § 2 et seq., 29 U.S.C.A. § 1001 et seq.

> Kemp v. Control Data Corp., 785 F.Supp. 74.

D.Md. 1974. Equal Employment Opportunity Commission v. Raymond Metal Products Co., 385 F.Supp. 907, stay granted E.E.O.C. v. Raymond Metal Products Co., Subsidiary of Raymond Intern., Inc., 1974 WL 10566, affirmed in part, reversed in part 530 F.2d 590, on remand 1978 WL 22437.

E.D.Mo. 1994. Factual dispute regarding whether provider of ERISA health benefit plan was fiduciary of plan precluded dismissal of claims against it for breach of fiduciary and cofiduciary duties, and for equitable estoppel under federal common law. Employee Retirement Income Security Act of 1974, § 3(21)(A), as amended, 29 U.S.C.A. § 1002(21)(A).

> Mathis v. American Group Life Ins. Co., 873 F.Supp. 1348.

E.D.Mo. 1983. Hechenberger v. Western Elec. Co., Inc., 570 F.Supp. 820, affirmed 742 F.2d 453, certiorari denied 105 S.Ct. 1182, 469 U.S. 1212, 84 L.Ed.2d 330.

D.Mont. 1987. Action brought by former railroad employees against railroad, based upon common-law fraud, fraudulent misrepresentation, and promissory estoppel grounds, did not require dismissal nor did motion for class certification require denial on basis that complaint failed to clearly allege that claims of each named plaintiff exceeded $10,000 or that claims of each member of putative class exceeded $10,000; rather, appropriate action would be to permit amendment of complaint. 28 U.S.C.A. § 1332.

> Polich v. Burlington Northern, Inc., 116 F.R.D. 258.

S.D.N.Y. 1993. District court would not dismiss for lack of subject matter jurisdiction complaint for sexual harassment of employee of instrumentalities of foreign sovereign, even though employee erroneously alleged that jurisdiction was based on diversity of citizenship rather than on fact that action was against foreign state; although pleading was undeniably defective, there was prima facie showing of subject matter jurisdiction, and, therefore, employee would be allowed to amend complaint. 28 U.S.C.A. §§ 1330, 1330(a), 1332; Fed.Rules Civ.Proc.Rule 8(a), 28 U.S.C.A.

> Zveiter v. Brazilian Nat. Superintendency of Merchant Marine, 833 F.Supp. 1089, opinion supplemented on reconsideration 841 F.Supp. 111.

S.D.N.Y. 1990. Federal employee's Title VII suit did not have to be dismissed due to fact that his counsel, retained after employee was granted leave to amend original pro se complaint to name head of national office of employing agency as sole defendant, inadvertently copied caption of initial pro se complaint that did not name proper defendant; body of second amended complaint filed by counsel contained necessary allegations against head of national office, and employing agency was served within period of limitations. Civil Rights Act of 1964, § 717(c), as amended, 42 U.S.C.A. § 2000e–16(c).

> McGuire v. U.S. Postal Service, 749 F.Supp. 1275.

S.D.N.Y. 1977. Stewart v. Wappingers Central School Dist., 437 F.Supp. 250, opinion amended 493 F.Supp. 791.

W.D.N.Y. 1978. Gill v. Monroe County Dept. of Social Services, 79 F.R.D. 316, motion denied 95 F.R.D. 518.

N.D.Ohio 1996. Employee's § 1981 race discrimination claim against supervisor would be dismissed as frivolous where there was no arguable basis in fact for claim. 42 U.S.C.A. § 1981.

> Czupih v. Card Pak Inc., 916 F.Supp. 687.

N.D.Ohio 1982. Easter v. Jeep Corp., 538 F.Supp. 515, reversed 750 F.2d 520, appeal after remand 896 F.2d 553.

D.Or. 1994. Whether facts giving rise to fraudulent conveyance claim of pension trusts against employer in action under ERISA and LMRA were known at time of previous action against employer as to which defendant was alleged to be alter ego or successor, for purpose of res judicata, was factual matter and not appropriate as basis for motion to dismiss for failure to state claim on which relief could be granted. Employment Retirement Income Security Act of 1974, §§ 502, 515, as amended, 29 U.S.C.A. §§ 1132, 1145; Labor Management Relations Act, 1947, § 301(a), 29 U.S.C.A. § 185(a); Fed.Rules Civ.Proc.Rule 12(b)(6), 28 U.S.C.A.

> Oregon Laborers-Employers Health & Welfare Trust Fund v. All State Indus. and Marine Cleaning, Inc., 850 F.Supp. 905.

E.D.Pa. 1995. Any contractual defense that state transportation authority might rely on through collective bargaining agreement was susceptible to factual arguments, and thus authority's contention that procedures used to dismiss employee, as set forth in union contract, met requirements of due process, and that employee's post-termination hearing satisfied due process, did not allow dismissal of employee's § 1983 claim, alleging that authority failed to grant him pre-termination hearing, in violation of his due process rights. 42 U.S.C.A. § 1983; Fed.Rules Civ.Proc. Rule 12(b)(6), 28 U.S.C.A.

> Frederick v. Southeastern Pennsylvania Transp. Authority, 892 F.Supp. 122.

Discharged state employee's failure to oppose state's motion to dismiss with respect to employee's state law wrongful discharge and contract claims warranted dismissal of those claims. Fed.Rules Civ.Proc. Rule 12(b)(6), 28 U.S.C.A.

> Frederick v. Southeastern Pennsylvania Transp. Authority, 892 F.Supp. 122.

E.D.Pa. 1995. Third-party beneficiary claim of husband of former executive director of county opportunity board against board had to be repled, providing missing information if possible, as board had no basis on which to admit or deny allegations; neither amended complaint nor brief in opposition to motion to dismiss or for more specific complaint made any allegations to support assertion of third-party beneficiary status, or provided terms of employment contract in which husband allegedly had interest, what that interest was, how he obtained it, or any other facts relevant to show third-party beneficiary status. Fed.Rules Civ.Proc.Rule 12(e), 28 U.S.C.A.

> Pierce v. Montgomery County Opportunity Bd., Inc., 884 F.Supp. 965.

Former public employee stated claim for wrongful discharge on which relief could be granted, where she alleged that she was terminated on account of her participation in Republican Party politics and for utilizing her right of freedom of speech in her off hours. U.S.C.A. Const.Amend. 1; Fed.Rules Civ.Proc.Rule 12(b)(6), 28 U.S.C.A.

> Pierce v. Montgomery County Opportunity Bd., Inc., 884 F.Supp. 965.

E.D.Pa. 1994. In the context of pro se hostile work environment sexual harassment pleading, defects, consisting of complaint listing inconsistent home addresses for plaintiff, failure of plaintiff to attach Equal Employment Opportunity Commission (EEOC) "right-to-sue" letter to which complaint referred, and complaint's requesting improper relief, were not sufficient to compel dismissal of claim.

> Pittman v. Correctional Healthcare Solutions, Inc., 868 F.Supp. 105.

E.D.Pa. 1994. Where count against individual defendant seeking to pierce corporate veil for purposes of ERISA claim was sufficient in all other respects, dismissal was not required because plaintiffs had failed to specify which of individual defendants initiated actions complained of; parties were only at pleading stage, and it was possible that plaintiffs did not know which defendant actually took alleged actions and would not know until discovery was conducted; defendants had adequate notice of claims, and they could simply deny allegations that they did not pertain to particular individual.

> Killian v. McCulloch, 850 F.Supp. 1239.

E.D.Pa. 1994. Former employee's claim for sex plus pregnancy discrimination would be dismissed as duplicative of her claims in earlier counts alleging discriminatory intent by employer and failure to accommodate her during her pregnancy. Civil Rights Act of 1964, § 701, as amended, 42 U.S.C.A. § 2000e.

> Brennan v. National Telephone Directory Corp., 850 F.Supp. 331.

Former employee's discrimination claim against codefendant whom other defendant asserted was not her employer would not be dismissed, where various documents sent to former employee included both defendants on letterhead, defendants admitted that they were interrelated, and no discovery had yet been conducted. Civil Rights Act of 1964, § 701, as amended, 42 U.S.C.A. § 2000e; Fed.Rules Civ. Proc.Rule 12(b)(6), 28 U.S.C.A.

> Brennan v. National Telephone Directory Corp., 850 F.Supp. 331.

M.D.Pa. 1992. Issue of whether multiple employer welfare arrangement was "employee benefit plan," for purpose of determining whether ERISA preempted Pennsylvania regulation of arrangement as insurance company, could not be resolved on motion to dismiss, due to lack of facts before court as to characteristics of arrangement. Employee Retirement Income Security Act of 1974, §§ 3, 3(1), 29 U.S.C.A. §§ 1002, 1002(1).

> Atlantic Health Care Benefits Trust v. Foster, 809 F.Supp. 365, affirmed 6 F.3d 778, certiorari denied 114 S.Ct. 689, 510 U.S. 1043, 126 L.Ed.2d 656.

D.Puerto Rico 1997. Dismissal of former employees' age discrimination claim against former employer under Puerto Rico law also required dismissal of employees' derivative claim under tort damages statute. 29 L.P.R.A. § 148.

> Dominguez v. Eli Lilly and Co., 958 F.Supp. 721, affirmed 141 F.3d 1149.

D.Utah 1997. Disparate treatment employment discrimination claim was subject to dismissal, where claim was only mentioned in a heading in the complaint, and employees provided neither evidence nor argument in support of claim in complaint, memoranda, or oral argument on summary judgment motion. Civil Rights Act of 1964, § 701 et seq., as amended, 42 U.S.C.A. § 2000e et seq.

> Metcalf v. Metropolitan Life, Inc., 961 F.Supp. 1536.

D.Vt. 1997. Former employee's failure to allege in her complaint that she had exhausted her administrative remedies and that her former employer was "employer" for purposes of Title VII, ADEA and Vermont Fair Employment Practices Act (FEPA) did not require dismissal of her age and sex discrimination claims under such statutes; rather, former employee would be granted leave to amend her complaint to make such allegations. Age Discrimination in Employment Act of 1967, § 2 et seq., 29 U.S.C.A. § 621 et seq.; Civil Rights Act of 1964, § 701 et seq., as amended, 42 U.S.C.A. § 2000e et seq.; 21 V.S.A. § 495.

> Gadbois v. Rock-Tenn Co., Mill Div., Inc., 984 F.Supp. 811.

S.D.W.Va. 1989. District court would not dismiss complaint alleging violations of state labor law where claim was not patently without merit.

> Shiveley v. Tri-State Greyhound Park, 724 F.Supp. 421.

⨂**1794. —— Fair Labor Standards Act cases.**

For other cases see earlier editions of this digest, the Decennial Digests, and WESTLAW.

⨂**1795. Governmental bodies or officers, actions involving.**

Library references

C.J.S. Federal Civil Procedure § 832.

C.A.D.C. 1991. Same standard applicable to motions to dismiss for failure to state a claim in other cases are applicable to a case challenging surveillance under Foreign Intelligence Surveillance Act (FISA). Fed.Rules Civ.Proc.Rule 12(b)(6), 28 U.S.C.A.; Foreign Intelligence Surveillance Act of 1978, §§ 101–111, 50 U.S.C.A. §§ 1801–1811.

> ACLU Foundation of Southern California v. Barr, 952 F.2d 457, 293 U.S.App.D.C. 101, rehearing denied.

C.A.D.C. 1976. McSurely v. McClellan, 553 F.2d 1277, 180 U.S.App.D.C. 101, certiorari granted 98 S.Ct. 260, 434 U.S. 888, 54 L.Ed.2d 173, certiorari dismissed McAdams v. McSurely, 98 S.Ct. 3116, 438 U.S. 189, 57 L.Ed.2d 704, appeal after remand 697 F.2d 309, 67 A.L.R. Fed. 614, 225 U.S.App.D.C. 67, appeal after remand 753 F.2d 88, 243 U.S.App.D.C. 270, certiorari denied 106 S.Ct. 525, 474 U.S. 1005,

88 L.Ed.2d 457, certiorari denied Brick v. McSurely, 106 S.Ct. 525, 474 U.S. 1005, 88 L.Ed.2d 457.

C.A.10 (Kan.) 1986. Dismissal of claim by borrowers against the Farmers Home Administration and its employees in their capacity as federal officials on common-law tort claims was warranted absent use of proper procedures under Federal Tort Claims Act, and where no federal question arose considering acts of defendants as individuals. 28 U.S.C.A. §§ 1346, 2671 et seq.

> Munk v. Federal Land Bank of Wichita, 791 F.2d 130.

C.A.10 (Utah) 1985. Where district court concluded that plaintiff's First Amendment claim might have had merit but that it was too conclusory to allow judgment on its merit, and where court gave plaintiff ample opportunity to remedy inadequacies of the complaint, which plaintiff failed to do, district court was not in error in dismissing the First Amendment claim made by plaintiff. U.S.C.A. Const.Amend. 1; Fed.Rules Civ.Proc.Rule 12(b)(6), 28 U.S.C.A.

> Eames v. City of Logan, Utah, 762 F.2d 83.

D.Ariz. 1994. Material issue of fact whether Department of Economic Security employee's liberty interest was implicated when he was suspended and reassigned on charge that he endangered health, safety and welfare of a child precluded dismissal of action for failure to state claim upon which relief may be granted.

> Lara v. Cowan, 848 F.Supp. 1456.

E.D.Cal. 1993. Material issue of fact as to whether water district granted landowners extension of time in which to file suit under California Tort Claims Act precluded dismissal of landowners from action brought against water district which alleged that water district caused flooding of property. West's Ann.Cal. Gov.Code § 810 et seq.

> Sumner Peck Ranch, Inc. v. Bureau of Reclamation, 823 F.Supp. 715.

Breach of contract action brought by landowners who alleged water distribution and drainage system caused flooding of their lands would not be dismissed, although federal defendants asserted impossibility defense; issue could not be resolved on pleadings, as neither party provided sufficient evidence to allow adjudication of impossibility defense as to fulfillment of duties created by statute, and neither party identified specific language from reclamation contracts which they contended created or failed to create contractual drainage obligation owed by United States.

> Sumner Peck Ranch, Inc. v. Bureau of Reclamation, 823 F.Supp. 715.

D.D.C. 1992. Inmate's failure to serve individual prison officials with process in civil rights action mandated dismissal of *Bivens* claims for lack of personal jurisdiction over officials in their individual capacities. Fed. Rules Civ.Proc.Rules 12(b)(2), 4(d)(1), 28 U.S.C.A.

Huskey v. Quinlan, 785 F.Supp. 4.

D.D.C. 1988. Dismissal of case involving mooted Settlement Act claims, not transfer to United States District Court for District of Massachusetts where related case was pending, was appropriate.

James v. Hodel, 696 F.Supp. 699, affirmed 893 F.2d 1404, 282 U.S.App.D.C. 255.

D.D.C. 1987. Question of whether United States Attorney General's interest in proper exercise of prosecutorial responsibilities outweighed Department of Justice attorney's allegedly protected interest in speaking concerning matter of public concern raised fact questions not susceptible of resolution on motion to dismiss, in attorney's action alleging wrongful termination of his employment, in violation of First Amendment, based on his "whistleblowing" activities. U.S.C.A. Const.Amend. 1.

Twist v. Meese, 661 F.Supp. 231, affirmed 854 F.2d 1421, 272 U.S.App.D.C. 204, certiorari denied 109 S.Ct. 2066, 490 U.S. 1066, 104 L.Ed.2d 631, rehearing denied 109 S.Ct. 3267, 492 U.S. 927, 106 L.Ed.2d 612.

M.D.Fla. 1989. Failure to allege compliance with notice of claim requirements of Florida law warranted dismissal without prejudice of pendent cause of action based on Florida law. West's F.S.A. § 768.28(6).

Redner v. Citrus County, Fla., 710 F.Supp. 318.

S.D.Fla. 1995. Government was not entitled to dismiss federal appointee's estoppel claims after his appointment was withdrawn.

Klaskala v. U.S. Dept. of Health and Human Services, 889 F.Supp. 480.

N.D.Ill. 1995. Mere fact that plaintiffs sued city officials in their individual capacities, and yet sought injunctive relief, was not grounds in itself to invoke dismissal.

Dertz v. City of Chicago, 912 F.Supp. 319, on reconsideration in part 1997 WL 85169.

N.D.Ill. 1994. Whether city franchise and zoning ordinances, authorizing city officials to prohibit and/or remove public pay telephones within city limits, violated substantive due process rights of pay telephone companies because they had no deterrent effect on crime and were simply irrational were issues which could not be resolved on motion to dismiss complaint in companies' action against city, its zoning administrator, and its director of revenue, challenging validity of ordinances. U.S.C.A. Const.

Amend. 14; Chicago, Ill., Municipal Code, Titles 10–28–265, 17–44–220(12).

Independent Coin Payphone Ass'n, Inc. v. City of Chicago, 863 F.Supp. 744.

N.D.Ill. 1994. District court would dismiss as seeking duplicative recovery federal government's alternative claim of unjust enrichment in action in which federal government prevailed in its claim that food store operator who violated food stamp program violated False Claims Act. Food Stamp Act of 1977, §§ 2–23, as amended, 7 U.S.C.A. §§ 2011–2032; 28 U.S.C.A. 1345; 31 U.S.C.A. § 3729(a), (a)(1).

Brooks v. U.S. Dept. of Agriculture, 841 F.Supp. 833, affirmed 64 F.3d 251.

S.D.Iowa 1980. Health Care Equalization Committee of Iowa Chiropractic Soc. v. Iowa Medical Soc., 501 F.Supp. 970, affirmed 851 F.2d 1020, rehearing denied.

D.Minn. 1988. Whether employing federal agency and other defendants were absolutely immune from federal employee's claims for money damages for defamation, tortious interference with contractual relations, and intentional infliction of emotional distress involved disputed fact questions, making motion for dismissal inappropriate.

Moreno v. Small Business Admin., 681 F.Supp. 1370, reversed in part 877 F.2d 715.

S.D.Miss. 1987. Qualified immunity defense of public officials may be considered on motion to dismiss.

Sorey v. Kellett, 673 F.Supp. 817, reversed 849 F.2d 960, rehearing denied.

In determining whether plaintiff had overcome defense of qualified immunity, court would consider allegations in plaintiff's brief in response to motion to dismiss, allegations that were more specific than those made in complaint and amended complaint.

Sorey v. Kellett, 673 F.Supp. 817, reversed 849 F.2d 960, rehearing denied.

Court would consider whether members of Mississippi Board of Trustees of State Institutions of Higher Learning were entitled to qualified immunity, although plaintiff attempted to reserve right to amend her complaint if court found it insufficient to overcome qualified immunity defense; plaintiff, who had filed both complaint and amended complaint along with extensive briefs, had made her best case, so qualified immunity issue could properly be considered.

Sorey v. Kellett, 673 F.Supp. 817, reversed 849 F.2d 960, rehearing denied.

E.D.N.Y. 1987. Under both the convention on the privileges and immunities of the United Nations and the International Organizations and Immunities Act, the General Assembly of the United Nations had absolute immunity with respect to Title VII employment discrimination claim, absent any evidence of express waiver of such immunity; however, action would not be dismissed due to remote possibility that General Assembly, if it were aware of suit, might choose to waive its immunity, and copy of complaint and district court's memorandum would be ordered served on legal department of General Assembly to provide opportunity to do so. Civil Rights Act of 1964, § 701 et seq., as amended, 42 U.S.C.A. § 2000e et seq.; International Organizations Immunities Act, §§ 1–12, as amended, 22 U.S.C.A. §§ 288–288f–2.

> Boimah v. United Nations General Assembly, 664 F.Supp. 69.

E.D.N.Y. 1987. Complaint alleging that funds were fraudulently transferred from credit union to defendants and used to purchase and develop numerous real properties, sufficiently put defendants on fair notice of Government's claim; complaint identified relationships among four individual moving defendants in its allegation that they were engaged in the acquisition, development, and management of real property and that latter three were associated with former, and identified defendant realty corporations and property they owned, and alleged relationships four individuals had with those corporations. Fed.Rules Civ.Proc.Rule 9(b), 28 U.S.C.A.

> U.S. v. Rivieccio, 661 F.Supp. 281 1987 WL 15271.

Although complaint by United States Government charging constructive trust for conspiracy to defraud credit union by diverting millions of dollars to individuals on behalf of realty corporations was not phrased in terms of four factors that New York courts considered prior to impressing a constructive trust, lack of such phrasing was not a pleading defect warranting dismissal. Fed.Rules Civ.Proc.Rule 12(b), 28 U.S.C.A.

> U.S. v. Rivieccio, 661 F.Supp. 281 1987 WL 15271.

Fact that two corporate defendants were named as recipients of certain real property in original complaint but omitted in supplemental and amended complaint did not establish that Government no longer had claim against defendants and that they should be dismissed where Government contended that corporations had received money from credit union which had not been repaid. Fed.Rules Civ.Proc.Rule 12(b)(6), 28 U.S.C.A.

> U.S. v. Rivieccio, 661 F.Supp. 281 1987 WL 15271.

M.D.N.C. 1986. Plaintiffs were entitled to dismissal of their claim against named defendant after discovery showed she acted within scope of her authority in accordance with established policies and procedures of city board of education, where dismissal did not deny defendant board of education an opportunity to refute claim that former defendant acted pursuant to either stated or unstated official policy, and plaintiffs were not pursuing claim on basis of respondeat superior, but were directly attacking board's official policy.

> S-1 By and Through P-1 v. Spangler, 650 F.Supp. 1427, vacated 832 F.2d 294, appeal after remand 6 F.3d 160, rehearing granted, opinion vacated, on rehearing S-1 and S-2 By and Through P-1 and P-2 v. State Bd. of Educ. of North Carolina, 21 F.3d 49, certiorari denied 115 S.Ct. 205, 513 U.S. 876, 130 L.Ed.2d 135.

E.D.Pa. 1994. Complaint may be dismissed for failure to state claim where defendant contends that under facts alleged he is entitled to immunity, even though immunity is generally characterized as affirmative defense. Fed.Rules Civ.Proc.Rule 12(b)(6), 28 U.S.C.A.

> Frazier v. Southeastern Pennsylvania Transp. Authority, 868 F.Supp. 757.

E.D.Tex. 1987. Unless plaintiff's allegations state claim of violation of clearly established law, defendant pleading qualified immunity is entitled to dismissal before commencement of discovery.

> Sherrell By and Through Wooden v. City of Longview, 683 F.Supp. 1108.

N.D.Tex. 1988. Plaintiff must plead specific facts to support claim against governmental official who is entitled to protection of immunity in order to survive motion to dismiss.

> Starks v. Bowles, 682 F.Supp. 891, affirmed 851 F.2d 1419.

If plaintiff is given ample opportunity to plead his best case against governmental official and still fails to meet heightened pleading requirement, district court must dismiss complaint as it relates to defendants who assert protection of immunity.

> Starks v. Bowles, 682 F.Supp. 891, affirmed 851 F.2d 1419.

S.D.Tex. 1993. When considering motion to dismiss complaint against governmental official on qualified immunity grounds, court must determine whether plaintiffs' allegations, if accepted as true, state claim for violation of any rights secured under Constitution.

> McDonald v. City of Freeport, Tex., 834 F.Supp. 921.

To withstand motion to dismiss complaint against governmental official on qualified immunity grounds, plaintiff must state with factual detail and particularity basis for claim which necessarily includes why defendant-official cannot successfully maintain defense of immunity.

McDonald v. City of Freeport, Tex., 834 F.Supp. 921.

To withstand motion to dismiss complaint against governmental official on qualified immunity grounds, plaintiff invoking § 1983 must plead specific facts, not merely conclusory allegations; if plaintiff fails to specifically claim constitutional violation, then court must dismiss plaintiff's case. 42 U.S.C.A. § 1983.

McDonald v. City of Freeport, Tex., 834 F.Supp. 921.

Upon motion to dismiss complaint against governmental official under § 1983 on qualified immunity grounds, if plaintiff's complaint specifically states constitutional violation, court must then consider whether right which governmental official allegedly violated was clearly established. 42 U.S.C.A. § 1983.

McDonald v. City of Freeport, Tex., 834 F.Supp. 921.

Upon motion to dismiss complaint against governmental official under § 1983 on qualified immunity grounds, if plaintiff cannot demonstrate clear establishment of alleged right which official allegedly violated, then district court must dismiss. 42 U.S.C.A. § 1983.

McDonald v. City of Freeport, Tex., 834 F.Supp. 921.

Upon motion to dismiss complaint against governmental official under § 1983 on qualified immunity grounds, if constitutional right which official allegedly violated is clearly established, then court must examine objective reasonableness of defendant's conduct in reference to established law. 42 U.S.C.A. § 1983.

McDonald v. City of Freeport, Tex., 834 F.Supp. 921.

E.D.Wis. 1985. Fact that government might not be entitled to all relief it sought in conversion complaint, in particular, that government's request for damages might be inconsistent with proper measure of damages for conversion, did not make complaint one upon which no relief could be granted.

U.S. v. Fullpail Cattle Sales, Inc., 617 F.Supp. 73.

⚷1796. Injunction actions.

Library references

C.J.S. Federal Civil Procedure § 833.

C.A.9 (Alaska) 1995. Claim brought by voter and third party candidate for United States Congress, which sought injunction prohibiting competing congressional candidates from accepting out-of-state campaign contributions on ground that such contributions violated candidate's and voter's rights to free associa-

tion, equal protection, and republican form of government, was frivolous; candidate and voter offered no precedent in any judicial decision to support their claim, and district court could not have granted injunction because it would have abridged people's constitutionally protected liberty to contribute to candidates of their choice. U.S.C.A. Const.Amends. 1, 14.

Whitmore v. Federal Election Com'n, 68 F.3d 1212, as amended, certiorari denied 116 S.Ct. 1543, 517 U.S. 1155, 134 L.Ed.2d 646.

C.A.7 (Ill.) 1989. Injunction ordering insurer to dismiss its California fraud action against investment advisor, entered by Illinois district court in investment advisor's breach of contract action, was improper, where such relief was not requested, and there was no showing that California action was brought to harass advisor.

Asset Allocation and Management Co. v. Western Employers Ins. Co., 892 F.2d 566, on remand Anbar, Inc. v. Western Employers Ins. Co., 1991 WL 139862.

C.A.8 (Neb.) 1989. On former employer's motion for preliminary injunction to enforce noncompetition covenant with former employees, district court, subsequent to finding that covenant was unenforceable as matter of law, properly dismissed employer's claim based on covenant.

Ecolab, Inc. v. Morisette, 879 F.2d 325.

On former employer's motion for preliminary injunction to enforce noncompetition covenant with former employees, district court abused its discretion, subsequent to finding that covenant was unenforceable, in dismissing employer's other claims based on misappropriation of trade secrets, misuse of confidential information, unfair competition, and tortious interference with contractual relations; employer was entitled to have such claims considered in proceeding independent from preliminary injunction hearing.

Ecolab, Inc. v. Morisette, 879 F.2d 325.

C.A.2 (N.Y.) 1981. Complaint by Commodity Futures Trading Commission for preliminary and permanent injunctive relief against corporations and named individuals who engaged in business of commodity futures trading and who refused access to books and records relating to their trading activity was prematurely dismissed, notwithstanding production of all documents requested, where necessity for a permanent injunction based on a finding of reasonable likelihood of future violations was an issue which was not yet resolved. Fed.Rules Civ. Proc. Rules 52(a), 65(a)(2), 28 U.S.C.A.

Commodity Futures Trading Commission v. Incomco, Inc., 649 F.2d 128, on remand 559 F.Supp. 529.

S.D.N.Y. 1993. Claims seeking injunctive relief against state and federal judicial officers, alleging misconduct and corruption, would be dismissed as patently frivolous; only basis for conclusory allegations of misconduct was that defendants issued decisions or rendered orders adverse to plaintiff, who was merely attempting to relitigate adjudicated matters by suing judges who continued to dismiss his frivolous complaints.

Sassower v. Abrams, 833 F.Supp. 253.

S.D.N.Y. 1991. Challenge to government's requested injunctive relief in action under Racketeer Influenced and Corrupt Organizations Act (RICO), that new general election be held at defendant labor organization, was premature on motion to dismiss. 18 U.S.C.A. § 1964.

    U.S. v. District Council of New York City and Vicinity of United Broth. of Carpenters and Joiners of America, 778 F.Supp. 738.

Bkrtcy.E.D.N.Y. 1987. Claims for injunctive relief do not require more particularized and detailed pleading than do other claims in order to survive motion for dismissal for failure to state claim upon which relief can be granted. Fed.Rules Civ.Proc.Rules 8(a), 12(b)(6), 28 U.S.C.A.; Rules Bankr.Proc.Rules 7008(a), 7012(b), 11 U.S.C.A.

    In re Baptist Medical Center of New York, 80 B.R. 637.

⚷**1797. Insurance actions.**

Library references

C.J.S. Federal Civil Procedure § 834.

C.A.11 (Ala.) 1986. Sua sponte dropping of insured's principal stockholder as a plaintiff in insured's action against insurer did not constitute dismissal for failure to state a claim upon which relief could be granted. Fed.Rules Civ. Proc.Rules 12(b)(6), 21, 28 U.S.C.A.

    Lampliter Dinner Theater, Inc. v. Liberty Mut. Ins. Co., 792 F.2d 1036.

C.A.7 (Ill.) 1987. Amended complaint of trustee in bankruptcy of unnamed beneficiary of fire insurance policy issued on three land trusts failed to allege either general or specific performance of conditions precedent in policies, and absent such allegations, amended complaint failed to state cause of action for breach of three fire insurance contracts and required dismissal without prejudice. Fed.Rules Civ.Proc.Rule 9(c), 28 U.S.C.A.

    Redfield v. Continental Cas. Corp., 818 F.2d 596.

N.D.Cal. 1995. Complaint by school district's general commercial liability insurer against district's excess workers' compensation and employers liability insurers would be dismissed without leave to amend, where underlying complaint by employee, which was based on allegations that defendants wrongfully failed to defend and indemnify district in action by district employee and her children, did not trigger duty to defend or indemnify under either defendant's policy, and plaintiff could point to no facts known by defendants that could have created duty to defend. Fed.Rules Civ.Proc.Rule 12(b)(6), 28 U.S.C.A.

    General Star Indem. Co. v. Schools Excess Liability Fund, 888 F.Supp. 1022.

S.D.Cal. 1994. Plaintiff insurer seeking to recover through contribution amounts it paid in settlement of securities litigation, sufficiently pled primary liability of accountants for purposes of 10b–5, to avoid motion to dismiss even though the liability alleged was not for statements made in reports certified by the accountants. Securities Exchange Act of 1934, § 10(b), 15 U.S.C.A. § 78j(b); 17 C.F.R. § 240.10b–5.

    Employers Ins. of Wausau v. Musick, Peeler, & Garrett, 871 F.Supp. 381, opinion amended on reconsideration 948 F.Supp. 942.

C.D.Ill. 1981. Peoria Union Stock Yards Co. v. Penn Mut. Life Ins. Co., 518 F.Supp. 1302, reversed 698 F.2d 320.

N.D.Ill. 1993. Dismissal of complaint would be improper in action for breach of insurance contract under Illinois law if any set of facts existed under which insured could recover interest costs it sought as damages as part of its action. Fed.Rules Civ.Proc.Rule 12(b)(6), 28 U.S.C.A.

    Heller Intern. Corp. v. Sharp, 839 F.Supp. 1297.

N.D.Ill. 1989. Undeveloped factual circumstances precluded resolution within context of a motion to dismiss of issue of whether insured gave timely notice of occurrence to comprehensive general liability insurer.

    W.E. O'Neil Const. Co. v. National Union Fire Ins. Co. of Pittsburgh, Pa., 721 F.Supp. 984.

E.D.Ky. 1989. Court would not dismiss claims of lender, who was insured under blanket bond policy, that fraudulent loans made by employees of lender to corporations should have been aggregated under Kentucky law, even though aggregation law did not apply to corporations; if court pierced corporate veil of corporate entities, loans could be aggregated. KRS 287.280.

    Federal Deposit Ins. Corp. v. Reliance Ins. Corp., 716 F.Supp. 1001.

E.D.La. 1988. Grant of dismissal without prejudice of an action of insurer to permit bankruptcy debtor to pursue the action in bankruptcy court was not justified, where debtor failed to follow court orders to amend petition to substitute bankruptcy trustee as proper party plaintiff and to allege cause of action on negotiated instrument, although debtor alleged it had not been able to acquire permission from additional payees to represent them as additional plaintiffs and alleged it would be in best interest of all parties to have lawsuit dismissed without prejudice to further resolution of any other disputes in bankruptcy court.

> Transload & Transport, Inc. v. American Marine Underwriters, Inc., 94 B.R. 416.

E.D.La. 1988. Complaint alleging almost complete failure on insurance company's part to comply with its various contract obligations with insurance salesman satisfied Rule 11's good faith pleading requirements and was not so vague as to preclude responsive answer by defendants; thus, neither dismissal of pleadings on grounds of impermissible vagueness, nor order requiring plaintiffs to plead more definite statement, was warranted. Fed.Rules Civ.Proc. Rules 9(f), 11, 28 U.S.C.A.

> Cowan v. Fidelity Interstate Life Ins. Co., 89 B.R. 564.

D.Me. 1990. Whether protections for insurance purchasing groups included in Federal Product Liability Risk Retention Act were violated by Maine statutes requiring purchasing groups to buy insurance from insurers licensed by Maine or from licensed agent or broker acting pursuant to surplus lines laws and regulations as Maine statutes were applied could not be determined without factual record, for purposes of preemption as applied argument, so complaint allegations were sufficient to withstand motion to dismiss for failure to state a claim on which relief can be granted. 24–A M.R.S.A. §§ 404, 6097, 6099, subd. 1; Products Liability Risk Retention Act of 1981, § 4(a), 15 U.S.C.A. § 3903(a); U.S.C.A. Const. Art. 6, cl. 2.

> City Cab Co. v. Edwards, 745 F.Supp. 757.

D.N.J. 1980. Fidelity & Deposit Co. of Maryland v. Hudson United Bank, 493 F.Supp. 434, reversed 653 F.2d 766.

N.D.Tex. 1992. It is appropriate to examine face of insurance contract which forms basis of suit on motion to dismiss for failure to state claim upon which relief can be granted; if contract sued upon unambiguously reveals that claimant is not entitled to coverage, then dismissal is proper. Fed.Rules Civ.Proc.Rule 12(b)(6), 28 U.S.C.A.

> Bartley v. National Union Fire Ins. Co. of Pittsburgh, Pa., 824 F.Supp. 624.

On motion to dismiss for failure to state claim, court had to determine not merely whether insureds' cause of action existed as one capable of supporting suit, but whether insureds had valid claim against insurer under any possible theory. Fed.Rules Civ.Proc.Rule 12(b)(6), 28 U.S.C.A.

> Bartley v. National Union Fire Ins. Co. of Pittsburgh, Pa., 824 F.Supp. 624.

⬤**1798. Land, actions involving in general.**

Library references

> C.J.S. Federal Civil Procedure § 839.

C.A.9 (Cal.) 1990. Motions to dismiss and motions for summary judgment must be viewed with particular skepticism when property owner contends that it has been deprived of property through governmental regulation in violation of due process. U.S.C.A. Const.Amends. 5, 14.

> Del Monte Dunes at Monterey, Ltd. v. City of Monterey, 920 F.2d 1496, appeal after remand 95 F.3d 1422, rehearing granted 118 F.3d 660, rehearing en banc denied 127 F.3d 1149, certiorari granted 118 S.Ct. 1359, 140 L.Ed.2d 509.

E.D.N.Y. 1987. Government's cross claim in quiet title action would not be dismissed for failure to state an actionable claim in bank's action seeking foreclosure of mortgages on three properties which were subject of constructive trust claims by United States although defendants could request more definite statement of pleading. Fed.Rules Civ.Proc.Rule 12(e), 28 U.S.C.A.

> U.S. v. Rivieccio, 661 F.Supp. 281 1987 WL 15271.

⬤**1799. Leases, actions involving.**

Library references

> C.J.S. Federal Civil Procedure §§ 829, 839.

⬤**1800. Libel and slander, actions for.**

Library references

> C.J.S. Federal Civil Procedure § 835.

N.D.Ill. 1990. Failure to plead exact words used by employer, as required to state defamation claim under Illinois law, did not require dismissal of claim, but required employee to give more definite statement of words allegedly used within ten days. Fed.Rules Civ. Proc.Rule 12(b)(6), (e), 28 U.S.C.A.

> Hoth v. American States Ins. Co., 735 F.Supp. 290.

N.D.Ind. 1984. Lepucki v. Van Wormer, 587 F.Supp. 1390, affirmed 765 F.2d 86, certiorari denied Hyde v. Van Wormer, 106 S.Ct. 86, 474 U.S. 827, 88 L.Ed.2d 71.

D.Kan. 1997. General rule of liberally construing complaint when considering motions to dismiss for failure to state a claim is inapplicable to certain traditionally disfavored causes of action, including defamation; in such instances, courts tend to construe complaint by somewhat stricter standard. Fed.Rules Civ. Proc.Rules 8(a), 12(b)(6), 28 U.S.C.A.

Classic Communications, Inc. v. Rural Telephone Service Co., Inc., 956 F.Supp. 910, reconsideration denied 1997 WL 231087.

E.D.Mo. 1985. In ruling on motion under Federal Civil Rule 12(b)(6) to dismiss libel suit for failure to state claim for relief, court must determine whether particular words or statements are libelous. Fed.Rules Civ.Proc.Rule 12(b)(6), 28 U.S.C.A.

Quartana v. Utterback, 609 F.Supp. 72, reversed 789 F.2d 1297.

⚩1801. Mortgages, actions involving.

Library references

C.J.S. Federal Civil Procedure §§ 829, 839.

N.D.Ind. 1990. Defendant failed to state cause of action against judge upon which relief could be granted in that claim against judge was irrelevant to mortgage foreclosure action and judge was not party to the action. Fed. Rules Civ.Proc.Rule 12(b)(6), 28 U.S.C.A.

Federal Nat. Mortg. Ass'n v. Cobb, 738 F.Supp. 1220.

W.D.Tex. 1994. Trust beneficiary's allegations of standing based on trustee's waiver of compliance with trust agreement's procedures for presentment of claims to trustee were sufficient to overcome mortgage company's motion to dismiss for failure to state a claim in beneficiary's action against mortgage company for its performance under trust agreement. Fed.Rules Civ.Proc.Rule 12(b)(6), 28 U.S.C.A.

Teacher Retirement System of Texas v. Reilly Mortg. Group, Inc., 154 F.R.D. 156.

⚩1802. Negligence, actions for in general.

Library references

C.J.S. Federal Civil Procedure § 836.

S.D.N.Y. 1992. Conclusory allegations of ineffective assistance in civil suit against criminal defense attorney were subject to dismissal, though dismissal should be stayed for 45 days to permit plaintiff to make showing of facts in support of allegations not previously adjudicated.

D'Souza v. Howell, 794 F.Supp. 517.

E.D.Wis. 1994. Multiple counts of patient's complaint against surgeon were not subject to dismissal for failure to state a claim on grounds that, under Wisconsin law, there was but one cause of action where there was but single unit of negligent medical treatment and that such cause of action was stated in first count of complaint; case law cited by surgeon merely provided that patient did not have to bring more than one lawsuit where continuum of negligent medical treatment was alleged, and various counts of complaint adequately presented patient's negligence claims based on surgeon's alleged continuum of wrongful treatment. Fed.Rules Civ.Proc.Rule 12(b)(6), 28 U.S.C.A.

Nunley v. Kloehn, 158 F.R.D. 614.

Bkrtcy.S.D.Ohio 1991. Whether doctrine of in pari delicto should bar Chapter 7 trustee's claim that attorneys committed malpractice by advising and assisting debtor in certain real estate transactions and conveyances could not be determined only from complaint, and therefore attorneys' motion to dismiss could not be granted. Fed.Rules Civ.Proc.Rule 12(b)(6), 28 U.S.C.A.; Fed.Rules Bankr.Proc.Rule 7012, 11 U.S.C.A.

In re Dow, 132 B.R. 853.

⚩1803. Negotiable instruments, actions involving.

Library references

C.J.S. Federal Civil Procedure §§ 829, 839.

S.D.N.Y. 1988. Determination of whether individual is holder in due course generally raises subjective factual issues of individual's actual knowledge, which are ill-suited for resolution on motion to dismiss. Fed.Rules Civ. Proc.Rule 12(b)(6), 28 U.S.C.A.; N.Y.McKinney's Uniform Commercial Code § 3–305.

Leeming v. Dean Witter Reynolds Inc., 676 F.Supp. 541.

⚩1804. Personalty, actions involving in general.

Library references

C.J.S. Federal Civil Procedure § 839.

C.A.2 (N.Y.) 1992. Pro se petition for return of property seized at time of arrest should not have been dismissed without hearing as untimely motion under Criminal Procedure Rule 41(e); whether petition was treated as Rule 41(e) motion or complaint under Tort Claims Act, court should have taken evidence, determined if any of property was still in Government's possession, and, if not, whether Government's conduct with respect to property rendered Government liable for damages. Fed. Rules Cr.Proc.Rule 41(e), 18 U.S.C.A.; 28 U.S.C.A. § 2671 et seq.

Mora v. U.S., 955 F.2d 156.

⚩1805–1806. ***For other cases see earlier editions of this digest, the Decennial Digests, and WESTLAW.***

Library references

C.J.S. Federal Civil Procedure.

⚷**1807. Rescission of contracts.**

Library references

C.J.S. Federal Civil Procedure § 829.

D.Kan. 1988. Practicability of rescinding portion of settlement agreement in class action was not before district court at pleading stage; thus, dismissal of rescission claim would be premature.

Raymark Industries, Inc. v. Stemple, 714 F.Supp. 460.

⚷**1808. Specific performance.**

Library references

C.J.S. Federal Civil Procedure § 839.

⚷**1809. Stockholders', investors, and other class actions.**

Library references

C.J.S. Federal Civil Procedure § 827.

C.A.D.C. 1986. Complaint under Racketeer Influenced and Corrupt Organizations Act which alleged predicate acts in form of misstatements and omissions in proxy statement that were insufficient for liability under securities laws would be dismissed. 18 U.S.C.A. §§ 1961–1968.

Berg v. First American Bankshares, Inc., 796 F.2d 489, 254 U.S.App.D.C. 198.

C.A.2 (Conn.) 1995. Magistrate should not have incorporated securities fraud claim against officer of English corporation, being sued for stock fraud, with claims against corporation, and dismissed claim against resident officer, without considering whether cause of action was stated for stock fraud involving officer's sale of shares of English corporation on same day that securities fraud claimant had purchased shares on London exchange, as a possible insider trading violation. Securities Exchange Act of 1934, §§ 10(b), 20, 15 U.S.C.A. §§ 78j(b), 78t; 17 C.F.R. § 240.10b–5.

Itoba Ltd. v. Lep Group PLC, 54 F.3d 118, certiorari denied Berkley v. Itoba Ltd., 116 S.Ct. 702, 516 U.S. 1044, 133 L.Ed.2d 659, certiorari denied 116 S.Ct. 703, 516 U.S. 1044, appeal after remand 930 F.Supp. 36.

C.A.11 (Ga.) 1985. In class action brought on behalf of minority shareholders of one corporation alleging that second corporation and several other corporate and individual defendants had entered into a conspiracy to "freeze out" first corporation's minority shareholders at an unconscionably unfair price through fraud and deception, plaintiff deliberately chose to forego his opportunity to cure the defects of his complaint against second corporation, despite specific and repeated warnings from the trial judge that such amendment was necessary to avoid dismissal, and the trial judge thus properly granted second corporation's motion to dismiss for failure to state a claim and for failure to plead fraud with particularity. Fed.Rules Civ. Proc.Rules 9(b), 12(b)(6), 28 U.S.C.A.

Friedlander v. Nims, 755 F.2d 810.

C.A.10 (Okl.) 1986. The dismissal of complaint or counterclaim for failing to satisfy the pleading with particularity requirements of Federal Rule of Civil Procedure is treated as a dismissal for failure to state a claim upon which relief can be granted. Fed.Rules Civ.Proc.Rules 8, 9(b), 12(b)(6), 28 U.S.C.A.

Seattle-First Nat. Bank v. Carlstedt, 800 F.2d 1008, on remand 678 F.Supp. 1543.

N.D.Cal. 1986. Count in securities fraud suit seeking rescissionary damages, but not injunction, for alleged violation of California statute providing only for injunctive relief or other orders in support of injunction was required to be dismissed, notwithstanding that court might have ordered rescission or restitution as ancillary remedy. West's Ann.Cal.Bus. & Prof.Code §§ 17500 et seq., 17535.

David K. Lindemuth Co. v. Shannon Financial Corp., 637 F.Supp. 991.

S.D.Cal. 1994. Court would dismiss fraud claims asserted under laws of California and New York, requiring that securities fraud be pled with particularity, after dismissing federal securities fraud claims on same grounds. Securities Exchange Act of 1934, § 10(b), 15 U.S.C.A. § 78j(b); Fed.Rules Civ.Proc.Rule 9(b), 28 U.S.C.A.

Steiner v. Hale, 868 F.Supp. 284.

D.Del. 1988. Under Delaware law, shareholders' pendent state law claims of violation of fiduciary duty, waste of corporate assets, and improper purpose were properly brought as derivative claims and were dismissed where similar derivative claims were already pled in petition.

In re General Motors Class E Stock Buyout Securities Litigation, 694 F.Supp. 1119, reargument granted 790 F.Supp. 77.

N.D.Ill. 1993. Failure to plead compliance with statute of limitations applicable to federal securities claims justified dismissal of investors' securities claims. Securities Exchange Act of 1934, §§ 9(e), 10(b), 15 U.S.C.A. §§ 78i(e), 78j(b); Securities Act of 1933, § 12(2), 15 U.S.C.A. § 77l (2).

Tregenza v. Great American Communications Co., 823 F.Supp. 1409, affirmed 12 F.3d 717, certiorari denied 114 S.Ct. 1837, 511 U.S. 1085, 128 L.Ed.2d 465.

N.D.Ill. 1991. Claims of purchasers of interests in real estate investments against investment advisor for violation of ERISA, common-law fraud, violation of Illinois Securities Law, violation of Illinois Consumer Fraud and Deceptive Business Practices Act, breach of fiduciary duty, and negligent misrepresentation would be dismissed for failure to allege loss causation, even though no authority was asserted that loss causation was essential element of any of those claims, where purchasers had effectively conceded such requirement. Employee Retirement Income Security Act of 1974, § 2 et seq., 29 U.S.C.A. § 1001 et seq.; Ill.S.H.A. ch. 121½, ¶¶ 137.1 et seq., 261 et seq.

> Lewis v. Hermann, 775 F.Supp. 1137, reconsideration denied 783 F.Supp. 1131, reinstatement denied 1992 WL 57939.

N.D.Ill. 1990. Federal district court would not dismiss minority shareholder's derivative claim on behalf of corporation where minority shareholder adequately alleged demand upon corporation in his complaint, which was only source of facts on which court could rely for purposes of motion to dismiss; consideration of other, potentially undisputed facts, which allegedly entitled defendants to dismissal pending findings of corporation's special litigation committee, could not be considered unless presented by appropriate motion. Fed.Rules Civ.Proc. Rules 12(b), 23.1, 28 U.S.C.A.

> Grafman v. Century Broadcasting Corp., 743 F.Supp. 544.

N.D.Ill. 1987. Plaintiff in derivative action maintained on behalf of corporation was required to verify his complaint, but his failure to do so did not entitle defendants to summary dismissal when failure was curable by amendment. Fed.Rules Civ.Proc.Rule 23.1, 28 U.S.C.A.

> Halsted Video, Inc. v. Guttillo, 115 F.R.D. 177.

N.D.Ill. 1986. Investor's securities fraud claim would not be dismissed as "sham" under Rule 11, though broker's testimony that he had participated in churning of investor's accounts was rendered virtually worthless by investor's promise to pay him up to 20% of recovery, where broker's testimony was allegedly corroborated by his personal trading records. Fed. Rules Civ.Proc.Rule 11, 28 U.S.C.A.

> Wagner v. Lehman Bros. Kuhn Loeb Inc., 646 F.Supp. 643.

D.Mass. 1991. Dismissal of investor's individual claim under § 10(b) and Rule 10b–5 required dismissal of entire class action on claim, where class had not been certified at time of dismissal and individual investor failed to allege that he was member of class of purchasers who relied on misrepresentations in connection with purchase of stock. Securities Exchange Act of 1934, § 10(b), 15 U.S.C.A. § 78j(b).

> Boyle v. Merrimack Bancorp, Inc., 756 F.Supp. 55.

W.D.Mich. 1988. Failure of securities broker and its principal to retain counsel and amend complaint to comply with requirements for shareholder derivative suit as ordered by court warranted dismissal of complaint against NASD and officials. Fed.Rules Civ.Proc.Rule 23.1, 28 U.S.C.A.

> Prevatte v. National Ass'n of Securities Dealers, Inc., 682 F.Supp. 913.

D.N.H. 1996. On motion to dismiss securities claim based on statements of industry analyst for failure to state cause of action, court will determine whether complaint contains allegations which, favorably construed and viewed in context of entire pleading, could establish significant and specific, not merely casual or speculative, entanglement between defendants and analysts with respect to statements at issue. Securities Exchange Act of 1934, § 10(b), 15 U.S.C.A. § 78j(b); Fed.Rules Civ.Proc.Rule 12(b)(6), 28 U.S.C.A.

> Schaffer v. Timberland Co., 924 F.Supp. 1298.

D.N.J. 1991. Motion to dismiss shareholder's derivative complaint for failure to meet demand requirement is determined by reviewing the sufficiency of the allegations of the complaint. Fed.Rules Civ.Proc.Rule 23.1, 28 U.S.C.A.

> Abrams v. Koether, 766 F.Supp. 237.

Dismissal of shareholder's derivative complaint because of inadequacy of demand does not implicate the merits of the complaint and is based only on the sufficiency of the pleadings. Fed.Rules Civ.Proc.Rule 23.1, 28 U.S.C.A.

> Abrams v. Koether, 766 F.Supp. 237.

E.D.N.Y. 1986. Customer's claims that brokerage firm was liable for acts of salesman on basis of principal and agent law were duplicative of respondeat superior claims and would be dismissed.

> Morris v. Gilbert, 649 F.Supp. 1491.

E. & S.D.N.Y. 1991. Court need not dismiss entire class action for lack of subject matter jurisdiction of certain individual class members.

> In re Joint Eastern and Southern Dist. Asbestos Litigation, 129 B.R. 710, vacated 982 F.2d 721, opinion modified on rehearing 993 F.2d 7.

S.D.N.Y. 1996. Dismissal on materiality grounds of securities fraud complaint alleging misrepresentation or nondisclosure of a fact is appropriate only if plaintiff could prove no facts under allegations of pleading that would permit trier to find fact material. Securities Act of 1933, § 12(2), 15 U.S.C.(1994 Ed.) § 77l(2);

Securities Exchange Act of 1934, § 10(b), 15 U.S.C.A. § 78j(b); 17 C.F.R. § 240.10b–5.

L.L. Capital Partners, L.P. v. Rockefeller Center Properties, Inc., 921 F.Supp. 1174.

S.D.N.Y. 1995. Complaint alleging control person liability under Securities Exchange Act would not be dismissed, based upon statements made by plaintiffs in motion papers; plaintiffs had made allegations sufficient to state cause of action for control person liability in complaint, shifting burden to prove otherwise to defendants in later stage of proceedings. Securities Exchange Act of 1934, § 20(a), 15 U.S.C.A. § 78t(a).

Miele v. Greyling, 892 F.Supp. 107.

S.D.N.Y. 1995. Assertion by corporation and its current sole shareholder that former officer breached his fiduciary duty to corporation through alleged diversion of corporate assets to improvement of former officer's property stated colorable claim for breach of officer's fiduciary duty under New York law and joined material issues of fact, thus precluding dismissal or summary judgment; corporation and shareholder did not have to show that they could not have uncovered alleged diversion with reasonable diligence. Fed.Rules Civ.Proc.Rules 12(b)(6), 56, 28 U.S.C.A.

Red Ball Interior Demolition Corp. v. Palmadessa, 874 F.Supp. 576.

S.D.N.Y. 1990. Shareholder's attempt to prosecute direct class action and derivative action simultaneously did not provide basis for dismissal for failure to state claim, even though attempt could serve as reason to refuse class certification. Fed.Rules Civ.Proc.Rules 12(b)(6), 23, 28 U.S.C.A.

Brickman v. Tyco Toys, Inc., 731 F.Supp. 101.

S.D.N.Y. 1990. Partnership that qualified as investment company with more than 100 beneficial owners under Investment Company Act was not entitled to have dismissed as moot action by closed-end management investment company whose stock partnership held in violation of the Act, although partnership claimed it had abandoned tender offer, severed ties to other limited partnerships which were a part of tender vehicle, and avowed that no agreements or understandings existed between those limited partnerships and defendant partnership. Investment Company Act of 1940, § 12(d)(1)(A), 15 U.S.C.A. § 80a–12(d)(1)(A).

Clemente Global Growth Fund, Inc. v. Pickens, 729 F.Supp. 1439.

S.D.N.Y. 1988. Amended complaint which failed to specify circumstances constituting fraud in connection with sale of securities with requisite particularity justified dismissal with prejudice; despite explicit instructions from court, amended complaint failed to identify representative who sold purchasers certificates, time that sales were made, and commissions or representations which were misleading by virtue of omissions. Fed.Rules Civ.Proc.Rule 9(b), 28 U.S.C.A.

Sanderson v. Roethenmund, 682 F.Supp. 205.

S.D.N.Y. 1986. Courts should be particularly hesitant to dismiss a securities law complaint on grounds of immateriality of an omission or misstatement. Fed.Rules Civ.Proc.Rule 12(b)(6), 28 U.S.C.A.; Securities Exchange Act of 1934, § 10(b), 15 U.S.C.A. § 78j(b); Securities Act of 1933, §§ 11, 12(2), 15 U.S.C.A. §§ 77k, 77*l* (2).

In re Union Carbide Class Action Securities Litigation, 648 F.Supp. 1322.

S.D.N.Y. 1985. On motion to dismiss, plaintiffs who alleged that account managers liquidated large positions of other customers in abrupt, unreasonable and disorderly fashion shortly before liquidating plaintiffs' account, artificially depressing market price, and that managers profited from malicious liquidation in market manipulation, pleaded requisite facts with sufficient particularity to sustain claim for fraud. Securities Exchange Act of 1934, § 10(b), 15 U.S.C.A. § 78j(b); Fed.Rules Civ. Proc.Rule 9(b), 28 U.S.C.A.

Modern Settings, Inc. v. Prudential-Bache Securities, Inc., 603 F.Supp. 370.

S.D.N.Y. 1981. Kirshner v. Goldberg, 506 F.Supp. 454, affirmed 742 F.2d 1430.

E.D.Pa. 1991. Fact that named plaintiffs in securities fraud class action could not demonstrate reliance did not require dismissal of action; given fact that complaint alleged that there were over 1,000 class members, class attorneys were entitled to opportunity to find acceptable named plaintiffs. Securities Exchange Act of 1934, § 1 et seq., 15 U.S.C.A. § 78a et seq.; Fed.Rules Civ.Proc.Rule 23, 28 U.S.C.A.

Gruber v. Price Waterhouse, 776 F.Supp. 1044.

W.D.Pa. 1993. Conclusory allegation that defendants sold or solicited purchase of securities will withstand motion to dismiss in action brought under section of Securities Act of 1933 regarding false prospectuses only if accompanied by allegations of fact that defendants did sell or solicit purchase of securities. Securities Act of 1933, § 12(2), as amended, 15 U.S.C.A.

§ 77*l* (2);   Fed.Rules Civ.Proc.Rule 9(b), 28 U.S.C.A.

> In re Westinghouse Securities Litigation, 832 F.Supp. 948, affirmed in part, reversed in part 90 F.3d 696, on remand 1998 WL 119554.

D.Utah 1994.   Complaint alleging violations of Racketeer Influenced and Corrupt Organizations Act (RICO), securities law and various pendent state claims, would be dismissed for failure to comply with Civil Procedure Rule 8 requiring that pleadings contain short and plain statement of claim and that averments be simple, concise and direct; despite warning issued in rejection of earlier complaints, claimants continued to advance irrelevant and redundant allegations and consistently make repetitive legal conclusions unsupported by relevant facts, and to utilize sentences with passive verbs and awkward sentence construction making it difficult to read and identify wrongs complained of, perpetrators and victims.   Fed.Rules Civ. Proc.Rule 8, 28 U.S.C.A.

> Arena Land & Inv. Co., Inc. v. Petty, 906 F.Supp. 1470, affirmed 69 F.3d 547.

Bkrtcy.W.D.Mich. 1991.   Suit filed as class action is not subject to dismissal, even though it fails to meet requirements for class certification, if suit also states claim for relief against named defendant or defendants individually.   Fed. Rules Civ.Proc.Rule 23, 28 U.S.C.A.

> In re Check Reporting Services, Inc., 133 B.R. 392.

⚷**1810. Tax actions.**

Library references

> C.J.S. Federal Civil Procedure § 837.

C.D.Cal. 1993.   Despite substantial doubt with which district court viewed state taxpayers' prospects for actually generating triable issue of material fact as to purpose and effect prongs of *Lemon* test, with respect to their complaint that university's reimbursing professor for his participation at conferences that allegedly attacked particular religion violated establishment clause, allegations in complaint did not fail in these respects for purposes of 12(b)(6) dismissal.   Fed.Rules Civ.Proc.Rule 12(b)(6), 28 U.S.C.A.; U.S.C.A. Const.Amend. 1.

> Van Dyke v. Regents of University of California, 815 F.Supp. 1341.

For purposes of 12(b)(6) dismissal, state taxpayers failed to allege facts showing excessive government entanglement with religion, so as to violate establishment clause, with respect to university's reimbursing its professor for his participation at conferences that allegedly attacked particular religion; to grant taxpayers' request and bar university from reimbursing professor for such activities would require state to evaluate whether various activities were anti-religious, pro-religion, or neutral, thereby producing very entanglement that establishment clause prohibits.   Fed.Rules Civ.Proc.Rule 12(b)(6), 28 U.S.C.A.; U.S.C.A. Const.Amend. 1.

> Van Dyke v. Regents of University of California, 815 F.Supp. 1341.

D.Hawai'i 1992.   Claim for injunction based on allegation in complaint that government has been issuing collections summonses to corporations' financial institutions as means of collecting tax assessments was not so vague as to require dismissal; discovery or motion for more definite statement may clarify allegations. 26 U.S.C.A. § 7426.

> Kersting v. U.S., 818 F.Supp. 297.

N.D.Iowa 1992.   Internal Revenue Service (IRS) was not entitled to dismissal, on limitations grounds, of taxpayer's conservator's action for refund of "advance deposits" or "unclassified collections" for certain years; conservator alleged that taxpayer suffered from mental illness when she made those remittances, and mental illness, if legally proven, could toll statute of limitations.   26 U.S.C.A. § 6511(b)(2)(A).

> Wiltgen v. U.S., 813 F.Supp. 1387.

E.D.Mich. 1995.   Pro se civil litigant's complaint, which was apparently intended to challenge tax laws, was insufficient to meet federal pleading requirements and would be dismissed; complaint did not set forth basis for jurisdiction, did not contain sufficient facts to give notice of nature of claims, and did not contain prayer for relief.   Fed.Rules Civ.Proc. Rules 8(a), 12(b)(1, 6), 28 U.S.C.A.

> Anderson v. Office of Atty. Gen., Dept. of Justice, 890 F.Supp. 648.

9th Cir.BAP (Cal.) 1994.   Allegations in tax protestor's complaint, that federal income tax assessments were constitutionally impermissible since Congress never intended U.S. citizens earning only ordinary wages to be liable for personal income tax, were patently frivolous and warranted dismissal of complaint for failure to state claim upon which relief could be granted.

> In re Robnett, 165 B.R. 272.

⚷**1811. Tort actions in general.**

Library references

> C.J.S. Federal Civil Procedure § 838.

C.A.11 (Ala.) 1989.   Dismissal of Racketeer Influenced and Corrupt Organizations Act claim against offerors of tax exempt bonds issued to finance residential and medical facility for elderly were properly dismissed, where predicate acts required for RICO claim consisted of fraudulent sale of bonds, and federal securities fraud claim was dismissed. (Per Anderson, Circuit Judge, with Roney, Chief Judge, and three Circuit Judges concurring and one Circuit Judge

For later cases see same Topic and Key Number in Pocket Part

concurring in result.) Securities Exchange Act of 1934, § 10(b), 15 U.S.C.A. § 78j(b); 18 U.S.C.A. § 1961 et seq.

> Ross v. Bank South, N.A., 885 F.2d 723, certiorari denied 110 S.Ct. 1924, 495 U.S. 905, 109 L.Ed.2d 287.

C.A.9 (Alaska) 1988. Dismissal of complaint for failure to plead fraud with particularity was proper when, after plaintiffs failed to comply with initial order to amend, but instead improperly appealed order, plaintiffs were given another chance to amend complaint, but merely refiled proposed amended complaint which trial court had already found defective. Fed.Rules Civ.Proc.Rule 8(a), 28 U.S.C.A.

> Sparling v. Hoffman Const. Co., Inc., 864 F.2d 635.

C.A.2 (Conn.) 1994. District court did not abuse its discretion in dismissing securities fraud claim for failure to plead fraud with sufficient particularity, even though court did not grant plaintiff leave to amend her complaint; plaintiff had already substantively amended her complaint once before, and she did not ask district court for leave to amend it further. Securities Exchange Act of 1934, § 10(b), 15 U.S.C.A. § 78j(b); Fed.Rules Civ. Proc.Rule 9(b), 28 U.S.C.A.

> Shields v. Citytrust Bancorp, Inc., 25 F.3d 1124.

C.A.2 (Conn.) 1992. District should grant motion to dismiss Racketeer Influenced and Corrupt Organizations claim only if it is clear that no relief could be granted under any set of facts that could be proved consistent with allegations. 18 U.S.C.A. § 1961 et seq.

> McLaughlin v. Anderson, 962 F.2d 187.

C.A.11 (Fla.) 1990. Issue of material fact as to whether government agent was acting within scope of his employment when he attended Christmas parties and afterwards was involved in automobile accident precluded dismissal of other driver's Federal Tort Claims Act suit against United States for lack of subject matter jurisdiction. Fed.Rules Civ.Proc.Rules 12(b)(1), 56, 28 U.S.C.A.; 28 U.S.C.A. § 1346(b).

> Lawrence v. Dunbar, 919 F.2d 1525.

C.A.7 (Ill.) 1993. Medical malpractice plaintiff who pled specific failures of three named doctors, unnamed residents and hospital employees in her first three complaints waived claims of hospital's negligence based on additional negligent acts and failures not alleged in first three complaints. Fed.Rules Civ.Proc. Rules 8(a), 56(e), 28 U.S.C.A.

> Johnson v. Methodist Medical Center of Illinois, 10 F.3d 1300, rehearing and suggestion for rehearing denied, certiorari denied 114 S.Ct. 2102, 511 U.S. 1107, 128 L.Ed.2d 664.

C.A.7 (Ill.) 1988. Steel buyer's claim that steel was negligently and defectively manufactured by supplier and that tanks and bins manufactured from the steel and sold by buyer accordingly sustained severe cracking and splitting was properly dismissed under Illinois law on theory tort remedies were not available in suits for economic loss arising from breach of contract; *Maxfield* decision upholding action by home builder against manufacturer and supplier of roof trusses alleging tortious conduct on theory of implied contract for indemnification would be interpreted as narrow exception arising as solution to situation where statute of limitations applicable to implied warranty provisions had elapsed, and steel buyer was not barred by statute of limitations from bringing its warranty claims against steel supplier. Ill.S.H.A. ch. 26, ¶ 2–725; ch. 70, ¶ 302.

> Bethlehem Steel Corp. v. Chicago Eastern Corp., 863 F.2d 508.

C.A.7 (Ill.) 1985. If false, statement to television reporter that judge said that customer of appliance repair company had a good case against company was actionable, and it was premature to dismiss that claim at the pleading stage on the ground that it was just one person's opinion.

> Action Repair, Inc. v. American Broadcasting Companies, Inc., 776 F.2d 143.

C.A.8 (Iowa) 1988. Debtor's failure to allege time, place and content of all false representations allegedly made by bank's collection employee, even after having been given both opportunity to amend and court warning that dismissal would result, warranted dismissal of debtor's RICO and Fair Debt Collection Practices Act. 18 U.S.C.A. §§ 1961–1968; Consumer Credit Protection Act §§ 102–817, as amended, 15 U.S.C.A. §§ 1601–1692o.

> Lally v. Crawford County Trust & Sav. Bank, Denison, Iowa, 863 F.2d 612.

C.A.6 (Ky.) 1994. Where product itself is unavailable as evidence in products liability action, dismissal of case or granting of summary judgment is not necessarily mandated; if case is based on design defect, plaintiff could demonstrate through expert testimony that product's design was defective and therefore each product was defective, and, even if case was not based on design defect, plaintiff would not be prohibited from trying to prove its case without specific product.

> Beil v. Lakewood Engineering and Mfg. Co., 15 F.3d 546.

C.A.4 (Md.) 1995. Fact that woman labeled her claim as one for "sexual molestation," which was not recognized as separate tort in Nevada, did not warrant dismissal of woman's claim that, when she was 17, her brother-in-law engaged in nonconsensual sexual relations with her in his home in Nevada, where complaint pleaded cause of action for battery and where brother-in-law was aware throughout proceedings of legal and factual basis for action. Fed. Rules Civ.Proc.Rules 8(a)(2), 12(b)(6), 28 U.S.C.A.

Labram v. Havel, 43 F.3d 918.

C.A.1 (Mass.) 1994. Because each of three counts of complaint alleging RICO violations required different element of proof, judgment for defendants is a matter of law and count alleging association-in-fact enterprise did not require dismissal of other counts. 18 U.S.C.A. § 1962(c, d).

Aetna Cas. Sur. Co. v. P & B Autobody, 43 F.3d 1546.

C.A.2 (N.Y.) 1998. Plaintiffs failed to make prima facie showing that Japanese automobile manufacturing corporation was subject to personal jurisdiction under New York long-arm statute, based on presence there of its American subsidiary, and thus were not entitled to discovery on issue in connection with corporation's motion to dismiss products liability action for lack of jurisdiction; allegations failed to show that subsidiary was either agent or mere department of Japanese corporation, as required under statute. N.Y.McKinney's CPLR 301; Fed. Rules Civ.Proc.Rule 12(b)(2), 28 U.S.C.A.

Jazini v. Nissan Motor Co., Ltd., 148 F.3d 181.

C.A.2 (N.Y.) 1991. Allegations of fraud which were made upon information and belief, and which did not identify with particularity the facts upon which that belief was founded, were not sufficient to survive motion to dismiss. Fed. Rules Civ.Proc.Rule 9(b), 28 U.S.C.A.

Stern v. General Elec. Co., 924 F.2d 472, on remand 1992 WL 8195.

C.A.6 (Ohio) 1995. Intentional infliction of emotional distress claims may entirely appropriately be dealt with on summary judgment or on motion to dismiss.

Miller v. Currie, 50 F.3d 373.

C.A.1 (Puerto Rico) 1991. To avert dismissal for failure to state a claim, civil and Racketeer Influenced and Corrupt Organizations Act (RICO) complaint must, at a bare minimum, state facts sufficient to portray specific instances of racketeering activity within reach of RICO statute and causal nexus between that activity and harm alleged. 18 U.S.C.A. §§ 1961–1968.

Miranda v. Ponce Federal Bank, 948 F.2d 41.

C.A.5 (Tex.) 1994. Borrowers' allegation that president of management company that lender hired to manage its mortgaged properties and company's attorney misrepresented ef-

fect of company's appointment as fiduciary of borrowers' properties was sufficiently specific to survive dismissal for failure to plead claim of fraudulent misrepresentation with particularity, where there was evidence that attorney represented that management company would serve as borrowers' fiduciary, and written agreements drafted by attorney repeatedly refer to management company's independent fiduciary powers and that borrowers would entrust their properties to management company. Fed.Rules Civ. Proc.Rule 9(b), 28 U.S.C.A.

Castillo v. First City Bancorporation of Texas, Inc., 43 F.3d 953.

C.A.4 (Va.) 1993. On motion to dismiss libel suit for no actionable statement, court must credit plaintiff's allegation of factual falsity of statement.

Chapin v. Knight-Ridder, Inc., 993 F.2d 1087.

C.A.7 (Wis.) 1979. Preston v. U. S., 596 F.2d 232, certiorari denied 100 S.Ct. 228, 444 U.S. 915, 62 L.Ed.2d 169, appeal after remand 696 F.2d 528, rehearing denied 709 F.2d 488, appeal after remand 776 F.2d 754.

M.D.Ala. 1993. Whether Alabama law would recognize claim for intentional interference with business relations based on interference with relations between local cable operator and potential subscribers was novel issue not subject to resolution on motion to dismiss.

Storer Cable Communications, Inc. v. City of Montgomery, Ala., 826 F.Supp. 1338, vacated 866 F.Supp. 1376.

C.D.Cal. 1991. In order to avoid dismissal for failure to state a claim, RICO plaintiff must plead specific facts, not mere conclusory allegations, which establish existence of enterprise. 18 U.S.C.A. § 1961 et seq.; Fed.Rules Civ.Proc. Rule 12(b)(6), 28 U.S.C.A.

Comwest, Inc. v. American Operator Services, Inc., 765 F.Supp. 1467.

RICO claims based on predicate acts of mail and wire fraud must be dismissed where alleged predicate acts fail to state claim for violation of mail and wire fraud statutes. 18 U.S.C.A. §§ 1341, 1343, 1961 et seq.

Comwest, Inc. v. American Operator Services, Inc., 765 F.Supp. 1467.

N.D.Cal. 1993. Plaintiffs need not conclusively establish by offer of proof the prima facie elements of intentional infliction of emotional distress claim to overcome motion to dismiss; plaintiffs need only allege sufficient facts, which if proved true, would entitle them to relief.

Palm v. U.S., 835 F.Supp. 512.

N.D.Cal. 1989. Complaints, which alleged breach of contract, payment under mistake of fact, and unjust enrichment were sufficiently specific to withstand motion to dismiss for failure to state claim, in action arising out of alleged fraud in connection with contract to monitor and review hospital discharge payments under the Medicare program; complaint provided details about allegedly false certifications, identified false documents, and explained precisely what work defendant was obligated to perform. 31 U.S.C.A. § 3729 et seq.; Fed.Rules Civ.Proc.Rule 12(b)(6), 28 U.S.C.A.

U.S. ex rel. McCoy v. California Medical Review, Inc., 723 F.Supp. 1363.

D.Colo. 1995. Chapter 11 debtor's claim for relief based on alleged "bad faith" was subsumed in her first claim for breach of contract to purchase debtor's commercial property and, thus, had to be dismissed, because under Colorado law breach of covenant of good faith and fair dealing that is implied in every contract does not give rise to independent tort claim.

In re Mullaney, 179 B.R. 942.

D.Colo. 1987. Malicious prosecution complaint of numerous plaintiffs which was based on events allegedly occurring on December 31, 1984, but which asserted that claim did not arise until one plaintiff's acquittal on criminal charges on July 23, 1985, would be dismissed without prejudice to amendment to firmly identify the party or parties for whom the claim was brought and to allege facts avoiding the time bar of the notice provision of the Colorado Governmental Immunity Act. C.R.S. 24–10–109.

Martinez v. El Paso County, 673 F.Supp. 1030.

D.Conn. 1993. Action under Racketeer Influenced and Corrupt Organizations Act (RICO) alleging that defendants fraudulently obtained various mortgages in derogation of demand promissory notes used to finance purchase of real estate from plaintiff generally pled fraud with sufficient particularity; although complaint filled only the haziest outline concerning interstate affect of defendants' enterprise, dismissal was not required, rather, better approach was to permit amendment. 18 U.S.C.A. § 1962(a); Fed.Rules Civ.Proc.Rule 9(b), 28 U.S.C.A.

Young v. Morrissey, 151 F.R.D. 22.

D.D.C. 1986. There was fact question as to whether buyer was reasonably unaware of misrepresentation that he would receive long-term financing within three years of filing of action or whether he could invoke doctrine of "fraudulent concealment," precluding granting of motion to dismiss on ground of District of Columbia's statute of limitations for fraud claims.

Lawson v. Nationwide Mortg. Corp., 628 F.Supp. 804.

M.D.Fla. 1989. Under Florida law, owners of chicken farm alleged facts sufficient, for purposes of dismissal, to raise question concerning qualified or conditional privilege with respect to libel claim against well testing company for advising EPA in written publication that chicken farm's well was contaminated, by asserting that appropriate testing procedures were not followed and that testing was done in negligent manner.

Brenner v. Professional Service Industries, Inc., 710 F.Supp. 1336.

S.D.Fla. 1990. Songwriter alleged that wrongful conduct on part of singer/coauthor in depriving her of royalties from song continued up until after time of trial, and, thus, singer's motion to dismiss songwriter's claim for civil theft on statute of limitation grounds was denied. West's F.S.A. § 772.17; Fed.Rules Civ.Proc.Rule 9(b), 28 U.S.C.A.

Korman v. Iglesias, 736 F.Supp. 261.

N.D.Ill. 1993. Given federal courts' requirement of notice pleading, plaintiff's claim under Illinois law for intentional infliction of emotional distress with respect to defendant's alleged numerous and vulgar phone calls to plaintiff would survive motion to dismiss, despite fact that specific content of calls was unknown. Fed.Rules Civ.Proc.Rule 12(b)(6), 28 U.S.C.A.

Otterbacher v. Northwestern University, 838 F.Supp. 1256.

N.D.Ill. 1993. Allegations in securities fraud complaint adequately set forth time, place, contents, and consequences of any misrepresentations by corporation, officers, and directors, and thus, complaint could not be dismissed for "lumping together" defendants, under civil rule requiring fraud to be alleged with particularity; buyers had no way of knowing which defendant made which representations or omitted which material facts. Fed.Rules Civ.Proc.Rule 9(b), 28 U.S.C.A.

Endo v. Albertine, 812 F.Supp. 1479, reconsideration denied 1995 WL 170030.

N.D.Ill. 1988. Paragraph of RICO civil action complaint stating that in furtherance of allegedly fraudulent tax shelter scheme, defendants used or caused to be used the telephone on numerous occasions and thereby violated wire fraud statute would be dismissed, where complaint nowhere gave any details about purported telephone calls, such as approximately when they were made, for what purpose, or who was called, and there was no allegation that telephone calls were interstate calls. 18 U.S.C.A. §§ 1343, 1961–1968; Fed.Rules Civ. Proc.Rule 9(b), 28 U.S.C.A.

Balabanos v. North American Inv. Group, Ltd., 708 F.Supp. 1488.

N.D.Ill. 1969. Shakman v. Democratic Organization of Cook County, 310 F.Supp. 1398, reversed 435 F.2d 267, certiorari denied 91 S.Ct. 1383, 402 U.S. 909, 28 L.Ed.2d 650, on remand 356 F.Supp. 1241.

N.D.Ind. 1994. Federal Tort Claims Act (FTCA) plaintiff's allegation that government negligently committed other acts or omissions provided no opportunity for government to respond and, thus, even under the generous standard of notice pleading, was insufficient and could not withstand government's motion to dismiss.

    Bailor v. Salvation Army, 854 F.Supp. 1341, affirmed 51 F.3d 678.

S.D.Ind. 1990. Even though complaint's allegation that consumer, while operating riding lawn mower, sustained severe and permanent injury to his right foot as result of defective condition of tractor or negligence of manufacturer and seller was inadequate to inform defendants concerning claims against which they must defend, complaint would not be dismissed in best interest of justice; in response to defendants' initial motion to dismiss, consumer adequately set forth facts on which claims were based, thereafter filed contentions which added further detail to claims, and defendants did not claim prejudice based on insufficiency of allegations. Fed.Rules Civ.Proc.Rule 8(f), 28 U.S.C.A.

    Spangler v. Sears, Roebuck and Co., 752 F.Supp. 1437, on reconsideration 759 F.Supp. 1337.

D.Kan. 1997. Court was required to accept plaintiff's allegations as true for purposes of motion to dismiss, and thus could not grant dismissal for failure to state claim based on defendant's assertion, unsupported by any authority, that it could not be held vicariously liable for torts of other defendants. Fed.Rules Civ.Proc.Rule 12(b)(6), 28 U.S.C.A.

    Wesley v. Don Stein Buick, Inc., 985 F.Supp. 1288, vacated in part 996 F.Supp. 1299.

E.D.La. 1994. Defendant's complete failure to address allegations in amended Racketeer Influenced and Corrupt Organizations Act (RICO) complaint that he used mails to fraudulently give appearance that he and other defendants were conducting school board's activities in legitimate manner precluded granting of his motion to dismiss for failure to state a claim. 18 U.S.C.A. § 1961 et seq.; Fed.Rules Civ.Proc. Rule 12(b)(6), 28 U.S.C.A.

    Dammon v. Folse, 846 F.Supp. 36.

D.Me. 1988. "False light" claim of invasion of privacy under Maine law could be resolved in motion to dismiss. Fed.Rules Civ. Proc.Rule 12(b)(6), 28 U.S.C.A.

    Dempsey v. National Enquirer, Inc., 687 F.Supp. 692, reconsideration denied 702 F.Supp. 927.

D.Me. 1987. Trial court would not grant involuntary dismissal of products liability case at close of plaintiffs' evidence where it was not manifestly clear that plaintiffs had not proved their case based upon negligence in design. Fed.Rules Civ.Proc.Rule 41(b), 28 U.S.C.A.

    Central Maine Power Co. v. Foster Wheeler Corp., 116 F.R.D. 339.

Breach of warranty claim would not be involuntarily dismissed at close of plaintiffs' evidence where it was not "manifestly clear" that disclaimer of warranties was effective; applicable law remained in doubt and, because disclaimer was matter of affirmative defense, defendants bore burden of proof with respect to its ineffectiveness. Fed.Rules Civ.Proc.Rule 41(b), 28 U.S.C.A.

    Central Maine Power Co. v. Foster Wheeler Corp., 116 F.R.D. 339.

D.Mass. 1993. Even if patient's pro se claim for misdiagnosis at Veterans Administration (VA) hospital had been timely, patient could not prevail against motion to dismiss, where patient produced nothing beyond his unsupported contention that he suffered from "brain lesion" to show that VA diagnosis of chronic meningitis was incorrect.

    Gaudreault v. U.S., 835 F.Supp. 684, affirmed Guadreault v. U.S. Dept. of Veteran Affairs, 7 F.3d 218, certiorari denied 114 S.Ct. 1308, 510 U.S. 1197, 127 L.Ed.2d 659, rehearing denied 114 S.Ct. 1666, 511 U.S. 1078, 128 L.Ed.2d 382.

D.Mass. 1987. Possibility that Massachusetts would not permit parents to maintain independent cause of action for loss of consortium when tortious injury was inflicted upon their adult, but unemancipated child, did not mandate dismissal of parents' loss of consortium claim against vehicle manufacturer.

    Wood v. General Motors Corp., 673 F.Supp. 1108, remanded 865 F.2d 395, certiorari denied 110 S.Ct. 1781, 494 U.S. 1065, 108 L.Ed.2d 782.

E.D.Mich. 1993. Where investors asserting claims under Racketeer Influenced and Corrupt Organizations Act (RICO) against stockbroker failed to plead predicate acts of securities fraud, mail fraud, or wire fraud with any specificity, district court would use its discretion to dismiss claims. 18 U.S.C.A. §§ 1341, 1343, 1962(c).

    Arioli v. Prudential-Bache Securities, Inc., 811 F.Supp. 303.

W.D.Mich. 1991. Defamation claim under Michigan law which lacks requisite pleading specificity as to special damages may be subject to dismissal. Fed.Rules Civ.Proc.Rule 9(g), 28 U.S.C.A.

Parker v. Aetna Life and Cas., 791 F.Supp. 175.

S.D.Miss. 1987. Action would not be dismissed on ground that specific amount of damages was claimed against licensed physician in violation of Mississippi statute; the statute does not require dismissal of complaint, and plaintiff had requested to be allowed to amend her complaint to cure the defect. Miss.Code 1972, § 11–1–59.

Sorey v. Kellett, 673 F.Supp. 817, reversed 849 F.2d 960, rehearing denied.

E.D.N.Y. 1993. Although franchisees asserting Racketeer Influenced and Corrupt Organizations Act (RICO) claims against franchisor and its principal bore burden to prove at trial that members of alleged RICO enterprise participated in some conduct other than business of franchisor, that burden was not basis for dismissal of complaint for failure to state claim. 18 U.S.C.A. §§ 1961 et seq., 1962(c); Fed.Rules Civ.Proc.Rule 12(b)(6), 28 U.S.C.A.

Giuliano v. Everything Yogurt, Inc., 819 F.Supp. 240.

E.D.N.Y. 1992. Under New York law, fraud claim may be dismissed when plaintiff's deposition testimony reveals that plaintiff is unable to produce factual support for claim.

Celi v. Canadian Occidental Petroleum Ltd., 804 F.Supp. 465.

E.D.N.Y. 1992. Notice pleading requirements are applicable to RICO, and failure to place defendant and court on adequate notice of plaintiff's claim generates basis for dismissing complaint. 18 U.S.C.A. § 1961; Fed.Rules Civ.Proc.Rule 8(a), 28 U.S.C.A.

U.S. v. Private Sanitation Industry Ass'n of Nassau/Suffolk, Inc., 793 F.Supp. 1114.

E.D.N.Y. 1988. Even if organized crime family were erroneously alleged to be both RICO "enterprise" and "person" violating RICO in single claim, such defect in pleading was not grounds to dismiss civil RICO claims against individual defendants. 18 U.S.C.A. § 1962(c).

U.S. v. Bonanno Organized Crime Family of La Cosa Nostra, 683 F.Supp. 1411, affirmed 879 F.2d 20.

Failure to satisfy notice pleading requirements may be grounds to dismiss RICO complaint for failure to state claim. Fed.Rules Civ.Proc.Rules 8(a), (a)(2), 9(b), 12(b)(6), 28 U.S.C.A.

U.S. v. Bonanno Organized Crime Family of La Cosa Nostra, 683 F.Supp. 1411, affirmed 879 F.2d 20.

Complaint that fails to allege one or more of RICO's statutory elements is subject to dismissal for failure to state claim. Fed.Rules Civ.Proc.Rules 8(a), (a)(2), 12(b)(6), 28 U.S.C.A.

U.S. v. Bonanno Organized Crime Family of La Cosa Nostra, 683 F.Supp. 1411, affirmed 879 F.2d 20.

E.D.N.Y. 1985. Dismissal without prejudice was appropriate sanction for claim for interference in business relationships asserted under New York law without the pleading of any basis for application of New York law.

Liamuiga Tours, Div. of Caribbean Tourism Consultants, Ltd. v. Travel Impressions, Ltd., 617 F.Supp. 920.

S.D.N.Y. 1995. Pro se complaint that contained little more than conclusory allegations of "oral, wire and electronic" eavesdropping, false imprisonment and defamation failed to meet applicable pleading standards, thus requiring its dismissal; even after careful review of complaint, it was impossible to tell when any alleged conduct took place or in what manner defendants allegedly imprisoned plaintiff, and plaintiff did not recite, paraphrase, or identify alleged defamatory statements. Fed.Rules Civ. Proc.Rule 8(a)(2), (e)(1), 28 U.S.C.A.

Jones v. Capital Cities/ABC Inc., 874 F.Supp. 626, motion denied 168 F.R.D. 477.

Defamation claim completely failed to identify with specificity allegedly defamatory words used, thus requiring dismissal of that claim; plaintiff identified defamation only generally as being "of a highly offensive nature that any person of ordinary sensibilities would have been offended at the disclosure, of such matters of a private nature, matters such as private relationships, nudiety [sic], and other personal relationships, such as her sexual proclivities." Fed. Rules Civ.Proc.Rule 9, 28 U.S.C.A.

Jones v. Capital Cities/ABC Inc., 874 F.Supp. 626, motion denied 168 F.R.D. 477.

S.D.N.Y. 1995. Failure to adequately allege that defendant's predicate acts under Racketeer Influenced and Corrupt Organizations Act (RICO) proximately caused plaintiff's injury is defect of pleading and is grounds for dismissal at pleading stage. 18 U.S.C.A. § 1964(c); Fed. Rules Civ.Proc.Rule 12(b)(6), 28 U.S.C.A.

Red Ball Interior Demolition Corp. v. Palmadessa, 874 F.Supp. 576.

S.D.N.Y. 1994. Claim for fraud must be dismissed for failure to state a claim if it does not satisfy requirements of rule requiring fraud to be pled with particularity. Fed.Rules Civ. Proc.Rules 9(b), 12(b)(6), 28 U.S.C.A.

> MTV Networks, a Div. of Viacom Intern., Inc. v. Curry, 867 F.Supp. 202.

S.D.N.Y. 1994. Whether allegedly libelous statement constitutes fact or opinion is matter of law, and thus may be resolved by court on motion to dismiss.

> Coliniatis v. Dimas, 848 F.Supp. 462.

S.D.N.Y. 1992. Claims of investors in limited partnerships for conversion, arising from allegedly fraudulent roll-up transaction and connected mortgage refinancing, would be dismissed, where plaintiffs failed to allege that general partner, any of his corporate affiliates, or any related defendants actually exercised ownership, possession or control of proceeds from refinancing of limited partnership mortgage.

> Ackerman v. National Property Analysts, Inc., 887 F.Supp. 494.

S.D.N.Y. 1992. Borrowers' allegations of mail fraud and wire fraud as predicate acts under Racketeer Influenced and Corrupt Organizations Act (RICO) were sufficiently particularized to withstand motion to dismiss, even if borrowers would have difficulty proving allegations; borrowers alleged that lender's officers presented borrowers with incomplete documents and fraudulently represented that obligations would be the same as prior loans, that borrowers were induced to borrow additional money based on misrepresentations about interest rate, that one officer used borrowers' debt obligations to pressure borrowers into selling automobile below cost, and that lender repeatedly refused to provide regular statements documenting nature of obligations. 18 U.S.C.A. § 1962; Fed.Rules Civ.Proc.Rule 9(b), 28 U.S.C.A.

> Center Cadillac, Inc. v. Bank Leumi Trust Co. of New York, 808 F.Supp. 213, affirmed 99 F.3d 401.

S.D.N.Y. 1992. In assessing sufficiency of libel complaint, court could consider the allegedly defamatory article. Fed.Rules Civ.Proc. Rule 12(b)(6), 28 U.S.C.A.

> Church of Scientology Intern. v. Time Warner, Inc., 806 F.Supp. 1157.

S.D.N.Y. 1992. For purposes of motion to dismiss for failure to allege fraud with particularity, court must read complaint generously and draw off inferences in favor of pleader; however, time, place, speaker, and sometimes even content of alleged misrepresentation must be alleged specifically. Fed.Rules Civ.Proc. Rules 8(a), 9(b), 28 U.S.C.A.

> Pompano-Windy City Partners, Ltd. v. Bear Stearns & Co., Inc., 794 F.Supp. 1265.

S.D.N.Y. 1991. Where investor's securities fraud claims were well-pled, Racketeer Influenced and Corrupt Organizations Act (RICO) claims grounded on the securities fraud claims would not be dismissed. 18 U.S.C.A. § 1962(a-d).

> Parnes v. Mast Property Investors, Inc., 776 F.Supp. 792.

S.D.N.Y. 1991. Counterclaim by signers of note which counterclaim defendant asserted was based on intentional infliction of emotional distress and should be dismissed for failure to plead requisite elements of that tort would be dismissed, where signers alleged they had properly pled claim for pain, suffering, and emotional distress as unintentional, but predictable, result of counterclaim defendant's fraudulent conduct, but signers would be permitted to seek damages on another counterclaim for their alleged pain and suffering.

> Citicorp Intern. Trading Co., Inc. v. Western Oil & Refining Co., Inc., 771 F.Supp. 600.

S.D.N.Y. 1991. Dismissal of Racketeer Influenced and Corrupt Organizations (RICO) claim is warranted where pleadings merely repeat words of statute in conclusory and general fashion. 18 U.S.C.A. § 1962(a-c).

> Varnberg v. Minnick, 760 F.Supp. 315.

S.D.N.Y. 1989. Failure to connect allegations of fraudulent representation to particular defendants and to allege specific facts to support claims of fraud is sufficient grounds for dismissal. Fed.Rules Civ.Proc.Rule 9(b), 28 U.S.C.A.

> Kuczynski v. Ragen Corp., 732 F.Supp. 378.

S.D.N.Y. 1989. RICO claims arising out of sale of limited partnerships would be dismissed for failure to adequately plead continuity of activity; there was no allegation of a tie to organized crime, and the partnerships were by their terms limited to a duration of slightly more than five years and there was nothing in the complaint which suggested the possibility of further investment. 18 U.S.C.A. § 1962(c).

> Bruce v. Martin, 712 F.Supp. 442.

S.D.N.Y. 1989. Statute of limitations claim, and other issues regarding whether defendant's negligence was cause of plaintiffs' harm, could not be disposed on motion to dismiss.

> Cohen v. Abrahams, 710 F.Supp. 981.

S.D.N.Y. 1989. Union and individuals associated with it were not entitled to dismissal of Government's RICO complaint on ground that allegations of complaint could not support requested equitable relief, which included, inter alia, ouster of members of union's general executive board, and orders permanently enjoining board members from participating in affairs of any labor organization; if Government prevailed at trial, it would be court's responsibility to fashion equitable remedy to restrain future violations of RICO. 18 U.S.C.A. § 1964(a).

U.S. v. International Broth. of Teamsters, 708 F.Supp. 1388.

"First to file rule" did not require dismissal of RICO civil action against defendant, even though he had action pending in different district court; subject matter of cases was not identical, parties in two cases were different, and, while allegations in latter case involved activities of organized crime family's activity in New York, including its alleged influence over union local, RICO complaint alleged nationwide enterprise whose nature far exceeded scope of other case. 18 U.S.C.A. § 1961 et seq.

U.S. v. International Broth. of Teamsters, 708 F.Supp. 1388.

S.D.N.Y. 1989. Plaintiff's failure to amend and plead properly its fraud and RICO counts, even after having been given opportunity to do so after court specified defects to be cured, warranted dismissal with prejudice. Fed.Rules Civ.Proc.Rule 9(b), 28 U.S.C.A.; 18 U.S.C.A. §§ 1961(1), 1962(c).

Sendar Co., Inc. v. Megaware Inc., 705 F.Supp. 159.

S.D.N.Y. 1986. Complaint filed by investors in government securities who suffered losses resulting from dealer's hypothecation of investors' securities alleging aiding and abetting of common law of fraud would not be dismissed, even though issue of whether such cause of action existed was not free from doubt, because keeping common law aiding and abetting claim in case would not require proof of any facts at trial additional to facts necessary for aiding and abetting claims as to securities fraud. Securities Act of 1933, § 17(a), 15 U.S.C.A. § 77q(a); Securities Exchange Act of 1934, §§ 8(b), 10(b), 15(c)(1), 15 U.S.C.A. §§ 78h(b), 78j(b), 78o (c)(1); NMSA 1978, § 58–13–39.

First Federal Sav. and Loan Ass'n of Pittsburgh v. Oppenheim, Appel, Dixon & Co., 629 F.Supp. 427.

S.D.N.Y. 1981. Kirshner v. Goldberg, 506 F.Supp. 454, affirmed 742 F.2d 1430.

M.D.N.C. 1985. State counterclaims alleging assault, battery, and libel were sufficient to withstand motion for dismissal.

Waller v. Butkovich, 605 F.Supp. 1137.

W.D.N.C. 1985. Where contract claim was coupled with identifiable tort of intentional infliction of emotional distress, which contained element of aggravated conduct, claim for punitive damages survived motion to dismiss.

Deen v. Great Atlantic & Pacific Tea Co., Inc., 608 F.Supp. 783.

N.D.Ohio 1990. In light of ambiguity as to place of injury and jurisdiction whose law controlled question, negligence action against product endorser for failure to exercise reasonable care in performing testing procedures or inaccurately communicating testing results to others could not be dismissed for failure to state a claim. Fed.Rules Civ.Proc.Rule 12(b)(6), 28 U.S.C.A.

U.S. Lighting Service Inc. v. Llerrad Corp., 745 F.Supp. 426, vacated 807 F.Supp. 439.

S.D.Ohio 1989. Court would not dismiss plaintiff's RICO claim based on alleged failure of plaintiff's attorney to investigate acts allegedly committed by defendant which comprised the required second episode of racketeering activity, inasmuch as court was required to presume that all material factual allegations in complaint were true for purposes of motion to dismiss, and signature of plaintiff's attorney on complaint constituted certificate that complaint was well-grounded in fact. 18 U.S.C.A. § 1961(5); Fed.Rules Civ.Proc.Rules 11, 12(b)(6), 28 U.S.C.A.

Developer's Mortg. Co. v. TransOhio Sav. Bank, 706 F.Supp. 570.

D.Or. 1990. Allegation of defamation is subject to dismissal if it fails to set out actual words published.

Rice v. Comtek Mfg. of Oregon, Inc., 766 F.Supp. 1539.

When false light privacy claim alleges defamatory, as opposed to nondefamatory, statement, it is duplicative of defamation claim and must be dismissed if both are pleaded.

Rice v. Comtek Mfg. of Oregon, Inc., 766 F.Supp. 1539.

Under Oregon law, false light action was akin to defamation and, because of close connection between two actions, dismissal of defamation claim warranted dismissal of false light privacy claim.

Rice v. Comtek Mfg. of Oregon, Inc., 766 F.Supp. 1539.

E.D.Pa. 1994. New Jersey Superior Court, Appellate Division's reading of definition of "pattern" in New Jersey Racketeer Influenced and Corrupt Organizations statute (New Jersey RICO) as not requiring continuity was reasoned and not contradicted by other persuasive data, and, therefore, federal district court would not dismiss New Jersey RICO claims for failing to sufficiently allege continuity in pattern of racketeering activity. N.J.S.A. 2C:41–1 to 2C:41–6.2.

> Philadelphia Reserve Supply Co. v. Nowalk & Associates, Inc., 864 F.Supp. 1456.

E.D.Pa. 1993. Complaint should be dismissed for failure to state claim only where, taking all allegations of complaint as true, and making all reasonable inferences in plaintiffs' favor, it appears beyond doubt that plaintiffs can prove no set of facts in support of their claims which would entitle them to relief; standard is same for RICO as for non-RICO claims. Fed.Rules Civ.Proc.Rule 12(b)(6), 28 U.S.C.A.; 18 U.S.C.A. § 1961 et seq.

> Gurfein v. Sovereign Group, 826 F.Supp. 890.

E.D.Pa. 1992. Buyer's allegation of seller's intentional interference with contracts that buyer had with "unnamed parties" did not provide fair notice to seller, supporting dismissal of claim without prejudice.

> Tersco, Inc. v. E.I. DuPont de Nemours and Co., 879 F.Supp. 445.

E.D.Pa. 1992. Parent's claim for loss of consortium of injured child would not be dismissed for failure to state claim upon which relief could be granted; although applicable Pennsylvania law did not recognize such cause of action, it was foreseeable that law could change at any time. Fed.Rules Civ.Proc.Rule 12(b)(6), 28 U.S.C.A.

> Fields v. Graff, 784 F.Supp. 224.

E.D.Pa. 1991. Products liability plaintiff's tort law claims to recover goodwill damages were subject to dismissal for failure to state cause of action for which relief could be granted, even if plaintiff could properly recover goodwill damages under contract theory; tort complaint did not inform defendant with reasonable particularity that cognizable contract claims might exist against it for such damages and plaintiff's contract-based counts requested same damages as tort counts. Fed.Rules Civ.Proc. Rules 8, 12(b)(6), 28 U.S.C.A.

> Lucker Mfg. v. Milwaukee Steel Foundry, a Div. of Grede Foundries, 777 F.Supp. 413, appeal dismissed 983 F.2d 1051.

E.D.Pa. 1988. Sufficiency of allegations under Racketeer Influenced and Corrupt Organizations Act section which prohibits any person employed by or associated with enterprise from conducting or participating in enterprise's affairs through pattern of racketeering activity may be examined on motion to dismiss. 18 U.S.C.A. § 1962(a-c).

> Schwartz v. Philadelphia Nat. Bank, 701 F.Supp. 92, affirmed 879 F.2d 859.

E.D.Pa. 1987. Attorney's claim that persons involved in underlying criminal investigation and prosecution of attorney for witness tampering violated Racketeer Influenced and Corrupt Organizations Act required dismissal with leave to amend, where attorney failed to allege role of any person in alleged RICO violation and also failed to allege violation of predicate offenses listed in his complaint. 18 U.S.C.A. § 1961 et seq.

> Syre v. Com., 662 F.Supp. 550, affirmed 845 F.2d 1015, certiorari denied 109 S.Ct. 139, 488 U.S. 853, 102 L.Ed.2d 112, rehearing denied 109 S.Ct. 521, 488 U.S. 976, 102 L.Ed.2d 554, affirmed Appeal of Syre, 845 F.2d 1015, certiorari denied 109 S.Ct. 139, 488 U.S. 853, 102 L.Ed.2d 112, rehearing denied 109 S.Ct. 521, 488 U.S. 976, 102 L.Ed.2d 554.

M.D.Pa. 1993. Products liability suit against manufacturer of allegedly miswired engine block heater would be dismissed on public policy grounds where heater had been repaired, and thus was unavailable for manufacturer's inspection.

> Sipe v. Ford Motor Co., 837 F.Supp. 660.

W.D.Pa. 1994. Liberal standard which applies to a motion to dismiss non-Racketeer Influenced and Corrupt Organizations Act (RICO) claims for failure to state a claim also applies to RICO claims. 18 U.S.C.A. § 1961 et seq.; Fed. Rules Civ.Proc.Rule 12(b)(6), 28 U.S.C.A.

> Dugan v. Bell Telephone of Pennsylvania, 876 F.Supp. 713.

W.D.Pa. 1993. Standard of review applicable to motion to dismiss for failure to state claim upon which relief can be granted does not distinguish between Racketeer Influenced and Corrupt Organizations Act (RICO) and non-RICO claims. Fed.Rules Civ.Proc.Rule 12(b)(6), 28 U.S.C.A.; 18 U.S.C.A. § 1961 et seq.

> Portland General Elec. Co. v. Westinghouse Elec. Corp., 842 F.Supp. 161.

W.D.Pa. 1993. Dismissal or summary judgment in products liability action in which product is lost or destroyed is defensive mechanism used by courts to protect party who would otherwise be forced to prepare its case without ever having opportunity to inspect very subject matter of case.

> Shultz v. Barko Hydraulics, Inc., a Div. of Pettibone Corp., 832 F.Supp. 142.

D.R.I. 1995. Allegation of pain and suffering in complaint alleging intentional infliction of emotional distress, without more, was just the kind of bald assertion that could not pass muster on motion to dismiss for failure to state claim, especially where plaintiff was specifically ordered by judge to set forth particulars as to the facts on which claims were based. Fed. Rules Civ.Proc.Rule 12(b)(6), 28 U.S.C.A.

> Socha v. National Ass'n of Letter Carriers Branch No. 57 (Merged), 883 F.Supp. 790.

E.D.Tenn. 1988. Strict liability plaintiffs' failure to allege manufacturer's insolvency at time suit was filed against seller, as required under Tennessee law, did not warrant dismissal of complaint where seller had failed to object and manufacturer's insolvency was subsequently demonstrated. T.C.A. § 29–28–106(b).

> Seals v. Sears, Roebuck and Co., Inc., 688 F.Supp. 1252.

D.Utah 1988. It is proper to dismiss an action for intentional infliction of emotional distress if all the elements of the tort are not alleged and, in addition, dismissal of claim is proper if the alleged conduct of defendant does not rise to the level of outrageousness required under state law. Fed.Rules Civ.Proc.Rule 12, 28 U.S.C.A.

> Boisjoly v. Morton Thiokol, Inc., 706 F.Supp. 795.

E.D.Va. 1992. Plaintiffs' allegations of factual falsity must be accepted as true, for purposes of motion to dismiss a defamation action.

> Chapin v. Greve, 787 F.Supp. 557, affirmed 993 F.2d 1087.

Upon a motion to dismiss a defamation action, question presented was whether or not a reasonable fact finder could conclude that the article or statements in the article stated or implied, in their plain and natural sense, the defamatory meanings ascribed to them by plaintiffs in their complaint.

> Chapin v. Greve, 787 F.Supp. 557, affirmed 993 F.2d 1087.

S.D.W.Va. 1995. In suit by insured against agent and insurer, tort and contract claims against agent would not be dismissed for failure to state claim where agent's role in denial of insurance coverage was unclear and insurer's denial of insurance claim appeared upon agent's stationery and agent's name was listed directly below insurer's name on policy.

> Pen Coal Corp. v. William H. McGee and Co., Inc., 903 F.Supp. 980.

E.D.Wis. 1992. Defendant accounting partnership was not entitled to dismissal of plaintiffs' Wisconsin law fraud, negligent mis-

representation, strict liability, and racketeering claims on proximate cause grounds prior to trial; factual issues were complex.

> Grove Holding Corp. v. First Wisconsin Nat. Bank of Sheboygan, 803 F.Supp. 1486.

Defendant accounting partnership was not entitled to dismissal of Wisconsin law negligent misrepresentation claim on public policy grounds prior to trial; factual issues were complex.

> Grove Holding Corp. v. First Wisconsin Nat. Bank of Sheboygan, 803 F.Supp. 1486.

Bkrtcy.D.Dist.Col. 1993. To extent that borrower's claims against Federal Deposit Insurance Corporation (FDIC), as receiver for failed bank, for tortious interference with existing contract and for tortious interference with prospective business were nothing more than borrower's allegation that bank breached its oral promise that it would consent to purchase of another business, disguised as different cause of action, claims had to be dismissed.

> In re Beitzell & Co., Inc., 163 B.R. 637.

Bkrtcy.N.D.Ill. 1991. Application of business judgment rule was question of fact and wholly inappropriate for consideration on motion to dismiss breach of fiduciary duty claims against Chapter 11 debtor's officers and directors in connection with prepetition leveraged buyout transaction wherein debtor acquired assets and liabilities of aluminum corporation.

> In re Aluminum Mills Corp., 132 B.R. 869.

~1812. Trusts, actions involving.

Library references

> C.J.S. Federal Civil Procedure § 839.

D.Utah 1988. Rather than go through wasted effort of dismissing suit against trustee defendant, sued only in his capacity as trustee, but named in complaint as being sued in his individual capacity, and then requiring plaintiff to refile suit against trustee in his capacity as trustee, district court struck phrase "an individual" on pleadings which referred to defendant. Fed.Rules Civ.Proc.Rule 9(a), 28 U.S.C.A.

> Castleglen, Inc. v. Commonwealth Sav. Ass'n, 118 F.R.D. 515.

Bkrtcy.D.Mass. 1993. Plaintiffs' labeling of count in complaint as "Constructive Trust" was not substantive defect requiring dismissal, but merely one of semantics, despite defense contention that constructive trust is a remedial device rather than cause of action; whether constructive trust was a claim to be brought or merely remedy to be obtained for another claim such as breach of fiduciary duty was irrelevant.

In re Curran, 157 B.R. 500.

Key Numbers 1821 et seq. in Next Volume

For later cases
see
Same Topic and Key Number
in Pocket Part